THE CAMBRIDG

EIGHTEENTH-CE

The eighteenth century arguably boasts a m ... ...ni-cant musical figures, and a more engaging con ... ...yles and aesthetic orientations, than any century before ... ...ge swathes of its musical activity remain under-appreciated. ... ...nbridge History of Eighteenth-Century Music* provides a comprehensive survey, examining little-known repertories, works and musical trends alongside more familiar ones. Rather than relying on temporal, periodic and composer-related phenomena to structure the volume, it is organized by genre; chapters are grouped according to the traditional distinctions of music for the church, music for the theatre and music for the concert room that conditioned so much thinking, activity and output in the eighteenth century. A valuable summation of current research in this area, the volume also encourages readers to think of eighteenth-century music less in terms of overtly teleological developments than of interacting and mutually stimulating musical cultures and practices, thus pointing to ways in which eighteenth-century music studies will evolve in the future.

SIMON P. KEEFE is James Rossiter Hoyle Chair of Music and Head of Department at the University of Sheffield. He is the author of *Mozart's Piano Concertos: Dramatic Dialogue in the Age of Enlightenment* (2001) and *Mozart's Viennese Instrumental Music: A Study of Stylistic Re-Invention* (2007), and editor of four volumes for Cambridge University Press: *The Cambridge Companion to Mozart* (2003) and *The Cambridge Companion to the Concerto* (2005); *Mozart Studies* (2006); and (with Cliff Eisen) *The Cambridge Mozart Encyclopedia* (2006). He is a member of the Akademie für Mozartforschung, Salzburg.

THE CAMBRIDGE HISTORY OF EIGHTEENTH-CENTURY MUSIC

*

EDITED BY
SIMON P. KEEFE

CAMBRIDGE
UNIVERSITY PRESS

CAMBRIDGE
UNIVERSITY PRESS

University Printing House, Cambridge CB2 8BS, United Kingdom

One Liberty Plaza, 20th Floor, New York, NY 10006, USA

477 Williamstown Road, Port Melbourne, VIC 3207, Australia

4843/24, 2nd Floor, Ansari Road, Daryaganj, Delhi - 110002, India

79 Anson Road, #06-04/06, Singapore 079906

Cambridge University Press is part of the University of Cambridge.

It furthers the University's mission by disseminating knowledge in the pursuit of education, learning and research at the highest international levels of excellence.

www.cambridge.org
Information on this title: www.cambridge.org/9781107643970

First published 2009
First paperback edition 2014

A catalogue record for this publication is available from the British Library

ISBN 978-0-521-66319-9 Hardback
ISBN 978-1-107-64397-0 Paperback

Contents

Illustrations

Contributors

GREGER ANDERSSON is Professor of Music at Lunds Universitet, Sweden. His recent publications include *Musik i Norden* (1997), and articles in *Musik, Wissenschaft und ihre Vermittlung: Bericht über die internationale musikwissenschaftliche Tagung der Hochschule für Musik und Theater Hannover* (2002), and *Zur Geschichte und Aufführungspraxis der Harmoniemusik* (2006)

DAVID BLACK is Junior Research Fellow at Homerton College, Cambridge. He was awarded a PhD from Harvard University in 2007, and has published articles in the *Mozart-Jahrbuch*, *Acta Mozartiana* and elsewhere. He is presently writing a monograph on Mozart's sacred music and preparing a new edition of the Mozart Requiem.

CHARLES E. BREWER is Associate Professor of Musicology at the College of Music of The Florida State University and Director of the Program in Early Music. He is an active researcher on the musical traditions and interrelationships of the early American colonies and Europe, especially the cultural meanings of music during the American Revolution. He is also a passionate singer from the Sacred Harp.

MICHAEL BURDEN is Reader in Music at the University of Oxford, and Fellow in Music and Opera Studies at New College, Oxford, where he is also Dean. His published research is on the stage music of Henry Purcell, and aspects of dance and theatre in London theatre in the seventeenth, eighteenth and nineteenth centuries; it includes an analytical catalogue of Metastasio's operas as performed in London. He is currently completing books on the staging of opera in London from 1660 to 1860, and on the London years of the soprano Regina Mingotti. He is Vice President of the British Society for 18th-Century Studies.

MARGARET R. BUTLER is Assistant Professor of Musicology at the University of Florida and holds a PhD from The Ohio State University. A grant from the

Fulbright Foundation led to research for *Operatic Reform in Turin: Aspects of Production and Stylistic Change in the 1760s* (Lucca, 2001). Other publications include articles and reviews in the *Cambridge Opera Journal*, *Eighteenth-Century Music* and in proceedings of conferences held in Würzburg, Naples and Valencia. She is a founding member and serves on the board of directors of the Society for Eighteenth-Century Music.

ANKE CATON studied at Kassel University before undertaking postgraduate studies at Cardiff University. She is currently pursuing a PhD at Cardiff on the political implications of Schubert's songs.

JEN-YEN CHEN is Assistant Professor in the Graduate Institute of Musicology at National Taiwan University. He has published essays in the *Journal of Musicological Research*, *Ad Parnassum* and *Musiktheorie*, and has edited volumes of music for the Johann-Joseph-Fux Gesamtausgabe and A–R Editions. His research focuses on eighteenth-century Austria, and his interests include sacred music, aristocratic patronage and performance practice.

CLIFF EISEN is Professor of Music at King's College London. He is the editor of a number of volumes on Mozart, including *Mozart Studies* (1991), *Mozart Studies 2* (1997), *Mozart: A Life in Letters* (2006), Hermann Abert, *W.A. Mozart* (2007) and (with Simon P. Keefe) *The Cambridge Mozart Encyclopedia* (2006). He is a member of the Akademie für Mozartforschung, Salzburg.

MICHAEL FEND is Senior Lecturer at King's College London and Privatdozent at the University of Bayreuth. His research focuses on issues in the intellectual history of music. Together with Michel Noiray (CNRS, Paris) he has edited *Musical Education in Europe (1770–1914): Compositional, Institutional, and Political Challenges*, 2 vols. (2005). He is also the author of *Cherubinis Paris Opern (1788–1803)* (*Beihefte zum Archiv für Musikwissenschaft*, vol. 59) (2007).

JOHN IRVING is Professor of Music History and Performance Practice at the University of Bristol. He specializes in the keyboard and chamber music of Mozart (especially reception and performance practice). His published research includes three books on Mozart's piano sonatas, string quartets and piano concertos (another book on the piano sonatas is forthcoming), as well as numerous journal articles and book chapters. Current projects include a facsimile edition of Mozart's Piano Concerto in A, K. 488 and a recording on historic keyboard instruments of keyboard sonatas by Leopold Mozart and his Salzburg contemporaries.

BERTA JONCUS is Lecturer in Music at St Anne's College and St Hilda's College, Oxford. She specializes in the music and practices of the Georgian London stage, European popular music before 1750 and eighteenth-century vocal music more generally. She also created the electronic resource Ballad Operas Online (www.odl.ox.ac.uk/balladopera). Her monograph, *Kitty Clive, Goddess of Mirth: Creating a Star through Song (1728–1765)* is to be published in 2009. She reviews recordings regularly for the BBC.

SIMON P. KEEFE is James Rossiter Hoyle Chair of Music and Head of Department at the University of Sheffield. He is the author of *Mozart's Piano Concertos: Dramatic Dialogue in the Age of Enlightenment* (2001) and *Mozart's Viennese Instrumental Music: A Study of Stylistic Re-Invention* (2007), and editor of four volumes for Cambridge University Press: companions to Mozart (2003) and the concerto (2005); *Mozart Studies* (2006); and (with Cliff Eisen) *The Cambridge Mozart Encyclopedia* (2006). He is a member of the Akademie für Mozartforschung, Salzburg, and is currently at work on a monograph on Mozart's Requiem for Cambridge University Press.

RAINER KLEINERTZ is Chair in Musicology at Saarland University (Universität des Saarlandes) in Saarbrücken, Germany, having previously been visiting professor at Salamanca University (1992–4), reader and professor at Regensburg University (1994–2006) and visiting fellow at Oxford University (2000–1). His main areas of interest are the music and writings of Franz Liszt and Richard Wagner, and Spanish music theatre. He is co-editor of the Complete Writings of Franz Liszt (*Sämtliche Schriften*, 1989–) and author of two volumes on eighteenth-century Spanish music theatre (*Grundzüge des spanischen Musiktheaters im 18. Jahrhundert. Ópera – Comedia – Zarzuela* (2003)).

PAUL R. LAIRD is Professor of Musicology at the University of Kansas, where he teaches courses in music history and directs the Instrumental Collegium Musicum. His scholarly specialties include the Spanish villancico, the music of Leonard Bernstein, musical theatre and early string instruments. He is the author of *Towards A History of the Spanish Villancico* (1997), *Leonard Bernstein: A Guide to Research* (2001), *The Baroque Cello Revival: An Oral History* (2004), and is the co-editor with William A. Everett of *The Cambridge Companion to the Musical* (2nd edn., 2008).

JEAN-PAUL C. MONTAGNIER holds a PhD from Duke University. He is currently Professor of Musicology at the University of Nancy, France, Adjunct Professor at McGill University and member of the Institut de

Recherche sur le Patrimoine Musical en France (CNRS). He specializes in the sacred music of the French Baroque, and serves on the advisory board of the journal *Eighteenth-Century Music*.

SIMON MCVEIGH is Professor of Music at Goldsmiths, University of London. He has published extensively on eighteenth-century instrumental music and on music in London, including *Concert Life in London from Mozart to Haydn* (1993) and, with Jehoash Hirshberg, *The Italian Solo Concerto 1700–1760: Rhetorical Strategies and Style History* (2004). He also co-edited with Susan Wollenberg a volume of essays entitled *Concert Life in Eighteenth-Century Britain* (2004). Current research projects include a study of the British symphony in the eighteenth century and a book with Leanne Langley on London concert life around 1900.

STEPHEN ROSE is Lecturer in Music at Royal Holloway, University of London. His research focuses on German music of the seventeenth and eighteenth centuries in its social, material and performing contexts. He has published articles in journals such as *Early Music*, *Early Music History*, *German History*, the *Journal of the Royal Musical Association*, *Music & Letters* and the *Schütz-Jahrbuch*, and is currently completing a book on the musician-novels of the German Baroque. He is currently Reviews Editor of *Early Music*.

LOIS ROSOW, Professor at the Ohio State University, specializes in French opera of the seventeenth and eighteenth centuries. She has published articles on the administrative history and scribal workshop of the Opéra in Paris, Lully's reception in eighteenth-century Paris, performance-practice issues and the interplay of dramaturgy with poetic and musical form. Her critical edition of Lully's *Armide* is found in *Jean-Baptiste Lully: Oeuvres complètes*, series 3, vol. 14 (2004), and she was guest editor for the *Journal of Seventeenth-Century Music*, 10/1 (2004), devoted to Lully's *Persée*. A chapter on the descending tetrachord in France is forthcoming in *New Perspectives on Marc-Antoine Charpentier* (Ashgate Publishing).

DAVID SCHROEDER is University Research Professor at Dalhousie University in Halifax, Canada, in the Department of Music. He has published extensively on Haydn, Mozart, Schubert, music and film, Berg, and eighteenth-century aesthetics. His books include *Haydn and the Enlightenment* (1990), *Mozart in Revolt* (1999), *Cinema's Illusions, Opera's Allure* (2000) and *Our Schubert* (Scarecrow Press, forthcoming).

ROHAN STEWART-MACDONALD obtained his PhD from the University of Cambridge in 2001. He specializes in British music of the eighteenth and nineteenth centuries; his book on Clementi's keyboard sonatas, *New Perspectives on the Keyboard Sonatas of Muzio Clementi*, was published by Ut Orpheus Edizioni (2006). Current projects include an article on the symphonies of Charles Villiers Stanford for *Ad Parnassum* and a chapter for the forthcoming book *Domenico Scarlatti*, ed. W. Dean Sutcliffe and Massimiliano Sala. He is currently Director of Music at New Hall, Cambridge and Director of Studies in Music at both New Hall and Fitzwilliam College.

STEFANIE TCHAROS is Assistant Professor of Musicology at the University of California, Santa Barbara, where she specializes in early modern Italian musical culture, opera and related dramatic vocal types, aesthetics and genre theory. She holds a PhD in musicology from Princeton University, and received an Alvin Johnson AMS 50 Dissertation Fellowship in 2001–2. Her book, *Opera's Orbit: Conceptions of Musical Drama in Pre-Enlightenment Rome*, is forthcoming with Cambridge University Press. She has published articles and review essays in the *Journal of Musicology*, the *Cambridge Opera Journal* and *Music & Letters*.

RICHARD WILL is the author of *The Characteristic Symphony in the Age of Haydn and Beethoven* (2002), and of articles on eighteenth- and nineteenth-century music in *Music & Letters*, the *Journal of the American Musicological Society*, the *Beethoven Forum*, the *Musical Quarterly* and elsewhere. He is Associate Professor of Music at the University of Virginia.

CLAUDIA MAURER ZENCK is Professor of Music History at the University of Hamburg. She is the author of *Versuch über die wahre Art, Debussy zu analysieren* (1974), *Ernst Krenek – ein Komponist im Exil* (1980), *Vom Takt. Untersuchungen zur Theorie und kompositorischen Praxis im ausgehenden 18. und beginnenden 19. Jahrhundert* (2001) and *Dramma giocoso und deutsches Singspiel. Mozarts 'Così fan tutte' in frühen Abschriften und frühen Aufführungen* (2007). Her numerous edited books include *Der Orpheus-Mythos von der Antike bis zur Gegenwart* (2004) and *Musiktheater in Hamburg um 1800* (2005).

STEVEN ZOHN is Associate Professor of Music History at Temple University. He has published extensively on eighteenth-century topics, with an emphasis on Telemann and the Bach family, and is active as a performer on historical flutes. He is the author of *Music for a Mixed Taste: Style, Genre, and Meaning in Telemann's Instrumental Works* (2008).

EVA ZÖLLNER holds a PhD from the University of Hamburg with a dissertation on English oratorio after Handel. Currently working as a freelance lecturer, author and editor, she continues her research on music and musicians in eighteenth-century Britain, contributing to, among other publications, *The New Grove Dictionary of Music and Musicians, Revised Edition* and *The New Dictionary of National Biography*.

Editor's preface

The eighteenth century perhaps boasts a more remarkable coterie of totemic musical figures, and a more engaging combination of genres, styles and aesthetic orientations, than any century before or since. Modern Western audiences probably esteem more profoundly the collective accomplishments of great eighteenth-century musical figures than comparable accomplishments of great figures from both earlier and later. Yet huge swathes of its musical activity remain under-appreciated by musicians of all kinds – performers, composers, students and scholars (including eighteenth-century specialists) alike. The traditional dividing point at 1750 has been both scourge and inspiration, validating Bach and Handel, then Haydn and Mozart, as supreme practitioners of the late Baroque and high Classical styles, respectively, while implicitly or explicitly relegating others to an ill-defined periphery. Indeed, many eighteenth-century histories from recent times treat the Baroque and Classical periods in discrete volumes.[1] Whatever the merits of an approach determined by a mid-century partition, the sense of musical continuity across the century as a whole is invariably lost as a result, as is the inter-generic and intra-generic ebb and flow of musical development.[2] By rejecting Baroque and Classical periodizations as a means of organizing this volume – though not adopting a censorious approach to the use of the culturally embedded terms

1 See, for example, the Prentice Hall History of Music series – Claude Palisca, *Baroque Music* (3rd edn., Englewood Cliffs, NJ, 1991) and Reinhard G. Pauly, *Music in the Classic Period* (4th edn., Englewood Cliffs, NJ, 1999); the Macmillan Man & Society series – George J. Buelow (ed.), *The Late Baroque Era: From the 1680s to 1740* (London, 1993) and Neal Zaslaw (ed.), *The Classical Era: From the 1740s to the End of the Eighteenth Century* (London, 1989); and the Thames & Hudson series – Nicholas Anderson, *Baroque Music from Monteverdi to Handel* (London, 1994) and Julian Rushton, *Classical Music: A Concise History from Gluck to Beethoven* (London, 1986). Richard Taruskin brings the seventeenth and eighteenth centuries together in a single volume in *The Oxford History of Music, Volume 2: The Seventeenth and Eighteenth Centuries* (Oxford and New York, 2005). For an important edited volume dealing with the eighteenth century in its entirety, see Carl Dahlhaus (ed.), *Die Musik des 18. Jahrhunderts* (Laaber, 1985).

2 For a new perspective on periodization, focusing on a 'long' eighteenth century divided into three periods (*c.* 1670–1720, *c.* 1720–80 and *c.* 1780–1830), see James Webster, 'The Eighteenth Century as a Music-Historical Period?', *Eighteenth-Century Music*, 1 (2004), pp. 47–60. Daniel Heartz provides a magisterial assessment of European music from 1720 to 1780 in *Music in European Capitals: The Galant Style, 1720–1780* (New York, 2003).

themselves – it is hoped that eighteenth-century musical activities will be portrayed as richer, more diverse and more complex than is often the case in single- or multi-authored historical volumes. By eschewing a chronological approach across the volume as a whole, we encourage our reader to think less in terms of overtly teleological developments than of interacting and mutually stimulating musical cultures and practices.

Great men may have ensured the century's special place in our collective musical consciousness, but organizing a history primarily around their achievements would be no less problematic than structuring it around Baroque and Classical periods and ideals. Fundamentally, such an approach would run counter to the spirit of the eighteenth century, when the composer as a valorized, single-minded creative artist played second fiddle to the composer as a more down-to-earth provider of music, at least until notions of 'genius' came to the fore in late-eighteenth-century German-speaking countries.[3]

Instead of relying on temporal, periodic and composer-related phenomena, then, we organize our volume by genre; chapters are grouped according to traditional distinctions of music for the church, music for the theatre and music for the concert room that conditioned so much thinking, activity and output in the eighteenth century. As a counterbalance – and potential respite for those reading from cover to cover – we include 'interludes' on topics relevant to all genres (listening, thinking and writing; and performance), as well as a 'prelude' and 'postlude' on musical orientations and predilections in general at either end of the century (and, with an eye on historical continuity, a little earlier and later as well).

Complete comprehensiveness in the treatment of any given musical period is, of course, a historical chimera. But it remains our aspiration to cover as much ground as realistically possible in a single volume on eighteenth-century music, above all ground that has typically received less than its fair share of coverage in English-language publications, in an attempt to portray eighteenth-century musical life in a balanced, broad-based fashion. Thus, entire chapters (opera in Sweden and the serenata, for example) and sections of chapters (sacred music in Iberia and Latin America, the zarzuela, *Harmoniemusik* and so on) are devoted to areas that have generally been under-researched in comparison to traditional *loci* of scholarly focus, and numerous musicians illuminated who are often consigned to the dimly lit background. Nor are momentous musical monuments by compositional giants marginalized as a result. An approach that foregrounds norms of the day ultimately helps to explain the greatness of individual composers rather than to detract from it. At any rate, it is hoped that our volume will

3 On the latter point see, in particular, Mary Sue Morrow, *German Music Criticism in the Late Eighteenth Century: Aesthetic Issues in Instrumental Music* (Cambridge, 1997).

bring to life for the twenty-first-century reader the extraordinary diversity of eighteenth-century musical activities.

I am very grateful to David Wyn Jones for his planning of the volume and his solid advice throughout, both of which played a crucial role in bringing the project to fruition. I also record my thanks to the volume's contributors, and to Vicki Cooper and her team at Cambridge University Press, for their patience, tolerance and good humour. My wife, Celia Hurwitz-Keefe, and children, Abraham and Madeleine, have long endured my fascination with all things eighteenth century, and have willingly – and generously – shared much of it.

Simon P. Keefe
The University of Sheffield

• PRELUDE •

· 1 ·

The musical map of Europe *c.* 1700

STEPHEN ROSE

At the start of the eighteenth century, Europe displayed a panorama of musical styles and an array of performing opportunities. When Wolfgang Caspar Printz described a musical tour through central Europe in his *Phrynis Mytilenaeus* (1696), his account consisted of the names of leading musicians in each place. Certainly the achievements of individuals were important; but equally significant were the environments in which they worked. As Charles Burney wrote: 'Music, indeed like vegetation, flourishes differently in different climates; and in proportion to the culture and encouragement it receives.'[1] This chapter outlines some of the 'different climates' encountered by early eighteenth-century musicians, ranging from courtly patronage to the entrepreneurial possibilities in large towns. The connection between music and place is also seen in the national styles of composition and performance that were central to musicians' vocabulary in the period.

A crucial factor in the awareness of music's geography was the growth in international travel by the eighteenth century. Increasing numbers of musicians went abroad to work or to learn foreign styles. Aristocrats and connoisseurs also journeyed, particularly on the Grand Tour that English and German tourists took to France and Italy. For Johann David Heinichen, travel was a way to gain musical experience and nurture that 'rarest jewel', good taste. 'Why do we go through effort, danger and expense to travel around from nation to nation ...? ... Simply and solely to develop our good taste.'[2] International exchange also occurred in the trade in sheet music, particularly as the main music-publishing centres (Amsterdam and London) specialized in music from France and Italy.

Full consideration of two important aspects of this musical panorama, however, are beyond the scope of the present chapter. First, everywhere in Europe there was popular or traditional music, heard on the street, in the

1 Charles Burney, *A General History of Music from the Earliest Ages to the Present* (London, 1776–89), 4 vols., vol. 1, Preface.

2 Johann David Heinichen, *Der General-Bass in der Composition* (Dresden, 1728), p. 23. English trans. in George J. Buelow, *Thorough-Bass Accompaniment According to Johann David Heinichen*, 2nd edn. (Lincoln, NB, 1992), p. 325.

tavern and in the countryside. Much of this popular music circulated orally and was documented only when it intersected with the literate tradition; for this reason it is often overlooked by historians. Yet it was a constant aural backdrop to life, noted by travellers and irking or stimulating elite musicians. Elite and popular musicians sometimes quarrelled for reasons of economic rivalry; but other musicians found inspiration in the popular traditions. Franz Benda learned many new ideas about violin-playing from a Jewish tavern musician in Prague,[3] and Georg Philipp Telemann's fascination with the traditional music of Poland will be discussed at the end of this chapter.

A second topic largely absent from this chapter is the dissemination of Western musical culture beyond Europe. An array of missionaries, merchants, diplomats and colonists with musical talents took Western music to the New World and the Far East, often along routes established in previous centuries.[4] Domenico Zipoli (1688–1726) was an Italian organist recruited by the Jesuits to work in South America, where his compositions circulated widely; Roque Ceruti (c. 1683–1760; born in Milan) served a viceroy in Peru, writing dramatic works for the court, and later acted as *maestro de capilla* at cathedrals in Trujillo and Lima; Teodorico Pedrini (1671–1746) was a Lazarist missionary who became court musician to Emperor Kangxi of China. Such individuals added a cross-cultural dimension to the international exchange described in this chapter.

Types of musical environment

European musicians worked in a variety of environments, including churches, courts, theatres and charitable institutions such as orphanages. Some were employed as municipal musicians and some freelanced in major cities. Of these various places, the most significant in the eighteenth century were the courts and the emergent 'public sphere' in large towns and cities; both will be examined in the following section.

Courts, the personal households of aristocrats and rulers, remained among the most important centres for music throughout the eighteenth century, particularly in German-speaking lands. The musical lives of courts varied as much as the personalities and tastes of individual rulers. Although some courts were provincial backwaters, others were internationally famous for their music and hired performers from across Europe. The young Johann Joachim Quantz,

3 Douglas A. Lee, *A Musician at Court: An Autobiography of Franz Benda* (Warren, MI, 1998), p. 15.
4 Victor A. Coehlo, 'Music in New Worlds', in Tim Carter and John Butt (eds.), *The Cambridge History of Seventeenth-Century Music* (Cambridge, 2005), pp. 88–110.

as a trainee municipal musician, wanted to go to a court such as Dresden or Berlin, because he believed he 'could hear much more beautiful music there and learn much more' than in a town.[5] The Dresden court employed French and Italian as well as German musicians, and its orchestra pioneered the practice of each member performing exclusively on a single instrument, raising the standard of the playing.[6] Courts were also centres for opera, which by the early eighteenth century was prized by aristocrats as a way to show their education and status.

The life of a court musician – often hectic, dictated entirely by their relationship with their patron – is portrayed in the diary and other writings of the Weissenfels concertmaster Johann Beer (1655–1700). In his posthumously published *Musicalische Discurse*, he recounts: 'Today one must go with the court there, tomorrow somewhere else. There is no difference between day and night. Come storm, rain or sunshine it is all the same. Today one must be at church, tomorrow at table, the next day at the theatre.'[7] His diary records the swirl of events, night and day, with his young patron, Johann Georg of Saxony-Weissenfels (reigned 1698–1712). On 23 August 1698 Beer supplied a serenade for the princess and was rewarded with a silver watch. That night at 3 a.m. he went riding with his prince, resting under a tree in an oat-field. On 10 February 1699 the prince came to Beer's house at 5 a.m. after a gala, presumably expecting entertainment, and stayed for two hours with the oboists.[8] Beer had a strong personal relationship with his patron and consequently enjoyed many rewards such as the aforementioned silver watch. Indeed, it may have been with such gifts in mind that Beer wrote a chapter in his *Musicalische Discurse* on whether musicians could be ennobled.[9]

Despite all its advantages, court employment could also be very unpredictable. Musicians were at the whim of their patron, liable to be sacked when tastes changed or when their overlord died. As Beer explained: 'there are not a few courts which at the least disruption reduce their establishment, or merely dismiss their servants so that the court structure is dissolved by itself. Hence there are many court musicians who would like to move to the cities, and who would go there immediately if the cities paid as well as court. For what is more splendid in anything than constancy? ... I say: constant poverty could be more

5 Autobiography in Friedrich Wilhelm Marpurg, *Historisch-kritische Beyträge zur Aufnahme der Musik*, 1 (1754–5), p. 202; trans. with some inaccuracies in Paul Nettl, *Forgotten Musicians* (New York, 1951), p. 284.
6 Ortrun Landmann, 'The Dresden Hofkapelle During the Lifetime of Johann Sebastian Bach', *Early Music*, 17 (1989), pp. 19–20.
7 'Heute muß man mit dem Hof da/morgen dorthin. Tag und Nacht leiden da keinen Unterscheid. Sturmwind/Regen und Sonnenschein/gilt da eines wie das andere. Heute muß man in die Kirche/morgen zu der Tafel/übermorgen aufs *Theatrum*.' Johann Beer, *Musicalische Discurse* (Nuremberg, 1719), pp. 18–19.
8 Johann Beer, *Sein Leben, von ihm selbst erzählt*, ed. Adolf Schmiedecke (Göttingen, 1965).
9 James Hardin, *Johann Beer* (Boston, MA, 1983), pp. 13–14.

blissful than transitory riches.'[10] Similar opinions were held by Telemann, who moved to the stability of a municipal post in Frankfurt am Main after working at the Sorau and Eisenach courts. As he recollected in his 1740 autobiography: 'Whoever wants a lifetime position should settle in a republic.'[11] In an earlier autobiography he captured the fickle nature of court life: 'In the morning the weather seems calm and cheery, but in the evening cloudy and dreary.'[12] How drastically the courtly climate could change is evident from J. S. Bach's experience at the Cöthen court, where Prince Leopold lost his enthusiasm for music on marrying an unmusical wife.

The patron's absolute power over the court was symbolized by the strict hierarchy imposed on courtiers and court servants. Often this ranking was listed in ordinances and enacted at mealtimes or in processions.[13] Telemann proudly recorded how at Eisenach he made his way up the hierarchy, gaining the title of secretary and a seat at the dining table of the marshals.[14] Court employees often jostled for rank, with drawn-out disputes about precedence. Printz's novel *Pancalus* (1691) recounts how, at the fictitious court of the Marquis of Pomponio, the court-tailor, the wine-steward, the cooks, the barber and the gardener all try to leap-frog the musicians in the court hierarchy. Much later in the century at the court of the Archbishop of Salzburg, Mozart resented being made to eat at the same table as the servants, below the valets, but above the confectioner and cooks.[15] Mozart's experience symbolized the limited personal freedom of many court musicians: although they contributed in indispensable ways to the prestige of courts, musicians were liable to be treated as the feudal property of their patron.

The opposite pole from court music was found in the 'public sphere' emerging in large towns and cities. Traditionally towns had employed musicians in churches and schools or as municipal instrumentalists; thus J. S. Bach served as organist in Arnstadt and Mühlhausen, and as cantor (school music teacher) and

10 'sind derer Höfe nicht wenig/welche bey der geringsten *ruptur* den Staat *reduci*ren/oder doch ihren Dienern dergestalt abbrechen/daß die Hof-Staat/*vel sua sponte* zerfliessen muß. In *regard* dessen sehnen sich viel Fürstliche *Musici* nach denen Städten/würden auch/im Fall die Städte so starck als der Hof/bezahleten/ sich dort bald einfinden. Denn was mag wol vortrefflicher in einer Sache seyn/als der Bestand? ... Ich sage: Die beständige Armuth könne glückseeliger geheissen werden/als ein unbeständiger Reichthum.' Beer, *Musicalische Discurse*, p. 18.

11 'Wer Zeit Lebens fest sitzen wolle, müsse sich in einer Republick niederlassen.' Autobiography published in Johann Mattheson, *Grundlage einer Ehren- Pforte* (Hamburg, 1740), p. 363, reprint Kassel, 1969.

12 'Qu'au matin l'air pour nous est tranquille & sérein, /Mais sombre vers le soir & de nuages plein.' Quoted in Johann Mattheson, *Grosse General-Bass-Schule oder exemplarische Organisten- Probe* (Hamburg, 1731), p. 168.

13 John Spitzer and Neal Zaslaw, *The Birth of the Orchestra: History of an Institution, 1650–1815* (Oxford and New York, 2004), pp. 214–15, 229.

14 Mattheson, *Grundlage einer Ehren-Pforte*, p. 363.

15 Emily Anderson (ed. and trans.), *The Letters of Mozart and His Family*, 3rd edn. (London, 1985), pp. 713–14 (letter of 17 March 1781).

civic music director in Leipzig. Increasingly, however, musicians tapped the collective market of urban dwellers for concerts, music theatre, sheet music and tuition. The best example of this new market for music was in early-eighteenth-century London, although elements of it were also found in cities such as Hamburg, Leipzig, Paris and Venice. The term 'public sphere' was coined by Jürgen Habermas, who studied the processes whereby 'the sphere of private people come together as a public', giving rise to public debate on cultural and political matters.[16] In London, the critical factors included the dwindling power of the royal court and the rise of alternative institutions where the powerful or wealthy could meet or communicate with each other, such as coffee-houses and newspapers. Similar trends occurred in musical life: by 1690 the English court ceased to be the major patron of music, partly owing to its weak finances, partly owing to the indifference of the new monarchs. Already in the late seventeenth century court musicians were regularly moonlighting from their regular employment, augmenting their court stipends by running concert series (as with John Banister) or working for the theatre (as with Henry Purcell).[17] Public musical life continued to develop in the early eighteenth century in the form of concert series and music-meetings, and music played an important part in the theatres and pleasure-gardens.

Harold Love has analyzed the public market for music in London, showing that the 'public sphere' as defined by Habermas could be more accurately described as a multitude of tightly knit groups that sometimes interlocked.[18] Different concert series attracted different types of clientele. Thomas Southerne in his play *The Wives' Excuse* (1692) portrayed a concert-room as the place where the *beau monde* of London go to gossip and flirt. Other concert series were run on subscription with deliberately high prices to ensure social exclusivity. As *The Female Tatler* reported in September 1709: 'at *Consorts* of Note the Prices are extravagant purposely to keep out inferiour People.'[19] Musical connoisseurs and enthusiasts, by contrast, attended the private clubs known as music-meetings. From 1724 a musical society met for concerts every Wednesday evening at the Castle Tavern in Paternoster Row. The serious tone of the society is evident from its by-laws of 1731, which divide the membership into performers and auditors (a maximum of 160 of the latter). Only members and their guests could attend concerts. New members could join only if they

16 Jürgen Habermas, *The Structural Transformation of the Public Sphere: An Inquiry into a Category of Bourgeois Society*, trans. Thomas Burger with the assistance of Frederick Lawrence (Cambridge, MA, 1989), p. 27.

17 Stephen Rose, 'Music in the Market-Place', in Tim Carter and John Butt (eds.), *The Cambridge History of Seventeenth-Century Music* (Cambridge, 2005), pp. 56, 61.

18 Harold Love, 'How Music Created a Public', *Criticism*, 46 (2004), pp. 257–71.

19 Quoted in Rosamund McGuinness, 'Musical Provocation in Eighteenth-Century London: The *British Apollo*', *Music & Letters*, 68 (1987), p. 340.

were nominated by an existing member and if the majority of the membership approved the nomination. The by-laws specified who was responsible for organizing each aspect of the weekly concert, and fines were imposed on members who arrived late, or who changed seats or spoke during a performance.[20] Such strict regulations suggest a different clientele from the gossipy audience satirized by Southerne. Other musical societies specialized in particular repertories: the Academy of Ancient Music (originally the Academy of Vocal Music, founded in 1726) performed sacred polyphony from the sixteenth and seventeenth centuries.

Although the public market for music in London was fragmented, its vibrancy attracted many continental musicians. As Johann Mattheson declared in 1713: 'anyone who wants to be eminent in music at the present time takes himself to England.'[21] Musicians who travelled to London included Germans (notably George Frideric Handel, but also Jakob Greber, Melchior Hoffmann, Jakob Kremberg, Johann Sigismund Kusser and Johann Christoph Pepusch); musicians born or trained in France (Charles Dieupart, Jean-Baptiste Loeillet); and, above all, hundreds of Italian singers and instrumentalists. Italian singers included the castratos Farinelli (visited 1734–7), Nicolini (visited 1708–12, 1714–17) and Senesino (visited 1720–8, 1730–6), and the sopranos Faustina Bordoni (visited 1726–8) and Francesca Cuzzoni (visited 1722–8). Italian instrumentalists and composers included Nicola Cosimi (visited 1701–5), Francesca Geminiani (in England 1714–32 and intermittently thereafter), Nicola Francesco Haym (resident 1701–29) and Nicola Porpora (visited 1733–6). The main reason for this influx of Italians was the lucrative remuneration available in London. Nicolini, for instance, was paid 800 guineas for the 1708–9 season and would have earned still more from benefit concerts and private performances.[22] Such high fees reflected the competition between London theatres, whose impresarios relied on famous or novel virtuosos to entice an audience. Most Italians stayed for only a few seasons before moving on to other engagements, another indication of the premium placed on novelty.[23]

Many of the foreign performers coming to London were unaccustomed to the entrepreneurial ingenuity required in its musical world. Johann Siegmund Kusser, arriving from Germany in 1704, wrote down a list of advice apparently

20 *The By-Laws of the Musical Society, at the Castle-Tavern in Pater-Noster-Row* [London, 1731], British Library, classmark 557*.d.43.(2).
21 'Wer bey diesen Zeiten etwas in der *Music* zu *præsti*ren vermeinet/der begibt sich nach Engelland.' Johann Mattheson, *Das neu-eröffnete Orchestre* (Hamburg, 1713), p. 211.
22 Lowell Lindgren, 'Handel's London – Italian Musicians and Librettists', in Donald Burrows (ed.), *The Cambridge Companion to Handel* (Cambridge, 1997), p. 89.
23 *Ibid.*, p. 83.

given to him by Jakob Greber.[24] Kusser noted which impresarios to contact (John Rich and Thomas Betterton) and how to negotiate a contract ('At the signing of the contract, announce that you cannot remain longer than about six weeks ... Don't sign a new contract before the old one has elapsed, and in the meantime point out to them occasionally how they are profiting from you ... Retain your freedom and have it in the contract that you are permitted to perform outside the theatre whenever you wish'). Kusser's list also recommends suitable behaviour ('Be proud but greet everyone politely, for the English like to be flattered'), choosing music that fits English taste ('no pathos, certainly, and short, short recitatives'; 'sing an English aria from time to time') and flattering English sensibilities ('Praise the deceased Purcell to the skies and say there has never been the like of him'). Later Kusser moved to Dublin, where he described the requisites for a concert: tickets had to be printed and sold; change was required, along with a pair of scales to weigh coins; guards had to be hired for the entrance, and the upper doors of the theatre should be nailed shut (presumably to prevent non-payers entering). Musicians had to consider all these practicalities in the new world of public concerts.

Yet patronage remained important in the musical life of early-eighteenth-century London; as much as at court, musicians needed to cultivate the favour of powerful individuals. The opera-companies depended on royal and aristocratic support: the Royal Academy of Musick received an annual subsidy of £1,000 from the monarch and most of its shareholders were aristocrats. Several foreign musicians lived in the household of aristocrats: Cosimi and Haym received food and lodging from Wriothesley Russell, 2nd Duke of Bedford; and Handel, in his early years in London, was the private guest of the Earl of Burlington and 'Mr Andrews of Barn-Elms'. Performances at noble households and private teaching could make up a large part of a musician's income. Indeed the violinist Geminiani 'was seldom heard in public during his long residence in England. His compositions, scholars, and the presents he received from the great, whenever he could be prevailed upon to play at their houses, were his chief support.'[25] Kusser's advice included recommendations on etiquette when dining and conversing with the nobility after performing at their homes. As Simon McVeigh notes, the appearances of musicians at public concerts acted as 'both advertisement and validation' for these private activities of teaching and house-concerts.[26]

The defining feature of the public sphere in Habermas' analysis is the emergence of coherent public opinion from an array of individual viewpoints.

24 Harold E. Samuel, 'A German Musician Comes to London in 1704', *Musical Times*, 122 (1981), pp. 591–3.
25 Burney, *A General History of Music*, vol. 4, p. 643.
26 Simon McVeigh, 'Italian Violinists in Eighteenth-Century London', in Reinhard Strohm (ed.), *The Eighteenth-Century Diaspora of Italian Music and Musicians* (Turnhout, 2001), p. 153.

In the case of England, Habermas identified moral weeklies such as *The Spectator* and *The Tatler* as a 'key phenomenon', educating the public with essays on philosophy, literature and art.[27] In musical life, too, the periodical press helped to shape public taste. The moral weeklies covered music among other topics, with Joseph Addison writing a series of critical essays on opera in *The Spectator*. In England, however, the discussion of music was scattered across a range of publications from short essays to learned treatises;[28] there was no journal dedicated specifically to the critical discussion of music until the early nineteenth century.

It was in northern Germany that the first periodical devoted to the discussion of music appeared, Johann Mattheson's *Critica musica* (1722–5). Mattheson was the secretary to the British ambassador in Hamburg and was heavily influenced by literary developments in London such as the moral weeklies. Indeed, his weekly magazine *Der Vernünftler* (1713) contained German translations of articles from *The Tatler* and *The Spectator*. Many of his musical writings share the moral weeklies' mission to speak to the lay reader. His first musical treatise, *Das neu-eröffnete Orchestre* (1713), is intended to demystify music theory for the amateur: the title-page promises 'instruction whereby a *galant homme* can gain a complete grasp of the majesty and worth of noble music, form his taste in the same, understand technical terms, and argue skilfully in this splendid branch of knowledge'.[29] Mattheson's musical periodical *Critica musica* is aimed at more specialist readers. It contains an annotated translation of the Raguenet–Le Cerf dispute over French versus Italian styles (see p. 20); discussion of compositional techniques such as canon; and musical news from European cities (reports of opera performances, obituaries of distinguished musicians and reviews of new publications). Much of *Critica musica* is filled with Mattheson's own polemics, defending his previous treatises and publishing the opinion of other musicians on them; consequently the journal is somewhat inward-looking, more like a learned journal than a moral weekly.[30] Yet *Critica musica* paved the way for subsequent periodicals in Germany, such as Mattheson's own *Der Musicalische Patriot* (1728), Scheibe's *Der critische Musikus* (1737–40), Mizler's *Musikalische Bibliothek* (1736–54) and Marpurg's *Historisch-kritische*

27 Habermas, *The Structural Transformation*, pp. 41–2.
28 Thomas McGeary, 'Music Literature', in H. Diack Johnstone and Roger Fiske (eds.), *The Blackwell History of Music in Britain: The Eighteenth Century* (Oxford, 1990), pp. 397–421, at 397.
29 'Anleitung/Wie ein *Galant Homme* einen vollkommenen Begriff von der Hoheit und Würde der edlen *Music* erlangen/seinen *Gout* darnach *formiren*/die *Terminos technicos* verstehen und geschicklich von dieser vortrefflichen Wissenschafft *raisonniren* möge.'
30 Imogen Fellinger, 'Mattheson als Begründer der ersten Musikzeitschrift (*Critica musica*)', in George J. Buelow and Hans Joachim Marx (eds.), *New Mattheson Studies* (Cambridge, 1983), pp. 179–97.

Beyträge zur Aufnahme der Musik (1754–62). These serials pioneered many features of music journalism, including reviews of new publications, biographical articles and reports from leading musical centres; they helped shape a collective sense of musical taste, first among connoisseurs and then across wider circles of music-lovers.

During the eighteenth century the public sphere increased in significance for musicians, although courtly employment remained important. To take some examples from the second half of the century: Joseph Haydn spent the 1750s as a freelance musician in Vienna, worked for the next three decades at the Esterházy court, then in the 1790s freelanced in London. Wolfgang Amadeus Mozart served at the Salzburg court until 1781 (albeit with many journeys to perform at other courts and cities), then worked as a freelance musician in Vienna. Like countless other musicians, Haydn and Mozart sought in their career choices to profit from the diversity of environments for music-making that Europe offered.

National styles

The varied musical geography of Europe in the early eighteenth century was symbolized by the styles of composition and performance associated with different countries. In the sixteenth century there seem to have been fewer differences between national traditions, with a *lingua franca* of polyphonic vocal composition. By 1700, however, Italy, France and Germany each had a distinctive musical style; there was also an awareness of the traditional music of such peoples as the Poles and Scots. (Although Italy and Germany did not exist as nation-states at the time, they were still recognised as territories with distinctive cultures.) The national styles were disseminated by foreign musicians on their travels and were studied by apprentice musicians who went abroad. Around 1700 the Italian style was dominant in Europe, with countless Italian expatriates promoting opera and string-playing north of the Alps. But national styles were not the exclusive property of musicians from the relevant country; they could also be learned by foreigners, as one of the many resources in a composer's vocabulary. Some musicians adopted wholesale the style of another country: Handel was born in Germany, but spent most of his career bringing Italian opera to London; and the violinist Jean Baptiste Woulmyer was of Flemish origin, but learned French techniques of string-playing in Paris, Frenchified his surname to Volumier, and then brought the French styles of performance to the Berlin and Dresden courts. Other musicians promoted a synthesis of French and Italian styles, notably François Couperin and several German musicians including Quantz and J. S. Bach.

The characteristics of the different national styles can be observed in the surviving repertory, and were also discussed by writers of the time. Appraisal of national styles was a mainstay of the emergent critical literature on music. In France, François Raguenet and Jean-Laurent Le Cerf de La Viéville debated fiercely the merits of French and Italian styles. In Germany, authors such as Beer, Mattheson and Quantz described national styles as part of their advice to listeners on how to judge music; their tone was less polemical than the French writers, perhaps because Germany – sandwiched between France and Italy – was more sympathetic to foreign styles. All such discussions, however, were liable to stereotype either musical or national characteristics.

Italian music had a dual appeal, based on the success of Italian opera-singers (epitomized by castratos) and the power of Italian violin-playing (epitomized by such figures as Corelli and Vivaldi). Many early-eighteenth-century writers acknowledged that the Italians excelled over other nations as musicians: 'no folk under the sun are more inclined by nature to music than the Italians.'[31] A key factor in this supremacy was the innate musicality of the Italian language. 'They are naturally disposed more to singing than us Germans, because their language is full of vowels, whereas German is full of consonants.'[32] As for composition, the Italian style was characterized by its bold modulations and lively expression of affections;[33] these could be seen in the extravagant harmonic progressions of an instrumental Adagio, or in the alternation of contrasting sections in a Corelli concerto grosso. In instrumental and vocal music alike, Italian performers were renowned for their solo virtuosity and profuse ornamentation. Beer reported that 'out of twenty bars, scarcely half are without coloraturas or trills'.[34] Antonio Vivaldi specialized in pyrotechnics on the violin: 'He got with his fingers so close to the bridge that there was not the width of a straw left and no room for the bow – and this happened on all four strings with fugues and at an incredible speed.'[35] Quantz, however, bemoaned that the violin virtuosity of Vivaldi and Tartini had taken them away from a true singing style.[36]

The French style was virtually synonymous with the music of Jean-Baptiste Lully (1632–87). Even though Lully was Italian by birth, his close relationship

31 'kein Volck unter der Sonnen von Natur der *music* mehr ergeben/als eben die Italiener.' Beer, *Musicalische Discurse*, p. 60.

32 'Zu dem seynd sie von *natur disposter* zum singen als die Teutsche/weil ihre Sprache voller *vocalen*, hingegen die unsere voller *consonanten* ist.' *Ibid.*, p. 60.

33 Oliver Strunk and Leo Treitler (eds.), *Source Readings in Music History*, rev. edn. (New York, 1998), pp. 675–6.

34 'Unter zwantzig *Tacten* kaum einen halben ohne *collor*iren oder *trillo* aushalten.' Beer, *Musicalische Discurse*, p. 60.

35 Walter Kolneder, *Antonio Vivaldi: Documents of His Life and Works*, trans. Kurt Michaelis (New York, 1982), p. 10.

36 Johann Joachim Quantz, *Versuch einer Anweisung die Flöte traversiere zu spielen* (Berlin, 1752); trans. Edward R. Reilly as *On Playing the Flute* (London, 1985), p. 325.

with Louis XIV and his control of the court musical apparatus meant that his style gained official status. Aspects of the French style epitomized by Lully's output included the French overture (with its grand dotted rhythms marking the entry of the monarch) and an array of dance movements (including the bourrée, gavotte, loure, minuet and rigaudon). As Quantz wrote, French compositions are much better suited to dancing than those of any other nation.[37] French melodies were often lyrical, with a simple and sweet (*douceur*) quality; ornaments were frequently specified by the composer.[38] For Le Cerf de La Viéville, in his 1704 comparison of Italian and French music, French music was defined by its sense of beauty and good taste (*bon goût*), achieved via an orderly, natural yet reasoned manner.[39]

The French were also known for their performance styles. The string-players were renowned for their disciplined ensemble and bowing techniques (in particular, the down-bow on the first beat of the bar); Quantz commented that the 'distinct execution' of French instrumentalists made them better ripienists in an orchestra than Italians.[40] French musicians were also recognized across Europe as pioneers on wind instruments, notably the oboe and bassoon, but also new versions of the recorder and transverse flute.

Between the two poles of Italian and French music lay the German style. Traditionally German music was regarded as grave and contrapuntal. According to the Jesuit scholar Athanasius Kircher, the Germans favoured 'a style that is serious, moderate, sober and choral'.[41] Heinichen noted the German love of 'artful counterpoint' and their belief that 'art is only that which is difficult to compose'.[42] As for performance, Beer declared that the Germans held their own on certain wind and brass instruments such as the trumpet, trombone, cornett (*Zinck*) and recorder (*Flöte*); he also noted the virtuosity of Germanic violin solos such as Biber's.[43]

By the 1720s, however, German musicians gained a reputation for a mixed style of composition and performance that combined elements of French and Italian music. Such a style had already been pioneered by Georg Muffat in his *Armonico tributo* (1682), where the texture of the Corellian concerto grosso is joined with the rhythms and forms of French dances. Mattheson may have had Muffat's example in mind when he commented in 1713 that Germans strive to combine

37 Quantz, *On Playing the Flute*, p. 329.

38 David Tunley, *François Couperin and 'The Perfection of Music'* (Aldershot, 2004), pp. 23–37.

39 Strunk and Treitler (eds.), *Source Readings*, pp. 679–82.

40 Quantz, *On Playing the Flute*, p. 328.

41 Athanasius Kircher, *Musurgia universalis* (Rome, 1650), quoted in Strunk and Treitler (eds.), *Source Readings*, p. 709.

42 Heinichen, *Der General-Bass in der Composition*, pp. 10, 12.

43 Beer, *Musicalische Discurse*, pp. 60, 64.

the Italian and French styles.[44] The Dresden court was an important crucible in the formation of the mixed style: its ensemble included French, German and Italian performers, and the concertmaster Johann Georg Pisendel (who had travelled widely abroad) was later credited by Quantz with developing such a mixed style. Quantz studied with Pisendel and subsequently expounded the benefits of a mixed style of composition and performance in his *Versuch* (1752).

Germans saw several advantages in the mixed style. In the dedication to *Florilegium primum* (1695) Muffat saw his mingling of national styles as 'a prelude to the unity, the dear peace, desired by all people' – a poignant hope in a century when the Habsburg powers had frequently been at war with France.[45] On a more pragmatic level, Heinichen suggested that 'a felicitious mélange of Italian and French taste would affect the ear most forcefully and must succeed over all other tastes of the world'.[46] Quantz regarded the mixed style of composition as having a universal appeal while also being intrinsically German: 'If one has the necessary discernment to choose the best from the styles of different countries, a *mixed style* results that, without overstepping the bounds of modesty, could well be called *the German style*.' In such a mixed style, 'each nation finds something with which it has an affinity, and which thus can never displease it'. Quantz proudly asserted that this mixed style 'must certainly be more universal', 'more pleasing' and 'the very best';[47] in his pride, we might detect shades of early German nationalism, possibly stemming from his place at the powerful Prussian court.

Some writers of the time attributed the different national styles to the climate of individual countries. Kircher argued that musical styles reflected the 'natural temperament' of a people, which in turn depended on 'the spirit of a place and natural tendency'. Thus 'the Germans for the most part are born under a frozen sky and acquire a temperament that is serious, strong, constant, solid and toilsome, to which qualities their music conforms'. By contrast 'the most temperate clime' of Italy produces 'a style completely perfect and temperate'. According to Kircher's essentialist view, one nationality cannot appreciate another's music: 'the style of the Italians and French pleases the Germans very little, and that of the Germans hardly pleases the Italians or French.' He attributed these prejudices to 'patriotism and inordinate affection to both nation and country'; he also noted that each country was accustomed by long-standing habit to enjoy only its own music.[48]

44 Mattheson, *Das neu-eröffnete Orchestre*, p. 208.

45 David K. Wilson (ed.), *Georg Muffat on Performance Practice* (Bloomington, IN, 2001), pp. 86–7.

46 Heinichen, *Der General-Bass in der Composition*, pp. 10–11; trans. Buelow, *Thorough-Bass Accompaniment*, p. 316.

47 Quantz, *On Playing the Flute*, pp. 341–2.

48 Strunk and Treitler (eds.), *Source Readings*, pp. 709–10.

Contrary to Kircher's assertion, foreign styles were often highly popular, particularly in England and Germany. By far the dominant style was the Italian, although French music also appealed to some areas and patrons. The dominance of the Italian style is evident in the employment of Italian musicians all over Europe and beyond, as well as the travels of numerous musicians to study in Italy. Opera-singers and virtuoso violinists were the dual ambassadors of Italian music abroad. In particular, as Reinhard Strohm explains, 'Italian opera, and the patronage which supported it, became the main basis for the Italian musical diaspora'.[49] Around 1700, many courts and aristocrats considered the cultivation of Italian opera a sign of learning and prestige. Numerous German courts staged operas: the Ansbach court employed the castrato Francesco Antonio Mamiliano Pistocchi to organize operas (1697–9); the Munich and Hanover courts staged operas by Agostino Steffani in the 1680s and 1690s; and the wedding of crown prince Friedrich August II of Saxony in 1719 was marked by several Italian operas at Dresden. Courts on the peripheries of Europe were particularly keen to prove their cultural credentials by staging opera. From the mid-1730s the Russian court at St Petersburg sponsored Italian operas, hiring a succession of Italian *maestri di cappella* such as Francesco Araja, Vincenzo Manfredini, Baldassare Galuppi, Tommaso Traetta and Giovanni Paisiello.[50] Cities in central Europe also hosted Italian opera, with Italian troupes performing in Prague from 1724 and in Breslau (present-day Wrocław) from 1725.[51]

Italian opera singers rarely stayed in the same place for more than a few seasons. One reason for this mobility was the intermittent nature of most operatic productions. Court opera was usually arranged for festivals such as dynastic marriages, and many productions in towns ran in short seasons during trade-fairs or holidays. At towns and courts alike, opera companies were liable to be dissolved when they ran into financial trouble. Another reason for the rapid turnover of Italian singers was the audiences' clamour for novelty, seen particularly in the London theatres discussed above. Hence many Italian opera singers travelled extensively, whether as individuals or as part of a troupe; usually their journeys radiated out from northern Italian cities such as Venice, where musicians were recruited and new repertory obtained.

The value placed on Italian opera was evident in the high salaries paid to singers. I have already mentioned the substantial fees that Italian castratos and

49 Reinhard Strohm, 'Italian Operisti North of the Alps *c.*1700–1750', in Strohm (ed.), *The Eighteenth-Century Diaspora*, p. 6.

50 Marina Ritzarev and Anna Porfireva, 'The Italian Diaspora in Eighteenth-Century Russia', in Strohm (ed.), *The Eighteenth-Century Diaspora*, pp. 211–53.

51 Daniel E. Freeman, *The Opera Theater of Count Franz Anton von Sporck in Prague* (Stuyvesant, NY, 1992); Renate Brockpähler, *Handbuch zur Geschichte der Barockoper in Deutschland* (Emsdetten, 1964), pp. 98–104.

sopranos received from London theatres, which competed to attract audiences with famous or novel singers. A similar premium was paid to the Italian opera singers recruited by the Dresden court in preparation for the wedding celebrations of 1719. On being hired in 1717, the Kapellmeister Antonio Lotti and his wife (the singer, Santa Stella) received 10,500 thalers, the castrato Senesino 7,000 thalers and the soprano Margherita Catarina Zani 4,000 thalers. By comparison, in 1719 the German Kapellmeister Johann Christoph Schmidt and the concert master Jean Baptiste Volumier each received 1,200 thalers.[52] Such a disparity in pay was resented by the non-Italians, but reflected the competitive international market for opera singers. Indeed, lengthy negotiations and the intervention of agents were often necessary before the leading castratos could be hired. In 1719 Handel went to Dresden to recruit singers such as Senesino for London; in 1734 Lord Essex, British ambassador to the king of Sardinia at Turin, helped negotiate Farinelli's transfer to London.

Italian instrumentalists also travelled north of the Alps. As might be expected from the land of Corelli and Vivaldi, many of these instrumentalists were violinists (such as Locatelli, Geminiani and Veracini), although there were also cellists and double-bass players. Such Italians might be employed as orchestral leaders: in 1698 Torelli was employed as *maestro di concerto* by the Margave of Brandenburg at the Ansbach court; in 1749 Giuseppe Passerini was hired as the leader of the Edinburgh musical society. Francesco Maria Veracini made his name in London by playing solos in the theatre, while Geminiani made a living there from private recitals, publishing his compositions and teaching. Italian violinists were particularly popular in England, for they offered the prized Italian style without the problematic associations of opera. The diaspora of Italian string players also reflected the surfeit of well-trained instrumentalists supplied by the conservatories of Naples and Venice; many young Italians took advantage of the excellent training available in their country, then sought their fortune north of the Alps.[53]

Although Italian musicians were popular in England and Germany, they also raised patriotic hackles. Writers in both countries bemoaned the premium placed on foreign styles simply because of their novelty. As Beer explained: 'the foreign donkey is valued more highly than the native horse.'[54] Johann Kuhnau satirized the Germans' susceptibility to the Italian style in his novel *Der musikalische Quacksalber* (1700): here, the eponymous musical quack is an incompetent German musician, who hides his deficiencies by pretending to be

52 Moritz Fürstenau, *Zur Geschichte der Musik und des Theaters am Hofe zu Dresden* (Dresden, 1861–2), 2 vols., vol. 2, pp. 105, 134.

53 Spitzer and Zaslaw, *The Birth of the Orchestra*, p. 179.

54 '*asinus peregrinus*, höher *æstimi*rt wird/als *equus domesticus*.' Beer, *Musicalische Discurse*, p. 61.

that most desirable of commodities, a visiting Italian virtuoso. In England, Joseph Addison lamented in *The Spectator* that 'at present, our Notions of Musick are so very uncertain, that we do not know what it is we like; only, in general, we are transported with any thing that is not *English*'.[55] Another issue of *The Spectator* satirized a woman who is 'a great Pretender to Musick, and very ignorant of it; but far gone in the *Italian* Taste'. Her ignorance is exposed when she hears a setting of lines by the classical author Tully and assumes that the words are Italian rather than Latin. 'To be short, my Wife was extremely pleased with it; said the *Italian* was the only Language for Musick ... and how pretty the Accent is of that Language; with the rest that is said by Rote on that occasion.'[56]

Italian opera in London sparked off a further range of anxieties, ranging from fear of the destabilizing influence of Catholics to disgust at the unmanliness of castratos.[57] Richard Steele described opera as 'unadorn'd Effeminacy' and 'Popery in Wit' (epilogue to his comedy *The Tender Husband*, 1705). John Dennis, who was known for his hostility to Catholic Europe, saw Italian opera as a threat to English morals, particularly during the current war with the Continent: 'At a time when we are contending with our Enemies for our very Being, we are aukwardly Aping their Luxuries and their Vices.' Invoking the dichotomy of sense versus reason, Dennis worried that, without the manly rationality of English poetry, opera was 'meer sensual Delight, utterly incapable of informing the Understanding, or of reforming the Will'.[58] But Dennis' qualms were not widely shared by theatre-goers or impresarios in London, where Italian opera remained popular until the 1730s.

The musical dominance of Italy in the early eighteenth century was reinforced by the many journeys made there by northern aristocrats, scholars and musicians. The cities of Italy were among the main destinations on the Grand Tour, undertaken by many young men and a few women to broaden their culture and for general amusement. Italy, according to Addison, 'is the great School of Musick and Painting, and contains in it all the noblest Productions of Statuary and Architecture both Ancient and Modern'.[59] But alongside its classical and cultural heritage, Italy offered more sensual pleasures to the young traveller. One guidebook warned that Italy can 'turne a *Sainte* into a *Devill* and deprave the best natures, if one will abandon himselfe to pleasure, and become

55 *The Spectator*, 21 March 1711.

56 *The Spectator*, 2 November 1711.

57 Lowell Lindgren, 'Critiques of Opera in London, 1705–1719', in Alberto Colzani *et al.* (eds.), *Il melodramma italiano in Italia e in Germania nell'età barocca* (Como, 1995), pp. 143–65.

58 John Dennis, *Essay on the Operas After the Italian Manner* (London, 1706), pp. 1–2.

59 Joseph Addison, *Remarks on Several Parts of Italy, &c. in the Years 1701, 1702, 1703* (London, 1705), Preface.

a prey to dissolute courses & wantonnes'.[60] Most travellers headed to Venice (especially for the carnival season) and to Rome (to view the Classical remains, the papal court and the religious observances), although Turin, Bologna and Naples also featured on many itineraries. Music was a major source of interest and amusement, including performances at the opera-houses and the *ospedali* (orphanages) of Venice, as well as private concerts and outdoor serenades in Rome. Indeed, foreign tourists were vital to the Italian musical economy, being a mainstay of the Venetian opera-houses as well as buying sheet music and tuition. Vivaldi was adept at tapping the market of visiting dilettantes. In 1739 Charles de Brosses, a visiting French jurist, remarked that 'Vivaldi has entered into a close friendship with me, in order to sell me his concertos at a rather high price', while in 1715 the German visitor Johann Friedrich Uffenbach was sold concertos and also tuition by Vivaldi. 'To let me hear [the concertos] better, he wanted to teach me how to play them and visit me occasionally for this purpose, starting this day.'[61] Another foreign dilettante, the young Scottish gentleman Sir John Clerk of Penicuik, studied with Corelli and Pasquini during his stay in Rome in 1697–8.

Visits to Italy were crucial in forming the taste of young connoisseurs, who might then recruit Italian musicians for home. Wriothesley Russell, soon to be 2nd Duke of Bedford, visited Rome in 1698–9, where he enjoyed serenatas and purchased musical scores, and on his return to England he employed the Italian instrumentalists Nicola Cosimi and Nicola Francesco Haym (see p. 9 above).[62] The crown prince of Saxony, Friedrich August II, visited Venice in 1712, 1713 and 1716–17; on the third visit he was instructed by his father to recruit opera singers for the 1719 wedding celebrations. This led to Lotti, Senesino and other singers being employed by Dresden; the crown prince also hired the opera composer Heinichen and the violinist Veracini, despite his father's opposition.[63]

Many German musicians also travelled to Italy to work or study there, including George Frideric Handel, Johann Adolf Hasse, Johann David Heinichen, Georg Muffat, Johann Georg Pisendel, Wolfgang Caspar Printz, Johann Joachim Quantz and Sylvius Leopold Weiss, to name but a few. Often such visitors sought out different parts of Italy for their musical specialities: Venice for its opera-houses and for Vivaldi; Rome for the Corellian school of violin-playing; Naples for its traditions of opera seria and opera buffa. Many northern

60 James Howell, *Instructions and Directions for Forren Travell* (London, 1650), p. 84.

61 Kolneder, *Antonio Vivaldi*, pp. 81–2.

62 Lowell Lindgren, 'Nicola Cosimi in London, 1701–1705', *Studi musicali*, 11 (1982), p. 232.

63 Fürstenau, *Zur Geschichte*, vol. 2, pp. 98–101; John Walter Hill, *The Life and Works of Francesco Maria Veracini* (Ann Arbor, MI, 1979), pp. 18–19, 435–6.

musicians visited Italy in the company or with the support of aristocratic patrons. In 1661 Printz toured Rome, Venice and Naples as the chamber servant of a Dutch nobleman.[64] In 1716–17 the Dresden violinist Pisendel visited Venice in the retinue of the crown prince of Saxony, and was then sent on to Rome at Saxon command to learn from violinists such as Antonio Montanari.[65]

Many of these northerners said they had studied in Italy, and it is useful to explore what 'study' might have meant for musicians who had already reached considerable accomplishment in their homeland. Some Germans had composition lessons in Italy: Hasse studied counterpoint with Alessandro Scarlatti and Quantz studied counterpoint with Francesco Gasparini. Gasparini also offered to correct Quantz's compositions, giving an insight into how free composition was taught.[66] More commonly, northern musicians were keen to learn Italian manners of performance, whether via formal lessons, playing in ensembles, or listening to soloists and ensembles. Quantz's autobiography is full of detailed accounts of performers he heard on his travels (such as Farinelli and Carestini in Parma) and in his *Versuch* he emphasized the value of listening to different ensembles.[67] Some Germans also found jobs at Italian opera-houses. In two novels by Printz the musician-protagonists travel to Italy where they work at the opera, presumably playing in the orchestra.[68] In 1709 Handel wrote *Agrippina* for the Teatro S Giovanni Grisostomo in Venice, and in 1713 Heinichen wrote two operas for the Teatro S Angelo in Venice. The examples of Handel and Heinichen show how successfully northern musicians could assimilate Italian styles and adapt to Venetian conditions.

For northerners who did not travel south of the Alps, it was still possible to learn about the Italian style from sheet music. The concertos of Albinoni, Corelli and Vivaldi were published in Amsterdam, immediately lending an international dimension to their dissemination. J. S. Bach never travelled outside Germany, but encountered Vivaldi's music in 1713 when one of his patrons in Weimar brought back printed copies from Amsterdam. Quantz and Johann Gottfried Walther also acquired their initial knowledge of Italian concertos from printed or manuscript copies.

The Italian style was not completely dominant in Europe. France resisted the Italian style for a long time and indeed acted as a counter-pole, attracting musical pilgrims from England and Germany. Louis XIV (personal rule

64 Mattheson, *Grundlage einer Ehren-Pforte*, pp. 266–7.

65 Kai Köpp, *Johann Georg Pisendel (1687–1755) und die Anfänge der neuzeitlichen Orchesterleitung* (Tutzing, 2005), pp. 96–7.

66 Quantz, Autobiography, pp. 223–4; given in Paul Nettl, *Forgotten Musicians* (New York, 1951), p. 300.

67 Quantz, *On Playing the Flute*, p. 208.

68 Wolfgang Caspar Printz, *Musicus magnanimus oder Pancalus* ('Freyburg, 1691'); Printz, *Musicus curiosus oder Battalus* ('Freyburg, 1691').

1661–1715) was keen for France to be culturally distinct from its foreign rivals, a policy implemented in music by Lully. Lully discouraged study abroad and excluded Italians from the musical establishment at court; after his death in 1687, his style and output were upheld by a clique of his followers. Gradually Italian music began to infiltrate Paris, particularly in the form of songs, cantatas and chamber sonatas for private performance. Even at court there were isolated performances of Italian music, but the King's preference for Lully was well known. When a violin pupil of Corelli played an Italian piece before Louis, the King commanded one of his own violinists to play an air from Lully's *Cadmus et Hermione*, stating 'that is my taste'.[69] The antagonism between adherents of French and of Italian music reached a climax early in the eighteenth century in the polemic between Raguenet and Le Cerf de La Viéville. Raguenet's *Paralèle des italiens et des françois, en ce qui regarde la musique et les opéra* (1702) asserted that the Italian style was superior, on account of its striking modulations and range of passions, as well as the musicality of the Italian language. Le Cerf's reply, the *Comparaison de la musique italienne et de la musique françoise* (1704), defended such features as the simplicity and moderation of the French style. For Le Cerf, French music was superior because it adhered to good taste (*bon goût*) as shaped by reason, rather than submit to raw sensuality, as in Italian music. The dispute between Raguenet and Le Cerf thus touched not only on surface features of national styles, but also on different ideals of musical expression.[70]

The distinctiveness of French culture attracted many foreign visitors to Paris in the last decades of the seventeenth century. There were close links between France and the courts of central Germany: trips to Paris were made by German princes such as Ernst Ludwig, Landgrave of Hesse-Darmstadt; count Erdmann II of Promnitz at Sorau; Anton Ulrich, duke of Brunswick-Wolfenbüttel; and Friedrich August I of Saxony (August the Strong). Such aristocratic visitors were keen to replicate the ceremony, dancing and music of the French court on their return home. At the time, Lully's musical power was at a peak, and his style was rapidly copied by small German courts. Already in the 1660s and 1670s Lully's music had circulated widely in Germany, and German musicians such as Kusser and Muffat spent time in Paris absorbing his style. French dancing-masters and musicians were employed at many German courts, including Hanover, Schwerin and Sorau. One of the most Francophile courts was that of Georg Wilhelm, duke of Celle. Influenced by his French wife, Eléonore Desmier

69 Jean-Laurent Le Cerf de la Viéville, *Comparaison de la musique italienne et de la musique françoise* in Pierre Bourdelot, *Histoire de la musique* (Amsterdam, 1725), 4 vols., vol. 3, pp. 320–1.
70 Georgia Cowart, *The Origins of Modern Musical Criticism: French and Italian Music 1600–1750* (Ann Arbor, MI, 1981), pp. 61–85.

d'Olbreuse, he employed a French director of music, Philipp La Vigne, and a band of around sixteen French musicians. (As a teenager J. S. Bach heard this orchestra and was thus exposed to the French style of performance.[71]) The Dresden court was also Francophile during the reign of Friedrich August I, who had made a formative visit to Paris and Versailles as a young man in 1687. On succeeding to the throne in 1696 he introduced a French troupe of actors, and in 1709 hired Volumier to drill the orchestra in the French manner of playing.

In the early eighteenth century Paris still attracted some musical pilgrims, particularly those wishing to study the instrumental techniques cultivated there. Between 1698 and 1701 the German viol player Ernst Christian Hesse studied with the Parisian virtuosos Antoine Forqueray and Marin Marais. Quantz visited Paris in 1726–7, where he had a second key added to his flute to improve intonation. But by this date many foreigners felt that the French style had ossified. Even Quantz complained that 'the French are too constant and slavish in [music] ... What is new among them often seems to be old'.[72] Indeed, several French musicians sought to depart from the stultifying legacy of Lully by combining the French and Italian styles, thus taking a similar course to the German mixed style. François Couperin's 1724 publication of ensemble sonatas, *Les goûts-réünis*, juxtaposes French dances with Italianate fugues and sicilianos; it ends with a homage to Corelli, *La Parnasse ou L'Apothéose de Corelli*, a sonata da chiesa depicting the Italian composer entering Parnassus. The following year Couperin issued a counterweight in the form of another trio sonata, *L'Apothéose de Lully*. Here the first seven movements are Lullyian, culminating in him being raised to Parnassus. Corelli then makes an appearance in a sonata da chiesa, whereupon 'Apollo persuades Lully and Corelli that the union of French and Italian styles must create musical perfection'. This union is symbolized by a French overture, two airs for violin duet and a trio finale. In the first air 'Lully plays the subject and Corelli accompanies', while in the second 'Corelli takes his turn playing the subject and Lully accompanies'.[73] Lully's subject is a sweet flowing melody, adorned with *coulades* that fill the gaps in the tune; Corelli, by contrast, favours the pathos of the minor key and a more angular melody. Couperin's sonata is a witty response to the debate over national styles, but its programmatic concept and its strong sense of taste mark it as distinctly Gallic.[74]

71 Hans T. David and Arthur Mendel (eds.), *The New Bach Reader*, rev. Christoph Wolff (New York, 1998), p. 300.

72 Quantz, *On Playing the Flute*, p. 328.

73 Modern edn.: François Couperin, *Oeuvres complètes IV/4: Musique de chambre*, ed. Kenneth Gilbert and Davitt Moroney (Monaco, 1992).

74 Tunley, *François Couperin and 'The Perfection of Music'*, pp. 86–94.

In Western Europe the awareness of national styles of music extended to popular or traditional music such as Scots songs and Polish dances. These orally circulated repertories sounded intriguingly exotic to the cultural elite. At the end of the seventeenth century, ballads of apparently Scottish origin were popular among London high society. In c. 1691, Queen Mary reportedly requested, after hearing several songs by Purcell, that the 'old Scots ballad *Cold and raw*' be sung.[75] A few decades later the Scottish singer William Thomson enjoyed the favour of the royal court: his collection *Orpheus Caledonius* (1725), dedicated to the Princess of Wales, includes fifty Scots songs with Thomson's own figured bass and melodic ornaments. 'Scots songs' of fake parentage also circulated: ''Twas within a Furlong of *Edinborough* Town' by Thomas d'Urfey (with music by Henry Purcell) features a stereotyped Scotsman 'Jockey', with fake dialect. The appeal of such songs lay, to quote John Dryden, in their 'rude Sweetness ... which is natural and pleasing';[76] such an attitude reflected England's changing relationship with Scotland, which after the Act of Union (1707) no longer posed a political threat. In Edinburgh, by contrast, the publication of such collections of Scots songs as Allan Ramsay's *The Tea-Table Miscellany* (1723) served a growing interest in Scottish identity.[77]

Germans held similar attitudes to the peasant music of Poland. Whereas Wolfgang Caspar Printz had scorned the sound of bagpipes and hurdy-gurdies in his *Phrynis Mytilenaeus* (1696), Telemann was entranced by the Polish music he heard 'in its true barbaric beauty' on travels with courtly retinues to upper Silesia and Kraków. 'One can hardly believe what wonderful ideas such bagpipers or fiddlers have when they improvise while the dancers rest. In eight days an attentive listener could gain enough ideas from them to last a lifetime,'[78] and he subsequently evoked Polish dance rhythms in many of his instrumental works. There were political undertones to Telemann's use of the Polish style. In 1697 Elector Friedrich August I of Saxony had converted to Catholicism and gained the Polish throne. Poland was thus annexed to German lands, and Polish dances and instruments were used at the Dresden court as a symbol of the Elector's political empire.

The eighteenth-century preoccupation with national style shows how music could represent both peoples and places. Whereas at the start of the century

75 Sir John Hawkins, *A General History of the Science and Practice of Music* (London, 1776), 5 vols., vol. 2, p. 564, reprint London (1875), 2 vols.

76 Quoted in David Johnson, *Music and Society in Lowland Scotland in the Eighteenth Century* (London, 1972), p. 131.

77 *Ibid.*, pp. 132–3.

78 'Man sollte kaum glauben, was dergleichen Bockpfeiffer oder Geiger für wunderbare Einfälle haben, wenn sie, so oft die Tantzenden ruhen, fantaisiren. Ein Aufmerckender könnte von ihnen, in 8. Tagen, Gedancken für ein gantzes Leben erschnappen.' Mattheson, *Grundlage einer Ehren-Pforte*, p. 360.

national styles sometimes aroused rivalry and xenophobia, increasingly they were valued as symbols of the diversity of European music. Travel played a vital role in fostering awareness of the panorama of musical environments and styles. As Charles Burney wrote: 'by travelling, musicians lose, among other local partialities, that veneration for a particular style, which ... keeps them in such subjection.'[79] With these broadened perspectives, musicians and music-lovers reflected the Enlightenment's growing curiosity about the diversity of mankind.

Select Bibliography

Addison, Joseph. *Remarks on Several Parts of Italy, & c. in the Years 1701, 1702, 1703*. London, 1705

Anderson, Emily (ed. and trans). *The Letters of Mozart and his Family*. 3rd edn., London, 1985

Beer, Johann. *Musicalische Discurse*. Nuremberg, 1719

Sein Leben, von ihm selbst erzählt, ed. Adolf Schmiedecke. Göttingen, 1965

Brockpähler, Renate. *Handbuch zur Geschichte der Barockoper in Deutschland*. Emsdetten, 1964

Buelow, George J. *Thorough-Bass Accompaniment According to Johann David Heinichen*. 2nd edn., Lincoln, NB, 1992

Burney, Charles. *The Present State of Music in Germany, the Netherlands and United Provinces*. 2 vols., 2nd edn., London, 1775

A General History of Music from the Earliest Ages to the Present. 4 vols., London, 1776–89

Coehlo, Victor A. 'Music in New Worlds'. In Tim Carter and John Butt (eds.), *The Cambridge History of Seventeenth-Century Music*. Cambridge, 2005, pp. 88–110

Cowart, Georgia. *The Origins of Modern Musical Criticism: French and Italian Music 1600–1750*. Ann Arbor, MI, 1981

Dennis, John. *Essay on the Operas After the Italian Manner*. London, 1706

Fellinger, Imogen. 'Mattheson als Begründer der ersten Musikzeitschrift (*Critica musica*)'. In George J. Buelow and Hans Joachim Marx (eds.), *New Mattheson Studies*. Cambridge, 1983, pp. 179–97

Freeman, Daniel E. *The Opera Theater of Count Franz Anton von Sporck in Prague*. Stuyvesant, NY, 1992

Fürstenau, Moritz. *Zur Geschichte der Musik und des Theaters am Hofe zu Dresden*. 2 vols, Dresden, 1861–2

Habermas, Jürgen. *The Structural Transformation of the Public Sphere: An Inquiry into a Category of Bourgeois Society*. Trans. Thomas Burger with the assistance of Frederick Lawrence. Cambridge, MA, 1989

Hardin, James. *Johann Beer*. Boston, MA, 1983

Hawkins, Sir John. *A General History of the Science and Practice of Music*. 5 vols., London, 1776. Reprint London, 1875, 2 vols

Heinichen, Johann David. *Der General-Bass in der Composition*. Dresden, 1728

Hill, John Walter. *The Life and Works of Francesco Maria Veracini*. Ann Arbor, MI, 1979

79 Charles Burney, *The Present State of Music in Germany, the Netherlands and United Provinces*, 2nd edn. (London, 1775), 2 vols., vol. 2, p. 338.

Howell, James. *Instructions and Directions for Forren Travell.* London, 1650

Johnson, David. *Music and Society in Lowland Scotland in the Eighteenth Century*. London, 1972

Kolneder, Walter. *Antonio Vivaldi: Documents of His Life and Works*. Trans. Kurt Michaelis. New York, 1982

Köpp, Kai. *Johann Georg Pisendel (1687–1755) und die Anfänge der neuzeitlichen Orchesterleitung*. Tutzing, 2005

Landmann, Ortrun. 'The Dresden Hofkapelle During the Lifetime of Johann Sebastian Bach'. *Early Music*, 17 (1989), pp. 17–30

Le Cerf de la Viéville, Jean-Laurent. *Comparaison de la musique italienne et de la musique françoise*. In Pierre Bourdelot, *Histoire de la musique*. 4 vols., Amsterdam, 1725

Lee, Douglas A. *A Musician at Court: An Autobiography of Franz Benda*. Warren, MI, 1998

Lindgren, Lowell. 'Nicola Cosimi in London, 1701–1705'. *Studi musicali*, 11 (1982), pp. 229–48

'Critiques of Opera in London, 1705–1719'. In Alberto Colzani *et al.* (eds.), *Il melodramma italiano in Italia e in Germania nell'età barocca*. Como, 1995, pp. 143–65

'Handel's London – Italian Musicians and Librettists'. In Donald Burrows (ed.), *The Cambridge Companion to Handel*. Cambridge, 1997, pp. 78–91

Love, Harold. 'How Music Created a Public'. *Criticism*, 46 (2004), pp. 257–71

Mattheson, Johann. *Das neu-eröffnete Orchestre*. Hamburg, 1713

Grosse General-Bass-Schule oder exemplarische Organisten-Probe. Hamburg, 1731

Grundlage einer Ehren-Pforte. Hamburg, 1740. Reprint Kassel, 1969

McGeary, Thomas. 'Music Literature'. In H. Diack Johnstone and Roger Fiske (eds.), *The Blackwell History of Music in Britain: The Eighteenth Century*. Oxford, 1990, pp. 397–421

McGuinness, Rosamund. 'Musical Provocation in Eighteenth-Century London: The *British Apollo*'. *Music & Letters*, 68 (1987), pp. 333–42

McVeigh, Simon. 'Italian Violinists in Eighteenth-Century London'. In Reinhard Strohm (ed.), *The Eighteenth-Century Diaspora of Italian Music and Musicians*. Turnhout, 2001, pp. 139–76

Nettl, Paul. *Forgotten Musicians*. New York, 1951

Printz, Wolfgang Caspar. *Musicus curiosus oder Battalus*. 'Freyburg, 1691'

Musicus magnanimus oder Pancalus. 'Freyburg, 1691'

Quantz, Johann Joachim. *Versuch einer Anweisung die Flöte traversiere zu spielen*. Berlin, 1752. Trans. Edward R. Reilly as *On Playing the Flute*. London, 1985

Ritzarev, Marina and Anna Porfireva. 'The Italian Diaspora in Eighteenth-Century Russia'. In Reinhard Strohm (ed.), *The Eighteenth-Century Diaspora of Italian Music and Musicians*. Turnhout, 2001, pp. 211–53

Rose, Stephen. 'Music in the Market-Place'. In Tim Carter and John Butt (eds.), *The Cambridge History of Seventeenth Century Music*. Cambridge, 2005, pp. 55–87

Samuel, Harold E. 'A German Musician Comes to London in 1704'. *Musical Times*, 122 (1981), pp. 591–3

Spitzer, John and Neal Zaslaw. *The Birth of the Orchestra: History of an Institution, 1650–1815*. Oxford and New York, 2004

Strohm, Reinhard. 'Italian Operisti North of the Alps *c.*1700–1750'. In Strohm (ed.), *The Eighteenth-Century Diaspora of Italian Music and Musicians*. Turnhout, 2001, pp. 1–60

Strunk, Oliver and Leo Treitler (eds.). *Source Readings in Music History*. Rev edn., New York, 1998

The By-Laws of the Musical Society, at the Castle-Tavern in Pater-Noster-Row [London, 1731]

The New Bach Reader, ed. Hans T. David and Arthur Mendel. Rev. Christoph Wolff, New York, 1998

Tunley, David. *François Couperin and 'The Perfection of Music'*. Aldershot, 2004

Wilson, Daniel K. (ed.). *Georg Muffat on Performance Practice*. Bloomington, IN, 2001

· PART I MUSIC FOR THE CHURCH ·

· 2 ·

Catholic church music in Italy, and the Spanish and Portuguese Empires

PAUL R. LAIRD

From J. S. Bach's cantatas and Handel's oratorios to Mozart's operas and Haydn's string quartets, the eighteenth century includes a great deal of familiar music, and many unknown works from the century are in styles that we intuitively understand. It is unsettling, then, to find large corners lacking illumination, including religious music composed in Italy, Spain, Portugal and Latin America. We encounter the occasional famous composer – usually a master of opera such as Alessandro Scarlatti or Giovanni Battista Pergolesi who also wrote sacred works – but most extant religious music was by local composers. The vast majority of these works were never printed, and many are extant only as *unica* in one archive. When we start to consider the number of archives at religious institutions in these countries, and that few have been investigated in detail, we begin to appreciate how much remains to be discovered about eighteenth-century sacred music in Roman Catholic countries.

Isolated pieces, such as Pergolesi's *Stabat Mater* and Vivaldi's *Gloria*, RV 589, are well known, but placing them in a vivid historical context is problematic because analogous compositions remain largely unstudied. There are useful dissertations and articles on a number of less-celebrated composers, but little about them in textbooks. John Walter Hill's *Baroque Music* excavates new ground in his coverage of marginalized repertories, but his material on Latin church music in Italy for the second half of the seventeenth century through to the end of the Baroque is confined to six pages.[1] His consideration of formal procedures in arias is instructive, and he also covers church music in Spain, Portugal and their colonies.[2] Philip G. Downs, in his textbook *Classical Music*, concentrates on the works of Haydn, Mozart and Beethoven with some mention of less-important composers. The section entitled 'Religious Music in Roman Catholic Europe', which primarily names Austrian composers, is less

1 John Walter Hill, *Baroque Music: Music in Western Europe, 1580–1750* (New York, 2005), pp. 414–19.
2 *Ibid.*, pp. 257–68.

than one page long.[3] Giorgio Pestelli dedicates fewer than five pages to sacred music, besides that by the Classic era's most famous composers, in *The Age of Mozart and Beethoven*.[4]

A major part of the sacred music performed in Roman Catholic institutions during the eighteenth century was composed by chapel-masters who directed musical ensembles at the cathedrals, basilicas, churches, monasteries, *ospedali* and other institutions. Chant remained a large part of the church's musical practices at the time, but for many institutions it was customary to have a musician directing the chapel who was capable of writing polyphonic works. Fray Antonio Soler (1729–83) is a good case in point, a Catalan composer trained as a choirboy at the monastery at Montserrat who then spent most of his life at the royal monastery of San Lorenzo de El Escorial, where for years he was *maestro de capilla*. Soler studied with Domenico Scarlatti and José de Nebra, members of the royal household and among Spain's leading musicians, and became well known for his keyboard sonatas, Latin works and villancicos; the vocal works primarily survive in the Escorial archive. An example of a long-time *maestro di cappella* at important Italian institutions is Nicola Fago (1677–1745), who held the position from 1709 until 1731 at the Cappella del Tesoro di San Gennaro of Naples Cathedral and then from 1736 until his death at San Giacomo degli Spagnuoli. Fago wrote numerous religious works for these and other institutions, many extant in manuscript form.

Our understanding of eighteenth-century Catholic sacred music in Italy, Spain, Portugal and Latin America is assisted by the large amount of research that has been carried out on Italian opera. The most celebrated composers of Italian church music were often opera composers as well, and they brought into the church the same style of elaborate solo vocal music. Italian musical taste was also highly influential in the Spanish and Portuguese Empires at the beginning of the eighteenth century.

Roman Catholic church music in Italy, Spain, Portugal and Latin America represents the intersection of four different styles: *stile antico*, polychoral writing, homorhythmic textures and operatic solo music. The term *stile antico* had been in use since the early seventeenth century, referring to music in a traditional style associated with Palestrina and his contemporaries. Palestrina's successors in Rome included Felipe Anerio and Gregorio Allegri, who also wrote in an imitative, smooth style, but often with added basso continuo. By the second half of the seventeenth century, the *stile antico* (also called *da cappella*) had become nearly obligatory for various types of church music,

3 Philip G. Downs, *Classical Music: The Era of Haydn, Mozart, and Beethoven* (New York, 1992), pp. 174–5.
4 Giorgio Pestelli, *The Age of Mozart and Beethoven*, trans. Eric Cross (Cambridge, 1984), pp. 96–100.

especially Mass Ordinary movements and psalms, and it remained so for many later musicians as well. Johann Joseph Fux demonstrated the continuing importance of the *stile antico* in his contrapuntal treatise *Gradus ad Parnassum* (1725). The style remained current into the nineteenth century in church music by Rossini and Verdi, where we find unaccompanied, contrapuntal choral writing in *alla breve*.

References to polychoral writing usually appear in the context of the Renaissance and early Baroque, but the texture remained important in seventeenth- and eighteenth-century sacred music as well. Italian composers often used it through the Baroque and into the Classic era, with reduced frequency as the century progressed; on the Iberian Peninsula and in Latin America, polychoral textures were favoured well into the eighteenth century. The distinctive configuration of voices in Spanish and Portuguese music was SSAT in the first choir (usually soloists) and SATB in the second, sometimes with a third choir (SATB) as well. Polychoral music was often homorhythmic, allowing for block chords that produced powerful contrasts between opposing forces. When instruments were introduced, these oppositions were all the more striking. Homorhythmic textures had also been used for contrast by Renaissance composers as an antidote to continuous points of imitation, and eighteenth-century composers of Roman Catholic church music, with their hearts partly pledged to the *stile antico*, continued to use chordal passages in order to effect contrast. By adding operatic solo and duet passages, composers created the *stile misto* ('mixed style').

Operatic writing became especially popular in motets, occasional pieces outside the usual liturgical realm. Most motets composed in Italy after 1700 were for solo voice, strings and basso continuo. Vivaldi's generation standardized the genre's form, relating it to the solo secular cantata, with two or three arias of contrasting moods separated by recitatives, usually concluding with an 'Alleluia'. Aspects of this form remain in late eighteenth-century solo motets, such as Mozart's famous *Exsultate, jubilate*, K. 165 (1773).

The *concertato* style included soloists, one or more choirs and various groups of accompanying instruments, and was a feature of church music from the late sixteenth century. As Hill has noted, in the first two-thirds of the seventeenth century, instrumental parts in such pieces were similar to the vocal lines, functioning as another choir.[5] Around 1680 a new orchestral style emerged, inspired by the nascent concerto genre. Strings played rapid figurations, with repeated notes, scalar passages and memorable melodic snippets that comprised the ritornellos, separating homorhythmic choral passages and solo

5 Hill, *Baroque Music*, p. 415.

entrances. Many scholars have classified this as a Neapolitan style, also heard in opera, but Hill traces its development to Bologna, a city influential in the concerto's development. Alessandro Scarlatti, one of the most important composers in Naples, did not actually write in this style until his *St Cecilia Mass* (1720), by which time it was well established in religious institutions in Bologna and Venice. Francesco Durante, perhaps Naples's most important composer of sacred music, did not embrace the new style until 1740. It would remain popular for much of the eighteenth century, helping to create one of the truly striking aspects of eighteenth-century Roman Catholic church music in its entirety, because certain stylistic features remained consistent throughout. Solo music based on operatic models and concertato textures, for example, remained evident in Haydn's late masses.

There were, to be sure, stylistic changes between the Baroque and Classic eras that played out in sacred music as well. Counterpoint, terraced dynamics, orchestral accompaniment of primarily strings and basso continuo with winds used occasionally for colour and irregular melodic phrase lengths appear more often in the first half of the century. Music from later in the century includes a wider dynamic palette, more gradual changes in volume, a larger orchestra with varied use of winds, a generally slower harmonic rhythm and balanced phrase lengths.

Sacred music in eighteenth-century Italy

The most significant composers worked in major centres, especially Bologna, Naples, Venice, Rome and Milan. Part of the importance of major cities was that opera houses were located there, and many successful composers of dramatic music also worked in churches, where they composed for what might be called the relaxed liturgical standards of the day. Polyphonic practices varied locally, but items such as motets with non-liturgical texts and instrumental music were often substituted for liturgical segments in both the Proper and Ordinary of the Mass, and in major Offices, such as Vespers and Compline. Liturgical observance became so lax that in 1749 Pope Benedict XIV noted that 'on certain days of the year, sacred buildings are the theatre for sumptuous and resounding concerts, which in no way agree with the Sacred Mysteries'.[6] Around 1700, most composers in Venice writing a concerted mass set only the Kyrie and Gloria texts, with the remainder of the Ordinary filled with semi-liturgical substitutes. This was by no means universal in Italy because we still encounter full Mass Ordinaries, such as Alessandro Scarlatti's *St Cecilia Mass*

6 Quoted in *ibid.*, p. 414.

with its separate settings of the Kyrie, Gloria, Credo, Sanctus and Agnus Dei, composed for St Cecilia's day in 1720 in Rome.[7] The outputs of numerous composers, however, demonstrate the incompleteness of Mass Ordinaries. Giacomo Antonio Perti, *maestro di cappella* for sixty years (1696–1756) at Bologna's Basilica of San Petronio, for example, left twenty-eight masses, all of them featuring only a Kyrie and Gloria, but he also left eleven extant settings of the Credo.[8] Eighteenth-century Italian composers wrote psalms, canticles, hymns and motets as well as mass movements, often selling new motet texts just as they sold opera librettos. The arias of motets tended to be da capo, as was so common in operas, but often only the opening ritornello and/or first vocal phrase was repeated. The motet's popularity is revealed by the stipulated requirements for the *maestro di coro* at the Ospedale della Pietà in Venice, who had to compose two motets each month.[9] The motets appeared first in northern Italian centres such as Bologna and Venice, eventually spreading to Rome, Naples and elsewhere.

Bologna

Musicians and composers active at the Basilica of San Petronio in the seventeenth century played a major role in establishing the sacred musical style that came to dominate eighteenth-century Italian church music. There were other religious institutions in Bologna, of course, but none could rival the size of the musical chapel of San Petronio, which in 1687 had three to five singers per part, greatly augmented for major feast days, and accompanied by an orchestra of more than twenty strings.[10] Orchestral music at the basilica became especially important during the chapel-mastership of Maurizio Cazzati (1657–71), and the concerted style appears in the religious works of Giovanni Paolo Colonna (1637–95, chapel-master 1674–95). Colonna printed his *Motetti sacri*, Op. 2 in 1681, revealing many devices that became associated with the Italian solo motet. His *O lucidissima dies*, for example, is scored for soprano or tenor soloist, two violins, *bassetto viola* (violoncello) and organ, and features an alternation of recitatives and arias.[11] The violinists play music based on the vocal lines, but they also sound as an independent entity both when the voice rests and in a separate ritornello. Colonna's use of concertato procedures for works with more vocal parts can be observed in his *Messe e salmi concertate*, Op. 10 (1691). Colonna's music also shows his great concern for counterpoint, certainly an

7 Alessandro Scarlatti, *St Cecilia Mass (1720)*, ed. John Steele (Sevenoaks, Kent, 1968), p. i.

8 Anne Schnoebelen (with Marc Vanscheeuwijck), 'Perti, Giacomo Antonio', in Laura Macey (ed.), *New Grove Online* (accessed 24 May 2007).

9 Hill, *Baroque Music*, p. 419. 10 *Ibid.*, p. 416.

11 Peter Smith, *Concerted Sacred Music of the Bologna School*, vol. 57 of *Recent Researches in Music of the Baroque Era* (Madison, WI, 1987), pp. 51–66.

interest of all Bolognese composers who were members of the conservative Accademia Filarmonica.

Colonna's successor as San Petronio chapel-master was Giacomo Antonio Perti (1661–1756), who showed more interest in vocal music than his predecessors had done. Instrumentalists were dismissed in 1696, and the departure helped to widen the city's stylistic preferences. Perti, who also wrote operas, left an enormous output of all kinds of sacred vocal pieces, including elaborate works for Vespers such as the *Magnificat*, and the psalms *Beatus vir*, *Laudate pueri* and *Laudate Dominum*. We can observe his mastery of *stile antico* in a setting of *Ave regina coelorum*, and of the concerted style in his *Laudate pueri* scored for solo voice, violin, viola and basso continuo.[12] Perti had many students, among them Padre Giovanni Battista Martini (1706–84). For many years *maestro* at the Bolognese church of San Francesco, Martini also left a large volume of church music. His conventional continuation of the concertato style may be seen in his *Domine, ad adjuvandum me festina*, for SATB chorus and string orchestra.[13] Solo sections alternate with choral passages that are both homorhythmic and imitative, propelled throughout by active orchestral writing.

Venice

Venice was an economic and imperial political power during the seventeenth century, but began a period of decline around 1700. Still, it remained a wealthy centre of commerce, and its rare political structure – with a doge elected from a legislature that included all adult male nobles – allowed for a wide distribution of musical patronage. The leading centre was St Mark's Basilica, where splendid music for worship praised God and furthered the city's prestige. In addition, Venice was home to hundreds of churches with choirs, and often pairs of organs. The four *ospedali* (Mendicanti, Pietà, Incurabili and Ospedaletto), which housed and educated thousands of female orphans, were major musical centres because of the significance they placed on a musical education. Many of Venice's greatest musicians, such as Vivaldi, worked at the *ospedali* (later called *conservatorios*), where regular concerts of sacred music, oratorios and concertos were popular among Venetians and those visiting the city. This elaborate sacred music was often heard in vespers performances on Saturday and Sunday, especially in psalms, canticles and solo motets.

Major composers of sacred music working in Venice during the eighteenth century included Francesco Gasparini (1661–1727), Antonio Lotti (1667–1740),

12 Musical examples of these works and others by Perti can be seen in Jean Berger, 'The Sacred Works of Giacomo Antonio Perti', *Journal of the American Musicological Society*, 17 (1964), pp. 370–7.
13 Padre Giovanni Battista Martini, *Lord, My God, Assist Me Now (Domine, ad adjuvandum me festina)*, ed. John Castellini (St Louis, MO, 1958).

Antonio Vivaldi (1678–1741), Benedetto Giacomo Marcello (1686–1739), Baldassare Galuppi (1706–85) and Fernando Bertoni (1725–1813). In addition, other musicians of international importance spent time in Venice, such as Antonio Sacchini (1730–86) and Johann Adolf Hasse (1699–1783). The majority of these composers also wrote operas; indeed some of the genre's most successful figures are among them.

Lotti's Requiem, representing the first generation of eighteenth-century Venetian composers, carries the expected mixture of styles.[14] Written for SATB chorus and an orchestra of strings and winds and organ, the work includes *stile antico* (such as in the opening movement and 'Inter oves', both with instruments doubling voices), concerted textures with active orchestral accompaniment in the 'Christe eleison' and elsewhere, operatic solos such as the 'Mors stupebit' for soprano and strings and evocative trios as in the 'Juste judex', for SAB *soli*, oboe and strings.

From the next generation, Vivaldi's famous and highly accessible *Gloria*, RV 589, offers a rich stylistic blend.[15] The opening 'Gloria' shows the power of homorhythmic choral entrances, with accompaniment similar to the ritornellos in Vivaldi's concertos. 'Et in terra pax', an Andante in B minor, is contrapuntal with closely spaced choral entrances. The 'Laudamus te', for two sopranos and strings, is operatic, moving between imitative entrances and duet passages in thirds. 'Gratias agimus tibi' opens chordally, with a brief fugue later on. The 'Domine Deus, Rex coelestis' is a *siciliano* for soprano, oboe and continuo, and is operatic in conception. We should note the concertato writing in the seventh movement, 'Domine Deus, Agnus Dei', where Vivaldi interrupts the plaintive alto continuo aria with choral interjections accompanied by strings. Vivaldi recalls the opening segment's ritornello in the 'Quoniam tu solo sanctus', and the closing 'Cum Sancto Spiritu' is fugal. Vivaldi mirrors this sectional treatment of the text in his antiphon *Salve Regina*, RV 616, for alto soloist and orchestra, a work demonstrating many of the typically operatic techniques of writing for solo voices, including lengthy melismas based on difficult, sequential lines in the opening movement on 'salve' and word-painting, such as rests in his setting of 'suspiramus' in the Larghetto third movement.[16] Vivaldi's psalm settings are for varied forces. The *Dixit Dominus*, RV 594 (Psalm 109), scored for SSTB soloists, two SATB choirs, two trumpets, two oboes and strings (with orchestra divided into two choirs),[17] includes florid vocal writing for both soloists and choir and brilliant

14 See the modern edition of Antonio Lotti, *Requiem* (Vienna, 2001).
15 Antonio Vivaldi, *Gloria*, RV 589, ed. Michael Talbot (Milan, 2002).
16 Antonio Vivaldi, *Salve Regina*, RV 616, ed. Michael Talbot (Milan, 1998).
17 Antonio Vivaldi, *Dixit Dominus*, RV 594, ed. Paul Everett (Rome, 2002).

use of instruments, a strong contrast to *Laudati pueri Dominum*, RV 601 (Psalm 112), scored for soprano and small orchestra.[18]

Baldassare Galuppi, famed in opera as a founder of the *dramma giocoso*, served for over two decades as chapel-master at St Mark's and was associated with various *ospedali*. He studied with Lotti and even late in his career produced music not unlike that of his teacher. This may be heard to an extent in Galuppi's setting of the *Dixit Dominus*, first composed in 1775 as a piece for SSAA, chorus and orchestra at the Ospedali degli Incurabili.[19] It is one of Galuppi's few sacred choral works that does not have lengthy solo movements. He then reset the piece for St Mark's in 1781, with SATB choir, and added pairs of oboes and horns to the string orchestra. (With many works sung by female choirs at the *ospedali* and convents, it was common in Venice for SATB pieces to be recast as SSAA works, and vice versa.) Galuppi's assertive, triadic opening material, presented in dotted rhythms with a gentle descending scale reminiscent of light operas, reappears in each of the three movements, including in the Doxology for 'sicut erat in principio' ('as it was in the beginning'), a common musical pun. In the first movement, Allegro, e con spirito, in 4/4, the string orchestra pushes forward with repeated quavers, semi-quavers and arpeggios; the choir sings primarily homorhythmically; the harmonic rhythm is mostly a minim or semibreve per chord. The second movement, a Largo in 4/4, begins with the text 'Juravit Dominus' ('The Lord has sworn'), set by Galuppi in C minor in crotchets. The choral parts approach the *stile antico* with deliberate motion, paired imitation and effective use of dissonance. At the text 'Tu es sacerdos' ('You are a priest'), Galuppi begins a contrapuntal passage based on two subjects. The opening material from the first movement (in the subdominant) returns at 'Dominus a dextris tuis', reminiscent of the opening phrase 'Dixit Dominus'. The finale opens in a Largo sostenuto, with a distinctive figure with grace notes and a dotted rhythm introducing the fearsome 'Judicabit in nationibus' ('He will judge among the nations'), presented stridently in strong chords, moving to an Allegro. After the Doxology begins, the work's opening material appears a third time at 'Sicut erat in principio', in B-flat major, but modulates quickly to the home key of E-flat major for the 'Amen'. An example of Galuppi's writing for solo voice is *Cantate, jubilate* for tenor, strings and two horns,[20] a proud Allegro assai with a high tessitura for the soloist (to c'') and first violins doubling the tenor line through much of the work.

18 Antonio Vivaldi, *Laudate pueri Dominum*, RV 601, ed. Michael Talbot (Rome, 2002).
19 Baldassare Galuppi, *Dixit Dominus*, ed. David Larson (Dayton, OH, 1995).
20 Galuppi, *Cantate, jubilate*, ed. Hermann Müller (Adliswil, 1985).

Naples

The perceived international dominance of Neapolitan opera has made Naples seem like the pre-eminent musical city in Europe by the early seventeenth century but, as discussed above, the principles behind the concertato style actually appeared earlier in Bologna and Venice. The most important composers of religious music in Naples during this period, in chronological order, include: Alessandro Scarlatti (1660–1725), Nicola Fago (1677–1745), Francesco Durante (1684–1755), Nicola Porpora (1686–1768), Leonardo Leo (1694–1744) and Giovanni Battista Pergolesi (1710–36).

In 1700, the population of Naples worshipped at more than 500 churches.[21] Of these, twenty-three had a *cappella musicale*, with the major institutions including the Spanish viceroy's Cappella Reale, the Duomo, the Oratorio dei Filippini, the Santissima Annunziata and four conservatories.[22] The latter provided musicians for other institutions, and different musicians ran the schools and taught at them. Composers working for the various religious institutions in the city wrote masses, psalms and motets for services, but also music for sacred concerts that celebrated Spanish royal events. Military victories resulted in the commissioning of *Te Deum* settings, and when a noble lady entered a convent there would be a sacred concert in her honour. The death of a prominent citizen would occasion a new *Missa defunctorum*. Special days during the year called for an elaborate Mass, set of vesper psalms, or *Magnificat*, and composers penned settings of Lamentations and Lessons for Holy Week and the *Stabat Mater* and/or *Salve Regina* for Good Friday.[23] A look at representative compositions by Scarlatti, Pergolesi, Fago and Durante traces Neapolitan church music across three generations.

Scarlatti spent much of his life in Naples, including two decades as chapelmaster of the Cappella Reale, and then most of the remainder of his life after several tempestuous years in Rome. He maintained contacts in Rome, but most of his compositional efforts are tied stylistically to Naples. Although the date of Scarlatti's setting of the *Stabat Mater* for the Confraternita dei Cavalieri della Vergine dei Dolori in Naples is unknown, it appears to be a mature work.[24] Scarlatti scored it for soprano and alto soloists, two violins and basso continuo, and brought his operatic style wholesale into the piece, writing in

21 Carolyn Gianturco, 'Naples: A City of Entertainment', in George J. Buelow (ed.), *The Late Baroque Era From the 1680s to 1740* (Englewood Cliffs, NJ, 1993), p. 115.

22 *Ibid.*, p. 115.

23 This summary of liturgical practices in Naples derives from Stephen M. Shearon, 'Latin Sacred Music and Nicola Fago: The Career and Sources of an Early Eighteenth-Century Neapolitan *maestro di cappella*', PhD thesis (The University of North Carolina at Chapel Hill, 1993), pp. 89–90.

24 Alessandro Scarlatti, *Stabat Mater per soprano, contralto, due violini e basso continuo*, ed. Maria Luisa Baldassari (Bologna, 1998), p. i.

eighteen brief movements solos for each voice, duets of varied tempos and affects and accompanied recitatives. The musical content is driven by the text, as can be seen in the Adagio fourth movement, a setting of 'Quae maerebat' for full forces. Scarlatti expresses the word 'tremebat' through repeated semiquavers in the violins and in the voices, with quaver rests on the beat and each syllable of 'et tremebat' on the off-beat. The virtuosic solo writing for which Scarlatti became famous can be seen in the following movement, a setting for soprano, violins and continuo of 'Quis est homo', an Andante in duple meter with long, convoluted melismas on the word 'tanto' and considerable chromaticism. All combines effectively to render the sense of the text 'Who is the man who would not weep if seeing the Mother of Christ in such agony?'. As noted above, Scarlatti composed his *St Cecilia Mass* for performance in Rome in 1720. Written for soloists, five-part chorus (SSATB), string orchestra and organ continuo, it is a striking example of a concerted Mass, with solo movements (such as the 'Gratias agimus tibi' for alto), *stile antico* ('Agnus Dei') and many concerted movements with alternation between soloists in various combinations and the full choir. Some moments recall the kind of textural contrast we hear in Haydn's symphonic masses written more than seven decades later. A number – but by no means all – of Scarlatti's masses have been published in modern editions and several of his motets have been subjected to detailed study,[25] effectively demonstrating the relative paucity of material available on eighteenth-century Italian church music. Scarlatti was one of the most famous composers of the first half of the century, but even his sacred output is barely known.

Giovanni Battista Pergolesi wrote a great deal of church music during his short life, but the true nature of his output is clouded by doubtful attributions. Helmut Hucke finds Pergolesi's masses – of which only two are extant – more ambitious than those of Durante, Leo and others, particularly in the solo movements where 'buffo-like melodies capture the situations and the psychological states of the text'.[26] Each work is a large-scale setting of the Kyrie and Gloria, with various versions existing for one, two and four choruses. Pergolesi's knack for writing for solo voices can be seen in his *Stabat Mater* in F minor for two solo voices, strings and basso continuo (1736).[27] Breathing the air of the *style galant*, the piece was controversial, eliciting comment from Padre Martini among others. Pergolesi also wrote his setting of the *Salve Regina* in

25 Paul Allen Brandvik, 'Selected Motets of Alessandro Scarlatti', DMA thesis (University of Illinois at Urbana–Champaign, 1969).

26 Helmut Hucke, 'Pergolesi's *Missa S. Emidio*', in Allan W. Atlas (ed.), *Music in the Classic Period: Essays in Honor of Barry S. Brook* (New York, 1985), p. 113.

27 Pergolesi, *Sequenze: Stabat Mater–Dies Irae*, ed. Duke Filippo Caffarelli (Rome, 1942), pp. 1–46.

C minor, scored for soprano, strings and basso continuo, in the last year of his life (1736).[28] The work comprises contrasting movements and transmits a feeling of resignation, seldom leaving the minor mode and featuring many affective, descending intervals in the soprano and upper string voices.

One of Pergolesi's teachers, Francesco Durante, outlived his student by nearly two decades and produced some of the greatest Neapolitan works of sacred music in the middle of the century, perhaps partially influenced by his student. In 1746, for example, he composed his *Messa di'morti* for use in Rome, a work for eight voice parts and orchestra, described by Hanns-Berthold Dietz as 'the most important orchestral requiem of the early 18th century'.[29] Other significant works include his *Missa in afflictionis tempore* (1749) and the *Magnificat* in B-flat for four vocal parts and orchestra, the latter based on chant tones for the canticle used as the basis for various textures and styles.[30]

Among Nicola Fago's finest sacred works is his *Missa pro defunctis*, where he took the Requiem text from the *Missale Romanum* (1570) and set it in forty-six separate sections for two five-part choruses (probably soloists and ripienists), mostly with string accompaniment but also with brass. Fago uses the *stile antico*, but the Sequence texts include his most interesting writing in the work, with nine solos, one duet and seven choruses comprising the seventeen brief movements.

Rome

As the centre of Roman Catholic orthodoxy, the Eternal City seldom nurtured progressive musical trends in the church, but sacred music in Roman religious institutions was in fact more varied than is sometimes thought. As in previous centuries, the major musical institutions were the papal choir in the Sistine Chapel, the Cappella Guilia in St Peter's Basilica and the musical chapels at Santa Maria Maggiore and St John Lateran, but at any given time other chapels might present elaborate music for a particular liturgical occasion.

There was no shortage of attempted musical regulation by popes and other officials, but even within Rome observance of these edicts was mixed. In 1692 Pope Innocent XII called for music that was 'ecclesiastical, grave, and devout', sung only by males who could not be seen by the congregation, and no lengthy solo passages.[31] The only truly permissible instrument was the organ. The

28 Helmut Hucke and Dale E. Monson, 'Pergolesi, Giovanni Battista', in Laura Macey (ed.), *Grove Music Online* (accessed 7 May 2007).

29 Hanns-Berthold Dietz, 'Durante, Francesco', in Macey (ed.), *Grove Music Online*, (accessed 21 May 2007).

30 See David William Barnett, Jr, 'Francesco Durante's "Magnificat in B-flat": A Conductor's Analysis', DMA thesis (University of Miami, 1980).

31 Malcolm Boyd, 'Rome: The Power of Patronage', in Buelow (ed.), *The Late Baroque Era* (Englewood Cliffs, NJ, 1993), p. 41.

Pope's authority barely extended beyond Vatican City in such matters. In the Cappella Sistina, one customarily heard the *stile antico* of Palestrina and composers imitating him, whereas at St Peter's the Cappella Giulia more commonly made use of organs and polychoral textures. Elsewhere in Rome, one often heard orchestral instruments along with extensive solo singing. Musical activities at other churches and chapels in Rome fell under the regulatory eye of the musicians's guild, the Congregazione (later Accademia) di Santa Cecilia.

Even if Roman churches did not feature the most innovative music of the period, there was no shortage of fine musicians. The first decade of the eighteenth century saw an utterly remarkable group of composers in Rome, including Alessandro and Domenico Scarlatti, Arcangelo Corelli and George Frideric Handel, among others. The elder Scarlatti was more interested in composing opera when he moved to Rome in 1702, but it was during a period when operas were rare in Rome and the composer found only assistant positions at major institutions. Domenico Scarlatti failed to obtain a major position in Rome in the first decade of the century, but from 1714 to 1719 was chapel-master of the Cappella Giulia. The vast majority of his sacred vocal output is undated, but four works that he wrote for Santa Maria Maggiore in 1708–9 (when he was chapel-master for the exiled Queen of Poland) remain in the archive there, including some of his most successful uses of the *stile antico*.[32] It is thought that D. Scarlatti's famous *Stabat Mater* for ten voices dates from his time at the Cappella Giulia,[33] and he also wrote some church music while working later in Portugal and Spain. Corelli was the reigning violin virtuoso in Rome; no vocal music by him survives, however. Handel was in the employ of Francesco Maria Ruspoli, Marquis of Cerveteri, and he wrote some splashy music for church performance, including his memorable *Dixit Dominus* (April 1707) and Vespers music for the Feast of Our Lady of Mount Carmel at Santa Maria di Montesanto (July 1707).[34]

Another apex in eighteenth-century Roman church music occurred between 1750 and 1753, when Niccolò Jommelli was chapel-master at the Cappella Giulia. Up to this point, his career had been primarily in opera, but he wrote an oratorio for Rome in 1749, allowing him to gain the favour of important cardinals. The Pope named him *maestro coadiutore* of St Peter's, assisting *maestro* Pietro Paolo Bencini.[35] After writing more operas for Vienna, he returned to Rome and St Peter's for Corpus Christi in 1750, and embarked

32 For an example, see Malcolm Boyd, 'Die Kirchenmusik von Domenico Scarlatti', *Kirchenmusikalisches Jahrbuch*, 72 (1988), p. 119.

33 Domenico Scarlatti, *Stabat Mater; a dieci voce e basso continuo*, ed. Jürgen Jürgens (Mainz, 1973).

34 For a score of these works, see Handel, *The Roman Vespers of 1707*, ed. Ian Cheverton, Robert Court (principal ed.), Robin Stowell and H. C. Robbins Landon (Cardiff, n.p.).

35 Wolfgang Hochstein, *Die Kirchenmusik von Niccolò Jommelli (1714–1774)* (Hildesheim, 1984), p. 32.

on an intensive three-year period of writing materials for Mass and Offices, especially Vespers. Jommelli composed in *stile antico*, such as in his full cycle of Holy Week responsories – twenty-seven movements in all – but he more commonly wrote in a more modern style featuring soloists, perhaps two SATB choirs and a string orchestra, forces heard to good advantage in his *Dixit Dominus* in F (1751), and his *Aurea luce* (1750) for solo voices, double choir and continuo, which is said to have been performed with eleven groups of performers spread throughout the huge basilica.[36] He also wrote highly virtuosic works for soloists, such as his *Domus mea* (1750) for soprano and alto soloists and continuo.[37] Among the important sacred composers in Rome following Jommelli were Giovanni Battista Costanzi (1704–78), who became *maestro di cappella* at St Peter's in 1755 and left an output of twenty-one masses and other works, and Giovanni Battista Casali (1715–92), who held several positions at major Roman churches and has an extant output of twenty-four masses among other pieces.

Milan

The capital of Lombardy was closely linked to Austria for most of the eighteenth century, meaning that its musicians tended to follow the Viennese lead. Milanese musical standards rivalled those of other major Italian centres, and the most important composer there during the century was Giovanni Battista Sammartini (1700/1–75). Sammartini was also *maestro* at an unusual number of Milanese religious institutions; documents from the 1760s and 1770s list him in such positions at eight and eleven different churches, respectively.[38] There were many important performances of church music within the city for which Sammartini wrote music and directed, and his extant output includes mass movements, psalm settings and eight Lenten cantatas, among other works, written in styles already covered in detail in this chapter. Charles Randall Verble's study and transcription of five of Sammartini's psalm settings offers convincing proof of the composer's abilities in large-scale sacred works.[39] Other important church musicians in Milan during the century included Johann Christian Bach, who was in the city from 1755 to 1762 and worked for a time as an organist at the Duomo. The *cappella* at the latter institution was active throughout the century, led by such musicians as Giuseppe Sarti (1778–87).

36 Marita P. McClymonds, *et al.*, 'Jommelli, Niccolò', in Macey (ed.), *Grove Music Online* (accessed 23 May 2007).

37 Jommelli, *Sieben kleine Kirchenkompositionen für 1–5 Solostimmen und Generalbass*, ed. Wolfgang Hochstein (Zurich, 1986), pp. 6–7.

38 Bathia Churgin, 'Sammartini, Giovanni Battista', in Macey (ed.), *Grove Music Online* (accessed 24 May 2007).

39 Charles Randall Verble, 'Five Psalm Settings by Giovanni Battista Sammartini', PhD thesis (Northwestern University, 2003).

Sacred music in eighteenth-century Iberia and Latin America

Spain and Portugal, and their colonies, carved out proud musical histories during the seventeenth century. In the area of setting Latin texts for sacred use, composers in these countries continued to cultivate the *stile antico* while also moving confidently into concertato writing, directions followed in Italy and elsewhere in Europe as well. Spanish and Portuguese composers were influenced by composers such as Giovanni Gabrieli in concertato writing, but also built upon the traditions of their own countries in the *stile antico*, represented by the Spaniard Tomás Luis de Victoria (1548–1611) and the Portuguese Manuel Cardoso (1566–1650). The continued presence of the *stile antico* in the works of Mexican composer Manuel de Zumaya (*c.* 1678–1755) has been discussed by Craig H. Russell.[40]

There was a strain of independence in Iberian sacred music that had started in the sixteenth century, based upon a tradition of vernacular texts in worship music. The villancico first appeared in the late fifteenth century as a courtly song that from its beginnings included examples of devotional texts. During the sixteenth century it became a religious genre with vernacular texts performed as a substitute for Latin responsories in Christmas and Epiphany matins services and for Corpus Christi processions and services, celebration of saints' days and other occasions. The genre became ubiquitous throughout the Spanish and Portuguese Empires during the seventeenth century, becoming a large part of the compositional duties of a *maestro de capilla* and part of much-anticipated events at cathedrals, churches, chapels and monasteries.[41] The musical style of these works during the seventeenth century was based mainly on theatrical music, often with primarily chordal textures, triple meter with rich use of hemiola and vocal parts within fairly narrow ranges. This constituted a Spanish musical style for the setting of vernacular texts that remained prevalent into the eighteenth century, but not without significant challenge from Italian opera in the decades around 1700.

The Spanish and Portuguese acceptance of Italianate music around 1700 was long portrayed as a blot on Iberian musical history. As Juan José Carreras has noted, 'late nineteenth-century Spanish musicology centred on the recovery of a lost golden past in which the foreign, especially Italianate, eighteenth century

40 Craig H. Russell, 'Manuel de Sumaya: Reexamining the *a Cappella* Choral Music of a Mexican Master', in David Crawford and G. Grayson Wagstaff (eds.), *Encomium Musicae: Essays in Memory of Robert J. Snow* (Hillsdale, NY, 2002), pp. 91–106.
41 For a detailed consideration of the genre, see Paul R. Laird, *Towards a History of the Spanish Villancico* (Warren, MI, 1997).

was looked upon as playing a key antagonistic role'.[42] Carreras substitutes a notion of Iberian music in a process of modernization, a useful perspective given the international popularity of Italian opera at this time. Louise Stein has also placed this process within 'the modernization of institutions' which 'brought a devaluation of traditional Spanish music and its assumptions'.[43]

The adoption of monody and the concertato style by Iberian composers in the early seventeenth century shows that they had already looked to Italy, as had musicians in several European countries in the early Baroque. The style associated with Italian opera of the later seventeenth century, however, was a subsequent acquisition. Juan Hidalgo (1614–85), harpist for the Real Capilla, wrote scores for musical theatre in Spain in the 1660s, works in which he made use of recitatives, usually of a *secco* variety and with little dissonance.[44] Villancico performances usually coincided with the publication of the texts sung in the service,[45] and the appearance of Italianate music in this most Spanish of genres may be studied through attention to these sources, usually called *pliegos sueltos* in Spanish. One section of a text is identified as a *relación en recitativo* in a Christmas service at Toledo Cathedral in 1678,[46] and further examples appeared in Toledan Christmas services in the 1680s and 1690s.[47] We witness Italianate musical styles at the Spanish court in *pliegos sueltos* from the Real Capilla, such as from Christmas 1703.[48] Six of the seven villancicos in the *pliego suelto* are in traditional forms, with an *estribillo* and *coplas*, and sometimes an *introducción*, but in the third villancico the *estribillo* divides into the following sections: *Arieta Ital.*, *Coro*, *Recit. Ital.*, *Ariet. Recit.*, *Ariet.* and *Alegre*. The text even refers to Italian influence at the court of Spain's new French king, with the line 'nuestro Italiano en metro Francés'. Subsequent *pliegos sueltos* from the Real Capilla become even more explicit concerning the Italian influence.[49]

42 Juan José Carreras, 'Introduction', in Malcolm Boyd and Carreras (eds.), *Music in Spain during the Eighteenth Century* (Cambridge, 1998), p. 2.

43 Louise K. Stein, 'The Iberian Peninsula', in Buelow (ed.), *The Late Baroque Era* (Englewood Cliffs, NJ, 1993), p. 423.

44 See William Muir Bussey, *French and Italian Influence on the Zarzuela, 1700–1770* (Ann Arbor, MI, 1982), p. 19. The most detailed consideration of Hidalgo's musical theatre pieces is found in Louise K. Stein, *Songs of Mortals, Dialogues of the Gods: Music and Theatre in Seventeenth-Century Spain* (Oxford, 1993).

45 For a description of these *pliegos sueltos* as sources for the study of villancicos, see Laird, *Towards a History*, pp. 63–7.

46 Madrid, Biblioteca Nacional, *siglum* VE 88–43.

47 See Biblioteca Nacional, *Catálogo de villancicos de la Biblioteca Nacional: Siglo XVII* (Madrid, 1992), pp. 195–200.

48 Madrid, Biblioteca Nacional, *siglum* VE 1306–4.

49 Juan José Carreras, 'From Literes to Nebra', in Boyd and Carreras (eds.), *Music in Spain during the Eighteenth Century*, pp. 13–14; Alvaro Torrente, 'Italianate Sections in the Villancicos of the Royal Chapel', in Boyd and Carreras (eds.), *Music in Spain during the Eighteenth Century*, pp. 72–9; *Catálogo de villancicos de la Biblioteca Nacional: Siglos XVIII–XIX* (Madrid, 1990), pp. 263–329.

Some in Spain condemned this attraction to Italian music, such as the critic and essayist Benito Jerónimo Feijóo y Montenegro (1676–1764), a Benedictine monk. In *La música de los templos*, he criticized operatic music in church, placing full blame on the shoulders of Sebastián Durón (1660–1716), Spain's leading composer in the years around 1700: 'This is the species of music, with which Italians, by the hand of their beloved master Durón, has regaled us; for he was the man, who first introduced foreign modes into the music of Spain.'[50] Feijóo's objections are legion, such as those concerning the 'diminution of figures', causing such rapid passages that do 'not give space for the ear to perceive the melody'.[51] He goes on to condemn Durón and the Italian composers who served as his models for excessive word-painting. Feijóo might have fretted about Italian musical influence, but, as will be shown in our consideration of sacred music in the Spanish and Portuguese Empires, he might as well have been shouting at the rain.

The Spanish Empire

Spain witnessed a brand new era at the beginning of the eighteenth century when King Charles II, the last of the Spanish Hapsburgs, died without issue in 1700. Louis XIV of France promptly placed his grandson Philip, who had survived the War of Spanish Succession, on the throne in Madrid. Philip V brought Spain new influences with French court fashions and dances, and an additional dose of Italian opera. Musical taste within the Spanish church, and for the entire Empire, was determined in Madrid, where there were three royal chapels: the crown's Real Capilla, and the chapels at the monasteries of Descalzas and Encarnación.[52] Spain's most famous musicians worked at least part of their careers at one of these institutions, and if one was hired at one of them he seldom thereafter left Madrid, and his musical works often circulated in manuscript throughout the Empire.

Chapel-masters at major cathedrals were also important in the Spanish musical hierarchy, including major institutions in Latin America. In Spain, especially significant posts included those at Toledo, Seville, Santiago de Compostela, Salamanca, Barcelona, Valencia and Zaragoza. Musicians in these positions composed new villancicos and Latin works every year, and

50 Feijóo's essay in the original Spanish may be found in his *Theatro crítico universal. Discursos varios en todo género de materias, para desengaño de errores communes* (Madrid, 1726–40), 9 vols, vol. 1, pp. 273–96. I have quoted Feijóo from a contemporary English translation: *Three Essays or Discourses on the following Subjects. A Defence or Vindication of the Women. Church Music. A Comparison between Antient and Modern Music. Translated From The Spanish of Feyjóo By A Gentleman* (London, 1778), p. 149.

51 *Ibid.*, pp. 145–6.

52 Craig H. Russell, 'Spain in the Enlightenment', in Neal Zaslaw (ed.), *The Classical Era From the 1740s to the End of the 18th Century* (Englewood Cliffs, NJ, 1989), p. 351.

exchanged villancico texts and musical works on a regular basis.[53] Much of the music that they wrote could have been produced by composers active in Italy.

There were many outstanding musicians in Spain during the eighteenth century, but few native Spaniards have become well known. The most famous musicians were Italians, including Domenico Scarlatti, the castrato Farinelli (Carlo Broschi) and Luigi Boccherini. Another important foreign-born musician active in Madrid but less famous today was Francisco Courcelle (1705–78), born in Italy of French parents, who became *maestro de capilla* of the Real Capilla in 1738. Among the best-known Spanish composers of the period were: Sebastián Durón (Real Capilla *maestro* from 1702 who fled to France in 1706 after supporting the enemy Austrian faction), José de Torres y Martínez Bravo (1670–1738, functionally *maestro* from Durón's departure until his own death), Antonio Literes (1672–1748, a court composer) and José de Nebra (1702–68, organist and vice-chapel-master at the Real Capilla). Fabián García Pacheco (*c.* 1725–*c.* 1808) was a theatre music composer in Madrid whose religious music circulated widely throughout the Spanish Empire. Among the many noted musicians working in religious institutions outside of Madrid during the century were: Francesc Valls (1671–1747, *maestro* at Barcelona Cathedral), Antonio Rodríguez de Hita (1722–87, *maestro* at Palencia Cathedral before becoming chapel-master at Encarnación), Antonio Soler (discussed above) and Francisco Jávier García Fajer (1730–1809, nicknamed 'El Españoleto' and long-time *maestro* at La Seo Cathedral in Zaragoza, from where he engineered a major reform that helped remove villancicos from Spanish churches).[54]

As Spain and Portugal colonized the New World, they transferred their religious system there, including the establishment of forty-three dioceses and major cathedrals, along with hundreds of monasteries, convents, oratories and other institutions. In Lima alone, for example, in the early eighteenth century, there were fifty-four churches, twenty monasteries and twelve convents.[55] Although colonial music in Latin America has become a subject of interest in the last five decades or so – led by the protean efforts of Robert Stevenson[56] – large lacunae remain, and we can only begin here to capture the breadth of

53 Laird, *Towards a History*, pp. 179–84.

54 For an excellent survey of church music in Spain during the eighteenth century, see Antonio Martín Moreno, *Siglo XVIII*, vol. 4 of *Historia de la música española*, ed. Pablo López de Osaba (Madrid, 1985), pp. 23–210.

55 For a splendid survey of music in Latin American institutions, see Daniel Mendoza de Arce, *Music in Ibero-America: A Historical Survey* (Lanham, MD and London, 2001), p. 311. Latin American religious institutions are discussed on pp. 277–363.

56 Robert Stevenson contributed some of the first books on music in colonial Spanish America: see *Music in Mexico: A Historical Survey* (New York, 1952); and *The Music of Peru: Aboriginal and Viceroyal Epochs* (Washington, DC, 1960). He also provided catalogues of a number of important Latin American archives in his *Renaissance and Baroque Musical Sources in the Americas* (Washington, DC, 1970), and published musical editions and many useful articles in his journal *Inter-American Music Review*.

activity. There were, however, certain musicians active in Spanish America during the 1700s who have garnered attention from scholars, identified here as we move south from Mexico and the Caribbean. The most important composers in Mexico during the period worked as *maestros* at Mexico City Cathedral, including Antonio de Salazar (*c.* 1650–1715), the *criollo* Manuel de Zumaya (*c.* 1678–1755, who also served at Oaxaca Cathedral), Italian violinist Ignacio de Jerusalem (1707–69) and organist Matteo Tollis de La Roca (*c.* 1710–81). The most important musician at Santiago de Guatemala Cathedral during the century was the *maestro* Rafael Antonio Castellanos (*c.* 1730–91). Esteban Salas y Castro Montes de Oca (1725–1803) was a noted chapel-master at Havana Cathedral in Cuba, as was Francisco Pérez Camacho (1659–1725) at Caracas Cathedral. The most important musicians at Santafé de Bogotá Cathedral in Colombia were Juan de Herrera (*c.* 1665–1738) and Francisco Jiménez de Alarcón (*c.* 1675–1724). Lima Cathedral boasted three of Latin America's finest musicians of the century: Tomás de Torrejón y Velasco (1644–1728), Roque Ceruti (*c.* 1683–1760) and José de Orejón y Aparicio (1705–65). In Bolivia, at Chuquisaca, also known as La Plata Cathedral (now Sucre), the following made significant compositional contributions: Juan de Araujo (1646–1714), Manuel Mesa y Carrizo (*c.* 1725–73), Eustaquio Franco Rebollo (*c.* 1710–86) and Estanislao Miguel Leyseca (*c.* 1715–95). Also in Bolivia, at Potosí Cathedral, Antonio Durán de la Mota (*c.* 1680–1752) served as *maestro*. In Córdoba, Argentina, a major musician at the cathedral and a Jesuit missionary in the area was Domenico Zipoli (1688–1726), one of the finest musicians to work in South America during the period; he had previously had a significant career in Rome.

The villancico and cantada in the Spanish Empire

As noted above, the villancico was semi-liturgical. Several aspects of the genre violated church teachings concerning acceptable sacred music, and there were voices in the Iberian world and their colonies from the sixteenth century onwards that condemned the villancico.[57] But its popularity as a devotional vehicle that reflected the lives and interests of the typical member of society outweighed the disadvantages. Given their equally ubiquitous presence in monasteries and convents, it would seem that the average priest, monk and nun also enjoyed villancicos. This seems predictable in the case of villancicos for Corpus Christi, which usually remained devotional in tone, but less expected for many of the villancicos for the Christmas season, which often included stereotypical characters from the popular theatre and would be sung

57 See, for example, Laird, *Towards a History*, pp. 29–31, 146–51.

in outrageous dialects reflecting how the ruling *castellanos* heard Spanish being spoken by people from other provinces and countries.[58] These included *villancicos negros* that transmitted a pidgin dialect of Spanish as spoken by people of African descent.

The principal musical issues for the villancico in the eighteenth century are continued interest in the *estilo español*, which had dominated settings of Spanish and Portuguese vernacular texts during the seventeenth century,[59] and a growing interest in modern, Italianate music. The traditional style had been current in villancicos since Francisco Guerrero's publication of his *Canciones y villanescas espirituales* (1589),[60] and the persistence of a pervasive triple meter with rich use of syncopation and hemiola, mostly syllabic declamation, and a fondness for chordal textures, continued well into the eighteenth century. These more traditional villancicos usually include a section identified as the refrain, or *estribillo*, and verses, or *coplas*, and often begin with an *introducción*.

Composers born in the middle of the seventeenth century, still active as mature musicians early in the eighteenth, demonstrate the transition from the *estilo español* to a more Italianate style. Tómas de Torrejón y Velasco, active in Lima, began his career writing in the former, as heard in the villancico *A este solo peregrino* (1679); the text includes *estribillo* and *coplas*.[61] Sebastián Durón, working in Spain, also wrote villancicos and theatrical music in this style.[62] His villancico *Volcanes del amor* contains the standard use of triple meter with frequent hemiola and features a texture more imitative than chordal, producing a charming textural contrast.[63] Durón becomes more Italianate in *Dulcísimo dueño*, a Christmas villancico that appears to have been composed for Christmas 1705 at the Real Capilla.[64] This piece includes extensive chromaticism, uncommon in the genre during the eighteenth century, and has a concerted texture with a tenor soloist backed by an SSTB choir singing

58 For consideration of the texts of villancicos, see *ibid.*, pp. 153–84.

59 For a brief discussion of the *estilo español*, see Stein, 'The Iberian Peninsula', pp. 412–13.

60 See Laird, *Towards a History*, pp. 27–9.

61 The piece can be heard on the compact disc *Musique à la cité des Rois: Torrejón y Velasco*, Coro de Niños Cantores de Córdoba, Ensemble Elyma/Gabriel Garrido, K617 035, 1993.

62 For an example of Durón's theatrical music, see Durón, *Salir el amor del mundo* (1696), ed. Antonio Martín Moreno (Malaga, 1979).

63 Miguel Querol Gavaldá (ed.), *Villancicos polifónicos del siglo XVII*, vol. 42 of *Monumentos de la música española* (Barcelona, 1982), pp. 89–98.

64 The manuscript for this villancico is at the Real Biblioteca de San Lorenzo de El Escorial, *siglum* 32-5. A concordant text is in the *pliego suelto* at Madrid, Biblioteca Nacional, *siglum* VE 1306-9. The score for the villancico is given in Paul R. Laird, 'The Villancico Repertory at San Lorenzo del Escorial, *c.* 1630–*c.* 1715', 2 vols., PhD thesis (The University of North Carolina at Chapel Hill, 1986), vol. 2, pp. 50–80. Consideration of the work, with musical examples appears in Laird, *Towards a History*, pp. 98–102 and Laird, '*Dulcísimo Dueño* by Sebastián Durón: A "Poster Child" for the Baroque Villancico', in David Crawford and G. Grayson Wagstaff (eds.), *Encomium Musicae: Essays in Memory of Robert J. Snow* (Hillsdale, NY, 2002), pp. 493–507.

similar material. Metrically, the villancico is traditional. An example of a villancico from Mexico written by a composer of Durón's generation is *Tarará qui yo soy Antoniyo*, a delightful *villancico negro* by Antonio de Salazar for two sopranos and continuo in which phrases begin imitatively, but the majority of the work is homorhythmic.[65]

We witness the full adoption of Italian recitatives and arias in the decades around 1700 in Juan de Torres' *O quién pudiera alcanzar?*, scored for solo soprano, two violins, oboe and basso continuo. The composer's identity is uncertain, but one by this name worked in Madrid in the 1690s.[66] Torres uses the instruments in active, independent lines, and the solo soprano sings operatic vocal material in both arias and recitatives. In Spanish-speaking countries, such works became known as cantadas.

A Mexican composer who exemplifies the transition to writing cantadas is Manuel de Zumaya. One of his more traditional villancicos is *Sol-fa de Pedro*, written in 1715 as he competed to become *maestro* at Mexico City Cathedral. Full of word-painting based on musical puns, *Sol-fa de Pedro* is in the genre's traditional meter and has the imitative texture found in works by Durón.[67] Zumaya's transition to the cantada can be heard in many works, such as *Hoy sube arrebatada* for two treble instruments, soprano and continuo,[68] or appreciated in score study in Aurelio Tello's useful edition.[69] The variety of scoring found in villancicos from this generation appears in the output of Pedro Rabassa (1683–1767), *maestro* at the cathedrals in Vich, Valencia and Seville. His villancico *Que habeis visto pastorcillos* (1722) is scored for twelve voices in three choirs, cello and continuo; a tenor recitative and aria from it have been published.[70] The aria includes an unusual duet texture between the tenor and cello with continuation of the traditional metric nature of the genre with alternation between 3/2 and 6/4.

Roque Ceruti (1683–1760), born in Milan and *maestro* at Lima Cathedral from 1728 to 1757, wrote elegant Italianate works.[71] Worthy examples include *Hoy que Francisco reluce*, scored for four voices, two violins and continuo, and filled with rapid semiquavers in the violins on account of the frequent vocal

65 See Robert Stevenson, *Christmas Music in Baroque Mexico* (Berkeley, 1974), pp. 160–2. The villancico appears on the recording *Spain in the New World: Renaissance, Baroque and Native American Music from New Spain*, Hesperus/Scott Reiss, Golden Apple 9768-77552-2, 1990.

66 For more on this piece and its possible attribution, see Laird, *Towards a History*, pp. 113–15.

67 *Sol-fa de Pedro* can be heard on *Mexican Baroque*, Chanticleer/Joseph Jennings, Teldec 4509-96353-2, 1994. Craig H. Russell prepared the editions for this recording and wrote the excellent programme notes.

68 A recording of this charming piece appears on the disc *Spain in the New World*.

69 Aurelio Tello (ed.), *Cantadas y villancicos de Manuel de Sumaya*, vol. 7 of *Archivo musical de la Catedral de Oaxaca, Tesoro de la música polifónica en México* (Mexico City, 1994).

70 See Vincenç Ripollès, *El villancico i la cantata del segle XVIII a València* (Barcelona, 1935), pp. xiii–xx.

71 Four of his villancicos and cantadas appear on a compact disc directed by Gabriel Garrido, *Musique Baroque en la Real Audiencia de Charcas: Le style italien à la Plata*, Ensemble Elyma/Gabriel Garrido, K617 064, 1996.

references to 'fuego' (fire), and *Según veo el aparato*, an *xácara* for two voices, two violins and continuo. An *xácara* was a type borrowed from popular theatre based upon the exploits of a young braggart, set by composers with especially rich use of hemiola.[72] This rhythmic character appears in both movements, the second of which closely approximates a *giga*. A composer of the same generation active in Spain whose music is comparable is José Pradas Guillén (1689–1757), chapel-master of Valencia Cathedral during the precise years that Ceruti was at Lima.[73] Another local composer whose villancicos have been studied in detail is Juan Francés de Iribarren (1698–1767), *maestro* at Málaga Cathedral from 1733 until his death.[74]

Examples of villancico composers from the Classic era include Esteban Salas y Castro Montes de Oca (1725–1803), Antonio Soler and Rafael Antonio Castellanos (1725–91). Salas y Castro, working in Havana, left villancicos, pastorelas and cantatas for Christmas, genres in which he showed marked interest after 1783.[75] The pastorela *Oh, niño soberano!*, scored for three vocal parts, two violins and continuo, opens with a gentle instrumental introduction, followed by a pastorela in 6/8 based on the *siciliano*, associated with shepherds in operas. The text includes reference to Christ as the 'good shepherd'. The voices sing in various combinations, mostly homorhythmically, and then often all together in the brief Allegro that follows, accompanied by active violin lines. Salas y Castro's gifts as a melodist appear as well in his solo cantata with violins, *Tú, mi Dios, entre galas*, including one *recitado* and an aria (Andante). The recitative is undistinguished, but the aria is based on a charming melodic idea in balanced phrases. The villancico *Claras luces* is long and multi-sectioned, scored for four voice parts and violins in the *estribillo*, with solo *coplas*.

Antonio Soler, as noted above, was *maestro* at San Lorenzo de El Escorial, where his 125 villancicos survive at the Escorial archive, 114 of them complete.[76] A representative work by Soler is *Fuego y agua en lid plausible* (1754), composed for SSAT soloists, SATB choir accompanied by organ, oboe, two

72 Laird, *Towards a History*, pp. 171–2.

73 His 300 extant villancicos and cantadas are the subject of a monograph, José Luis Palacios Garoz, *El último villancico barroco valenciano* (Castelló de la Plana, 1995).

74 Marta Sánchez, *XVIII Century Spanish Music: Villancicos of Juan Francés de Iribarren* (Pittsburgh, 1988). Two of Iribarren's villancicos appear on the compact disc, *Barroco español, 1: Villancicos, cantatas, et al.*, Al Ayre Español/Eduardo López Banzo, Deutsche Harmonia Mundi 77325, 1994.

75 Robert Stevenson, 'Salas y Castro, Esteban', in Macey (ed.), *New Grove Outline* (accessed 18 May 2007). Examples of his vernacular religious works appear on the compact disc, *Cuban Baroque Sacred Music: Esteban Salas*, Exaudi Choir of Cuba with Benedictine Monks of Santo Domingo de Silos/María Felicia Pérez, Jade 73138–35808–2, 1997.

76 Soler's villancicos have been considered in a monograph: Paulino Capdepón Verdú, *El P. Antonio Soler y el cultivo del villancico en El Escorial* (Real Monasterio de El Escorial, 1993). Capdepón has published a number of Soler's villancicos, see Soler, *Villancicos*, ed. Paulino Capdepón Verdú (Madrid, 1992–), 4 vols. Three of Soler's cantatas appear in *P. Antonio Soler (1729–1783), I. Música religiosa*, vols. 2 and 3, ed. José Sierra Pérez (San Lorenzo del El Escorial, 1997).

horns in D, two violins and basso continuo.[77] Soler wrote the work for the feast day of St Lawrence. The *obertura* is a Vivace and in rounded binary form, followed by a brief, harmonically ambiguous *introducción* in which the voices announce a contest between Fire and Water. The *estribillo*, in a triumphant D major with bows towards F-sharp major and B minor, highlights the contest, with soloists at times urging on Fire while the choir calls for Water's victory. The villancico concludes with a *recitado* and *aria*, the former predictable but with interesting chromaticism. The da capo aria is for solo tenor, usually doubled by the oboe. The tempo is unmarked, but apparently an Andante, with a florid vocal line. There are long melismas and ornaments on appropriate words, and the B section is in the relative minor with vocal trills and semiquavers in the violins to emphasize the word 'fire'. The polychoral forces join the tenor and orchestra for the repeat of the A section, providing effective punctuation to the elaborate tenor line. One aspect of Soler's villancicos not found in this work is the use of dance-like rhythms, which give some of his pieces a folk-like flavour. A fascinating contemporary of Soler working in Guatemala was Rafael Antonio Castellanos, also an effective exponent of the genre, whose villancicos have been studied by Dieter Lehnhoff.[78]

In the decades around 1800, the oratorio gradually replaced the villancico as the primary Spanish vernacular religious expression. A major figure in the gradual demise of the villancico was Zaragoza chapel-master Francisco Jávier García Fajer. The villancico had originally replaced the Latin responsories for Christmas and Epiphany matins a few centuries earlier, and García Fajer worked to reverse the process, writing Latin responsories that he sent to other Spanish cathedrals, convincing several of them to discontinue their use of the villancico in various services.[79] In the early nineteenth century it ceased to be a compositional expectation for *maestros* in the Spanish Empire.

Latin liturgical music in the Spanish Empire

The villancico was Iberia's unique contribution to religious vocal music. Many settings of Latin sacred texts in the Spanish Empire during the eighteenth

77 The villancico appears in Capdepón's edn., vol. 2, pp. 13–76. For an extended analysis with musical examples, see Laird, *Towards a History*, pp. 128–36.

78 See Dieter Lehnhoff, *Rafael Antonio Castellanos: Vida y obra de un músico guatemalteco* (Guatemala City, 1994), pp. 102–27 and Dieter Lehnhoff, 'The "Villancicos" of the Guatemalan Composer Raphael Antonio Castellanos (d. 1791): A Selective Edition and Critical Commentary', PhD thesis (The Catholic University of America, 1990). A number of Castellanos' villancicos appear on the recording *Capilla Musical: Música Histórica de Guatemala/Cantadas, Villancicos y Tocatas del Siglo XVIII*, Cristina Altamira and Quinteto MILLENIUM/Dieter Lehnhoff, 1992. For scores, see Alfred E. Lemmon (ed.), *La música de Guatemala en el siglo XVIII/Music from Eighteenth-Century Guatemala* (Antigua, Guatemala and South Woodstock, VT, 1986), pp. 57–123, and Dieter Lehnhoff, *Música de la época colonial en Guatemala* (Antigua and Guatemala, 1984), pp. 23–32.

79 Capdepón, *El P. Antonio Soler*, p. 45.

century, though, could have been written by one of any number of Italian church musicians. Far more famous than the actual sacred music written for church use in the eighteenth-century Spanish-speaking world is the controversy over a dissonance that Barcelona Cathedral chapel-master Francesc Valls used in his *Missa Scala Aretina* (1702) and the Madrid Royal Palace fire in 1734 that destroyed the Real Capilla's archive. In his mass, Valls had the temerity to bring in the second soprano on an unprepared ninth on 'miserere nobis' in the Gloria, an offence that caused printed comment from over fifty Spanish composers after 1715.[80] Valls defended himself and also wrote the lengthy treatise *Mapa armónico*. The 1734 palace fire destroyed valuable music that would have told us a great deal about the Real Capilla in earlier centuries, and it also left the institution without its repertory. The king commissioned royal musicians Antonio Literes, José de Nebra and José de Torres to write works to replenish the archive. Torres died two years later, but Francesco Courcelle also played a major role in the process. It is significant that these composers were also active in producing music for Madrid's theatres.

The amount of music in the Real Capilla archive remained a concern almost two decades later. In 1751 King Ferdinand VI ordered that works written by Torres and Courcelle be placed in the archive. At some point, Courcelle produced a document in which he proposed the quantity and quality of works needed for the archive, in the process providing a fascinating survey of the required genres, similar to practices in cathedrals.[81] Courcelle calls for the following: six dozen complete Masses; six each of Vespers of the Virgin and Common Vespers of the Saints; six each of hymns to the Virgin, the saints and other annual feasts; twelve Marian Litanies; twelve *Salves*; six settings of the *Te Deum*; four each of the sequences or proses for Easter, Pentecost, Corpus Christi and the Sorrows of Mary; four each of settings of the Lamentations for eight, four, three and two voices parts, and solos for SATB; a dozen settings of the *Miserere*; and four of the Offices for the Dead (with the texts for Martyrs) and Requiem masses with their sequence and necessary motets. Courcelle then suggested that the Real Capilla could acquire works from other musical centres, including Madrid, Rome, Naples, Bologna, Barcelona, Zaragoza, Córdoba, Toledo, Seville (he notes that all Spanish cathedrals possess music by *maestros especiales*) and Lisbon. Among the composers he mentions in these cities are: A. Scarlatti, Leo, Durante, Pergolesi, Valls, Palestrina, Benevoli, Carissimi, Morales, Victoria and D. Scarlatti (suggesting his music written in Rome).

80 See Craig H. Russell, 'Valls, Francisc', in Macey (ed.), *Grove Music Online* (accessed 20 May 2007) and Stein, 'The Iberian Peninsula, p. 423.
81 Martín Moreno, *Siglo XVIII*, pp. 48–9.

A brief survey of sacred musical works by composers from across the Spanish Empire provides a representative illustration of their collective efforts. Valls' *Missa Scala Aretina* (1702) reflects music from the end of the seventeenth century.[82] Valls scored the Mass for eleven voices (distributed SAT, SSAT, SATB) with a fourth choir of two violins, two oboes, two trumpets and cello, and includes a continuo part for each choir. The name of the mass is derived from Guido d'Arezzo's hexachord, used freely in various movements in both ascending and descending forms, and with chromatic alteration. (Rare for Spanish Masses, Valls did not set the Benedictus text.) Valls used his varied forces masterfully, optimizing the opportunity for contrasts of timbre. A few Italianate features appear, especially in lengthy melismas (such as early in the Gloria) and the presence of the violins and oboes, instruments associated in Spain at this time with the more modern sound.[83] Only a decade earlier, an instrumental choir in a polychoral work would have likely included shawms and sackbuts.

At least seventy-two Latin works by Sebastián Durón survive in archives in Spain and Latin America, among them most of the types listed by Courcelle.[84] Martín Moreno explains that Durón did not tend to use Italianate gestures in his religious music, as he did in his theatrical output.[85] The presence of violins in some of his Latin works indicates a marginal Italian influence, but many of Durón's Latin works are polychoral and reflect the same techniques of textural manipulation heard in Valls. Durón's *Lamentación segunda* for the Friday of Holy Week shows a composer with his heart in the seventeenth century.[86] It is scored for soprano solo, three violins and continuo, not unlike some of the more forward-looking motets written in Italy at this point, but the work breathes the air of earlier Italian monody stretching back to late Monteverdi and Carissimi. The work is profoundly beautiful, with the violin lines providing the equivalent of three other voice parts. Somewhat more mixed in style is Durón's *Lección de difuntos Taedet animam meam*, for two choirs (SSAT, SATB), two flutes, two violins and continuo, which includes *stile antico* where the instrumental parts are similar to those of the voices, but also at times more active.[87]

82 See Valls, *Missa Scala Aretina*, ed. José López-Calo (London, 1978); José López-Calo, 'The Spanish Baroque and Francisco Valls', *The Musical Times*, 113 (1972), pp. 353–6; and for a recording, *Francisco Valls: Mass 'Scala Aretina'*, The London Oratory Choir, Thames Chamber Orchestra/John Hoban, CRD 3371, 1994.

83 For a consideration of the oboe's entrance into Spanish ecclesiastical music, see: Joseba-Endika Berrocal Cebrián, '"Y que toque el abuè": una aproximación a los oboístas en el entorno eclesiástico español del siglo XVIII', *Artigrama*, 12 (1996–7), pp. 293–312.

84 Martín Moreno, *Siglo XVIII*, p. 39. 85 *Ibid.*, p. 40.

86 For a recording of this work, see *Barroco español, III: 'Quando muere el sol': Música penitencial en la Capilla Real de Madrid*, Al Ayre Español/Eduardo López Banzo, Deutsche Harmonia Mundi 77376, 1997.

87 Paulino Capdepón Verdú (ed.), *La música en la Real Capilla de Madrid* (Madrid, 1992), pp. 29–56.

Philip V's second wife, Isabel de Farnesio, pushed musicians of the Real Capilla in a more Italianate direction. Her favourite musician was Filippo Falconi, an inferior talent, whom she installed as director of a second chapel at the Palacio at La Granja. José de Torres followed Durón as chapel-master, and his music illustrates the turn of Spanish composers to the Italian.[88] When needed, he embraced the *stile antico*, as can be seen in his *Himno Pange lingua* for two choirs (SSAT, SATB) and continuo.[89] His setting of the *Miserere* is from earlier in his career, perhaps *c.* 1700,[90] and is scored for four voice parts (SATB), two violins, viola da gamba and continuo. The instrumental parts provide bold contrast with the voice parts in sections for all four voices and in solo passages, where arias and recitatives appear to emerge. The dual nature of the work is represented in the notation, a traditional alternative common in seventeenth-century Spain for the *antico* style, and a more modern style for the newer music. Torres' move to Italian musical styles is evident in many of his works, including his *Lamentación segunda*, for Holy Thursday, scored for solo soprano, two violins, obbligato cello and continuo.[91] The vocal and instrumental lines in this work are independent of each other, each contributing to the tragic affect. Other outstanding works by Torres, typifying his musical style later in life, are a mass and Requiem composed in 1724, the year that Philip V abdicated in favour of his son Luis, who died before his coronation. Both demonstrate that Torres had fully adopted the concertato Italian style, and that he was writing solo lines for his sacred music that would be appropriate in an opera seria.[92]

One of the finest Spanish composers of the generation was José de Nebra. His sacred output includes many pieces written for the eight voice parts and instruments popular at the Real Capilla, but he also composed works for other cathedrals. His tendency to place a choir in block chords appears in his *Principio de Maitines de Navidad* (1751) and *Responsorium I* for Christmas Matins (1752), both available in an excellent recording.[93] These works feature wide contrasts between solo and choral sections, and a highly operatic dimension is evident in the tenor solo 'Quoniam Deus Magnus Dominus', energetically accompanied

88 For a brief consideration of Torres' style and a catalogue of his works at the archive of the Real Palacio, see Begoña Lolo, *La música en la Real Capilla de Madrid: José de Torres y Martínez Bravo (h. 1.670–1.738)* (Madrid, 1988), pp. 127–91.

89 Capdepón Verdú (ed.), *La música en la Real Capilla de Madrid*, pp. 57–74.

90 *Barroco español, III* also includes a recording of Torres' *Miserere*. 91 *Barroco español, III*.

92 This Mass and *Misa de Difuntos* have been recorded: *Días de Gloria y Muerte: Dos misas de José de Torres (1670–1738)*, Estil Concertant/Josep R. Gil-Tárrega, Comunidad de Madrid Dirección General de Investigación, Consejería de Educación and Sociedad Español de Musicología, 2001.

93 *Madrid 1752: Sacred Music from the Royal Chapel of Spain*, Madrid Barroco/Grover Wilkins, Dorian 93237, 2001.

by trumpets and strings. Nebra's *Misa Breve* for two choirs (SSAT, SATB), two violins, two oboes, trumpet and organ continuo and *Letanía de Nuestra Señora* for two choirs and continuo further demonstrate his mastery of the polychoral idiom and idiomatic writing for instruments.[94] Working in Madrid at the same time was the Italian Francesco Courcelle, a composer of the first rank in both sacred and theatrical music, who left thirty masses and other church music. He was more interested in counterpoint than Nebra, but there are few differences in their musical styles, as can be heard in Courcelle's *Responsorium II* and *III* for Christmas Matins.[95] These works possess a wide emotional range and gloriously decorative solo writing, such as the 'Stella, quam viderunt Magi', with satisfying and delicate interplay between solo soprano and trumpet. A brief work by Courcelle is *Letanía de Nuestra Señora* for two choirs (SSAT, SATB), two oboes, two violins, two violas, cello, bass and organ, which uses the concertato principle throughout in the voices and has an active instrumental accompaniment.[96] From the next generation of Spanish composers, several of Antonio Soler's liturgical works have been published, ranging from one- and two-choir works with basso continuo accompaniment to others that include a small orchestra.[97]

One of the better, and most studied, composers working in Latin America during the century was the Italian Ignacio de Jerusalem.[98] The Polychoral Mass in D major and the psalm *Dixit Dominus* are excellent examples of Jerusalem's music,[99] both showing his elegant grasp of the *style galant*. From a later generation, Esteban Salas y Castro Montes de Oca, based in Havana, left a sizeable output of Latin works, including worthy examples of *Salve Regina* settings in C minor and D minor, a Mass in G minor and a Requiem Mass, all of which have been recorded.[100] His orchestral writing includes active woodwind participation, especially in several movements from the Requiem Mass.

94 Capdepón Verdú (ed.), *La música en la Real Capilla de Madrid*, pp. 75–200. 95 *Madrid 1752*.

96 Capdepón Verdú (ed.), *La música en la Real Capilla de Madrid*, pp. 201–20.

97 See. *P. Antonio Soler, II. Música religiosa*, ed. Eutimio Bullón Pastor (San Lorenzo de El Escorial, 1983) and *P. Antonio Soler (1729–1783), II. Música religiosa*, vols. 2 and 3, ed. José Sierra Pérez (San Lorenzo de El Escorial, 1998–9).

98 In addition to Craig H. Russell's entry on the composer in *Grove Music Online*, see his 'Hidden Structures and Sonorous Symmetries: Ignacio de Jerusalem's Concerted Masses in Eighteenth-Century Mexico', in Paul R. Laird and Craig H. Russell (eds.), *Res Musicae: Essays in Honor of James W. Pruett* (Warren, MI, 2001), pp. 136–60.

99 Both works appear on *Mexican Baroque*. For more works by Jerusalem, see another Chanticleer disc, *Matins for the Virgin of Guadalupe*, Teldec 21829, 1998 and *México Barroco Vol. I*, Schola Cantorum, Conjunto de Cámara de la Ciudad de México/Benjamín Juárez Echenique, Urtext 2001, 1995.

100 See *Cuban Baroque Sacred Music*.

Portuguese Empire

The general outlines of sacred music in Portugal and Brazil resemble those for Spain and its colonies, especially the increasing interest in Italian music, but there are also significant differences. Portugal gained its political independence from Spain in 1668, after which it was necessary for them to re-build their economy and re-establish national objectives related to the management of Brazil.[101] These goals were largely realized – partly through the discovery of gold in Brazil – helping to make possible a musical flowering at the royal court under King João V, who reigned from 1706 to 1750. This ran parallel with a growth in musical opportunities around Portugal, meaning that, as in Spain, there were many local composers writing villancicos and Latin liturgical music. Similar cases existed in a number of Brazilian centres as well, including Salvador de Bahia, Olinda, Recife, Rio de Janeiro, São Paulo, Vale de Paraiba and the region of Minas Gerais, where a mulatto society developed with rich sacred music traditions in Vila Rica and other centres.[102]

Italian opera was also popular in Lisbon, but Italianate influence remained in the royal chapel under João V on account of the monarch's desire to model his court's sacred music on that in Rome. The *stile antico* was highly favoured in Portugal, especially by a number of seventeenth-century composers. Portugal boasted little significant activity in sacred music in the decades before 1700, and what little occurred was overshadowed by that of Spanish composers who wrote in similar genres and styles.[103]

King João V increased the number of musicians involved in his celebration of divine services and in 1713 founded a musical seminary. In 1710 his chapel was named a collegiate church, and in 1716 he managed to raise it to the level of a patriarchal chapel. The king also supported music in other churches in Lisbon, sent some of his best musicians to Rome for study, including António Teixeira (1707–post-1769), João Rodrigues Esteves (*c.* 1700–51) and Francisco António de Almeida (fl. 1722–52). João V ordered copies of Roman choirbooks and banned the performance of villancicos in his chapel in order to increase further the acceptance of Vatican orthodoxy. When he hired Domenico Scarlatti in 1719, he took him from the directorship of the Cappella Giulia at St Peter's Basilica. An excellent example of Italianate music by an important Portuguese composer is the Mass for Eight Voices by Esteves,[104] who in his one hundred

101 See Stein, 'The Iberian Peninsula', pp. 427–32.
102 Mendoza de Arce, *Music in Ibero-America*, pp. 326–41.
103 For a demonstration of similarities between Portuguese and Spanish villancicos, see José Augusto Alegria (ed.), *António Marques Lésbio (1639–1709)*, vol. 46 of *Portugaliae Musica, Série B* (Lisbon, 1985).
104 See the compact disc *Domenico Scarlatti, Stabat Mater a dieci voci e basso continuo; João Rodrigues Esteves, Missa a oito voces*, Vocal and Instrumental Ensemble Currende/Erik van Nevel, Accent 9069, 1990

extant works moved through the *stile antico* to the updated counterpoint of the contemporary Roman school, and finally to the more concertato approach heard in this work.[105]

Among the best composers working in late-eighteenth-century colonial Brazil were José Joaquim Emérico Lobo de Mesquita (1746–1805) and José Maurício Nunes Garcia (1767–1830). Both were mulattos.[106] Lobo de Mesquita spent most of his career in Arraial do Tejuco (now Diamantina, Minas Gerais), where he was an organist. Many pieces by him survive, most not unlike the compositions of Leo and Pergolesi. Lobo de Mesquita in particular shows fine command of interactive possibilities between solo voices and a four-part homophonic choir. A representative work is the Mass for Four Voices for Ash Wednesday, which includes a violoncello obbligato part and organ continuo.[107] José Maurício served as chapel-master at Rio de Janeiro Cathedral, and took the same position with the Portuguese royal chapel in 1808, when King João VI escaped to Brazil during Napoleon's conquest of Portugal. There are 237 extant works by Maurício, including nineteen extant masses and a Requiem Mass from 1816, perhaps his most famous composition.[108]

Select Bibliography

Augusto Alegria, José (ed.), *António Marques Lésbio (1639–1709)*, vol. 46 of *Portugaliae Musica, Série B*. Lisbon, 1985

Barnett, David William, Jr. 'Francesco Durante's "Magnificat in B-flat": A Conductor's Analysis'. DMA thesis, University of Miami, 1980

Berger, Jean. 'The Sacred Works of Giacomo Antonio Perti'. *Journal of the American Musicological Society*, 17 (1964), pp. 370–7

Berrocal Cebrián, Joseba-Endika. '"Y que toque el abuè": una aproximación a los oboístas en el entorno eclesiástico español del siglo XVIII'. *Artigrama*, 12 (1996–7), pp. 293–312

Biblioteca Nacional. *Catálogo de villancicos de la Biblioteca Nacional: Siglo XVII*. Madrid, 1992

Catálogo de villancicos de la Biblioteca Nacional: Siglos XVIII-XIX. Madrid, 1990

105 See Pieter Andriessen's notes in *ibid*.

106 See the compact disc *Sacred Music From 18th-Century Brazil*, Ensemble Turicum/Luiz Alves Da Silva, Claves 50–9521, 1995; Sérgio Dias' notes are a useful source of information.

107 See Antônio Lincoln Campos de Andrade, 'Critical Edition of the Missa a 4 Vozes para Quarta-feira de Cinzas para Coro Misto, Violoncello Obbligato e Órgão by the Brazilian colonial composer José Joaquim Emerico Lobo de Mesquita (1746–1805)', DMA thesis (University of Kansas, 2002). Several works by Lobo de Mesquita appear on *Sacred Music From 18th-Century Brazil*.

108 José Maurício M. Nunes Garcia, *Requiem*, ed. Cleofe Person de Mattos, Kirchheim/Teck, Hänssler Edition, 1989. The work has been recorded, for example, on the LP *Columbia Records Black Composers Series*, CBS Special Products, P 19425–P 19433, 1987. Eight motets by the composer appear on *Sacred Music From 18th-Century Brazil*.

Boyd, Malcolm. 'Die Kirchenmusik von Domenico Scarlatti'. *Kirchenmusikalisches Jahrbuch*, 72 (1988), pp. 117–25

'Rome: The Power of Patronage'. In George J. Buelow (ed.), *The Late Baroque Era*. Englewood Cliffs, NJ, 1993, pp. 39–65

Boyd, Malcolm and Juan José Carreras (eds.). *Music in Spain during the Eighteenth Century*. Cambridge, 1998

Brandvik, Paul Allen. 'Selected Motets of Alessandro Scarlatti'. DMA thesis, University of Illinois at Urbana-Champaign, 1969

Bussey, William Muir. *French and Italian Influence on the Zarzuela, 1700–1770*. Ann Arbor, MI, 1982

Campos de Andrade, Antônio Lincoln. 'Critical Edition of the Missa a 4 Vozes para Quarta-feira de Cinzas para Coro Misto, Violoncello Obbligato e Órgão by the Brazilian Colonial Composer José Joaquim Emerico Lobo de Mesquita (1746–1805)'. DMA thesis, University of Kansas, 2002

Capdepón, Paulino. *El P. Antonio Soler y el cultivo del villancico en El Escorial*. Real Monasterio de El Escorial, 1993

Capdepón Verdú, Paulino (ed.). *La música en la Real Capilla de Madrid*. Madrid, 1992

Downs, Philip G. *Classical Music: The Era of Haydn, Mozart, and Beethoven*. New York, 1992

Feijóo y Montenegro, Benito Jerónimo. *Theatro crítico universal. Discursos varios en todo género de materias, para desengaño de errores communes*. 9 vols., Madrid, 1726–40

Three Essays or Discourses on the following Subjects. A Defence or Vindication of the Women. Church Music. A Comparison between Antient and Modern Music. Translated From The Spanish of Feyjóo By A Gentleman. London, 1778

Gianturco, Carolyn. 'Naples: A City of Entertainment'. In George J. Buelow (ed.), *The Late Baroque Era From the 1680s to 1740*. Englewood Cliffs, NJ, 1993, pp. 94–128

Hill, John Walter. *Baroque Music: Music in Western Europe, 1580–1750*. New York, 2005

Hochstein, Wolfgang. *Die Kirchenmusik von Niccolò Jommelli (1714–1774)*. Hildesheim, 1984

Hucke, Helmut. 'Pergolesi's *Missa S. Emidio*'. In Allan W. Atlas (ed.), *Music in the Classic Period: Essays in Honor of Barry S. Brook*. New York, 1985, pp. 99–115

Laird, Paul Robert. 'The Villancico Repertory at San Lorenzo del Escorial, *c.* 1630–*c* 1715', 2 vols. PhD thesis, The University of North Carolina at Chapel Hill, 1986

Laird, Paul R. *Towards a History of the Spanish Villancico*. Warren, MI, 1997

'*Dulcísimo Dueño* by Sebastián Durón: A 'Poster Child' for the Baroque Villancico'. In David Crawford and G. Grayson Wagstaff (eds.), *Encomium Musicae: Essays in Memory of Robert J. Snow*. Hillsdale, NY, 2002, pp. 493–507

Lehnhoff, Dieter. *Música de la época colonial en Guatemala*. Antigua and Guatemala, 1984

'The 'Villancicos' of the Guatemalan Composer Raphael Antonio Castellanos (d. 1791): A Selective Edition and Critical Commentary'. PhD thesis, The Catholic University of America, 1990

Rafael Antonio Castellanos: Vida y obra de un músico guatemalteco. Guatemala City, 1994

Lemmon, Alfred E. (ed.). *La música de Guatemala en el siglo XVIII/Music from Eighteenth-Century Guatemala*, Antigua, Guatemala and South Woodstock, VT, 1986

Lolo, Begoña. *La música en la Real Capilla de Madrid: José de Torres y Martínez Bravo (h. 1.670–1.738)*. Madrid, 1988

López-Calo, José. 'The Spanish Baroque and Francisco Valls'. *The Musical Times*, 113 (1972), pp. 353–6

Martín Moreno, Antonio. *Siglo XVIII*, vol. 4 of *Historia de la música española*, ed. Pablo López de Osaba. Madrid, 1985

Mendoza de Arce, Daniel. *Music in Ibero-America: A Historical Survey*. Lanham, MD and London, 2001

Palacios Garoz, José Luis. *El último villancico barroco valenciano*. Castelló de la Plana, 1995

Pestelli, Giorgio. *The Age of Mozart and Beethoven*. Trans. Eric Cross, Cambridge, 1984

Querol Gavaldá, Miguel (ed.). *Villancicos polifónicos del siglo XVII*, vol. 42 of *Monumentos de la música española*. Barcelona, 1982

Ripollès, Vincenç. *El villancico i la cantata del segle XVIII a València*. Barcelona, 1935

Russell, Craig H. 'Spain in the Enlightenment'. In Neal Zaslaw (ed.), *The Classical Era From the 1740s to the end of the 18th Century*. Englewood Cliffs, NJ, 1989, pp. 350–67

'Hidden Structures and Sonorous Symmetries: Ignacio de Jerusalem's Concerted Masses in Eighteenth-Century Mexico'. In Paul R. Laird and Craig H. Russell (eds.), *Res Musicae: Essays in Honor of James W. Pruett*. Warren, MI, 2001, pp. 136–60

'Manuel de Sumaya: Reexamining the *a Cappella* Choral Music of a Mexican Master'. In David Crawford and G. Grayson Wagstaff (eds.), *Encomium Musicae: Essays in Memory of Robert J. Snow*. Hillsdale, NY, 2002, pp. 91–106

Sánchez, Marta. *XVIII Century Spanish Music: Villancicos of Juan Francés de Iribarren*. Pittsburgh, OH, 1988

Shearon, Stephen M. 'Latin Sacred Music and Nicola Fago: The Career and Sources of an Early Eighteenth-Century Neapolitan *maestro di cappella*'. PhD thesis, The University of North Carolina at Chapel Hill, 1993

Smith, Peter. *Concerted Sacred Music of the Bologna School*, vol. 57 of *Recent Researches in Music of the Baroque Era*. Madison, WI, 1987

Stein, Louise K., 'The Iberian Peninsula'. In George J. Buelow (ed.), *The Late Baroque Era*. Englewood Cliffs, NJ, 1993, pp. 411–34

Songs of Mortals, Dialogues of the Gods: Music and Theatre in Seventeenth-Century Spain. Oxford, 1993

Stevenson, Robert. *Music in Mexico: A Historical Survey*. New York, 1952

The Music of Peru: Aboriginal and Viceroyal Epochs. Washington, DC, 1960

Renaissance and Baroque Musical Sources in the Americas. Washington, DC, 1970

Christmas Music in Baroque Mexico. Berkeley, 1974

Tello, Aurelio (ed.). *Cantadas y villancicos de Manuel de Sumaya*, vol. 7 of *Archivo musical de la Catedral de Oaxaca, Tesoro de la música polifónica en México*. Mexico City, 1994

Verble, Charles Randall. 'Five Psalm Settings by Giovanni Battista Sammartini'. PhD thesis, Northwestern University, 2003

· 3 ·

Catholic sacred music in Austria

JEN-YEN CHEN

Some idea of the centrality of religious music in eighteenth-century life in Austria and southern Germany can be garnered from the following passage from Charles Burney's description of his visit to Vienna in 1772:

> there is scarce a church or convent in Vienna, which has not every morning its *mass in music*: that is, a great portion of the church service of the day, set in parts, and performed with voices, accompanied by at least three or four violins, a tenor and base, besides the organ, and as the churches here are daily crowded, this music, though not of the most exquisite kind, must in some degree form the ear of the inhabitants.[1]

Undoubtedly a principal reason for this prevalence of *musica da chiesa* was the intimate association of the Roman Catholic faith with the political rule of the Holy Roman Emperors, whose cultural and ideological imprint radiated outwards from the Austrian capital to far-flung territories of the Empire as well as to lands with close ties to Vienna, such as Salzburg, Bavaria and Saxony. Therefore the concept of an 'imperial style' (*Reichstil*) broadly characterizes the subject matter of the present chapter,[2] though it is not intended to deny the regional and institutional diversity of sacred music practices and repertories. Furthermore, the *Reichstil* enjoyed its heyday particularly during the reigns of Joseph I (1705–11) and Charles VI (1711–40)[3] but became a less quintessentially defining element of society and culture in subsequent decades as the Enlightenment movement began to transform Austria. Indeed, the notion of a paradigmatic break around 1740 occurs in important studies by Ludwig von Köchel, Otto Ursprung and Ernst Tittel, which all argue that Catholic sacred music underwent a precipitous decline following the deaths of Charles VI

1 Charles Burney, *The Present State of Music in Germany, The Netherlands and United Provinces*, 2nd edn., (London, 1773, repr. 1969), 2 vols., vol. 1, pp. 226–7.
2 Friedrich Wilhelm Riedel, 'Der "Reichstil" in der deutschen Musikgeschichte des 18. Jahrhunderts', in Georg Reichert and Martin Just (eds.), *Bericht über der Internationalen Musikwissenschaftlichen Kongress Kassel 1962* (Kassel, 1963), pp. 33–6 discusses the concept as one originating from the field of architecture but with a strong relevance to music as well. See also Hans Sedlmayr, 'Die politische Bedeutung des deutschen Barocks (der Reichstil)', in *Gesamtdeutsche Vergangenheit. Festgabe für Heinrich Ritter von Srbik zum 60. Geburtstag* (Munich, 1938), pp. 126–40.
3 Riedel, 'Der "Reichstil"', p. 33.

and his long-time Hofkapellmeister Johann Joseph Fux, in 1740 and 1741, respectively.[4]

Against this viewpoint, Bruce MacIntyre has offered substantive evidence for sustained vigorous activity in the composition and performance of masses and other church genres into the latter part of the century.[5] A balanced consideration of the complex intertwining of forces of continuity and change thus represents a historiographical challenge for researchers of sacred music between the reigns of Charles VI and Maria Theresa (1740–80). The conventional interpretation favouring change, applied not only to *musica da chiesa* but to music as a whole and resulting in a bifurcation of the century into two sharply differentiated halves is especially problematic with respect to a careful assessment of religious music during the later, 'Classical' period.[6] An opportunity arises here to explore critically some of the assumptions of nineteenth- and twentieth-century accounts regarding the value and success of sacred compositions in the age of Haydn and Mozart, especially when these contributions diverge from the evident high respect for the music accorded to it by those living in the era itself. Above all, dichotomies of old/new, sacred/secular, vocal/instrumental, Baroque/Classical and the like, which form a sometimes tacit aspect of historiographical discourses of style development in eighteenth-century music, need to be examined for their appropriateness to individual repertories and locales.

The Viennese imperial court chapel in the era of Fux and Caldara

The existence of a full-fledged *Kapelle* at the court of the Habsburg monarchs dates back to no later than the reign of Maximilian I (1493–1519), though the

4 Ludwig von Köchel, *Die kaiserliche Hof-Musikkapelle in Wien von 1543 bis 1867 nach urkundlichen Forschungen* (Vienna, 1869), p. 12; Otto Ursprung, *Die katholische Kirchenmusik*, vol. 10 of Ernst Bücken (ed.), *Handbuch der Musikwissenschaft* (Wildpark-Potsdam, 1931), p. 241; Ernst Tittel, *Österreichische Kirchenmusik: Werden, Wachsen, Wirken* (Vienna, 1961), p. 173, as cited in Bruce MacIntyre, *The Viennese Concerted Mass of the Early Classic Period* (Ann Arbor, MI, 1986), p. 684, n. 1.

5 MacIntyre, *The Viennese Concerted Mass*, *passim*.

6 See David Wyn Jones, 'Introduction: New Challenges, New Perspectives', in Jones (ed.), *Music in Eighteenth-Century Austria* (Cambridge, 1996), pp. 1–10: 'the labels Baroque and Classical tend to declare two fixed points of stylistic development at the beginning and end of the century. This has had two unfortunate consequences. It implies that there was a sudden switch of direction, even a revolution in musical language in the middle of the century; such a dramatic view has some plausibility in musical development in other parts of Europe, notably in the musical taste of London and Paris in the 1760s, but stylistic development in Austria throughout the century is strongly evolutionary with conservative and progressive elements continually intermingling…' (p. 8); 'If musicians did think about the relative importance of genres then they would have placed opera at the top of their ambitions… and then, because of its central place in a deeply Catholic society, church music' (p. 9). Among the most influential negative evaluations of late eighteenth-century sacred music is that of Charles Rosen, *The Classical Style: Haydn, Mozart, Beethoven*, rev. edn. (New York, 1997), pp. 367–75.

institution acquired the name by which it is usually designated today, the *Hofmusikkapelle*, only in 1855.[7] Already in the earliest period of its history, the chapel included among its members some of the most distinguished musicians of the day such as Heinrich Isaac, who held an appointment as court composer from 1496 until 1517, and his successor Ludwig Senfl. A key development occurred in 1498, when a reform of the *Kapelle*, then under the direction of Georg von Slatkonia, formalized the practice of music in relation to the structure of court life as a whole and ensured its long-term continuity.[8] During the subsequent centuries, the chapel's musicians assumed a broad set of responsibilities that encompassed not only liturgical music but also *Tafelmusik* and opera, the latter featuring particularly at grand imperial festivities. This diversity of activity reached its high point during the years of Charles VI's rule.

The *Kapelle* attained a remarkable level of artistic eminence in certain periods before the eighteenth century, including the latter half of the seventeenth century, during which Johann Heinrich Schmelzer, Johann Jacob Froberger, Antonio Draghi, Antonio Cesti and Johann Caspar Kerll (among others) were employed at the court, even if only briefly in the case of Cesti. Nevertheless, it remains true that the tenure of Johann Joseph Fux as imperial Kapellmeister, which lasted from 1715 to 1741 and thus corresponded almost exactly with the reign of Charles VI, has received special praise from historians.[9] For Köchel it marked 'the time of the highest flowering of the imperial court chapel' (*die Zeit der höchsten Blüthe der kais. Hofkapelle*), while Theophil Antonicek characterizes these years as 'the close and culmination of the age of courtly magnificence',[10] and Daniel Heartz writes that 'Under Charles VI [the chapel] acquired an opulence that was never again equalled'.[11] The extent to which such lofty assessments may contribute to an exaggerated sense of the chapel's decline following the death of Charles will be considered later in this chapter.

7 Köchel, *Die kaiserliche Hof-Musikkapelle*, pp. 6–7. Köchel's history is based principally upon his examination of surviving imperial account books now housed in the Austrian State Archive (Vienna). For a description and inventory of these account books, see Christian Sapper, 'Die Zahlamtsbücher im Hofkammerarchiv 1542–1825', in *Mitteilungen des Österreichischen Staatsarchivs*, 36 (1983), pp. 329–73.

8 Rudolf Wran, 'Eröffnung', in Theophil Antonicek, Elizabeth Theresia Hilscher and Hartmut Krones (eds.), *Die Wiener Hofmusikkapelle I: Georg von Slatkonia und die Wiener Hofmusikkapelle* (Vienna, 1999), pp. 13–14. Wran emphasizes the *myth* of the founding of the *Kapelle* in this year by noting the existence of singers employed by the Habsburg rulers in the preceding decades.

9 The correspondence becomes even closer when one takes into account Fux's appointment as Vice-Kapellmeister in 1711, the same year as Charles' ascension to the throne of the Holy Roman Empire. However, he had served at the imperial court since 1698, at the latest.

10 Köchel, *Die kaiserliche Hof-Musikkapelle*, p. 10; Theophil Antonicek, 'Vienna 3. The Baroque Era', in Stanley Sadie (ed.), *The New Grove Dictionary of Music and Musicians, Revised Edition* (London, 2001), vol. 26, p. 552.

11 Daniel Heartz, *Haydn, Mozart and the Viennese School 1740–1780* (New York and London, 1995), p. 5.

Harry White nicely captures the distinctive flavour of musical culture at Charles' court through the designation 'Austro-Italian Baroque'.[12] The presence of the Venetian Antonio Caldara, who served alongside Fux as Vice-Kapellmeister from 1716 to 1736, represents most tangibly the Italian element of the compound adjective. The idea of these two musicians as the dual quintessential figures of the Viennese court music, contrasting yet complementary in ways beyond mere nationality, derives a measure of justification from Caldara's virtual equality to Fux in all but official title.[13] Appointed to his post by the Emperor against Fux's recommendations in favour of Giuseppe Porsile and Francesco Scarlatti, Caldara assumed primary responsibility for the composition of operas, eventually writing dozens for the most significant festive events at the court, though he also contributed an important body of sacred works. His ever-increasing salary, which began initially at 1,600 florins but had reached the astronomical sum of 3,900 florins by 1729, gives a good indication of how deeply the Emperor valued him.[14] Caldara's more melodic-homophonic orientation paired with Fux's preference for a weighty contrapuntal manner furnished an effective basis from which the *Kapelle* could develop and elaborate a richly diversified, comprehensive *Imperialstil* mirroring Charles' universalist aspirations. Neither stylistic direction was the exclusive domain of the one or other composer, however, and Fux achieved probably his finest moment as Kapellmeister on Caldara's 'territory' of opera in his composition of *Costanza e fortezza* for the coronation of Charles as King of Bohemia in Prague in 1723. By this year, the personnel of the chapel had reached an impressive 134, a number maintained at a nearly constant level until the end of Charles' reign.[15]

The various repertories, styles and genres of sacred music that flourished during the era of Fux and Caldara include composers from the sixteenth century to contemporary times; concerted and *a cappella* idioms; and masses, motets, offertories, psalms, antiphons, hymns, oratorios and instrumental works (church sonatas). This breadth of musical material served a particular functional purpose, namely the accompaniment of a comparably diverse liturgy. Friedrich Wilhelm Riedel has employed the concept of 'historical architecture' in order to account for the tendency of a single worship service to feature a highly disparate and even incongruous set of sacred compositions – so

12 Harry White (ed.), *Johann Joseph Fux and the Austro-Italian Baroque* (Aldershot, 1992).

13 See Jen-yen Chen, 'Fux, Caldara, and Their Canonic Masses as Evidence of Professional Rivalry', in Thomas Hochradner and Susanne Janes (eds.), *Fux-Forschung. Standpunkte und Perspektiven. Bericht des wissenschaftlichen Symposions auf Schloss Seggau 14.–16. Oktober 2005* (Tutzing, 2008), pp. 159–70.

14 Brian Pritchard, 'Caldara, Antonio', in Sadie (ed.), *The New Grove Dictionary of Music and Musicians, Revised Edition*, vol. 4, p. 821.

15 Köchel, *Die kaiserliche Hof-Musikkapelle*, p. 10.

that, for example, works by Palestrina and Georg Christoph Wagenseil (court composer from 1739) might be placed next to one another.[16]

Riedel's exhaustive study of sacred music at the court of Charles VI, published in 1977, made use of a broad range of primary documentary sources, including protocols, calendars and newspaper reports, in order to reconstruct the musico-liturgical structure of the church year.[17] Chief among these sources, from a specifically musical standpoint, is the *Rubriche generali per le Funzioni Ecclesiastiche Musicali di tutto l'anno*, compiled by the 'Konzertmeister' Kilian Reinhardt in 1727.[18] Reinhardt, uncle of the court organist and composer Johann Georg Reinhardt, had entered imperial service in 1683 under Emperor Leopold I (reigned 1657–1705) as librarian and copyist; his title of concertmaster, granted by Leopold in 1699, seems to have resulted from an effort to raise him above the status of servant, and he apparently possessed no skills as a practical musician. Nevertheless, his importance in the administration of the *Hofmusikkapelle* was such that in 1712 Charles VI included him on a commission charged with the re-organisation of the chapel.[19] By 1727, two years before Reinhardt's death, few members of the court could match his extraordinary ability to describe the imperial liturgical customs with a deep sense of their tradition and historical continuity; indeed the inscription on the title page of the *Rubriche* makes mention of his accumulation of knowledge 'Nell'interrotto corso di 50 anni' (in the interrupted course of fifty years).

For scholars of church music, the immense value of Reinhardt's document lies in its detailed information on the musical requirements for the many different sections of the complex court liturgy. Beginning with 1 January, the *Rubriche* chronologically catalogues a series of services, rituals and festivities taking place over the course of the church year, often specifying location, appropriate musical style and even individual compositions when these were written by members of the Habsburg imperial family;[20] works by Leopold I appear with particular

16 Friedrich Wilhelm Riedel, *Kirchenmusik am Hofe Karls VI. (1711–1740)* (Munich and Salzburg, 1977), pp. 222–8. Riedel specifically invokes the title of the treatise by Johann Bernhard Fischer von Erlach, *Entwurff einer historischen Architectur* (Vienna, 1721), the relevance of which here consists in its linking of a powerful consciousness of tradition with the ideology of contemporary Viennese imperial culture. See also Paul Naredi-Rainer, 'Johann Bernhard Fischer von Erlach und Johann Joseph Fux: Beziehungen zwischen Architektur und Musik im österreichischen Barock', in Götz Pochat and Brigitte Wagner (eds.), *Barock-regional-international* (Graz, 1993), pp. 275–90.

17 Riedel, *Kirchenmusik am Hofe Karls VI.*, pp. 14–20.

18 Austrian National Library (Vienna), S.m. 2503.

19 Elizabeth Roche, 'Reinhardt (1) Kilian Reinhardt', in Sadie (ed.), *The New Grove Dictionary of Music and Musicians, Revised Edition*, vol. 21, p. 162.

20 A summary of the contents of the *Rubriche* appears in Köchel, *Die kaiserliche Hof-Musikkapelle*, pp. 135–44.

frequency, illustrating the tendency of the *Kapelle* to maintain a more or less stable repertory through a period of decades. Undoubtedly the most significant aspect of the *Rubriche* is the distribution throughout the year of the three musical types that correspond to the different grades of liturgical event: *solenne*, for festive occasions such as birthdays and name-days of members of the imperial family and feasts of the Order of the Golden Fleece; *mediocre* (that is, ordinary), for the majority of liturgical observances; and *in contrapunto* (that is, *a cappella*), for the two penitential seasons of Advent and Lent.[21]

Solenne music featured the immediately recognizable timbre of clarinos and trumpets and frequently also included timpani as components of a luxuriant orchestration; the bright, soprano tessitura of the clarinos in particular functioned as the unique sonic marker of liturgical celebrations of the foremost rank at the court.[22] Because of the defining role of these instruments, most *solenne* compositions were written in the key of C major. The *Missa solemnis* and *Vesperae solennes* represent exceptional types of the mass and vespers genres, while the *Te Deum* took on its special character through its exclusive setting in *solenne* style. Intradas at the opening and close of services of the highest grade, taking the place of the more usual organ preludes and postludes, further indicate the importance of these instruments in articulating the hierarchical structure of worship. As suggested by the name, music of the *mediocre* category was 'middling' in nature, of shorter length than *solenne* compositions, with less obbligato writing and with a typically modest concerted instrumentation of first and second violins in both solo and ripieno roles, doubling winds and continuo (a scoring known as *Kirchentrio* or church trio). Sacred works *in contrapunto* constitute the other 'extraordinary' manifestation of Viennese liturgical music. Fux's *Gradus ad Parnassum* of 1725 in fact details two distinct types of *stylus a capella*, the first for voices alone and the second employing continuo and doubling instruments.[23] The latter, because of the support provided for the singers, featured a greater freedom of chromatic writing. Reinhardt also differentiates these two types, making a special point of noting non-participation by organ and other instruments (especially prevalent during Lent). By implication, a designation *in contrapunto* without the further qualification *senz'organo e senza stromenti* indicates music in the second *a cappella*

21 Exceptions to this general rule include the Introit, which was performed *a cappella* throughout the church year at Charles' court.

22 For detailed discussions of music with trumpet at the Habsburg court in the late Baroque era, see A. Peter Brown, 'The Trumpet Overture and Sinfonia in Vienna (1715–1822): Rise, Decline, and Reformulation', in Jones (ed.), *Music in Eighteenth-Century Austria*, pp. 13–69 and Brown, 'Caldara's Trumpet Music for the Imperial Celebrations of Charles VI. and Elisabeth Christine', in Brian Pritchard (ed.), *Antonio Caldara: Essays on His Life and Times* (Aldershot, 1987), pp. 3–48.

23 Johann Joseph Fux, *Gradus ad Parnassum* (Vienna, 1725), pp. 243–73.

style. This convention of musical terminology underscores the exceptional character of *a cappella* compositions wholly without accompaniment by instruments.

Pure vocal sonority had of course long been associated with Palestrina, whose centrality in the history of Catholic sacred music offered a means for consolidating the Italianate aspect of Viennese musical culture in the early eighteenth century. Works by the Roman master and other significant representatives of the classical vocal polyphony such as Giovanni Animuccia and Gregorio Allegri entered the liturgical repertory of the Habsburg court during the reign of Ferdinand III (1637–57).[24] This material helped to satisfy the musical requirements of the penitential seasons, though contemporary composers also contributed *a cappella* music of their own. Indeed, in 1733 the court hired, on Fux's recommendation, Matteo Palotta, whose sole obligation was to write works in *stile antico*. Thus the high value placed upon a predominantly vocal idiom continued into the closing years of the reign of Charles VI. In general, however, versatility was the *sine qua non* for a composer employed at the court, who had to demonstrate competence in all of the *solenne*, *mediocre* and *in contrapunto* categories. This situation provides a starting point for considering the output of Fux and Caldara, as well as that of their most noteworthy colleagues.

The mass represented the core of the Roman Catholic liturgy; in this genre Fux and Caldara easily overshadowed the other composers of the Habsburg chapel in their production of approximately one hundred Ordinary cycles each. Of the ninety-five settings by the former,[25] only two, the *Messa di San Carlo*, K. 7, and the *Missa Quadragesimalis*, K. 29, are in the unaccompanied *a cappella* style, which has played a disproportionate role in defining Fux's reputation, though one unjustified only from a quantitative standpoint given the importance of the vocal polyphonic aesthetic to his oeuvre.[26] The *Messa di San Carlo* of *c.* 1718, named after St Charles Borromeo and also known as the *Missa canonica*, is particularly remarkable for its elaborate contrapuntal edifice consisting of a gradually diminishing interval of canonic imitation across the different sections of the work (a rationalistic procedure comparable to that of

24 Riedel, *Kirchenmusik am Hofe Karls VI.*, pp. 72–107, discusses a group of large manuscript codexes prepared for the court that contains music by these composers.

25 This is the number of works listed in the most up-to-date catalogue of Fux's oeuvre: Thomas Hochradner, Martin Czernin and Géza-M. Vörösmarty, *Johann Joseph Fux: Thematisches Verzeichnis der musikalischen Werke* (forthcoming). For a summary of this catalogue, see the work-list in Harry White, 'Fux, Johann Joseph', in Sadie (ed.), *The New Grove Dictionary of Music and Musicians, Revised Edition*, vol. 9, pp. 370–1. In the discussion below, 'K.' numbers refer to the earlier inventory that appears in Ludwig van Köchel, *Thematisches Verzeichniss der Compositonen von Johann Josef Fux* (Vienna, 1872).

26 See Jen-yen Chen, 'Palestrina and the Influence of "Old" Style in Eighteenth-Century Vienna', *Journal of Musicological Research*, 22/1–2 (2003), pp. 1–44.

J. S. Bach's *Goldberg Variations*).[27] Manuscript copies by Jan Dismas Zelenka and Michael Haydn confirm the deep impression made by this *tour de force* of compositional technique, and exemplify the transmission of the *Reichstil* northwards to Dresden and westwards to Salzburg.[28]

Fux's concerted masses (*solenne* and *mediocre*) integrate Italian Baroque melodic–harmonic elements with the composer's general predilection for counterpoint. In the *Missa Sanctissimae Trinitatis*, a work from 1695 dedicated to Leopold I and possibly marking Fux's entry into imperial service, the Italianate manner assumes a 'colossal Baroque' character in its predominant use of double choirs.[29] The later masses demonstrate a greater textural variety, including the *Missa Corporis Christi*, K. 10, a *solenne* composition from 1713 in which tutti choruses (homophonic or fugal) and passages for solo voices typically accompanied by obbligato instruments follow one another in rapid succession. The Kyrie movement offers a good example. The first Kyrie begins with an introduction for trumpets, trombones and continuo and then alternates choral homophony (with *colla parte* accompaniment) and vocal–instrumental solos (alto–violin, tenor–trombone, and bass–violin). The Christe is a duet for soprano and alto with ritornelli featuring obbligato first and second violins and trombone in active contrapuntal interaction. Finally, Fux casts the second Kyrie as a choral fugue (a convention for this section of the mass text and for 'Cum Sancto spiritu' and 'Et vitam venturi' in the Gloria and Credo, respectively). This diversity of texture, here encompassed within a time span of only about five minutes, also characterizes Fux's writing for voices in other sacred genres such as Vespers, as well as in the quasi-liturgical genre of oratorio.

The mastery of modern affective Baroque techniques reaches a high point in the Requiem Mass of 1720, K. 51–53, known as the *Kaiserrequiem* or Emperor's Requiem, even though it was originally written for Eleanor Margaret Theresa, the widow of Leopold I.[30] This work, which Harry White praises for 'its madrigalian intensity of expression',[31] vividly underscores the limitations of a view of Fux as a conservative musician rigidly beholden to the *stile antico*, a

27 Ed. Johannes Evangelist Habert and Gustav Adolf Glossner, in *Denkmäler der Tonkunst in Österreich* 1 (Vienna, 1894), a volume that also contains the *Missa Quadragesimalis*, the *Missa Purificationis* (an example of the second *a cappella* style) and the *Missa Sanctissimae Trinitatis*.
28 Zelenka's copy, dated 18 October 1719 and formerly in the Sächsische Landesbibliothek (Dresden), is now lost; it was described by Köchel in his thematic catalogue. Haydn's, dated 5 September 1757, is in the Austrian National Library, Mus. Hs. 15556, MusA/Haydn, Michael/3.
29 White, 'Fux, Johann Joseph', in Sadie (ed.), *The New Grove Dictionary of Music and Musicians, Revised Edition*, vol. 9, p. 368. The mass is edited by Hellmut Federhofer in *Johann-Joseph-Fux: Sämtliche Werke I/1* (Graz, 1959).
30 Ed. Klaus Winkler, *Johann-Joseph-Fux: Sämtliche Werke I/7* (Graz, 1972).
31 White, 'Fux, Johann Joseph', in Sadie (ed.), *The New Grove Dictionary of Music and Musicians, Revised Edition*, vol. 9, p. 368.

consequence primarily of the extraordinary fame of the *Gradus ad Parnassum* coupled with the relative obscurity of his music in later centuries. Within a near-continuous stream of imitative polyphony, the Requiem presents a succession of memorably plangent melodies occasionally contrasted with declamatory passages highlighting theologically or dramatically significant text (for example 'Dies irae', 'Rex tremendae majestatis', 'Confutatis maledictis'). This mass unquestionably made a profound impact on the Viennese court, to judge from its selection in later years for the funerals of such luminaries as Leopold Joseph of Lothringen (father of Emperor Francis Stephen, the consort of Empress Maria Theresa) in 1729, Prince Eugene of Savoy in 1736 and Charles VI in 1740.[32]

Though he had sought a post at the Viennese court for several years prior to his appointment as Vice-Kapellmeister in 1716, Antonio Caldara faced great challenges of adjustment on his arrival at the imperial capital, for he possessed little previous experience in composing church music, his earlier work consisting mostly of operas, oratorios and cantatas. However, he seems to have rapidly achieved fluency in the diverse sacred genres and idioms that constituted the court's liturgical repertory.[33] The apparent ease of transition underscores the degree of cross-fertilization between secular vocal music and Latin liturgical music in the Catholic domain. Caldara's output of masses for Vienna, consisting of some 110 works including mass sections, ranges from full-fledged *Missae solemnes* to works in a strict vocal polyphonic style. Belonging to the latter category is a *Missa canonica* (1720) that, on the basis of notable similarities of contrapuntal procedure, may represent a self-conscious response to Fux's *Messa di San Carlo* from two years earlier. However, the Mass eschews the abstract structuring of its putative model, and in addition manifests a more progressive conception of harmony in the service of text expression, as in the 'Et incarnatus est', where vivid chromaticism exceeds the norm even for this portion of the Credo text conventionally set by composers in a highly affective manner.[34]

32 Riedel, *Kirchenmusik am Hofe Karls VI.*, p. 182.

33 Christoph Wolff, 'Bach and the Tradition of the Palestrina Style', in Wolff, *Bach: Essays on His Life and Music* (Cambridge, MA, 1991), pp. 96–99, discusses Caldara's significance for Bach as a principal master of the classical vocal polyphony, illustrated in particular through a copy of the Magnificat in C which supplements the original four-part *a cappella* vocal scoring with two violin parts. The adaptation is available in an edition prepared by Wolff (Kassel, 1969).

34 See Chen, 'Fux, Caldara, and Their Canonic Masses', example 6 of which reproduces the opening of the 'Et incarnatus est'. Caldara's mass is floridly titled *Missa artificiosissimae compositionis in contrapuncto canonico sub duplici canone inverso contrario et cancrizante* in a number of its sources, though the set of performance parts originating from the archive of the *Hofmusikkapelle* (now the Austrian National Library) provides the simpler designation *Missa a 5. con canoni diversi*. The work is misattributed to Caldara's pupil, Georg Reutter (or possibly his identically named father), in a manuscript in the archive of Kremsmünster Abbey, Lower Austria. This misattribution has unfortunately made its way into the scholarly literature,

Other court composers who contributed to the mass repertory of the *Hofmusikkapelle* under Charles VI include Francesco Bartolomeo Conti, with five works in concerted style, Matteo Palotta and Georg Christoph Wagenseil and Georg Reutter, both members of a younger generation who exemplify the transition to and consolidation of the next phase of the history of Viennese music. A pupil of Fux, Wagenseil demonstrated an early mastery of contrapuntal writing such that the aging Hofkapellmeister believed he would preserve the legacy of a dignified polyphonic idiom, not anticipating the later concentration upon instrumental genres.[35] An output of around eighteen masses evidently belongs mostly to the 1730s and 1740s; during much of the 1740s Wagenseil served as organist in the private chapel of Elizabeth Christine, Charles' widow. (The securely dated works span the period 1736–46.) The chronology of most of the approximately eighty masses by Reutter remains uncertain, but the *Missa Sancti Caroli* from 1734 is an exception.[36] Performed in this year for the Emperor's name-day, it features a *solenne* scoring of clarinos and timpani as well as active violins that became an oft-noted and sometimes disparaged hallmark of the composer's orchestral writing. Reutter later occupied the Kapellmeister and Vice-Kapellmeister posts not only of the imperial chapel but also of St Stephen's Cathedral, thereby elevating himself to a central and controversial position in Viennese musical life. Because he has often been associated with a perceived decline of music at both institutions during the period following the death of Charles VI, his work and significance will be considered in greater depth in the following section of this chapter.[37]

Among the sections of the Mass Proper, the Offertory in particular developed a rich musical style comparable to that of settings of the Ordinary, probably due largely to its intimate connection with the ritual core of the Mass, the celebration of the Eucharist.[38] While the Gradual and Alleluia comprised instrumental sonatas except during the penitential seasons (when the Tract took the place of the Alleluia), the Offertory was a vocal, figural composition occurring throughout the church year. During the late seventeenth century, the genre developed a distinctive, motet-like type based on the use

beginning with Norbert Hofer's *Die beiden Reutter als Kirchenkomponisten*, PhD dissertation (University of Vienna, 1915), where the Mass is number 6 in the thematic catalogue. See also David Wyn Jones, 'Haydn's *Missa Sunt bona mixta malis* and the *a cappella* Tradition', in Jones (ed.), *Music in Eighteenth-Century Austria*, p. 92; Chen, 'Palestrina and the Influence of "Old" Style', pp. 23–31; and Chen, correspondence, *Journal of Musicological Research*, 24 (2005), pp. 85–7.

35 Heartz, *Haydn, Mozart and the Viennese School 1740–1780*, pp. 89–90.

36 Ed. Norbert Hofer, *DTÖ* 88 (Vienna, 1952).

37 For a broad survey of the mass genre in early eighteenth-century Vienna, see Georg Reichert, *Zur Geschichte der Wiener Messenkomposition in der ersten Hälfte des 18. Jahrhunderts*, PhD dissertation (University of Vienna, 1935).

38 Gabriele Krombach, *Die Vertonungen liturgischer Sonntagsoffertorien am Wiener Hof* (Munich and Salzburg, 1986), p. 7.

of non-liturgical text and intended for performance outside of Advent and Lent.[39] A terminological differentiation, 'Offertorium' versus 'Motetto', helped to clarify this nascent type, though the two designations became virtually interchangeable after the middle of the eighteenth century.[40] In its newer form, the Offertory featured a mixture of ripieno and solo textures as well as alternating recitatives and arias, thereby evincing a notably secular dramatic character. Rudolf Walter has noted the similar process by which the Protestant cantata evolved from an earlier liturgical Offertory repertory.[41]

At the court of Charles VI, the Offertory received settings in all of the three stylistic idioms, though examples belonging to the *solenne* category are in fact rare. Fux provided a total of nineteen liturgical compositions for the penitential seasons, self-evidently in *a cappella* style; two of these, *Ad te, Domine levavi*, K. 153, and *Ave Maria*, K. 151, for the first and fourth Sundays in Advent, respectively, appeared in full in the *Gradus ad Parnassum*.[42] A further fifty works of the non-liturgical type, twelve of them no longer extant, complete Fux's activity in the genre.[43] A consideration of Caldara's Offertories again illuminates the complementary relation of the two leading musicians at the imperial court. In contrast with his senior colleague, Caldara furnished a complete cycle for the church year, but with the notable omission of the Sundays of Advent and Lent (so that the *stile mediocre* predominates in this body of work). The intensive concentration on a single form of church music reflected in the production of thirty-four compositions in 1718 and 1719 alone[44] indicates the importance of the Offertory in facilitating Caldara's assimilation into the cultural and ideological milieu of Vienna, since the stylistically similar genres of cantata and oratorio had been two of his primary focuses prior to his appointment as Vice-Kapellmeister. Conversely, the long-standing affinity of the Catholic North for Italian music received a powerful new impetus through Caldara's spectacular productivity in the realm of dramatic vocal music – liturgical, quasi-sacred and secular – upon arrival in the Habsburg capital. His Offertories accordingly demonstrate a co-ordination of diverse approaches in their mixture of solo and tutti vocal passages, obbligato violins and active basses on the one hand[45] and highly polyphonic concluding Alleluias on the other.

39 Rudolf Walter, 'Bemerkungen zu den Kompositionen von Johann Joseph Fux zum Offertorium', in White (ed.), *Johann Joseph Fux and the Austro-Italian Baroque*, p. 232.

40 Krombach, *Die Vertonungen liturgischer Sonntagsoffertorien*, p. 18.

41 Walter, 'Bemerkungen zu den Kompositionen von Johann Joseph Fux', p. 232.

42 Fux, *Gradus ad Parnassum*, pp. 247–54, 256–61.

43 See Walter, 'Bemerkungen zu den Kompositionen von Johann Joseph Fux zum Offertorium', pp. 256–60, for a full accounting of Fux's Offertory output.

44 *Ibid.*, p. 233. 45 Krombach, *Die Vertonungen liturgischer Sonntagsoffertorien*, p. 116.

During the early seventeenth century in Catholic domains and especially in Italy, the Vespers service achieved pre-eminence as the most musically elaborate of the Office Hours. A century later, this pre-eminence remained a significant feature of Austrian sacred music as demonstrated above all in the eighty-three settings by Fux and over one hundred by Caldara.[46] Drawing on earlier precedents but also expanding them, Vespers at the Habsburg court incorporated a carefully structured arrangement of diverse components, consisting of five Psalms, a hymn, the Canticum Mariae or *Magnificat*, a Marian antiphon and the Lauretanian Litany. Two groupings of Psalms, exemplified by the *Vesperae de confessore* and the *Vesperae de Beatae Mariae Virginis*, acquired particular importance as the basis for the groupings employed at numerous other Vespers celebrations:[47]

Vesperae de confessore	*Vesperae de Beatae Mariae Virginis*
Dixit Dominus (109)	Dixit Dominus (109)
Confitebor (110)	Laudate pueri (112)
Beatus vir (111)	Laetatus sum (121)
Laudate pueri (112)	Nisi Dominus (126)
Laudate Dominum (116)	Lauda Jerusalem (147)

The powerfully affective quality and vivid imagery of the texts of these (and other) Psalms undoubtedly provides the most convincing explanation for the increased importance of the Vespers genre in the Baroque era, for these traits represented a natural focus of the modern *concertato* techniques formulated in early-seventeenth-century Italy. This observation applies as well to the text of the *Magnificat*, from the Gospel of Luke (chapter 1, verses 46–55). By contrast, the hymn that stood in between the Psalms and the *Magnificat* was usually in *a cappella* style (throughout the year); in fact contemporary composers rarely provided music for this portion of the Vespers liturgy, for which older works especially by Palestrina were employed instead.[48] Following the *Magnificat*, one of the four Marian antiphons was heard, chosen according to the season: *Alma redemptoris Mater* (Advent to 1 February), *Ave Regina coelorum* (2 February to the Wednesday of Holy Week), *Regina coeli* (Easter Sunday through Pentecost week) and *Salve Regina* (remainder of the year). Finally, the Lauretanian Litany, the invocation of the Virgin Mary associated with the Annunciation

46 These settings are catalogued in Walter Gleissner, *Die Vespern von Johann Joseph Fux: Ein Beitrag zur Geschichte der Vespervertonung*, PhD dissertation (University of Mainz, 1981), pp. 89–99.

47 *Ibid.*, pp. 14–15. The numbering of the Psalms is that of the Latin Vulgate.

48 Riedel, *Kirchenmusik am Hofe Karls VI.*, pp. 101–2. The term 'Vespers', when used to refer to a musical work, frequently denotes settings of the Psalms and Magnificat in particular (hence reflecting their perceived relative importance). This is the convention by which Gleissner reckons the number of eighty-three Vespers compositions by Fux. He does not count Fux's Marian antiphons and Litanies.

shrine in the Italian town of Loreto,[49] concluded Vespers on Sundays and most high feast days. Fux and his colleagues generally furnished their own compositions for these last two components of the service.

With respect to the Psalms and the *Magnificat*, two organizational principles prevailed: either all six items were set together as a coherent group for use in the same liturgical observance ('Vespere intiere'), or a single text was set to comprise an individual composition. In his study of Fux's Vespers, Walter Gleissner observes that while declamatory homophony predominates in the former type, a highly diversified concerted idiom characterizes the latter, with pronounced variety of compositional technique, rhythm, meter, vocal and instrumental scoring and formal segmentation. Gleissner further notes the use of these and other style elements in the service of a highly developed sensitivity to text expression, appropriately perpetuating the aesthetic ideal of the *seconda pratica* through which Vespers moved to a central position in the domain of sacred music.[50]

The most important para-liturgical genre cultivated at the Habsburg court, the oratorio, had functioned as a kind of dramatic substitute for opera during Lent since the mid-seventeenth century in Vienna. A special type of oratorio – known as the *sepolcro*, because performances of it took place in front of a replica of the Holy Sepulchre placed in the chapel of the imperial palace – became the hallmark of a distinctive Viennese tradition. The *sepolcro* stood apart from *oratorio volgare* through the meditative, speculative character of its texts and as a result of comprising a single *parte* instead of two. However, the differentiation of the types had blurred by the early eighteenth century, so that the former took on the character of a Passion oratorio.

In its eighteenth-century manifestation, the *sepolcro* assumed a form of two parts (in between which a sermon in Italian was given), and featured librettos that placed emphasis upon emotional reflection. The authors of these librettos include a number of those court poets now famed for their seminal role in the history of opera seria – Pietro Pariati, Claudio Pasquini and Pietro Metastasio. Not unexpectedly, their work in the domain of *sepolcro* shares the Arcadian ideals of their opera texts.[51] This Italian and specifically Roman imprint extended to the music as well, and the stylistic similarities between the oratorios of Alessandro Scarlatti and those of Fux are notable, above all the

49 John Harper, 'Litany 5. Litaniae Lauretanae', in Sadie (ed.), *The New Grove Dictionary of Music and Musicians, Revised Edition*, vol. 14, p. 880.

50 Gleissner, *Die Vespern von Johann Joseph Fux*, pp. 230–1.

51 Harry White, 'The *Sepolcro* Oratorios of Fux: An Assessment', in White (ed.), *Johann Joseph Fux and the Austro-Italian Baroque*, p. 214. See also Erika Kanduth, 'The Literary and Dramaturgical Aspects of the Viennese Sepolcro Oratorio, with Particular Reference to Fux', in White (ed.), *Johann Joseph Fux and the Austro-Italian Baroque*, pp. 153–63.

dominance of da capo arias. The individuality of the Viennese tradition lies in its prominent choruses, especially those at the end of each *parte*.

The court composers who were active in writing oratorios include Fux (ten surviving works), Caldara (twenty-six Viennese works) and Conti (ten works), as well as Giuseppe Porsile (thirteen works) who, though not attaining an imperial post until 1720, had already served under Charles prior to 1711 while Charles pursued his ultimately unsuccessful claim to the Spanish crown. Harry White classifies the ten wholly extant oratorios by Fux composed between 1714 and 1728 into three groups – biblical, allegorical and *sepolcro*.[52] Pariati provided the texts for at least two of the biblical works and for five of the six that belong to the *sepolcro* category; his collaboration with Fux represents yet another example of a specific librettist–composer pairing that yielded extraordinarily fruitful results. The sixth and last of the *sepolcro* oratorios, *La deposizione dalla Croce di Gesù Cristo Salvator Nostro* from 1728, employs a text by Pasquini that depicts Christ's descent from the Cross through a combination of vivid expressions of grief and moral commentary on the sins of humanity. This culminating composition of Fux's oeuvre (he evidently wrote very little during the 1730s, having settled into a kind of semi-retirement) stands as a conclusive illustration of a mastery of Italianate expressiveness that contradicts notions of a style dominated by 'dry' counterpoint. Indeed, White argues that it is precisely Fux's contrapuntal inventiveness that offsets the schematicism inherent in the prevalence of da capo arias. For example, the aria 'Aveva ancor bambino', sung by the Virgin Mary in the *seconda parte* of *La deposizione dalla Croce*, achieves a notable pathos through a careful deployment and interweaving of vocal and instrumental motifs highlighting graphic vocabulary such as 'piagato' (wounded), 'svenato' (bleeding), 'lacero' (torn), 'pesto' (battered) and 'infranto' (crushed).[53] This aria in C minor, an emotional high point of the oratorio lasting about ten minutes, also features a prominent obbligato part for chalumeau, a single-reed precursor of the clarinet common in eighteenth-century Viennese music up to the 1770s; Colin Lawson has noted the affective similarities between this solo (and others for the instrument in Fux's works) and those for oboe and oboe d'amore in J. S. Bach's Passions and cantatas.[54]

In addition to the vocal genres surveyed thus far, instrumental music played a significant role in shaping the Viennese imperial court liturgy. Celebrations of mass generally opened and concluded with organ preludes or with intradas for trumpet and timpani on high feast days, while sonatas accompanied the

52 White, 'The *Sepolcro* Oratorios of Fux: An Assessment', p. 165. 53 *Ibid.*, pp. 217, 205–6.
54 Colin Lawson, 'The Chalumeau in the Works of Fux', in White (ed.), *Johann Joseph Fux and the Austro-Italian Baroque*, pp. 78, 90.

Gradual except during Advent and Lent. The substantial repertory of these sonatas reflected their importance as the pre-eminent form of sacred instrumental music in early eighteenth-century Austria. The division of style according to liturgical rank applied to them as well, though this self-evidently resulted in only two types, the *sonate solenne* and the *sonate ordinarie* or *mediocre*. The former featured obligatory trumpets and an otherwise variable instrumentation consisting most usually of violins, violas, cornets, trombones and continuo. In fact, the court chapel seems to have made use primarily of older, seventeenth-century *sonate solenne*, for few such works dating from the reign of Charles VI have survived, among them two by Caldara and one by the court organist Wenzel Birck.[55] By contrast, Fux and his colleagues actively produced a large body of *sonate ordinarie* for liturgical use. The Hofkapellmeister alone composed at least thirty-one such sonatas,[56] which adopt the Corellian model of alternating slow and fast movements, though usually in a three- rather than four-movement format, Adagio–Allegro–Adagio. On the basis of the extant source material, Martin Eybl has argued that the performance of this music by the *Kapelle* employed four first violins, four second violins and a continuo ensemble of cello, bassoon, violone and organ, thereby evincing little of the chamber music conception suggested by the label *sonata à tre* and reflecting a more appropriately imperial luxuriance. Eybl furthermore notes a pronounced stylistic variety, including a tendency towards the striking and the bizarre (the chromaticism of the Presto of K. 386), *battaglia* themes (the openings of K. 381 and K. 387) and dance movements (the Passacaglia of K. 377).[57]

Viewed in its entirety, the culture of sacred music at the Habsburg court in the late Baroque era presents a picture of highly diverse, co-existing styles and genres that nevertheless achieve consistency as a whole through their mutual reinforcement of the Roman Catholic universalism of Charles VI's reign. Of a deeply conservative ideological cast (perhaps a stumbling block to the appreciation by modern listeners of the music of Fux and Caldara), this culture also assimilated the most up-to-date techniques of Italian musical style, especially from the realm of opera, and charges of traditionalist blandness do not stand up to close scrutiny. Daniel Heartz has described life under Charles as a constant

55 Riedel, *Kirchenmusik am Hofe Karls VI.*, pp. 212, 215.
56 This is the number of works for which there exist manuscript sources in the former archive of the *Hofmusikkapelle*; see *ibid.*, pp. 217–18. Hochradner's work-list for the Fux entry of *The New Grove Dictionary of Music and Musicians* gives a figure of fifty-three (including eight lost compositions), obviously taking account of material in other archival collections. Twenty-five of the sonatas are printed in volumes VI/3 (ed. Josef-Horst Lederer) and VI/4 (ed. Martin Eybl) of *Johann-Joseph-Fux: Sämtliche Werke*, and an additional sonata (K. 370) is included as part of the trio partita K. 320 in volume VI/2 (ed. Erich Schenk and Theophil Antonicek). The remaining works will appear in the forthcoming volume VI/6 (ed. Martin Eybl).
57 Eybl, *Joseph-Joseph-Fux: Sämtliche Werke*, vol. VI/4, p. viii.

religious pageant.[58] This representational splendour in fact had much to do with the difficult political situation of the early eighteenth century, during which Habsburg power experienced especially severe challenges to its hegemony. In particular, the disastrous loss of Spain to the Bourbon dynasty of France permanently marked the Emperor's outlook, and the intensive cultivation of symbols of imperial might in the following decades reflected the urgent need for a psychological counterweight to the fragile, troubling reality. Charles' eldest daughter and successor, Maria Theresa, likely shared her father's mindset, but by the time she ascended to the throne in 1740 the earlier sense of dynastic inevitability had irrevocably passed. This would lead unavoidably to the profound transformation of the character of the *Hofmusikkapelle*.

Sacred music at the Viennese imperial court following the death of Fux

The significance of the end of Charles' rule is elegantly expressed in Riedel's metaphor 'mit dem Leichnam Karls VI. [wurde] die imperiale Kultur des Barock feierlich zu Grabe getragen' (with the body of Charles VI the imperial culture of the Baroque was festively carried to the grave).[59] The reduction in support for opera seria and the growing interest in French music during the reign of Maria Theresa most clearly illustrate the court's departure from its former, quintessentially Italianate orientation. However, the Empress' impassioned assertion in 1759, despite the distraction of the ongoing Seven Years' War, that 'Spectacles must continue; without them one cannot stay here in such a great Residence'[60] and Charles Burney's observation in 1772 about the Viennese predilection for processions[61] provide strong indications that pageantry had not vanished completely. The conventional historiographical view of mid-eighteenth-century music as a period of paradigmatic change has contributed to an unbalanced view of the Habsburg imperial chapel under Fux's successors, Luca Antonio Predieri and Georg Reutter. According to this interpretation, the *Kapelle* declined pitiably following the heights of the 1720s and 1730s, becoming virtually moribund by the time of Reutter's death in 1772, but managed to regain some of its former glory under the next Kapellmeister, Florian Leopold Gassmann.

58 Heartz, *Haydn, Mozart and the Viennese School 1740–1780*, p. 5.

59 Friedrich Wilhelm Riedel, 'Liturgie und Kirchenmusik', in Gerda Mraz, Gottfried Mraz and Gerald Schlag (eds.), *Joseph Haydn in seiner Zeit* (Eisenstadt, 1982), p. 121.

60 Derek Beales, 'Vienna 4. 1740–1806', in Sadie (ed.), *The New Grove Dictionary of Music and Musicians, Revised Edition*, vol. 26, p. 555.

61 Burney, *The Present State of Music in Germany, The Netherlands and United Provinces*, vol. 1, p. 309.

This narrative of extreme waning followed by partial revival originates in Köchel's 1869 study of the *Hofmusikkapelle* and appears as recently as 1995 in Daniel Heartz's *Haydn, Mozart and the Viennese School 1740–1780*. Köchel's account notes both the appointment as Kapellmeister of Predieri, who in 1746 had succeeded Caldara, only five years after Fux's death (evidently on account of the financial difficulties that Maria Theresa inherited from her father and the turmoil of the War of Austrian Succession), and the simultaneous appointment as Vice-Kapellmeister of Reutter; responsibilities were divided in such a way as to leave Reutter in charge of sacred music. As a result of a new contract in 1751, Predieri entered into retirement while officially retaining his title and Reutter became *de facto* Kapellmeister. The most striking feature of this contract was the annual sum of 20,000 florins provided to Reutter for the management of all aspects of the chapel's activities, including the hiring of new musicians to fill vacancies created by the deaths of current members. Unlike their predecessors, however, these musicians would not belong officially to the imperial court (*Hofstaat*), which in practical terms meant that they did not enjoy lifelong positions and could not receive pensions. Köchel especially emphasizes the apparent fact that by 1772 the chapel's numbers had dwindled to a mere twenty and included no violoncellist or contrabassist, not even an organist. He censures Reutter as energetically as he praises Gassmann, whose dedicated efforts purportedly prevented the complete dissolution of the *Kapelle* by restoring a conviction that no truly great court could tolerate such neglect of the musical art.[62] Although Gassmann died only two years after becoming Kapellmeister, the personnel of the chapel doubled to forty under his direction and the old administrative regime was restored so that the musicians once again comprised official employees of the court.

In an essay from 1999, Elizabeth Theresia Fritz-Hilscher persuasively exposed the myth of the chapel's decline, a decline that had assumed near-axiomatic status in the musicological literature.[63] Drawing on a careful examination of the relevant documentary sources, including the 1751 contract itself,[64] Fritz-Hilscher argued that the need for cost-saving measures motivated a radical reform in which the *Kapelle* was removed from the court bureaucratic structure and thereby privatized for the only time in its long history. The provision of 20,000 florins per year therefore anticipated a future point in time when all of the musicians hired before 1751 had passed away, and the twenty chapel members remaining in 1772 represented only those

62 Köchel, *Die kaiserliche Hof-Musikkapelle in Wien*, pp. 12–14.

63 Elizabeth Theresia Fritz-Hilscher, 'Die Privatisierung der kaiserlichen Hofmusikkapelle unter Maria Theresia 1751–1772', in Antonicek, Hilscher and Krones (eds.), *Die Wiener Hofmusikkapelle I*, pp. 161–70.

64 Vienna, Haus-, Hof-, und Staatsarchiv, Oberhofmeisteramt Protokol (OMeA Prot) 21, fos. 105v–111r.

appointed under the former administrative system, not the full personnel. Indeed, the names of Reutter's selections to fill vacancies occasionally appear in the imperial account books alongside that of the Kapellmeister himself.[65] Fritz-Hilscher surmises that the abandonment of the 'privatization experiment' upon the death of Reutter concerned the lack of actual savings and the confusion resulting from the ambiguous place of the chapel's musicians within the court organization.

In spite of the indisputable sea change that occurred in the cultural life of the Habsburg imperial court after 1740, important continuities linked the reigns of Charles VI and Maria Theresa. And the central place of the *Hofmusikkapelle* in Viennese sacred music must count among these continuities.

The fundamentally ceremonial aspect of the threefold division of liturgical music into *solenne*, *mediocre* and *in contrapunto* categories had allowed this classification scheme to maintain a firm, well-defined structure during the years of Charles' rule. In the following decades, though, the boundaries became increasingly blurred. The distinction between the two concerted idioms, *solenne* and *mediocre*, essentially disappeared by the end of the century as a new 'symphonic' manner characterized by massed sonorities gradually replaced the *concertante* textures of earlier *solenne* music,[66] and clarinos lost much of their former symbolic power.[67] The *stylus a capella* remained indispensable to the penitential seasons, and its special province, counterpoint, retained its significance as a musical marker of sacredness. At the same time, skill in polyphonic writing became less of a fundamental necessity for church music composition (even granting the persistence of conventions such as fugal endings of the Gloria and Credo movements of masses) as the *galant* style pervaded the realm of *musica da chiesa*. As the century progressed, the practice of vocal counterpoint in particular took on increasing pedagogical significance, so that Viennese composers whose mature outputs evince predominantly homophonic textures, such as Wagenseil and Giuseppe Bonno, not only undertook rigorous courses of polyphonic study but also provided such courses to their own pupils.[68] And even where *a cappella* writing fulfilled continuing liturgical

65 Fritz-Hilscher, 'Die Privatisierung der kaiserlichen Hofmusikkapelle unter Maria Theresia', pp. 166–8.
66 Krombach, *Die Vertonungen liturgischer Sonntagsoffertorien*, pp. 116–17.
67 Riedel, 'Liturgie und Kirchenmusik', p. 132.
68 Wagenseil's training under Fux was touched upon earlier; the most significant product of his lessons in strict counterpoint is a *Messa da quattro a Capella* of *c.* 1735, available in a modern edition in Jen-yen Chen (ed.), *Three Masses from Vienna: A Cappella Masses by Georg Christoph Wagenseil, Georg Reutter, and Leopold Hofmann* (Middleton, WI, 2004). Testimony of Wagenseil's later use of this pedagogical approach in his own teaching is provided by one of his last students, Johann Baptist Schenk ('Autobiographische Skizze', printed in *Studien zur Musikwissenschaft*, 11 [1924], pp. 75–85). Bonno, a Viennese-born Italian, spent a decade in Naples for the purposes of study, beginning in 1726; despite this extended preparation, his application upon return to the imperial capital for a post as court composer failed because Fux deemed his

needs, the actual works (with the major exception of Mass Ordinary cycles) frequently featured a primarily chordal, hymn-like style, as in Reutter's and Johann Georg Albrechtsberger's settings of sections of the Mass Proper. Reutter's *De profundis clamavi*, well known for its former attribution to Mozart (K. 93/Anh. A22), who had made a copy during the late 1780s,[69] exemplifies the later 'non-contrapuntal' manifestation of sacred music *in contrapunto*. But the changed functions of vocal polyphony in the second half of the eighteenth century in no way imply that counterpoint represented an insignificant facet of the musical language of the period. Rather, they simply underscore the weakening of the earlier symbolic and ceremonial connotations of the *a cappella* style in the specific context of liturgical practice.

The transformation of this practice assumed its most immediately tangible musical form in a large-scale substitution of Fux and Caldara's works by those of the next generation of composers, above all Reutter, whose music would achieve such widespread distribution as to constitute a new *Reichstil*.[70] Reutter is a controversial figure in eighteenth-century Viennese music, for a number of reasons: his monopolization of the leading church music posts and his eagerness to hinder the career advancement of perceived rivals;[71] his sycophantism, as in the naming of his children after Emperor Charles and Empress Elizabeth Christine; his 'neglect' of the court and cathedral music; his reputation for a shallow and boisterous compositional style, originating in Burney's description of a *Te Deum* by him as 'great noise and little meaning';[72] and his perhaps excessive facility in producing an enormous oeuvre.[73]

Not all of these accusations are merited. We have seen how earlier historians exaggerated the decline of the *Hofmusikkapelle* under Reutter's management, and David Wyn Jones has proposed that Burney's derogatory comment derived from having heard a work not by the imperial Kapellmeister but by his father, former music director at the cathedral.[74] Most significantly, Mozart

contrapuntal mastery insufficient. Only after three years as a court scholar, with lessons from the Kapellmeister himself to address the shortcoming, did Bonno achieve his goal. During the 1750s he offered a young Karl Ditters similar lessons. For a consideration of the appropriateness of the Fuxian method as preparation for composition in the *galant* idiom, see Chen, 'Palestrina and the Influence of "Old" Style', pp. 10–17.

69 Karl Pfannhauser, 'Mozart hat kopiert!', *Acta mozartiana*, 1 (1954), pp. 21–5, 38–41.

70 See the thematic catalogue in Hofer, *Die beiden Reutter als Kirchenkomponisten*.

71 This eagerness is well illustrated by the famous dispute of 1760–1 with Count Giacomo Durazzo, the director of the court theatres, one aspect of which involved Reutter's complaint against Gluck's involvement in chamber music and *Tafelmusik* at the court and his apparent appointment as a Kapellmeister. For a general account of the dispute, see Heartz, *Haydn, Mozart and the Viennese School 1740–1780*, pp. 137–42.

72 Burney, *The Present State of Music in Germany, The Netherlands and United Provinces*, vol. 1, p. 361.

73 The large collection of Reutter's autograph scores, now preserved in the archive of Heiligenkreuz Abbey in Lower Austria (brought there by his son), hints at this facility in their few revisions and the hurried nature of their calligraphy.

74 David Wyn Jones, 'Reutter, (Johann Adam Joseph Karl) Georg (von) (ii)', in Sadie (ed.), *The New Grove Dictionary of Music and Musicians, Revised Edition*, vol. 21, p. 236.

and Beethoven both seem to have viewed Reutter's compositions as models of court taste in church music when they considered seeking (and in Mozart's case actually applied for and obtained) positions as Kapellmeister.[75] The performances of the Kyrie and Gloria from Reutter's Mass in E-flat major on the occasion of Pope Pius VI's 1782 visit to Vienna and of one of his six Requiems for the observance of the tenth anniversary of Maria Theresa's death in 1790 provide further evidence of Reutter's status as a paradigmatic representative of imperial sacred style. Such a status had little to do with aesthetic matters, and even less with ideas of 'greatness'; rather, it concerned the suitability of a given body of work to fulfil the symbolic and practical functions of *musica da chiesa* at the Habsburg court.

Reutter's output includes approximately eighty masses, making him the most prolific composer of the genre in the mid to late eighteenth century, ahead of Franz Tuma (*c.* sixty-five settings) and Johann Baptist Vanhal (*c.* fifty).[76] Among the eighty are some of the final examples of *Missae solemnes* featuring clarinos as well as two works in *a cappella* style.[77] Though the concerted style dominates, an excessive focus on Reutter's predilection for busy instrumental accompaniments – and the resultant 'noisy' character of certain of his church works – disregards his small but not negligible contribution to the liturgical repertory of *a cappella* music. As usual, functional necessity motivated the writing of such music; in this instance, however, the necessity encompassed a consideration that went beyond the long-standing prohibition of obbligato instruments during Advent and Lent, for during the middle of the century various ecclesiastical and political authorities attempted to check what they perceived as a growing secularization of sacred musical style. (The concluding section of this chapter will discuss in greater depth controversies surrounding the 'encroachment' of instrumental and operatic elements.) The constraints that confronted Reutter and his contemporaries took shape in a series of edicts from the late 1740s and early 1750s: the encyclical *Annus qui* issued in February 1749 by Pope Benedict XIV which, among other things, criticized theatricality in religious music and urged that instruments aid rather than obscure the comprehension of text; the December 1753 decree of the Viennese archiepiscopal *Konsistorium* forbidding trumpets and timpani in churches and processions; and the imperial *Hofreskript* of January 1754, which reinforced and broadened this ban. While the precise impact of these measures

75 See Christoph Wolff, *Mozart's Requiem*, trans. Mary Whittall (Berkeley and Los Angeles, 1994), pp. 36, 119–20 and David Black, 'Mozarts Anstellung am Stephansdom', *Acta mozartiana*, 53 (2006), pp. 109–26.

76 Bruce MacIntyre, 'Johann Baptist Vanhal and the Pastoral Mass Tradition', in Jones (ed.), *Music in Eighteenth-Century Austria*, p. 114.

77 One of these two works is edited in Chen, *Three Masses from Vienna*. See also Jones, 'Haydn's *Missa Sunt bona mixta malis*', pp. 91–7.

remains unclear,[78] they certainly contributed to the persistent belief that vocal sonority represented the quintessential medium for the expression of pious feeling through music. This pronounced aspect of tradition, continuity and conservatism must balance an understanding of the stylistic transformations of the later eighteenth century that imparted an increasing instrumental character to sacred works.

Bruce MacIntyre lists Reutter among a group of 'progressive' Viennese composers whose masses reflect strong influences from secular genres.[79] The others he includes are Albrechtsberger, Carl Ditters von Dittersdorf, Gassmann, Johann Adolf Hasse, Leopold Hofmann, Ignaz Holzbauer, Christoph Sonnleithner and Vanhal. To this list should be added Antonio Salieri, whose concerted masses lie outside the chronological limits of MacIntyre's study, as well as Haydn and Mozart, of course.[80] Albrechtsberger, Dittersdorf, Gassmann, Hofmann, Mozart and Salieri held court positions at some point in their careers, though not necessarily at the *Hofmusikkapelle* – as in the case of Dittersdorf, who served as violinist in the orchestra of the Burgtheater for three years during the 1760s. Hasse enjoyed close connections with the imperial family, becoming 'Kapellmeister in all but name'.[81] Despite the heated criticisms that it sometimes engendered in the late eighteenth century, the assimilation of operatic styles within Viennese sacred music certainly did not begin in this period, as the earlier examination of the work of Fux and Caldara clearly demonstrates.[82] The more genuine innovation lay in the 'instrumentalization' of the mass. This process did not simply involve a greater foregrounding of the orchestra, but also related to specific facets of compositional procedure such as thematic–harmonic recapitulation, long-range continuity and motivic unity.

78 See below for a more detailed consideration of this question. Hofer, *DTÖ* 88, p. 15, notes the composition by Reutter of a number of vocally orientated works, evidently in the wake of the measures; one of these is a *Miserere in B a due chori all uso Romano* with no instrumental accompaniment.

79 MacIntyre, *The Viennese Concerted Mass*, p. 733, n. 3.

80 Salieri's Mass in D major (1788) and Mass in D minor (1805) are available in modern editions prepared by Jane Schatkin Hettrick (Middleton, WI, 1994, 2002).

81 Heartz, *Haydn, Mozart and the Viennese School 1740–1780*, p. 135. These connections are epitomized by the *Litania della B.V.M.* composed for the imperial family and performed by them on 5 August 1762, with Maria Theresa and several of her daughters participating as vocalists and the future Joseph II on organ. Especially notable is the difficulty of the arias, including the two for the Empress that include wide ranges and melismas. A *Salve Regina* in E-flat major of 1766 for soprano and alto, possibly also written for Vienna, likewise exemplifies the application of Hasse's quintessentially operatic bent to his music for the church. See Sven Hansell, 'Hasse (3) Johann Adolf Hasse', in Sadie (ed.), *The New Grove Dictionary of Music and Musicians, Revised Edition*, vol. 11, p. 107.

82 What was new, though, was the 'entry' of comic opera into the church. Cf. Friedrich Nicolai, *Beschreibung einer Reise durch Deutschland und die Schweiz* (Berlin, 1784), vol. 4, pp. 544–5: 'With respect to composition, Catholic Church music up until several years ago still had much of its own special character. But nowadays operatic music also forces its way into churches everywhere, and, what is worse, [it is] the insipid Italian opera music of the new style. In Vienna, too, I found it all too conspicuous. During many a Credo or Benedictus I knew not whether perhaps I was hearing music from an Italian *opera buffa*.' Cited (in translation) in MacIntyre, *The Viennese Concerted Mass*, p. 54.

The more forward-looking masses of the second half of the century feature, in the first place, an increased degree of obbligato instrumental writing. The work of Hofmann and Dittersdorf (in addition to that of Reutter) exemplifies this characteristic, and the status of both men as outstanding violinists of their day as well as active composers of concertos (and symphonies) cannot be coincidental. Indeed, Dittersdorf himself likely played the numerous violin solos in his Mass in C performed at the coronation of Joseph II as Holy Roman Emperor in 1765.[83] The adaptation of elements of sonata form such as the double reprise and thematic functionalism represents a further progressive trait of the late-eighteenth-century mass,[84] as does the tendency towards less frequent sectionalization of individual movements through a closer integration of vocal solos with surrounding choral passages (in contrast to the earlier prevalence of discrete arias).

Finally, motivic concision and repetition as a means of linking together disparate materials helped to bring about the symphonic type of mass best known through the six late works of Haydn. This technique can be illustrated by two sub-genres, the Credo Mass and the *Missa pastoralis*. The first, typified by Mozart's *Missa brevis* in F major, K. 192 (1774) and Mass in C major, K. 257 (1776), employs a specifically textual–vocal motif in its restatements of the word 'Credo' and the associated melody throughout the movement. The second forms a component of the Christmas Eve liturgy and presents a musical style characterized by a simplified, limited vocabulary of motifs with well-established semiotic connotations related to the nativity theme. Vanhal's *Missa Pastoralis* in G (composed by 1782) epitomizes this style, which helped 'to simplify, consolidate and unify a mass' and thereby contributed to 'the gradual change from the sprawling, multi-movement number mass of the Baroque to the more concise, symphonic, and unified mass at the end of the eighteenth century'.[85]

An attempt to achieve coherence at the broadest structural level is evident in Reutter's *Missa Sancti Placidi*, which stands as an exceptional work for its use of a common accompanimental figure in all five of its movements.[86] The

83 Heartz, *Haydn, Mozart, and the Viennese School 1740–1780*, p. 442. Margaret Grave and Jay Lane, 'Dittersdorf, Carl Ditters von', in Sadie (ed.), *The New Grove Dictionary of Music and Musicians, Revised Edition*, vol. 7, p. 387, suggest that the mass is no. 327 in the works catalogue in Carl Krebs, *Dittersdorfiana* (Berlin, 1900).

84 MacIntyre, *The Viennese Concerted Mass*, p. 30. Martin Chusid, 'Some Observations on Liturgy, Text, and Structure in Haydn's Late Masses', in H. C. Robbins Landon and Roger E. Chapman (eds.), *Studies in Eighteenth-Century Music: A Tribute to Karl Geiringer on His Seventieth Birthday* (London, 1970), pp. 129–30, discusses Haydn's use of other instrumental forms such as rondo and sonata rondo in his six final masses.

85 MacIntyre, 'Johann Baptist Vanhal and the Pastoral Mass Tradition', p. 132. Vanhal's mass is designated XIX:G4 in Alexander Weinmann, *Themen-Verzeichnis der Kompositionen von Johann Baptiste Vanhal* (Vienna, 1987), part 1, p. iv.

86 MacIntyre, *The Viennese Concerted Mass*, p. 121. The mass is no. 33 in Hofer's thematic catalogue.

investigation of cyclic coherence in the eighteenth-century mass, however, must confront the matter of the liturgical uses of the music, whose most tangible consequence was the separation of the movements of the Ordinary by other ritual events (with the exception of the Kyrie and Gloria, which occurred successively). As long as composers intended their masses for the church rather than the concert hall, the kind of macro-cohesion exemplified by Beethoven's *Missa solemnis* of 1823 could not constitute an essential trait of the genre. That unifying techniques do nevertheless make a significant impact despite the 'unfavourable' conditions indicates the force of the new aesthetic that emerged over the course of the second half of the eighteenth century.

Among liturgical genres other than the Mass Ordinary, the Offertory demonstrated a particular musical richness, just as in the first half of the century, and it too reflected a similar development towards a symphonic style. Gabrielle Krombach's study of the Offertory at the Viennese court in the eighteenth and nineteenth centuries especially notes the trend in works by Salieri, whose traits include a predominance of homophonic texture in both voices and instruments and an enriched orchestration of five-part strings, oboes, bassoon, continuo and occasionally trumpets and timpani (but, significantly, without the high sonority of clarinos).[87] One of these works, the *Populi timete* of 1778, maintained a place in the repertory of the *Hofmusikkapelle* even as late as the twentieth century.[88]

Liturgical instrumental music in the second half of the eighteenth century continued to include organ preludes for the beginning and conclusion of mass services,[89] and a further organ prelude or a trio sonata for the Gradual and the Alleluia outside of the penitential seasons. However, the middle of the century began to see symphonies being used as the accompanying music for these sections of the Proper. Neal Zaslaw has discussed the prevalence of the *sinfonia da chiesa* throughout Austria, southern Germany, Italy and Spain, while Riedel has detailed an illuminating example of the liturgical functions fulfilled by some of Joseph Haydn's symphonies at Göttweig Abbey in the province of Lower Austria.[90] In an essay of 1978, Jens Peter Larsen proposed that both the typical four-movement structure of the church sonata, with alternating slow and fast tempos, and the trumpet intrada in the key of C major represent

87 Krombach, *Die Vertonungen liturgischer Sonntagsoffertorien*, p. 117.

88 Jane Schatkin Hettrick and John A. Rice, 'Salieri, Antonio', in Sadie (ed.), *The New Grove Dictionary of Music and Musicians, Revised Edition*, vol. 23, p. 153.

89 See n. 168 below on the uncertain status, following the 1754 *Hofreskript*, of the traditional trumpet intradas for high feasts.

90 Neal Zaslaw, 'Mozart, Haydn, and the *Sinfonia da Chiesa*', *The Journal of Musicology*, 1/1 (1982), pp. 95–124; Friedrich Wilhelm Riedel, 'Joseph Haydns Sinfonien als liturgische Musik', in Karlheinz Schlager (ed.), *Festschrift Hubert Unverricht zum 65. Geburtstag* (Tutzing, 1992), pp. 213–20.

essential stylistic sources of the symphony, balancing the more conventional view of the genre as derived from the secular domain of opera.[91] He identified Haydn's symphonies nos. 5, 11, 18, 21, 22 and 49 as belonging to a 'church' type and nos. 20, 32, 33 and 37 as belonging to an 'intrada' type.[92] However, Zaslaw's study reveals that the *da chiesa* form had little if any impact upon the selection of works for use in the church, which as often as not began with fast rather than slow openings.[93] Furthermore, a single movement of a symphony usually sufficed as the Gradual music for a given celebration of mass,[94] in contrast to trio sonatas where briefer durations called for complete performances. A crucial distinction is thus necessary between function and *topos*, which manifested 'sacredness' in differing ways.

In Vienna, compositions by Hofmann and by Carlo d'Ordoñez, among others, likely featured as *sinfonie da chiesa* in the city's worship services. Burney heard several symphonies (probably individual movements) by Hofmann when he attended mass in the cathedral on 8 September 1772.[95] D' Ordoñez, a violinist employed at the Habsburg court, wrote no liturgical vocal music that has survived, so a report in the *Wiener Theater Almanach* of 1794 praising his sacred works may actually refer to church symphonies,[96] of which a possible example is the seven-movement *Sinfonia solenna* with a contrapuntal conclusion.[97] The *sinfonia da chiesa* remains a topic for further research. The relative lack of earlier investigation has much to do with historiographically conditioned notions of the symphony first as theatre music and then later as concert music; however, as Zaslaw has noted, in the eighteenth century the genre partook of all three categories of the tripartite division of style, and not just two of them.[98]

The re-orientations of Viennese musical culture that occurred over the successive reigns of Charles VI, Maria Theresa and Joseph II are nowhere more vividly embodied than in the oratorio. Wholly cultivated within a formal court liturgical context under Charles, the oratorio entered the secular milieu of the concerts that took place in the Burgtheater, one of the two court theatres, during the early years of Maria Theresa's rule. These concerts,

91 Jens Peter Larsen, 'Zur Entstehung der österreichischen Symphonietradition (ca. 1750–1775)', in *Haydn-Jahrbuch*, 10 (1978), p. 76. Larsen additionally notes the affinity between the *sonata da chiesa* structure and the slow fugal sectionalization common in organ preludes.

92 *Ibid.*, p. 78. 93 Zaslaw, 'Mozart, Haydn, and the *Sinfonia da Chiesa*', pp. 114–15.

94 This was the case at Göttweig, for example; see Riedel, 'Joseph Haydns Sinfonien', pp. 214–18.

95 Burney, *The Present State of Music in Germany, The Netherlands and United Provinces*, vol. 1, p. 326.

96 A. Peter Brown, *Carlo d'Ordoñez: Seven Symphonies* (New York and London, 1979), p. xii (cited in Heartz, *Haydn, Mozart and the Viennese School 1740–1780*, p. 473).

97 David Young, 'Ordoñez, Karl (Rochus) von', in Sadie (ed.), *The New Grove Dictionary of Music and Musicians, Revised Edition*, vol. 18, p. 551. The work is designated D5 in A. Peter Brown, *Carlo d'Ordoñez, 1734–1786: A Thematic Catalog* (Detroit, MI, 1978).

98 Zaslaw, 'Mozart, Haydn, and the *Sinfonia da Chiesa*', p. 95.

initiated in 1745, occurred during the Lenten season when performances of drama and opera were forbidden. The surviving documentation indicates the presence of oratorios on programmes no later than the 1750s.[99] The featured works included compositions by Andrea Bernasconi, Niccolò Jommelli and Baldassare Galuppi as well as by Wagenseil and Holzbauer, all in Italian (for example Wagenseil's *Gioas, re di Giuda* of 1755); only around 1780 did German oratorio begin to emerge, at around the same time as the founding of a German opera company by Joseph II. In 1759, the Burgtheater concerts suffered a temporary cessation as a result of the financial difficulties caused by the Seven Years' War. However, a performance on 18 March of Bonno's *Isaaco figura del redentore* held at the Palais Rofrano (later the Palais Auersperg), the residence of Prince Joseph Friedrich von Sachsen-Hildburghausen, evidently aimed at compensating the loss.[100] The audience included the Empress and Emperor and seven of their children, hence reflecting the continued imperial associations of the oratorio. At the same time, the aristocratic sponsorship marked the beginnings of a shift in patronage that would culminate some forty years later in the commissioning by the Baron Gottfried van Swieten's Gesellschaft der Associierten Cavaliere (discussed in the following section) of Joseph Haydn's two masterpieces, *The Creation* and *The Seasons*.

In the intervening decades, however, the court remained institutionally significant for the cultivation of the genre. Only several months before he succeeded Reutter as imperial Kapellmeister, Gassmann founded the Tonkünstler-Societat for the charitable purpose of supporting the widows and children of deceased musicians. The society presented benefit concerts featuring oratorios during the Advent and Lenten seasons in the second of the court theatres, the Kärntnertortheater. A contemporary report stated that the musicians gathered together for these occasions numbered up to 400;[101] even if somewhat exaggerated, the claim nevertheless suggests the increasingly communal aspect of oratorio performance in the second half of the eighteenth century and hints at a displacement of the cultural centre of gravity away from the court towards a new bourgeois public.[102] During the 1770s and 1780s a

99 *Répertoire des Theatres de la Ville de Vienne depuis l'Année 1752 jusqu'à l'Année 1757* (Vienna, 1757); Philipp Gumpenhuber, *Repertoire de tous les Spectacles qui ont été donné au Theatre de la Ville* (Harvard College Library, Theatre Collection, MS Thr. 248–248.3, 1758–63); Gumpenhuber, *Repertoire de tous les Spectacles qui ont été donné au Theatre pres de la Cour* (Austrian National Library, Mus. Hs. 34580a-c. Mus R/XVIII/ Gumpenhuber/1, 1761–3).

100 Heartz, *Haydn, Mozart and the Viennese School 1740–1780*, p. 48. A report of the event appeared in the *Wiener Diarium*, 21 March 1759.

101 Johann Kaspar Riesbeck, *Briefe eines reisenden Franzosen über Deutschland an seinen Brüder zu Paris* (Zürich, 1783). The relevant passage of this source is cited in Heartz, *Haydn, Mozart and the Viennese School 1740–1780*, p. 61.

102 See Jürgen Habermas, *Strukturwandel der Öffentlichkeit* (Darmstadt and Neuwiedt, 1962), trans. Thomas Burger and Frederick Lawrence as *The Structural Transformation of the Public Sphere* (Cambridge, MA, 1989).

noteworthy proportion of the major composers working in or around Vienna provided music for the society's benefits including Gassmann (*La betulia liberata*, 1772); Hasse (*Sant'Elena al Calvario*, 1772, revived in 1773 and 1781, *Il cantico de' tre fanciulli*, 1774); Dittersdorf (*Esther*, 1773, *Giob*, 1786); Bonno (*Il Giuseppe riconosciuto*, 1774); Haydn (*Il ritorno di Tobia*, 1775, revived in 1784 in a much revised version); Joseph Starzer (*La passione di Gesù Cristo*, 1778); Albrechtsberger (*Die Pilgrime auf Golgotha*, 1781); Mozart (*Il Davidde penitente*, 1785, the re-working of the incomplete 'Great' Mass in C minor K. 427).[103]

As a whole, sacred music during the reigns of Charles VI's immediate successors presents a diversified picture in which the court chapel remained a centrally important institution yet did not carry the same symbolic weight as in earlier times in reflecting an ideology of monolithic power. The re-distribution of this weight, as it were, manifested itself in part through the cultivation of liturgical and para-liturgical music by Austria's aristocratic houses, among which the Esterházys unquestionably occupied the pre-eminent position.

Aristocratic patrons of sacred music: the Esterházy family and Joseph Haydn

Of Hungarian stock, the Esterházy family established their principal residence in Eisenstadt (Hungarian Kismarton), approximately 50 km southeast of Vienna, and already maintained a *Kapelle* in the early seventeenth century.[104] The history of the chapel during the eighteenth century is distinguished by the lengthy tenures of Gregor Werner (1728–66) and Joseph Haydn (1766–90) as successive directors. Werner possibly studied with Fux in Vienna shortly before he was appointed Kapellmeister by Princess Maria Octavia (regent during the minority of her son, Paul Anton, who reigned from 1734 to 1762). Several circumstances hint at this possibility. The one-month preparation time granted to Werner before he took up his new duties, which he devoted partly to arranging for the copying of sacred works by Fux, Caldara and Marc'Antonio Ziani (Fux's predecessor), suggests that he specifically received the charge of cultivating the *Reichstil* at Eisenstadt.[105] If Maria

103 Carl Ferdinand Pohl, *Denkschrift aus Anlass des hundertjährigen Bestehens der Tonkünstler-Societät* (Vienna, 1871) provides the complete programmes of the concerts. Many of the oratorios are edited in the series *The Italian Oratorio: 1650–1800* (New York, 1986–7), 31 vols.

104 Harald Dreo, 'Die fürstliche Esterházysche Musikkapelle von ihren Anfängen bis zum Jahre 1766', *Jahrbuch für österreichische Kulturgeschichte*, 1/2 (1971), p. 81.

105 Richard Moder, 'Gregor Joseph Werner, ein Meister des ausgehenden musikalischen Barock in Eisenstadt', *Burgenländische Heimatblätter*, 21/2 (1959), pp. 146ff. (cited in Dreo, 'Die fürstliche Esterhazysche Musikkapelle', p. 99). A 1721 catalogue of the Esterházy sacred music repertory, titled *Prothocolum inventationis Tempore Incepti Tutoratus*, includes many works by Viennese court composers; see János Hárich, 'Inventare der Esterházysche-Hofmusikkapelle in Eisenstadt', *Haydn Yearbook*, 9 (1975),

Octavia strove musically to emulate the Habsburg rulers, then she may well have sought candidates with connections to the *Hofmusikkapelle*. Also supporting the likelihood of a period of instruction under Fux is Werner's mastery of vocal counterpoint, evident in his five masses and numerous shorter church works in *a cappella* style. David Wyn Jones has described him as 'the most important composer of such music after Fux'.[106] In fact, Werner's sacred oeuvre as a whole reflects the diversity of the imperial musical liturgy. Eighteen masses and three Requiems with orchestral accompaniment survive, as do nineteen oratorios intended for performance, like their Viennese counterparts, during Lent.[107] A highly significant difference lies, however, in the setting of German rather than Italian texts; in the absence of an Arcadian literary tradition furnished by poet–librettists such as Pariati and Metastasio, the Eisenstadt *Kapelle* could not foster the brand of representational symbolism associated with Italian language and culture in the capital.

Prince Paul Anton appointed Haydn to the post of Vice-Kapellmeister in 1761. The contract of employment specified a clear division of duties with Werner: 'Gregorius Werner, in consideration of his long service, shall continue to retain the post of *Ober-Capel-Meister*, while the said Joseph Heÿden, as *Vice-Capel-Meister* at Eÿsenstadt, shall in regard to the choir music depend upon and be subordinate to the said Gregorio Werner; but in everything else, whenever there shall be a musical performance, and in all required for the same in general and in particular, said *Vice-Capel-Meister* shall be responsible.'[108] Thus Haydn initially had little or no reason to write church music, and though the several years following his promotion to Kapellmeister in 1766 saw the production of a notable body of liturgical works which included at least three complete masses, the *Stabat Mater* of 1767 and the *Salve Regina* of 1771, not all of these were intended for use at the Esterházy court. Haydn did not become a regular church music composer like Fux, Caldara, Reutter and his younger brother Michael,[109] even though his temperament and inclinations would surely have enabled him to head in such a direction, to judge from the six late masses, had he so wished. The reason he did not do so lay in the increasing focus of Prince

p. 21 and James Armstrong, Jr, 'Towards a History of the Esterházy Church Music Archive', in Georg Feder (ed.), *Internationales Musikwissenschaftliches Symposium 'Dokumentarische Grundlagen in der Haydnforschung'* (Tutzing, 2006), p. 112.

106 Jones, 'Haydn's *Missa Sunt bona mixta malis*', p. 98.

107 Dreo, 'Die fürstliche Esterhazysche Musikkapelle', p. 102. János Hárich, a long-time Esterházy archivist, prepared a thematic catalogue of Werner's sacred music that lists over 460 compositions (not including oratorios). A transcription of this catalogue appears in Róbert Árpád Murányi, 'Thematischer Katalog der Werke G. J. Werners in Budapest', *Studia Musicologica Academiae Scientarium Hungaricae*, 38/1–2 (1997), pp. 151–228 (cited in Armstrong, 'Towards a History of the Esterházy Church Music Archive', p. 110, n. 13).

108 A translation of the entire contract, from which the quoted passage is taken, appears in H. C. Robbins Landon, *Haydn: Chronicle and Works I: Haydn: The Early Years, 1732–1765* (Bloomington, IN, 1980), pp. 350–2.

109 Riedel, 'Liturgie und Kirchenmusik', p. 121.

Nicholas 'the Magnificent' (reigned 1762–90) – Paul Anton's younger brother and successor – on his new summer palace at Esterháza, where the extraordinary cultivation of opera occupied much of the Kapellmeister's energies. Back in Eisenstadt, the requirements for liturgical music were largely fulfilled by other members of the *Kapelle*, among them Franz Novotny and Carl Schiringer, or through compositions imported from elsewhere.[110]

Haydn's sacred works up to 1782 still observed the liturgically determined *solenne*, *mediocre* and *a cappella* style categories, and thus range from the *Missa Sunt bona mixta malis* (1768) in *stile antico* to the monumental *Missa Cellensis in honorem Beatissimae Virginis Mariae*, a *solenne* setting begun in 1766.[111] The latter, Haydn's second extant mass (after the *Missa brevis* in F major of 1749),[112] has also come to be known as the *Cecilia Mass*, resulting in some uncertainty regarding its origins. 'Cellensis' refers to the pilgrimage church of Mariazell in the province of Styria, to the southwest of Vienna. However, Otto Biba has pointed out the impossibility of a performance at this church, given its limited musical resources, and given that the mass is an enormous work featuring a Gloria movement that exceeds in length those of J. S. Bach's Mass in B minor and Mozart's Mass in C minor, K. 427 (821 bars versus 785 and 737). Haydn more likely composed the *Missa Cellensis* as a result of a commission from the Styrian Confraternity of Vienna, which each year celebrated a feast of Our Lady of Mariazell on 8 September with a solemn mass in St Augustine's Church, located in the imperial palace complex. However, the alternate name of *Cecilia Mass* suggests a different possibility, namely that the work featured in an annual observance by the Viennese Brotherhood of Saint Cecilia of the feast day of its patron saint on 22 November.[113] Whatever the specific occasion on which the *Missa Cellensis* received its first performance, those present experienced music of exceptional ambitiousness, especially in the extended choral fugues that conclude the Kyrie, Gloria, Credo and Agnus Dei. Furthermore, despite its breadth and the contingencies of liturgical practice, the Mass demonstrates a close integration of its diverse material through the

110 Otto Biba, 'Die kirchenmusikalischen Werke Haydns', in Mraz, Mraz and Schlag (eds.), *Joseph Haydn in seiner Zeit*, p. 142.

111 Riedel, 'Liturgie und Kirchenmusik', p. 121. An 1805 thematic catalogue of concerted masses in the Esterházy sacred music collection that divides the works into 'Missa Solennis' and 'Kleine Meßen' lists the early *Missa brevis* in F and the *Missa brevis Sancti Joannis de Deo* of *c.* 1775 under the latter category and the remaining settings under the former (the *Missa Cellensis*, the *Missa Rorate caeli desuper* and the *Missa Sunt bona mixta malis* do not appear in the catalogue); see Armstrong, 'Towards a History of the Esterházy Church Music Archive', pp. 120–1.

112 The *Missa Rorate caeli desuper*, attributed to Haydn in a manuscript in Göttweig Abbey and published as his work by H. C. Robbins Landon (London, 1957), is of uncertain authorship, as other sources identify the composer as Reutter or Ferdinand Arbesser, organist at the imperial court.

113 Biba, 'Die kirchenmusikalischen Werke Haydns', pp. 142–3; Heartz, *Haydn, Mozart and the Viennese School 1740–1780*, pp. 296–8.

deployment of unifying motifs first presented in the slow introduction to the Kyrie, such as the dissonant interval of E-flat–B-natural (later richly elaborated in the 'Qui tollis', 'Et incarnatus est' and particularly the deeply expressive Benedictus). Heartz compares this slow introduction to those of Haydn's symphonies of the same period that were similarly 'pregnant with meaning for the entire cycle to follow'.[114] This link provides another illustration of the cross-fertilization of sacred and instrumental genres discussed above.

The *Missa Sunt bona mixta malis* survives in a fragmentary state, breaking off in the middle of the Gloria after the 'Gratias agimus tibi'. Indeed, its music remained unknown until the rediscovery of the autograph manuscript in 1983. The vocal polyphonic idiom of the work, while certainly fulfilling the liturgical requirements of the penitential seasons, probably also reflects a conscious pedagogical aim. Contemporary composers who wrote *a cappella* masses evidently with a similar purpose in mind include Hofmann (*c.* 1760) and Salieri (1767). In a study of Haydn's Mass, David Wyn Jones points out that the curious designation, 'Sunt bona mixta malis', or 'the good mixed with the bad', was added as an afterthought on the title page of the autograph.[115] This may have occurred after the (apparent) abandonment of the composition, as a pronouncement upon its equivocal results. Such a possibility gains credence in view of the lack of affinity for a manifestly *antico* brand of counterpoint in Haydn's later work, in contrast to the music of his brother Michael. The impact of an early intensive training in strict polyphony took on a much subtler form in the mature style of the elder sibling, as a complete assimilation within a fully *moderno* idiom, illustrated in the sophisticated contrapuntal mastery of the concerted masses, the oratorios, the Op. 20 string quartets and many other works.

Haydn's next complete mass, the *Missa in honorem Beatissimae Virginis Mariae* of *c.* 1768–9, is also known as the Great Organ Solo Mass because of its obbligato organ part which the composer may have written for himself.[116] The floridness of the organ writing, becoming 'a veritable concerto' in the Benedictus, exemplifies the delicate ornateness of the work as a whole. Daniel Heartz persuasively links this quality with a culture of Rococo Catholicism in late-eighteenth-century Austria and southern Germany, notable for its light, graceful expression of popular religious sentiment.[117] Heartz's sympathetic

114 *Ibid.*, p. 297.

115 Jones, 'Haydn's *Missa Sunt bona mixta malis*', p. 99. The title page is reproduced on p. 104 of this essay.

116 Armstrong, 'Towards a History of the Esterházy Church Music Archive', pp. 128–30, discusses the possibility that Haydn revised the mass some time between 1772 and 1774, adding trumpet and timpani parts only at this time.

117 Heartz, *Haydn, Mozart and the Viennese School 1740–1780*, p. 312.

viewpoint contrasts strikingly with Charles Rosen's censure of a comparably ornate passage in a later work, the 'Christe eleison' of the *Missa in tempore belli* of 1796, which 'can only have sounded as trivial to Haydn's contemporaries as they do to us today'.[118] Rosen's failure to engage in a 'hermeneutic recognition of others',[119] evident in the easy assumption of how listeners of Haydn's time must have reacted, underscores the dangers of an insufficiently developed sensitivity to cultural experiences vastly different from those of contemporary people but no less valid as a result. With respect to eighteenth-century music, these dangers have particularly plagued the subject matter of the present chapter.

Towards the end of 1772 Haydn composed the *Missa Sancti Nicolai* evidently at breakneck speed, in order to have the work ready for the celebration of Prince Nicholas' name-day on 6 December. H. C. Robbins Landon suggests that the mass was intended as an expression of thanks for the return of the *Kapelle* to Eisenstadt following a particularly prolonged stay at Esterháza;[120] as such, it may stand as a kind of companion piece to the Symphony No. 45 in F-sharp minor, 'Farewell', written shortly before the return. As with the Great Organ Solo Mass, a delicate quality pervades the *Missa Sancti Nicolai*, a *missa pastoralis* liturgically appropriate to the season and demonstrating such characteristic features of the genre as the key of G major and the lilting 6/4 meter of the opening Kyrie.[121] Haydn had occasion to write only two further masses before the inception in 1796 of the impressive series of six large-scale compositions: the *Missa brevis Sancti Joannis de Deo* (*c.* 1775), also called the Little Organ Solo Mass and, like the earlier, larger work, containing an elaborate organ obbligato part in the Benedictus movement; and the second *Missa Cellensis*, composed in 1782. Biba reasonably links this near-total lack of activity in church music to the liturgical reforms promulgated by Emperor Joseph II in 1783, an Enlightened measure that drastically curtailed the lavishness of Catholic religious observance throughout the empire.[122]

Though Leopold II, Joseph's younger brother, ascended to the throne in 1790 and reversed many of his elder sibling's radical edicts, a resumption of mass composition by Haydn did not commence until 1796 on account of his two London trips. A commission by the Viennese Piarist order shortly after the final return to Austria, leading to the writing of the *Missa in tempore belli* (also known as the *Paukenmesse* for its famous timpani solo in the Agnus Dei),

118 Rosen, *The Classical Style*, p. 369.
119 Gary Tomlinson, *Music in Renaissance Magic: Towards a Historiography of Others* (Chicago, 1993), pp. 20–7.
120 H. C. Robbins Landon, *Haydn: Chronicle and Works II: Haydn at Esterháza* (Bloomington, IN, 1978), p. 182.
121 See table 5.1, *Pastoral Traits in Eighteenth-Century Masses*, in MacIntyre, 'Johann Baptist Vanhal and the Pastoral Mass Tradition', pp. 117–18.
122 Biba, 'Die kirchenmusikalischen Werke Haydns', p. 149.

provides an indication of the marked shift in political climate. Even more dramatically Haydn, who had been pensioned in 1790 following the death of Prince Nicholas and the consequent dissolution of the Esterházy *Kapelle* by his son and successor, Paul Anton, resumed in 1794 his post as director of a chapel re-constituted by the next prince, Nicholas, son of Paul Anton. Under his latest employer, a passionate devotee of sacred music, Haydn had but the single obligation of providing a mass annually for the celebration of the name-day on 12 September of Princess Maria Hermenegild, Nicholas' wife. These favourable conditions of Haydn's renewed appointment resulted in the greatest concentration on sacred music in the composer's career, bringing six masses in the six-year period from 1796 to 1802: the *Missa Sancti Bernardi von Offida* (1796, also known as the 'Heiligmesse'), the *Missa in tempore belli* ('Paukenmesse', first performed at Eisenstadt in 1797), the *Missa in angustiis* (1798, also known as the 'Nelsonmesse'), the *Theresienmesse* (1799), the *Schöpfungsmesse* (1801) and the *Harmoniemesse* (1802).[123] Whereas Esterházy patronage of liturgical music under Nicholas 'the Magnificent' had had a rather diffuse character, with opera carrying the greatest representational burden (so to speak), the more focused support of the younger Nicholas, though hardly matching that of the Viennese *Hofmusikkapelle*, nevertheless adumbrates the growing de-centralization of influence discussed earlier. With respect to Haydn, though, this process took on landmark significance only with the sponsorship of the two great oratorios by the Gesellschaft der Associierten Cavaliere.

The transformation of the genre of *Missa solemnis* from a *concertante* to a symphonic type reaches a high point in the six late settings, with which Beethoven's Mass in C major, Op. 86 (1807), also commissioned by Prince Nicholas, shares a close affinity. The temporal proximity between an intensive

123 The *Missa Sancti Bernardi von Offida* derives its name from a seventeenth-century Capucin monk who had been beatified by Pope Pius VI on 19 May 1795, and is also called the *Heiligmesse* because of the citation of the German church lied 'Heilig, heilig' at the opening of the Sanctus. According to legend, Haydn intended the Benedictus of the *Nelsonmesse* as an acclamation to lord Horatio Nelson, admiral of the British navy and later hero of the Battle of Trafalgar. The name of the *Theresienmesse* evidently refers to Empress Marie Therese (not the daughter of Charles VI, but the consort of the then-reigning Franz II), though for uncertain reasons. However, the Empress' enthusiasm for sacred music, comparable to that of Prince Nicholas, may help to explain the link, and it is perhaps not insignificant that the *Te Deum* of 1800 was written for Marie Therese during the one-year hiatus in Mass composition between the *Theresienmesse* and the *Schöpfungsmesse*. In any event, the active patronage of church music at the turn of the century by both Empress and Prince strikingly illustrates the need for some re-thinking of the traditional historical focus on the secular music of the period; see Armstrong, 'Towards a History of the Esterházy Church Music Archive', p. 124. The 'Qui tollis' of the *Schöpfungsmesse* quotes a theme from the duet 'Holde Gattin, dir zur Seite', from the third part of *The Creation*, and the *Harmoniemesse* is so called on account of its rich instrumentation featuring an elaborate woodwind complement; *Harmonie* was the German term for the wind bands that proliferated in Austria at the end of the eighteenth century and frequently provided entertainment at aristocratic dinners (as unforgettably depicted at the end of Mozart's *Don Giovanni*); see also Chapter 20 in this volume.

preoccupation with writing symphonies and the production of church music, discussed above in connection with the first *Missa Cellensis*, came to fruition once again, as the London experiences undoubtedly remained vividly in Haydn's musical consciousness up until the end of his compositional life. Examples of the enriched orchestration of the six masses include the conspicuous timpani part of the Agnus Dei of the *Missa in tempore belli*; the solo for cello, a rare instrument in sacred music up to that time, in the 'Qui tollis' of this same mass; and the luxuriant woodwind writing of the *Harmoniemesse*. The first of these examples demonstrates the profoundly personal quality that sacred music had assimilated, as indeed does the *Missa in belli tempore* as a whole and also the *Missa angustiis*: both works are shadowed by the ongoing war with France, and the triumphant 'Dona nobis' of the earlier mass, with the timpani now joined by martial trumpets, expresses a hope for peace with an especially graphic vigour that later served as a model for a similar passage in Beethoven's *Missa solemnis*. Riedel asserts that in Haydn's last masses the remaining vestiges of the liturgical ceremonial so fundamental in the earlier part of the century finally disappeared for good, supplanted by a heroic element; the trumpets and timpani of the *Missa in tempore belli* epitomize the transformed significance of the genre.[124]

Other notable sacred vocal works by Haydn include the *Stabat Mater* (1767); the *Salve Regina* in G minor (1771), written on the occasion of the composer's recovery from a serious illness;[125] and the *Te Deum* (*c.* 1800) for Empress Marie Therese, consort of Francis II (reigned 1792–1806 as Holy Roman Emperor and 1806–35 as Austrian Emperor Francis I). Haydn sent a copy of the *Stabat Mater* to Hasse, who offered generous praise of the work. The links between these two figures, both stylistic and personal, underscore the continuing importance of an Italian impact upon Viennese music, now augmented by a significant new influence from Naples. Though Haydn never visited the city, his involvement with its style, characterized by delicately expressive, often chromatic melody and thin homophonic texture, took on manifold forms. During the 1750s he had studied under Nicola Porpora, one of the outstanding Neapolitan masters, who resided in Vienna at the time. In composing the *Stabat Mater*, he undoubtedly had in mind the most famous of all settings of this poetic text, that of another Neapolitan master, Giovanni Battista Pergolesi; Heartz points out the particularly Pergolesian flavour of Haydn's music for the sixth stanza, 'Vidit suum dulcem'.[126] Finally, the approval of Hasse, himself not from Naples but nevertheless a major exponent of its

124 Riedel, 'Liturgie und Kirchenmusik', p. 133.
125 Biba, 'Die kirchenmusikalischen Werke Haydns', p. 146.
126 Heartz, *Haydn, Mozart, and the Viennese School 1740–1780*, p. 306.

musical tradition, was likely inspired to a certain extent by the satisfaction of observing his compositional idiom practiced by the pre-eminent representative of the younger generation.[127] A final aspect of the Neapolitan character of Haydn's *Stabat Mater* requires a brief mention here, since it is a central topic in the concluding section of this chapter, namely the quintessentially operatic nature of the style, one that 'intruded' increasingly into Austrian sacred music and that helped to fuel the secularization controversies of the later decades of the century.

The patronage conditions under which *The Creation* and *The Seasons* came into being provide a paradigmatic example of the aristocracy's increasing centrality in the musical practice of late-eighteenth- and early-nineteenth-century Austria. In fact, Haydn's first oratorio, *Il ritorno di Tobia*, for the 1774–5 season of the Tonkünstler-Societät, already hints at the displacement of influence away from the Habsburg court. As an institution under imperial auspices, the society employed the court's musicians for its benefit events; however, for the premiere of *Il ritorno*, Haydn brought seven members of the Esterházy *Kapelle* to Vienna, stirring up professional resentment in the process.[128] Some time in the mid-1780s van Swieten established another society devoted to oratorio, but without the explicit charitable purpose of the Tonkünstler-Societät. This new organization, the Gesellschaft der Associierten Cavaliere (often abbreviated to the 'Associierten') evidently aimed to satisfy the musical interests of a number of prominent Austrian aristocrats, including members of the Esterházy, Schwarzenberg, Lobkowitz, Liechtenstein and Batthyany families (the 'cavaliers'), as well as to mark the growing cultural power of these noblemen by means of music. The Associierten also sponsored annual Lenten oratorio performances, with private hearings in the Viennese palaces of Prince Esterházy or Schwarzenberg sometimes followed several days later by public presentations in the Burgtheater. Joseph Starzer initially directed the society and, following his death in 1787, was succeeded by Mozart.[129] From the beginning, the music of Handel represented a special focus of the Associierten; arrangements by Starzer of *Judas Maccabaeus* (1786) and by Mozart of *Acis and Galatea* (1788), *Messiah* (1789, 1790), the *Ode for St. Cecilia's Day* (1791) and *Alexander's Feast* (1791) featured in the earliest concerts. 'Old' music, a passion for which van Swieten had cultivated during his

127 Hasse may also have heard a performance of the first *Missa Cellensis* in Vienna; on this possibility and the Neapolitan traits of the mass, see *ibid.*, pp. 298, 304–5.

128 *Ibid.*, pp. 380–2.

129 Mary Sue Morrow, *Concert Life in Haydn's Vienna: Aspects of a Developing Musical and Social Institution* (Stuyvesant, NY, 1989), pp. 10–11.

years as Austrian ambassador in Berlin (1770–7), clearly enjoyed a high social currency in Vienna, much as it did in London in the same period.[130]

Haydn's ties with the Associierten began with *The Seven Last Words*, originally an orchestral composition commissioned in 1784 or 1785 by the church of Santa Cueva in Cádiz, Spain, for performance during Holy Week and consisting of seven individual movements in slow tempo depicting each of the last words of Christ. Shortly after his return in 1795 from his second London trip, Haydn learned of a choral version of the work prepared by Joseph Friebert, music director for the prince-bishops in Passau. Whatever he felt about this unauthorized appropriation of his music, he seems not to have thought badly of Friebert's arrangement itself, for he used much of its material for his own version in a performance sponsored by van Swieten's group in 1796.[131] This event helped to set the stage for *The Creation* and *The Seasons*.

The extraordinary and extensive support received by Haydn from the Associierten for the two oratorio projects is vividly illustrated by the financial expenditures of one of the members of the society, Prince Joseph von Schwarzenberg. In an essay published in 1973–4, Gerhard Croll presented a transcription with commentary of documents in the Schwarzenberg family archive (now part of the state archive in Český Krumlov, in the Czech Republic) that detail these expenditures.[132] Croll's study demonstrated that in 1798 the Prince contributed one-tenth of the impressively munificent sum of 2,250 florins paid to Haydn for the composition of *The Creation*; by comparison, none of the musicians regularly employed by Joseph in his *Kapelle* earned a salary of more than 450 florins in the same year.[133] Following the dress rehearsal of the oratorio in the Schwarzenberg Palace on 29 April, during which he heard Haydn's music for the first time, the Prince rewarded Haydn with a further 450 florins, an indication of the profound impression made upon him by the work. He also provided 90 florins 8 kreuzer for expenses associated with the premiere a day later as well as additional performances on 7 and 10 May, again at the Palace.[134] A new set of performances took place in 1799, including the first public presentation of the work on 19 March in the Burgtheater. In this year, the Prince's outlay amounted to 339 florins 24 kreuzer. The score of *The Creation* first appeared in print in 1800, for six copies of which Joseph paid 81 florins to

130 Simon McVeigh has discussed the aristocratic aspect of the Concert of Ancient Music series in London; see his *Concert Life in London from Mozart to Haydn* (Cambridge, 1993), pp. 22–4 and also William Weber, *The Rise of Musical Classics in Eighteenth-Century England: A Study in Canon, Ritual, and Ideology* (Oxford, 1992).

131 Nicholas Temperley, *Haydn: The Creation* (Cambridge, 1991), pp. 6–7.

132 Gerhard Croll, 'Mitteilungen über die *Schöpfung* und die *Jahreszeiten* aus dem Schwarzenberg-Archiv', in Georg Feder (ed.), *Haydn-Studien*, 3 (Munich, 1973–4), pp. 85–92.

133 *Ganzjährige Hauptkasse Rechnung Für das 1798te Jahr* (Schwarzenberg account book for 1798, CZ-K ÜP 276), p. 73.

134 There were 60 kreuzer in one florin.

the Viennese music dealer Artaria. Performances of the oratorio continued in the meantime, with the Prince supplying a total of 159 florins 57 kreuzer towards logistical costs. The premiere of *The Seasons* occurred on 24 April 1801 in the Schwarzenberg Palace, followed by the public premiere on 29 May in the Redoutensaal, located in the imperial palace. Joseph's contribution to the organizational expenses of these events and also of a benefit performance of *The Creation* on 27 December, as well as to Haydn's fee for the new work, totalled 1103 florins 7 kreuzer.[135] All in all, then, a single member of the Associierten devoted the very considerable sum of 2,448 florins 36 kreuzer over four years to support Haydn's two late masterpieces.

The Creation, arguably Haydn's most beloved work, represented a new direction in the Viennese oratorio tradition. While continuing to draw upon Italian stylistic sources, it reflected more significantly the powerful impact that Handel's oratorios had made on Haydn during his London visits. The encounter with Handel's music was probably not entirely new, given the performances organized by the Tonkünstler-Societät and the Associierten;[136] however, Haydn's experience of attending the 1791 Handel Festival, where *Israel in Egypt* and *Messiah* were rendered by colossal forces in the setting of Westminster Abbey, undoubtedly inspired a new understanding of the affective potency of massed sonority: 'He meditated on every note and drew from those most learned scores the essence of true musical grandeur'.[137] The most celebrated moment of *The Creation*, at the words, 'und es ward Licht' (and there was light), owes its overwhelming force to its effect of the Sublime, an aesthetic category that in commentaries of the late eighteenth and early nineteenth centuries encompasses traits such as incommensurability, boundlessness and transcendence.[138] At the same time, this passage stands as the musical *locus classicus* of the Enlightenment ideology of the triumph of light over darkness, an ideology articulated in earlier work such as

135 The Schwarzenberg account book for 1801 (CZ-K ÜP 279) records payments on 11 April of 58 florins 49 kreuzer for lighting and on 25 April of 32 florins 18 kreuzer for police guard and 27 florins for the clearing of vendors from the Neuer Markt, the square that the Schwarzenberg Palace abutted. To account for the early date of the first payment, Croll speculates that these costs may relate to yet another performance of *The Creation*, rather than to the premiere of *The Seasons* ('Mitteilungen über die *Schöpfung* und die *Jahreszeiten* aus dem Schwarzenberg-Archiv', pp. 91–2).

136 Starzer's German version of *Judas Maccabaeus* (1779) for the Tonkünstler-Societät, later presented by the Associierten in 1786, belongs (along with the Mozart arrangements noted above) to the early history of oratorio in the vernacular in Vienna.

137 Giuseppe Carpani, *Le Haydine* (Milan, 1812), pp. 162–3, trans. by H. C. Robbins Landon in *Haydn: Chronicle and Works III: Haydn in England, 1791–1795* (Bloomington, IN 1976), p. 84 (cited in Temperley, *Haydn: The Creation*, p. 121, n. 9).

138 See James Webster, 'The Creation, Haydn's Late Vocal Music, and the Musical Sublime', in Elaine Sisman (ed.), *Haydn and His World* (Princeton, NJ, 1997), pp. 57–102, for a discussion of the central importance of the sublime in Haydn's late oratorios and masses.

Mozart's *Die Zauberflöte* and the 'Dissonance' Quartet, K. 465.[139] Its status as a landmark in the history of music is clear. The oratorio however also features a pastoral pictorialism that contrasts effectively with the frequent tone of exaltation, as in the accompanied recitative from the second part that colourfully depicts the creation of various animals, 'Gleich öffnet sich der Erde Schoß'. Such balancing of the sublime and the popular also characterizes *The Seasons*.

The libretto of *The Creation* draws upon two principal sources, the Book of Genesis and John Milton's *Paradise Lost*, and was translated and adapted by van Swieten from an earlier English text almost certainly intended for Handel. Georg August Griesinger's record of Haydn's telling of his life gives 'Lidley' as the author of the original libretto, by whom historians have identified one Thomas Linley the Elder.[140] However, Edward Olleson has suggested that this Linley, who had inherited the management of Handel's oratorio series from several predecessors, merely possessed the manuscript of the text at the time it was offered to Johann Peter Salomon, the impresario who arranged Haydn's visits to London.[141] The true author will likely remain unknown.

No such mystery surrounds the provenance of the libretto for *The Seasons*, arranged by van Swieten from a poem of the same name by the Scottish author James Thomson. Not so tangibly dramatic as *The Creation*, *The Seasons* presents tableaux of peasant life lived in each of the four seasons, manifestly a less dynamic scenario than the day-by-day recounting of the world's creation. Elements of the sublime nevertheless occur also in this second oratorio, as in the massive invocation of the Almighty towards the end of the Spring section. On the whole, though, the balance tilts more towards the pastoral, a cause perhaps of the somewhat lesser popularity of the work, though not a reflection of the aesthetic superiority of the earlier oratorio, as is sometimes suggested.[142] The different emphasis of *The Seasons* is apparent especially in the trio of peasant narrators, Simon, Jane and Lucas, in place of the archangels Gabriel, Uriel and Raphael. Examples of vivid and 'popular' pictorialism include the Summer storm, the dense fogs of Winter and the successive hunt (featuring horn calls and double grace notes depicting the baying of hounds), celebration

139 An informal performance in February 1785 in Mozart's home of the last three 'Haydn' Quartets, including the 'Dissonance', had of course prompted Haydn to pronounce Mozart 'the greatest composer known to me either in person or by name'.

140 Georg August Griesinger, *Biographische Notizen über Joseph Haydn* (Leipzig, 1810), p. 37 (cited in Temperley, *Haydn: The Creation*, p. 122, n. 2).

141 Edward Olleson, 'The Origin and Libretto of Haydn's Creation', *Haydn Yearbook*, 4 (1968), pp. 150–1 (cited in Temperley, *Haydn: The Creation*, p. 122, n. 2).

142 For example, see Temperley, *Haydn: The Creation*, p. 8, which simplistically asserts that a 'gain in intimacy and charm' comes 'at the expense of greatness'.

and drinking chorus at the close of Autumn.[143] The chorus in particular surely counts among Haydn's finest compositional achievements: a miraculous integration of disorder (drunkenness) and discipline (fugue) every bit as impressive as the Representation of Chaos that opens *The Creation*, on the one hand rowdy and vulgar, with its 'whirling' country dance and 'intoxicated' vocalisms, and on the other transcendent and exalted in its profoundly sympathetic humanism.

Haydn's intense involvement with sacred vocal music at the end of his career, resulting in the stupendous output over six years of the two oratorios, the six masses and the *Te Deum*, underscores the fallacy of viewing 'Classical' style as 'in all essentials an instrumental one'[144] (even recognizing the impact of instrumental idioms upon vocal composition). As will be discussed below, such involvement also characterizes the last few years of Mozart's life, though to a lesser extent. The persistent interest of two figures of the 'triumvirate' in church music reflects the generally high prestige of *musica da chiesa* in a devoutly Catholic society, certainly greater than that of *musica da camera* (subsequent historiography notwithstanding), if not of music for the theatre. Herein lies another point of continuity between the earlier and later parts of the eighteenth century. Yet what precisely constituted 'religious music' did not remain fixed, as a result fuelling the secularization controversies from the mid-century onwards. From a strictly liturgical and ceremonial genre, *musica da chiesa* developed to embrace much more personalized idioms reflecting the humanistic ideals of the Enlightenment. The approaching extinction of the Holy Roman Empire, whose throne the Habsburg clan had occupied since the reign of Frederick III (1440–93), epitomized the paradigm shift, as did the increasing intertwining of aristocratic and bourgeois interests that helped to engender *The Creation* and *The Seasons*.[145]

Sacred music in eighteenth-century Salzburg

A similar process of transition marks the history of sacred music in eighteenth-century Salzburg which, though nominally an autonomous political entity, in fact fell within the orbit of Viennese influence. The ruling archbishops of the territory had enjoyed a status as imperial princes since Rudolf of Habsburg granted them this privilege in 1278, so that they embodied the same kind

143 James Webster, 'Haydn, Joseph', in Sadie (ed.), *The New Grove Dictionary of Music and Musicians, Revised Edition*, vol. 11, p. 196.
144 Rosen, *The Classical Style*, p. 366.
145 See also Tia DeNora, *Beethoven and the Construction of Genius: Musical Politics in Vienna, 1792–1803* (Berkeley and Los Angeles, 1995).

of integrated temporal and spiritual power as the Viennese monarchs. Accordingly, they too embraced an orthodox and universalist Catholic ideology, such that, for example, the Archbishop Firmian (reigned 1727–44) carried out a forcible expulsion of Protestants in 1731–2. As a member state of the Holy Roman Empire, independent Salzburg came to an end in the same year as the Empire (1806).

A court music was formally established in 1591 by the Archbishop Wolf Dietrich von Raitenau (reigned 1587–1612).[146] Outstanding musicians active in Salzburg before the eighteenth century include Georg Muffat, court organist from 1678 to 1692, and Heinrich Ignaz Franz von Biber, Kapellmeister from 1684 to 1704. Biber's *Missa Salisburgensis*, an epic *solenne* setting formerly attributed to Orazio Benevoli but in fact written for the celebration in 1682 of the eleven-hundredth anniversary of the archiepiscopate's founding, is a high-point in the history of Austrian sacred music. It is scored for seven choirs, suiting the multiple galleries of Salzburg Cathedral where the first performance certainly took place. Two of the choirs feature clarinos, trumpets and timpani, instruments that – here as in Vienna – symbolically transmitted an ideology of everlasting might.

Later Kapellmeisters, up to the year of Mozart's birth, were Matthias Siegmund Biechteler (1706–43), Carl Heinrich Biber, son of Heinrich Ignaz Franz (1743–9) and Johann Ernst Eberlin (1749–62). The second half of the eighteenth century represents a distinguished period of musical accomplishment in Salzburg, as embodied in the work of Eberlin, Anton Cajetan Adlgasser, both Mozarts and Michael Haydn, though none of these figures (except Eberlin) ever attained the post of Kapellmeister. In the liturgical compositions of the younger Mozart and Haydn in particular, church music at the archiepiscopal court achieved a standard comparable to that in Vienna, Eisenstadt and elsewhere in the Austrian domains.

Eberlin had joined the court music as fourth organist in 1726, and by the time of his death in 1762 had a voluminous output to his name that included fifty-eight masses. Leopold Mozart, in his (unattributed) report of the Salzburg musical establishment that appeared in the third volume of Friedrich Wilhelm Marpurg's *Historisch-kritische Beyträge zur Aufnahme der Musik* (1757), wrote of the Kapellmeister: 'He is entirely in command of the notes, and he composes with such quickness that many people would take for a fairy tale the manner in which this profound composer brings this or that important composition to the music-stand. As far as the number of musical compositions that he has composed is concerned, one can compare him to the

146 Cliff Eisen, 'Salzburg under Church Rule', in Zaslaw (ed.), *The Classical Era*, p. 166.

two very famous and industrious composers, [Alessandro] Scarlatti and Telemann.'[147] Eberlin's sacred music reflects the typical stylistic diversity of the period: a late Baroque *stile antico* on the one hand, and a harmonically conservative *stile moderno* on the other. This music remained a significant component of the active liturgical repertory in Salzburg at least until the late 1770s, and thus was well known to Haydn and to W. A. Mozart.[148] In particular, the formal conventions that Eberlin established for the *Missa brevis* guided the work of younger composers up to the early years of the reign of Prince Archbishop Hieronymus Colloredo (1772–1803), whose liturgical reforms drastically altered the character of sacred music practice in Salzburg: in the Kyrie, a slow introduction to the main part of the tutti; solo and tutti writing in the Gloria and Credo, with fugal endings to both; a three-section Sanctus and a solo quartet Benedictus; and a simple, chordal tutti Agnus followed by a lively triple-time 'Dona nobis pacem'.[149] Mozart's early *Missae breves*, K. 49 and K. 65, exemplify this type of construction.

Michael Haydn, younger brother of Joseph, was a model eighteenth-century Austrian church music composer, much like Fux and Reutter. Over the course of his career, which included more than four decades in Salzburg (1763 until his death in 1806), he produced some 600 sacred works. Many of these were widely disseminated, with many manuscript copies surviving in ecclesiastical archives in Vienna and elsewhere.[150] The best known is the *Missa pro defuncto Archepiscopo Sigismundo*, on account of its musical links with Mozart's Requiem. Haydn wrote this setting at high speed, completing it in time for the funeral masses that took place on 2–4 January 1772 for Archbishop Sigismund von Schrattenbach, who had died on 16 December. Both Leopold and Wolfgang Mozart took part in these observances, and the son clearly recalled the experience nearly twenty years later, in the closing months of his life. The two Requiems open with material that shares contrapuntal and accompanimental features; both cite a plainchant at 'Te decet hymnus', the *Lamentatio* or first psalm tone in the case of Haydn and the *tonus peregrinus* or ninth psalm tone in the case of Mozart;[151] and the subjects of the 'Quam olim Abrahae' fugues

147 [Leopold Mozart], 'Nachricht von dem gegenwärtigen Zustande der Musik Sr. Hochfürstlichen Gnaden des Erzbischoffs zu Salzburg im Jahr 1757', in Friedrich Wilhelm Marpurg, *Historisch-kritische Beyträge zur Aufnahme der Musik* (Berlin, 1757), vol. 3, p. 183. The entire report is translated in Neal Zaslaw, *Mozart's Symphonies: Context, Performance Practice, Reception* (Oxford, 1989), pp. 550–7; the above passage is taken from page 550.

148 Eisen, 'Salzburg under Church Rule', p. 170.

149 Cliff Eisen and Stanley Sadie, 'Mozart (3) Wolfgang Amadeus Mozart', in Sadie (ed.), *The New Grove Dictionary of Music and Musicians, Revised Edition*, vol. 17, p. 296.

150 See Charles Sherman and T. Donley Thomas, *Johann Michael Haydn (1737–1806): A Chronological Thematic Catalogue of His Works* (Stuyvesant, NY, 1993).

151 Wolff, *Mozart's Requiem*, pp. 49–50.

closely resemble each other in their declamatory character and insistent pitch repetitions. More generally, however, the two composers differ in significant ways that help to account for Haydn's greater centrality as an Austrian composer of church music. Haydn remained firmly rooted in his native traditions, in sharp contrast to Mozart who cultivated an international and cosmopolitan orientation in his sacred works, as in the rest of his oeuvre. Furthermore, the self-conscious ambition to achieve an idiosyncratically 'difficult' style, so manifest in the music of both Joseph Haydn and Mozart, quite evidently did not align with Michael's musical temperament. Highly individualized genius, though about to move centre stage in musical aesthetics, was not a necessary attribute of *musica da chiesa* in the conventional, functional sense, and probably detracted from it instead. Hence, a work such as Mozart's Mass in C minor, K. 427, widely regarded as 'better' than anything Michael Haydn produced, was in fact 'worse' in terms of its suitability for church use; or, rather, this profound masterwork intimated a new meaning of *musica da chiesa*. Around fifteen years later Joseph Haydn's six late masses demonstrate considerably less tension between 'expression' and function, revealing the extent to which the essential character of sacred music had changed in the interim.

The election of Count Hieronymus Colloredo as Prince Archbishop led to changes that actually enhanced Michael Haydn's position in certain respects. Colloredo, a native Viennese, sympathized profoundly with the Enlightened outlook of Emperor Joseph II, whose intervention helped to ensure that the son of the imperial state Vice-Chancellor, rather than one of several local candidates seen as more likely to succeed Schrattenbach, became the new ruler of Salzburg. Shortly after the beginning of his tenure, the archbishop initiated a series of modernizing and secularizing reforms that greatly affected numerous aspects of society, including religious observance.[152] Colloredo's demand for the simplification and rationalization of liturgical practice, effectively dismissing as useless superstition the opulence, sumptuousness and mystery that had marked Catholic worship for centuries, manifested itself most famously in the limitation of masses to forty-five minutes, Ordinary and Proper included. The impact of this measure, which Mozart described in a letter of 4 September 1776 to Padre Martini,[153] is felt in the pronounced brevity

152 In 1787, Colloredo added a sword to his family coat of arms, thereby demonstrating the extent to which he conceived of his power as secular in nature; see Eisen, 'Salzburg under Church Rule', p. 179.

153 This letter is in fact in Leopold's hand, with the exception of Wolfgang's signature at the end; see Zaslaw, 'Mozart, Haydn, and the *Sinfonia da Chiesa*', p. 107, n. 38. Manfred Hermann Schmid, 'Mozart und die Salzburger Kirchenmusik', *Mozart-Jahrbuch 1978–79*, p. 27, notes that nearly all of Eberlin's solemn masses, as well as two by Michael Haydn composed before 1768, suit the time limit, so that lengthy settings seem not to have been a widespread characteristic of earlier Salzburg church music. Furthermore, Zaslaw questions the extent to which the measure was actually enforced in the 1770s and later (p. 108), and cites studies by Walter Senn that share his viewpoint (n. 40): 'Beiträge zur Mozartforschung', *Acta musicologica*,

of his Ordinary cycles of the 1770s, especially K. 192 ('Little Credo' Mass), K. 194, K. 220 ('Sparrow' Mass), K. 258 ('Spaur' Mass), K. 259 ('Organ Solo' Mass) and K. 275, several of which last for only about fifteen minutes. The reform of the liturgy also called for the replacement of instrumental music for the Gradual with simple choral pieces and the introduction of hymns in the vernacular.

Among eighteenth-century composers, Michael Haydn exhibited an affinity for the *stile antico* matched only by a handful of others, including Fux, Werner and Albrechtsberger. This stylistic proclivity quite naturally accommodated the archbishop's desire for a simpler and more restrained church music. Haydn's interest in vocal counterpoint revealed itself early on, as illustrated by his copying out of Fux's *Messa di San Carlo* in 1757, and remained with him throughout his career. The specific character of his *stile antico* compositions differed markedly from that of similar music by Fux, however. Rather than functioning as a symbolically loaded reference to the central musical figure of the Counter-Reformation, thereby reinforcing an Italianate orientation as part of a dynastic ideological programme, works by Haydn in strict polyphony instead epitomized a simplified, transparent expressiveness as a particular manifestation of *musica da chiesa*. This conception of sacred style did not always entail elaborate counterpoint: the one hundred or more Graduals and Offertories composed by Haydn during the 1780s to fulfil the new liturgical prerequisites of 'Enlightened' Salzburg feature predominantly homophonic textures.

Johann Kohlbrenner's hymnal, *Der heilige Gesang zum Gottesdienste in der römisch-katholischen Kirche*, published in 1777 in Landshut (Bavaria), marked a crucial step in the greater use of the vernacular in the musical portions of the liturgy. This collection included the *Singmesse*, a setting of the mass with texts in German; for the second printing (Salzburg, 1790) of the hymnal's second edition, Haydn revised the setting, thereby producing its best-known version and frequently earning himself the mistaken attribution as the original author of the work.[154] Two church lieder by Mozart, 'O Gottes Lamm' and 'Als aus Aegypten', K. 343, appear also to represent contributions to the emerging tradition of vernacular hymns.[155]

The greater part of Mozart's substantial sacred oeuvre belongs to the years 1773–80, and is closely connected with the liturgical requirements of the

47 (1976), pp. 205–27 and 'Mozarts Kirchenmusik und die Literatur', *Mozart-Jahrbuch 1978–79*, pp. 14–18. Publicly pronounced ideals and actual cultural practice constitute distinct (if almost always interconnected) objects of scholarly investigation, needless to say.

154 Reinhard Pauly, 'The Reforms of Church Music Under Joseph II', *The Musical Quarterly*, 43/3 (1957), p. 375.

155 Otto Biba, 'Mozarts Wiener Kirchenmusikkompositionen', in Ingrid Fuchs (ed.), *Internationaler musikwissenschaftlicher Kongreß zum Mozartjahr 1991* (Tutzing, 1993), 2 vols., vol. 1, pp. 47–8.

Salzburg court. Only a handful of works were composed for other locales (including Vienna and Milan). This unbalanced distribution does not imply a lack of deeper interest in the writing of church music, however, as the concluding section of this chapter will explain. Mozart's earliest sacred compositions date from his grand tour of Northern Europe as a young child (June 1763–November 1766), and include the anthem 'God is Our Refuge', K. 20 (1765) and the Kyrie in F major, K. 33 (1766). The closing months of the subsequent Viennese trip (September 1767–January 1769) produced the first large-scale liturgical works, the *Missa brevis*, K. 49, and the impressive *Missa solemnis*, K. 139, intended for the consecration of the Waisenhauskirche (Orphanage Church) and therefore known as the *Waisenhausmesse*. The breadth and expressive range of the latter setting, particularly in its opening slow introduction in C minor, understandably caused Köchel to assign it to the early 1770s instead of to its true date. The interval spent in Salzburg between the return from Vienna and the departure for Italy in December 1769 saw the composition of two further masses, K. 65 and K. 66, the 'Dominicus Mass', for the ordination as Pater Dominicus of St Peter's Abbey of Cajetan Hagenauer, son of the Mozarts' landlord.

The three Italian visits, which spanned the years 1769–73, provided Mozart with plentiful opportunities to familiarize himself with Roman and Neapolitan church music,[156] as well as to become acquainted with Giovanni Battista Martini ('Padre Martini'), who in 1770 administered and corrected an examination in *a cappella* polyphony submitted by Mozart in order to gain membership (successfully) to the Accademia Filarmonica in Bologna. The immediate musical impact of this famous encounter with one of the preeminent representatives of traditional counterpoint is disputable, however, given the ready availability of comparable stylistic models in the works of Eberlin and other local figures. The intensive preoccupation with opera, resulting in *Mitridate, rè di Ponto* (1770), *Ascanio in Alba* (1771) and *Lucio Silla* (1772), had greater consequences for the active composition of sacred music upon which Mozart would embark shortly after his return to Salzburg in 1773. The motet *Exsultate, jubilate*, K. 165, already exemplified such an influence before he had left Italian soil. Written in January 1773 during the first performances of *Lucio Silla* for the castrato Venanzio Rauzzini, the opera's *primo uomo*, this popular work features a solo vocal part manifestly derived from the secular world of the theatre, with prominent melismas in its opening and concluding movements.

156 Karl Gustav Fellerer, 'Liturgische Grundlagen der Kirchenmusik Mozarts', in Erich Egg (ed.), *Festschrift Walter Senn zum 70. Geburtstag* (Munich and Salzburg, 1975), p. 68.

During the seven years prior to the Munich journey of 1780–1 for the premiere of *Idomeneo* followed by the permanent move to Vienna in 1781, Mozart composed no fewer than eleven masses for Salzburg: K. 167 (*Missa in honorem Sanctissimae Trinitatis*, 1773), K. 192 ('Little Credo' Mass, 1774), K. 194 (1774), K. 220 ('Sparrow' Mass, 1775?), K. 262 (*Missa longa*, 1775), K. 257 ('Credo' Mass, 1776), K. 258 ('Spaur' Mass, 1776), K. 259 ('Organ Solo' Mass, 1776?), K. 275 (1777), K. 317 ('Coronation' Mass, 1780) and K. 337 (1780).[157] He also contributed significantly to other liturgical genres, including the two Vespers settings of 1780, K. 321 (*Vesperae de Dominica*) and K. 339 (*Vesperae solennes de confessore*). The stylistic orientation illustrated by *Exsultate, jubilate* makes itself felt in this music. The Agnus Dei movements of K. 259, K. 317 and K. 337 feature solo singing that is operatic in flavour, as does the 'Laudate Dominum' of the Vespers, K. 321. To this list should be added the 'Et incarnatus est' of the unfinished Mass in C minor, K. 427, begun in Vienna probably in 1782 but first performed in St Peter's Abbey in Salzburg in October 1783 (probably with material from other masses filling out the incomplete portions). Not by coincidence, all of these examples reflect the tender, amorous type of aria epitomized by the Countess' 'Porgi, amor' and 'Dove sono' from *Le nozze di Figaro* (1786). Indeed, the Agnus Dei of K. 337 conspicuously resembles the former and that of K. 317 the latter.[158] Delicate orchestration featuring obbligato woodwinds and pizzicato strings reinforces the similarity. This particular style trait reflects not so much an Italian influence as one from native sources, for it constitutes a quintessential feature of the instrumental serenade music actively cultivated by Salzburg composers, including Mozart himself (as in the 'Haffner' Serenade, K. 250 and the 'Posthorn' Serenade, K. 320).[159] The distinctive orchestral idiom of the serenade genre made its way into Mozart's operatic work, as in Sandrina's cavatina 'Geme la tortorella' from *La finta giardiniera* (1775), and then into his sacred music (hence most of the above examples from the masses date from 1776 or later). The interaction of different musical domains thus did not flow only in a

157 The *Missa brevis* in G major, K. 140/C1.12, a pastoral mass, is probably spurious. It has been attributed to Mozart because of the existence of a set of parts in Augsburg with corrections in Mozart's hand. Bruce MacIntyre, in a paper titled 'Missa brevis in G, K. 140: Mozart or Kracher?', presented at the third biennial conference of the Mozart Society of America, 'Mozart's Choral Music: Composition, Contexts, Performance', Indiana University, 10–12 February 2006, discussed the evidence in favour of the authorship of Matthias Kracher, who served as an organist in the Austrian towns of Seekirchen and Kuchl, near Salzburg.

158 Heartz, *Haydn, Mozart and the Viennese School 1740–1780*, pp. 664, 669.

159 See Maynard Solomon, *Mozart: A Life* (New York, 1995), pp. 115–35 (the chapter titled 'A Composer's Voice') for a sensitive and insightful interpretation of the affective significances embodied in Mozart's serenades and related compositions such as the violin concertos. Clearly, these significances could enter fruitfully into the sacred domain, restrictive views about 'authentic' religious expression (whether from the eighteenth century or from later times) notwithstanding.

single direction; as with the rest of his work, Mozart's music for the church embodies a richly multi-faceted, international character.

Nevertheless, the compositional gains of the Italian sojourns encompassed instrumental writing as well as vocal writing, as is demonstrated by the brilliant *sinfonia* that opens *Lucio Silla*. With respect to Mozart's sacred music of the ensuing period, the strength of the instrumental element takes at least three different forms, beyond the employment of the serenade *topos*: lengthy introductory passages for orchestra alone, such as occur in the Benedictus of K. 167 and the Kyrie of K. 220; the incorporation of dance movements, illustrated by the minuet at 'Et in Spiritum Sanctum' of K. 167 (with another extended orchestral introduction) and the gavotte that closes K. 275;[160] and, most significantly, the developed sense of formal organization provided by large-scale repetition and the intensive working-out of motivic material. K. 220, the popular 'Sparrow' Mass, presents the same beginning and ending music in the Kyrie movement and in the work as a whole, while the Magnificat of the *Vesperae solennes de confessore*, K. 339, outlines a sonata form prefaced by an Adagio introduction. Particularly remarkable is the reprise in the 'Coronation' Mass, K. 317, of the 'Christe eleison' for the 'Dona nobis'; here, at the close, the soprano restates her earlier melody and is directly echoed by the chorus, which presents the melody for the very first time in a modified and accelerated version. This surprising and ingenious touch climactically unites solo and tutti voices, which previously had alternated regularly throughout the mass, a typical enough procedure in concerted sacred music yet in this work a dynamic source of propulsion exemplifying the essential meaning of *concertare* ('to contend'). By virtue of the motto technique to which their designation refers, the 'Credo' Masses, K. 192 and K. 257, provide two of the best examples of the use of a single motif to unify an entire movement. The motif for K. 192 consists of scale degrees 1–2–4–3, a figure better known as the *fugato* subject of the finale of the 'Jupiter' Symphony, K. 551. That for K. 257, initially 5–3–6–5, appears at all significant points of formal articulation and undergoes manifold transformations in these recurrences, functioning variously as confirmation of key or means of modulation.[161] Mozart's fluid integration of a single idea within the fabric of a complex musical structure is exceptionally impressive here.

Mozart completed no more masses after K. 337 (1780), but his two best-known sacred works, the C minor Mass, K. 427, and the Requiem, K. 626, belong to the final decade of his life. The circumstances under which Mozart

160 Heartz, *Haydn, Mozart and the Viennese School 1740–1780*, pp. 645–6, 661–2.
161 *Ibid.*, pp. 656–8.

began composition of the Mass and then failed to finish it, having only reached the 'Et incarnatus est' of the Credo and having not even begun the Agnus Dei, remain uncertain. It seems reasonable however to suggest a personal dimension to this deeply moving masterwork that is connected to recent turbulent events in the composer's life – the move from Salzburg to Vienna and the marriage to Constanze Weber, both bitterly opposed by Leopold. In contrast to nearly everything else Mozart wrote, no obvious occasional use is associated with the Mass, the great length of which (even in its incomplete state) hardly suited the streamlined Salzburg liturgy of the 1780s. In any event, this monumental *solenne* setting unquestionably represents the *summa* of Mozart's achievement in the mass genre. Its choruses, in particular, attain a grandeur unsurpassed in music of the late eighteenth century. The encounter with the works of Bach and Handel at the Sunday matinees of Baron van Swieten, which Mozart began attending in 1782, came to fruition here. Handel in particular makes his presence felt, nowhere more so than in the magnificent 'Qui tollis', which features a plethora of late-Baroque compositional techniques: double-choir texture, dotted rhythms as a marker of nobility (here in reference to Jesus Christ) and a descending bass-line pattern signifying lament.[162] In the arias of the Mass, the operatic quality already evinced in the earlier settings reaches a high point in its development, as in the 'Christe eleison', the 'Laudamus te' and the 'Et incarnatus est', with their predilection for wide tessituras and extended melismas. By the time Mozart actively renewed an interest in church music at the end of the 1780s, he had clearly assimilated the trend towards simplification evident also in Michael Haydn's sacred compositions; the Requiem features little of the elaborate solo vocal writing of the Mass, for example.

Mozart, like the elder Haydn, had few opportunities to compose music for the church during the decade of Joseph II's reign, to a large extent on account of the Emperor's sweeping reforms of liturgical practice. These reforms took shape most tangibly in the famous *Gottesdienstordnung*, a decree issued in February 1783 which severely limited the extent and elaborateness of religious observance throughout the Empire, though it did not, as sometimes alleged, ban instrumentally accompanied sacred music. Joseph's 'Enlightening' of traditionally devout Austrian society threw into doubt the continued centrality of one of the principal means of manifesting this devoutness, *musica da chiesa* – or,

162 The chorus notably resembles 'The people shall hear, and be afraid' from Part 3 of *Israel in Egypt*, among other similarities with Handel's oratorio; see Silke Leopold, 'Händels Geist in Mozarts Händen: Zum Qui tollis aus der c-Moll Messe KV 427', *Mozart-Jahrbuch 1994*, pp. 84–111. Mozart would again draw upon material from this same work for his Requiem, the opening of which adapts 'The sons of Israel do mourn' from Part 1. Or, perhaps, he employed as his model Handel's Funeral Anthem for Queen Caroline, 'The ways of Zion do mourn' (1737), which was later recycled as the first part of the 1739 version of the oratorio; see Wolff, *Mozart's Requiem*, pp. 74–8.

more specifically, figural church music. The general movement towards a rationalization of religious culture had diverse impacts upon the work of contemporary composers: Michael Haydn's production of liturgical music remained uninterrupted but shifted its stylistic orientation to accommodate the prescriptions of the political rulers; Joseph Haydn occupied himself wholly with other genres (opera, string quartet and symphony, above all), not returning to sacred music until the former luxuriant manner had become acceptable again. Mozart's activities in the 1780s seem upon casual consideration to resemble those of the elder Haydn, yet in fact they represent a particularly complex reaction to a fundamental question raised by the full development of the Enlightenment in Austria: what place could *pietas austriaca*[163] maintain in the new, radically modern society?

Conclusion: the Enlightenment and Mozart's late sacred music

The multiplicity of religious expression through music in eighteenth-century Austria will be evident from the foregoing discussion of genres, styles and composers. This characteristic underscores music's potency as an affective complement to the diversified ritual forms of Catholic worship. The matter of which specific affects properly represented the sphere of the sacred, though an age-old question, assumed greater urgency during this period as stylistic heterogeneity increasingly became the defining feature of musical practice. The numerous debates concerning the perceived problem of secularization constitute a particular culture's negotiations over the basic meanings of what had long formed one of its essential domains, even as this culture was undergoing rapid transformation. Evaluations of historical processes by scholars of later eras are themselves negotiations of meaning, of course, as in the common judgement about the weakness of much Catholic church music of the late eighteenth century even by the most outstanding composers. These scholars, however, carry the additional burden of a self-critical acknowledgement of their own partiality as the precondition of a genuine understanding of a past society.

The encyclical *Annus qui* issued by Pope Benedict XIV on 19 February 1749 offers a notably lucid statement regarding the qualities of an 'authentic' sacred music.[164] This papal bull, which sought to produce an exemplary liturgy in anticipation of the many pilgrims who would visit Rome during the jubilee

163 See Anna Coreth, *Pietas Austriaca: Österreichische Frömmigkeit im Barock*, 2nd edn. (Vienna, 1982).
164 See Karl Gustav Fellerer, 'Die Enzyklika "Annus qui" des Papstes Benedict XIV', in Fellerer (ed.), *Geschichte der katholischen Kirchenmusik* (Kassel, 1976), 2 vols., vol. 2, pp. 149–52.

year of 1750, gave concrete form to the principle of *nihil profanum* through its call for greater comprehensibility of text, avoidance of noisy orchestration and limitation of instruments to the organ, strings and oboes. On the whole, the measure adopted a balanced and tolerant attitude towards figural church music, recognizing such music as a valuable resource for the promotion of religious sentiment yet also as a potentially dangerous means of encouraging the opposite outcome. In fact, its emphasis on restraint and on voices rather than instruments encapsulated a general trend of thought about *stylus ecclesiasticus* that is found throughout the century. For example, Burney's record of his visit to Vienna in 1772 includes the following remark: 'The first time I went to the cathedral of St. Stephen, I heard an excellent mass, in the true church style, very well performed; there were violins and violoncellos though it was not a festival.' And in 1781 another traveller to the Austrian capital, Friedrich Nicolai, expressed a similar viewpoint but on the basis of a contrasting experience: 'Seldom did I hear anything moving or sublime. What was supposed to be magnificent was mostly only noisy.'[165]

Decrees originating from Rome did not have an impact upon the Austrian lands unless publicized by the Habsburg monarchs.[166] The first attempt to apply the policies of the *Annus qui* within the empire did not occur for nearly five years, until 24 December 1753, when the archiepiscopal *Konsistorium* of Vienna announced a ban on trumpets and timpani in churches and processions. Several weeks later, on 26 January 1754, Maria Theresa issued a *Hofreskript* that seems to have extended the prohibition to all of her territories.[167] However, the Empress' relative indifference to the issues raised by the encyclical, already evident in the long delay in making any effort at enforcement, quickly manifested itself again in an exception to the *Hofreskript* – namely permitting trumpets and timpani at the ceremony of baptism of her son, the Archduke Ferdinand, on 2 June 1754. By 1755 trumpets and timpani had become generally acceptable once again, though the ban was officially reversed only in 1767,[168] the same year in which a service of thanksgiving for Maria Theresa's recovery from a serious illness took place in the cathedral and featured the

165 Burney, *The Present State of Music in Germany, The Netherlands and United Provinces*, vol. 1, p. 218; Nicolai, *Beschreibung einer Reise durch Deutschland und die Schweiz*, p. 545, as trans. Heartz in *Haydn, Mozart and the Viennese School 1740–1780*, p. 17. See MacIntyre, *The Viennese Concerted Mass*, pp. 41–6, for a discussion of a broad range of eighteenth-century views on the role of church music.

166 Biba, 'Mozarts Wiener Kirchenmusikkompositionen', p. 44.

167 MacIntyre, *The Viennese Concerted Mass*, p. 43.

168 See Biba, 'Mozarts Wiener Kirchenmusikkompositionen', p. 44, which cites the journals of the court chamberlain Rudolf Khevenhüller-Metsch, ed. Hans Schlitter, Maria Breunlich-Pawlik and Hans Wagner as *Aus der Zeit Maria Theresias* (Vienna, 1907–72), 8 vols. Riedel, 'Liturgie und Kirchenmusik', p. 123, proposes that the ban aimed only to eliminate the intradas played at the beginning and end of a solemn mass.

performance of a *Te Deum*. Clearly, then, the old ceremonial music of the *solenne* type could not so readily be abandoned and maintained some of its former symbolic importance. In the Austrian realms, at least, the increasing sense of a firm divide between the sacred and the profane remained primarily theoretical and had as yet limited effect on the actual working of composers.

During the decade of Joseph II's sole regency following the death of his mother in 1780, politico-religious ideals and musical practice intertwined to a far greater extent. The Enlightened mindset that prevailed in this period demonstrated a rather different attitude towards church music than that reflected in the *Annus qui* and other similar pronouncements. Joseph's radical worldview motivated an attempt at a wholesale redefinition of the place of religious faith in society, with the effective elimination of spiritual mystery and clerical authority in favour of a pragmatic morality directed towards the public good. This aspiration did not concern itself principally with safeguarding the integrity of a religious sphere in need of 'protection' against incursions by 'lower', worldly domains, and as such lacked a strongly reverential aspect. The polemical attacks on the operatic character of contemporary church music by Rationalist critics of the day might seem to suggest otherwise, as in the following passage from Joseph Richter's *Bildergalerie katholischer Misbräuche* of 1784:

> there soon slipped into the church style unnoticed a trio from a menuet, then the thrum-thrum of a symphony, then again fragments of waltzing music, and finally half and whole opera arias; moreover, they thought nothing of profaning God's temple with the crowing of Italian capons. Comic opera singers of both sexes exchanged the theatre for the church with regularity. The primo buffo who played the Marchese Villano in the carnival opera took the role of Saint Peter in Lent, and the prima donna who sang to us instilling love and voluptuousness in the theatre wished now to make up for our sins, and hers, with a touching *Stabat Mater*.[169]

However, Richter also published a *Bildergalerie weltlicher Misbräuche* (as well as a *Bildergalerie klosterlicher Misbräuche*), whose disparagement of Viennese secular life includes a censure of the excessively socializing nature of concerts, with their drinking, gambling, card-playing and the like.[170] Like other proponents of the Enlightenment, he sought to promote rationalist values in all areas of society and to uncover dissolution and corruption wherever they occurred, whether in the church or outside it.

169 Obermayr [Joseph Richter], *Bildergalerie katholischer Misbräuche* (Frankfurt, Vienna and Leipzig, 1784), trans. in Heartz, *Haydn, Mozart and the Viennese School 1740–1780*, pp. 15–16.
170 See Heartz, *Haydn, Mozart and the Viennese School 1740–1780*, p. 56 and the illustration on p. 57.

The *Gottesdienstordnung* promulgated on 25 February 1783 consisted of several discrete measures, each intended to help bring about the reformed, practical Catholicism envisioned by Joseph, among them the dissolution of most of Austria's monasteries, with the release of their wealth to the state; a drastic cutback in the number of liturgical observances; and an increased use of the vernacular.[171] Instrumentally accompanied music did not vanish from the church altogether, and concerted masses could still be performed on Sundays and high feast days at those institutions with sufficient remaining resources.[172] In fact, the material impact upon sacred music in Vienna can be precisely determined thanks to the survival of an invaluable historical document, a listing of the salaries of the city's church musicians before and after the issuance of the order. This listing, prepared in fulfilment of a request by the Emperor whom the musicians had petitioned to lessen the harshness of his decree, reveals that a former payroll total of 27,944 florins 24 kreuzer had fallen precipitously to 14,030 florins 42½ kreuzer through a combination of income reduction and cancelling of positions.[173]

The impact of the *Gottesdienstordnung* upon church music composition is less easily determined, apart from the obvious effect of a significant reduction in the number of concerted works. A new type of 'organ mass', with a solo organ comprising the only instrumental element and acting as a kind of substitute orchestra, seems to have partially satisfied a continued desire for concerted masses. Albrechtsberger's *Missa Sancti Augustini* of 1784, written for a feast that occurred on a Saturday in this year, exemplifies this manner of adapting to the changed conditions of liturgical practice.[174] Numerous historians have noted the virtual silence of Joseph Haydn and Mozart in the field of sacred music after 1783. This silence, in the case of Haydn quite literally for over a decade, less accurately characterizes Mozart's creative activities of the 1780s, though earlier accounts regarded the Corpus Christi motet, *Ave verum corpus*, K. 618 and the Requiem, K.626, both dating from the second half of 1791, as the only sacred works composed by Mozart in the final eight years of his life. Alan Tyson's paper studies have offered persuasive evidence, however, that five mass fragments once assigned to the 1770s and early 1780s in fact reflect a renewal of interest in the writing of church music on Mozart's part that began in 1787 or

171 See Pauly, 'The Reforms of Church Music Under Joseph II'. 172 *Ibid.*, p. 378.

173 Biba, 'Mozarts Wiener Kirchenmusikkompositionen', p. 45. The listing is transcribed with commentary in Biba, 'Die Wiener Kirchenmusik um 1783', *Jahrbuch für Österreichische Kulturgeschichte*, 1/2 (1971), pp. 1–79.

174 Karl Pfannhauser (ed.), *Johann Georg Albrechtsberger: Messe in Es-dur (Missa Sancti Josephi)* (Vienna, 1951), p. 46 (cited in Pauly, 'The Reforms of Church Music Under Joseph II', p. 378). The alternate name of the mass appears in a catalogue begun in 1824 of the archive of St Stephen's Cathedral.

1788.[175] Around this time Mozart also copied three sacred compositions in *a cappella* style by Reutter,[176] requested that his sister send him manuscripts of two 'tutti-Messen' and the Graduals of Michael Haydn[177] and familiarized himself with the Requiem of Gassmann.[178]

Thus Mozart had clearly begun to revive a major outlet for his creative energies from his Salzburg days, following several years of preoccupation with the genres of piano concerto and opera buffa. His search for a regular church music post in Vienna provides a further indication of the strength of the new (or old) direction. In 1790 he drafted a petition to an unspecified archduke (perhaps Francis, eldest son of Leopold II and future Emperor) for an appointment as second court Kapellmeister, writing that 'Salieri, that very skilful Kapellmeister, has never devoted himself to the church style, while I have made this style my very own since I was a youth'.[179] The same evident pride in his mastery of sacred music appears again in his application the following year to the Viennese municipal council to be named adjunct Kapellmeister and successor to Leopold Hofmann at St Stephen's Cathedral: 'I believe that I may claim to be better fitted for [the office] than many others, in view of the knowledge of church style that I have cultivated alongside my other accomplishments.'[180] Mozart's earlier remark in a letter of 12 April 1783 to his father that, on account of rapid changes of taste, 'true church music is to be found *only* in attics and in worm-eaten condition'[181] can also be read as a continued commitment to the 'kirchen Styl'.

The notion of 'wahre Kirchenmusik' would come to define the Cecilian movement of the nineteenth century, but in the context of Mozart's letter does not imply the same exaltation of older liturgical repertories (chiefly Gregorian chant and Renaissance vocal polyphony) as paradigms of sacred

175 Alan Tyson, *Mozart: Studies of the Autograph Scores* (Cambridge, MA, 1987), pp. 26–8. The fragments are a Kyrie in G major, K. Anh. 16/196a; a Kyrie in C major, K. Anh. 13/258a; another Kyrie in C major, K. Anh. 15/323; a Gloria in C major, K. Anh. 20/323a; and a Kyrie in D major, K. Anh. 14/422a. Tyson speculates that the Kyrie in D minor, K. 341/368a, traditionally connected to the Munich visit of November 1780–March 1781 for the premiere of *Idomeneo*, may also belong to these years.

176 The Reutter works are two Psalm settings, *De profundis clamavi*, K. 93/Anh. 22 and *Memento Domine David*, K. 93a/Anh. 23, and a Kyrie in G, K. 91/186f. See Pfannhauser, 'Mozart hat kopiert!' and Monika Holl, 'Nochmals: "Mozart hat kopiert!"', *Acta mozartiana*, 30 (1983), pp. 33–6.

177 Letter of 2 August 1788; given in Emily Anderson (trans. and ed.), *The Letters of Mozart and His Family*, 3rd edn. (London, 1985), p. 918.

178 Biba, 'Mozarts Wiener Kirchenmusikkompositionen', pp. 49–50 and also n. 27, where the author cites Franz Kosch, 'Florian Leopold Gassmann als Kirchenkomponist', *Studien zur Musikwissenschaft*, 14 (1927), pp. 1–213 (based on a dissertation of the same title completed at the University of Vienna in 1924) as the first instance of the frequently observed resemblance between the openings of the Requiems by Gassmann and Mozart.

179 Biba, 'Mozarts Wiener Kirchenmusikkompositionen', p. 51. Translation from Heartz, *Haydn, Mozart and the Viennese School 1740–1780*, pp. 527–8.

180 Translation from Wolff, *Mozart's Requiem*, p. 120.

181 Anderson (ed. and trans.), *The Letters of Mozart*, p. 845.

style.[182] Nevertheless, Mozart's decision to copy *a cappella* compositions by Reutter and to become acquainted with two 'tutti masses'[183] and the Graduals of Michael Haydn indicates a fundamental reshaping of his conception of church music in his Viennese years in favour of simplicity and austerity. This re-orientation bore fruit in the *Ave verum corpus* and the Requiem. Christoph Wolff has observed that choral texture dominates in the motet and that orchestral accompaniment fulfils a largely subsidiary role.[184] Indeed, this work exemplifies the freer *a cappella* style in the way that the instrumental parts essentially double the voices, adhering to the *colla parte* conventions of the day (for example, first and second violins proceeding with soprano and alto, respectively). Wolff further argues that the same primacy of the chorus characterizes the Requiem.[185] The unfinished state of Mozart's final composition notwithstanding, the manifest difference with the Mass in C minor is apparent in the much more restrained and distinctly 'un-theatrical' writing for the solo voices. The orchestration likewise assumes a notably subdued quality, particularly as a result of the dark timbre of the basset horns.

Mozart's late sacred music superficially corresponds to the simplified liturgical style promoted by Joseph II, Archbishop Colloredo and other major figures of the Austrian Enlightenment. However, this seems more a fortuitous circumstance than a direct consequence of a close sympathy with Rationalist ideals, even though Mozart may indeed have supported such ideals. Throughout his life Mozart attached importance to music for the church,[186] and the creative products of his final years reveal a deepened and refined conception of his compositional activities in this area. The early Cecilianists recognized the special achievement of the Requiem, in particular. E. T. A. Hoffmann, in a seminal essay of 1814, 'Old and New Church Music', offered the following assessment of the work:

> In the last half of the eighteenth century increasing enfeeblement and sickly sweetness finally overcame art; keeping step with so-called enlightened attitudes, which killed every deeper religious impulse, it eventually drove all gravity and dignity from church music ... In one church work, however, [Mozart] revealed his innermost feelings; and who can remain unmoved by

182 For an excellent collection of primary documents related to Cecilianism, see Winfried Kirsch (ed.), *Palestrina und die Idee der klassischen Vokalpolyphonie im 19. Jahrhunderts: Zur Geschichte eines kirchenmusikalischen Stilideals* (Regensburg, 1989).

183 'Tutti mass' is essentially equivalent to '*a cappella* mass' because of the prevalence of pieno textures (with respect to both voices *and* instruments) in the *a cappella* style.

184 Wolff, *Mozart's Requiem*, pp. 33–6. 185 *Ibid.*, p. 37.

186 See also David Black, *Mozart and the Practice of Sacred Music, 1781–1791*, PhD dissertation (Harvard University, 2007), whose discussion of the range of Mozart's sacred music activities during the 1780s includes consideration of a possible close association with St Michael's Church, where an obsequies was held on 10 December 1791 for the recently deceased composer.

> the fervent devotion and spiritual ecstasy radiating from it? His Requiem is the sublimest achievement that the modern period has contributed to the church.[187]

In the last analysis, however, Mozart was no Cecilian, and Hoffmann's comments illuminate early-nineteenth-century culture far more than late-eighteenth-century culture. There is no compelling reason to believe that Mozart or his contemporaries regarded the Requiem as in any way a 'correction' or a 'rejection' of the liturgical music traditions of preceding decades. Though the work drew on 'antique' sources, as illustrated by the citations of Handel and of plainchant in the Introit, it also benefited from an awareness of the modern sacred style of Michael Haydn and Gassmann. The seamless continuity of old and new is one of the outstanding features of Mozart's final compositional effort.

The church music of Mozart, like that of Fux earlier in the century, does not fit comfortably within clearly and simplistically defined categories: *antico*, *moderno*, instrumental, vocal, dignified, sweet, etc. The idealizing tendencies of historical interpretation have often worked to stabilize these categories, resulting in the exaltation of some repertories and the devaluation of others. Such differentiations in the reception of a diverse range of music are both inevitable and legitimate, to the extent that they shape the distinctive cultural experiences of particular milieus (and are recognized as engaging in this process). Equally inevitably, they change over time but in no way automatically engender superior viewpoints in later eras as a consequence.

Select Bibliography

Armstrong, James, Jr. 'Towards a History of the Esterházy Church Music Archive'. In Georg Feder (ed.), *Internationales Musikwissenschaftliches Symposium 'Dokumentarische Grundlagen in der Haydnforschung'*. Tutzing, 2006, pp. 107–41

Biba, Otto. 'Die Wienerkirchenmusik um 1783'. *Jahrbuch für Österreichische Kulturgeschichte*, 1/2 (1971), pp. 1–79

'Die kirchenmusikalischen Werke Haydns'. In Gerda Mraz, Gottfried Mraz and Gerald Schlag (eds.), *Joseph Haydn in seiner Zeit*. Eisenstadt, 1982, pp. 142–51

'Mozarts Wiener Kirchenmusikkompositionen'. In Ingrid Fuchs (ed.), *Internationaler musikwissenschaftlicher Kongreß zum Mozartjahr 1991*. 2 vols., Tutzing, 1993, vol. 1, pp. 43–55

Chusid, Martin. 'Some Observations on Liturgy, Text, and Structure in Haydn's Late Masses'. In H.C. Robbins Landon and Roger E. Chapman (eds.), *Studies in*

187 E.T.A. Hoffmann, 'Alte und Neue Kirchenmusik', *Allgemeine musikalische Zeitung*, 16 (1814), cols. 577–584, 593–603, 611–619, trans. Martyn Clarke as 'Old and New Church Music', in David Charlton (ed.), *E.T.A. Hoffmann's Musical Writings* (Cambridge, 1989), p. 370.

Eighteenth-Century Music: A Tribute to Karl Geiringer on His Seventieth Birthday. London, 1970, pp. 125–35

Croll, Gerhard. 'Mitteilungen über die *Schöpfung* und die *Jahreszeiten* aus dem Schwarzenberg-Archiv'. In Georg Feder (ed.), *Haydn-Studien* 3. Munich, 1973–4, pp. 85–92

Fellerer, Karl Gustav. 'Liturgische Grundlagen der Kirchenmusik Mozarts'. In Erich Egg (ed.), *Festschrift Walter Senn zum 70. Geburtstag*. Munich and Salzburg, 1975, pp. 64–74

'Die Enzyklika "Annus qui" des Papstes Benedict XIV'. In Karl Gustav Fellerer (ed.), *Geschichte der katholischen Kirchenmusik*. 2 vols., Kassel, 1976, vol. 2, pp. 149–52

Fritz-Hilscher, Elizabeth Theresia. 'Die Privatisierung der kaiserlichen Hofmusikkapelle unter Maria Theresia 1751–1772'. In Theophil Antonicek, Elizabeth Theresia Hilscher and Hartmut Krones (eds.), *Die Wiener Hofmusikkapelle I: Georg von Slatkonia und die Wiener Hofmusikkapelle*. Vienna, 1999, pp. 161–70

Gleissner, Walter. *Die Vespern von Johann Joseph Fux: Ein Beitrag zur Geschichte der Vespervertonung*. PhD thesis, University of Mainz, 1981

Heartz, Daniel. *Haydn, Mozart and the Viennese School 1740–1780*. New York and London, 1995

Hofer, Norbert. *Die beiden Reutter als Kirchenkomponisten*. PhD thesis, University of Vienna, 1915

Holl, Monika. 'Nochmals: "Mozart hat kopiert!"', *Acta mozartiana*, 30 (1983), pp. 33–6

Jones, David Wyn. 'Haydn's *Missa Sunt bona mixta malis* and the *a cappella* Tradition'. In Jones (ed.), *Music in Eighteenth-Century Austria*. Cambridge, 1996, pp. 89–111

Keefe, Simon P. '"Die Ochsen am Berge": Franz Xaver Süssmayr's Orchestration of Mozart's Requiem, K. 626'. *Journal of the American Musicological Society*, 61 (2008), pp. 1–65

Köchel, Ludwig von. *Die kaiserliche Hof-Musikkapelle in Wien von 1543 bis 1867 nach urkundlichen Forschungen*. Vienna, 1869

Krombach, Gabrielle. *Die Vertonungen liturgischer Sonntagsoffertorien am Wiener Hof*. Munich and Salzburg, 1986

Leopold, Silke. 'Händels Geist in Mozarts Händen: Zum Qui tollis aus der c-Moll Messe KV 427'. *Mozart-Jahrbuch* 1994, pp. 84–111

MacIntyre, Bruce. *The Viennese Concerted Mass of the Early Classic Period*. Ann Arbor, MI, 1986

'Johann Baptist Vanhal and the Pastoral Mass Tradition'. In David Wyn Jones (ed.), *Music in Eighteenth-Century Austria*. Cambridge, 1995, pp. 112–32

Pauly, Reinhard. 'The Reforms of Church Music Under Joseph II'. *The Musical Quarterly*, 43 (1957), pp. 372–82

Pfannhauser, Karl. 'Mozart hat kopiert!', *Acta mozartiana*, 1 (1954), pp. 21–5, 38–41

Pohl, Carl Ferdinand. *Denkschrift aus Anlass des hundertjährigen Bestehens der Tonkünstler-Societät*. Vienna, 1871

Riedel, Friedrich Wilhelm. 'Der "Reichstil" in der deutschen Musikgeschichte des 18. Jahrhunderts'. In Georg Reichert and Martin Just (eds.), *Bericht über der Internationalen Musikwissenschaftlichen Kongress Kassel 1962*. Kassel, 1963, pp. 33–6

Kirchenmusik am Hofe Karls VI. (1711–1740). Munich and Salzburg, 1977

'Liturgie und Kirchenmusik'. In Gerda Mraz, Gottfried Mraz and Gerald Schlag (eds.), *Joseph Haydn in seiner Zeit*. Eisenstadt, 1982, pp. 121–33

'Joseph Haydns Sinfonien als liturgische Musik'. In Karlheinz Schlager (ed.), *Festschrift Hubert Unverricht zum 65. Geburtstag*. Tutzing, 1992, pp. 213–20

Schmid, Manfred Hermann. 'Mozart und die Salzburger Kirchenmusik'. *Mozart-Jahrbuch* 1978–79, pp. 26–9

Temperley, Nicholas. *Haydn: The Creation*. Cambridge, 1991

Walter, Rudolf. 'Bemerkungen zu den Kompositionen von Johann Joseph Fux zum Offertorium'. In Harry White (ed.), *Johann Joseph Fux and the Austro-Italian Baroque*. Aldershot, 1992, pp. 231–61

Webster, James. 'The Creation, Haydn's Late Vocal Music, and the Musical Sublime'. In Elaine Sisman (ed.), *Haydn and His World*. Princeton, NJ, 1997, pp. 57–102

White, Harry. 'The *Sepolcro* Oratorios of Fux: An Assessment'. In White (ed.), *Johann Joseph Fux and the Austro-Italian Baroque*. Aldershot, 1992, pp. 164–230

Wolff, Christoph. *Mozart's Requiem*. Trans. Mary Whittall, Berkeley and Los Angeles, 1994

Zaslaw, Neal. 'Mozart, Haydn, and the *Sinfonia da Chiesa*'. *The Journal of Musicology*, 1/1 (1982), pp. 95–124

· 4 ·

Catholic church music in France

JEAN-PAUL C. MONTAGNIER

From the time of Francis I and the Concordat of Bologna (1516) onwards, the Church of France continuously defended its independence from the Holy See, notably by reducing papal interferences in temporal matters. Thanks to his *Declaration of the Clergy of France* (1682), in which the privileges of the Gallican Church were officially codified, Jacques Benigne Bossuet (1627–1704) succeeded in widening the prerogatives of the French king, and even managed to protect him against excommunication. But the Gallican Church intended by Louis XIV did not survive the revolutionary storm, being completely destroyed by the *Civil Constitution of the Clergy* in July 1790. Two years later (21 September 1792) the *Musique* of the Chapelle Royale, reorganized in 1683, was suppressed alongside the abolishment of the Absolute Monarchy. Between 1682–3 and 1790–2 French religious music underwent profound changes, while remaining firmly anchored in established traditions.

In matters of fashion and taste, the Court of Versailles, and then Paris, set the requisite tone and attracted the best musicians. Numerous provincial *maîtres de musique*, whose duties included composing and conducting motets as well as training *pueri chori* (boy choristers), were *vicariants* (itinerant musicians) who criss-crossed the country to secure a position at a major *maîtrise* (choir school). From there, some even tried to reach the capital in order to make a name for themselves at the Concert Spirituel (where motets were regularly performed), and in the case of the most gifted to enter the Chapelle Royale. Henry Madin (1698–1748) is a prime example: born at Verdun into a poor family, he directed in turn the *maîtrises* of Meaux, Verdun, Bourges, Tours and Rouen before being named *sous-maître de la Musique* of the king's chapel, the most sought-after musical position of the *ancien régime* together with the superintendence of the king's *Musique de la Chambre*. To gain fame, musicians had to compose either stage works or *grands motets*. Some like André Campra (1660–1744), Charles-Hubert Gervais (1671–1744), Jean-Philippe Rameau (1683–1764) and Jean-Joseph Cassanéa de Mondonville (1711–72) did both, while others such as Nicolas Bernier (1665–1734), Madin or Antoine

Blanchard (1696–1770) wrote only motets, receiving high praise in the process from their contemporaries.

Grands motets

The *motet à grand chœur* or *grand motet* was the most important French sacred genre in the eighteenth century. This multi-movement work for soloists (gathered in the *petit chœur*), five-part choir (D, HC, T, BT and B regrouped in the *grand chœur*)[1] and (often five-part) orchestra was performed in those churches of the kingdom that could afford to hire extra musicians, and was originally conceived by Henry Dumont (1610–84), Jean-Baptiste Lully (1632–87) and Pierre Robert (*c.* 1618–99) to accompany the king's mass.

At 10 a.m. during the reign of Louis XIV, at one o'clock in the afternoon under Louis XV and at noon under Louis XVI, a procession of courtiers was led by the monarch to his two-storied chapel of the Versailles château. The monarch attended mass from the royal tribune and walked down to the centre of the nave only for major liturgical ceremonies. The nave was occupied by the courtiers, who remained standing while the ladies of the court filled the lateral galleries. The service lasted roughly thirty minutes. The Sun King and his successors attended daily but preferred a low mass spoken by the celebrant, not a high mass chanted and sung by clergy and choir. At the beginning of Louis XIV's reign, our knowledge of the place and nature of the music accompanying this ceremony derives from a single paragraph from the foreword to Pierre Perrin's *Cantica pro Capella Regis*. (This book is a collection of neo-Latin texts intended to be sung in the Chapelle Royale.) According to this testimony published by Ballard in 1665, the chapel musicians usually performed three motets during the mass, including first of all a substantial *grand motet* of approximately fifteen minutes in length that concluded before the elevation of the Sacred Host; if the priest saying the mass in a low voice arrived at the consecration before the musicians were finished, he was obliged to wait. Then, a briefer *petit motet* on a Eucharistic text (appropriately called an *Élévation*) was performed by a handful of singers and instrumentalists at the elevation of the Sacred Host. At the end of the mass, a *Domine salvum fac Regem* (a sort of choral prayer for the king's good health setting the last verse of Psalm 19) was sung by all the available musical forces during the withdrawal of the prince. Almost nothing is known for certain, though, about the celebration of the king's mass after *c.* 1682; it cannot definitely be said that established

1 *Dessus* (D, soprano), *haute-contre* (HC, high tenor), *taille* (T, tenor), *basse-taille* (BT, baritone), *basse* (B, bass).

practices at the beginning of Louis XIV's reign were retained during those of his two successors.

Upon Dumont's and Robert's retirement in 1683, a national competition was organized to recruit four new *sous-maître de la Musique du Roi*. Michel-Richard de Lalande (1657–1726), Pascal Collasse (1649–1709), Nicolas Goupillet (pre-1650–post-1713) and Guillaume Minoret (pre-1650–1720) were selected and served a quarter of the year (*quartier*) each. Among them, Lalande – Louis XIV's personal choice, the three others having been appointed under pressure from Lully and ecclesiastical dignitaries – quickly became the most prolific and gifted sacred music composer of the time, and one of the most frequently performed up until the end of the *ancien régime*.

Lalande's first *grands motets* follow the pattern established by Dumont's generation, in which the instrumental introduction (*symphonie*), the first solo section (*récit*) and the following chorus share the same musical material and the same words. This first episode is then continued in a series of unbroken sections in which solo voices and ensembles dialogue with the *grand* and *petit chœur*. The words set to music – rarely selected in connection with the liturgy of the day, but rather for their laudatory rhetoric to the monarch – are Latin texts used by the Gallican liturgy, mostly psalms, canticles, sequences and hymns (notably the *Te Deum*, a sort of 'state motet' performed to celebrate military victories and events related to the royal family). Lalande's *Beati quorum remissæ sunt* (S5),[2] likely composed for the 1683 competition, is a good example: the fourteen verses of Psalm 31 are roughly distributed into five large, tonally contrasted sections (C major, G minor, C minor, C major/A minor/C major, C major) set apart by *symphonies* and/or choruses; each section comprises a mosaic of barely self-contained segments in which *récits*, ensembles and choir alternate.

By the turn of the century, and under the influence of the fashionable Italian style cultivated in several Parisian circles – including those of Philippe, Duke of Orléans and Regent-to-be, and of the Stuart court at Saint-Germain-en-Laye – Lalande started to incorporate more Baroque-orientated stylistic features into his motets: autonomous and contrasting clear-cut movements or *numéros* (usually one per verse, but with the possibility of re-grouping verses according to their word-content); aria-like *récits*; more independent and concertante instrumental writing; and larger polyphonic choruses. This rationalization of the style and form of the individual movement – and for that matter, of the motet as a whole – suited Louis XIV's hierarchical organization of his kingdom

2 'S' numbers refer to Lionel Sawkins, *A Thematic Catalogue of the Works of Michel-Richard de Lalande (1657–1726)* (Oxford and New York, 2005).

Table 4.1. *Lalande*, Confitebor tibi *(S56)*

symphonie and duet	chorus	*récit* HC	*récit* BT	chorus	*récit* BT	*récit* D	quartet	chorus	chorus
v. 1	v.2	v.3	v.4	v.5	v.6	v.7	v.8	v.9	L. Doxology
B minor———————				G major	B minor———————				

Note: HC: *haute-contre* (high tenor); BT: *basse-taille* (baritone); D: *dessus* (soprano).

and the ceremonial grandeur of his court. For example, in his *Confitebor tibi* (S56), composed in 1699 but subsequently revised, Psalm 110 (111) is divided into nine concentrically arranged movements framed by a fourteen-bar *symphonie* and a majestic choral setting of the Lesser Doxology (see table 4.1).

Lalande's *Confitebor tibi*, like most *grands motets* of the period, is quite unadventurous in tonal terms: variety is achieved by means of contrasting tempos, textures, scorings and contrapuntal fabrics. Among these nine *numéros*, movement 3 ('Confessio et magnificentia opus ejus') is a beautiful show-piece for *haute-contre* (high tenor), obbligato violin and continuo unfolding smoothly through numerous harmonic sequences and melismas; movement 4 ('Memoriam fecit') set for *basse-taille* (baritone) and orchestra is a *rondeau*-like aria whose typically French choreographic swaying nicely renders the mercifulness of God. As for the central chorus ('Memor erit in sæculum'), it is one of the most beautiful contrapuntal passages Lalande wrote, alongside the 'Requiem æternam' chorus that closes his *De profundis* (S23): a subject in minims, more or less modelled on a plainchant psalmody, contrasts with a vivid counter-subject to extol God's – and by implication King Louis' – grandeur and might.

In the *grands motets* of Lalande's followers the progressive secularization of French church music that began as early as *c.* 1683 becomes more and more marked, as in Campra's *Notus in Judæa Deus* (*c.* 1737) or Gervais' *Deus noster refugium* (*c.* 1722–44) in which some typical features of the contemporary tragédie en musique are found – sleep (*sommeil*), battle scene, tempest and earthquake in particular. In the hands of Mondonville, this new stylistic trend reached its height. His *grands motets* were indeed no longer conceived as church works to be sung at Louis XV's mass (although they were performed in this context), but rather as genuine Latin entertainments to appear in public concerts, such as the *Concert Spirituel* founded by Philidor in 1725. Mondonville's *grands motets* were, with those of Lalande, the most frequently performed and successful of the eighteenth century, probably on account of their oratorio-like design. For example, Mondonville's *Venite exultemus* (1743) met with unprecedented success, and was given sixty-one times at the *Concert Spirituel* between 1743 and 1762. After a short (three- or four-part) *symphonie*, the motet continues with an ABA aria for *dessus* (soprano) and choir (no. 1, Ps. 94 (95) vv. 1–2) in the Rameau tradition. A majestic *récit* for *basse-taille*, reminding us of the greatness of God (no. 2, vv. 3–4), follows. After a ternary aria with a 'liquid' instrumental accompaniment imitating the maritime streams (no. 3, v. 5) an 'adoration' for *dessus* ensues, underlining the allegiance of believers to their God (no. 4, v. 6). This movement attracted particular praise and assured notoriety for the motet on account of the many harmonic subtleties that were used to depict the holy tears. A brief pastoral evoking the ewes that the Lord feeds in his pastures (no. 5, v. 7), and a tender recitative-like transition (v. 8) lead to a repetition of the sixth verse set for solo soprano and choir (no. 6). A sort of *aria di bravura*, preceded and followed by a slower section for *haute-contre*, illustrates the temptation in the desert (no. 7, vv. 10–11). The motet concludes with a jubilant choral section on the Lesser Doxology (no. 9). This Latin divertissement divides into five parts (movements 1, 2–3, 4–6, 7–8 and 9), and can be regarded as a prototype for Mondonville's forthcoming oratorios. In this respect, his motets seemed to have been more sought after by the public and the king's courtiers than those of François Giroust (1737–99) who nevertheless remained the most influential *sous-maître de la Musique de la Chapelle du Roi* up to the Revolution. Giroust's *grands motets* distinguished themselves from those of his predecessors by a large orchestra (strongly influenced by the classical symphonies performed at that time at the Concert Spirituel), by instrumental word-paintings, regular phrases and clear structures: the 'Fidelia omnia' movement from his *Confitebor tibi* (1773), for example, is cast in sonata form. In *c.* 1780, Giroust also abandoned the traditional five-part choral texture by dropping the baritone part.

Oratorios

The first Latin oratorios (*histoires sacrées*; *motets dramatiques*) composed in France were by Marc-Antoine Charpentier (1643–1704), a former student of Carissimi at Rome. Following this lead, some minor composers then wrote isolated and mostly undated works, such as *L'Histoire de la femme adultère* by Louis-Nicolas Clérambault (1676–1749), the *Oratorio de nativitate Christi* (1701) by Jacques-François Lochon (the only one printed during the first part of the eighteenth century), the *Oratorio sopra l'immaculata conceptione della B. Vergina* by Sébastien de Brossard, and even two oratorio-like motets sung in French (Jacques Morel's 1706 *Te Deum* and Alexandre de Villeneuve's 1727

Concert-Spirituel ... sur une traduction Françoise du Pseaume 96 Dominus regnavit). In spite of being roughly comparable to the sung *tragédies* performed in some Jesuit colleges, the oratorio barely had an impact in France – perhaps because of the increasing number of divertissement-like *grands motets* written by the king's *sous-maîtres* – until Mondonville undertook to compose works in the genre.

Mondonville's two sacred *oratorios français* (or 'motet français en forme d'oratorio'), *Les Israëlites à la montagne d'Oreb* (1758) and *Les fureurs de Saül* (1759) were welcomed at the time as two genuinely innovative works. The librettist, Claude-Henri de Fuzée, abbot of Voisenon (1708–76), arranged the two Biblical episodes with numerous alternations between soloists and chorus, suggesting that the music (now lost) was to all intents and purposes continuous rather than split into separate movements. Mondonville's immediate followers, Jean-Nicolas Loiseau de Persuis (*Le passage de la Mer Rouge*, 1759) and Pierre-Just Davesne (*La conquête de Jéricho*, 1760) were soon forgotten, and no prominent sacred oratorios by French composers were performed in France until works by Nicolas-Jean Lefroid de Méreaux (1745–97), and by François-Joseph Gossec (1734–1829) attained more long-lasting success.

At the end of the eighteenth century, the twenty-six year-old Jean-François Le Sueur (1760–1837) composed four 'Mass-oratorios', hybrids of the two genres; his *Oratorio de Noël*, however, survives only in a version that alters the original. In order for a mass to be appropriate to one particular feast, Le Sueur explains in his *Essai de musique sacrée* (1787), it 'must have its own mood, brought about chiefly by two means: the quotation of familiar music associated with the feast in question and the addition of texts suitable to it. Two kinds of music could be quoted, chants and traditional sacred songs. They should always be familiar so that the congregation, upon hearing them, would realize that they were linked to the subject of the day.' As for the added Biblical or other sacred Latin texts, they took place in and between the items of the Ordinary. Since all these texts 'were given to soloists in arias, recitatives, duets, trios and the like, the masses became veritable oratorios, each incorporating the entire text of the Ordinary, but placing it in a different dramatic situation'.[3]

Petits motets and *Leçons de ténèbres*

The first book of *petits motets* published in France was Henry Dumont's *Cantica sacra* (1652). This new genre may be related to the refined French

3 Donald H. Foster, 'The Oratorio in Paris in the 18th Century', *Acta musicologica*, 47 (1975), pp. 52–3.

art of the melismatic *air de cour* – in which flexible melody as well as rhythmic freedom reflect improvisatory practices – and to the influence of the contemporary Italian style. The genre soon became fashionable, Dumont issuing approximately one hundred works between 1652 and 1689. From *c.* 1695 onwards, *petits motets* were usually set for one or two solo voices (often *dessus*) and *basse-continue*, and at times with one or two treble instruments whose accompaniment could be quite idiomatic. Alongside the traditional liturgical and Biblical texts (hymns, canticles, psalms, etc.), an original repertory of verses by neo-Latin poets, such as Jean Santeul and Pierre Portes, became commonplace.

Thanks to their small format, *petits motets* were ideal for accompanying Vespers, *Saluts* (a typically Gallican afternoon service during which the Holy Sacrament was worshipped), as well as processions (Corpus Christi, Assumption, Rogation days, etc.) where a motet was performed at each *reposoir* (altar of repose). They also made up the basic repertory of small churches and of most religious houses (including the Royal institution of Saint-Cyr, the 'Cent Filles de la Miséricorde' in Paris, and the monastery of Saint-Bonaventure in Lyons), at which resources for lavish performances were insufficient. They were usually sung at the Offertory and at (or after) the elevation, in order to heighten the liturgy. By *c.* 1784 in Metz, there was even a tradition of singing a *petit motet* after Compline on certain occasions.

By *c.* 1695, the first composers of *cantates françaises* (Campra, Bernier and Jean-Baptiste Morin (1677–1745)), much influenced by the fashionable Italian style, had published their first books of *petits motets*, works that could be labelled 'Latin cantatas': *airs à devise* and recitatives alternate in a style close to that of secular *cantates*. Thus, the overall form of Bernier's *Congratulamini con gaudete* (from his 1703 book) resembles that of Carissimi's or Cesti's cantatas: A (aria) – B (recitative) – C (aria) – A (da capo) – D (aria) – A (da capo). As for Campra's *Tota pulchra es* (1695) for two sopranos, it directly borrows its vocabulary from the contemporary tragédies en musique. In order to depict the mystic love between the sinner's soul and God, the motet opens with a long and tender dialogue in A minor supported by a ground bass, a traditional device to underline the affection of two lovers. It continues with a tight, almost canonic, dialogue in A major with numerous parallel thirds and sixths, extended melismas and many very sensual – if not erotic – repetitions of the word 'Veni' ('come').

The genre reached its apex with these authors, to whom we should add François Couperin (1668–1733) whose bright motets (including the in-turn playful and serious *Motet pour le jour de Pâques*) stand comparison with Campra's. *Petit motets* also appeared regularly in private and public concerts.

Works by Jean-Joseph Mouret (1682–1738), Louis Lemaire (*c.* 1693–*c.* 1750) and François Martin (1727–57) – to name but a few – achieved lasting success, directing the *petit motet* towards a profane genre in the service of avid professional singers keen to vie in skill with one another at the Concert Spirituel.

During the first nocturns of the Matins of Maundy Thursday, Good Friday and Holy Saturday – in some fashionable convents in Paris, these offices often took place the previous afternoons, which were more convenient for the nobles and bourgeois – three *Leçons de Ténèbres* were sung on the 'Lamentations of Jeremiah', mourning the destruction of Jerusalem while the candles were gradually extinguished. The style of these *tenebræ* lessons is akin to that of the *petits motets* of the period, but distinguishes itself by the long and lavish melismas heard on the Hebrew letters beginning each verse. These melismas, often modelled on the original Gregorian melody, give birth at times to a sort of 'prelude' that features writing similar to that in trendy Italian sonatas, as in Couperin's third *Leçon pour le Mercredi*. In some settings composed before *c.* 1730, such as Couperin's, Bernier's and Lalande's, the outdated *air de cour* art remains easily perceptible. It can be surmised from these works, and those by Joseph Michel (1679–1736), Michel Corrette (1707–95) and even Jean-Jacques Rousseau (1712–78), that eighteenth-century *Leçons de Ténèbres* were, unlike most *petits motets* of the day, primarily intended for actual offices and not for private or public concerts.

The abundant repertory of French or Latin pious songs (*cantiques spirituels*), often set as parodies of secular tunes, were originally designed to counteract Protestant vernacular melodies, and provided believers with appropriate spiritual amusements. However, in the hands of Jean-Noël Marchand (1666–1710), Jean-Baptiste Moreau (1656–1733), Collasse, and Lalande, who set to music the famous *Cantiques spirituels* by Jean Racine (1639–99), this sub-genre became a kind of sacred cantata, more or less in keeping with the *Cantates françaises sur des sujets tirés de l'Écriture* (1708 and 1711) by Élisabeth Jacquet de La Guerre (1665–1729).

It must not be forgotten – in light of the discussion above – that the daily choral singing in most French churches of the eighteenth century still consisted mainly of psalmody, plainchant and harmonized chant (*faux-bourdon* or *chant-sur-le-livre*), sometimes sung in alternation with the organ; the *Cæremoniale Episcoporum* (published in 1600 and revised in 1752; book 1, chapter 28) recommended recitation or even singing of the words while the organ played the melody as well. Polyphonic masses and motets accompanied only by the continuo (*musique figurée*) could also be performed during services.

Plainchant and improvised polyphony

In 1754, Philippe-Joseph Caffiaux could still hold plainchant to be 'the mother of music',[4] because there was a time when it was the only type of music available. As a result of the development of the Catholic Reformation and of its related ecclesiastical strategies, a newly composed *plain-chant 'musical'* was conceived around 1610. This mensural chant without melismas, simple enough to be sung by every ecclesiastical member of a community, was composed in a more or less tonal system and included some leading-notes and ornaments. By publishing his five *Messes royales* in 1669, Dumont provided the most successful examples of this new plainchant, and thus created a new sub-genre of monodies: not only were they reprinted several times during the eighteenth century and distributed in all French dioceses, but they were also imitated by prominent composers such as Campra, Lalande and Jean-François Lallouette (1651–1728). The neo-Gallican reforms also led to the revision of the traditional liturgical melodies. In the 1680s, Guillaume-Gabriel Nivers (1632–1714) undertook with royal support a scholarly revision of the Roman Antiphonary and Gradual so that his editions became reference points for all convents and churches complying with the Roman rite.

Starting in *c.* 1736, however, most French dioceses, eager to preserve their local rites, followed the lead of the Parisian reformers (including Jean Lebeuf (1687–1760)), who greatly modified the liturgical books under the supervision of Archbishop Charles de Vintimille (1655–1746). Various plainchants were then newly composed on neo-Latin texts – particularly hymns and *proses* – to fulfil the request of some religious houses and dioceses as a consequence of the revisions undertaken in provincial liturgies. The *Graduale Tullense* (1752), for example, supplies new melodies for the Proper, different from those of the *Graduale Romanum*; common monodies with the Roman rite – like the *prose* for Easter – are rare (see table 4.2).

At times, and in order to enhance the solemnity of certain festivals, choirboys and choristers could improvise on the melodies of the Proper and of the Ordinary, either by placing the plainchant in the tenor part and harmonizing it in a note-against-note style (*faux-bourdon*), or by extemporizing a simple counterpoint above the plainchant, this time located in the lowest part of the polyphony and sung isochronically without pause or ornament (*chant-sur-le-livre*). The latter practice progressively disappeared during the eighteenth century, but was still in use as late as *c.* 1830. (Interestingly, *faux-bourdon* was

4 Philippe-Joseph Caffiaux, 'Dissertation sur la musique d'Église', in *Histoire de la musique* (1754), *F-Pn* fr. 22536, fol. 235r.

Table 4.2. *Examples of differences between the Toul Gradual and the* Graduale Romanum

Graduale Tullense (1752)	*Graduale Romanum*
In nativitate Domini,	Ad missam in die
Int. *Parvulus natus est nobis*	Int. *Puer natus est nobis*
Gr. *Misericordia & veritas*	Gr. *Viderunt omnes*
All. *Per viscera*	All. *Dies sanctificatus*
Prose *Votis Pater annuit*	[none]
Off. *Memor sit*	Off. *Tui sunt cœli*
Co. *Recordatus est*	Co. *Viderunt omnes*
In die sancto	Paschae
Int. *Nunc Christus*	Int. *Resurrexi*
Gr. *Hæc dies ... Ecce vicit*	Gr. *Hæc dies ... Confitemini Domino*
All. *Tua est, Domine*	All. *Pascha nostrum*
Prose *Victimae paschali laudes*	Prose *Victimae paschali laudes*
Off. *Habebitis*	Off. *Terra tremuit*
Co. *Exurgat Deus*	Co. *Pascha nostrum*

performed at Louis XV's chapel, and even perhaps some sort of *chant-sur-le-livre*, as Henry Madin seems to suggest in his 1742 *Traité du contrepoint simple, ou chant sur le livre*.)

Masses and Requiems

Concertante masses for soloists, chorus and orchestra were uncommon in France before Charpentier. By the turn of the eighteenth century, though, numerous minor *maîtres de musique* active in large cathedrals started lavishly to set the text of the Ordinary to music, as did Antoine Hugues (*c.* 1720–*c.* 1773), Jean Clavis (*c.* 1700–post-1752), Laurent Belissen (1693–1762) and Joseph-Antoine Lorenzitti (*c.* 1740–*c.* 1789). These scores were never published, and most are now lost. It can nonetheless be inferred that their style was comparable to that of contemporary *grands motets*, as Giroust's masses – including the Coronation Mass for Louis XVI (1775) – bear witness.

From 1725 onwards, Jean-Baptiste Christophe Ballard began to re-issue seventeenth-century *a cappella* four- and five-part masses (notably by François Cosset, Charles d'Helfer and Jean Mignon), which found a reliable market in the *maîtrises* of the kingdom. It cannot be determined whether these out-of-fashion scores were actually put to use in church: according to Brossard's testimony, Charles d'Helfer's *Missa Deliciæ regum* (1664) still made 'the delights of all people of good taste' as late as 1725,[5] but this sentence remains too ambiguous to constitute firm proof. It is known, however, that they were employed by *maîtres de musique* to teach composition (and Latin prosody?) to their choirboys. Some of the most talented of them even managed to have their own masses printed by Ballard. With his apprenticeship barely finished, Pierre Hugard (*fl.* 1744–61), then *senior puer* ('spé') at Notre Dame in Paris, published his masterwork, the *Missa Laudate, pueri, Dominum* (1744), dedicated to the cathedral canons. Between 1729 and 1761, ten four-part masses came out with the Ballard press, works remarkably refined in style and indebted in turn to the old *stile ecclesiastico* and the theatrical trends of the day. While some were composed by otherwise unknown figures (Claude Mielle, Nicolas Pacotat and Hugard), others were the work of famous musicians: Lallouette, Lully's former secretary whose *Missa Veritas* was published posthumously in 1729; Louis-Joseph Marchand (1698–1774), who was the first French eighteenth-century theorist to publish a treatise of counterpoint (1739) at a time when Rameau's harmonic theories were heatedly debated; and above all Henry Madin, whose four masses (*Vivat Rex*, 1741; *Dico ego opera mea Regi*, 1743; *Velociter currit sermo ejus*, 1746; *Fiat Pax*, 1747) must rank among the finest sacred pieces produced during the period. Between 1772 and the end of the century, other publishers (notably Richomme and Montulay) brought out several other insipid mass settings by composers such as Henri Hardouin (1727–1808) and Claude Hermant de Saint-Benoist (1723–1802).

Even though they were published in open scores and without instrument parts, evidence shows that *maîtres de musique* were required to provide (in addition to an unavoidable basso continuo, better described as a *basso seguente*) the necessary instrumental lines by extracting them from the printed vocal parts. Depending on the *maître*'s skill, this process of 're-writing' could result in strict doubling of the voices (at times with octave transpositions), or in a genuine and idiomatic instrumental accompaniment. In other words, these apparently *a cappella* masses were seldom – perhaps never – sung as such, retaining at least the support of a continuo. This practice actually follows the practice observed in the contemporaneous four-and five-vocal-part motets, such as Louis Homet's *Exurge Deus* (1711) and Jean Audiffren's *Magnificat* (*c.* 1730), which were always accompanied by an instrumental bass.

Performances of polyphonic settings of the *Missa pro defunctis* were also very frequent, and provincial authors, like Hardouin and Jean-Marie Rousseau (d. 1784), continued the tradition of the Renaissance by writing archaic

5 Yolande de Brossard (ed.), *La Collection Sébastien de Brossard 1655–1730. Catalogue (Département de la Musique, Rés. Vm[8] 20)* (Paris, 1994), p. 88.

Requiem masses right up to the end of the *ancien régime*. Some outmoded settings even remained in the repertory throughout the seventeenth and eighteenth centuries. One example is the *Missa pro defunctis* by Charles d'Helfer (d. 1661), published in 1656: it was sung in 1726 at the funeral of Lalande, again in 1729, and forty-eight years later at the solemn funeral service for Louis XV, held at the royal Abbey of Saint-Denis on 27 July 1774. Thus, Helfer's mass became a classic which underwent several arrangements and even inspired Giroust's own mass setting (1775). The renewal of the Requiem mass in France is probably attributable to Charpentier and Jean Gilles (1668–1705), who composed the first French Requiems with instrumental accompaniment. As late as 1776, John Hawkins still said of Gilles' *Messe des morts* that it was his 'capital work',[6] one that had been performed twelve years earlier at the eglise de l'Oratoire at the memorial service for Rameau (1764).

The most magnificent of these Requiem masses, however, is probably Campra's *Messe de morts*, composed in all likelihood for the memorial service for Philippe II d'Orléans held at Saint-Eustache some time in 1724. This work achieved a certain popularity in Provence, where it was performed several times between *c.* 1748 and *c.* 1754. The score is divided into seven by-and-large symmetrical movements. In the 'Introïte', the Gregorian plainchant is used as a cantus firmus sung by the lowest voices of the choir, a technique that revises the centuries-old practice of '*chant-sur-le-livre*', which Campra learned as a choirboy. In four places in the mass, there is a bell-motif, a common effect in funeral works including Campra's own *De profundis* (1723). In the operatic Offertory, the composer makes use of repeated crotchets ('slurred' with wavy lines) to depict the deceased believers trembling with fear before the King of Glory, not yet certain that they will be delivered from the agonies of hell and the fathomless lake. It is a theatrical device borrowed from the chorus 'L'hiver qui nous tourmente' in Lully's *Isis* (1677) and frequently imitated thereafter by Lalande and others.

The beautiful and imposing *Grande messe des morts* (1760) by Gossec must also be mentioned; its spectacular sound effects (especially in the 'Tuba mirum') may have inspired Mozart's and Berlioz's own settings. It seems to have enjoyed some success during the Revolution, being performed on 6 August 1789 for the memory of the dead of the Bastille siege, and in several other ceremonies until 1792.

'Although church music should be noble in general, and [should] preserve a tone of impressive grandeur, all the grand subjects of Religion can also be

6 John Hawkins, *A General History of the Science and Practice of Music* (London, 1776), 5 vols., vol. 5, p. 44.

adapted to a piquant and graceful music.'[7] Indeed eighteenth-century French sacred music certainly had to balance a kind of dignity with the worldly spirit of its time. But beyond a natural evolution towards the 'international' style of the late eighteenth century, church-music composers managed to conform to the proper French rhetorical declamation of Latin texts, and almost always retained in their works a number of seventeenth-century idiosyncrasies, including elegant and refined melodies, a mastery of (often five-part) choral writing, and, above all, dance rhythms.

Select Bibliography

Anthony, James R. *French Baroque Music from Beaujoyeulx to Rameau*. Rev. and expand. edn., Portland, OR, 1997

Bisaro, Xavier. *Une Nation de fidèles. L'Église et la liturgie parisienne au XVIIIe siècle*. Turnhout, 2006

Davy-Rigaux, Cécile. *Guillaume-Gabriel Nivers. Un art du chant grégorien sous le règne de Louis XIV*. Paris, 2004

Dompnier, Bernard (ed.). *Maîtrises & chapelles aux XVIIe et XVIIIe siècles. Des institutions musicales au service de Dieu*. Saint-Étienne, 2003

Eby, Jack. 'A Requiem Mass for Louis XV: Charles d'Helfer, François Giroust and the *Missa pro defunctis* of 1775'. *Early Music*, 29 (2001), pp. 218–32

Foster, Donald H. 'The Oratorio in Paris in the 18th Century'. *Acta musicologica*, 47 (1975), pp. 67–133

Gaudelus, Sébastien. *Les Offices de Ténèbres en France 1650–1790*. Paris, 2005

Higginbottom, Edward. 'French Classical Organ Music and the Liturgy'. *Proceedings of the Royal Musical Association*, 103 (1976–7), pp. 19–40

Kotylo, Joseph A. 'A Historical and Stylistic Study of the *Petit Motet* 1700–1730'. PhD thesis, University of Colorado, 1979

Launay, Denise. *La Musique religieuse en France du Concile de Trente à 1804*. Paris, 1993

Maral, Alexandre. *La Chapelle royale de Versailles sous Louis XIV: cérémonial, liturgie et musique*. Sprimont, 2002

Mongrédien, Jean and Yves Ferraton (eds.). *Actes du colloque international de musicologie sur le grand motet français (1663–1792)*. Paris, 1986

Montagnier, Jean-Paul C. 'Chanter Dieu en la Chapelle Royale: le grand motet et ses supports littéraires'. *Revue de musicologie*, 86 (2000), pp. 220–60

'Le *Chant sur le Livre* en France aux XVIIe et XVIIIe siècles: de la survivance d'une tradition orale ancienne à l'avènement d'un genre écrit'. In Giulio Cattin and F. Alberto Gallo (eds.), *Un Millennio di polifonia liturgica tra oralità e scrittura, Quaderni di 'Musica e storia'*. Venice, 2002, pp. 257–89

'Le *Te Deum* de Jacques Morel et le *Concert spirituel* d'Alexandre de Villeneuve comme exemples de divertissements sacrés'. *Revue de musicologie*, 88 (2002), pp. 265–96

7 Jean-François Le Sueur, *Exposé d'une musique une, imitative, et particulière à chaque solemnité. Suite de l'Essai* (Paris, 1787), p. 71: 'Quoique la Musique d'église doive être noble en général, & conserver un ton de grandeur imposante, tous les grands sujets de la Religion peuvent aussi s'accommoder à une musique piquante & gracieuse.'

'French *grands motets* and Their Use at the Chapelle Royale from Louis XIV to Louis XVI'. *The Musical Times*, 146 (2005), pp. 47–57

'La messe polyphonique imprimée en France au XVIIIe siècle: survivance et décadence d'une tradition séculaire'. *Acta musicologica*, 77 (2005), pp. 47–69

Sawkins, Lionel. *A Thematic Catalogue of the Works of Michel-Richard de Lalande (1657–1726)*. Oxford and New York, 2005

· 5 ·

Lutheran church music

STEPHEN ROSE

The history of Lutheran church music in the eighteenth century is often described as a culmination and then a decline.[1] Johann Sebastian Bach is regarded as the pinnacle of Lutheran music; then, according to Georg Feder, 'there is unanimity of opinion that Protestant church music after Bach declined in comparison to the achievements of earlier days'.[2] Certainly church music underwent a crisis in the second half of the eighteenth century. Changed religious ideals, inspired by the Enlightenment, increasingly sought simple and intelligible music, eschewing worldly or learned elements. Furthermore, with the rising secularization of society, the church became less important in musical life; composers and performers instead focused on public concerts, music-publishing and other secular enterprises. The very institutions of Lutheran church music were also undermined, with the dissolution of most of the school choirs that had formerly sung in churches.

Yet it is hard to assess these major changes in Lutheran church music, mainly because most researchers and performers concentrate on J. S. Bach to the exclusion of his contemporaries and successors. Until there are more recordings and modern editions of the church music of composers such as Johann Friedrich Doles, Gottfried August Homilius, Johann Philipp Krieger, Gottfried Heinrich Stölzel and Georg Philipp Telemann, it is inevitable that Bach's output will look like an isolated summit. Gradually the situation is changing, with selected works of Homilius, Stölzel and Telemann undergoing a revival via new editions and recordings.[3] By examining Bach in the context of such

1 Friedhelm Krummacher, 'Kulmination und Verfall der protestantischen Kirchenmusik', in Carl Dahlhaus (ed.), *Musik des 18. Jahrhunderts* (Laaber, 1985), pp. 108–21.

2 Georg Feder, 'Decline and Restoration', in Friedrich Blume (ed.), *Protestant Church Music* (London, 1975), p. 319.

3 A sample of recent editions includes Gottfried August Homilius, *Ein Lämmlein geht*, ed. Uwe Wolf (Stuttgart, 2006); Homilius, *Motetten*, ed. Uwe Wolf (Stuttgart, 2000); and Georg Philipp Telemann, *Geistliches Singen und Spielen: Kantaten vom 1. Advent bis zum Sonntag nach Weihnachten*, Werke vol. 39, ed. Ute Poetzsch-Seban (Kassel, 2004). Several of Stölzel's cantatas and his *Brockes-Passion* have been recorded by Ludger Rémy on the cpo label.

figures, it is possible to see how his output is representative in some ways and idiosyncratic in others.

A survey of Lutheran church music across the whole century shows that, despite the many changes, there were two notable continuities: first, the desire of composers to communicate with a congregation and, secondly, the debate over the use of secular styles in church. The importance of communication is evident when one considers that, until the rise of the public concert, the church cantata was the genre that reached the largest number of listeners.[4] During the seventeenth century music was seen as a way to project and enhance a sacred text. By the eighteenth century church music was also regarded as a means to manipulate the emotions of the congregation. Doles and Johann Mattheson argued that church music should move the emotions like operatic arias; other writers saw music as a way to enhance a devotional mood. Musicians also discussed how to communicate with less-educated members of the congregation, recommending simpler styles such as popular hymns or syllabic word-setting. In the second half of the eighteenth century, this concern for intelligibility mirrored the creation of simpler repertories for less learned listeners (for *Liebhaber* as well as *Kenner*, in C. P. E. Bach's words).

Related to the importance of communication was the debate over the use of secular styles in church. Traditional notions of musical style preserved a distinction between theatre, church and chamber music. At the start of the eighteenth century, however, Erdmann Neumeister provocatively advocated using aspects of operatic music (such as recitatives and arias) in church. Also introduced were such features as dance metres and the ritornello techniques associated with arias and instrumental concertos. These secular elements even infiltrated the relatively cloistered world of organ music. Supporters of such secular features saw them as a way to hold the attention of listeners, but many theologians and musicians regarded them as frivolous or sacrilegious. Increasingly in the second half of the eighteenth century, the notion arose of a 'true church music' – implying styles (such as unaccompanied singing) segregated from the mainstream of secular music.

This chapter avoids applying the narrative of climax and decline to eighteenth-century Lutheran music. Instead, it places the works of Bach and other composers within the debates about the communicative power and secularization of church music. Bach's output can consequently be seen as an individual response to these debates, not as the universal that its subsequent reception seems to have made it.

4 Krummacher, 'Kulmination und Verfall', p. 110.

Lutheran music *c.* 1700: repertories and institutions

At the start of the eighteenth century, Lutheran music was cultivated with particular intensity at court chapels and town churches. The courts were centres of cultural innovation in the first half of the century, fostering church music in operatic styles; but it was in towns that the full scope of the Lutheran repertory was evident. In most towns, church music was performed by choirs from local schools (under the direction of the cantor, the school music teacher) with the support of civic instrumentalists. Three distinct repertories were used, corresponding to different levels of musical accomplishment among the pupils.[5] At the most basic level were chorales, the body of hymns dating back in some cases to the Reformation. Chorales were sung in unison by the congregation during services, as well as being performed by the choirboys with the most limited musical abilities (in J. S. Bach's words, 'those who do not understand music at all'). Chorales were also used outside church, being sung during the daily domestic life of Lutherans, and being performed on the streets by the *Currende*, the choir of schoolboys who sang for alms. The second repertory comprised motets, settings of a Biblical text or chorale for choir with no obbligato instruments apart from continuo. Motets were performed by the schoolboys able to sing in parts; at the start of the eighteenth century, they were regarded as somewhat old-fashioned, although they still carried residual prestige as a genre sanctioned by Lutheran ordinances of the late sixteenth century. As we shall see, the motet regained popularity in the second half of the eighteenth century. Finally, the most prestigious repertory comprised concerted music for voices (usually soloists) and obbligato instruments.[6] Vocal concertos were described with a variety of terms, including *Concerto*, *Dialogo*, *Kirchen-Stück* and *Kirchen-Music*; nowadays they are often dubbed 'cantatas' (an anachronistic term that is appropriate only for Italianate works with alternating recitatives and arias). The concerted repertory required highly trained singers and instrumentalists; here the town choirs aspired to the standard of performance of courts and opera-houses. Besides these three levels of vocal music, organ music was also used in church, and will be considered at the end of this chapter.

The multi-levelled nature of the church repertory in the eighteenth century was a continuation of the inclusive spirit that Martin Luther brought to music

5 These layers of repertory are described by J. S. Bach in his *Entwurff* of 1730; see Hans T. David and Arthur Mendel (eds.), *The New Bach Reader*, rev. Christoph Wolff (New York, 1998), pp. 145–51 and Andrew Parrott, *The Essential Bach Choir* (Woodbridge and Rochester, NY, 2000), pp. 17–28, 163–70.

6 On the solo-voice performance of this repertory – a contentious but increasingly accepted approach – see Parrott, *The Essential Bach Choir*.

in the Reformation. Although Luther fostered congregational singing via chorales, he also valued motets such as Josquin's that were for trained singers only; such an inclusive attitude helped create the richness of Lutheran music in the eighteenth century, although there could be tensions between congregational and choral repertories. A church service in Leipzig in the early eighteenth century included all three types of vocal music – congregational chorales, simple motets and vocal concertos – plus organ preludes, as Bach noted in an order of service of 1723.[7] Moreover, the motets and vocal concertos often quoted chorales, as a way to communicate with the congregation and assert their Lutheran lineage.

Another legacy of the Reformation was the ecumenical nature of the Lutheran liturgy. Luther retained much of the cycle of the Catholic church year, including Marian festivals such as Candlemas and the Annunciation, as well as some saints' days.[8] Biblical readings for each Sunday were prescribed by the lectionary, giving church musicians a huge stock of texts for setting. Although one hallmark of reformed worship was the use of the vernacular, Luther authorized a Latin mass (1523) as well as a German liturgy (1526).[9] During the first half of the eighteenth century, many town churches still recited the Kyrie eleison and Gloria at the start of the Communion service. In Leipzig, the service usually began with a Latin motet, typically from the collection *Florilegium portense* (1603–21) that contained pieces by such composers as Andrea Gabrieli, Jakob Handl (Gallus) and Orlande de Lassus.[10] Bach also set several Latin texts, including the Magnificat, BWV 243 (which could be sung annually on at least fifteen high feasts in Leipzig) and the Missa Brevis (the Kyrie and Gloria, BWV 233–236). Many of the movements of Bach's B minor Mass BWV 232, could be used within Lutheran worship – the Sanctus was performed on several occasions in Leipzig between 1724 and the 1740s – although the purpose of the entire Mass remains unclear. In short, the rich eclecticism of the Lutheran liturgy increased the choice of texts for church composers.

In the first half of the century, Lutheran cantors and organists focused their energies on concerted music, the most prestigious sacred style of the time. The vocal concertos from around 1700 constitute a richly inventive repertory, where almost every surviving piece is unique in some way. One characteristic of this repertory is the mixing of texts within a single piece. Composers

7 David and Mendel (eds.), *The New Bach Reader*, p. 113.

8 Nicholas Hope, *German and Scandinavian Protestantism 1700–1918* (Oxford, 1995), pp. 165–7.

9 Joseph Herl, *Worship Wars in Early Lutheranism: Choir, Congregation and Three Centuries of Conflict* (Oxford, 2004), pp. 23–35.

10 The motets set for each Sunday are listed in Charles S. Terry, *Joh. Seb. Bach: Cantata Texts Sacred and Secular* (London, 1926).

combined Biblical excerpts with chorales and devotional strophic poetry ('odes'). Such a technique allowed different texts to comment on each other and add layers of meaning. The layering of texts is seen in *Der Himmelreich ist gleich einem Könige*, a vocal concerto by the organist Georg Böhm. Here the main text is the parable of the royal wedding feast and the ungrateful guests (Matthew 22:2–14), interspersed with verses from Philipp Nicolai's chorale 'Wachet auf', an Advent hymn that uses the wedding feast as a metaphor for Christ's first and second coming. The chorale would be easily recognized by listeners, and its words link the Biblical story to a rich tradition of allegories and glosses. Johann Sebastian Bach used a similar layering of texts in his earliest vocal pieces, written around 1707–8. The funerary cantata *Gottes Zeit ist die allerbeste Zeit* (BWV 106) sets a mosaic of Biblical sayings on death and resurrection, starting with Old Testament passages that stoically accept death, and moving to New Testament extracts that speak of the eternal life of the resurrected. The Biblical texts are reinforced by chorales (some sung, some played instrumentally with the words implied).

Composers set these mosaics of texts in a variety of imaginative and individual ways. Most vocal concertos are a patchwork of short sections of contrasting affect or imagery. Böhm's *Der Himmelreich* is in seventeen sections, with much painting of individual words: the music falls silent on 'verstummet' ('made speechless'), a rhetorical device repeated four times for good measure. In Bach's *Gottes Zeit*, each Biblical passage is set to a new theme, with contrast between words such as 'leben' (live) and 'sterben' (die). Such attention to individual words was recommended by Johann Kuhnau in 1709. When setting prose texts such as the Bible, he advised that composers maintain interest by seizing 'every opportunity for invention and variation'. As an example he took the opening of Psalm 1, suggesting how each word or clause could be characterized (for instance, by using a variety of voices or choruses for 'blessed is the man', and by repeating a passage in many keys for 'walketh').[11] Instruments also have a major role in vocal concertos, amplifying and enhancing the sung sections. Frequently an instrumental sinfonia is used to set the scene; the scoring may be expressive or symbolic, as with Bach's choice of the veiled sound of recorders and viola da gambas for his funerary cantata, BWV 106. Throughout, though, the text determines the structure of the piece, reflecting the vocal concerto's main function as a vehicle for the sacred words.

11 Bernhard F. Richter, 'Eine Abhandlung Joh. Kuhnaus', *Monatshefte für Musikgeschichte*, 34 (1902), pp. 151–3; trans. Ruben Weltsch as 'A Treatise on Liturgical Text Settings', in Carol K. Baron (ed.), *Bach's Changing World: Voices in the Community* (Rochester, NY, 2006), pp. 222–4.

Theatrical music in church: the Neumeister reform

From about 1700 concerted church music was transformed by the introduction of elements from opera and the Italian cantata. By this date, opera was a fashionable yet controversial entertainment in Protestant Germany. Opera-houses had opened at the courts of Weissenfels and Naumburg and in towns such as Hamburg and Leipzig. Many younger musicians were intoxicated by the lively charm of operas and secular cantatas: in the 1690s the teenage Telemann named Agostino Steffani and Antonio Caldara as two of his compositional models, along with Arcangelo Corelli and Johann Rosenmüller.[12] The decisive impulse in introducing such operatic elements into church, however, came from devotional poets (notably Erdmann Neumeister) who supplied church composers with libretti modelled on secular cantatas and opera. The resultant sacred music was immensely popular, but also provoked bitter attacks from theologians and conservative musicians.

Erdmann Neumeister (1671–1756), pastor and poet, popularized the use of libretti that included verse for recitatives and arias. In 1702 he published a cycle of cantata texts for the whole church year, written for the Weissenfels court. Unlike most previous texts for Lutheran church music, Neumeister excluded Biblical extracts and chorales; the cycle uses entirely his own free poetry, meditating on the scriptural readings of the day. His revolutionary step was to use madrigalian verse ('madrigalian' denoting a freedom in the rhymes and length of lines) that was suitable for arias and recitatives. As Neumeister explained, 'a cantata resembles a piece from an opera, assembled from recitatives and arias'. In addition, he favoured a high literary style with many metaphors (describing death as a 'sweet hour', or the believer as a storm-ravaged ship seeking a safe harbour) and heavy use of the first-person voice. Neumeister signalled his break from Lutheran tradition by calling his cycle *Geistliche Cantaten statt einer Kirchen-Music* (Sacred cantatas instead of a church music). This was one of the first times that the term 'cantata' had been used in German church music; the title also implies that Neumeister intended his texts for private devotional music rather than public worship.

Neumeister's reform had several musical implications. His libretti created a polarity between recitatives (where the text was set without repetition, but with the potential to highlight individual words) and arias (where the composer could write an extended movement with a self-sufficient musical structure, projecting a single Affect). This division between two types of word-setting was entirely different from the vocal concerto of the previous century, which rarely contained

12 Johann Mattheson, *Grundlage einer Ehren-Pforte* (Hamburg, 1740), p. 357; reprint Kassel, 1969.

extended sections and was throughout responsive to individual words. The original setting of Neumeister's cycle by Johann Philipp Krieger (Kapellmeister at the Weissenfels court) does not survive; but his performance diary shows that the cantatas were scored modestly, usually for solo voice and about five instrumentalists.[13] This intimate scale suited Neumeister's conception of the texts as his private meditation, and also underlined the affinities with the secular solo cantata. Something akin to Krieger's settings may perhaps be found in the few solo cantatas by Bach such as BWV 54 or BWV 199 (see below).

Neumeister's subsequent cycles of cantata texts still used arias and recitatives, but made concessions to Lutheran tradition by including choruses, chorales and Biblical excerpts. In his cycle published in 1708 (set by P. H. Erlebach at the Rudolstadt court), he used 'Tutti' markings to indicate that some movements should be sung chorally. In his cycle *Geistliches Singen und Spielen* (1711; set by Telemann for the Eisenach court) Neumeister included chorales and Biblical extracts, as well as free poetry for the recitatives and arias. This cycle thus offered a mix of texts similar to that of the late seventeenth-century vocal concerto; such mixing became the norm for cantatas in the first half of the eighteenth century, allowing an interplay of scripture and interpretative passages, and encouraging a wide variety of musical textures. Similar mixed texts (including Biblical passages, chorales, arias and recitatives) were already being used at the Meiningen court by 1704, possibly written by Ernst Ludwig, Duke of Saxe-Meiningen.[14]

It was no coincidence that Neumeister's musico-poetic experiment developed at the courts of central Germany. These courts were open to Italian musical influence and were also centres for opera. By the 1690s operas in German were being performed at the Weissenfels court under Krieger's musical direction, and at the Rudolstadt court with music by Erlebach. The aristocratic patrons doubtless encouraged the application of these theatrical styles to sacred music. Moreover, several of the court composers of sacred cantatas had studied operatic writing in Italy, notably Gottfried Heinrich Stölzel who subsequently served at the Gotha court from 1720. On a pragmatic level, the small-scale Italianate cantata was an ideal model for sacred music at the courts, which tended to have a small but select group of virtuoso musicians. A court composer did not have to contend with the variable quality of town choirs, nor make music intelligible to a large urban congregation.

Following Neumeister's example, many German poets published cycles of cantata texts for the liturgical year. The mixed type of libretto, with chorales

13 Johann Philipp Krieger, *21 ausgewählte Kirchenkompositionen*, ed. Max Seiffert, Denkmäler Deutscher Tonkunst 53–4 (Leipzig, 1916), pp. xxiv–lii.
14 Konrad Küster, 'Meininger Kantatentexte um Johann Ludwig Bach', *Bach-Jahrbuch*, 73 (1987), pp. 159–64.

and Biblical excerpts as well as recitatives and arias, was most popular. In the vanguard of this movement were the Weimar court poet Salomo Franck (*Evangelisches Andachts-Opffer*, 1715) and the Darmstadt court poet Georg Christian Lehms (five cycles, 1711–16). Such poets now had an unprecedented role in the creation of church music, since their libretti determined the overall structure of a cantata. The creation of annual cycles of texts also demanded an increased productivity by composers, implying that a new piece would be written each Sunday. Church music now began to be created on a vast scale: Stölzel wrote twelve annual cycles of cantatas (a total of about 1,150 works, of which about 450 survive); Telemann wrote at least twenty annual cycles, comprising about 1,700 works (of which around 1,400 survive). Such mass production was facilitated by the standardized nature of the libretti, which usually imposed the same sequence of movements on each Sunday in a cycle. Moreover, the movements of a church cantata used formulaic structures and stereotyped representations of affections, unlike the highly individual vocal concertos of the previous century. Yet because the cantata cycles were written for the whole church year, they reinforced the Lutheran awareness of the liturgical calendar: each libretto usually alluded to the Biblical readings for the relevant Sunday.

Neumeister's fusion of operatic and sacred elements was a provocative step. In previous decades there had been much controversy about the morality of opera, notably when the Hamburg opera house opened. In addition there was long-standing disquiet about worldly or over-complex elements in church music, which might obscure the words or disturb the congregation's devotion.[15] Neumeister anticipated that his innovation would raise hackles: 'It might be supposed that many will be vexed in spirit and ask how sacred music and opera can be reconciled, any more than Christ and Belial, or light and darkness.' In justification, he pointed to the example of secular songs that had been converted into sacred ones, arguing that his theatrical verse was sanctified by being dedicated to the honour of God.[16] One of his supporters, Gottfried Tilgner, defended Neumeister's texts by arguing they had brought church music to 'a better state', attracting the interest of 'private people', 'high potentates' and also the foremost composers of the day.[17]

15 Summarised in Joyce L. Irwin, *Neither Voice Nor Heart Alone: German Lutheran Theology of Music in the Age of the Baroque* (New York, 1993).

16 'so dürffte fast muthmassen/daß sich mancher ärgern möchte/und dencken: Wie eine Kirchen-Music und Opera zusammen stimmeten? Vielleicht/wie Christus und Belial? Etwan/wie Licht und Finsternis?', Preface to *Geistliche Cantaten*, quoted in Henrike Rucker (ed.), *Erdmann Neumeister (1671–1756): Wegbereiter der evangelischen Kirchenkantate* (Rudolstadt, 2000), p. 64.

17 Unpaginated preface to Erdmann Neumeister, *Fünffache Kirchen-Andachten bestehend in theils eintzeln, theils niemahls gedruckten Arien, Cantaten und Oden* (Leipzig, 1717).

As operatic styles became more widespread in church, another argument emerged in their favour: that sacred music had fundamentally the same purpose as opera, namely to move the emotions of the listener. Johann Mattheson, who worked in both the opera-house and the cathedral at Hamburg, declared that 'in church I have ... precisely the same intention with the music as in opera, namely: I want to stir the listener's mind and get it moving in a certain way, whether towards a feeling of love, compassion, joy or sadness etc. ... Especially here, during worship, intense, serious, long-lasting and extremely profound emotions are needed.'[18] Similar statements were made by the Breslau theologian Gottfried Ephraim Scheibel: 'I don't know why operas alone should have the privilege of extracting tears from us. Why shouldn't that apply in church? ... If a composer can move my affections in theatrical and secular music, he will be able to do the same in sacred matters, as the examples of Monsieurs Keiser, Mattheson and Telemann show.'[19] Such a concern for the affections signalled a new conception of church music, supplanting the earlier view of sacred music as a vehicle for holy words.

Yet the theatrical style aroused fierce opposition from conservative musicians and theologians. Joachim Meyer, a cantor and academic in Göttingen, complained that the words were rarely intelligible (indeed, the instrumental passages had no words to direct the thoughts of the congregation). He also criticized the fast-moving lines of the new style, recommending instead that church composers use semibreves, minims and crotchets as in the older style of motets.[20] Other listeners objected to the recitatives (which they associated with comedies), the unison instrumental writing and the repetition of text.[21] Friedrich Erhardt Niedt criticized church musicians who unthinkingly copied any style from Italy. Instead he advised that cantatas be 'entirely serious', with no skips or leaps in the recitative, and that melismas and runs be avoided 'because our mother tongue cannot stand such Italian humbug'.[22]

In Leipzig the dispute between old and new styles took the form of rivalry between the churches. The theatrical style was cultivated at the Neukirche

18 'Ich habe sonst in der Kirche ... eben die Absicht mit der Music, als in der Opera, nehmlich diese: Daß ich die Gemüths-Neigungen der Zuhörer rege machen, und auf gewisse Weise in Bewegung bringen will, es sey zur Liebe, zum Mitleid, zur Freude, zur Traurigkeit &c. ... Hier allein, nehmlich bey dem Gottes-Dienst, sind gar hefftige, ernstliche, dauerhaffte, und höchst-angelegentliche Gemüths-Bewegung nöthig.' Johann Mattheson, *Der musicalische Patriot* (Hamburg, 1728), pp. 105–6.

19 Gottfried Ephraim Scheibel, *Zufällige Gedancken von der Kirchen-Music* (Frankfurt and Leipzig, 1721), pp. 40–1; excerpts trans. Joyce L. Irwin as 'Random Thoughts About Church Music', in Baron (ed.), *Bach's Changing World: Voices in the Community*, p. 241.

20 Joachim Meyer, *Unvorgreiffliche Gedancken über der neulich eingerissene theatralische Kirchen-Music* (n.p., 1726); summarised in Irwin, *Neither Voice Nor Heart Alone*, pp. 134–5.

21 Gottfried Tilgner, unpaginated preface to Neumeister, *Fünffache Kirchen-Andachten*.

22 Friedrich Erhardt Niedt, *Musicalische Handleitung III* (Hamburg, 1717), pp. 37–8; trans. Pamela L. Poulin and Irmgard C. Taylor as *The Musical Guide* (Oxford, 1989), pp. 258–9.

(under the direction of Telemann and later Melchior Hoffmann), while older styles of church music were maintained by the cantor Johann Kuhnau at the Nikolaikirche and Thomaskirche. Kuhnau resented the popularity of the performances at the Neukirche, which enticed congregations and singers away from his own efforts. He also voiced scepticism about the new style in a 1709 preface to a set of texts for church music. In this collection he had avoided 'the madrigalian style [of poetry] that is suitable for arias and recitatives' because he did not want to be accused of writing theatrical music; he instead limited himself to 'plain words in prose'. Yet he admitted that he was not opposed to the use of madrigalian verse *per se* in church. Rather, he perceived the difference between sacred and theatrical music in terms of their effect on listeners. Church music should aim to arouse 'sacred devotion, love, joy, sadness, wonder and the like in the listener', whereas theatrical music may arouse 'innocent pleasure' among 'pure and innocent music-lovers', but may also excite 'carnal desires in the worldly-minded'.[23] Later Kuhnau's attitude softened: he used madrigalian poetry and recitatives alongside chorale verses in *Wie schön leuchtet der Morgenstern*. He even set one of Neumeister's texts, *Weicht ihr Sorgen aus dem Hertzen*, as a cantata for solo soprano, oboe and string ensemble: here he wrote recitatives and a da capo aria, and the lilting charm of the melodies seems inspired by opera. Thus Kuhnau was deeply ambivalent towards the operatic style: he understood its appeal, but was also wary of blurring the distinction between secular and sacred music, not least because of the rivalry between churches in Leipzig.

Bach's church cantatas

Of the church cantatas written in Germany in the first half of the eighteenth century, Bach's are the best known today, and hence will here serve as examples (if idiosyncratic) of prevalent tendencies in church music at the time. Most of Bach's sacred cantatas date from two short periods of his career: as Konzertmeister at the Weimar court (1714–17) and as Thomaskantor – his first years in the role at least – in Leipzig (1723–*c.* 1727). The Weimar pieces show Bach learning how to use libretti like Neumeister's and working with a small ensemble for an intimate court chapel. By contrast, most of his Leipzig cantatas are on a larger scale, using the forces available to a civic music director, and maintain a careful balance between the latest trends and the Lutheran heritage of choruses and chorales.

23 Richter, 'Ein Abhandlung', p. 149.

Bach's Weimar cantatas coincide not only with the Neumeister reform; they also show him applying ritornello principles that he had learned from Italian repertory such as Vivaldi's concertos.[24] During this period Bach mainly used libretti by the Weimar court poet Salomo Franck, plus a few by Lehms and Neumeister. Two of his Weimar cantatas – BWV 54 and BWV 199, both to texts by Lehms – may give an insight into Neumeister's original conception of the sacred cantata, for they are for solo voice and use almost exclusively free poetry, with no words from the Bible. *Mein Herze schwimmt im Blut*, BWV 199, opens with a graphic first-person account of a sinner's inner turmoil, set as a soprano recitative accompanied by strings:

Mein Herze schwimmt im Blut,	My heart swims in blood,
weil mich der Sünden Brut	because the brooding sin
in Gottes heilgen Augen	turns me into a monster
zum Ungeheuer macht ...	in God's holy eyes ...

Such a focus on subjective experience was typical of the poetry inspired by Neumeister.

The text of *Widerstehe doch der Sünde*, BWV 54, is more impersonal, urging the believer to resist the outward allure of sin. Although the libretto is written in the third person, the elaborate metaphors (comparing sin to Sodom's apples or a white sepulchre) exemplify the high literary style encouraged by Neumeister. The cantata consists of two alto arias, separated by a recitative. The first aria starts boldly, with an unprepared entry of one of the most dissonant chords conceivable at the time; the subsequent chain of suspensions in the violins may suggest the discord of the sinful world or the struggle to resist sin (see example 5.1). The sensuality and intensity of expression – partly

Ex. 5.1. J. S. Bach, from 'Widerstehe doch der Sünde', BWV 54

24 Christoph Wolff, *Bach: Essays on His Life and Music* (Cambridge, MA, 1991), pp. 72–83.

achieved via the instrumental ritornello that recurs throughout the aria – is typical of cantatas written in the Neumeister mould.

Bach's other Weimar cantatas have a more extended sequence of movements, including chorales and choruses as well as arias and recitatives. *Komm, du süsse Todesstunde*, BWV 161 (*c.* 1715–16), starts with two arias, each followed by a recitative, and ends with a chorus and a chorale. It was written for the 16th Sunday after Trinity, when the Gospel reading recounts the raising of the boy of Nain from the dead (Luke 7:11–17). Franck interpreted this story as a parable of the new life promised in heaven, and his libretto expresses the believer's yearning to die. Much of it is written in the first person ('I wish to kiss my Saviour'), although there are also allusions to Biblical sentences used at funerals (Philippians 1.23) and to the Old Testament story of the honey that flowed from the dead lion (Judges 14.8, suggesting the sweetness of death). Bach's opening aria – scored for two recorders, alto and continuo – has an intimacy typical of the Weimar cantatas; the movement is dominated by a downward slurred figure, a wistful sigh of longing for death. Over this aria, however, Bach superimposes the melody of 'Herzlich thut mich verlangen' (played wordlessly on the organ); this chorale expresses a desire for death, reinforcing the message of Franck's poetry. Another strophe of the same chorale is used at the end of the cantata, sung to the words 'Der Leib zwar in der Erden/von Würmen wird verzehrt' (Though worms devour our flesh/ buried deep in the earth); here the tune is harmonised in four parts with a florid descant for recorders. Bach usually ended a cantata with a succinct harmonisation of a chorale for all performers, and in BWV 161 the return of the melody heard earlier gives a pleasing sense of closure.

Compared to his cantatas for Weimar, Bach's church music for Leipzig is on a more ambitious scale. It was written for churches that could accommodate up to 3,000 worshippers in a service.[25] Bach seems to have had larger forces at his disposal, although the exact numbers are unclear. (In 1730, Bach complained that his ensemble was of insufficient size and standard; there has been an extensive musicological debate about the size of his choir in Leipzig.[26]) Most of his Leipzig cantatas use a four-part chorus, and when he repeated his earlier cantatas in Leipzig, he sometimes augmented the scoring (as, for instance, in BWV 4, 21 and 161). Furthermore, Bach's Leipzig cantatas are often longer than his previous vocal works, notably in the opening choruses. Although on taking up the post Bach promised to 'arrange the [church] music that it shall

25 Tanya Kevorkian, 'The Reception of the Cantata During the Leipzig Church Services, 1700–1750', *Early Music*, 30 (2002), p. 27.

26 Summarized in Parrott, *The Essential Bach Choir*.

not last too long',[27] his first two cantatas (BWV 75 and 76) are in fourteen movements, half to be performed before the sermon and half after it.

As cantor in Leipzig, Bach was subject to conflicting demands from two factions on the town council. On the one hand there was pressure for church music in the latest secular idiom, to satisfy those citizens and visiting merchants who wanted to hear the same styles as at the opera or the coffee-house concerts. Indeed the council's original choice of cantor had been Telemann, who had made his name in Leipzig as a student by working at the opera and performing theatrical styles of music at the Neukirche. On the other hand, conservatives on the town council insisted that Bach sign the same undertaking made by Kuhnau in 1701, that the church music be 'of such a nature as not to make an operatic impression, but rather incite the listeners to devotion'.[28]

Bach was well aware of the pace of stylistic fashion, commenting in 1730 that 'the former style of music no longer seems to please our ears'.[29] Accordingly he included many up-to-date secular elements in his Leipzig church music, and several of his Leipzig cantatas are based on his secular compositions. In the spring of 1724 he reworked a series of secular cantatas originally written for the Cöthen court to create sacred cantatas such as BWV 66, 134, 173 and 184. In 1734 he adapted several homage cantatas written for the Saxon royal family to make the Christmas Oratorio (BWV 248). These parodies show the points of contact between secular and sacred styles. Both styles share celebratory choruses, often in a 3/8 dance metre (as with the opening movement of the Christmas Oratorio, derived from *Tönet ihr Pauken*, BWV 214); such festal movements typically include trumpets and drums, instruments reserved for the celebration of earthly rulers or of Christ the King. Another common element is the love duet, a favourite feature of opera. The third part of the Christmas Oratorio includes a duet that pleads for God's compassion: 'Tröstet uns und macht uns frei' (Console us and set us free). This is a re-working of a duet from the 'Hercules' Cantata, BWV 213, where Hercules and Virtue celebrate their erotic union by singing 'Küsse mich'/'Ich küsse dich' (Kiss me/I kiss you). Love duets on an operatic model also appear in Bach's sacred cantatas that are not parodies, usually to express the ecstatic union between Christ and the Soul (as in BWV 140 and 152).

Yet Bach's sacred parodies of secular cantatas also highlight the elements unique to his church music. Most obvious are the chorales, which Bach added when assembling the Christmas Oratorio or the sacred version of Cantata 66. The sacred versions of the Cöthen cantatas also tend to use a greater number of soloists (BWV 173 and 184 were duos in their secular incarnation, but in Leipzig

27 David and Mendel (eds.), *The New Bach Reader*, p. 105. 28 *Ibid.*, p. 105. 29 *Ibid.*, p. 149.

Bach re-distributed the parts for a quartet, presumably because more voices were available). Furthermore, many of the movements with secular origin tend to be in major keys or with a celebratory feel, whereas Bach's sacred cantatas include many movements in minor keys or with a bittersweet Affect.

Bach's sacred re-workings of secular compositions have aroused a long-running scholarly debate that is too extensive to explore here.[30] It is worth noting, though, the attitude of his contemporaries. Scheibel, a staunch supporter of theatrical styles in church, used parody to prove his point that 'religious and secular music have no distinctions as far as the movement of the affections is concerned'. He showed how opera arias by Telemann and Johann Gottfried Vogler could be adapted for church use by replacing the expressions of profane love with those of sacred love.[31] This would seem to be similar to Bach's use of love duets within his cantatas. Other writers, however, saw such parodies as infringing the distinction between sacred and secular styles. Johann Adolph Scheibe satirized a (doubtless fictional) musician who 'had a sheaf of opera arias stocked up from Italy, so whenever he needed a sacred aria for the Gloria, he made a parody out of a lovesick and voluptuous opera aria, and performed it with all devotion, just as if opera and church music were one and the same, and as if one could sigh just as voluptuously, tenderly and basely over the highest being as an insensible beauty'.[32]

Bach signalled that his Leipzig cantatas were fundamentally sacred works by incorporating two features unique to Lutheran traditions: the long opening choruses and the frequent chorales. Most of his Leipzig cantatas open with choruses of impressive length, often lasting more than one hundred bars. At first Bach used scriptural mottos for the choruses (for instance, Psalm 22:26 for BWV 75; Psalm 19:1, 3 for BWV 76); this was a traditional choice of text for choral movements. But rather than follow the old method of setting each line of text separately, he structured the choruses as a fugue or with a ritornello. From June 1724 he wrote chorale cantatas, where the opening and closing choruses set the first and last strophe of the chorale, and the intermediate recitatives and arias refer to the chorale's words or tune. In these pieces the opening chorus is typically a large-scale fantasia on the chorale melody, often with a ritornello that returns between each line of the chorale melody. In *Mit Fried und Freud*, BWV 125, the opening chorus sets Luther's version of the 'Nunc dimittis'. The movement is framed by a fourteen-bar ritornello, segments of which recur

30 See Hans-Joachim Schulze, 'The Parody Process in Bach's Music: An Old Problem Reconsidered', *Bach: The Quarterly Journal of the Riemenschneider Bach Institute*, 20 (1989), pp. 7–21.

31 Scheibel, *Zufällige Gedancken*, pp. 33–42.

32 Johann Adolph Scheibe, *Der Critische Musikus* (Leipzig, 1745), pp. 175–6; trans. in Schulze, 'The Parody Process in Bach's Music', p. 12.

between and during the lines of the chorale. In combining a ritornello structure with a chorale, the Leipzig chorale cantatas bear comparison with Bach's organ chorales known as the 'Eighteen' (discussed on pp. 164–5).

Bach's use of the chorale may have reflected his musical and religious convictions, but it was also a good way to ensure intelligibility to the large congregation in Leipzig. In 1728 Martin Fuhrmann suggested that it was better to perform chorale-based movements or straightforward motets before 'simple people', rather than Telemann's cantatas with unknown verse and long recitatives.[33] Indeed, there was a tradition in Leipzig of using chorales to make the concerted music comprehensible. In 1688–9 the then-Thomaskantor, Johann Schelle (1648–1701), made a cycle of chorale cantatas to complement weekly sermons by the pastor, Johann Benedikt Carpzov, that explicated a chorale to the congregation. Schelle performed his concerted setting of the hymn before the sermon, and the congregation sang the hymn after the sermon.[34] Bach's congregations were undoubtedly familiar with the chorales; the text booklets sold to worshippers included all the words of the arias and recitatives, but sometimes only the first line of the chorales.[35] It is uncertain, however, whether the congregation sang along with the chorales in the cantatas. Daniela Garbe suggests this was 'rather unlikely', because Bach often varied the chorales melodically or rhythmically, and chose pitches too high for most untrained singers.[36] On the other hand, Scheibel's account of a Passion performance and Hiller's account of Doles' figured chorales (both quoted below) describe congregations who joined in with the chorales in concerted music. Whatever was the case with Bach, his use of the chorale was a way to forge a link with the congregation, as well as to prove that his cantatas (despite all their modern features) were fundamentally Lutheran works.

Passion music

Musical settings of the Passion story were a particular flashpoint for disputes about theatrical church music. Traditionally Lutheran churches had recited the Biblical story of Christ's trial and crucifixion on Good Friday. The Passion story is inherently dramatic – with its scenes of anger and betrayal, and its narrative pushing inexorably to Jesus' death – and so it would seem suited to an

33 Martin Fuhrmann, *Gerechte Wag-Schal* (Altona, 1728), quoted in *Erdmann Neumeister: Wegbereiter der evangelischen Kirchenkantate*, p. 45.

34 Johann Schelle, *Six Chorale Cantatas*, ed. Mary S. Morris (Madison, WI, 1988).

35 Kevorkian, 'The Reception of the Cantata', p. 36.

36 Daniela Garbe, 'Gemeindegesang: iii', in *Musik in Geschichte und Gegenwart* (Kassel, 1995), vol. 3, col. 1180.

operatic presentation. Moreover, the use of free poetry and affecting arias could express the strong emotions aroused by the Passion. Yet churches were wary of theatrical treatments of this most solemn and sacred of stories, partly because of the ecclesiastical restrictions on non-liturgical poetry. Elaborate settings of the Passion aroused polarized opinions, as shown by two anecdotes from the time. Scheibel, an advocate of theatrical music in church, regarded a concerted Passion as a way to attract a large congregation:

> The people certainly would not have come to church so promptly and in such numbers because of the preacher but rather presumably because of the music. The libretto was simply the account of Christ's suffering from one of the Gospels, into which frequent chorales and also two or three arias were introduced. I marvelled how diligently people listened and how devoutly they sang along; it was the moving music that contributed the most to this, and even though the service lasted more than four hours, everyone stayed until it was over.[37]

By contrast, Christian Gerber, an opponent of elaborate church music, reported a hostile response:

> But gradually the Passion story, which had formerly been sung in simple plainchant, humbly and reverently, began to be sung with many kinds of instruments in the most elaborate fashion … When this Passion music was performed for the first time in one of our great cities with twelve violins [i.e. strings], many oboes, bassoons and other instruments, many people were shocked and didn't know what to make of it. In the pew of a noble family in church, many ministers and noble ladies were present and sang the first Passion hymn from their books with great devotion, but when this theatrical music commenced, all these people were filled with the greatest amazement, looked at one another, and said, 'May God preserve us, children. It's as if a person were at the opera or the theatre'. Everyone thoroughly disapproved of the music and registered justified complaints about it. But of course there were also such spirits as take pleasure in such vain aberrations, especially if they are of a sanguine nature and are given to voluptuousness.[38]

It is not known which performances Gerber and Scheibel describe, but their anecdotes symbolize the divided attitudes to operatic Passions in central Germany.

In Hamburg, although the city had the first public opera-house in Germany, theatrical Passion music was so contentious that eventually a local tradition developed of performing Passion oratorios outside church services. In 1704–5

37 Scheibel, *Zufällige Gedancken*, pp. 30–1; trans. adapted from Irwin, 'Random Thoughts About Church Music', p. 237.

38 Christian Gerber, *Geschichte der Kirchen-Ceremonien in Sachsen* (Leipzig, 1732), pp. 283–4; trans. adapted from David and Mendel (eds.), *The New Bach Reader*, pp. 326–7.

the clergy and city council objected to performances (both in and outside services) of Reinhard Keiser's *Der blutige und sterbende Jesus* (text by Christian Friedrich Hunold), complaining that it was too theatrical and that the entire text was free poetry, omitting the Evangelist's words. In 1710 the Hamburg senate vetoed a proposed church performance of Georg Bronner's Passion oratorio *Der gottliebenden Seelen Wallfahrt zum Kreuz und Grabe Christi*, on the grounds that it was unedifying and unduly theatrical.[39] Such opposition was a backdrop for the creation of the most popular Passion libretto in the first half of the century, *Der für die Sünde der Welt gemarterte und sterbende Jesus* by Barthold Heinrich Brockes (*Brockes-Passion*). Brockes did not quote the Biblical text at all, although he included an Evangelist who sings a paraphrased account synthesized from all four Gospels. In addition, his libretto includes many emotional responses to the story, as arias, ariosos or recitatives for Biblical characters (such as Peter and Judas) or allegorical figures (such as the Daughter of Zion and the Believer). Like the cantata libretti inspired by Neumeister, Brockes included extravagant metaphors to move the listener. In the aria 'Die Rosen krönen', for instance, the drops of blood on Jesus's brow are described as 'erbärmliche Rubinen' (pitiful rubies) and 'Schmuck der Seelen' (jewellery of the soul).

Brockes' libretto was immensely popular with composers, with settings by Keiser (1712), Telemann (1716), Handel (1716–17), Mattheson (1718), Johann Friedrich Fasch (1723) and Stölzel (1725), among others. Given that Brockes' libretto was a devotional poem rather than a liturgical text, it is unsurprising that many of these settings were performed outside worship, sometimes as concerts. In 1712 Keiser's setting was performed at Brockes' home, attended by 'the entire foreign nobility, all the ministers and residents with their ladies, but also the major part of the most eminent citizens of Hamburg, so that over 500 persons were present'.[40] In 1716 Telemann performed his setting in the cathedral in Frankfurt am Main, but in circumstances that resembled more a concert than a church service. Although 'members of the Reverend Ministry took their place at the altar fully robed', the performance was intended to raise funds for an orphanage; guards on the doors of the church admitted only those who had purchased a printed libretto.[41]

By contrast, Stölzel's 1725 setting of the *Brockes-Passion* was performed in a Good Friday service at the court chapel of Gotha; at a court there were fewer restrictions on liturgical music, and Stölzel's patron, Duke Friedrich II, was enthusiastic about the Passion poetry of Hunold and Brockes. Stölzel's setting

39 Howard E. Smither, *A History of the Oratorio Vol. 2: The Oratorio in the Baroque Era: Protestant Germany and England* (Chapel Hill, NC, 1977), pp. 107–10.
40 Quoted in *Ibid.*, p. 111
41 Mattheson, *Grundlage einer Ehrenpforte*, p. 365.

shows his operatic experience (he had written operas for several German courts, and had made a study-trip to Venice), notably in dramatic rage-arias such as 'Was Bähren-Tatzen' or 'Erweg, ergrimmte Nattern Bruth', as well as the serene melodiousness of 'Was Wunder!'. Yet Stölzel also included traditional Lutheran features, such as choruses in the motet style (that is, without independent instrumental parts); the use of the special sound of the viola da gamba as Jesus carries the cross in 'Es scheint, da den zerkerbten Rücken'; and the frequent chorales (three of which were added by Stölzel to Brockes' libretto).[42]

In Leipzig in Bach's time, concerted settings of the Passion were performed as part of the Vespers service on Good Friday. The first concerted setting in the Thomaskirche was that by Kuhnau in 1721; although this does not survive complete, it contrasted greatly with the simple chanted Passion by Johann Walter (*c.* 1530) that had formerly been sung. The Leipzig cantors seem to have been instructed to retain the Biblical account of the Passion, but they also included contemplative poetry and chorales to give a rich tapestry of texts. In Bach's St Matthew Passion, BWV 244 (first performed 1727), the Gospel text is complemented by many strophes from chorales and also by madrigalian verse by Christian Friedrich Henrici (pen-name 'Picander'). Picander's poetry uses metaphors as vivid as Brockes' (for example, 'Only bleed, you dear heart', 'My heart swims in tears', etc.), and he also borrows the allegorical figures of the Daughter of Zion and the Believer. The resultant mosaic of textual layers recalls the mingling of texts in vocal concertos or 'mixed' cantatas; it creates levels of allusion and commentary that immeasurably enrich the piece. For example, the first recitative of the piece – the Biblical passage where Jesus prophesizes his death – is immediately followed by the chorale 'Herzliebster Jesu', which expresses incredulity that Jesus should die ('Dearest Jesus, what have you done wrong/That so cruel a sentence has been pronounced?').

The different texts can also be layered simultaneously, as in the opening chorus. Here, Choir 1 represents the Daughters of Zion, singing 'Come ye daughters, help me lament, see the bridegroom' (a reference to a Biblical tradition of representing Christ's coming as a wedding, except that here Christ will be taken to his death). Choir 2 represents the believers, who (as in Brockes' libretto) interject questions about what is happening: 'Whom?', 'How?', 'What?', 'Where?'. Over all this, a group of trebles sing the German Agnus Dei ('O Lamm Gottes, unschuldig'); this sixteenth-century chorale was used at Communion services and refers to Christ's innocence at his crucifixion.

42 Axel Weidenfeld, 'Die Brockes-Passion von Gottfried Heinrich Stölzel', in Kathrin Eberl and Wolfgang Ruf (eds.), *Musikkonzepte – Konzepte der Musikwissenschaft* (Kassel, 2000), pp. 301–7.

Bach sets the two main choirs as a 12/8 pastorale in E minor, whereas the Agnus Dei is sung in G major. This dual tonality epitomizes the musical and textual richness of the movement.

The arias of the St Matthew Passion draw on operatic convention: Peter's sorrow at betraying Jesus is expressed in the lament of 'Erbarme dich'; Judas' anger at his own treachery is voiced in a rage-aria, 'Gebt mir meinen Jesum wieder'. Yet unlike the *Brockes-Passion*, these arias are not for named characters. 'Erbarme dich' is sung by an alto, not by the bass who sang Peter's words in the preceding recitative. The change of singer may have been required by the limitations of Bach's performers (the aria may have been too hard for the bass in choir 1); but it also universalizes the message of the arias, showing that the experience of repentance is not specific to a single singer.[43] Further dissipating any impression of opera are the large choruses that frame the Passion and the many chorales. As with Bach's cantatas, it is unclear if the congregation sang the chorales, but the familiar tunes would draw the laity into the musical action, as well as proclaiming the Lutheran lineage of Bach's setting.

The crisis of church music after 1750

The second half of the eighteenth century is one of the least-studied and least-understood periods of Lutheran church music. Superficially there are many similarities with the previous fifty years. Many church composers continued to focus their energy on the cantata, notably Gottfried August Homilius (1714–85), cantor at the Kreuzkirche in Dresden, whose output of almost 200 cantatas was widely copied and performed.[44] In 1758 Johann Ernst Bach remarked that 'there are few Protestant churches in Germany where Telemann's cantata cycles are not performed';[45] in 1767 Johann Adam Hiller noted that cantatas were performed in towns of all sizes and even in villages, although the standard of performance was often unsatisfactory.[46] Even Bach's cantatas continued to be performed in a few places with which the composer had close connections (Leipzig, Halle via W. F. Bach, Hamburg via C. P. E. Bach), contradicting the stereotype that his vocal music was completely forgotten after his death.[47]

43 John Butt, 'Bach's Vocal Scoring: What Can it Mean?', *Early Music*, 26 (1998), pp. 99–107.

44 Hans John, *Der Dresdner Kreuzkantor und Bach-Schüler Gottfried August Homilius* (Tutzing, 1980), p. 165.

45 Preface to Jakob Adlung, *Anleitung zu der musikalischen Gelahrtheit* (Erfurt, 1758), p. 15.

46 Johann Adam Hiller (ed.), *Wöchentliche Nachrichten und Anmerkungen die Musik betreffend*, 1 (Leipzig, 1767), p. 395.

47 Peter Wollny, 'Wilhelm Friedemann Bach's Halle Performances of Cantatas by his Father', in Daniel Melamed (ed.). *Bach Studies 2* (Cambridge, 1995), pp. 202–28; Andreas Glöckner, 'Bach-Aufführungen unter Johann Friedrich Doles', *Händel-Jahrbuch*, 47 (2001), pp. 239–50.

Yet it was a period when church music was weakened institutionally and when the styles of church music were fiercely debated. Underlying this crisis were the gradual changes in society and religion that today are labelled as the Enlightenment. Religious beliefs and public worship mutated in ways that are hard to summarize; but the growing emphasis on rationality led to a conviction that church services should be simplified and intelligible to all. Increasingly, the service focused on a strong and moving sermon, with less emphasis on the liturgy.[48] Writers of the 1780s discussed liturgical reforms, with many opposing the ceremonies and formulae that Lutheranism had inherited from Catholicism.[49] From 1785 in Leipzig, the new Church Superintendent Johann Georg Rosenmüller introduced a variety of liturgical simplifications: the service was shortened, Latin chants and prayers were phased out and by 1810 the scriptural readings no longer needed to be taken from the lectionary.[50] Hence the calendar of prescribed readings lost the controlling importance that it had in the first half of the century; as will be seen below, this reduced emphasis on the lectionary was evident in church music, with a cantor such as Hiller using extracts from oratorios rather than pieces related to the scripture for each Sunday.

The changing religious sentiments of the period are particularly evident in sacred poetry. Whereas the cantata texts of the first half of the century emphasize God's power to terrify mortals – the believer is portrayed as a ship tossed by the storm, or as a pus-filled wound – there increasingly appeared a mood of equanimity in sacred poetry. In 1727, Picander's libretto for Bach's St Matthew Passion emphasized the believer's anguish at Christ's suffering, and the bittersweet redemption achieved via Christ's death. About fifty years later, Ernst August Buschmann's libretto for Homilius' Passion cantata *Ein Lämmlein geht und trägt die Schuld* struck a much more self-assured note:

Nun sterb ich Sünder nicht	Now I, a sinner, will not die
Der Vater will verzeihn ...	The Father will grant pardon ...
Mein ganzes Herz freut sich	My whole heart rejoices
Ich soll den Tod nicht sehn!	I shall not see death!

Homilius set these lines to an aria in A major marked 'Fröhlich' (Cheerful), which opens with confident two-bar phrases and then breaks into jubilant melismas.

The desire for intelligible, rational poetry also extended to the chorale repertory. For much of the eighteenth century, many towns used relatively

48 Hope, *German and Scandinavian Protestantism 1700–1918*, pp. 285–8, 296–8, 355.

49 Herl, *Worship Wars in Early Lutheranism*, pp. 127–9.

50 Günther Stiller, *Johann Sebastian Bach and Liturgical Life in Leipzig* (St Louis, MO, 1984), pp. 158–63.

old hymnals (in Hamburg, an edition of 1700); but from 1780 a wave of new hymnals appeared (in Prussia in 1780, in Hamburg in 1787–8 and in Leipzig in 1793). Generally these collections make many changes to the traditional texts; in the Hamburg hymnal, the alterations are so substantial that the names of the authors can no longer be indicated.[51] Hiller's 1793 hymnal for Leipzig reflects the liturgical simplifications of Superintendent Rosenmüller, in that it abandons the old ordering of chorales according to the church year and instead groups them by line-length.

Enlightenment ideals also undermined the place of music in the schools that had formerly supplied the choirs for town churches. Musical training was increasingly seen as an unnecessary burden in the curriculum. Such arguments had already been rehearsed in the late 1730s between J. S. Bach and the rector of the Thomasschule, Johann August Ernesti. The two men came to loggerheads over the question of who appointed the prefects who acted as Bach's musical assistants;[52] but their clash stemmed from a deeper tension about the place of music in education. Educational reformers such as Ernesti wanted to revise the curriculum, reducing the role of music to make space for such subjects as physics, physiology and French. The reformers also saw the traditional activity of singing in the streets and at funerals as demeaning, tantamount to beggary. Reportedly when Ernesti encountered a pupil practising an instrument, he exclaimed: 'What? You want to be a beer-fiddler too?'[53] In this climate it was unsurprising that cantors lost social status, with their name being regarded as an insult by 1805.[54] Eventually many towns lost their choirs and cantors. In Lüneburg, choral singing was abolished from the Michaelisschule in 1789 and from the Johannisschule in 1796. Choral music in church ceased after the deaths of the Michaeliskantor (1792) and the Johanniskantor (1813).[55] In Flensburg, the cantorate was dissolved in 1797, and church music became the responsibility of the municipal instrumentalists and organist.[56]

Even where cantorates survived, they were increasingly marginalized in an era when musical life centred on concerts and chamber music. In 1768 C.P.E. Bach succeeded Telemann as cantor of the Johanneum in Hamburg and director of music in the city's main churches. Standards of performance were low: in 1772 Charles Burney heard 'some very good music' by C. P. E. Bach,

51 Ulrich Leisinger, 'C. P. E. Bach and C. C. Sturm: Sacred Song, Public Church Service, and Private Devotion', in Annette Richards (ed.), *C. P. E. Bach Studies* (Cambridge, 2006), p. 139.

52 David and Mendel (eds.), *The New Bach Reader*, pp. 172–85, 189–96. 53 *Ibid.*, p. 172.

54 Georg Christian Friedrich Schlimbach, 'Ideen und Vorschläge zur Verbesserung des Kirchenmusikwesens', *Berlinische musikalische Zeitung*, 1 (1805), p. 272n.

55 Horst Walter, *Musikgeschichte der Stadt Lüneburg* (Tutzing, 1967), p. 84.

56 Hans Peter Detlefsen, *Musikgeschichte der Stadt Flensburg bis zum Jahre 1850* (Kassel, 1961), pp. 53–4.

'very ill performed, and to a congregation wholly inattentive ... There is a fluctuation in the arts of every city and country where they are cultivated, and this is not a bright period for music at Hamburg.'[57] Yet C. P. E. Bach did not seek to reform the Hamburg institutions for church music; rather, he accepted the weaknesses of the existing system and instead channelled his energy into secular enterprises such as running concert series and publishing his music by subscription. Whereas Telemann had composed two new cantatas each Sunday in Hamburg, C. P. E. Bach reserved his own compositions for high feast days (Christmas, Easter, Pentecost, Michaelmas). Otherwise he performed pieces by other composers and as a consequence was criticized by the church authorities for conducting his 'office by commission'.[58] C. P. E. Bach may have been forced into this route by his relatively slow pace as a composer, for he lacked the fluency of his father or of Telemann. But it also showed that his compositional priorities lay outside the liturgy. Of his sacred vocal pieces, several can be performed outside services. In his oratorio *Die Israeliten in der Wüste* (published 1775) he explained that the piece 'can be performed not for just one kind of ceremony, but at all times, within and without the church'.[59] His setting of the Sanctus, *Heilig* (*c.* 1776) was performed at Michaelmas services in Hamburg, but it also appeared in concerts, and Bach may have intended its striking choral effects as a compositional legacy ('so that I may not so soon be forgotten in the future').[60]

New institutions were developing for the performance of sacred vocal music outside church. We have already seen how settings of the *Brockes-Passion* were performed outside church services in Hamburg and Frankfurt, and similar extra-liturgical outlets for sacred music developed in other cities. Between 1749 and 1756 *concerts spirituels* were held in Leipzig's Inn zu den drei Schwanen during Lent. Many of the programmes included Italianate oratorios by Johann Adolf Hasse, originally performed in nearby Dresden a few years earlier; the charm of Hasse's melodies doubtless appealed to Leipzigers, but his pieces could not be performed in the town's churches on account of their Catholicism.[61] Concerts of sacred music were also held in Berlin (where Johann Friedrich Reichardt began *concerts spirituels* in 1783), Frankfurt am Main, Magdeburg and Schwerin. With the decline of the school choirs that had

57 Charles Burney, *The Present State of Music in Germany, the Netherlands and United Provinces*, 2nd edn. (London, 1775), 2 vols., vol. 2, p. 251.

58 Stephen L. Clark (trans. and ed.), *The Letters of C. P. E. Bach* (Oxford, 1997), p. 22.

59 Quoted by Howard E. Smither, *A History of the Oratorio Vol. 3: The Oratorio in the Classical Era* (Chapel Hill, NC, 1987), p. 348.

60 Paul Corneilson, 'Zur Entstehungs- und Aufführungsgeschichte von Carl Philipp Emanuel Bachs *Heilig*', *Bach-Jahrbuch*, 92 (2006), pp. 273–89; Clark, *The Letters of C. P. E. Bach*, p. 124.

61 Arnold Schering, *Johann Sebastian Bach und das Musikleben Leipzigs im 18. Jahrhundert (Musikgeschichte Leipzigs: iii)* (Leipzig, 1941), pp. 268–9.

once supplied church music, these concerts sometimes featured newly founded choral societies. In Berlin in 1791, Carl Friedrich Christian Fasch established the Sing-Akademie to train vocalists and maintain standards of choral singing. Sacred music was prominent in its repertory, including a performance of Bach's motet *Komm, Jesu, komm* (BWV 229) in 1794.

Alongside these changes to the religious and institutional foundations of church music, there was also a crisis in the styles of church music. A fierce debate developed about the purpose and nature of ecclesiastical music, conducted in such periodicals as Hiller's *Wöchentliche Nachrichten und Anmerkungen die Musik betreffend* and Reichardt's *Musikalisches Kunstmagazin*. Most writers agreed that church music should be intelligible to all members of the congregation, but they disagreed whether this intelligibility was best achieved via simple songs or operatic formulae. Increasingly writers spoke of a 'true church music', as if the increased strength of secular musical life made church musicians seek exclusively ecclesiastical styles.[62]

In the late 1760s Hiller's *Wöchentliche Nachrichten* ran a campaign against the older style of church cantata. It complained about the madrigalian texts, criticizing 'the arid and frosty Neumeister style of poetry' (presumably a reference to the elaborate metaphors in cantata libretti).[63] It also criticised incompetent and insensitive performers, such as 'the singer who, from immature pride in his art, disturbs our devotion with endless runs, trills, cadenzas and suchlike'.[64] Indeed, 'in most places the cantatas do little or nothing to awake devotion, nor to adorn the service, but arouse the most disagreeable emotions of boredom and disgust, if not utter annoyance'.[65] Instead of the cantata, Hiller's journal suggested that small churches use 'odes' – strophic songs for solo voice and continuo such as the *Lieder zum unschuldigen Vergnügen* (1757) by Johann Heinrich Hesse (a cantor and organist in Eutin) and the 50 *Psalmen, geistlichen Oden und Lieder* (1760) by Johann Friedrich Gräfe (an amateur poet, postal official and court secretary in Brunswick).[66] These modest pieces were suitable for domestic use, epitomizing the new trend for simplicity.

62 On these debates, see Feder, 'Decline and Restoration' and Jürgen Heidrich, *Protestantische Kirchenmusikanschauung in der zweiten Hälfte des 18. Jahrhunderts: Studien zur Ideengeschichte 'wahrer' Kirchenmusik* (Göttingen, 2001).

63 *Wöchentliche Nachrichten*, 3 (1768), pp. 51–2.

64 'der Sänger, durch einen unzeitigen Stolz seine Kunst zu zeigen, mit ewigen Läufern, Trillern, Cadenzen, und dergleichen Dingen, unsere Andacht wegscheuchte …' *Wöchentliche Nachrichten*, 1 (Leipzig, 1767), p. 395.

65 'sie an den meisten Orten wenig und gar nichts, weder zur Erweckung der Andacht, noch zur Zierde des Gottesdienstes beytragen, sondern gar oft die widerwärtigsten Empfindungen der langen Weile, des Ekels, wo nicht des Aergernisses erregen.' *Wöchentliche Nachrichten*, 4 (Leipzig, 1769), p. 134.

66 *Wöchentliche Nachrichten*, 1 (Leipzig, 1766), pp. 195–7, 1 (1767), p. 397; 4 (1769), p. 134.

Hiller and Doles also advocated using chorales to engage the full attention of congregations. In the mid-1740s Doles, working as cantor at Freiberg, observed that the cantata bored the congregation, who read during it or left the service altogether. His solution was to work chorales into the cantatas; it is likely that the chorale cantatas of Bach and Schelle (mentioned above) were a similar attempt to hold the congregation's attention with familiar melodies. In 1756 Doles became Thomaskantor in Leipzig, where he again encountered a jaded congregation. His initial solution was to perform chorales during the communion on feast-days, with a forceful accompaniment of cornetts, slide-trumpets, trombones, oboes, bassoons and horns; he reported 'the special attentiveness' that this scoring aroused on the faces of the congregation.[67]

In 1769 Hiller described a 'new kind of church music' created by Doles at Leipzig – what would become known as the 'figured chorale':

> The chorale is sung in four parts by the choir, reinforced by an ensemble of trombones. The rest of the orchestra plays ritornellos at the start and end, and also interludes that make the harmonic transition from one line to another … Our soul rejoiced most deeply when we heard the whole congregation joining in with the chorale; we have never ever heard such a moving church music as this.[68]

Such figured chorales comprised a significant proportion of Doles' church compositions, to judge from the list of works assembled by Helmut Banning in 1939. Many of these pieces are now lost, making it hard for us to assess Doles' innovation. Nonetheless, the simplicity and communicative power of the chorale were similarly utilized in cantatas by other composers such as Daniel Gottlob Türk.[69]

In 1790, the year after he resigned as Thomaskantor, Doles reiterated his desire for church music that was intelligible to all members of the congregation. Writing in the preface to his valedictory cantata *Ich komme vor dein Angesicht*, he declared that the purpose of 'true church music' is to stir the

67 Hans-Joachim Schulze, 'Über den Endzweck der Kirchenmusik in Leipzig nach 1750', *Bach-Jahrbuch*, 81 (1995), pp. 191–3.

68 'Der Choral wird von dem Chore nach der gewöhnlichen Melodie vierstimmig gesungen, und zur Verstärkung desselben nimmt der Componist ein Chor Posaunen zu Hülfe. Das übrige Orchestre spielt außer dem Anfangs- und Schlußritornelle, zwischen jeder Zeile einige aus jenem hergenommene Tacte, um die harmonischen Uebergänge von einer Zeile zur andern zu machen … Wir haben uns in dem Innersten der Seele gefreut, da wir die ganze Gemeine in den Gesang einstimmen hörten, und nie, ja nie hat uns eine Kirchenmusik so sehr gerührt, als diese.' *Wöchentliche Nachrichten*, 4 (Leipzig, 1769), p. 134.

69 Helmut Banning, *Johann Friedrich Doles: Leben und Werk* (Leipzig, 1939). Banning's works-list (the basis of that given in *The New Grove Dictionary of Music and Musicians, Revised Edition*) erroneously includes sixty-eight cantatas from Telemann's 1745 cycle *Musikalisches Lob Gottes in der Gemeinde des Herrn*. See also Franziska Seils, 'Die Choralkantaten Daniel Gottlob Türks im Spiegel ihrer Gattungsgeschichte', in Kathrin Eberl, Konstanze Musketa and Wolfgang Ruf (eds.), *Daniel Gottlob Türk: Theoretiker, Komponist, Pädagoge und Musiker* (Halle, 2002), pp. 157–64.

heart. 'Church music must express and arouse love, trust and joyful thankfulness in God, compassion and gentle goodwill for other men, joy at our blessings, deep sadness at our moral transgressions ... enthusiastic delight at the joyful prospect of heavenly life, etc.'[70] So far, this might seem similar to Mattheson's or Scheibel's position on sacred music, but Doles went on to argue that for church music to have such emotional power, it must be comprehensible to the diversity of listeners in a congregation:

> Hence it is clear that those church pieces which contain only artful fugues, or which are fugal and nervously devised following the rules of double counterpoint, should not belong in church ... It is far from my intention, as a pupil of the late Sebastian Bach and having composed much in the fugal style myself, to decry the value of this higher art of composing, still less to dispense with it. No, I merely disapprove of its untimely application. If I had a collection of learned composers as listeners, I would happily let them hear deeply thought-out fugues on the organ, but not for church music for the public honour of God and with the intention of stirring unlearned listeners.[71]

Instead Doles recommended that church music possess 'the easy intelligibility of rhythms, the simple and strong harmonies, and the heart-melting melodies that one often finds in recent operas'.[72] Doles did not name any composers as models, but it is significant that he dedicated the cantata to Wolfgang Amadeus Mozart and to the Dresden Kapellmeister Johann Gottlieb Naumann (1741–1801), both of whom wrote opera buffa as well as opera seria.

Doles' cantata *Ich komme vor dein Angesicht* satisfies some of his demands for intelligibility. The first chorus may be an example of his 'heart-melting melodies': a tune mainly moving by step, supported by 'simple and strong harmonies' of tonic and dominant chords. The parallel thirds and sixths are particularly characteristic of his writing (see example 5.2). A similar emphasis on melodic clarity can be found in Homilius' arias, where the theme is usually carried in the first violins (and when the voice enters, its melody is often

70 'Die Kirchenmusik muß Liebe, Vertrauen, freudige Dankbarkeit gegen Gott, Mitleid, sanftes Wohlwollen gegen andere Menschen, Freude über ihre Glückseligkeit, tiefe Traurigkeit über unsere moralischen Vergehungen ... begeisterndes Entzücken über die frohen Aussichten in die Ewigkeit &c. ausdrücken, und erwecken.' Johann Friedrich Doles, *Kantate über das Lied des seel. Gellert: Ich komme vor dein Angesicht* (Leipzig, 1790), Preface.

71 'Hieraus ist klar, daß diejenigen Kirchenmusiken, welche nur künstliche Fugen enthalten, oder fugenartig und zu ängstlich nach den strengen Regeln und Künsteleien des doppelten Kontrapunkts ausgearbeitet sind, nicht in die Kirche gehören ... Fern sey es von mir, der ich ein Schüler des sel. Sebastian Bachs bin, und selbst viel im Fugenstil componirt habe, die höhere Tonsetzkunst herabzuwürdigen, oder wohl gar zu verwerfen: Nein! Ich mißbillige nur deren unschickliche Anwendung. Wenn ich eine Versammlung gelehrter Tonkünstler zu Zuhörern habe, so würde ich mich freilich gern mit einer tief durchdachten Fuge auf der Orgel &c. hören lassen, aber nicht so in der Kirchenmusik bei der öffentlichen Gottesverehrung, und in der Absicht ungelehrte Zuhörer zu rühren.' *Ibid.*

72 'die leichte Faßlichkeit und Folge der Rhythmen, die simple und kräftige Harmonie, und die herzschmelzende Melodie, die man oft, besonders in den neuern Opern antrifft'. *Ibid.*

Ex. 5.2. Johann Friedrich Doles, from 'Ich komme vor dein Angesicht'

doubled by instruments). Other aspects of Doles' cantata, however, are more traditional. Although the text by Gellert is a simple ode in thirteen strophes, Doles does not respect this form, instead transforming it into a cantata in the early-eighteenth-century mould with arias, recitatives and choruses. His use of recitatives is a link with opera and defies Hiller's dislike of this type of word-setting. The cantata, in a nod to Leipzig tradition, concludes with a chorale where Gellert's words are set to a melody loosely based on 'Nun lob, mein Seel, den Herren'. With its mix of Lutheran and operatic elements, the cantata is less radical than Doles' manifesto suggests.

Whereas Doles advocated the use of operatic styles for intelligibility, other writers promoted a simple choral style to give dignity and purity to church music. Here we may detect a proto-Romantic view of church music as isolated from the world of the profane. Johann Friedrich Reichhardt (1752–1814), Kapellmeister of the royal Berlin opera and a prolific music journalist, pioneered just such an attitude in his *Musikalisches Kunstmagazin*. In a 1782 article on church music, he condemned its 'desecration' and 'degradation' with 'silly trifles and cheap sentimentality'. 'That art so noble, so sublime, so divine, which surely has the power to improve and ennoble mankind, is now reduced to sensational thrills and fashionable frivolities!'[73] This appears to be a reference to secular elements, perhaps the operatic tunes that Doles recommended for church. Instead Reichardt printed a selection of pieces that he believed to have 'the true, noble character of church music'. These included choral compositions by Leonardo Leo and Johann Abraham Peter Schulz, a duet by Kirnberger, and Handel's aria 'He shall feed his flock' (with German words) from *Messiah*. Commenting on this selection, Reichardt explained that 'of all our usual forms, the chorus is best suited to the church'; recitative, by contrast,

73 'Sie, die edle, die erhabene, die göttliche Kunst, die mit ihrer Allgewalt so sicher den Menschen bessern und veredeln kann, sie soll sich ist begnügen mit Nervenküßel und Geschmackverschönerung!' *Musikalisches Kunstmagazin*, 1 (1782), p. 179.

is 'too empty and characterless', while many arias are 'too diverting, charming and pleasing to allow devout feelings'.[74] He permitted the Kirnberger duet and the Handel aria because they are 'closer to the simple song than the voluptuous aria'; indeed the Handel aria, he claimed, resembled a choral piece on account of its four-part accompaniment.

Another piece that exemplified Reichardt's ideal of church music was C. P. E. Bach's *Heilig*. In a review of the *Heilig* he again asserted that 'neither arias nor recitatives belong in the church ... Only choruses seem appropriate, for they alone instil in the assembled people the devotion and reverence that should fill the heart in God's temple.'[75] Reichardt felt that his ideals were fulfilled entirely by Bach's piece, which consists of antiphony between an angelic choir and an earthly choir, with both choruses uniting for a final fugue. He expressly excluded from his praise the opening Ariette for solo alto and strings; this introductory movement is in the light and melodious style of Doles, contrasting greatly with the grandeur of the subsequent choruses. Interestingly, Reichardt's advice for an effective performance – recommending at least fifty singers for each of the two choirs – implied concert rather than church performance, for such forces exceeded those of the few remaining church choirs.[76]

In 1783 and 1790 Reichardt travelled to Italy, and thereafter his ideal of church music centred on Palestrina. In 1791 he praised Palestrina as 'the greatest exponent known to us of the noble, solemn church style'. He perceived Palestrina's music in harmonic rather than contrapuntal terms, as 'emphatic and often bold progressions of mainly consonant chords, whose resolute effect is not modified or weakened by melodic ornaments or rhythmic diversity'.[77] Indeed, he detected a similar 'bold sequence of consonant chords' in the juxtaposition of angelic and earthly choirs in C. P. E. Bach's *Heilig*.[78] Reichardt's admiration of Palestrina and other Roman composers influenced his Berlin colleague, Fasch, who increasingly composed in a contrapuntal style after Reichardt showed him a mass by Orazio Benevoli in 1783. Reichardt's

74 'das Chor sich vorzüglich vor allen unseren übrigen Formen für die Kirche schicke. Das Rezitativ ist zu leer, zu charakterlos ... die Arie ist ... zu zerstreuend, zu reizend, zu vergnügend, als daß bey ihr Andachtgefühle statt haben könnte.' *Ibid.*, p. 193.

75 'Eigentlich schicken sich weder Arien noch Recitative in die Kirche... Die Chöre scheinen sich allein für die Kirche zu schicken, sie allein flößen dem versammelten Volke die Andacht und Ehrfurcht ein, die das Herz im Tempel Gottes erfüllen sollen.' *Musikalisches Kunstmagazin*, 1 (1782), pp. 84–5.

76 For more comments on Bach's *Heilig*, see Heidrich, *Protestantische Kirchenmusikanschauung*, pp. 112–15.

77 'der nachdrücklichen und oft kühnen Folge von größtentheils konsonirenden Accorden besteht, deren ganz bestimmter Eindruck weder durch melodische Verzierungen noch durch rhythmische Mannigfaltigkeit modificirt oder geschwächt wurde'. See *Musikalisches Kunstmagazin*, 2 (1791), p. 55.

78 *Musikalisches Kunstmagazin*, 2 (1791), p. 57.

attitudes also anticipated the revival of Palestrina's music that would occur in Germany during the nineteenth century.[79]

Reichardt's preference for simple choral music was echoed by Johann Nicolaus Forkel (1749–1818) in his *Allgemeine Geschichte der Musik* (1801). But whereas Reichardt discussed repertory, Forkel wanted to improve the institutions of church music (particularly the school choirs) and make the music intelligible to a congregation. He, too, advised against the use of recitative and aria, less because of their secular connotations but rather because the average singer could not perform these movements in an edifying or tasteful manner. Moreover, recitative and aria might be appreciated by connoisseurs, but would not go down so well with the less-educated members of a congregation. Instead Forkel recommended choral settings of well-known Biblical texts – in other words, motets (a genre discussed below): 'If the common man understands the words, he thinks he understands the music as well ... Public devotion loses nothing when instead of the aria a pure, four-voiced, solemn and reverent chorale is sung by a choir.'[80] Forkel's concern for a pragmatic church repertory led him to emphasize simplicity in a similar way to other musicians and writers of the period.

A final example of a manifesto for church music at the end of the eighteenth century is supplied by Johann Adam Hiller. We have already encountered Hiller's views on church music from his journalistic days in the late 1760s on the *Wöchentliche Nachrichten*. Thirty years later, he succeeded Doles as Leipzig Thomaskantor; by this date, Leipzig was one of the few cities that still had an active cantorate. In 1789 Hiller issued his own statement on 'What is true church music?', with significant similarities to the views of Reichardt and Forkel.[81] He argued that church music should be appropriate – 'serious, solemn and suiting the moods with which one should appear before God in his temple' – and that it should 'behave with the noblest simplicity, avoiding all empty noise, all attempts to arouse admiration, and all immature pretensions to individual skill'. Like Reichardt and Forkel, Hiller recommended choruses and chorales as textures for church music, with occasional solos or arias for variety; recitative should be avoided. Indeed, during his time as Thomaskantor he made increasing use of motets for four-part chorus, a genre that served his demand for succinct pieces with comprehensible words.

79 James Garratt, *Palestrina and the German Romantic Imagination* (Cambridge, 2002).

80 'Wenn [der gemeine Mann] die Worte versteht, so glaubt er auch die Musik verstanden zu haben ... die öffentliche Erbauung verliere nichts, wenn statt ihrer ein recht rein vierstimmiger, feyerlicher und andächtiger Choral vom Musikchor gesungen wird'. Johann Nicolaus Forkel, *Allgemeine Geschichte der Musik* (Berlin, 1801), vol. 2, pp. 67–8.

81 Issued as the preface to his first set of texts of church music (1789); here I quote from the revised reprint in the *Berlinische musikalische Zeitung*, 2 (1806), pp. 189–92.

Despite Hiller's quest for 'noble simplicity' in church music, he thought it unnecessary to renounce all that is 'sensuous and new'. Church music could be cheerful if the occasion demanded, although it should not resemble comic sinfonias. Moreover, in his performances at Leipzig he often included movements from oratorios, which could be in an operatic style. Many of these extracts were by Handel – whose oratorios were increasingly performed in Germany, following their popularity in England – or by Hasse. In 1791 Hiller published a miscellany of movements from Hasse's oratorios and operas, newly supplied with sacred texts in German.[82] Hasse's originals had been written for Dresden in the 1740s, so their *galant* writing was fifty years old; yet they retained some of the melodious appeal that had doubtless charmed audiences when they were performed in the 1750s at the Leipzig *concerts spirituels*. Hiller's use of oratorio extracts in the services reflected two significant trends. First, it signalled the diminishing importance of the lectionary, as already seen in the reforms of Superintendent Rosenmüller. Indeed, Hiller wrote in his Hasse edition that the texts for church music did not need to refer to the Sunday Gospel reading, a complete change of approach from the cantatas of the first half of the century. Secondly, Hiller's preference for selections from oratorios recognized that many of the innovations in sacred music were now occurring in concerts rather than in worship.

The motet

The resurgence of the motet after decades of neglect was a sign of how church music had changed in the second half of the eighteenth century; the genre benefited from the renewed interest in choral singing without obbligato instruments. Previously, at the start of the century the motet represented an older or more provincial repertory. Until the 1790s the Leipzig cantors continued to perform Latin-texted motets from the sixteenth century (taken from Erhard Bodenschatz's anthology *Florilegium portense*) as introits to the morning service. This older music was valued by conservative members of the congregation and was suitable for the secondary choir of less experienced singers. German-texted motets were also used at small churches that did not have the instrumentalists or skilled singers necessary for cantatas. Often these were simple homophonic settings of Biblical words, sometimes with a chorale melody superimposed (as in *Fürchte dich nicht* by Johann Christoph Bach

82 *Meisterstücke des italiänischen Gesanges in Arien, Duetten und Chören mit deutschen geistlichen Texten*, ed. Johann Adam Hiller (Leipzig, 1791).

(1642–1703); further examples can be seen in the Gotthold ms.13661, formerly in the library of Königsberg University.[83]) Given the prestige of obbligato instruments in church music at the start of the eighteenth century, such pieces were often seen as lowly or unpolished. Niedt remarked: 'I leave the explanation of the motet to the Thuringian peasants, who retain such pieces from the days of Hammerschmidt (just as the farmers' daughters from Altenburg inherit their boots from their ancestors).'[84]

The marginal significance of the motet for most early-eighteenth-century composers is evident in Bach's output. The number of his authenticated motets is disputed – between five and eight pieces[85] – but in any case only a tiny proportion of his 200 surviving church cantatas. Moreover, Bach's motets are enigmatic and highly idiosyncratic pieces, indebted to the traditions of the genre but also exceeding its customary bounds. As might be expected, Bach's motets require no obbligato instruments apart from continuo, and their words are usually taken from the Bible, chorales and sacred songs. Also recalling the central German tradition are the double-choir textures (heard with particular clarity in the chordal interjections at the start of *Komm, Jesu, komm*, BWV 229) and the quotation of chorale melodies. In the closing section of *Fürchte dich nicht*, BWV 228, the chorale 'Herr, mein Hirt, Brunn aller Freuden' is sung by the trebles, while the remaining parts weave polyphony below; in the middle section of *Singet dem Herrn*, BWV 225, a four-part setting of the chorale 'Wie sich ein Vater erbarmet' alternates line-by-line with the other four parts singing a sacred aria.

Yet the scale of Bach's motets exceeds anything in the central German repertory: *Der Geist hilft*, BWV 226, is in four movements, lasting a total of 268 bars; *Singet dem Herrn* is in three movements (fast–slow–fast, like an Italian concerto). Moreover, the vocal writing is as virtuosic as in his cantatas and – despite the absence of obbligato instruments – often seems to mimic instrumental writing. Daniel Melamed has argued that the melismatic opening of *Der Geist hilft* resembles a vocal duet with continuo.[86] As for the exuberant melismas in *Singet dem Herrn*, Mozart remarked that the piece 'should have a whole orchestra added to it'.[87]

83 Modern edition, Max Seiffert (ed.), *Thüringische Motetten der ersten Hälfte des 18. Jahrhunderts*, Denkmäler Deutscher Tonkunst 49–50 (Leipzig, 1915).

84 Niedt, *Musicalische Handleitung III*, p. 34; trans. Pamela L. Poulin and Irmgard C. Taylor as *The Musical Guide*, p. 255. Andreas Hammerschmidt (1611/12–75) was a prolific composer of simple motets.

85 On questions of authenticity, see Daniel Melamed, *J. S. Bach and the German Motet* (Cambridge, 1995).

86 *Ibid.*, p. 71.

87 Mozart's comment on his score of *Singet dem Herrn*: Gesellschaft der Musikfreunde, Vienna, A169b (III 31685).

Despite their idiosyncratic style and technical difficulty, Bach's motets were performed regularly in Leipzig after his death.[88] This survival possibly reflected the inherent historicity of the motet repertory; after all, sixteenth-century motets from *Florilegium portense* were still being sung in Leipzig during these decades. But the continued use of Bach's motets also indicated the resurgence of the genre from the 1760s: increasingly it gained a significant place in the output of church composers. Whereas Bach had focused almost exclusively on the cantata, Doles wrote about thirty-five motets, Homilius wrote over sixty and the Magdeburg music director Johann Heinrich Rolle wrote about sixty-five. This new focus on the motet reflected the preference for choral writing expressed by writers such as Forkel and Reichardt. A further advantage of the motet was that it usually set Biblical texts, therefore avoiding the distaste felt towards the high poetic style of Neumeister. Indeed, Christian Friedrich Michaelis (a professor of aesthetics and metaphysics at Leipzig University, and known for his musical interests) declared in 1806 that

> the motets by Bach, Doles, Homilius, Hiller, Haydn, Rolle and others, sung without instruments, constitute a not insignificant part of church music ... Often these motets make a greater impression on the listener than the artful cantatas accompanied with instruments. On hearing a cantata the listener's feelings are easily distracted by the display of the individual performers, whereas in the motets all manifold diversity is beautifully and movingly united in human voices.[89]

The new status of the motet was evident in the six-volume anthology edited by Hiller, *Vierstimmige Motetten und Arien in Partitur, von verschiedenen Componisten* (Leipzig, 1776–91). Like most of Hiller's publications, it had a pedagogical purpose, being intended for the declining numbers of school choirs. It includes pieces by Doles, Hiller, Homilius, Christian Friedrich Penzel and Christian Gotthilf Tag. The final volume (1791), issued shortly after Hiller became Thomaskantor, indicates his intention to abandon the Latin eight-voice motets of the *Florilegium portense* (which by then was over 170 years old). 'Instead it is better to adorn the service with a German motet, although on high festivals I prefer to use a Latin hymn, reinforced with

88 Uwe Wolf, 'Zur Leipziger Aufführungstradition der Motetten Bachs im 18. Jahrhundert', *Bach-Jahrbuch*, 91 (2005), pp. 301–9.

89 'Die ohne Instrumente gesungenen Motetten, die von J. S. Bach, Doles, Homilius, Hiller, Haydn, Rolle u. a. machen nicht den unbedeutensten Theil der Kirchenmusik aus ... Sie haben dann nicht selten eine noch mächtigere Wirkung, als manche mit Instrumenten begleitete kunstreiche Cantaten, bei deren Anhören das Gemüth leichter zerstreut, und auf einzeln glänzende Partieen abgelenkt wird, als in den Motetten, wo alle Mannichfaltigkeit sich in der Menschenstimme so schön und rührend vereinigt.' Christian Friedrich Michaelis, 'Über den Charakter der Kirchenmusik', *Berlinische musikalische Zeitung*, 2 (1806), p. 140.

trombones.'[90] He thus echoed the move to German in the liturgical reforms of the period.

The motets of the late eighteenth century mix old and new musical features. Like Thuringian motets from a century earlier, they often combine a chorale with a Biblical text. Homilius' setting of Psalm 12, *Hilf Herr, die Heiligen haben abgenommen*, begs for God's help with plaintive sighs of a descending semitone; then, to reinforce the psalmist's message, the chorale melody 'Ach Gott, vom Himmel sieh darein und lass dich dess erbarmen' (O God, look down from heaven and have pity on us) is sung over a return of the opening. Doles favoured the more dramatic texture of a declamatory solo over a harmonised chorale. At the end of his motet *Wer bin ich?*, the chorale 'Wer nun den lieben Gott läßt walten' is sung in minims by *divisi* sopranos, alto and bass, while the tenor declaims the words 'Herr, ich bin zu gering aller Barmherzigkeit' (Lord, I am unworthy of the least of all the mercies – Genesis 32:10). As Doles observed in his 1790 manifesto on church music, using 'good and appropriate chorales' in a motet could win 'unusual approval' from listeners.[91]

Compared to the earlier repertory, the motets of the late eighteenth century tend to use a thinner texture of four voices (although some double-choir pieces by Doles and Homilius circulated in manuscript). Doles' motets often have solo–tutti markings, giving the soloists delicately ornamented lines that recall the lieder of the period. At their strongest, the composers of motets found a powerful expressivity within the discipline of choral writing. Hiller's motet on the death of Maria Antonia of Saxony, *Alles Fleisch ist wie Gras* (1780), sets a text from 1 Peter 1:24–5 that contrasts the transience of earthly life ('For all flesh is as grass') with the everlasting power of scripture ('The word of the Lord endureth for ever'). The piece opens in A minor with falling melodies illustrating the withering of the grass and flowers (see example 5.3); then a vigorous fugue in A major evokes the endurance of scripture, and the piece ends with a chorale. The use of multiple sections recalls Bach's motets, whereas the dramatic switch to the major mode is a technique of the later eighteenth century.

Although the motets of the late eighteenth century drew on Lutheran compositional traditions, their performance practice pointed to a new ideal of unaccompanied singing. In the first half of the century Bach performed his motets with continuo (and sometimes with instruments doubling the voices: instrumental parts survive for *Der Geist hilft*, BWV 226, with strings doubling choir 1 and woodwind doubling choir 2). In the second half of

90 'Besser ist es doch, den Gottesdienst mit einem deutschen Motett einzulauten, welches ich, an hohen Festen, lieber mit einem lateinischen Hymnus, und dazu geblasenen Posaunen thun möchte.' Johann Adam Hiller, *Vierstimmige lateinische und deutsche Chorgesänge* (Leipzig, 1791), Preface.

91 Doles, *Kantate über das Lied des seel. Gellert: Ich komme vor dein Angesicht*, Preface.

Ex. 5.3. Johann Adam Hiller, from 'Alles Fleisch ist wie Gras'

the eighteenth century such instrumental participation seems to have declined. To be sure, Hiller occasionally used trombones to reinforce his performances of motets; but the manuscript parts of Homilius' motets do not indicate the use of continuo.[92] The reduced use of instruments paralleled Reichardt's admiration of Palestrina: as he noted, unaccompanied choral singing was practised in the papal chapel and known as *alla Palestrina* after its most famous exponent.[93]

Organ music

The strand of church music that remains to be considered is organ music. The organist's role in church included playing continuo in vocal concertos and cantatas, and guiding the congregational chorales (by introducing them and, in some places, accompanying them). The organist's solo repertory divided into two categories: chorale-based works and free works (such as preludes and fugues). It is usually assumed that the chorale-based works were used in church, to introduce or frame congregational singing. It is harder to know where the free works were performed (possibilities include the trials of new organs, auditions of prospective organists, or concerts given by visiting

92 See Uwe Wolf, Preface, in Homilius, *Motetten* (Stuttgart, 2000).
93 *Musikalisches Kunstmagazin*, 2 (1791), p. 55.

virtuosi);[94] indeed, some organ music was played outside church, on chamber instruments.

Throughout the century, improvisation remained an important skill of organists. Niedt began his treatise on figured bass by satirizing a novice organist who (among other deficiencies) could not improvise.[95] Mattheson described auditions for organists in Hamburg that required improvisations upon a chorale, a fugal subject and a chaconne theme.[96] Given the importance of improvisation, it is likely that the surviving repertory of notated organ music is just the tip of the iceberg. George Stauffer observes that 'only thirty-three Bach free organ preludes have been handed down, a figure that represents an average of less than one work for each year of the composer's career. As an organist famous throughout Germany for his fruitful invention, Bach must have improvised countless other pieces.'[97] All the same, improvisations probably stood in close relationship to notated compositions. The 1725 Hamburg organ trials described by Mattheson required the candidates to show their skill in composition by submitting a notated version of their improvised fugue within two days. Türk commended Homilius' practice of devising a plan for his chorale preludes 'and apparently writing it down ... I prefer a good prelude prepared in advance to a mediocre one which is extemporized only during the performance'.[98]

Some organ pieces were written down to demonstrate a player's skill. In 1741 Homilius submitted five chorale settings, three for organ solo and two for organ plus obbligato horn, when applying for an organist post in Bautzen.[99] The most common reason to notate organ music was for use in teaching, to supply pupils with a basic repertory and to give specimens of improvisation and composition. Bach's *Orgelbüchlein* (BWV 599–644), his collection of condensed chorale harmonizations, outlines its didactic purpose on the title-page: 'a beginner at the organ is given instruction in developing a chorale in many diverse ways, and at the same time in acquiring facility in the study of the pedal.'[100] The pedagogical role of notated compositions is also evident in the typical pattern of transmission via pupils. Much of Bach's organ music survives

94 Peter Williams, *The Organ Music of J. S. Bach*, 3 (Cambridge, 1984), pp. 1–54; Siegbert Rampe, 'Abendmusik oder Gottesdienst? Zur Funktion norddeutscher Orgelkompositionen des 17. und frühen 18. Jahrhunderts', *Schütz-Jahrbuch*, 25 (2003), pp. 7–70, and 26 (2004), pp. 155–204.

95 Niedt, *Musicalische Handleitung I* (Hamburg, 1700), fol. 1–2 trans. as *The Musical Guide*, pp. 20–1.

96 Mattheson, *Grosse General-Bass-Schule oder exemplarische Organisten-Probe* (Hamburg, 1731), pp. 34–7.

97 George Stauffer, *The Organ Preludes of Johann Sebastian Bach* (Ann Arbor, MI, 1980), p. 173.

98 Daniel Gottlob Türk, *Von den wichtigsten Pflichten eines Organisten in Beytrag zur Verbesserung der musikalischen Liturgie* (Halle, 1787), p. 127, trans. Margot Ann Greenlimb Woolard as *Daniel Gottlob Türk on the Role of the Organist in Worship (1787)* (Lanham, MD, 2000), p. 65.

99 John, *Der Dresdner Kreuzkantor*, p. 15.

100 David and Mendel (eds.), *The New Bach Reader*, p. 80.

in copies by such pupils as Johann Caspar Vogler, Johann Christian Kittel and Johann Tobias Krebs.

In its compositional techniques, organ music has affinities with the keyboard genres discussed in chapter 16 of this volume. Here I merely relate organ music to two of the main concerns of church composers in the period, namely the legitimacy of secular elements and the importance of communicating a text or mood.

The traditional idiom of Lutheran organ music was bound closely to the unique qualities of the instrument. Because the organ gave such power to a single player, there was a strong improvisatory element, best seen in the fantastical flourishes (for single-line manuals or pedal solo) of Dieterich Buxtehude's praeludia. At the same time, the ability of the organ to sustain simultaneous independent lines made it an ideal medium for fugues and also for the combination of dissonances and suspensions (*durezze e ligature*) found in the middle section of Bach's *Pièce d'orgue*, BWV 572. Obligatory pedal writing was another characteristic of the Lutheran organ style: the pedal lines do not necessarily resemble continuo parts, instead having a zig-zag contour that can be easily played by alternate feet.

The idiom of organ music thus described stands at some distance from the styles of contemporary vocal or chamber music. Yet in the eighteenth century, organ music was increasingly infiltrated by aspects of the Italianate string concerto, French dance or *galant* aria. Early in the century it was common to transcribe Italian concertos for the organ. Mattheson described how Jan Jacob de Graaf, the blind organist at the Nieuwe Kerk in Amsterdam, played 'all the most recent Italian concertos and sonatas' by heart on the organ;[101] Johann Gottfried Walther transcribed concertos by Albinoni, Torelli and other Italian composers;[102] and Bach arranged concertos from Vivaldi's Op. 3, *L'estro armonico*, for organ as BWV 593 and 596. Much of the figuration in these concertos was new to the organ, such as the repeated-note bass-lines or the percussive quaver chords (indeed, the rapidly repeated notes are hard to play effectively on the organ).

Bach then deployed aspects of the concerto in his own compositions such as the Praeludium in G major, BWV 541. It opens, like the previous generation of organ pieces, with a long single-line flourish roaming across the keyboard compass, but rather than the whimsical freedom of a Buxtehude *passaggio*, this flourish has an insistent motor rhythm and a careful harmonic plan (the tonic is arpeggiated in every bar except bars 4 and 6, which arpeggiate the

101 Johann Mattheson, *Das beschützte Orchestre* (Hamburg, 1717), pp. 129–30.
102 Modern edn., Denkmäler Deutscher Tonkunst, 26–27, ed. Max Seiffert (Leipzig, 1906).

Ex. 5.4. J. S. Bach, from 'Schübler chorale', BWV 645

dominant). When all the parts enter in bar 12, it is like the tutti entering after a concertist's solo, and indeed this tutti has the features of a ritornello (including a clear opening motif, here stated in the pedals; sequential passages; and a drive towards the eventual cadence). In the rest of the piece, short versions of the solo *passaggio* alternate with the full texture, and Bach follows a clear tonal plan, with cadences in the dominant (bar 29), mediant (bar 46) and tonic (bar 79, after a long dominant pedal from bar 63). Bach thus achieves the same forward momentum as a Vivaldi concerto, partly through the exhilarating figuration, but also through the solo–tutti alternation and the use of a ritornello.[103]

The gradual secularization of musical culture in the middle of the eighteenth century could have left the organ stranded in an ecclesiastical backwater. Yet several organists followed the fashion for singable or *galant* melodies. In *c.* 1748–9 Bach's so-called 'Schübler chorales' were published (BWV 645–650), five of which are transcriptions of arias from his Leipzig cantatas. In most of the original versions, a chorale is sung against an obbligato instrumental melody with continuo. Transcribed for organ, this produces a transparent texture unlike any of Bach's other organ works: there is a sharp distinction between the unadorned chorale, the aria-like counter-melody and the cello-like bass line (example 5.4). Similar trio writing occurs in some of the settings in Georg Friedrich Kauffmann's *Harmonische Seelenlust* (1733–40) (for instance, his second setting of *Man lobt dich in der Stille*) and many of Homilius' organ chorales. Just as the Schübler transcriptions blur the boundary between organ and concerted music, both Homilius and Kauffmann experimented with incorporating a horn or oboe into some of their organ chorales.

Inevitably there was a long-running debate about whether secular traits such as *galant* melodies or French dances were suitable in church. Niedt asked organists to play 'very devoutly and not too merrily'.[104] In 1767 Hiller's

103 For further analyses, see Peter Williams, *The Organ Music of J. S. Bach*, 2nd edn. (Cambridge, 2003), pp. 81–5; Stauffer, *The Organ Preludes*, pp. 51–5.
104 Niedt, *Musicalische Handleitung III*, p. 45; trans. as *The Musical Guide*, p. 262.

Wöchentliche Nachrichten complained about organists who introduced hymns with dances such as minuets and polonaises.[105] In 1805 Johann Christian Kittel explained that his *Vierstimmige Choräle mit Vorspielen* were written in 'the true church style, without the adornment of theatrical or dance styles that today so often are clumsily used to disrupt devotion in church'.[106] On the other hand, Doles claimed in his *Singbare und leichte Choralvorspiele* (1794–7) to use an 'arietta-like style, not the strict, forced church style that most listeners cannot grasp, still fewer understand, and that moves nobody to devotion'.[107]

The belief that the organist should foster devotion through his playing was particularly relevant for chorale settings. Many of these were played before congregational singing, and thus might not only remind the congregation of the tune of the chorale, but also prepare them for its mood and text. In 1739 Scheibe outlined two main approaches when preluding upon a chorale. 'First, one can take the melody of the chorale as the basis, and treat this fugally, or link it in a free and lively way with a freely invented counter-melody that at first dominates, until eventually the chorale melody is heard. Secondly, one can prelude upon the chorale in such a way that the main melody is omitted, but instead one follows the content and words of the song, observing only in the invention of the prelude's main theme a passing similarity with the start of the chorale melody.'[108] In fact, the most successful chorale settings of the century combine elements of both approaches, using the chorale as a basis for counterpoint and also for evoking an appropriate mood. But because the words of the chorale are un-stated, the mood is often hard to describe, as is the case with many of J. S. Bach's organ chorales.

Bach's *Orgelbüchlein* (BWV 599–644) contains rich and condensed harmonizations of chorale tunes. Originally he intended the collection to contain 164 pieces for every occasion in the church year, but he never finished it. Most of the settings are short (between ten and twenty bars), with the chorale being stated a single time (usually in the upper part). The accompanying parts are

105 *Wöchentliche Nachrichten*, 1 (1767), p. 262.

106 'ohne von dem Schmucke theatralischer oder Tanzmusik, der heutiges Tages oft so unschicklich zur Störung der Andacht in den Kirchen angewandt wird, etwas zu entlehnen, im wahren Kirchenstyle gearbeitet sind.' Johann Christian Kittel, *Vierstimmige Choräle mit Vorspielen* (Altona, 1805), p. 2.

107 'Ariettenmäßig und nicht im strengen zwangartigen Kirchenstile geschrieben, den die meisten Zuhörer nicht fassen, viel vielweniger verstehen, und der nicht zur Andacht vorbereitet.' Quoted in Banning, *Johann Friedrich Doles: Leben und Werk*, p. 164.

108 'Erstlich kann man die Melodie des Chorals zum Grunde legen, und dieselbe entweder auf Fugenart ausführen, oder auch auf eine freye und lebhafte Art mit einem ungezwungenen melodischen Gegensatze verbinden, doch daß dieser letztere gleichsam am meisten herrschet, und sich die Choralmelodie nur dann und wann hören läßt. Zweytens kann man auch das Präludiren auf den Choral so einrichten, daß man zwar von der Hauptmelodie desselben abgeht, sich aber vornehmlich nach dem Inhalte und nach den Worten des Gesanges richtet, und nur in der Erfindung des Hauptsatzes eines solchen Vorspiels, eine mittelmäßige Aehnlichkeit mit dem Anfange der Melodie des Chorals beobachtet.' Scheibe, *Der Critische Musikus*, p. 424.

Ex. 5.5. J. S. Bach, from 'Nun komm der Heiden Heiland', BWV 599

contrapuntal, generally saturated by a short motive or rhythmic figure in quavers or semiquavers. Occasionally the motives have a clear interpretative significance – in *Durch Adams Fall ist ganz verderbt* (BWV 637), the downward leaps in the pedal suggest Adam's fall from grace. More typically, the motives create a mood that is hard to capture in words. In *Nun komm der Heiden Heiland* (BWV 599) a figure perhaps inspired by the *brisé* technique for rolling chords on a harpsichord gives a sense of rapt mystery, appropriate for an Advent chorale that speaks of the miraculous birth of Christ. Yet the lower neighbour notes in the figuration allow Bach to tonicize almost every chord, intensifying the harmonic richness and also accommodating an ancient modal tune to the tonal vocabulary of the early eighteenth century (example 5.5).

Whereas in the *Orgelbüchlein* Bach restricted himself to a single statement of the chorale tune, his larger settings transform the chorale into another genre altogether. Many of Bach's so-called 'Eighteen' chorales (BWV 651–668) sound like trios, fugues or ritornello movements, until the entry of the chorale adds another level of complexity. *Nun komm der Heiden Heiland* (BWV 661) starts as a vigorous fugue on a subject derived from the chorale; the cantus firmus then enters in minims and semibreves on the pedal. Subsequently the fugal theme is stated in keys determined by the tonal shape of the chorale (G minor, D minor, B flat major), giving an effect similar to a ritornello. Indeed, the piece is comparable with the opening choruses of Leipzig chorale cantatas where a ritornello structure is combined with a chorale.

In another of the 'Eighteen' chorales, *Schmücke dich, O liebe Seele* (BWV 654), a Communion hymn is transformed into a gentle sarabande. Perhaps from a sense of ecclesiastical propriety, Bach restrains the sarabande rhythms: although he stresses the second beat of each bar, his piece lacks the regular cadences of a simple dance. Further veiling the dance character are the many interrupted cadences; such harmonic evasiveness is a response to the chorale tune (which, published in 1649, embodies the tonal language of the previous century) and the cadential pull of its opening (g'–f'–e-flat'), which Bach repeatedly weakens by harmonizing with an interrupted cadence. *Schmücke dich* is not structured with ritornellos as such, but there is still a strong sense of return when Bach brings back the opening in bar 116.

As with sacred vocal music, organ music suffered an exodus of creative talent after 1750. C. P. E. Bach is a case in point: in 1772 he refused to play the organ in front of Charles Burney, claiming to have 'lost the use of the pedals, which are thought so essential throughout Germany, that no one can pass for a player worth hearing, who is unable to use them'.[109] Unlike his father, C. P. E. Bach wrote only a few pieces specifically for the organ, and there is little evidence that these were used in church.[110] Organ composition was also stifled by the demands for simplicity in church music. As Johann Abraham Peter Schulz declared, 'Anything on the organ that isn't a simple chorale becomes a musical hocus-pocus, which disturbs the holy state of devotion and diverts attention away from God and religion to the decadent affectations of the so-called organist'.[111] Despite such attitudes, the organ and church music of the late eighteenth century should not be discounted entirely. Much of the repertory is little known and thus hard to evaluate accurately until it is properly explored. Above all, the repertory shows how musicians responded to the debates about the nature and purpose of sacred music. As in the first half of the century, church music stood at the confluence of musical, religious and social currents; it is thus a unique document of how composers reacted to their immediate environment, and also to wider-ranging changes.

Select Bibliography

Adlung, Jakob. *Anleitung zu der musikalischen Gelahrtheit.* Erfurt, 1758

Banning, Helmut. *Johann Friedrich Doles: Leben und Werk.* Leipzig, 1939

Berg, Darrell M. 'C. P. E. Bach's Organ Sonatas: A Musical Offering for Princess Amalia?' *Journal of the American Musicological Society*, 51 (1998), pp. 477–519

Burney, Charles. *The Present State of Music in Germany, the Netherlands and United Provinces.*, 2nd edn., 2 vols., London, 1775

Butt, John. 'Bach's Vocal Scoring: What Can it Mean?', *Early Music*, 26 (1998), pp. 99–107

Clark, Stephen L. (ed. and trans). *The Letters of C. P. E. Bach.* Oxford, 1997

Corneilson, Paul. 'Zur Entstehungs- und Aufführungsgeschichte von Carl Philipp Emanuel Bachs *Heilig*'. *Bach-Jahrbuch*, 92 (2006), pp. 273–89

109 Burney, *The Present State of Music*, vol. 2, p. 275.

110 Darrell M. Berg, 'C. P. E. Bach's Organ Sonatas: A Musical Offering for Princess Amalia?', *Journal of the American Musicological Society*, 51 (1998), pp. 477–519.

111 'Alles, was nicht simpler Choral ist, wird auf der Orgel leicht zu musikalischer Gaukeley, die an heiliger Stätte die Andacht stört, und die Aufmerksamkeit von Gott und der Religion ab- und auf die luxuriösen Künsteleyen eines sogenannten Orgelspielers zieht.' Quoted in Gerhard Hahne, 'Johann Abraham Peter Schulz' "Gedanken über den Einfluß der Musik auf die Bildung eines Volkes"', in Carl Dahlhaus and Walter Wiora (eds.), *Musikerziehung in Schleswig-Holstein* (Kassel, 1965), p. 59.

David, Hans T. and Arthur Mendel (eds.). *The New Bach Reader*. Rev. Christoph Wolff, New York, 1998

Detlefsen, Hans Peter. *Musikgeschichte der Stadt Flensburg bis zum Jahre 1850*. Kassel, 1961

Feder, Georg. 'Decline and Restoration'. In Friedrich Blume (ed.), *Protestant Church Music*. London, 1975, pp. 319–404

Garbe, Daniela. 'Gemeindegesang: iii'. In *Musik in Geschichte und Gegenwart*, vol. 3. Kassel, 1995, cols. 1174–81

Garratt, James. *Palestrina and the German Romantic Imagination*. Cambridge, 2002

Gerber, Christian. *Geschichte der Kirchen-Ceremonien in Sachsen*. Leipzig, 1732

Glöckner, Andreas. 'Bach-Aufführungen unter Johann Friedrich Doles'. *Händel-Jahrbuch*, 47 (2001), pp. 239–50

Hahne, Gerhard. 'Johann Abraham Peter Schulz' "Gedanken über den Einfluß der Musik auf die Bildung eines Volkes"'. In Carl Dahlhaus and Walter Wiora (eds.), *Musikerziehung in Schleswig-Holstein*. Kassel, 1965, pp. 58–67

Heidrich, Jürgen. *Protestantische Kirchenmusikanschauung in der zweiten Hälfte des 18. Jahrhunderts: Studien zur Ideengeschichte 'wahrer' Kirchenmusik*. Göttingen, 2001

Herl, Joseph. *Worship Wars in Early Lutheranism: Choir, Congregation and Three Centuries of Conflict*. Oxford, 2004

Hiller, Johann Adam (ed.). *Wöchentliche Nachrichten und Anmerkungen die Musik betreffend*, 1–4. Leipzig, 1767–9

Hope, Nicholas. *German and Scandinavian Protestantism 1700–1918*. Oxford, 1995

Irwin, Joyce L. *Neither Voice Nor Heart Alone: German Lutheran Theology of Music in the Age of the Baroque*. New York, 1993

John, Hans. *Der Dresdner Kreuzkantor und Bach-Schüler Gottfried August Homilius*. Tutzing, 1980

Kevorkian, Tanya. 'The Reception of the Cantata During the Leipzig Church Services, 1700–1750'. *Early Music*, 30 (2002), pp. 27–45

Krummacher, Friedhelm. 'Kulmination und Verfall der protestantischen Kirchenmusik'. In Carl Dahlhaus (ed.), *Musik des 18. Jahrhunderts*. Laaber, 1985, pp. 108–21

Küster, Konrad. 'Meininger Kantatentexte um Johann Ludwig Bach'. *Bach-Jahrbuch*, 73 (1987), pp. 159–64

Leisinger, Ulrich. 'C. P. E. Bach and C. C. Sturm: Sacred Song, Public Church Service, and Private Devotion'. In Annette Richards (ed.), *C. P. E. Bach Studies*. Cambridge, 2006, pp. 116–48

Mattheson, Johann. *Das beschützte Orchestre*. Hamburg, 1717

Der musicalische Patriot. Hamburg, 1728

Grosse General-Bass-Schule oder exemplarische Organisten-Probe. Hamburg, 1731

Grundlage einer Ehren-Pforte. Hamburg, 1740. Reprint Kassel 1969

Melamed, Daniel. *J. S. Bach and the German Motet*. Cambridge, 1995

Michaelis, Christian Friedrich. 'Über den Charakter der Kirchenmusik'. *Berlinische musikalische Zeitung*, 2 (1806), pp. 137–40

Niedt, Friedrich Erhardt. *Musicalische Handleitung*. 3 vols., Hamburg, 1700–17. Trans. Pamela L. Poulin and Irmgard C. Taylor as *The Musical Guide*. Oxford, 1989

Parrott, Andrew. *The Essential Bach Choir*. Woodbridge and Rochester, NY, 2000

Rampe, Siegbert. 'Abendmusik oder Gottesdienst? Zur Funktion norddeutscher Orgelkompositionen des 17. und frühen 18. Jahrhunderts'. *Schütz-Jahrbuch*, 25 (2003), pp. 7–70 and 26 (2004), pp. 155–204

Reichardt, Johann Friedrich (ed.). *Musikalisches Kunstmagazin*, 1–2. Berlin, 1782–91

Richter, Bernhard F. 'Eine Abhandlung Joh. Kuhnaus'. *Monatshefte für Musikgeschichte*, 34 (1902), pp. 147–54. Trans. Ruben Weltsch as 'A Treatise on Liturgical Text Settings'. In Carol K. Baron (ed.), *Bach's Changing World: Voices in the Community*. Rochester, NY, 2006, pp. 219–26

Rucke, Henrike (ed.). *Erdmann Neumeister (1671–1756): Wegbereiter der evangelischen Kirchenkantate*. Rudolstadt, 2000

Scheibe, Johann Adolph. *Der Critische Musikus*. Leipzig, 1745

Scheibel, Gottfried Ephraim. *Zufällige Gedancken von der Kirchen-Music*. Frankfurt and Leipzig, 1721. Excerpts trans. Joyce L. Irwin as 'Random Thoughts About Church Music'. In Carol K. Baron (ed.), *Bach's Changing World: Voices in the Community*. Rochester, NY, 2006, pp. 227–49

Schering, Arnold. *Johann Sebastian Bach und das Musikleben Leipzigs im 18. Jahrhundert (Musikgeschichte Leipzigs: iii)*. Leipzig, 1941

Schlimbach, Georg Christian Friedrich. 'Ideen und Vorschläge zur Verbesserung des Kirchenmusikwesens'. *Berlinische musikalische Zeitung*, 1 (1805), pp. 271–3

Schulze, Hans-Joachim. 'The Parody Process in Bach's Music: An Old Problem Reconsidered'. *Bach: The Quarterly Journal of the Riemenschneider Bach Institute*, 20 (1989), pp. 7–21

'Über den Endzweck der Kirchenmusik in Leipzig nach 1750'. *Bach-Jahrbuch*, 81 (1995), pp. 191–3

Seils, Franziska. 'Die Choralkantaten Daniel Gottlob Türks im Spiegel ihrer Gattungsgeschichte'. In Kathrin Eberl, Konstanze Musketa and Wolfgang Ruf (eds.), *Daniel Gottlob Türk: Theoretiker, Komponist, Pädagoge und Musiker*. Halle, 2002, pp. 157–64

Smither, Howard E. *A History of the Oratorio Vol. 2: The Oratorio in the Baroque Era: Protestant Germany and England*. Chapel Hill, NC, 1977

A History of the Oratorio Vol. 3: The Oratorio in the Classical Era. Chapel Hill, NC, 1987

Stauffer, George. *The Organ Preludes of Johann Sebastian Bach*. Ann Arbor, MI, 1980

Stiller, Günther. *Johann Sebastian Bach and Liturgical Life in Leipzig*. St Louis, MO, 1984

Terry, Charles S. *Joh. Seb. Bach: Cantata Texts Sacred and Secular*. London, 1926

Türk, Daniel Gottlob. *Von den wichtigsten Pflichten eines Organisten in Beytrag zur Verbesserung der musikalischen Liturgie*. Halle, 1787. Trans. Margot Ann Greenlimb Woolard as *Daniel Gottlob Türk on the Role of the Organist in Worship (1787)*. Lanham, MD, 2000

Walter, Horst. *Musikgeschichte der Stadt Lüneburg*. Tutzing, 1967

Weidenfeld, Axel. 'Die Brockes-Passion von Gottfried Heinrich Stölzel'. In Kathrin Eberl and Wolfgang Ruf (eds.), *Musikkonzepte – Konzepte der Musikwissenschaft*. Kassel, 2000, pp. 301–7

Williams, Peter. *The Organ Music of J. S. Bach*, 3. Cambridge, 1984

The Organ Music of J. S. Bach, 2nd edn. Cambridge, 2003

Wolf, Uwe. 'Zur Leipziger Aufführungstradition der Motetten Bachs im 18. Jahrhundert'. *Bach-Jahrbuch*, 91 (2005), pp. 301–9

Wolff, Christoph. *Bach: Essays on his Life and Music*. Cambridge, MA, 1991

Wollny, Peter. 'Wilhelm Friedemann Bach's Halle Performances of Cantatas by his Father'. In Daniel Melamed (ed.), *Bach Studies 2*. Cambridge, 1995, pp. 202–28

· 6 ·

Protestant church music in England and America

CHARLES E. BREWER

Throughout the eighteenth century, the musical traditions of the Protestant churches in the United Kingdom and its New World Colonies were part of an extremely complex and at times fraying fabric. Their diversity was not limited to differing religious traditions but also included varying cultural, social and economic factors within similar traditions that created at times radically dissimilar musical repertories. As the state-sanctioned religion since the Restoration and the Act of Uniformity of 1662, The Church of England (together with the revised Book of Common Prayer) were strong influences on both sides of the Atlantic, and this influence had both positive and negative ramifications. One negative influence was that Catholics, though now tolerated, still had to rely primarily on Latin plainsong disseminated in manuscript copies, many prepared by John Francis Wade (1711/12–86).[1]

Although open to influences from Italian opera, English oratorio and the newer musical styles from Germany and Austria, the dominant musical style of church music during the Georgian era (1714–1830) always maintained a clarity, gravity and restraint partly based on the antiquated language and rhetoric of the authorized Bible, Prayer Book and the newer repertories of English hymns, but also upon the Enlightenment search for order and balance in all things.[2] Given the privileged role of the Church of England in both ecclesiastical and secular society, those institutions most closely associated in London with the royal court and the political life of the nation cultivated the most elaborate and expensive musical styles. Whether at St Paul's Cathedral, Westminster Abbey, or the Chapel Royal (and employment was not restricted to only one institution), organists and composers – including William Croft (1678–1727), Maurice Greene (1696–1755), William Boyce (1711–79) and Thomas Attwood (1765–1838) – created a repertory of church music built

1 Bennett Zon, *The English Plainchant Revival* (Oxford, 1999).
2 For an overview of enlightenment aesthetics, see Rémy G. Saisselin, *The Enlightenment Against the Baroque: Economics and Aesthetics in the Eighteenth Century* (Berkeley, 1992).

upon the traditions of the Restoration that also eschewed newer, more theatrical, musical styles.

Related to the elaborate musical traditions of the 'cathedral' style, the long-established choirs of the university colleges were also able to support an active musical life. Composers such as William Hayes (1708–77) at Oxford not only promoted the newest works from London through local performances, but also were able to emulate these works in their own compositions. To varying degrees, the network of Anglican cathedrals and urban parish churches outside of London and in the New World also attempted to copy the 'cathedral' style of the capital, although lack of financial resources and trained personnel often restricted their repertory.[3] English composers and performers also travelled to the Colonies, including William Selby (1738–98), who emigrated in 1773 to become the organist of Trinity Church, Rhode Island, and later held similar positions in Boston.[4]

The genre of the verse anthem, with its use of instrumental support (either as simple as basso continuo only or as complex as a full orchestra) and the alternation of solos with simple choruses, was of primary significance to the establishment of the 'cathedral' style. Composers in this style also helped establish a durable model for setting the short service, consisting of only the *Te Deum*, *Jubilate*, *Magnificat* and *Nunc dimittis*. Throughout the century, large anthologies containing examples of older repertory from the seventeenth century alongside newer works helped to establish the tradition of 'cathedral music'. Examples range from Thomas Tudway's manuscript collection of service music and anthems (British Library, Harley MSS. 7337–42) from the late seventeenth and early eighteenth century to Samuel Arnold's *Cathedral Music* of 1790, which was, however, poorly received.[5]

The tradition of singing prose translations of the Psalms in the Book of Common Prayer to short harmonized formulas, otherwise known as Anglican chant, was prevalent throughout the eighteenth century.[6] A number of manuscript and printed sources, including Granville Sharp's *Fifty Double and Single Chants being the Most Favourite, as performed at St Paul's, Westminster and Most of the Cathedrals in England* (*c.* 1770), document its significance not only to the 'cathedral' practice but also to those smaller parishes that had trained choirs.

3 Christopher Dearnley, *English Church Music, 1650–1750, in Royal Chapel, Cathedral and Parish Church* (Oxford and New York, 1970), pp. 75 and 82–95; Nicholas Temperley, *The Music of the English Parish Church*, 2 vols. (Cambridge, 1979), vol. 1, pp. 100–40; and Ruth Wilson, 'Episcopal Music in America: The British Legacy', *The Musical Times*, 124/1685 (1983), pp. 447–8 and 450.

4 David P. McKay, 'William Selby, Musical Emigré in Colonial Boston', *Musical Quarterly*, 57 (1971), pp. 609–27 and Nicholas Temperley, *Bound for America: Three British Composers* (Urbana, IL, 2003), pp. 12–51.

5 Dearnley, *English Church Music*, p. 108.

6 Ruth Wilson, *Anglican Chant and Chanting in England, Scotland, and America, 1660 to 1820* (Oxford, 1996).

That this tradition was also known in the New World is demonstrated by a manuscript copied in 1809 by Jacob Eckhard, organist of St Michael's Episcopal Church in Charleston, South Carolina, which includes nineteen formulas, many entitled 'Chaunt', and a special setting of the *Jubilate Deo*.[7]

In contrast to the traditions of reformed churches on the Continent, the Anglican churches did not develop an elaborate tradition of independent instrumental music. The most significant genre was that of the organ voluntary, which was often used after the psalms and the second lesson at Matins and Evensong, as an Offertory, or as a prelude or postlude to a service.[8] Though these works were often improvised, composers such as Croft, Greene, Boyce and John Stanley (1712–86) published a number of model sets. Greene seems to have established the commonly used pattern of a slow movement followed by one in a faster tempo. Even though the cathedral churches could not support elaborate musical performances on a regular basis, the choral festivals established in the eighteenth century – such as the St Cecilia Festivals at Salisbury and the Three Choirs Festival at Gloucester, Hereford and Worcester – provided ample opportunities for the performance of more elaborate musical works, including oratorios.

In a number of respects, George Frideric Handel represents an exception among the Protestant composers in England, in that most of his music for religious use came into being through specific commissions for particular political events, such as his Coronation Anthems or the so-called 'Utrecht' and 'Dettingen' *Te Deums*. Even his few anthems for the Duke of Chandos and the Chapel Royal were never part of the common repertory of eighteenth-century Anglican church music.

While Handel occupied a unique position, the most influential, widespread and popular repertory of church music in the eighteenth century was that associated with psalmody and hymnody. Since the Reformation in the sixteenth century, the singing of metrical psalms has been an important component in the services of the Church of England (especially outside the major urban centres in the smaller parish churches) and the other reformed traditions in both the United Kingdom and its New World colonies.[9] Throughout the eighteenth century, many independent churches continued to use the so-called 'Old Version' from the sixteenth century by Thomas Sternhold (d. 1549) and John Hopkins (d. 1570), though the 'New Version' by Nahum

7 George W. Williams, *Jacob Eckhard's Choirmaster's Book of 1809: A Facsimile with Introduction and Notes* (Columbia, SC, 1971).

8 Temperley, *The Music of the English Parish Church*, vol. 1, pp. 135–8.

9 Robin Leaver, *'Goostly Psalmes and Spirituall Songes': English and Dutch Metrical Psalms from Coverdale to Utenhove, 1535–1566* (Oxford, 1991) and John Richard Watson, *The English Hymn: A Critical and Historical Study* (Oxford, 1999), pp. 42–132.

Tate (1652–1715) and Nicholas Brady (1659–1726) from 1696 was also beginning to gain in popularity. However, towards the end of the seventeenth century, independent preachers, such as the Baptist Benjamin Keach (1640–1704), began to promote the usefulness of 'hymns of human composure' in addition to the psalms.[10] The hymn writers of the eighteenth century – including Isaac Watts (1674–1748), John Wesley (1703–91), Charles Wesley (1707–88), John Newton (1725–1807) and William Cowper (1731–1800), among many others – set a long-lasting standard for all later reformed hymnody.[11]

The traditional psalm tunes, some as old as the sixteenth century but others newly composed, were just as important as the text for the metrical psalms and hymns.[12] At the beginning of the eighteenth century, many parish and independent churches still practised monophonic lined-out psalmody, in which a song leader or precentor, often the parish clerk, would recite a line or two of the text and set one of the established tunes to which the congregation would respond.[13] 'Turns and flourishes' were added to the original tunes in many churches in what came to be termed 'the old way of singing'.[14] Already in 1671, John Playford was advocating a reform in the singing of psalmody, and a number of works were soon published by Playford and others that sought to provide musical instruction and a new repertory.[15] By the early eighteenth century, even the independent churches were beginning to allow part singing, and composers and compilers, such as John Chetham (1688–1746), whose *A Book of Psalmody* appeared in eleven editions from 1718 to 1787, supplied practical collections for this new expanding market.[16]

As in Great Britain, the Calvinist churches of the British colonies also experienced conflicts over the introduction of both hymns and, more particularly, part singing. Some members of the New England clergy – such as Cotton Mather (1663–1728), Thomas Symmes (1677–1725), John Tufts (1689–1750) and Thomas Walter (1696–1725) – provided theological support in printed sermons as well as practical collections of music and musical

10 James C. Brooks, 'Benjamin Keach and the Baptist Singing Controversy: Mediating Scripture, Confessional Heritage, and Christian Unity', PhD thesis (The Florida State University, 2006).

11 Watson, *The English Hymn*, pp. 133–299.

12 Dearnley, *English Church Music*, pp. 135–55; Nicholas Temperley, *The Music of the English Parish Church*, vol. 1, pp. 141–203; and David Hunter, 'English Country Psalmodists and Their Publications, 1700–1760', *Journal of the Royal Musical Association*, 115/2 (1990), pp. 220–39.

13 For an anecdotal history, see Peter Hampson Ditchfield, *The Parish Clerk* (New York, 1907).

14 Nicholas Temperley, 'The Old Way of Singing: Its Origins and Development', *Journal of the American Musicological Society*, 34 (1981), pp. 511–44.

15 Aspects of this reform are summarized in Rebecca Louise Burkart, '"Young Men and Maidens, Old Men and Children May Praise the Name of the Lord": A Comparative Study of Eighteenth-Century English Books of Psalmody with Special Emphasis on *A Book of Psalmody* by John Chetham (1688–1746)' PhD thesis (The Florida State University, 2001), pp. 26–46 and 88–119.

16 For a biography of Chetham, see Burkart, '"Young Men and Maidens"', pp. 47–87.

instructions to support what they termed 'regular singing' (that is, the ability to read notes on a staff, or *regulus*).[17]

In both the Old and New Worlds, this reform movement also led to the establishment of religious and singing societies, part of whose rationale was to teach music.[18] Itinerant teachers would hold singing schools, often during the winter when children would not be otherwise employed, or the parish clerks in the larger churches would occasionally be responsible for teaching choirs of charity children who would then participate in the services. This movement also led to churches establishing choirs from these newly trained singers who would lead the congregational music, and in England they were often placed in the West Gallery of the churches.

Outside the larger urban centres, the parish churches supported a large network of singing masters and often purchased their collections of 'country psalmody'.[19] Composers such as William Knapp (1698–1768) and William Tans'ur (*c.* 1699–1783) were especially influential on both sides of the Atlantic. Tans'ur's collection, *The Royal Melody Compleat* (1754–5), was frequently reprinted both in Great Britain and America and was significant enough still to be included under a revised title as part of *The American Harmony* (Newburyport, MA, 1769), a change attributable to the increasing tensions between England and the Colonies. The typical collection of 'country psalmody' contained an introductory section explaining basic musical notation and theory, plain tunes (simple syllabic settings), 'fuging' tunes (compositions which included a section in loose imitative style) and anthems (extended settings, generally of biblical texts). In America, the first local anthology to rival Tans'ur was compiled by Rev. James Lyons (1735–94), *Urania* (Philadelphia, 1761) which, in addition to works copied from earlier anthologies, also included five compositions that can be ascribed to Lyons himself.[20]

Perhaps the dominant figure of the parish tradition in the New World was William Billings (1746–1800), who most likely learned music at a singing school, and according to an advertisement on 2 October 1769, was already at a tender age co-leading a singing school with John Barry (b. 1735), the choir

17 For short summaries of this controversy in New England, see David P. McKay and Richard Crawford, *William Billings of Boston: Eighteenth-Century Composer* (Princeton, NJ, 1975), pp. 3–22 and Alan Clark Buechner, *Yankee Singing Schools and the Golden Age of Choral Music in New England, 1760–1800* (Boston, 2003), pp. 1–40.

18 Temperley, *The Music of the English Parish Church*, vol. 1, p. 103. For a more extensive discussion of the singing schools, see Buechner, *Yankee Singing Schools*, pp. 41–113.

19 Hunter, 'English Country Psalmodists and Their Publications, 1700–1760', pp. 233–5.

20 Oscar G. Sonneck, *Francis Hopkinson, The First American Poet-Composer (1737–1791) and James Lyon, Patriot, Preacher, Psalmodist (1735–1794): Two Studies in Early American Music* (Washington, DC, 1905; reprint New York, 1967).

leader at New South Church in Boston.[21] Throughout his life, Billings pursued other occupations, including tanner, scavenger, hogreeve and sealer of leather, but by 1789 was listed in *The Boston Directory* solely as 'musician'. At the age of twenty-four, he published his first collection, *The New-England Psalm-Singer* (1770), whose frontispiece, depicting a domestic musical scene, was engraved by the great American Revolutionary Paul Revere. Not only did Billings compose all the music, but he also wrote some of the texts, including that for the tune 'Chester'. In the midst of the American Revolution, Billings published his second collection, the *Singing Master's Assistant* (1778), which was so popular that a second edition appeared in the same year, and it was subsequently reprinted at least four more times. Not only did this collection include a number of Billings' more overtly political compositions (such as his parody of Psalm 137, the 'Lamentation over Boston'), it also included his satirical text, 'To the Goddess of Discord', a response to those critics who thought his music too consonant, a trait shared with most composers, English and American, in the country psalmody tradition. He published four further collections: *Music in Miniature* (1779), a collection of psalm tunes, many 'borrowed' from other composers; the *Psalm-Singer's Amusement* (1781), containing 'A Number of Fuging Pieces and Anthems'; the *Suffolk Harmony* (1786), which included a number of works for the Universalist tradition; and *The Continental Harmony* (1794), a retrospective collection of Billings' previously unpublished works. Though musical tastes changed rapidly in Boston after the end of the American Revolution, Billings' music was still featured in concerts and benefits, including one organized by William Selby on 22 September 1787 – also showcasing works by Selby, Anton Filtz as well as Handel's 'Hallelujah' chorus – to support the rebuilding of the Hollis Street Church after a fire.

In addition to the popularity of his music, Billings' most lasting legacy arose from his work as a travelling singing master throughout New England, from Rhode Island to Maine. His work inspired a younger generation of composers, sometimes termed song- or tune-smiths, to take the country psalmody tradition to the frontiers of the new nation: among these composers were Daniel Read (1757–1836), Timothy Swan (1758–1842), Jacob Kimball, Jr (1761–1826), Supply Belcher (1751–1836), David Belknap (1771–1815), Jacob French (1754–1817), Stephen Jenks (1772–1856), Abraham Maxim (1773–1829) and Justin Morgan (1747–98). Like Billings, many of these tune-smiths were trained only in the singing schools and pursued other careers; for example, Justin Morgan was a school teacher and farmer, and the first breeder of the

21 McKay and Crawford, *William Billings of Boston*, provide a detailed documentary biography of the composer.

Morgan horse.[22] This style of psalmody was prevalent through the early nineteenth century among English Canadians and the Loyalists who emigrated to Canada at the end of the Revolution.

While most independent religious traditions (Presbyterians, Baptists and Congregationists, for example) and rural Anglican parish churches had not traditionally used instruments, one or two were initially included as a result of the reform movements in the later eighteenth century; full-scale church bands were subsequently formed, often mixing wind and string instruments.[23] By the end of the century, some churches in Great Britain that could not support a choir or band had installed barrel organs, whose mechanical mechanisms were pinned to play the most popular psalm and hymn tunes.[24]

During the last decades of the eighteenth century in both Great Britain and North America, however, the style of country psalmody came increasingly under criticism both for its often-raucous performance and its frequent transgressions of the established rules of musical composition. In Great Britain, clerics such as William Tattersall (1751–1829) proposed reforms of both the texts and musical style of traditional psalmody, and in 1791 he published a collection of tunes marked by their simplicity and comparatively lively musical style.[25] In the New World, composers and tune-book compilers like Andrew Law (1748–1821), Oliver Holden (1765–1844) and Samuel Holyoke (1762–1820) also advocated musical reform and provided collections that were corrected according to the most proper European musical standards.[26]

Among the protestant traditions of the New World, those associated with immigrants from Central Europe are of particular interest. The Quaker colony of Pennsylvania granted religious freedom to all and even advertised in German newspapers to solicit settlers for its western frontiers. Mennonites and other Anabaptist groups came to escape religious persecution as early as

22 Betty Bandel, *Sing the Lord's Song in a Strange Land: The Life of Justin Morgan* (Rutherford, NJ, 1981).

23 Temperley, *The Music of the English Parish Church*, vol. 1, pp. 147–51 and 196–201. For the American perspective, see Frederick R. Selch, 'Instrumental Accompaniments for Yankee Hymn Tunes: An Investigation of the Evidence Relating to the Use of Musical Instruments for the Accompaniment of New England's Protestant Worship Music between 1760 and 1850', PhD thesis (New York University, 2003).

24 Lyndesay G. Langwill and Canon Noel Boston, *Church and Chamber Barrel-Organs: Their Origins, Makers, Music and Location, A Chapter in English Church Music*, 2nd edn. (Edinburgh, 1970); Temperley, *The Music of the English Parish Church*, vol. 1, pp. 234–8; Allan Phillip, 'An Old Sussex Barrel Organ', *The Musical Times*, 94/1329 (1953), p. 517; Christopher Turner, '"Miserable Machines": The Role of the Barrel Organ within Georgian Psalmody', in Turner (ed.), *Georgian Psalmody 2: The Interaction Between Urban and Rural Practice, Papers from the Second International Conference organised by The Colchester Institute* (Grantham, 1999), pp. 65–72.

25 Temperley, *The Music of the English Parish Church*, vol. 1, pp. 204–43.

26 McKay and Crawford, *William Billings*, pp. 190–6; and Richard Crawford, '"Ancient Music" and the Europeanizing of American Psalmody', in Richard Crawford, Allen R. Lott and Carol J. Oja (eds.), *A Celebration of American Music: Words and Music in Honor of H. Wiley Hitchcock* (Ann Arbor, MI, 1990), pp. 225–55.

the late seventeenth century. Among these, the most conservative were the Amish, who still practice a form of lined-out monophonic hymnody based upon a restricted repertory of early hymns. Their basic eighteenth-century hymnbook, nicknamed the *Ausbund*, is still in print.[27]

The New World also gave rise to new developments within these German traditions. Johann Kelpius (1673–1708) led a group of Pietists to settle in the Wissahickon Valley near Philadelphia, and a music manuscript associated with these hermits was copied in 1705 with texts in German and English: *The Lamenting Voice of the Hidden Love at the Time when She Lay in Misery & forsaken; and oprest by the multitude of Her Enemies.*[28] Another unique group within the German traditions of the New World was inspired by Georg Conrad Beissel (1691–1768), who arrived in Pennsylvania in 1720.[29] He eventually established a cloister for Seventh-Day Baptists or 'New Dunkards' in 1732 at Ephrata, near Lancaster, Pennsylvania. In addition to his own ascetic teachings, Beissel helped to promote and compose a unique repertory of hymnody, whose texts are preserved in prints from the cloister's own press and whose music is preserved in elaborately illuminated manuscripts.[30] For example, *Das Gesäng der einsamen und verlassenen Turtel-Taube Nemlich der Christlichen Kirche* (The Song of the Solitary and Forsaken Turtle-Dove namely the Christian Church), was completed at the cloister in 1747 and contained printed texts and manuscript music for 750 original hymns.[31] Beissel even developed a compositional theory based on a hierarchical division of pitches into 'Masters and Servants'.[32] A further group of immigrants from Silesia, who arrived in Pennsylvania in 1734, were followers of Kaspar Schwenkfeld von Ossig

27 *Ausbund das ist: Etliche schöne Christliche Lieder, Wie sie in dem Gefängnis zu Passau in dem Schloß von den Schweizer-Brüdern und von anderen rechtgläubigen Christen hin und her gedichtet worden. Allen und jeden Christen, Welcher Religion sie seien, unpartheiisch sehr nützlich. Nebst einem Anhang von sechs Liedern*, 41 *Bekannte Auflage* (Lancaster County, PA, 1997). See also George Pullen Jackson, 'The Strange Music of the Old Order Amish', *Music Quarterly*, 31 (1945), pp. 275–88 and Rupert Karl Hohmann, 'The Church Music of the Old Order Amish of the United States', PhD thesis (Northwestern University, 1959).

28 Philadelphia, Historical Society of Pennsylvania, MS Ac.189; see Albert G. Hess, 'Observations on "The Lamenting Voice of Hidden Love"', *Journal of the American Musicological Society*, 5 (1952), pp. 211–23, for more detailed information on this source. For more general background, see Williard M. Martin, 'Johannes Kelpius and Johann Gottfried Seelig: Mystics and Hymnists on the Wissahickon', PhD thesis (The Pennsylvania State University, 1973).

29 Jeff Bach, *Voices of the Turtledoves: The Sacred World of Ephrata* (University Park, PA, 2003).

30 Concerning the musical traditions at Ephrata, see Julius Friedrich Sachse, *The Music of the Ephrata Cloister; also Conrad Beissel's Treatise on Music as set forth in a Preface to the 'Turtel-Taube' of 1747, Amplified with Fac-simile Reproductions of Parts of the Text and Some Original Ephrata Music of the Weyrauchs Hügel, 1739; Rosen und Lilien, 1745; Turtel Taube, 1747; Choral Buch, 1754, etc.* (Lancaster, PA, 1903; reprint New York, 1971) and Betty Jean Martin, 'The Ephrata Cloister and its Music, 1732–1785: The Cultural, Religious, and Bibliographical Background', PhD thesis (University of Maryland, 1974).

31 Carl T. Holmes, 'A Study of the Music in the 1747 Edition of Conrad Beissel's *Das Gesaeng der einsamen und verlassenen Turtel-Taube*', MA thesis (University of Southern California, 1959).

32 Lloyd G. Blakely, 'Johann Conrad Beissel and Music of the Ephrata Cloister', *Journal of Research in Music Education*, 15/2 (1967), pp. 120–38.

(1489–1561); in addition to several large folio manuscripts, a 1762 collection of their hymns was printed in Philadelphia by Christopher Sauer.[33]

Among the most musically active groups in the British colonies were the members of the *Unitas Fratrum*, also known as Moravians or the Bohemian Brethren, who first travelled to Savannah, Georgia (along with John Wesley) in 1735, but established their first permanent settlements at Nazareth, Bethlehem and Lititz, Pennsylvania in 1740 and 1741, later also founding Salem, North Carolina (1753). The Moravians promoted a rich tradition of vocal and instrumental music both within and outside of their traditional religious services, extensively documented in the extant diaries kept at each settlement.[34] In 1744 a *Collegium musicum* of instrumentalists was founded, which by 1788 included four violins, one viola, two violoncellos, two flutes, two oboes, two horns and two trumpets. In addition to an original tradition of hymnody (often played instrumentally by a choir of trombones), both immigrants and Moravians born in the New World contributed to an extensive repertory of anthems, including Jeremias Dencke (1725–95) and Johannes Herbst (1735–1812). Though born in Pennsylvania, John Antes (1740–1811) spent most of his life abroad, and composed his *Tre Trii, per due Violini e Violoncello* in Cairo, Egypt (1779–81). Johann Friedrich Peter (1746–1813), who arrived in Bethlehem in 1770, was not only a prolific composer and arranger of sacred music, but after his move to Salem was also the composer of six *Quintetti Due Violini, Due Viole e Violoncello* in 1789. By the end of the century, David Moritz Michael (1751–1825) was composing anthems and sacred arias and *Harmoniemusik* for winds. Another Moravian, David Tannenberg (1728–1804) was a prolific organ-builder, completing approximately fifty instruments during his lifetime for churches within and outside his own community.[35]

The rich diversity of Protestant traditions in both Great Britain and the New World, encompassing theological and aesthetic attitudes that ranged from a strong conservative retention of tradition to radical innovation, demonstrate the vitality and popular significance of music to the religious practices on both sides of the Atlantic Ocean. A composer such as William Billings could even bridge apparent contradictions, blending his adherence to the traditional musical styles typical of country psalmody with his more radical use of the traditions to support the patriot cause in the American Revolution. Perhaps

33 Allen Anders Seipt, *Schwenkfelder Hymnology and the Sources of the First Schwenkfelder Hymn-Book Printed in America* (Philadelphia, PA, 1909; reprint New York, 1971).

34 Hans Theodore David, *Musical Life in the Pennsylvania Settlements of the Unitas Fratrum* (Winston-Salem, NC, 1959).

35 William H. Arnold, *Organs for America: The Life and Works of David Tannenberg* (Philadelphia, PA, 1967).

the most significant aspect of the diverse musical styles is that they collectively formed a firm foundation for all later Protestant music, whether in the practices of established churches or in the more folk-like *Sacred Harp* traditions of the American south.

Select Bibliography

Arnold, William H. *Organs for America: The Life and Works of David Tannenberg*. Philadelphia, 1967

Ausbund das ist: Etliche schöne Christliche Lieder, Wie sie in dem Gefängnis zu Passau in dem Schloß von den Schweizer-Brüdern und von anderen rechtgläubigen Christen hin und her gedichtet worden. Allen und jeden Christen, Welcher Religion sie seien, unpartheiisch sehr nützlich. Nebst einem Anhang von sechs Liedern, 41 Bekannte Auflage. Lancaster County, PA, 1997

Bach, Jeff. *Voices of the Turtledoves: The Sacred World of Ephrata*. University Park, PA, 2003

Bandel, Betty. *Sing the Lord's Song in a Strange Land: The Life of Justin Morgan*. Rutherford, NJ, 1981

Blakely, Lloyd G. 'Johann Conrad Beissel and Music of the Ephrata Cloister'. *Journal of Research in Music Education*, 15/2 (1967), pp. 120–38

Brooks, James C. 'Benjamin Keach and the Baptist Singing Controversy: Mediating Scripture, Confessional Heritage, and Christian Unity'. PhD thesis, The Florida State University, 2006

Buechner, Alan Clark. *Yankee Singing Schools and the Golden Age of Choral Music in New England, 1760–1880*. Boston, 2003

Burkart, Rebecca Louise. '"Young Men and Maidens, Old Men and Children May Praise the Name of the Lord": A Comparative Study of Eighteenth-Century English Books of Psalmody with Special Emphasis on *A Book of Psalmody* by John Chetham (1688–1746)'. PhD thesis, The Florida State University, 2001

Crawford, Richard. '"Ancient Music" and the Europeanizing of American Psalmody'. In Richard Crawford, Allen R. Lott and Carol J. Oja (eds.), *A Celebration of American Music: Words and Music in Honor of H. Wiley Hitchcock*. Ann Arbor, MI, 1990, pp. 225–55

America's Musical Life: A History. New York, 2001

David, Hans Theodore. *Musical Life in the Pennsylvania Settlements of the Unitas Fratrum*. Winston-Salem, NC, 1959

Dearnley, Christopher. *English Church Music, 1650–1750, in Royal Chapel, Cathedral and Parish Church*. New York, 1970

Ditchfield, Peter Hampson. *The Parish Clerk*. New York, 1907

Georgian Psalmody 1: The Gallery Tradition, Papers from the First International Conference organised by The Colchester Institute, ed. Christopher Turner. Grantham, 1997

Georgian Psalmody 2: The Interaction Between Urban and Rural Practice, Papers from the Second International Conference organised by The Colchester Institute, ed. Christopher Turner. Grantham, 1999

Gleason, Harold and Warren Becker. *Early American Music: Music in America from 1620 to 1920*. 2nd edn., Bloomington, IN, 1986

Hamlin, Hannibal. 'Psalm Culture in Early Modern England'. PhD thesis, Yale University, 2000

Hess, Albert G. 'Observations on "The Lamenting Voice of Hidden Love"'. *Journal of the American Musicological Society*, 5 (1952), pp. 211–23

Hohmann, Rupert Karl. 'The Church Music of the Old Order Amish of the United States'. PhD thesis, Northwestern University, 1959

Hunter, David. 'English Country Psalmodists and Their Publications, 1700–1760'. *Journal of the Royal Musical Association*, 115/2 (1990), pp. 220–39

Jackson, George Pullen. 'The Strange Music of the Old Order Amish'. *Music Quarterly*, 31 (1945), pp. 275–88

Langwill, Lyndesay G. and Canon Noel Boston. *Church and Chamber Barrel-Organs: Their Origins, Makers, Music and Location, A Chapter in English Church Music*. 2nd edn., Edinburgh, 1970

Lowens, Irving. *Music and Musicians in Early America: Aspects of the History of Music in Early America, and the History of Early American Music*. New York, 1964

McKay, David P. 'William Selby, Musical Emigré in Colonial Boston'. *Musical Quarterly*, 57 (1971), pp. 609–27

McKay, David P. and Richard Crawford. *William Billings of Boston: Eighteenth-Century Composer*. Princeton, NJ, 1975

Martin, Betty Jean. 'The Ephrata Cloister and its Music, 1732–1785: The Cultural, Religious, and Bibliographical Background'. PhD thesis, University of Maryland, 1974

Martin, Williard M. 'Johannes Kelpius and Johann Gottfried Seelig: Mystics and Hymnists on the Wissahickon'. PhD thesis, The Pennsylvania State University, 1973

Nicholls, David (ed.). *The Cambridge History of American Music*. Cambridge, 1998

Owen, Barbara. 'The Other Mr. Selby'. *American Music*, 8 (1990), pp. 477–82

Phillip, Allan. 'An Old Sussex Barrel Organ'. *The Musical Times*, 94/1329 (1953), p. 517

Sachse, Julius Friedrich. *The Music of the Ephrata Cloister; also Conrad Beissel's Treatise on Music as set forth in a Preface to the 'Turtel-Taube' of 1747, Amplified with Fac-simile Reproductions of Parts of the Text and Some Original Ephrata Music of the Weyrauchs Hügel, 1739; Rosen und Lilien, 1745; Turtel Taube, 1747; Choral Buch, 1754, etc.* Lancaster, PA, 1903; reprint New York, 1971

Saisselin, Rémy G. *The Enlightenment Against the Baroque: Economics and Aesthetics in the Eighteenth Century*. Berkeley, 1992

Seipt, Allen Anders. *Schwenkfelder Hymnology and the Sources of the First Schwenkfelder Hymn-Book Printed in America*. Philadelphia, PA, 1909; reprint New York, 1971

Selch, Frederick R. 'Instrumental Accompaniments for Yankee Hymn Tunes: An Investigation of the Evidence Relating to the Use of Musical Instruments for the Accompaniment of New England's Protestant Worship Music between 1760 and 1850'. PhD thesis, New York University, 2003

Sonneck, Oscar G. *Francis Hopkinson, The First American Poet-Composer (1737–1791) and James Lyon, Patriot, Preacher, Psalmodist (1735–1794): Two Studies in Early American Music*. Washington, DC, 1905; reprint New York, 1967

Spink, Ian. *Restoration Cathedral Music, 1660–1714*. Oxford, 1995

Stevenson, Robert. *Protestant Church Music in America: A Short Survey of Men and Movements from 1564 to the Present*. New York, 1966

Temperley, Nicholas. *The Music of the English Parish Church*. 2 vols., Cambridge, 1979

'The Old Way of Singing: Its Origins and Development'. *Journal of the American Musicological Society*, 34 (1981), pp. 511–44

Bound for America: Three British Composers. Urbana, IL, 2003

Turner, Christopher. '"Miserable Machines": The Role of the Barrel Organ within Georgian Psalmody'. In *Georgian Psalmody 2: The Interaction Between Urban and Rural Practice, Papers from the Second International Conference organised by The Colchester Institute*, ed. Christopher Turner. Grantham, 1999, pp. 65–72

Watson, John Richard. *The English Hymn: A Critical and Historical Study*. Oxford, 1999

Williams, George W. *Jacob Eckhard's Choirmaster's Book of 1809: A Facsimile with Introduction and Notes*. Columbia, SC, 1971

Wilson, Ruth. 'Episcopal Music in America: The British Legacy'. *The Musical Times*, 124/1685 (1983), pp. 447–8 and 450

Anglican Chant and Chanting in England, Scotland, and America, 1660 to 1820. Oxford, 1996

Woodforde, James. *The Diary of a Country Parson*. 5 vols., ed. John Beresford. London, 1924–31

Zon, Bennett. *The English Plainchant Revival*. Oxford: Oxford University Press, 1999

Zuckerman, Shelley P. Sanders. 'Spiritual Formation through Psalm-Singing Worship: A Study of the Piety Nurtured by the Annotations in John Brown of Haddington's *The Psalms of David in Metre with Notes* (1775)'. PhD thesis, Drew University, 2005

• INTERLUDE •

· 7 ·

Listening, thinking and writing

DAVID SCHROEDER

The emergence of new audiences in the eighteenth century spawned different ways of thinking about music, resulting in modes of writing not evident in the previous century. Some of the traditional audiences, of course, remained intact, such as those for liturgical music and opera, as did the venues provided by wealthy patrons, but over the course of the century one no longer necessarily had to go to a church to hear religious music or be invited to a court to hear operas or symphonies. Concert societies and organizations sprang up across the Continent and in Britain that in some cases engaged listeners other than aristocrats, running on either a profit or a non-profit basis. In part, the new audience arose from a new breed of music-makers, both amateurs and connoisseurs, women who played keyboard instruments, and others who could play chamber music, solo pieces, or the orchestral repertory.

With audiences now larger and more numerous than they had been, embracing musically sophisticated listeners as well as those with less developed tastes and coming from a much broader social spectrum (although still primarily from the upper classes), those who wrote about music often considered themselves on a special mission. Along with a burgeoning listening audience came a similar explosion in the numbers prepared to read about music, and writers on the subject could therefore write with the assurance that their thoughts would reach a significantly sized readership. More importantly, these writers saw a large cross-section of society that they could influence, in matters of taste, improvement, standards, the past in relation to the present, the development of skills – and, for many above all else, in issues of morality.

Writing strategies

Numerous types of writing on music emerged, starting early in the eighteenth century, reflecting the new concert venues as well as the more diversified nature of the audience. Much of this writing ran parallel to other types of writing, either gaining a foothold in the eighteenth century or in some cases carrying over from the previous century. With the tenets of the Enlightenment firmly established by the end of the seventeenth century, in the work of the Third Earl of Shaftesbury and others, it became natural to place music among those things that could make society better, through improvement of taste, through acquiring refinement and through the ways that these together could promulgate morality. The writing of treatises became a favourite vehicle in this process, giving not only practical instruction but underlying moral principles as well. Writing on music could follow the well-established paths of philosophical discourse, in the sub-discipline of aesthetics comparing music with the other arts and examining its means of expressiveness through traditional philosophical and literary means. The first histories of music originated in the eighteenth century, reflecting a new interest in music of the past. A type of distance education in practical matters of skill-building sprang up, educating teachers to become better teachers of instruments and of the practices of ornamentation in 'how-to' treatises; these books usually managed to offer moral instruction at the same time. Concert reviews became common, namely reviews of performances usually intended for the local community, and reviews of composers and their works that would appear in local newspapers or were circulated abroad, as with the Paris-based *Correspondance littéraire*. With this proliferation of writing, composers got in on the act as well, often feeling they had to set the record straight, or at least to give an impression they would wish to be carried into posterity, now that music of the past could be regarded seriously.

We have no shortage of sources for eighteenth-century writing on music, and of course have welcomed them with open arms, delighted to have some means other than the music itself to come to terms with the music. Sometimes this enthusiasm has led to curious misuses of the source material, resulting from a lack of understanding of the strategic purposes of eighteenth-century writers. Often writers are prompted to publish because of their disagreements with other writers, for example; instead of an objective assessment of a particular situation, then, we have a highly polarized point of view, revealing much about the polemics of the time, but less about the actual nature of the issue or phenomenon concerned. We see this in virtually all areas of writing about music, from aestheticians, reviewers, music historians and composers themselves. Rousseau had much to say about music, in the *Dictionnaire de musique* as well as the *Encyclopédie*, but his preference for melody over harmony should not be taken as the full measure of the French view of music. Instead, it reveals above all Rousseau's position in the *Querelle des Bouffons* – his objection to the views of Rameau and his inclination towards Italian music that prompted him to disparage almost all French music. Forkel could find few composers in the 1770s to admire, with the exception of C. P. E. Bach, but instead of revealing an actual problem with the music of his contemporaries it exposed his own aesthetic view as being roughly half a century out of date. Many other writers of treatises in Germany were in a similar position.

The comments of composers late in the century can be similarly misleading. In an autobiographical letter from 1776 Haydn listed his best works by name as vocal works, lumping all his instrumental music together under the heading of the 'chamber style', giving the impression that only his vocal works mattered.[1] Haydn knew perfectly well that writers on music thought more highly of vocal music than of instrumental, and in self-promotion at the time subscribed to the prevailing view, in fact telling us little about what he actually thought. By the time he spoke to biographers at the beginning of the nineteenth century, instrumental music had come to the fore in aesthetic opinion, and his more specific comments to Georg August Griesinger and Albert Christoph Dies about his instrumental works reflect the shift. Similarly, Mozart had much to say to his father about the function of opera when writing *Idomeneo*, including the view that 'in an opera the poetry must absolutely be the obedient daughter of the music'.[2] This comment came amid other negative ones about Gluck, and in contradicting Gluck's (or more accurately Calzibigi's) famous dictum about music serving the text in opera, Mozart, hoping to mend fences with his father Leopold, gave Leopold some satisfaction in his long-held grudge against Gluck. Again, it tells us little about Mozart's actual views. In examining writings about music in the eighteenth century, we ignore the axes that writers had to grind at our peril, and this necessitates awareness not only of the writings themselves but also their contexts. The categories of writing to be covered in this chapter – and by no means mutually exclusive ones – include treatises both practical and aesthetic, audience formation, histories and literary writing. Some similar issues arise in all categories, for example matters of taste for listeners and creators; all eighteenth-century writers wished to influence their readers, in effect prompting them to adopt views on music and the world consistent with their own, using the most persuasive practices of eighteenth-century writing.

Practical treatises

The eighteenth century, in contrast to the seventeenth, saw an explosion in the writing of treatises, both practical and theoretical. Unlike writing on music in

1 H. C. Robbins Landon, *The Collected Correspondence and London Notebooks of Joseph Haydn* (London, 1959), pp. 19–20.

2 Wilhelm A. Bauer, Otto Erich Deutsch and Joseph Heinz Eibl (eds.), *Mozart: Briefe und Aufzeichnungen* (Kassel, 1963), 7 vols., vol. 3, p. 167. My translation.

much of the twentieth century, which tended to be driven by music itself and its composers, eighteenth-century writing on the subject owed much more to other types of writing, and the objectives pursued by their authors. In many cases the writers themselves were not experts on music, although they may have been musically talented; as music came to play a prominent role in the life of their communities and society in general, writers recognized the need to give musical activity its due, considering the influence it could have in shaping the taste and outlook of the multitudes experiencing it. In most countries writers late in the seventeenth century or early in the eighteenth century, such as Shaftesbury in England and Johann Christoph Gottsched in Germany, had pointed the way forward in their respective approaches to the Enlightenment, especially in advancements in the use of literary language;[3] the recognition that music could be a shaping force not unlike literature prompted writers to attempt to persuade others how that should happen. In many instances the philosophical and literary foundations remained prominent in writings on music, with writers adhering to the customary categories of aesthetics, such as mimesis, the sublime and beautiful, and genius, or literary fundamentals such as rhetoric.

Even writing of the most practical kind, the 'how-to' books for aspiring performers, teachers, or composers, retained elements of the literary and philosophical grounding, and the writers who wrote these books, almost always sophisticated musicians, still revealed their leanings to other writing traditions. A deluge of these kinds of treatises came from the beginning of the century to the end, from all countries but with a preponderance of them from Germany, offering instruction in thorough-bass, harmony, basic counterpoint and the fugue, the playing of every possible instrument (but especially piano and violin) and vocal technique, on all aspects of performance practice, and on composition itself. Writers include professional musicians such as Johann Joseph Fux (*Gradus ad Parnassum*, 1725), Pier Francesco Tosi (*Opinioni de' cantori antichi e moderni*, 1723), Carl Philipp Emanuel Bach (*Versuch über die wahre Art das Clavier zu spielen*, 1753–62), Johann Joachim Quantz (*Versuch einer Anweisung die Flöte traversiere zu spielen*, 1752), Jean-Philippe Rameau (*Traité de l'harmonie*, 1722), Giambattista Martini (*Esemplare a sia saggio fondamentale di contrappunto sopra il canto fermo*, 1774) and Johann G. Albrechtsberger (*Gründliche Anweisung zur Composition*, 1790). They also include more philosophically orientated writers, some of whom actively wrote in fields other than music before writing their music treatises, as Johann Mattheson did as editor of *Der Vernüfftler* (1713–14), a moral weekly modelled on those of Addison

3 See Eric Blackall, *The Emergence of German as a Literary Language* (Cambridge, 1959), pp. 88–9.

and Steele and published in Hamburg. With his *Exemplarische Organisten-Probe* (1719), *Grosse General-Bass-Schule* (1731) and *Der vollkommene Capellmeister* (1739), among other works, he provided inspiration for the likes of Friedrich Marpurg (*Abhandlung von der Fuge*, 1753; *Anleitung zum Clavierspielen*, 1755; and *Anleitung zur Singcomposition*, 1758), Johann Adolph Scheibe (*Über die musikalische Composition*, 1773), and William Crotch (*Elements of Musical Composition*, 1812).

One of the notable writers not yet identified, Leopold Mozart, illustrates well in his *Versuch einer gründlichen Violinschule* (1756) – published in the same year as the birth of his son Wolfgang – the pull between the nuts and bolts of musical instruction and the more lofty aspirations of the Enlightenment. On the surface, this treatise on the fundamental principles of violin playing, with its illustrations and numerous musical examples, seems practical in the extreme, designed for teachers instead of pupils, with detailed descriptions of notation, holding the violin, the nature of bowing, positions and all facets of ornamentation. Behind this enterprise, though, lay a higher purpose, to cultivate good taste in youth, expressed most clearly in the dedication to the Archbishop of Salzburg: 'How many young people, often endowed with the fairest gifts of Nature, would have grown to maturity, untended as the seedlings run wild in the forest, if your right fatherly help had not in good time brought them under the supervision of judicious persons for their upbringing ... I may, therefore, surely venture to present to Your Grace in deepest loyalty, a book in which I have endeavoured, according to my poor powers, to pave a way for music-loving youth which shall guide them with certainty to good taste in music.'[4] Good taste in music implies the same in life; for Leopold, educated in jurisprudence and a deep admirer of Gottsched and Christian Fürchtegott Gellert, all writing served an edifying function, and the refinement of taste could be equated with the cultivation of morality. Other writers make this principle abundantly clear, including Mattheson, noting in part 1, chapter 3 of *Der vollkommene Capellmeister* that 'it is the true purpose of music to be, above all else, a moral lesson [*Zucht-Lehre*]'.[5]

In order to have an impact on listeners, music had to appeal to the emotions, and performers had to understand the means for accomplishing this, especially in ornamentation. In large measure this could be conveyed through the affections, referred to early in the century as the *Affektenlehre*, but by no means an eighteenth-century invention, going back at least as far as the Florentine

4 Leopold Mozart, *A Treatise on the Fundamental Principles of Violin Playing*, trans. E. Knocker, 2nd edn. (Oxford, 1951), p. 6.

5 Quoted in Hans Lenneberg, 'Johann Mattheson on Affect and Rhetoric in Music', *Journal of Music Theory*, 2 (1959), p. 51.

Camerata. Melodic figures or ornaments were designed to move the emotions, and not only did Leopold Mozart write about them at the middle of the century, but so too did C. P. E. Bach and Johann Joachim Quantz in their treatises, making them a matter of greater concern for practical musicians than aestheticians. The focus on the single affect, uncluttered by competing material, gave way in the later part of the century to duelling ideas as they occur in sonata form.

Aesthetics

The purest form of thinking about music in the eighteenth century lay in the branch of philosophy that Alexander Baumgarten first called 'aesthetics' in 1750, and a lack of musical skill proved no serious impediment to this type of writing. In the hands of these writers, especially in Germany, who preferred the usual apparatuses on philosophical discourse and also treatises, dictionaries and other distinctive eighteenth-century modes of writing such as correspondences, an eerie cleft between theory and practice emerged, as one could often see little connection between the music of the time and aesthetic opinion. Johann Georg Sulzer (1720–79) is a good example, attending university in Zurich and falling under the influence of Johann Jakob Bodmer and Johann Jakob Breitinger, academics who moved away from the strict rationalism of Gottsched and the Leipzig intellectuals towards a greater role for the imagination.[6] As a student of theology with a keen interest in the natural sciences, Sulzer developed his aesthetic views with special attention to pedagogy and morality, undoubtedly influenced by his Calvinist upbringing and education in his native Switzerland. His academic career started in Magdeburg, but he soon moved to Berlin to teach mathematics and restructure the educational system in Prussia. In the highly progressive domain of Frederick the Great, he found himself increasingly out of step with his colleagues as a result of his more conservative traditionalism.

Music did not stand foremost among his interests, but his writings on the subject became remarkably influential, in his own time as well as subsequently. Charles Burney for one, visiting him in the 1770s, seemed impressed by his attachment to music: '[he is] not only well-read in books concerning music, but an ingenious and refined thinker on the subject.'[7] His most enduring work, the *Allgemeine Theorie der schönen Künste*, appeared in 1771 and 1774 in dictionary form, not unrelated to similar efforts by the French *philosophes*; unlike their

6 Nancy Kovaleff Baker and Thomas Christensen (eds.), *Aesthetics and the Art of Musical Composition in the German Enlightenment* (Cambridge, 1995), p. 7.

7 Quoted in Matthew Riley, *Musical Listening in the German Enlightenment* (Aldershot, 2004), p. 64.

more collaborative works though, Sulzer wrote his almost single-handedly.[8] In this tome he tackled the big subjects of interest to aestheticians, one of the most central being mimesis, or the imitation of nature and human characteristics in art works. In music this posed a special challenge, one that writers struggled with until the end of the century, concerning the distinctive properties of vocal and instrumental music. Vocal music, with intelligible texts, generally took precedence, the music gaining intelligibility by supporting the text in imitative or affective ways. Instrumental music, aestheticians like Sulzer believed, could not be imitative since it lacked these properties, and as a result was judged to be very much inferior to vocal music until near the end of the century when the *Frühromantiker* writers such as Jean Paul, Wackenroder, Tieck, August Wilhelm Schlegel and E. T. A. Hoffmann made a virtue of notions of the infinite and indefinite, which in their view could only be achieved by music lacking texts.[9] Earlier writers often disparaged instrumental music to the point of calling it trash or worthless, certainly considering it incapable of achieving the moral qualities of vocal music.[10] Sulzer built his argument on aesthetic moral principles; if music was to be edifying to an audience, it must be imitative, since any other type of music would involve disinterested contemplation, and would exist for sensory instead of edifying purposes.

For thoughtful aestheticians such as Sulzer or his younger colleague Johann Nikolaus Forkel at the University of Göttingen, this did not mean that instrumental music should be rejected out of hand. After all, the greatest composer of all time (certainly in Forkel's view), J. S. Bach, had written much instrumental music, and Forkel's own aesthetic scheme required that this music should be given its due. To do this, Forkel and Sulzer turned to the long-standing principles of rhetoric, associated since antiquity with the art of persuasion and revived in the Enlightenment because of its capacity to play a strong role in moral persuasion. In this way, they could take music that otherwise seemed to lack intelligibility and endow it with the properties of the great literary tradition, taking music more or less out of the realm of the sensory and placing it in the same category as literature through the observation of similar methodologies. These were not new thoughts, since they went back at least to Mattheson early in the century if not further, although Mattheson had not succeeded in developing a rigorously analytical way of demonstrating the

8 On the musical articles for which he received help from Johann Philipp Kirnberger and Johann Abraham Peter Schulz, see Baker and Christensen, *Aesthetics and the Art of Musical Composition*, p. 14.

9 See John Neubauer, *The Emancipation of Music from Language* (New Haven, CT and London, 1986), pp. 193–210 and Bellamy Hosler, *Changing Aesthetic Views of Instrumental Music in 18th-Century Germany* (Ann Arbor, MI, 1981), p. 189.

10 Hosler, *Changing Aesthetic Views*, pp. 160–4.

presence of the parts of oratory in music, namely the invention, disposition, style, memory and delivery.[11] In fact, his efforts at it proved unconvincing and, recognizing this, Sulzer attempted something more subtle and less prone to failure, focusing with a more generalized approach on the ways that the creation of an art work could parallel the composition of a speech.[12] As a result, his view on the subject proved to be more enduring, but in many respects remained – as was also true of Forkel – an apologia for the music of the past, out of touch with the great works emerging in the later part of the century. Composers such as Haydn would ably demonstrate that instrumental music could achieve the highest moral objectives without having to be grounded in outdated methods.[13]

The fascination with rhetoric by aestheticians in part sparked interest in the contrast between the sublime and the beautiful, since the sublime was initially thought of as a device for persuasion through the emotions. It also allowed an element of mimesis since it focused on objects or phenomena of nature that could awaken a sense of grandeur. Through the arousal of terror and ecstasy, the incomprehensible greatness of the divine could be approached. With his *Philosophical Enquiry into the Origin of our Ideas of the Sublime and Beautiful* (1747), Edmund Burke moved the discussion in a different direction, still emphasizing emotions, but now as part of an aesthetic theory, and obscurity, solitude and power came into sharper focus. Burke also extended the discussion beyond literature, bringing in music and the other arts. Immanuel Kant added another dimension in his *Beobachtungen über das Gefühl des Schönen und Erhabenen* (1764), emphasizing the perceiver instead of the object or the capacity of the imagination of the observer to be aroused. Like most writers, he considered both the sublime and the beautiful, noting the limits that apply to beauty, and the role of form and understanding in defining those limits. The limits themselves do not impinge on the sublime, thus placing it beyond the complete comprehensibility of the imagination, and for many at the time this put it in a negative category, unlike beauty. Sulzer, for one, could not take this notion of the sublime as far as some others, insisting that restraints remain in place and that the raw emotions of the *Sturm und Drang* should be avoided. For Sulzer, nature necessarily remained benevolent, and his view was criticized by Goethe, among others, who recognized that our awe of nature can be the awe of its destructive power.[14] Despite his more traditional leanings, Sulzer could

11 See Peter Hoyt, 'The Classical Oration as a Model for Musical Form in the Eighteenth Century', in K. Eberl and W. Ruf (eds.), *Musikkonzepte – Konzepte der Musikwissenschaft* (Kassel, 1998), pp. 26–8.

12 Baker and Christensen, *Aesthetics and the Art of Musical Composition*, p. 18.

13 See my *Haydn and the Enlightenment: The Late Symphonies and Their Audience* (Oxford, 1990), pp. 110–11.

14 Baker and Christensen, *Aesthetics and the Art of Musical Composition*, p. 15.

appreciate the efforts of those who were original creators instead of imitators, and that their genius of invention deserved special recognition. The phenomenon of genius drew much attention, with credit now going to individuals who could direct society or the arts along previously untrodden paths.[15]

Audience formation

Unlike the aestheticians writing in the first instance for fellow philosophers and students – continuing the thrust of Descartes and others in the seventeenth century – a new type of writing emerged in the eighteenth century to accommodate the emergence of the new audience and the perceived need to educate this audience, with the hope of transforming the taste of individuals from the level of the amateur to that of the connoisseur. While some of this might appear in treatises, it was much more likely to occur in more accessible modes of writing, most notably reviews that could appear in daily or periodic magazines and newspapers, in literary correspondences, or in the great projects of the *philosophes* intended to give a large cross-section of humanity access to information and opinions, still considered subversive and dangerous by the *ancien régime*, in the form of dictionaries or the *Encyclopédie* itself. The anonymous reviewers of the morning newspapers in London at the end of the century continued the role that reviewing had had for much of the century, namely to improve taste among its readers. In referring specifically to the last of Haydn's symphonies presented in London, the review for the *Morning Chronicle* on 6 May 1795 agreed with the opinion of a gentleman 'eminent for his musical knowledge, taste, and sound criticism', that 'for fifty years to come Musical Composers would be little better than imitators of Haydn'.[16] Similar views turned up in memoirs and other personal reflections, for example that of George Dance who painted Haydn's portrait; he wrote that the 'beneficial influence [of Salomon's Concerts] upon the taste and judgement of the rising generation cannot be doubted'.[17]

Reviewers had to be able to respond quickly to new works, making a determination about whether these works did indeed cultivate taste, and of course they often could be wrong, predisposed to their own preferences or biases. Others enshrined their opinions in more enduring forms of writing, publications of their own lectures perhaps, or book-length studies about issues

15 See Peter Kivy, *The Possessor and the Possessed: Handel, Mozart, and Beethoven, and the Idea of Musical Genius* (New Haven, CT and London, 2001), esp. chapter 3, 'Breaking the Rule'.
16 Quoted in H. C. Robbins Landon, *Haydn: Chronicle and Works. Haydn in England 1791–1795* (London, 1976), p. 308.
17 George Dance, *A Collection of Portraits Sketched from the Life*, vol. 2 (London, 1814), n.p.

of musical taste. Haydn elicited positive responses from many in England, including the outstanding writers Charles Burney, Thomas Holcroft, Christian Ignatius Latrobe and Thomas Twining, but not all shared their views, with the most vitriolic criticism coming from William Jackson. His *Observations on the Present State of Music in London* was published in 1791, the year of Haydn's arrival in his city, and with composers such as Haydn in mind, he complained that 'later Composers, to be grand and original, have poured in such floods of nonsense, under the sublime idea of *being inspired*, that the present Symphony bears the same relation to good Music, as the ravings of a Bedlamite do to good sense'.[18] Jackson appears neither to have spoiled Haydn's sojourns in England nor the next English generation's adoring view of him.

Jackson may have been a lightweight in the relative scheme of things, but when such stinging views are expressed by the leading intellectuals of a country, the result can be much more influential, or can provoke a great controversy with heavyweights lining up on either side. This is what happened in the middle of the century in France, with Jean-Jacques Rousseau setting off one of the greatest musical battles ever waged with his diatribes against the leading French composer earlier in the century, Jean-Philippe Rameau. As Enrico Fubini reminds us, this *querelle* proved decisive not only for France but for all of European culture.[19] The controversy took shape as an opposition between French and Italian music, and became so widespread that it encompassed the divisions between rationalists and empiricists, the classical and the new *galant*, even harmony against melody and, depending on one's perspective, the past against the present. Rameau set the stage with his *Traité de l'harmonie* (1722) and *Nouveau système de musique théoretique* (1726), in which he argued the principle that music is founded on harmony and not on melody. Harmony offers a rational foundation for music, recognized as a mathematical principle by Pythagorus and reiterated among others by Descartes. This recognition took the arbitrariness out of music, freeing it from the whims of texts, aligning it with other great human achievements founded on science, and Rameau saw this approach as fundamentally French.

Rousseau argued against this position not only with passion but also with contempt for anyone who supported Rameau. It ran contrary to everything he believed, and he distanced himself from any notion of a confluence between art and science. Art must speak to our primitive urges, and can do this only with melody. French composers, he believed, had been notoriously incompetent at writing good melody, while the Italians had excelled at it, certainly in song but

18 William Jackson, *Observations on the Present State of Music in London*, 2nd edn. (London, 1791), pp. 16–17.
19 Eurico Fubini (ed.), *Music and Culture in Eighteenth-Century Europe: A Source Book*, trans. W. Freis, L. Gasbarrone and M. L. Leone (Chicago and London, 1994), p. 4.

especially in opera. It took only a small leap for Rousseau to deem all French music bad and all Italian music good, and the matter came to a head with the performance in Paris in 1752 of a relatively inconsequential work, *La serva padrona* by Pergolesi, launching the *Querelle des Bouffons*. In Rousseau's mind this was no mere argument about musical preferences, but struck at the core of society itself, shaping not only civil liberties but the very principles of democracy.[20] He made his views known in every possible format, from tracts and newspapers to dictionaries and articles in the *Encyclopédie*, and even in music itself, with his own one-act opera *Le Devin du village*. Spearheading the vast undertaking of the *Encyclopédie*, Denis Diderot also wrote at length about music; in total 1,600 articles on the subject appeared in the *Encyclopédie*. Much less trenchant in his views than Rousseau, Diderot rescued harmony from its detractors, but joined Rousseau in regarding music as a 'cri animal' in opposition to the old views of classicism, leaving Voltaire as one of the few holdouts in France.[21] The argument quickly spilled beyond the French border, assisted by Baron Grimm in his *Correspondance littéraire* and the dissemination of other letters and documents, and Sulzer took an especially keen interest in the matter, adapting it to his own argument about how music can civilize the savage, in effect re-directing the argument back to a classicism that Rousseau had rejected.

No country could match the boundless energy of the French for these types of arguments, and with the spread of these ideas similar debates emerged in virtually every other European country. When other composers came to France, as did one of the leading composers of opera Christoph Willibald von Gluck, despite what he may have actually thought about the relationship between words and music, his pronouncements on the subject fell into line with prevailing French thought, as in the famous dedication to *Alceste*: 'I have striven to restrict music to its true office of serving poetry by means of expression.'[22] When Mozart spent half a year in Paris in 1778, his father advised him to study well the taste of the French before composing for the Parisian audience, even discussing his works with people like Grimm and Jean-Georges Noverre.[23] The arguments composers had to contend with came from the pens of literati, musical connoisseurs in the cases of Rousseau and Diderot, but not from professional musicians, as Rameau had been, with philosophical aspirations. Musicians had little choice but to take these arguments very seriously, and adapt their styles and pronouncements accordingly, fearful of stirring up the intellectual beasts. Paris may have remained the centre of debate

20 *Ibid.*, pp. 15–16. 21 *Ibid.*, p. 17.
22 Oliver Strunk (ed.), *Source Readings in Music History* (New York, 1950), p. 674.
23 *Mozart: Briefe und Aufzeichnungen*, vol. 2, pp. 354 and 365.

on music, but perhaps it is not surprising that Mozart did not stay, that Gluck became something of a musical dead end and, with the exception of opera (leading lights including Lully and Cherubini, both Italians), that Paris did not emerge as the centre of the musical world. Vienna and Berlin became such centres, with their abundance of home-grown composers, as did London, which welcomed foreign composers without forcing them into a national mould.

Despite the pervasiveness of the French *philosophes*, the approaches to audience education in Germany moved in decidedly different directions. Here the tension between past and present unfolded with a general bias towards the past, and in many respects developed more as a tension between theory and practice than anything else. In some respects, arguments in France could develop as they did because eighteenth-century France could not boast many of the world's greatest composers; those on French soil who fitted the bill tended to be foreigners. Italy, Germany and Austria had many more leading composers, of course, and writers on music, often with philosophical backgrounds and a preoccupation with morality, who could not reconcile their views with the often more sensory types of music coming from the outstanding eighteenth-century practitioners. Forkel is an interesting figure in this regard, as a musician unlike Sulzer, and also as an academic at the University of Göttingen, one who had a strong philosophical inclination. In Forkel's scheme of things, the new *galant* style with all its emphasis on sound itself could not be taken seriously, since it lacked the means for edifying an audience. He made much of the distinction between *Kenner* and *Liebhaber* (expert/connoisseur and dilettante), and saw his own role as a music educator as one of transforming a dilettante into an expert.[24] He saw little of value in the music of the present, specifically the 1770s, which is when he wrote works such as *Ueber die Theorie der Musik, insofern sie Liebhabern und Kennern nothwendig und nütlich ist* (1777), with the exception of the music of C. P. E. Bach. Music needed to serve an intellectual function, but even though the sensory elements did not have to be entirely absent, music based on dance *topoi* would be inferior to music in which the principles of rhetoric could be recognized.[25] One can easily see how the music of Mozart and Haydn, if in fact Forkel knew any of it, would fare poorly in his scheme of things, whereas J. S. Bach would stand as the best possible musical model. His ambitious biography of Bach showed where his sentiments lay, and as a life-long resident of the university town of Göttingen, he attempted to educate the home audience. His preference for music roughly half a century old indicated where his priorities lay, and his failure to come to terms

24 Riley, *Musical Listening*, pp. 88–9. 25 See *ibid.*, p. 104.

with the present, like many writers on music in Germany, widened the gulf between theory and practice.

Music histories

Few writers on music were able to avoid the polemics of present versus past, as they became the champions of one side or the other. With the exception of England, the audiences of few countries had any interest in music of the past. Composers wrote new music for their patrons, for churches, or later in the century for concert or opera organizations, and that music usually had a very short shelf life. Most works vanished from sight after their initial performances, and with the exception of especially popular operas, there seemed little reason to revive works as new works would quickly replace them. Consequently works such as Bach's cantatas disappeared into dusty storage rooms, and when interest in them revived in the nineteenth century, many could not be found. Exceptions existed, when a composer had as profound an impact on audiences – as Handel did in England, for example – and organizations such as the Academy of Ancient Music came into being to keep alive these musical treasures from half a century earlier (although nothing before then).

In countries with no venues for the performance of earlier music, the option of exclusively new music did not sit well with all observers. Writers on music who were proponents of the Enlightenment generally welcomed the new, subscribing to notions of progress that saw the best of the latest achievements as the pinnacles in a larger continuum. For others, new music seemed to get progressively worse, in their view exploring novelty for novelty's sake alone, regrettably abandoning the great traditions of the past and failing to offer audiences anything intelligible or edifying. To some extent these contrasting views of the present in relation to the past gave rise to an entirely new way of thinking and writing about music in the eighteenth century, the venture into historiography. As with other types of writing, issues of taste remained central to the endeavour, but now attitudes about taste could be shaped by considerations of the past. Some of the first attempts to write histories of music may be attributed simply to their novelty value, perhaps being of interest to a segment of the reading public, as was true of the history started early in the century by Pierre Bourdelot and continued by his nephew Jacques Bonnet, who actively wondered whether this new type of enterprise would be a success.[26] These early attempts in France in the end had much less to do with revealing the origins and development of music than with casting light on the

26 Fubini, *Music and Culture*, p. 27.

controversy of French versus Italian music by putting the familiar argument into an historical context.

In England, two distinguished writers of music histories emerged at about the same time in the second half of the century, Charles Burney (1726–1814) and John Hawkins, and their strongly contrasting approaches to their monumental undertakings illustrate very nicely the differing attitudes to the past and the present. Thoroughly grounded in the Enlightenment, Burney looked at the great achievements of the present with delight, and became a champion of outstanding new composers. When Haydn, for example, came to England, he had no greater supporter than Burney, who paid Haydn the ultimate English compliment as the Shakespeare of music,[27] and Burney also gave high praise to other composers whom he believed deserved it, including Mozart. No armchair historian, Burney went to as many concerts as he could in order to have the widest possible knowledge of the music of his time, and he set out on arduous journeys across Europe to discover the music of other countries as well. He had two main purposes in making these journeys: one was to hear the latest music and meet the composers; the other was to uncover documentation of the past. His approach to historiography was clearly motivated by the present, as he wished to show the progression that had led to the great (indeed highest) achievements of the present. His *General History of Music from the Earliest Ages to the Present Period* in four volumes (1776–89), turned out to be exactly what the title said, giving a very comprehensive view of the music of the present period. He developed methodologies for talking about music of the past, methodologies that still remain of interest today, but the prior lack of engagement with music of the past did not make his task an easy one. For example, on his trip to Italy in 1772, he could find no documentation in Venice to support Vivaldi's existence.[28]

As a by-product of his main historical project, Burney wrote two other notable works, perhaps of even greater interest to us now than his *General History*, namely his musical travelogues or diaries compiled while collecting his material on the Continent, *The Present State of Music in Italy and France* (1771) and *The Present State of Music in Germany, the Netherlands and United Provinces* (1773). Here of course a long writing tradition already existed, especially in England where a trip to the Continent was a major undertaking and seemed exotic to many English readers. A curiosity about how people lived in other parts of the world fed the appetite for this type of writing, and many major writers indulged as well, including Goethe with his vivid descriptions of Italy in his *Italian Journey*. Writers of travel books would often slant them towards

27 See Landon, *Haydn in England*, p. 34. 28 Fubini, *Music and Culture*, p. 26.

their own fields or special interests, in the arts or sciences, and Burney's observations about music proved to be especially useful since they gave a slice of eighteenth-century musical life that provided major sources of information. Burney's humanity and the keenness of his observations shine through.

Whereas Burney directed his history to the present, in both content and attitude, Hawkins, in his *General History of the Science and Practice of Music* (1773), as the title suggests, took a very different tack. Hawkins had little interest in music of the present, most of which he did not like, and his history consequently focuses on music of the past. He did no travelling to gather his material, but instead went to books, treatises and other documents available to him in England. With his interest in the science of music, he focused on the music of the past for which it was possible to show science, unlike (in his view) the more frivolous music of the present. Burney revealed himself to be an empirical humanities scholar with the social outlook of the Enlightenment, while Hawkins, in contrast, took a rationalist approach, continuing in the older view that the arts needed to remain grounded in science. This older view of methodologies coincided with his view of music itself, namely that it was on a steady decline after the great achievements of the past, a past that could better illustrate than the present foundational principles such as rhetoric.[29] Both Hawkins and Burney found readers for their differing approaches.

Burney may have been something of an exception in undertaking such a huge project in order to extol the virtues of the present. Writers in other countries who were prepared to spend the time and effort on such projects usually did so because they had axes to grind in favour of the past. Padre Martini, the great musician and friend of the Mozarts in Bologna, published the first volume of his three-volume history (*Storia della musica*) in 1757, and did not even come close to the present in any of his work. He preferred the polyphonic rigour of music of the past, but in his history fell far short of his favourite subject, the counterpoint of Palestrina. In Palestrina's case he put together an exceptional collection of documents and manuscripts from the distant past that has been preserved in its entirety to the present day. In Germany, Forkel's orientation towards the past has already been noted, and developed most clearly in his *Allgemeine Geschichte der Musik* (1788–1801). He, too, did not get beyond the distant past, but his work has special relevance on account of his approach to periodization, which left a lasting legacy to German historiography and musicology.[30] In the passage through periods he did perceive a sense of development, but could see little evidence of that progressing beyond the work of J. S. Bach to the present. Progress need not be linear, and

29 *Ibid.*, pp. 28–9. 30 *Ibid.*, pp. 30–1.

Forkel believed that the time in which he lived represented a regression. Progress could once again be made when the past was understood, and he saw his own writing as helping that along.

Poets and novelists

Music or musical instruments became powerful images for poets and novelists during the eighteenth century, a trend that in fact offered one of the most interesting new ways of thinking about music. Far removed from the polemics of those who are more philosophically inclined, literary writers give us a different type of insight into the role of music in society and, more importantly, into the lives of individuals. Some of these writers were themselves excellent musicians, such as the pianist Jane Austen, who incorporated piano playing and piano music into a number of her novels, while others went more on instinct, responding to music and using it to enrich their imagery. Friedrich Schiller, for one, found the piano and its music to be a potent image in his poem *Laura am Klavier*, in which he allows Petrarch's muse Laura to speak in a modern, erotically provocative voice through the piano, at the same time retaining her sense of spiritual mystery. She keeps the latter with her angelic harmonies, 'like new-born seraphim from their heaven',[31] but Schiller also calls her 'Zauberin' (enchantress), capable of enticing and tempting with 'ein wollustig Ungestum' (a sensual impetuousness). Laura had become a familiar figure in late-eighteenth-century German poetry, but she could now sing with the seductive silvery tones of the fortepiano.

This seductive element of music proved especially useful for novelists, in part since musical instruments such as the piano, as a woman's instrument at the time, had specific gender associations. Nowhere does this work more effectively than in Goethe's *Die Leiden des jungen Werther* (1774), in which Werther's unrequited passion for Lotte smoulders because of the way her piano playing stirs him. Decorum prevents Goethe from exploring an actual relationship between an engaged or married woman and another man, but in the relationship that does emerge, in his response to her piano playing, he gets at something even more interesting and erotically charged, made possible by music. In this epistolary novel Werther reflects on his dilemma: 'Why couldn't I throw myself at her feet? Why couldn't I counter with an embrace and a thousand kisses? She escaped to the piano and sang to her own accompaniment in her sweet, low voice, and so melodiously. Never were her chaste lips more enchanting. It was as though they parted thirsty for the sweet tones that swelled forth

31 Trans. Richard Wigmore in *Schubert: The Complete Song Texts* (New York, 1988), p. 260.

from the instrument and only a furtive echo escaped them.'[32] Lotte herself is not entirely unconscious of the effect her playing can have, recognizing a parallel in dancing: 'if passion for dancing is sinful, then I cheerfully admit to it.'[33] Steven Huff sums up the effect she has on Werther: 'Given this context, the nexus between Lotte and the *Klavier*, the religious/erotic overtones of Lotte's music, and its ambiguous effect upon Werther all become understandable.'[34]

While discussions of music in literary works may not be the predominant mode of writing about music in the eighteenth century, they surely represent one of the most important, taking music out of the debates concerning morality or melody versus harmony and into an entirely different realm. Writers who insist on music serving an edifying role would probably have little use for the sensuality of its treatment in the works of Schiller and Goethe, but the sensuality clearly points to the romantics and the direction in which music itself would move in the nineteenth century. Writers such as Goethe genuinely understood the best music of the present, and in the end they carried the day, pointing vividly to the future, and perhaps even having an influence on it.

Select Bibliography

Baker, Nancy Kovaleff and Thomas Christensen (eds.). *Aesthetics and the Art of Musical Composition in the German Enlightenment*. Cambridge, 1995

Bauer, Wilhelm A. and Otto Erich Deutsch (eds.). *Mozart: Briefe und Aufzeichnungen*. 7 vols, Kassel, 1962–75

Blackall, Eric. *The Emergence of German as a Literary Language*. Cambridge, 1959

Bonds, Mark Evan. *Wordless Rhetoric: Musical Form and the Metaphor of the Oration*. Cambridge, MA, 1991

Christensen, Thomas. *Rameau and Musical Thought in the Enlightenment*. Cambridge, 1993

De Bolla, P. *The Discourse of the Sublime: Readings in the History, Aesthetics, and the Subject*. Oxford, 1989

Fubini, Enrico. *The History of Music Aesthetics*. Trans. M. Hartwell, London, 1990

(ed.). *Music and Culture in Eighteenth-Century Europe: A Source Book*. Trans. W. Freis, L. Gasbarrone and M. L. Leone, Chicago and London, 1994

Goethe, Johann Wolfgang von. *The Sorrows of Young Werther*. Trans. Catherine Hutter, London, 1962

Heartz, Daniel. *Music in European Capitals: The Galant Style, 1720–1780*. London and New York, 2003

Hosler, Bellamy. *Changing Aesthetic Views of Instrumental Music in 18th-Century Germany*. Ann Arbor, MI, 1981

32 Johann Wolfgang von Goethe, *The Sorrows of Young Werther*, trans. Catherine Hutter (London, 1962), p. 95.

33 *Ibid.*, p. 37.

34 Steven Huff, 'Lotte's Klavier: A Resounding Symbol in Goethe's *Die Leiden des jungen Werthers*', *The Germanic Review*, 59 (1984), p. 47.

Hoyt, Peter. 'The Classical Oration as a Model for Musical Form in the Eighteenth Century'. In K. Eberl, and W. Ruf (eds.), *Musikkonzepte – Konzepte der Musikwissenschaft*. Kassel, 1998

Huff, Steven. 'Lotte's Klavier: A Resounding Symbol in Goethe's *Die Leiden des jungen Werthers*'. *The Germanic Review*, 59 (1984), pp. 43–8

Kivy, Peter. *The Possessor and the Possessed: Handel, Mozart, Beethoven, and the Idea of Musical Genius*. New Haven, CT and London, 2001

Landon, H.C. Robbins. *Haydn: Chronicle and Works. Haydn in England, 1791–1795*. London, 1976

Le Huray, Peter and James Day (eds.). *Music and Aesthetics in the Eighteenth and Early-Nineteenth Centuries*. Cambridge, 1981

Lenneberg, Hans. 'Johann Mattheson on Affect and Rhetoric in Music'. *Journal of Music Theory*, 2 (1958), pp. 47–83 and 193–236

Morrow, Mary Sue. *German Music Criticism in the Late Eighteenth-Century: Aesthetic Issues in Instrumental Music*. Cambridge, 1997

Mozart, Leopold. *A Treatise on the Fundamental Principles of Violin Playing*. Trans. E. Knocker, 2nd edn., Oxford, 1951

Neubauer, John. *The Emancipation of Music from Language*. New Haven, CT and London, 1986

Riley, Matthew. *Musical Listening in the German Enlightenment*. Aldershot, 2004

Schroeder, David. *Haydn and the Enlightenment: The Late Symphonies and their Audience*. Oxford, 1990

Mozart in Revolt: Strategies of Resistance, Mischief, and Deception. New Haven, CT and London, 1999

Strunk, Oliver (ed.), *Source Readings in Music History*. New York, 1950

• PART II MUSIC FOR THE THEATRE •

· 8 ·

Italian opera in the eighteenth century

MARGARET R. BUTLER

The history of Italian opera in the eighteenth century is as much the history of theatres, cities and performers as it is the history of composers, genres and works. Its study has benefited from a number of masterful recent inquiries that take a variety of approaches.[1] The present summary views the history of Italian opera in the eighteenth century through the lens of the opera theatre, focusing on genres and their venues, seeking to elucidate categories of opera theatres – within and extending outside of Italy, in places where Italian opera was favoured – and exploring the implications of these varieties for the style of repertory represented by them. By no means a comprehensive overview of the history of all eighteenth-century theatres, nor a survey organized strictly according to cultural centres, composers, genres, or works (although these play integral roles), it highlights specific theatres and works, placing them in the context of the production process. Composers of eighteenth-century opera sought to 'tailor' their arias to an individual singer like a suit of clothes.[2] Applied more broadly, this famous metaphor might be expanded to entire

1 See, among others, Franco Piperno, 'L'opera in Italia nel secolo XVIII', in Alberto Basso (ed.), *Musica in scena. Storia dello spettacolo musicale*, 6 vols., vol. 2 (Turin, 1996), pp. 96–199; *idem*, 'Opera Production up to 1780', in *Operatic Production and its Resources*, trans. Lydia G. Cochrane (Chicago, IL, 1998), pp. 1–79 (orig. pub. as *Storia dell'opera italiana* 4: *Il sistema produttivo e le sue competenze*, eds. Lorenzo Bianconi and Giorgio Pestelli [Turin, 1987]); *idem*, 'State and Market, Production and Style', in Victoria Johnson, Jane E. Fulcher and Thomas Ertman (eds.), *Opera and Society in Italy and France from Monteverdi to Bourdieu* (Cambridge, 2007), pp. 138–59; Reinhard Strohm, *Dramma per Musica: Italian Opera Seria of the Eighteenth Century* (New Haven, CT, 1997); Daniel Heartz, *Music in European Capitals: The Galant Style, 1720–1780* (New York and London, 2003); Martha Feldman, *Opera and Sovereignty: Transforming Myths in Eighteenth-Century Italy* (Chicago, IL, 2007).

2 Leopold Mozart commented about Mozart's desire to compose arias that would best showcase the singer's abilities, 'so as to fit the costume to [the] figure' (24 November 1770), and a few years later Mozart stated that an aria should 'fit a singer as perfectly as a well-made suit of clothes' (28 February 1778). See Emily Anderson (ed. and trans.), *The Letters of Mozart and His Family*, 3rd edn. (London, 1985), pp. 497, 171. Several years before Leopold's observation about his son's compositional practice, Antonio Sacchini had expressed the same desire for arias he would compose for Turin's Teatro Regio. Turin, Archivio storico della città di Torino, Libri ordinati della Nobile Società dei Cavalieri, vol. 6, pp. 50, 22 December 1764: 'Sacchini … intends to set aside the most important arias and to compose them in Turin in order to better adapt them to the abilities of the leading singers' (Sacchini … intende riservarsi i pezzi d'arie più importanti, e comporli poi in Torino per adattarsi meglio all'abilità de' primi soggetti). Quoted in Margaret Ruth Butler, *Operatic Reform at Turin's Teatro Regio: Aspects of Production and Stylistic Change in the 1760s* (Lucca, 2001), p. 200.

operatic works themselves, allowing us to explain them as whole, integrated entities – they are manifestations of the preferences, status, conditions, background and identities of the patrons and audiences for whom they were produced and the facilities for which they were designed.

Theatres: organization and categories

Theatrical organization

A theatre's organization and administration were decisive for the shape of its works and many aspects of style. Examining these considerations requires us to appreciate factors such as a theatre's production season and performance schedule, the decision-making process that determined its repertory and personnel, its audiences, patronage, finances and subsidies. Such factors, traditionally considered 'external', are hardly of lesser importance than so-called 'internal' factors such as poetic and musical style; instead, they are crucial for understanding the identities and functions of different eighteenth-century operatic genres and of particular works.

The character of an Italian state influenced that of its cities and, in turn, that of its theatres. For the most part, eighteenth-century Italy's numerous theatres can be described in terms of broad categories that are determined by a complex of factors. Perhaps the most important distinction, and one that gave rise to other distinguishing features, is the extent to which a theatre more closely resembled in its seventeenth-century origins a court theatre or a public theatre, and the degree to which it combined elements of both.

Seventeenth-century origins

In that they were artistic products of the states that produced them, seventeenth-century court operas necessarily affirmed the power and prestige of the sovereign and utilized the facilities and resources of the court that sponsored them.[3] The musical and technical personnel involved constituted standing bodies of salaried people (a feature of court opera that was to be decisive in the production of the reform of public opera in the eighteenth

3 The following discussion highlights just some of the basic features of seventeenth-century opera. For a fuller overview see, for example, Ellen Rosand, *Opera in Seventeenth-Century Venice: The Creation of a Genre* (Berkeley, 1991); Lorenzo Bianconi and Thomas Walker, 'Production, Consumption, and Political Function of Seventeenth-Century Opera', *Early Music History*, 4 (1984), pp. 209–96; Beth L. Glixon and Jonathan E. Glixon, *Inventing the Business of Opera: The Impresario and His World in Seventeenth-Century Venice* (Oxford, 2006). A concise summary of opera's beginnings in Venice and its conventions is presented in Ellen Rosand, 'Venice, the Cradle of (Operatic) Convention', in Roberta Montemorra Marvin and Downing A. Thomas (eds.), *Operatic Migrations: Transforming Works and Crossing Boundaries* (Aldershot, 2006), chapter 1, pp. 7–20.

century). The decisive shift from court to commercial opera – famously inaugurated and represented by the Venetian performance in 1637 of *Andromeda* at the public Teatro di San Cassiano – coincided with the shift of the role and function of the audience. The role of a court opera's audience – that of its 'public', the anachronism of this term notwithstanding[4] – was to enhance the prestige of the ruler by its presence, the members thereby at once fulfilling their duties as courtiers and contributing to the elaborateness of the spectacle itself with their attendance. The public's role in court opera was a secondary and passive one, the primary and active role being that of the sovereign. In public opera the audience became the point of focus, took on an active role and assumed a distinctive identity. In their function as consumers, buying tickets and theatre boxes and supporting the works financially, audiences for public opera now possessed power and gained influence. The distinction between the role and function of audiences in seventeenth-century court and public opera was one that persisted to a certain extent into the eighteenth century and one that contributed to the differing character of the century's theatres.

Court and commercial opera in the seventeenth century were by no means mutually exclusive, and the latter by no means eclipsed the former at its inception. Examples abound of overlap and co-existence in these modes of production and consumption. Production systems were among their crucial distinguishing features and, like their audiences, were to influence the theatrical types of the eighteenth century as well.[5]

Commercial theatres were generally owned by families, individuals, or collectives comprising groups of nobles, who rented them out to impresarios. On the impresarial model, professional personnel that included commercial troupes of performers were recruited and engaged by the impresario. Admission to performances was charged, the impresario being held responsible for financial losses. The rise of the impresario's significance over the second half of the seventeenth and into the eighteenth century coincided with the increasingly public nature of opera fuelled by the gradual development of a circulation of repertory as well as that of an international production circuit, by means of which the era's leading singers, dancers and other personnel moved among Italy's many theatres.[6]

4 Bianconi and Walker, 'Production, Consumption, and Political Function'.
5 Points from the foregoing discussion are drawn from Franco Piperno, 'Opera Production up to 1780', pp. 2–7.
6 On the activities of a particular impresario, see William C. Holmes, *Opera Observed: Views of a Florentine Impresario in the Early Eighteenth Century* (Chicago, IL and London, 1993). On production practices that include the significance, function and role of impresarios, see John Rosselli, *The Opera Industry in Italy from Cimarosa to Verdi: The Role of the Impresario* (Cambridge, 1984) and *idem*, *Singers of Italian Opera: The History of a Profession* (Cambridge, 1992), chapter 4, pp. 79–90.

Principal and secondary houses

Most of the theatres of eighteenth-century Italy may be thought to fall into two broad categories: principal houses and secondary houses.[7] In Venice and Naples the categories were perhaps more fluid than in other places, and theatres in these cities did not always fit neatly within a single one. Certain theatres in fact occupied different categories over the course of their existence. But for theatres in other cities these categories may yield useful information that can be used better to understand their artistic products. The two theatrical types contrasted in size, prestige, patronage, function, administration and, to some degree, genre and repertory as well.

A principal theatre was a state theatre, the most prestigious in its city. Principal theatres descended from the tradition of the court theatre, from which they retained distinctive features. Their character was most pronounced in cultural centres with absolutist governments, although they existed in cities exhibiting other modes of government, too. They could be expansive in size and were patronized by large, relatively homogeneous audiences comprising the nobility and prosperous upper classes. Principal theatres played an integral role in a city's culture. They were the prime spots for patrons to meet, interact, see and be seen, the hub of the city's cultural and commercial activity – in other words, the beating heart of its body.

Their management sometimes involved an impresario, but many principal theatres, for all or part of their history, were managed by collective associations of nobles or patrician sponsors who incorporated elements of the impresarial system. Collective management worked differently in different principal theatres. Either the group of sponsors would engage an impresario to oversee production, or the members of the group themselves might make production-related decisions on their own, functioning as a sort of collective impresario. Carnival was the main performance season for principal theatres, although in certain cities opera was performed at other times as well; in cities lacking multiple theatres, opera might be given all year round. Leading personnel were hired by means of the international production circuit, with local personnel filling out the ranks of solo singers and other performers. Principal theatres generally presented works of opera seria, although works of other genres might be given according to the circumstances of a particular theatre. In cities in which the principal theatre was the only one, seasons certainly included both serious and comic operas, as well as other types of entertainment.

By contrast, secondary theatres were generally smaller, although their public varied more greatly, drawn from broader strata of society. Such theatres were

7 Piperno, 'Opera Production up to 1780', p. 42.

secondary in that they played a subordinate role relative to principal theatres and were less prestigious. Travelling companies usually comprised the performers, and works were presented in seasons other than Carnival (in cities possessing both principal and secondary theatres). Their management was closer to the seventeenth-century impresarial tradition. If a collective management were at all involved, that group would engage an impresario to oversee production. The repertory at secondary theatres included comic operatic genres, although opera was sometimes just one of many types of entertainment presented in a given season, which might encompass non-musical genres as well.

A dichotomy thus emerges between two complexes of qualities: court/principal/nobility/serious and impresarial/secondary/bourgeois/comic. These complexes can be considered to occupy opposite ends of a continuum, most theatres being situated at different points along it. Principal theatres generally blended features of court and impresarial models more than secondary theatres did and thus might be characterized as hybrids, neither strictly one nor the other but possessing qualities of both. The nature of the blend and degree of balance among the qualities determined a theatre's particular identity and its position along the continuum.

The designations 'principal' and 'secondary' by no means imply a value judgement. Secondary theatres were hardly secondary in importance in certain places, particularly Naples and Venice, and principal theatres in different cities in relation to each other might not be comparable in terms of influencing the development of musical style; for instance, Naples' Teatro di San Carlo and Palermo's Teatro di Santa Cecilia, both principal theatres, contrasted greatly in their significance during the eighteenth century.

Any broad generalizations necessarily have limitations. While it is useful to identify contrasting categories, it is equally important to recognize that the distinctions embedded in them were not always pronounced; strict separation among these categories was not the rule. Some principal houses sponsored opera buffa and other genres of entertainment as well as opera seria, sometimes on a regular basis and sometimes on rare occasions, depending on specific circumstances. Furthermore, different cities had theatres that can be understood in the context of the above mentioned dichotomy at different times in their histories; from 1740 onwards Turin had two main theatres dedicated to different genres and catering to different publics, but Milan did not have them until after 1776 and the destruction by fire of the Teatro Regio Ducale, which presented both opera seria and opera buffa. Milan's Teatro alla Scala, reserved for opera seria, was built in 1778 and the comic theatre, Teatro della Cannobiana, was built in 1779. Finally, it is important to keep in mind that certain cities – Rome, for example – were home to more than one court, and in certain others – Venice, most importantly, as we shall see – the court (of the doge, in this case) did not have the extent of involvement in the theatres and their activities as in other places.[8]

Circumstances affecting production in Italian theatres: performance seasons, the circuit, character types

Seasons

Performance seasons, like theatres of a particular city, had their own hierarchy. The regularity of their schedule, with their annual repetitions, facilitated the mechanisms of the international circuit and provided the temporal context in which it functioned. The existence of recurring periods of the year during which opera would be performed, applying to a broad geographic area, reflects the distinctly public character of eighteenth-century opera. Part of the framework of a city's culture, operatic seasons arose because of circumstances shaping the life of eighteenth-century people that varied as widely as the occurrence of good weather to the arrival of religious holidays. They were an important part of the structure and flow of the social life of a city's residents. Understanding performance seasons helps elucidate the particular rhythm of a city's musical life and the richness of its character, and that of its theatres as well.

Carnival comprised the period between Christmas and Lent, beginning on 26 December and ending on Shrove Tuesday (the date of which fell anywhere between early February and early March). This was the oldest season, associated with public opera from the time of its inception, its Venetian sponsors having capitalized on Carnival's festive atmosphere and heightened tourism to achieve commercial success. It was the main season for opera seria, during which the larger principal theatres primarily operated; it was consequently the most prestigious. Another with seventeenth-century roots, arising from the popularity of trade fairs, was the fair season, which ran for several weeks between April and October; certain cities such as Reggio and Padua maintained lucrative fair seasons during the eighteenth century.

The spring season took advantage of the continued pleasant weather of the spring months. Occurring sometime after Easter, running between April and the end of June, it especially benefited the smaller principal houses, which might hire the prominent singers engaged by the larger theatres for Carnival operas, like Parma's Teatro Ducale, and other larger ones as well, such as Bologna's Teatro Malvezzi and later the Teatro Comunale.

8 Heartz, *Music in European Capitals*, p. 1,000.

Principal theatres generally avoided the summer months, their noble patrons tending to abandon the city for their country estates, both to escape the heat and to oversee their harvests. Small-scale summer operatic performances were sometimes staged in suburban residences, such as the 1787 performance of Mozart's *Le nozze di Figaro* at Monza, Archduke Ferdinand's villa, outside Milan. The patrician sponsors' return from the leisure of the countryside tended to happen gradually, causing their sparse attendance at works performed during the autumn season, running from late August or September to the end of November, and contributing to this season's lower rank in prestige. Secondary theatres generally operated and flourished during the autumn season, however, their patrons being routinely present in the city year round. Religious holidays prevented the performance of opera in most places, during which times other genres dominated.[9]

Naples operated on a different schedule. The performance season at the Teatro di San Carlo was determined by name days and birthdays of the sovereigns, the months of performances naturally varying during the course of the century. Important months during large portions of the century were January, May, July, August, November and December, with opera occurring at other times as well, but varying considerably in frequency. In parts of the last decades of the eighteenth century, opera was given almost all year round.[10]

The circuit: principal theatres

Theatres functioned in the context of an international production circuit, by means of which the leading singers, dancers, designers, choreographers and other personnel trafficked among Italy's various theatres and those abroad. Difficult to study, since most of the materials that might provide information about it are either sparse and dis-unified or no longer survive, the circuit and its operation in the eighteenth century remains largely a mystery. Informal contact among impresarios and people involved in theatrical production in different places certainly facilitated it and allowed it to flourish. The *Indice de' teatrali spettacoli* attests to its vitality in the second half of the century; this theatrical periodical, printed successively in Milan, Venice and finally Rome, between 1764 and 1823, listed programmes and casts of companies of singers

9 The foregoing discussion is indebted to John Rosselli, 'Season', in Stanley Sadie (ed.), *The New Grove Dictionary of Opera*, vol. 4 (London, 2001), pp. 281–3; Thomas Bauman, 'The Eighteenth Century: Serious Opera', in Roger Parker (ed.), *The Oxford Illustrated History of Opera* (Oxford, 1994), pp. 49 and 50; Paolo-Emilio Ferrari, *Spettacoli Drammatico-Musicale e Coreografici in Parma dall'anno 1628 all'anno 1883* (Bologna, 1969; reprint of Parma, 1884).

10 See Paologiovanni Maione and Francesca Seller, *Il teatro di San Carlo di Napoli (1739–1777). Cronologia degli spettacoli (1737–1799)* (Naples, 2005), vol. 1.

and dancers engaged in Italy and abroad.[11] Theatres competed against each other for the most renowned performers of the era. They hired leading singers and dancers for operas of a given Carnival season to perform vocal and choreographic roles of the same rank in each opera. They sometimes hired designers for several seasons at a time. They engaged composers for individual operas, either the first or second of the Carnival season. The choice of operas came later; composers committed themselves to a work for a given theatre without usually knowing what that work would be. All of these personnel would be sent contracts (known as either 'scritture' or 'contratti'), which they signed and returned to the theatre. Theatres tended to fill out their rosters with local personnel for the lowest-ranking roles.

Vocal types and character types: principal theatres

Opera seria singers usually specialized in character types occupying different ranks. The higher-ranking roles were more prestigious and commanded the highest fees. The leading singers and dancers were usually among the most expensive components of a production and were the first to be chosen and contacted. This was certainly the case in Turin and probably in other places as well; the amounts spent on the singers of first rank sometimes influenced subsequent choices of singers for the remaining ranks. The highest rank comprised the primo uomo, usually a soprano castrato, the prima donna, usually a soprano, and the tenor. Second- and third-ranking characters followed – secondo and terzo uomo, seconda and terza donna, generally hired in order of importance. There might be an 'ultima parte', played by a man or woman, usually a local singer.

Principal/state theatres

Principal theatres varied as widely as the cities they inhabited. The metaphor of a state theatre as 'the flower in the city's buttonhole'[12] was perhaps nowhere more fitting than in capital cities of absolutist states, especially those with kings, or regents governing for emperors, as their heads of state.

Royal Theatres: Naples, Milan, Turin

The absolutist governments of Naples, Milan and Turin sponsored large state theatres that gave lavish operatic productions. Naples' Teatro San Carlo, Milan's

11 Roberto Verti, 'The Indice de' teatrali spettacoli, Milan, Venice, Rome 1764–1823: Preliminary Research on a Source for the History of Italian Opera', *Periodica Musica*, 3 (1985), pp. 1–7. Cited in Piperno, 'Opera Production up to 1780', p. 44. The *Indice* is published as *Un almanacco drammatico. L'indice de' teatrali spettacoli, 1763–1823*, ed. Roberto Verti (Pesaro, 1996), 2 vols.
12 Piperno, 'Opera Production up to 1780', p. 43.

Teatro Regio Ducale and Turin's Teatro Regio bear intriguing resemblances. A brief introduction to their significance and circumstances associated with their creation will facilitate comparison of their administrations and artistic products.

The Kingdom of Naples (or, Kingdom of the Two Sicilies) was ruled during the early eighteenth century by Spain until 1707 and then by the Hapsburgs until 1734. Subsequently Charles Bourbon, son of Philip V of Spain, regained control, established the kingdom as a monarchy, and ruled as Charles III until 1759, when he succeeded to the Spanish throne. His rule was a prosperous period in Neapolitan history and one during which Neapolitan opera began to achieve international prominence. His son then reigned as Ferdinand IV almost to the end of the century, the short-lived but artistically significant period of the Parthenopean Republic being followed by the brief return of the Bourbons and the arrival of Joseph Bonaparte in 1806.

During its eighteenth-century history Naples possessed two principal theatres, the Teatro di San Bartolomeo in the early part of the century, which was later replaced by the Teatro di San Carlo, one of the most illustrious theatres in all of Europe.[13] Works presented at the Teatro di San Bartolomeo and other theatres in the city established Naples as the pre-eminent centre for the era's most modern musical developments. Built around 1620, the San Bartolomeo was the venue for the operas of Alessandro Scarlatti, who directed them there and who came to prominence in Naples as the Spanish viceroy's *maestro di cappella* around the turn of the century.[14] The theatre grew in prominence when the Spanish viceroys began attending the opera. The opere serie set at the San Bartolomeo by Leonardo Vinci, Johann Adolph Hasse and other composers around 1720 helped further to establish the century's international operatic language. The broad appeal and wide dissemination of this new vocal style led opera seria to become synonymous with Neapolitan opera. Giovanni Pergolesi's *La serva padrona* (1733) was performed between acts of Pergolesi's own *Il prigoniero superbo*; it was commissioned for the birthday of Empress Elisabeth Christina, consort of Charles VI. The relationships among the theatres, the vice-regal chapel and the city's four conservatories, renowned and internationally known training grounds for many of the era's leading composers, significantly shaped Neapolitan theatrical works in both the principal and the secondary theatres.

In 1737 the Teatro di San Bartolomeo was demolished and replaced by the Teatro di San Carlo, one of the era's most prestigious and influential theatres. Built by Charles III, King of the Two Sicilies, it featured one of the largest

13 Franco Mancini, *Il teatro di San Carlo, 1737–1987* (Naples, 1987), 3 vols.; Michael F. Robinson, *Naples and Neapolitan Opera* (Oxford, 1972).
14 Bauman, 'The Eighteenth Century: Serious Opera', p. 53.

stages to date, an opulent interior and advanced technical capabilities. It hosted the era's most sought-after composers, singers, choreographers and dancers.

Turin was the capital of the Savoyard state, which comprised the principality of Piedmont and duchies and territories on both sides of the western Alps. It became a kingdom after the Savoy duke Vittorio Amedeo II acquired Sicily in 1713, which he was forced to exchange for Sardinia in 1720 as a result of negotiations connected with peace treaties following the War of the Austrian and Spanish Successions, the state consequently losing status. Piedmont, a geographically precarious state, exhibited a militaristic culture shaped in part in response to the state's constant challenge of defending its borders against larger, surrounding powers. It consequently developed into one of the strongest of the Italian states in the eighteenth century, with correspondingly lavish cultural products.

Turin's Teatro Regio, built in 1740, three years after the Teatro di San Carlo, exhibits the hybrid character typical of principal theatres, which merges aspects of both court and public theatre traditions. Like the San Carlo, it was internationally known during the century for its lavish productions of opere serie by the era's leading composers. It attracted many leading solo singers, dancers, choreographers and designers. Its spacious, opulent theatre boasted the latest technical advances and presented two original opere serie every Carnival season. Its repertory reflected the latest stylistic trends affecting opera seria throughout the century and it was a leader among Italian theatres not only in the production of new works but also in the integration of innovative elements drawn from the style of the tragédie-lyrique that began to influence the style of opera seria as a result of mid-century reform efforts.[15]

Under Spanish rule from the sixteenth century, Lombardy became part of the Austrian Empire in the early eighteenth century. Milan was then ruled by governors appointed by Vienna. A long-standing tension between the Milanese nobility and the Austrian governors marked not only the city's politics but also the history of its theatres.

Milan's Regio Teatro Ducale was among the oldest of Italy's principal theatres, having been inaugurated in 1717. At the time of its construction it was one of the largest, and was Milan's only public theatre. Although one of the most prestigious of Italy's theatres, it did not compare until the 1770s with most other state theatres – Naples, Venice, Turin, Rome and Parma – in the production of original works.[16] It rose to prominence for the attention lavished on its theatrical ballets, becoming a major centre for innovations in

15 Butler, *Operatic Reform at Turin's Teatro Regio*.
16 Kathleen Kuzmick Hansell, 'Opera and Ballet at the Regio Ducal Teatro of Milan, 1771–1776: A Musical and Social History', PhD thesis (University of California at Berkeley, 1980), 2 vols.

dance towards the end of its history. It burned in 1776 and was soon replaced by the Teatro alla Scala. Given the close geographical proximity between Milan and Turin, there were many points of contact, including much overlap in personnel and numerous similarities in repertory.[17] Like Turin and Naples, Milan sought to engage the leading performers of the era. The famous scenographers, the Galliari brothers Ferdinando and Bernardino, designed the scenery. Perhaps the biggest difference between Milan on the one hand and Turin and Naples on the other came in the variety and type of repertory. While Turin's Teatro Regio and Naples's Teatro di San Carlo presented exclusively opere serie, Milan's Teatro Ducale presented both serious and comic works – entirely consistent for a principal theatre in a city without multiple theatres.

Milan's Teatro Ducale was the one Italian theatre where Wolfgang Amadeus Mozart's operatic works enjoyed great success, the premieres of his opere serie *Mitridate, rè di Ponto* and *Lucio Silla* having benefited from the relationship between Hapsburg Emperor Joseph II and his brother, Archduke Ferdinand, ruler of Milan. Count Karl Joseph von Firmian, a regent appointed in Vienna, determined the works to be performed at the Teatro Ducale and upon hearing some of Mozart's arias in a private performance gave the composer a contract for the first opera of Carnival 1771. This resulted in *Mitridate, rè di Ponto* (1770), the libretto of which came from Turin – it was an original work by the Teatro Regio's house poet and had been set there in 1767 by Quirino Gasparini. On the basis of *Mitridate*'s success Mozart received the commission for another opera seria, which became *Lucio Silla* (1772). Mozart's third opera for Hapsburg Milan, *Ascanio in Alba*, was one of the operas for the nuptials of Archduke Ferdinand and Princess Maria Beatrice of Modena in 1771.[18] A serenata on a libretto by Giovanni De Gamerra, it was on a smaller scale and was not given in the Teatro Ducale, but in the cathedral.[19]

Running the royal theatres: societies of nobles

Several principal theatres during the century utilized a collective assembly of individuals who had varying degrees of control over the theatres' management

17 Similarities in repertory at Turin and Milan are given in Mercedes Viale Ferrero, *La Scenografia dalle origini al 1936, Storia del Teatro Regio*, ed. Alberto Basso (Turin, 1980), vol. 3, p. 240.

18 See Daniel Heartz, 'Three Operas for Habsburg Milan', in *Haydn, Mozart and the Viennese School, 1740–1780* (New York and London, 1995), pp. 544–55. See also Kathleen Kuzmick Hansell, 'Mozart's Milanese Theatrical Works', in Susan Parisi (ed.), *Music in the Theatre, Church, and Villa: Essays in Honor of Robert Lamar Weaver and Norma Wright Weaver* (Warren, MI, 2000), pp. 195–212 and John A. Rice, 'A Dispute Involving the Musico Manzoli and Mozart's *Ascanio in Alba*', *Fonti Musicali Italiane*, 9 (2004), pp. 85–97.

19 Alberto Basso, *I Mozart in Italia: Cronistoria dei viaggi, documenti, lettere, dizionario dei luoghi e delle persone* (Rome, 2006) provides a compendium of the Mozarts' Italian travels and activities. The Italian theatres Mozart visited and the productions he attended at them (in Milan and elsewhere), with information on performers, are listed in appendix VI; Milan house poet Giuseppe Parini's account of the 1771 wedding festivities appears in appendix IV.

and administration. This was a feature common to Milan's Teatro Regio Ducale, Turin's Teatro Regio and Naples' Teatro di San Carlo.

From the time of its inauguration in 1740, Turin's Teatro Regio was run by the Nobile Società dei Cavalieri, a group of about forty Piedmontese noblemen (a total that varied slightly throughout the century) selected by the Duke of Savoy. Their statutes show that the Cavalieri were charged with decisions about all aspects of production, were responsible for drawing up a financial projection and budget in advance of each season and for accounting for all expenses, and would receive an annual subsidy from the duke. The constitution of the Cavalieri resembled other centralizing reforms undertaken by Vittorio Emanuele II at around the same time.[20]

Turin's Cavalieri elected seven directors from among its membership, five of whom were in charge of a different sector of production: music, dance, scene design, costume design and libretto (the remaining offices were secretary and treasurer). These powerful men assumed the financial responsibility for their sectors and made all decisions for related aspects of production, subject to the approval of the other directors. They decided on pre-existing librettos and subject matter for new ones, chose, contacted, drew up contracts for and hired personnel, and approved payments to them and purchases of materials; they also performed many other duties related to production and the running of the theatre. The directors functioned as a collective impresario for the Teatro Regio, with each selecting, contacting and engaging the personnel in his sector. Although they had the occasional help of an envoy, whom they called an 'agent' and sometimes sent out to recruit performers, the directors themselves communicated on an ongoing basis with all personnel, conducting negotiations and issuing contracts and payments, and making all other decisions for every aspect of production. After the dismissal of the last impresario at the court theatre, the Teatro Regio never operated on the single impresarial model.

The treasurer drew up a summary of all expenditures and profits from the previous year, which was presented to the entire body at their annual meeting, and used to make production decisions for the coming year. The directors met periodically to deliberate and report on matters of production, keeping meticulously detailed records of their conversations and of all expenditures. The body of documents they produced exhibits a uniformity and survives with a consistency greater than for perhaps any other eighteenth-century theatre, affording a unique glimpse into its production practices and their influence on style.

20 Vittorio Amedeo II actually created the Nobile Società dei Cavalieri in 1727, before the establishment of the Teatro Regio. This body managed the theatre until 1792, whereupon the French invasion of the city forced its temporary closure. On the activities of the Cavalieri and the early history of Turin's Teatro di Corte and Teatro Regio, see Marie-Thérèse Bouquet, *Il teatro di corte. Dalle origini al 1788*, *Storia del Teatro Regio di Torino*, ed. Alberto Basso (Turin, 1976), vol. 1.

Turin's Nobile Società dei Cavalieri administered the Teatro Regio (and the Teatro Carignano, Turin's main comic theatre, as well as other, smaller theatres) throughout the century, except during the years of the Napoleonic occupation of the city, demonstrating a regularity and efficiency in its management structure and style that seems not to be paralleled elsewhere. News of Turin's management's efficiency evidently spread during the second half of the century; Turin's directors received requests from several Italian theatres for copies of their administrative statutes, including one from Naples.

The Teatro di San Carlo in Naples was administered differently at different times in its history, and attempted to combine the impresarial and collective management models. Groups of nobles (known as a Deputazione or Giunta de' teatri) governed the theatre periodically, engaging an impresario and holding him accountable. Evidence suggests that in a restructuring of administrative management in the late 1770s, Naples modelled its new administration on Turin's, having requested a copy of their governmental statutes and seems to have tried – temporarily and unsuccessfully – a variation of their organizational model.[21]

Additional points of contact and similarity between Turin and Naples facilitate their comparison. The two cities' aspirations to royal status shaped their artistic products including but not limited to their operas, such as architecture and fine arts, suggesting that a 'spirit of competitiveness' might have existed between them.[22] Mutual enrichment certainly marked their relationship in any case. Their repertories were similar, with many of the same librettos receiving settings by different composers, and they often employed the same musical personnel. Well-known non-Italian composers included both theatres in their Italian tours, a testament to the venues' shared renown. Turin's directors chose certain librettos specifically because of the success they had enjoyed in Naples. The theatres were similar in shape and general design although the size and capacity of the San Carlo exceeded those of the Regio. Finally, their managements differed significantly in consistency and in form, although both blended public and court-derived models.

Societies of nobles were important to the history of Milan's Teatro Regio Ducale, especially at its inception. But they played a minor role here in comparison to their role in Turin. During the first forty years of its history, the theatre was run by the Collegio dei Vergini Spagnuoli, as the court theatre had been in the seventeenth century; established by Philip II of Spain, this

21 This point and some of the following points are drawn from Margaret R. Butler, 'Opera Fit for Kings: Royal Theatres in Turin and Naples in the Eighteenth Century', in Alberto Basso (ed.), *Miscellanea di Studi 6, Il Gridelino 23* (Turin, 2006), pp. 197–212. On administration at the San Carlo, see Michael F. Robinson, 'A Late 18th-Century Account Book of the San Carlo Theatre, Naples', *Early Music*, 18 (1990), pp. 73–81 and Anthony R. DelDonna, 'Production Practices at the Teatro di San Carlo, Naples, in the Late 18th Century', *Early Music*, 30 (2002), pp. 429–45.

22 Robert Oresko, 'Culture in the Age of Baroque and Rococo', in George Holmes (ed.), *The Oxford Illustrated History of Italy* (Oxford, 1997), p. 161.

college educated girls and women whose fathers had died in the service of Spain, and received all profits from entertainments. After Hapsburg rule was established, the Regio Ducale was managed by the Collegio who were answerable to governors appointed by Vienna. They imported many works previously performed elsewhere, especially in Naples and Venice. In 1737 the new Austrian governor charged a council of Cavalieri Direttori with the running of the theatre. They engaged various impresarios and in 1752 oversaw restoration and improvements to the theatre. New works began to appear with more frequency. In 1755, an influential impresario, Gaetano Crivelli, received an eighteen-year contract, consequently playing a decisive role in the shift the Teatro Ducale was to take. It was in an impresario's interest to engage the finest performers available, since he was responsible for any financial losses incurred from unsuccessful works. Crivelli's contract makes this very clear, even specifying cities whose theatres were to be emulated by Milan. The singers engaged in Milan were to be the same as, or on par with, those who had performed in Naples, Venice, Turin and Reggio [Emilia] in similar roles[23] – testimony to the prestige and influence of the theatres in these four cities.

After the construction of the Teatro alla Scala in 1778, dedicated solely to opera seria, Milan's opera began to achieve the status shared by that of the principal European centres. And upon the establishment the following year of a smaller, comic theatre, the Teatro della Cannobiana, the distinction, by now witnessed in Italian cities generally, between a principal theatre dedicated to opera seria and a secondary one dedicated to comic works, became more pronounced in Milan.

These three royal theatres can be compared in other respects as well: for example their size and structure, hierarchical seating arrangement and significance of the gambling establishments in the theatrical building (both as a component of entertainment as well as a profitable enterprise influencing the theatres' prosperity). Their schedules demonstrate the function they served within their respective social frameworks. While Turin's Teatro Regio and Milan's Teatro Regio Ducale both presented two opere serie in each Carnival season (comic works being presented at the Ducale during spring and, later, autumn) the schedule at Naples' Teatro di San Carlo involved performances on birthdays and name days of its sovereigns and other members of the noble family. From 1745 onwards the numbers of productions per year varied, increasing gradually from four to five or six, and decreasing to two in the last decade. Each work was performed for a certain number of nights that remained consistent regardless of financial success. Connections among the theatres illustrate the functioning of the

23 The foregoing discussion draws on Hansell, 'Opera and Ballet at the Regio Ducal Teatro of Milan', chapter 1, pp. 15–63 (see esp. pp. 21–3).

Italian production circuit, especially regarding repertory and performers. All three showcased lavish productions of Metastasian works to the end of the century and beyond (La Scala of course supplanting the Ducale in Milan and continuing this aspect of the Ducale's tradition). The three theatres kept up with each other's activities; certain librettos were chosen for setting in Turin after their Naples successes, and a few of the many connections in repertory between Turin and Milan have already been mentioned. Although in administrative terms all three were hybrids, incorporating aspects of impresarial and court theatre traditions, and although all instituted a collective management system at one stage or another, Turin's artistic directors were much more involved in the actual production process than were Milan's Cavalieri or Naples's Deputazioni, who engaged impresarios to handle the actual production. Turin exhibited a greater consistency in its administration over time, which led, in certain respects, to a greater stylistic consistency as well.

Other principal/state theatres: ducal theatres in Parma, Florence, Reggio Emilia

In that they were also state theatres, the principal theatres in the cities at the seats of ducal power in Italy bore many similarities to those of Italy's kingdoms. Perhaps the greatest differences lay in their management, as well as variety in repertory and audience.

The Duchy of Parma's strong ties with France influenced the repertory and style of Italian opera presented at its principal theatre, the Teatro Ducale. The tastes of the Bourbon court and the cosmopolitan view and innovative direction of the minister of theatres, Guillaume du Tillot, shaped the works at the Teatro Ducale. The theatre's eighteenth-century repertory was eclectic, including opere buffe and French tragédies-lyrique as well as traditional and experimental opera seria. More significantly than any other theatre in the Italian states, Parma's Teatro Ducale participated in the path-breaking French-inspired reform efforts affecting opera seria at mid-century. Du Tillot oversaw theatrical activity and engaged impresarios. Financial support from the Bourbon court was essential to the theatre's success.

Florence's principal theatre, the Teatro di via della Pergola ('the Pergola'), had opened in 1657;[24] its eighteenth-century history begins with its re-opening in

24 Robert Lamar Weaver and Norma Wright Weaver, *A Chronology of Music in the Florentine Theatre 1751–1800* (Warren, MI, 1993), vol. 2. For a discussion of Pietro Leopoldo's theatrical regulations and the subsequent shifts in the policy governing the city's theatres, leading first to the profusion and then to the curtailment of their activities, see pp. 35–49; for a discussion of the Pergola and its activities see pp. 14–22 and 45–9. A chronology integrating all of the known Florentine theatres and their productions from the second half of the century comprises vol. 2 of this series; vol. 1 provides the same survey for the first half. Robert Lamar Weaver and Norma Wright Weaver, *A Chronology of Music in the Florentine Theatre 1590–1750* (Detroit, MI, 1978), vol. 1.

1718. The prominence of Florence's many academies influenced operatic culture at the Pergola especially because the theatre was owned by the Accademia degli Immobili and many of its impresarios from the first half of the century came largely from their ranks. One of the most influential, Luca Casimiro degli Albizzi, promoted works by Vivaldi and his contemporaries. His personal papers and related documents provide a rare glimpse into the activities of an impresario and the day-to-day workings of the Pergola in the 1720s and 1730s.[25] The theatre received financial support from the academicians as well as an annual subsidy from the grand-ducal government, a situation similar to other principal theatres.

Two factors combined to influence the nature and quality of the works at the Pergola during much of the century. One was the regular turnover of impresarios during the first half, and the resulting inconsistent management that led to the general decline in the quality of works. Another, during the second half of the century, was the transition in the political control of Tuscany – upon the death of the last Medici grand duke – to the Hapsburgs of Austria. Francis I ruled as regent, remaining in Vienna. Starting in 1765, with the reign of the Grand Duke Pietro Leopoldo of Tuscany, and lasting until 1790, the Pergola rose to prominence, presenting many works by leading composers that illustrated the most up-to-date late eighteenth-century stylistic trends. In the last decades of the century comic operas were added to the theatre's repertory.

The principal theatre in Reggio Emilia received a subsidy from the Este court in Modena, whose dukes supported the theatre primarily because of its importance to the state's economy. It represents a merging of court and public theatrical models and a combination of impresarial and absolutist management.[26] Unlike many other principal theatres that operated during Carnival or at other times, the theatre's performance season was linked to the popular fair held during the spring months, which attracted many visitors to the mutual benefit of each. Reggio's theatre was clearly of high rank; as previously mentioned, it was listed in Crivelli's contract for Milan's Teatro Ducale as one of the theatres to be emulated by Milan in terms of the prominent singers hired.

Principal/state theatres: city theatres in the Republics of Venice, Bologna, Genoa

The character of the cities that were seats of government within republics, rather than in monarchies, varied greatly from those of absolutist governments. Their character in turn affected that of their theatres.

25 Holmes, *Opera Observed*.
26 Piperno, 'Opera Production up to 1780', p. 37. On Reggio, see also Paolo Fabbri and Roberto Verti, 'Struttura del repertorio operistico reggiano nel Settecento', in Susi Davoli (ed.), *Civiltà teatrale e Settecento emiliano* (Bologna, 1986), pp. 257–99.

Venice ranked close to Naples in the early decades of the century as a thriving and influential operatic centre. Power lay in the 'widespread network' of noble families who owned Venice's theatres.[27] Like Naples, Venice possessed a broad mosaic of theatres that varied so widely in their management, public and character that the dichotomy already mentioned – principal/seria contrasted with secondary/buffa – applies less well to Venice than to other centres. Not surprisingly, in the city where impresarial theatre developed and from which it spread, secondary theatres were more numerous than in other major cities and in some respects of greater importance.

The Teatro di San Giovanni Grisostomo, which can be considered a principal theatre or a highly ranked secondary theatre attracting an aristocratic audience, flourished in the early years of the century. It hosted many of the most famous singers and mounted works by the most prominent composers; two of Metastasio's librettos received their first settings here. Hasse's setting of *Artaserse* for the theatre (1730) became one of the best-known early-eighteenth-century serious works.

Two theatres played a crucial role in the city's theatrical life later in the century: the Teatro di San Benedetto and the Teatro La Fenice. The San Benedetto, the 'noblest and most luxurious in Venice'[28] was eighteenth-century Venice's principal theatre, presenting opere serie almost exclusively. Catering to an elegant and exclusive audience, it resembled in this respect the Teatro di San Giovanni Grisostomo, but was smaller in size. Built by the Grimani family in the early 1750s, its period of greatest importance occurred between its rebuilding after destruction by fire in 1774 and the opening of La Fenice in 1792; during the 1770s and 1780s it put on three or four productions each year.

The construction of the Teatro La Fenice – an elegant theatre built in 1792 specifically for opera seria and ballet – is only one example of an expensive new theatre being built during the eighteenth century for the purpose of cultivating the genre.[29] After its advent and dedication to opera seria, the San Benedetto began to present comic opera. La Fenice's establishment, at the time that opera seria was supposedly in decline, testifies to the genre's endurance and longevity as well as to the privileged role of the theatre within the city's civic and cultural life. Controversies between its patrician sponsors and the impresarios who ran it highlight some of the central issues affecting eighteenth-century operatic production. For example, the constant demand for ever-more extravagant

27 Piperno, 'Opera Production up to 1780', p. 8.
28 Thomas Bauman, 'The Society of La Fenice and Its First Impresarios', *Journal of the American Musicological Society*, 39 (1986), p. 333.
29 Bauman, 'The Eighteenth Century: Serious Opera', p. 48.

productions often forced impresarios to over-extend the subvention they received from a theatre's sponsor, sometimes resulting in grave consequences. One of La Fenice's impresarios poisoned himself when, in serious financial distress and having resigned his post under pressure from the theatre's administrative directors, he was passed over for renewal of his contract.[30] The Teatro La Fenice witnessed a crucial stage in opera seria's transformation and revitalization at the end of the century, as we shall see.

Bologna's principal theatre before its destruction by fire in 1745 was the Teatro Malvezzi. A group of noblemen organized a move to establish a new theatre, which received financial backing from the senate and the papal government. The new, prestigious theatre, the Teatro Comunale (also known as the Teatro Pubblico), featured a design by Antonio Galli-Bibiena and opened ceremonially with Gluck's *Il trionfo di Clelia*. It was leased to various impresarios during the century, resulting in presentation of a mixed repertory in three annual seasons. In 1778 the Teatro Comunale mounted a production of Gluck's *Alceste* in which the production staff and theatrical administration wrestled with the logistics of incorporating the work's integrated choral and danced episodes, elements of French-inspired operas that often challenged the resources and staff at Italian theatres.

Genoa was the capital of an independent republic. Its musical theatre was strongly influenced by Venice from the sixteenth century onwards in both repertory and the strength of the impresarial administrative model. The principal theatre was the Teatro Sant'Agostino, built in 1703 and owned by the Pallavicino family, which rivalled the old Teatro Falcone that had been in existence since the 1640s and owned by the Durazzo family. The two families reached an agreement in which their theatres would function on alternate years, but in 1770 the Durazzo family bought the Sant'Agostino (as they had done with minor theatres as well). In 1772 the city's enterprising citizens formed an association, the Impresa dei Teatri di Genova, in order to manage all of the city's theatres. The senate of the republic granted the society both an exclusive right to sponsor spectacles and a right prohibiting other theatres from opening.

Theocratic state theatre: the Teatro Argentina in Rome

Rome was a vibrant operatic centre in the seventeenth century and in the eighteenth boasted numerous theatres, several of which presented serious and comic works. The Teatro Argentina presented opera seria most often. Its management varied between corporate and individual control until a

30 Bauman, 'The Society of La Fenice', pp. 341–2.

shareholders' society composed of some thirty Roman noblemen, the Società e Compagnia di Cavalieri, ran it from 1761 to 1764; for a few years, therefore, it resembled Turin's Teatro Regio and also Venice's Teatro La Fenice at its founding in 1792, which were also run by groups of nobles. The Argentina's status as a principal theatre important to the city's identity was reflected in the charter drawn up for the society.

Opera seria was a prominent product in Rome, at the Argentina and elsewhere. At the Teatro delle Dame, for example, the first performances of five of the seven serious operas Metastasio penned during his years in Italy (before his move to Vienna in 1730) were given at this theatre, and others soon followed. The works of other librettists who imitated Metastasio's style were also featured, including Mattia Verazi's *Ifigenia in Aulide* set by Jommelli for the Teatro Argentina in 1751. The Argentina, with its six tiers of boxes, was comparable in size to other leading Italian theatres; Denis Diderot and Jean Le Rond d'Alembert included it in their comparison of theatres in the *Encyclopédie*, which presents designs, diagrams of the layout and construction, size and dimensions of Turin's Teatro Regio, Naples's Teatro San Carlo and Rome's Teatro Tordinona and Teatro Argentina.[31]

The principal Italian theatres discussed above are just some of those that formed the international circuit, which could not have operated without the participation of many others as well. Those assuming prominence from mid-century onwards include the Teatro Santa Cecilia in Palermo, the Teatro Nuovo in Padua (1751), the Teatro Nazari in Cremona (1747), the Teatro Condominiale (Pubblico) in Senigallia (1752), the Teatro dell'Accademia Filarmonica in Verona (1754) and the Teatro Nuovo in Novara (1779).

Opera seria: origins and conventions

The genre that reigned supreme on the stages of Italy's principal theatres was opera seria. Although theatres often competed more for famous singers and dancers, as a composer's reputation grew he became increasingly sought after by leading theatres. Principal theatres looked to hire *maestri di cappella*; those without court appointments were not high in demand. The leading opera seria composers in the first part of the century were Leonardo Vinci, Johann Adolph Hasse, Leonardo Leo, Giovanni Pergolesi, Niccolò Jommelli and Baldassare Galuppi. Emerging slightly later were Tommaso Traetta, Gian Francesco

31 Denis Diderot and Jean Le Rond d'Alembert, *Encyclopédie, ou Dictionnaire raisonné des Sciences, des Arts et des Métiers, par une Société de gens de Lettres. Recueil de planches, sur le sciences, les arts libéraux, et les arts méchaniques, avec leur explication* (Paris, 1772), vol. 10. The comparison of the theatres is discussed briefly in Robinson, *Naples and Neapolitan Opera*, p. 8; Franco Mancini, *Il Teatro di San Carlo 1737–1987: la storia, la struttura*, vol. 1 of *Il Teatro di San Carlo 1737–1987* (Naples, 1987), 3 vols., p. 28.

de Majo, Antonio Sacchini, Niccolò Piccinni and Pasquale Anfossi, followed by Domenico Cimarosa, Giovanni Paisiello and Niccolò Zingarelli. Many of these figures feature in the development of comic opera, thus making their mark in both genres.

Opera seria's origins lie in the literary reform undertaken by the Roman Accademia dell'Arcadia in the 1690s.[32] 'Dramma per musica' was the name most often used from the seventeenth to the early nineteenth century to refer to Italian operas, appearing on librettos and reflecting the genre's identity as a form of dramatic literature. In 1740 a comic libretto carried the label 'dramma giocoso per musica'. 'Opera', the more colloquial term, appeared in sources other than literary ones and over time 'opera buffa' and 'opera seria' began to be used as designations. In the later eighteenth century 'opera seria' emerged as the standard term for serious opera, differentiating the serious from the comic variety.

The Arcadian reformers were grounded in the tradition of seventeenth-century French drama – of Pierre Corneille and of Jean Racine – which exemplified the principles of classical Greek drama. The Aristotelian unities of time, place and action provided more a theoretical than a practical foundation, lending consistency and verisimilitude to the dramatic action of the dramma per musica. Dramas were intended to 'enlighten and instruct' through interaction among characters who faced – and resolved – a moral dilemma involving a conflict between love on the one hand and duty and honour on the other. Historical events and the people in them, as opposed to mythological events and characters, provided the genre's backdrop and materials, earning it the moniker 'heroic opera'. Heroes representing actual people from significant historical events wrestling with psychological and emotional conflict were thought to be more appropriate models than mythological characters for provoking the sympathy and compassion of spectators. The norms of behaviour followed by the dramma per musica's characters were linked to the aristocratic culture in which the genre developed and which cultivated and sponsored it. The virtue of the enlightened ruler and the decorous conduct of those around him were to be witnessed in the rational outcome of the opera's action and the reasoned series of events that lead to the conflict's resolution. The victorious emergence of the hero at the opera's conclusion was an allegory for the triumph of the enlightened sovereign. The members of the Arcadian Academy sought to improve the literary quality of libretto poetry through a simplification of its structure along classical lines. Comic elements (scenes and characters) were deemed to contribute to the disorderly nature of the libretto and were thus purged, a crucial factor in the development of the intermezzo.

32 On opera seria, see Reinhard Strohm, 'Introduction: The dramma per musica in the Eighteenth Century', in *Dramma per Musica*, pp. 1–29, to which the following discussion is indebted.

The Accademia dell'Arcadia included both librettists and composers. While Apostolo Zeno (1668–1750) emerged as the leading figure, other librettists included Silvio Stampiglia and Antonio Salvi; the composers, some of whom were leading figures in the genre's early history, included Alessandro Scarlatti and Francesco Gasparini. Many librettos emanating from this group in the early 1700s were modelled on French classical plays. An example is Zeno's *Lucio Vero*, which enjoyed long-standing success, being set numerous times throughout the century and eventually reworked as *Vologeso*, after which both continued to circulate. Zeno's librettos dominated opera in Venice in the early years of the century; in part his emergence as the leading figure of the Arcadian reform can be attributed to the recognition given him in Pier Jacopo Martello's writings on opera.

Zeno was appointed poet to the Hapsburg court in 1718, and was succeeded by Pietro Metastasio (Pietro Trapassi) in 1730. Metastasio's elegant and mellifluous verses and their associated conventions became emblems of the dramma per musica. His librettos circulated widely, receiving hundreds of settings until the end of the eighteenth century and beyond by composers in Italy and across Europe. 'Metastasian opera' became synonymous with aristocratic patronage and enhanced the prestige of the sovereigns who sponsored it. As a high-class, refined art form it was the hallmark of the principal Italian theatres. Among Metastasio's most popular librettos were *Artaserse*, *Alessandro nelle Indie*, *L'Olimpiade*, *Adriano in Siria*, *Demetrio*, *Demofoonte*, *Didone abbandonata*, *Nitteti* and *Antigono*. *Il trionfo di Clelia* and *La clemenza di Tito* also received important settings during the century.

Since opera seria emerged from the context of a specifically literary reform, many of its conventions stem from aspects of poetic structure and form. An eighteenth-century opera is rightly considered to be 'the musical garment in which the drama is presented'.[33] The poem was primary in importance, as evident in the genre's name. A 'Metastasian' dramma per musica (hereafter opera seria) emphasized a streamlined structure eschewing extraneous characters, action and sub-plots; the interactions of between five and eight characters occurred over about twenty scenes, which took the form of three acts, ending with a *lieto fine*. The position of each character within the hierarchy that determined their status, actions and dramatic function also determined the frequency and order of their arias. The structural consistency of the poem was highly valued, and occurred through the regular alternation of verses of recitative in *versi sciolti* with those of arias in a variety of poetic meters. Arias served a wide array of expressive functions, as Metastasio himself explained. The

33 Reinhard Strohm, 'Towards an Understanding of the opera seria', in *Essays on Handel and Italian Opera* (Cambridge, 1985), p. 96.

variety of aria types that emerged as part of his oeuvre were labelled and understood according to their function, such as the *aria d'affetto* and *aria di bravura*, among others. The subtlety and variety of moods Metastasio created in his arias is an essential feature of his artistry.

Arias had to be carefully and properly distributed among the characters, according to a set of conventions governing their types, placement and frequency of occurrence. They generally consisted of two stanzas of lines equal in length and in number; stanzas increased in number and length over the course of the century. The action occurring during passages of recitative culminated in an aria, which occurred at the end of a scene and was followed by the character's exit. Scenes did not always end with an aria, but new scenes always began at the entrance of a new character (stemming from the genre's roots in French classical drama). Cavatinas – short, one-stanza arias after which the character remained on-stage – also occurred. Ensembles, which had no parallel in spoken drama, and choruses received less emphasis. An opera's final 'coro' was a chorus of the solo singers. When choral groups were present they usually stood apart from and commented on the action rather than participating in it, and the structure of their poetry was simple, resembling that of an aria. Love duets between the primo uomo, the heroic, first-ranking lead male character, and the prima donna, his love interest, occasionally occurred, usually positioned like arias at the conclusions of scenes.

Musical conventions arose from poetic ones. Recitative poetry was set as *recitativo semplice*, with continuo accompaniment, or *recitativo accompagnato*, with orchestral accompaniment. The dramatic situation determined the type of musical setting that recitative received; composers reserved orchestral accompaniment for highly charged moments of dramatic intensity, usually but not always preceding arias. The primary musical interest in the genre lay in the aria, its two stanzas set in da capo form, the proportions of which expanded as the century progressed. Opera seria's dramaturgy privileged the aria, and thus the solo singer. Composers lavished great care on arias, crafting them so as to highlight the abilities of the singers who were to perform them. Singers often took active roles in creating the music they sang, exerting an influence that extended beyond mere additions of embellishments. The 'suitcase aria' convention (*aria di baule*) was facilitated both by the abruptness of the transition between the end of a recitative passage and the aria that followed it and from the sometimes generic emotional states expressed in aria texts. This practice came to be considered one of the 'abuses' of opera seria that required reform, according to mid-century writers. Others were the notorious behaviour of solo singers and their sometimes unreasonable demands. Singers gained great power during the century as they seized control as professionals in an open market, and as their reputations, status and earning potential grew.[34] They became increasingly able to influence factors ranging from the actual libretto a composer was to set to the number of times that an aria that displeased them would be re-composed. But star singers also played a decisive and positive role in opera seria, in its growth and development. And audiences and the star singers they admired entered into a mutually beneficial relationship, a 'dynamic, self-propagating system', in which both stars and spectators facilitated the genre's longevity.[35] The privileged status of the opera seria aria within its genre, held since the genre's inception, was a factor in the criticism heaped on opera seria in later decades. Opera seria's many conventions, and the regularity they engendered, led to a common critical assessment of the genre as static, formulaic, repetitious and uninteresting.[36]

Other opera seria conventions concerned spectacular elements. Opera seria featured sumptuous stage settings, ornate costumes and elaborate stage machinery used for special effects. Stage spectacle was man-made, rather than supernatural; it was associated with battles, processions, conflagrations and similar events connected to a particular opera's historical subject. Ballets given between opera seria's acts (and at the end) always entailed lavish spectacle. The practice of presenting dances with operas as an essential part of an evening's entertainment had become the norm by the early eighteenth century. With the rise of the intermezzo, information about ballets began to disappear from librettos, but dances continued to remain popular throughout Italy. By the mid-1730s ballets had once again become the favoured entertainments for intervals between the acts of an opera. The use of intermezzos as entr'acte entertainments therefore constituted a 'short-lived historical parenthesis', a brief exception to the rule of about two hundred years, which was that ballets typically filled this role.[37]

Chronicles of foreign visitors criticize audiences at Italian theatres for their inattentiveness, noise and general unruliness – another 'abuse' to be 'reformed'. During an opera performance audiences might converse, eat and drink and

34 On this topic see Rosselli, *Singers of Italian Opera*, chapters 2 (pp. 32–55), 3 (pp. 56–78) and 4 (pp. 79–90).

35 Berta Joncus, 'Producing Stars in Dramma per Musica', in Melania Bucciarelli and Berta Joncus (eds.), *Music as Social and Cultural Practice: Essays in Honour of Reinhard Strohm* (Woodbridge and Rochester, NY, 2007), p. 287.

36 For an examination of the genre's experiential dimension and the role of the audience in creating the spectacle, and a re-evaluation of the ritual paradigm through which the genre is traditionally viewed, see Martha Feldman, 'Magic Mirrors and the Seria Stage: Thoughts Toward a Ritual View', *Journal of the American Musicological Society*, 48 (1995), pp. 423–84.

37 Kathleen Kuzmick Hansell, 'Eighteenth-Century Italian Theatrical Ballet: The Triumph of the *Grotteschi*', in Rebecca Harris-Warrick and Bruce Alan Brown (eds.), *The Grotesque Dancer on the Eighteenth-Century Stage: Gennaro Magri and His World* (Madison, WI, 2005) p. 19. See also *idem*, 'Theatrical Ballet and Italian Opera', in Lorenzo Bianconi and Giorgio Pestelli (eds.), *Opera on Stage* (Chicago, IL, 2002), esp. pp. 192–241.

engage in other activities, lending more attention to the stage during arias and dances and less during portions of recitative. Patrician patrons were served meals in their boxes, which were prepared in advance and brought by their servants (who could themselves watch the entertainment, but from the very top tier of the theatre).[38] Audiences' behaviour was partially connected to opera's social function. Opera was the context in which aristocratic patrons interacted socially in boxes that they owned or rented. They attended nightly and heard the same works numerous times (runs varied according to circumstances, but a single opera could expect anywhere between about twelve and several dozen performances). Librettos contained familiar plots and stories; erudite theatre-goers likely knew Metastasio's verses by heart. Under these conditions, eighteenth-century audience behaviour is perhaps understandable, even as it highlights a central irony of opera seria: few in this environment likely benefited from the 'enlightenment and instruction' intended by the genre's creators.

Opera seria in practice: adaptation, reform, revitalization

Metastasian librettos were subject to revision and adaptation as they received settings by different composers at different theatres. This was an established and respected tradition and an expected part of the opera seria production process. Either the house poet, or the composer, or the two in collaboration, undertook the alterations. Arias or passages of recitative could be cut, and texts shortened, lengthened, or completely re-written. Substitute arias frequently occurred; sometimes the substitute texts appeared in the libretto (in the body of the text or at the end). Alterations were sometimes even more extensive, involving re-arrangements of scenes and deletions or additions of characters, for example. Ensembles might be created by conflating several aria texts, such as in Galuppi's setting of *Artaserse* for Vienna's Burgtheater in 1749, in which the texts of four arias combine to form a great quartet that concludes Act 1. One of the foremost ensembles in opera seria repertory, it did not meet with the approval of the imperial poet, for whom poetry was to take precedence over music. Galuppi later undertook a similar activity in his *Adriano in Siria* for Venice's Teatro San Salvatore in 1760, in which he created a magnificent trio by telescoping three arias, an ensemble praised by the poet Carlo Goldoni.

The elements that led to opera seria's overwhelming popularity early in the century were the same elements that led it later to receive criticism. In part arising from the genre's conventions, and in part fuelled by economic

38 Audiences did not always behave in this manner, however. For example, spectators at Venice's Teatro San Salvatore in 1760 were transfixed by the power of Galuppi's great trio in *Adriano in Siria* and listened intently, as Carlo Goldoni reports in a dialect poem published after he heard the performance. See Heartz, *Music in European Capitals*, p. 271.

circumstances involving audiences' preferences for virtuoso singing, increased focus was placed on the solo singer, coinciding with the decline of emphasis on other aspects of the drama. Several writers on opera from around 1750 issued calls for the reform of the genre, the best-known and broad-ranging of which was Francesco Algarotti's *Saggio sopra l'opera in musica* from 1755 (reprinted in 1765). Algarotti's manifesto of operatic reform addresses many 'abuses' of opera seria that he and others observed. He encouraged poets to expand their palette of resources from which to draw their material and to engage with subjects that provided richer opportunities for visually striking, spectacular display. He urged designers to create settings that focused on the details of the locale, heightening opportunities for the presentation of local colour. Algarotti envisioned a more visually exciting theatre, whose emphasis on spectacle would result in a concomitant de-emphasizing of soloistic display. He advocated the integration of choral and danced episodes in the style of the tragédie-lyrique into opera seria's scenes in order to vary their structure and to provide opportunities for spectacular display. His essay concluded with two models: an outline for a sample libretto on Enea in Troia and a full-length libretto on the subject of Ifigénie in Aulide.

Parma's Teatro Ducale was probably the Italian theatre that put these ideas most tangibly into action. Guillaume du Tillot, Parma's director of theatres and a proponent of French culture, assembled a creative team that included Tommaso Traetta and the court poet Carlo Innocenzo Frugoni. At great expense to the duchy, this group produced four operas that represented the merging of Italian and French operatic style, on texts that comprised re-workings of French librettos: *Ippolito ed Aricia* (1759), *I Tindaridi* (1760), *Le feste d'Imeneo* (1760) and *Enea e Lavinia* (1761). *Ippolito ed Aricia* was widely publicized and highly touted as one of the finest, original and most spectacular works of the time.[39] These works presented French-inspired choral and danced episodes, flexible scene structures, multiple ensembles and other innovative features integrated into Italianate librettos. The choruses presented challenges that were perhaps more easily met at Parma than elsewhere. While opera choruses during this period often comprised chapel singers or local amateurs, Parma hired several professional opera buffa soloists for the reform opera choruses, who were brought from Bologna and rehearsed by the composer himself.[40] Gluck's *Le feste d'Apollo* for Parma in 1769, for the royal marriage of Maria Amalia, daughter of Maria Theresa of Austria, to Ferdinand IV of

39 Daniel Heartz, 'Traetta in Parma: *Ippolito ed Aricia*', in John A. Rice (ed.), *From Garrick to Gluck: Essays on Opera in the Age of Enlightenment* (Hillsdale, NY, 2004), pp. 271–92.
40 Margaret R. Butler, 'Producing the Operatic Chorus at Parma's Teatro Ducale, 1759–1769', *Eighteenth-Century Music*, 3 (2006), pp. 231–51.

Bourbon, can be considered the last of the mid-century reform efforts. But the taste for French-inspired Italian opera never completely left Parma: Giuseppe Sarti's *Alessandro e Timoteo* (1782) exhibited many stylistic features of the Parmesan reform operas.

Italian cities responded in different ways to the French-inspired reforms at Parma, and to revisionist reforms taking place at Mannheim and Stuttgart.[41] Turin's Teatro Regio mounted several productions that illustrate that the directors of the Nobile Società dei Cavalieri were well aware of developments in these cities and eager to participate in them. *Enea nel Lazio* (1760), an original libretto by Turin's house poet Vittorio Amedeo Cigna-Santi, integrated the entre'acte ballets into the action of the scenes in innovative ways, illustrating the progressive orientation that the choreographer, Giuseppe Salomoni, had acquired from his experience in Vienna. Tommaso Traetta's music sought to heighten the libretto's dramatic potential by creating numerous expressive passages of accompanied recitative intensifying its dramatic high points and battle scenes.

Ifigenia in Aulide (1761) was a direct, positive response to Parma's French-inspired reform operas. Algarotti's Ifigenia libretto concluding his *Saggio* was greatly to influence Turin's presentation of the subject. Integrating choral and danced episodes to a degree unprecedented in Turin's operatic style, the work is a compilation of several different librettos on the subject, including one by Mattia Verazi. Several passages are direct translations of Algarotti's and the ensembles reveal the influence of his libretto as well. *Ifigenia in Aulide* illustrates a comfortable co-existence between conventional Italianate and French-style features. Turin's directors unsuccessfully attempted to engage Traetta for this opera, as well as other composers associated with reform opera elsewhere. They eventually hired Ferdinando Bertoni from Venice to set the libretto rather late in the process. The work exhibits a high number of passages of orchestrally accompanied recitative in comparison to other operas in Turin, and their smooth connection with preceding and ensuing arias and choruses demonstrates an awareness of French operatic stylistic features. The relative simplicity of the choral music reflects the limited time available for preparing and rehearsing the choristers. Turin hired the leading singers for this season, those who had just enjoyed great success in Parma. The complex and elaborate stage machinery contributed greatly to the stage spectacle.

Turin's adaptations of two librettos from Mannheim illustrate that choruses presented resource-related problems. Italian theatres did not generally maintain a standing body of choristers, which made incorporating choruses

41 Points from the following discussion are drawn from Butler, *Operatic Reform at Turin's Teatro Regio*.

from French-inspired and revisionist librettos difficult. Choral singers in Turin had to be hired opera by opera, and the numerous extra sets of costumes for them incurred additional expenses. Choral poetry was cut from Galuppi's setting of Mattia Verazi's *Sofonisba* (1764) when an insufficient number of performers were available, but was later reinstated; it was cut altogether from Turin's revision of Verazi's *Ifigenia in Tauride* (Carlo Monza's *Oreste*, 1766). Choristers were paid little, and different musicians co-ordinated them at different times and in different ways. Integrating the dances into the scenes of opera seria posed various problems, which had more to do with co-ordination than lack of personnel (since dancers for opera seria's entr'acte ballets were generally available). Turin's dancers demanded extra payment for the dances they performed as part of the opera's scenes, and they required extra costumes as well. Yet Turin put many of Algarotti's principles into practice, producing new works that frequently exhibited the visually striking spectacle he envisioned.[42]

Major composers set works for Florence's Teatro di via della Pergola that illustrated many of the stylistic trends influencing opera seria towards the end of the century. Significant works exhibiting French-influenced and reform-inspired features such as choruses, scene complexes and dance, appeared from the late 1760s onwards and escalated in the 1770s and 1780s, including *Ifigenia in Tauride* (1767); and *I Tindaridi* (1768); *Enea e Lavinia* (1768); *Motezuma* (1771), with its exotic subject matter; *Armida* (1772) with its mythological spectacle; and *Erifile* (1779) featuring multi-sectional finales.[43]

Reform was one of a number of trends affecting opera seria in the second half of the century; another was exoticism. Librettists increasingly turned to non-European locales and subjects as material for new plots and actions.[44] Stage settings, costumes and other aspects of the stage spectacle were enhanced in operas featuring exotic material. In presenting images of the non-Western world, theatres inserted themselves into a broader, cosmopolitan context. *Motezuma* proved a popular choice, attractive to Italian theatres for its opportunities for heightened spectacle. The subject emerged early in the century, with Vivaldi's setting of Alvise Giusti's libretto in 1733, and Frederick the Great's libretto created for Berlin, set by Carl Heinrich Graun in 1755. Cigna-Santi produced his *Motezuma* in 1765, set for Turin's Teatro Regio by

42 Marita Petzoldt McClymonds, 'Opera Reform in Italy, 1750–80', in Bianca Maria Antolini, Teresa M. Gialdroni and Annunziato Pugliese (eds.), *'Et facciam dolçi canti': Studi in onore di Agostino Ziino in occasione del suo 65° compleanno* (Lucca, 2003), 2 vols., vol. 2, pp. 895–912.

43 Marita Petzoldt McClymonds, 'The Role of Innovation and Reform in the Florentine Opera Seria Repertory, 1760 to 1800', in Colleen Reardon and Susan Parisi (eds.), *Music Observed: Studies in Memory of William C. Holmes* (Warren, MI, 2004), pp. 281–99.

44 Francesco Cotticelli and Paologiovanni Maione (eds.), *Le arti della scena e l'esotismo in età moderna* (Naples, 2006) contains essays on this topic.

Gian Francesco de Majo. This libretto received eight additional settings in many leading cities, Florence included, in the remainder of the century. Librettists began to explore other opportunities for dramatic situations towards the end of the eighteenth century. A group of Venetian librettists was especially influential in the revitalization of opera seria at this time, infusing it with new energy by enriching older features and introducing new ones, such as on-stage death and tragedy, enhanced choral participation, increasingly integrated and expressive dances, complex and active ensembles and expansive scene complexes, frequently involving all these elements.[45] Much of this coincided with the opening and initial activity of the Teatro La Fenice, inaugurated in 1792 and, until the end of the Venetian Republic in 1797, a monument to civic pride.[46] A series of impresarios held tenures at the theatre, hired by a patrician society who served as the theatre's administrative directors, and whose existence recalls the societies of nobles who directed Turin's Teatro Regio, and for a short period, Rome's Teatro Argentina. The impresarios tended to shuttle between the Fenice and the San Benedetto, thus linking the institutional histories of the theatres. Their unfortunate and consistent failure illustrated the financial difficulties that accompanied the heightened spectacle of the new librettos, whose impassioned subjects were infused with a populism and idealistic fervour that linked them with the French Revolution. The Teatro La Fenice, rather than being a bastion of conservatism sponsoring a moribund genre, was in fact the 'preeminent theatrical institution in Venetian civic life', promoting a genre that had not only undergone a transformation but that was capable of arousing cultural sympathies of deep significance.[47]

Secondary theatres and comic opera

'Secondary theatres' were hardly secondary in importance in the development of eighteenth-century Italian opera. They were the venues for the wide-ranging dissemination of a repertory that consisted of some of the era's most influential and highly acclaimed works. They hosted the most prominent and renowned composers of the day and the popularity of works they presented rivalled those of opera seria, appealing to an increasingly broad and influential public. They were secondary in other ways: they were managed by single impresarios, and

45 Marita Petzoldt McClymonds, 'The Venetian Role in the Transformation of Italian Opera Seria during the 1790s', in Maria Teresa Muraro (ed.), *I vicini di Mozart 1: Il teatro musicale tra Sette e Ottocento* (Florence, 1989), pp. 221–40.

46 Bauman, 'The Society of La Fenice', pp. 332–54, from which points in the following discussion are drawn.

47 Other opere serie from the end of the century reflect such sentiments; see Lorenzo Mattei, 'Metastasio con il berretto frigio: Sui *Veri amici repubblicani* di Niccolò Zingarelli (Torino 1799)', *Fonti Musicali Italiane*, 8 (2003), pp. 31–52.

compared to the principal theatres generally had smaller audiences composed of a more varied public; and they were comparatively less prestigious, in some cities playing a subordinate role to the city's principal theatre, as in the case of the Teatro Nuovo in Naples, which paid a fee to the Teatro San Carlo.[48] Their repertory was more varied in comparison to principal theatres, consisting of comic opera (the varieties of which included various, sometimes overlapping genres, such as intermezzo, farsetta, burletta, commedia per musica, opera buffa, and dramma giocoso), spoken drama and other types of entertainment. While Carnival was the main season for principal theatres, secondary theatres operated primarily during autumn or spring; their performance schedules were different as well. The production and organizational model was that of impresarial theatre, by which impresarios, hired by the management of secondary theatres, engaged troupes of comic singers. The character types of comic singers reflected a ranking similar to that of opera seria, including prima and seconda buffa and primo and secondo uomo (or musico).

Comic genres

The intermezzo occupies a unique position in the history of opera, sharing that of both principal and secondary theatres. In that it was a comic opera performed between acts of an opera seria, its venue was the principal theatres of Italy in the early part of the century; in that it plays a vital role in the development of opera buffa, its link to the secondary theatres is crucial. The intermezzo developed from a confluence of sources including comic scenes of opera before the pre-Arcadian reforms, and stock characters from the improvised comic theatre of the commedia dell'arte.[49] Character types recognizable in the intermezzo include the wily servant girl, who tricks her male partner into marriage, the old man, the doctor and the mute servant possessing some sort of physical deformity. Audiences relished the physical comedy of the performers as well as the music. Some of opera seria's musical conventions – several da capo arias for each of the characters separated by passages of simple recitative – as well as plots that parodied dramatic conventions of opera seria, characterize the intermezzo. Its musical features have been acknowledged as a primary source for the Classical style.[50]

48 Piperno, 'Opera Production up to 1780', p. 43.

49 Charles E. Troy, *The Comic Intermezzo: A Study in the History of Eighteenth-Century Italian Opera* (Ann Arbor, MI, 1979). On the intermezzo and its origins, see also Robinson, *Naples and Neapolitan Opera*, pp. 178–86; on the influence of the commedia dell'arte, see pp. 190–4.

50 The seminal article on this topic, engendering one of the central debates in eighteenth-century musicological scholarship, is Daniel Heartz, 'Opera and the Periodization of Eighteenth-Century Music', in *Report of the 10th Congress of the International Musicological Society, Ljubljana, 1967* (1970), pp. 160–8; *idem*, *Haydn, Mozart and the Viennese School, 1740–1780*, p. xviii. See Eric Weimer, *Opera Seria and the Evolution of the Classical Style, 1755–1772* (Ann Arbor, MI, 1984), for an analytical discussion of Classical-style features in arias by Hasse, Jommelli and J. C. Bach.

Venetian theatres provided venues in which the intermezzo flourished, although the genre appeared everywhere, in theatres of all categories and ranks. Repertory circulated widely, and its performers achieved great fame. The genre's rise to popularity was facilitated by the conventions of the production system in which it operated.[51] In contrast to the expensive opera seria, the more economical intermezzo was easy for theatres to present, with modest orchestral and scenographic requirements and singers whose fees were comparatively lower than those of opera seria. The Teatro di San Cassiano was one of its major centres, presenting in 1706 the first known intermezzo between the acts of an opera seria by Francesco Gasparini. The San Cassiano continued to present the most popular intermezzi. The earliest surviving score of an intermezzo is Tomaso Albinoni's *Pimpinone* (1708). The Teatro Sant' Angelo briefly participated in the diffusion of the intermezzo, and in 1734 Goldoni singled out the director of the comic troupe at the Teatro San Samuele, Giuseppe Imer, for its introduction in this theatre (even accounting for its cultivation there and elsewhere in earlier years).[52]

The Neapolitan theatres handled the intermezzo differently. Before 1720, comic scenes were integrated into operas that were performed without them elsewhere. The peak of the genre's cultivation occurred in the 1720s and 1730s in Naples with works such as Giovanni Pergolesi's *La serva padrona* (1733), the best known of all intermezzi; as mentioned above, the work was presented at the Teatro di San Bartolomeo, performed between acts of Pergolesi's own opera seria, *Il prigoniero superbo*. Intermezzi were also composed by Johann Adolf Hasse, Domenico Sarro and other leading composers. The fact that librettists of these works were concurrently providing libretti for full-length comic operas being performed elsewhere, among other considerations, has long raised questions about the chronology of the development of the two genres.[53] The controversial Paris performance in 1752 of *La serva padrona* (and other intermezzi and opere buffe between 1752 and 1754) in part stimulated the famous Querelle des Bouffons, perhaps one of the main reasons why the intermezzo, and this work in particular, is known today.

In Naples in 1741 Charles III ordered the performance of ballets instead of intermezzi during opera seria at the Teatro di San Carlo. By mid-century the practice of presenting dances, rather than intermezzi, between opera seria's acts had become broadly speaking conventional. However, some intermezzi – now

51 Franco Piperno, 'Appunti sulla configurazione sociale e professionale delle "parti buffe" al tempo di Vivaldi', in Lorenzo Bianconi and Giovanni Morelli (eds.), *Antonio Vivaldi: Teatro musicale, cultura e società* (Florence, 1982), 2 vols., vol. 2, pp. 483–97.

52 Troy, *The Comic Intermezzo*, p. 5.

53 Comic opera and intermezzo represented 'two distinct but at times interrelated forms'. Piperno, 'Opera Production up to 1780', p. 60.

called farsette – continued to appear between acts of spoken plays. These co-existed with contemporaneous opere buffe, with which they were essentially identical; many of the former were simply condensed versions of the latter, the proportions and resources being dictated by the circumstances of a given theatre.

Opera buffa developed from a long tradition of comic opera, centred first in Venice. In the context of the intermezzo's cultivation and popularity, opera buffa's emergence is associated with librettos by the Venetian poet Carlo Goldoni comprising full-length pieces usually in three acts for several singers. It eventually displaced the intermezzo.[54] The growth of opera buffa depended on many things, not the least of which was an 'institutional phase' of its development in which impresarios, employing 'a mix of tried and true stylistic conventions and professional devices borrowed from the intermezzi', produced it in certain secondary theatres that already possessed stable companies specializing in comic repertory. A later, 'free -market' phase saw the burgeoning activities of performers and composers independent of, but co-existing with, travelling performing companies.[55] In the case of the commedia per musica, a genre designating full-length comic operas in local dialect performed by local companies that attracted a broad public within a given city, works that first enjoyed strictly local success were eventually exported (and translated), contributing to opera buffa's appeal on a national and international scale. Its performers correspondingly became more independent as well, increasingly functioning outside the context of the itinerant unified company.

Opera buffa eventually adopted elements associated with opera seria, giving it more variety, in a process that resulted in a sub-type of opera buffa libretto referred to by Goldoni as the dramma giocoso. Its blend of comic and serious elements offered greater opportunities for varying degrees of subtlety and led to characters of greater depth and richness. Goldoni and Baldassare Galuppi collaborated in different Venetian secondary theatres on a series of path-breaking works over the course of which they created a hallmark of comic opera, the buffo finale, a multi-sectional final ensemble involving numerous characters and allowing for a rapid succession of varying states of emotion and action.[56] For the effectiveness of their collaboration and the broad acclaim of their works, Goldoni and Galuppi resemble another great creative team in the history of comic musical theatre, with whom they have been rightly compared: William Schwenk Gilbert and Arthur Sullivan.[57]

54 Piero Weiss, 'La diffusione del repertorio operistico nell'Italia del Settecento: Il caso dell'opera buffa', in Susi Davoli (ed.), *Civiltà teatrale e Settecento emiliano* (Bologna, 1986), pp. 241–56.

55 Piperno, 'Opera Production up to 1780', pp. 64–5.

56 On the buffo finale, see Heartz, *Music in European Capitals*, pp. 278–83 and *idem*, 'The Creation of the Buffo Finale', in *From Garrick to Gluck*, ed. Rice, pp. 40–51.

57 Heartz, *Music in European Capitals*, p. 278.

Venetian secondary theatres: S Angelo, S Salvador, S Samuele, S Cassiano, S Moisè, S Luca

Cities varied in the number of secondary theatres they sponsored. The major centres in the development of comic opera – Venice, Naples and Rome – possessed numerous secondary theatres. As mentioned above, the complexity of theatrical life in Naples and Venice means that the dichotomy of principal/secondary–seria/buffa works less well here than elsewhere. Venice's theatres sometimes offered combined seasons in which opera seria and opera buffa both appeared; moreover, the status of certain theatres and the types of opera they presented, in Venice especially, changed at different times during the century. Some of Venice's theatres can be considered closer to principal theatres; several buffa venues were theatres of importance and could thus be considered among the city's principal theatres.

Except for the San Giovanni Grisostomo and San Benedetto, most of Venice's theatres shifted from featuring opera seria to featuring opera buffa during the first decades of the eighteenth century. Six major comic theatres operated in the early part of the century, all of which functioned during the three production seasons of Carnival, spring and autumn. Three of them had mixed seasons, in which opera buffa was only one of several entertainment types. These were the Teatro di Sant'Angelo, Teatro San Salvatore (San Salvador) and Teatro San Samuele. The Sant'Angelo was one of Venice's oldest theatres, having opened in 1676, and presented spoken drama and opera. Zeno's first libretto, *Gli inganni infelici*, was set to music here in 1695 by Carlo Francesco Pollarolo; it was also one of the theatres at which Antonio Vivaldi functioned as impresario early in the eighteenth century.[58] Goldoni and Galuppi's first collaboration on an original work was done for the theatre in 1749, *L'Arcadia in Brenta*, with a comic action finale that represented the first in a series they were to create.[59] The San Salvador (San Salvatore) gave spoken drama and opera seria, hosting works by Galuppi and other prominent composers of the day. The San Samuele, founded in 1710, presented comic works and spoken drama.

Three Venetian theatres had seasons consisting entirely of musical works. The Teatro San Cassiano, famous for being the first theatre to open its doors to the public for the premiere of Antonio Cesti's *Il pomo d'oro* in 1637, hosted many important intermezzi in the early eighteenth century. The Teatro San Moisè was the smallest of Venice's theatres, presenting many comic works by Vivaldi and others. Galuppi and Goldoni's other comic hits that led to the

58 Strohm, 'Vivaldi's Career as an Opera Producer', in *Essays on Handel and Italian Opera*, pp. 122–63.
59 Daniel Heartz, 'Vis Comica: Goldoni, Galuppi, and *L'Arcadia in Brenta*', in Heartz, *From Garrick to Gluck*, ed. Rice, pp. 11–39.

creation of the buffo finale, *Arcifanfano re dei Matti* (1749) and *Il mondo della luna* (1750), were given at the Teatro San Moisè. The San Teatro Luca presented opera seria during the 1760s.

Neapolitan secondary theatres: Fiorentini, Nuovo, Pace, Fondo

The numerous secondary theatres of Naples were home to some of the most crucial developments in Italian opera, in both serious and comic domains. Naples' four conservatories provided training grounds from which scores of Neapolitan-trained composers emerged and subsequently shaped the city's theatrical life and Europe's musical language. The abiding influence of Neapolitan-trained composers on international musical style was so widespread and of such great significance that eighteenth-century Italian opera was long referred to as 'Neapolitan opera'.

Naples' secondary theatres benefited from several generations of composers who emerged from the conservatories and comprised the so-called 'Neapolitan school'.[60] Those prominent in the first half of the century included Leonardo Vinci, Leonardo Leo, Giovanni Pergolesi, and Niccolò Jommelli. (Johann Adolph Hasse belongs among Neapolitan-trained composers as well, although his Neapolitan operas flourished at the San Bartolomeo and he is better known for his triumphs in Venice and Dresden.) Among their contemporaries were Gaetano Latilla, Nicola Logroscino, Gioacchino Cocchi, Domenico Fischietti, Vincenzo Ciampi and Pietro Auletta. Leading Neapolitan composers coming to the fore around mid-century included Niccolò Piccinni, Pasquale Anfossi, Tommaso Traetta, Pietro Guglielmi, Giacomo Insanguine, Fedele Fenaroli, Antonio Sacchini and Gian Francesco de Majo.[61] Rising to prominence after this group were figures such as Domenico Cimarosa, Giovanni Paisiello and Niccolò Zingarelli.

The significant Neapolitan comic theatres in the eighteenth century were the Teatro de' Fiorentini, the Teatro Nuovo, the Teatro della Pace and the Teatro del Fondo. They offered a variety of entertainments, including intermezzi and the commedia per musica (sometimes referred to as the commedia musicale) in Neapolitan dialect, championed by Niccolò Piccinni and others.[62]

Leonardo Vinci established his reputation within the context of the commedia per musica, a genre whose origins are linked with the rivalry between the Teatro de' Fiorentini, which produced many of them, and the nearby Teatro di

60 The idea of a 'Neapolitan School' has long been a subject of debate. See Robinson, *Naples and Neapolitan Opera*, pp. 34–5 for a brief summary and Heartz, *Music in European Capitals*, pp. 75, 157.

61 These groupings are drawn from Heartz, *Music in European Capitals*, p. 156.

62 Francesco Degrada, '*Lo frate 'nnamorato* e l'estetica della commedia musicale napoletana', in Bianca Maria Antolini and Wolfgang Witzenmann (eds.), *Napoli e il Teatro Musicale in Europa tra Sette e Ottocento: Studi in Onore di Friedrich Lippmann* (Florence, 1993), pp. 21–35.

San Bartolomeo. When serious opera at the Fiorentini was eclipsed by that at the San Bartolomeo, the Fiorentini's management responded by offering comic works in Neapolitan dialect that appealed to a broader public. The success of these works was in part due to nationalistic sentiments of the Neapolitan public, expressed after their city came under Hapsburg control in 1707.[63] Distinctly different from the intermezzo, these works were full-length, three-act operas, with a cast of several characters; their librettos formed a newly flourishing literary tradition in the first decades of the century.

The flexibility of the Teatro de' Fiorentini is evident in its presentation of comedies in Tuscan as well as Neapolitan. Alessandro Scarlatti's *Il trionfo di onore* of 1718–19 received a high number of performances there, followed in 1722 by Vinci's commedia per musica *Li zite 'ngalera*. Another early commedia is Leonardo Leo's *La semmeglianza di chi l'ha fatta* (1726).

With Piccinni's commedie per musica the histories of the Fiorentini and the Teatro Nuovo (opening in 1724) overlap, the latter eventually becoming a rival of the former. Starting in the mid-1750s, Piccinni set a successful series of comic operas with Neapolitan dialect roles for the Fiorentini and the Nuovo, receiving approbation at both theatres that continued into the 1770s. He subsequently obtained important commissions at the San Carlo, and elsewhere, that further served to establish his reputation as a leading composer. (He wrote his best-known comic work, *La buona figliuola* (1760) not for Naples, but for Rome's Teatro delle Dame.) But he continued composing commedie per musica for the Fiorentini; two of his later works for that theatre were *Gelosia per gelosia* (1770) and *I furbi burlati* (1773; a revised version of his *La furba burlata* from 1760, also for the Fiorentini). The Teatro Nuovo presented some of his commedie, along with those of Paisiello; Charles Burney heard performances of the composers' works at both theatres.[64] Other secondary theatres were the Teatro della Pace, also inaugurated in 1724, which gave comic works until opera production ceased there in 1751, and the Teatro del Fondo, opening in 1779, which also produced comic operas and plays. Piccinni enjoyed the spotlight as the major figure in the theatres of Naples and Rome (as we shall see), until the rise to prominence of younger composers such as Anfossi and Paisiello.[65]

63 The motivations of the Fiorentini's management in the promotion of comic opera in dialect may be interpreted in slightly different ways. While Heartz (*Music in European Capitals*, p. 79) views it as a result of the competition with the San Bartolomeo over the production of serious opera, to Robinson it is both 'a piece of opportunism to capitalize on nationalistic feelings and also as a way of avoiding a further direct (and financially damaging) competition with the S. Bartolomeo'. Robinson, *Neapolitan Opera*, pp. 10–11.

64 Burney's evaluation of Piccinni's and Paisiello's comic operas at the Fiorentini and the Nuovo are given in Heartz, *Music in European Capitals*, pp. 163–5.

65 For further discussion of Neapolitan opera, see Francesco Degrada, 'L'opera napoletana', in Guglielmo Barblan and Alberto Basso (eds.), *Storia dell'opera* (Turin, 1977), 6 vols., vol. 1, part 1, pp. 237–332.

Rome, Florence and Turin: Capranica, Alibert (Dame) and Carignano

The vibrancy of Rome's theatrical life with its numerous theatres make it difficult to determine a single principal theatre and secondary theatres, a situation similar to Venice. The Teatro Argentina, more than any of Rome's other theatres, consistently exhibits qualities that place it in the category of principal theatre. But others, like the Teatro Alibert – renamed the Teatro delle Dame in 1726 – demonstrate the flexibility exhibited by Roman theatres in terms of repertory and public. This flexibility was of course a reflection of the city's political climate; its theatres were subject to governmental edicts overseen by papal authorities that influenced the genres of opera that could be presented. Such edicts permitted the performance of opera seria at either two or three theatres at different times in the first half of the century; these were the Argentina, which presented opera seria most often, the Capranica, and the Alibert (Dame). The last two presented opera seria in combination with comic genres. In the second half of the century, the distinction between serious and comic theatres became more pronounced, with the Argentina almost exclusively occupying the role of a seria theatre.

The Teatro Alibert/Teatro delle Dame put on an intriguingly varied series of works. It played a vital role in bringing Metastasio's early librettos to prominence and in maintaining his dominance in Rome even after his move to Vienna as poeta caesareo. The first settings of most of Metastasio's early drammi per musica were given here in the 1720s and 1730s and settings of his other texts followed later as well.[66] The theatre was renamed after its enlargement in 1726, the Carnival season of which featured one of these Metastasio premieres, Vinci's setting of *Didone abbandonata*. Works by Porpora and other leading early eighteenth-century composers reinforced the theatre's significance. Its mixed character and excellence in comic opera were to develop later; Piccinni, as we have seen, established his reputation in the secondary theatres of Naples (confirmed with a commission from its primary theatre), and achieved prominence with *La buona figliuola* (1760) for the Teatro delle Dame. The same theatre commissioned from him two settings of *L'Olimpiade*, the first in 1761, and the second in 1768; the latter's favourable reception led to a revival in Naples in 1774.

Rome's Teatro Capranica came to prominence in the first half of the century, presenting works by Vivaldi and Leo. Staging opera seria during the 1720s and 1730s, it gave almost exclusively comic and spoken theatre works in the second

66 Piperno, 'Opera Production up to 1780', p. 50. Five of the seven drammi per musica written by Metastasio in Italy were set at the Teatro delle Dame.

half of the century. The Argentina, Dame and Capranica were among the larger and more prestigious theatres of the city. Rome's other theatres were generally smaller. Presenting comic works and spoken theatre, they included the Teatro Valle (which did give a season of opera seria in 1730), the Teatro Pace, the Pallacorda, Granari and the Rucella. The Teatro Tordinona was the city's government-run theatre.

Florence's main secondary theatre was the Teatro di via del Cocomero, which also staged opera seria;[67] later on, the Pergola began giving opera buffa. Other secondary theatres active in the early part of the century included the Coletti and the Tintori. More minor theatres opened later as the theatrical life of the city continued to blossom; after restrictions were imposed to limit their activities, two of them survived, joining the Pergola and Cocomero as the established theatres of the city: the Teatro di via Santa Maria and the Teatro della Piazza Vecchia di Santa Maria Novella (or simply the Piazza Vecchia), both of which presented a varied repertory.[68]

The Teatro Carignano, inaugurated in 1715, occupied an older theatrical building that was modernized by Turin's Carignano princes. From 1727 onwards Turin's secondary theatre was run by the same society of nobles that ran the Teatro Regio, the Nobile Società dei Cavalieri. In the early years of its existence the repertory at the Carignano included settings of librettos by Zeno, Salvi, and Stampiglia set mostly by local composers. The repertory became more varied after the Teatro Regio opened in 1740 and became the domain of opera seria. The directors of the Cavalieri eventually began to hire individual impresarios who brought in comic troupes for performances at the Carignano. The repertory was mixed, encompassing opere buffe, spoken dramas, public viewings of exotic animals and travelling acts of various sorts.[69]

Italian opera outside Italy: Vienna

Italian opera was the international musical language of the eighteenth century. It graced the stages of both court and public theatres in cities ranging from the large and cosmopolitan to the small and provincial and those in between: among others, London, Vienna, Berlin, Prague, Mannheim, Stuttgart, Dresden,

67 Weaver and Weaver, *A Chronology of Music in the Florentine Theatre 1751–1800*, vol. 2, pp. 23–8 and 50–7, discuss the Cocomero and its activities.

68 Weaver and Weaver, *A Chronology of Music in the Florentine Theatre 1751–1800*, vol. 2, pp. 58–72.

69 On the Teatro Carignano, see Marie-Thérèse Bouquet-Boyer, 'Public et Répertoire aux Théâtres Regio et Carignano de Turin', *Dix-Huitième Siècle*, 17 (1985), pp. 229–40; *idem*, 'Role du Théâtre Carignan dans l'histoire des spectacles à Turin au XVI-IIe siècle', in Gianni Mombello, Lionello Sozzi and Louis Terreaux (eds.), *Culture et Pouvoir dans le États de Savoie du XVIIe siècle à la Révolution, Actes du colloque d'Annecy-Chambéry-Turin, 1982* (Geneva, 1985), pp. 161–75.

Munich, St Petersburg, Madrid, Lisbon, Esterháza, Salzburg, Stockholm and Copenhagen. The Italian production circuit significantly influenced Italian opera outside Italy. Theatres in non-Italian courts generally engaged personnel for several years at a time. These performers, remaining in the service of their patrons, would form the standing company associated with that theatre, although in the leading non-Italian cities the top-ranking singers of the era were often hired season by season, as in Italy. Composers were engaged for periods that ranged from a single season, as in Italy, to several years at a time.

Vienna's venues for Italian opera

Eighteenth-century Vienna has appropriately been called a 'musical melting pot',[70] in which Italian opera was a main ingredient. The court theatres in the most cosmopolitan cultural centre of all of Europe in the eighteenth century were the Burgtheater and the Kärntnertortheater.[71] Their institutional histories were profoundly influenced by political events that shaped the history of the Hapsburg Empire. Briefly, the Kärntnertortheater was the larger of the two, and an actual civic theatre. By contrast, the Burgtheater was smaller and more elegant. While neither of them compared in size and capacity to the great theatres of Italy,[72] some of the works presented at them were among the most influential in the history of opera. Other places where Italian opera was performed in Vienna included imperial residences outside the city such as the Schönbrunn palace theatre (Schlosstheater), and the garden theatre at the palace at Laxenburg as well as the palace theatre of Prince Auersperg. The main venue for Italian opera from the beginning of the century up to 1740 was the ballroom (Tanzsaal) of the imperial palace (Hofburg), refurbished and ornamented in Baroque magnificence by Francesco Galli-Bibiena. Italian opera's popularity in Vienna dates back to the preceding century, however. Venetian operas were often imported to Vienna, when they were performed during Carnival and for

70 John A. Rice, *Empress Marie Therese and Music at the Viennese Court, 1792–1807* (Cambridge, 2003), p. 2.

71 The literature on Viennese opera, especially concerning Mozart, is vast. A fuller account of Viennese operatic institutions and their function may be found in the following studies, to which the ensuing discussion is indebted: Bruce Alan Brown, *Gluck and the French Theatre in Vienna* (Oxford, 1991), chapter 1; Daniel Heartz, *Haydn, Mozart and the Viennese School, 1740–1780* (Norton, 1995), chapter 1, pp. 3–78; Dorothea Link, *The National Court Theatre in Mozart's Vienna: Sources and Documents, 1783–1792* (Oxford, 1998); and John A. Rice, *Antonio Salieri and Viennese Opera* (Chicago, IL, 1998), chapter 2, pp. 32–60. The Burgtheater and Kärntnertortheater's dimensions, capacities and facilities are mentioned in Malcolm S. Cole, 'Mozart and Two Theatres in Josephinian Vienna', in Mark A. Radice (ed.), *Opera in Context: Essays on Historical Staging from the Late Renaissance to the Time of Puccini* (Portland, OR, 1998), pp. 111–45. John A. Rice, *Mozart on the Stage* (Cambridge, 2009) treats in detail many aspects of production surrounding Mozart's operas.

72 The dimensions of the court theatres are discussed in Mary Sue Morrow, *Concert Life in Haydn's Vienna: Aspects of a Developing Musical and Social Institution* (Stuyvesant, NY, 1989), pp. 71–81; cited in Rice, *Antonio Salieri and Viennese Opera*, p. 35.

festive occasions celebrating important events in the lives of the sovereigns, such as birthdays, name-days and weddings. They were given in rooms in the Hofburg and other residences. Antonio Cesti's *Il pomo d'oro*, for example, was presented in 1668.[73]

Emperor Charles VI, himself a musician, was a dedicated patron of Italian opera, attracting the foremost Italian librettists to his court opera and spending great sums of money on the cultivation of opera seria until his death in 1740. Apostolo Zeno initially held the post of imperial poet, Pietro Metastasio succeeding him in 1729 as his librettos began to enjoy increasing success. The poets Pietro Pariati and Giovanni Pasquini were also in residence at the Viennese court in these years. Operas there represented the splendour and grandeur of the Baroque, principal composers including Johann Joseph Fux and Antonio Caldara. Metastasio's *La clemenza di Tito* received its first setting at the Viennese court in 1734, by Caldara. The 'Bibiena Theatre' was used only once after Charles's death, for Johann Adolph Hasse's setting of *Ipermestra*, and dismantled later in the 1740s.

The Kärntnertortheater was not a venue of great importance for Italian opera, although some Italian works were presented there. Known as the German theatre on account of the German troupes engaged, it was decidedly secondary in importance to the Burgtheater in operatic terms. Built in 1709, it burned in 1761. It was promptly rebuilt in 1763, closing again in 1788. Leopold II had it reopened in the 1790s. There is evidence that some works by Vivaldi were performed there in the 1730s, and one opera by him premiered in the 1740s. During these early decades, the repertory consisted largely of improvised plays derived from the commedia dell'arte with intermezzi and dances. In the early 1730s the theatre presented works by Hasse and Vinci. Later, Sarti's *Giulio Sabino* was staged when the Burgtheater was unavailable, and some of Salieri's works were given as well.

In contrast, artistic events at Vienna's Burgtheater were closely tied to political events surrounding the Hapsburg rulers. These affected not only the occasions for which operas were given but the circumstances under which they occurred. Maria Theresa, daughter of Charles VI, reigned as empress from 1745 to 1780 and many of the significant works in the theatre's history occurred during her reign.

The Burgtheater was built as a new palace theatre in 1741 to serve as a venue for celebration of events important to the imperial family. Erected on the site of a former tennis court, the small and elegant theatre was designed

73 Connections between Venice and Vienna remained strong into the later years of the century, as witnessed in the Viennese activities of Venetian composers, librettists and singers. See Rice, *Antonio Salieri and Viennese Opera*, pp. 12–13.

by Nicolas Jadot. A court theatre open to the public, which included Vienna's bourgeoisie, the Burgtheater stood in stark contrast to the court theatre of Charles VI with its exclusively aristocratic audience. Known as the French theatre because of the residence of French performing troupes, its eclectic offerings reflected the city's cosmopolitanism. Over the course of the century it presented works in a wide variety of genres including spoken plays, ballet, opéra-comique, opera buffa, and opera seria, witnessing formative events in the history of Italian opera. It participated in the most influential stylistic trends affecting opera, in some cases spearheading them. It engaged the century's renowned composers, both those in residence and those who came from abroad, including Galuppi, Traetta, Gluck, Paisiello, Salieri and Martín y Soler. Two of Mozart's Italian operatic masterpieces (*Le nozze di Figaro* and *Così fan tutte*) were premiered there.

After renovations the Burgtheater re-opened in 1748 both in celebration of the empress's birthday and in recognition of newly gained strength resulting from the Peace of Aix La Chapelle in May of that year, after the War of the Austrian Succession. Gluck's first opera for Vienna, *La Semiramide riconosciuta*, was premiered to mark the occasion. In 1752 the empress brought the Viennese theatres under the control of the court. The substitution of a company of French actors for an Italian company laid the foundation for path-breaking innovations in Italian opera. The wedding of Archduke Joseph and Isabella of Bourbon-Parma in 1760 was celebrated both in Parma (with Traetta and Frugoni's *Le feste d'Imeneo*, one in a sequence of Italian works for the Teatro Ducale inspired by and adapted from French models, as discussed above) and in Vienna. Metastasio's *Alcide al bivio* was set by Hasse and given at the Burgtheater as part of the wedding festivities.[74] A French-inspired spectacle opera, Traetta's *Armida* (1761), was also given at the Burgtheater in celebration of Isabella's birthday.[75]

Theatrical dance and Italian opera at the Burgtheater

The history of theatrical dance intersects with that of Italian opera throughout the century and at all the leading operatic centres within and outside Italy. Profound changes in its character occurred in mid-century productions at Vienna's Burgtheater.

Presented together with opera as entr'acte entertainments up until c. 1710, dances began to be replaced by intermezzos in theatres around Italy in a

74 On the imperial wedding festivities, and the very different goals and characters of the Parmesan and Viennese works, see Brown, *Gluck and the French Theatre in Vienna*, chapter 7, pp. 263–81.

75 Daniel Heartz, 'Traetta in Vienna: *Armida* and *Ifigenia in Tauride*', in *From Garrick to Gluck*, ed. Rice pp. 293–312.

practice that lasted until c. 1740. A reverse occurred at this point, when ballets displaced the intermezzos and dance was once again considered an integral part of the evening's stage spectacle. Theatrical administrations expended vast sums in the engagement of leading opera seria singers, as we have seen; they did so for leading dancers and choreographers as well. Theatrical dance traditions were among the strongest in the centres for Italian opera that enjoyed strong ties with France, where the art of ballet developed, where it was a vital component of opera and where it was vigorously cultivated in the eighteenth century – primarily Vienna (and by political association Milan and Naples, as we have seen), Venice, Turin, Parma, Mannheim and Stuttgart.

Of the many points of contact between dance and Italian opera during the century, perhaps the most significant was the development of dramatic pantomime and its influence on both dances integrated into the scenes of reform opera and on entr'acte ballets for opera seria, formative developments in which occurred in Vienna. The choreographer Franz Hilverding began to introduce interpretive pantomime into theatrical dance in the 1740s, a tradition that was perpetuated and enhanced by Gasparo Angiolini, his successor as ballet-master at the Burgtheater. Angiolini produced a sequence of revolutionary danced dramas with programmes and collaborated with Gluck and Traetta along with Giacomo Durazzo, director of the Viennese theatres, to produce French-inspired works such as *Armida* (1761), *Orfeo ed Euridice* (1762) and *Ifigenia in Tauride* (1763). Italian choreographers with whom Angiolini worked, such as the Salomoni family, carried his innovations south, linking entr'acte ballets – by convention, separate from the opere serie they adorned – with an opera's action.

Angiolini's rival, French-Swiss choreographer Jean-Georges Noverre, was at the time working with pantomime ballet in Stuttgart. Succeeding Angiolini in Vienna, Noverre choreographed Gluck and Calzabigi's *Alceste* (1767); the Italian reform operas at the Burgtheater drew upon the ample resources and institutional support available for French-influenced opera, not the least of which were strong dancers and innovative choreographers. Earlier Noverre himself had claimed to have invented the *ballet en action*, and published his revolutionary ideas on the nature and function of theatrical dance in writings such as *Lettres sur la Danse et sur les Ballets* (Stuttgart, 1760). Angiolini responded with *Lettere di Gasparo Angiolini a Monsieur Noverre sopra i balli pantomimi* (Milan, 1773). The polemic between Noverre and Angiolini, following on from the latter's ballets for Milan's Teatro Regio Ducale during the 1770s, had a decisive impact on the future of theatrical dance. Gennaro Magri, an Italian dancer and choreographer who performed in Vienna between 1759 and 1764, authored the *Trattato teorico-prattico di ballo* (Naples, 1779), one of the few surviving treatises on dance in the eighteenth century.[76]

Operatic reform at the Burgtheater

The interplay of international politics and stylistic innovation had a profound impact on Gluck's Italian operas for the Burgtheater in the 1760s.[77] Both were set to librettos by Calzabigi: *Orfeo ed Euridice* (1762), the *festa teatrale* composed in celebration of the emperor's name day, and *Alceste* (1767), the tragic drama in which the title character evoked the devoted, grieving Maria Theresa, a widow after the death of her husband, Franz I, in 1765. Gluck's preface to the printed score of *Alceste* was one of the century's widely known manifestos of operatic reform. With their intermingling of choral and danced episodes, flexible scene structures, simpler and more direct musical language and other innovative features, these works sought to de-emphasize the solo singer and restore dramatic unity to Italian opera.[78]

Prince Wenzel Anton Kaunitz was a powerful minister of state who exerted a significant influence on Italian opera at the Burgtheater. A champion of French culture, he was ambassador to Paris and planned an alliance between Austria and France. As advisor to Maria Theresa, he influenced her appointment of Count Giacomo Durazzo as director of the city's theatres. Durazzo was also the court's Musikgraf (supervisor of musical activities).[79] Before his dismissal in 1764 for political reasons, Durazzo masterminded the French-inspired reform of dance and theatre that was profoundly to influence Italian opera in Vienna and elsewhere. His involvement in these reform efforts demonstrates how crucial three factors – 'artistic talent, material circumstances, and effective management' – are

76 On theatrical dance and Italian opera, see Marian Hannah Winter, *The Pre-Romantic Ballet* (London, 1974); Hansell, 'Opera and Ballet at the Regio Ducal Teatro of Milan, 1771–1776'; Salvatore Bongiovanni, 'Gennaro Magri e il "ballo grottesco"', in Giovanni Morelli (ed.), *Creature di Prometeo: Il ballo teatrale dal divertimento al dramma* (Florence, 1996), pp. 239–45; Ingrid Brainard, 'The Speaking Body: Gasparo Angiolini's *rhétorique muette* and the *ballet d'action* in the Eighteenth Century', in John Knowles (ed.), *Critica Musica: Essays in Honor of Paul Brainard* (Amsterdam, 1996), pp. 15–56; Kathleen Kuzmick Hansell, 'Theatrical Ballet and Italian Opera', in Lorenzo Bianconi and Giorgio Pestelli (eds.), *Opera On Stage* (The History of Italian Opera, part II: Systems, vol. 5) (Chicago, 2002), chapter 2, pp. 177–308; and Rebecca Harris-Warrick and Bruce Alan Brown (eds.), *The Grotesque Dancer on the Eighteenth-Century Stage: Gennaro Magri and His World* (Madison, WI, 2005).

77 For a broad view of the intersecting political, geographical and theatrical circumstances affecting Viennese opera around 1760, see Brown, *Gluck and the French Theatre in Vienna*, chapter 1, pp. 1–25.

78 On *Orfeo ed Euridice*, and on the influence of the opéra-comique on aspects of its style, see Brown, *Gluck and the French Theatre in Vienna*, chapter 9, pp. 358–81.

79 The Musikgraf was the director of the theatre, working with others who assisted him. Later individuals assuming the role of Musikgraf were Count Sporck (Count Rosenberg fulfilled the duties although he never actually held the title) and Count Wenzel Ugarte. This individual's crucial function and his place in court bureaucracy, as well as his ranking and that of others in the hierarchy of theatrical administration, is explored in Link, *The National Court Theatre*, pp. 481–5.

in order for reform efforts at a theatre to have any effect.[80] Durazzo, as director of the Kärntnertortheater and the Burgtheater was able to combine the resources of both, which aided his efforts. Evidence that the court subsidized the production of *Alceste* comes in the form of a letter from Calzabigi to Kaunitz about its preparations, the language of which implies the court's support.[81]

The face of Italian opera in Vienna changed after the death of Francis. Maria Theresa's son Joseph became co-regent, and the court loosened its control somewhat over operatic production. From 1766 to 1776 the court hired a string of impresarios consisting of Franz Hilverding (1766–7), Giuseppe Affligio (Afflisio) (1767–70), Johann Kohary (1770–2) and Joseph Keglevich (1772–6).[82] These individuals were caught in a precarious position. Although the court no longer maintained direct control over all aspects of production, it nevertheless monitored very closely the activities of the impresarios; they ran the theatres at their own financial risk, were forced to abide by the regulations the court imposed and could be – and in some cases were – dismissed if the court was not pleased with the products they offered. The court's Musikgraf had a supervisory role with respect to the impresarios, possessing the ability to influence repertory and personnel. Durazzo was Musikgraf until 1764 whereupon Count Johann Wenzel Sporck took over until 1775. Apart from the performers assembled by a given impresario, the court sometimes brought singers to Vienna for specific purposes, and impresarios sometimes had to abide by arrangements the court made independently with other members of operatic personnel. They could benefit from court subsidy, but there were always many strings attached.

Joseph II and the changing scene in the 1770s and 1780s

Antonio Salieri wrote his first ten operas for Vienna in the context of the impresarial management system. His stature at court as music director of its theatres in 1774 might have played a role in him securing his commission from the impresario at that time, Keglevich, who was perhaps reluctant to engage a composer other than the court music director.[83] In 1776 Joseph II dismissed the last impresario, who was bankrupt and had fallen out of favour for offering sub-standard productions, and brought opera back under court control. His new Musikgraf, Count Orsini-Rosenberg, operated essentially as

80 Brown, *Gluck and the French Theatre in Vienna*, p. 9: 'only with the right combination of artistic talent, material circumstances, and effective management could any theatre afford to listen to such basic criticism.'
81 Rice, *Antonio Salieri and Viennese Opera*, p. 39 and Heartz, *Haydn, Mozart and the Viennese School 1740–1780*, pp. 729–32.
82 Rice, *Antonio Salieri and Viennese Opera*, p. 38. The rapid turnover of impresarios is comparable to that of the King's Theatre in London; see below.
83 Rice, *Antonio Salieri and Viennese Opera*, p. 40.

a court-appointed impresario. Joseph's reform of the Viennese theatres in 1776 ended the court monopoly on them, other companies now staging works there. The Burgtheater was now the Nationaltheater and Joseph installed German performers.[84] Opera buffa gained in popularity and, after 1780, opera seria was no longer performed, because of Joseph's distaste for the genre itself and for the costs entailed in producing works. Ballets by Noverre appeared frequently on the Burgtheater (Nationaltheater) stage from 1767 to 1773.

At various times between 1763 and 1788, the Burgtheater (Nationaltheater) and the Kärntnertortheater operated concurrently, the city's burgeoning operatic activity producing some of eighteenth-century opera's most influential works. Antonio Salieri was one of the leading figures in Viennese opera in the last three decades of the century. With important works for the Burgtheater, both serious and comic, such as *Armida* (1771), *La fiera di Venezia* (1772), *La grotta di Trofonio* (1785) and *Axur, re d'Ormus* (1788) – as well as other works in several Italian cities – he also ranked as one of the late eighteenth century's most significant composers of Italian opera anywhere in Europe. So, too, did Giovanni Paisiello, who set the popular *Il re Teodoro in Venezia* (1784) for the Burgtheater (his *Il barbiere di Siviglia*, written for St Petersburg in 1782, had a Viennese performance in 1783, leading to *Il re Teodoro in Venezia*'s commission). Giuseppe Sarti's *Fra i due litiganti il terzo gode* was given at the Burgtheater as a benefit for the composer in 1784 as he passed through Vienna en route to Russia in 1784; his *Giulio Sabino* (which had its premiere at Venice's Teatro di San Benedetto in 1781) celebrated the Kärntnertortheater's re-opening in 1785. Sarti's *I finti eredi* and Francesco Bianchi's *La villanella rapita* were both comic hits in 1786. Also making his mark in Vienna was the Spanish composer Vicente Martín y Soler, whose drammi giocosi for the Burgtheater are among the century's finest. Martín's *Il burbero di buon cuore* (1786), *Una cosa rara* (1786, from which Mozart quoted in *Don Giovanni*) and *L'arbore di Diana* (1787) took Vienna by storm and brought the composer great acclaim. Martín and Salieri owed part of their success to the librettist with whom they collaborated, Lorenzo Da Ponte who, engaged by Joseph as chief poet to the imperial theatre, authored some of the century's best-known comic librettos. They were also able to exploit the talents of the first-rate

84 The Nationaltheater was a 'court-financed, public theatre that presented stage works in the language of the nation' (Link, *The National Court Theatre*, p. 1). Although its emphasis was on German spoken plays, its significance for Italian opera lies in its production of important opere buffe. A brief overview of Josephinian Theatre is provided in Link, *The National Court Theatre*, pp. 1–4, followed by a detailed performance calendar, information on private performances that included Italian opera (at Laxenburg and the palace of Prince Auersperg and elsewhere), and extensive reports on production materials and associated expenses at the Nationaltheater.

comic singers Durazzo recruited for Joseph, such as Michael Kelly, Nancy Storace and Francesco Benucci, for whom they created memorable roles.

This was the environment in which Mozart composed *Le nozze di Figaro* (1786) for the Burgtheater. The work formed part of Viennese entertainment culture, participating in an 'operatic conversation' that involved contemporaneous pieces and their conventions, in the context of a broad-ranging repertory.[85] Mozart's leading singers were those brought in by Durazzo; the arias he composed for them were elements in the 'conversation' with his contemporaries.[86] The work enjoys a privileged status today; although it received few performances at the time of its premiere, it is unsafe to assume that it was therefore poorly received.[87] It had a very favourable reception at its Prague performance later in 1786 (in German translation), where it was given by Pasquale Bondini's company and led to the commissioning of *Don Giovanni* (1787) for the same theatre.

Le nozze di Figaro moved down to Italy with two fairly unusual performances. The first, in 1787, took place at the palace theatre of Monza, near Milan, the villa of Archduke Ferdinand, governor of Lombardy. Angelo Tarchi re-set the last two acts and made other revisions. Florence's Teatro di via della Pergola gave it the following year, with the acts split up and performed separately, the first two on one evening and the last two a few nights later. These performances might have resulted from Joseph's recommendations of the opera to his brothers, Archduke Ferdinand and Archduke Peter Leopold, Grand Duke of Tuscany (soon to re-locate to Vienna).[88]

Leopold II and events of the 1790s

Leopold II ascended to the throne in 1790, and in 1791 focused on opera. Among the many changes he made upon assuming power were the dismissal of Da Ponte and the engagement of Caterino Mazzolà and then Giovanni Bertati as chief poets of the imperial theatre, the re-opening of the Kärntnertortheater

85 Mary Hunter, *The Culture of Opera Buffa in Mozart's Vienna: A Poetics of Entertainment* (Princeton, NJ, 1999). On the relationship between contemporary spoken comedy and the theatre of masks to Mozart's comic works, see Paolo Gallarati, 'Mozart and Eighteenth-Century Comedy', in Mary Hunter and James Webster (eds.), *Opera Buffa in Mozart's Vienna* (Cambridge, 1997), pp. 98–111. See also *idem*, *Musica e maschera: Il libretto italiano del Settecento* (Turin, 1984) and 'Music and Masks in Lorenzo Da Ponte's Mozartian Librettos', *Cambridge Opera Journal*, 1 (1989), pp. 225–47. On the variety and richness of entertainments at the Burgtheater, see the performance calendar in Dorothea Link, *The National Court Theatre*, pp. 5–190.

86 Dorothea Link, *Arias for Nancy Storace: Mozart's First Susanna* (Middleton, WI, 2002) and *Arias for Francesco Benucci: Mozart's First Figaro and Guglielmo* (Middleton, WI, 2004).

87 More reliable than numbers of performances in determining an opera's success in Vienna is the total income an opera generated, which should then be considered in the context of general attendance patterns. See Dexter Edge, 'Mozart's Reception in Vienna, 1787–1791', in Stanley Sadie (ed.), *Wolfgang Amadè Mozart: Essays on His Life and His Music* (Oxford, 1996), pp. 66–117; see also Link, *The National Court Theatre*.

88 Tim Carter, *W.A. Mozart: Le nozze di Figaro* (Cambridge, 1987), p. 129.

and the re-establishment of opera seria with the engagement of a seria troupe at the Burgtheater. Although *La clemenza di Tito* had its premiere in Prague and not Vienna, it stands as the most significant work of those marking opera seria's return to Vienna under Leopold II. Certainly the many years Leopold had spent in Florence as Grand Duke of Tuscany shaped his preference for opera seria and influenced his desire to bring it back to Vienna. Two works, for example – Sebastiano Nasolini's *Teseo a Stige* and Alessio Prati's *La vendetta di Nino* – both first performed in Florence, were given performances at the Burgtheater under Leopold II.

Opera buffa continued to remain popular as well, as illustrated by Mozart's *Così fan tutte* (1790). The work's appeal lay in its employment and manipulation of familiar conventions, as well as in the rich network of associations it created and into which it drew its audience, which functioned on musical and extra-musical levels.[89] The commission for Mozart's third masterwork in the so-called 'Da Ponte trilogy' occurred after *Don Giovanni*'s success in Prague and *Le nozze di Figaro*'s successful revival in Vienna.[90] The emperor (Joseph) became ill and died after the first performances, which resumed later the same year.[91] Income generated by the performances demonstrates the increased popularity Mozart had begun to enjoy with Viennese audiences shortly before his death.[92] *Il matrimonio segreto* (1792), a libretto by Bertati set by the international celebrity Domenico Cimarosa, also achieved wide acclaim. Both *Le nozze di Figaro* and *Così fan tutte* benefited from continuities in the Burgtheater's personnel and treated themes common to other works in the theatre's repertory.[93]

At the end of the century Italian opera had a devoted patron in Empress Marie Therese (1792–1807), second wife of Emperor Franz II from 1790 onwards and empress from 1792 to her death in 1807. She compiled a large

89 Hunter, *The Culture of Opera Buffa in Mozart's Vienna*, chapters 8 (pp. 247–72) and 9 (pp. 273–98); Daniel Heartz, 'Citation, Reference and Recall in *Così fan tutte*', in *Mozart's Operas*, ed. Thomas Bauman (Berkeley, 1990), pp. 229–53.

90 The commission was long thought to have resulted from these factors. But as demonstrated in Bruce Alan Brown and John A. Rice, 'Salieri's *Così fan tutte*', *Cambridge Opera Journal*, 8 (1996), pp. 17–43, evidence shows that Salieri, who composed a fragmentary setting of the libretto, was its original recipient, which calls the previous assumption into question.

91 Perhaps because of verbal agreements not honoured after the emperor's death, or for other reasons, Mozart evidently only received half the payment owed to him for *Così fan tutte* (despite the custom of various alternative sorts of compensation enjoyed by other composers at the Burgtheater). See Dexter Edge, 'Mozart's Fee for *Così fan tutte*', *Journal of the Royal Musical Association*, 116 (1991), pp. 211–35.

92 Edge, 'Mozart's Fee', p. 215; box-office receipts indicate that *Così* was 'by far the most successful opera of 1789–90'. See *idem*, 'Mozart's Reception in Vienna, 1787–1791', p. 82.

93 Hunter, *The Culture of Opera Buffa in Mozart's Vienna*, p. 247. Pierpaolo Polzonetti, in 'Mesmerizing Adultery: *Così fan tutte* and the Kornman Scandal', *Cambridge Opera Journal*, 14 (2002), pp. 263–96, enriches the context of the opera's inception by exploring its relationship to a contemporary adultery scandal, to mesmerism and, through a transformation of that doctrine's theories, to a political radicalism that formed part of French pre-Revolutionary propaganda. Some possible frameworks within which *Così fan tutte* may be understood are explored in Edmund J. Goehring, *Three Modes of Perception in Mozart: The Philosophical, Pastoral, and Comic in 'Così fan tutte'* (Cambridge, 2004).

music library that included many scores of Italian operas. She organized both public and private concerts that included Italian operatic excerpts from works such as Domenico Cimarosa's *Gli Orazi e i Curiazi* (Venice, 1797), Giuseppe Sarti's *Armida and Rinaldo* (St Petersburg, 1786) – and Giovanni Simone Mayr's *Lodoiska* (Venice, 1796).[94] Count Karl Zinzendorf's diaries offer valuable information on other private music-making in Vienna during the last decades of the century, frequently providing commentary on Italian opera at private theatres and in concerts (as well as on Burgtheater performances).[95]

Italian opera outside Italy: Prague and Esterháza

As the capital city of Bohemia and part of the Hapsburg hereditary crown lands, Prague was a crucial centre for Italian opera at the end of the century, witnessing important events associated with the imperial court with which its operatic history is linked. As at the palace theatre in Vienna, Italian opera flourished in Prague early in the century, too. For the coronation of Charles VI as Emperor of Bohemia in 1723, Fux's *Costanza e fortezza* was given, with lavish set and designs by Giuseppe Galli-Bibiena. Members of the aristocracy in Prague staged Italian opera at their residences. Count Franz Anton Spork invited Antonio Denzio's Italian company to his summer palace, and the same company then performed in Prague from 1725 to 1734, presenting works by Vivaldi, Albinoni, Porta and others. The theatre in Prague gave performances of Italian operas that had their premieres and became popular in other cities, such as Galuppi's *L'Olimpiade*, which – fairly unusual for the time and attesting to the composer's celebrity – had its premiere at Milan's Teatro Regio Ducale and in 1747 circulated to Mannheim before coming to Prague in 1750 (and then moving to other theatres).

The Nostitzsches Nationaltheater (also referred to as the Nostitz Theatre and the National Theatre), Prague's main opera house, was built by Count F. A. Nostitz in 1783 and was approximately the same size as the Burgtheater.[96] It was leased at different times by two impresarios, Pasquale Bondini and Domenico Guardasoni, who were to play decisive roles in the history of Italian opera for the operas they commissioned from Mozart. *Don Giovanni* (1787) was Bondini's commission for the

94 Rice, *Empress Marie Therese*, chapter 4, pp. 90–106.

95 Dorothea Link, 'Vienna's Private Theatrical and Musical Life, 1783–92, as Reported by Count Karl Zinzendorf', *Journal of the Royal Musical Association*, 122 (1997), pp. 205–57. See also *The National Court Theatre*, pp. 191–398.

96 Another venue for Italian opera in Prague was the theatre at Kotce, which opened in the late 1730s and, until its closure in 1783, offered numerous opere buffe and the occasional opera seria with sponsorship by various impresarios.

wedding celebration of Maria Teresa and Prince Anthony of Saxony, and *La clemenza di Tito* (1791) was Guardasoni's for the coronation festivities of Leopold II.[97] Bondini had a history at Prague, having been invited to the Thun palace in 1781 to stage opera there, and he mounted productions of Mozart's *Le nozze di Figaro* in 1786. For nearly twenty years Guardasoni presented Italian opera in Prague and was the last impresario to do so; *La clemenza di Tito* was given alongside works by Paisiello, Cimarosa and others, and after Guardasoni's departure German opera displaced Italian.

Prague mounted a successful production of *Le nozze di Figaro* at the Nostitz Theatre six months after its Vienna premiere, and its positive reception delighted the composer. Mozart led another performance of *Figaro* in Prague in 1787, which exposed him to the singers and instrumentalists who were to perform *Don Giovanni* later in the year. The small group of seven singers comprised an itinerant troupe that had also performed in Dresden and Leipzig. Although the date of the commission is unknown, the idea for the subject might have come from one of the singers, Antonio Baglioni, who had just performed in a work whose libretto would serve as a model for Da Ponte, Giovanni Bertati's *Don Giovanni, o sia Il convitato di pietra*, a dramma giocoso set by Giuseppe Gazzaniga at Venice's Teatro San Moisè in 1787. Mozart's *Don Giovanni* formed part of a long-standing tradition of operatic settings of the Don Juan story given in Prague and in the smaller (public) theatres in Vienna. (The association of the subject with popular theatre might have been partially responsible for the failure of Mozart's opera at the Burgtheater when it was given there in 1788.) The planned date of its premiere was chosen to coincide with the arrival in Prague of Maria Teresa and her brother Francis from Florence, en route to Dresden where the princess was to become the wife of Prince Anthony of Saxony. Various delays ensued, causing the postponement of the work until after her departure.[98]

La clemenza di Tito, on a Metastasian libretto revised by Caterino Mazzolà,[99] was a political allegory glorifying the enlightened absolutism that Leopold was to represent to the Austrian people. It was given at the National Theatre in

97 There were three coronations with separate ceremonies spanning an extended period. Leopold was crowned Emperor of the Holy Roman Empire in October 1790, King of Hungary in November 1790 and King of Bohemia in 1791.

98 See Daniel Heartz, '*Don Giovanni*: Conception and Creation', in *Mozart's Operas*, ed. Bauman, pp. 157–77, from which points in the foregoing discussion are drawn. On *Don Giovanni*'s controversial ending in the context of contemporary dramatic convention, see Michael F. Robinson, 'The Alternative Endings of Mozart's *Don Giovanni*', in Hunter and Webster (eds.), *Opera Buffa in Mozart's Vienna*, pp. 261–85. On *Don Giovanni* in the context of Enlightenment morality and on the function of recognition as a dramatic convention within it, see Jessica Waldoff, '*Don Giovanni*: Recognition Denied', in Hunter and Webster (eds.), *Opera Buffa in Mozart's Vienna*, pp. 286–307. See also Waldoff, *Recognition in Mozart's Operas* (Oxford, 2006).

99 Sergio Durante, 'Mozart and the Idea of "vera opera": A Study of *La clemenza di Tito*', PhD thesis (Harvard University, 1993).

1791 to celebrate Leopold II's coronation. The opera had a special significance given political events of the time. Set years earlier in Vienna in 1734, it presents an idealized view of the Hapsburg ruler. A popular libretto for the next forty years or so and set by Italy's leading composers, it had fallen out of fashion by the early 1770s. It was likely chosen for the occasion of Leopold II's coronation on account of associations between the historical Titus and Leopold known in Florence and Germany at that time.[100]

Domenico Guardasoni's contract for the opera – an agreement with the Bohemian Estates, a group of members of the nobility and church officials – indicates that he would provide an opera for part of the coronation festivities and elucidates certain aspects of production.[101] It specifies that he was to engage a prima donna and primo musico of the first rank and names some singers considered appropriate (but makes no mention of a tenor). He was free to choose his own composer. Guardasoni travelled to Vienna and Italy for singers and composers. When Salieri was unavailable, he turned to Mozart.[102] The work was put together in haste, not only for the composer but for everyone involved; Guardasoni signed the contract on 8 July and the premiere was on 6 September. When it came time for the performances, Guardasoni's troupe was occupied with more than *Tito*, and they operated on a tight schedule. Other works for the coronation included Paisiello's *Pirro* on 29 August, and *Don Giovanni* on 2 September, in addition to the premiere of *Tito*. The opening night was unsuccessful; Mozart claimed that subsequent performances were more positively received, although Guardasoni was unhappy, claiming to have lost money because of poor attendance at all performances after the first.

Esterháza court theatre

Esterháza was one of the leading centres for the international cultivation of Italian opera in the 1780s.[103] Its strong links with Vienna and Venice significantly influenced the operas produced there by Joseph Haydn. The theatre

100 John A. Rice, *W. A. Mozart: 'La clemenza di Tito'* (Cambridge, 1991).

101 Questions and controversies over the opera's composition process and its chronology have long engendered conflicting hypotheses. Production practices and many other circumstances surrounding its genesis are re-evaluated by Sergio Durante, in 'The Chronology of Mozart's *La clemenza di Tito* Reconsidered', *Music and Letters*, 80 (1999), pp. 560–94. The author presents a transcription of Guardasoni's contract in an appendix.

102 One of the aforementioned controversies involves the circumstances of the commission and Guardasoni's contact with Salieri and Mozart. In addition, certain scholars believe Mozart accepted reluctantly and because he needed money. John A. Rice shows that the commission is better understood in light of Joseph II's rejection of the opera seria genre. He suggests that Mozart was in fact eager to take the commission, for some time having sought Leopold's patronage and anticipating the commission being to his advantage, given that opera seria was coming back into favour at court. See Rice, *La clemenza di Tito*, chapter 4, pp. 45–65; *Mozart on the Stage*, pp. 41–3.

103 Dénes Bartha, 'Haydn's Italian Opera Repertory at Eszterháza Palace', in William W. Austin (ed.), *New Looks at Italian Opera: Essays in Honor of Donald J. Grout* (Ithaca, 1968), pp. 172–219.

presented opera almost all year round (with the exception of the winter months), and although the most popular works were opere buffe or drammi giocosi, opera seria flourished briefly as well. Haydn's *Lo speziale* and *Il mondo della luna* (drammi giocosi on librettos by Goldoni), and *L'isola disabitata*, *Orlando paladino* and others illustrate the popularity of Italian comic genres at the theatre. Haydn revised and adapted previously performed opere serie for performance at Esterháza, and his admiration for certain composers – Giuseppe Sarti, Niccolò Zingarelli, Domenico Cimarosa and Francesco Bianchi, in particular – shaped the serious works chosen for performance. Haydn's single opera seria, *Armida*, is standard late-century fare in the genre.[104]

Esterháza's contact with other operatic centres undoubtedly influenced the theatre's productions of Italian opera. Vienna was not surprisingly the source for most of Esterháza's comic works, while the opere serie came from Italian cities such as Venice, Milan, Florence, Naples, Padua and Verona. Opera seria at Esterháza bore similarities to opera seria at certain Italian theatres, such as Turin's Teatro Regio; comparisons of repertory in terms of broad categories according to subject matter show that despite the genre's brief popularity at Esterháza, the theatre participated in all stylistic trends affecting the genre and its transformation towards the end of the century.[105]

Italian opera outside Italy: London

Italian opera in eighteenth-century London existed under an expansive, century-long cloud of multi-faceted controversies. The history of London's Italian opera is inseparable from the on-going history of the tensions among the city's aristocratic operatic sponsors, difficult liaisons among theatrical managers and members of the nobility and gentry and complex interactions between managements of both musical and non-musical venues for entertainment.

One of the earliest controversies led indirectly to the establishment of Italian opera in London, which occurred through a sequence of fits and starts.[106] Drury Lane, the established theatre for spoken plays, also occasionally presented musical works – mostly semi-operas in English although some

104 Marita P. McClymonds, 'Haydn and the Opera Seria Tradition: *Armida*', in Bianca Maria Antolini and Wolfgang Witzenmann (eds.), *Napoli e il Teatro Musicale in Europa tra Sette e Ottocento: Studi in Onore di Friedrich Lippmann* (Florence, 1993), pp. 191–206.

105 Margaret R. Butler, 'Annäherungen an eine Kontextualisierung der opera seria in Eszterháza: Rückschlüsse aus Turin', in Armin Raab and Christine Siegert (eds.), *Bericht über die Internationale wissenschaftliche Tagung 'Bearbeitungspraxis in der Oper des späten 18. Jahrhunderts', vom 18. bis 20. Februar 2005, Würzburg, Germany* (Tutzing, 2007), pp. 103–25.

106 Curtis Price, Judith Milhous and Robert D. Hume, *Italian Opera in Late Eighteenth-Century London*, vol. 1, *The King's Theatre, Haymarket, 1778–1791* (Oxford, 1995). Some points from the present discussion are drawn from chapter 1, pp. 1–54.

Italian works as well. The financial success of theatrical works offset the high costs of opera. John Vanbrugh built the King's Theatre in the Haymarket in 1705 (then called the Queen's Theatre for Queen Anne) seeking a monopoly on theatrical entertainment. Upset by continued competition from Drury Lane, he attempted a monopoly on musical entertainment with a separation of genres – musical works at his theatre and spoken plays at Drury Lane. Not having thought of producing works in a language other than English, and deprived of the opportunity to mount popular semi-operas thereby having to rely on less-popular all-sung operas, he resigned in the wake of considerable financial losses. The next manager, Owen Swiney, did somewhat better, recognizing the importance of a highly skilled Italian castrato to the success of Italian opera and hiring one, although his eventual losses soon caused him to leave as well.

The King's Theatre in the Haymarket was to become London's premier Italian opera house and a centre of international importance for opera seria in the early part of the eighteenth century. This occurred primarily through productions of many of Handel's operas (he wrote thirty operas in total for the theatre).[107] Handel arrived in the city in 1710 and during his first visit produced *Rinaldo* (1711), which was well received and enjoyed many successful revivals.[108] Handel had been appointed court composer to the Elector of Hanover in 1710. Despite being dismissed from his post, he later regained favour and became court composer to the elector, crowned George I of Great Britain in 1714. John Jacob Heidegger, the manager at the King's Theatre who was to become instrumental in Italian opera's success in London, mounted several performances of operas by Handel, but the company closed down in 1717.

The king's passion for Italian opera was decisive in its resurgence. The Royal Academy of Music was established in 1719, intended for the re-institution of Italian opera as entertainment for the nobility and upper classes.[109] The collaboration between Handel as music director and resident impresario – he travelled to the Continent and hired singers – and Heidegger as the enterprising theatre manager, made the venture work for almost a decade, and witnessed some of Handel's best-known and masterful operas, *Giulio Cesare* (1724), *Tamerlano* (1724), *Rodelinda* (1725) and *Siroe, re di Persia* (1728) among them. But the offerings were not limited to Handel's works; operas by

107 Lowell Lindgren, 'The Staging of Handel's Operas in London', in Stanley Sadie and Anthony Hicks (eds.), *Handel Tercentenary Collection* (Ann Arbor, MI and London, 1987), pp. 93–119, presents a description of the theatre and discusses Handel's interest in staging and scenography.

108 For technical information on the Haymarket Theatre and its stage facilities, and on the staging of *Rinaldo*, see Mark W. Stahura, 'Handel's Haymarket Theatre', in Mark A. Radice (ed.), *Opera in Context: Essays on Historical Staging from the Late Renaissance to the Time of Puccini* (Portland, OR, 1998), pp. 95–109.

109 See Elizabeth Gibson, 'The Royal Academy of Music (1719–28) and its Directors', in Sadie and Hicks (eds.), *Handel Tercentenary Collection*, pp. 138–64.

Giovanni Bononcini and Domenico Scarlatti were also given. Singers engaged included the early eighteenth century's leading trinity of stars: Senesino, Francesca Cuzzoni and Faustina Bordoni, famous for their brilliant voices and notorious for their personal squabbles and intrigues. The rivalry between the two prima donnas was particularly damaging and an important contributing factor to the demise of the company.

London audiences especially enjoyed the spectacular aspects of the Royal Academy's operas as well as the fantastic voices of the era's leading singers. Emphasis was placed on elements synonymous with opera seria's central conventions: heroic subject matter, elaborate stage machinery and lavish costumes and dances. The Royal Academy replicated features of court-sponsored opera in its royal subsidy and noble patronage, but was a joint-stock company, relying on outside investments for success. It ran into deficit every year. Tensions and in-fighting occurred not only among the academy's financial backers but among the performers as well, which was compounded by the increasing impression that opera was no longer worthy of support by the aristocracy. The Royal Academy collapsed in 1728.

For the next five years Handel and Heidegger's collaboration continued, after the Royal Academy's bankruptcy, with a 'Second Academy'. Handel maintained his dual role of composer and impresario, travelling and engaging high-quality Italian singers from the Continent. He composed new works, some of which were poorly received, turning subsequently to pasticcios and revivals. Several of his new operas in these years were settings of Metastasian librettos: *Siroe, re di Persia* (1728), *Poro, re dell'Indie* (1731) and *Ezio* (1732). *Poro* was well received; it was superior to those he had set in the years immediately preceding and following and was to enter the tradition of Italian settings of Metastasio's popular *Alessandro nell'Indie*. Handel revised and adapted the libretto, which had its premiere a year earlier at Rome's Teatro delle Dame (set by Vinci).[110] The era of the 'Second Academy' represented a decline in originality in response to changing public tastes, during which revivals and pasticcios were generally produced. It also coincided with the rise of the oratorio and the beginning of Handel's shift towards it and away from Italian opera, occurring gradually by way of a complex series of events and being influenced by a combination of inter-related political, artistic and personal circumstances. The Opera of the Nobility, a rival company, was founded in 1733 and received financial sponsorship from a group of noble patrons; it took over at the King's Theatre, employing some of Handel's singers. A competition between the theatres ensued when Handel continued to mount operas, moving

110 Strohm, 'Metastasio's *Alessandro nell'Indie* and Its Earliest Settings', in *Essays on Handel and Italian Opera*, pp. 232–48.

to Covent Garden and producing some of his greatest works, including *Alcina* (1735). The Opera of the Nobility had hired Farinelli, an important factor in their success. By 1741 Handel had composed his last Italian opera.

From the 1740s onwards, the King's Theatre continued to present Italian opera but through a succession of differently organized and sponsored attempts ranging from those by independent noble financial backers to those by proprietors and investors who competed against each other, owning and being bought out by others.[111] The King's Theatre operated according to a private entrepreneurial system, individual impresarios being largely responsible for the productions, the types and quality of which varied considerably. Until the late 1770s conditions of financial and managerial controversy and inconsistency – sometimes verging on a state of collapse – dogged the theatre.[112] There were mixed seasons composed of opera seria, opera buffa and ballet, offering varied activities that helped to protect against complete financial failure in a given season. Handel's dominating presence resulted in a lacuna in the London opera scene upon his departure that no later composer could fill, although other composers of stature visited the King's Theatre and produced excellent works.[113]

The relationship between two of the leading composers at the King's Theatre in the following decades, Johann Christian Bach and Antonio Sacchini, and the impresarios who came in contact with them, shaped the circumstances of their engagements in significant ways.[114] Johann Christian Bach was one of the house composers during the 1760s and the late 1770s but his tenure was discontinuous; he was hired by different management teams at different times. The first team who hired him consisted of the soprano Colomba Mattei and her husband, Bach perhaps having been recommended to Mattei by Filippo Elisi, a fellow high-ranking singer who was pleased with the composer's music when he sang it earlier in Milan.[115] Mattei and her husband were shrewd managers and also benefited from Bach's skill in

111 Price *et al.* make a useful attempt to sort out the various organizational models on which opera companies in London were run, defining four of them: the impresario, the board of directors, partner-impresarios or managers and the noble patron. See *Italian Opera in Late Eighteenth-Century London*, vol. 1, p. 113.

112 Ian Woodfield, *Opera and Drama in Eighteenth-Century London: The King's Theatre, Garrick and the Business of Performance* (Cambridge, 2001), p. 1. This point and others in the ensuing discussion derive from the Introduction to Woodfield's volume. For specifics from the years up to 1775, see Elizabeth Gibson, 'Italian Opera in London, 1750–1775: Management and Finances', *Early Music*, 18 (1990), pp. 47–59.

113 Price *et al.* and Woodfield concur that London opera declined in quality after Handel's withdrawal from opera, whether because of conditions being such that 'no other composer of similar stature could be recruited to replace him' (Price *et al.*, *Italian Opera in Late Eighteenth-Century London* vol. 1, p. vii) or because 'no other composer of stature stayed long enough in London to make an impact' (Woodfield, *Opera and Drama in Eighteenth-Century London*, p. 1). In his praise of J. C. Bach and Sacchini's operas for London, however, Daniel Heartz reassesses the quality of London opera after Handel; see *Music in European Capitals*, pp. 894–904 and 920–6 (esp. pp. 904 and 922).

114 Points from the following discussion are taken from Heartz, *Music in European Capitals*, pp. 883–929.

115 Heartz, *Music in European Capitals*, p. 895.

assessing a singer's talents: Mattei hired the prominent De Amicis family of singers to perform comic works, but Bach recognized different potential in Anna De Amicis, casting her in the role of prima donna in his opera seria and first major contribution to the London stage, *Orione* (1763), a move that contributed significantly to its success. Despite his opera's positive reception, with the change of impresario after his first season Bach was not re-engaged by the new management team, which included Felice Giardini, one of London's best violinists. Bach was passed over for a little-known Italian composer, reflecting the generally negative disposition on the part of Italian musicians in London towards non-Italian composers, despite the favour Bach enjoyed at court.[116] Bach was hired for the season that included his *Adriano in Siria* (1765) by new managers, former partners of Giardini. Ferdinando Tenducci, one of the singers, may have recommended Bach to the managers, who also secured the first-rate musico Giovanni Manzuoli, recognizing the prestige that such a famous singer would bring. One of the revivals at the King's Theatre in the late 1760s was Bach's *Orione*. *La clemenza di Scipione*, Bach's last London opera, from 1778, was not only the best of his London works but one of the greatest to be staged in the city in the second half of the century.

Despite the generally short tenure of composers at the King's Theatre during the second half of the century, the various management teams were able to attract many of the most prominent ones. In addition to Bach and Sacchini, Pietro Guglielmi and Tommaso Traetta both mounted works; others, respected but less highly ranked, included Ferdinando Bertoni, Pasquale Anfossi and Francesco Bianchi. In the years before Bach's arrival, the King's Theatre also gave works by Gluck and Galuppi, among others.

The 1770s, the decade before the King's Theatre's 'golden age' of the 1780s when it regained its former international status, was marked by yet another series of managerial controversies that coincided with improved quality in the theatre's artistic products.[117] Antonio Sacchini was house composer during the 1770s, with a length of tenure that surpassed that of Bach and any other composer in the second half of the century. Recruited by the King's Theatre proprietor, George Hobart, Sacchini went to London in 1772. He dominated the city's opera for the ensuing nine years (his presence extending into the next administration of the King's Theatre), and his works for the city comprised new operas and previously performed ones re-worked for the new resources at hand. The newly composed works outnumbered the revisions, and included

116 Heartz, *Music in European Capitals*, p. 897.

117 Woodfield, *Opera and Drama in Eighteenth-Century London* examines this decade and its history, which set the stage for the decades and events explored in Price *et al.*, *Italian Opera in Late Eighteenth-Century London*, vol. 1. Details from the following discussion are drawn from Woodfield's Introduction, pp. 1–18.

Tamerlano (1773), *Montezuma* (1775), *Erifile* (1778), *L'amore soldato* (1778) and *Mitridate* (1781). The revisions include *Il Cid* (1773), adapted from *Il Cidde* given in Rome's Teatro Argentina in 1769, and *Rinaldo* (1780), revised from his *Armida* for Milan's Teatro Regio Ducale in 1772.

A confluence of circumstances that included Sacchini's tenure, further engagements of prestigious singers and a revolution in management led to the theatre's renewed prosperity. The theatre now enjoyed a period of strong management that demonstrated a greater degree of continuity than hitherto, leading to increased stability that contributed to its success. Circumstances influencing the theatre's activities in this period illustrate the intriguing intersection, possible only in a cosmopolitan cultural centre such as London, of the operatic world with those of literature and spoken theatre. In 1773 a team of five partners, which included three managers, assumed control of the King's Theatre. Two of the managers were actors, Mary Ann and Richard Yates, and the third a writer, Frances Brooke, clearly the leader of the enterprise. Brooke's proprietorship revitalized the King's Theatre.

During her tenure at the theatre, from 1773 to 1778, Brooke instituted a well-organized administrative policy and made smart, calculated moves to help the theatre hold its own against competing venues. She gained control of the King's Theatre to access a venue for performances of her own spoken plays, upon rejection of her petitions to David Garrick, the actor and major figure of the English stage, to have them performed at Drury Lane, where he was proprietor. In so doing she attempted to circumvent restrictions imposed by the Licensing Act of 1737, which gave Drury Lane and Covent Garden a monopoly on spoken theatre, planning to present her own works at the King's Theatre on the off-season when operas were not performed. Although she never received the desired permission to stage her plays, the fortunate by-product of her attempt was flourishing Italian opera at her theatre. In 1778 managers from Drury Lane and Covent Garden joined forces to acquire the theatre, effectively putting an end to Brooke's petitions (by then, she had turned her attentions elsewhere). They purchased the theatre and its resident company, and had bankrupted it by 1783.

Brooke's management worked for a variety of reasons. She instituted a sound and well-organized financial policy, carefully controlling costs. She sought no major alterations to the existing structure, always a major financial undertaking. The stable and substantial financial resources of her partners also contributed to her success. She had her finger on the pulse of Italian opera elsewhere in Europe, maintaining contact with English artists in Italy who reported on successes of particular works and facilitating the purchase of scores for adaptation at her theatre. When the Pantheon, a stylish concert venue that featured Italian operatic singers, began to emerge early in her tenure, she rose to the challenge. The Pantheon hired a wildly popular prima donna, Lucrezia Agujari, and Brooke countered with the engagement of one of equal if not higher stature, Caterina Gabrielli. Brooke recognized not only the value of attracting star singers to ensure success, but of having an excellent composer in residence to provide high quality works, holding on to Sacchini as house composer. She also commissioned original works from other internationally prominent composers; J. C. Bach composed his *La clemenza di Scipione*, already mentioned as the best London opera in the second half of the century, in April 1778, during the last year of her proprietorship. Brooke's critic, David Garrick, confirmed what her tenure at the King's Theatre had come to demonstrate: 'the Opera House would prove a mine of gold, if conducted with ability.'[118]

If the 1780s can be described as a sort of renaissance for opera at the King's Theatre, the preceding decade must be considered integral to its success, exceeding it in terms of strength and continuity of management. The theatre by the 1780s had gained international prominence and thus attracted the attention of proprietors, individuals and teams, who competed for its control and who hoped to be associated with its prestige and remuneration. During the 1780s the King's Theatre became interested in innovative trends in entertainment that had been popular in Continental opera for several decades, while continuing earlier trends as well.

The first half of the decade was marked by the prominence of theatrical dance, with many of the era's finest and most creative choreographers spending seasons at the King's Theatre. Soon after they took over, the management team of Sheridan and Harris imported a ballet master who was a disciple of Jean-Georges Noverre, and eventually brought in Gaétan Vestris and his son Auguste, who considerably raised the level of theatrical dance in London and cultivated a taste not only for pantomime but for the revolutionary ballet en action. Noverre himself arrived in 1781, stayed for one season and was succeeded by Charles Le Picq and Jean Dauberval. Thereafter the focus turned away from dance, other priorities commanding the attention of the next manager.

Giovanni Andrea Gallini, the theatre's last proprietor (1785–9), continued to maintain the high level of opera production established in the previous decade, although his tenure was marked by ongoing disputes with the aristocracy and

118 Reported as Garrick's advice to Edward Vanbrugh in 1777, quoted by Robert Bray O'Reilly, *An Authentic Narrative of the Principal Circumstances Relating to the Opera-House in the Hay-market; from its Origins to the Present Period; but more particularly including the transactions from the year 1778* (London, 1791), p. 5. Quoted in Price *et al.*, *Italian Opera in Late Eighteenth-Century London*, vol. 1, p. 57 and Woodfield, *Opera and Drama in Eighteenth Century London*, p. 223.

other managerial crises.[119] Under his leadership the theatre became in many ways more cosmopolitan and up to date. Gallini forged connections with Vienna that resulted in the arrival of popular Viennese repertory. Rather than focusing on commissioning new works, he imported operas that had enjoyed success in Vienna, such as Martín y Soler's *Una cosa rara*, Paisiello's *Il barbiere di Siviglia*, and works by Giuseppe Sarti and Domenico Cimarosa, Angelo Tarchi, Luigi Cherubini and Giuseppe Gazzaniga. He attracted top-notch singers of international prestige such as Luigi Marchesi and Francesco Benucci, his Viennese connections significantly raising the level of comic opera in London. He managed to attract the Burgtheater's leading comic singer Nancy Storace from Vienna to London, accompanied by her brother, Stephen Storace. With Gallini's tenure London's King's Theatre kept pace with the most cosmopolitan opera centre in all of Europe.

Similar to certain Italian theatres built early in the century and still in use later, the King's Theatre was eventually enlarged. Enhancements made in 1782 doubled its capacity. After the destruction by fire in 1789, and ensuing controversies that arose over its re-building, the King's Theatre in the Haymarket re-opened in 1791, again enlarged from its former size. Haydn's last opera, *L'anima del filosofo*, was commissioned for it, but was not performed there.

London's Pantheon, which opened in 1772, was an elite venue that gave performances of Italian arias by Italian singers. It offered to a certain stratum of London audiences the spectacular vocal dimension of Italian opera without its costly spectacle, in a casual, relaxed and elegant setting.[120] It caused concern for various managements of the King's Theatre, competing as it did for the high-class audiences that patronized Italian opera. It rivalled the re-built King's Theatre in the 1790s and Mozart received an invitation to become its house composer in 1790. But the Pantheon was eventually plagued by its own financial problems, and in 1792 was destroyed by fire.[121]

Italian opera outside Italy: Dresden, Berlin, Stuttgart, Mannheim, Munich, Salzburg

A strong Venetian influence characterized music in Dresden, the Saxon capital, from the seventeenth to the early years of the eighteenth century. Production of serious opera coincided with court celebrations, while smaller-scale comic

119 See Price *et al.*, *Italian Opera in Late Eighteenth-Century London*, vol. 1, chapter 6, 'Opera under Gallini', pp. 335–436.

120 Price *et al.* describe the Pantheon as 'conceived as a kind of a court opera, a small, exclusive, heavily subsidized venture in which artistic decisions would not be dictated by popular appeal and ticket sales'. *Italian Opera in Late Eighteenth-Century London*, vol. 1, p. viii.

121 Judith Milhous, Gabriella Dideriksen and Robert D. Hume, *Italian Opera in Late Eighteenth-Century London*, vol. 2, *The Pantheon Opera and its Aftermath, 1789–1795* (Oxford, 2000).

performances were given by an itinerant troupe in residence at the court. Activities involving Italian opera took place as part of the wedding celebration of 1719. King Augustus I had a large and lavish opera house built next to the Zwinger Palace to mark the occasion, and musicians were imported from Venice, most notably the composer Antonio Lotti and the musico Senesino. Lotti's *Teofane* of 1719 was the official wedding opera, although the theatre was inaugurated with a different opera set by Lotti. Handel came to Dresden for the event, seeking out singers to engage for his London operas. Although at first unsuccessful, Handel succeeded in luring Senesino away, temporarily affecting opera seria production in Dresden. Improvised Italian comedies continued, given by a troupe of Italian comedians directed by Tommaso Ristori.

Serious opera production was soon rejuvenated with a fresh wave of Venetian singers preceding the arrival in 1731 of Johann Adolf Hasse and his Venetian wife Faustina Bordoni, one of Europe's reigning prima donnas. The ensuing period of intense activity made Dresden the leading centre for Italian opera in Germany. The Hasses' trips to Dresden resulted in important works, and after moving there permanently in 1734 the composer regularly produced new operas for Carnival and for other occasions, with roles that highlighted his wife's magnificent range and flexibility. His *Cleofide* (1731), on a revision of Metastasio's *Alessandro nell'Indie*, was one of his works that achieved great approbation. Others that might be considered part of a Metastasian opera canon include his *Artaserse* (originally set for Venice's San Giovanni Grisostomo in 1730 which, together with Vinci's setting for Venice soon after, launched 'the single most substantial tradition in eighteenth-century opera seria'[122]), and *Didone abbandonata*, given at a small theatre at Hubertusburg (1742), near Dresden; all these operas circulated widely. Metastasio's *Antigono* had its first setting in Dresden, by Hasse, in 1743. In Dresden for political negotiations in 1742, King Frederick heard a performance of Hasse's new opera, *Lucio Papirio*. Former Dresden musicians Johann Joachim Quantz and Carl Heinrich Graun, who were to play influential roles in the cultivation of Italian opera in Berlin in the next decade and were by then in the king's service, knew Hasse and perhaps introduced his music to the king. Frederick was so taken with the Dresden performances that he had Hasse's works produced regularly thereafter in Berlin. Around 1750 Giuseppe Galli-Bibiena renovated and redecorated the opera theatre at Dresden, productions continuing until the Seven Years' War (1756–63).

122 Strohm, *Dramma per Musica*, p. 78; Heartz, *Music in European Capitals*, p. 310.

Public, commercial theatre flourished briefly in Dresden during the closure of the Dresden opera house (1745–7). Angelo Mingotti, a Venetian impresario, had a temporary wooden theatre built near the Zwinger Palace, where he staged operas with his small company of Italian singers during summer months for the paying public. His troupe gave popular performances of Vinci's *Artaserse* and Hasse's *La clemenza di Tito*, and also performed there and in another nearby theatre for the wedding celebrations in 1747. These involved a festival opera by Gluck, which represents the composer's first known connection with a troupe that he later followed to Hamburg and Copenhagen. The dancers engaged included Jean-Georges Noverre, at that time at Berlin. Another tiny theatre, built in 1755, hosted the troupe of Giovanni Battista Locatelli, which performed comic operas by Galuppi and others in the early 1760s; the court later took it over, re-built it, and re-opened it as the Kleines Kurfürstliches Theater. Following the Seven Years' War, which had severe consequences for opera in Dresden, travelling troupes occasionally presented opera buffa, and serious opera was offered sporadically. Caterino Mazzolà was engaged in Dresden in 1780 and wrote opera buffa librettos for among others Johann Gottlieb Naumann (Oberkapellmeister from 1776).

The inauguration of Berlin's Königliches Opernhaus in 1742 was an auspicious occasion. It was a step in the process by which Berlin became a capital city of international significance, the result of the artistic vision and political will of Frederick II of Prussia ('Frederick the Great' on assuming the throne in 1740). A massive, lavishly designed structure, it featured a canal system for cascades and waterfalls that also provided fire protection.[123] Frederick devoted much attention and resources to the cultivation of opera at his court, actively involving himself in the production process. He exerted control over all its components, from the selection of pre-existing librettos and subjects for new ones, to the rehearsal schedule, the scene design and stage machinery, costume design and other aspects. He engaged Italian singers and French dancers, reflecting his cosmopolitan tastes. His appreciation of French poetry and theatre in particular coincided with his preference for French subject matter as material for opera; his court poet, Leopoldo de Villati, authored a series of Italian librettos adapted from French plays or operas. The king himself provided scenarios and sketched opera plots in French.

Frederick intervened in musical matters as well, demanding that his singers closely follow the written score, dictating the style of overtures to be performed and even composing insertion arias. His preference for Hasse led to the performance of his works in Berlin. In 1741, Carl Heinrich Graun received the

123 Bauman, 'The Eighteenth Century: Serious Opera', p. 48.

appointment of Kapellmeister when Frederick acceded to the throne, setting the librettos the king created and that the court poet (Giampietro Tagliazucchi replaced de Villati after his death in 1752) translated into Italian and then versified. *Montezuma* (1755) is an Italian version of Frederick's prose libretto written in French, which Graun set to music. It represents the height of operatic achievement during Frederick's reign. A work with large numbers of supernumeraries, choruses and dramatic scenes requiring special stage effects, it must have benefited from its lengthy production period in Berlin, a luxury that most Italian theatres had to do without: rehearsals of *Montezuma* began in autumn 1754 and the opera had its premiere in January 1755. An unusual subject for an opera seria in this decade, *Montezuma* deals with events surrounding the conquest of Mexico by the Spaniards, and the subsequent destruction of Montezuma's ancient civilization. Frederick, an atheist, conceived the opera as an expression of his hatred for Christian barbarity. The king sympathized with the critical view of Italian opera held by his friend Francesco Algarotti and set forth in the *Saggio sopra l'opera in musica*, published in the year of *Montezuma*'s premiere. Because of its many opportunities for spectacular stage effects, the Montezuma subject was attractive to Italian theatres, and other librettos on the topic and their musical settings became popular all over Italy.[124] In the following year the situation in Berlin changed abruptly; the Seven Years' War began and operatic activity was curtailed.

Stuttgart, capital of the duchy of Württemberg, had a forceful presence on the European operatic scene, primarily for its French-inspired Italian operas of the 1760s. Before he became Duke of Württemberg in 1744 at the age of sixteen, Carl Eugen travelled to Berlin under the protection of Frederick the Great. After spending three years at the Berlin court, Carl Eugen returned to his capital and modelled his reign on that of his mentor. This choice had significant implications for opera: Carl Eugen assumed total control over music and theatre, as did Frederick at his own court. He had developed a taste for French music and culture not only during his Berlin stay but also from his travels to Paris and Versailles. He built a company of singers, hired Ignaz Holzbauer from Vienna as his Oberkapellmeister in 1751 (he stayed only two years) and had the court theatre in the Lusthaus re-modelled along Italian lines. He eventually hired his own corps de ballet, investing in dance on the same scale as opera. After Niccolò Jommelli's arrival in 1753 to take up the position

124 Graun's *Montezuma* was revived in 1771 in Berlin, with dances by the choreographer who had created them for Turin's *Motezuma* in 1765 (a libretto by Vittorio Amedeo Cigna-Santi set by Gian Francesco de Majo). This and other points of contact between Turin and Berlin are discussed in Margaret R. Butler, 'Exoticism in Eighteenth-Century Turinese Opera: *Motezuma* in Context', in Mara E. Parker (ed.), *Music in Eighteenth-Century Life: Cities, Courts, Churches* (Ann Arbor, MI, 2006), pp. 105–24. Cigna-Santi's libretto was set eight different times outside Turin after 1765, in Italian cities and in London.

of Kapellmeister, Stuttgart's Italian operatic activity escalated. Jommelli enjoyed almost complete autonomy over operatic production. He worked briefly there with the dramaturgically adventurous court poet Mattia Verazi, who created a series of works for Stuttgart, Mannheim and elsewhere that challenged traditional conventions of opera seria.[125] His first two librettos, on mythological subjects and integrating French-inspired features such as chorus, pantomime and spectacular stage effects accompanying the appearance of deities, were *Pelope* and *Enea nel Lazio* of 1755. Their *Vologeso* (1766, Verazi's revision of Zeno's *Lucio Vero*) heightens the dramatic impact of the traditional libretto with the expansion of several ensembles. Taking advantage of the technical sophistication of the renovated theatre at the palace of Ludwigsburg near Stuttgart, Verazi and Jommelli collaborated on the most elaborate of French-inspired spectacle operas, *Fetonte* (1768), which featured all of these elements as well as flexible ensembles and extensive integrated danced episodes, derived from the subject of the opera.[126] Jean-Georges Noverre, the innovative French-Swiss choreographer and rival of Angiolini in Vienna, was in Stuttgart from 1760 to 1767, and played a role in the development of dance in the city similar to that which Jommelli played for opera. For Carl Eugen's corps de ballet Noverre created lavish dramatic pantomimes, some of them entr'acte ballets performed with opere serie by Jommelli and some independent pieces.

Theatrical production in Stuttgart doubled when the theatre at Ludwigsburg was built in 1764. To the company of seria performers was added a comic troupe, engaged in 1766. Gaetano Martinelli, poet and author of numerous comic works (who would later be Jommelli's correspondent in Lisbon) arrived in 1767. Martinelli and Jommelli collaborated on several Italian comedies for Stuttgart during the 1760s. Jommelli also composed settings of Metastasian librettos, *L'Olimpiade* (1761) and *Didone abbandonata* (1763). At his death Jommelli (who had left Stuttgart in 1769) was considered one of the greatest composers of his era.

Italian opera at Mannheim, as in other German centres with affinities for French culture, stood out in the years around 1760 for opere serie by Tommaso Traetta and Gian Francesco de Majo; these incorporated French-inspired elements such as choral and danced episodes, large, active and flexible ensembles and spectacular stage effects, all combined in expansive, dramatic scene complexes.

125 Marita Petzoldt McClymonds, 'Transforming Opera Seria: Verazi's Innovations and Their Impact on Opera in Italy', in Thomas Bauman and Marita Petzoldt McClymonds (eds.), *Opera and the Enlightenment* (Cambridge, 1995), pp. 119–32. See also *idem*, 'Mattia Verazi and the Opera at Mannheim, Stuttgart, and Ludwigsburg', *Studies in Music from the University of Western Ontario*, 7 (1982), pp. 99–136.

126 This work should not be confused with an earlier *Fetonte* (1753) also performed at Stuttgart; the arias were by Jommelli but Holzbauer was responsible for the performance. Heartz, *Music in European Capitals*, p. 446.

Elector Carl Theodor, nephew and successor to Elector Palatine Carl Philipp, began his reign in Mannheim in 1742. He imported works by the era's leading European composers for performance at the Hoftheater, Mannheim's court theatre, which was situated in the palace. Built between 1737 and 1741, it was designed by Alessandro Galli-Bibiena, the architect who had advised Benedetto Alfieri on the construction of Turin's Teatro Regio (built 1740). The Hoftheater shares certain features with the Regio including the large staircase for use by live horses that sometimes appeared on-stage. Seating 2,000 spectators, the Hoftheater was the largest theatre in Germany at the time and was comparable in size to the largest contemporaneous Italian theatres.[127]

Opera thrived in Mannheim, where seven or eight works were offered in a given season, which began on Carl Theodor's name day (4 November) and lasted through Carnival to Shrove Tuesday. After Easter, operatic activity shifted to Schwetzingen, where during the summer the court enjoyed comic operas by Galuppi, Piccinni, Salieri and Sacchini.

Kapellmeister Ignaz Holzbauer set three Metastasian librettos for the Hoftheater in the 1750s. After collaborating with Jommelli in Stuttgart, Verazi took up the post of court poet in Mannheim in 1756, producing two innovative librettos.[128] These were *Sofonisba* (1762), set by Traetta, well versed by then in French-style Italian opera from his activities in Parma, and *Ifigenia in Tauride* (1764), set by de Majo, both of which infused heightened dramatic action and tragic intensity with large scene complexes involving choruses, flexible ensembles and spectacular events such as storms, shipwrecks, breaching of city walls, processions involving chariots drawn by tamed beasts, caged wild animals, battles, gladiatorial games, conflagrations and collapsing temples. A pantomime introduction opens both of them, linking the overture with the opening scenes. Both end tragically, contrary to convention. Turin's Teatro Regio mounted performances of revised settings of these librettos soon after their Mannheim premieres (*Sofonisba* by Galuppi in 1764 and *Ifigenia in Tauride*, re-titled *Oreste*, by Carlo Monza in 1766). As mentioned above, the circumstances surrounding the deletion of certain innovative elements and the preservation of others in Turin illustrate both the difficulties posed by French-inspired works for Italian theatres and the ways in which obstacles presented by the works could be overcome.[129]

Renovations between 1767 and 1768 enlarged the Hoftheater's seating capacity and added dressing rooms for the performers. Mannheim opera

127 Paul Corneilson, 'Reconstructing the Mannheim Court Theatre', *Early Music*, 25 (1997), pp. 63–81, from which points in this discussion are drawn.
128 McClymonds, 'Transforming Opera Seria', pp. 121–3.
129 Margaret Butler, 'Administration and Innovation at Turin's Teatro Regio: Producing *Sofonisba* (1764) and *Oreste* (1766)', *Cambridge Opera Journal*, 14 (2002), pp. 243–62.

continued to flourish into the 1770s, while the activities of court theatres at Dresden and Stuttgart were hampered in the 1760s by the effects of war. After Mannheim's unconventional productions of the early 1760s, more conservative opere serie followed, composed by Piccinni and J. C. Bach. One of them was *Lucio Silla*, on the libretto by Giovanni De Gamerra that Mozart had set for Milan in 1772, and which Bach had composed in London. Part of the score went astray during its shipment from London, resulting in a year's delay in its Mannheim performance, eventually given in 1775.[130] *Lucio Silla* was the last opera seria commissioned at Mannheim before Carl Theodor left Mannheim for Munich in 1778, transferring his famous *Hofkapelle* there – orchestra, singers and theatrical company. Although some musicians stayed, most followed him to Munich, which effectively brought an end to Italian operatic activity in Mannheim.

Munich, the capital city of Bavaria, had a well-established, lively court opera tradition dating from long before the arrival of Carl Theodor. Farinelli and Faustina Bordoni had visited in the 1720s, and Vinci's *Alessandro nell'Indie*, performed first in Rome, was later produced as a pasticcio for Munich (1735). In 1753 the Residenztheater, the city's grand theatre dedicated to opera seria, opened with great ceremony. Count Joseph Anton Graf von Seeau served as Intendant of the city's theatres, which included at least five others as well as smaller venues for operatic performances. One of the comic theatres was the Opernhaus am Salvatorplatz, where Mozart's dramma giocoso *La finta giardiniera* had its premiere in Carnival 1775, given in a series of disjointed performances on account of the complicated Munich theatrical calendar, a singer's illness that forced the cancellation of one performance and the subsequent re-location of the production to a different venue, the Redoutensaal. Carl Theodor attended the opera's second performance.

Carl Theodor brought from Mannheim to Munich not only his *Hofkapelle* but his French tastes as well. The result was Mozart's magnificent French-inspired opera seria, *Idomeneo*, performed at the Residenztheater in 1781. Rich in flexible scene structures, choruses and ballets integrated into the opera's action, crowd scenes and expansive stage tableaux, its original libretto by Gianbattista Varesco is drawn from Antoine Danchet's tragédie en musique *Idoménée* (set by André Campra in 1712).[131] For the dramatic impact of its music (the most orchestrally-conceived of Mozart's operas, in which the composer took full advantage of the superb Mannheim orchestra), the intensity of

130 Paul Corneilson, 'The Case of J. C. Bach's *Lucio Silla*', *Journal of Musicology*, 12 (1994), pp. 206–18.
131 Lois Rosow, '*Idomeneo* and *Idoménée*: The French Disconnection', in Michelle Biget-Mainfroy and Rainer Schmusch (eds.), *'L'esprit français' und die Musik Europa/Entstehung, Einfluss und Grenzen einer ästhetischen Doktrin,'L'esprit français' et la musique en Europe: Émergence, influence et limites d'une doctrine esthétique. Festschrift für Herbert Schneider* (Hildesheim, Zürich and New York, 2007), pp. 434–45.

its characterization and the masterful manipulation of its materials, *Idomeneo* is rightly considered 'nothing less than the greatest lyric tragedy of its century'.[132] The contract for *Idomeneo* was negotiated through Count Seeau. Mozart was in Salzburg at the time of the commission, and collaborated on the opera's composition there with Varesco, a chaplain in the Salzburg cathedral. Three of the leading singers were his friends from Mannheim, Dorothea and Elizabeth Wendling and Anton Raaff. Again the rehearsal period, long by Italian standards (1 December 1780 to 27 January 1781), likely aided the complex staging of the opera's numerous dramatic choruses and dances, and the scenes involving pantomime and spectacle. In comparison to Mozart's other Italian operas, more is known about *Idomeneo*'s production process, including the dates of and circumstances surrounding the rehearsals, the dealings with the singers, the collaborations with members of the personnel and the compositional process.[133]

Italian opera was also given in Mozart's home town of Salzburg, at the archbishop's palace, on special occasions such as the arrival of visiting dignitaries and installation ceremonies. Salzburg witnessed some of Mozart's earliest essays in Italian opera, the first being *La finta semplice*, a dramma giocoso by Carlo Goldoni. Mozart had composed the work in Vienna; Leopold had taken him there in 1767 in the hopes of securing Mozart a commission for an opera connected to festivities for the wedding of the Archduchess Maria Josepha and King Ferdinand of Naples. On account of various obstacles – including Leopold's obstinacy in dealing with Joseph II – the opera was never given there.[134] The Mozarts returned to Salzburg and presented the work to the archbishop. Although no musical materials survive, the opera was probably performed in Salzburg, in 1769. Also, for the celebration of the birthday of Archbishop Schrattenbach, Wolfgang set Metastasio's azione teatrale *Il sogno di Scipione*. He composed it in 1771, soon after his return from Milan (and soon after his first Italian operas composed for an Italian theatre). The archbishop's subsequent death forced cancellation of the festivities. The work was then planned for the installation of his successor, Archbishop Colloredo, a year later, but did not receive a performance.

The visit of Archduke Maximillian to Salzburg in 1775 resulted in settings of two Metastasian works, the serenata *Il rè pastore*, which Mozart set soon after

132 Heartz, *Haydn, Mozart and the Viennese School 1740–1780*, p. 716.

133 Daniel Heartz, 'The Genesis of Mozart's *Idomeneo*', in Bauman (ed.), *Mozart's Operas*, pp. 15–35. See also Rice, *Mozart on the Stage*, pp. 30; 40, 76–81.

134 The complicated controversy surrounding the commission and cancellation of *La finta semplice*, involving the emperor, the impresario Giuseppe Affligio, Leopold Mozart, Gluck and Chancellor Kaunitz, has been subject to at least two different interpretations; see Heartz, *Haydn, Mozart and the Viennese School 1740–1780*, pp. 512–16; Rice, *Antonio Salieri and Viennese Opera*, p. 41; *Mozart on the Stage*, pp. 56–7.

his return from Munich where he had given *La finta giardiniera*, and the azione teatrale *Gli orti esperidi*, set by the court of Salzburg's *maestro di cappella* at the time, Domenico Fischietti. Other *maestri di cappella* set Italian librettos in Salzburg later in the century, such as Giacomo Rust, Fischietti's successor, with Metastasio's festa teatrale *Il Parnaso confuso* (1778) for the consecration of the Archbishop of Olmütz.

Italian opera outside Italy: St Petersburg, Portugal, Madrid

Peter I (the Great) founded St Petersburg in 1703, a city that was to become the capital of Russia and another major centre for Italian opera and theatrical ballet outside Italy. Court opera at the Imperial Theatre under Catherine II was comparable to other prominent European opera theatres. Many of the finest Italian composers of the day had Russian sojourns as *maestri di cappella* at her court, and some of their operas for St Petersburg are distinguished by a strong choral component, attesting to the expertise of the Russian choral singers (men and boys from the Imperial Chapel). One of these is Galuppi's setting of Marco Coltellini's *Ifigenia in Tauride* (set first by Traetta for Vienna in 1763). Gasparo Angiolini staged pantomime ballets between 1766 and 1772, one of them using the score and sets of Galuppi's *Didone*.[135] Coltellini moved to St Petersburg in 1772 and remained there as theatre poet until his death in 1777. Among the works Traetta composed during his stay include two choral operas, *L'Olimpiade* (a revision of an earlier setting), and his masterpiece *Antigona* (1772). In essence a reform opera, on a libretto by Coltellini with the highly esteemed prima donna Caterina Gabrielli in the title role (a singer for whom Traetta had composed many times before, in Parma and Turin), *Antigona* exhibits all the standard features of French-inspired reform works seen earlier in other locations. Traetta composed the ballet music himself. Paisiello was Catherine's favourite composer. His *Nitteti* for St Petersburg (1777) has inserted choral episodes. His *Il barbiere di Siviglia* (1782), to become one of the most renowned comic works of the century, had its premiere in St Petersburg and was performed in Vienna the next year. Following Paisiello, Sarti, Cimarosa and Martín y Soler had appointments as court composers. The regular turnover of composers – most of whom were issued three-year contracts – was attributable to the court's wish to discourage them from settling in Russia. Although renewals of contracts sometimes

135 Heartz, *Music in European Capitals*, p. 936; Bruce Alan Brown, 'Metastasio und das Ballett', *Händel-Jahrbuch 1999*, pp. 43–5 (cited by Heartz).

occurred, only Sarti stayed for more than seven years.[136] In the 1780s one theatre was newly built and one was renovated to accommodate the increasing demand for opera.

Italian opera took hold in Lisbon in the early eighteenth century, although it was seriously cultivated only on the arrival of David Perez as *mestre de capela* in 1752. His setting of *Alessandro nell'Indie* (1755) inaugurated the magnificent Casa da Ópera (Ópera do Tejo), designed by Giovanni Galli-Bibiena. Despite the theatre's destruction in an earthquake later the same year, the court persisted in sponsoring Italian opera, constructing two new theatres, the Ajuda and the Salvaterra, also by Galli-Bibiena. Theatres at the summer palace at Queluz near Lisbon, and several public theatres repaired after the earthquake also gave Italian opera. The favoured repertory consisted of opere serie by Perez, Antonio Mazzoni and Niccolò Jommelli and opere buffe by Piccinni. In the 1750s the Portuguese court, under José I, a dedicated patron of music and of Italian opera in particular, competed unsuccessfully with those of Mannheim and Stuttgart to hire Niccolò Jommelli. After the composer left the Duke of Württemberg's service in 1769 and before he moved to Naples, the Portuguese court re-established contact with him, which resulted in an agreement whereby for an annual pension he would send copies to Lisbon of existing operas as well as new works. Correspondence between Jommelli and two individuals – his friend, Gaetano Martinelli, whom he sent to Lisbon to oversee production in his absence, and the director of the royal theatres in the 1760s, Pedro da Silva Bottelho – reveals much about the production process in Lisbon. The court ultimately sponsored performances of twenty of Jommelli's works between 1767 and 1780. Its resources for opera, understandably diminished from the middle of the century onwards on account of the destructive earthquake, resulted in revisions of Jommelli on a smaller scale; the massive French-inspired work from Stuttgart, *Fetonte*, was significantly revised. Others from the Stuttgart years revised for Lisbon were *Enea nel Lazio*, *Pelope*, *Vologeso* and settings of several Metastasian librettos. Three of Jommelli's late operas were written for Lisbon, among them a second version of *Ezio* (1772), revised by the *mestre de capela*, the Portuguese, Neapolitan-trained composer João Cordeiro da Silva, and *Il trionfo di Clelia* (1774), his final work.[137]

Italian opera in Madrid flourished at different times, primarily at the Teatro de los Caños del Peral and the Teatro Coliseo del Buen Retiro. During the

136 Rice, *Antonio Salieri and Viennese Opera*, p. 10.
137 Marita Petzoldt McClymonds, *Niccolò Jommelli: The Last Years, 1769–1774* (Ann Arbor, MI, 1980), esp. chapters 2 (pp. 19–57) and 4 (pp. 127–50); Manuel Carlos de Brito, *Opera in Portugal in the Eighteenth Century* (Cambridge, 1989).

early and middle years of the century productions were given at the Buen Retiro and the Aranjuez, both court theatres, and at Los Caños del Peral. Farinelli had come to the city in 1737, remaining a central fixture in Italian opera in Madrid until his departure in 1759. He served as manager of the court theatres. Metastasio's *Nitteti* had its first setting, by Nicola Conforto, at the Buen Retiro in 1756 under Farinelli's direction. Conforto came to Madrid in 1755, having received an appointment to compose opera for the court as a result of earlier works, and remained an important presence in Italian opera there until 1759. Conforto and Farinelli's collaboration played a crucial role in establishing Spain's mid-century taste for Italian opera. Los Caños del Peral reopened ceremonially as the Italian opera theatre in 1787 with a production of Sarti's *Medonte*. Thereafter the repertory consisted of comic works until 1790, when seria works appeared until the end of the century. Most operas presented at Los Caños del Peral were based on scores brought from elsewhere with few new works being presented. Pantomime ballet became an essential part of the theatre's repertory late in the century.[138]

In his *A Treatise on Theatres* (1790), George Saunders wrote: 'When a foreigner arrives at a town, his curiosity naturally leads him in the first place to visit the theatre. Here he receives his first impressions of the state of the arts, of the genius and the manners of the people.'[139] A town or a city's character and identity was inextricably linked with its opera theatres, with the works they produced, with the creators and performers they hosted and with the traditions they cultivated. Italian opera in the eighteenth century was a variegated tapestry, as multi-faceted and dynamic as the theatrical landscape that sponsored it.

Select Bibliography

Antolini, Bianca Maria and Wolfgang Witzenmann (eds.). *Napoli e il Teatro Musicale in Europa tra Sette e Ottocento: Studi in Onore di Friedrich Lippmann*. Florence, 1993

Bauman, Thomas. 'The Society of La Fenice and Its First Impresarios'. *Journal of the American Musicological Society*, 39 (1986), pp. 332–54

Bauman, Thomas and Marita Petzoldt McClymonds (eds.). *Opera and the Enlightenment*. Cambridge, 1995

138 The effect of patronage and broad-ranging economic factors on Italian opera's fortune in eighteenth-century Spain, along with aspects of management and finances at the Teatro de los Caños de Peral, are discussed in Michael F. Robinson, 'Financial Management at the Teatro de los Caños del Peral, 1786–99', in Malcolm Boyd and Juan José Carreras (eds.), *Music in Spain during the Eighteenth Century* (Cambridge, 1998), pp. 29–50. On Italian operatic activity in public theatres, see Xoán M. Carreira, 'Opera and Ballet in Public Theatres of the Iberian Penninsula', pp. 17–28 in the same volume.

139 George Saunders, *A Treatise on Theatres* (London, 1790; reprint New York, 1968), p. vi, quoted in Corneilson, 'Reconstructing the Mannheim Court Theatre', p. 63.

Bianconi, Lorenzo and Georgio Pestelli (eds.). *Opera Production and Its Resources.* (The History of Italian Opera. Part 2: Systems. Vol. 4.) Trans. Lydia G. Cochrane. Chicago, IL, 1998

(eds.). *Opera On Stage.* (The History of Italian Opera. Part 2: Systems. Vol. 5.) Trans. Kate Singleton. Chicago, IL, 2002

Bianconi, Lorenzo and Renato Bossa (eds.). *Musica e Cultura a Napoli dal XV al XIX Secolo.* Florence, 1983

Bouquet, Marie-Thérèse. *Il teatro di corte. Dalle origini al 1788, Storia del Teatro Regio di Torino.* Vol. 1. ed. Alberto Basso, Turin, 1976

Brown, Bruce Alan. *Gluck and the French Theatre in Vienna.* Oxford, 1991

W. A. Mozart: Così fan tutte. Cambridge, 1995

Brown, Bruce Alan and John A. Rice. 'Salieri's *Così fan tutte*'. *Cambridge Opera Journal*, 8 (1996), pp. 17–43

Bucciarelli, Melania and Berta Joncus (eds.). *Music as Social and Cultural Practice: Essays in Honour of Reinhard Strohm.* Woodbridge and Rochester, NY, 2007

Butler, Margaret Ruth. *Operatic Reform at Turin's Teatro Regio: Aspects of Production and Stylistic Change in the 1760s.* Lucca, 2001

'Administration and Innovation at Turin's Teatro Regio: Producing *Sofonisba* (1764) and *Oreste* (1766)'. *Cambridge Opera Journal*, 14 (2002), pp. 243–62

'Producing the Operatic Chorus at Parma's Teatro Ducale, 1759–1769'. *Eighteenth-Century Music*, 3 (2006), pp. 231–51

Carter, Tim. *W. A. Mozart: 'Le nozze di Figaro'.* Cambridge, 1987

Corneilson, Paul. 'Reconstructing the Mannheim Court Theater', *Early Music*, 25 (1997), pp. 63–81

Cotticelli, Francesco and Paologiovanni Maione (eds.). *Le arti della scena e l'esotismo in età moderna.* Naples, 2006

Davoli, Susi (ed.). *Civiltà teatrale e Settecento emiliano.* Bologna, 1986

Degrada, Franco and Maria Teresa Muraro (eds.). *Antonio Vivaldi da Venezia all'Europa.* Milan, 1978

DelDonna, Anthony R. 'Production Practices at the Teatro di San Carlo, Naples, in the Late 18th Century'. *Early Music*, 30 (2002), pp. 429–45

Durante, Sergio. 'The Chronology of Mozart's *La clemenza di Tito* Reconsidered'. *Music and Letters*, 80 (1999), pp. 560–94

Feldman, Martha. 'Magic Mirrors and the Seria Stage: Thoughts Toward a Ritual View'. *Journal of the American Musicological Society*, 48 (1995), pp. 423–84

Opera and Sovereignty: Transforming Myths in Eighteenth-Century Italy. Chicago, 2007

Goehring, Edmund J. *Three Modes of Perception in Mozart: The Philosophical, Pastoral, and Comic in 'Così fan tutte'.* Cambridge, 2004

Hansell, Kathleen Kuzmick. 'Opera and Ballet at the Regio Ducal Teatro of Milan, 1771–1776: A Musical and Social History', 2 vols. PhD thesis, University of California, Berkeley, 1980

Harris-Warrick, Rebecca and Bruce Alan Brown (eds.). *The Grotesque Dancer on the Eighteenth-Century Stage: Gennaro Magri and His World.* Madison, WI, 2005

Heartz, Daniel. *Mozart's Operas.* Ed. Thomas Bauman, Berkeley, 1990

Haydn, Mozart and the Viennese School, 1740–1780. New York and London, 1995

Music in European Capitals: The Galant Style, 1720–1780. London and New York, 2003

From Garrick to Gluck: Essays on Opera in the Age of Enlightenment. Ed. John A. Rice, Hillsdale, NY, 2004

Holmes, William C. *Opera Observed: Views of a Florentine Impresario in the Early Eighteenth Century*. Chicago and London, 1993

Hunter, Mary. *The Culture of Opera Buffa in Mozart's Vienna: A Poetics of Entertainment*. Princeton, NJ, 1999

Hunter, Mary and James Webster (eds.). *Opera Buffa in Mozart's Vienna*. Cambridge, 1997

Link, Dorothea. *The National Court Theatre in Mozart's Vienna: Sources and Documents, 1783–1792*. Oxford, 1998

Maione, Paologiovanni and Francesca Seller. *Teatro di San Carlo di Napoli (1739–1777). Cronologia dei spettacoli (1737–1799)*. Vol. 1, Naples, 2005

Mancini, Franco. *Il Teatro di San Carlo, 1737–1987*. 3 vols., Naples, 1987

McClymonds, Marita Petzoldt. *Niccolò Jommelli: The Last Years, 1769–1774*. Ann Arbor, MI, 1980

'The Venetian Role in the Transformation of Italian Opera Seria during the 1790s'. In Maria Teresa Muraro (ed.), *I vicini di Mozart 1: Il teatro musicale tra Sette e Ottocento*. Florence, 1989, pp. 221–40

'Opera Reform in Italy, 1750–80'. In Bianca Maria Antolini, Teresa M. Gialdroni and Annunziato Pugliese (eds.), *'Et facciam dolçi canti': Studi in onore di Agostino Ziino in occasione del suo 65° compleanno*. 2 vols., vol. 2, Lucca, 2003, pp. 895–912

'The Role of Innovation and Reform in the Florentine Opera Seria Repertory, 1760 to 1800'. In Colleen Reardon and Susan Parisi (eds.), *Music Observed: Studies in Memory of William C. Holmes*. Warren, MI, 2004, pp. 281–99

Milhous, Judith, Gabriella Dideriksen and Robert D. Hume. *Italian Opera in Late Eighteenth-Century London*, vol. 2, *The Pantheon Opera and its Aftermath, 1789–1795*. Oxford, 2000

Parisi, Susan (ed.). *Music in the Theater, Church, and Villa: Essays in Honor of Robert Lamar Weaver and Norma Wright Weaver*. Warren, MI, 2000

Piperno, Franco. 'L'opera in Italia nel secolo XVIII'. In Alberto Basso (ed.), *Musica in scena. Storia dello spettacolo musicale*. 2 vols., vol. 2, Turin, 1996, pp. 96–199

'State and Market, Production and Style'. In Victoria Johnson, Jane E. Fulcher and Thomas Ertman (eds.), *Opera and Society in Italy and France from Monteverdi to Bourdieu*. Cambridge, 2007, pp. 138–59

Polzonetti, Pierpaolo. 'Mesmerizing Adultery: *Così fan tutte* and the Kornman Scandal'. *Cambridge Opera Journal*, 14 (2002), pp. 263–96

Price, Curtis, Judith Milhous and Robert D. Hume. *Italian Opera in Late Eighteenth-Century London*. Vol. 1. *The King's Theatre, Haymarket, 1778–1791*. Oxford, 1995

Rice, John A. *W. A. Mozart: 'La clemenza di Tito'*. Cambridge, 1991

Antonio Salieri and Viennese Opera. Chicago, IL, 1998

Empress Marie Therese and Music at the Viennese Court, 1792–1807. Cambridge, 2003

Mozart on the Stage. Cambridge, 2009

Robinson, Michael F. *Naples and Neapolitan Opera*. Oxford, 1972

'A Late 18th-Century Account Book of the San Carlo Theatre, Naples'. *Early Music*, 18 (1990), pp. 73–81

Rosselli, John. *The Opera Industry in Italy from Cimarosa to Verdi*. Cambridge, 1984

Singers of Italian Opera: The History of a Profession. Cambridge, 1992

Rushton, Julian. *W. A. Mozart: 'Don Giovanni'*. Cambridge, 1981

Sadie, Stanley (ed.). *Wolfgang Amadè Mozart: Essays on His Life and His Music*. Oxford, 1996

Strohm, Reinhard. *Essays on Handel and Italian Opera*. Cambridge, 1985

Dramma per Musica: Italian Opera Seria of the Eighteenth Century. New Haven, CT, 1997

Waldoff, Jessica. *Recognition in Mozart's Operas*. Oxford, 2006

Weaver, Robert Lamar and Norma Wright Weaver. *A Chronology of Music in the Florentine Theater 1590–1750*. Vol. 1, Detroit, MI, 1978;

A Chronology of Music in the Florentine Theater 1751–1800, vol. 2, Warren, MI, 1993

Weimer, Eric. *Opera Seria and the Evolution of the Classical Style, 1755–1772*. Ann Arbor, MI, 1984

Woodfield, Ian. *Opera and Drama in Eighteenth-Century London: The King's Theatre, Garrick and the Business of Performance*. Cambridge, 2001

· 9 ·

Opera in Paris from Campra to Rameau

LOIS ROSOW

'The clock is striking four; let's go to the Opéra. We shall need at least an hour to get through the throng crowding the door.'[1] Dufresny's evocative remark underscores the popularity of the Académie Royale de Musique, familiarly known as 'the Opéra', at the turn of the eighteenth century. A half-century later this Parisian institution remained a favourite gathering place for high society, a preoccupation of intellectuals and a symbol of the glory of the French monarchy.[2] The discussion that follows focuses on the offerings of that theatre, with an occasional glance at the royal court and the early development of the Opéra-Comique. Two important and representative works are treated as case studies: Campra's *L'Europe galante* and Rameau's *Hippolyte et Aricie*.

The death of Jean-Baptiste Lully in 1687 signalled the end of an era for French opera. While the Opéra had been Lully's personal fiefdom, where he was both impresario and sole composer, administration of the company now passed to his son-in-law, Jean-Nicolas Francine, who extended the opportunity to compose new works to several musicians and poets. In addition, Louis XIV no longer wished the Académie to bring its productions routinely to the royal court. Various reasons have been given, especially Louis's preoccupation with religion and morality during this phase of his life, and his decision to embark on a costly war of aggression (the War of the League of Augsburg, 1688–97). Whatever the case may be, though concert readings certainly occurred, fully-staged opera almost disappeared from Louis' court after 1686. Thus, after Lully's death the Académie functioned almost exclusively as a public opera company in Paris. The troupe continued to occupy the theatre in the Palais Royal that had been given to Lully by the King, but the days of re-using costumes and scenery paid for by the court, and otherwise profiting from royal largesse, were over.

1 Charles Rivière, called Dufresny, *Amusemens sérieux et comiques* (Paris, 1699), p. 57; see Caroline Wood and Graham Sadler (eds.), *French Baroque Opera: A Reader* (Aldershot, 2000), pp. 24–5.
2 See Neal Zaslaw, 'At the Paris Opéra in 1747', *Early Music*, 11 (1983), pp. 515–16; Daniel Heartz, *Music in European Capitals: The Galant Style, 1720–1780* (New York, 2003), pp. 602–5.

Nonetheless, the company persevered in the 1690s, weathering a series of financial crises as well as a flurry of moralistic tracts by clergymen and poets, who denounced the Opéra as a threat to public virtue. At issue were both the off-stage sexual liaisons of the female singers and the poetic and musical enticements to youthful love that reigned on stage. Patronage by the royal family continued in a new vein. Both the Dauphin (Louis de France, known as 'Monseigneur'), who had been a regular member of Lully's audience throughout the 1680s, and his cousin Philippe II d'Orléans (Duke of Chartres, future Duke of Orléans and future Regent of France) took a keen interest in the Opéra and supported Francine's activities. It is probably no coincidence that some of the new operas of the 1690s were composed by musicians who were under the protection of the Orléans family, notably Marc-Antoine Charpentier, Charles-Hubert Gervais and André Campra. Other principal composers came from Lully's circle: his sons Louis and Jean-Louis, Pascal Collasse, Henry Desmarest, Marin Marais and Theobaldo di Gatti. The repertory mingled new works, generally two or three per year, with revivals of operas by Lully.[3]

Events towards the end of the century at another venerable theatre in Paris had important repercussions for the future direction of French opera. On 14 May 1697, a royal seal appeared on the door of the Hôtel de Bourgogne, the theatre of the 'Italian comedians of the King'. Overnight Louis XIV had banished this institution, which had long flourished in Paris under royal protection and had occupied that building since 1660. Over the years it had evolved from a simple commedia dell'arte troupe to one performing fully written-out plays as well as improvised sketches, in French freely mingled with Italian and with musical numbers interspersed. Moreover, its members included highly skilled musicians. Louis' reasons for this act of repression were complex. They involved the troupe's use of the French language (perceived by the Comédie-Française as competition) and its drain on the royal pension fund, but the last straw was its offensive satire of Madame de Maintenon (the King's morganatic wife) in a play called *La fausse prude*. Other Parisian theatres naturally rushed to fill the void, each in a way appropriate to its own repertory and style. New troupes imitating the Italian comedians sprang up at the two Parisian trade fairs, the Foire Saint-Germain and the Foire Saint-Laurent. There the public could continue to enjoy the costumes and irreverent antics of Arlequin (Harlequin), Pierrot, Columbine and the other familiar figures of

3 Louis Ladvocat and Jérôme de La Gorce, *Lettres sur l'Opéra à l'abbé Dubos suivies de Description de la vie et moeurs, de l'exercise et l'état des filles de l'Opéra* (n.p., 1993), pp. 7–18; Jean-Paul Montagnier, *Un mécène-musicien: Philippe d'Orléans, Régent (1674–1723)* (n.p., 1996), pp. 18–21. For librettos and overview of repertory, see *Recueil général des opéra, representez par l'Académie royale de musique depuis son établissement*, 16 vols. (Paris, 1703–45; 3-vol. facsimile edn., Geneva, 1971.)

the French-styled Italian comedy.[4] Even the Opéra, where poetry and stage action unfailingly followed the rules of decency and decorum, found ways to incorporate *commedia dell'arte* characters and themes in its scores and librettos.

L'Europe galante and the 'opéra-ballet'

The Dauphin and Philippe II d'Orléans, along with the Dauphin's half-sister Marie-Thérèse de Bourbon, Princess of Conty, led a social circle that gravitated to the various chateaux and town-houses of its members, thus avoiding the now-repressive atmosphere at Versailles. Several among them were fine amateur musicians, whose amusements included private performances of divertissements (brief occasional pieces). Among the composers favoured with commissions for these modest works was André Campra, a well-established provincial church musician who in 1694 had become *maître de musique* at the cathedral of Notre Dame in Paris. In July 1697 a divertissement by Campra, dedicated to Philippe II, was performed at the Paris home of the Duke of Sully. A young poet named Antoine Houdar de La Motte provided the text, a dispute between Apollo and Mars that satirizes Louis XIV's bellicosity. Three months later, on 24 October 1697, Campra and Houdar de La Motte made their debut at the Opéra, with one of the most successful and influential works of the ensuing century, *L'Europe galante*. In all likelihood, Campra had been brought to Francine's attention by the Dauphin or Philippe II; indeed, the idea for the new opera might have come from the authors' aristocratic supporters.[5]

Houdar de La Motte called *L'Europe galante* a 'ballet' and gave each act (labelled 'entrée') an independent plot, tying the *entrées* together with an overarching theme, namely the different styles of love-making in four nations of Europe – the 'fickle, indiscreet, and coquettish' French lovers; the 'faithful and romantic' Spanish; the 'jealous, shrewd, and violent' Italians; and finally, the 'haughty' sultan and 'passionate' sultanas of Turkey. Thus, the characters and settings belonged to contemporary Europe, not to the mythological or chivalric past. ('*Galante*' meant amorous; it also meant stylish and well mannered.) The structural division into a series of separate but related plots had been tried

4 Maurice Barthélemy, 'L'opéra-comique des origines à la Querelle des Bouffons', in Philippe Vendrix (ed.), *L'Opéra-Comique en France au XVIIIe siècle* (Liège, 1992), pp. 8–78; William Brooks, 'Louis XIV's Dismissal of the Italian Actors: The Episode of *La fausse prude*', *The Modern Language Review*, 91 (1996), pp. 840–7.

5 Don Fader, 'The "cabale du dauphin", Campra, and Italian Comedy: The Courtly Politics of French Musical Patronage around 1700', *Music & Letters*, 86 (2005), p. 397; Alain Niderst, 'L'Europe galante de La Motte et Campra', in Irène Mamezarz (ed.), *Le Théâtre et l'Opéra sous le signe de l'histoire* (Paris, 1994), pp. 75–80. For the score, see André Campra, *L'Europe galante, ballet* (Paris, 1724; facsimile edn. Farnborough, 1967); and for the libretto: *Recueil général des opéra*, vol. 6, pp. 121–70; facsimile edn., vol. 1, pp. 628–40.

before, but contemporary characters and settings were a novelty. Surely the recent silencing of the Italian comedians had something to do with this choice.

Only the prologue takes place in a mythological setting: a *forge galante*, where a troupe of 'Pleasures, Graces, and Laughters', urged on by Venus, make arrows for Cupid (L'Amour, whose name also means Love). This is ironic, for the allegorical prologue, which traditionally linked the fictional world of the opera to the real world of French politics, is the one place where the Opéra audience might have expected a contemporary setting – as in, for instance, the prologue to Lully's *Alceste*, set in the Tuileries Gardens. Majestic *tirades* announce the arrival of Discord (La Discorde), who claims to have banished Cupid from all of Europe. Venus assures her that she claims a false victory: thanks to the King, Europe no longer listens to Discord's voice and is ruled only by Love. The Treaty of Ryswick, signed on 20 September 1697, had ended the lengthy War of the League of Augsburg between France and most of Western Europe. (War in the east would end in 1699, with the Treaty of Carlowicz between the Austrian Hapsburgs and Ottoman Turks. Louis XIV had unsuccessfully invited Turkey's participation in the earlier treaty.) Thus, *L'Europe galante* may be understood in part as a political allegory, a celebration of peace. In a brief epilogue at the end of the opera, Discord admits defeat, and Venus commands the Pleasures and Games to spread the empire of Love far and wide. To an accompaniment of running quavers, these creatures (who would have been represented in this scene by stage props) fly off in all directions.

The choice of foreign nations reflects not the major players in the war so much as the long-standing favourite 'exotic' locations in French drama. Each *entrée* parodies a standard dramatic genre, reducing it to miniature proportions. In a French pastorale an unfaithful shepherd pursues an indifferent shepherdess, leaving his jilted sweetheart to hope that his unfaithfulness will return him to her in the end. In a Spanish romantic comedy two gentlemen intent on serenading their sweethearts pause to argue with each other over who is the more faithful lover. In a Venetian commedia dell'arte, a tale of smouldering jealousy and feigned murder unfolds against the festive backdrop of a masked ball. In a tragicomedy that turns momentarily violent, the new favourite of the Turkish sultan expresses her love for him, after which his former favourite flies into a jealous rage and draws a dagger on her rival. She is removed from the seraglio, to everyone's relief. Doleful and joyful endings alternate: 'France' and 'Italy' end unhappily with emotionally charged monologues in orchestrally accompanied recitative; 'Spain' and 'Turkey' end with group celebrations. As was normal for French opera, the work progressed from one act to the next without pause, the scenery (on side-flats and a backdrop) changing instantaneously and spectacularly during brief orchestral entr'actes.

Extended group actions (divertissements) in each *entrée* are sprinkled with local colour. In 'France' a tuneful rigaudon for strings and double reeds, both danced and sung, evokes imagery of the Provençale countryside. 'Spain' offers a stage band for a nocturnal serenade and a soulful love song in Spanish. 'Italy' presents a troupe of 'gallant and comic maskers' at Carnival. Their songs include a tiny da capo aria in Italian, with motto opening, internal word repetition, obbligato treble part and melismas, all in the Italian manner. The divertissement ends with a Venetian dance called a 'forlana'. 'Turkey' presents a series of songs in *lingua franca*, as well as pantomime 'games' for the '*bostangis* or gardeners of the Sultan'. 'Turkey' has a secondary divertissement in addition to the final celebration, and there the sultanas demonstrate their love for the sultan in a passacaille that is French through and through.

Exoticism notwithstanding, these divertissements are structured in the conventional manner – loosely symmetrical arrangements of dances, solo songs, choruses and reprises of these items, the dancers representing the bodies of the collective characters and the singers representing their voices. For instance, the tiny da capo aria in 'Italy' ('Ad un cuore'), sung by an entertainer at the masked ball, contains in its entirety a stanza of poetry, divided musically into 'A' and 'B' segments. A second stanza ('Un bel viso') is sung to identical music, and the two stanzas are presented in alternation with a dance for the maskers having the same rhythmic character as the aria. That set of pieces, in Italianate giga rhythms, is followed immediately by a thoroughly French 'chaconne en rondeau' set, performed by another group of masked Italians. In this manner the divertissement progresses through a series of contrasting sets, mimicking the series of dances at a ball. The poetry of each set addresses in some way the overarching theme of the *entrée*: the triumph of Love over jealousy. A final group of dances, without sung text, signals the end of the scene: the Venetian forlana, a minuet and a reprise of the forlana. The libretto calls for action near the end of the divertissement, involving the main characters of the *entrée* – a dance between Olimpia and a mysterious masked stranger, which arouses Octavio's already inflamed jealousy. In all likelihood, Campra intended his minuet for this purpose. The minuet was a traditional French courtship dance, and the Parisian audience would have understood its erotic signals.[6]

Two of the *entrées* open with dialogues and the other two with monologues, but variety overshadows that parallelism. In 'France' the shepherd Silvandre and his confidant enter in mid-conversation as the reprise of the overture

6 Rebecca Harris-Warrick, 'Staging Venice', *Cambridge Opera Journal*, 15 (2003), pp. 313–14; see also pp. 307–12.

concludes (the 'forge galante' of the prologue having been replaced by a grove, with a hamlet in the background); their recitative dialogue is suffused with lyricism. In 'Italy' a slow, serious entrance prelude for the couple reveals the tension between them before they utter a word. In 'Turkey' the sultana's orchestrally accompanied monologue begins with a brief air apostrophizing her eyes ('Mes yeux', composed by Campra's student André Cardinal Destouches[7]); it then turns to impassioned recitative and concludes with a repeated invocation of Love. In 'Spain' Dom Pedro serenades his beloved under her balcony in a traditional *sommeil* (sleep piece) with gently rocking two-note phrases for flutes and strings. A descending minor tetrachord in the bass line (a device found also in 'Mes yeux' and in Silvandre's first recitative utterance) adds a melancholy flavour to the *sommeil*, in keeping with the text:

> Que Lucile soit inhumaine
> Ou sensible à l'ardeur que je viens declarer,
> Il faudra toujours expirer
> De mon plaisir, ou de ma peine.
>
> (Whether Lucile is unfeeling or sympathetic to the ardour I have just declared, I must die either way, of my pleasure or of my pain.)

In short, La Motte and Campra's first foray into composition for the Opéra reveals a thorough familiarity with French operatic conventions.

L'Europe galante was enormously successful and influential. It was performed numerous times at the Opéra through the 1750s, and portions could still be found on programmes of excerpts in the 1760s and 1770s. Its innovative subject matter, the activities of contemporary Europeans, remained in vogue at the Opéra for about two decades (perhaps not coincidentally, the same years as Campra's heyday as an opera composer) and continued to appear occasionally after that. Moreover, 'ballets' having several *entrées* with separate plots soon overtook the venerable tragédie en musique in popularity. Around the 1760s aestheticians gave the genre a specific name, 'opéra-ballet'.[8] A variant type, called 'ballet-héroïque', developed from the 1720s. It combined a series of separate plots with subject matter featuring classical or exotic heroes, often drawn from ancient mythology (and thus conducive to supernatural spectacle). In 1754 Louis de Cahusac drew an evocative analogy between opéra-ballet, as conceived by Houdar de La Motte and Campra, and Antoine Watteau's paintings of elegant flirtation by upper-class Parisians. After calling the tragédie en

7 Evrard Titon du Tillet, *Second supplément du Parnasse français, ou suite de l'ordre chronologique des poëtes et des musiciens que la mort a enlevés depuis le commencement de l'année 1743 jusqu'en cette année 1755* (n.p., n.d.), p. 54.

8 For instance, Nicolas Bricaire de la Dixmerie and Pierre-Jean-Baptiste Nougaret, quoted in Wood and Sadler (eds.), *French Baroque Opera: A Reader*, pp. 43 and 48, respectively.

musique 'a vast canvas, like those of Raphael and Michelangelo', he characterized the several acts of 'the entertainment discovered by La Motte' as 'pretty Watteaus, piquant miniatures that demand precise design, graceful brushstrokes, and brilliant colour'.[9]

The era of Campra and Destouches[10]

Campra published three editions of the score of *L'Europe galante* (1697–9), all of them 'partitions réduites' (scores lacking inner choral and string parts, the new norm for opera prints). They appeared anonymously in deference to his position at Notre Dame, though his authorship was no secret. A satirical song predicted that 'De sa Cathédrale/Campra décampera' (Campra will clear out of his cathedral),[11] and indeed, in 1700 he quit his post, to devote himself full-time to opera. Between 1699 and 1718 he composed numerous tragédies en musique, opéra-ballets and works in various other light genres, such as 'ballets' on continuous plots (sometimes referred to nowadays as 'comédies-lyriques') and collections of 'fragments' (individual acts from different works). He continued to compose, sporadically and less successfully, in later years. His most enduring successes, after *L'Europe galante*, were the tragédie en musique *Tancrède* (1702) and the opéra-ballet *Les fêtes vénitiennes* (1710). Both had librettos by Antoine Danchet, Campra's principal librettist.

Campra's student André Cardinal Destouches rose to prominence as well. Destouches, the son of a wealthy landowner, had given up a military career to pursue music. On 7 October 1697 – in the same month as the premiere of *L'Europe galante* – his friend Antoine de Grimaldi, future Prince of Monaco, escorted him to the royal court at Fontainebleau, where his pastorale-héroïque *Issé*, on a libretto by Houdar de La Motte, was given a concert performance before an illustrious audience. The King declared that no music since Lully's had pleased him so much.[12] On 17 December performers from the Opéra gave a staged performance of *Issé* at the Grand Trianon near Versailles, as part of the festivities surrounding the wedding of the Duke of Burgundy (the Dauphin's eldest son) and Marie-Adélaïde of Savoy. The authors eventually reworked *Issé*

9 Louis de Cahusac, *La danse ancienne et moderne, ou Traité historique de la danse*, 3 vols. (The Hague, 1754; facsimile edn., Geneva, 1971), vol. 3, p. 108.

10 General studies of this era include Jérôme de La Gorce, *L'opéra à Paris au temps de Louis XIV: histoire d'un théâtre* (Paris, 1992), *passim*; James R. Anthony, *French Baroque Music from Beaujoyeulx to Rameau*, rev. and expanded edn. (Portland, OR, 1997), pp. 140–82.

11 James R. Anthony, 'Printed Editions of André Campra's *L'Europe galante*', *The Musical Quarterly*, 56 (1970), p. 59, quoting 'Chansonnier de Maurepas'.

12 Titon du Tillet, *Second supplément du Parnasse français*, p. 55. For score and libretto, see André Cardinal Destouches, *Issé: pastorale héroïque*, facsimile edn., with Introduction by Robert Fajon and contributions by Jérôme de La Gorce and Wendy Hilton (New York, 1984).

from its original three acts to five, for its premiere at the Opéra in 1708. That version had numerous revivals in the course of the eighteenth century. In 1724 the printer Jean-Baptiste-Christophe Ballard honoured two well-loved works from the operatic repertory by publishing them in large-format full-score editions; they were *L'Europe galante* and *Issé*.[13]

The adjective 'héroïque' in this context indicates the presence of high-born characters, whether human or supernatural. The protagonists of an operatic pastorale-héroïque include gods as well as the usual shepherds and other rustic mortals. Here the nymph Issé falls in love with Apollo disguised as a shepherd. Only after he is certain of her love does he reveal himself, bringing about a spectacular scenic transformation. While the stage at the Grand Trianon lacked complex machinery, at the Opéra the instantaneous transformation of a pastoral 'solitude' into a 'magnificent palace', the Hours descending from Heaven on clouds, must have been breathtaking. Yet the music at the moment of revelation is intimate, an exchange in unadorned yet affective recitative, which conveys the couple's feelings far more effectively than orchestral bombast or vocal virtuosity would have done.

Between 1698 and 1703 four operas by Destouches, with librettos by Houdar de La Motte, had their premieres at the royal court before appearing soon thereafter at the Opéra. These included his two most successful tragédies en musique, *Amadis de Grèce* and *Omphale*, as well as a comic 'ballet', *Le Carnaval et la Folie*. Yet at court only *Omphale* had modest scenery and costumes; the other three were performed in concert readings. If the success of *Issé* led the administration of the Opéra to hope for a return to royal patronage like that in Lully's day, those hopes were dashed. Moreover, after attending the first three, the King declared himself weary of sitting through complete operas. With that, his brief flurry of renewed interest came to an end. As for Destouches, he composed no new operas during the next eleven years, and only a small number after that. Nevertheless, his importance increased in other ways. In 1713, in an administrative re-organization, the King appointed Destouches 'inspecteur général' (*Surintendant*) of the Opéra – in effect, music director and chief administrator – a position he retained until 1728, at which time he became 'directeur' (*maître de musique*), thus obtaining financial interest in the company as well. He retired in 1730.[14]

Other principal composers for the Opéra in the early decades of the century included Collasse, Marais, Gatti, Gervais, Michel de La Barre, Louis de La Coste, Battistin Stück, Joseph François Salomon and Jean-Joseph Mouret. (Mouret's

13 Anthony, 'Printed Editions', pp. 62–73; facsimile edns. of both are cited above.
14 Wood and Sadler (eds.), *French Baroque Opera: A Reader*, pp. 3, 14–16.

operatic career started in 1714–15 in the brilliant salon of Anne, Duchess of Maine, at Sceaux.) The 1720s also saw the early works of François Colin de Blamont and the collaborators François Francoeur and François Rebel.

Additional aspects of style and genre

Although none of the era's authors slavishly copied the style developed by Lully and his librettist, Philippe Quinault, they adopted its essential formal components. The stately 'French overtures'; the dialogues that unfold in melodious recitative,[15] brief airs and brief duets; the introductory monologues in refrain forms; the allegorical prologues (though the allegory might now focus on genre and aesthetic issues as much as royal encomium); the entrance preludes and other orchestral passages that accompany stage movement;[16] the familiar dance types, voice types, textures and orchestral colours – all remained in use and served as a framework for traditional expression and new departures. Moreover, the new rules for the Opéra promulgated by the King in 1713–14 enshrined the practice of mingling new works with revivals of those by Lully, and aestheticians tended to judge new compositions, especially tragédies en musique, by the standard of Lully's.

Despite the overwhelming popularity of 'ballets', the tragédie en musique remained the most prestigious operatic genre – or at any rate, the one commanding the highest fees for the composer and librettist, perhaps simply because it contained five acts rather than three or four. Most plots are drawn from mythology, some from chivalric legend. Endings are usually joyous but sometimes tragic. In either case, the vicissitudes of tender love and heroic adventure among high-born heroes and heroines are the main concerns, not the great political and moral dilemmas of French classical tragedy.[17]

A principal characteristic of tragédies en musique and other 'heroic' operatic genres (pastorales-héroïques and most ballets-héroïques) is the presence of the

15 On terminology, see Charles Dill, 'Eighteenth-Century Models of French Recitative', *Journal of the Royal Musical Association*, 120 (1995), pp. 232–50.

16 On stage movement, see Antonia L. Banducci, 'Staging a *tragédie en musique*: A 1748 Promptbook of Campra's *Tancrède*', *Early Music*, 21 (1993), pp. 180–90; and *idem*, 'Staging and Its Dramatic Effect in French Baroque Opera: Evidence from Prompt Notes', *Eighteenth-Century Music*, 1 (2004), pp. 5–28; Thomas Betzwieser, 'Musical Setting and Scenic Movement: Chorus and *choeur dansé* in Eighteenth-Century Parisian Opera', *Cambridge Opera Journal*, 12 (2000), pp. 1–28; Mary Cyr, 'The Dramatic Role of the Chorus in French Opera: Evidence for the Use of Gesture, 1670–1770', in Thomas Bauman and Maria Petzoldt McClymonds (eds.), *Opera and the Enlightenment* (Cambridge, 1995), pp. 105–18.

17 See Laura Naudeix, *Dramaturgie de la tragédie en musique (1673–1764)* (Paris, 2004); Catherine Kintzler, *Poétique de l'opéra français, de Corneille à Rousseau* (Paris, 1991). On musical style, see Geoffrey Burgess, 'Ritual in the tragédie en musique from Lully's *Cadmus et Hermione* (1673) to Rameau's *Zoroastre* (1749)', PhD thesis (Cornell University, 1998); and Caroline Wood, *Music and Drama in the tragédie en musique, 1673–1715: Jean-Baptiste Lully and His Successors* (New York and London, 1996).

merveilleux – the supernatural element. Demons and deities display human behaviour and interact directly with mortals, yet they wield immense power over humankind. Enchantments, psychological torments and dreams are enacted, typically in dance. In *L'Europe galante*, set in the contemporary world, Dom Pedro's *sommeil* is simply a serenade by a man to a sleeping woman. In *Issé* the same musical genre signals a supernatural intervention (Act 4, scene 2). As the shepherdess Issé concludes a lengthy monologue, the bass line descends from the treble to the bass range, and the sounds of gently rocking two-note phrases announce the approach of Somnus (Le Sommeil), the god of sleep, along with the Dreams and a retinue of zephyrs and nymphs. In a chorus for high voices (*petit choeur*) and a sarabande, they urge Issé to give in to the 'charms of repose'. As she sinks into sleep, Somnus commands the troupe to demonstrate Apollo's love to her in an enchanted dream. The gently rocking 'sleep' music resumes in an extended postlude, during which the dancers carry out the god's instruction and the group makes its exit.

Perhaps in response to the profusion of dances in opéra-ballets, the divertissements of tragédies en musique grew very long (and recitative scenes grew correspondingly shorter). Indeed, in the librettos of Houdar de La Motte the massive divertissement is often the centre of gravity for the act. Instead of just one or two dances and their repetitions, intertwined with musically related vocal solos and choruses, a divertissement might now contain a long string of dance pieces, punctuated occasionally by vocal numbers and indicated in the libretto only by the repeated instruction, 'They dance'. A consistent tonal centre throughout contributes to a feeling of stasis. Stage directions (for instance, 'The people show their joy in new dances'), sung poetry and dancing still work together to create meaning, but the relationship is more diffuse than in Lully's operas. Though the group action – such as a celebration, ritual, or supernatural intervention – is addressed to a main protagonist, its sheer length offsets its relationship to the central plot. Ironically, as the linear unfolding of plot gives way to extended ceremony and to aural and visual delights, the divertissement may simultaneously prolong and diffuse dramatic tension.

In all genres, while retaining essentially syllabic text-setting, Lully's successors favoured a more decorative melodic surface. A filigree of *agréments* grace many vocal melodies, and selected airs have delicate instrumental counterpoint, for violin, oboe, or flute. By 1713 two transverse flutes had been added to the two violins and continuo instruments in the highly paid solo group of the Opéra orchestra; the pair of flutes played ornate solos and duets in orchestral movements as well as delicate obbligato accompaniments. In eighteenth-century scores a distinction is usually apparent between the larger group of unison or *divisi* 'flutes' (recorders) and the soloistic 'flutes allemandes' (transverse flutes). Another favourite timbre, related to the *petit choeur*, is a bass line in the treble or alto range supporting one or more high-pitched voices. This sound came to be associated with the pastoral, especially Cupid and the delights of pastoral love.[18]

Sounds inspired by Italian sonatas and cantatas entered French opera as well (to the distress of conservative aestheticians[19]). They are particularly evident in descriptive 'noise' pieces, representing storms, battles, or Underworld rumblings, and in so-called 'ariettes'. Collasse's *Thétis et Pelée* (1689), a work revived numerous times in the eighteenth century, contains the first instance of Italianate string figuration meant to represent noise, here a storm at sea. The score calls for fast scalar runs and tremolos (explicitly notated) and also for swelling and receding percussion (*batterie de tambour*, indicated by verbal cue), all imitating the sound of the winds and the waves. The printer Christophe Ballard inserted the storm into the published score on engraved pages, for he lacked appropriate type-pieces for printing fast runs requiring four or more beams. (Soon engraving would overtake typesetting as the principal mode of music printing in France, so the problem was only a temporary one.) The celebrated tempest in Marais' *Alcyone* (1706) served as the principal model of the genre for later composers.[20] As for ariettes – the French name for bravura arias in da capo form – their function is narrow and decorative. Limited to divertissements, they most often concern romantic love. Most draw on a small vocabulary of words for elaborate melismas ('voler', 'regner', 'briller', 'chaîne', 'triomphe', among others). Ariettes and virtuosic dances, intended as showcases for star performers, were sometimes added to existing operas as occasional pieces.

While musical Italianisms entered all types of opera, they dovetailed particularly nicely with the desire for local colour in pieces set in contemporary Italy. French fascination with Venice, especially its reputed sexual freedom at Carnival time, made that city a popular setting for operas, where masked balls and commedia dell'arte characters and situations could be interwoven with familiar French operatic conventions.[21] In one case, *Le Carnaval de Venise* (1699), Campra and librettist François Regnard (formerly a playwright for the

18 Deborah A. Kauffman, '*Violons en basse* as Musical Allegory', *Journal of Musicology*, 23 (2006), pp. 153–85; Sylvette Milliot and Jérôme de La Gorce, *Marin Marais* (Paris, 1991), pp. 172–3. On the Paris Opéra orchestra, see John Spitzer and Neal Zaslaw, *The Birth of the Orchestra: History of an Institution, 1650–1815* (Oxford and New York, 2004), pp. 184–90.

19 Wood and Sadler (eds.), *French Baroque Opera: A Reader*, pp. 95–9.

20 See Caroline Wood, *Music and Drama*, pp. 334–45. On dramaturgical function of storms, see Sylvie Bouissou, 'Mécanismes dramatiques de la tempête et de l'orage dans l'opéra français à l'âge baroque', in Jean Gribenski, Marie-Claire Mussat and Herbert Schneider (eds.), *D'un opéra l'autre: Hommage à Jean Mongrédien* (Paris, 1996), pp. 218–30.

21 Harris-Warrick, 'Staging Venice'.

banished Italian comedians) wrote an entire miniature opera-within-an-opera in the Italian language and style, entitled *Orfeo nell' inferi*. The setting is a Venetian opera house, complete with an on-stage audience enjoying that opera, which is set in the realm of Pluto. This bellicose god of the Underworld bears an uncanny resemblance to the war-mongering Pluto in the tragédie en musique *Orphée* (1690) by Lully's son Louis; might both have been covert satires of Louis XIV, intended for the pleasure of the Dauphin and his circle?[22] This Pluto does seem to invite an undignified performance. The play-within-a-play ploy permitted the authors to present an Olympian god as a clownish figure, an approach that otherwise would have broken the rule of *bienséance* (appropriateness and decorum) required of French opera.[23]

The Opéra-Comique

Louis XIV died in 1715, and Philippe II d'Orléans served as Regent until 1723. One of his first official acts was to invite the return of the Italian comedians (a new troupe now, led by Luigi Riccoboni, the original company having disbanded). The reinstatement of an official Italian troupe, soon to be installed in the Hôtel de Bourgogne, clearly posed a threat to the small privately run company of comedians that performed at the Foire Saint-Laurent in summer and the Foire Saint-Germain in winter, for this was yet another state-sponsored theatre, with the weight of royal privilege supporting its interests. The fair theatres (by this time known as the Opéra-Comique) had managed to thrive over the years, despite continual efforts by the Comédie-Française to unseat them. When told that they were forbidden to use spoken dialogue, the actors had combined monologues with mime. When told that they could not use speech, they had unfurled banners so that the audience and actors could sing the written text as vaudevilles (familiar tunes set with new words). In 1718, with the new Comédie-Italienne adding its voice to the threats, the Regent attempted to shut down the fair theatres entirely. Once again ingenuity prevailed: denied the right to use actors, the company used marionettes. Ultimately the fair theatres survived. A large part of the reason was a long-standing alliance with the Opéra, which had the right to control the use of music in other French theatres. Starting in 1708, in exchange for the privilege of using music and dance extensively, the entrepreneurs of the fair theatres had

22 Georgia Cowart, 'Carnival in Venice or Protest in Paris? Louis XIV and the Politics of Subversion at the Paris Opéra', *Journal of the American Musicological Society*, 54 (2001), pp. 277–85; André Campra, *Le Carnaval de Venise: comédie lyrique*, facsimile edn., with Introduction by James R. Anthony with a section on stage designs and costumes by Jérôme de La Gorce (Stuyvesant, NY, 1989), pp. xxv, lviii–lxi, 227–93.
23 On relevant literary theory, see Wood and Sadler (eds.), *French Baroque Opera: A Reader*, pp. 73–7.

negotiated a series of financial arrangements with the debt-ridden Opéra. In 1721 a new contract of this type received royal sanction, and the Opéra-Comique resumed its complex relationship with its powerful rivals.[24]

From an artistic point of view, the ongoing arrangement with the Opéra was fortunate. While presenting its social satires mainly in vaudevilles, which permitted multiple layers of comic innuendo,[25] the Opéra-Comique had purely musical satire at its disposal as well. For instance, in *Arlequin Deucalion* by Alexis Piron (1722), a satirical retelling of a myth from Ovid, Apollo awakens a character by playing 'the *sommeil* from *Issé* on a flute'. The brilliant parodies of serious operas that appeared at the fairs profited from the company's good relationship with the Opéra; for example, *Télémaque* by Alain Lesage (1715) quotes the overture and tempest from Marais' *Alcyone* as well as Destouches' score for the parodied work itself (*Télémaque*, tragédie en musique, 1714). The company employed a small orchestra, and a number of composers of serious opera also wrote airs for the Opéra-Comique.[26]

During the next generation, from 1732 to 1745, the principal poet of the Opéra-Comique was Charles-Simon Favart, who continued the tradition of satirizing the offerings of the Opéra in clever parodies, but is best remembered for applying the vaudeville technique to sentimental tales of love in idealized rustic villages.[27]

Rameau's first opera

Despite the prestige of the tragédie en musique, it was a genre in decline in the 1720s. New works appeared, but few succeeded. Nonetheless, this was the operatic genre that most attracted Jean-Philippe Rameau, who presented his first opera at the age of fifty. Rameau was well known as a music theorist, he had composed music in a number of small genres and, as he later said, he had been attracted to the theatre for most of his life, yet he had never written an opera. His first effort, *Hippolyte et Aricie* (1733), was at the time an astonishing work – not for its formal components, which were quite traditional, but for the

24 Barthélémy, 'L'opéra-comique'; Robert M. Isherwood, *Farce and Fantasy: Popular Entertainment in Eighteenth-Century Paris* (Oxford, 1986), pp. 60–80.

25 Thomas Betzwieser, 'Text und "Subtext" in der frühen Opéra-comique: Zur Semantik des Vaudevilles', in Hermann Danuser and Tobias Plebuch (eds.), *Musik als Text: Bericht über den internationalen Kongress des Gesellschaft für Musikforschung Freiburg im Breisgau 1993* (Kassel, 1998), 2 vols., vol. 2, pp. 431–6; Michel Noiray, 'Hippolyte et Castor travestis: Rameau à l'Opéra-Comique', in Jérôme de La Gorce (ed.), *Jean-Philippe Rameau: Colloque international organisé par la Société Rameau, Dijon 21–24 septembre 1983: actes* (Paris and Geneva, 1987), pp. 109–25.

26 Barthélémy, 'L'opéra-comique', pp. 42, 66–8; Heartz, *Music in European Capitals*, p. 702. On parody, see Dörte Schmidt, *Armide hinter den Spiegeln: Lully, Gluck und die Möglichkeiten der dramatischen Parodie* (Stuttgart and Weimar, 2001), pp. 70–151; as well as Noiray, 'Hippolyte et Castor travestis'.

27 Heartz, *Music in European Capitals*, pp. 703–9.

sheer inventiveness and complexity of the music. Reactions ranged from bafflement to admiration. 'When by accident two bars were encountered that could make a pleasant song, the key, mode, and meter were quickly changed', complained an anonymous critic.[28] Yet Campra is said to have remarked: 'There is enough music in that opera to make ten of them.'[29]

Having tried unsuccessfully to interest Houdar de La Motte in providing him with a libretto, Rameau turned to the elderly Simon-Joseph Pellegrin, who had most recently written the libretto for Montéclair's *Jephté* (the first French opera on a Biblical subject, 1732). Pellegrin took a bold step: he based his new libretto on Jean Racine's great tragedy *Phèdre* (1677), as well as on Racine's classical sources. Knowing that he could be accused of debasing a revered classic, he wrote an extended preface, valuable to us especially for its comments on dramaturgical convention – for instance, the circumstances under which a god may undo the work of another god.[30]

The plot revolves around three elements: the illicit love of Phèdre, Queen of Athens, for her stepson Hippolyte (*haute-contre*); the star-crossed but ultimately happy love of Hippolyte and Aricie, a princess of rival lineage; and the tragic reaction of the King, Thésée (bass), to the events around him. The conventions of opera naturally differentiate Pellegrin's work from Racine's. Thus, his setting moves from the earth to the Underworld and back; his story focuses on the pastoral lovers and introduces a happy ending; and he inserts spectacular divertissements, gives an important role to the chorus, shows horrific supernatural events on stage and makes the gods corporeal. Still, Pellegrin included far more truly tragic poetry than is typical of the genre. It is perhaps not surprising that the great monologue air for Phèdre that began Act 3, 'Cruelle mère des Amours' – an invocation of Venus in which the Queen pours out her feelings of guilt – was quickly cut and replaced by a more conventional expression of tender desire, 'Espoir, unique bien d'une fatale flamme'.[31] Nevertheless, the Queen's final outpouring of guilt at the end of Act 4 (following Hippolyte's apparently fatal encounter with a sea-monster) remained in place. Here she expresses her despair in recitative over an unusually rich and varied orchestral accompaniment. While the chorus had registered its horror of the sea-monster in a shocking chromatic modulation, it sets Phèdre's powerful

28 'Lettre de M. X … sur l'origine de la musique', *Mercure de France* (May 1734), pp. 867–69: 'et lorsque par hasard il se rencontrait deux mesures qui pouvaient faire un chant agréable, l'on changeait bien vite de ton, de mode et de mesure.' The passage is allegorical but obviously about *Hippolyte et Aricie*.

29 Cuthbert Girdlestone, *Jean-Philippe Rameau: His Life and Work*, rev. edn. (New York, 1969), p. 191 (quoting Hughes Maret, *Eloge historique de Monsieur Rameau* [1766]). For the score and libretto, see Jean-Philippe Rameau, *Hippolyte et Aricie*, ed. Sylvie Bouissou, *Opera omnia Rameau*, gen. ed. Sylvie Bouissou, series IV, vol. 1 (Paris, 2002).

30 Wood and Sadler (eds.), *French Baroque Opera: A Reader*, pp. 79–82.

31 Charles Dill, *Monstrous Opera: Rameau and the Tragic Tradition* (Princeton, NJ, 1998), pp. 74–5.

passage in relief with a more measured response, the final statement of a simple yet haunting choral refrain: 'O remords superflus!/Hippolyte n'est plus.' (O vain remorse! Hippolyte is no more.)[32]

Rameau's skill in painting character, mood and setting is evident throughout the opera. As the first act begins, for instance, we see Aricie (dressed as a huntress) in the Temple of Diana, where she is to be cloistered against her will. The extended entrance prelude, marked 'tenderly', allows the audience to take in both the setting and the heroine's mood, presumably suggested by the actress's gestures as well as the music. In key, meter, timbre and harmony, the prelude recalls the goddess Diana's pastoral entrance air from the prologue, 'Sur ces bords fortunés', and that similarity reinforces the setting. When the flutes take over the melody, the low bass drops out, and a bass line in the treble range slowly unfurls a descending major tetrachord – not a lament *topos* like the minor tetrachord, but certainly a venerable symbol of love, a reflection of Aricie's thoughts of Hippolyte. The music of the prelude prefigures that of the ensuing monologue air, 'Temple sacré', and is interwoven with it as well. Together the music, poetry and setting paint a scene of pathos and thinly veiled eroticism. The immediate tonicization of the relative minor as Hippolyte enters (without prelude), addressing Aricie in recitative, provides a sudden jolt, the end of a reverie. None of this was revolutionary in 1733; yet the novice Rameau handled these conventions with consummate skill.[33]

Elsewhere Rameau astonishes with his rhythmic vigour, not only in dance music of all types but in certain vocal settings, such as the air for the Fury Tisiphone (*haute-contre*), 'Non, dans le séjour ténébreux' (beginning of Act 2). That air follows an equally vigorous entrance prelude, with just enough of the conventional running semiquavers to assure the listener that this is 'monster or Fury' music, and to support the obvious staging: Tisiphone attempting to chase Thésée away from Pluto's realm. Later, when the chorus of infernal divinities joins Pluto in invoking the rivers of Hades ('Que l'Avergne, que le Ténare'), vigorous rhythms are joined by string and oboe figuration in perpetual motion, painting the roiling rivers. The normal position of the chorus in French opera, in two lines on opposite sides of the stage, leaving centre-stage for the dancers, must have been particularly effective in such Underworld scenes, where the voices seemed to echo through the caverns of Hades.

Certainly the barbarity of the Underworld reaches its climax in the second Trio des Parques, 'Quelle soudaine horreur', where the Fates (three male

32 Charles Dill, 'Rameau's Imaginary Monsters: Knowledge, Theory, and Chromaticism in *Hippolyte et Aricie*', *Journal of the American Musicological Society*, 55 (2002), pp. 455–9; on harmony in the refrain, see Heartz, *Music in European Capitals*, p. 625.

33 See Dill, *Monstrous Opera*, pp. 50–6; Burgess, 'Ritual in the tragédie en musique', pp. 172–3.

voices) command Thésée to tremble with fear, for he 'will find Hell at home'. Here Rameau wrote a passage of enharmonic modulation, intended (as he later explained) to evoke in the listener a reaction of 'repulsion and horror'. Whereas eighteenth-century aestheticians understood the 'pity and terror' of Aristotelian tragedy as an intellectual response, a moral identification with the hero, they understood 'horror' as a visceral, physical response.[34] Unfortunately the singers could not manage the quarter-tone distinctions Rameau required, and the passage was simplified in performance.

Rameau skilfully manipulated the genre's decorative and spectacular elements so that they might contribute directly to the human tragedy. At the end of Act 3, for instance, Thésée finds his son and wife in a compromising position, and readily believes his son guilty. (Pellegrin, in his preface, declared Racine's Thésée too credulous; he added the earlier encounter with the Fates to provide a reason for that credulity.) Before the King can investigate, however, sailors arrive to welcome him home in a maritime celebration comprising, in Rameau's setting, an enormous fugal chorus ('Que ces rivages'), a tuneful air and a profusion of colourful dances. An audience may lose itself in the celebration, but it also sees Thésée, sitting in silence and pretending to be pleased as he endures inner turmoil. Only after the troupe departs does he react, invoking Neptune over evocative string figuration ('Puissant maître des flots'), and imploring the god to kill Hippolyte. Though Neptune makes no personal appearance in this scene, the shuddering of the orchestral waves demonstrates that the King has been heard.

Yet that version of these scenes might never have been performed. By the time the *Mercure de France* published its initial review of the production (in the month immediately following the premiere), the divertissement had been moved to the end of the act – a more conventional location for an extended celebration, and one probably more immediately pleasing to the segment of the Opéra audience that attended performances primarily to enjoy the ballet and spectacle.[35] The authors cannot have been happy. Pellegrin, quite proud of his creation, had described this episode in detail in his preface; Rameau, in a supplement to the printed edition of the score, grudgingly accepted the alteration for the theatre but insisted that the divertissement remain in its original location in concert performances.

In this opera the traditional Corneillian combination of weak king and young hero, found in many tragédies en musique, is given a twist. Thésée is

34 Downing A. Thomas, *Aesthetics of Opera in the ancien régime, 1647–1785* (Cambridge, 2002), pp. 162–9.
35 Graham Sadler, 'Rameau, Pellegrin, and the Opéra: The Revisions of *Hippolyte et Aricie* during Its First Season', *The Musical Times*, 124 (1983), pp. 535–6.

flawed rather than weak, and Hippolyte rejects political ambition altogether; moreover, as originally written, the final act treats both father and son as heroes, one tragic and the other fortunate. Yet the first two scenes of that act, featuring Thésée's remorse and punishment, were suppressed shortly after performances began (a decision that eliminated some of Rameau's most powerful music). The review in the *Mercure* claimed that 'the public' had been offended by the violation of unity of place, for after those scenes the seashore gives way to a lovely garden, where the goddess Diana has arranged the reunion of Hippolyte and Aricie. To be sure, transformations of scenery at moments other than the entr'acte do occur in this repertory, and this one is clearly justified by a supernatural intervention; nonetheless, dramaturgical convention called for the scenes within an act to be seamlessly elided, without temporal rupture, and this transformation is unsettling from that point of view. In any case, whatever the motivation for the deletion of Thésée's scenes, it had the effect of clarifying the focus on a single hero: Hippolyte, given to the shepherds by Diana as their new ruler. The final divertissement includes a chaconne, danced not by the usual heroic character but by a pastoral character. Thus, instead of celebrating the union of masculine heroic love and political triumph, the customary role of a chaconne at the end of a tragédie en musique, this dance celebrates love as a reward for virtue, in a pastoral atmosphere suffused with supernatural marvels and tender gallantry.[36]

The era of Rameau: a time of change

Rameau lived another three decades; he composed operas for the rest of his life. The 1730s saw additional masterpieces (the tragédies en musique *Castor et Pollux* and *Dardanus*, the opéra-ballets *Les Indes galantes* and *Les fêtes d'Hébé*); the 1740s, a profusion of works in every genre then known to French opera (though only one new tragédie en musique); the 1750s, a string of charming one-act miniatures (actes de ballet), which had begun in 1748 with the exquisite *Pigmalion*. A final masterpiece, *Les Boréades*, was never performed.[37] Rameau's music remained controversial until mid-century for its textural and harmonic complexity. Because conservatives cited the long-dead Lully as their ideal, the factions came to be called 'lullistes' and 'ramistes'.[38] In

36 Geoffrey Burgess, 'Le théâtre ne change qu'à la troisième scène: The Hand of the Author and Unity of Place in Act V of *Hippolyte et Aricie*', *Cambridge Opera Journal*, 10 (1998), pp. 275–87; see also Sadler, 'Rameau, Pellegrin, and the Opéra', pp. 536–7.

37 Sylvie Bouissou, *Jean-Philippe Rameau, Les Boréades: la tragédie oubliée* (Paris, 1992).

38 Wood and Sadler (eds.), *French Baroque Opera: A Reader*, pp. 99–105.

1748, in the allegorical novel *Les bijoux indiscrets*, Denis Diderot aptly summarized the situation: 'The ignoramuses and the graybeards were all in favor of Utmiutsol [Lully]; the youth and the virtuosi were all for Uremifasolasiututut [Rameau]; and the people of good taste, young as well as old, had a high opinion of them both.'[39] Nonetheless, Rameau was prolific, the dominant composer at the Opéra by the late 1740s.

Rameau eventually expanded the orchestra with the occasional use of French horns and clarinets (instruments he had encountered at the home of his principal patron, Alexandre-J.-J. Le Riche de La Pouplinière), and he developed an increasingly flexible approach to orchestration. His mid-century style bears traces of the style galant (which came to France later than elsewhere). From the mid-1740s he prefigured the action of the opera in his overtures, which varied in form. Starting with the tragédie en musique *Zoroastre* (1749), he abandoned the traditional operatic prologue.

Zoroastre reflects the preoccupations of the librettist, dance theorist Louis de Cahusac, who attempted to re-energize a near-moribund genre by radically subordinating narrative to spectacle and virtually eliminating tender love intrigue. (The revised version, 1756, restores a more traditional sentimental narrative.) Here and in other operas, Cahusac introduced the magical world of genies and sprites (*la féerie*) in plots set in the ancient Near East; he incorporated Masonic themes, most obviously in the battle between the forces of darkness and light that dominates *Zoroastre*; and like other mid-century poets, he used pantomime to integrate ballet more fully into dramatic plots.[40]

In 1745 Rameau began composing operas for the royal court as well as the Opéra and received the title 'composer of the King's chamber music' (*compositeur de la Musique de la chambre du Roy*). His court appointment reflects a larger trend: the introduction of fully staged opera to the court of Louis XV, spurred initially by the festivities at Versailles in 1745 for the marriage of the Dauphin to Maria Teresa of Spain. Important sites would eventually include theatres at Fontainebleau and Choisy as well as Versailles. Court productions were the responsibility of the King's chamber music, which drew necessary personnel from the Opéra – a source of tension for the directors of the Opéra, who on occasion found themselves without cast or crew. Amateur productions occurred as well. Madame de Pompadour, the King's mistress and a gifted soprano, starred in the tiny Théâtre des Petits Cabinets at Versailles (1747–53). In addition to reviving old favourites, Pompadour commissioned a steady

39 Denis Diderot, *Oeuvres romanesques*, ed. Henri Bénac (Paris, 1962), p. 33.
40 Jean-Philippe Rameau, *Zoroastre*, ed. Graham Sadler, in *Opera omnia Rameau*, gen. ed. Sylvie Bouissou, series IV, vol. 1 (Paris, 1999), pp. l, lv–lvi; Paolo Russo, 'Les Incertitudes de la tragédie lyrique: *Zoroastre* de Louis de Cahusac', *Revue de musicologie*, 75 (1989), pp. 47–64; Dill, *Monstrous Opera*, pp. 112–21.

stream of new works from various composers, most of which were later produced professionally at the Opéra.[41]

In the early 1750s, malaise enfolded the Opéra. The institution was recovering from a period of financial mismanagement; the emphasis on Rameau's works had been reduced as part of that strategy;[42] and the trickle of ballets-héroïques and pastorales-héroïques from other fine composers (Joseph-Nicolas-Pancrace Royer, Jean-Joseph Cassanéa de Mondonville, and the collaborators François Francoeur and François Rebel, among others) failed to spark much enthusiasm. Moreover, musical taste had changed, and revivals of old works, once the bread and butter of the institution, seemed stale and uninteresting. Friedrich Melchior, Baron von Grimm, a German writer who had been living in Paris since 1748, urged in his *Lettre sur Omphale* (1752) that the old repertory be limited to a few masterpieces. It was in this atmosphere that Francoeur and Rebel, then co-inspecteurs général of the Opéra, invited a small troupe from Italy to stage several comic intermezzi, starting with Pergolesi's *La serva padrona*. The group created such a stir, in the extended pamphlet war known as the *Querelle des Bouffons* and eventually at the box office, that the Opéra extended their brief residency to two seasons (1752–4).

French audiences knew nothing of opera seria or Italian operatic conventions; nor did it occur to them to compare the Italian comedies, focused on music, with the parodies at the Opéra-Comique, focused on words. Rather, those sympathetic to the offerings of the Italian 'buffoons' perceived the intermezzi as free of constraint, spontaneous and relevant to daily life, in comparison with the convention-bound, staid offerings of the Opéra, which reflected an increasingly irrelevant monarchical culture.[43] For Grimm, whose allegorical *Le Petit prophète de Boehmischbroda* (1753) set off the pamphlet war, the Italian residency provided an opportunity to goad the French into developing an internationally relevant style of opera, as well as cover for a veiled political attack on monarchical repression. Jean-Jacques Rousseau (*Lettre sur la musique française*, 1753) used the dispute to call traditional French poetics into question and to set forth a new aesthetic programme. Each of those pamphlets led to a spirited debate.[44]

41 See François Lesure, *L'Opéra classique français* (Geneva, 1972), plates 4–5 (images of Versailles theatre, 1745); Paul F. Rice, *Fontainebleau Operas for the Court of Louis XV of France by Jean-Philippe Rameau (1683–1764)* (Lewiston, NY, 2004), pp. 5–27.

42 Rice, *Fontainebleau Operas*, pp. 24–5.

43 Andrea Fabiano 'Introduction', in Fabiano (ed.), *La 'Querelle des Bouffons' dans la vie culturelle française du XVIIIe siècle* (Paris, 2005), pp. 14–18.

44 Elisabeth Cook, 'Challenging the ancien régime: The Hidden Politics of the "Querelle des Bouffons"', in Fabiano (ed.), *La 'Querelle des Bouffons'*, pp. 141–60; Wood and Sadler (eds.), *French Baroque Opera: A Reader*, pp. 105–11; Heartz, *Music in European Capitals*, pp. 709–12; Denise Launay (ed.), *La Querelle des Bouffons: texte des pamphlets, 1752–54*, 3 vols. (Geneva, 1973).

The most enduring result of the 'Querelle' was the invention of a new type of opéra-comique (see chapter 10), but it affected the traditional repertory as well. Rameau emerged as the undisputed standard-bearer for traditional French opera. His revised tragédie en musique *Castor et Pollux* (first version, 1737) and his 'ballet bouffon' *Platée* (Versailles, 1745; Paris, 1749) both triumphed at the Opéra in 1754. *Platée*, a satirical farce that had earlier left critics cold, now seemed in some circles a model for French musical comedy. Its most successful scene, the divertissement for Folly (La Folie) – a vehicle for the brilliant Marie Fel, otherwise a performer of serious roles – features a carnivalesque reversal, a tragic text set as a lively Italianate ariette and a lighthearted text set as a graceful yet solemn French air.[45] As for the old repertory, it was reborn in a new guise: editors stripped Lully's masterpieces of their prologues, shortened their recitatives (now encrusted with ornaments), lengthened their divertissements, and replaced most dances, overtures and other instrumental movements with new ones in a more recent style.[46] Nonetheless, by the mid-1760s the type of French opera rooted in seventeenth- and early-eighteenth-century sensibilities had run its course.[47] Definitive change was on the way.

Select Bibliography

Anthony, James R. 'Printed Editions of André Campra's *L'Europe galante*'. *The Musical Quarterly*, 56 (1970), pp. 54–73

French Baroque Music from Beaujoyeulx to Rameau. Rev. and expanded edn, Portland, OR, 1997

Banducci, Antonia L.. 'Staging a *tragédie en musique*: A 1748 Promptbook of Campra's *Tancrède*'. *Early Music*, 21 (1993), pp. 180–90

'Staging and Its Dramatic Effect in French Baroque Opera: Evidence from Prompt Notes'. *Eighteenth-Century Music*, 1 (2004), pp. 5–28

Barthélémy, Maurice. 'L'opéra-comique des origines à la Querelle des Bouffons'. In Philippe Vendrix (ed.), *L'Opéra-Comique en France au XVIIIe siècle*. Liège, 1992, pp. 8–78

Betzwieser, Thomas. 'Text und "Subtext" in der frühen Opéra-comique: Zur Semantik des Vaudevilles'. In Hermann Danuser and Tobias Plebuch (eds.), *Musik als Text:*

45 Jean-Philippe Rameau, *Platée*, ed. M. Elizabeth C. Bartlet, *Opera omnia Rameau*, gen. ed. Sylvie Bouissou, series IV, vol. 10 (Kassel, 2005), pp. lxiv–lxvii; Downing A. Thomas, 'Rameau's *Platée* Returns: A Case of Double Identity in the Querelle des Bouffons', *Cambridge Opera Journal*, 18 (2006), pp. 1–20; Georgia Cowart, 'Of Women, Sex, and Folly: Opera under the Old Regime', *Cambridge Opera Journal*, 6 (1994), pp. 218–20.

46 Herbert Schneider, *Die Rezeption der Opern Lullys im Frankreich des Ancien régime* (Tutzing, 1982), pp. 75–122; Lois Rosow, 'How Eighteenth-Century Parisians Heard Lully's Operas: The Case of *Armide*'s Fourth Act', in John Hajdu Heyer (ed.), *Jean-Baptiste Lully and the Music of the French Baroque: Essays in Honor of James R. Anthony* (Cambridge, 1989), pp. 213–37; William Weber, '*La musique ancienne* in the Waning of the *ancien régime*', *The Journal of Modern History*, 56 (1984), pp. 58–88.

47 See Lois Rosow, 'French Opera in Transition: *Sylvie* (1765) by Trial and Berton', in John Knowles (ed.), *Critica musica: Essays in Honor of Paul Brainard* (Amsterdam, 1996), pp. 333–63.

Bericht über den internationalen Kongress des Gesellschaft für Musikforschung Freiburg im Breisgau 1993. Kassel, 1998, 2 vols., vol. 2, pp. 431–6

'Musical Setting and Scenic Movement: Chorus and *choeur dansé* in Eighteenth-Century Parisian Opera'. *Cambridge Opera Journal*, 12 (2000), 1–28

Bouissou, Sylvie. *Jean-Philippe Rameau, 'Les Boréades': la tragédie oubliée*. Paris, 1992

'Mécanismes dramatiques de la tempête et de l'orage dans l'opéra français à l'âge baroque'. In Jean Gribenski, Marie-Claire Mussat and Herbert Schneider (eds.), *D'un opéra l'autre: Hommage à Jean Mongrédien*. Paris, 1996, pp. 218–30

Brooks, William. 'Louis XIV's Dismissal of the Italian Actors: The Episode of *La fausse prude*'. *The Modern Language Review*, 91 (1996), pp. 840–7

Burgess, Geoffrey. 'Le théâtre ne change qu'à la troisième scène: The Hand of the Author and Unity of Place in Act V of *Hippolyte et Aricie*'. *Cambridge Opera Journal*, 10 (1998), pp. 275–87

'Ritual in the tragédie en musique from Lully's *Cadmus et Hermione* (1673) to Rameau's Zoroastre (1749)'. PhD thesis, Cornell University, 1998

Cahusac, Louis de. *La danse ancienne et moderne, ou Traité historique de la danse*. 3 vols. The Hague, 1754; facsimile edn., Geneva, 1971

Campra, André. *L'Europe galante, ballet*. Paris, 1724. Facsimile edn. Farnborough, 1967

Le Carnaval de Venise: comédie lyrique. Facsimile edn. with Introduction by James R. Anthony with a section on stage designs and costumes by Jérôme de La Gorce, Stuyvesant, NY, 1989

Cook, Elisabeth. 'Challenging the ancien régime: The Hidden Politics of the "Querelle des Bouffons"'. In Andrea Fabiano (ed.), *La 'Querelle des Bouffons' dans la vie culturelle française du XVIIIe siècle*. Paris, 2005, pp. 141–60

Cowart, Georgia. 'Of Women, Sex, and Folly: Opera under the Old Regime'. *Cambridge Opera Journal*, 6 (1994), pp. 205–20

'Carnival in Venice or Protest in Paris? Louis XIV and the Politics of Subversion at the Paris Opéra'. *Journal of the American Musicological Society*, 54 (2001), pp. 265–302

Cyr, Mary. 'The Dramatic Role of the Chorus in French Opera: Evidence for the Use of Gesture, 1670–1770'. In Thomas Bauman and Maria Petzoldt McClymonds (eds.), *Opera and the Enlightenment*. Cambridge, 1995, pp. 105–18

Destouches, André Cardinal. *Issé: pastorale héroïque*. Facsimile edn. with Introduction by Robert Fajon and contributions by Jérôme de La Gorce and Wendy Hilton, New York, 1984

Dill, Charles. 'Eighteenth-Century Models of French Recitative'. *Journal of the Royal Musical Association*, 120 (1995), pp. 232–50

Monstrous Opera: Rameau and the Tragic Tradition. Princeton, NJ, 1998

'Rameau's Imaginary Monsters: Knowledge, Theory, and Chromaticism in *Hippolyte et Aricie*'. *Journal of the American Musicological Society*, 55 (2002), pp. 433–76

Fabiano, Andrea. 'Introduction'. In Fabiano (ed.), *La 'Querelle des Bouffons' dans la vie culturelle française du XVIIIe siècle*. Paris, 2005, pp. 11–22

Fader, Don. 'The "cabale du dauphin", Campra, and Italian Comedy. The Courtly Politics of French Musical Patronage around 1700'. *Music & Letters*, 86 (2005), pp. 380–413

Girdlestone, Cuthbert. *Jean-Philippe Rameau: His Life and Work*. Rev. edn., New York, 1969

Harris-Warrick, Rebecca. 'Staging Venice'. *Cambridge Opera Journal*, 15 (2003), pp. 297–316

Heartz, Daniel. *Music in European Capitals: The Galant Style, 1720–1780*. New York, 2003

Isherwood, Robert M. *Farce and Fantasy: Popular Entertainment in Eighteenth-Century Paris*. Oxford, 1986

Kauffman, Deborah A. '*Violons en basse* as Musical Allegory'. *Journal of Musicology*, 23 (2006), pp. 153–85

Kintzler, Catherine. *Poétique de l'opéra français, de Corneille à Rousseau*. Paris, 1991

La Gorce, Jérôme de. *L'opéra à Paris au temps de Louis XIV: histoire d'un théâtre*. Paris, 1992

Ladvocat, Louis and La Gorce, Jérôme de. *Lettres sur l'Opéra à l'abbé Dubos suivies de Description de la vie et moeurs, de l'exercise et l'état des filles de l'Opéra*. N.p., 1993

Launay, Denise (ed.). *La Querelle des Bouffons: texte des pamphlets, 1752–54*. 3 vols., Geneva, 1973

Lesure, François. *L'Opéra classique français*. Geneva, 1972

Milliot, Sylvette and La Gorce, Jérôme de. *Marin Marais*. Paris, 1991

Montagnier, Jean-Paul. *Un mécène-musicien: Philippe d'Orléans, Régent (1674–1723)*. N.p., 1996

Naudeix, Laura. *Dramaturgie de la tragédie en musique (1673–1764)*. Paris, 2004

Niderst, Alain. 'L'Europe galante de La Motte et Campra'. In Irène Mamezarz (ed.), *Le Théâtre et l'Opéra sous le signe de l'histoire*. Paris, 1994, pp. 75–80

Noiray, Michel. 'Hippolyte et Castor travestis: Rameau à l'Opéra-Comique'. In Jérôme de La Gorce (ed.), *Jean-Philippe Rameau: Colloque international organisé par la Société Rameau, Dijon 21–24 septembre 1983: actes*. Paris and Geneva, 1987, pp. 109–25

Rameau, Jean-Philippe. *Platée*. Ed. M. Elizabeth C. Bartlet. *Opera omnia Rameau*, gen. ed. Sylvie Bouissou, series IV, vol. 10 Kassel, 2005

Hippolyte et Aricie. Ed. Sylvie Bouissou. *Opera omnia Rameau*, gen. ed. Sylvie Boissou, series IV, vol. 1. Paris, 2002

Zoroastre. Ed. Graham Sadler. *Opera omnia Rameau*, gen. ed. Sylvie Bouissou, Paris, series IV, vol. 10. Paris, 1999

Recueil général des opéra, representez par l'Académie royale de musique depuis son établissement. 16 vols. Paris, 1703–45. 3-vol. facsimile edn., Geneva, 1971

Rice, Paul F. *Fontainebleau Operas for the Court of Louis XV of France by Jean-Philippe Rameau (1683–1764)*. Lewiston, NY, 2004

Rivière, Charles, called Dufresny. *Amusemens sérieux et comiques*. Paris, 1699

Rosow Lois. 'How Eighteenth-Century Parisians Heard Lully's Operas: The Case of *Armide*'s Fourth Act'. In John Hajdu Heyer (ed.), *Jean-Baptiste Lully and the Music of the French Baroque: Essays in Honor of James R. Anthony*. Cambridge, 1989, pp. 213–37

'French Opera in Transition: *Sylvie* (1765) by Trial and Berton'. In John Knowles (ed.), *Critica musica: Essays in Honor of Paul Brainard*. Amsterdam, 1996, pp. 333–63

Russo, Paolo. 'Les Incertitudes de la tragédie lyrique: *Zoroastre* de Louis de Cahusac'. *Revue de musicologie*, 75 (1989), pp. 47–64

Sadler, Graham. 'Rameau, Pellegrin, and the Opéra: The Revisions of *Hippolyte et Aricie* during Its First Season'. *The Musical Times*, 124 (1983), pp. 533–7

Schmidt, Dörte. *Armide hinter den Spiegeln: Lully, Gluck und die Möglichkeiten der dramatischen Parodie*. Stuttgart and Weimar, 2001

Schneider, Herbert. *Die Rezeption der Opern Lullys im Frankreich des Ancien régime*. Tutzing, 1982

Spitzer, John and Neal Zaslaw. *The Birth of the Orchestra: History of an Institution, 1650–1815*. Oxford and New York, 2004

Thomas, Downing A.. *Aesthetics of Opera in the ancien régime, 1647–1785*. Cambridge, 2002

'Rameau's *Platée* Returns: A Case of Double Identity in the Querelle des Bouffons'. *Cambridge Opera Journal*, 18 (2006), pp. 1–20

Titon du Tillet, Evrard. *Second supplément du Parnasse français, ou suite de l'ordre chronologique des poëtes et des musiciens que la mort a enlevés depuis le commencement de l'année 1743 jusqu'en cette année 1755*. N.p., n.d

Weber, William. '*La musique ancienne* in the Waning of the *ancien régime*'. *The Journal of Modern History*, 56 (1984), pp. 58–88

Wood, Caroline. *Music and Drama in the tragédie en musique, 1673–1715: Jean-Baptiste Lully and His Successors*. New York and London, 1996

Wood, Caroline and Sadler, Graham. *French Baroque Opera: A Reader*. Aldershot, 2000

Zaslaw, Neal. 'At the Paris Opéra in 1747'. *Early Music*, 11 (1983), pp. 515–16

· 10 ·

An instinct for parody and a spirit for revolution: Parisian opera, 1752–1800

MICHAEL FEND*

This chapter first explains why 'revolution' is a central term for understanding French operatic culture in the period under investigation. It is historically organized and divided into four sections. The first deals with attempts to bring Italian opera to Paris in the 1750s. The second describes the vicissitudes at two theatres – the Comédie-Italienne and the Opéra-Comique – to establish French opera for a bourgeois and lower-middle-class audience. In the third section we follow the career of Christoph Willibald Gluck from Viennese to Parisian composer in the context of theatrical rivalries and in the final section observe the uncertainties that befell French opera in the Revolutionary period.

Using 'revolution' as the central concept for understanding Parisian opera in the second half of the eighteenth century might be regarded as either banal or far-fetched. For although the events of 1789 that have shaped our concept of 'revolution' took place within the time-frame of our topic, the question of whether music was one of the causes of those political events, or whether the events in turn brought about a simultaneous revolution in music, remains a subject of debate. Certainly, historic upheavals of such magnitude do not happen overnight, nor could the participants instantly channel the collective energy that overpowered the Bastille on 14 July 1789 into a sustainable 'volonté générale', to use Rousseau's phrase. Searching for the historical thresholds of the origin and ending of the political revolution, though without pandering to the illusion of finding such all-decisive points, Roger Chartier saw royal powers already being shaken in three political crises of the 1750s, while François Furet dated the revolution's political conclusion to the establishment of a parliamentary democracy as late as the 1880s.[1] Extending the 'French Revolution' over such a long time-frame makes it necessary briefly to clarify

* I would like to thank David Charlton, Michel Noiray and Roger Parker for many corrections and improvements to an earlier draft of this chapter.

1 Roger Chartier, *Les Origines culturelles de la Révolution française* (Paris, 1990), pp. 55–8; Francois Furet, *La Révolution française de Turgot à Napoléon (1770–1814)* and *Terminer la Révolution de Louis XVIII à Jules Ferry (1814–80)*, 2 vols. (Paris, 1988).

the concept of 'revolution' in early modern Europe, so that we can appreciate its usage in French operatic history of the period under consideration.

From the seventeenth century, what had originally been an astronomical term for the description of a circular motion of planets was brought to bear upon a political turn of events, as in Britain's 'Glorious Revolution' of 1688, or in the perception of the American Declaration of Independence of 1776.[2] This new employment of the term 'revolution' was concurrent with a change in the conception of history, now seen less as a circular movement than as a progress towards a happy future, as the Anglo-Saxon experiences showed. Reforms, renovations and, indeed, revolutions, were now equally perceived as the means to achieve that goal.[3] A demand for reform also occurred in the development of knowledge and culture in eighteenth-century France. Given the term's association with reform and renovation, talking about revolutions could be naïve or daring, but in any case was highly fashionable. As such, it also infiltrated writings on music.

Is France the land without music?

If any quest for reform is naturally preceded by a sense of dissatisfaction, a pamphlet war, known as the 'Querelle des Bouffons' (1752–4),[4] fought in some sixty instalments, seeming at first to have been motivated by the performance of thirteen intermezzi and opere buffe at the Académie royale de musique in Paris, surely must have had a non-musical sub-text.[5] Or could a mere difference in musical taste have given so many people the urge to put pen to paper? When the inspectors of the Académie, the lifelong collaborators François Francœur and François Rebel took the decision – basically a novelty in French operatic history – to allow three Italian singers under their director Eustachio Bambini to perform just three intermezzi over two, three and eventually four months (August–November 1752), they were motivated to some extent by their empty purse: despite its most privileged position among France's cultural institutions, the Académie's average debt of half a million *livres* had become worse since 1749, when Louis XV had passed its ownership to the city of Paris to reduce his own household expenses.[6]

2 Abbé Guillaume-Thomas Raynal, *Révolution de l'Amérique* (Paris, 1781).

3 Reinhart Koselleck, Christian Meier, Jörg Fisch and Neithard Bulst, 'Revolution, Rebellion, Aufruhr, Bürgerkrieg', in Otto Brunner, Werner Conze and Reinhart Koselleck (eds.), *Geschichtliche Grundbegriffe* (Stuttgart, 1984), 8 vols., vol. 5, pp. 653–788.

4 '*Bouffon*' – 'comic' is an abbreviation for farcical theatre and bawdy language.

5 For a definition of musical genres see the preceding article in this volume, by Lois Rosow, and see Michel Noiray, *Vocabulaire de la musique de l'époque classique* (Paris, 2005).

6 Martine de Rougemont, *La vie théâtrale en France au XVIIIe siècle* (Paris, 1988), p. 255.

The *bouffons*' three intermezzi at the Académie and their more serious French counterparts, together with premiere dates and box-office receipts,[7] were as follows:

1. Lully, *Acis et Galathée* (1686) (pastorale-héroïque) – Pergolesi, *La serva padrona* (1733), 1 August 1752, 4,091 *livres*
2. Campra, *Alphée et Arethuse* (1701) (ballet) (deuxième acte) – Orlandini, *Il giocatore* (1715) (pasticcio) – Montéclair, *Les Festes d'été* (1716) (opéra-ballet) (prologue), 22 August 1752, 2,966 *livres*
3. Campra, *Alphée et Arethuse* (1701) (ballet) (deuxième acte) – Auletta, *Il maestro di musica* (1737) – Montéclair, *Les Festes d'été* (1716) (opéra-ballet) (prologue), 19 September 1752, 1,856 *livres*[8]

Thus, the Parisian nobility and upper middle class that constituted the audience at the Académie could watch on 1 August the myth of the uncouth giant Polyphemus killing in a fit of jealousy the shepherd Acis whose lover Galathée, a goddess of the sea, escapes into her element. This was followed by the story, sung in Italian, of a maid manipulating her elderly master into marrying her. Whenever the Académie mounted one of the intermezzi in the next couple of years, it avoided combining them with the performance of a tragédie-lyrique, the musical counterpart to the classical French tragedy, which 'represented an abstraction of the tragic from everyday reality to the highest degree ever achieved in European literature'.[9] The Académie chose instead to combine the intermezzi with pastorals, ballets or opera-ballets on mythological plots. But these were as far removed from everyday reality as spoken French tragedy.

Pergolesi's *La serva padrona* became the most successful intermezzo of Bambini's troupe, and it conquered many European stages before and after. His orchestra consisted of strings and continuo only and had no more than a two-part texture, with first and second violins playing in unison and violas doubling the cellos. While the hapless couch-potato of an elderly *signore* and his beguilingly clever maid, supported by a mute second servant, were familiar to the audience from the commedia dell'arte tradition, the musical characterization of their respective emotional weakness and strength was original and direct and could not fail to be comprehensible to the general public.

From October 1752 the Académie enhanced the position of the Italian intermezzi in their repertory by combining Campra's *Alphée* with Auletta's *Il Maestro* as well as with Pergolesi's *La serva padrona*, while in November

7 Subscriptions, for which there are no records, are discounted.
8 See Andrea Fabiano, *Histoire de l'opéra italien en France (1752–1815): Héros et héroïnes d'un roman théâtral* (Paris, 2006), pp. 236–8.
9 Erich Auerbach, *Mimesis* (Bern, 1982), p. 364.

Dauvergne's newly composed ballet-héroïque *Les Amours de Tempé* was performed before Auletta's *Il Maestro*. All these works were usually performed three times per week. Bambini's troupe were paid a mere 200 *livres* for each performance, leaving the Académie with a substantially greater total income than enjoyed in the three previous seasons, since staging intermezzi incurred a fraction of the cost required for a ballet, let alone a tragédie lyrique.[10] Furthermore, the intermezzi had a more obvious human touch than the learned French repertory and, as many dealt with human frailty in the shape of older men coming to grief in their pursuit of young women, they made the audience laugh out loud, a behaviour previously unheard of at the Académie. In view of the *bouffons*' developing success, in November 1752 Francœur and Rebel signed a new contract with Bambini for a further full year of his services, upon which the latter enlarged his cast from three to nine singers and his repertory by another ten intermezzi and opere buffe.[11]

As the 1752–3 season progressed with high revenues and an increased number of performances, Baron Grimm, a thirty-year-old German critic and later diplomat who settled in Paris in 1749, published anonymously a pamphlet entitled *Le petit prophète de Boemischbroda* attacking the French repertory at the Académie, which he chastized for its 'childish' operatic plots, a 'monotony in their singing' and 'plainsong'-like recitatives. Imitating the rhetoric of a biblical prophet in thrall to 'revelations', Grimm wanted to provoke a sea-change in French opera, the failure of which he warned would result in the Académie's demise. He named Manelli, the *bouffons*' outstanding singer and actor, as his 'emissary', whose performing skills in the intermezzi of the 'divine' Pergolesi had already 'enraptured' the Parisians. Nonetheless, Grimm also praised the acting and singing of Marie Fel and Pierre de Jélyotte who, over many years, had not only created the leading roles in Rameau's operas at the Académie, but had also just performed in the successful premiere of Rousseau's intermède *Le devin du village* ('The Village Soothsayer') at the court theatre in Fontainebleau in October 1752, in which Grimm's 'prophet' claimed to have had a governing hand.[12]

In Rousseau's intermède a soothsayer persuades a shepherd that he should abandon an amourous liaison with the lady of the manor and return to his shepherdess while he teaches her the benefits of playing the game of 'hard-to-get' with the shepherd and thus they are happily reunited. Set among a village

10 Elizabeth Giuliani, 'Le Public de l'Opéra de Paris de 1750 à 1760. Mesure et définition', *International Review of the Aesthetics and Sociology of Music*, 8 (1977), pp. 161ff.

11 Fabiano, *Histoire de l'opéra italien en France*, pp. 25–36, 235–8.

12 Friedrich Melchior Grimm, *Le petit prophète de Boehmischbroda* (Paris, 1753); reprint in Denise Launay (ed.), *La Querelle des Bouffons* (Geneva, 1973), vol. 1, pp. 132–92; excerpts in Oliver Strunk (ed.), *Source Readings in Music History: The Classic Era* (New York, 1965), pp. 45–61.

community, Rousseau's own textbook had the advantage over the intermezzi of being in French. In line with the *bouffons*, he benefitted from the Académie's privilege as the only theatre institution to stage pieces that were sung throughout. His recitatives surprisingly followed the French tradition in their use of metrically free declamation. The employment of what he later called *récitatif obligé* was unheard of in this genre. With its use of flutes, oboes and bassoons, the violins, too, usually playing in unison, the violas doubling the continuo and the winds performing in parallel thirds or sixths with the strings, Rousseau's orchestra was richer than Pergolesi's. Although less vivid in his melodic invention, Rousseau was able to add pantomimic comments to the score for the singers which made it theatrically successful. In its avoidance of vocal ornamentation and orchestral virtuosity, so conspicuous in Rameau, the overall tone of Rousseau's arias and duets was clearly inspired by Italian opera, which he had come to know when acting as secretary to the French ambassador in Venice in 1744 and which by 1753 was very much in the Parisians' ears.[13] In performance Rousseau's intermède had been coupled since its premiere at the Académie with the opéra bouffon, *Le jaloux corrigé*, by Michel Blavet who was the orchestra's first flautist and a well-known composer. In contrast to Rousseau's original, though stylistically derivative composition, Blavet took a far more economical route by simply parodying arias from *La serva padrona*, *Il giocatore*, *Il maestro di musica* and arias from other composers to an excellent new French libretto, by Charles Collé, with Blavet adding an overture, recitatives in an Italian manner and a *divertissement*.[14]

A number of Parisians had been annoyed by Grimm's letter with its sarcastic tone and hostility towards French opera and the French in general, whom he accused of being arrogant and vain. If Grimm had not made opera a target for his nationalist attack, it is likely that fewer people would have responded so indignantly. Within a couple of months, and before the successful debut of *Le devin du village* at the Académie on 1 March 1753 had demonstrated the practical compatibility of French verse and Italianate music, eleven authors joined the fray in hotly debating the relevant merits and flaws of the two nations' opera.[15] Instead of taking Rousseau's example as proof that musical style was a writing-skill open to learning, they chose to see opera as a national *apanage*.

13 Rousseau's original critique of Italian opera and surprising defence of French opera is clear from his fragmentary manuscript published only posthumously (*Lettre sur l'opéra italien et français*), *Œuvres complètes*, ed. Bernard Gagnebin, Marcel Raymond *et al.* (Paris, 1959–95) (hereafter, *OC*), vol. 5, pp. 249–57.

14 Lionel de La Laurencie, 'Deux Imitateurs français des bouffons', *L'Année musicale*, 2 (1913), pp. 66–91.

15 Daniel Heartz, 'Italian by Intention, French of Necessity: Rousseau's *Le devin du village*', in Marie-Claire Mussat, Jean Mongrédien and Jean-Michel Nectoux (eds.), *Échos de France et d'Italie: Liber amicorum Yves Gérard* (Paris, 1997), pp. 31–46.

Most astonishingly, Rousseau himself championed the idea of a nation's music as all-important. The slurs against Italian music permeating the writings of Grimm's opponents in turn annoyed him, despite his own musical success – *Le devin* would remain in the Académie's repertory until 1829. With his hostile and finally vicious *Lettre sur la musique française*, published in November 1753, Rousseau 'set all parts of Paris on fire' and 'created a terrible sequence' of rebuttals, according to Grimm, who himself could not overlook the paradox that the composer of *Le devin* had undertaken the task of theoretically proving the superiority of Italian over French music to the extent that he famously concluded: 'The French don't have music and could not have any; or if they ever have, it will be so much the worse for them.'[16] Such an aphorism makes a jolly read, but how could Rousseau the writer contradict in such flagrant terms the achievement of Rousseau the composer? Indeed, he feared for his life after musicians of the Académie burnt his effigy.

In an autobiographical note written three years later Rousseau claimed that the performance of French and Italian music side-by-side, as practised at the Académie since the arrival of the *bouffons*, had finally disenchanted his and many others' view of French opera.[17] While his *Lettre* is ostensibly about French music, it is in fact his manifesto about the unsuitability of the French language for musical setting. For Rousseau, the perfect example of a perceived French deficiency was Lully's opera *Armide*, in which the composer continuously employs the key of E minor for the heroine's central monologue, although she softens and transforms her iron determination to massacre her powerless enemy Renaud into yearning for him.[18] Rousseau's critique, against which Rameau pointed to Lully's metrically sophisticated text declamation as a means of showing Armide's agitation,[19] loses some of its startling eccentricity if it is understood as part of Rousseau's fundamental critique of contemporary society, first formulated in his *Discours sur les sciences et les arts* (1750). In this prize-winning discourse he maintained that the development of culture in general alienated man from the natural, happy, virtuous life enjoyed in earlier times. A fundamental component of that mythical era lay, for Rousseau, in people communicating their needs and desires with sincerity and directness. He believed that the sonorous, vowel-saturated and mellifluous

16 Friedrich Melchior Grimm *et al.*, *Correspondance littéraire, philosophique et critique*, ed. Maurice Tourneux (Paris, 1877), vol. 2, p. 307 (15 December 1753); Jean-Jacques Rousseau, *Lettre sur la musique française*, *OC*, vol. 5, p. 328.

17 Jean-Jacques Rousseau, 'Fragment biographique', *OC*, vol. 1, pp. 1116–17; see also the extended account in *Les Confessions*, *OC*, vol. 1, p. 383.

18 Rousseau, *Lettre sur la musique française*, *OC*, vol. 5, pp. 323–7.

19 Jean-Philippe Rameau, 'Observations sur notre instinct pour la musique' (1754), in *La Querelle des Bouffons*, vol. 3, pp. 1801–82.

Italian language provided an unrivalled basis for harnessing the traces of such unbridled expression of feeling, while in the French language many words were unusable for musical setting because of their mute syllables and nasal sounds. Moreover, the comparative paucity of vowels in French words would cause musical exclamations to be shrill and hard. He maintained that the lack of expression at the heart of French music was meant to be supplemented historically by the development of harmony, epitomized at his time by Rameau's theory and operas. Yet, because of its refinement and artificiality French music had little effect on its audience. In short, Rousseau tried to explain in a slightly complex way, why the unpretentious, funny and swift intermezzi caught fire with the Parisian public while their own allegorical and sophisticated tragédies lyriques and ballets were losing their appeal.

In his philosophically related *Essai sur l'origine des langues*, written in the same years but published only posthumously in 1781, Rousseau extended his view of the different aptitude of languages for music to consider the superiority of music above language in general in its ability 'directly to imitate emotive phenomena'.[20] Music could communicate emotions and it could strengthen the expressiveness of emotions:

> Melody, by imitating the inflexions of the voice, expresses complaints, cries of sadness or of joy, threats, and moans; all the vocal signs of the passions are within its scope. It imitates the accents of languages, and the turns of phrase appropriate in each idiom to certain movements of the soul; it not only imitates, it speaks, and its language, inarticulate but lively, ardent, passionate, has a hundred times more energy than speech itself. Here is from whence the strength of musical imitation arises.'[21]

Rousseau's ideas gained extremely wide currency not only through his entries on music for the *Encyclopédie*, which he revised for his own *Dictionnaire de musique* (1768), but in particular through his sentimental novel *la Julie, ou La nouvelle Héloïse* (1761), the evocation of sensual personalities in his educational treatise *Emile* (1762) and its sequel *Emile et Sophie* (1780) and his autobiographical writings. It was in the *Confessions* that Rousseau constructed a link between the musical *Querelle* and a contemporaneous constitutional crisis that has been interpreted by some historians as the real non-musical sub-text for the

20 Catherine Kintzler, *Poétique de l'opéra français de Corneille à Rousseau* (Paris, 1991), p. 461.

21 Jean-Jacques Rousseau, 'Essay on the Origin of Languages', in J. T. Scott (ed. and trans.), *The Collected Writings of Rousseau* (Hanover, 1998), vol. 7, p. 322; and *OC*, vol. 5, p. 416: 'La mélodie en imitant les inflexions de la voix exprime les plaintes, les cris de douleur ou de joye, les menaces, les gémissemens; tous les signes vocaux des passions sont de son ressort. Elle imite les accents des langues, et les tours affectés dans chaque idiome à certains mouvemens de l'ame; elle n'imite pas seulement, elle parle, et son langage inarticulé mais vif, ardent, passionné a cent fois plus d'énergie que la parole même. Voilà d'où nait la force des imitations musicales.'

Querelle: the appearance of his infamous *Lettre sur la musique française* 'did perhaps prevent a revolution of the state, unlikely as it may seem', since it distracted the public from a theological dispute that was raging between clergy and parliament.[22]

In March 1754 the *bouffons* were made to leave the country without, however, vanishing from the audience's memory. Audience familiarity with the *bouffons*' repertory had already been enhanced through its pasticcio character, as certain arias and ensembles of one intermezzo would be re-used in another, but also through the publication and circulation of their music. In addition, between 1754 and 1756 the Comédie-Italienne and the Opéra-Comique mounted no fewer than eleven parodies of the *bouffons*' repertory. Pergolesi's prime historical position as capturer of the musical spirit of the *Querelle des Bouffons* is justifiable not only on the basis of a total of thirty-six performances for *La serva padrona*, the positive reception of which was enormously augmented by a French version, *La Servant maitresse*, written by Pierre Baurans and premiered on 13 August 1754 at the Comédie-Italienne.[23] A number of the pasticci were concocted in part from Pergolesi's tunes. 'One cannot deny that there has been a revolution in musical taste since the sojourn of the *bouffons*, which one can only attribute to them. All operas brought on the stage since *Castor et Pollux* have failed.'[24] The departure of the *bouffons* did the opposite of liberating the Académie from its competitors. Instead it drove its audience into the theatres of the Comédie-Italienne and the Opéra-Comique.

Opera as a happy school for bourgeois life

The cut-throat competition between the companies had been the second probable motive (after an empty purse) behind the decision of the Académie's inspectors to hire the *bouffons*. For, in terms of genre and language, the intermezzi concerned would have fitted better into the repertory of the Comédie-Italienne or the Opéra-Comique. The bad feelings between the four main theatre troupes – the Comédie-Française also reckoned in the equation – were ingrained in their constitution. The Académie was used to rent free housing in the Palais Royal furnished for some 1,300 visitors. As mentioned

22 Jean-Jacques Rousseau, *Les Confessions*, *OC*, vol. 1, p. 384; the issue is discussed in Robert Wokler, '"La Querelle des Bouffons" and the Italian Liberation of France: A Study of Revolutionary Foreplay', *Eighteenth-Century Life*, 11 (1987), pp. 94–116; Elisabeth Cook, 'Challenging the *Ancien Régime*: The Hidden Politics of the 'Querelle des Bouffons"' in Andrea Fabiano (ed.), *La 'Querelle des Bouffons', dans la vie culturelle française du XVIIIe siècle* (Paris, 2005), pp. 141–60.

23 Fabiano, *Histoire de l'opéra italien en France*, p. 235.

24 Grimm, *Correspondance littéraire*, vol. 2, p. 176 (19 August 1754). In its second version, premiered on 8 January 1754, Jean-Philippe Rameau's *Castor et Pollux* was set to become his most successful opera in the eighteenth century.

above, the Académie was the only French theatre to enjoy the privilege to mount lyric drama on the scale of its choosing. Other companies trespassing on the Académie's privilege could be virtually destroyed by drastic fines and have their buildings and even costumes confiscated. The Comédie-Italienne, which daily performed Italian farces, French plays, ballets and opéras-comiques for up to 1,500 spectators in the Hôtel de Bourgogne, situated in rue Mauconseil near St Eustache in the Les Halles area, was itself plagued by non-paying noble visitors, often poor attendance and a dilapidated building, despite receiving annual royal subsidies of 15,000 *livres* from 1723 onwards.[25]

Thirdly, after a seven-year suppression for having flouted the Académie's privileges, for which it had been fined 10,000 *livres*, the seasonal Opéra-Comique theatre had just come back in 1752 and was also competing for audiences. Complying with the Académie's privilege meant that at the Opéra-Comique musical numbers had to be interspersed with spoken dialogue and no more than six musicians could play at a time, while musical accompaniment was recommended in order to avoid infringement of the Comédie-Française's privilege in the area of spoken plays.[26] The influence of the system of privileges on the development of theatrical forms can hardly be overestimated. The Opéra-Comique's impresario, the zestful Jean Monnet, who took a dim view of his colleagues' administrative skills, had succeeded in obtaining a new lease for six years paying the city 12,000 *livres* for the first three years, and 15,000 *livres* for the last three.[27] Monnet's newly constructed theatre was situated at the Foire Saint-Laurent near today's Gare de l'Est.[28] It usually staged comedies with some musical accompaniment and also dances, pantomimes or even acrobatics from the beginning of August to the end of September, while at the second big market, the Foire Saint-Germain, Monnet's troupe performed from the beginning of February until Palm Sunday. Both the Comédie-Italienne and the Opéra-Comique had profited for decades from mounting parodies of tragédies lyriques created at the Académie.

In the course of the *Querelle des Bouffons* Monnet realised that his own company was well placed to exploit a market niche. He writes in his

25 Clarence D. Brenner, *The Théâtre Italien: Its Repertoire, 1716–1793* (Berkeley, 1961), pp. 6–7, 16–17.
26 An upper limit of two vocal and six instrumental parts had been decreed by Louis XIV in 1673 for performances outside the Académie royale de musique. Charlton has calculated that around 1760 the orchestra at the Comédie-Italienne had risen to about twenty players and was to increase to forty-eight instrumentalists by the end of the century. See David Charlton, 'Orchestra and Chorus at the Comédie-Italienne (Opéra-Comique), 1755–1799', in *French Opéra, 1730–1830: Meaning and Media* (Aldershot, 2000), pp. 94–103.
27 Jean Monnet, *Mémoires*, ed. Henri d'Alméras (Paris, 1909), pp. 164 and 171.
28 For illustrations of temporary, wooden buildings, scenery and the Foires' topographical surroundings, see Raphaëlle Legrand and Nicole Wild, *Regards sur l'opera-comique: Trois siècle de vie théâtrale* (Paris, 2002), pp. 12–23; for illustrations of Monnet's theatre, see Daniel Heartz, *Music in European Capitals: The Galant Style, 1720–1780* (New York and London, 2003), p. 707.

Mémoires: 'I had the idea to have a piece made roughly in the same taste [as the *bouffons*'] by a musician from our own country'.[29] In plain prose, he was looking for a composer who could imitate Rousseau's *Devin*. Although Monnet's *Mémoires* grant his idea a role that was in reality performed by the commercial system of Parisian operas, the task he set was superbly filled by Antoine Dauvergne, violinist at the Académie's own orchestra. By then he had gained over a year's experience in performing intermezzi. Dauvergne's intermède, *Les troqueurs* (The swappers) was premiered at the Foire Saint-Laurent on 30 July 1753. His librettist, Jean-Joseph Vadé, used not an Italian but a French literary source: La Fontaine. Somewhat related to the plot of Mozart's and Da Ponte's *Così fan tutte*, *Les troqueurs* tells the story of two men abandoning their project of wife-swapping, after one finds his new woman a little too lively and the other finds his a little slow. As in the Italian models, Dauvergne has his first and second violins play in unison, he uses the Pergolesian fingerprint of a drum bass, tremoli preceded by large interval jumps and symmetrical phrasings to give clarity to text settings especially in ensembles. His recitatives often change meter in line with French tradition and his arias are mostly in da capo form, except where dramatic continuity makes this inappropriate. Margot's potential temper is musically as unmistakable as is Lucas' dismay that he could become its target. The final quartet 'was one of the earliest examples of an ensemble designed to further the action of an opéra-comique. It opened with four characters still locked in disagreement, but allowed them to resolve their differences as the music progressed and, finally, to reach an amicable solution.'[30]

Engaging with Rousseau's thesis that 'the French do and could not at all have a music', Monnet spread rumours that *Les troqueurs* had been written by an Italian composer resident in Vienna and only revealed its true author once success was assured.[31] Confronted with Blavet's and Dauvergne's 'works' as evidence of Italian music by French composers and in their own language at a point when his *Lettre sur la musique française* had been written but was still awaiting publication, Rousseau condemned Blavet's, without mentioning him by name, as having produced a 'disgusting combination [which] is too monstrous to be allowed' while snobbishly alluding to Dauvergne as 'a man of talent , who seems to have listened to good music with good ears'.[32] In fact, *Les troqueurs* was to hold the stage for thirty years.

29 Monnet, *Mémoires*, p. 174.
30 Elisabeth Cook, *Duet and Ensemble in the Early Opéra-Comique* (New York, 1995), p. 82.
31 Monnet, *Mémoires*, p. 174. Monnet may have invented this story.
32 Rousseau, 'Letter on French Music', in *Collected Writings of Rousseau*, vol. 7, p. 174.

Next to Jean-Michel Sedaine and Jean François Marmontel, Charles-Simon Favart was the most successful French writer for the musical stage of the eighteenth century and the only one to have created a 'European vogue'.[33] His libretti and musical concoctions were translated and adapted as far away as Scandinavia. In Paris, the domicile of the Opéra-Comique had been called 'Salle Favart' since 1784 (granting some interruptions along the way). His career was temporarily blighted by real-life drama. Thrown out of business by the closure of the Opéra-Comique in 1745, he and his eighteen-year-old wife, the actress, singer, dancer and dramatist Marie-Justine-Benoîte Favart, found employment in the private theatre company of Marechal de Saxe. The Marechal had the cruel idea of making his actors perform on both sides of a war campaign he was then conducting in the Netherlands, but he was equally busy on another kind of campaign. When Marie-Justine took refuge from the stalking Marechal in a monastery, Favart had to make his own escape from fabricated debt-charges. Conveniently, the Marechal died in 1750 and the couple were reunited.

This unpleasant encounter of a lower-class artist couple with a member of the nobility was no doubt still in Favart's mind when he translated and adapted the bouffons' second most successful intermezzo, *Bertoldo in corte*. Based on a play by Goldoni, *Bertoldo in corte* was, so to speak, born as a pasticcio at its Venetian premiere in 1748. Probably lacking leisure activities, Vincenzo Ciampi had set Goldoni's text to existing melodies from arias by fellow Neapolitan composers Leo, Vinci, Sellitto, Jommelli and others. As part of the bouffons' repertory at the Académie, *Bertoldo in corte* became such a success in November 1753 that Monnet's Opéra-Comique brought out its own French version under the title *Bertholde à la ville* in September 1754, revised by Anseaume and LaSalle d'Offemont. Only at this point did Favart link his Comédie-Italienne with this gold mine. He translated the Italian text afresh, used existing French and Italian arias and vaudevilles and performed it as *Le caprice amoureux, ou Ninette à la cour* from February 1755 onwards.[34]

With Favart we encounter the parody-industry of French opera feeding on the success of the *bouffons*' intermezzi. Unencumbered by copyright issues, Favart exploited the popularity of a master plot in which the nobility were usually cast in a bad light and were rejected, while the lower class came to realize and express their moral superiority over, as well as their social independence from, the nobility. For well over a decade Favart had parodied French and Italian serious and comic operas and ballets, such as Rameau's

33 Alfred Iacuzzi, *The European Vogue of Favart: The Diffusion of the Opéra-Comique* (New York, 1932).

34 For a list of musical attributions, see Kent Maynard Smith, *Egidio Duni and the Development of the 'Opéra-Comique' from 1753 to 1770* (Ann Arbor, MI, 1980), pp. 56–9. The political aspect of the plot is emphasized in Fabiano, *Histoire de l'opéra italien en France*, pp. 31ff. and Heartz, *Music in European Capitals*, p. 727.

Hippolite et Aricie. Working mostly for the Comédie-Italienne or Monnet's Foire Theatres, Favart recreated mythological plots from the Académie among peasants, or translated Italian operas into French and substituted arias with popular songs (vaudevilles). He also added his texts to existing dance tunes, especially minuets.[35] In his parody of Rameau's *Hippolite* Favart ridiculed Phaedra's wrath in a sixteen-bar melisma on 'fureur' of the utmost musical banality.[36] His parody of Rousseau's *Le devin du village*, performed as *Les amours de Bastien et Bastienne* at the Comédie-Italienne in August 1753, is best known in Mozart's Singspiel adaptation *Bastien und Bastienne* (1768). Favart was not the inventor of parody as a musical practice and, although he parodied many Italianate airs for his opéras-comiques himself, he did not publish orchestral scores and instead usually added 'his' *timbres* – that is songs, without instrumental accompaniment, at the end of his printed libretti to ensure maximum popularity, or he sold them separately.

That three theatres staged basically the same opera within fifteen months indicates competition in a confined market, competition made possible by audience fascination with plots such as *Bertoldo* and *Ninette*. It was also based on a 'mania of interpolation' that allowed the audience to hear one version as a commentary on another.[37] Authors demonstrated their originality by varying pre-existing models. For the literary scholar Jean-François de La Harpe writing some fifty years after the event, with *Ninette à la cour*, opéra-comique 'for the first time came close to a good comedy that is one which teaches through amusing us and edifies in dallying'.[38]

Outside Paris, music theatre had been staged by travelling troupes in major French cities, such as Marseille, Montpellier, Toulouse, Rouen, Lyon, Bordeaux and Rennes. Across the Italian border the duchy of Parma had become very active since 1748 when wars between the Papal State, Spain, Austria and France were settled for the benefit of Duke Don Philip of Bourbon, whose wife Louise Elizabeth was the oldest daughter of Louis XV. The general intendant of the royal household, Guillaume du Tillot, engaged a French troupe to perform tragédies lyriques by Rameau, including ballets, French plays and opéras-comiques. Du Tillot also engaged Italian composers,

35 David Charlton, '"Minuet-scenes" in Early opéra comique', in *French Opera 1730–1830: Meaning and Media* (Aldershot, 2000), pp. 256–91.

36 See Michel Noiray, '*Hippolyte* et *Castor* travestis: Rameau à l'opéra-comique', in Jérôme de la Gorce (ed.), *Jean-Philippe Rameau: Colloque international organisé par la Société Rameau, Dijon, 21–24 Septembre 1983* (Paris, 1987), pp. 109–25.

37 Oscar George Theodore Sonneck, 'Ciampi's "Bertoldo, Bertoldino e Cacasenno" and Favart's "Ninette à la Cour"', *Sammelbände der Internationalen Musik-Gesellschaft*, 12/1911, p. 539.

38 Jean-François de La Harpe, *Lycée, ou Cours de littérature ancienne et moderne* (Paris, an VII – an XIII [1798–1804]), vol. 12, p. 336, quoted in Herbert Schneider and Reinhard Wiesend (eds.), *Die Oper im 18. Jahrhundert* (Laaber, 2001), p. 261.

such as Tommaso Traetta, who became court composer (*maestro di capella*) in 1758, and Egidio Duni. Originally from Matera and trained in Naples, Duni had almost a dozen opere serie performed from the 1730s onwards and was the first composer to set Goldoni's *La buona figliuola* – after Richardson's novel – in Parma. Subsequently however, Duni abandoned Italian opera altogether and requested from Monnet a French libretto to be set by him with a view to performance in Paris. This became *Le peintre amoureux de son modèle* based on a libretto by Louis Anseaume and premiered at the Foire Saint-Laurent on 26 July 1757. It tells the story of an elderly painter and his young apprentice both falling in love with the 'model'. Although the elderly painter attempts to bribe her, he musically resembles less the corrupt courtiers in the previously discussed operas than the hapless *signore* in *La serva padrona*. Of course, the model goes for the oppressed apprentice. Duni's score is 'a hybrid of French and Italian elements'; in its revised version seventeen Italian ariettes stood next to ten vaudeville timbres, and he also imitated two airs from Rousseau's *Le devin du village*.[39] With unmistakable reference to Rousseau's polemic against French opera Duni, or somebody close to him, wrote in his dedicatory letter to du Tillot: 'While an author in Paris exerts himself to show that the country's language is unfit for musical setting, I, an Italian from Parma, only use French words for musical setting.'[40] As Dauvergne had done in *Les troqueurs*, Duni and his librettist Anseaume accelerated the dramatic flow through ensembles and, especially, a first-act quartet finale. He was publicly hailed by Grimm as a model for French composers to follow.

Duni used the commission for *Le peintre* as a reason to settle in Paris for good, although his next works were less successful. By 1760 Monnet had retired from the Opéra-Comique and Duni had affirmed his allegiance to the Comédie-Italienne. There he brought out *L'isle des fous*, also based on a play by Goldoni and written by Anseaume. The plot brings an array of predictably eccentric characters on stage, such as a strong man, a miser, a forgetful person whose musically imitative features Duni partly explores in a variety of aria forms and partly incorporates into developmental action ensembles. These musically continuous scenes, which usually concluded one act or the opera as a whole, had been Goldoni's real and wide-reaching gift to opera buffa composers in the 1750s. Through Duni, the ensemble finale was now transferred to Paris. Strong dynamic contrasts, a ubiquitous parlando style and instrumental ostinatos were some of the techniques he exploited. One particular scene, in which the heroine reveals her secret love while sleepwalking, could not have

39 Smith, *Egidio Duni*, pp. 94–101.
40 Egidio Duni, *Le peintre amoureux de son modèle* (Paris, [1757]), n.p.

failed to entice the audience, just as the dialogical structure of Duni's action-style ensemble would have given the audience a sense of musical continuity that was unheard of in this genre.

Despite Duni's personal success, the Comédie-Italienne was troubled by low financial returns, often attracting fewer than 200 spectators. With hindsight it relied too much on divertissements and semi-improvised Italian comedies involving Harlequins. The ensuing hardship stood in stark contrast to the Foire Theatres' success under Favart's directorship and their two home-grown youngsters, Pierre-Alexandre Monsigny and François-André Danican Philidor, who initially rode on Duni's coat-tails and were soon to supersede him. Monsigny's first intermède, *Les aveux indiscrets*, as well as Philidor's second opéra-comique, *Blaise le savetier*, were premiered in 1759. In the former, two related couples confess to their extra-marital affairs and in the latter a young cobbler-couple, much in arrears with their rent-payments, succeed in feigning amorous interest for the angry but quickly mollified proprietor-couple. As they leave squabbling among each other, the cobbler has won another day. Both operas show excellent musical characterization in fully developed arias which, in crucial distinction to Favart, were newly composed (except, perhaps, for a final vaudeville). Monsigny and Philidor also explored dialogical duets and ensemble finales.

The exciting success of the Foire Theatres was a thorn in the side of the Premiers Gentilhommes of the king's private household who in 1760 commissioned the administrator of the Comédie-Italienne, Denis Pierre Jean Papillon de la Ferté, to put an end to its disastrous performance, as debts had mounted to more than 700,000 *livres*. De la Ferté's solution was brutal. He ordered the Foire Theatres to hand over their repertory to the Comédie-Italienne and to discharge their personnel with the exception of five singers who would transfer to the Comédie. Shareholders in the Foire Theatres were to be indemnified but, crucially, the Comédie-Italienne would be forbidden to mount sung plays on Tuesdays and Fridays, performance-days of the Académie. In one stroke the unruly Foire Theatres were brought under control of a royal theatre and the privileges of the Académie confirmed.[41] The merger with the Comédie-Italienne was to the advantage of the audience to the extent that it could now enjoy three shows on a performance night, instead of the double-bills that were previously the norm. The Italian actors and actresses of the troupe hoped to receive a major boost to their repertory with the arrival of Goldoni in Paris in August of the same year (1762) although he proved less successful with his new plays and libretti in Paris than in Italy. For a fee of 30,000 *livres* per year

41 See Fabiano, *Histoire de l'opéra italien en France*, pp. 45–69.

paid to the Académie, the Théâtre Italien was now also officially granted the privilege to stage operas. This sum represented around 15 per cent of the Théâtre's gross annual income. The enlargement in size, depth and theatrical means of its productions in the following years was a direct consequence of these institutional changes.

In the year of the theatres' merger Monsigny, who came from noble background such that his name never appeared on his printed scores, continued his partnership with Sedaine in *Le Roi et le fermier* (The King and the Farmer). Although Sedaine called his libretto a 'comédie mélée des morceaux de musique', its humour was of a daring kind. It concerns the story of a king, who is rescued by a farmer after he had lost his way on a hunt, and disguising his identity hears from him candidly about the corruption at court. Just a little earlier the audience had witnessed the report from the farmer's beloved Jenny that she had escaped a courtier's clutches at the expense of abandoning her only piece of dowry: a flock of sheep. Sedaine built up the audience's empathy with the oppressed couple by melodramatically intensifying their expression of fear through the simultaneous outbreak of a storm. Such a coincidence of turmoil in outer and inner nature required an intensification of musical expressivity when compared with operas in the commedia dell'arte tradition and their popular songs. The lovers' pathos of expression was temporarily lightened in the original idea of a spoken dialogue between a king on stage and his critical subject. A later scene, in which the farmer's mother gives her illustrious guest a square meal, derives audience interest less from the plain music than from the novel effect of a humble king on stage. Still, Sedaine had to minimize his more outspoken English model, in which the young woman had consented to her 'own Undoing' by the courtier, erroneously believing that her lover had himself been unfaithful.[42] In both versions she pleads with the king who restores the moral and social order. The ensemble-scene of recognition by his subjects was to prove a model for later operas, such as Beethoven's *Fidelio*, Wagner's *Lohengrin*, or Verdi's *Rigoletto*, without the composers necessarily knowing Monsigny's work. Sedaine's preface to one of his librettos makes the point that in spoken drama the protagonists' divergent feelings – the courtiers' flattery, the king's inquisitiveness, Richard's fears for his outspokenness, the mother's, the daughter's and the guard's surprise – would have been expressed by the protagonists in succession and 'in order to render them plainly and with dignity as well as in good grace would have weakened the mood. Music, which allows them to speak simultaneously, asserts the right to make the picture [of

42 Robert Dodsley, *The King and the Miller of Mansfield* (London, 1737), p. 17. See Michel Noiray, 'Quatre rois à la chasse: Dodsley, Collé, Sedaine, Goldoni', in David Charlton and Mark Ledbury (eds.), *Michel-Jean Sedaine (1719–1797): Theatre, Opera and Art* (Aldershot, 2000), pp. 97–118

emotions] motionless and to keep it longer under the eyes.'[43] The creation of such a 'tableau', in which the action gives way to a 'contemplative ensemble' distinguishes opera as the theatre of emotion. However, most ensembles in *Le Roi et le fermier* proved controversial in the contemporary press because the increase in dramatic verisimilitude, especially in *duos dialogués*, came at the expense of the contrapuntal writing employed and the fear of the imperfect rendering of the ensembles.[44] Goldoni, whose facility in writing librettos for intermezzi and opere buffe had come to be admired all over Europe, praised Monsigny's music for its expressiveness and harmoniousness, while admitting a sense of defeat in competition with Sedaine and other French librettists.[45]

Philidor's and his librettist Antoine Poinsinet's *Tom Jones* (1765) represents a further attempt at the Comédie-Italienne to look for inspiration no longer exclusively in Italian theatre, as had been the case with the intermezzi, and instead to appropriate the vogue for sensibility in English literature or exploit the French literary tradition, such as Jean de La Fontaine's *Fables*. Only successful after some revisions by Sedaine and the composer, Fielding's complex novel was reduced to the casting of the wedding plan for Mr Western's daughter Sophie with Mr Alworthy's nephew Blifil, which sends Sophie into despair (Act 1), the confession of love between her and foundling Tom Jones, for which he is thrown out of Western's house (Act 2), and the reconciliation between all parties at the Upton Inn, after Tom is revealed as Blifil's blood brother (Act 3). *Tom Jones* shares with Goldoni's original Parma libretto of *La buona figliuola* (1756), set by Piccinni in 1760, not only its origins in an English novel – *La buona figliuola* was adapted for the theatre by Goldoni from Richardson's *Pamela, or Virtue Rewarded* (1740) – but also its fashionable subject: in Paris where, during the last quarter of the eighteenth century every third baptized child had been abandoned, seeing those outcasts' social aspirations fulfilled without moral compromises must have represented the audience's own dreams coming true. Removing a social obstacle to marriage represents one of the ways in which the genre of opéra-comique as well as contemporary opera buffa acted out their master-plot of match-making.[46]

43 Michel Sedaine, 'L'Auteur au lecteur', *Rose et Colas* (Paris, 1764), pp. vi–vii, in Charlton and Ledbury (eds.), *Michel-Jean Sedaine*, p. 246.
44 See Cook, *Duet and Ensemble*, pp. 271–5.
45 Carlo Goldoni, *Mémoires pour servir à l'histoire de sa vie et à celle de son théâtre*, ed. Norbert Jonard (Paris, 1992), p. 496.
46 In a comparative study of 150 opéras-comiques composed between 1757 and 1789, and opere buffe composed between 1746 and 1792, 89 per cent and 95 per cent, respectively, dramatize the removal of some problem before marriage; see Ruth Müller-Lindenberg, *Weinen und Lachen. Dramaturgie und musikalisches Idiom der Opéra-comique im Vergleich zur Opera buffa (1750–1790)* (Münster, 2006), 2 vols., vol. 1, pp. 27 and 46.

Philidor's sound is more distinctive than Duni's on every level. He adopted, for example, the rocket-effect from the Mannheim symphonists in the overture and, as Daniel Heartz has pointed out, employed a tonal plan in the first four numbers of *Tom Jones*. They are all in B-flat or F and make ample use of oboes, horns and bassoons in dialogue with the strings, culminating in an air sung by the pompous Mr Western, 'D'un cerf dix cors'. This through-composed, multi-sectional aria (Maestoso, Allegretto, Andantino, Allegro assai and Allegro) amounts to a dramatic scene created in Western's own fertile imagination recalling his glorious pursuit of a stag. It is pervaded by hunting *topoi* and, in particular, the exchange of horns in F with horns in D marks the pack of dogs closing in on the stag in Western's account. Philidor's persistence in composing in keys directly related to F makes the change to D all the more striking.[47] Although eight out of the thirteen arias overall are in da capo form, tempo changes in some of the middle sections enhanced their dramatic pace. Four 'duos dialogués' directly translated the conflict between the protagonists. A multi-sectional septet closed the second act, though the ensemble merely presented a frozen picture of its emotions. Preceding the dramatic resolution in spoken dialogue, the musical climax was reached in Sophie's outbreak of despair and longing for Jones at the Inn. In her 'chant entrecoupé' in a *recitative accompagnée* ('Respirons un moment', Act 3, scene 3), the uneven instrumentation combined with an unusual degree of chromaticism and the following aria's through-composed form echoes some of Diderot's recommendations for the setting of emotive scenes.[48] Yet, in the manner of a Shakespearean comedy, this scene of high drama had followed a typical pub scene with brutish drunkards. In similar fashion, its spell was derided immediately afterwards, when a group of actors rehearse the abduction of a cross-dresser. These comic interludes can be understood as a remnant of the genre's tradition – one that has taken on more substantial plots with more conflicting voices.

In *Le Deserteur* (1769), Monsigny and Sedaine strove for a more exciting kind of music theatre, designated as drame. The audience's delayed appreciation confirms a pattern that applies to all of the most successful French operas in the period under investigation. *Le Deserteur* enjoyed 250 performances in Paris and became, like many other opéras-comiques, a European success. As in *Le Roi et le fermier* Sedaine's plot originates in the misdemeanour of a member of the nobility who was overcome by a benevolent king, but in *Le Deserteur*, in contrast to the earlier libretto, only members of the third estate appear on stage, creating the fiction of being in charge of their own destiny, although

47 See Heartz, *Music in European Capitals*, p. 756f.

48 Denis Diderot, 'Entretiens sur "Le fils naturel"', *Œuvres esthétiques*, ed. Paul Vernière (Paris, 1965), pp. 101–2.

only the king's benevolence avoids the misfortune: a cruel duchess dupes a peasant family into staging a wedding ceremony with a simulated groom in order to 'test' the real groom's faith. He is a soldier returning home on a visit and, seeing the ceremony, deserts but soon finds himself in prison. Eventually, he escapes capital punishment only because his remorseful bride begs the king for mercy.

Sedaine and Monsigny constructed *Le Deserteur* around a series of dramatic and musical contrasts with the aim of heightening audience expectations. As funny and sad scenes followed in quick succession, the audience was never allowed to settle into one mood. In Act 1, for example, the heroine Louise worries about the prank to be played on her lover (scene 1); a carefree shepherdess muses about her lost 'spindle' and attests his sweetheart to do 'everything with his knife' (scene 3); the homeward-bound Alexis looks forward to being reunited with his betrothed but is upset by the sight of a wedding procession in the distance (scenes 4 and 5); the frivolous shepherdess enlightens him about his bride's U-turn (scene 6); he vents his disbelief in an accompanied recitative that is likewise a model of the 'chant entrecoupé' advocated by Rousseau and Diderot with changing tempi and dynamics and instrumental solos in the orchestra (scene 7); and in the multi-section finale the looming conflict begins to engulf the public as soldiers chase the fugitive Alexis.

The two other acts follow a similar scheme at a heightened dramatic pace. Sedaine's resourcefulness in creating dramatic intensity within the unchanging surroundings of a prison cell involves recurring references to time, especially the time running out before Alexis' execution. All the more shocking was the distraught Louise's dishevelled appearance brandishing the king's letter of mercy in her hand but fainting before she could communicate its content. Monsigny, too, appropriated a wider variety of expression by contrasting scenes of high pathos with drinking songs, such as a scene in which two drunkards first intone a stanza in two different melodies before singing it in contrapuntal fashion, a technique copied later in Cherubini's *Lodoïska* (1791). Monsigny also used off-stage drum-rolls to announce Alexis' execution but continues with a final chorus (instead of a vaudeville) celebrating the king's clemency in a tune already heard at the close of the overture.

Monsigny's presentation of impassioned human action in *Le Deserteur* contrasts with the stately display and fabulous dénouement of an earlier stage work he had written for the Académie, confirming the differences in the aesthetic experience associated with the Académie and the Opéra-Comique in the mid-1760s. In 1766, Monsigny took the decisive step with his ballet-héroïque *Aline, reine de Golconde* to inherit the deceased Rameau's position at the Académie and to exploit his success with *Les Indes galantes* (1735) in the genre of exotic opera.

His commission for *Aline, reine de Golconde* shows that the Académie hoped to build on the career of a composer who had begun at the Opéra-Comique. It was part of the Académie's programme after a fire in 1762 had prevented it commissioning new works for two to three years. However, it turned out to be Monsigny's only successful attempt to infiltrate France's most prestigious musical institution. His librettist, Sedaine, had rewritten the plot from Stanislas-Jean de Bouffler's enormously successful *conte* of the same name from 1761, thereby proving to be as helpful in the design of a ballet-héroïque as he had been to Philidor's *Tom Jones*. In Bouffler's plot, a noble teenage boy seduces the shepherdess Aline between meadows and pastures. The pregnant girl is thrown out of her home by her parents and soon turns into a Parisian courtesan. Subsequently her elderly marquis-husband is killed in a duel, and after some further vicissitudes she becomes enslaved to an Indian merchant, is married to the king of Golconde, only to be miraculously reunited with the first lover of her youth. Sedaine, by contrast, purified Aline of her libertine youth as well as its unwanted consequences focussing instead on the events in Golconde, which between the thirteenth and seventeenth century was a kingdom in south-east India with a lively diamond industry where France had a trading station. From the start Aline appears as the queen of Golconde, while her erstwhile lover, unsuspecting her fate, is introduced as the general of a French army-unit on a mission to protect her exotic kingdom. As Aline, she re-stages the pastoral scene of their youthful encounter in her royal park and reveals herself, but, subsequently, as the veiled queen of Golconde offers herself in marriage to him in order to test his resolve. Yet he would rather wed the shepherdess; her identity as the queen is then disclosed. Grimm reprinted Bouffler's *conte* in his *Correspondance littéraire* at the time of the premiere of the ballet-héroïque and, thus, made Sedaine's idealization of the characters' constancy of sentiment all the more transparent.[49]

In accordance with the Académie's needs, Monsigny wrote for *Aline* a massive score of some 320 pages, twice as bulky as *Tom Jones*. It is built up from innumerable small units to enable a constant change between simple recitative, *récitatif obligé* and expressive arias and, in particular, the display of royal pomp in choruses and many, many dances. They overshadow the main plot, which is devoid of conflict. The score, with few exceptions, also lacks references to its exotic setting and its successful run of forty-five performances must primarily have been due to its visual effects.

If in this ballet-héroïque Monsigny and Sedaine sought to give pleasure to his audience and to respond to criticism of the genre's traditionally disparate

49 See Stanislas de Boufflers, *Contes*, ed. Alex Sokalski (Paris, 1995), pp. 132ff.

plots by clinging to the thread of one continuous action,[50] Philidor's *Ernelinde, princesse de Norvège* (1767; revised 1769, 1773, 1777) to a libretto by Poinsinet aimed to absorb the audience's emotions through a brutal drama in a pre-Christian setting. Although *Ernelinde* was performed just over a year after *Aline, reine de Golconde* at the Académie, it represents a major shift not only in dramatic structure but also in the audience attitude that would be required to appreciate it. The number and scale of the revisions for *Ernelinde*, yet again carried out by Sedaine, mirror the distance to be covered before the success of this tragédie lyrique was eventually secured. These measures included scrapping the divertissements, tightening the recitatives, and turning metaphorical diction into direct diction while also making their settings metrically regular. A number of commentators have seen Philidor's and Sedaine's work as a first realization of Diderot's ideas for the reform of French serious opera, which he may well have developed in conversation with Rousseau and which he first published in 1757. Based on the assumption that the process of civilization has weakened people's poetic customs, Diderot stated that 'poetry requires something out of the ordinary, barbaric and wild'. Although he did not provide any proposals for a compositional technique to fulfil such a request, he made some suggestions about the singer's delivery: 'If the singer would confine himself at the cadence to only imitate the inarticulate tone of passion in airs bound up with feeling, or the main objects of nature in airs bound up with description, and if the poet realised that his ariette forms the conclusion of the scene, then the reform would be well advanced.'[51]

Considering the genre's history, Philidor might have taken Diderot's suggestion to heart to furnish his protagonist with music that could render an 'inarticulate tone of passion'. The plot did help: a Norwegian king is conquered by a Swedish king who is helped by a Danish prince. They are both in love with the Norwegian king's daughter Ernelinde, but she loves only the Danish leader. A series of broken loyalties ensues, culminating in the Swedish king's demand that she chooses between the death of her father or her lover. This gives rise to the musical climax of the opera, Ernelinde's accompanied

50 For Heartz 'the word "plaire" alone would be our choice to sum up the age, if faced with so drastic a choice', *Music in European Capitals*, p. 705. Rousseau wished to ban dances from opera as they 'interrupt the action' and 'weaken the interest' of the audience, unless they are placed at the end of the performance; see Rousseau, 'Opéra', *Dictionnaire de musique*, *OC*, vol. 5, p. 961.

51 Denis Diderot, 'De la poésie dramatique', *Œuvres esthétiques*, ed. Paul Vernière (Paris, 1965), pp. 74ff. and 260ff; 'Entretiens sur "Le fils naturel"', *ibid.*, p. 162: 'Si le chanteur s'assujettissait à n'imiter, à la cadence, que l'accent inarticulé de la passion dans les airs de sentiment, ou que les principaux phénomènes de la nature, dans les airs qui font tableau, et que le poète sût que son ariette doit être la péroraison de sa scène, la réforme serait bien avancée.' Manuel Couvreur points out that the starting point for Diderot's aesthetics of opera was French classical drama; see Manuel Couvreur, 'Diderot et Philidor: Le philosophe au chevet d'*Ernelinde*', *Recherches sur Diderot et sur l'Encyclopédie*, 11 (1991), p. 98.

recitative and aria 'Ou suis je? Quel épais nuage'. The recitative has chromatic orchestral figures, abrupt changes of tempo and keys with the vocal and orchestral phrases commenting on each other, while in the aria the vocal line remains to considerable extent independent from the orchestral accompaniment, a common feature of serious French opera later in the century by which a protagonist's expressivity was significantly heightened.[52]

Although they lived until 1795 and 1817, respectively, neither Philidor nor Monsigny achieved similar success with their works in the 1770s or 1780s. Philidor's reputation was damaged by the discovery of his perhaps unintentional plagiarism from Gluck's *Orfeo ed Euridice*, which in 1764 he had edited for a Parisian publisher. He also pursued a lifelong career at the chessboard.[53] Given the widespread practice of parody encountered earlier, it would be intriguing to find out why Philidor was accused of crossing a line in regard to what was permissible. That Monsigny virtually ended his career at the age of forty-eight with the comédie *Félix, ou l'enfant trouvé* (1777) can be attributed to his suffering from a cataract but was perhaps also due to his over-sensitivity. In his funeral eulogy Quatremère-de-Quincy reports that 'the composition of *Le Deserteur* made him weep many tears to the effect that the libretto was twice taken from him. Long after, when talking about the scene in which Louise gradually came back to her senses, thinking of her suffocated voice that is almost chopped by the orchestra, he would burst into tears and fall into the despondency that he had musically depicted.'[54] Another reason for Philidor's and Monsigny's gradual eclipse was the rise of a slightly younger rival André-Ernest-Modeste Grétry which began with *Le Huron* (1768) and continued with a string of works mostly for the Comédie-Italienne, lasting even beyond the Revolution of 1789.

Despite an early domestic accident, the nineteen-year old Grétry walked in 1760 from his birth-town Liège to Rome to take up a place at the Collège Darchis for the study of counterpoint with Giovanni Battista Casali. Through his own determination but also with some good fortune, Grétry obtained first commissions to write for the theatre in Rome in 1765 and, as he was heading back north, in Geneva in 1766, before appearing on the Parisian scene in 1767. Although he later collaborated with Sedaine, just as his rivals Monsigny and

52 François-André Danican Philidor, *Ernelinde*, ed. Julian Rushton (New York, 1991), pp. 206–21.
53 See Charles Michaël Carroll, *François-André Danican Philidor: His Life and Dramatic Art*, PhD thesis (Florida State University, 1960), pp. 190ff.
54 'Ainsi la composition du Déserteur lui coûta tant de pleurs, qu'on fut obligé deux fois de lui retirer le poëme. Long-temps encore après, en parlant de la scène où Louise revient par degrés de son évanuissement, et en se rappelant le jeu de ses paroles étouffées et comme coupées par des traits d'orchestre, on le vit fondre en larmes et tomber lui-même dans l'accablement qu'il avait depeint.' A.-C. Quatremère-de-Quincy, *Notice historique sur la vie et les ouvrages de M. de Monsigny* (Paris, 1818), p. 44f.

Philidor had done, in his early career Grétry's main provider of libretti was Jean François Marmontel, his senior by almost a generation, who since the 1750s had made his own intellectual journey from librettist for Rameau, to author of *Contes moraux*, editor of *Mercure de France* and collaborator on the *Encyclopédie*. In *Le Huron* (1768) both Marmontel and Grétry paid tribute to their hero Voltaire whose politically contentious *conte philosophique L'Ingénu* (The Innocent) was used as its source. Voltaire's title could serve for many opéras-comiques, based on the authors' agenda to show 'virtue rewarded', quoting once again the subtitle of Richardson's novel *Pamela*. In *Le Huron* the hero is an uneducated Canadian who was brought up among Huron Indians but who has recently returned to Brittany and is revealed as a relative of its community. After some turmoil and his demonstrations of courage he is allowed to marry into a French family. While *Le Huron* had only moderate success with the public, it demonstrates to the historian the growing similarity between the Académie and the Comédie-Italienne, based on the common model of Italian opera seria, and the way in which the opéra-comique appropriated the 'grand goût'. For, like Ernelinde, the heroine in *Le Huron* undergoes a time of anguish, in which she imagines the death of her lover, set by Grétry in an accompanied recitative fifty bars long using hemidemisemiquaver tremolando strings, abrupt dynamic changes and chromatic chord sequences. Her scene culminates in an aria.

Three years later, in 1771, Grétry obtained his first international success with *Zémire et Azor*, an operatic version of the myth of 'Beauty and the Beast'. It was not staged only in central Europe, but also as far afield as Moscow and Philadelphia. Set in oriental Persia, Grétry made gentle use of musical exoticism and, above all, exploited his compositional technique to evoke a family's trauma concerning their father who had been captured by Azor and had selfishly pledged his daughter in return for his own freedom. The most admired scene introduces a supernatural element to the opera, by staging in the background an event that is taking place simultaneously, far away in Zémire's family home, enabling Zémire to watch a 'magic picture' or mimed scene of her grieving family. The subsequent successes that Grétry enjoyed in the 1770s with his opéras-comiques should have enabled him also to try his luck in the genre of tragédie lyrique. Before we consider this phase of his career we need to investigate the developments at the Académie royale in the 1770s.

Homeric and other mythological tales at the Académie

On 19 April 1774 a Parisian audience witnessed the premiere of Gluck's tragédie opéra *Iphigénie en Aulide*. However, it would be misleading to think that his so-called Italian reform operas in Vienna, *Orfeo ed Euridice* (1762), *Alceste* (1767) and *Paride ed Elena* (1770) to librettos by Raniero Calzabigi, were seamlessly followed by a triumphant reception of *Iphigénie en Aulide* in Paris four years later. In fact, Gluck and many collaborative supporters had worked towards his arrival at the Académie for almost twenty years. In 1755 he had assumed the musical directorship of the Viennese court theatre (Burgtheater), which since 1752 had included a troupe of French actors and used the Genoese diplomat Giacomo Durazzo as *intendant des spectacles*. In a similar way to the arrangements and re-compositions of intermezzi by Blavet and Favart in the wake of the *Querelle des Bouffons* in Paris, Gluck adapted French operas for the Burgtheater imported through the offices of Durazzo, and between 1758 and 1764 Durazzo commissioned Gluck to compose eight opéras-comiques which successfully held the stage in competition with the new works by Monsigny and Philidor. In this way Gluck gained inside knowledge of French diction and theatrical practice and contributed to the appreciation of this new genre of opera at courts connected to the Habsburg monarchy, such as Mannheim, Stuttgart and even Brussels. Furthermore, in 1759 Durazzo enlisted Favart to report regularly to Vienna on all Parisian theatrical matters, not unlike Grimm's *Correspondance littéraire*, and to use his widespread personal contacts with singers and actors for the benefit of the Burgtheater.[55]

The collaboration with the playwright Raniero Calzabigi furnished Gluck with weighty librettos based on a new aesthetic outlook described in the preface to *Alceste* in 1769. Calzabigi's and Gluck's dramaturgical and musical ideas, namely to 'strip [opera] of all those abuses ... which have for so long disfigured Italian opera',[56] had one common goal: intellectually and emotionally to enhance the audience's interest in the story to an unprecedented extent. For this purpose da capo arias and any whiff of vocal bravura in cadenzas were banned and the middle sections of arias received greater attention. The distinction between recitatives and arias should be reduced and the orchestral accompaniment should be shaped according to the text rather than according to principles of symmetry associated with instrumental music. However, the surprising number of da capo arias in his Parisian operas shows that Gluck did not slavishly follow his own principles, although his widespread practice of borrowing music from earlier works needs to be taken into account in this respect.[57]

55 C. S. Favart, *Mémoires et correspondence littérarires, dramatiques et anecdotiques*, ed. A. P. C. Favart, 3 vols. (Paris, 1808).

56 Quoted in Patricia Howard, *Gluck: An Eighteenth-Century Portrait in Letters and Documents* (Oxford, 1995), p. 84.

57 See Klaus Hortschansky, *Parodie und Entlehnung im Schaffen Christoph Willibald Glucks* (Cologne, 1973).

The ambitious idea of bringing Gluck to Paris may have originated with François Louis Gand Leblanc du Roullet. He was connected to the French embassy in Vienna and provided Gluck with a libretto adapted from Racine's tragedy *Iphigénie* (1674). The Italian poet and writer on opera Francesco Algarotti had already published a prose libretto version of the same plot in the annex to his book on opera reform and Diderot had singled out the same story for operatic setting.[58] Both writers, and most vociferously Calzabigi, shared a rejection of the bland and flowery style of Metastasio's librettos. Homer's *Iliad* was the oldest source for the myth of Agamemnon, commander of the Greek army, being forced by an oracle and his savage soldiers to sacrifice his daughter, Iphigénie, in order to pacify the Gods and ensure prosperous winds for his fleet's departure from Aulis to the Trojan war. Diderot, to prove his point, quoted from Racine the lines in which Clitemnestra despairs in seeing her daughter led to the slaughter and commented: 'Clitemnestra is in a state that must wrest a cry of nature from her entrails. And the musician will bring it to my attention in all its nuances ... I no longer hear the mother of Iphigénie; it's the thunderbolt that is growling, it's the earth that is shaking, it's the air which echoes the terrifying noise.'[59]

To overcome French opposition to a Bohemian composer, Gluck could count on support from the highest echelons of society. The daughter of the Austrian Empress Maria Theresia and his former pupil, Marie Antoinette, had married the future king Louis XVI in 1770. Du Roullet launched the bid on Gluck's behalf in October 1772 by way of an open letter published in the *Mercure de France* and addressed to Antoine Dauvergne, celebrated composer of *Les troqueurs* during the *Querelle des Bouffons* and of a further dozen stage works in the intermittent years, as well as co-director of the Concert Spirituel, and co-director of the Académie (from 1769). Although du Roullet repeated some of the composer's aims from the *Alceste* preface, emphasized the enormous financial gains of an earlier Gluck opera in Bologna and praised him as a partisan of French music against Rousseau's calumny, the letter was to no avail.[60] Five months later Gluck sent his own letter to the *Mercure de France*, in which he expressed the hope of collaborating with Rousseau in developing a universal music and thus to 'do away with the ridiculous differentiation

58 Francesco Algarotti, *Saggio sopra l'opera in musica. Le edizioni di Venezia (1755) e di Livorno (1763)*, ed. Annalisa Bini (Rome, 1989), pp. 33–90; Diderot, 'Entretiens sur "Le fils naturel"' (1757), *Œuvres esthétiques*, ed. Paul Vernière (Paris, 1965), pp. 168–71.

59 'L'état de Clytemnestre doit arracher de ses entrailles le cri de la nature; et le musicien le portera à mes oreilles dans toutes ses nuances ... Ce n'est plus la mère d'Iphigénie que j'entends; c'est la foudre qui gronde, c'est la terre qui tremble, c'est l'air qui retentit de bruits effrayants.' Diderot, 'Entretiens sur "Le fils naturel"', pp. 168–70.

60 See Howard, *Gluck: An Eighteenth-Century Portrait*, pp. 102–5.

between national musical styles'.[61] At some point Gluck also sent the first act of *Iphigénie* to Dauvergne who agreed to a production of the opera on the condition that Gluck supply five more works. He was to write eight operas in total, of which four were revisions. After an intervention by Marie Antoinette, a contract was agreed. Gluck arrived in Paris in November 1773 and rehearsed the opera for five months.

It would be an exaggeration to describe the premiere as a triumph. Even Marie Antoinette's letter home, which has been quoted in support of this impression, provides a more nuanced picture[62] and the court's collective hand-clapping after most numbers is ridiculed in the *Mémoires secrets* as an involuntary gesture of the nobility obliged to follow the dauphine's lead.[63] If Rousseau had an overwhelming sense of the deficiencies of French music upon hearing the Italian intermezzi next to French ballets and pastorales in 1752, the sense of shock cannot have been less for an audience confronted with Gluck's opera having been accustomed to the style of Rameau and his followers for nearly forty years. The dramas of bourgeois life staged at the Comédie-Italienne did not have those 'moments of terror and pathos' that Gluck exploited with a higher degree of musical intensity. Within a short period of time Rousseau was reported to have become 'tout Gluck'.[64] With Louis XV out of the way after he had supposedly become infected with smallpox in a pleasure session and subsequently died on 10 May 1774,[65] Voltaire imagined the dawn of a new epoch for France: 'It seems to me that you Parisians are about to witness a great and peaceful revolution both in your government and in your music. Louis XVI and Gluck will found a new French nation.'[66]

After the success with *Iphigénie en Aulide* Gluck consolidated his position in Paris by adapting his first Viennese reform opera, *Orfeo ed Euridice* (1762/1774) for the Académie, as well as staging new versions of two French works he had originally written in Vienna, the opéra-comique *L'arbre enchanté* (1759/1775)

61 Quoted in *ibid.*, p. 107.

62 'M. le Dauphin was roused from his composure, and found something to applaud throughout. But at the performance, as I expected, whenever there were affecting passages, there was a general air of holding back; this new approach needs getting used to after being so accustomed to the old one.' In Paul Vogt d'Hunolstein (ed.), *Correspondance inédite de Marie-Antoinette* (Paris, 1864), pp. 48–50, quoted in Howard, *Gluck: An Eighteenth-Century Portrait*, p. 114.

63 'The Chevalier Gluck did not have as complete a success as his supporters had predicted. The greater part of the applause lavished on him could well be attributed to the audience's desire to please the dauphine. This princess seemed to have manipulated the acclaim, and would not stop clapping, which obliged the Countess de Provence, the princes, and all those in the boxes to do the same.' See *Mémoires secrets*, vol. 7, pp. 185–6 (26 April 1774), quoted in Howard, *Gluck: An Eighteenth-Century Portrait*, pp. 113ff.

64 See letter of François de Chambrier to Konrad Reinhard von Koch (6 May, 1774), in Ralph A. Leigh (ed.), *Correspondance complète de Jean Jacques Rousseau* (Oxford, 1981), vol. 39, p. 249.

65 Robert Darnton, *The Forbidden Bestsellers of Pre-Revolutionary France* (London, 1996), p. 385.

66 François-Marie Arouet de Voltaire, Letter of 28 July 1774, *Œuvres complètes*, vol. 67, pp. 352–3; quoted in Howard, *Gluck: An Eighteenth-Century Portrait*, p. 122.

and the opera-ballet *Cythère assiégée* (1759/1775). But aware of the opera-going public and of the coffers of the Académie, his re-composition of his second reform opera, *Alceste* (1767/1776), was of far greater importance, not least because of the inherent confrontation with Lully's and Quinault's tragédie of the same protagonist, entitled *Alceste, ou Le triomphe d'Alcide* (Alceste, or the triumph of Hercules) (1674). Calzabigi's and Gluck's Viennese version had been attacked by Rousseau and others for its lugubrious monotony.[67] The opera centred on Admetus being mysteriously condemned to death and, according to an oracle, only released from his fate when his wife Alceste, Queen of Pherae in Thessaly, sacrifices herself on his behalf. She fulfils her promise, but in desperation he then commits suicide. However, both are ultimately restored to life by the intervention of a *deus ex machina*. It should be noted that, as in *Orfeo*, operatic 'reform' did not extend to the exclusion of supernatural powers. The Parisian version of *Alceste* offers a far greater versatility of mood, due primarily to the re-introduction from Lully's opera of the lay-about manners of Hercules who fetches Alceste back from the underworld with his sheer strength, so that the final appearance of Apollo merely preserves a façade of divine supremacy. In the French version, Gluck aims at a greater degree of drama by generally treating the chorus as another protagonist, enhancing the main characters' expression of feeling through accompanied recitatives, as well as subverting singers' pronouncements in the orchestral commentaries, and even adding a surprising number of ballets and divertissements – surprising, because they had been considered at least by Rousseau to represent the height of boredom.[68]

Only a year later Gluck took it upon himself to challenge the inner sanctum of French operatic tradition, its ultimate *chef d'œuvre*, Lully and Quinault's *Armide* (1686). In the course of the eighteenth century it had been subjected to a number of parodies, such as Gluck's own *Cythère assiégée* to a libretto by Favart.[69] Yet Gluck's score of *Armide* (1777) was entirely based on Quinault's text (apart from the omission of his prologue), and he accepted at face value the conflation of poetic characters from medieval crusades, allegories and demons with the expressed intention of providing each with musical individuality, such as a dotted and syncopated rhythm for Armide, melodic progressions in thirds associated with the figure of Hatred and syllabic text-settings for Armide's magician uncle. Likewise at the beginning of Act 5 Armide and Renaud each adopt a melodic formula that sometimes borders on the mechanical. In view of the commotion surrounding Lully's setting of Armide's monologue during the

67 Rousseau, 'Lettre à M. Burney et Fragmens d'observations sur l'Alceste de Gluck', *OC*, vol. 5, p. 442.
68 Rousseau, *Dictionnaire de musique*, *OC*, vol. 5, pp. 648–50, 960–2.
69 Dörte Schmidt, *Armide hinter den Spiegeln: Lully, Gluck und die Möglichkeiten der dramatischen Parodie* (Stuttgart, 2001).

Querelle des Bouffons, which was surely familiar to him, Gluck not only employed a wide range of keys and orchestral figures in his version (Act 2, scene 5), but also transformed the last part of Armide's monologue into a two-tempo aria which integrates her soliloquy into the drama.

Ever since Marie-Antoinette's partisanship for Gluck at the premiere of *Iphigénie en Aulide* and even more so after the premiere of his *Alceste* and *Armide*, the French audiences had divided into admirers and detractors. 'At this point [the premiere of *Iphigénie en Aulide*] Mme. Du Barry, who was hardly the Dauphine's friend, was persuaded by her entourage (including Marmontel and the Neapolitan ambassador, Caraccioli) to find a rival or imitator of Gluck in the person of Piccinni. This was therefore a rather political affair which was to encourage competition between Germany and Italy.'[70] Piccinni arrived in Paris at the end of 1776 but, in contrast to Gluck, who had almost twenty years of preparation for his trip, Piccinni had never been abroad and, crucially, had no French. Marmontel not only coached Piccinni in the language, but also adapted a total of five librettos for him to set, beginning with *Roland* (1778) and *Atys* (1780) after Quinault. Through these choices Piccinni moved into the position of inheritor to the French operatic tradition as personified in Lully and in direct competition with Gluck, especially his *Armide*. With its twenty extended arias in varied ABA forms and even occasionally long coloraturas *Roland* has often been considered to closely follow opera seria conventions. There is a dramaturgical problem in the coquettish Angelique's ability to make herself magically invisible in front of her stern suitor Roland who nevertheless proceeds with his mighty aria. The inward problem of the protagonist remains musically unexplored until Act 3 by virtue mainly of the fixed musical forms that Piccinni could not easily abandon. Even Roland's tryst with Angelique in a forest cave, where he, however, has to learn of her elopement with Medor, is set as a multi-sectional scene but ends in an aria to represent Roland's fury, though Piccinni's fury was more civilized than the relatively raw emotion musically realized by Gluck. *Atys* shares with *Roland* the topic of an over-emotional hero. His suicide was substituted by a happy ending in a revival of the opera in 1783. To render Atys' state of emotions Piccinni employs two specific traits: startling dynamic contrasts and striking textures. For example, the Andantino section of the overture begins with a semibreve chord in the strings with crescendo marking and is joined halfway by the winds in *forte* but equally to be played crescendo. This is contrasted in bar 2 by a repeated sighing figure to be played *piano* and *smorzando*. More than *Roland*, *Atys* also has various far-reaching harmonic sequences touching unconventional keys, and Piccinni

70 François Lesure (ed.), 'Introduction', *Querelle des Gluckistes et des Piccinnistes* (Geneva, 1984), vol. 1, n.p.

appropriated some typically 'French' features, such as a dream sequence of song, chorus and dance.

On the performance of Piccinni's *Didon* (1783) Grimm's *Correspondance littéraire* reported: 'Never has anything been reported with such enthusiasm. The fanatic followers of Gluck, these unjust and demoralizing enemies of his rival's talent are the greatest partisans of *Didon* claiming that Piccinni has become a Gluckist.'[71] This view is not altogether surprising, as the triangular affair between the irascible Numidian King Iarbas in pursuit of Dido's bed and Carthagian empire and her new lover, Aeneas, is rendered in vivid accompanied recitatives continually alternating with arias and ensembles of different sizes. Even in the duet between the two testosterone-charged men, though, which effectively concludes the first act, a symmetrical periodicity is preserved in the orchestral accompaniment. Supported by the congenial lead singer Mme De Saint-Huberty, Piccinni found a far more declamatory melodic line than customary in contemporary opera seria.

His librettist, Marmontel, also became the chief ideologist of a group known as the 'Piccinnistes'. In his central 'Essai sur les révolutions de la musique en France', Marmontel rejected a primarily emotive reaction to opera, as such an effect could easily be encountered when hearing the suffering of ordinary people but ultimately would lack beauty. He also reproached Gluck for, among other things, his 'bold and rugged harmony' and the 'broken and incoherent modulations' in his arias.[72] Marmontel advocated instead a compositional technique that he found in Piccinni and like-minded Italian composers: 'The musical phrase and melodious song that is well shaped and refined, describing its circle with grace, finally a tune once it is known, will everywhere and always create delight in the ear ... The Italians say, and one must believe them: greatness in music lies in song, and melody is its soul.'[73] The 'chant périodique' in the manner of Marmontel's own loose description became the war cry of the Piccinnistes, while Gluckistes fully indulged in the emotional experience that this 'prosateur en musique' had to offer: 'Meanwhile the opera [*Alceste*] began ... Every piece hit me longer and moved me more deeply. Yet

71 'jamais rien n'a été applaudi avec tant de transports. Les zélateurs de Gluck, ces ennemis si injustes et si décourageants du talent de son rival, sont les plus grands partisans de *Didon* et prétendent que Piccinni s'est fait Gluckiste.' Grimm, *Correspondance littéraire*, vol. 13, p. 410–15; quoted in Elisabeth Schmierer, *Die Tragédies lyriques Niccolò Piccinnis* (Laaber, 1999), p. 287.

72 Jean-François Marmontel, 'Essai sur les révolutions de la musique en France' (1777), in Lesure (ed.), *Querelle des Gluckistes et des Piccinnistes*, vol. 1, pp. 167 and 179.

73 'La période musicale, le chant mélodieux, dessiné, arrondi, décrivant son cercle avec grace, l'air enfin une fois connu, fera par-tout et dans tous les tems les délices de l'oreille ... Les Italiens le disent et l'on doit les en croire: l'excellence de la musique est dans le chant, et la mélodie en est l'ame.' Jean-François Marmontel, 'Opéra', in Denis Diderot *et al.* (eds.), *Encyclopédie, ou dictionnaire raisonné des sciences, des arts et des métiers, par une société de gens de lettres* (Paris and Neuchâtel, 1751–80), 35 vols.; *Supplément* (Amsterdam, 1777), vol. 4, p. 158.

the third performance truly was the unravelling of the chaos. It created a complete revolution in me. I saw everything at its place. I had the sweetest and most vivid feelings one by one. My neighbours were not quiet anymore. And the same happened to a large number of people in the audience. The Abbé … congratulated himself on seeing our thrill and tears.'[74]

When the triumph of his *Iphigénie en Tauride* (1779) could not prevent the failure of his drame lyrique *Echo et Narcisse* (1780), Gluck decided to depart Paris for ever. In the long run, *Iphigénie en Tauride* became Gluck's most famous Parisian work, unhindered by the fact that Piccinni had his own version of the plot performed in 1781, which suffered nonetheless from an unclear characterization of protagonists in spite of the composer's persistent search for effective orchestral devices.[75] Gluck left behind him not only the pamphleteers but also his first historian: Leblond took Marmontel's description of French operatic changes or 'revolutions' in the plural, and made it into a singular event achieved by one man – Gluck's musical revolution.[76] This grammatical change represents in musical parlance the advance from the astronomical to the political usage of the term 'revolution' mentioned at the beginning of the chapter. Leblond's title did not do justice to Piccinni but also, with hindsight, did not do justice to the successors of both composers in serious opera of the 1780s, namely Antonio Salieri in *Les Danaïdes* (1784), *Les Horaces* (1786), *Tarare* (1787) and Johann Christoph Vogel in *La toison d'or* (1786), *Démophon* (1789), as well as Antonio Sacchini in *Renaud* (1783), *Chimène* (1783), *Dardanus* (1784), *Oedipe à Colone* (1786), *Arvire et Eveline* (1788), and Jean-Baptiste Lemoyne in *Electre* (1782) and *Phèdre* (1786), though all had to contend with the continued presence of Gluck's and Piccinni's works in the Académie's repertory.[77] During the same period (1780–5) Marie-Antoinette participated in a number of performances of rustic opéras-comiques at the Trianon palace of Versailles, such as Monsigny's *Le Roi et le fermier*, discussed earlier. It is worth remembering that Rousseau's *Le devin du village*, likewise, had had its premiere

74 'Cependant l'Opéra commença; … Chaque chose me frappa davantage, et m'émut plus vivement; mais la troisième répresentation fut véritablement le débrouillement du chaos. Il se fit en moi une entière révolution. Je vis chaque chose à sa place: j'éprouvai successivement les émotions les plus douces et les plus véhémentes. Mes voisins n'étoient pas plus tranquilles. Il en étoit de même du plus grand nombre de spectateurs. L'Abbé qui nous regardoit de temps en temps, s'applaudissoit en voyant nos transports et les larmes qui couloient de nos yeux.' Anon., 'Le Souper des enthusiastes', in Lesure (ed.), *Querelle des Gluckistes et des Piccinnistes*, vol. 1, p. 69.

75 Julian Rushton, 'Iphigénie en Tauride: The Operas of Gluck and Piccinni', *Music and Letters*, 53 (1972), pp. 411–30; Elisabeth Schmierer, *Die Tragédies-lyriques Niccolò Piccinnis* (Laaber, 1999), pp. 178–220.

76 Abbé Gaspard Michel Leblond, *Mémoires pour servir à l'histoire de la révolution opérée dans la musique par M. le chevalier Gluck* (Naples, 1781), in Lesure (ed.), *Querelle des Gluckistes et des Piccinnistes*, vol. 1.

77 See Michel Noiray, 'The Pre-Revolutionary Origins of "Terrorisme musical"', in Melania Bucciarelli and Berta Joncus (eds.), *Music as Social and Cultural Practice: Essays in Honour of Reinhard Strohm* (Woodbridge and Rochester, NY, 2007), pp. 294–311.

at court. While the Académie put on stage plots in which absolute rulers were challenged or even reduced to pity, the operas at court, which queried behaviour of the nobility, 'represented some sort of wish to make these urgent social issues unreal, to tame them by having them absorbed into their own frivolous way of life'.[78]

In the roughhouse

On 14 July 1789 about 2,000 Parisians stormed the Bastille, an event that encapsulated our understanding of the French Revolution. There is no similarly revolutionary act in a musical score written or performed in that year, but a power-shift surrounding the foundation of a music theatre was significant. On the surface, the establishment of the Théâtre de Monsieur merely institutionalized a long-lasting French appetite for Italian opera that had been on display ever since the *Querelle des Bouffons*. It had been re-kindled by a season of opere buffe at the Académie (1778–80) under the artistic directorship of Piccinni and by a summer season at Versailles in 1787 where, on Marie Antoinette's invitation, a troupe of Italian singers from the Haymarket Theatre in London performed operas by Paisiello, Cimarosa and Sarti-Mengozzi.[79] But despite the concomitant calls in the contemporary press for Italian opera's fixed presence in Paris, the foundation of the Théâtre de Monsieur itself was a revolutionary act in legal and in financial terms. This theatre took its name from the king's brother, the comte de Provence (the Monsieur) and later Louis XVIII and, fittingly, it performed first in the Palais des Tuileries. In this way the royals themselves fetched the wood for the pyre on which their own system of privileges soon went up in smoke. As explained earlier, only the Académie royale de musique had been granted the privilege to stage theatrical performances with continuous musical accompaniment. Other theatres with similar ambitions had to pay a fee to the Académie and trespassers could be severely punished. Yet a royal institution was, of course, above the jurisdiction of the Académie. Moreover, two men of Marie Antoinette's inner court, her hairdresser Léonard-Alexis Autié and her chamber-musician Giovanni Battista Viotti, acted as administrators and co-owners in this 'enterprise'.[80] A financial enterprise it surely was, for the backing did not come from the court, let alone from the 'co-owners', but entirely from a group of

78 Walter Rex, *The Attraction of the Contrary: Essays on the Literature of the French Enlightenment* (Cambridge, 1987), p. 165.
79 See Fabiano, *Histoire de l'opéra italien en France*, pp. 71–87, 105–15.
80 Alessandro Di Profio, *La Révolution des Bouffons: L'opéra italien au Théâtre de Monsieur 1789–1792* (Paris, 2003), pp. 41–97.

anonymous 'speculators'. In the process they daringly bid also to take over the Académie, for which they offered the tidy sum of 3 million in bonds, with Viotti's final aim being to bring the entire system of privileges in France under his control. Although his bid failed and although the Académie initially received a license fee of 30,000 *livres*, the foundation of the Théâtre de Monsieur represents a decline in royal power and financial control. The plans of ruthless entrepreneurs coincided with the interest of the general musical public and the wishes of the royal household who were dissatisfied with the repertories of the two opera houses already in existence.

The operations of the Théâtre de Monsieur were no less unusual. Until its forced closure during the massacre of royalists in September 1792, the mostly Italian troupe staged thirty-four Italian operas that had already been successfully performed at an Italian theatre on the Continent and thus carried little risk. This was in complete contrast to the custom of constantly performing new works, usually associated with Italian stagione-opera. Moreover, their topics had often become familiar to the audience in similar versions, sometimes in French; they were consequently prepared to put up with performances in Italian. The Théâtre de Monsieur set up a 'confrontation' between competing houses by performing on Tuesdays and Fridays, days that the Académie had enjoyed exclusively in the past.[81] It also attempted to avoid paying the recently granted 'droits d'auteur' by translating a French opera into Italian and substituting existing music with an Italian pasticcio. Such strategies were resented by the other troupes, for the law of the freedom of theatre in 1790, which allowed anyone to open a theatre, had made competition far more intense. The Théâtre de Monsieur hired the poet Antonio Andrei and the composer Luigi Cherubini to adjust the Italian operas for Parisian taste by removing dialect passages, shortening dialogues and elevating the tone of the arias. For an annual income of 4,000 *livres* (half a top French and a quarter of a top Italian singer's salary), Cherubini composed about fifty new arias; if an aria was considered insufficient, however, unrelated music from a different opera and composer was used as a replacement.[82]

Although a foreigner until 1794, Cherubini became embroiled in the revolutionary process in a number of ways. His first independent opera for the Théâtre de Monsieur, *Marguerite d'Anjou* (1790), had to be shelved after Act 1 because of its monarchical sympathies. His second, *Lodoïska* (1791), became an international success generating a 'revolution in French music and instigating the powerful music [*musique d'effet*] which all composers have imitated to some

81 Fabiano, *Histoire de l'opéra italien en France*, pp. 129–33.
82 See the statistics in Di Profio, *La Révolution des Bouffons*, pp. 60ff., 437–85.

extent'.[83] *Lodoïska* also contains the clearest example of Cherubini applying developmental techniques to opera that were familiar especially from Haydn's symphonies and that certainly provided a counterfoil to the relatively free declamatory style of writing for the voice.[84] A year later, all his Italian colleagues, including his house-mate Viotti, fled the country. His third Parisian opera, the anti-royalist *Koukourgi* (1793), remained unperformed for unknown reasons, while he spent most of the year in hiding. His fourth opera, *Le congrès des rois* (1794) was written in collaboration with Méhul among others and was not considered worth mentioning later in the composer's catalogue. *Eliza, ou Le voyage au glaciers du mont St Bernard* (1794), his fifth, required a completely new ending before it reached the stage. From 1794 onwards he composed hymns for revolutionary festivities and after 1795 became one of the four inspectors of the newly founded Conservatoire. He may already have received the libretto to his sixth opera, *Médée*, by 1790 and definitely by 1793, but it was premiered only in 1797. In 1798–9 he composed three comic operas with varied success for different stages, as his contractual obligations with the Théâtre Feydeau (as the Théâtre de Monsieur became in 1791) came to an end and its proprietor, Sageret, filed for bankruptcy. Still, at the same theatre he premiered his tenth, *Les Deux Journées*, which was to be performed all over Europe throughout the nineteenth century.

In age and musical technique Cherubini was closest to Étienne-Nicolas Méhul. Méhul occupied a position at the Comédie-Italienne (from 1793, the Opéra-Comique) that was similar in importance to Cherubini's at the Théâtre de Monsieur. Méhul triumphed first with *Euphrosine, ou Le tyran corrigé* (1790), but his *Cora* (1791) disappointed and his *Adrien, empereur de Rome* (1792) was banned by the Paris commune; an almost entirely new version was likewise banned after two performances in 1799. Cherubini considered the comédie-héroïque *Stratonice* (1792) Méhul's best work. Yet Méhul's harmonically most advanced score, the experimental *Mélidore et Phrosine* (1794), later came under harsh attack from Cherubini. In 1795, like Cherubini, he was made an inspector of the Conservatoire, though he contributed little to the establishment of a curriculum of textbooks. After 1797 Méhul participated in the vogue for a lighter fashion in opera with his *Epicure* (1800), in collaboration with Cherubini, and above all with *L'Irato* (1801) dedicated to Napoleon. He ordered the merger of the Théâtre Feydeau and the Opéra-Comique in 1801, but neither composer could maintain the position in Parisian opera that they had enjoyed in the previous decade.

83 François Fétis, *Biographie universelle des musicians* (Paris, 1860–5), 8 vols., vol. 2, p. 266.
84 Carl Dahlhaus (ed.), *Die Musik des 18. Jahrhunderts* (Laaber, 1985), pp. 351–4.

Despite occasional official patronage, this decline is most conspicuous in the career of Jean François LeSueur. From a provincial background and evidently headstrong, he came to Paris in 1786 as director of Notre Dame but had already left a year later, because his church music was decried as essentially theatrical. LeSueur created a stir with the relentless dissonances, harsh melodies and ostinato orchestral motives of his *La Caverne*, performed at the Théâtre Feydeau in 1793 at the height of the *terreur*. He succeeded in bringing together serious drama with ariettes in opéra-comique tradition. Subsequent operas at the same theatre, namely *Paul et Virginie* (1794) and *Télémaque* (1796), were no less effective, in part on account of the ample stage and singing directions he incorporated into his scores. Still, they did not enjoy a great reputation and his career as inspector at the Conservatoire ended in a quarrel with its director Bernard Sarrette in 1802. An intriguing figure, LeSueur became one of Napoleon's main protégés.

The dramatic style of opera, which focused on plots full of pathos, a declamatory vocal melody contending with an increasingly 'noisy' orchestra, ostinato motives and dissonant harmonies, was abandoned by virtually all composers working in France after 1797. A reviewer of Cherubini's *Médée* (1797) brought audiences' growing wariness to a head by complaining that the composer was guilty of *terrorisme musical*.[85] '[Speaking] of *terrorisme*, in allusion to the Terror of 1793–4, was … a way of associating [the librettist] Hoffman and Cherubini's opera with a historical phase which French society was struggling to eliminate from its collective psyche.'[86] This rupture in operatic writing indicates the extent to which composers were dependent on audiences and critics, but it may also have been a result of their own thought processes. Grétry markedly reduced his productivity after 1790, as he was out of step with revolutionary fervour, and transferred his activities to the analyses of his own works as well as to the development of a poetics of opera whose chief plea was for a return to simplicity. The extraordinary success of Dominique Della Maria's *Le prisonnier* (1798), which parodied the heavy-going genre of 'rescue-opera', and *L'opéra comique* (1798), where a love story is dressed up as preparation for an opera performance, motivated Cherubini, Méhul and many others to follow. Della Maria's recipe was funny plots featuring a string-based orchestra with violins shadowing the singers' vocal line, almost in the manner of Pergolesi and certainly with similar verve. Viewed from up close it could have appeared that theoretical and compositional toils in Paris between the *Querelle des*

85 See David Charlton, 'Cherubini: A Critical Anthology, 1788–1801', *Royal Musical Association Research Chronicle*, 26 (1993), p. 116.
86 Noiray, 'The Pre-Revolutionary Origins of "Terrorisme musical"', p. 295.

Bouffons and the merger of the Opéra-Comique and the Théâtre Feydeau in 1801 had all gone up in smoke.

By way of conclusion, several points come to light:

1. In the French system, opera was conditioned by the fact that its institutions were run by the state.
2. The creation of opera in both genres was consistently experimental, in part thanks to a lively debate in journals and pamphlets.
3. The debates were led by men of letters (Rousseau, Diderot, Sedaine and many others) who were often involved in spoken theatre.
4. Authors' obsession with the integration of music into the action should be seen as part of the goal to make opera an emotionally absorbing experience for the musicians as well as the audience. In pursuit of this goal, composers developed techniques that allowed orchestral gestures to be understood as contradicting singers' utterances. Building on Sedaine's theatrical experience, composers also developed techniques to manipulate dramatic time.
5. France maintained a national musical idiom because of the emphasis put on declamation at the expense of legato singing.
6. The visual aspect was incorporated into the action as well. Ballets unrelated to the plot were unpopular for a period of time, while pantomime and stage sets became increasingly significant.

Select Bibliography

Algarotti, Francesco. *Saggio sopra l'opera in musica. Le edizioni di Venezia (1755) e di Livorno (1763)*. Ed. Annalisa Bini, Rome, 1989

Betzwieser, Thomas. *Exotismus und Türkenoper in der französischen Musik des Ancien Régime. Studien zu einem ästhetischen Phänomen*. Laaber, 1993

Brenner, Clarence D. *The Theatre Italien: Its Repertoire, 1716–1793*. Berkeley, 1961

Calella, Michele. *Das Ensemble in der Tragédie lyrique des späten Ancien Régime*. Eisenach, 2000

Carroll, Charles Michaël. *François-André Danican Philidor: His Life and Dramatic Art*. PhD thesis, Florida State University, 1960

Charlton, David. *Orchestration and Orchestral Practice in Paris, 1789–1810*. PhD thesis, University of Cambridge, 1974

Grétry and the Growth of Opéra-Comique. Cambridge, 1986

French Opera 1730–1830: Meaning and Media. Aldershot, 2000

Charlton, David and Mark Ledbury (eds.). *Michel-Jean Sedaine (1719–1797): Theatre, Opera and Art*. Aldershot, 2000

Chartier, Roger. *Les Origines culturelles de la Révolution française*. Paris, 1990

Cook, Elisabeth. 'Challenging the *Ancien Régime*: The Hidden Politics of the "Querelle des Bouffons"'. In Andrea Fabiano (ed.), *La 'Querelle des Bouffons' dans la vie culturelle française du XVIIIe siècle*. Paris, 2005, pp. 141–60

Duet and Ensemble in the Early Opéra-Comique. New York, 1995

Couvreur, Manuel. 'Diderot et Philidor: Le philosophe au chevet d'*Ernelinde*'. *Recherches sur Diderot et sur l'Encyclopédie*, 11 (1991), pp. 83–107
Dahlhaus, Carl (ed.). *Die Musik des 18. Jahrhunderts*. Laaber, 1985
Darnton, Robert. *The Forbidden Bestsellers of Pre-Revolutionary France*. London, 1996
Diderot, Denis. *Œuvres esthétiques*. Ed. Paul Vernière, Paris, 1965
Di Profio, Alessandro. *La Révolution des Bouffons: L'opéra italien au Théâtre de Monsieur 1789–1792*. Paris, 2003
Fabiano, Andrea. *Histoire de l'opéra italien en France (1752–1815): Héros et héroïnes d'un roman théâtral*. Paris, 2006
(ed.). *La 'Querelle des Bouffons' dans la vie culturelle française du XVIIIe siècle*. Paris, 2005
Favart, Charles Simon. *Mémoires et correspondence littéraires, dramatiques et anecdotiques*. Ed. A. P. C. Favart. 3 vols., Paris, 1808
Furet, François. *La Révolution française de Turgot à Napoléon (1770–1814)* and *Terminer la Révolution de Louis XVIII à Jules Ferry (1814–80)*. 2 vols., Paris, 1988
Giuliani, Elizabeth. 'Le Public de l'Opéra de Paris de 1750 à 1760. Mesure et définition'. *International Review of the Aesthetics and Sociology of Music*, 8 (1977), pp. 159–81
Goldoni, Carlo. *Mémoires pour servir à l'histoire de sa vie et à celle de son théâtre*. Ed. Norbert Jonard, Paris, 1992
Grétry, André-Ernest-Modeste. *Mémoires, ou Essais sur la musique*. 3 vols., Paris, 1797; reprint 1971
Grimm, Friedrich Melchior. *Le petit prophète de Boehmischbroda* (1753). Reprint in Denise Launay (ed.), *La Querelle des Bouffons*. Geneva, 1973, vol. 1, pp. 132–92. Excerpts in Oliver Strunk (ed.), *Source Readings in Music History: The Classic Era*. New York, 1965, pp. 45–61
Heartz, Daniel. *Music in European Capitals: The Galant Style, 1720–1780*. New York and London, 2003
Hortschansky, Klaus. *Parodie und Entlehnung im Schaffen Christoph Willibald Glucks*. Cologne, 1973
Howard, Patricia. *Gluck: An Eighteenth-Century Portrait in Letters and Documents*. Oxford, 1995
Iacuzzi, Alfred. *The European Vogue of Favart: The Diffusion of the Opéra-Comique*. New York, 1932
Kintzler, Catherine. *Poétique de l'opéra français de Corneille à Rousseau*. Paris, 1991
Launay, Denise (ed.). *La Querelle des Bouffons*. 3 vols., Geneva, 1973
Laurencie, Lionel de La. 'Deux Imitateurs français des bouffons'. *L'Année musicale*, 2 (1913), pp. 66–91
Legrand, Raphaëlle and Nicole Wild. *Regards sur l'opéra-comique: Trois siècle de vie théâtrale*. Paris, 2002
Lesure, François (ed.). *Querelle des Gluckistes et des Piccinnistes*. 2 vols., Geneva, 1984
McClellan, Michael E. *Battling over the Lyric Muse: Expression of Revolution and Counterrevolution at the Théâtre Monsieur*. Ann Arbor, MI, 2000
Mongrédien, Jean. *Jean-François le Sueur: contribution à l'étude d'un demi-siècle de musique française (1780–1830)*. 2 vols., Bern, 1980
French Music from the Enlightenment to Romanticism. Portland, OR, 1996
Monnet, Jean. *Mémoires*. Ed. Henri d'Alméras, Paris, 1909
Müller-Lindenberg, Ruth. *Weinen und Lachen. Dramaturgie und musikalisches Idiom der Opéra-comique im Vergleich zur Opera buffa (1750–1790)*. 2 vols., Münster, 2006

Noiray, Michel. '*Hippolyte* et *Castor* travestis: Rameau à l'opéra-comique'. In Jérôme de la Gorce (ed.), *Jean-Philippe Rameau 1983*. Paris, 1987, pp. 109–25
Noiray, Michel. *Vocabulaire de la musique de l'époque classique*. Paris, 2005
'The Pre-Revolutionary Origins of "Terrorisme musical"'. In Melania Bucciarelli and Berta Joncus (eds.), *Music as Social and Cultural Practice: Essays in Honour of Reinhard Strohm*. Woodbridge and Rochester, NY, 2007, pp. 294–311
Philidor, François-André Danican. *Ernelinde*. Ed. Julian Rushton, New York, 1991
Rougemont, Martine de. *La vie théâtrale en France au XVIIIe siècle*. Paris, 1988
Rousseau, Jean-Jacques. *Œuvres complètes*. Ed. Bernard Gagnebin, Marcel Raymond *et al.*, 5 vols., Paris, 1959–95
The Collected Writings. Ed. and trans. J. T. Scott, 30 vols., Hanover 1998
Rushton, Julian. 'Iphigénie en Tauride: The Operas of Gluck and Piccinni'. *Music and Letters*, 53 (1972), pp. 411–30
Schmidt, Dörte. *Armide hinter den Spiegeln: Lully, Gluck und die Möglichkeiten der dramatischen Parodie*. Stuttgart, 2001
Schmierer, Elisabeth. *Die Tragédies-lyriques Niccolò Piccinnis*. Laaber, 1999
Schneider, Herbert and Reinhard Wiesend (eds.). *Die Oper im 18. Jahrhundert*. Laaber, 2001
Smith, Kent Maynard. *Egidio Duni and the Development of the 'Opéra-Comique' from 1753 to 1770*. Ann Arbor, MI, 1980
Taïeb, Patrick. *L'Ouverture d'opéra en France de Monsigny à Méhul*. Paris, 2007
Vendrix, Phillippe (ed). *Grétry et l'Europe de l'Opéra-Comique*. Liège, 1992
Wokler, Robert. '"La Querelle des Bouffons" and the Italian Liberation of France: A Study of Revolutionary Foreplay'. *Eighteenth-Century Life*, 11 (1987), pp. 94–116

· 11 ·

German opera from Reinhard Keiser to Peter Winter

CLAUDIA MAURER ZENCK

TRANSLATED BY ANKE CATON AND SIMON P. KEEFE

Neither in music historical publications nor in major compendiums or encyclopaedias do we find chapters or articles on eighteenth-century German opera. Instead, the Italian dramma per musica (later called opera seria) and the French tragédie lyrique appear as stand-ins for the serious German Baroque opera, and opera buffa, also called commedia per musica by contemporaries and later dramma giocoso, alongside opéra-comique, as designations for the lighter comic complement. There is also the German 'Singspiel', but is a singspiel an opera? And why does German Baroque opera, which has received substantial scholarly attention, not appear in digests of the history of opera?

These are just a few of the questions resulting from the particularities and difficulties of German opera that do not apply in the same way to Italian or French opera in the eighteenth century. We will approach very pragmatically the problem of what constitutes 'German' within the 'Holy Roman Empire of German Nations' whose Emperor was crowned in Frankfurt, resided in Vienna, was King of Bohemia and Hungary and also reigned in Upper Italy: we will include operas where at least the recitative texts were written in German and where the libretto was set by a German composer for performance on a German stage. The second problem arises from the fact that the German Empire was split into more than thirty principalities and also included several free imperial cities. Their musical life has only been partially explored thus far, making a comprehensive account at present virtually impossible. Where required in this chapter, the term 'opera' is replaced by other terms in accordance with common practice at the time – a practice far removed from today's predilection for specifying terms as accurately as possible.[1] In the first half of the eighteenth century the terms 'Musikalisches Schau-Spiel' (musical play),

1 For details, see Herbert Schneider, 'Das Singspiel vor Mozart', in Schneider and Reinhard Wiesend (eds.), *Die Oper im 18. Jahrhundert. Handbuch der musikalischen Gattungen*, vol. 12 (Laaber, 2001), pp. 301–22. The usual substitute expression 'deutschsprachiges Musiktheater' ('German-speaking music theatre' or 'German-speaking opera') can be used for the genre as a whole, but not for single works.

'Singe-Spiel' (sung play) and 'Oper' (opera) were generally synonymous; after 1750 '(komische) Oper' (comic opera), 'Singspiel' (musical comedy) and 'Schauspiel mit Gesang' (drama with singing) were the standard, interchangeable terms. When necessary the terms *Serenata* (serenade) and *Operette* (operetta) were used for shorter pieces. But these terms were also used to describe operas from other countries, such as the serious Italian dramma per musica, and later (above all) the Italian commedia per musica and the French opéra-comique.[2] All of these not only influenced German productions, but also played a significant role in performance practice. At places like Hamburg, Braunschweig and Weißenfels opere serie were given in German translations (at least for texts of recitatives) at the beginning of the eighteenth century. But they were presented in completely translated form, too, including Handel's Italian *Rinaldo* in Hamburg in 1715.[3] In the second half of the century non-courtly theatres as well as travel groups performed Italian and French operas in German. For Italian buffa operas this meant inserting spoken texts in place of sung recitatives. (The process of transference happened the other way round too, but much less frequently.[4]) Joseph Haydn was received as a composer of singspiele – for example *Der Äpfeldieb*, which had been fabricated as a pasticcio from two of his Italian operas, and *Ritter Roland* (originally *Orlando Paladino*), at which even the Emperor was present at the Viennese performance. However, Haydn's original singspiele, which are no longer extant, were seemingly never played outside Vienna, or rather outside Castle Esterháza.

German Baroque opera from Keiser to Telemann

From the end of the seventeenth century until the 1730s, the German variant of baroque opera did not feature on all stages in German-speaking areas. Most were court theatres and had Italian operas in their repertory. But German operas were performed at the municipal theatre at the Brühl in Leipzig, until it closed in 1720. At the beginning of the eighteenth century they were temporarily on the programme at the theatre of Braunschweig (not a courtly theatre),

2 The tragédies-lyriques were not performed at court theatres. Exceptions, however, were performances of operas that were translated into German, such as Lully's *Acis et Galatée* in 1695 (first performed in French in 1689) and Desmaret's *Vénus et Adonis* in Hamburg in 1725.

3 Robert D. Lynch compiled a list of operas that followed the language of their original texts; see *Opera in Hamburg, 1718–1738: A Study of the Libretto and the Musical Style* (Ann Arbor, MI, 1980), part 1, p. 24.

4 From the 1790s onwards, successful German singspiele were occasionally translated into Italian (for example Süßmayr's *Der Spiegel von Arkadien*) or French, and then played in Italy and France. Haydn's *La vera costanza* was staged in Paris in 1791 under the title *Laurette, opéra-comique en trois actes* and *Die Zauberflöte* was also performed there, at the Théâtre des Arts, as *Les mistères d'Isis* in four acts. In 1819, it was performed in English at the Haymarket Theatre in London and in the same year printed in two languages, Italian and English.

and on the court stages of Weißenfels, as well as some other small residences in Saxony-Thuringia. Even the court of the Bavarian Electoral Prince in Munich performed them, albeit as the exception not the rule. Above all, German Baroque opera was cultivated at the opera house at the Gänsemarkt (Goose Market) in the Imperial City of Hamburg. The opera house was established in 1678 at the behest of Duke Albrecht of Holstein-Gottorf, and supported financially by rich merchants. The following discussion therefore focuses on the city and its stage; most surviving German Baroque operas were composed for this location. Later, some were also repeated in Braunschweig and Weißenfels. The changes in location also worked the other way around as well, as duke Anton Ulrich of Braunschweig-Wolfenbüttel endeavoured to develop a German variety of ballet and opera at the turn of the century. Fairly early on he employed Friedrich Christian Bressand, whose libretti were also set in Hamburg, as court poet. Likewise, there could have been a connection to Leipzig, as five of the six composers whose works were certainly performed in Leipzig (little material, unfortunately, has survived) were also heard in Hamburg. When, for financial reasons, the resident ensemble of the Hamburg Opera House had to be dissolved in 1738, and the theatre was visited only by touring companies who performed Italian operas (if anything musical), the history of German Baroque opera gradually came to a close.

German Baroque opera *c.* 1700–40 is distinctive in various ways that distinguishes it from German opera of the preceding two decades. The interest in drammi per musica, which started in Hamburg in 1693, and led to the performance of eleven works until 1699, decreased abruptly from 1700 onwards. Until 1714 exclusively German works by seven composers were performed (most from Keiser; others from Bronner, Mattheson, Schieferdecker, Grünewald, Handel and Graupner). One exception was an opera by Agostino Steffani, which was translated into German. From 1715–17, Keiser's operas continued to dominate, but each year brought a new production of an Italian opera. Italian operas were already in the majority in 1718, and in 1719 about sixty evenings with (five) Italian operas can be confirmed from performance dates, but only twenty-four evenings with (three) German operas. While the reverse was true in 1721 (the newest operas by Georg Caspar Schürmann were often staged from 1719 on), the performances of Italian opera dominate once again in 1722. Thereafter, numbers of performances equalized.[5]

Another difference between pre- and post-1700 German Baroque opera is that the biblical themes that dominated before 1700 gave way to mythological

5 Based on the published performance dates in Hans Joachim Marx and Dorothea Schröder, *Die Hamburger Gänsemarkt-Oper: Katalog der Textbücher (1678–1748)* (Laaber, 1995), pp. 469–507.

and historical ones. The latter also provided the material for the particularly long phase of political festive operas in Hamburg.[6] From 1718 onwards it can also be observed that operas no longer relied on modern history, but rather turned to old history instead.[7] In addition, heroic themes are often found, but comic and pastoral ones seldom. With Telemann's activity in Hamburg (from 1721 on), German Baroque opera changed textually as well as musically. Telemann was very interested in comic scenes, which were now regularly integrated – and on a larger scale – into serious plots. This also applied to older operas that were revived.

Barthold Feind, one of Hamburg's most important librettists – others were Christian Heinrich Postel, Johann Philipp Praetorius, Hinrich Hinsch and Christian Friedrich Hunald (*nom de plume*: Menantes)[8] – tried to replace 'artificially chosen words' ('künstlich zusammengesuchte Wörter') with expressive action in his 1708 libretto *L'Amore ammalato. Die kranckende Liebe. Oder: Antiochus und Stratonica*. From this point onwards, action was important to all eighteenth-century operatic stages as well as music and decoration.[9] The art especially of French actors and singers, admired across Europe, was regarded as exemplary.

Reinhard Keiser, who was active as Kapellmeister at the opera at the Gänsemarkt from approximately 1697 onwards, had already been joined *c.* 1700 at the Hamburg Opera by the composers Mattheson and Handel. Although Handel stayed for only a short period, it was here that he started his career as an opera composer. Later, his Italian operas were often played in adapted versions in Hamburg. Between 1699 and 1711 Mattheson composed six operas and an act for a pasticcio for the Hamburg stage, on which he had already performed as a child singer. But Keiser was by far the most productive opera composer, and active in Hamburg for the longest period. From 1696 to 1728 he delivered around sixty operas for the local stage. When Telemann came to Hamburg in 1721, the city gained a composer who not only provided church music in his function as cantor of the Johanneum and music director of the five main churches but who also composed around twenty stage works for the opera house at the Gänsemarkt. (He took over as musical director of the opera house as early as 1722.[10])

6 Festive operas appeared throughout the eighteenth century, Mozart's *La clemenza di Tito* (1791) being a late and typically Italian example. Michael Haydn, on the other hand, composed the festive German opera *Andromeda und Perseus* four years earlier, which is still linked to Baroque opera in structural terms, but is entirely contemporary in its musical language.

7 Lynch, *Opera in Hamburg, 1718–1738*, part 1, pp. 27 and 31.

8 Bressand from Braunschweig was also asked on several occasions to co-operate on Hamburg operas.

9 Hellmuth Christian Wolff, *Die Barockoper in Hamburg (1678–1738)* (Wolfenbüttel, 1957), 2 vols., vol. 1, pp. 56ff. (Quote by Feind on p. 57.)

10 From 1701 until 1719 he had composed only seven operas. In Hamburg he composed at least sixteen operas in a comparable time period, as well as three intermezzi; sometimes he also composed interludes for operas by other composers.

Thus, from *c.* 1700 onwards, there was a concentration of forces in Hamburg unrivalled elsewhere in the world of German Baroque opera. Additionally, a big ensemble was available: the orchestra comprised over sixty instruments[11] and was predominantly formed by *Ratsmusiker*, musicians paid by the city council, and students. The singers were mainly of German nationality. This also meant that the heroic parts were not written for soprano or alto castratos, as in Italian operas, but for tenors and basses. When the first castrato was engaged at the Gänsemarkt Opera in 1720, the event was directly related to the rising interest in the performances of Italian operas, noticeable from 1718 onwards. However, the operatic style adapted by composers from Keiser's predecessor Johann Sigismund Kusser onwards was that of Italian opera. Kusser was the first to instruct the singers in the Italian style of singing. Some, like Margaretha Susanna Kayser, the later long-standing Hamburg prima donna, gained fame nationwide. From Keiser's 1703 opera *Der verführte Claudius* onwards, it was also customary – in Hamburg as well as in Leipzig and Braunschweig – for recitatives to be sung in German. However, the same did not always apply to arias. Barthold Feind reasoned that the Italian language would entice the audience 'with hidden titillation' ('durch eine verborgene Kitzlung').[12] From then onwards a linguistic 'mishmash' prevailed. Operas with added French texts, like Telemann's *Orpheus* in the 1726 and 1736 performed versions were the exception not the rule. Here, Telemann served as his own librettist and used a French model. He integrated choruses and great processions into the plot, modelled the necromancy on Lully's *Armide* and composed two songs for the spurned Orasia on French texts and as airs. These are all characteristic compositional deviations of German Baroque opera from Italian Baroque opera, as are the numerous single-strophe songs, strophic songs and the *vaudeville* at the end of Telemann's satire *Die verkehrte Welt*, which premiered two years later and was also based on a French model.[13]

Reinhard Keiser composed only two operas on French models in the 1720s, when a French acting company performed in Hamburg. Yet his *Ulysses*, composed for Copenhagen in 1722, shows clearly that the composer and his

11 In Joachim Wenzel, *Geschichte der Hamburger Oper 1678–1978* (Hamburg, 1978), p. 21 the number is still mistakenly given as the number of musicians. The *Ratsmusiker*, however, were trained to play several instruments, in which case the thirty-seven wind instruments would have been played by considerably fewer musicians.

12 See Feind's introduction to his libretto *Octavia* (1705), quoted in Dorothea Schröder, 'Die Einführung der italienischen Oper in Hamburg durch Johann Georg Conradi und Johann Sigismund Kusser (1693–1696)', in A. Colzani, N. Dubowy, A. Luppi and M. Padoan (eds.), *Il melodramma italiano in Italia e in Germania nell'età barocca* (Como, 1995), p. 52.

13 See Peter Huth, 'Telemanns Hamburger Opern nach frz. Vorbildern', in Friedhelm Brusniak and Annemarie Clostermann (eds.), *Französische Einflüsse auf deutsche Musiker im 18. Jahrhundert* (Cologne, 1996), pp. 133–9.

German librettist endeavoured to conform to the typical shape of Italian opera. Keiser had already encountered the tragédie lyrique during his time in Braunschweig. In any case, his early operas demonstrate a number of peculiar features, traceable to French influence: the choice of opening overtures instead of symphonies, and choruses instead of arias; ballet insertions; the tendency to use smaller forms; two-part arias; strophic arias and dance arias; and a syllabic setting of the text.[14]

Mattheson's suggestion in the *Critica Musica* (1722–5), that the Germans should develop a 'mixed taste' ('vermischten Geschmack') from the Italian and the French style, could have been based on his experiences with German Baroque opera in Hamburg. Here it was exposed to strong Italian and, to a lesser degree, French influences. In addition, it contained more and more 'German' songs, which were modelled after folk songs and recitatives adapted for the German language.

Although many of the printed texts of German Baroque operas, especially those from Hamburg, are preserved (and are even catalogued and partly available in newer reprints[15]) most scores were unfortunately lost or are preserved only in parts (in the form of printed arias). This is true for all of the cities mentioned so far, including Hamburg. Thus, only one of the three operas by the young Handel is preserved in score.[16] When Handel composed his first opera, *Der in Krohnen erlangte Glücks-Wechsel oder: Almira, Königin von Castilien* in 1704, he had already been active for two years as a violinist and substitute harpsichord player at the Gänsemarkt orchestra. The work is strongly influenced by the model provided by his Kapellmeister, Reinhard Keiser, who already had ten years' experience as an opera composer. The piece has a French overture and French dances (five in a row in Act 1, scene 11), is written in the Italian manner with great coloratura arias and rather 'instrumental' handling of vocal lines, as well as a declamation that does justice to the German language, and has a grammatically meaningful fragmentation of the sentences in the recitative. (According to Mattheson, this conforming to the German language was first found in the compositions of Keiser.) Moreover,

14 See Klaus-Peter Koch, 'Reinhard Keisers Schaffen im Hinblick auf französische Einflüsse', in Brusniak and Clostermann (eds.), *Französische Einflüsse*, pp. 77–91, especially pp. 80–5.

15 They are primarily preserved in the 'Theater-Bibliothek' collection of the Staats- und Universitätsbibliothek Hamburg Carl von Ossietzky. Concerning the catalogue, see annotation 5. Twenty-one libretto texts in facsimile are provided in the three volumes of Reinhard Meyer's *Die Hamburger Oper: Eine Sammlung von Texten der Hamburger Oper aus der Zeit 1678–1730* (Munich, 1980), as well as printed scores of Keiser's *Desiderius* and Mattheson's *Der edelmüthige Porsenna*; the *Boris Goudenow* print includes a reprint of the libretto.

16 The unsuccessful *Nero* (also from 1705) was lost, as was his last opera, which was premiered as late as 1708 and had to be performed in two parts on account of its considerable length (*Der beglückte Florindo* and *Die verwandelte Daphne*).

Handel set German and Italian texts in the arias, which the librettist Friedrich Christian Feustking had kept in the original language. Handel's score has only been preserved in a copy, which Telemann used for the reproduction of the opera in 1732. It therefore carries traces of Telemann's adaptation, including two inserted German arias and a new overture.[17] At the time it was common for the librettist to choose the text of another writer as a model, and even to adapt parts of it. Similarly, it was common practice in the field of opera in the eighteenth century to adapt works to suit new performance conditions, which explains why there is often more than one version of an opera, famous operas in particular. Either the composer himself or a local colleague adapted the work, mostly by inserting arias from other works or by composing new ones. But the practice of incorporating arias by other composers also occurred in newly composed operas and was similar to another practice that featured throughout the eighteenth century – the creation of a pasticcio from a variety of compositions in order to produce a new opera, or the creation of a piece by several composers intended as such right from the start. Schieferdecker, Mattheson and Bronner for example quickly composed *Victor, Hertzog der Normannen* (1702) for an approaching festive day. *Der Stein der Weisen* (1790) was accomplished through the collaboration of five musicians linked to the Freihaustheater in Vienna – Schikaneder, Henneberg, Gerl, Schack and Mozart – who wanted quickly to present a new piece to the audience.

Reinhard Keiser, whom Mattheson praised as the 'greatest opera composer in the world' in 1740,[18] is especially noteworthy for his long and fruitful accomplishments in German Baroque opera. His stage works, approximately one-third of which have been preserved, are divisible into a first experimental phase to *c.* 1710, a middle phase and a final phase from 1718 onwards. In the first phase he composed great solo scenes, a considerable variety of different aria forms (from those without basso continuo, to a completely unaccompanied aria in *La forza della virtù oder: Die Macht der Tugend* (1700), that substitutes the ritornelli with long vocalizations), inserted arias with Italian texts and composed comic scenes in Low German.[19] With da capo arias dominating, the works of his middle phase are influenced in more prominent fashion by Italian opera. In his final phase, Keiser increasingly interpolated arias from popular works of other composers. He also concentrated more on the composition of buffo arias, attaching less importance to consistency of structure. All

17 See Dorothea Schröder, introduction to Handel, *Almira, Königin von Kastilien*, in *Hallesche Händel-Ausgabe*, Series II, vol. 1 (Kassel, 1994), pp. vii–xii.

18 Johann Mattheson, *Grundlage einer Ehren-Pforte* (Hamburg, 1740; reprint Kassel *et al.* 1969), p. 133.

19 Low German songs from comic figures can already be found in Johann Wolfgang Franck's *Der glückliche Groß-Vezier Cara Mustapha* (1686).

of this was probably a combined result of his unsuccessful attempts around 1720 to attain regular employment elsewhere, his return to the opera that was then under Telemann's direction,[20] Telemann's own interests and the changed taste of the audience.

In 1709 Keiser set Feind's libretto *Desiderius*. With this opera the free Imperial City of Hamburg wanted to celebrate the birthday of Emperor Joseph I. As customary for festive operas, the plot made reference to political events, in this case to the ongoing controversy of the Emperor with the Pope about the supremacy in Parma and the recognition of Joseph's brother Karl as Spanish king. Consequently, the opera has an extensive homage prologue, connects the political action with love intrigues, portrays the figure of the sovereign in a very refined way and manages completely without comic figures. It provided an opportunity for many glamorous dances but, according to custom, most were not composed by Keiser, but rather chosen or written by the ballet-master. A large number of choruses, higher than in the operas that were not composed for a special event, contributed to the spread of glory and symbolically represented the audience on stage through acclamations and congratulatory ovations. As in Italian Baroque opera, most scenes of this large-scale opera consist of recitatives and arias. Yet the arias and ariettas are very different in form, length and instrumentation. In this respect this opera, and Keiser's additional four preserved festive operas, are similar to his other works. As in most other operas, the propaganda choruses are mainly short, which means that they are composed homorhythmically and without major repetitions.[21]

In contrast to *Desiderius*, Keiser's 'singspiel' *Der hochmüthige, gestürtzte und wieder erhabene Croesus*, which was composed two years later, has comic scenes and is influenced by Venetian opera. Uncommonly, it features aria texts that are written exclusively in German as well as many strophic arias instead of da capo arias (of which there are few). The instrumentation is also unusual in that it calls for the first time in a Hamburg opera for three chalumeaux. In the second version of the opera (1730) Keiser left out the ballet, wrote a new overture and a ritornello for the second act and re-composed thirty-seven arias (comprising two-thirds of the sung numbers). He also reworked others: instead of accompanying the solo voice with the basso continuo, he integrated it into a polyphonic setting, and in some unison arias abandoned the parallel voice-leading of the outer voices. Overall he almost completely abandoned the basso continuo – even the simple song of the farmers' children in Act 2 has a final

20 See Klaus Zelm, *Die Opern Reinhard Keisers* (Munich and Salzburg, 1975), esp. pp. 202ff.

21 See Dorothea Schröder, *Zeitgeschichte auf der Opernbühne. Barockes Musiktheater in Hamburg im Dienst von Politik und Diplomatie (1690–1745)* (Göttingen, 1998), pp. 292–6, esp. p. 293.

ritornello with two oboes – and related the voices more directly to the instrumental sound. Even the coloraturas were designed instrumentally. He also differentiated instrumental colours very clearly.

Similar tendencies are evident in the 1717 premiere of *Die großmüthige Tomyris*. The plot, based on an Italian libretto translated into German, concentrates on a single theme and manages without minor comic characters. This should have contributed to a reduction in the opera's numbers and to a sense of compositional unification. Aside from the thirty arias, there is only one trio after the opening concerto, four short choruses, four dances and two symphonies, the second of which frames a recitative scene with allegorical figures. Keiser composed all solos except one as da capo arias – whether provided with an Italian or a German text. Compared to the Italian arias, however, they are relatively short. In *Desiderius* and the first version of *Croesus*, arias with basso continuo accompaniment and arias with obligato instruments balance each other. In this work the arias with basso continuo disappear altogether. Instruments used for solo purposes include all strings, even the contrabass. They accompany the pleading aria of the love struck Policares (No. 33) in unison and pizzicato, for example. The refinement of this opera lies in its contrasts of colours and registers, as well as the mostly four-part setting of the strings, and the diverse string and wind instrumental combinations in accompanying the voice parts. In contrast to this diversity is a strong sense of formal unification.[22] For the performances in 1723 and 1724 Keiser substituted two of the arias for two from a Bononcini opera that had been premiered in London in 1721,[23] which is typical of his last period and of the revivals of his earlier operas carried out at that time.

Handel and his slightly older friend Johann Mattheson of Hamburg were great admirers of Keiser. From childhood, Mattheson received a comprehensive musical education, and sang his first role at the opera house, then directed by Kusser, at the age of nine. Under Keiser he already sang principal parts. Under the influence of both composers, the young Mattheson was soon successful in his first 'Singspiele'. Even after he had left the opera house in 1705 and worked mainly as a diplomat for an English envoy (from 1718, he was director of the cathedral choir in his secondary occupation and also began activities as a music theorist), he composed his two last stage works for the opera house at the Gänsemarkt (1710 and 1711). Thereafter, until he lost his hearing in the middle of the 1730s, he mostly composed vocal music. His last oratorios in particular should be characterized as theatrical church music. In his

22 Klaus Zelm, introduction to Reinhard Keiser, *Die Großmütige Tomyris*, ed. Zelm (Munich, 1975), p. vi.
23 *Kritischer Bericht* to *Tomyris* (Munich, 1996), pp. 21ff.

theoretical works he captured the essence of much of his compositional experience, in order to pass it on to his readers. Direct influence as an opera composer, at least on the young Handel, can also be demonstrated in the context of numerous borrowings on Handel's part. This also featured in the opera *Der edelmüthige Porsenna*, which implies that it was not given only in Hamburg in the year of its premiere (1702).[24]

Five of Mattheson's seven operas composed in full or in part have historical contents, and four have been preserved to the present day, *Der edelmüthige Porsenna* from 1702 and *Boris Goudenow* from 1710 (with the libretto by the composer himself) among them. *Boris Goudenow* was his penultimate opera, and like the last one had negligible impact. But whereas his last opera was performed in 1711, *Boris Goudenow* was not. This could have been connected to the political background of the libretto, which Mattheson might have written originally as a festive opera. Mattheson, independent from the City of Hamburg through his employment by an English envoy, renamed the contemporary princes in anagram form Johannes of Denmark (Josennah) and Gustav of Sweden (Gavust), in order to portray them as alternately positive and negative figures on the stage – a disguise that was regarded as sufficient for historical princes.[25] Hamburg had been entangled in political power struggles with Denmark for a long time, but during 1702 and 1708 in particular three homage operas for the Danish King by Keiser were repeatedly performed in the city.[26] Whether it was the transparent disguise of living Princes or the figure of Tsar Feodor on-stage that led to objections, remains an open question. The plot illustrates that Mattheson had dramaturgical shortcomings as a librettist – it is intricate and not always well reasoned. This was not the case in his second opera *Der edelmüthige Porsenna*, composed eight years earlier. It is based on a text that Bressand had written for a Keiser composition in 1695, and can be traced back to a Livius legend depicting the fight between the Etruscans and the inhabitants of Rome for the town. As usual, Bressand combined the legend with love intrigues and added a comic figure in the form of the simple soldier Bibellus. He structured the text in five acts and on several occasions joined several of the standard 'Italian' recitativo-cum-aria sets into larger scenes. In his 1702 setting of the libretto, Mattheson left out the first act, which did not cause a problem from the point of view of content. The division into four acts, though, was uncommon – the first three acts were subsumed

24 Hansjörg Drauschke, introduction to Johann Mattheson, *Der edelmütige Porsenna*, ed. Drauschke (Beeskow, 2006), p. vii.
25 For the manifestation of this practice in the festive opera *Victor Hertzog der Normannen*, which Mattheson produced with others in 1702, see Schröder, *Zeitgeschichte auf der Opernbühne*, p. 221.
26 *Ibid.*, pp. 257–62.

into two for the printed libretto, resulting in a first act that contained more numbers than the other two together. Mattheson's preference for the unusual four-act design speaks well of his dramaturgical instincts. The imprisonment of Clelia (who was disguised as a man) and the remorse aria of Bibellus (who had done justice to the wine) are still placed at the end of the first act, and both Mutius' extremely dramatic test of courage, with which he regains his liberty, and his 'honour' aria, remained at the end of the opera's second act.

The overture and the arias of *Der edelmüthige Porsenna* are mostly set in four parts. They show that Mattheson liked to introduce the numbers with extensive soggetti (short fugal subjects) which, in most cases, were imitated by the voice (in contrast to Keiser, who preferred to keep ritornellos and soggetti apart). They also illustrate that Mattheson reserved for the comic Bibellus simple and song-like melodies with two repeated passages. Nevertheless, in his aria at the end of the first act, he was allocated a regular (if five-part) da capo aria, even if it is short and melodically as simple as his songs. Most of the arias and duets of the other characters are written in da capo form and their sung parts are differentiated rhythmically as well as melodically. They are smoother than those by Keiser and have fewer coloraturas. The instrumentation remains conventional: the violins are often doubled by the oboes, but the jubilation choruses for the Etruscan king Porsenna at the opening of the plot and shortly before the *lieto fine* are symbolically scored for clarini, as is Porsenna's entry aria ('Ihr muntern Trompeten'). Mattheson elaborated this short da capo aria as an effective duet between the solo instrument and the voice in the A section. It shows the imitation of the soggetto as well as the parallel movement in sixths in the coloraturas. The voice part in this aria is thus conceived instrumentally; it can be presumed that Mattheson knew some of the numerous trumpet arias of Italian provenance.

That Mattheson still translated and arranged some 'imported' operas for the performance in Hamburg in the 1720s (among other things providing Handel's *Radamisto* with German recitatives) relates to the continued interest in the Italian dramma per musica witnessed from 1718 onwards. The aforementioned integration of arias by Italian contemporaries into Keiser operas, performed under Telemann's direction in the 1720s, relates to the same phenomenon. In the sixteen years of his direction at the Gänsemarkt Theatre Telemann was responsible for the performance of over forty German Baroque operas; although the number of newly staged Italian operas was lower, they were performed more often. Telemann put special emphasis on operas by Handel, who on his own had twelve works in the repertory. For some of them (like the German *Almira*) Telemann composed extensive supplementary material. His own stage works composed for Hamburg, however, did not apparently contain filler or substitute arias, although the most successful ones were revived several times.

When Telemann came to Hamburg, he had already managed the Leipzig opera house for three years and had also composed operas for Leipzig during his time in Frankfurt. Only for the last one from 1719, a 'Satyra' (satyr), have single arias been preserved, as Telemann performed an altered version of it in Hamburg five years later. His works for the opera house at the Gänsemarkt range from a few prologues and epilogues, to contributions to a pasticcio, two intermezzi and seventeen operas, from *Der geduldige Sokrates* (presumably premiered by Telemann himself in Hamburg at the beginning of 1721, before his election as church music director) to *Der Weiseste von Sidon* from 1733. Most operas are comic in content. Even the serious opera *Adelheid*, written for the Bayreuth court in 1725 rather than for Hamburg, has a range of comical scenes. They are grouped around a teacher with the descriptive name of Tumernix. Although barely connected to the main action, they collectively form an intermezzo; Telemann later published its arias separately. This parallels the development of the first opera buffa (*La serva padrona*, 1733) created by Pergolesi from two intermezzi originally interpolated into an opera seria.

Apart from a number of arias left in the original language, the libretto for *Sokrates* is mainly based on Johann Ulrich König's translation of an Italian libretto. König also wrote a few German texts, which he added to the libretto. His interest in a German comic opera with a popular character met Telemann's preference for cheerful and satirical plots. It is not only the humorous servant that accounts for its comic value, but also the depiction of Aristophanes as 'conceited court poet' (selbstgefälligen Hofpoeten).[27] An essential element is the confrontation of the philosopher – who is idealised as passionless and patient – with bourgeois private life, and is conveyed by a governmental implementation of bigamy that must have come across as extremely comical to the Hamburg audience.

König created a dramaturgically diverse libretto, with scenes that could contain numerous ensembles in a variety of situations. The result is not only closed numbers, but also recitatives with up to six participants (No. 46), including a short two-voiced passage (No. 41). Telemann used the full orchestra to accompany the voice, as well as common obligato solo instruments such as flute, oboe and violin, but also the less common viola da gamba and violoncello. In addition to the da capo arias, he composed vocal pieces featuring strophic structure or a (choral) refrain, cavatinas and dance songs, and parodied serious arias through comic repetitions of the text and coloraturas (as

27 Bernd Baselt, 'Bemerkungen zum Opernschaffen Georg Philipp Telemanns', *Musica*, 35/1 (1981), p. 22.

in the revenge aria of the court poet). In order to characterize the characters or the situation he exploited various styles: in No. 31 the rivalling women sing in canon (at most imitating an initial three-note figure); and in a dispute scene with Aristophanes the four pupils of Sokrates sing a mock canon (No. 28).

Considering his preference for comic opera, it is not surprising that the eighty-year-old Telemann made a contribution to the nascent German singspiel of the 1750s. One of his former pupils from the Johanneum, the twenty-year-old Daniel Schiebeler – who had already written prologues for Koch's company and later contributed significantly to the development of the new serious style in German opera – featured as librettist. Telemann's and Schiebeler's *Don Quichotte auf der Hochzeit des Comacho* was premiered as a concert piece in Hamburg in 1761, but the designation 'Serenate' on the autograph preserved in Berlin, makes clear that a scenic performance as a one-act play was also possible.[28] Like his earlier operas, Telemann treated Schiebeler's 'Singegedicht' (literally 'sung poem') – which he had heavily edited – in through-composed fashion, setting the dialogues as recitatives. The German expression marks are new; otherwise all of the distinctive features of Telemann's comic style are to be found. The two knights are given da capo arias, which contain baroque melodic structures and rhythms and clearly reveal elements of parody. The rural population and shepherds sing simple song-like melodies, and an ensemble of fife, violin, bassoon/basses and drum add interesting 'Spanish' colour.

Thus Telemann, significantly in the history of eighteenth-century opera, bridges the gap between German Baroque opera (which was drawing to a close in compositional and performance respects in the 1730s) and the singspiel of the 1750s. However, Telemann's operatic works composed after 1729 are lost and according to Sulzer a German opera of which nothing is known was last performed in Danzig in May 1741. Nor is anything known of Johann Adolph Scheibe's 'weak attempt to save it [with his *Thusnelde*]' (schwachen Versuch, sie [mit seiner *Thusnelde*] zu retten).[29] The situation in the history of Italian and French opera is very different, where the development of the comic genre is closely connected to the serious genre: it was initially intended as a parody; both types then existed side by side for several decades. The German counterpart, however, was a later product of vernacular comic opera, which was independent of baroque opera. The short-lived phase of serious German

28 See Bernd Baselt, 'G. Ph. Telemanns Serenade "Don Quichotte auf der Hochzeit des Comacho": Beiträge zur Entstehungsgeschichte von Telemanns letztem Hamburger Bühnenwerk', in Constantin Floros, Hans Joachim Marx and Peter Petersen (eds.), *Studien zur Barockoper. Hamburger Jahrbuch für Musikwissenschaft* (Hamburg, 1978), vol. 3, pp. 85–100, esp. p. 92.

29 See the article 'Oper' in Johann Georg Sulzer (ed.), *Allgemeine Theorie der schönen Künste* (reprint of the 2nd edn., Leipzig, 1792–4), vol. 3, pp. 601ff. (This is not mentioned in the earlier edition of the treatise.)

opera in the second half of the century is also unrelated to it. The desire to parody serious opera thus played no role in the development of the singspiel, in contrast to opera buffa and opéra-comique.

Aesthetic debates about German opera

The caesura in German operatic history is filled by the beginning of aesthetic debate about the genre led mainly by literary figures rather than by composers. Johann Christoph Gottsched paved the way in 1737 when he criticized the 'linguistic mishmash' of German opera, in his *Versuch einer Critischen Dichtkunst.* He rebuked the audience, moreover, for foolishly believing that everything it did not understand was bound to be beautiful. This criticism included the German text, which Gottsched regarded as incomprehensible on account of the many sung ornaments. He castigated in particular the belief that the Italian language sounds better than German when sung by a castrato.[30] (In aesthetic debates about French opera in the eighteenth century enemies of French opera also put forward the view that Italian would be more melodious and better suited than French for musical settings.) Gottsched went further, too, accusing librettists of trying to make their libretti as miraculous as possible even if not taking them from old fables, in order to 'dazzle the rabble'.[31] All in all, then, he denounced opera as a genre entirely lacking consistency, doing so for general reasons, such as that it did not aspire to nature and therefore did not comply with reality, but also in specific terms, perceiving a lack of imitation of human action that would have vindicated a moralistic doctrine.[32] Even in 1774 Johann Georg Sulzer repeated these arguments in the article 'Oper' from his *Allgemeine Theorie der schönen Künste*, albeit directing his remarks only at opera seria.

In this way, Gottsched took up a position diametrically opposed to the aesthetic position at the beginning of the century. In 1710 the poet Menantes (on whose texts Bach composed some of his worldly cantatas, called 'dramma per musica') as well as his teacher Erdmann Neumeister and the librettist Johann Ulrich König celebrated an opera text as the 'most gallant', the 'masterpiece', or even the 'main piece' of dramatic poetry and regarded it as genuinely poetic. At the time, librettists were orientated towards contemporary Baroque literature and poetics and demanded that opera composers accept the primacy of poetry.[33]

30 Johann Christoph Gottsched, *Versuch einer Critischen Dichtkunst* (4th edn., Leipzig, 1751; reprint Darmstadt, 1962), section 2, 'Hauptstück', iv, §12, p. 742.

31 *Ibid.*, section 1, 'Hauptstück', v, §18, p. 185. 32 *Ibid.*, section 2, 'Hauptstück', iv, §9, p. 739.

33 See Bodo Plachta, '"Die Vernunft muss man zu Hause lassen, wenn man in die Oper geht": Die literaturkritische Debatte über Oper und Operntext in der Aufklärungsepoche', in Eleonore Sent (ed.), *Die Oper am Weissenfelser Hof* (Rudolstadt, 1996), pp. 171–89.

This viewpoint still surfaces in the practical Mattheson's recommendations for a composer to actualize 'the intention of a sung play' (Absicht eines Sing-Spiels).[34]

At the same time as the decline of German Baroque opera and the abolition of most opera houses, the libretto slipped from the realm of poetics, and with the onset of the Age of Enlightenment conceptions of opera changed as well. This is exemplified by Gottsched's attack, which was not only directed against the German variety of opera, but also against German practices in performing Italian operas. From his bourgeois position, he condemned the increasingly mannerist qualities of opera (which was also obvious from titles such as *Boris Goudenow oder Der Durch Verschlagenheit Erlangte Thron oder Die mit der Neigung glücklich verknüpfte Ehre* [Boris Goudenow or The Throne Obtained through Trickiness or The Honour fortunately connected with the Inclination]); its purpose of praising a prince or appealing to his virtues; and serious opera's claim to pre-eminence. In 1743 the author of the article 'Singespiel' in the 37th volume of Johann Heinrich Zedler's *Grossem vollständigem Universal-Lexicon aller Wissenschaften und Künste* welcomed operatic decline in Germany as a sign of the increasingly good taste of the audience. The author, seemingly, was Gottsched himself.[35]

Gottsched's critique was fiercely debated only a few years after its first publication and would remain a topic for discussion until the 1770s. His opponents' strategies differed in form and content. Gotthold Ephraim Lessing chose satire to cultivate his line of argument, with a contribution to Friedrich Wilhelm Marpurg's journal *Critischer Musicus an der Spree* and, almost contemporaneously, with his 'PoßenOper' (operatic farce) *Tarantula*, which remained a fragment. Here he voiced his opposition to the idea that the productive spirit should be subjected to binding rules. He also fought against the notion of condemning a work without a sound basis for critique and left the summary of opera's plots, seen as incomprehensible, to the aesthetically low figure of Hanswurst. In 1750 Lessing also countered the apparent inconsistency and lack of reason in opera with the argument (thus taking into consideration the effect on the audience) that opera should not be about reason, but rather about sensual pleasure provided to the senses by the mutually supportive arts of poetry and music. He therefore took up the same

34 Johann Mattheson, *Der vollkommene Capellmeister* (Hamburg, 1739; reprint Kassel and Basel, 1954), trans. and ed. Ernest C. Harriss (Ann Arbor, MI, 1981), p. 219.

35 In the volume that was released in Halle and Leipzig in 1743, the anonymous author used exactly the same formulations as Gottsched in 1739 about the necessary imitation of a human action for the confirmation of a moral doctrine, but does not refer to Gottsched.

position as the supporters of Italian opera and opponents of French opera in 1760s France.[36]

When in 1761 the writer Justus Möser protested against Gottsched's position that art should imitate nature, the position had basically already been superseded. Möser refined Lessing's arguments (that a productive spirit could not follow given rules and that only the sensuous impact of opera is significant) by appealing to certain principles. The demand that opera imitate reality is way off the mark, as opera is not a play with music. It cannot be judged therefore according to the rules of dramatic theory. The poet should have the right and the opportunity to invent other worlds; hence the unnatural in opera is immanent and necessary, and its musical execution not an impediment to aesthetic success. He therefore emphasized productive fantasy, which would soon become the core of the *Sturm und Drang* movement (see below).

In 1775 Gottsched's critique once again came under attack, this time from Christoph Martin Wieland, a poet who had already had practical experience with German opera, as the librettist of *Alceste*. In the essay *Versuch über das Deutsche Singspiel und einige dahin einschlagende Gegenstände*, he argued in pragmatic fashion against the ideal of opera imitating nature by focusing on the notion of delusion. The theatre as location for performance already requires the audience to accept delusion; thus the singspiel's attempt to present musically a simple and interesting plot is built on a delusion. Every listener knows, for example, that nobody can die while singing. It is not reality that is to be achieved, then, but pleasure, a pleasure of the noblest kind, which agitates the heart and moves the audience to tears. It aims at the improvement of taste and morality – in short, the advancement of humanity. Based on precepts of the Enlightenment, Wieland argues for a moral purpose for the singspiel, thereby linking it with the (albeit exaggerated) attempts in the Vienna of Joseph II to establish a German National Theatre[37] and a German National-Singspiel.

In spoken theatre, delusion and imitation of nature were not contradictory: plot and action, roles, characters, costumes that fit the era, stage design and especially the facial expressions and gestures of the actors could come close to reality, in order to strive for veracity and to persuade the audience to identify with the figures on stage. Dramas by Shakespeare, Molière, Lessing, Schiller and

36 See Elisabeth Schmierer, 'Die deutsche Rezeption der Querelle des Gluckistes et Piccinnistes', in Herbert Schneider (ed.), *Studien zu den deutsch-französischen Musikbeziehungen im 18. und 19. Jahrhundert* (Hildesheim, 2002), pp. 196–217.

37 See Reinhart Meyer, 'Die Idee eines deutschen "Nationaltheaters"', in Alena Jakubcová, Jitka Ludvová and Václav Maidl (eds.), *Deutschsprachiges Theater in Prag. Begegnungen der Sprachen und Kulturen* (Prague, 2001), pp. 15–30, esp. pp. 15 and 18. The Hamburg repertory was not very nationalistically inclined: there are twice as many original pieces in French as in German (Martina Switalski, 'Wandlungen im Theater des 18. Jahrhunderts am Beispiel von Köln', in Frank Günter Zehnder and Werner Schäfke (eds.), *Der Riss im Himmel. Clemens August und seine Epoche* [Cologne, 2000], p. 72).

Goethe, but also so-called 'Familiengemählde' (pieces in which the audience is presented with appropriate moral behaviour between parents and children, and husband and wife, for example, and were by authors who wrote for daily needs, such as Kotzebue), were required to 'emotionalize and moralize'[38] the audience. On the opera stage this was neither possible nor desirable to the same degree, as can be determined from the debates about opera. However, it was not only sensual pleasure that was to be achieved with the agitation of the heart through music, as there had also been a didactic dimension to the singspiel from its inception. (But for this purpose the 'irrational' plot was not much help.)

With the development of the German singspiel, true pragmatism ruled the day: singspiel aspired to create situations for the singing of simple lieder on the stage and to make it possible to perform these songs at home with piano accompaniment.[39] Already in Middle German singspiele by Johann Adam Hiller from the 1760s and 1770s, all the figures on stage drew their conclusions from the plot in the final sung roundelay (that is, chorus with refrain);[40] and when the pit was addressed in the last couplet (as was customary), the audience was directly confronted with the practical application of these conclusions.[41] Also the German national singspiel in Joseph II's Vienna demanded that a final moral be preached, as witnessed for example in the libretti of the most successful singspiele of Umlauf and Dittersdorf and in Mozart's *Die Entführung aus dem Serail* ('Nothing is as ugly as revenge' [Nichts ist so hässlich wie die Rache]). (Reason already featured in the traditional *lieto fine* of the dramma per musica, but only the sovereign's virtue was praised.) After the conclusion of the second phase of what can be called the 'national singspiel experiment' in 1788, this form of instruction continued in the suburban theatres, occasionally in a tiresome manner, such as in Schikaneder's libretto for *Die Zauberflöte*, studded with aphorisms and wise clichés.[42]

38 Susanne Eigenmann, *Zwischen ästhetischer Raserei und aufgeklärter Disziplin. Hamburger Theater im späten 18. Jahrhundert* (Stuttgart and Weimar, 1994), p. 71.

39 Strophic songs in particular were not supposed to be sung in full on stage, as they held up the action. See Christian Felix Weiße, 'Vorbericht', in *Komische Opern* (Karlsruhe, 1778), n.p. See also Gudrun Busch, '"Die Aura des Intimen": Interdependenzen des empfindsamen Klavier-, Roman- und Bühnenliedes zwischen 1766 und 1800', in Bernhard R. Appel, Karl W. Geck and Herbert Schneider (eds.), *Musik und Szene. Festschrift für Werner Braun zum 75. Geburtstag* (Saarbrücken, 2001), pp. 223–55.

40 In Hiller's *Poltis* (libretto 1773; piano arrangement printed 1782), a summary was already given in the third last number: 'Wenn Kleider Leute machen,/sind Leute selbst nicht schön ... Freylich haben viele, leider!/ihren Werth von ihrem Schneider ... Freylich sind es seltne Gaben,/beim Befehlen Welt zu haben.' (When clothes make people, the people themselves are not good-looking ... Sure enough, many unfortunately are valued by their dressmaker ... Sure enough, it is seldom a gift to own the world when giving orders.) With 'Wenn böse Männer Weiber plagen' (When bad men harass women), a different aspect was addressed in the final song.

41 This was also the case when the last couplet was re-written in order to fit the circumstances of a different performance venue. An example is Hiller's *Die Jagd*, when re-staged in Hamburg after a long absence. (See the review in *Hamburgischer Briefträger*, 25 January 1794, p. 154f.).

42 See Claudia Maurer Zenck, 'Einige ungewohnte Bemerkungen zur Zauberflöte, oder: Pamina walzt, Tamino sitzt im Bierzelt', *Musikforschung*, 57/1 (2004), pp. 36–55.

The other important element at the end of works was the presentation of the cast, their summing-up and their address to the audience. This custom spread across the nation in folk theatre, but the German singspiel ultimately adopted it from the opéra-comique (which adapted it in turn from the comédie-en-vaudeville.

The singspiel: introduction

The history of the singspiel in the eighteenth century can be divided roughly into two phases that are determined geographically as well as institutionally. The beginnings of this new type of music theatre occurred in northern and central Germany in the context of touring companies. Its further development was influenced by a characteristic type of singspiel production in South Germany and Austria at the end of the 1770s that spread across Germany in the 1790s. It was mainly cultivated at standing theatres and often at court theatres, as a lot of smaller courts had to dismiss their Italian opera groups for financial reasons and therefore employed cheaper German acting companies. This was the case in Stuttgart in 1774 and in Mannheim in 1777.[43]

But it is hard to tell when exactly the German singspiel came into being. Thomas Bauman subsumes all pieces written before 1766 as 'Before the Beginning', and Jörg Krämer starts his list of singspiele in 1760.[44] Recalling one of the standard terms for these pieces, 'Schauspiel mit Gesang' (see above), it is likely that the term itself signifies an early source of singspiele. It was long customary for theatrical pieces to be loosened through the introduction of familiar songs or new texts sung to familiar melodies. In England and France this popular medium resulted in new generic terms – comédies-en-vaudeville and ballad operas[45] – and in France provided a source for the development of comic opera. The date of 1760 is arbitrary as a starting point, if the practise of songs on stage and the similarly early occurrences of musical introductions and interludes between acts[46] are both taken into consideration. We can assume

43 Meyer, 'Die Idee', pp. 21ff. In Mannheim, the 'German court comedians' had been part of the theatre since 1768, and in 1777 their principal Marchand was instructed to organize the acting company for the newly founded Court and National Theatre. (See Thomas Betzwieser, 'Zwischen Kinder- und Nationaltheater: die Rezeption der Opéra-comique in Deutschland (1760–1780)', in Erika Fischer-Lichte and Jörg Schönert (eds.), *Theater im Kulturwandel des 18. Jahrhunderts. Inszenierung und Wahrnehmung von Körper, Musik, Sprache* [Göttingen, 1999], pp. 254ff.).

44 Thomas Bauman, *North German Opera in the Age of Goethe* (Cambridge, 1985), pp. 21–6; Jörg Krämer, *Deutschsprachiges Musiktheater im späten 18. Jahrhundert. Typologie, Dramaturgie und Anthropologie einer populären Gattung* (Tübingen, 1998), 2 vols., vol. 2, pp. 783ff.

45 For the ending of his *Beggar's Opera* John Gay planned a vaudeville with violin ritornelli and a final chorus. Johann Christoph Pepusch added only an overture in 1729 and put a bass line underneath the melodies.

46 By 1745 Johann Adolph Scheibe had already demanded that overture and interludes between the acts refer to the dramatic context, *Critischer Musikus* (2nd edn., Leipzig, 1745, pp. 611ff.); see Detlef Altenburg, 'Von den Schubladen der Wissenschaft. Zur Schauspielmusik im klassisch-romantischen Zeitalter', in Michael Berg, Helen Geyer and Matthias Tischler (eds.), *'Denn in jenen Tönen lebt es'. Wolfgang Marggraf zum 65.* (Weimar, 1999), p. 433.

then that the transition to the singspiel is as fluid as the retention of key terminology and the early repertories of travel companies imply. These companies travelled to the big centres of trade and commerce like Frankfurt (the city where the Emperor was crowned), but also performed their programmes elsewhere, such as in Mainz and Mannheim.

The early repertory of travel companies

The repertories of most travel companies performing at Frankfurt are well documented for the fifty-year span beginning in 1741 and ending with the construction of a permanent theatre. The 'High German comedians' (Hoch-Teutsche Comödianten), who gave guest performances there in the 1740s, performed a so-called 'Operette-Comique' approximately twice a week. It did not constitute the main item performed, but usually followed the performance of a play.[47] Typical titles of these musical pieces include: *Der in die Länder reisende dumme Peterl* (The stupid little Peter who travels to different countries); *Die lustige Jägerey* (The cheerful hunt); and *Das lustige Elend zwischen zwey versoffenen Eheleuten* (The hilarious misfortune of a pair of drunks, husband and wife). *Das lustige Elend* was written by Franz Anton Nuth, who was responsible for the music in this particular company, and was so successful that it was still being performed in the mid-1750s. They all betray the principal's central concern: namely to provide ample singing opportunities for the figure of Hanswurst, who was indispensable as the main actor in improvised plays with their musical and dance interludes. The plays themselves were described as 'Haupt- und Staats-Action', 'Pièce-Comique', or 'Bourlesque'. As shown in announcements the participants were 'our singer' (unsere Sängerin) or 'our first female agent' (unsere Primier Agentin), both actress and singer. She was part of the company and could sing well, although was probably not a specially trained singer. Nevertheless, she often sang artistically, even in plays, and performed not only German but also Italian arias ('our singer will distinguish herself best in good arias' [Unsere Sängerin wird sich in guten Arien bestens signalisieren]).

We can assume that the differences between such a spoken piece decorated with songs and dances and an 'Operette-Comique' were only minor ones; the texts of the spoken pieces were therefore also offered in printed form. But there seem to be two small differences. One involves the number of songs, totalling only around eight to ten in the plays.[48] And second, the 'arias' of the

47 For evidence, see Elisabeth Mentzel, *Geschichte der Schauspielkunst in Frankfurt am Main: von ihren ersten Anfängen bis zur Eröffnung des Städtischen Komödienhauses* (Frankfurt, 1882), pp. 439–69.

48 Georg Joseph Vogler's 'Operette' *Der Kaufmann von Smyrna*, composed in 1771, admittedly had only nine sung numbers (later extended to eleven), not a large number even for a single-act singspiel.

spoken pieces were more often taken from other pieces ('from an operetta newly composed here' [aus einer allhier erst componirten Operette]) rather than composed anew ('six new extra funny German arias' [6 neue extra lustige teutsche Arien]). The musical numbers for an 'Operette-Comique' could also be borrowed (explaining the occasional Italian aria), but more commonly were provided by a skilful member of the company. In the case of the 'High German actors' this task was fulfilled by Nuth, who was even mentioned by name on some of the announcements. An absence of surviving evidence makes it difficult to determine if other pieces – such as those advertised as 'extraordinary amusing action, decorated with amusing musical arias' (mit lustigen Musicalischen Arien decorirte, extra-ordinair lustige Action) or as a similarly equipped 'Comique-Piece' – adopted French vaudevilles and if they distinguished themselves from the spoken piece with amusing arias or from the Operette-Comique.

The first singspiele at Leipzig

In 1743 Johann Friedrich Schönemann certainly adapted the melodies from the popular English ballad opera *The Devil to Pay* to perform this novelty in translation in Berlin. (Schönemann succeeded the famous Neuberin, after she and her company moved to Russia in 1740.) *Der Teufel ist los*, the German title of the ballad, was so successful on German stages that Heinrich Gottfried Koch, who founded his own drama company in Leipzig in 1750, wanted to profit from it, too. As he could not get hold of the German text (Schönemann did not print it in order to ward off competition), he charged the Leipzig poet Christian Felix Weiße with the responsibility of providing a new translation. One of the violinists of his group, Johann Standfuß, composed the music. From its premiere in 1752 onwards the piece enjoyed such remarkable success that a number of years later Weiße even translated its sequel, *The Merry Cobbler* (*Der lustige Schuster*). Koch meanwhile was expelled from Leipzig during the Seven Years' War and got his company underway in the area around Hamburg. The highly successful sequel was again composed by Standfuß and premiered in Lübeck in 1759.

The fact that thirteen songs are preserved from *Der Teufel ist los* shows that more music was provided than was customary, especially as Standfuß had composed at least another four numbers. For the sequel, thirty-two numbers by Standfuß are preserved. This state of affairs can be attributed to Hiller, who adopted and presumably adapted the numbers, when providing the two libretti[49] with additional (and new) compositions in 1766. He contributed

49 Weiße meanwhile revised them with new titles for Koch, who came back to Leipzig in 1763.

another twenty-four numbers for *Die verwandelten Weiber, oder Der Teufel ist los, Erster Teil*[50] and another seven for *Der lustige Schuster, oder Der Teufel ist los, Zweyter Teil.* Both singspiele have survived in the piano score from 1770 and 1771 co-produced by Standfuß and Hiller. It is not, then, the first Leipzig performance in 1766 that marks the beginning of the history of German singspiel; its history had already begun in 1752 – as a contemporary observes[51] – with Standfuß's setting of *Der Teufel ist los.* (The theatre directors and even Koch himself remained interested in this setting and its sequel for a long while.[52]) It has to be remembered that dating depends on the material that survives and that the practice of equipping spoken texts with insertions mentioned above was standard practice both before and after 1752. Since temporal and structural transitions are to be expected, the suggested caesura at 1752 should not be considered a rigidly fixed date.

The lighter, established types of opera from other countries became influential during the transitional phase. They were performed in translation by travel companies and their translated texts newly set by German composers, as there were initially no original libretti. The use of vaudevilles at the end shows the clear influence of opéra-comique, and is already evident in Standfuß's *Der Teufel ist los* sequel from 1759. Opéra-comique became familiar in Germany in the 1750s, first in the cities close to the central area of the Rhein (Mainz, Frankfurt, Mannheim, Straßburg). The acting company of F. J. Sebastiani and his successor Theobald Marchand frequently translated and performed them. Later they were also played in Dresden, Hamburg and Vienna and frequently in the 1780s in Rheinsberg, but not in Berlin.[53] Apart from the final roundelay it was the romance that particularly influenced the early singspiele. The romance became popular as a narrating stage song, and provided an example of the most effective way of overcoming an obstacle in the plot. It therefore represented the pragmatic counterpart to the parable aria in serious operas. The song-like lieder were a characteristic feature not only just of opéra-comique, as strophic lieder were usually chosen for vocal solos and were even performed as duets. The da capo aria and even the opening sinfonia (with its three movements and fast–slow–fast tempi) moved into the singspiel from Italian opera burlesca or comedia per musica, Hiller already using a sinfonia for each of the two pieces

50 Four of these replaced first versions by Standfuß, and twenty set new texts; cf. Bauman, *North German Opera*, p. 29. Bauman is mistaken by one, however, in terms of the number of texts that Standfuß adopted.

51 Schneider, 'Das Singspiel vor Mozart', p. 305.

52 Bauman, *North German Opera*, p. 29 (citing the preface to the print of Weiße's *Komische Opern* [Leipzig, 1768], vol. 1, p. vii) and p. 32.

53 Betzwieser, 'Zwischen Kinder- und Nationaltheater', p. 246.

that together comprise his adaptation of Standfuß's *Der Teufel ist los*.[54] The form of the songs, whether set as a strophic song, da capo or ABA' aria, or through-composed with tempo changes, depended on the text and the mood of the character.

Hiller's next singspiel was *Lisuart und Dariolette, oder Die Frage und die Antwort*, which he composed in the same year (1766). It was based on a French model adapted by the law student Daniel Schiebeler, who had written a libretto for his former teacher Telemann five years earlier, as explained above: Charles-Simon Favart's *La Fée Urgèle*, composed by Duni in 1765 and including a number of elements incorporated later by Schindler into *Die Zauberflöte*. Schiebeler strove for a more serious type of singspiel; Hiller composed few strophic songs and more dal-segno and fully written-out da capo arias instead, in order to enhance the genre's serious credentials. He also drew on a French element for the same purpose: whereas the first *Teufel*-singspiel begins with Lene's comic and desperate debut song 'Immer Bier und Brandtewein' (always beer and brandy), here the first act opens with a roundelay addressed to the month of May and with couplets for each of the queen's three court ladies. The ending of the third act is appropriately extended: a chorus with a long introduction is placed before the vaudeville; it is an extension of the build-up to the ending, which Hiller retained in similar fashion for his subsequent singspiele. The solo numbers often reveal harmonic and formal sophistication.[55] Even in Queen Ginevra's first aria, the final A' does not return to the E-flat from the beginning after the B-flat major middle section, but moves to C minor instead. The B-flat major aria of the court lady Olinde is similar. Also, the 'Andante affettuoso' (B-flat) of the enchanted princess Dariolette, in which she addresses the young knight Lisuart, is already interspersed with echo effects and other elaborations in its A section, where the voice takes up and pursues the short echo motif. The repetition of the first four verses results in variant versions (even the beginning of the A' section is new), and the B section finishes with a meaningful Phrygian cadence (at 'oder ists die Liebe?' [or is it love?]) before an A'' section ensues. Knight Lisuart's agitation is revealed in his E-flat major aria in Act 3: the adagio from the opening question ('Auf ewig würde sie die Meine?' [She would become mine forever?]) is abandoned by the second verse and

54 It is not known how Standfuß introduced his two settings. The first opera buffa in its German translation appears to have been performed in Berlin in 1775, namely Pietro Guglielmo's *La sposa fedele*, which was widely disseminated across Europe. Its translation as *Robert und Kalliste* was carried out by Johann Joachim Eschenburg.

55 This sophistication is also demonstrated in the way that the setting is constructed: the usual series of four-bar phrases ('Vierer'), with occasional elisions of beats, is loosened by extended phrases or even by three-bar phrases ('Dreier') – for example, in the Act 1 song of the ladies, at the instrumental and vocal opening of Madasine and Derwin's duet. For further details, see below.

continued in an allegro with dynamic contrasts and marked leaps. Hereafter, the same changes take place respectively a fifth and fourth higher set to the same text. Again the largo B section begins with the first verse and in C minor, but on this occasion follows the question with different, more joyful verses, the tonality soon returning to E-flat major. The falling, sigh figures in the question are no longer interrupted, but merge into a continuous melodic line, before all of the first part is repeated. The introduction to Act 3 is similarly imaginative, with the knight initially singing the first and fourth lines twice. Each time he continues musically and texturally in a different way, before presenting the entire first strophe that also incorporates an interlude.

But Hiller did not want to follow such compositionally challenging procedures. He rewrote the piece as a three-act opera, expanded it by nine numbers and performed it only six weeks after the original two-act version was performed. For half of the new numbers, he expanded the female title role of Dariolette, who was transmogrified into an old woman. As the title vignette for the piano arrangement (engraving by Geyser) illustrates[56] she is not to be perceived solely as a serious character. The comic character of the squire Derwin is also expanded. The final vaudeville already showed in the first version of the singspiel (mentioned above) that Hiller and his librettist wanted humour to assume an important role: while the preceding chorus is connected with the singspiel's plot, the opening couplet of the final song is pure parody. The audience no doubt enjoyed it, but it concerns the subtitle of the singspiel (the question and the answer) rather than the plot *per se.*[57]

Hiller's next three singspiele (1767–70), once again collaborations with Weiße, were his most successful. They are based on plots that were especially popular in French plays or as opéras-comiques. *Lottchen am Hofe*, *Die Liebe auf dem Lande* and *Die Jagd* also have in common the fact that rural innocence is set and defended against the courtly world, a topic of interest in French and Italian circles. But now the topic was aired in a German-speaking work and later employed in other singspiel libretti as well. For understandable reasons, Weiße maintained the French name of the aristocratic opponent in *Lottchen am Hofe*, who tries to seduce the country girl Lottchen. In the two subsequent libretti the girls are more grounded than Lottchen who, at the beginning, is dazzled at

56 Here the old woman approaches Lisuart, who smiles disdainfully. His squire Derwin is highly amused by the situation.

57 'Elmire weint auf ihres Gatten Bahre,/die weisse Hand tobt in dem schönsten Haare,/es bringt ihr klagendes Geschrey/die ganze Nachbarschaft herbey./Doch fühlt der jungen Wittwe Herz/auch in der That so grossen Schmerz?/Und währt ihr Kummer viele Tage? – Chor: O schwere Frage! o schwere Frage! o schwere Frage!' (Elmire cries at the bier of her husband, her white hand goes wild in her most beautiful hair, her wailing screams bring over the whole neighbourhood. But does the heart of the young widow indeed feel such great pain? And does her grief last for many days? – Chorus: Oh, difficult question! difficult question! difficult question!)

the prospect of a life at court ('Gürge, now I forsake you. I only like it at the court' [Gürge, nun entsag ich dir. Nur am Hof gefällt es mir]). And in both plays Weiße softened the precarious class distinction: in *Die Liebe auf dem Lande*, the prospective seducer was scaled down to a tax collector, while the count was represented as the gracious one at the end, in spite of the abduction of Lieschen. In *Die Jagd*, the count's seduction attempt is narrated only in the song of the rural beauty Hannchen, albeit in two different versions. In the manner of a romance, both songs are interrupted after each strophe by the remarks and the questions of the sympathetic Röschen, and later by the worried beloved. The count is punished in the end – by the king himself. The king is portrayed in a fashion typical of German singspiel: as an unknown person, mingling among the village people; in a brotherly duet with the village judge Michel at the end of Act 2; singing reasonably about conceited but weak human beings earlier in Act 2 ('Was sind die Menschen doch für Thoren' [Oh what fools human beings are]); and doing good deeds at the end. Thus, the village judge opens the final divertissement with 'Wer sollte nicht sein Leben / für einen solchen König geben' (Who would not give his life for such a king) while the others answer in an accompanied four-part canon in buoyant 3/8 time 'Es lebe der König' (Long live the king).[58]

Musically these three singspiele are considerably simpler than their immediate predecessor and are connected to both *Teufel* pieces. They consist mainly of solo numbers, for the most part (strophic) songs, and a few small ensembles with which the first acts end. They often divide the finale into two numbers, the characters changing the nature of their participation.[59] In *Die Liebe auf dem Lande*, the final roundelay follows a divertissement, where the pattern of couplet and chorus arises from alternate singing of one and two characters. In this piece Hiller uses the 'tempo di menuetto' to characterize the love-struck Schösser, but not at the beginning, when he extols the virtues of his adored country-maiden, Lieschen. It appears subsequently when he sings about the rival he has to outmanoeuvre, Hänschen. (Johann André uses the 'tempo di menuetto' in similarly mocking fashion for Bernardo's No. 3 'Hin ist hin und tot ist tot' [broken is broken and dead is dead], where this fatherly friend seems to allay Elmire's fears about Erwin. Through the choice of tempo he conveys at least to his audience the tongue-in-cheek nature of the words.)

58 In Ernst Wilhelm Wolf's *Ehrlichkeit und Liebe* from 1776, the prince asks in a strophic song for understanding in regard to his duties. He points out the enviably quiet life of his subjects and even takes part in the final roundelay. The portrayal of the tender-hearted prince shows the tacit acceptance of political circumstances, as is also discernible in 'private' spoken pieces. It was only in the *Sturm und Drang*, in Schiller's *Kabale und Liebe*, that such pieces became political.

59 Compare sung numbers for *Die Liebe auf dem Lande* and *Die Jagd* as given in Schneider, 'Das Singspiel vor Mozart', pp. 308ff. and 313ff.

This work brings to an end Hiller's vital contribution to what Thomas Bauman describes as the first phase of the North German singspiel and 'birth of the Saxon Opera'.[60] The next phase of development, the dissemination of this type of opera between 1770 and 1773, includes four further singspiele by Hiller. *Die Jubelhochzeit*, composed at the end of the second phase in 1773, distinguishes itself only in detail from his earlier compositions – for example, by presenting the roundelay as early as the end of the first act and by placing two instrumental interludes between the acts. The first interlude is cast in ABA' form, the A section containing two frequently repeated elements and the A' being significantly shortened. The second interlude consists of two minuets, the first dependent upon numerous repetitions again, while the second – written for oboe with accompaniment and therefore constituting a trio positioned before the repeated first minuet – is through-composed.

Meanwhile – from 1768 to be precise – Ernst Wilhelm Wolf, 'Hofkonzertmeister' (court concert master) at the music-loving Weimar Court, also dabbled in the new genre. And Hiller wakened the interest of his pupils Christian Gottlob Neefe and Johann Friedrich Reichardt in 'low-comic' one-act pieces. First Hiller left Neefe to compose ten of the twenty-four numbers for *Der Dorfbarbier*. Next Neefe had success with his two-act *Die Apotheke*, while Reichardt's two attempts apparently remained unperformed. From compositional perspectives, Neefe orientated himself around the singspiele of his teacher (three-part symphony; aria forms that featured frequent tempo changes; strophic songs and ariettas; 'tempo di menuetto' for a courting song; choruses at the end of acts). Most interesting are probably the da capo aria (with shortened A') of the infuriated pharmacist Enoch ('Komm du mir wieder, verdammtes Thier!' [Just come back to me, damned beast!]), in which he staggers between Furioso, Molto Allegro and Allegretto in major and minor, as well as the farce-like song of the hypochondriac barber Trist relaying his digestive problems.[61] In each strophe, Lamentoso (D minor), Tumultuoso (F major) and Lamentoso (E-flat major–D minor) once again, he describes these problems by using forceful harmonies, no doubt to amuse the audience.

This singspiel was not performed again at Leipzig, but was taken to Berlin at the end of 1771. After gaining performance privilege for Prussia and also acquiring the Schuchische Theater in the Behrenstraße, Koch moved his group bit by bit to Berlin. In Berlin and in the Prussian province he and his successor Carl Döbbelin performed a number of new German singspiele. Aside

60 The association of the years 1766–70 with this phase has been disregarded here, for reasons demonstrated above.

61 Bauman's statement (*North German Opera*, p. 71) that Neefe wanted to satirize the barber's allergy through the classical languages contained therein, does not get to the heart of the humour.

from Hiller, music directors from Berlin were most present in the repertory; for Koch it was Holly, who hailed from Prague, and for Döbbelin it was Johann André.

The autodidact Johann André from Offenbach, who worked later as a music-seller and publisher, translated a variety of opéras-comiques for Marchand's company, before writing his first opera *Der Töpfer* in 1773 stimulated by his involvement with Marchand. André's friend Goethe, who lived in nearby Frankfurt, was also interested in the new genre, although he mocked the then prevalent 'Handwerksopern' (trade operas).[62] Goethe had already in childhood experienced Marchand's company in Frankfurt and during his studies heard Hiller's first singspiele in Leipzig. When André asked him for a libretto in 1775, he adapted the long ballad of Edwin and Angelina from the eighth chapter of Oliver Goldsmith's novel *The Vicar of Wakefield*. It was the first of a number of libretti that Goethe wrote (just under a third of his dramatic work comprises libretti, libretto-related projects and hybrid types, such as the melodrama[63]) and the only one that was set a number of times – by André, the duchess Anna Amalia, Carl David Stegmann, Ernst Wilhelm Wolf and Anton Schweitzer (although his was not performed). The last person to take it up was Reichardt, who used the setting that Goethe revised during his second tour of Italy and set it with recitatives, but did not have it performed.

Goethe's *Erwin und Elmire* and his concept of the singspiel

Goethe's choice of *Erwin und Elmire* shows that he was interested in characters with an upper-middle-class background. He linked an intrigue, one not initiated by a third party but solely the result of the behaviour of two lovers, with a discussion of different educational concepts. The exposition in the house of a residential city continues in a rural scenario (including a supposed hermitage). Unlike at the court, forthrightness is possible here, and the lovers' entangled feelings can be resolved. Goethe fashioned their reunification through exclamations and planned eloquent pauses: 'Music may dare to express the feelings of these rests' (Die Musik wage es, die Gefühle dieser Pausen auszudrücken). Not every composer could comply with this wish, least of all probably André.

62 Goethe, *Dichtung und Wahrheit*, 4th part, book 17 (Munich, 1962), vol. 24, p. 229.

63 Bodo Plachta, '"*Wir müssen nun auf alle teutsche Opern Theater Anschläge machen*". Goethes Versuche der Literarisierung von Oper und Singspiel', in Michael Zywietz (ed.), *Grenzgebiete. Festschrift Klaus Hortschansky zum 65. Geburtstag* (Eisenach, 2000), p. 119 (with reference to Dieter Borchmeyer). In 1816 Goethe was still looking in vain for a composer for his libretto *Feradeddin und Kolaila* and therefore left it as a fragment (Wolfram Huschke, *Musik im klassischen und nachklassischen Weimar 1756–1861* [Weimar, 1982], p. 32).

He set the exclamations as recitatives and filled the pauses with lombardic accompanying figures in downward-moving triadic arpeggios; Elmire's 'weh mir' (woe for me), when she recognizes Erwin as the hermit,[64] is not very plausibly set as a simple deviation from the antecedent upbeat-jumping third at 'Erwin'. Stegmann, however, demonstrating manifold qualifications as an actor, singer, violinist and harpsichord player and employed at the time at the Schuchische company at Königsberg, proceeds with a fiery presto at the recognition scene. He continues with an appropriate fall of a fifth on the downbeat at 'weh mir' and a stretched and sustained 'Du bist's' (it is you), in a lyrical Adagio with descending figures. Here he probably had in mind Elmire bending down to Erwin, who kneeled in front of her. Duchess Anna Amalia,[65] who was trained in Italian opera and was concerned with differentiated character portrayals,[66] chose an accompagnato with key, time and tempo changes as well as wandering harmonies. She regarded Elmire's sensitive 'weh mir' as dispensable, but set Elmire's three 'Erwin' cries according to her emotional ups and downs. In the ensuing Adagio Anna Amalia incorporates modulations with strong dynamic contrasts and upward-directed instrumental figures, as they occur in a free fantasia and as they correspond to the emotional flight of fancy of the two lovers at the end. This climax, which Goethe left to the music, was thus interpreted as emotionally confusing by Anna Amalia and conceived on a broad scale while Stegmann, like André, favoured the touching solution. Stegmann, however, did not compose it as simply as André, focusing on the scene where Elmire gives full vent to her feelings in natural surroundings and finds herself 'full of breath' (Mit vollen Atemzügen). He also set the text very accurately, employing rich compositional devices – intermissions in the middle of the strophe featuring a ritornello; tempo, key and time changes; dynamic contrast; and varied settings of repeated strophes.

Goethe's subsequent singspiele and the duchess' setting of *Erwin und Elmire* were made possible by Anna Amalia's establishment of a private theatre in Weimar in the autumn of 1775. The palace theatre had burned down in 1774 and the company of Abel Seyler that was employed there had to be dismissed. The private theatre remained until 1783, playing on four improvised stages and

64 Tina Hartmann (*Goethes Musiktheater. Singspiele, Opern, Festspiele, 'Faust'* [Tübingen, 2004], p. 66) interprets the ending from a gender perspective and wrongly proceeds from the assumption that Elmire does not identify Erwin as the hermit. Countering her interpretation are not only Elmire's multiple 'Erwin'-cries, but also the final trio, in which Erwin departs from the monastery in her presence.

65 Her singspiel contains five further numbers at the beginning of the action as well as some text changes, which were probably made by the duchess herself, but which Goethe did not include in the printed version.

66 Concerning the different compositional portrayals of Olimpia and her daughter Elmire, see Annie Janeiro Randall, *Music and Drama in Weimar 1776–1782: A Social-Historical Perspective* (Ann Arbor, MI, 1996), pp. 134–40.

remaining open to experiments.[67] Goethe, who arrived at the court at the end of 1775, wrote among other things *Lila*, *Claudine von Villa Bella*, *Jery und Bätely* and *Die Fischerin* for this theatre. His highly pragmatic attitude was that a singspiel should have three types of songs: stage songs; arias as expression of feelings; and a 'rhythmical dialogue',[68] which was to be composed very flexibly, according to action and movement. Thus, Goethe was basically describing a musical scene. He changed his conception of the singspiel on two more occasions, though, apparently attributable both times to the impression Mozart's operas made on him. Listening to *Die Entführung aus dem Serail*, a popular piece in Weimar from 1785 onwards, he realised the advantages of using choruses as a counterpart both to the small number of acting figures and to arias, which put the emphasis on the operatic features of the singspiel. During his second tour of Italy, Mozart's *Le nozze di Figaro* discouraged him from finishing his libretto *Die Hausgenossen*, which was likewise inspired by Beaumarchais' play. For the setting of his singspiel *Scherz, List und Rache* Goethe also looked for a composer who would model his work on opera buffa. As librettist he strove for a natural flow of speech when deemed necessary; on other occasions he included forms from the serious dramma per musica. In consequence he reworked his three earliest singspiele, simplifying their plot and versifying their dialogues, so that they could be set as recitatives. But this did not prove productive in 1790. Reichardt's settings of the new versions were relatively unsuccessful, or were not even performed, and Goethe for the time being did not take his operatic plans any further. When he became director of the Weimar Court Theatre in 1791, however, he staged a multitude of contemporary operas. He even returned to the simple concept of the singspiel with sung numbers and spoken texts when starting to write a sequel to *Die Zauberflöte*,[69] admittedly emphasizing the declamatory setting of his words in the manner of Gluck's French operas.

It was André's setting of Goethe's singspiel *Erwin und Elmire* that brought him success. *Claudine von Villa Bella*, André's first setting of Goethe's second singspiel with its *Sturm und Drang* theme and its big finale,[70] remained unperformed. Twelve of his singspiele, however, were performed by Döbbelin's company in Berlin, and most were successful. André thereby dominated the local music scene until the end of the 1770s, when his works gradually fell from

67 Randall, *Music and Drama in Weimar*, pp. 122 and 212–15. The municipal audience was allowed into the Redoutenhaus and, from 1780 onwards, the Komödienhaus. In the castles of Ettersburg and Tiefurth only the court was present (see Huschke, *Musik im klassischen und nachklassischen Weimar*, p. 24).

68 Goethe's letter to Philipp Christoph Kayser from 29 December 1779, quoted in Plachta, 'Goethes Versuche der Literarisierung', p. 130f.

69 Hartmann, *Goethes Musiktheater*, p. 313.

70 According to Bauman (*North German Opera*, p. 171), it is the first finale for a North German opera.

favour. Among the acclaimed singspiele are *Der Alchymist* (1778) and *Elmine* (1782). *Elmine* has quite a few interesting compositional traits, even if traits not altogether compatible with the plot.[71] There is still a finale in the style of a vaudeville, but now with couplets that have been texturally constructed in very different ways than previously; the singspiel opens with a single sonata movement as an overture (and no longer with a three-movement sinfonia); the principal character has a da capo aria with concerted instruments; hide-and-seek activities are acted out with spoken 'Still' and 'Bst' on the stage in an Andante grazioso (ending with sung laughter); and the ending of the first act consists of an emotional solo scene that finally culminates in a wordless action – Elmine dropping into an armchair. For the purpose of intensifying the situation on the stage, André turns to a relatively new dramatic device at the end of this first act – the melodrama.[72] It emerged independently and experienced immediate success.

The melodrama

Towards the end of 1774 the theatrical genre of melodrama was developed by Jiří (Georg) Antonín Benda, who hailed from Bohemia and had been Hofkapellmeister in Gotha since 1750.[73] In Gotha he presumably witnessed a performance of Rousseau's 'scène lyrique' *Pygmalion* (written in 1762) in a new setting by the composer Anton Schweitzer in 1772[74] and it probably acted as a stimulus for his own work. In the melodrama one or two dramatic, and mostly tragic, scenes are connected to one or two characters (monodrama or duodrama) in the context of a new type of music, where the text is not sung but declaimed. The audience were attracted to this new genre because, in contrast to opera, it ensured that the verses were understood and because actors would act continuously throughout. In opera, they usually performed only during the spoken passages or recitatives and sang their arias standing on the forestage.

71 Bauman's harsh judgement about the inadequacies of the composition is at least partially overstated: he takes a mostly silent scene for a melodrama and criticizes the laughter as 'imbecilic' (*ibid.*, p. 185).

72 Here contemporary usage is followed: the word is used to denote the particular type of setting (in German: 'Melodram') associated with this term today, as well as the scenic whole, which in turn is determined by the setting and defined as (in German) 'Melodrama'.

73 See Zdeňka Pilková, 'Georg (Jiří) Bendas Melodramen', in Hermann Danuser and Tobias Plebuch (eds.), *Musik als Text. Bericht über den Internationalen Kongress der Gesellschaft für Musikforschung, Freiburg 1993* (Kassel, 1998), vol. 1, pp. 374–6.

74 Rousseau had his text set to music in 1770, a version premiered at the Paris Opéra in 1772. (Concerning dates, see Gerhard Sauder, 'Rousseau und das Melodram', in Danuser and Plebuch (eds.), *Musik als Text*, vol. 1, p. 369.) It seems that Benda was influenced, moreover, by the tradition of the Latin school drama, in which context we must also view the first surviving Latin drama *Sigismund* by Johann Ernst Eberlin, with its musical accompaniment to a spoken text. Other early forms of melodrama are mentioned in Werner Braun, 'Das Gebrauchsmelodram', in *ibid.*, vol. 1, pp. 382ff.

The melodrama was of interest to poets, because their words had absolute primacy; the music had to follow the poetry, but could lend it greater expressivity as well. Likewise, the melodrama benefited theatre companies, as they mostly had better actors than singers. It was therefore two famous actresses who launched Benda's first melodramas *Ariadne auf Naxos* and *Medea* in 1775: Charlotte Brandes, whose husband Johann Christian had written the former text with *Pygmalion* as his model (the latter was written by Friedrich Wilhelm Gotter), and Sophie Seyler, a famous tragic actress. As members of Abel Seyler's company they had come shortly before from Weimar to Gotha, where the court theatre was soon to be established. Goethe also wrote a melodrama in 1776, *Proserpina*. It was presumably written for Corona Schröter, the famous actress and singer, whom he had just called to Weimar (and who also set his libretto *Die Fischerin*). The actresses (names indicate that it involved mainly female characters; the speakers of Theseus and Jason, for example, remained secondary roles) were likely enthusiastic about the pieces, as they allowed them to pull out all the stops, not only in declamatory terms, but also in terms of mastery of gesture.[75] The scenes were less about the events, which were simply narrated, than about the inner action. These mental processes were supposed to be elucidated through pantomime, a kind of physical action not generally seen in music theatre.[76] A number of other composers were similarly enthusiastic about the novelty of melodrama; about sixty-five were written and set to music up to 1800. Cannabich, for example, composed an *Electra*, Meißner and Neefe each a *Sofonisbe*, Peter Winter three melodramas with several acts (1778–80) and Seckendorf Goethe's *Proserpina* (1779). Neefe's *Sofonisbe* was premiered in Mannheim in 1778, again by Seyler's company. Mozart missed this event when he was in Mannheim at the end of that year, but he listened to and watched Benda's melodramas, and when the theatre manager von Dalberg gave him the commission for a duodrama for Mannheim he reacted enthusiastically. *Semiramis*, set to a text by Otto Heinrich von Gemmingen, was apparently a 'declaimed opera'[77] in several acts, but even if it was finished it is now lost.

75 The unusually numerous stage directions in melodramas apply mostly to appearance and to body language.
76 On this point, see Sabine Henze-Döring, '"Ausdruck" und "Körperlichkeit": das deutsche Melodram des späten 18. Jahrhunderts', in Fischer-Lichte and Schönert (eds.), *Theater im Kulturwandel*, pp. 215–26. The copper engraving of Charlotte Brandes as Ariadne (in a garment vaunted as Greek) bequeaths a specific gesture to – and an unusual perspective on – the character. Similar to the engraving of Madame Koch as the desperate Alceste from Schweitzer's opera, she is shown lifting her arms above her head and twisting the upper part of her body (in contrast to Sophie Huber as a joyful Elmire experiencing nature, who stands up straight with outstretched arms).
77 See Mozart's letter to his father of 3 December 1778, in Emily Anderson (ed. and trans.), *The Letters of Mozart and His Family*, (3rd edn., London, 1985), p. 638. For further details, see, for example, Peter Branscombe, 'The Relationship between Spoken Theatre and Music-Theatre', in Moritz Csáky and Walter Pass (eds.), *Europa im Zeitalter Mozarts* (Vienna, Cologne and Weimar, 1995), p. 360.

The librettists of the early melodramas favoured themes from Greek and Roman antiquity. As with the development of opera around 1600 they took inspiration from ancient theatre. (Rousseau had similar intentions for his *Pygmalion*, in which he tried once again to overcome the deficiencies of French declamation and thus demanded a setting 'in the style of Greek chant' (dans le genre de la melopée des Grecs).[78] The reference to antiquity was all the more desirable as the new melodrama, with its way of connecting text and music, was reclaimed as a genuine German invention, allowing us to apprehend 'the German bourgeois theatre consequently as the legacy of the Greek theatre' (das deutsche bürgerliche Theater mithin als Erbe des griechischen Theaters).[79]

The librettists first worked their material into a very elaborate plot, encompassing a single act. Soon this dimension was exceeded; it was not only Mozart's intended *Semiramis* that had several acts. Linguistically they included vivid metaphors from nature as well as 'wild exclamations and ecstacy' (wilde Ausrufungen und Verzuckungen).[80] They therefore had at their core frenetic emotional outbursts and the oscillation between extreme affects. They did not follow modern operatic aesthetics in this respect, rather (Italian) Baroque opera, which was dominated by the da capo aria with its principal and secondary affects. The old gradation of affects was sharpened, however, to the contrast of emotions, resulting in the invention of a new kind of presentation. A scene highly charged in affective terms was introduced by a short instrumental passage; the monologues were spoken in sentences or paragraphs, and were commentated upon or refuted (through feelings hidden beneath the surface) by musical insertions. These short musical inserts, often only a single bar of music, were imitated speech and relied on rhetorical figures. Whenever a climax was reached, music as well as gestures and miming accompanied the declamation '[which] produces the finest effect' (welches alsdann die herrlichste wirckung thut), as Mozart wrote enthusiastically to his father.[81] As a result of the shortness of these episodes, there was no formal or harmonic development, but abrupt change instead. In order to balance the fragmentary nature of the form, Benda on the one hand relied on a number of recurrent main motifs, and on the other often put in a longer passage after a climax that

78 See Sauder, 'Rousseau und das Melodram', p. 369.

79 For evidence see Siegfried Bushuven and Michael Huesmann, 'Gesteuerter Affekt. Die Instrumentalisierung von Musik im deutschen Melodrama des 18. Jahrhunderts', in Fischer-Lichter and Schöhnert (eds.), *Theater im Kulturwandel*, p. 237f.

80 Critique of the melodrama *Electra* in *Allgemeine deutsche Bibliothek*, vol. 43 (Berlin and Stettin, 1780), p. 108, quoted in Wolfgang Schimpf, *Lyrisches Theater. Das Melodrama des 18. Jahrhunderts* (Göttingen, 1988), p. 177.

81 Letter of 12 November 1778, in Anderson (ed. and trans.), *Letters of Mozart and His Family*, p. 631.

contrasted in tempo, key and instrumentation. It accompanied the character's exhaustion after her or his outburst and was contemplative in character.

In this form, however – as an independent scene, a sequence of scenes, or even as a sequence of several acts, which on their own can reasonably denote a genre – the melodrama was short-lived. In the nineteenth century it continued mainly under the influence of French popular theatre in German-speaking areas.[82] The relationship between music and spoken text proved fruitful in a different way, though, for music theatre of the eighteenth century. There is, for example, not only a melodrama in Mozart's incidental music to *Thamos*, but also two melodramas called 'Melologo' for his unfinished singspiel *Zaide* from 1779–80. By integrating this type of setting as an opera scene (or in an opera scene) he opened up a new way of utilizing the melodrama on the stage – a way immediately imitated by other composers. Johann André in Berlin seized the opportunity to diversify his music for plays and singspiele by introducing melodramatic passages. He arranged the witch scene of Act 4 of Shakespeare's *Macbeth*,[83] for example, to include six bars of spoken evocation above sustained chords by the wind players, before the witches start singing.[84] (Incidental music for the same drama from 1794 by Johann Gallus Mederitsch even contains a newly written and composed melodrama at the beginning of Act 4.[85]) André's singspiel *Elmine* contains not only the one melodramatic scene already mentioned, but two. In the 1790s the melodrama is sometimes combined with the eerie and numinous, as is the case in Stegmann's *Der Triumpf der Liebe, oder: Das kühne Abenteuer* (1796), Wenzel Müller's extremely popular singspiel *Das Sonnenfest der Braminen* (1790) and Peter Winter's *Das unterbrochene Opferfest* (1796). In Winter's work it is reserved for the announcement of the forthcoming feast of sacrifice during thunder and lightning, and in Müller's melodrama for the (feigned) ill-fated oracle of the gods. In contrast, Reichardt decided in his *Geisterinsel* (1798) to mark Ariel's first entry by a spoken comment from Prospero over a brief instrumental segment, whereas Johann Rudolf Zumsteeg in Stuttgart eschewed melodrama in his setting of the same libretto.

82 See Monika Schwarz-Danuser, 'Die Rezeption des französischen Boulevard-Melodrams im deutschen Sprachraum', in Danuser and Plebuch (eds.), *Musik als Text*, vol. 1, pp. 397–401. Whether Carl David Stegmann's *Moses Errettung* (*c.* 1807) can legitimately be included with the melodramas mentioned hitherto requires further investigation.

83 Shakespeare's dramas – promoted in particular by Schröder in Hamburg from 1776 onwards – seem to have provided a challenge for incidental music; see Ursula Kramer, 'Zur Bedeutung Johann Andrés für die Herausbildung einer neuartigen, "analogen" Schauspielmusik. Seine Kompositionen zu *Macbeth* und *King Lear*', in Dagmar Beck and Frank Ziegler (eds.), *Carl Maria von Weber und die Schauspielmusik seiner Zeit* (Mainz, 2003), pp. 61–74 and Joachim Veit, 'Georg Voglers "Beiträge zur Gattung Schauspielmusik"', in *ibid.*, pp. 75–102. (It is the performance of *Hamlet c.* 1778 that is discussed in Veit's article.)

84 See the illustration in Kramer, 'Andrés "analoge" Schauspielmusiken', p. 70.

85 Wolfgang Schimpf, 'Hekate als Medea. Beobachtungen zu einer melodramatischen Szene in *Macbeth*', in Danuser and Plebuch (eds.), *Musik als Text*, vol. 1, pp. 365ff.

In the context of compositional activity, the melodrama plays a similar role to *recitativo accompagnato* in Italian opera and could be considered its analogue in a non-singing context; for it is mostly melodramatic passages that prepare an aria, as in No. 9 of Mozart's *Zaide*. But with the increasing compositional distinctiveness of singspiele, genuine accompagnato introductions (with German texts) were also gradually composed for arias, and melodrama regarded as an additional option for a setting. André, for example, employed melodrama for the dramatic conflict of the main character in his singspiel *Elmine*. He built up the finale of the first act by portraying inner indecision through smooth alternation of compositional devices – repeated melodramatic passages and sung parts, in different tempi, meters and keys.

In the period that followed, opera would remain the place for meaningful use of melodrama. Spoken passages with music were seen as a particularly effective expressive mechanism in opera, and mostly as an alarm signal for forthcoming disaster, well into the twentieth century.[86]

Serious German Opera or 'courtly singspiel'

Two years before launching the new operatic genre of melodrama in Gotha in 1775, Seyler's company had taken part in a novelty in Weimar that aroused great curiosity. This time the singers also took part.

In a way, melodrama followed on from baroque opera, which was possible in the mid-1770s, as composers still wrote operas about great mythical figures for court theatres in the second half of the eighteenth century. Customarily, they were performed at the court as a dramma per musica with an Italian libretto. (Pietro Metastasio, the celebrated Viennese court poet and author of dramas numerously set in the eighteenth century, some over fifty times, died only in 1782, three months before the première of Mozart's *Entführung*.) The singspiel enabled the creation of a German counterpart: a serious German opera, also called a 'höfisches Singspiel' (courtly singspiel).[87] The first successful work aspiring to this status was instigated by Christoph Martin Wieland. He wrote the libretto *Alceste* in 1773 and convinced the music director of Seyler's company, Anton Schweitzer, to set it to music. Attempts to create a courtly singspiel had been made earlier, Metastasio's libretti representing important examples for the company as they did for Wieland's *Alceste*. The young Daniel

86 See also Daniela Kaleva, 'Melodrama Insertions in Opera', in Schneider (eds.), *Studien zu den deutsch-französischen Musikbeziehungen*, pp. 228–39.

87 According to Jörg Krämer, 'Metastasio und das deutsche Singspiel', in Laurenz Lütteken and Gerhard Splitt (eds.), *Metastasio im Deutschland der Aufklärung* (Tübingen, 2002), pp. 85–102, esp. pp. 92ff. The title is misleading, however, as it appears to refer to all singspiele.

Schiebeler admired Metastasio so much that he sometimes quoted entire scenes from the poet's works; the influence of Metastasio's texts is striking then in his libretto *Lisuart und Dariolette* for Hiller in 1766. Hiller, also a great admirer of Metastasio, met the need to implement a more serious kind of opera by composing more demanding forms than in his two early singspiele, thus uncompromisingly enforcing them against Koch's will. The expectations of the Leipzig theatre audience, however, centred on the comic, such that when approbation was not forthcoming, Schiebeler and Hiller had to adapt the work with comedy in mind (see above).

Metastasio's influence on Wieland in *Alceste* was less apparent in the choice of the mythological plot and dramaturgical conception than in overall layout. He divided the text into five acts, structured the scenes mainly from recitatives and arias and provided only four ensembles: a duet; a further duet with chorus; a trio; and a quartet as a finale. The Metastasio model is also notable in the poetic text, especially in the parable aria of Alceste 'Zwischen Angst und zwischen Hoffen' (between fear and hope). But he carried out 'a sensitive conversion of the model',[88] wanting to show 'great moral characters, sublime dispositions, noble fights between virtue and passions',[89] therefore replacing Metastasio's 'reason' (ragion) with 'heart' (Herz). He aimed at a 'lyrical scene' (lyrische Scene)[90] relying on the emotion of the audience and intended to foster 'most reputable entertainment' (anständigste Unterhaltung) for the court, 'most noble recreation' (edelste Erholung) for the tradesmen and 'delights for the mind' (Gemüthsergötzung) and a 'school of good manners' (Schule guter Sitten) for the rest.[91] This resulted in crucial changes to the model, but also led to a clear differentiation from the ordinary singspiel: Wieland rejected both 'an overly artificial complication' (einen allzu künstlichen Knoten) of the plot as unsuitable for the musical setting and a 'particularly tragic' (äußerst tragisches) piece. Instead, he trusted 'greatest possible simplicity in the plan' (möglichste Einfalt im Plan). He therefore agreed with the critique of his Mannheim colleague C. F. Schwan, who in 1771 voiced the concern that the construction of most operettas was uninteresting and irregular and moreover 'devoid of all morals' (leer von aller Moral), such that hardly any scene would be endurable

88 Krämer, 'Metastasio und das deutsche Singspiel', p. 95.

89 Christoph Martin Wieland, 'Versuch über das Teutsche Singspiel, und einige dahin einschlagende Gegenstände', in Wieland, *Singspiele und Abhandlungen* (Leipzig 1796; reprint Hamburg, 1984), p. 245.

90 This explains the subtitle that is similar to Rousseau's for his melodrama *Pygmalion* (see above).

91 Wieland, 'Theatralische Nachrichten. Weimar', in *Der Teutsche Merkur* (March 1773), part 3, p. 264, quoted from Gabriele Busch-Salmen, '"Übrigens ein Werk voll Fehler und Nachlässigkeiten": Wieland/Schweitzers Singspiel *Alceste* in der opernästhetischen Debatte', in Beatrix Borchard and Claudia Maurer Zenck (eds.), *Alkestis: Opfertod und Wiederkehr. Interpretationen. Hamburger Jahrbuch für Musikwissenschaft* (Frankfurt, 2007), vol. 23, p. 97.

without the music.[92] Wieland renounced strong affective contrasts in favour of the psychological motivation of the action. (The fact that he had just translated Shakespeare's dramas, which were enjoying an enhanced reputation on German stages in the 1770s, no doubt played a part in this.) The poet was certainly aware of the fact that 'the lyric drama' (das lyrische Drama) could have a 'dull and soporific' (matt und einschläfernd) effect, especially as he only chose recitatives for parts of the action ('action cannot be sung' [Handlung kann nicht gesungen werden]).[93]

This last point was also a focus for the critics of his libretto, Johann Friedrich Reichardt (1774) and the *Sturm und Drang*'s Joseph Martin Kraus (1777) – both were composers and authors themselves. (Kraus' critique also illustrates the declining reputation of Metastasio in the *Sturm und Drang* period, whereby the hopes for a serious German opera soon foundered.) They missed individual characterizations – especially the formation of passions – and action that evolves from it. Kraus, for example, found fault with the implausibility of the parable aria in Alceste's psychological situation at the beginning of the drama, and Reichardt with the extra-long secco-recitative of her death scene. But both authors also criticized the musical setting. For this scene in particular, Reichardt criticized the choice of secco rather than accompagnato recitative as well as the mistaken characterization of Herkules. Kraus slated the unending repetition and variation of two single lines, scoffing at this attempt at musical eloquence.

The opera came with Seyler to Gotha in 1774 and went to all the bigger theatres as well, creating a sensation wherever it was staged and encouraging similar compositional attempts. In 1776 Benda composed the 'serious operetta' *Walder* and the 'serious singspiel' *Romeo und Julie*. Compared with *Alceste* (and the opera of Holzbauer that was to follow), these two are rather short: the first is a one-act opera with thirteen sung pieces. The second has as many numbers, but spread out over three acts. Accordingly, the *recitativo accompagnato*, with which the action of *Romeo und Julie* begins, is prepared only by a twenty-four-bar long 'Entry' and not by a fully worked-out overture, reminiscent of the introductions to Benda's melodramas. Strikingly, even the 'entry' of the one-act opera *Walder* is longer. *Walder* attracts our attention as a result of its strange ending: the quartet (and biggest ensemble used) does not function as the finale, but the main character Hannchen (not exactly a fitting name for a character in a serious opera) sings a very elaborate dal-segno aria instead. Both

92 C. F. Schwan, 'Vorbericht', to *Das Milchmädgen und die beiden Jäger, eine Operette* (Mannheim, 1771) pp. 3ff., quoted in Herbert Schneider, 'Übersetzungen französischer Opéras-comiques für Marchands *Churpfälzische Deutsche Hofschauspielergesellschaft*', in Ludwig Finscher, Bärbel Pelker and Rüdiger Thomsen-Fürst (eds.), *Mannheim: Ein 'Paradies der Tonkünstler'? Kongressbericht Mannheim 1999* (Frankfurt *et al.*, 2002), p. 396f.

93 Wieland, 'Versuch über das Teutsche Singspiel', pp. 257ff.

works, which are not through-composed, do not convey the impression that Benda made a concerted effort to build on Schweitzer's attempt.

In 1778, when the Dresden court opera was dissolved and was to be substituted by a German travelling company, August Gottlieb Meißner translated Metastasio's *L'Isola disabitata* into German for the local Kapellmeister Joseph Schuster. In the following year Haydn composed the Italian original for Esterháza. Meißner followed Metastasio's dramaturgical design and also took on the recitatives, but transferred the aria texts into unrhymed verses. The opera was not premiered in Dresden, however, but in Leipzig in 1779.

In Schwetzingen and Mannheim *Alceste* met with patriotic responses, those that had already expressed themselves in the foundation of a society for the fostering of German language and literature. The performance may in fact have given rise to two further operas of this type[94] – *Rosamunde*, Wieland's and Schweitzer's commissioned work for Mannheim, and *Günther von Schwarzburg* from the Mannheim Hofkapellmeister Ignaz Holzbauer and the professor Anton von Klein. The latter had already published his views about the German language in 1769.

With *Rosamunde*, Wieland decided on a topic from English history. But he was not content with his work, only being encouraged to complete it in the hope that Schweitzer's composition would compensate for the deficiencies of his libretto. Perhaps it was Reichardt's critique of his *Alceste* that made him admit in 1777 that he had neither the sense nor the talent for dramatic composition.[95]

As this work dragged on, a crucial step towards a 'national' opera was being taken by Klein and Holzbauer, who were adapting a topic from German history. Their work was staged in Mannheim just before the Electoral Prince Carl Theodor moved to Munich, while at the same time *Rosamunde* was being rehearsed but could not be performed before the move. *Günther von Schwarzburg* retained a strong Metastasian influence in dramaturgical and topical terms, thus containing homage to the prince, a dominating sovereign and an intriguing character (the only one for whom we cannot account in historical terms), who initiates the entanglements of the love story as well as the political story, determines the progression of the plot and dominates it. From the point of view of compositional requirements, the librettist also remained within the realm of the familiar, providing no more than a duet, trio and an aria with chorus. For novelty value, Klein included more monologue scenes than was

94 Just after *Alceste*, Wieland wrote two more libretti. He wrote an opera again for Schweitzer in 1773, *Die Wahl des Herkules*, which followed a 'festa teatrale' by Metastasio. One year later he wrote *Medor und Angelica* for Wolf after a 'serenata' by Metastasio. But it was given only in a concert performance in Berlin not before 1788.

95 See Wieland's letter dated 26 May 1777, in *Wielands Briefwechsel* (Berlin, 1983), vol. 5, p. 619, quoted in Busch-Salmen, 'Wieland/Schweitzers Singspiel *Alceste*', p. 111.

customary and constructed whole scenes from alternating sections of recitatives and arias (as in the entry scene, for example). Holzbauer, who had thus far earned his reputation in music theatre exclusively with drammi per musica, did not always follow Klein in this respect. Although Holzbauer composed monologues as impressive accompagnati throughout, he changed smoothly in some scenes between the three vocal types, secco, accompagnato and aria, and also included stage directions in his composition. Nevertheless, his arias do not go beyond the forms already adopted (including in singspiele) from Italian operas. Holzbauer discarded a planned recitative after an aria, with which Klein had tried to make the exit of a figure seem more plausible, returning instead to the old model of the exit aria.

It is not surprising, then, that Klein and Holzbauer returned completely to the (Italian) dramma per musica in Mannheim, when Carl Theodor assumed the governance of Bavaria in Munich and took his court theatre with him. They returned to ancient subjects; before choosing *Tancredi* (premiered in 1783), for example, they decided on an episode from Roman mythology that had been popular for decades, namely the fate of Dido who had been abandoned by Aeneas. In autumn 1779 the new Mannheim Theatre, which Carl Theodor financed in compensation for the town's loss of its status as a residential city, was opened with the one-act piece *La morte di Didone*. The Italian text, however, was supplemented with a German translation, as was customary, and both authors soon seem to have come to the agreement that the opera should also be performed with a German text. Holzbauer could not have actually witnessed this: it took until 1784 for a performance to come to fruition in Mannheim. The German libretto, *Die Zerstörung von Karthago*, includes further aria texts and is designed to culminate in a key scene after which all characters leave the stage one after the other, until the abandoned Dido embraces death while singing in unrhymed verses.

In the form of an Italian dramma per musica, but one provided with a singable German translation in the score, the serious 'German' opera seems to have taken a detour. First, this recalls the detour taken by German Baroque opera. Second, it is not contradictory since in the meantime 'Italian' arias were composed with coloraturas. Third, singspiele translated not only from opéras-comiques but also from opere buffe had long been commonplace. The 'mixed taste' demanded by Mattheson was still demonstrable in opera's mixture of styles, which would not have been experienced as contradictory. (A perceived German idiom was discovered only in 1821 in the celebrated *Freischütz*, even though the 'German' hunting chorus in particular was very similar to French opera choruses.) A good case in point in this respect is Peter Winter.

In 1778 Winter moved with the Electoral Prince from Mannheim to Munich as an orchestral musician. There he was appointed music director and composed his first German opera in 1782, *Helena und Paris*, in the tradition of Holzbauer's serious opera. As it failed to achieve success, he mainly composed singspiele after that, some to great acclaim (see below), and also experimented with serious Italian and French operas. In 1798 he tried once again to write a German opera: the 'große Oper' (grand opera) *Marie von Montalban* (premiered in Munich in 1800) had a libretto based on a sequel to the much-performed tragic play *Lanassa*. Two years later his dramma per musica *La grotta di Calipso*, with a libretto by Da Ponte, was premiered in London. This opera features a translation that conforms with the music; Winter ensured that the recitatives were congruent with the German text, by matching the music with the vocal inflection or by simply composing them afresh.[96] This was a practice that had also been carried out when adapting Italian Baroque operas for the German stage. The aim of the translations in both cases was to enable the work to be performed in German theatres. In its translation, *Calipso* was performed as a German opera in Munich in 1807. With this variability of practice Winter effectively brought to a close the history of German opera in the eighteenth century. At the same time, his attempts to create a serious German opera represent a point of connection with the history of opera in the nineteenth century.

Repertory and performances

Contemporaries agree that from the 1770s onwards audience predilection for music theatre increased dramatically.[97] If we investigate the relationship between music theatre and spoken theatre, in terms of the repertory and programmes of established, regular theatres and travel companies, as well as the proportion of original German singspiele in programmes and repertories, a confusing picture emerges that allows for few generalizations. The repertory of the court actors of the Electoral Palatinate (Kurpfälzische Hofschauspieler) under Theobald Marchand, who performed regularly in Frankfurt between 1771 and 1777, contained thirty-three plays and comedies, mainly adaptations of French dramas, among which were five with inserted arias, and ninety operas.[98] What is interesting here is the relationship among singspiele, opéras-comiques and opere buffe which, it is important to note, were also performed in German and with inserted spoken texts. The group played six Italian pieces, about fifty of French origin (their importance also being documented in the collections of

96 Both versions of the recitative are printed next to each other in the piano score published around 1809.
97 The widespread popularity of opera across Germany is described for the year 1788 by Johann Friedrich Schütze (*Hamburgische Theater-Geschichte* [Hamburg, 1794], p. 619) among others.
98 See Mentzel, *Geschichte der Schauspielkunst in Frankfurt*, pp. 517–21.

printed libretti translated by Johann Heinrich Faber, a University professor at Mainz[99]), and thirty-five by German composers (whose libretti were often modelled on French ones). Hiller was most prominently represented with nine singspiele and a prologue; five singspiele were by Ernst Wilhelm Wolf and four by Carl David Stegmann. Christian Gottlob Neefe, Georg Benda and Johann André had three singspiele each in the repertory.

For companies that did not specialize in operas, such as the Neuhausische Schauspieler-Gesellschaft, the exact opposite occurred: at the end of 1778 they had ninety-two plays in their repertory, supplemented by twenty-seven epilogues and only thirty-two operas. Among these, there were twenty French opéras-comiques and only six Italian and six German operas, as well as two melodramas.[100] Between these extremes in repertory terms there were a number of intermediate stages, dependent on the staff at a particular company and on the preferences of particular directors. The Kurcölnische Gesellschaft under Gustav Friedrich Wilhelm Großmann and Johann Friedrich Helmuth performed twenty plays at Easter 1780 (and another three prologues and epilogues, of which at least one contained arias and choruses), a melodrama and ten singspiele, of which seven were French, one Italian and two German. In the autumn of 1780 Frankfurt audiences could experience nineteen plays, three ballets, one melodrama and another twelve pieces fitted out with music performed by the Böhmische Gesellschaft. Strikingly, seven pieces connected with a particular composer were all of German provenance. Seyler's company also had nine singspiele exclusively by German composers in their repertory when touring Lower Saxony from autumn 1769 to autumn 1771. When they were employed at the Weimar court in 1771, they performed twenty-six German singspiele, including Benda's melodramas, and also five Italian and French singspiele. At the court in Gotha (1775–9) they only performed sixteen German singspiele and two melodramas, but thirteen adaptations.[101] This difference can probably be attributed to the differing tastes of the princes.

Where the Böhmische Gesellschaft is concerned, the relationship between pieces and performances in the aforementioned time span was *c.* 2:3 (19:28) for plays and almost 1:2 (13:24) for singspiele, which meant that on average a singspiel was played twice, and a play one and a half times. This changed according to the society concerned and their speciality,

99 Compare Schneider, 'Das Singspiel vor Mozart', pp. 389–94. Schubart criticized Marchand's 'undeutsches' (un-German) repertory in his 'Teutsche Chronik' from 1774 (Augsburg and Ulm).

100 Mentzel, *Geschichte der Schauspielkunst in Frankfurt*, pp. 526–9.

101 The numbers in Bauman (*North German Opera*, pp. 92ff.) and Reinhart Meyer ('Der Anteil des Singspiels und der Oper am Repertoire der deutschen Bühnen in der zweiten Hälfte des 18. Jahrhunderts', in Renate Schusky (ed.), *Das deutsche Singspiel im 18. Jahrhundert* [Heidelberg, 1981], p. 27–76, esp. pp. 50ff.) are slightly different, as one survey starts in September, and the other one in October 1775.

as=well as to the time-frame under consideration. If we were just to compare the evenings when only spoken pieces were given (often two at a time) with those when a singspiel was heard (excepting one-act pieces or burlesques that traditionally followed most music theatre pieces, as a final dance, although not for the longest and most successful ones) we would come to the following conclusion: for most established theatres and travel companies that specialized in German language works, there were about two to three times more spoken theatre evenings than music theatre evenings from the mid-1770s onwards.[102] The great court theatres could have a completely different ratio, on account of the presence of an Italian opera ensemble. The Burgtheater in Vienna, for example, which from 1783 to 1792 at least usually presented spoken and music theatre pieces alternately,[103] offers a more even balance. And if one includes the times when the Kärntnertortheater staged operas only, the ratio shifts in favour of music theatre.

The singspiele of the 1780s

The German audience's increased interest in opera in the 1780s is linked to changes undergone by the singspiel itself. These changes involved the libretti as well as the music.

At the end of the 1770s, a Leipzig businessman appeared before the public as a talented librettist: Christoph Friedrich Bretzner. His comedies, which immediately achieved great success, were set more often than those of anyone else up to the end of the eighteenth century. Bretzner did not draw on the rural and sentimental subject matter that originated in French topics and that Weiße had used in his texts for the early singspiele. His strength was that he invented comical intricacies in plots, and introduced some entirely new elements. Even in his early *Der Äpfeldieb* – the anonymous first print in 1769 did not feature sung numbers and the first musical setting is dated 1780 – there is theft, a professional swindler, a nobleman trying himself out as a treasure seeker, his adulterous wife and, finally, blackmailing on account of the compromising behaviour, which leads ultimately to a solution to all problems but is also responsible for the fact that the frequent lapses are not punished. Behaviour that was inappropriate, dishonest, or deceitful was adopted by other librettists

102 Meyer ('Der Anteil des Singspiels und der Oper') has also put together statistics for disparate geographical areas and time periods, but unfortunately does not differentiate between the number of performed plays and singspiele on the one hand and the programmes with only spoken pieces versus those with a singspiel on the other. For present purposes, then, his numbers are of very limited relevance.

103 See the tabular survey of programmes compiled by Dorothea Link in *The National Court Theatre in Mozart's Vienna: Sources and Documents, 1783–1792* (Oxford, 1998), pp. 23–190. It was also common here for two plays to be given on the same evening.

and time and again used in the context of blackmail as the solution to the plot: in Stephanie's text for Dittersdorf's *Der Apotheker und der Doktor* (Vienna, 1786) both characters mentioned in the title put each other under pressure on account of professional lapses; in the singspiel libretto that Dittersdorf wrote himself, *Hieronymus Knicker* (Vienna, 1789), and which was later adapted by August Vulpius, a simulated treasure hunt and a broken marriage vow work together to produce a happy ending; and in Joachim Perinet's libretto to Wenzel Müller's *Die Schwestern von Prag* (Vienna, 1794) it is the planned infidelity of both parents of the bride, on account of which they have to agree, like it or not, to the love match of their daughter. The motive of a threatening compromise or of the deceived swindler comes from the Italian burlesque tradition. Goethe also used it when he started to work on his new libretto *Scherz, List und Rache* in 1784. That this motive was first included by Bretzner in his libretti and later among Viennese libretti demonstrates the gradual cultural exchange in the 1780s between North/Middle Germany and Vienna. This exchange led to the reception and musical setting of four of Bretzner's libretti that had been published in an operetta collection in 1779 (*Der Äpfeldieb*, *Adrast und Isidore*, *Der Irrwisch* and *Das wütende Heer*)[104] – also in Vienna. Shortly after the period of his greatest influence in Berlin where, in the span of just two years (1779–81), five singspiele set to his early libretti were premiered, he also established a strong presence in Vienna. The demand for his libretti is especially clear when we look at his *Der Irrwisch* which, between 1779 and 1791, was chosen by ten composers.[105] Ignaz Umlauf's setting, under the title *Das Irrlicht*, was premiered in Vienna in 1782 and staged again at the Kärtnertortheater in 1786, where it was highly successful; it was then widely disseminated, especially in southern Germany (but also in Hamburg). At the same time Otto Carl Erdmann von Kospoth's *Irrwisch* setting was popular in North Germany in particular. In those days, Umlauf was the Kapellmeister responsible for German opera performances in Vienna, and also a well-known composer of singspiele. With his *Bergknappen*, he inaugurated the Emperor Joseph II's 'National-Singspiel' in 1778, and wrote one singspiel after another until 1788, including some highly acclaimed ones (*Die Apotheke*, 1778; *Die schöne Schusterin oder Die pücefarbenen Schuhe*, 1779).

Gottlieb Stephanie, who had revised Bretzner's *Der Irrwisch* to *Das Irrlicht*, was also involved in the adaptation of a Bretzner operetta that was undoubtedly one of the best known: *Belmont und Constanze, oder: Die Entführung aus dem*

104 On this period and these works, see Bauman, *North German Opera*, p. 191.

105 See Claudia Maurer Zenck, 'Die Tugend in der Hütte. Umlaufs *Irrlicht* – ein frühes Wiener Singspiel in Hamburg', in Zenck (ed.), *Musiktheater in Hamburg um 1800. Hamburger Jahrbuch für Musikwissenschaft* (Frankfurt *et al.*, 2005), vol. 22, pp. 61ff.

Serail. Bretzner wrote it for Johann André in Berlin in 1780, who premiered his singspiel of the same name in May 1781 at Döbbelin's theatre. It is possible that the famous actor Friedrich Ludwig Schröder, who was employed at the Burgtheater at the time (and who after his return to Hamburg initiated Mozart reception at the Comödienhaus), brought the text from Berlin to Vienna afterwards and gave it to Mozart, for whom he was instructed by the imperial director to find a 'booklet'.[106] In any case, the text ended up in the hands of Stephanie who, commissioned by the Nationalsingspiel, continually searched for usable libretti and, if required, also translated French and Italian texts so that they could be set to music. He worked on Bretzner's libretto and Mozart composed a new version to it, which appeared under its original subtitle at the Burgtheater in 1782. It was frequently performed there until the end of the Nationalsingspiel in 1788. A few months after its première in Vienna it had already been given in Prague and after that was performed in all of the main European opera houses.[107] The travelling companies included it in their repertory and performed it wherever they went from 1783 onwards; they continued to perform it to the acclaim of their audiences in the 1790s. *Die Entführung aus dem Serail* was a great success for Mozart, in part on account of its plot.

Plots

The first plots of German singspiele are to be found in burlesques and coarse 'ballad operas'. From these a fashion developed for trade operas (*Der lustige Schuster*, *Die Liebe unter den Handwerkern*, *Der Töpfer*, *Der Hufschmied*), about which Goethe complained. Very soon the French librettists of the opéra-comique, Favart, Michel-Jean Sedaine and Jean-François Marmontel, became the model, and with them arrived the pastoral environment, sentimental love affairs and matters relying on the contrast between country people and courtiers. Ambitious German librettists, who strove for a more serious German opera, continued to favour ancient plots until the turn of the century. In this respect, serious German opera as a bourgeois genre did not really distinguish itself from the courtly opera seria.

After the 'French period' two areas of focus stand out among the great variety of plots – a third follows from *c.* 1790 onwards (see below) – as can

106 See Claudia Maurer Zenck, *Così fan tutte: dramma giocoso und deutsches Singspiel. Frühe Abschriften und frühe Aufführungen* (Schliengen, 2007), pp. 152ff.

107 Occasionally it was translated into the relevant national language for the location in which it was being performed, as was the case in Warsaw in 1783. (It was also performed in Warsaw with the German text in the same year.)

be gathered from the list of performed operas in Jörg Krämer's comprehensive study of the singspiel.[108] Hiller's later libretti are no longer based on libretti by Weiße, but had names such as *Das Grab des Mufti, oder: Die beyden Geizigen* (1779) and *Poltis, oder das gerettete Troja*. In spite of its ancient characters (the main female character is called Euridice and on one occasion 'father Orpheus' is addressed in song; the other names are also of Greek provenance), this singspiel contains the familiar ingredients of a nobleman in love, who tries to seduce a simple girl. Indirectly through French models, then, ancient models came to be of interest for librettists in North Germany from *c.* 1777 onwards. In the south, evidence of such interest is witnessed a few years earlier – for example, in Haydn's singspiele *Die reisende Ceres* and *Philemon und Baucis* with the prologue *Der Götterrat*. He composed these works at the beginning of the 1770s and *Philemon und Baucis* and *Der Götterrat* were performed in 1773 in honour of Empress Maria Theresia, who was visiting Eisenstadt. In 1794, a trace of antiquity is still present in Schikaneder's confused and dramaturgically unconvincing libretto *Der Spiegel von Arkadien*. It was set by Süßmayr, who was clearly dependent on the model of Mozart's *Zauberflöte*, and performed very frequently in Vienna – the figures of Jupiter and Juno participate. As this particular example illustrates, singspiele represent trivial adaptations of antiquity far removed from themes of serious melodramas as well as from Wieland's libretto of *Alceste*, and far removed from Wieland's view that opera is heir to the great mythological plots of ancient tragedy. It is more reminiscent instead of the popular parodies of elevated stage works.

The second area of focus – the attraction of 'foreignness' – was already present in Hiller's earlier work, and also influenced the idyllic 'Arkadien'. Its French prototype was composed by André-Ernest-Modeste Grétry in 1770, and first appeared in the German singspiel in 1776, illustrating the early popularity and rapidly increasing and long-lasting attraction of remote and exotic peoples and locales on stage. In 1796, the librettist Franz Xaver Huber chose Peru and the Inkas for Peter Winter's 'heroisch-komische Oper' (heroic-comic opera), *Das unterbrochene Opferfest*. Wenzel Müller in his popular *Das Sonnenfest der Braminen* (libretto by Carl Friedrich Hensler) from 1790, and Karl Regers in his serious text *Marie von Montalban* for Winter ten years later, opted for India with his native inhabitants and Brahmins alike. In the dramas on which some libretti are based the 'conquest' of exotic places is already tangible a decade earlier. At the same time 'Turkish' colour dominated singspiele. In 1771, it can be found in the German adaptation of Gluck's last, and frequently performed, opéra-comique, *La rencontre imprévu* (1764) with the title *Unvermuthete*

108 Krämer, *Deutschsprachiges Musiktheater*, vol. 2, pp. 783–847, 848–55.

Zusammenkunft, oder die Pilgram zu Mekka. It is also evident in Vogler's *Der Kaufmann von Smyrna* (premiered 1771; also set by Franz Andreas Holly in 1773 and, more successfully, by Stegmann), in Holly's singspiel *Der Bassa von Tunis* (1774), in Hiller's *Das Grab des Mufti* (1779) and in Neefe's *Adelheit von Veltheim* (1780), based on a libretto by Großmann. Bretzner certainly knew the latter when he wrote his text *Belmont und Constanze* for André shortly thereafter, and it is also likely that Stephanie consulted it in his adaptation of Bretzner's libretto for Mozart in 1781. In 1783 André's *Barbier von Bagdad* was performed (though it garnered little success), and also the *Oberon*-operas, which were composed in 1789 by Friedrich Ludwig Emilius Kunzen, Karl Hanke, Franz Danzi and Paul Wranitzky to a fairy tale by Wieland, and were set in Baghdad and Tunis. (And in 1790 Lorenzo Da Ponte played ironically with the 'Turkish fashion' in his libretto for Mozart's Italian dramma giocoso *Così fan tutte*.)

These exotic subjects served two main aims – exciting the curiosity of the audience and luring them into the theatre, and also providing contrast with the familiar, the exotic figures serving individually and collectively as accessories to the principal European characters who had ended up far from home. The fact that the latter ultimately won their conflicts goes without saying. It was standard practice for the Turkish element to have a comical side-line, making effective use of foreign manners (the harem guard) and religion (the prohibition of alcohol). Thus Hiller composed a roundelay for drunken Janissaries in the second act of his *Das Grab des Mufti*; and Bretzner and Stephanie combined both elements in the figure of Osmin.

The Viennese singspiel

With the abduction scene, Bretzner had already designed the kind of great musical finale for *Belmont und Constanze* that was customary in opera buffa, but not yet customary in singspiele from North and Middle Germany. The endings of the second and third act of Stephanie's and Mozart's version (see below) are extended further and exit arias not provided by Bretzner are given at the end of some scenes. Bretzner, enraged about his Viennese rival Stephanie's adaptation, put great emphasis on the poetic quality of his sung verses (in contrast to Stephanie's adaptation), which was more important to him than dramaturgical improvements, as they were for Weiße and Goethe.[109] Changes in the adaptation also emphasize differences in content between singspiele from the North and the South. The modified ending, for example, sheds light on the situation: for the urban audience in Berlin or Leipzig, for

109 Krämer, *Deutschsprachiges Musiktheater*, vol. 1, p. 414.

whom Bretzner was writing, the father–son relationship suddenly discovered by Bassa Selim and Belmonte must have made sense as a solution to the conflict. In the court theatre in Vienna the emphasis was placed on the generosity of the sovereign – not only in serious Italian operas, then, but also in the singspiel – a generosity that prevailed over deeply personal thoughts of revenge and that portrayed him as the sole guider of destiny.[110] But dramaturgical improvement is evident in the characterization of Stephanie's and Mozart's Osmin – who is simply a 'bad' character in Bretzner's version – demanding unconventional compositional solutions on Mozart's part, as witnessed in Osmin's entry and closing scenes.

In Osmin's F-major aria 'Solche hergelaufne Laffen', the text of the first two strophes is repeated, but is varied musically in different ways – first through a shift into an unrelated key (D major), and second by returning as usual from the dominant key to the main key but providing a melodic variation and a considerable extension at the end. Osmin is then provoked by a sentence from his adversary Pedrillo (an interruption between single strophes typical of romances in the North and Middle German singspiel), such that he adds a third strophe constructed in a completely different way from the first two. Here he loses control through endless textual and musical repetitions in a third key (A minor), which must have been highly comical for the contemporary audience. In the vaudeville, just before the final chorus of the Janissaries that Mozart and Stephanie, like many before them, adapted from the opéra-comique tradition (granting each character the opportunity to speak to the same music, punctuated by the general refrain), Blonde deviates from the regular pattern, changes the text of the first two verses of the refrain and thereby insults the only loser, Osmin ('only look at the animal, if we can endure it' [denn seh er nur das Tier dort an,/ob man so was ertragen kann]). Before everybody can join in, Osmin interrupts, takes up the melody of the refrain, returns the insult ('the dogs should be burned' [verbrennen sollte man die Hunde]) and thereafter falls into the last strophe of his aforementioned entry aria. The vaudeville comes off the rails in this way – but the construction provides the opportunity for a contrasting chorus of the two pairs. After singing in calm acquiescence about the reprehensible nature of revenge, they close the roundelay with the last refrain.

While Umlauf's *Bergknappen* was staged from time to time outside Vienna from 1780 onwards, and his singspiel *Die pücefarbenen Schuhe* and *Das Irrlicht* frequently performed (*Das Irrlicht* from 1786), the influence of the South

110 An analogous observation can be made for the adaptation of Bretzner's *Irrwisch* to Stephanie's *Irrlicht*; see Krämer, *Deutschsprachiges Musiktheater*, vol. 1, pp. 402–10 and Maurer Zenck, 'Die Tugend in der Hütte', pp. 70–6.

German, more precisely Viennese, singspiel on the North and Middle German singspiel really began only with the widespread dissemination of Mozart's *Die Entführung aus dem Serail*. It continued with Dittersdorf's *Der Apotheker und der Doktor*, which was premiered in Vienna in 1786, and paved the way up north for his subsequent singspiele, *Die Liebe im Narrenhause* (1787) and *Hieronoymus Knicker* (1789). Compared to the earlier singspiel, they both put greater emphasis on humour associated with mental and physical defects, not appreciated in Hamburg among other places. All in all Dittersdorf favoured topics concerning the bourgeoisie and dealing with love affairs. Stephanie, as the librettist of the highly successful *Der Apotheker und der Doktor*, followed the well-established pattern of two young pairs of lovers, one of which is jeopardized through a marriage arranged by the parents who want their daughter paired off with an old but affluent wooden-legged suitor. Stephanie develops all sorts of comical and other effective manoeuvres from this, leading Dittersdorf to pull out all the stops – from a parody of Gluck to a coloratura aria. (Mozart obviously found the work memorable, drawing two stimuli from it for his *Zauberflöte*.[111])

Paul Wranitzky's *Oberon, König der Elfen* (1789) also played in numerous venues and remained in German repertories up to the time of Carl Maria von Weber's opera of the same name. Its quick success provided a popular third, and typically Viennese, area of focus for the singspiel: the world of magic, fairies and ghosts. The predilection for this topic was not limited to Vienna – it was responsible, for example, for Shakespeare's *Sturm* (*The Tempest*) being adapted as a libretto by Friedrich Wilhelm Gotter in Gotha at the beginning of the 1790s. In 1798 it was set by Reichardt in Berlin (including male choirs standard for this city) as well as by Zumsteeg in Stuttgart. For both composers, the resulting *Geisterinsel* was their most successful singspiel.

The adaptation of demanding literature, however, remained exceptional; there would not have been enough high-quality works to fulfil the considerable demand in any case. Most of the more than 200 singspiele Wenzel Müller, Kapellmeister at Marinelli's theatre in Vienna's Theater in der Leopoldstadt, wrote for this suburban stage were magic operas. Müller was a versatile pragmatist, who also arranged burlesques with music, wrote parodies of well-known operas and later also contributed music to Ferdinand Raimund's folk plays. Considering his mass productivity, it is not surprising that the author of the *Hamburgischer Briefträger*, a weekly paper that appeared from 1791 onwards, described his music on the occasion of his singspiel *Eigensinn und Launen in der Liebe* as 'quite agreeable, although not new. We rediscover some old acquaintances there' (recht artig, obgleich nicht neu. Man findet in

111 See Maurer Zenck, 'Einige ungewohnte Bemerkungen über die "Zauberflöte"', pp. 43ff.

derselben so manchen alten Bekannten wieder).[112] Müller had his greatest successes before 1800. The first was *Das Sonnenfest der Braminen* (1790), although the same critic described it as a 'motley potpourri' (buntscheckiges Allerley), 'magic lantern' (Laternamagika) and a box office draw to fill the cash boxes, solely focused on fun and therefore 'inappropriate for the true purpose of art' (dem eigentlichen Zweck der Kunst nicht angemessen). In spite of the content-related criticism he nevertheless called it 'one of the most perfect German operas' (eine der vollkommensten deutschen Opern), on account of its music and actions.[113] Most remarkable are three extended and variedly constructed numbers: the introduzione to the first act, which begins with a chorus of the Brahmins together with a melodrama of their high priest; the dynamic ensemble of five of the main characters that follows, and takes more than ten minutes; and both of the diverse finali which last about 20–25 minutes.[114] The last finale ends with a chorus of rejoicing, but there is no longer any sign of a vaudeville. (Both finali from Müller's similarly popular singspiel *Die Schwestern von Prag*, which he wrote four years later, are distinguished by many quick changes in situation. The first involves a window scene with several serenades, mix-ups and fights, ending with the night watchman leading off the servant Kaspar. The other one brings the love affair to a happy conclusion – but beforehand the two servants appear in disguise as the 'sisters of Prague'. They sing falsetto, are of course unmasked, and the extramarital deviations of the parents are disclosed, too.)

A lot shorter and clearly more traditional was the chorus finale with an initial instrumental number, which Mozart dismissed disparagingly when he witnessed it at the performance of Müller's *Kaspar, der Fagottist, oder: Die Zauberzither* in the summer of 1791. Mozart's judgement does not come as a surprise in relation to the overdone plot. He himself was setting Schikaneder's libretto *Die Zauberflöte* at the time; both composers therefore hoped to profit from the popularity of the genre. As a matter of fact, *Zauberflöte* was as colourfully constructed as Wranitzky's *Oberon*, and, similarly to Karl Ludwig Giesecke, Schikaneder combined the magical elements with the exotic: what was 'Turkish' there, was 'Egyptian' here. The colourfulness of the pieces satisfied the 'visual pleasure' of the audience, and up to the turn of the century Mozart's and Müller's singspiele were equally popular.

112 'Theater-Artikel./(Fortsezzung)', *Hamburgischer Briefträger*, 2/3 (1792), p. 469 (for the performance on 21 May).

113 'Theater-Artikel./(Fortsezzung)', *Hamburgischer Briefträger*, 3/3 (1793), pp. 520ff. (for the performance on 3 July 1793).

114 At the end of this number '12 Mi' is written with a graphite pencil in the Hamburg transcription of this singspiel (Staats- und Universitätsbibliothek Hamburg Carl von Ossietzky, ND VII 279, vol. 1); presumably it does not date back to 1793. In contrast, the other numbers that are mentioned in the text are written in brown ink and the '20' is later corrected to '24' or perhaps '27' with graphite pencil.

A 'box office hit' of a special kind was Ferdinand Kauer's singspiel *Das Donauweibchen*, which premiered in Vienna in 1798. It created such a stir that, after only a short period of time, it garnered a number of sequels as well as 'counterparts' written by other composers. Amongst these was Wenzel Müller's *Die Teufelsmühle am Wienerberg*, already composed by 1799. (Even at this time it was customary to exploit a singspiel's success by writing a sequel. Benedikt Schack followed this line of attack in 1790 with the second part to his *Lilla*, the German version of Vicente Martín y Soler's *Una cosa rara*; and the three composers who wrote sequels to the *Zauberflöte* did likewise.) The more precise description of *Donauweibchen* as a 'romantic–comical folk fairy tale' (romantisch-komisches Volksmährchen) clarifies the cultural–historical relation between magic and ghost operas. There are the figures of the knight and of the mastersinger Minnewart (first taken up in Sedaine's and Grétry's *Richard Cœur-de-lion* that had its first performance in Hamburg in 1787), as reminiscences of the middle ages, to which the romantics were so often drawn. As part of the intrigue (the freshly married knight has to fall in love with the water nymph Hulda) the essence of the Undine plot comes to light, albeit differently clothed, leading us today to perceive the success of the *Donauweibchen* as rather suspect. The libretto of Carl Friedrich Hensler is not only higgledy-piggledy, but also highly confused, such that it would require great effort to put together just a synopsis from the many short and often burlesque fragments contained therein; it should suffice to know that the Donauweibchen transforms into ten (!) different figures. But the contemporary audience was not only used to this kind of thing in Vienna (with its long-standing 'Hanswurst' tradition in improvised theatre), but also in other German cities. The performances of tragedies and tragic dramas usually ended with a burlesque, in order to leave the departing audience in a happy frame of mind. In Hamburg, too, the muddled libretto did not deter the musical public at large: 'Wherever this *Donauweibchen* was performed on a German stage it received extraordinary acclaim and many admirers, and also received the very best reception among the local audience.'[115] This praise appears from the author of the *Hamburgischer Briefträger* after the premiere in 1801 in spite of malfunctioning stage machinery. It is not surprising, then, that the subsequent sequels to the work were greatly acclaimed up until 1810. But the quoted critic was not as positive as he may at first appear: he characterized the librettist Hensler, for example, as one of the 'opera manufacturers of the Marinelli theatre in Vienna'. The true meaning of this statement can be determined from his complaint about the

115 'Dieses *Donauweibchen* hat überall, wo es auf den deutschen Bühnen erschienen ist, ausserordentlich viel Beyfall und Verehrer gefunden, und auch bey dem hiesigen Publikum hat es die beste Aufnahmen erhalten.' See 'Über das Hamburgische Theater/Februar, 1801', *Hamburgischer Briefträger*, 11/1 (1801), pp. 87ff.

prevailing taste in opera ten years earlier, on the occasion of Dittersdorf's *Demokrit der Zweite*: if we are unwilling to seek refuge in the texts of the Italian and the French, we will unfortunately depend in part on the pitiful concoctions of the 'Viennese opera manufacturers' (Wiener Opernfabrikanten).[116]

Summary: musical forms

In the singspiele of the 1770s musical forms were expanded in relation to their simpler manifestations in the comical pieces of the 1750s and 1760s. Several general trends are significant:

- Up to the late 1770s all of the introductory symphonies were three movements in length. In *Alceste*, which Schweitzer began as a musical tragedy, he chose a French overture. Single-movement overtures in sonata form began to appear only around 1780.[117]
- Strophic songs, which include the popular narrating romances (to which Pedrillo's 'Im Mohrenland gefangen war' from Mozart's *Die Entführung* belongs), were initially dominant, sometimes being sung as duets.[118] Otherwise, duets followed a standard pattern: several verses were initially sung by one character, then by the other, after which the sections performed alternately became shorter until both sang one or two final verses together at the end. On most occasions several sections were subsequently repeated.
- Even at the beginning of the singspiel's history, ariettas and arias were written in ABA' form, and were very simple, short and built on the repetition of small segments. Their scope increased over time, which was partly connected to better training that singing actors received as well as the specializations of singers. Concerting instruments, coloraturas (including for the male voices) and other highly technical demands subsequently made their way into arias. For passionate excitement and emphasis on a particular statement, a lot of big jumps in a short time-span came into effect, as in the Italian seria aria. Seldom were they related to the social position of a character, much more to the situation.
- Aria forms included three-part (rarely five-part) da capo or dal-segno arias, regularly written out in full. They usually featured a rather short middle

116 'Theater-Artikel. (Fortsezzung)', *Hamburgischer Briefträger*, 1/4 (1791), p. 598f.

117 Kramer has pointed out that André wrote single-movement overtures to his music for Shakespeare's plays at the end of the 1770s. However, they did not employ sonata form ('*Macbeth* und *King Lear*', p. 66).

118 The number of strophes was sometimes very high, not unusually six or seven. But they were intended for music-making at home from the piano edition score; only a small selection would have been performed on the stage.

section in a different tempo and often a shortened reprise, and were differentiated formally, when musical and textual repetition did not coincide. Often we find bipartite arias with several changes of tempo. Arias could be demanding, especially those with serious pretensions, as illustrated in Hiller's early singspiel *Lisuart und Dariolette*.

- While the overall quantity of numbers in individual singspiele decreased over time, ensembles and choruses increased in frequency and in significance, more and more characters taking part in the former in particular. At one end of the scale the early singspiel *Die verwandelten Weiber oder Der Teufel ist los*, which was composed by Standfuß and adapted by Hiller, comprises thirty-seven numbers, among which is a duet at the end of the second act and a roundelay at the end of the third. (All the other numbers are solos.) At the other end of the scale, thirty years later, we find singspiele such as Stegmann's *Der Triumpf der Liebe*, a 'fairy opera' premiered in Hamburg in 1796, that confirms the dissemination of Viennese magic operas in Northern Germany. Its first two acts have six numbers each, the two following five numbers each, of which more than half are ensembles. The solo numbers are in part song-like and in part arioso, dependent on character, situation and the character's frame of mind. Each finale on its own is approximately as long as the preceding part of the act, and brings together everybody who has taken part in the action, as well as the chorus.
- Finali with a lot of action and large-scale introductions at the beginning of the first act became standard features of sophisticated singspiele from 1790 onwards. By the end of the eighteenth century these singspiele were often referred to as 'heroic–comic' (heroisch-komisch), irrespective of from where the composer concerned hailed. The Oberon singspiel *Holger Danske* (1789), however, is unusual; the second act, set exclusively in the palace of the sultan, is almost completely through-composed by the composer Kunzen.[119]
- A 'Ballo' and a gavotte at the beginning of *Holger Danske* indicate another new characteristic of the later singspiel.[120] With the increasing distinctiveness of numbers, more instrumental pieces were interpolated, not only the oft-criticized and seemingly obligatory 'thunderstorm music' of early singspiele, but also finali and other big scenes, which became more and more diverse as a result. Depending on the situation, interpolations mostly involved

119 After the two opening dances (eighteen pages in the score), all the scenes up to the end of No. 48 are through-composed (eighty-four pages, counting not only closed numbers but also larger sections). As No. 49 is harmonically connected to No. 48, the last thirty-two pages could be included as well.

120 Hiller's short thunderstorm 'symphony' in the second act of *Die Jagd* (1770), to which we have to imagine pantomimic action, constitutes as much of an exception as the entr'acte he composed for his *Jubelhochzeit* in 1773.

dances or marches that were sometimes accompanied by pantomimes. All of these features appear in Schikaneder's and Mozart's *Die Zauberflöte*.

Conclusion: *Die Zauberflöte*

To the present day, the best-known and best-loved of Mozart's singspiele is *Die Zauberflöte*. As it is surely his most thoroughly researched opera, its position in the history of the German opera can only be briefly outlined in the present context.

When Schikaneder drafted the libretto of *Die Zauberflöte* in 1791, he had already worked on a similar subject a year earlier with *Der Stein der Weisen*. Both works belong to the genre of magic-, ghost- and fairy-operas, which had just surfaced in Wranitzky's *Oberon* (1789), a work premiered in Schikaneder's theatre. Schikaneder obviously tried to profit from this success, not only in his position as an entrepreneur, but also as a librettist. With his two libretti, especially that of *Zauberflöte*, he contributed considerably to the popularity of the genre. It was not unusual for subject matter to be drawn from many sources (in the first instance from the same one used by Karl Ludwig Giesecke for *Oberon*), or for motives from other operas to be redeployed. To be sure this contributed to the colourfulness of the libretto, which is a lot more pronounced than in *Oberon* and provoked an educated listener such as Count Zinzendorf to refer disparagingly to the 'unbelievable farce' (une farce incroyable).[121] For Schikaneder took his suburban audience even more into consideration than Giesecke had. Like Joachim Perinet (who was himself a folk actor at the Leopoldstädter Theater) with his libretto to *Kaspar, der Fagottist*, Schikaneder brought together figures from folk theatre with those from great Italian opera. In this way a chain of activity began in Vienna, initiated by Schikaneder himself with *Das Labyrinth oder der Kampf mit den Elementen* written for Peter Winter and explicitly marked as a sequel to *Die Zauberflöte* (by contrast, *Die Zauberflöte* is rather severe), which was irreparably broken with Hensler's incredibly clumsy *Donauweibchen*. Schikaneder satisfies the enduring desire of his audience for exotic motives in a different way from his contemporaries. In the singspiele of Wranitzky and Müller, the exotic motives are still supplied by familiar Turkish features. Schikaneder, however, sought lasting pleasure for the audience in the characterization of Tamino and with symbols of freemasonry, as belonging to an as-yet-unknown foreign environment: Egypt. In 1790, the Viennese audience encountered a remote India with Wenzel Müller's

121 '*Le soir au théâtre*: From the Diary of Count Karl Zinzendorf, 1783–92', in Link, *The National Court Theatre*, p. 386.

Das Sonnenfest der Braminen, and further remote regions were to be exploited in the 'heroic-comic operas' of the late 1790s. (The term for this type of singspiel apparently emerged only in the 1790s; *Die Zauberflöte* was called 'große Oper' (grand opera) by Schikaneder and 'deutsche Oper' (German opera) by Mozart.)

Mozart, with his affinity for crude jokes, would have readily accepted Schikaneder's offer to write an opera for his suburban theatre. In 1790 he had participated in the collective work *Der Stein der Weisen*. The stylistic variety of *Die Zauberflöte* was greeted compositionally with strophic songs that were to be sung either as a solo or a duet, with great coloratura as well as sentimental arias, with choruses and march parades, ensembles, scenes that alternate between recitative and arioso and extensive finali with plenty of action. Other composers had similar command of all of this, and many of the musical details in *Die Zauberflöte* can be found in other contemporary singspiele. But the similarities with Dittersdorf's *Der Apotheker und der Doktor*, in particular, demonstrate the greater richness of Mozart's compositional invention. He relied much less on catchy repetitions than on interesting continuations, as can also be recognized in formal contexts. Examples include his combination of the French overture with the Sinfonia in sonata form; the two-part or through-composed coloratura arias, which no longer follow da capo or ABA' form; the oft-admired chorale-like and intricately textured duet of the armoured men; and the scene between Tamino and the Priest in the first act, which is longer and more diverse than comparable contemporary scenes. And Stegmann probably learned how long and diverse finali could be directly from *Die Zauberflöte*.

Mozart wanted to compensate for the stylistic breadth of the opera as well, and achieved this – for example, by orchestrating the simple and song-like vocal numbers in as thoroughly distinctive a fashion as the more demanding arias and ensembles. So he represents the end of the line for eighteenth-century German opera and, in contrast to his contemporaries, stands out as a concise composer of singspiele – dramaturgically and compositionally – who would not have got involved in the escalation of magic- and ghost-plays of this type had he lived beyond 1791. The consequence for us today of *Die Zauberflöte* outliving all attempts to outdo it is that we miss points of comparison; and its colourfulness is probably more apparent to us than to Mozart's contemporaries. It is not surprising, then, that it has found its place in children's theatre.

Select Bibliography

Altenburg, Detlef. 'Von den Schubladen der Wissenschaft. Zur Schauspielmusik im klassisch-romantischen Zeitalter'. In Michael Berg, Helen Geyer and Matthias Tischler (eds.), *'Denn in jenen Tönen lebt es'. Wolfgang Marggraf zum 65*. Weimar, 1999, pp. 425–49

Anderson, Emily (ed. and trans.). *The Letters of Mozart and His Family*. 3rd edn., London, 1985

Baselt, Bernd. 'G. Ph. Telemanns Serenade "Don Quichotte auf der Hochzeit des Comacho": Beiträge zur Entstehungsgeschichte von Telemanns letztem Hamburger Bühnenwerk'. In Constantin Floros, Hans Joachim Marx and Peter Petersen (eds.), *Studien zur Barockoper. Hamburger Jahrbuch für Musikwissenschaft*. Hamburg, 1978, vol. 3, pp. 85–100

'Bemerkungen zum Opernschaffen Georg Philipp Telemanns'. *Musica*, 35/1 (1981), pp. 19–23

Bauman, Thomas. *North German Opera in the Age of Goethe*. Cambridge, 1985

Betzwieser, Thomas. 'Zwischen Kinder- und Nationaltheater: die Rezeption der Opéra-comique in Deutschland (1760–1780)'. In Erika Fischer-Lichte and Jörg Schönert (eds.), *Theater im Kulturwandel des 18. Jahrhunderts. Inszenierung und Wahrnehmung von Körper, Musik, Sprache*. Göttingen, 1999, pp. 245–64

Branscombe, Peter. 'The Relationship between Spoken Theatre and Music-Theatre'. In Moritz Csáky and Walter Pass (eds.), *Europa im Zeitalter Mozarts*. Vienna, Cologne and Weimar, 1995, pp. 359–64

Brusniak, Friedhelm and Annemarie Clostermann (eds.). *Französische Einflüsse auf deutsche Musiker im 18. Jahrhundert*. Cologne, 1996

Busch-Salmen, Gabriele. '"Übrigens ein Werk voll Fehler und Nachlässigkeiten": Wieland/Schweitzers Singspiel *Alceste* in der opernästhetischen Debatte'. In Beatrix Borchard and Claudia Maurer Zenck (eds.), *Alkestis: Opfertod und Wiederkehr. Interpretationen. Hamburger Jahrbuch für Musikwissenschaft*. Frankfurt, 2007, vol. 23, pp. 97–111

Colzani, A., N. Dubowy, A. Luppi and M. Padoan (eds.). *Il melodramma italiano in Italia e in Germania nell'età barocca*. Como, 1995

Eigenmann, Susanne. *Zwischen ästhetischer Raserei und aufgeklärter Disziplin. Hamburger Theater im späten 18. Jahrhundert*. Stuttgart and Weimar, 1994

Gottsched, Johann Christoph. *Versuch einer Critischen Dichtkunst*. 4th edn., Leipzig, 1751; reprint Darmstadt, 1962

Hartmann, Tina. *Goethes Musiktheater. Singspiele, Opern, Festspiele, 'Faust'*. Tübingen, 2004

Huschke, Wolfram. *Musik im klassischen und nachklassischen Weimar 1756–1861*. Weimar, 1982

Krämer, Jörg. *Deutschsprachiges Musiktheater im späten 18. Jahrhundert. Typologie, Dramaturgie und Anthropologie einer populären Gattung*. Tübingen, 1998, 2 vols

'Metastasio und das deutsche Singspiel'. In Laurenz Lütteken and Gerhard Splitt (eds.), *Metastasio im Deutschland der Aufklärung*. Tübingen, 2002, pp. 85–102

Link, Dorothea. *The National Court Theatre in Mozart's Vienna: Sources and Documents, 1783–1792*. Oxford, 1998

Lynch, Robert D. *Opera in Hamburg, 1718–1738: A Study of the Libretto and the Musical Style*. Ann Arbor, MI, 1980

Mattheson, Johann. *Der vollkommene Capellmeister*. Hamburg, 1739; reprint Kassel and Basel, 1954, trans. and ed. Ernest C. Harriss. Ann Arbor, MI, 1981

Grundlage einer Ehren-Pforte. Hamburg, 1740; reprint Kassel *et al.*, 1969

Marx, Hans Joachim and Dorothea Schröder. *Die Hamburger Gänsemarkt-Oper: Katalog der Textbücher (1678–1748)*. Laaber, 1995

Mentzel, Elisabeth. *Geschichte der Schauspielkunst in Frankfurt am Main: von ihren ersten Anfängen bis zur Eröffnung des Städtischen Komödienhauses*. Frankfurt, 1882

Meyer, Reinhart. 'Der Anteil des Singspiels und der Oper am Repertoire der deutschen Bühnen in der zweiten Hälfte des 18. Jahrhunderts'. In Renate Schusky (ed.), *Das deutsche Singspiel im 18. Jahrhundert*. Heidelberg, 1981, pp. 27–76

'Die Idee eines deutschen "Nationaltheaters"'. In Alena Jakubcová, Jitka Ludvová and Tomaz Maidl (eds.), *Deutschsprachiges Theater in Prag. Begegnungen der Sprachen und Kulturen*. Prague, 2001, pp. 15–30

Pilková, Zdeňka. 'Georg (Jiří) Bendas Melodramen'. In Hermann Danuser and Tobias Plebuch (eds.), *Musik als Text. Bericht über den Internationalen Kongress der Gesellschaft für Musikforschung, Freiburg 1993*. Kassel, 1998, vol. 1, pp. 374–6

Plachta, Bodo. '"Die Vernunft muss zu Hause bleiben, wenn man in die Oper geht": Die literaturkritische Debatte über Oper und Operntext in der Aufklärungsepoche'. In Eleonore Sent (ed.), *Die Oper am Weissenfelser Hof*. Rudolstadt, 1996, pp. 171–89

'"*Wir müssen nun auf alle teutsche Opern Theater Anschläge machen*". Goethes Versuche der Literarisierung von Oper und Singspiel'. In Michael Zywietz (ed.), *Grenzgebiete. Festschrift Klaus Hortschansky zum 65. Geburtstag*. Eisenach, 2000, pp. 117–48

Randall, Annie Janeiro. *Music and Drama in Weimar 1776–1782: A Social-Historical Perspective*. Ann Arbor, MI, 1996

Sauder, Gerhard. 'Rousseau und das Melodram'. In Hermann Danuser and Tobias Plebuch (eds.), *Musik als Text. Bericht über den Internationalen Kongress der Gesellschaft für Musikforschung, Freiburg 1993*. Kassel, 1998, vol. 1, pp. 369–73

Scheibe, Johann Adolph. *Critischer Musikus*. 2nd edn., Leipzig, 1745

Schneider, Herbert. 'Übersetzungen französischer Opéras-comiques für Marchands *Churpfälzische Deutsche Hofschauspielergesellschaft*'. In Ludwig Fischer, Bärbel Pelelker and Rüdiger Thomsen-Fürst (eds.), *Mannheim: Ein 'Paradies der Tonkünstler'? Kongressbericht Mannheim 1999*. Frankfurt *et al.*, 2002, pp. 387–434

(ed.). *Studien zu den deutsch-französischen Musikbeziehungen im 18. und 19. Jahrhundert*. Hildesheim, 2002

Schneider, Herbert and Reinhard Wiesend (eds.). *Die Oper im 18. Jahrhundert, Handbuch der musikalischen Gattungen*. Laaber, 2001, vol. 12

Schröder, Dorothea. *Zeitgeschichte auf der Opernbühne. Barockes Musiktheater in Hamburg im Dienst von Politik und Diplomatie (1690–1745)*. Göttingen, 1998

Schütze, Johann Friedrich. *Hamburgische Theater-Geschichte*. Hamburg, 1794

Sulzer, Johann Georg (ed.). *Allgemeine Theorie der schönen Künste*. Reprint of the 2nd edn., Leipzig, 1792–4

Switalski, Martina. 'Wandlungen im Theater des 18. Jahrhunderts am Beispiel von Köln'. In Frank Günter Zehnder and Werner Schäfke (eds.), *Der Riss im Himmel. Clemens August und seine Epoche*. Cologne, 2000, pp. 67–85

Wenzel, Joachim. *Geschichte der Hamburger Oper 1678–1978*. Hamburg, 1978

Wieland, Christoph Martin. 'Versuch über das Teutsche Singspiel, und einige dahin einschlagende Gegenstände'. In Wieland, *Singspiele und Abhandlungen*. Leipzig, 1796; reprint Hamburg, 1984, pp. 229–67, 321–42

Wolff, Hellmuth Christian. *Die Barockoper in Hamburg (1678–1738)*. Wolfenbüttel, 1957, 2 vols

Zelm, Klaus. *Die Opern Reinhard Keisers*. Munich and Salzburg, 1975

Zenck, Claudia Maurer. *Musiktheater in Hamburg um 1800. Hamburger Jahrbuch für Musikwissenschaft*. Frankfurt *et al.*, 2005, vol. 22

Così fan tutte: dramma giocoso und deutsches Singspiel. Frühe Abschriften und frühe Aufführungen. Schliengen, 2007

The lure of aria, procession and spectacle: opera in eighteenth-century London

MICHAEL BURDEN*

In 1789, Charles Burney described the operas of Henry Purcell – *Dioclesian*, *King Arthur* and *The Fairy-Queen* – as 'differing from real operas, where there is no speaking'.[1] Burney's remark reflected his expressed preference for Italian music and (sub-consciously) his own failure as a composer to do anything other than produce a few insignificant ditties while apprenticed to the theatre composer Thomas Arne.[2] But it is also a remark that has contributed to a skewed historical picture of late-seventeenth- and eighteenth-century opera in England that persists to this day – skewed, because for the majority of English theatre-goers, 'real opera' *had* spoken dialogue, and was a genre they preferred to the 'foreign' all-sung version. Yet despite this self-evident fact, it is Burney's view that has come to dominate both English and non-English writings about opera in England. This situation has been compounded by the country's inability to nurture to an internationally recognized level the musical talent that it clearly possessed, making it easy for those viewing England both from without and within the Austro-German tradition to dismiss the country as 'the land without music', and English opera as 'a mass of insincerity' lacking 'the pure ideal which had been the guiding spirit of Peri and Monteverdi', or (at best) as 'light opera' relying on 'dramatic principles'.[3]

This is an approach which reflects a focus on works that are the product of a single composer (usually white, male and canonic) and has overlooked the fact that the notion of the 'work' is less important when considering a repertory that largely consisted of a constant stream of new spectacles many of which were got up at short notice, and old works which required (as a matter of course) alteration and adaptation to make them acceptable. The result has encouraged a gross under-estimation of the importance of London as an

* I am grateful to Roger Savage for reading a draft of this chapter.

1 Charles Burney, *A General History of Music*, 4 vols. (London, 1789), vol. 4, p. 191.

2 Burney even blamed Arne; see Slava Klima, Garry Bowers and Kerry S. Grant (eds.), *Memoirs of Dr Charles Burney, 1726–1769* (Lincoln, NE and London, 1988), p. 43.

3 Oscar Adolff Schmitz and R. A. Streatfield, 'Das Land Ohne Musick', *The Opera* (London, 1896), p. 18; and Eric Walter White, *The Rise of English Opera* (London, 1951), p. 65.

operatic centre for it was a vast, wealthy, commercial melting pot for singers, composers and instrumentalists, and was, into the bargain, a major publishing and distribution centre for music of all kinds.[4]

In any case, the essential truth of opera in eighteenth-century London is that – whether Italian or English (or of any other origin) – it was first and foremost a performative genre. Obviously, this is not unique to London, nor indeed alien to the conception of opera as a high art form. But London was alone in the monarchical capitals of Europe in having opera performed entirely on a commercial footing, where the three principal theatres were reliant on what came in at the box-office or was paid as a subscription.[5] Two of these theatres were Theatres Royal operating under a royal patent – one in Drury Lane, the other variously in the eighteenth century at Lincoln's-Inn-Fields (in 1700) and in Covent Garden (from 1732) – at which opera, both all-sung and with spoken dialogue, was staged in English. Both theatres relied on the effectiveness of their respective and competing managements to keep the doors open and the bills paid. The third venue – the Queen's Theatre (from 1705 then, from 1711, the King's Theatre), colloquially, the 'Opera' or the 'Opera House' – was one that performed, after a few early mis-steps, all-sung Italian operas in their original language. It relied similarly on the management for its survival, but did have a subscription system to support the overall season. But even here, the subscribers had to be kept entertained each season, for their patronage had to be retained for the succeeding ventures. A high level of audience attendance, then, was not just a matter of prestige, or pride, or desire, but one of economic necessity, and the London opera repertory was not subject to the imposition of one person's taste – as, say, in a princely court – but had to capture or reflect the audiences' desires and whims.[6] To help satisfy these, the bill at the London theatres always included extra entertainment. At the King's Theatre, the operatic main-piece was nearly always followed by dance, and was sometimes supplemented with further dances between the acts. At the playhouses, the main-piece was usually a spoken drama (which frequently contained songs, dances and even large-scale musical events such as incantations and, as we shall see later, processions) and was followed by a shorter work – an after-piece, known as the 'farce' – which was the slot in

4 See Robert D. Hume, 'The Economics of Culture in London, 1660–1740', *Huntington Library Quarterly*, 69 (2006), pp. 487–533.

5 See William Weber, 'Musical Culture and the Capital City: The Epoch of the Beau Monde in London 1700–1870', in Susan Wollenberg and Simon McVeigh (eds.), *Concert Life in 18th-Century Britain* (Aldershot, 2004), pp. 71–89.

6 For a fuller discussion of the division of repertory between the two theatres, see Michael Burden, 'Opera and Theatre', in Jane Moody and Daniel O'Quinn (eds.), *The Cambridge Companion to the British Theatre 1730–1830* (Cambridge, 2007), pp. 205–17.

which works that were sung throughout most frequently appeared. Towards the end of the century, further items were added to the bill, greatly extending the length of the evening's entertainment.

And in this climate, novelty was all. Novelties at the playhouses included all-sung, free-standing masques (on and off from 1700, starting with Congreve's *The Judgment of Paris*), pantomimes (in quantity from Weaver's *The Loves of Mars and Venus*, 1717), ballad operas (from 1728, Gay's *The Beggar's Opera*), one-composer dialogue operas (from 1764, Rush's *Capricious Lovers*[7]) and burlettas (from 1760, Kane O'Hara's *Midas*). Each extra genre was devoured by the ever-hungry audience, and then abandoned almost as quickly when the novelty wore off. At the Opera, dance and dancers of all kinds were used to lure in the audience, at times overtaking opera as the central attraction; Thomas Harris, who in the 1745–6 season had felt that 'the dancers are magnifique and make amends for the music' by Galuppi,[8] later in the same season could 'foresee the downfall of the operas this year because they have lost their best dancers, which was their sheet-anchor'.[9] However, there were only a few full-length narrative dance works staged, and none before the 1770s; despite the popularity of dance, opera always re-asserted itself as the dominant genre.

The central dynamic force on the scene was, of course, the singer whose looks, acting ability, salary, personality, sexual identity and nationality were the subject of tittle-tattle, critical report and press comment. Nicolini was said to have set 'off the character he bears in an opera by his action' with 'every limb, and every finger',[10] Farinelli earned £1,501, 1,500 guineas, £2,500, or 2,500 guineas depending on who was reporting the figure,[11] and Gertrud Mara offended everyone by remaining seated during the 1785 Handel Commemoration performance of *Messiah*'s Hallelujah chorus.[12] The real scandals were sensations. When the soprano Susanna Cibber (née Arne) was (almost) forced by her appalling husband Theophilous to have an affair with William Sloper, it was reported everywhere, as were the scurrilous but probably true revelations that the great English soprano Elizabeth Billington (see ill. 12.1) had had a series of liaisons while working in Dublin.[13] And when the

7 See Roger Fiske, *English Theatre Music in the Eighteenth Century*, 2nd edn. (Oxford, 1986), chapter 9, for a discussion of this genre.

8 From a letter to James Harris given in Donald Burrows and Rosemary Dunhill, *Music and Theatre in Handel's World: The Family Papers of James Harris 1732–1780* (Oxford, 2002), p. 222.

9 From a letter to Elizabeth Harris given in *ibid.*, p. 232.

10 Isaac Bickerstaff, *The Tatler; or the lucubrations of Isaac Bickerstaff Esq*. (London, 1754), vol. 3, p. 4.

11 For an account of the matter, see Judith Milhous and Robert D. Hume, 'Construing and Misconstruing Farinelli in London', *British Journal for Eighteenth-Century Studies*, 28 (2005), pp. 361–85.

12 *Morning Herald and Daily Advertiser*, 10 June 1785, issue 1443.

13 [James Ridgway], *The Memoirs of Mrs Billington* (London, 1792).

Illustration 12.1. 'A bravura air'. The great soprano Elizabeth Billington, famous for her singing, vocal ornaments, and *embonpoint*, pictured in the role of Mandane from Thomas Arne's *Artaxerxes*. Gillray's image captures Billington's much noted stately manner and encapsulates the English public's cult of celebrity that surrounded the singer. Billington was the subject of a scurrilous 1792 'memoir' and found it prudent to spend some time on the Continent. She returned triumphantly to London, introduced Mozart to the London audience through a performance of *La clemenza di Tito* in 1806, and died (probably) at the hands of her violent second husband at her villa in Italy.

James Gillray. Coloured engraving, published 1801 by Hannah Humphrey. © Courtesy of the Warden and Scholars of New College, Oxford/Bridgeman Art Library.

soprano Teresa Cornelys, the 'Empress of Pleasure', included an unlicensed performance of Mattia Vento's 1771 setting of Metastasio's libretto *Artaserse* among the entertainments at her house in Soho, the results reverberated around the town, through the courtroom and beyond, for the stylishness of her parties only lent credence to the possibility that she ran an up-market whorehouse.[14] Such tales reflected the preoccupation of the London audience with personality, something that both arose from and was reflected in a singer's performance.[15] And this performance centred on the aria.

Aria: 'a thousand exquisite passages'

Although English opera and Italian opera (as seen in London) were unlike each other in conception, musical context and most aspects of performance, the aria (or air, in the more modest English offerings) was the musical unit on which both operatic edifices were constructed. For much of the period, imported opera seria repertory consisted of a three-act structure that had at its centre the da capo aria, a tripartite form in which the third section was an ornamented version of the first. The plot of the opera was advanced though recitative; there were few ensembles, although a duet could usually be found, and the opera always closed with a 'chorus' frequently sung only by the principals. As the century wore on, composers tried to soften this somewhat rigid recitative–aria pattern, at first by a greater use of orchestrally accompanied recitative and then by gradually increasing the number of ensembles. Finally, towards the end of the century the da capo and dal-segno arias were out-numbered by a range of through-composed forms, and the number of acts was reduced to two. Thus, a London opera-goer of, say, sixty years' experience could have seen Giovanni Lampugnani's three-act *Alessandro* in 1746, hearing twenty da capo arias, an act-closing duet and two choruses in the last scene; in 1761, another three-acter, this time *Tolemeo*, a pasticcio directed by Gioacchino Cocchi, with nine da capo arias, twelve solo numbers in other forms, a duet and two choruses, both in the final scene; in 1786, the two-act *Virginia* with music by Angelo Tarchi, which had some seven da capo arias, five other pieces, a couple of accompanied recitatives, a duet, a quartet and chorus; and, finally, in 1802, Paisiello's *Elfrida*, which offered only six arias, but two scena, three duets, two trios, two quartets, one septet and nine accompanied recitatives, one of

14 Judith Summers, *Empress of Pleasure: The Life and Adventures of Teresa Cornelys – Queen of Masquerades and Casanova's Lover* (London, 2003), pp. 210–30 and Patricia Howard, 'Guadagni in the Dock: A Crisis in the Career of a Castrato', *Early Music*, 27 (1999), pp. 87–95.

15 Berta Joncus, 'Producing Stars in *Dramma per musica*', in Melania Bucciarelli and Berta Joncus (eds.), *Music as Social and Cultural Practice: Essays in Honour of Reinhard Strohm* (Woodbridge and Rochester, NY, 2007), pp. 275–93.

which Paisiello used to close the opera, a circumstance that would have been unthinkable twenty years earlier, except in the few cases (such as Metastasio's *Didone abbandonata*) which eschewed the *liete finale*.

The gradual employment of more flexible musical forms in London Italian opera had much to do with the popularity of opera buffa, a genre not only new to London, but one newly contrived. Although some comic operas were written in the seventeenth century, it was only at the beginning of the eighteenth century that Neapolitan comic opera made its appearance, to be honed in Rome during the 1720s and 1730s, and to spread throughout Europe in the following years. As in other centres, the London audience immediately took the genre to heart. Among the early works to be staged were Leo's *La finta frascatana* in 1749, Cocchi's *Gli amante gelosi* in 1753 and Goldoni's and Galuppi's *Il mondo della luna* in 1760.[16] But it was with the arrival in 1761 of Goldoni's and Galuppi's most popular opera buffa, *Il filosofo di campagna* (1754), that the genre became a staple in every season (apart from one or two in the mid-1760s), and the dominant type in many of them; indeed, the 1769 and 1792 seasons consisted of nothing else. Subjects for opera buffa were satirical and contemporary, and unlike serious operas which only lasted one season, or two at the most, some were performed again and again; Piccini's setting of *La buona figliuola*, for example, played in every season (apart from 1784–5) between its premiere and the end of the century. Other opera buffa appearing in more than one season over a number of years include *Il filosofo di campagna*, Piccini's *La Schiava*, Guglielmi's *I viaggiatori ridicoli* and Paisiello's *La Frascatana*.

Although buffa and seria genres were – and remained – distinct in both their presentation and in the London audience's perception, there was a limited amount of cross-over between them. The satirical nature of opera buffa, combined with the custom of aria replacement, meant that opera seria arias sometimes appeared in dramatically appropriate situations which reflected not only on the characters in the drama, but on opera seria itself. The version of 'Quel labbro adorato' from Metastasio's *Demetrio* which appears in Sacchini's 1782 *La Contadina in Corte*, is the choice of Dr Stoppino (who believes that his song will have more of an effect on his beloved Sandrina than 'all the eloquence of Cicero') to 'try this efficacious power of harmony'; it is, predictably enough, beyond his vocal capabilities.[17] As the turn of the

16 See Saskia Willaert, 'Italian Comic Opera at the King's Theatre in the 1760s: The Role of the Buffi', in David Wyn-Jones (ed.), *Music in Eighteenth-Century Britain* (Aldershot, 2000), pp. 17–71, esp. p. 20.

17 Antonio Sacchini, *La Contadina in Corte* (London, 1782), pp. 27–8; see Michael Burden, 'Metastasio on the British Stage to 1840: A Catalogue', *Royal Musical Association Research Chronicle*, 40 (2007), for a listing of the re-use of Metastasio's arias in both comic and serious London opera.

century approached, the division of the genres, musically at least, became less obvious as opera seria adopted the more fluid musical forms of – or ones very similar to – those of its comic counterparts, and its subjects began to be taken less from the ancient world and more from contemporary literature and recent history.

Meanwhile, English opera, which used a wide variety of subjects, also employed a wider variety of musical forms, showing both a flexible approach to the drama and a desire to connect with its audience. Representative of the mix of forms and styles that could often be found in an English opera are those musical numbers from Congreve's masque of *The Judgment of Paris*, in a setting by Arne, from 1742: there are three da capo arias, a da capo trio, a through-composed trio and a number of other songs (mostly in ABB form), together with a couple of accompanied recitatives; there were also five choruses, showing the English predilection for grand choral numbers. Typical of the kind of music provided for both grand and humble dramas at the playhouses is Thomas Arne's 'Come Britannia' from his all-sung English opera *Eliza* (1754); this six-verse strophic air has a refrain and a simple tune capable of the all-important decoration.

The central role played by the solo aria in both English and Italian opera, as both a unit of composition and a vehicle for performance, is clearly witnessed in the negotiations between the diva Regina Mingotti and King's Theatre manager Francesco Vanneschi over what she should sing in Hasse's setting of Metastasio's *Ipermestra* in 1754:

> On my Arrival in *London*, *Vanneschi* came to me, and brought me, according to Custom, the Manuscript of *Ipermestra*, not as *Metastasio* originally writ it, and as it is exhibited in *Vienna* and all other Places, but curtailed and changed by himself in a most unskilful and absurd manner. Amongst other stupid Mutilations, he had not only cut out the Duetto, which is, without doubt, the most pleasing Part of an Opera; but taken the Air *Tu sai ch'io sono Amante* from the Character of *Ipermestra*, and given it (against all Theatrical Rules, and yet more against common Sense) to that of *Lineco*; that is, he took from me my capital Air to give it to Signor *Ricciarelli*, and when I remonstrated against his Folly and Injustice, and insisted upon his restoring many Parts to the Drama, especially the Duetto, he sent me word by Signor *Lampugnani* that he was *Manager* and *Master*, and would have me sing what he pleased, and nothing else.[18]

The impresario could be desperate, as indeed Vanneschi was the next season when the new setting of Metastasio's *Siroe, re di Persia* arrived, newly penned by the House's musical director, Lampugnani:

18 Regina Mingotti, *An Appeal to the Public* (London, 1755), p. 2.

> When *Vanneschi* heard me privately sing the Songs that were allotted me in this Opera, he found them so little to his Taste, that he begged of me as a Favour, to substitute other Songs of other Masters, knowing that I had better Compositions in my Possession.[19]

Mingotti's 'better compositions' were classic arie di biaggolo, 'suitcase arias' that travelled around with the diva to be unpacked in moments such as these; both Vanneschi and Mingotti expected such a proceeding as a matter of course. It was possible because aria texts were not 'opera-specific', but reflected on the dramatic content of the preceding recitative; so as long as the sentiment of the aria was appropriate to its context, any setting of any text could be (and was) used.

The extent to which Mingotti's probably self-serving account of these particular negotiations is accurate is not important; what is of concern to us is the fact that they took place at all, and the manner in which they did so. On the one hand, Vanneschi was attempting to alter the opera to please the public (thereby maximising the box office); on the other hand, Mingotti, despite her appeals to sense and dramatic verisimilitude, was trying to arrange for it to be a suitable vehicle for her performance (thereby nurturing her image with the public). Neither she nor Vanneschi was paying the slightest heed to 'composer intentions', 'authorship', 'characterization', or 'continuity of drama', not because they were actively ignoring them, or because in the choices ultimately made these aspects did not play a part, but because, in the overall picture, they were irrelevant. Both impresario and singer were dealing with what was essentially a pool of performing material, and they fished out whatever items suited them at any given moment. What either of them managed to achieve in such situations depended entirely on the balance of power between them within the company; had the discussion been with the 'third woman singer' and not with prima donna Mingotti, that lady might very well have found herself singing just what Vanneschi desired. Such negotiations tended to form part of the preparation for the performance of Italian works at the Opera where not all imports were new works; while there is record of a similar process in the preparation of English opera, the composer was more likely to be present at rehearsals of operas at the playhouses, where he was more often than not in charge of the rehearsal and able to re-write or re-cast the music without the singer importing something of his or her own.

Throughout this period in both English and Italian opera, one of the great performative aspects employed was ornamentation. A London singer not only defined his or her image in the choice and complexity of the aria chosen, but in

19 *Ibid.*, pp. 3–4.

the complexity of the ornaments applied to it in performance. Indeed, it was commented that a singer 'who does not vary [the repeat section of a da capo aria] for the better is no great master' and that 'from the nature and quality of the variations, it will easily be discerned in two of the greatest singers which is best'.[20] Skill in ornamentation was a real measure of a singer's standing and, as always, 'taste' and 'style' were the measures of its final success. The great Pacchiarotti was thought 'though perhaps the best singer in Europe in his style', to be 'in danger of injuring his reputation by fringing and ornamenting every note with too much extravagance',[21] while Nancy Storace's 'taste' was bad, for 'she utterly disregards simplicity, and will introduce the *capricioso* cadence with its *ruffle* and *frill* of close and open shake, in defiance of feeling, either as it refers to the *subject* of the song or the *music*'.[22]

Naturally enough perhaps, singers did not reveal either their methods or their ornaments; many sets of ornaments were probably never written down, and those that were recorded were probably guarded jealously, not just to curb pirate performances but because they might also reveal how little a singer needed to add to the music to make it sound vocally splendid, elaborate and taxing. But if the singer was famous enough, then publicising such techniques could only enhance her or his reputation, and could then be part of a published 'version' on which the singer's name appeared; this was a fine way of bolstering an image. Elizabeth Billington's 'graces, variations and embellishments' to the aria 'Let not rage' from Arne's *Artaxerxes*, is one such example; in her case, she was so widely admired that anyone able to sing her ornaments would benefit by association.[23]

But as important as the added ornamentation was, the singer had to be able to 'act', that is to 'perform' the aria:

> Nothing can be more deeply affecting than the interesting scenes of the serious opera, when to good Poetry and good Music, to the poetry of Metastasio and the Music of Pergolese, is added the execution of a good actor.[24]

The audience wanted to be engaged, moved and uplifted by the performance, caring little otherwise for the composer, librettist, music, or singer's ornaments. Eighteenth-century London recognized three broadly different approaches

20 Piero Francesco Tosi, *Observations on the Florid Song; or, Sentiments on the Ancient and Modern Singers*, trans. J. E. Galliard (London, 1742), pp. 94, 95.
21 In Bertoni's *Ezio*; see *The Westminster Magazine*, 9 (November 1781), p. 610.
22 [James Haslewood], *The Secret History of the Green Room* (London, 1795), vol. 1, p. 128.
23 *Let not Rage*, Sung by M^RS BILLINGTON *In the Celebrated Opera of* ARTAXERXES. *With all the Graces, Variations & Embellishments introduced by her, at the* Theatres Royal Drury Lane & Covent Garden. *Arranged with an accompaniment For the Piano Forte from the Original Score by Dr Busby* (London, 1797–1806).
24 Adam Smith, 'Of the Nature of that Imitation which Takes Place in what Are Called the Imitative Arts', in Smith, *Essays on Philosophical Subjects*, ed. William P. D. Wightman and J. C. Bryce (Oxford, 1980), p. 194.

to performance in different locations which might be summarised as follows: a lively and various style in the theatre; a delicate and finished style in the chamber; and a moving and grave style in church.[25] Even if these categories were not consciously employed, their application by critics can be detected in much of the commentary on individual singers. The account of Mrs Billington's performance in Stephen Storace's opera, *The Duenna*, for example, suggests an inappropriate use of Tosi's 'moving and grave' church style:

> MRS BILLINGTON is a very fine lady, a great deal too much so, to be interesting. She sings too well, she dresses too well, and knows all this too well to give the audience that kind of satisfaction that the heart longs for. Mrs Mountain's easy yet scientific notes, diffused much more general pleasure than the laboured tones of Mrs Billington, to which nature is, in a manner of speaking, obliged to do reluctant homage.[26]

Billington's vocal abilities were appreciated, but were too 'laboured'; she does seem to have been mis-cast in such a comedy. A further aspect of performance was what we might call 'acting technique'. Reports suggest that the Italian and English singers were perceived throughout the century as having different acting styles – the English tended to be described as 'natural' and have a more fluid manner than their Continental counterparts, while the Italians appear to have been given to grand gestures and more formal attitudes – but both were criticized when their efforts failed to convey meaning. More was required in the theatre than just the notes of the aria, as singers of both nationalities discovered.

As this narrative suggests, the singers and promoters were faced not with prescribed certainties, but with choices: arias, both text and music, may (or may not) have been replaced, added, or subtracted; ornaments may not (or may) have been added, tastefully or otherwise; the possibilities suggested by such choices combined to create a marvellously reflexive genre which could respond to the needs of individual performers, public demands and changing tastes.

Procession: 'a shilling's worth of show'

As we have seen, the aria in Italian opera came under pressure from many directions as the English public (like their Continental counterparts) began to demand a less formal, more integrated approach to musical drama. The variety of musical forms used in the English-language productions was already wide, and something new was needed to enhance the musical content. There were new practical needs, too; all the London theatres were rebuilt with larger

25 Tosi, *Observations on the Florid Song*, p. 92. 26 [Anon.], *The Prompter*, No. 6; 2 November 1789, p. 33.

auditoria, new performing spaces that required new strategies to attract and hold the audience's attention. The Opera House was the first to expand in this way; it was enlarged in 1782 and then, after a disastrous fire in 1791, was rebuilt with the seating capacity increased from 1,800 to 3,300. Over at Covent Garden, Shepherd's 1732 auditorium was rebuilt in 1782 and again ten years later; here capacity increased from 2,200 to 3,000. Drury Lane's rebuild by Henry Holland in 1794 raised the capacity from 2,300 to 3,611.

Naturally, complaints followed such expansion. In 1792, Anna Larpent commented that in the evening 'we all went to hear Mrs Siddons in *Macbeth*. The house is too large [and] attention becomes a werisome task to my eyes and ears';[27] in 1808, the Earl of Carlisle remarked that both the playhouses were now too large for 'the gratification of the eye and ear', and that 'more than half the verse [was] entombed in the performer's stomach';[28] and in the supplement to his 1806 *Memoirs*, Richard Cumberland wrote of the loss of theatrical effect resulting from these modifications:

> Since the stages of Drury Lane and Covent Garden have been so enlarged in their dimensions as to be hence forward theatres for spectators rather than playhouses for hearers ... there can be nothing very gratifying in watching the movement of an actor's lips, when we cannot hear the words that proceed from them.

Precisely how serious the problems were is difficult to gauge, for similar complaints were made on every occasion the buildings were altered from the 1690s onwards, as Colley Cibber's memoirs of that decade attest.[29] But it is clear that at this point, one theatrical effect was gained:

> it is hardly to be wondered at if their managers and directors encourage those representations, to which their structure is best adapted. The splendour of the scenes, the ingenuity of the machinist and the rich display of dresses, aided by the captivating charms of the music, now in a great degree supercede the labours of the poet ... when the animating march strikes up, and the stage lays open its recesses to the depth of a hundred feet for the procession to advance, even the most distant spectator can enjoy his shilling's worth of show.[30]

For the 'distant spectators', the aria was no longer enough; the London public needed something spectacular to catch their eye as well as to entertain their ears, and while the Opera had the advantage of the now fashionable ensemble

27 Anna Larpent's Diary, US-Cn HM 301201, I, 20 March 1792.
28 [Earl of Carlisle], *Thoughts upon the Present Condition of the Stage and Upon the Construction of a new Theatre* (London, 1808), pp. 4–5.
29 Colley Cibber, *An Apology for the Life of Mr Colley Cibber* (London, 1740), p. 241.
30 Richard Cumberland, *Memoirs of Richard Cumberland* (London, 1806, supplement, 1807), pp. 57–8.

and chorus numbers, the playhouse managers, as Cumberland suggests, increased the use of and focused attention on the procession. This was an extravagant operatic sequence whose employment was not confined to operas but which also appeared in plays and ballets. It is, of course, true that spectacle of all types had long been an integral part of the London operatic experience. In 1709, for example, the sets at the Opera were 'beautiful to behold, because they presented whole fortresses, attacks and perfect noises of war, underground prisons, castles, temples, and everything looked both splendid and pleasant', an obviously elaborate set designed to catch the eye.[31] And the primary reason for the popularity and continued production of pantomime at the two patent theatres was the almost unbridled licence for the production of spectacle of all kinds including jewelled clockwork eggs, sea monsters and chariots drawn by dragons.[32] But such spectacle as this was simply staged as a backdrop to (most) opera seria or remained confined within the structure of pantomime; the processions were something else, moments of 'splendour', 'show', ingenuity and (often) patriotic display that could be grafted on to any drama, serious or comic, all-sung or with spoken dialogue.

As a theatrical device, the procession had a long history both inside and outside the theatre. But as a regular event, it came into its own in 1750 when both Covent Garden and Drury Lane staged *Romeo and Juliet* on the same night. Covent Garden's was performed with Arne's 'Solemn Dirge' to accompany Juliet's supposedly dead body as it was borne across the stage; the ensuing sensation caused Garrick at Drury Lane to demand a similar procession from William Boyce.[33] Unlike many such operatic scenes from eighteenth-century London, the music for both survives. Arne's opened with the instruction 'at the Beginning of the procession the Trumpets advance with the Kettle Drums and sound the following Solemn notes between which the Bell tolls, till they are off the Stage'; the closing instruction directs the performers to 'Repeat the foregoing movement Viz. Hark, Hark, till the procession is Over'. The sequence of numbers began with an opening flourish, with the second trumpet and kettle drums muffled; then followed the Solemn Dirge – Chorus: 'Hark, Hark' – Adagio chorus – Chorus: 'Hark, Hark'.[34] Boyce's was very similar in conception; his sparse opening was accompanied by a striking bell that continued to sound throughout the procession, with the musical structure

31 Georg Wallin, Diary, IHRS report 1999–2000.

32 See M. Roger, *Persus and Andromeda* (London, 1728), p. 4; and *idem*, *The Rape of Prosperine* (London, 1727), p. 5.

33 See Fiske, *English Theatre Music*, p. 217; Charles Haywood, 'William Boyce's "Solemn Dirge" in Garrick's Romeo and Juliet Production of 1750', *Shakespeare Quarterly*, 11 (1960), pp. 173–87; and Robert J. Bruce, 'William Boyce: Some Manuscript Recoveries', *Music and Letters*, 55 (1974), pp. 437–43.

34 Thomas Arne, *A Complete Score of the Solemn Dirge in Romeo and Juliet* (London, *c.* 1767).

involving a repeating chorus: Chorus: 'Rise, rise, heartbreaking sighs' – Trio: 'She's gone, the sweet flow'r of May' – Chorus: 'Rise, rise, heartbreaking sighs' – Trio: 'Thou spotless soul look here below' – Chorus 'Rise, rise, heartbreaking sighs.'[35] This popular procession scene continued to be performed with the play well into the nineteenth century, although using other music.

From this point on, the number of processions staged rose exponentially, with a parallel increase in elaborate staged effects. Subsequent processions in the theatre included that in David Garrick's 1769 spectacular afterpiece *The Jubilee* (ill. 12.2), a theatre version of the pageant intended for (but never realised at) his Stratford-upon-Avon Shakespeare fest the same year.[36] The pageant, 'with bells ringing, fifes playing, drums beating and cannon firing' closed the Act 1 of the drama, and consisted of what might be called 'pageant standards' – dancers with tambourines, furies, black-boys and perhaps more unusually, eunuchs – and a representation of each of Shakespeare's plays.[37] Garrick's earlier *Cymon*, of 1767, contains one of the most frequently performed processions. As I have argued elsewhere, the key to understanding the construction of the London repertory is an appreciation of the process of adaptation;[38] here the entertainment was an adaptation of John Dryden's *Cymon and Iphigenia*, itself derived from Boccaccio's *Decameron*. Garrick's version had some 160 performances between 1767 and 1793, and had a second life as an 'opera' for twenty-two performances in 1792. The 1767 procession (with music by Michael Arne) opened with a march, with enchanters, with a procession of knights of the different orders of chivalry and so on, who arranged themselves in a semi-circle around the back of the stage; Merlin (with a nod to Purcell's *King Arthur*), Cymon and Sylvia are then brought forward in triumph by the Loves, and finally Arcadian shepherds and shepherdesses entered.[39] A descent of Merlin, Cymon and Sylvia in a car was probably added to the performance during rehearsals, for it is not included in the stage descriptions until the 3rd edition.[40] The procession was designed to be followed immediately by a chorus, and the play itself closed with a series of solos and choruses.

35 William Boyce, 'Dirge, for Romeo and Juliet', *GB-Ob* MS. Mus. *c.* 3, ff. 9^r-20^r.

36 See Isabel Roome Mann, 'The Garrick Jubilee at Stratford-upon-Avon', *Shakespeare Quarterly*, 1 (1950), pp. 129–34, and John A. Parkinson, 'Garrick's Folly or, the Great Stratford Jubilee', *The Musical Times*, 110 (1969), pp. 922–6.

37 No contemporary text survives. The manuscript copy at the Huntington Library, San Marino, US-Cn Larpent 298 was edited in *Three Plays by David Garrick*, ed. Elizabeth P. Stein (New York: William Edwin Rudge, 1926), pp. 55–111.

38 Burden, 'Opera and Theatre'.

39 David Garrick, *Cymon* (London, 1767), p. 57.

40 David Garrick, *Cymon*, 3rd ed. (London, 1767), p. 83.

Illustration 12.2. 'The Procession, Drury Lane'. The procession illustrated is that which appeared in David Garrick's *Jubilee* of 1769. Each of the banners carries the name of one of Shakespeare's plays, and is followed by the key characters in each drama. The use of procession as an extra attraction, which provided audiences with an 'operatic moment' in spoken drama, grew in importance with the enlargement of the London theatres towards the end of the century.

Anon. Black and white engraving, published 1 November 1770 by J. Johnson and J. Payne. © The Folger Shakespeare Library, Washington, DC

When the piece was altered to an opera, the procession was much expanded.[41] No longer was it simply a confirmation of the virtue of Cymon and of his fitness to rule; it became a bombastic event of immense proportions. The procession – now accompanied by war-like instrumental music – also included a number of on-stage bands dispersed throughout the procession; four heralds with trumpets, a 'warlike band' of eighteen performers, a double drum and cymbals, and another on-stage band to play a 'grand march'. Throughout the procession, the pit orchestra was given

41 David Garrick [adapter anon.], *Cymon: an Opera in Five Acts* (London, 1792), pp. 50–4.

directions, including 'orchestra silent', 'soft music in the orchestra', and so on. When the procession was assembled on stage, there followed a series of 'combats' – including a joust between an Englishman and a Spaniard on white horses – which were accompanied by 'both the Orchestra and the Martial Band introduced in the Procession'. A speech by Merlin and a choral finale closed the opera. The outcome of the joust – the Englishman won, naturally – serves to emphasize that it was impossible to divorce even such operatic extravaganzas from notions of being 'British'. Merlin's closing speech praises the virtue of the couple Cymon and Sylvia, who will set a guiding example; 'the people will make their Sovereign's bliss their own'.

But despite their popularity, it would be a mistake to believe that such grandiose theatrical events were always favourably received. Ultimately (and predictably), they were seen as yet another indication of the decline in the standards of opera and drama in England. Cumberland saw it in almost Jonsonian terms, a situation in which the poet's efforts were seen as entirely secondary to those of the scene-builder and the machinist; even Garrick described his *Cymon* as 'Some theatrical Trash which I have Exhibited to ye Public this winter'.[42] As Mrs Abbington said in Keate's epilogue to the 1767 *Cymon*, the intelligentsia moaned that legitimate drama was lost as the management exhausted the audience 'with *Op'ras*, *Monkies*, *Mab* and *Dr Faustus*'. But, she went on, the public taste was fickle; it needed 'variety to make the feast'.[43] And such variety did not mean that the drama itself was worthless; the critic writing in *The Theatrical Repertory* commented of another late eighteenth-century piece, Prince Hoare's *Chains of the Heart*, that 'the opera before us, considered merely as the vehicle for song and spectacle, is far from wanting in its recommendations'.[44]

Conclusion

The attitude of London audiences to both aria and procession emphasizes that they thought not in terms of opera as something all-sung, but in terms of operatic moments. The aria could appear in all-sung imported Italian operas, in ballad operas, in English opera with spoken dialogue, or as a musical moment in a spoken play. In all-sung works, the moment for the aria was prepared in

42 *The Letters of David Garrick*, ed. David M. Little and George M. Kahrl (London, 1963), II, Letter 449, p. 561.
43 Garrick, *Cymon* (1767), Epilogue (by George Keate).
44 *The Theatrical Repertory*, 14 December 1801, p. 197.

recitative. In works with spoken dialogue, the moment had to be equally well prepared, for playhouse audiences required dramatic verisimilitude and it was this requirement that was mostly responsible for the English detestation of recitative; how could singing dialogue of action be thought 'rational' or 'natural'? As a summation of a whole litany of complaint, Chesterfield's remark that whenever he went to an opera he left his sense and reason at the door with his half-guinea, and delivered himself up to his eyes and ears, cannot be bettered.[45] But a procession, as a version of the 'play-within-the-play', offered another version of *vraisemblance*; it was also related either closely or loosely (depending on circumstance) to the drama, but in whatever genre it appeared it provided a possible vehicle for a scene of operatic extravagance and, as in *Cymon*, national pride. Most important in the overall picture, though, both aria and procession were phenomena in which the singers – such an essential part of an audience's attraction – could shine and, hopefully, fill the manager's coffers in what was a fiercely competitive, essentially free-wheeling, commercial market.

Select Bibliography

Aspden, Suzanne. '"An Infinity of Factions": Opera in Eighteenth-Century Britain and the Undoing of Society'. *Cambridge Opera Journal*, 9/1 (1997), pp. 1–19

Barnett, Dene. *The Art of Gesture: The Practices and Principles of 18th-Century Acting*. Heidelberg, 1987

Burden, Michael. 'Metastasio's "London Pasties": Curate's Egg or Pudding's Proof?' In Elisabeth Theresia Hilscher und Andrea Sommer-Mathis (eds.), *Pietro Metastasio (1698–1782), 'uomo universal'*. Vienna, 2000, pp. 293–309

'Metastasio on the British Stage to 1840: A Catalogue'. *Royal Musical Association Research Chronicle*, 40 (2007)

'Opera and Theatre'. In Jane Moody and Daniel O'Quinn (eds.), *The Cambridge Companion to the British Theatre 1730–1830*. Cambridge, 2007, pp. 205–17

Burrows, Donald and Rosemary Dunhill. *Music and Theatre in Handel's World: The Family Papers of James Harris 1732–1780*. Oxford, 2002

Dean, Winton. *Handel and the Opera Seria*. Berkeley and Los Angeles, 1969

Handel's Operas, 1726–1741. Woodbridge and Rochester, NY, 2006

Dean, Winton and J. Merrill Knapp. *Handel's Operas 1704–1726*. Oxford, 1987

Dircks, Phyllis T. *The 18th-Century English Burletta*. Victoria, BC, 1999

Donohue, J. 'Burletta and the Early Nineteenth-Century English Theatre'. *Nineteenth-Century Theatre Research*, 1 (1973), pp. 29–51

Fenner, Theodor. *Opera in London: Views of the Press, 1785–1830*. Carbondale, IL, 1995

Fiske, Roger. *English Theatre Music in the Eighteenth Century*. 2nd edn. Oxford, 1986

45 Bonamy Dobrée (ed.), *The Letters of Philip Dormer Stanhope, 4th Earl of Chesterfield* (London, 1932), vol. 5, p. 1822.

Howard, Patricia, 'Guadagni in the Dock: A Crisis in the Career of a Castrato'. *Early Music*, 27 (1999), pp. 87–95

Hume, Robert D. 'Theatres and Repertory' [1660–1776]. In Joseph Donohue (ed.), *The Cambridge History of British Theatre*, vol. 2. Cambridge, 2004, pp. 53–70

'Drama and Theatre in the Mid and Later Eighteenth Century'. In John Richetti (ed.), *The Cambridge History of English Literature, 1660–1780*. Cambridge, 2005, pp. 316–39

'The Economics of Culture in London, 1660–1740'. *Huntington Library Quarterly*, 69 (2006), pp. 487–533

Joncus, Berta. 'Producing Stars in *Dramma per musica*'. In Melania Bucciarelli and Berta Joncus (eds.), *Music as Social and Cultural Practice: Essays in Honour of Reinhard Strohm*. Woodbridge and Rochester, NY, 2007, pp. 275–93

Lindgren, Lowell. '*Camilla* and *The Beggar's Opera*'. *Philological Quarterly*, 59 (1980), pp. 44–61

'Venice, Vivaldi, Vico and Opera in London, 1705–17: Venetian Ingredients in English Pasticci'. In A. Fanna and G. Morelli (eds.), *Nuovi studi vivaldiani*. Florence, 1988, pp. 633–66

Milhous, Judith. 'The Economics of Theatrical Dance in Eighteenth-Century London'. *Theatre Journal*, 5 (2003), pp. 481–508

Milhous, Judith, Gabriella Dideriksen and Robert D. Hume. *Italian Opera in Late Eighteenth-Century London. Vol. 2. The Pantheon Opera and its Aftermath 1789–1795*. Oxford, 2001

Milhous, Judith, and Robert D. Hume. 'Opera Salaries in Eighteenth-Century London'. *Journal of the American Musicological Society*, 46 (1993), pp. 26–83

'Construing and Misconstruing Farinelli in London'. *British Journal for Eighteenth-Century Studies*, 28 (2005), pp. 361–85

Petty, Frederick C. *Italian Opera in London, 1760–1800*. Ann Arbor, MI, 1980

Price, Curtis A. 'Opera and Arson in 18th-Century London'. *Journal of the American Musicological Society*, 42 (1989), pp. 55–107

'Unity, Originality and the London Pasticcio'. *Harvard Library Bulletin*, 2/4 (1991), pp. 17–30

Price, Curtis A., Judith Milhous and Robert D. Hume. *The Impresario's Ten Commandments. Royal Musical Association Monographs*, 6 (London, 1992)

Italian Opera in Late Eighteenth-Century London. Vol. 1. The King's Theatre, Haymarket 1778–1791. Oxford, 1995

Smith, W. C. *The Italian Opera and Contemporary Ballet in London, 1789–1820*. London, 1955

Strohm, Reinhard. *Essays on Handel and Italian Opera*. Cambridge, 1985

Toft, Robert. *Heart to Heart: Expressive Singing in England 1780–1830*. Oxford, 2000, pp. 147–81

Weber, William. 'Musical Culture and the Capital City: The Epoch of the Beau Monde in London 1700–1870'. In Susan Wollenberg and Simon McVeigh (eds.), *Concert Life in 18th-Century Britain*. Aldershot, 2004, pp. 71–89

Willaert, Saskia. 'Italian Comic Opera at the King's Theatre in the 1760s: The Role of the Buffi'. In David Wyn-Jones (ed.), *Music in Eighteenth-Century Britain*. Aldershot, 2000, pp. 17–71

White, Eric Walter. *A History of English Opera*. 2nd edn., London, 1983

· 13 ·

Music theatre in Spain

RAINER KLEINERTZ

The establishment of a new dynasty

From the beginning of the eighteenth century Spanish music theatre was distinguished by two features above all: the literary and musical tradition of the previous century, especially the plays ('comedias', 'zarzuelas' and operas) of Pedro Calderón de la Barca (1600–81); and the dynastic change from the House of Habsburg to the House of Bourbon and the subsequent War of the Spanish Succession (*c.* 1703–14). For Spain, this was not simply a war between European powers such as France, England and Austria, but rather a civil war, in which parts of the population and nobility favoured the young Bourbon King Philip V, grandson of Louis XIV of France, while others supported the Habsburg pretender Archduke Charles (later Emperor Charles VI). These internal conflicts could not fail to affect the political, social and cultural order of the relatively young Spanish state, which was still moving tentatively towards its own national identity.

Indeed, the War of the Spanish Succession had consequences that affected not only the territorial shape of Spain, but also the state's very identity. Dynastic succession, for example, had turned out to be a problem solvable not by reason or law but only by force, and affected the legitimacy of the Bourbon King of Spain (who was only accepted by the Viennese court as late as 1748 in the Treaty of Aix-la-Chapelle); similarly affected were claims to the thrones of Naples and Sicily, which were occupied from 1707 (Naples) and 1713 (Sicily) by a Habsburg Viceroy, and from 1734 and 1735 by a Bourbon King, the Spanish *infante* Charles (later Spanish King Charles III). Also, after his final victory, Philip V did everything in his power to turn Spain into a modern nation-state that followed the French model. With the help of French advisers, Philip V changed Spain from a feudal conglomeration of counties into a modern absolutist monarchy, with a unified system of legislation and taxes and without internal customs barriers. Paradoxically, the loss of the Flemish and Italian possessions in the Treaty of Utrecht was not an insignificant factor in allowing Spain to pursue this goal.

Of particular relevance for music theatre in Spain was the fact that Philip tried to 'hispanicize' the court as much as possible, apparently avoiding cultural imports such as Italian opera in an attempt to gain the trust of his subjects. At the same time, Italy was the main focus of Spanish foreign policy, since Philip wanted to recover the Italian territories as well as their associated influence in the Mediterranean.

These contextual features are reflected almost paradigmatically in one of the most significant Spanish works of the early eighteenth century, Pablo Escuder's *comedia* (Spanish play) *Los desagravios de Troya* ('The Atonement for Troy'), which includes operatic scenes and musical interludes composed by Joaquín Martínez de la Roca (*c.* 1676–*c.* 1756). The work – a dramatization of Aeneas' arrival in Italy, following Virgil's *Aeneis* – was performed in 1712 in the palace of the Spanish field-marshal José Carrillo de Albornoz, Conde de Montemar in Saragossa to celebrate the birth of the *infante* Felipe. While at first glance it might seem an ephemeral production, it was actually a significant 'event' for the new Bourbon dynasty in Spain. Both libretto and score were printed and included a dedication to Anne Marie de la Tremoïlle, Princesse des Ursins (1642–1722), the Queen's First Lady-in-waiting (*camarera mayor*) and the most important French person at the Spanish court. Even though the music by Martínez de la Roca was quite conventional, the fact that it was printed was significant. The most interesting pieces are the prologue in the tradition of the French tragédie lyrique with its appraisal of 'Louis the Great' (the French King Louis XIV) and the new-born *infante*, and the Intermedio cómico-músico between Act ('jornada') 2 and 3. Here the music of France, Portugal, Italy and Spain – represented by women in the respective national costumes – dispute who would be the worthiest to praise the birth of the *infante*. The prize is conceded to Spanish music for its ability 'to absorb the music of other nations'.

These efforts of the Bourbon side to create a genuine Spanish music theatre contrasted sharply with the attitude of the Habsburg pretender Charles, who resided in Barcelona from 1705 until 1713.[1] Charles brought with him musicians from Vienna and Naples (his chapel-master was Giovanni Porsile) and performed Italian opera just as in Vienna. Thus 1708 and 1709, for example, saw the dramma per musica *Zenobia in Palmira* by Apostolo Zeno and Pietro Pariati, with music by Fortunato Chelleri or Andrea Fiorè, and 1710 *Scipione nelle Spagne* by Zeno, as

1 Charles left for Frankfurt am Main in 1711, when he succeeded his brother Joseph I to the throne of the Holy Roman Empire. His wife Elisabeth Christina of Brunswick remained in Barcelona until early 1713.

well as *L'Atenaide* by Zeno with music by Andrea Fiorè, Antonio Caldara and Francesco Gasparini.[2]

Spanish opera 'in the Italian style'

The fundamental changes in the Spanish political situation inevitably impinged upon music theatre and affected the introduction of Italian opera. After the death of his first wife in 1714 Philip V married the Italian princess Elisabetta (Isabel) Farnese and the idea of recapturing the Italian territories – above all, Naples and Sicily – consequently became even more of a priority than it had before; the Spanish throne, it was thought, should not be limited to the Iberian peninsula (and Spain's overseas possessions), but should also be the legitimate heir of the Aragonese Mediterranean empire.

Even though a first military intervention in 1718 failed, political ambitions continued to be reflected in courtly music theatre. So, for example, in the prologue of *Las amazonas de España*, the first of a series of Spanish court operas performed in Madrid (1720), the allegorical figures of 'Music' and 'Representation' are a reflection of the royal couple: Italian music and Spanish drama shall form a new genre of Spanish opera, ideally unifying the Italian and the Iberian peninsula. As 'Circe' tells us in the same prologue, Madrid aspires to something almost impossible in this new genre, namely a spectacle 'Italian in its music and Castilian in its words' ('En la Musica Italiana,/Y Castellana en la letra'). Indeed, the libretto was written by the leading Spanish poet José de Cañizares (1676–1750), and the music by the Italian Giacomo Facco (1676–1753), teacher of the crown prince Luis and violinist in the Royal chapel. The plot, too, is significant, representing an episode in Hannibal's campaign against Rome when – on his way from Spain to Italy – he was held up by a Celtic army. After personal negotiations (featuring an inevitable love affair), he continued on his way. This artistic and political 'programme' was continued in the following year (1721) with the opera *Amor es todo invención, Júpiter y Amphitrión* ('Love is all invention, Jupiter and Amphitryon'), again with music by Facco. Although the librettist – again Cañizares – apparently knew the Italian dramatization of this subject by Zeno and Pariati (*Anfitrione*, 1707), the drama is characteristically Spanish in the tradition of Calderón in both its language and form, and in its plot.

The aim of the Spanish court was not to import Italian opera, but rather to create a new genre of Spanish opera with Italianate music. Artistic aims merged

2 For detailed information, see the appendix by Daniele Lipp in Andrea Sommer-Mathis, 'Entre Nápoles, Barcelona y Viena. Nuevos documentos sobre la circulación de músicos a principios del siglo XVIII', *Artigrama* 12 (1996–7), pp. 70–7.

with political ones. It was certainly no coincidence that for the wedding of crown prince Fernando with the Portuguese princess of Asturias Bárbara de Braganza (1728) the Spanish ambassador in Lisbon, the Marqués de los Balbases, had performed in his palace *Las amazonas de España* (6 January 1728) as well as the specially composed *Amor aumenta el valor*, a melodrama by Cañizares with music by three members of the Royal chapel: José de Nebra (Act 1), Felipe Falconi (Act 2) and Giacomo Facco (Act 3). For the first time, a Spanish composer (Nebra) participated in the composition of a court opera.

Towards the 'dramma per musica': the beginnings of Metastasio reception

When the clinically depressed King Philip V and his court stayed far from Madrid in Seville between 1729 and 1733, Spanish opera entered the traditional Spanish theatres of Madrid, the so-called *corrales de la Cruz* and *del Príncipe* (named after the streets in which they were situated). Apparently the Spanish nobility tried to maintain a sort of courtly entertainment during the absence of the court itself. The first opera to surface was *Con amor no hay libertad* ('With love there is no freedom'), initially performed in January 1731, repeated later the same year and in at least 1732 and 1734 as well. The librettist was again Cañizares and the composer was Francesco Corradini (*c.* 1700–69), a Venetian who had worked in Naples and since 1728 had been in the service of the Prince of Campofiorito (Campoflorido) in Valencia. In 1735 in Madrid a sort of Spanish opera company was formed with (almost exclusively) female singers assembled from the two municipal theatre companies. The productions took place in the Teatro de los Caños del Peral, constructed in 1708 at the place where the Plaza Isabel II and part of the Teatro Real stand today. The first opera staged was *Trajano en Dacia, y cumplir con amor, y honor* ('Trajan in Dacia, or To comply with love and honour'), attributed to José de Cañizares, a two-act adaptation of the dramma per musica *Trajano* by the Abbate Giovanni Biavi, performed in Naples in 1723 with music by Francesco Mancini. While the Neapolitan libretto was dedicated to the Austrian Viceroy Cardinal Michael Friedrich von Althann, the Spanish libretto bears a dedication to Bárbara de Braganza.[3] The plot of the drama concerns the Roman emperor Trajan, who twice defeats the Parthian king Cosroa and finally adopts his nephew Adriano as his successor to the throne. The ruler is shown as a magnanimous conqueror

3 The full title is: '*Trajano en Dacia, y cumplir con amor, y honor*. Drama, de un ingenio matritense, para representarse en Musica en el Theatro de los Caños del Peral, de esta Corte. Dedicada a S. A. S. la Princesa de Asturias, Nuestra Señora. Con licencia: En Madrid, en la Oficina de Don Gabriel del Barrio, impressor de la Real Capilla de su Magestad. Año de 1735.'

whose virtue assures the continuation – albeit a problematic one – of the dynasty. Thus Biavi's *Trajano* offers an ideological justification of the Pragmatic Sanction of 1713, in which Charles VI appointed his own descendants heir to all the Habsburg countries (which went to his eldest daughter Maria Theresia, born in 1717) in opposition to the claims of the daughters of his elder brother, Joseph I. Just as the Neapolitan libretto evidently identified the Roman emperor of its plot with the actual emperor of the Holy Roman Empire in Vienna, so the Madrid libretto of 1735 offered a clear answer to the ideological claim of dynastic succession and supremacy in Italy.

While the plot in the Spanish libretto is almost identical to the original, the setting of the drama – following an old tradition of Spanish drama in place since the Golden Age – is changed from Asia Minor to Dacia, the region between today's Hungary and Romania. It does not seem to have been coincidental that this new setting was on the banks of the Danube and in the eighteenth century formed part of the Habsburg lands. Because the emperor Trajan was born on the Iberian peninsula, like his successor Hadrian, at the Roman city of Italica near Seville, he is explicitly described several times in the libretto as a 'Spaniard'.[4] In this way, the original story, now with music by the Italian composer Francesco Corradini and dedicated to the future queen of Spain, became a justification for Spanish claims on Italy, identifying the Habsburg court not as the legitimate successor to, but as the barbaric enemy of, the Italian–Iberian Empire.[5]

This sort of ideological appropriation went well beyond the adaptation of a single plot: for the Spanish public it provided access to historical subjects from the Roman Empire as well as an identification with persons who until then had been unfamiliar to Spanish literature. When Pietro Metastasio's *Adriano in Siria* was given to the Madrid public only two years later – in Spanish translation as *Mas gloria es triunfar de sí. Adriano en Siria* ('It is greater glory to triumph over oneself') – the acclamation of the ruler at the beginning of the drama could be understood perfectly as a demonstration of Spanish dynastic rights in Italy.[6]

4 In the libretto Trajan refers to 'mi Patria Española', and a few scenes later his wife Plotina explains that 'Trajano es Español'. See *Trajano en Dacia* (Madrid, 1735), pp. 16, 19.

5 Unfortunately, the music to this opera is lost, as is that of all other Spanish operas of the 1730s; thus the comparison cannot be extended to the music. Nonetheless, the fact that an Italian composed the music is in itself remarkable.

6 'According to Metastasio's *argomento*, the drama accomplishes a development: that of Hadrian from an emperor freshly elevated by the troops to an emperor worthy of his glory ... It was a suitable *sujet* – from the poet's point of view – to honour the emperor who had commissioned the libretto.' See Reinhard Strohm, *Dramma per Musica: Italian Opera Seria of the Eighteenth Century* (New Haven, CT and London, 1997), p. 241. After Trajan and Hadrian had been claimed in Spain as Spanish-born emperors, the libretto of *Adriano in Siria* could be taken to be part of Spanish history and thus used to make dynastic claims. Originally written for the Viennese court, this libretto in its Spanish translation was given some specifically Spanish characteristics along with music by the Spanish composer José de Nebra.

Besides the political dimension, this was a cultural event of the greatest significance: in the immediate context of the recovery of Naples and Sicily, Spain seized upon the genre of dramma per musica as a means of proclaiming its hold over Italy and its supremacy in the Mediterranean. When in 1738 the rebuilt Teatro de los Caños del Peral was solemnly inaugurated with Johann Adolf Hasse's *Demetrio* (again setting a libretto by Metastasio),[7] this was rather the end than the beginning (as usually interpreted in Spanish historiographical contexts) of a long process of cultural assimilation. It was perhaps not a coincidence that this first dramma per musica performed in Madrid in Italian dealt yet again with the problems of dynastic succession. This and the following Italian operas, sung in Italian, were no longer performed by Spanish actresses, but by an Italian opera company that the Marchese Annibale Scotti had brought to Madrid. The first impresario was Giovanni Antonio Pieracini, followed by Giovanni Maria Mazza from 1739. The singers included the sopranos Rosa Mancini and Elisabetta Uttini and the famous tenor Annibale Pio Fabri. In 1739, three excellent singers were added: the Neapolitan castrato Gaetano Majorano, called Caffarelli, arriving from London, the soprano Anna Maria Peruzzi, called 'la Perrucchiera' and the contralto Vittoria Tesi.

Spanish opera did not disappear completely with the arrival of Italian opera proper, but was considerably reduced (see table 13.1). During the two decades from 1738 to 1758, the dramma per musica (that is, opera seria) was to become the leading genre at the Spanish court. Thus the wedding of the King of Naples (the future Spanish King Carlos III) with Maria Amalia of Saxony in 1738 was celebrated in Madrid with Metastasio's *Alessandro nell'Indie* with music by the *maestro* of the Royal chapel Francesco Corselli (1705–78). The following year it was again an Italian opera, *Farnace* (text by Antonio Maria Lucchini, music by Corselli), that was performed for the wedding of the *infante* Philip with the French princess Louise-Élisabeth. And in 1744 the wedding of the *infante* María Teresa with the French crown prince Louis was celebrated with Metastasio's *Achille in Sciro*, again set to music by Corselli.[8]

The splendour of Italian opera

The arrival of the famous castrato Farinelli in Madrid and his appointment as the King's personal servant ('criado familiar') in 1737 at first had little or

7 Hasse's *Demetrio* had been performed in 1732 in Venice, in 1734 in Vienna (as *Cleonice*), and in 1737 again in Venice. The Madrid performance retained the original recitatives and several of the arias; other arias were written by various authors, including in all likelihood Francesco Corselli.

8 Cf. Reinhard Strohm, 'Francesco Corselli's Operas for Madrid', in Rainer Kleinertz (ed.), *Teatro y Música en España (siglo XVIII), Actas del Simposio Internacional Salamanca 1994* (Kassel and Berlin, 1996), pp. 79–106.

Table 13.1 *Opera performances (premieres) in Madrid, 1731–46*

Year		Title	Acts	Librettist	Composer	Theatre	Company
1731	22 January	*Con amor no hay libertad*	2	Cañizares	Corradini	Cruz	Orozco
	9 September	*Con amor no hay libertad* [R]	2	Cañizares	Corradini	Príncipe	Orozco
1732	23 February	*Con amor no hay libertad* [R]	2	Cañizares	Corradini	Príncipe	Orozco
1734	6 August	*Con amor no hay libertad* [R]	2	Cañizares	Corradini	Príncipe	Zerquera
1735	July	*Trajano en Dacia, y cumplir con amor y honor*	2	Cañizares [?]	Corradini	Caños del Peral	Spanish actresses ('Compañía de músicas')
	July	*La cautela en la amistad y Robo de las Sabinas*	2	Agramont y Toledo	Corselli	Caños del Peral	Spanish actresses
1736	31 January	*Dar el ser el hijo al padre* [= *Artaserse*]	2	Metastasio	Corradini	Príncipe	Zerquera
	31 January	*Por amor y por lealtad recobrar la magestad y Demetrio en Syria*	2	Metastasio	Mele	Cruz	San Miguel
	1 November	*El ser noble es obrar bien*	2	Cañizares	Corradini	Caños del Peral	Spanish actresses
1737	Carnival	*Amor, constancia y muger* [= *Siface*]	3	Metastasio	Mele	Caños del Peral	Spanish actresses
	30 May	*Mas gloria es triunfar de si. Adriano en Syria*	3	Metastasio	Nebra	Cruz	Spanish actresses
	21 July	*Mas gloria es triunfar de si. Adriano en Syria* [R]	3	Metastasio	Nebra	Cruz	Spanish actresses
	23 August	*El ser noble es obrar bien* [R]	2	Cañizares	Corradini	Cruz	Spanish actresses

	21 September	*Trajano en Dacia, y cumplir con amor y honor* [R]	2	Cañizares [?]	Corradini	Cruz	Spanish actresses
	6 October	*La Casandra*	2	Cañizares	de la Roca	Cruz	Spanish actresses
	10 November	*Amor, constancia y muger* [= *Siface*] [R]	3	Metastasio	Mele	Cruz	Spanish actresses
	7 December	*La Casandra* [R]	2	Cañizares	de la Roca	Cruz	Spanish actresses
1738	13 January	*El oraculo infalible*	2	?	Sisi Maestres	Cruz	Spanish actresses
	9 February	*Demetrio*	3	Metastasio	Hasse and various authors	Caños	Italian singers
	10 February	*La fineza acreditada vence el poder del destino*		?	Cifuentes	Cruz	Spanish actresses
	9 May	*Alessandro nell'Indie*	3	Metastasio	Corselli	Buen Retiro	Italian singers
	After 19 May	*Demofoonte*	3	Metastasio	Schiassi and various authors	Caños del Peral	Italian singers
	25 October	*Artaserse*	3	Metastasio	[Hasse/Vinci?]	Caños del Peral	Italian singers
	15 November	*Por amor y lealtad recobrar la majestad. Demetrio en Siria* [R]	2	Metastasio	Mele	Cruz	Orozco
1739	30 January	*La Clizie*	2	Cañizares	Corradini	Príncipe	Orozco
	29 March	*Siroe re di Persia*	3	Metastasio	Hasse	Caños del Peral	Italian singers
	6 May	*La cautela en la amistad y Robo de las Sabinas* [R]	2	Agramont y Toledo	Corselli	Cruz	San Miguel
	After 13 May	*La clemenza di Tito*	3	Metastasio	Hasse	Caños del Peral	Italian singers

Table 13.1 (*cont.*)

Year		Title	Acts	Librettist	Composer	Theatre	Company
	17 September	*La cautela en la amistad y Robo de las Sabinas* [R]	2	Agramont y Toledo	Corselli	Príncipe	San Miguel
	4 October	*Farnace*	3	Lucchini	Corselli	Buen Retiro	Italian singers
	12 October	*La Elisa* [*Burlas y veras de amor*]	2	Cañizares	Corradini	Cruz	San Miguel
	After 30 December	*La fede ne' tradimenti*	3	Gigli	? [pasticcio]	Caños	Italian singers
1743		*Domiciano*	2	?	?	Caños	Spanish actresses (Palomino)
1744	18 September	*No todo indicio es verdad y Alejandro en Asia*	2	González Martínez	Nebra	Cruz	Parra
	8 December	*Achille in Sciro*	3	Metastasio	Corselli	Buen Retiro	Italian singers
		El Thequeli	2	Solano y Lobo	Corradini	Caños	San Miguel
1745	11 August	*La mas heroica amistad* [*L'olimpiade*]	2	Metastasio	Corradini	Caños	San Miguel
	14 August	*La Briseida*	2	Cañizares	Corradini	Cruz	Jibajas

Notes: Buen Retiro – Teatro del Palacio del Buen Retiro; Caños del Peral – Teatro de los Caños del Peral; Cruz – Teatro de la Cruz; Príncipe – Teatro del Príncipe; [R] – revival.

nothing to do with these events. Coming from London, Farinelli no longer appeared in public, but limited himself to singing every evening for the depressed King to whom his chant brought considerable relief. Only when Philip V died in 1746, and his son Ferdinand VI succeeded to the throne, was Farinelli appointed as a sort of artistic director of the Madrid court theatre and of the court divertissements at the Palace of Aranjuez. In this capacity he led Italian opera in Spain to a splendour that surpassed that of probably all other European courts. His activities from 1747 onwards are documented in an illustrated manuscript from 1758.[9] Here, Farinelli describes the conditions under which the singers lived in Madrid (for example, that they had a carriage at their disposal so as not to catch colds from wet shoes), the make-up of the orchestra, the works performed (operas, serenatas and intermezzi), and finally in a second part the divertissements at Aranjuez, especially the evening entertainments on the river Tagus. Details on the latter include the distribution of musicians on different ships and an instruction that rowing had to stop when Farinelli sang.

The orchestra consisted of twenty-seven musicians, including one *maestro*, a copyist and a tuner, and comprising the following in 1758: Maestro Nicolò Conforto; Pablo Facco, Antonio Marquesini, Francisco Fayni, Esteban Hiseren, Francisco Lenzi, Feliz Vivencio (violins); Juan Ledesma, Francisco Guerra (violas); Domingo Porreti, Gabriel Ferri, Antonio Villanson (violoni[10]); Carlos Millorini, Bernardo Alberich (double basses); Joseph Nebra (harpsichord); Manuel Cabaza, Luis Mison, Francisco Mestris, Juan Lopez (oboes); Antonio Schefler, Joseph Pincraut (horns); Phelipe Crespo, Antonio Schariel (trumpets); Francisco Bordas, Domingo Oriolo (bassoons); Joseph Alaguero (copyist); and Phelipe Gaular (tuner).[11] The manuscript also marks the exact dates at which the members of the orchestra annually had to move to Aranjuez, beginning with the *maestro*, one violone (Porreti) and three violins (Facco, Ferri and Marquesini) – together with the King and the Queen – apparently for chamber-music purposes. The Queen, a pupil of Domenico Scarlatti (whom she had brought with her from Lisbon to Madrid), was a good harpsichord player,

9 The manuscript is preserved in the Library of the Royal Palace in Madrid. The complete title reads: *Descripcion del estado actual del Real Theatro del Buen Retiro. De las funciones hechas en el desde el año de 1747 hasta el presente: de sus yndividuos, sueldos, y encargos, segun se expresa en este Primer Libro. En el segundo se manifiestan las diversiones, que annualmente tienen los Reyes Nrs. Sers. en el Real sitio de Aranjuez. Dispuesto por Don Carlos Broschi Farinelo, Criado familiar de Sus Magestades. Año de 1758*. (Description of the present state of the Royal Theatre of the Buen Retiro. The productions that took place there from 1747 to the present, their individuals, honoraries and commissions, which are expressed in this First Book. In the second are manifest the divertissements which the royal couple enjoy every year in the royal estate of Aranjuez.)

10 The use of violoni instead of violoncelli is indicated not only by the term 'violon' but also by illustrations in the manuscript.

11 For many of these names the 'correct' spelling is unknown (probably 'Poretti' instead of 'Porreti', 'Scheffler' instead of 'Schefler' and so on); I have preserved the original spellings here as used in the manuscript.

and we should not forget that Scarlatti himself was present at the Madrid court, also – we must assume – at Aranjuez.[12] The copyist followed to Aranjuez on 23 April, two oboes and two horns on 2 May, the main part of the orchestra on 10 May and trumpets and bassoons on 28 May. Apparently all matters were planned in minuscule detail in order that the Royal chapel could always fulfil its religious and theatrical duties when necessary.

From 1747 to 1757 fifteen new drammi per musica were commissioned and performed at the Spanish court theatres:[13]

- 1747 *La clemenza di Tito*, libretto by Metastasio, music by Corselli (Act 1), Corradini (Act 2) and Giovanni Battista Mele (Act 3)
- 1748 *Angelica e Medoro*, libretto by Metastasio, music by Mele (premiered on 4 December 1747)
- 1748 *Il Polifemo*, libretto by Paolo Rolli, music by Corselli (Act 1), Corradini (Act 2) and Mele (Act 3)
- 1749 *Il vello d'oro conquistato*, libretto by Giovanni Pico della Mirandola, music by Mele
- 1749 *Artaserse*, libretto by Metastasio, music by Mele with arias by other composers
- 1750 *Armida placata*, libretto by Giovanni Ambrogio Migliavacca, music by Mele
- 1750 *Demetrio*, libretto by Metastasio, music by Niccolò Jommelli
- 1750 *Demofoonte*, libretto by Metastasio, music by Baldassare Galuppi
- 1752 *Didone abbandonata*, libretto by Metastasio, music by Galuppi
- 1752 *Siroe, re di Persia*, libretto by Metastasio, music by Nicolò Conforto
- 1754 *L'eroe cinese*, libretto by Metastasio, music by Conforto
- 1754 *Semiramide riconosciuta*, libretto by Metastasio, music by Jommelli
- 1756 *La Nitteti*, libretto by Metastasio, music by Conforto
- 1756 *Il re pastore*, libretto by Metastasio, music by Antonio Mazzoni
- 1757 *Adriano in Siria*, libretto by Metastasio, music by Conforto

The dominance of Metastasio's libretti is plain for all to see. Apparently Farinelli and the Spanish court were firmly behind the promotion of the

12 That Scarlatti is not mentioned in Farinelli's *Descripcion* is not surprising. Scarlatti was in the personal service of the Queen and not a member of the royal chapel. In regard to the 'private' sphere of chamber music at the Spanish court we know that María Barbara owned two precious harpsichords on which she even accompanied Farinelli. As Farinelli was on good terms with Scarlatti, we may assume that both frequently took part in the Royal chamber music. Farinelli's manuscript, however, is a document on official court 'functions'. And as far as we know, Scarlatti never composed any opera for Spanish theatres, nor participated in activities related to the royal chapel.

13 Years given are those taken from Farinelli's manuscript. For the exact dates see the catalogue in Rainer Kleinertz, *Grundzüge des spanischen Musiktheaters im 18. Jahrhundert – Ópera, Comedia, Zarzuela*, 2 vols. (Kassel and Barcelona, 2003), vol. 2.

drammi per musica of the Viennese court poet, the *poeta cesareo*, in Madrid. The treaty of Aix-la-Chapelle in 1748 had put relations between Austria and Spain on a new, friendly footing, continuing in the peaceful domain of opera seria.[14] However, the Metastasian drama, with its long recitatives, was difficult for a non-Italian public to follow, even when the original text sung on stage was translated in the libretto. As Farinelli did not allow tacit changes to Metastasio librettos (even though this was common practice in Italy and elsewhere), he asked his 'caro gemello' (his 'dear twin brother' as Farinelli and Metastasio called each other in their letters) to revise some of his librettos. Consequently Metastasio did something that he had never done before and revised four of his drammi per musica for Madrid: *Adriano in Siria*, *Didone abbandonata*, *Alessandro nell'Indie* and *Semiramide riconosciuta*. These four revised versions were even included by Metastasio in the first volumes of his *Poesie* (Paris, 1755) with the note 'Corretto dall' Autore'.[15] Volumes six and seven of the same edition then provided the original versions. Metastasio also wrote for Madrid at Farinelli's request the dramma per musica *La Nitteti* (1756), the *azione per musica L'isola disabitata* (1753) and the *componimento drammatico L'ape* (1756).

The zarzuela

Ever since the seventeenth century the zarzuela had been recognized as the authentically Spanish music theatre genre. With its extensive spoken dialogues (entire scenes, in fact) the zarzuela was almost a *comedia* (a Spanish play, although not necessarily 'comic') with music but, in contrast to the *comedia*, had two acts instead of three. The musical numbers were limited to only some of the *dramatis personae*, usually the two *graciosos* (comic persons) and those engaged in the amorous aspects of the plot. The action was usually pastoral in character.

As Philip V tried to gain the support of his people and of the Castilian nobility during the War of the Spanish Succession, the zarzuela played an

14 'Dramma per musica' and 'opera seria' were two denominations for the same genre. The libretto was usually entitled 'dramma per musica', whereas 'opera seria' was the colloquial expression for the musical work.

15 In vol. 9, pp. 423ff.: *Distribuzione dell' edizione*. In the preface to vol. 1 (*Lettera dell' autore*) Metastasio tells his readers: 'I add here four older dramas that I have recently changed and in my eyes largely improved. These are *Didone abbandonata*, *Adriano in Siria*, *Semiramide riconosciuta*, and *Alessandro nell' Indie* in which I believe I find either a certain slowness in the action, or some ambitious luxury in the ornaments, or some uncertainty in the characters, or some coldness in the catastrophe. These mistakes are easily the product of careless youth but cannot deceive maturity that comes from experience and age' ('Unisco all' antecedente [dramma] quattro miei antichi drammi da me nuovamente riformati, e per mio avviso migliorati in gran parte. Son questi la *Didone abbandonata*, l'*Adriano in Siria*, la *Semiramide Riconosciuta*, e l'*Alessandro nell' Indie*, ne' quali ho creduto ora di riconoscere, o qualche lentezza nell' azione, o qualche ozio ambizioso negli ornamenti, o qualche incertezza ne' caratteri, o qualche fredezza nella catastrofe: difetti che facilmente sfuggono all' inconsiderata gioventù; ma non ingannano così di leggieri quella maturità di giudizio che deriva dall' esperienza, e dagli anni' [vol. 1, p. xif.]).

important role in courtly celebrations. Thus, on the occasion of the birth of the crown prince Luis in 1707 the zarzuela *Todo lo vence el amor* ('Love is always victorious') by Antonio Zamora was performed; for the King's name day in 1708 the comedia with music *Ícaro y Dédalo* (called 'Fiesta de música') was given and on his birthday in the same year the zarzuela *Acis y Galatea* by José de Cañizares with music by Antonio de Literes.[16]

During the 1720s and 1730s the zarzuela was overshadowed by Spanish opera. In the 1740s – under the influence of the classical plots of Italian opera – it experienced a revival mainly through the co-operation of the important Spanish composer José de Nebra, organist in the Royal chapel, and the playwright Nicolás González Martínez. Fruits of this co-operation were several 'heroic' zarzuelas: *Donde hay violencia no hay culpa* ('The rape of Lucretia') (1744); *La colonia de Diana* (1745); *Para obsequio a la deydad, nunca es culto la crueldad, y Iphigenia en Tracia* ('Iphigenia in Tauris') (1747); and *No hay perjurio sin castigo* ('Hesione') (1747). The music consists mainly of Italianate da capo arias for the serious characters such as Lucretia, Iphigenia and Orestes, and strophic songs – sometimes called *seguidillas* – for the *graciosos*.[17]

During the reign of Ferdinand VI zarzuela and Spanish opera almost completely disappeared. Apart from the two zarzuelas with music by Nebra mentioned above, in 1747 only the dramma harmonica, *Antes que celos y amor la piedad llama al valor, y Achiles en Troya* seems to have been performed, a Spanish opera again on a libretto by González Martínez. It would appear that after 1747 only earlier works were repeated.

From the 1760s onwards, the zarzuela came under the influence of Italian comic opera. Two Italians – the bass buffo Michele del Zanca and the impresario Gaetano Molinari – asked the King for permission to produce 'óperas de Goldoni' in the Teatro de los Caños del Peral in 1760. The project seems to have failed but, surprisingly, Goldoni's comic operas were apparently known in Madrid at this time. Indeed, Goldoni's *La buona figliuola* with music by Piccinni was performed in Barcelona in 1761; and the first dramma giocoso by Goldoni in Madrid seems to have been *Gli uccellatori* with music by either Florian Gassmann or Piccinni. The work was first performed in the palace of the Neapolitan ambassador, but also in 1761 was produced by the company of María Hidalgo in the Teatro del Príncipe, entitled *En las selvas sabe Amor tender sus redes mejor* ('In forests Love can better cast its nets'). In the orchestral parts of this Spanish version, preserved in the Biblioteca Histórica Municipal de Madrid, we find the indication: 'para la Zarzuela de Napoles *Los Cazadores*' ('for

16 Antonio Literes, *Acis y Galatea*, ed. Luis Antonio González Marín (Madrid, 2002) (Música Hispana A, 37).
17 Music examples from these zarzuelas are published in Kleinertz, *Grundzüge des spanischen Musiktheaters*, vol. 1, pp. 246–66.

the zarzuela from Naples *Los cazadores*' [that is, *Gli uccellatori*]). In fact, from the 1760s onwards Italian comic operas performed in Spanish with spoken dialogues were routinely called 'zarzuelas'.

Also from the 1760s onwards the zarzuela proper came under the direct influence of the dramma giocoso and became a new genre of comic opera with spoken dialogues (similar to French opéra-comique). In 1765 the composer and playwright Pablo Esteve adapted Goldoni's and Piccinni's *La buona figliuola* for the Spanish stage (as *La buena muchacha*), in two acts and with several new arias. The plot of this 'zarzuela' was imitated by the playwright Ramón de la Cruz and the composer Antonio Rodríguez de Hita in their zarzuela *Las segadoras de Vallecas* ('The [female] reapers of Vallecas'). Esteve answered with a genuine Spanish zarzuela of his own *Los jardineros de Aranjuez* ('The gardeners of Aranjuez'), certainly one of the most interesting works of Spanish music theatre in the eighteenth century. In the preface to the libretto (*Prologo al que le coja*), he attacked Ramón de la Cruz severely for his mere imitations of Italian operas. And even if Esteve's 'jardineros' are formally influenced by the dramma giocoso, the plot and the ideas contained therein are self-evidently Spanish, relating in certain respects to problems encountered by the rural population in the broader environs of the capital. On the other hand, de la Cruz and Rodríguez de Hita's *Las labradoras de Murcia* ('The [female] peasants of Murcia') – often regarded by modern scholars as the 'starting point' of a characteristically Spanish zarzuela – is quite a conventional work in the dramatic and musical traditions of Italianate comic opera. The famous and perhaps over-rated *jota murciana* in the finale of the first act is a simple intercalation, continued by a menuet. Until the nineteenth century, then, few zarzuelas were produced, mostly comprising translations or imitations of Italian operas.[18]

Spanish music theatre between nationalism and the Enlightenment

The fundamental change in Spanish music theatre during the reign of Charles III (who followed his brother to the throne in 1759) has often been attributed to Charles' lack of interest in music. But why would a King who earlier in Naples had constructed one of the greatest opera houses in the world, the Teatro di San Carlo, subsequently neglect opera altogether in his new kingdom? The real reasons for the shift in emphasis in Spanish music theatre are

18 For example the very successful 'zarzuela' *La Isabela*, premiered in Madrid in 1794. The text is by the important playwright Luciano Francisco Comella, and the anonymous score preserved in the Biblioteca Histórica Municipal de Madrid. Juan Moliner is named as the adaptor; this sentimental drama seems to be a translation of an as yet unidentified French or Italian opera.

complex. Since the 1740s the new genre of dramma giocoso created by the Venetian playwright Carlo Goldoni and the composer Baldassare Galuppi, and continued by composers such as Niccolò Piccinni, had triumphed. Goldoni's and Piccini's *La buona figliuola*, premiered in Rome in 1760, was probably one of the most important events in eighteenth-century music history. At the same time, in Spain the earthquake of Lisbon in 1755 (Bárbara de Braganza was a Portuguese princess), the illness and death of the Queen in 1758 and of the King in 1759 put an end to the musical splendour of the previous years.

The gradual decline of opera seria was not just a Spanish, but a European-wide phenomenon. Even setting this aside, Charles III had serious politically based reasons to be cautious about the presence of Italian opera. Most serious in this regard was again a problem of a dynastic nature: the *Ley Sálica* of 1713 allowed as heirs to the Spanish throne only male descendants born in Spain. Charles himself fulfilled this condition, but his son – the future Charles IV – was born in Portici near Naples. As far as can be determined, succession did not ultimately turn out to be a problem, but Charles did well not to provoke serious opposition. Only after the coronation of Charles IV in 1789 was the *Ley Sálica* abolished in favour of the older *Partidas*.

It seems to have been mainly a consequence of these dynastic problems that during the reign of Charles III even royal weddings (1764 and 1785) and the birth of *infantes* (1783) were celebrated with Spanish *comedias*. Opera – and this meant comic opera – was limited mainly to public theatres. Here Italian operas were given in Spanish translation as 'zarzuelas' with spoken dialogues, as we have seen. Only in the 1780s did Spanish companies perform operas in Italian and with recitatives. In 1783, for example, members of the company of Juan Ponce sung Filippo Livigni's *La Frascatana* in Italian with the enormously successful music by Giovanni Paisiello. In 1786 the Junta de los Hospitales de Madrid obtained the right to perform operas, and Italian opera flourished again in the Teatro de los Caños del Peral, now in the guise of dramma giocoso. Indeed, a dramma giocoso was even performed for the coronation of Charles IV in 1789 – Lorenzo Da Ponte's *Una cosa rara* (based on a Spanish play by Luis Vélez de Guevara) with music by Vicente Martín y Soler, which had premiered in Vienna in 1786.

'Authentic' Spanish music theatre continued only in the more ephemeral genres of *tonadilla* and *sainete*, small plays with a few music numbers performed between acts and at the end. The music consisted of quite a few witty, mostly strophic songs sometimes in the form of Spanish dances (*seguidillas*, *jotas*, *fandangos*), sometimes with an Italian or French tune, and was often parodistic in intent. The number of actors ranged from one or two to four; only exceptionally were there more. In the second half of the century thousands of these small plays were written and produced, thus certainly constituting an important theatrical practice in Spain in the second half of the century.

In 1766 the Conde de Aranda – who had previously been based at the Prussian court and in Paris – became president of the Consejo de Castilla. Aranda founded the 'Compañía del los Reales Sitios' in 1767 designed to support the royal palaces in and around Madrid with Italian opera (especially drammi giocosi) and French theatre. The latter comprised mainly spoken theatre, but presumably opéras-comiques as well. We know very little about the repertory of this company, which remained in existence until 1777 – only some performances of Italian comic operas (in Italian) are documented by librettos – although we are able to determine from the repertory of a short-lived French theatre in Cádiz in 1768 and 1769 that 'French theatre' usually included performances of opéras-comiques.[19]

The manuscript librettos of the municipal theatres at Madrid also clearly indicate the presence of opéras-comiques. The Biblioteca Histórica Municipal de Madrid, for example, preserves a manuscript translation of Charles-François Panard's *La Critique de l'Opéra-Comique*,[20] dated 1768. Furthermore a manuscript libretto entitled *El cuadro hablador*, a translation of the opéra-comique *Le Tableau parlant* by Louis Anseaume with music by André-Ernest-Modeste Grétry, was certainly performed in 1781 in the Teatro del Príncipe.

The increasing presence of French opéra-comique was interrupted by the French Revolution in 1789, but continued after the pact between Spain and France against England in 1795 and the prohibition of opera performances in Italian in 1799. French operas with spoken dialogues were seemingly easier to translate into Spanish than Italian operas with their recitatives and large finales. The 'French' repertory performed in Madrid in 1801 is a good example:

- *Adolfo y Clara o Los dos presos* (*Adolphe et Clara, ou Les deux prisonniers*), text by Benoît-Joseph Marsollier des Vivetières (trans. Eugenio de Tapia), music by Nicolas-Marie Dalayrac (29 January, Príncipe)
- *Medea* (*Médée*), text by François-Benoît Hoffman (?), music by Luigi Cherubini (?) (11 February, Caños del Peral)
- *La opera comica* (*L'Opéra comique*), text by Joseph Alexandre de Ségur u. Emmanuel Dupaty (trans. Vicente Rodríguez de Arellano), music by Dominique Della-Maria (19 May, Príncipe)

19 This is also documented for French theatre in Seville after 1769. See Francisco Aguilar Piñal, *Sevilla y el teatro en el siglo XVIII* (Oviedo, 1974), pp. 92–104.

20 *La crítica*, trans. Ramón de la Cruz. See Francisco Lafarga, 'Traducciones de comedias francesas', in Lafarga (ed.), *El teatro europeo en la España del siglo XVIII* (Lérida, 1997), p. 247.

- *El califa* (*Le calife de Bagdad*), text by Claude Godard d'Aucourt de Saint-Just (trans. Eugenio de Tapia), music by François-Adrien Boieldieu (4 July, Caños del Peral)
- *La casa en venta* (*Maison à vendre*), text by Alexandre Duval (trans. Eugenio de Tapia [?]), music by Nicolas-Marie Dalayrac (?) (9 July, Caños del Peral)
- *Marcelino* (*Marcelin*), text by François Bernard-Valville (trans. Eugenio de Tapia), music by Louis-Sébastien Lebrun (25 August, de la Cruz)
- *El engañador engañado* (*Le Trompeur trompé*), text by François Bernard-Valville (trans. Vicente Rodríguez de Arellano), music by Pierre Gaveaux (4 November, de la Cruz)
- *Las tres sultanas* (*Soliman II, ou Les Trois Sultanes*), text by Charles-Simon Favart, music by Paul-César Gibert (?) (4 November, Caños del Peral)
- *El secreto* (*Le secret*), text by François-Benoît Hoffman (trans. Félix Enciso Castrillón), music by Jean-Pierre Solié (3 December, Caños del Peral)
- *El delirio* (*Le Délire, ou Les Suites d'une erreur*), text by Jacques Antoine Révéroni Saint-Cyr (trans. Dionisio Villanueva y Ochoa [pseud.: Dionisio Solís]), music by Henri-Montan Berton (9 December, Príncipe)

Indeed the prominent presence of French opera in Madrid continued until 1808, when the French occupation and the abdication of Charles IV and of his son Ferdinand VII in favour of Joseph Bonaparte provoked the bloody uprising in Madrid of 2 May (impressively recorded by Goya's famous painting) and subsequently the Spanish War of Independence. The repercussions of these events would disturb Spanish cultural life for years to come.

Select Bibliography

Andioc, René and Mireille Coulon. *Cartelera teatral madrileña del siglo XVIII (1708–1808).* 2 vols., Toulouse, 1996

Boyd, Malcolm and Juan José Carreras (eds.). *Music in Spain during the Eighteenth Century.* Cambridge, 1998

Bussey, William M. *French and Italian Influence on the Zarzuela 1700–1770.* Ann Arbor, MI, 1982

Carmena y Millán, Luis. *Crónica de la ópera italiana en Madrid desde el año 1738 hasta nuestros días.* Madrid, 1878

Carreras, Juan José. '"Terminare a schiaffoni": La primera compañía de ópera italiana en Madrid (1738/9)'. *Artigrama*, 12 (1996–7), pp. 99–121

Casares Rodicio, Emilio and Álvaro Torrente. *La ópera en España e Hispanoamérica*, Actas del Congreso Internacional. 2 vols., Madrid, 1999, 2001

Cotarelo y Mori, Emilio. *Orígenes y establecimiento de la ópera en España hasta 1800.* Madrid, 1917

Historia de la zarzuela o sea el drama lírico en España, desde su origen a fines del siglo XIX. Madrid, 1934

Kleinertz, Rainer. *Grundzüge des spanischen Musiktheaters im 18. Jahrhundert – Ópera, Comedia, Zarzuela.* 2 vols., Kassel and Barcelona, 2003

'Ruler-Acclamation in Spanish Opera of the 1730s'. In Melania Bucciarelli, Norbert Dubowy and Reinhard Strohm (eds.), *Italian Opera in Central Europe: Institutions and Ceremonies.* Berlin, 2006, pp. 235–51

'Zur Rezeption der Opéra comique in Spanien im 18. und frühen 19. Jahrhundert. In Michelle Biget-Mainfroy and Rainer Schmusch (eds.), *'L'esprit français' und die Musik Europas. Entstehung, Einfluss und Grenzen einer ästhetischen Doktrin/'L'esprit français' et la musique en Europe. Émergence, influence et limites d'une doctrine esthétique* (Essays in honour of Herbert Schneider). Hildesheim, 2007, pp. 446–57

(ed.). *Teatro y Música en España (siglo XVIII), Actas del Simposio Internacional Salamanca 1994.* Kassel and Berlin, 1996

Lafarga, Francisco (ed.). *El teatro europeo en la España del siglo XVIII.* Lérida, 1997

Leza, José Máximo. 'Metastasio on the Spanish Stage: Operatic Adaptations in the Public Theatres of Madrid in the 1730s'. *Early Music*, 26 (1998), pp. 623–31

Sommer-Mathis, Andrea. 'Entre Nápoles, Barcelona y Viena. Nuevos documentos sobre la circulación de músicos a principios del siglo XVIII'. *Artigrama*, 12 (1996–7), pp. 45–77

Strohm, Reinhard, 'Francesco Corselli's Operas for Madrid', In Rainer Kleinertz (ed.), *Teatro y Música en España (siglo XVIII), Actas del Simposio Internacional Salamanca 1994.* Kassel and Berlin, 1996, pp. 79–106

Subirá, José. *La tonadilla escénica*, 4 vols. Madrid, 1928–30

La tonadilla escénica: sus obras y sus autores. Barcelona, 1933

Virgili Blanquet, María Antonia (ed.). *Música y Literatura en la Península Ibérica: 1600–1750. Actas del Congreso Internacional Valladolid, 20–21 y 22 de febrero, 1995.* Valladolid, 1997

· 14 ·

Opera in Sweden

GREGER ANDERSSON

Interest in music as an art-form increased steadily in Sweden during the eighteenth century. In the 1730s public concerts were given for the first time in Stockholm by the orchestra of the royal court (the only professional orchestra in eighteenth-century Sweden), reinforced by amateur aristocratic performers under the leadership of the Kapellmeister and composer Johan Helmich Roman (1694–1758), known as 'the Father of Swedish Music'. In the 1760s the society *Utile Dulci* was founded in Stockholm and included a specialized music department counting among its members many amateur musicians, mostly noblemen and others from the upper classes. In the 1770s the Royal Academy of Music and the Gustavian Opera were founded (1771 and 1773, respectively). All these developments contributed to a new demand for music both inside and outside professional circles and led to a strong interest in contemporary music – the music of Carl Friedrich Abel, Christoph Willibald Gluck, André-Ernest-Modeste Grétry, Carl Heinrich Graun, Johann Adolph Hasse, Joseph Haydn, Franz Anton Hoffmeister, Johann Stamitz and others was soon introduced to Swedish audiences.

We can identify two principal periods of musical activity in eighteenth-century Sweden. The first was the so-called 'Age of Freedom' (*Frihetstiden*, 1720–70); Johan Helmich Roman served as Kapellmeister for the majority of this period. Virtually no musical repertory survives, even though it is known that Roman travelled extensively in order to purchase music. The second (1770–92), referred to as the 'Gustavian period' on account of Gustavus III's reign, is represented mainly by Gustavian Opera, a kind of national opera project. Composers mostly from abroad came to be associated with it, including Johann Gottlieb Naumann (1741–1801), Joseph Martin Kraus (1756–92), Georg Joseph ('Abbé') Vogler (1749–1814) and Johann Christian Friedrich Haeffner (1759–1833). Official musical interest was focused on opera, with many foreign works being performed – in fact at least thirty-two different operas and thirteen ballets were staged during this period. Christoph Willibald Gluck was best represented, but works by André-Ernest-Modeste Grétry and Niccolò Piccinni were frequently performed as well.

The 'Age of Freedom' (1720–70)

The many military campaigns of King Charles XII brought Sweden to the point of economic ruin at the onset of the eighteenth century, and his death in 1718 marked the beginning of the 'Age of Freedom', namely freedom from absolutism. Now the Estates were supposed to rule, the king constituting only a formal head of state.

In 1699–1706 a French theatre company, the Rosidor troupe, visited Stockholm and gave performances at court and at the Bollhuset (the Tennis Court Theatre). The troupe under the leadership of Claude de Rosidor (*c.* 1660–1718) comprised twelve actors, four singers, four dancers and five musicians – 'violinister och hautboister' – and was soon expanded with other actors and the musician couple named Renault (a singer and a violinist). The troupe introduced current French opera including Lully, Campra and Destouches, also performing French classical drama, comedies and ballets, but were dismissed in 1706. Indeed, the first decades of the eighteenth century were far from a golden period for institutionalized musical life in Sweden, with constant wars and political expansion severely affecting cultural activities. After the battle of Poltava (1709) in Charles XII's decisive war with Russia, the entire funding for the *Hofkapelle* in Stockholm was withdrawn; opera was performed only sporadically by a few visiting troupes; even the performance of military music was affected. Nonetheless some investments were made in music. Johan Helmich Roman was granted a stay in England between 1716 and 1721 by King Charles XII in order to 'perfectionera sig i musiquen' ('perfect himself in music'). During his visit he is supposed to have met Handel, perhaps performing with Handel's orchestra on several occasions and taking lessons on how to play basso continuo. Once appointed Kapellmeister to the *Hofkapelle* in 1727, Roman went on a second journey around Europe, visiting France (Paris), Italy (Naples, Padua, Florence, Bologna and Venice), Austria (Vienna) and Germany (Munich, Augsburg, Dresden and Berlin), not least in order to purchase music for his orchestra in Stockholm.

From the second quarter of the eighteenth century onwards musical life in Sweden came more and more to resemble musical life in other European countries. Public concerts increased in significance, modelled above all on the Concert Spirituel in Paris and the Bach–Abel concerts in London; the first public concert in Stockholm was Roman's performance of Handel's *Brockes-Passion* in the House of Nobles in 1731. Ballet and opera performances gradually became more frequent. Resources were still very limited, leading to co-operation between professional musicians and upper-class amateurs, a co-operation supported by Roman and his succesors.

After the disappearance of the Rosidor troupe in 1706, it was not until 1723 that a new company with a musical repertory reached Stockholm – a troupe of French origin called the Académie Royale de musique. It performed operas once a week, and spoken plays twice a week. Operas by Lully are known to have been performed, including *Phaëton* and *Roland*. Musicians from abroad actually contributed a great deal to the musical life of the capital throughout the eighteenth century. When Adolf Fredrik arrived in 1743 as prospective king and successor to the throne, for example, he was accompanied by his *Hofkapelle* from Schleswig-Holstein. The orchestra comprised eleven strings and woodwinds, two French horns and a harpsichordist. But it was not until 1744 and the arrival of the young Crown Princess Lovisa Ulrika, who would soon marry Adolf Fredrik, that the cultural life of Stockholm changed dramatically. In 1753 she engaged a French theatre troupe to perform at the royal palace of Ulriksdal (the Confidencen theatre, see below). This thirty-strong troupe of actors remained in Sweden for almost twenty years, presenting a substantial repertory of French vaudevilles and opéras-comiques. From 1742 onwards, the Princess's brother, Frederick the Great of Prussia, had supported a court opera house in Berlin, and Lovisa Ulrika arranged for him to send plays to Stockholm. Then in 1754 an Italian company was invited to Sweden, featuring the tenor Giovanni Croce, and later Rosa Scarlatti (1727–76). The latter was accompanied by her husband, the Italian composer Francesco Antonio Baldassare Uttini (1723–95). He was appointed conductor of the company and composed a series of operas, and became Kapellmeister to the Hofkapelle in 1755, remaining in Sweden until his death. Native opera composers were rare in the mid-eighteenth century; Arvid Niclas von Höpken (1710–78), who set two Metastasio librettos *Il re pastore* (1752) and *Cantone in Utica* (1753), as well as the comic intermezzo *Il bevitore* (1755), was one exception.

The arrival of the French troupe in 1753 had major consequences for Swedish music. The old Bollhuset theatre, next to the Royal Palace, was given a major facelift, and the architect Carl Fredrik Adelcrantz created a new theatre – the Confidencen (inaugurated 1753) – at Ulriksdal, the King's favourite palace. There were plans for a new theatre as well, but this project never came to fruition. The Confidencen is Sweden's oldest extant theatre, as early as 1754 staging little French opéras-comiques, with Jean-Jacques Rousseau's *Le Devin du Village* probably among them. A theatre was also built at the Palace of Drottningholm in 1754, but burned down in dramatic circumstances in 1762, being replaced by a new one a few years later and remaining under the direction of Adelcrantz. (A third theatre outside Stockholm was located at the royal palace at Gripsholm, but was designed solely for spoken drama and was never intended for the musical public at large.)

Sweden had Lovisa Ulrika to thank for the building of theatres at all these palaces.

Both the Confidencen and the theatre at Drottningholm are still in use today. The latter is one of the best-preserved Baroque theatres in Europe completely equipped with its original stage machinery, which can produce all of the magical effects demanded by the eighteenth-century repertory.

The 'Gustavian Period' (1772–90)

After the death of Adolf Fredrik in 1771, his son Gustav III (1746–92) succeeded him to the throne. (Bizarrely, Gustav received the news of his father's death in a box at the Paris Opéra.) With Gustav in charge theatrical life intensified considerably, resulting in perhaps Swedish opera's most successful period.

Gustav III's intention to use Swedish in performances – lending important historical colour, he believed – led directly to the dismissal of the French troupe. Instead of employing performers from abroad the king, often in a leading role, went on stage (at the Confidencen, in the early years of his reign) with other members of the royal family and other prominent figures from court. He often also acted as a kind of producer and playwright, writing the plots for several operas on national topics himself, but relying on foreign, mainly German, composers for the music. Gustav III has been called 'the Theatre King' and is regarded as a semi-professional dramatist;[1] at any rate he transformed Stockholm, then a little town of no more than 75,000 inhabitants, into one of Europe's most outstanding theatrical cities. He founded the Royal Academy of Music in 1771 and the Royal Swedish Opera in 1773, the first company in northern Europe to give regular performances in the vernacular, not just of singspiels and vaudevilles but also of great heroic operas. As Gustaf Johan Ehrensvärd, appointed as the first director of the new opera, explained:

> An opera which contains a pleasant and engaging music, a well-integrated ballet, brilliant costumes, pretty and well-painted scenery, has so much going for it, that the eye and remaining senses are all satisfied simultaneously. Eventually we shall be accustomed to the language … we shall eventually find words and expressions easier … and subsequently we shall come to like our own language.[2]

1 Erik Lönnroth, *Den stora rollen: kung Gustaf III spelad av honom själv* (*The Big Part: King Gustav III Acted by Himself*) (Stockholm, 1986).

2 Quotation from Bertil H. van Boer, Jr, 'Gustavian Opera: An Overview', in Inger Mattsson (ed.), *Gustavian Opera: An Interdisciplinary Reader in Swedish Opera, Dance and Theatre 1771–1809* (Stockholm, 1991), p. 161.

In 1773 Gustavian opera was initiated by Uttini's *Thetis och Pelée*, setting a libretto by Johan Wellander. Uttini had been Kapellmeister at the court since 1755 and was the most experienced Swedish-based composer in theatre and opera. *Thetis och Pelée* was the very first opera written in Swedish and was staged in the Bollhuset; unfortunately the music survives only in incomplete form. At any rate the première was a great success and was followed the next year by two very different types of opera: a pasticcio Swedish version of Handel's *Acis and Galatea* and a work based on a national subject, a play 'with music', *Birger Jarl*, with text by Gustav Frederick Gyllenborg and music by Hinrich Philip Johnsen and Uttini. The ensuing decades brought a wide repertory of French and Italian operas to Sweden all performed in Swedish translation, including several of Gluck's works.

Gustavian opera was not a single type of opera, but rather three different types: a classical one, based on Greek and Roman mythology; a historical-nationalist one, based on Nordic subjects; and a comic one, with comical or pastoral plots. As well as *Thetis och Pelée*, examples of the first type include Haeffner's *Electra* and Kraus' *Prosperin* and *Æneas i Carthago*. The second type includes *Birger Jarl*, mentioned above, and works such as Gustav's 'drama med sång' (drama with singing) *Drottning Christina*, Naumann's *Gustav Wasa*, Vogler's *Gustav Adolf och Ebba Brahe* and Olof Åhlströms *Frigga*. The third type was the most popular among the musical public. These operas, some of which were sketched out by Gustav III in his lighter moments, were usually staged at Stenborg's Munkbro theatre. When we add into the musical-theatrical equation the numerous dramas 'blandade med sång' (mingled with singing) and the performances of dramatic ballets, we get a sense of the very considerable output of musical dramas in Gustavian Stockholm.

The king soon realized that the Bollhuset theatre would be inadequate for his opera plans and that a new opera house with facilities for opera performances at an international level was needed. The Bollhuset was also a fire hazard, a fact probably welcomed by the king at least for the purposes of strengthening his argument for a new building. This risk was explained by the director of public buildings, Carl Fredrik Lagercrantz:

> The Bollhus' condition declines annually, and the danger of a catastrophe by fire is ever more evident, in as much as the Theatre [namely the stage] is now so much more crowded on account of the considerable increase in operatic sets. My humble duty does not permit me either to contemplate or to present in cold blood a circumstance so important to Your Majesty's precious person, but I must humbly request that it may please Your Majesty to the end of avoiding that danger which for so many years has caused the Estates of the Realm and

> every faithful subject so much concern, to permit this new building to be completed, the sooner the better.[3]

In 1782 the new opera house was in place, positioned close to the royal palace in the city, and designed by Adelcrantz; the auditorium was dominated by the large royal box and all the seating was in strictly hierarchical order. It was inaugurated with a performance of Naumann's *Cora och Alonzo*, setting a libretto by Adlerbeth, an event described in detail in the *Kongl. Theaterns almanack* for 1783:

> The inauguration of this new opera house took place in Their Majestie's and the Royal family's presence, with the opera *Cora och Alonzo*. The highest officials of the realm, Foreign Ministers, the present colleges and States, i.e., branches of the administration, as well as burghers of Stockholm, were invited to attend the occasion. The excellent taste both in song and action wherewith this Play was put on by the actors, supported by a numerous and well-conducted orchestra, by lavish costumes and magnificent Sceneries all of which, albeit commingled with earthquakes, firespouting mountains, etc. was presented with good order and swiftness; in a word, the noble and beautiful coherence everywhere evident, indicated the heights and perfection reached by our National Theatre. To the honour of Swedish Genius and the arts must also be mentioned the judgement which not merely those impartial foreigners who were present but also our more enlightened Compatriots were pleased to pass upon this Spectacle, namely that they had hardly seen one more brilliant or perfect.[4]

Since the king's main concern was to create a Swedish National Theatre, the librettists were mostly native Swedes, including Wellander and Johan Henrik Kellgren. (The king established the Swedish Academy in April 1786, based on the model of the Académie Française, in order primarily to promote the Swedish language and to stimulate nationalist sentiments.) Most of the composers, however, were foreign: Naumann and Vogler came from Dresden and Mannheim, respectively, and Kraus and Haeffner were both born in Germany, but became naturalized Swedes. Antoine Bournonville (1760–1843) was responsible for the ballet, while his fellow-Frenchman Louis Jean Deprez (1743–1804) created the sets. The orchestra, with more than sixty musicians, was an international one, with first-rate players including the trumpeter Lorenz Merckl (*c.* 1754–1800), the brothers Wilhelm (*c.* 1761–98) and Johann Joseph (1763–1808) Steinmüller, who were recruited from Esterháza and both played the French horn, and the woodwind player Johann Friedrich Grenser (d. 1795). Two of the lead singers, Carolina Müller

3 Quotation from Stig Fogelmarck, 'Gustaf III and his Opera House', in *Gustavian Opera: An Interdisciplinary Reader*, p. 49.
4 Given in *ibid.*, p. 61

(1755–1826) from Denmark and Franciska Stading (?1763–1836) from Germany, provided international support; native swedes included Elisabet Olin (1740–1828) and Carl Stenborg (1752–1813).

The goal of Gustavian opera was a *Gesamtkunstwerk*, not in a Wagnerian fashion but in terms of a combination and co-ordination of music and scenery based on Gluckian models. In addition to appearing on stage, and acting as a playwright and dramatist, the king himself was heavily involved in other activities, deciding which works should be produced and how stage designs should work. He also provided financial support for all participants. His involvement did not go unnoticed outside Sweden, Charles d'Aguila remarking in the *Histoire des événements mémorables du règne de Gustave III* (Paris, 1807):

> Knowing Gustaf III's genius, taste, and desires, you will easily believe me when I say that he is the creator of the opera which has been born in Stockholm. Decorations, costumes, machinery, ballet – all was, and still is, directed, sketched, planned, and protected by his brilliant inventive genius. The music is lively and moving and the Swedish language extremely adaptable to opera.[5]

National operas

Creating a Swedish opera company with operas that set Swedish libretti at its core, was of paramount importance to King Gustav and put a premium on works based on national topics. The most nationally orientated operas – *Gustav Wasa* (1786) and *Gustav Adolf och Ebba Brahe* (1788) – came into being at the king's own initiative, like so many others. In his namesakes he saw two heroic kings, and no doubt looked upon himself as the third in this heroic line. (In fact throughout his life he played up his association by name with the earlier Gustavs.)

The libretto to *Gustav Wasa* was written by Kellgren and based on a prose version by the king. Naumann composed the music and the scenery was set by Louis Jean Deprez. Gustav Vasa was elected King of Sweden in 1523 and was recognized as the founder of Sweden as a sovereign state. Since he liberated Sweden from the Danes and Gustav III himself planned to conquer Norway (a part of Denmark at that time) in the 1780s, the opera represented an important weapon in Gustav III's propaganda offensive. His plans were supported principally by the aristocracy, and in the new opera the people are represented by noblemen. The action for the opera revolves around the coronation banquet for the Danish King Christian II (known in Sweden as 'The Tyrant'), the Stockholm Bloodbath of 1520, Gustav Vasa's siege of the city in

5 Given in van Boer, Jr, 'Gustavian Opera: An Overview', p. 165.

1521–3, his election as king, and his coronation, and takes place over the course of a single twenty-four-hour period in Stockholm. Premièred to great acclaim in 1786, *Gustav Wasa* was performed 122 times at the Royal Opera between 1786 and 1823.

While the plot of *Gustav Wasa* is an authentically nationalist one, Swedish elements in the music are much more difficult to determine. Naumann was a German composer, but one strongly influenced by Gluckian ideals. *Gustav Wasa* therefore features magnificent ensembles, large choruses, ballets, *recitativo accompagnato*, arioso arias in various forms and a French overture. Perhaps influences of the Swedish language and its types of declamation can be detected in the melodic structures of the opera. At any rate, we must conclude that neither the king nor the composer had any obvious intention to create a distinctively Swedish musical style.

The second heroic-opera – *Gustav Adolf och Ebba Brahe* – first performed in 1788, concerns the liason between King Gustav II Adolf and a court lady. The scenery alternates between the halls of Kalmar Castle and the fishing village on Öland. As with *Gustav Wasa* the premiere took place on the King's birthday in January and represented the joint efforts of Kellgren, Deprez and the king; the composer was Vogler. The plot, however, is quite different from that of its predecessor, since the king is no longer supported by the aristocracy on account of the fact that his autocratic and despotic manner in ruling the country made him their opponent; for reasons of political propaganda, the focus moved from the noblemen to the peasants. The king himself is characterized as a gentle, high-minded and unselfish father of the country, admired by his people – for example, by those in the small fishing village. The light operatic scenes inspired by folk music are new to this opera – clearly Vogler wanted to create a Swedish folk tone. And he was well placed to do so, given his documented interest in folk music in general.

The relationship between the king and the commoners in *Gustav Adolf och Ebba Brahe* reflects a political reality. A few months after the opera's premiere war broke out between Sweden and Russia, to a large extent provoked by the king himself. He could now play to the full the role of heroic father figure to his people. He writes the following in a letter to his sister Sophia Albertina:

> I cannot conceal from you how excited I am at the thought of the brilliant prospect opening itself to me; my soul cannot withstand the glorious attractions of the thought that it is I who am to determine the fate of Asia, and that it is to Sweden that the Ottoman Empire will have to thank for its existence, and further that I alone among so many monarchs either too different or too astounded by the Empress' of Russia's successes, that I alone, I say, am going to resist her; thus I consider myself worthy of the throne once occupied by

> great kings and now by myself, and flatter myself on not belying at the end of my career the judgement which Europe at the outset of my reign was pleased to form of me.[6] (Signed at Haga castle, 13 June 1788)

The strongest opposition to King Gustav's stance came from the nobility. The war went badly, however, and would probably have ended in disaster if the Great Powers (England and Prussia) had not intervened. But the defeat was a defeat for the nobility, too, in that they failed ultimately to prevent the establishment of a new constitution that gave increased powers to the king. Instead, they planned a conspiracy that would ultimately cost the king his life.

Joseph Martin Kraus

Joseph Martin Kraus must be regarded as the most distinguished composer in Gustavian Stockholm. Although he completed only three major operas his musical output for the stage is quite extensive. His first major work, *Azire*, dates from his initial years in Stockholm, namely 1778–82, and is a *Sturm und Drang* singspiel written to a Swedish text. Kraus intended the work as his calling card – one that would allow him to become a well-established composer in the capital – but never actually had it performed. Crucially, though, the king noticed Kraus and asked him to complete a trial composition. The resulting operatic work was a one-act Classical drama *Prosperin*, based upon a sketch by the king and a text by Kellgren. A private performance was arranged at the Confidencen in 1781, Kraus relating the experience as follows:

> My work was finally performed before the King at… Ulriksdal, and I was permitted to conduct myself. The court was extraordinarily pleased with the work and the manner in which the King declared his satisfaction was beyond all my expectations. Immediately following the end of the music, the King talked to me for a quarter of an hour; he complimented me politely, asked me about this and that, and took my measure from head to toe with his large eyes, and I, in my usual fashion, did the same, which pleased him.[7]

Kraus was duly appointed Vice-Kapellmeister by Gustav III in 1781, having been deemed someone suitable to fulfil the king's plans; he was thus commissioned to write an opera for the inauguration of the new opera house. As Kraus explains:

> I have received the honor of composing the new work with which the new theater will be dedicated … the title of the work is Aeneas i Carthago, and the

6 As given in Anna Johnson, 'The Hero and the People: On National Symbols in Gustavian Opera', in *Gustavian Opera: An Interdisciplinary Reader*, p. 180.

7 As given in van Boer, Jr, 'The Operas of Joseph Martin Kraus', in *Gustavian Opera: An Interdisciplinary Reader*, p. 341.

> plot, staging, and episodes are all by the king himself, with only the versification by the poet who did my last opera.[8]

The opera turned out to be a huge work with five acts and a prologue. At the beginning of 1782, however, Kraus' lead soprano, Caroline Müller, and her husband fled Sweden in order to avoid debtor's prison, making it impossible to stage the opera at the inauguration of the new opera house. In fact it was not staged until 1799, seven years after the composer's death, further delays perhaps being explained by the high demands the opera made on librettist, scenographer, choreographer and stage manager alike.

The death of Gustav III

During a masked ball in the opera house in March 1792 Gustav III was shot (an event that provided operatic subject matter for both Auber and Verdi) bringing the era of Gustavian opera to an abrupt end. Kraus was commissioned to write the funeral music. The resulting cantata – *Begravningskantat* [funeral cantata] *över Gustav III* – can actually be regarded as a kind of heroic opera in memory of the King. Kraus' music is far more operatic than ecclesiastical, lacking an aura of religiosity. The lyrics by Carl Gustaf Leopold (perhaps better referred to as the libretto) is as dramatic as the music of Kraus. Both had been patronized by Gustav III for a lengthy period and would naturally have been shocked by his sudden assassination. The exclamatory introduction by the choir sets the mood: 'Heavenly power! What horrid fates! Oh, what an hour for Sweden strikes!' The 'stage' in the Riddarholmskyrkan (Riddarholm church) was also like that of a theatre, featuring décor, soloists, a large choir and orchestra. The newspaper *Stockholms Posten* wrote of the remarkable scenery:

> The décor in Riddarholmskyrkan on the occasion of the Most Blessed King's funeral resembled a dark forest or Grove of Cypresses, where gravestones were seen to have been raised over the most celebrated of Sweden's kings ... In the midst of these Monuments stood a high Ancestral Mound, on the topmost point of which stood the Most Blessed King's portrait bust, on a Pedestal surrounded by weapons of war, in front of which sat the image of a grieving Woman, representing Svea, with the Swedish Lion at her feet. Below the Funeral Mound were seen in four places Runestones, in which had been engraved in Runic Letters the eminent Qualities adorning the King's Person, and the most remarkable events of His life.[9]

Unfortunately for musical culture in Sweden, Gustav III's successor to the throne, his son Gustav IV Adolf, took little or no interest in theatre, and

8 *Ibid.*, p. 342. 9 Given in Johnson, 'The Hero and the People', p. 192.

operatic performances diminished significantly in number. It took until 1810 for the Royal Opera to emerge from its period of decline, and even then the works performed were all fashionable opéras-comiques suiting the tastes of the newly adopted crown prince, Marshal Bernadotte of France. That said, opera flourished elsewhere in Sweden in the last decade of the eighteenth century and first decade of the nineteenth, especially in private companies in smaller theatres. One such company was Nya Svenska Teatern (New Swedish Theatre), directed by Carl Stenborg between 1784 and 1801, which featured a large repertory of opéras-comiques and Swedish singspiels.

Select Bibliography

Books and articles

Andersson, Greger. 'Musikens miljöer'. In *Signums svenska kulturhistoria. Frihetstiden* (Signums Cultural History of Sweden. Time of Freedom: The Music). Stockholm, 2006, pp. 345–73

(ed.). *Musikgeschichte Nordeuropas. Dänemark-Finnland-Island-Norwegen-Schweden.* Stuttgart, 2001

Boer, Bertil H. van, Jr. 'Gustavian Opera: an Overview'. In Inger Mattsson (ed.), *Gustavian Opera: An Interdisciplinary Reader in Swedish Opera, Dance and Theatre 1771–1809*. Stockholm, 1991, pp. 159–72

'The Operas of Joseph Martin Kraus'. In Inger Mattsson (ed.), *Gustavian Opera: An Interdisciplinary Reader.* Stockholm, 1991, pp. 337–50

Engländer, Richard. *Johann Gottlieb Naumann als Opernkomponist (1741–1801): mit neuen Beiträgen zur Musikgeschichte Dresdens und Stockholms.* Leipzig, 1922

Joseph Martin Kraus und die gustavianische Oper. Uppsala, 1943

Fogelmarck, Stig. 'Gustaf III and his Opera House'. In Inger Mattsson (ed.), *Gustavian Opera: An Interdisciplinary Reader.* Stockholm, 1991, pp. 47–78

Hedwall, Lennart. *Svensk musikhistoria: en handbok* (Swedish Music History: A Handbook). Stockholm, 1996

Ivarsdotter, Anna. 'The Hero and the People: On National Symbols in Gustavian Opera'. In Inger Mattsson (ed.), *Gustavian Opera: An Interdisciplinary Reader.* Stockholm, 1991, pp. 173–95

'"Gustaf Wasa soll mein Meisterstück werden": Naumann and the National Swedish Opera'. In Hans-Günther Ottenberg and Ortrun Landmann (eds.), *Johann Gottlieb Naumann und die europäische Musikkultur des ausgehenden 18. Jahrhunderts.* Dresden, 2006, pp. 53–64

Jonsson, Leif and Anna Ivarsdotter-Johnson (ed.). *Musiken i Sverige, vol. II, Frihetstid och Gustaviansk tid* (Music in Sweden, vol. II, Time of Freedom and Gustavian Era). Stockholm, 1993

Karle, Gunhild. *Kungl. Hovkapellet i Stockholm och dess musiker 1772–1818* (The Royal Court Orchestra in Stockholm and its Musicians 1772–1818). Uppsala, 2000

Kungl. hovmusiken i Stockholm och dess utövare 1697–1771 (The Royal Court Music in Stockholm and its Musicians 1697–1771). Uppsala, 2002

Lönnroth, Erik. *Den stora rollen: kung Gustaf III spelad av honom själv* (*The Big Part: King Gustav III Acted by Himself*). Stockholm, 1986

Mattsson, Inger (ed.). *Gustavian Opera: An Interdisciplinary Reader in Swedish Opera, Dance and Theatre, 1771–1809*. Stockholm, 1991

Skuncke, Marie-Christine and Anna Ivarsdotter. *Svenska operans födelse: studier i gustaviansk musikdramatik* (The Birth of the Swedish Opera: Studies in Gustavian Drama). Stockholm, 1998

Tegen, Martin. 'Die Nationaloper als königliche Institution'. In Greger Andersson (ed.), *Musikgeschichte Nordeuropas. Dänemark-Finnland-Island-Norwegen-Schweden*. Stuttgart, 2001

Music Editions

Kraus, Joseph Martin. *Sorgemusik över Gustav III: bisättningsmusik och begravningskantat = Trauersinfonie und Begräbniskantate*. Ed. Jan Olof Rudén. Stockholm, 1979

Naumann, Johann Gottlieb. *Gustaf Wasa: lyrisk tragedi i tre akter*. Ed. Anna Johnson, Margareta Rörby and Claude Génetay, facsimile edn. Stockholm, 1991

Vogler, Georg Joseph. *Gustav Adolf och Ebba Brahe: lyriskt drama i tre akter*. Ed. Martin Tegen, facsimile edn. Stockholm, 1973

· INTERLUDE ·

· 15 ·

Performance in the eighteenth century

JOHN IRVING*

Take yourself back in time. It is 1700 and you are in the studio of your teacher, Arcangelo Corelli, in Rome. He has just demonstrated to you a passage from his newly-published *Sonate a Violino e Violone o Cimbalo*, and now asks you: '*non l'intendite parlare?*'

'Do you not hear it speak?' In that question, Corelli captures the essentials of musical performance in the eighteenth century. The composer (who in the eighteenth century was so often also the performer) expected his music to be rendered sensible, expressive, meaningful by *being spoken*. The performer (whether or not synonymous with the composer) had a duty to make that music speak by reading the signs it contained (whether notated or not) and applying performance conventions to them that differed widely across Europe, and were diversely recorded in vocal and instrumental treatises published throughout the century in many places and in many languages. All such treatises, though, presumed the same thing: that the performer will afford the music a way of being spoken. The instrument or voice was a related tool (combining with the performer's skill) that allowed the music to speak, and to speak appropriately.[1] Finally, the audience expected the music to speak to them. Music was a kind of Rhetoric.

* I would like to record my thanks to the following individuals who, either in performance or discussion (usually both) have helped me develop my ideas during the writing of this chapter: Tom Beghin, Jane Booth, Ronald Brautigam, Gary Cooper, Martin Knizia, Michael Latcham, Mark Padmore, Antony Pay, Rachel Podger, Joel Speerstra, Hans-Erik Svendsen, Oliver Webber and Brinley Yare.

1 That is, with a sound that the composer would have conceived. This includes, for example, the sound production of baroque bows on violins with gut strings, perhaps on instruments strung to equal tension, with smaller bridges and with shorter necks set at different angles from violins built later, or else adapted later to suit nineteenth-, twentieth- or twenty-first-century principles and purposes. Or it might include clarinets with only five keys, with wooden mouthpieces and producing a sound whose tuning, colour and intensity varies unequally across the range. Or it might include particular temperaments (by Vallotti, Young, Werckmeister or Kirnberger, say), enhancing the characteristics of tonal inter-relations in a piece, which are rendered uniform – and arguably diminished – in equal temperament. This is not a chapter on organology or a defence of using only original instruments or copies of historical fortepianos, violins, flutes, horns and timpani to perform eighteenth-century music. The music may be (and sometimes is) very well played on modern instruments, of course. But we restrict our opportunities to explore those eighteenth-century sound-worlds and the extent to which they highlight an *unwritten* part of the musical vocabulary of the time by playing the repertory on instruments built for later and different expressive purposes.

References to the rhetorical nature of eighteenth-century music are widespread in contemporary instrumental and vocal treatises. As early as 1702, Monsieur de Saint-Lambert explains:

> Just as a piece of rhetoric is a whole unit which is most often made up of several parts, each of which is composed of sentences, each having a complete meaning, these sentences being composed of phrases, the phrases of words, and the words of letters, so the melody of a piece of music is a whole unit which is always composed of several sections ... Each section is composed of cadences which have a complete meaning and are the sentence of the melody. The cadences are often composed of phrases, the phrases of measures, and the measures of notes ... One must be trained in music in order to be aware of them.[2]

Saint-Lambert's final point about musical training is reiterated in various guises throughout the century. Thus Johann Mattheson comments in 1739:

> The first and most important abuse in singing may well be when through too frequent and untimely breathing the words and thoughts of the performance are separated, and the flow is interrupted or broken. The second is when one slurs what should be detached; and detaches what should be slurred.[3]

Mattheson here introduces the important idea that technique in performance is not an end in itself, but a means through which the music may speak properly. In the former case, an element of the music's rhetorical sense (namely, its sentence structure) is ruined by inadequate technical control of the breathing. Mattheson's implication is that the precise expressive language of eighteenth-century music can quite easily be destabilized by a technical failing: listening according to the standards and expectations of the time, a listener would assume that breathing points indicate distinctions between different musical thoughts (undermined, of course, if a breath were inappropriately taken in the middle of a musical 'sentence'). In the second case, a convention (the slur) is wrongly applied, and once again the music is inappropriately spoken.

It seems, then, that there was such a thing in eighteenth-century music as a vocabulary that needed to be correct in both the usage and in the pronunciation in order to be understood correctly. This much we know from contemporary writings of various kinds – for example, on harmony and counterpoint and on form, aspects of musical understanding that came to fruition in the theories of Rameau, Kirnberger and Koch.[4] While a detailed understanding of the scientific underpinning of such theories was not something routinely

2 *Les Principes du Claveçin* (1702), trans. and ed. Rebecca Harris-Warwick (Cambridge, 1984), p. 32.

3 Johann Mattheson, *Der vollkommene Capellmeister* (Hamburg, 1739; reprint Kassel and Basel, 1954), trans. and ed. Ernest C. Harriss (Ann Arbor, MI, 1981), II.3.10.

4 See Jean-Philippe Rameau, *Traité de l'harmonie reduite à ses principes naturels* (1722), trans. Philip Gossett as *Treatise on Harmony* (New York, 1971); Johann Philip Kirnberger, *Die Kunst der Reinen Satzes in der Musik*, 2 vols. (Berlin and Königsberg, 1771–79), trans. David Beach and Jürgen Thym as *The Art of Strict Musical*

expected of a performer, the fact that the most important rules of melody and harmony were regularly outlined in vocal and instrumental treatises, too – most fundamentally the relationship between consonance and dissonance, and its consequent effect on gesture, accent and on correct hierarchical representation of stress patterns within the bar or phrase – shows that a knowledge of musical composition did indeed merge with the practice of the performer. Music was an art in search of a good speaker. The symbiotic relationship between composition and performance as separate but related stages in an act of expression is portrayed by Johann Joachim Quantz in 1752:

> [Y]ou must know how to make use of all the imaginable skills that your insight into the art of performance offers. Hence you must strive to learn to see clearly and grasp what constitutes a good musical phrase, and what must therefore hang together. You must be just as careful to avoid separating phrases that belong together, as you must be attentive not to link passages that contain more than one phrase, and hence must be divided; for a great part of true expression in performance depends on this matter.[5]

Quantz's comment is similar to Mattheson's, quoted above, and specifically relates technical skill to conceptual understanding. His recommendation that the performer should strive to achieve 'true expression [of the music] in performance' might easily be read in a modern sense whereby the music is an autonomous entity (perhaps even embodying cultural value of some sort) to which the performer (and, by extension, the performance) relate as external agents with a specific function: to represent that entity's essence. Hence we may speak of 'faithfulness to the score'. For eighteenth-century music, though, the Music is most definitely *not* the score. We can investigate this point further by returning to Corelli.

Corelli and beyond

> His music is the language of nature; and for a series of years all that heard it became sensible of its effects; of this there cannot be a stronger proof than that, amidst all the innovations which the love of change had introduced, it continued to be performed and was heard with delight in churches, in theatres, at public solemnities and festivities in all the cities of Europe for near forty years. Men remembered, and would refer to passages in it as to a classic author; and even at this day the masters of the science ... do not hesitate to pronounce of

Composition (New Haven, CT and London, 1982); Heinrich Christoph Koch, *Versuch einer Anleitung zur Composition*, 3 vols. (Rudolstadt and Leipzig, 1782–93), partial trans. Nancy Kovaleff Baker as *Introductory Essay on Composition – The Mechanical Rules of Melody, Sections 3 and 4* (New Haven, CT and London, 1983).

5 *Versuch einer Anweisung die Flöte traversiere zu spielen* (Berlin, 1752), trans. and ed. Edward J. Reilly as *On Playing the Flute* (2nd edn., London and Boston, 1985), p. 90.

the compositions of Corelli, that, of fine harmony and elegant modulation, they are the most perfect exemplars.[6]

Writing in 1776, Sir John Hawkins seems a little surprised at the durability of Corelli's music. Its 'fine harmony and elegant modulation' may have seen to that, of course, safeguarding it amid fickle changes of fashion and musical style across chronological periods as well as geographical areas during the eighteenth century. But taking Hawkins' account of Corelli as a whole,[7] these material qualities seem peripheral. Something else is driving this remarkable 'Corelli phenomenon': performance.

For all that Hawkins dutifully attempts a conspectus of Corelli, outlining his career, his personality, his influence, and itemizing his output of sonatas *da chiesa* and *da camera* (Opp. 1–5) along with the concertos Op. 6, the qualities of Corelli the man and Corelli the musician really come alive in the context of performance:

> The proficiency of Corelli on his favourite instrument, the violin, was so great, that the fame of it reached throughout Europe; and Mattheson has not scrupled to say that he was the first [foremost] performer on it in the world.
>
> The style of his performance was learned, elegant, and pathetic, and his tone firm and even; Mr Geminiani, who was well acquainted with and had studied it, was used to resemble it to a sweet trumpet. A person who had heard him perform says that whilst he was playing on the violin, it was usual for his countenance to be distorted, his eyes to become as red as fire, and his eyeballs to roll as in an agony.
>
> During the residence of Corelli at Rome, besides those of his own country, many persons were ambitious of becoming his disciples, and learning the practice on the violin from the greatest master of that instrument the world had then heard of.
>
> In the year 1730 an eminent master, now living [according to Charles Burney it was Charles Wiseman], was present [at an annual commemoration of Corelli in the Pantheon in Rome], who relates that at it the third and the eighth of his Concertos [Op. 6] were performed by a numerous band, among whom were many who had been the pupils of the author. He adds that these two pieces were performed in a slow, distinct, and firm manner, without graces [embellishments], and just as they are wrote; and from hence concludes that this was the manner in which they were played by the master himself.[8]

The reason that the issue of specifically *unembellished* performance arises here concerns a persistent vogue during the eighteenth century for embellishing

6 Sir John Hawkins, *A General History of the Science and Practice of Music*, 5 vols (London, 1776); this and subsequent quotations are taken from the Novello & Ewer reprint edn. (London, 1875), 2 vols., vol. 2, p. 677.

7 Hawkins, *A General History*, vol. 2, pp. 674–7.

8 *Ibid.*, pp. 674, 674–5, 675, 676. For Charles Burney's identification of Wiseman as the aforementioned 'eminent master', see *A General History of Music from the Earliest Ages to the Present* (London, 1776–89), 4 vols., vol. 3, p. 599.

the Adagio movements in particular of Corelli's solo sonatas, of which by far the most popular were those of Op. 5. Originally published by Gasparo Pietra Santa in Rome on 1 January 1700, Corelli's XII *Sonate a violino e violone o cimbalo ... opera quinta* underwent approximately fifty re-issues during the eighteenth century whose dawn it graced; indeed, it seems never to have been out of print to this day. Already by 1710 Estienne Roger in Amsterdam had published a text of Op. 5 incorporating not just any embellishments, but those of Corelli himself: *SONATE a Violino e Violone o Cimbalo DE ARCANGELO CORELLI Da Fusignano OPERA QUINTA ... Troisième Edition ou l'on a joint les agreemens [sic] des Adagio de cet ouvrage, composez [sic] par Mr. A. Corelli comme il les joue*. The final remark points to several strands of the early eighteenth-century practice of embellishment, which Roger was perhaps aiming to regulate (and, no doubt, to exploit) in his marketing:

- Embellished versions of notated texts (especially Adagios) were clearly a natural habit of good performers, leading to a distinction between how a piece *looked* on the page, and how it *sounded* in performance. (Roger printed both the plain and embellished versions together on the page, vertically aligned.)
- There was evidently a need to police the style of such embellishments – claiming the composer's own authority for those provided by Roger, for example – perhaps because all manner of embellishments, varying in taste, virtuosity and grammatical quality were already in circulation.[9]
- As the popularity of sonatas such as those of Corelli's Op. 5 established themselves principally through the medium of print, circulating widely and rapidly across musical Europe, and rubbing up against a variety of educationally, geographically and culturally localized traditions, so appropriate embellishments needed to be supplied in notated form for the benefit of purchasers who either may not have had the wherewithal to supply embellishments themselves or else risked adapting them inappropriately (to different national trends, for example).

Roger's advertisement, 'les agreemens [sic] des Adagio de cet ouvrage, composez [sic] par Mr. A. Corelli comme il les joue' (the embellishments for the

9 It is clear that a good command of the underlying harmonic framework was regarded as a prerequisite for tasteful 'agrémens'. The English commentator and Corelli enthusiast, Roger North, remarked that 'it is not possible to compose such a part with tolerable propriety or success without a sufficient knowledge of all the proper harmonious accords that belong to every bass note'; see John Wilson, *Roger North on Music* (London, 1959), pp. 162–3. North denounced the embellishments published by Roger as fabrications: 'Some presumer hath published a continuall course of this sort of stuff [that is, inappropriate 'graces'] in score with Corelly's solos ... Upon the bare view of the print any one would wonder how so much vermin could creep into the works of such a master' (p. 161).

Adagios in this opus, composed by Mr. A. Corelli, as he plays them) suggests something of the prevailing inseparability of composition and performance. What lies within his publication should not be regarded as texts in the sense ordinarily meant (typically configured as an authorial 'intention', conveyed to a performer through the medium of notation), but instead as traces of an aspect of the Adagios that arises spontaneously in performance and is only *retrospectively* conveyed through notation. Playing the Adagio is not separate from the compositional stage in this formulation, but part of an ongoing process, connected to and extending the act of composition *in performance*. This linkage of composition and performance within the ontology of the work is radically different in kind from ontological notions that developed during the nineteenth century and later. We succumb all too easily to the temptation to classify a composition such as a sonata from Corelli's *Opera Quinta* as an objective entity of fixed dimensions. Throughout the eighteenth century there were many such entities, all identifiable as Corelli's *Opera Quinta*, but inhabiting the realm of *performance*, each one continuing in subtly different ways the creative process begun, perhaps, in improvisation and subsequent notation.[10] Overall, there is a tendency towards greater complexity in the style and extent of embellishments applied to Corelli's sonatas as the century progresses but, even allowing for that, there is huge variation between relatively sparse versions that steer a course around the most important melodic or harmonic junctures of the original text, others that allow a hint of those structures to emerge and still others that submerge Corelli's basic text entirely beneath a torrent of shameless virtuosity.[11] In all these cases, however, the 'Work' named Corelli's *Opera Quinta* was something relatively unbound by textual authority, existing instead in a flexible relationship with many and varied performance situations.

Adaptability along these lines also extended to genre. In 1726, Geminiani published two sets of concertos:

> *Concerti Grossi con Due Violini, viola, e Violoncello di Concertino obligati, e Due altri Violini, e Basso di Concerto Grosso ... Da Francesco Geminiani Composti delli Sei Soli della prima parte dell'Opera Quinta d'Arcangelo Corelli.* London: Printed by Wm Smith ... and John Barrett, [1726].

10 For a comprehensive study of these, see Neal Zaslaw, 'Ornaments for Corelli's Violin Sonatas, Op. 5', *Early Music*, 24 (1996), pp. 95–116, which includes an extended example of seven such embellishments to the opening movement of Corelli's A major sonata, Op. 5 no. 9.

11 For example, those by Francesco Geminiani, reproduced by Hawkins in *A General History*, vol. 2, pp. 904–7, by Geminiani's pupil, Matthew Dubourg (apparently dating from before 1721 and recorded in a privately owned manuscript, 'Corelli's Solo's Grac'd by Doburg'); and by Giuseppe Tartini (Padua, Biblioteca Antoniana, Ms 1896). See Zaslaw, 'Ornaments', table 1, p. 99.

Concerti Grossi Con due Violini, Viola e Violoncello di Concertini Obligati, e due altri Violini e Basso di Concerto Grosso … Composti della Seconda Parte del Opera Quinta d'Arcangelo Corelli per Francesco Geminiani, etc. N.B. Where these are sold may be had the first Six Solos of Corelli made into Concertos by Geminiani, and Twelve celebrated Solos by the same Author for a Violin and a Bass. London: Printed for and sold by I. Walsh … and Ios. Hare, [1729].[12]

'[T]he first Six Solos of Corelli made into Concertos' involves a substantial amount of tinkering with Corelli's original, splitting the material between a concertino of two violins and cello and a ripieno section of two violins, viola and basso. Typically in Geminiani's arrangement, the 'Violino Primo del Concertino' retains pretty much all of Corelli's original (unadorned) solo violin text. But re-composition, or new composition, is sometimes required. At the opening of Op. 5 no. 9 in A (Preludio Largo), for example, the 'Violino Secondo del Concertino' has a newly composed line of dialogue with the 'Primo', both Concertino parts being doubled throughout the first section by the Ripieno ('Concerto Grosso') violins. In the second half, the 'Concerto Grosso' has more frequent rests, the pattern of Tutti and Solo alternations being clearly marked in the 'Concertino' parts (bars 12, beat 4–14, beat 4 and bars 16, beat 4–18, beat 4 being 'Solo'). In the famous Gavotta of Op. 5 no. 10 in F, the structure of each binary half maps out an equal division, 'Solo'/'Tutti', the contribution of the 'Concerto Grosso' representing a textural one, adding weight of sound as well as a sharp punctuation to the cadences, and thus underscoring Corelli's characteristically sure sense of tonal scope (and perhaps – retrospectively – suggesting a way of defining dynamic shading in solo performances of Op. 5). Clearly, such a disposition of forces is radically different from a solo presentation. There are added elements of dialogue, between both the two Concertino violins and between the Concertino group and the Concerto Grosso. Geminiani distributes the cello's continuo role between the 'Concertino' and 'Grosso' players, the Concertino cello fulfilling this function alone in passages marked 'Solo'. Additionally, a 'Concertino' (solo) cello may have been 'set up' differently to a 'Concerto Grosso' (Ripieno) cello, in which case the projection of the cello sound would differ as the music alternated between Concertino/Ripieno from phrase to phrase (likewise, of course, the sound would be different between the 'Concerto Grosso' – assuming more than one player per part – and the 'Concertino' violins, and may also have been affected subtly by differences in instrumental 'set up').[13] Finally, given that

12 Soon reprinted in Amsterdam, *c.* 1730 by Le Cène (nos. 1–6) and again in London by Le Prévost (nos. 7–12), on which editions the following remarks are based.
13 'Set up' might affect, for instance, the profile of string gauges and the string tensions (equal or unequal). See Oliver Webber, 'Strings', at www.themonteverdiviolins.org/strings.html, for more information on this topic.

figuring is appended both to the 'Violoncello del Concertino' and 'Basso del Concerto Grosso' parts, the implication is that a chord-playing instrument was envisaged for both Concertino and Concerto Grosso groups.[14]

All in all, then, Geminiani's concerto arrangements alter the sound effects of Corelli's sonata originals, transforming them not only generically, but also in terms of their practical production, physical setting (referring both to the number and disposition of the players within the performance space, and to the performance space itself), and their perception by listeners. Interaction happens *between* and *across* the ensemble in a concerto, whose sound emerges from a broader span of physical space than in the original solo setting, in which the dynamic relationship is between a *soloist* (rather than concertino group) and a harmonic texture produced by just one player ('Violone o Cimbalo'). The music is still Corelli's Op. 5; but it *sounds* different.

It sounds different again in an edition by Muzio Clementi, published in 1799 and advertised as:

> *A New Edition of Corelli's Twelve Solos, for the Violin & Violoncello with a Thoroughbass for the Piano Forte or Harpsichord, in which a simple method is adopted for facilitating the reading of the Tenor Clef* By Muzio Clementi Op. 5 London: Longman, Clementi & Comp^{y} N°. 26 Cheapside.

There is no question here of performing the continuo part on *either* cello *or* keyboard; indeed, the provision of the bass part on parallel staves notated in the bass clef where the line migrates into the tenor clef was presumably intended for the use of pianists unfamiliar with reading the tenor clef. Interestingly, Clementi leaves the figures unrealized, tacit testimony to the fact that 'thoroughbass', at least, was a skill still alive and kicking at the end of the eighteenth century. But he does not shrink from adding dynamics, albeit unobtrusively and generally with a clear structural purpose. He frequently inserts a *piano* marking for the repetition of cadential phrases, for example at the end of the second section of the Preludio Largo first movement of Op. 5 no. 9 in A. While the next movement of the same sonata (Giga Allegro) has no dynamics in its first section, the second begins *piano* (for four bars), and continues *forte* (for one-and-a-half bars), thereafter *piano* again (for three bars), *forte* (for fourteen-and-a-half bars), and finally *piano* for the closing cadential repetition. Whether Clementi's structural dynamic contrasts continue a tradition extending back

14 In the original publication of 1700, Corelli stated that his sonatas were for *Violino et Violone* [meaning violoncello] *o Cimbalo*, a much-discussed subject of performance practice. See David Watkin, 'Corelli's Op. 5 Sonatas: "Violino e violone o cimbalo"?', *Early Music*, 24 (1996), pp. 645–63 and Lars-Ulrich Mortensen, '"Unerringly Tasteful?": Harpsichord Continuo in Corelli's Op. 5 Sonatas', *Early Music*, 24 (1996), pp. 665–79. Examples of both cello and harpsichord continuo accompaniment may be heard on *Corelli 12 sonate a violino e violone o cimbalo op.* 5, Trio Veracini (John Holloway, David Watkin and Lars-Ulrich Mortensen), Novalis 150 128–2 (1996).

towards the era of Corelli is uncertain. There are some coincidental overlaps with the dynamic effects of Concertino versus Concerto Grosso dispositions in Geminiani's 1726 concerto adaptation of this same movement of Op. 5 no. 9, though there are plenty of discrepancies, too, the first four bars of the second section being bar-by-bar alternations between Tutti and Soli in Geminiani's version (rather than a consistent *piano* as in Clementi), and the phrase beginning midway through bar 25 being marked *piano* by Clementi but Tutti by Geminiani. Clementi's long *forte* beginning in bar 28 begins Soli in Geminiani and alternates back and forth between Concertino and Concerto Grosso for eight bars, only attaining a stable and extended Tutti at bar 35.[15]

Once again, the music printed by Clementi is still Corelli's Op. 5; but it *sounds* differently. Variety of sonorous potential was indeed fundamental to the eighteenth-century musician. Corelli's music was not conceptual, not even largely so. It lived in sound, in performance, whether in Corelli's own 1700 edition of Op. 5, with continuo supplied either by the cello improvising a chordal texture or by a harpsichord; or with embellishments by Corelli himself or by others (changing in density and style as the century progressed); or reconfigured as concertos; or for cello and harpsichord (or pianoforte) continuo, as provided by Clementi; or in any of another fifty or so ways in which it was rendered performable in eighteenth-century editions. Neal Zaslaw has noticed that

> [as] tastes varied from individual to individual and from place to place, or evolved from decade to decade, new ornaments permitted the music to be suited to new demands. This is demonstrated by Tartini's and Galeazzi's ornaments for Op. 5; Tartini's tend to break down the Baroque Fortspinnung into shorter segments resembling the galant style, whereas Galeazzi's introduce to the melody a kind of chromaticism quite alien to both Corelli's and Tartini's music, but idiomatic in music of the late 18th century.[16]

In this important sense, Corelli's Op. 5 defies categorization as a single entity that would allow us to consign it to a particular glass case in an imaginary museum of musical compositions. It is not one thing only, but many. What it is at any one time depends on performance.

This circumstance is borne out by Charles Burney's comment to his friend, Thomas Twining (21 January 1774), in which he claims that 'Corelli is

15 Clementi's edition was reprinted in 1805, and in *c.* 1811 an identical text (though from newly engraved plates) with an identical title page and price (10*s.* 6*d*). was issued by Robert Birchall 'at his Musical Circulating Library, N° 133, New Bond Street' (once again including parallel bass clef transcriptions of tenor clef passages).
16 Zaslaw, 'Ornaments', p. 112.

so plain & simple that he can always be made modern'.[17] At first glance, we might miss the important implication of Burney's remark that the modernization of which he speaks is *made* – that is, as an *action*, in performing the music. It is salutary to remind ourselves that this *tabula rasa* that Corelli allegedly left behind was something to be *made to speak* afresh in each performance situation, an action of which its author (meaning here the performer) might plausibly say to a listener (just as Corelli is purported to have said to his pupils): '*non l'intendite parlare?*' (Do you not hear it speak?). A conceptual interpretation of Burney's claim (benchmarking different styles to which Corelli's music was successively adapted, for example, as a prelude to historical classification and the writing of a reception history) is one that derives from a tradition of musicology developed about a century after Burney was writing. For Burney and his contemporaries, though, *making* probably meant *doing* (that is, performing). A generation or so later the tide had arguably begun to turn as the concept of canonization, already tentatively emerging in editions and re-editions of, for example, Haydn's string quartets during the 1780s and 1790s, together with the rise of the public concert and concomitant upsurge in professionalization of musical life in European capitals, led to a new view of music as something centred on a metaphysical 'Work', which fundamentally altered the prevailing relationship between composition and performance. The composition (notationally enshrined in the 'Work'), was a separate thing from the performance, which now became a means, *post factum*, by which that 'Work' *as concept* was represented to a public.

Such a state of affairs has now become known as a 'Work Concept'.[18] Whether the concept is situated in the composer's mind (purportedly) or in ours (actually), it is perhaps to be understood as an entity existing separately from any perceptions of it and in the form of a musical score embodying that concept, and to be regarded as a predetermined, permanent text accessible in relation to activities such as analysis, historiography or performance *only through that text*. Consequently, such a work concept sits uneasily with eighteenth-century repertories since it is formulated apart from the *action* that is so fundamental to what music actually was at that time. If, for the eighteenth century, music's identity lay in the flexible arena of performance, rather than in the abstract domain of an intellectual concept represented on paper, then we might consider that a work concept for an eighteenth-century

17 Quoted in *ibid*., p. 112.

18 Fundamental to this debate is Lydia Goehr's ground-breaking study, *The Imaginary Museum of Musical Works: An Essay in the Philosophy of Music* (Oxford, 1992). Subsequent contributions include Michael Talbot (ed.), *The Musical Work: Reality or Invention?* (Liverpool, 2000), specifically Reinhard Strohm, 'Looking Back at Ourselves: The Problem with the Musical Work-Concept', pp. 128–52 and Michael Talbot, 'The Work-Concept and Composer-Centredness', pp. 168–86.

musician would have made sense only in relation to the possibility of the concept being realized in the action of performance, rather than embodied in a notated score regarded as the 'last word'. By contrast, the work concept after about 1800 raises a piece of music to the status of an autonomous and integral work of art, expected to retain a lasting place in a musical canon. It possessed a certain cultural value, was approached respectfully and was performed within a public – usually civic – setting in which both the performers and the listeners adhered (and sometimes still do) to certain dress codes and, by extension, regulated the expectations and behaviour of the participants, whether performers, listeners, or critics. The eighteenth-century work of music was a more flexible creature and did not normally bear such a load. If it seems to us that a work such as Bach's B minor Mass did so, then that is our construct of its pretensions rather than an eighteenth-century aspiration or practice. It would be wrong to think of apparently more transient eighteenth-century 'Works' as being of a lesser quality, though. True, their modes of production *in performance* were both more central and more mobile than later museum-like practices of enshrining and representing the musical canon in concert culture and in intellectual traditions of pedagogy, criticism and scholarship – factors that acquired a normative as well as regulatory status for music during the nineteenth century. But those eighteenth-century modes of production were different, not unsatisfactory, and we ought to resist the temptation to benchmark them against a later intellectualizing culture. I will pursue this thought in two directions in the following section, dealing with performance as an identifier within eighteenth-century music: performance settings as generic markers; and textual realization.

Performance and genre

In contrast to the 'work concept' (*c.* 1800 onwards), the performative status of eighteenth-century musical repertories[19] was characterized by a diversity so marked as to dilute their regulative qualities across the whole spectrum, from materials (within a piece), through pieces (within a genre) to genres (within a practice). Today, when we perform one of Haydn's 'London' symphonies, for example, we will arouse a certain set of expectations in our listeners, initiating a framework for our actions (and theirs). For instance, the event will probably

19 For orientation here, it may be useful to keep in mind the ontological contrast between a notated text whose identity resides in its potential to be spoken in performance, and one that exists as a site for intellectual discourse. For the eighteenth century, the weighting was heavily in favour of the former; for the nineteenth century, the proportions were at least equal, and perhaps tended as the century progressed in favour of the latter, as composers wrote for (or were written into) history.

occur in a concert hall; the audience will be paying attention deliberately and perhaps carefully to the performance, which they will regard as a 'reading' or 'interpretation' of Haydn's symphony (a work that has become canonized in the context of a two-hundred-year-old tradition of public concert-giving); more specifically, they will probably regard it as the 'reading' of a particular *maestro* on the podium (and these days, this circumstance alone seems bizarrely fundamental to the cultural value of the situation); they may have particular expectations of the tempos (solidified, perhaps, in the same centuries-old tradition of public concert-giving, and distinctly at odds with eighteenth-century understandings of these tempo indications). And so on. This is a rather different set of pragmatics from those brought to a performance in Haydn's day[20] – pragmatics further complicated for the present-day performer by an important generic twist: the popularity of arrangements. After Haydn returned finally to Vienna from his London journeys, Johann Peter Salomon purchased the rights to the 'London' symphonies and promptly brought out *Haydn's Celebrated Symphonies Composed for and Performed at Mr. Salomon's and the Opera Concerts ... Adapted for the Piano-Forte, With an Accompaniment for a Violin & Violoncello-ad Libitum* (London, 1795).[21] While the textural possibilities of this particular ensemble might perhaps be felt too limited to capture adequately the range of Haydn's expressive and colourful orchestral palette, it is worth noting that in *c.* 1820 the piano trio version could still be purchased from Goulding, D'Almaine, Potter & Co., 20 Soho Square and 7 Westmoreland Street, Dublin. The arrangement of the 'Surprise' Symphony (Hob.I:94; no. 3 in the set of trio arrangements) is rather full in its piano textures throughout, the pianist being kept busy with sextuplet semiquaver passagework and full chords much of the time in the first movement (typically, the arrangement is performable by the solo piano, though doublings and colour enhancements are provided by the violin). The weighty textures (murky basses, albertis, broken octaves) are quite well suited to an English-action piano such as Haydn had encountered during his recent visits and for which he conceived his last solo keyboard sonatas such as that in C major, Hob. XVI:50. All in all, the trio arrangement is quite demanding technically for the pianist; while playable by a good amateur, it is perhaps a bit forbidding. That fact may explain why the piano trio arrangements were not as commercially

20 A crucial difference in eighteenth-century and current performers' engagement with audience expectations can be seen in the contrasting amounts of preparatory rehearsal given over to a performance of a symphony. One rehearsal was perhaps the norm in Haydn's day, whereas today's professional rehearsal schedules tacitly build in the fact that the audience will be listening against the benchmark of CD perfection.

21 Salomon's trio arrangements were soon available from rival firms, for example Corri, Dussek & Co. (Edinburgh, 1796).

successful as those first issued in London *c.* 1798 as *Haydn's grand Symphonies. Composed for Mr. Salomon's Concerts, and Arranged for five instruments, vizt. Two Violins, a German Flute, a Tenor* [viola], *and a Violoncello: With an Accompaniment for the Piano Forte ad Libitum. By J. P. Salomon.* Here the piano parts are relatively simple continuo realizations, the main interest lying in the flute part and in the strings, which inventively cover both the original string parts and some of the wind and brass parts (the viola sometimes mimics the horns and trumpets, for example).[22]

Each individual symphony among these extremely popular arrangements is titled SINFONIA OR QUINTETTO at the beginning, begging an important question for the performer, namely 'What kind of a work am I playing here?' Clearly the setting is one we recognize as chamber music. The music to be played, however, is that of a symphony. In the introduction to the 'Clock' Symphony (Hob.I:101), the performers are responsible for representing a situation originally specific to a public concert setting in which the expectations of the audience are deliberately exploited. At the opening of the symphony (Adagio), Haydn's music struggles for form, the registers, melodic profile, harmonic and tonal direction all deliberately vague even mystifying, teasing the audience to the point of exasperation before relaxing into the following D major Presto. To judge from contemporary newspaper reviews of Haydn's symphony performances in *The Times* and the *Morning Chronicle*, the English public flocked to the Salomon concerts at the Hanover Square Rooms to witness the elderly composer's seemingly inexhaustible novelty. And this is precisely what Haydn expected of his listeners. The audience, in other words, was a part of the musical experience. Haydn's symphony lives in performance, and a crucial part of its being is the involvement of the listener. One could have no more powerful demonstration than this opening Adagio of the fallacy that notation is music, that the score is the work. Genre and situation were inextricably linked in eighteenth-century music. Salomon's quintet arrangements transplant one kind of generic identity (that of the public concert hall space) into another (the domestic, private performance space). How is the player supposed to react, representing this music now in a chamber setting? How is the local contrast between the quiet opening of the Presto and its louder repeat to be managed minus the accentual punctuation of the wind, brass and timpani in the orchestral original? What is the role of the lopsided flute-and-strings dialogue in the Trio, downsized from a public to a domestic scale? Such

22 Other arrangements of Haydn's 'London' symphonies include one for piano duet, published by Robert Birchall (London, *c.* 1800) and *Trois grandes simphonies ... arrangées pour deux violons, deux violes, violoncello, contrebasse, flûte et deux cors ... ou deux violons, viola, violoncelle et flute, pour [par ?] Mr. Salomon* from Simrock (Bonn, *c.* 1801).

situations of generic displacement matter to the tempo; the style of ornamentation; whether or not to embellish repeats; dynamic contrast; articulation; shaping of phrases and separation between them. In all of these decisions, it is not simply the reduced size of performing forces but also the adjustment to the acoustics of different performance spaces and the engagement with audiences of particular types and sizes that are vital ingredients in the mix. Indeed, they are all part of the Music.

Going beyond the text

Frequently, the performance of eighteenth-century music means going beyond the notated text. This much is obvious in the realization of continuo figured basses, of course, whether in an aria from a Bach cantata or a tutti passage in a Mozart piano concerto. But there are more subtle senses in which performers must stray beyond the page. Three will be considered briefly here: embellishment, sound and representation.

Spontaneous embellishment as a factor within the ontology of music for the eighteenth-century musician has already been discussed in relation to Corelli's Op. 5 sonatas. It was an important aspect of any performer's training[23] and was practised throughout the eighteenth century. Perhaps its highest point of development was reached in the Baroque opera seria of Handel and Vivaldi, one of whose fundamental ingredients, the da capo aria, consisted of three sections (A–B–A), the last of which was a repeat of the first and provided an ideal opportunity for the singer to demonstrate his or her ability to add brilliant and expressive decorations to the original text. Advice on appropriate methods of embellishment was given by, among others, Pier Francesco Tosi (for singers) and C. P. E. Bach (for keyboard players).[24] According to C. P. E. Bach:

> No one disputes the need for embellishments. This is evident from the great numbers of them everywhere to be found. They are, in fact, indispensable. Consider their many uses: They connect and enliven tones and impart stress and accent; they make music pleasing and awaken our close attention. Expression is heightened by them; let a piece be sad, joyful, or otherwise, and they will lend a fitting assistance. Embellishments provide opportunities for fine performance as well as much of its subject matter. They improve mediocre

23 For some eighteenth-century writers, embellishment also meant ornamentation, not in the application of trills, turns, mordents, etc. to individual notes or beats, but rather in the art of wholesale decoration of melodic passages or sections.

24 Pier Francesco Tosi, *Opinioni de' cantori antichi e moderni* (Bologna, 1723), trans. J. E. Galliard as *Observations on the Florid Song* (London, 1742); C. P. E. Bach, *Versuch über die wahre Art das Clavier zu spielen*, 2 vols. (Berlin, 1753 and 1762), trans. William J. Mitchell as *Essay on the True Art of Playing Keyboard Instruments* (New York, 1949).

compositions. Without them the best melody is empty and ineffective, the clearest content clouded.[25]

Embellishment is an issue that especially affects the music of Mozart.[26] Without a doubt, it is incorrect to regard his texts as 'definitive' in any prescriptive sense, requiring absolute fidelity to every last detail.[27] It is abundantly clear from documentary evidence that in his own performances of his piano concertos Mozart habitually ornamented the melodic lines. In a follow-up to a letter of 9–12 June 1784, he supplied a specimen embellishment of bars 56–63 of the Andante of the concerto K. 451 in D to satisfy his sister's curiosity. For the published text of his F major sonata, K. 332 (1784) he provided extensive written-out embellishments for the Adagio that appear nowhere in the autograph. Conversely, the autograph of the C minor Fantasia and Sonata, K. 475 and 457 (1784–5 – long thought lost, but rediscovered in 1990) contains written-out embellishments to the reprises of the sonata's Adagio theme absent from any published version from Mozart's time.[28]

Such embellishments reinforce the centrality of performance to the identity of Mozart's music as understood in the eighteenth century. A performance belongs firmly within the continuing creative aspect of that identity (rather than standing outside of it), imaginatively deforming the notated text in the act of speaking it. In other words, the identity extends along a time-line that embraces performance, rather than just inhabiting the page. Nor was it restricted to Mozart's instrumental compositions. It plays a key role in the design of his vocal music, which he liked to match carefully to the vocal capabilities of his singers. In a letter to his father of 28 February 1778, he remarks, after describing in detail how he had adapted the aria, 'Se al labbro mi non credi/Il cor dolente', K. 295 for the aging tenor Anton Raaff (1714–97), that he liked an aria 'to fit a singer as perfectly as a well-made suit of clothes'.[29] But this did not stop him subsequently making alterations either for the same

25 C. P. E. Bach, *Essay on the True Art of Playing Keyboard Instruments*, p. 79.

26 For a penetrating study of this issue, see Robert J. Levin, 'Improvised Embellishments in Mozart's Keyboard Music', *Early Music*, 20 (1992), pp. 221–33.

27 This is not the same as saying that Mozart's notation does not matter, and that one can brazenly ignore his precise articulation markings and dynamic placements. His notated performance indications (tempo or *Affekt* markings, slurs, dynamics, dots, or strokes, etc.) might best be regarded as provisional, rather than prescriptive. While these always need to be considered very carefully in relation to their precise situation and context (remembering, too, that they are not always consistent in all contexts), they remain *symbols for sound*, showing in detail how pitches and durations *might* creatively be brought to life in performance (including leaving room for the embellishment of what Mozart troubled to write down). They are invitations rather than commands.

28 See John Irving, *Mozart's Piano Sonatas: Contexts, Sources, Style* (Cambridge, 1997), pp. 80–1 (exx. 6.3 (a) and (b)).

29 See Emily Anderson (ed. and trans.), *The Letters of Mozart and His Family*, (3rd edn., London, 1985), p. 497 (letter of 28 February 1778).

or for a different singer. In the same letter, Mozart explains that he had written a setting ('for practice') of the text 'Non so d'onde vieni', K. 294 as a concert aria for Aloysia Weber (then the object of his affections):

> When it was finished, I said to Mlle Weber: 'Learn the aria yourself. Sing it as you think it ought to go; then let me hear it and afterwards I will tell you candidly what pleases and what displeases me.' After a couple of days I went to the Webers and she sang it for me, accompanying herself. I was obliged to confess that she had sung it exactly as I wished and as I should have taught it to her myself.[30]

In this light, it is remarkable that Mozart later re-composed the same aria, inserting cadences of greater melodic and rhythmic complexity with additional embellishments, and generally enhancing the expressive content by means of passing notes, appoggiaturas and a succession of dotted rhythms (replacing even-note patterns).[31] By his statement that 'she had sung it exactly as I wished and as I should have taught it to her myself' Mozart clearly did not mean 'this is the definitive version to be replicated for all time'. We could not wish for a more pertinent illustration of both the provisionality of his texts and of the fact that they live not on the page alone, but rather in their performances. The centrality of embellishment to eighteenth-century expectations of performance clearly demonstrates that the act of performance resides at the heart of the music.

The opening page of Haydn's D major Sonata Hob. XVI:42 (1784) is assiduously notated in the first edition in respect not only of precise durations, but also of staccatos, dynamics and slurs. What Haydn's notation on the page does not immediately convey is how all of this will sound on a fortepiano of his time (one from either Wenzel or Johann Schanz, for example, whose instruments were specifically recommended by Haydn for their light touch). Knowledge in this area allows us to hypothesize the importance of *silence* in the expressive palette of the piece. Haydn notates silence, of course, as rests, especially at the opening. And the number of rests in relation to notes (whether chords or continuous themes) declines as the first section unfolds towards its cadence, regains our attention momentarily at the imperfect cadence on A, and again at the beginning of the second section (the B major arpeggio) before giving way once again to more continuous musical phrases (with still a hint of its presence at the very end). That much can be seen in the score. But its significance only really comes alive on a fortepiano of Haydn's day (or a good

30 *Ibid*., p. 497. In a letter to Aloysia of 30 July 1778, Mozart elaborates somewhat, stating that he had 'found nothing to criticize or correct – you sang it to me with the interpretation, with the method and the expression which I desired'. See *ibid*., p. 582.

31 The original and embellished versions (along with a musical example) may be savoured in a recording by Majella Cullagh and Elizabeth Futral and The Hanover Band, conducted by Sir Charles Mackerras (*Mozart the Supreme Decorator*, ORR232, 2005; tracks 4 and 5, with musical example at p. 34).

copy). Because of the immediacy of the fortepiano sound, beginning with a pitch, rather than the 'thud-then-note' of a modern piano, and also because of the much more rapid decay of the sound (on a modern piano, the sound 'blooms' well after the hammer has struck the massive, high-tension, overwound string, causing it to vibrate, and it then takes some time to die away), the rests Haydn notates so carefully in his score are much more noticeable as *silence in distinction to* sound. On a fortepiano, then, it becomes possible to 'speak' Haydn's music (that is, to interpret it in relation to the sonorous possibilities of an appropriate instrument) as a dialogue between sound and silence, in the course of which music first intrudes into silence's space, then fills it, retreating again at the mid-point before sound once more seems to triumph in the *fortissimos* (bars 17–19), before being cloaked finally in silence. All this is a prelude to what follows in the variations, of course. The textural range of that journey truly works only on a fortepiano, at least to the degree that was evidently attainable for Haydn and for his listeners. Moreover, the effect of the fortepiano's sound production on note-duration alerts us to a sophisticated interplay of actual silence (indicated by Haydn's rests) and near-silence that is not specifically notated, but which represents a crucial dimension of the discourse on the sonata's first page. This works on several levels, only one of which – slurring – will be considered here. Slurs play a crucial role in the articulation of eighteenth-century music in general; at the opening of Haydn's sonata their effect is sometimes coupled with that of the staccato (normally represented in the first edition by a dagger, rather than a dot), for instance on the main beats of bar 3, each time preceded by a *forzando*[32] marking. The slur always indicated a local decrescendo in the eighteenth century, accompanied by a slight shortening of the second note in each pair.[33] In context then, each demisemiquaver rest would be preceded by something rather shorter than a semiquaver (whose sound would have been both the end of a decrescendo and curtailed in value by perhaps half its length). But on a modern piano, the sound of the second note of each of these slurred pairs could not 'clear' so immediately and a different, more continuous effect results. At bars 6 and 7, the realization of the slurred semiquaver pairs again implies local decrescendo and slight separation between each pair, such that there is something

32 Shown as *forz* in the first edition, *Trois Sonates Pour le Pianoforte. Composées & Dediées A Son Altesse Madame La Princesse Marie Esterhazy ... Par Son Très-Humble & Très Obéissant Serviteur Joseph Haydn. Œuvre 37* (Speyer, 1784).

33 Leopold Mozart's *Versuch einer gründlichen Violinschule* (Augsburg, 1756), chapter VII, part 1, §20 states, for example, that 'the first of such united notes [i.e. connected by a slur] must be somewhat more strongly stressed, but the remainder slurred on to it quite smoothly and more and more quietly'. Translation from Leopold Mozart, *A Treatise on the Fundamental Principles of Violin Playing*, trans. Editha Knocker (Oxford, 1985), pp. 123–4. See also Antony Pay, 'Phrasing in Contention', *Early Music*, 24 (1996), pp. 291–321.

approaching silence intruding into what looks notationally like a continuous line (and which is, indeed, just that on a modern piano, which again cannot 'clear' the sound of each semiquaver quickly enough). So, while actual notated rests have temporarily disappeared from view, silence has not altogether disappeared from Haydn's music as it would have been heard on the instruments of his day. His notation does not represent this dimension, which comes across only in performance on an appropriate instrument. The music is not the score.

In this page of Haydn's D major sonata, the performer is required to behave as a judicious arbiter between contrasting and competing subtleties rather than as a virtuoso. Virtuosity nevertheless played a significant role in the eighteenth-century world of performance, and sometimes in surprising places. Looking at the score of the tenor aria, 'Frohe Hirten' from *Und es waren Hirten in derselben Gegend*, BWV 248-ii (the second cantata of Bach's 'Christmas Oratorio'), we are impressed by the word-painting at the phrase 'Geht, die Freude heißt zu schön ... geht und labet Herz und Sinnen', the exquisite joy of the text represented by overflowing demisemiquavers. So far, so good. But there is a dimension to this aria's expressive language that the pursuit of mere *Augenmusik* leaves untouched and which reveals itself only in performance. At this point, the tenor behaves *like an instrument*, partnering the obbligato flauto traverso in dialogic passagework that is hardly vocal in character, and which for the moment jolts out of the narrative mode of story-telling into virtuoso display. It is a dramatic juxtaposition of effect, but also of role: it is as if at one moment the singer is part of the story being pictured in the imagination; at the next, he appears to have stepped directly into the here and now, literally acting out the indescribable joy of the birth of the Christ-child, embodying the salvation that mankind cannot achieve for itself but which is instead God-given in this instant at Bethlehem. Is this conjoining of the vocal (representing the Divine?) with the instrumental (a 'lower', human form of expression, as still acknowledged in eighteenth-century music theory?) in fact Bach's cunning way of suggesting God-becoming-Man – a representation of Divine intervention into the human world? Perhaps. More significant in the context of this chapter, this is not at all apparent in the score but is a powerful (and unforgettable) moment in performance. Performance is the dimension that allows Bach's intention (if he had one) to come alive, inviting us to join in the creative action of the piece, perceiving its possible messages. As Corelli might have said: '*non l'intendite parlare?*'

Select Bibliography

Bach, C. P. E. *Versuch über die wahre Art das Clavier zu spielen*. 2 vols., Berlin, 1753 and 1762. Trans. William J. Mitchell as *Essay on the True Art of Playing Keyboard Instruments*. New York, 1949

Burney, Charles. *A General History of Music from the Earliest Ages to the Present*. 4 vols., London, 1776–89

Goehr, Lydia. *The Imaginary Museum of Musical Works: An Essay in the Philosophy of Music*. Oxford, 1992

Hawkins, Sir John. *A General History of the Science and Practice of Music*. 5 vols., London, 1776. Reprint London, 1875, 2 vols

Irving, John. *Mozart's Piano Sonatas: Contexts, Sources, Style*. Cambridge, 1997

Kirnberger, Johann Philip. *Die Kunst der Reinen Satzes in der Musik*. 2 vols., Berlin and Königsberg, 1771–9. Trans. David Beach and Jürgen Thym as *The Art of Strict Musical Composition*. New Haven, CT and London, 1982

Koch, Heinrich Christoph. *Versuch einer Anleitung zur Composition*. 3 vols. Rudolstadt and Leipzig, 1782–93. Partial trans. Nancy Kovaleff Baker as *Introductory Essay on Composition – The Mechanical Rules of Melody, Sections 3 and 4*. New Haven, CT and London, 1983

Levin, Robert D. 'Improvised Embellishments in Mozart's Keyboard Music'. *Early Music*, 20 (1992), pp. 221–33

Mattheson, Johann. *Der vollkommene Capellmeister*. Hamburg, 1739; reprint Kassel and Basel, 1954. Trans. and ed. Ernest C. Harriss, Ann Arbor, MI, 1981

Mortensen, Lars-Ulrich. '"Unerringly Tasteful?": Harpsichord Continuo in Corelli's Op. 5 Sonatas'. *Early Music*, 24 (1996), pp. 665–79

Mozart, Leopold. *Versuch einer gründlichen Violinschule*. Augsburg, 1756. Trans. Editha Knocker as *A Treatise on the Fundamental Principles of Violin Playing*. Oxford, 1985

Pay, Anthony. 'Phrasing in Contention'. *Early Music*, 24 (1996), pp. 291–321

Quantz, Johann Joachim. *Versuch einer Anweisung die Flöte traversiere zu spielen*. Berlin, 1752. Trans. and ed. Edward J. Reilly as *On Playing the Flute*. 2nd edn., London and Boston, 1985

Rameau, Jean-Philippe. *Traité de l'harmonie reduite à ses principes naturels*. Paris, 1722. Trans. Philip Gossett as *Treatise on Harmony*. New York, 1971

Saint-Lambert, Monsieur de. *Les Principes du Claveçin*. Paris, 1702. Trans. and ed. Rebecca Harris-Warwick, Cambridge, 1984

Strohm, Reinhard. 'Looking Back at Ourselves: The Problem with the Musical Work-Concept'. In Michael Talbot (ed.), *The Musical Work: Reality or Invention?* Liverpool, 2000, pp. 128–52

Talbot, Michael. 'The Work-Concept and Composer-Centredness'. In Michael Talbot (ed.), *The Musical Work: Reality or Invention?* Liverpool, 2000, pp. 168–86

Tosi, Pier Francesco. *Opinioni de' cantori antichi e moderni*. Bologna, 1723. Trans. J. E. Galliard as *Observations on the Florid Song*. London, 1742

Watkin, David. 'Corelli's Op. 5 Sonatas: "Violino e violone o cimbalo"?' *Early Music*, 24 (1996), pp. 645–63

Webber, Oliver. 'Strings' at www.themonteverdiviolins.org/strings.html

Wilson, John. *Roger North on Music*. London, 1959

Zaslaw, Neal. 'Ornaments for Corelli's Violin Sonatas, Op. 5'. *Early Music*, 24 (1996), pp. 95–116

· PART III MUSIC FOR THE SALON AND CONCERT ROOM ·

· 16 ·

Keyboard music from Couperin to early Beethoven

ROHAN STEWART-MACDONALD

Comparing the openings of the sarabande from J. S. Bach's English Suite No. 2 in A minor and the second movement of Muzio Clementi's Piano Sonata in A major, Op. 50 no. 1 reveals some striking similarities and differences (see example 16.1a and 16.1b).[1] Clementi appears to have borrowed a good deal from the earlier suite movement, including its key, time signature, thematic substance and sarabande style; but he has strenuously reinterpreted the material within the expanded possibilities of a later keyboard idiom, adorning it with chromaticism and intensifying the texture. These two excerpts, dating from 1715 and 1804–5, respectively,[2] represent the chronological boundaries of this chapter. The comparison evokes, in microcosm, both the degree of stylistic progress that undoubtedly took place in certain areas of solo keyboard music from the time of Couperin to early Beethoven, and the extent to which this progress was circumscribed – or stimulated – by earlier stylistic models.

The sound world of Clementi's slow movement exploits the sonorous possibilities of the English piano that he would undoubtedly have had at his disposal at this stage of his career.[3] Developments in the manufacture and distribution of keyboard instruments were certainly a major stimulus for (and indirect consequence of) stylistic change in eighteenth-century keyboard music, but such a strenuous recreation of an earlier style must also be attributed to broader changes in musical culture of the 1780s, 1790s and early 1800s. Tia DeNora writes of a 'shift ... toward values of musical seriousness and learnedness' in particular sectors of Viennese musical life towards the end of

1 The similarity was first observed by W. Dean Sutcliffe in 'Chopin's Counterpoint: The *Largo* from the Cello Sonata, Op. 65', *The Musical Quarterly*, 83 (1999), p. 115. See also Sutcliffe's examples 1 and 2 on pp. 116–17. I have discussed the relationship in detail in *New Perspectives on the Keyboard Sonatas of Muzio Clementi* (Bologna, 2006), pp. 283–93.

2 The precise dating of Clementi's sonata, the first of his final set of three sonatas Op. 50, is controversial. Although not published until 1821 it could have been composed as early as 1804–5 and withheld from publication. See Plantinga, 'Clementi: The Metamorphoses of a Musician', in Roberto Illiano, Luca Sala and Massimiliano Sala (eds.), *Muzio Clementi: Studies and Prospects* (Bologna, 2002), p. xxiii.

3 See Katalin Komlós, *Fortepianos and their Music: Germany, Austria and England, 1760–1800* (Oxford, 1995), pp. 53–68.

Ex. 16.1a. J. S. Bach, English Suite No. 2 in A minor, Sarabande, bars 1–4

Ex. 16.1b. Muzio Clementi, Piano Sonata in A major, Op. 50 no. 1, 2nd movement, bars 1–4

the century.[4] She attributes this to the influence of the musical tastes and values being cultivated in North Germany in the 1770s that revolved around the emerging notion of creative genius. These new tastes emphasized high seriousness and enshrined the prestige of music of the past, particularly that of J. S. Bach. This value system and associated tastes were transferred to Viennese musical life by figures such as Gottfried van Swieten who spent seven years in Berlin interacting closely with students and disciples of J. S. Bach such as Marpurg and Kirnberger before moving to Vienna in the early 1780s. Van Swieten's subsequent influence on Mozart after his move to Vienna is well known to have stimulated Mozart's admiration for the music of J. S. Bach and preoccupation with integrating contrapuntal forms into his own music, eventually epitomized by works such as *Die Zauberflöte*. The preoccupation was also exemplified by solo keyboard works such as the rondo K. 494, composed before the first two movements of the Sonata in F major, K. 533, and later added to them and revised through the insertion of additional counterpoint: the first two movements appear to date from before 3 January 1788, the rondo having been completed on 10 June 1786 and first published in 1788.[5]

4 See Tia DeNora, *Beethoven and the Construction of Genius: Musical Politics in Vienna, 1792–1803* (Berkeley, 1995), pp. 20–7.

5 See Hans Neumann and Carl Schachter, 'Mozart's Rondo, K. 494', in William J. Mitchell and Felix Salzer (eds.), *The Music Forum, vol. 1* (New York and London, 1967), pp. 3–34.

Although DeNora associates such shifts in value with the Viennese aristocracy, example 16.1 from Clementi, who was based in Britain for most of his career, indicates that such values were, or quickly became, more widespread. In fact, still more recent writers have argued that similar changes in Britain ran parallel to or preceded those taking place in Germany and Austria in the later decades of the eighteenth century. In his radical and provocative book *London und der Klassizismus in der Musik*, published in 2002,[6] Anselm Gerhard attempted to reconfigure musical Classicism as a British, rather than a Viennese, phenomenon, on the grounds that eighteenth-century British philosophy and aesthetics provided the true intellectual context for such a development. According to Gerhard, the main factor defining 'British' musical Classicism was the 'unity within diversity' that crystallized in Clementi's sonatas of the 1780s, manifested in a form of 'monothematicism' similar to what was practised by composers such as Haydn at this time, and occasionally by Mozart after 1780, when he was working under the archaic, Bachian influences transferred to him by van Swieten.[7] Despite Gerhard's insistence that 'unity within diversity' was a direct response to the British cultural climate in which Clementi spent most of his career, it seems more likely that the changes Clementi's style underwent in the early 1780s, leading to 'monothematicism' and also to the Bachian preoccupations that first surface in the fugues from Opp. 5 and 6 and later in sonatas like Op. 50 no. 1, originated partly, if not wholly, on his trip to Vienna in the early 1780s. Otto Biba has shown that Clementi's activities during this visit created opportunities for the close study of earlier, North German keyboard music.[8] As with Mozart, Clementi's engagement with such repertory led to a heightened preoccupation with Baroque contrapuntal models, more intensive thematic processing and, as we have seen, direct modelling on actual Baroque-period works.[9]

Archaic preoccupations were thus inherent in a range of late eighteenth-century keyboard music and were inextricably bound up with a set of shifting philosophical and aesthetic priorities which may have begun in northern Germany but which quickly expanded – or were echoed or independently paralleled – elsewhere. It is similarly possible to stress the 'modernity' of solo keyboard music dating from the first half of the century, in particular that of

6 Anselm Gerhard, *London und der Klassizismus in der Musik: die Idee der 'absoluten Musik' und Muzio Clementis Klavierwerk* (Stuttgart and Weimar, 2002).

7 Works by Mozart from the 1780s that exemplify the 'monothematic' principle include the first movements of the Sonata in F major, K. 533 and of the Piano Quartet in G minor, K. 478.

8 Otto Biba, 'Clementi's Viennese Sonatas', in Richard Bösel and Massimiliano Sala (eds.), *Muzio Clementi: Cosmopolita della musica. Atti del convegno internazionale in occasione del 250° anniversario della nascita (1752–2002), Rome, 4–6 December 2002* (Bologna, 2004) (Quaderni Clementiani, 1), pp. 185–99.

9 See Leon Plantinga, 'Clementi, Virtuosity and the "German Manner"', *Journal of the American Musicological Society*, 15 (1972), pp. 303–30.

Domenico Scarlatti (1685–1757). In its preoccupation with strenuous, often anarchic small-scale contrasts and strange juxtaposition of idioms, this music is much more conceptually 'Classical' than 'Baroque'. It is partly for this reason that, according to W. Dean Sutcliffe in his study of Scarlatti's keyboard sonatas, it is 'axiomatic ... that much about the Scarlatti sonatas demands to be considered in the light of [the] Classical style, for all the factors that might make us resist such a classification'.[10]

Stylistic change in keyboard music by all eighteenth-century composers, whether in the direction of archaism or of explicit modernity, was regulated to a significant extent by the popularity of keyboard playing in the upper – and, increasingly, the middle – classes that stimulated the production of a vast and diverse repertory of solo keyboard music. The largest market for solo keyboard music was created by amateurs whose values and predilections centred on the desire – and the practical need – for stylistic and technical approachability in the music that they consumed: DeNora argues that it was the perpetuation of this value system in areas of Viennese musical life apart from the aristocracy that reduced Mozart's popularity in the later stages of his career once he had begun to cultivate a more learned, less approachable style, and similar complaints were provoked by Beethoven's more advanced keyboard (and other) music. By and large, in the 1780s, 'categories of taste were still generally dominated by the concerns of the dilettante and general listener', reflecting the 'ubiquity of pleasingness as a value in late eighteenth-century European music', and the consequent preference for music that was 'relatively easy to comprehend and play':[11] such values were particularly dominant in the realm of solo keyboard music, and composers writing for this market had to be aware of the restrictions they imposed. This awareness in turn often led to composers' conscious preservation of the distinction between, for instance, large-scale, 'serious' sonatas (often intended for professional performance) and keyboard music aimed more for the popular market. This is encoded in a letter Clementi wrote to his publisher Gottfried Christoph Härtel on 20 December 1809 concerning the publication of three sonatas written in his 'better style'. The expression 'better style' implies a compartmentalized approach, whereby different areas of the composer's output were affiliated to different sectors of the market:

> having completed the education of three favourite children, I wish to send them ... out into the world; that is, having completed three sonatas <u>in my</u>

10 Sutcliffe, *The Keyboard Sonatas of Domenico Scarlatti and Eighteenth-Century Musical Style* (Cambridge, 2003), p. 323.
11 DeNora, *Beethoven and the Construction of Genius*, pp. 15–16.

better style, I would like to publish them, and you are the first to whom I wish to offer them for this purpose.[12]

Leon Plantinga hypothesizes that these 'three sonatas' are in fact Clementi's final set of sonatas, Op. 50, originally intended as the second half of Op. 40. Op. 40 and 50 both contain large-scale and ambitious works, exemplifying some of the most advanced features of Clementi's later keyboard style – for instance, his strong predilection for strict counterpoint, canon in particular, recalling Mozart's experiments in his Sonata K. 533 that eventually included the Rondo, K. 494. One of the high points in this respect is of course the second movement of Op. 50 no. 1, discussed at the start.

Composers' responsiveness to their own desire for linguistic experimentation, circumscribed by the need to preserve marketability, led to pronounced dichotomies in the realm of solo keyboard repertory between progressive and conservative stylistic orientations. Such dichotomies are partly visible at the level of genre. The relative consistency in the format of solo keyboard rondos (both independent and within sonatas) and in independent variation sets from the time of Couperin and Rameau through to Beethoven suggests a stronger preoccupation with approachability in these areas, whereas the more dynamic emergence, evolution and diversification of the keyboard sonata implies that, as a genre, the sonata came to serve more diverse ends. The opening example from Clementi's Op. 50 suggests that some of the more 'conservative' features of later keyboard music arose from a conscious, implicitly progressive heightening of the keyboard sonata: Clementi's Op. 50 was after all written in his 'better' – implicitly more advanced and progressive – style. In addition, as already implied, the 'monothematicism' of Haydn's and Clementi's keyboard sonatas can be linked with an essentially 'contrapuntal' mentality re-emerging in the 1770s and 1780s, and beyond; furthermore, use of the minor mode, although conventionally allied with more ambitious and apparently 'forward-looking' works, often seems to lead to a revival of earlier tendencies, a topic to be pursued below.[13] The most unambiguously progressive features to be considered here are generally associated with tonality and structure. The structural use of remote keys in keyboard music from later in the period, for example, informs to varying degrees all of the three genres to be discussed (sonata, variations, rondo), and is a factor connecting them with other, non-keyboard genres.

12 This letter, recently discovered, is in the Irving S. Gilmore Music Library at Yale University, New Haven, CT.

13 I have also explored this topic in 'The Minor Mode as Archaic Signifier in the Solo Keyboard Works of Domenico Scarlatti and Muzio Clementi', in Massimiliano Sala and W. Dean Sutcliffe (eds.), *Domenico Scarlatti* (Bologna, 2007), pp. 1–43. I am indebted to W. Dean Sutcliffe, Gareth Nellis and Helen Sartory for their stimulating additional comments on this topic.

My purpose is to explore the broad dichotomy between stylistic continuity and change in eighteenth-century solo keyboard music, and in particular to consider how this was shaped by the tensions between the value systems associated with the amateur sphere and with the more exalted realm of learnedness and transcendence whose geographical origins lay in North Germany and whose ultimate embodiment was J. S. Bach. Exploring this central dichotomy and the factors that surrounded it will involve establishing the earlier roots of stylistic features traditionally considered to be progressive (such as Beethoven's introduction of new themes into sonata development sections) and also exploring lesser-known examples of the use of remote keys for slow movements and the cultivation of harmonic links between movements – two of the most progressive stylistic features of instrumental music of the 1780s, 1790s and early 1800s in general. There will also be consideration of the effects of the popularity and wide cultivation of genres such as rondo and variations in stimulating, rather than curbing, stylistic change. Often, these changes seem to emanate from composers' desires to integrate 'progressive' features without violating the conventions that were the basis of the particular genre's popularity. My other major aim is to equalize the emphasis on music by Viennese- and London-based composers in order to illustrate the geographical breadth of certain stylistic developments. The weighting of the discussion towards the latter part of the period stems partly from the advanced stage that genres such as the solo keyboard sonata had reached in both Vienna and London by the final decades of the eighteenth century, and also from the fact that the later century is also propitious for investigating the – increasingly pronounced – tensions between the demands of the amateur market for keyboard music and the periodic desires of composers to transcend the limitations these demands imposed in the pursuit of ideals of originality and stylistic progress. Repertory from beyond the confines of the established canon is also included, both because it better exemplifies some of the principal concerns of the chapter and because a broad spectrum of works is effective in shedding new light on familiar narratives of stylistic progress and development.

Variations and rondos

As basic structural principles, variation and rondo remained relatively consistent during the eighteenth century. They were employed by a wide range of composers and infiltrated all levels of keyboard music, ranging from the smallest and most trivial specimens to the largest examples by J. S. Bach, C. P. E. Bach, Haydn, Mozart, Beethoven and others. The transformations that variation and rondo procedures *did* undergo ran parallel with the widespread popularity of these genres; although marketability entailed the need for composers to remain faithful to certain conventions it did not prevent, and in some respects may even have stimulated, attempts to modify and depart from these conventions, reconciling them with the desire to experiment and cultivate originality. The rondo, in particular, partook of trends established in non-keyboard genres, specifically those that led to the emergence of so-called 'sonata-rondo' form in the 1770s and 1780s.

The format of the French *rondeau*, upon which these later departures were built, is amply represented by the four harpsichord collections of Couperin, published between 1713 and 1730, and by Rameau in his three collections, published between 1706 and 1741. It had earlier roots in the two-couplet *rondeau*, probably devised by Lully: the multi-couplet 'rondo' is likely to have developed from Italian opera.[14] Rameau standardized the key structure of the two-couplet format: in the major, the refrain always appeared in the tonic; the first couplet was in the dominant; the second in the submediant minor. In the minor mode, the first couplet was in the relative major, the second in the dominant minor.[15] Couperin's deployment of the rondo scheme was more flexible. In *Les bergeries* the first return of the refrain is abbreviated and in *La badine* all couplets are in the same key; in *La triomphante* the couplets are greatly expanded. In the thirteen rondos from the 'Kenner und Liebhaber' collection, C. P. E. Bach often departs in an idiosyncratic manner from the conventions established and reinforced by Couperin and Rameau: in the Rondo in E major from vol. 3, for instance, he brings back the refrain in remote keys. One significant difference between the French *rondeau* and later Italianate rondos is the latter's greater continuity between couplets and refrain. Increasing and building on this continuity was a compositional 'problem' towards which composers directed progressively more elaborate solutions, 'sonata-rondo' being the principal outcome. Such continuity was sometimes strategically avoided in earlier *rondeaus*. In *Les tourbillons*, for example, Rameau marks off each section with a clear cadence and thick, homophonic chords, as if to accentuate the joins in the structure.

The high production of rondos in the eighteenth century reflected the genre's widespread popularity. Malcolm Cole has associated the height of this popularity with the 1770s and 1780s: 'The vogue of the rondo was established by approximately 1773 ... the form was accepted by the critics ...

14 Malcolm Cole, 'Rondo', in Stanley Sadie (ed.), *The New Grove Dictionary of Music and Musicians, Revised Edition* (London, 2001), vol. 21, p. 649.

15 A famous exception is Rameau's *Les cyclops*, which departs from the typical key structure and contains fantasia-like elements.

by 1778 and ... the vogue was passing by 1785 or 1786.'[16] Citing an essay by Johann Nikolaus Forkel (1749–1818) Cole also confirms that the popularity of *keyboard* rondos reached a peak slightly later, between 1778 and 1786.[17] One obvious reflection of the popularity of the rondo was the increasing frequency with which it was used for the finales of all types of multi-movement work – by Mozart, Haydn and also composers such as Jan Ladislav Dussek (1760–1812). Cole attributes the popularity of rondos to their origins in Italian opera buffa: French formal procedures were assimilated into this realm before then being disseminated and popularized further through the growing quantity of Italian keyboard and chamber music.[18] One could also attribute the rondo's (and variation's) popularity to the basic concept of generating familiarity with easily assimilated material through repetition, and also to their fundamental light-heartedness: as rondos became structurally more flexible and diverse, a 'readily identifiable theme' remained its 'one necessary requirement', and exactly the same could be said of theme and variation.[19]

Running parallel with the growing popularity and high production of rondos were reservations about their quality.[20] Surviving opinions generally emanate from critics, but similar attitudes on the part of composers are suggested by the changes that rondos underwent at this time, generally in the direction of greater structural intricacy. The injection into rondo of sonata-based techniques led to the emergence of 'sonata-rondo' in various chamber and orchestral works composed by Haydn and Mozart in the early 1770s;[21] it quickly infiltrated other genres. Despite the problems posed by 'sonata-rondo' as a theoretical model, a definite heightening of the rondo through the infusion of sonata-like characteristics did coincide with the apex of its popularity.

16 Malcolm Cole, 'The Vogue of the Instrumental Rondo in the Late Eighteenth Century', *Journal of the American Musicological Society*, 22 (1969), p. 436.

17 *Ibid.*, p. 433, quoting Johann Nikolaus Forkel's essay on rondo in *Musikalisch Bibliothek*, 2 (Gotha, 1778), pp. 281–94.

18 *Ibid.*, pp. 444–7.

19 Joel Galand, 'Form, Genre and Style in the Eighteenth-Century Rondo', *Music Theory Spectrum*, 17 (1995), p. 37.

20 See Johann Friedrich Reichardt, *Musikalisches Kunstmagazin* (Berlin, 1782), vol. 1, part 4, pp. 168–9, quoted in Malcolm Cole, 'The Vogue of the Instrumental Rondo', p. 433.

21 For an account of the history of the term 'sonata-rondo', see Malcolm Cole, 'Sonata-Rondo, the Formulation of a Theoretical Concept in the Eighteenth and Nineteenth Centuries', *The Musical Quarterly*, 55 (1969), pp. 180–92. Concerning the importance of orchestral and chamber works by Haydn and Mozart in the emergence of 'sonata-rondo', see Cole, 'The Rondo Finale: Evidence for the Mozart–Haydn Exchange?', *The Music Review*, 36 (1975), pp. 242–56. For a different interpretation of the evidence, see Stephen Fisher, 'Sonata Procedures in Haydn's Symphonic Rondo Finales of the 1770s', in Jens Peter Larsen, Howard Serwer and James Webster (eds.), *Haydn Studies* (New York, 1981), pp. 481–6.

The basic ramification of this infusion of sonata-like characteristics into the rondo, as already noted, was increased continuity between the separate sections. Often this was brought about by retaining refrain-based material in the episodes, as seen in Mozart's Rondo in A minor, K. 511 (1787). The *maggiore* section makes explicit contact with the dotted figure that opens the rondo refrain; it is quoted in bars 89–90 and processed contrapuntally in bars 97–100. In more sophisticated, sonata-like rondos transitional passages tended to expand, as again seen in Mozart's A minor rondo; and *minore* episodes were enlarged and complicated almost to the point of resembling fully-fledged development sections. The *minore* in the finale of Dussek's Sonata in D major, Op. 31 no. 2 lasts for seventy-five bars and is more concerned with processing existing material than with introducing new elements. The section begins by quoting a motif from bars 17–18 that is in turn related to bars 2 and 6 of the refrain (see example 16.2). In bars

Ex. 16.2. Jan Ladislav Dussek, Sonata in D major, Op. 31 no. 2, finale, bars 1–4, 17–18, 64–5, 79–80, 111–14, 137–40

Ex. 16.2. (cont.)

137–40 and 145–8 the *minore* expands a motif originating in the first couplet (bars 79–80 and 83–4), thus drawing together elements from various points earlier in the movement: a new theme is nonetheless introduced, in bars 119–22. The motif in bar 2 processed in the refrain also provides the basis for the melody of the first couplet in bars 64ff., confirming its central importance as an agent of continuity running through the movement. An even more expansive and intricate *minore*, lasting for some 103 bars, occurs in the finale of Clementi's Sonata in G major, Op. 40 no. 1 (1802).[22] The section has its own tri-partite scheme in which the opening material is partially reprised and a central part reaches keys as remote as F

22 I have discussed aspects of this *minore* in *New Perspectives*, pp. 206–8.

minor and A-flat major. The *minore* contrapuntally processes motifs relating both to the rondo's opening refrain and also, in fact, the previous movement, which is a canonic minuet and trio:[23] this makes the sonata one of the comparatively rare Classical-era works in which explicit inter-movement motivic relationships are cultivated. This could be seen as another facet of the 'better', implicitly more advanced style Clementi aimed at in these sonatas, mentioned in the letter to Härtel cited above.

Like the rondo, the solo, independent keyboard variation was cultivated at all stages of the eighteenth century, and by the full range of composers. Couperin's and Rameau's keyboard collections contain relatively few sets of variations, but there are some notable examples, including Couperin's *Les folies francoises, ou Les dominos* from the *Ordre* no. 13 (1722) and Rameau's Gavotte with six *doubles* from *Nouvelles suites de pieces* (*c.* 1728), his longest set. The most famous, extended set of variations from the first half of the eighteenth century is of course J. S. Bach's Goldberg Variations, BWV 988, generally considered to represent part 4 of the *Clavierübung*. The work dates from 1741 and its title derives from Forkel's claim, made in his 1802 biography of Bach, that the composer 'had written the work for his student Johann Gottlieb Goldberg, so that the latter could entertain his employer Count Keyserlingk during the Count's frequent sleepless nights'.[24] Peter Williams refutes this claim, noting the absence of any dedication to the count from the title page, as well as the 'age and putative abilities of young Goldberg, who was born in 1727' and would have been only fourteen years old at the time. Williams suggests instead that it was more likely that Bach simply brought the count an already published, signed copy of the variations during his visit to Dresden in 1741.[25]

The Goldberg Variations consist of thirty variations plus an 'aria' that is played at the beginning and at the end. The variations are a mixture of movement types: a number are canonic, some are fugal, many are non-contrapuntal and a number evoke dance styles.[26] It is tempting to compare the Goldberg Variations with later, 'great' sets of variations such as Beethoven's 'Diabelli' Variations, Op. 126, from the 1820s, but it differs from them in presenting a series of realizations of the fundamental bass-line – the descending G major scale introduced in the aria – rather than introducing a 'theme' and reworking it successively, which the 'Diabelli' Variations do in exhaustive fashion. The same principle prevails in Bach's two other most significant variation cycles, the chaconne from the second Partita in D minor for solo violin, BWV 1004

23 *Ibid.*, pp. 234–40.
24 David Schulenberg, *The Keyboard Music of J. S. Bach* (London, 1993), p. 319.
25 Peter Williams, *Bach: The Goldberg Variations* (Cambridge, 2001), p. 5.
26 For a summary of the structure, see table 17–1 in Schulenberg, *The Keyboard Music of J. S. Bach*, pp. 320–1.

and the passacaglia from the Passacaglia and Fugue in C minor for organ, BWV 582. David Schulenberg notes that the 'direction to repeat the aria after variation 30 suggests that the aria is not really *the* theme of the work but merely one of an infinite number of possible realizations of the *Fundamental-Noten*',[27] and material from the melody of Bach's aria is never directly evoked in any of the variations. The harmonically based approach generates considerable harmonic uniformity throughout the cycle, some variety emanating from occasional moves to the parallel minor[28] and the introduction of chromatic inflections, mainly during the minor-key variations. The frequent elision of phrases prevents 'the music from appearing to be trapped in a periodic vice'.[29]

A question surrounding the Goldberg Variations is whether they can legitimately be regarded as a 'true cycle, with a perceptible large structure'.[30] Certainly there are internal ordering features such as the regular appearance of canons in every third variation, and a pattern is established whereby a canon is followed by a 'free' variation and then a 'duet': this pattern is established in variation 3 and maintained until variation 29. The canons are also arranged so that there is a progressively widening series of intervals of imitation – again implying a strategic structural arrangement. Having acknowledged that these features may be 'intellectually satisfying but largely irrelevant to the way in which one plays or hears the work', Schulenberg offers suggestions as to why a 'good live performance' can nevertheless 'give an impression of the work as an integrated whole':

> It is conceivable that when the work is played in its complete form, the basic three-variation unit produces a certain large-scale rhythm audible to a sensitive listener. This rhythm is defined in particular by the canons, which tend to be relatively restrained in character, hence constituting regularly occurring points of repose. The work breaks out of this pattern toward the end, where the last half-dozen variations – all extraordinary in one way or another – together serve as the climax.[31]

It remains equally possible that the 'truly cyclic aspects of the work' are 'minimal'[32] and that the desire to perceive the Goldberg Variations in this way stems more from the backward projection of ideals prevalent in later eras relating to the modern prioritizing of the 'cycle' over the excerpt or fragment. It is worth bearing in mind that, at the time of composition, the work was not intended for public performance as a complete entity and that '[f]ew purchasers of the original print … would have regarded it primarily as something to be used for playing through from cover to cover'.[33]

27 *Ibid.*, p. 337. 28 Three variations are in the parallel minor, namely variations 15, 21 and 25.
29 Schulenberg, *The Keyboard Music of J. S. Bach*, p. 327. 30 *Ibid.*, p. 321.
31 *Ibid.*, pp. 321–2. 32 *Ibid.*, p. 322. 33 *Ibid.*

C. P. E. Bach wrote twelve independent sets of variations between 1735 and 1781 and had a characteristically inventive approach to the form, particularly in his later sets. It was Haydn, however, who contributed most to the development of variation form from the 1770s onwards, making use of it in all types of movements in his multi-movement works. A particular contribution of Haydn's was to introduce alternating variations on major and minor themes, as in the Variations in F minor Hob. XVII:6 (1793).[34]

Beethoven published nine sets of variations between 1795 and 1800 while establishing his career in Vienna (see table 16.1). His inventive treatment of the medium in his earliest sets has been eclipsed by the higher status of later examples such as the 'Eroica' Variations (1804) and ultimately the 'Diabelli' Variations. In prioritizing the independent solo keyboard variation at this stage of his career, Beethoven was clearly tapping into the buoyant Viennese market for easy piano music – and, in particular, for sets of variations on popular operatic themes; Glenn Stanley states that Beethoven 'arrived in Vienna in the middle of an "epidemic" of variations that were improvised and published by piano virtuosos with whom he had to compete for public recognition'.[35] As well as responding to market conditions, according to Stanley, Beethoven was also exploiting variation as a more accessible arena for compositional experimentation than the more 'fully explored' sonata or rondo; the objective of elevating 'the *piano* variation into a keyboard genre as serious (if not as large) as the sonata'[36] would explain why Beethoven periodically provoked charges of lacking accessibility in his earlier variation sets.[37] This did not mean that Beethoven dispensed totally with *all* of those elements that made the solo keyboard variation popular and marketable: rather, he 'instead chose a middle road, retaining the *Liebhaber* character of the genre but enriching his variations with *Kenner* detail'.[38] Thus, Beethoven's variation sets of the 1790s again embody the paradox central to this discussion of solo keyboard music that seeks to reconcile linguistic experimentation with the demands of marketability.

Some of the most striking innovations in Beethoven's early keyboard variations (as well as his rondos) seem to have been aimed at increasing the articulation of large-scale tonic closure by engaging with remote keys in a penultimate or final variation or coda. Such remote-key engagements can dramatize closure by transforming final units into developmental climaxes, whose heightened tension and dissonance requires emphatic resolution by the final cadence or set of

34 See Elaine Sisman, 'Tradition and Transformation in the Alternating Variations of Haydn and Beethoven', *Acta Musicologica*, 62 (1990), pp. 152–82. For a more extended account of Haydn's contribution to variation form, see Sisman, *Haydn and the Classical Variation* (Cambridge, MA, 1993).

35 Glenn Stanley, 'The "wirklich ganz neue Manier" and the Path to It: Beethoven's Variations for Piano, 1783–1802', *Beethoven Forum 3* (Lincoln, NB and London, 1994), p. 54.

36 *Ibid.*, p. 55. 37 *Ibid.*, p. 53, n. 1. 38 *Ibid.*, p. 57.

Table 16.1. *Sets of keyboard variations by Beethoven, 1782–1803*

Source of theme	Opus/WoO Number	Date	Notes
March by Dressler	WoO 63	1782	
'*Schweizer Lied*'	WoO 64	1790	
'*Venni amore*', Righini	WoO 65	1790	Extended coda, with remote keys
'*Es war einmal ein alter Mann*', from *Das rote Käppchen*, Dittersdorf	WoO 66	1792	
'*Menuett à la Viganò*', from ballet *Le nozze disturbate*, Haibel	WoO 68	1795	Extended final variation, with remote keys
'*Quan' è più bello*', from *La Molinara*, Paisiello	WoO 69	1795	
'*Nel cor più non mi sento*', from *La Molinara*, Paisiello	WoO 70	1795	
Russian dance, from the ballet *Das Waldmädchen*, Wranitzky	WoO 71	1796	Extended coda, with remote keys
'*Une fièvre brûlante*', from *Richard Coeur de Lion*, Grétry	WoO 72	1796	Extended coda, with remote keys
'*La stessa, la stessissima*', from *Falstaff*, Salieri	WoO 73	1799	Extended final variation, with remote keys
'*Kind, willst du ruhig schlafen*', from *Das unterbrochene Opferfest*, Winter	WoO 75	1799	Extended coda, with remote keys
'*Tändeln und scherzen*', from *Solimann II oder die drei Sultaninnen*, Süssmayr	WoO 76	1799	Extended final variation, with remote keys
Original theme	WoO 77	1800	
Original theme	Op. 34	1802	Key of each variation a minor third below the previous one
Original theme: 'Eroica' Variations	Op. 35	1802	
'God save the King'	WoO 78	1803	
'Rule Britannia'	WoO 79	1803	Extended coda, with remote keys

cadences. The procedure directly reflects the predilection for the 'structural' use of remote keys that surfaced in the late years of the eighteenth century (see table 16.1). The key shifts take place either in an expanded final variation (WoO 65, 68, 73, 76) or a coda (WoO 67, 72, 75). In the final variation of WoO 65, the shift to the flattened submediant is dramatized by the prolonged pause and changes of dynamic level, register and tempo; in WoO 68, the equivalent harmonic digression to D major generates less of a *non sequitur* (see bars 26–55). In each of the final variations of WoO 73 and 76, enharmonicism is used to approach the remote key – the enharmonic flattened second in WoO 73 (bars 133–161) and a chain of third-related keys in WoO 76. The cultivation of remote-key relations late on in structures also occurs in Beethoven's later variation cycles. A case in point is the second movement of the Sonata in C minor, Op. 111. The harmonic simplicity of the theme ('arietta') means that the harmonic world of the movement is dominated by tonic and relative-minor sonorities, a situation that remains until bars 106–130 when E-flat major is suddenly introduced. The effect of this remote-key engagement again seems to be to articulate the return of the tonic in the final units that follow and thus to assist indirectly with closure. In the earlier sets, such techniques appear also to have been used to facilitate free exploration of the theme's possibilities outside the more constrained environments of the previous variations. The coda of WoO 71 eventually reaches A-flat major (bar 72), but approaches it through an elaborate sequential modulation with imitation of the variation's opening motif. The coda of WoO 75 is even more extensive, containing contrapuntal development of the theme in D major (bars 67ff.) and D-flat major (bars 108ff.). Katalin Komlós suggests, in connection with such codas, that the 'rambling, improvisatory character and wide tonal scope surely reflect the extempore playing of the young Beethoven'.[39] Elaine Sisman believes that the extended final variations and codas of Beethoven's early sets distinguish them from the Mozartian style Beethoven inherited,[40] but Mozart employed comparable procedures in some of his independent sets. The flattened submediant surfaces, for example, in the tenth variation of K. 500 and the final variation of K. 613.

Similar dips into the extreme flat side occur late on in some of Beethoven's earlier rondos. Amongst the keyboard sonatas, Cole cites the shift to the flattened submediant in the finale of the Piano Sonata in A major, Op. 2 no. 2 and to the flattened second in that of Op. 7 in E-flat major.[41] Another, slightly later work that combines elements of variation and rondo and that contains periodic shifts to remote keys at significant joins in the structure is the 'Andante Favori', WoO 56, the original slow movement of the 'Waldstein' Sonata. Most of the shifts are to the flattened submediant, but the final one, close to the end, is to G-flat major, the flattened supertonic, producing an even more memorable effect.

39 Komlós, *Fortepianos and their Music*, p. 63.
40 Sisman, 'Tradition and Transformation', p. 166.
41 Cole, 'Rondos, Proper and Improper', *Music & Letters*, 51 (1970), pp. 398–9. For a further study of Beethoven's exploitation of codas for developmental purposes, see Joseph Kerman, 'Notes on Beethoven's Codas', in Alan Tyson (ed.), *Beethoven Studies 3* (Cambridge, 1982), pp. 141–59.

The frequency of remote-key engagements late on in the structures of variation sets and rondos by Beethoven and other composers[42] starts to reveal the technique as a grammatical agency connected to large-scale structural articulation rather than an idiosyncrasy of any particular figure. This technique also forges an important link with the more progressive keyboard sonatas of the period in which similar moves were used with greater frequency and in more diverse contexts.

The solo keyboard sonata

William Newman has dated the first known keyboard 'sonata' to 1641,[43] but the genre did not emerge fully until the 1740s with the appearance of a plethora of examples by Giovanni Battista (Padre) Martini (1706–84), Giovanni Platti (1697–1763), Baldassare Galuppi (1706–85) and C. P. E. Bach. Many mid-century keyboard works in fact seem poised between the sonata and the earlier suite. The six 'lessons' of the British composer James Nares (1715–83), for example, include a mixture of sonata-type and dance movements, and the *VIII Sonatas or Lessons for the Harpsichord* (1756) by Thomas Arne (1710–78) contains a fugue. An early example of a sonata-type opening movement appears in C. P. E. Bach's Sonata in F major no. 1 from his set of 'Prussian' Sonatas (1742). Although the movement has a relatively substantial development section and a clear 'double return' followed by a regular tonic recapitulation of the whole of the exposition, the scale remains compact, the keyboard style unadventurous. The range and scope of the keyboard sonata developed greatly during the second half of the eighteenth century, and the main objective here is to shed new light on some of the specific means by which the sonata was expanded while also revealing the extent to which these processes perpetuated existing techniques, or even resurrected archaic ones.

Expositions

Axiomatic to nineteenth-century sonata-form theory is the concept of an 'exposition' sub-divided by two contrasting 'subjects', of which the second is usually the more subdued and lyrical. Adolph Bernhard Marx expressed this

42 A case in point is the penultimate variation of the third movement of Schubert's *Forellenquintett*, D. 667. The link between it and the final variation contains a chain of third-relations and consequent brief encounters with distant keys that, rather like the move to E-flat in the second movement of Beethoven's Sonata Op. 111, acts as a foil for the harmonic conservatism of the movement thus far. See Stewart-MacDonald, *New Perspectives*, pp. 83–4.

43 William Newman, 'A Checklist of the Earliest Keyboard "Sonatas" (1641–1738)', *Notes*, 11 (1954), pp. 201–12. The work in question is a set of sonatas by Giovanni Pietro del Buono, see pp. 208–9.

view in his *Kompositionslehre*,[44] but the theory had already been formulated in Paris as early as 1826 in Anton Reicha's *Traité de haute composition musicale*, in which '[u]ne SECONDE IDÉE MÈRE ou un second motif' is mentioned.[45] Carl Czerny, possibly under the influence of Reicha,[46] noted in his *School of Practical Composition*, Op. 600, originally published in 1837, that the '[second] subject ... must be a new and more beautiful and pleasing melody than all which precedes; and it must be very different from the foregoing'.[47]

Research by twentieth-century theorists into the comparatively small body of *eighteenth*-century writings on what is recognizably 'sonata form' has revealed a lack of clear consensus concerning the importance of bi-thematicism in expositions or of the structural importance and distinctness of 'second subjects'. Obvious variants of bi-thematicism include so-called 'monothematicism', where the opening material predominates throughout the exposition and beyond, and 'polythematicism', in which more than one theme is associated with each key area.[48] It is in fact possible to find eighteenth-century identifications of 'second subjects', formulated in similar terms to those by Marx, Czerny and Reicha. In the *Elementi teorico-pratici di musica*, part 4, section 2 (1796), Francesco Galeazzi's explanation that the 'Characteristic Passage' or 'Intermediate Passage' introduced 'toward the middle of the first part' (exposition) 'must be gentle, expressive and tender in almost all kinds of compositions' ('Il *Passo Caratteristico*, *O Passo di mezzo* ... deve questo esser dolce, espressivo, e tenero quasi in ogni genere di composizione') is generally agreed to be the earliest authentic description of the 'second subject' before Reicha's in 1826.[49] Galeazzi's description does seem appropriate to the many eighteenth-century minor-key expositions that move to the relative major, allied as the relative major is with more lyrical material. A good example occurs in the first movement of Beethoven's Sonata in C minor, Op. 10 no. 2, dating from the mid-1790s.

Lyrical and clearly differentiated second themes in both minor- and major-key expositions were a noticeable trait of the keyboard sonatas of London-based composers from the second half of the eighteenth century and were first

44 Marx's comments can be found in the *Kompositionslehre* vol. 3, p. 282. See Leonard Ratner, 'Harmonic Aspects of Classic Form', *Journal of the American Musicological Society*, 2 (1949), pp. 159–60, n. 4.

45 Reicha's description of sonata form appears in *Traité de haute composition musicale* (Paris, 1826), vol. 2, pp. 296–300.

46 Bathia Churgin suggests that Czerny may have been familiar with Reicha's discussion of sonata form. See 'Francesco Galeazzi's Description (1796) of Sonata Form', *Journal of the American Musicological Society*, 21 (1968), p. 187, n. 20.

47 Carl Czerny, *School of Practical Composition*, Op. 600 (London, 1848), vol. 1, p. 35.

48 These variants of 'bi-thematicism' are discussed in Ratner, 'Harmonic Aspects of Classic Form'.

49 Galeazzi, *Elementi*, part 4, section 2, para. 30, given in Churgin, 'Francesco Galeazzi's Description (1796) of Sonata Form', p. 193.

witnessed in the keyboard sonatas of Johann Christian Bach (1735–82). Dussek, based in London during the 1790s, expanded the technique, which is also noticeable in the keyboard sonatas of the German-born Johann Baptist Cramer (1771–1858) and the native English composer George Frederick Pinto (1786–1806).[50] Komlós has suggested that the 'lyrical second themes' in the sonatas of J. C. Bach may have been inspired by the 'softer attack and sensitivity of the pianoforte'.[51] Subsequent increases in this type of theme may have been encouraged by the capacities of the English pianos themselves, whose distinguishing double action was introduced during the 1780s. By comparison with Viennese instruments, English ones had a 'fuller and thicker tone', facilitating a 'homogeneous texture, full sound, legato style and powerful virtuosity'.[52] A prototypical example of an expansively lyrical second theme that exploited such capabilities occurs in the first movement of Dussek's Sonata in B-flat major, Op. 45 no. 1. In the first movement of the earlier Sonata Op. 23 in B-flat major, a similar melody gains heightened expression through the brief engagement with the flattened third of the dominant (bars 37–40). Dussek frequently cultivated harmonic digressions of this kind, and when they coincide with expansive, lyrical themes they increase the expressive possibilities. The aim may have been to exploit further the capacities of the instruments for which the works were written, or as a pretext for a type of harmonic experimentation that is more frequently associated with the works of Schubert and other nineteenth-century composers. Similar 'Schubertian' tendencies can be found in the sonata-type movements of Pinto, some of which pre-date Dussek's more adventurous examples, and all of which were written before Pinto had reached the age of twenty. The second theme of the first movement of his Sonata in A major, Op. 3 no. 2 (1801) contains a brief digression to G major (bIII of V) in bar 45, followed by a slightly longer one to C major (bVI of V) during the codetta (bars 56–59): Nicholas Temperley suggests that the 'second subject' of this movement, as well as parts of the slow movement, 'remind one, sometimes to an almost incredible degree, of the mature Schubert'.[53] A more intricate case is the first movement of Pinto's Sonata in C minor (1802–3), whose second thematic group, beginning

50 For further information on Pinto, see Nicholas Temperley, 'George Frederick Pinto', *The Musical Times*, 106 (1965), pp. 265–9 and Alexander L. Ringer, 'Beethoven and the London Pianoforte School', *The Musical Quarterly*, 56 (1970), pp. 742–58.

51 Komlós, *Fortepianos and their Music*, p. 41. For a consideration of which Bach sonatas (and concertos) were composed for piano in London, see Richard Maunder, 'J. C. Bach and the Early Piano in London', *Journal of the Royal Musical Association*, 116 (1991), pp. 201–10.

52 Komlós, *Fortepianos and their Music*, p. 54. For a further discussion of the differences between Viennese and English instruments, see Malcolm Bilson, 'Keyboards', in Howard Mayer Brown and Stanley Sadie (eds.), *Performance Practice: Music After 1600* (London, 1989), pp. 223–38.

53 Temperley, 'George Frederick Pinto', p. 267.

in the relative major, contains a lengthy, subsidiary unit in A-flat major that introduces lyrical material and contains its own brief digression to E major, established as the enharmonic flattened submediant of the local tonic – creating what is in effect a 'digression within a digression'. E major (sometimes spelled as F-flat major) appears at other points in the movement as well, including early on in the development section. The coda is also extended with a repetition of the opening of the development that led initially to E, thus reproducing this tonal move late on. In the coda, E major is fully resolved to the tonic, providing the earlier chromatic modulation with a retrospective rationale or delayed resolution. Temperley associates the unusual nature of this explicit recollection of the development in the coda with its status as a structural device.[54] These periodic instances of E in the movement suggest that, in Pinto's works as in Dussek's – and, later, Schubert's – the small-scale harmonic digression could be assimilated into a systematically constructed network of remote-key relations sustained across a whole movement.

Despite the frequency of lyrical second themes in certain areas of the repertory – and other attendant characteristics that added to their effects, such as harmonic digressions – they were far from ubiquitous. Ratner advances the 'monothematic' expositions of Haydn as significant exceptions to the perceived norm of bi-thematicism,[55] and more recently there has been growing recognition of the importance of Clementi's use of 'monothematicism' in his keyboard sonatas of the 1780s and 1790s. Gerhard even goes so far as to suggest that Haydn was directly influenced by Clementi in his use of the technique. As pointed out earlier, it would appear that Clementi's new interest in it was stimulated, at least in part, by his visit to Vienna in the early 1780s and his likely encounter with music of the German Baroque.[56] Notably, his interest in monothematicism seems to have waned with the onset of the nineteenth century as the Viennese visit receded into the past. The expositions of the keyboard sonatas in the Op. 40 and Op. 50 sets – and also, in fact, of the later surviving symphonies (WO 32–35) – tend to contain clearly differentiated, often lyrical, 'second subjects'.[57]

54 *Ibid.*, p. 269. 55 Ratner, 'Harmonic Aspects of Classic Form', p. 159.

56 For details of Clementi's interaction with German music in the early 1780s and its possible ramifications for his musical style, see Alan Tyson, 'Clementi's Viennese Compositions, 1781–1782', *The Music Review*, 27 (1966), pp. 16–24; Plantinga, 'Clementi, Virtuosity and the "German Manner"' and Biba, 'Clementi's Viennese Sonatas'.

57 I have explored this aspect of the symphonies in 'Clementi's Orchestral Works, their Style and British Symphonism in the Nineteenth Century: S. Wesley, Crotch, Potter, Macfarren and Sterndale Bennett', *Ad Parnassum. A Journal of Eighteenth- and Nineteenth-Century Instrumental Music* 5 (2007), pp. 7–72.

The notion that monothematicism was more widespread in the eighteenth century than subsequently acknowledged, and that it basically represented a recovery – or continuation – of 'Baroque' syntax, fits with the favouring of it over bi-thematicism among the more conservative, late-eighteenth-century commentators. Newman calls the recognition of contrasting second themes in contemporary theory 'tangential', and notes the 'tendency still to think of only one main theme'.[58] He then cites Marpurg and Reichardt as theorists who strongly criticized second themes, and also Gerber who, as late as 1813, praised Haydn's monothematicism.

The main contribution of Ratner and his followers has been to restore the eighteenth-century theoretical conception of sonata form as a 'harmonic plan'[59] centring on the opposition of two key areas (rather than thematic 'subjects') in the exposition. As a model, this is less suited to minor-key expositions whose possibilities appear to have been more varied – possibly because of the stronger tenacity of archaic tendencies in the minor mode. The sub-division of the second-key area into more than one tonal region, producing the so-called 'three-key' exposition, is conventionally associated with the sonata structures of Beethoven, Schubert, Brahms, Mendelssohn and others,[60] but in 1988 Rey Longyear and Kate Covington uncovered an assortment of examples in keyboard sonatas from the mid and late eighteenth century, by Dussek, Clementi and also Georg Benda (1722–95), all of which are in minor keys[61] (see table 16.2). Rather than regarding these as anticipations of the major- and minor-key 'three-key' expositions of Schubert, Mendelssohn and Brahms, as Longyear and Covington do,[62] it may be preferable to see in them a retrospective type of syntax that generates motivic, contrapuntal and sequential continuity, and sometimes the *illusion* of multiple-key areas. The relationship between counterpoint, linear motivic processing (including monothematicism) and a multiple-key arrangement is clearly seen in the motivically intricate and heavily contrapuntal finale of Clementi's Sonata in G minor, Op. 34 no. 2 (1795), whose development section includes a two-part canon based on the opening theme just prior to the recapitulation.[63]

Minor-key, multiple-key expositions also generate an explicit archaism: the revival of the dominant minor as the goal of the exposition. This is seen

58 William Newman, *The Sonata in the Classic Era*, 2nd edn. (New York, 1972), p. 34.

59 Ratner, 'Harmonic Aspects of Classic Form', p. 161.

60 See Charles Rosen, *Sonata Forms* (New York, 1980) and James Webster, 'Schubert's Sonata Form and Brahms's First Maturity (I)', *19th-Century Music*, 2 (1978), pp. 18–35.

61 Rey Longyear and Kate Covington, 'Sources of the Three-Key Exposition', *The Journal of Musicology*, 6 (1988), p. 448.

62 *Ibid.*

63 For further discussion of Clementi's 'three-key' expositions including the finale of Op. 34 no. 2, see Stewart-MacDonald, *New Perspectives*, pp. 85–109.

Table 16.2. *Selection of eighteenth-century keyboard works with multiple-key expositions*

Composer	Work	Movement/Key-Scheme	Date
Benda	Sonatina XIII in C minor	I (Cm-Eb-Gm)	Published 1782
Benda	Sonatina XI in A minor	I (Am-[?]-C)	Published *c.* 1783
Benda	Sonatina XV in C minor	I (Cm-Eb-Gm)	Published *c.* 1788
Clementi	Sonata in F minor, Op. 13 no. 6	II (Cm-Eb-Gm)	1785
Clementi	Sonata in F# minor, Op. 25 no. 5	I (F#m-A-C#m)	1790
Clementi	Sonata in G minor, Op. 34 no. 2	III (Gm-Bb-Dm)	1795
Clementi	Sonata in B minor, Op. 40 no. 2	I (Bm-D-F#m)	1802
Clementi	Sonata in G minor, Op. 50 no. 3 ('*Didone abbandonata*')	I and Finale (Gm-Bb-Dm)	1804–5 [?] (published 1821)
Dussek	Sonata in E minor, Op. 10 no. 3	Finale (Em-G-Bm)	1785–88

frequently in early-to-mid-century Italian keyboard sonatas and less so after about 1770.[64] In Martini's minor-key movements, the dominant minor is more frequently chosen as the secondary key than is the relative major, just as it was by Scarlatti in his minor-key sonatas.[65] As in certain 'three-key' expositions by Clementi and Dussek, in the first movement of Platti's Sonata no. 5 in C minor, the exposition moves ultimately to the dominant minor, but quite strongly articulates III on the way, as do the first sections of Scarlatti's Sonatas in D minor, K. 18 (*Essercizi*), K. 69 in F minor and so on. Another later example of the relative major being suspended in favour of the dominant minor in the exposition but then released after the double bar is the finale of Beethoven's Sonata in F minor, Op. 2 no. 1. The relative rarity of minor-key expositions that end in the dominant minor, certainly in the later part of the century, is reflected in the infrequency with which the procedure is advocated by late-century theorists such as Heinrich Christoph Koch, August Kollmann and Galeazzi, all of whom only mention the relative major in this context: only Johann Adolph Scheibe appears to have admitted both possibilities.[66]

All of this would appear to indicate, first, that there was more diversity in the internal grammar of minor-key expositions than orthodox (that is, nineteenth-century) sonata-form theory easily encompasses and secondly, and perhaps

64 Longyear and Covington, 'Sources of the Three-Key Exposition', p. 449.

65 Martini's sonatas themselves contain strongly archaic elements. The second movement of No. 1 in B minor is fugal, as is that of No. 3 in D minor and No. 4 in C major; the fourth movement of No. 3 in D minor is canonic.

66 See Ray Longyear, 'The Minor Mode in Eighteenth-Century Sonata Form', *Journal of Music Theory*, 15 (1971), p. 189.

more significantly, that the sonata exposition, particularly of solo keyboard works, was another realm in which the minor mode became intertwined with archaism. This in turn suggests that, ultimately, eighteenth-century composers achieved a less varied set of strategies for the minor than for the major mode – stemming, perhaps, from its less frequent cultivation. It is therefore slightly ironic that minor-mode works from this period have conventionally been considered to be the most canonical as well as the most progressive works: the latter surfaces in Longyear's conception of the 'revitalization of the minor mode' in works by Clementi, Viotti and others as an anticipation of nineteenth-century tendencies.[67]

Development sections

Expansion of the size and scope of the 'development' section was central to all genres that used the sonata principle in the mid-to-late eighteenth century; it is an area of undisputed change and is considered central to the evolution of 'sonata form' from the more compact binary principle. This expansion was literal – development sections became much longer and internally more complex than they had been in the middle of the century – and it also entailed a broadening of the range of techniques used to process exposition material. The kind of literal restatements of exposition themes familiar from the mid-century was replaced by more sophisticated forms of reinterpretation, involving 'fragmentation of a theme into shorter motifs ...; contrapuntal combination of originally separate themes ...; juxtaposition of contrasting themes originally stated separately ...; increasing complexity of texture ...; extension by sequence ...; alteration of the rhythmic structure'.[68] From about the 1780s there was also an increasing use of remote keys, sometimes reached enharmonically. A comparatively early specimen (1781–2) is the finale of Clementi's Sonata in G minor, Op. 7 no. 3, in whose development section E-flat major is reinterpreted as the enharmonic dominant of G-sharp minor: the opening is then stated in G-sharp minor, in the manner of a 'false recapitulation'. A slightly later example is the first movement of Beethoven's Sonata in A major, Op. 2 no. 2 (1795). The section starts immediately in C major, approached through the dominant minor; the next stable key is A-flat major, a semitone away from the movement's home key. Following this is F major, before a sequential unit gradually restores the dominant for the re-transition. Comparing Beethoven's development section in this movement with, say, the equivalent in the first movement of C. P. E. Bach's 'Prussian' Sonata in F major, cited above,

67 See *ibid.*
68 James Webster, 'Sonata Form 3: The Classical Period, (ii) The Development', in Sadie (ed.), *The New Grove Dictionary of Music and Musicians, Revised Edition* (London, 2001), vol. 23, pp. 692–3.

reveals basic similarities of internal grammar but also shows the great changes that had taken place between the 1740s and the 1790s in this area of sonata structure.

Despite the historical significance assigned to the expansion of the development section, the theoretical understanding of its internal grammar has remained surprisingly imprecise, as if its possibilities were infinitely varied from work to work – which, of course, they were not. Charles Rosen's emphasis on the importance of the submediant in the second halves of developments dating from about the 1780s onwards, for example, has been neglected by subsequent writers, in spite of its frequency in a broad range of repertory.[69] William Caplin's broad sub-division of developments into a 'pre-core' and a 're-transition', emphasizing stable key areas, flanking an unstable and processive 'core' ('Kern der Durchführung') is of course a useful advance.[70] The purpose of what follows is to focus on two more specialized techniques that added to the scope and sophistication of development sections in solo keyboard sonatas as well as in other genres, namely false recapitulations and 'new' themes that are introduced.

False recapitulations

False recapitulations, whereby the opening of the movement reappears prematurely during the development and is then abandoned until the 'real' recapitulation sets in, are frequent in Haydn's works, keyboard and otherwise.[71] One well-known example occurs about halfway through the development of the first movement of the Sonata in C major, Hob. XVI:50 (1794). The key involved is A-flat major (bars 73ff.), and the effect enhanced by the downward shift in register, the *pianissimo* dynamic and the famous 'open-pedal' effect. Other examples are found in works by Clementi, Beethoven and Dussek, suggesting that the false recapitulation was employed quite widely, particularly in the larger-scale keyboard sonatas of the 1780s and 1790s. Michael Spitzer has noted that, in Clementi's keyboard sonatas, the development section is 'more discursive and episodic than in Haydn's and Mozart's sonatas and features more frequent off-tonic false or premature reprises of the first group'.[72]

69 Rosen, *Sonata Forms*, pp. 40–1.
70 William Caplin, *Classical Form: A Theory of Formal Functions for the Instrumental Music of Haydn, Mozart and Beethoven* (New York and Oxford, 1998), pp. 150–4.
71 See Mark Evan Bonds, 'Haydn, Laurence Sterne and the Origins of Musical Irony', *Journal of the American Musicological Society*, 44 (1991), p. 57 and Janet Levy, 'Texture as a Sign in Classic and Early Romantic Music', *Journal of the American Musicological Society*, 35 (1982), p. 482.
72 See Michael Spitzer, 'Review of Anselm Gerhard, *London und der Klassizismus in der Musik*', *Eighteenth-Century Music*, 3 (2006), pp. 330–6. I have discussed the irregularities in Clementi's recapitulations in *New Perspectives*, pp. 110–43.

As a technical category, the false recapitulation is ambiguous. Opinions differ as to the key in which a false recapitulation may take place in order to be classified as such, but James Webster clarifies that 'in later years, [it] may appear in a foreign key'.[73] Nevertheless, false recapitulations can occupy different positions in a development; they also vary in length[74] and in the extent of their harmonic preparation. Sisman questions the *purpose* of the false recapitulation and whether its effect is 'always to mislead the listener into thinking that it really is the recapitulation'.[75] A false recapitulation may seem to disrupt the continuity and logical unfolding of the development by 'proposing' recapitulation disproportionately early in the structure, but this would apply only if it were heard as a would-be recapitulation. Such a situation is less likely if the key is remote; and it is perhaps the case that false recapitulations can be sensed more as brief bouts of stability that recall familiar thematic material and stimulate further, often heightened, developmental processing before the re-transition occurs. It is in this respect that they contribute to the expansion in the size and scope of development sections. A good example of a false recapitulation apparently stimulating heightened developmental processes is found in the first movement of Haydn's Sonata in E-flat major, Hob. XVI:38. The false recapitulation itself, in the submediant, lasts for only three bars (32–34) and is followed by a fairly elaborate sequence with a three-part texture whose two upper parts exchange the semiquaver motif of the opening theme in imitation – during which, as from bar 37, the contour of the motif is altered to form a descending scale. Another example occurs in the first movement of Dussek's Sonata in B-flat major, Op. 35 no. 1, where the false recapitulation is in the remote key of B major (bars 119–124). The passage following it (bars 125–143) is a long, chromatically ascending sequence whose structural purpose is to link B major with the dominant. The sequence processes two motifs originating in the exposition's respective subject groups – one that reproduces the contour of the melody from bar 1 (recalled in bar 119) and another that reproduces the rhythm of part of the second theme. As the sequence proceeds, the two motifs alternate in a bass/treble dialogue either side of a semiquaver continuum, and are modified at various points. Whereas the start of the section contained literal restatements of exposition contents, the passage following the false recapitulation incorporates more subtle processes of extraction, transformation and re-combination.

73 Webster, 'Sonata Form 3, (ii)', p. 693.
74 Sisman renames shorter examples 'reprise-interludes'. See *Mozart: The 'Jupiter' Symphony No. 41 in C major, K. 551* (Cambridge, 1993), pp. 50–3.
75 *Ibid.*, p. 51.

'New' themes in development sections

Another significant technique used in the development sections of more adventurous late eighteenth-century works, including keyboard sonatas, is the introduction of new themes that are absent from the exposition. The most famous example occurs in the first movement of Beethoven's 'Eroica' Symphony when, halfway through the development, a new theme is heard in the remote key of E minor (bars 284ff.).[76] The introduction of new themes into developments is an apparently innovative feature of Beethoven's sonata-type movements that appears to anticipate nineteenth-century developments.[77] Bathia Churgin locates examples in Beethoven's piano, violin and cello sonatas, string quartets and quintets, and concertos from between *c.* 1793 and 1826, but examples are most frequent in the early and early-to-middle-period works, including the piano sonatas Op. 2 nos. 1 and 3; Op. 7; Op. 10 nos. 1, 2 and 3; Op. 14 no. 1; and Op. 49 no. 1.[78] Although associated with archetypically progressive works such as the 'Eroica' Symphony, the 'introduction of a new theme in the development ... is an old device',[79] and provision is made for the possibility by a number of eighteenth- (and nineteenth-) century theorists such as Koch, Galeazzi, Reicha and Czerny.[80] Churgin, citing Ratner, suggests that it may signify the influence of the da capo aria, where new material is introduced at the start of the B section,[81] and she is one among many writers to note Mozart's frequent use of the technique.[82] All of this would indicate that introducing new themes into development sections was well established in the eighteenth century and certainly not a 'bold disregard' of sonata convention that appeared suddenly in the nineteenth.[83]

Churgin's examples by Beethoven are diverse in terms of genre, function ('contrast, surprise, enrichment, intensification ... structural articulation')[84] and positioning within the section,[85] and it is often also debatable whether

76 See Rosen's discussion of this theme and its possible derivation from the movement's opening theme in *The Classical Style* (New York and London, 1971), p. 393.

77 Bathia Churgin, 'Beethoven and the New Development-Theme in Sonata-Form Movements', *The Journal of Musicology*, 16 (1998), p. 323. Two nineteenth-century sonata-type movements in which strikingly new themes are introduced into development sections are the first movement of Mendelssohn's Symphony no. 4 in A major, Op. 90 ('Italian') and the finale of Hubert Parry's Symphony no. 4 in E minor.

78 Churgin, 'Beethoven and the New Development-Theme', pp. 327–8. See esp. the table on p. 328.

79 *Ibid.*, p. 323.

80 *Ibid.*, pp. 325–6.

81 *Ibid.*, p. 325, citing Leonard Ratner, *Classic Music: Expression, Form and Style* (New York, 1980), pp. 229, 233.

82 See Kerman, 'Notes on Beethoven's Codas', p. 142 and Rosen, *Sonata Forms*, pp. 321–2. See also Webster, 'Sonata Form 3, (ii)', p. 693 and Ratner, 'Harmonic Aspects of Classic Form', p. 160, n. 6.

83 K. M. Knittel, 'The Construction of Beethoven', in Jim Samson (ed.), *The Cambridge History of Nineteenth-Century Music* (Cambridge, 2002), p. 138.

84 Churgin, 'Beethoven and the New Development-Theme', p. 325.

85 *Ibid.*, p. 329.

the material concerned is genuinely new or in fact derived from earlier material. The 'new' elements in the development sections of the first movements of Beethoven's Piano Sonatas Op. 2 no. 3 and Op. 10 no. 2 consist of figuration rather than of themes as such; and the 'new' theme in the development of Op. 7 in E-flat major (presumably the fragments of melody in bars 173–174 and 181–184) is interspersed with explicit references to the exposition's opening theme. More convincing examples are located by Churgin in the first movements of Beethoven's sonatas in C minor, Op. 10 no. 1 and in E major, Op. 14 no. 1 – both lyrical melodies that engage with remote keys,[86] like the E minor theme in the 'Eroica'. Even here, though, there are connections between the 'new' themes and the contents of the exposition: William Kinderman notes that the one in Op. 10 'brings together motifs from both principal themes'.[87]

Remote-key false recapitulations and new themes of the types just cited in Beethoven's Op. 10 and Op. 14 were two techniques through which composers could articulate distant keys in developments and heighten the level of thematic processing: remote-key false recapitulations emphasize the movement's harmonic 'point of furthest remove' while providing a springboard of (thematic) stability from which more intensive development could proceed; and new, lyrical themes distinct from the contents of the exposition dramatize the movement's most distant key by making it coincide with a new thematic event. Both techniques are implicitly progressive in that they expand the proportions and scope of the development section, but can be related to earlier practice, too; and they are associated with a wide range of composers of the period.

The 'late Classical' slow movement and 'cyclic' techniques

Existing histories of the evolution of sonata form tend to concentrate on opening movements. More neglected, but still crucial is eighteenth-century composers' cultivation of *inner* movements and their varied treatment of the harmonic and expressive relationships between inner and outer movements. Multi-movement instrumental works of the 1790s and early 1800s often contain expansive and highly expressive slow movements whose progressive feature is their distant key, most often related by third to the tonic. The cultivation of remote-key slow movements of this type was more frequent than is generally realized; examples can be found in all genres and by a wide variety of composers (including Beethoven, Dussek, Steibelt and Cramer).[88]

86 Churgin notes that the 'traditional lyrical theme' is the 'most common type' of new theme, and twenty-four of her examples use remote keys. *Ibid.*, pp. 327, 334.
87 William Kinderman, *Beethoven* (New York and Oxford, 1995), p. 38.
88 Ethan Haimo, 'Remote Keys and Multi-Movement Unity: Haydn in the 1790s', *The Musical Quarterly*, 74 (1990), pp. 267–8.

Some of the most audacious examples occur in solo keyboard sonatas, most notably in Haydn's Sonata in E-flat major, Hob. XVI:52, whose slow movement is in the chromatically related key of E major.[89] The fact that Haydn, in this case, may have traversed the limits of acceptability is confirmed by the following contemporary reaction:

> The first movement is in E-flat, the second in E. Nothing, I think, can exceed the disagreeable effect thus produced by the immediate succession of scales so unrelated to each other.[90]

A related feature of works with disparate large-scale tonal plans is the interlinking of individual movements, usually through harmonic, rather than melodic or motivic, means. Kinderman notes how the rondo of Beethoven's Sonata Op. 13 ('Pathetique') assimilates the key of the slow movement, A flat major, into the second episode and also at other points, even if A flat is rather less distant than in other cases.[91] A more explicit and daring example is Haydn's E-flat sonata mentioned above, the key of whose slow movement is anticipated in a capricious episode in the development of the first movement (bars 68–70) where E major emerges without harmonic preparation and after an extreme shift in register. The second movement of Beethoven's Sonata in C major, Op. 2 no. 3, also in E major, contains a reference to C major in bars 53–54; in Dussek's Sonata in A-flat major, Op. 70 ('Le retour à Paris'), dating from 1807, the slow movement's key, again E major, is anticipated more than once in the first movement. The most explicit anticipation occurs late on in the recapitulation, in bars 171–174.[92] This work expands the kind of systematic network of tonal digressions seen in the first movement of Pinto's C minor sonata to encompass relationships between movements.[93]

It is easy to interpret the cultivation of remote-key schemes and inter-movement harmonic links as an overt form of compositional experimentation or conscious 'modernization' that connects the solo keyboard sonata to the most prestigious chamber works, concertos and symphonies from the turn of the nineteenth century such as the 'Eroica' Symphony.[94] The *aesthetic*

89 A short analysis of this movement is provided by Ratner, *Classic Music*, p. 416.

90 Quoted in Thomas B. Milligan, *The Concerto and London's Musical Culture in the Late Eighteenth Century* (Ann Arbor, MI, 1983), p. 160.

91 Kinderman, *Beethoven*, pp. 47–8.

92 I have discussed this and other examples of inter-movement harmonic links in *New Perspectives*, chapter 3, pp. 145–208.

93 Stephan D. Lindeman has investigated the structural use of harmonic digressions in piano concertos of the early-to-mid-nineteenth century with occasional references to sonatas by Dussek. See 'An Insular World of Romantic Isolation: Harmonic Digressions in the Early Nineteenth-Century Piano Concerto', *Ad Parnassum: A Journal of Eighteenth- and Nineteenth-Century Instrumental Music*, 4 (2006), pp. 21–80.

94 Beethoven again experimented with the procedures in his Third and Fifth Piano Concertos and off and on in string quartets at all stages of his career.

significance of such techniques, however, is more difficult to gauge. The frequent conjunction of inter-movement links and disparate key schemes might suggest, following Haimo, that the links represented compensatory measures in the face of threatened fragmentation and incoherence; but this is highly questionable. Being thematically unsupported in most cases, and occurring sporadically over a wide expanse of music, the harmonic links can be hard to discern for anyone who is not intimately acquainted with the work (or who has no access to a score); furthermore, composers' handling of the techniques were diverse in terms of the varying explicitness or subtlety of the harmonic interconnections and their placement in the structure. It is also necessary to consider why such an obvious compositional technique as 'cyclic' thematic interlinking was used with relative infrequency in this period; it may have had to do with the extent to which ideals of cyclic 'unification' went against the grain of the prevailing aesthetic values of the period. Most contemporary theorists stress the need for the movements of a multi-movement work to be strongly differentiated. In 1755, Jean-Jacques Rousseau defined the 'sonata' as 'an instrumental piece consisting of three or four consecutive movements *of different character*', as did Schulz in almost identical fashion twenty years later.[95] Newman notes that the 'interrelationship of movements in sonata cycles received little attention from writers *beyond the requirement of contrast*' and goes on to observe the theoretical lack of interest in *thematic* links between movements that occasionally did emerge.[96] By the same token, writers like Vogler stressed the desirability of *small-scale* contrast and of unexpected *local* effects.[97] Within such a value system, then, it is possible either that highly explicit links between movements would have been regarded as features that detracted from the large-scale differentiation of movements, or that the techniques were there primarily, or even wholly, to create *local* effects of surprise or disjunction; any long-range connections may have been unplanned or designed to function on a subliminal level and/or as a form of 'hermetic' compositional wit, whose full significance was disclosed only to those on intimate terms with the work – like the composer or player(s). Certainly, the keyboard sonatas that display such features represent the extremes of compositional (and technical) audacity and, as the negative contemporary reaction to Haydn's E-flat sonata cited above would seem to indicate, the boundaries of what was considered acceptable. It is in this area that certain keyboard sonatas share objectives with advanced works from 'pre-eminent' genres such as the string quartet and symphony.

95 William Newman, *The Sonata in the Classic Era*, 2nd edn. (New York, 1972), p. 23. (Italics added.)
96 *Ibid.*, pp. 27–8.
97 See Jane Stevens, 'Georg Joseph Vogler and the "Second Theme" in Sonata Form', *Journal of Musicology* 2 (1983), pp. 287–8.

Conclusion: the turn of the nineteenth century and stylistic retrospection

It is tempting to regard the more advanced solo keyboard music of the 1790s and very early 1800s as anticipating nineteenth-century preoccupations such as further exploration of the possibilities of virtuosity, of structural expansion and of the cultivation of distant key relationships. This impulse underlies Rosen's argument, put forward in *The Classical Style*, that Beethoven's early keyboard works anticipate the 'early Romantic' idiom of composers such as Weber and Hummel more directly than his 'middle-period' and 'late' works. Noting that 'with age, Beethoven drew closer to the forms and proportions of Haydn and Mozart', Rosen suggests that in Beethoven's 'youthful works, the imitation of his two great precursors is largely exterior' and that 'in technique and even in spirit, he is at the beginning of his career often closer to Hummel, Weber, and to the later works of Clementi than to Haydn and Mozart'. Rosen goes on to cite the first movement of the Sonata in C major, Op. 2 no. 3, which has a 'rigid sectional structure' and a 'wealth of connecting material that is never found in the opening movement of a work of Haydn or Mozart'.[98] Dussek's compositions have long been considered 'prophetic'[99] and Clementi, with his multi-faceted career as composer, pianist, teacher and business entrepreneur, is frequently seen as a prototype of the nineteenth-century keyboard-virtuoso whose later works – such as the programmatic 'Didone Abbandonata', Op. 50 no. 3 – anticipate early Romanticism. This is of course a one-sided view, since Clementi was the composer whose keyboard works most explicitly embodied the paradox of innovatory and conservative instincts, in a manner that anticipates Beethoven's later works. The ultimate example is the work that appears to have occupied Clementi for the last two decades of his career and that became central to branches of keyboard training in the nineteenth and early twentieth centuries: the *Gradus ad Parnassum*, Op. 44. Although the first of the three volumes of the *Gradus* was not published until 1817, the work's origins apparently extend back to *c.* 1801.[100] The assembly of the *Gradus* involved a mixture of new composition and the revision and

98 Rosen, *The Classical Style*, p. 380.

99 See Eric Blom, 'The Prophecies of Dussek', in Blom, *Classics Major and Minor: With Some Other Musical Ruminations* (London, 1958), pp. 88–117.

100 In a letter to Paul Härtel dating from 1818, Clementi mentions his intention, in about 1801, to assemble a series of keyboard exercises and to call them 'Studio'. See Max Unger, *Muzio Clementis Leben* (New York, 1971), p. 213. While summarizing in detail the contents of Clementi's letter to Härtel of 12 April 1818, Unger writes the following: 'Ungefähr im Jahre 1801 habe [Clementi] dem Harfenbauer in London, der ihn um ein beteutendes Studienwerk für seine Pariser Nichten gebeten hatte, erzählt, dass er sich schon lang mit einer Sammlung von Übungen zur Bildung fertiger Klavierspieler getragen habe, und diese habe er "Studio" nennen wollen.'

insertion of existing works, some of which, like the fugues from Op. 5 and 6, dated from before 1800. The end result is an extremely large, heterogeneous work that embodies, and builds on, a full spectrum of formats assumed by solo keyboard music of the period, ranging from the most 'mechanical' exercises to the progressive and sophisticated treatment of forms like sonata and variation, as well as the cultivation of apparently new forms, some of which anticipate the pictorial or programmatic miniatures of Schumann and others. The imposing scale and heterogeneity of the *Gradus* make its central purpose difficult to determine, and it is probably for this reason that it was so often disseminated in compressed editions in the nineteenth and much of the twentieth centuries that included only the most 'mechanical' exercises.[101] At the heart of the *Gradus*, though, seems to be a preoccupation with contrapuntal possibility – and, in particular, counterpoint's potential to continue to act as a live agency within the contemporary style. The work contains a large number of fugal and canonic movements, but counterpoint also infiltrates some of the predominantly non-contrapuntal pieces in a similar manner to the canons of the later solo keyboard sonatas. In this and other respects the *Gradus* recalls earlier, Baroque-period works such as J. S. Bach's Goldberg Variations and also *Das Wohltemperierte Klavier*. Like the *Gradus*, both volumes of *Das Wohltemperierte Klavier* were assembled from a range of sources, and the contents (particularly of the second volume) were diverse as a result,[102] distinguishing the work from its models.[103] The Goldberg Variations are similarly varied in style and disposition while assigning central importance to the manipulation of canon.

These parallels seem all the more significant when Clementi's interaction with the music of J. S. Bach is considered. This was sufficient to make him, along with figures like Samuel Wesley (1766–1837), one of the central representatives of the 'Bach revival' in England at the turn of the nineteenth century. In 1972 Plantinga hypothesized that Clementi studied and ultimately came into possession of the 'London Autograph' of *Das Wohltemperierte Klavier*, one of the most important sources for the work, dating from 1738–42.[104] Clementi may have used this source when preparing part II of another of his pedagogical works, the *Introduction to the Art of Playing on the Piano Forte*.[105] This was not published until 1820, but Plantinga suggests that Clementi was aware of the

101 I have discussed the reception of the *Gradus ad Parnassum* and the question of its ultimate meaning and purpose in 'The Faces of Parnassus: Towards a New Reception of Muzio Clementi's *Gradus ad Parnassum*', in Therese Ellsworth and Susan Wollenberg (eds.), *The Piano in Nineteenth-Century British Culture: Essays on Instruments, Performers and Repertoire* (Aldershot, 2007), pp. 69–100.

102 See Schulenberg, *The Keyboard Music of J. S. Bach*, pp. 197–201.

103 *Ibid.*, p. 161.

104 For details of the contents of the 'London Autograph', see *ibid.*, p. 200, table 12–1.

105 Plantinga, 'Clementi, Virtuosity and the "German Manner"', p. 327.

'London Autograph' a good deal earlier, perhaps explaining some changes in Clementi's style in works of the 1780s and 1790s in terms of the direct influence of the music of J. S. Bach. At the same time Mozart was also coming under the influence of Bach's music, as mentioned above in the context of the Rondo, K. 494 and the Sonata, K. 533. One work by Clementi that seems (according to Plantinga) to contain direct echoes of a specific work by Bach, recalling the subject of the Fugue in D major from volume 2 of *Das Wohltemperierte Klavier*, is the Sonata in G minor, Op. 34 no. 2: the main theme of the first movement, featuring three repeated Ds, bears a resemblance to Bach's fugal subject, and further echoes are apparent in the finale.[106] This sonata, therefore, is particularly 'Janus-faced' in that the powerfully 'archaizing' influences are set against consciously modern features such as the highly irregular approach to the recapitulation of the opening movement,[107] and the exploration of remote keys in the development section of the finale. That Clementi's approach to style was not simply idiosyncratic and unrepresentative of general orientations is explained by Spitzer, who observes that Clementi's 'sonata journey foreshadows Beethoven's each step of the way':

> a classicizing turn *c*1802 (Clementi's Opp. 40 and 41; Beethoven's 'Waldstein', Op. 53, of 1804), followed by a dramatic falling-off of piano sonata production, a striking neobaroque tendency, with an embrace of counterpoint and canon (Clementi's *Gradus*; Beethoven's late style) and ending with a 'Recollection of Classical Models' (Clementi's Op. 50; Beethoven's Op. 135).[108]

Consideration of the 'later' styles of Clementi, Beethoven and to some extent Mozart reminds us of the centrality of 'Baroque' tendencies in solo keyboard music from the turn of the nineteenth century – just as examination of the work of earlier figures such as Scarlatti and C. P. E. Bach reveals artistic mentalities more commensurate with the 'Classical' idiom that, according to conventional accounts, was yet to crystallize. Interaction with solo keyboard repertory from both halves of the century, moreover, seems to render the traditional 'Baroque–Classical' distinction progressively more difficult to sustain, particularly when repertory beyond the confines of the established canon is included. Viewing the repertory purely in terms of the social developments that caused the vast growth of a keyboard-playing public and of a buoyant market for keyboard compositions is naturally inclined to emphasize the

106 Plantinga postulates another direct reference to Bach in Clementi's works in addition to the one under discussion – to the Prelude and Fugue in B-flat minor from volume 1 of *Das Wohltemperierte Klavier* in the third fugue from Clementi's Op. 5. See Plantinga, 'Clementi, Virtuosity and the "German Manner"', pp. 323, 325–6, 329.
107 I have discussed this matter in detail in *New Perspectives*, pp. 131–43.
108 Spitzer, 'Review of Gerhard, *London und der Klassizismus*', p. 334.

differences in style and priorities between keyboard music of the earlier and later eighteenth century; but, as this discussion has shown, acknowledging the importance of such developments does not necessarily obscure the extent to which preoccupations or conventions more immediately associated with one part of the century can appear strongly at another – such as late-century composers' use of the dominant minor in place of the relative major in expositions. Dispensing with the traditional bifurcated perception of the eighteenth century according to the 'Baroque' and 'Classical' eras and also centralizing repertory lying outside the established canon is likely to stimulate renewed debate about seemingly familiar issues, revealing as it does a landscape of eighteenth-century solo keyboard music that is disorientating in its diversification but extremely rich.

Select Bibliography

Biba, Otto. 'Clementi's Viennese Sonatas'. In Richard Bösel and Massimiliano Sala (eds.), *Muzio Clementi: Cosmopolita della Musica: Atti del convegno internationale in occasione del 250 anniversario della nascita (1752–2002), Rome, 5–6 December 2002*. Bologna, 2004 (Quaderni Clementiani, 1), pp. 185–98

Bilson, Malcolm. 'Keyboards'. In Howard Mayer Brown and Stanley Sadie (eds.), *Performance Practice: Music After 1600*. London, 1989, pp. 223–38

Bonds, Mark Evan. 'Haydn, Laurence Sterne and the Origins of Musical Irony'. *Journal of the American Musicological Society*, 44 (1991), pp. 57–87

Churgin, Bathia. 'Francesco Galeazzi's Description (1796) of Sonata Form'. *Journal of the American Musicological Society* 21 (1968), pp. 181–99

'Beethoven and the New Development-Theme in Sonata Form Movements'. *The Journal of Musicology*, 16/3 (1998), pp. 323–43

Cole, Malcolm. 'Sonata-Rondo, the Formulation of a Theoretical Concept in the Eighteenth and Nineteenth Centuries'. *The Musical Quarterly*, 55 (1969), pp. 180–92

'The Vogue of the Instrumental Rondo in the Late Eighteenth Century'. *Journal of the American Musicological Society*, 22 (1969), pp. 425–55

'Rondos, Proper and Improper'. *Music & Letters*, 51 (1970), pp. 388–99

'The Rondo Finale: Evidence for the Mozart–Haydn Exchange?' *The Music Review*, 36 (1975), pp. 242–56

'Rondo'. In Stanley Sadie (ed.), *The New Grove Dictionary of Music and Musicians, Revised Edition*. London, 2001, vol. 21, pp. 649–56

Czerny, Carl. *School of Practical Composition*, Op. 600. London, 1848, vol. 1

DeNora, Tia. *Beethoven and the Construction of Genius: Musical Politics in Vienna, 1792–1803*. Berkeley, 1995

Einstein, Alfred. *Mozart: His Character, His Work*. Trans. Arthur Mendel and Nathan Broder. New York and London, 1946

Fillion, Michelle. 'Intimate Expression for a Widening Public: The Keyboard Sonatas and Trios'. In Caryl Clark (ed.), *The Cambridge Companion to Haydn*. Cambridge, 2005, pp. 126–37

Fisher, Stephen. 'Sonata Procedures in Haydn's Symphonic Rondo Finales of the 1770s'. In Jens Peter Larsen, Howard Serwer and James Webster (eds.), *Haydn Studies*. New York, 1981, pp. 481–6

Forkel, Johann Nikolaus. *Musikalisch Bibliothek*, 2. Gotha, 1778

Galand, Joel. 'Form, Genre and Style in the Eighteenth-Century Rondo'. *Music Theory Spectrum*, 17 (1995), pp. 27–52

Gerhard, Anselm. *London und der Klassizismus in der Musik: die Idee der 'absoluten Musik' und Muzio Clementis Klavierwerk*. Stuttgart and Weimar, 2002

Haimo, Ethan. 'Remote Keys and Multi-Movement Unity: Haydn in the 1790s'. *The Musical Quarterly*, 74 (1990), pp. 242–68

Kerman, Joseph. 'Notes on Beethoven's Codas'. In Alan Tyson (ed.), *Beethoven Studies 3*. Cambridge, 1982, pp. 141–59

Knittel, K. M. 'The Construction of Beethoven'. In Jim Samson (ed.), *The Cambridge History of Nineteenth-Century Music*. Cambridge, 2002, pp. 118–56

Kollmann, August Frederick Christopher. *Essay on Practical Composition*. London, 1799

Komlós, Katalin. *Fortepianos and their Music: Germany, Austria and England, 1760–1800*. Oxford, 1995

Levy, Janet. 'Texture as a Sign in Classical and Early Romantic Music'. *Journal of the American Musicological Society*, 35 (1982), pp. 482–531

Lindeman, Stephan D. 'An Insular World of Romantic Isolation: Harmonic Digressions in the Early Nineteenth-Century Piano Concerto'. *Ad Parnassum: A Journal of Eighteenth- and Nineteenth-Century Instrumental Music*, 4 (2006), pp. 21–80

Longyear, Rey. 'The Minor Mode in Eighteenth-Century Sonata Form', *Journal of Music Theory*, 15 (1971), pp. 182–226

Longyear, Rey and Kate Covington. 'Sources of the Three-Key Exposition'. *The Journal of Musicology*, 6 (1988), pp. 448–70

Marshall, Robert. 'Bach and Mozart's Artistic Maturity'. In Michael Marissen (ed.), *Bach Perspectives, Volume 3: Creative Responses to Bach from Mozart to Hindemith*. Lincoln, NB and London, 1998, pp. 47–79

Maunder, Richard. 'J. C. Bach and the Early Piano in London'. *Journal of the Royal Musical Association*, 116 (1991), pp. 201–10

McVeigh, Simon. *Concert Life in London from Mozart to Haydn*. Cambridge, 1993

Moss, L. 'Haydn's Sonata Hob. XVI:52 in E-flat Major: An Analysis of the First Movement'. In Jens Peter Larsen, Howard Serwer and James Webster (eds.), *Haydn Studies*. New York, 1981, pp. 496–501

Neumann, Hans and Carl Schachter. 'Mozart's Rondo K. 494'. In William J. Mitchell and Felix Salzer (eds.), *The Music Forum. vol. 1*, New York and London, 1967, pp. 3–34

Newman, William. 'A Checklist of the Earliest Keyboard "Sonatas" (1641–1738)', *Notes*, 11 (1954), pp. 201–12

The Sonata in the Classic Era. 2nd edn., New York, 1972

Olleson, Edward. 'Gottfried van Swieten: Patron of Haydn and Mozart'. *Proceedings of the Royal Musical Association*, 89 (1962–3), pp. 63–74

Plantinga, Leon. 'Clementi, Virtuosity and the "German Manner"'. *Journal of the American Musicological Society*, 15 (1972), pp. 303–30

'Clementi: The Metamorphoses of a Musician'. In Roberto Illiano, Luca Sala and Massimiliano Sala (eds.), *Muzio Clementi: Studies and Prospects*. Bologna, 2002, pp. xxi–xxvii

Radcliffe, Philip. 'Keyboard Music'. In Egon Wellesz and Frederick Sternfeld (eds.), *The Age of Enlightenment*, The Oxford History of Music, 5. London, 1973, pp. 574–610

Ratner, Leonard. 'Harmonic Aspects of Classic Form'. *Journal of the American Musicological Society*, 2 (1949), pp. 159–68

Classic Music: Expression, Form and Style. New York, 1980

Ringer, Alexander L. 'Beethoven and the London Pianoforte School'. *The Musical Quarterly*, 56 (1970), pp. 742–58

Rosen, Charles. *The Classical Style*. London, 1971

Sonata Forms. New York, 1980

Schulenberg, David. *The Keyboard Music of J. S. Bach*. London, 1993

Sisman, Elaine. 'Tradition and Transformation in the Alternating Variations of Haydn and Beethoven'. *Acta Musicologica*, 62 (1990), pp. 152–82

Haydn and the Classical Variation. Cambridge, MA, 1993

Mozart: The 'Jupiter' Symphony No. 41 in C major, K. 551. Cambridge, 1993

'After the Heroic Phase: Fantasia and the "Characteristic" Sonatas of 1809'. *Beethoven Forum 6*. Lincoln, NB and London, 1998, pp. 67–96

Spitzer, Michael. 'Review of Gerhard, *London und der Klassizismus in der Musik*'. *Eighteenth-Century Music*, 3 (2006), pp. 330–6

Stanley, Glenn. 'The "wirklich ganz neue Manier" and the Path to It: Beethoven's Variations for Piano, 1783–1802'. *Beethoven Forum 3*. Lincoln, NB and London, 1994, pp. 53–79

Stevens, Jane. 'Georg Joseph Vogler and the "Second Theme" in Sonata Form'. *Journal of Musicology*, 2 (1983), pp. 278–304

Stewart-MacDonald, Rohan H. *New Perspectives on the Keyboard Sonatas of Muzio Clementi*. Bologna, 2006

'The Faces of Parnassus: Towards a New Reception of Muzio Clementi's *Gradus ad Parnassum*'. In Therese Ellsworth and Susan Wollenberg (eds.), *The Piano in Nineteenth-Century British Culture: Essays on Instruments, Performers and Repertoire*. Aldershot, 2007, pp. 69–100

'The Minor Mode as Archaic Signifier in the Solo Keyboard Works of Domenico Scarlatti and Muzio Clementi'. In Massimiliano Sala and W. Dean Sutcliffe (eds.), *Domenico Scarlatti*. Bologna, 2007, pp. 1–43

'Clementi's Orchestral Works, their Style and British Symphonism in the Nineteenth Century: S. Wesley, Crotch, Potter, Macfarren and Sterndale Bennett', *Ad Parnassum. A Journal of Eighteenth- and Nineteenth-Century Instrumental Music*, 5 (2007), pp. 7–72

Sutcliffe, W. Dean. 'Chopin's Counterpoint: The *Largo* from the Cello Sonata, Op. 65'. *The Musical Quarterly*, 83 (1999), pp. 114–33

The Keyboard Sonatas of Domenico Scarlatti and Eighteenth-Century Musical Style. Cambridge, 2003

Temperley, Nicholas. 'George Frederick Pinto'. *The Musical Times*, 106 (1965), pp. 265–9

'Piano Music: 1800–1870'. In Nicholas Temperley (ed.), *Music in Britain: The Romantic Age, 1800–1914*. The Athlone History of Music in Britain, 5. London, 1981

Tyson, Alan. 'Clementi's Viennese Compositions, 1781–1782'. *The Music Review*, 27 (1966), pp. 16–24

Vogler, Georg. *Mannheimischer Tonschule*, vol. 2. Mannheim, 1778

Webster, James. 'Schubert's Sonata Form and Brahms's First Maturity (I)'. *19th-Century Music*, 2 (1978), pp. 18–35

'Sonata Form 3: The Classical Period, (ii) The Development'. In Stanley Sadie (ed.), *The New Grove Dictionary of Music and Musicians, Revised Edition*. London, 2001, vol. 23, pp. 692–3

Williams, Peter. *Bach: The Goldberg Variations*. Cambridge, 2001

Unger, Max. *Muzio Clementis Leben*. New York, 1971

· 17 ·

The serenata in the eighteenth century

STEFANIE TCHAROS

The eighteenth-century serenata has long remained a conundrum – difficult to define in its many permutations and to distinguish from other genres, or seen as somewhat peripheral because of its ephemeral, occasional nature, often leaving little or no trace for historians. Yet the challenges it presents have encouraged a rich collection of scholarly investigation, mostly on a local level, the best perspective from which to interpret the serenata as musical practice, as performance event, and as a refractor of eighteenth-century history.[1] In many respects, divergences abound: the serenata in Italy influenced those produced in Italianate court societies in Vienna and in northern Europe; in England, however, analogous serenata events acquired different local customs as was also the case in locations such as Spain and Portugal. Variability was a feature of this genre, whose function and conditions for performance changed according to context and occasion.

The similarities found among serenatas of different locales teach important lessons. In a very general sense, the serenata was a musical performance commemorating an event, or presented in someone's honour. It was most typically an open-air performance, often done at night, but other modes of presentation also existed. In the eighteenth century, the serenata frequently functioned as both musical form and event, serving political rituals marked by symbolic modes of representation. Marking occasions such as royal births, marriages, military victories, or recoveries from illness, the serenata offered patrons an opportunity for social display and image-building. Such performances could be acts of dynastic consolidation or reinforcement of known political realities. Serenatas were especially effective, however, during times of instability when their allegorical portrayal of political ascendancy was meant to be self-validating.

1 Among the most recent serenata scholarship that studies various contexts for the serenata, as well as issues of the genre's music, text and staging in the seventeenth and eighteenth century, is a collection of essays published from the 2003 Reggio Calabria conference, *La Serenata tra Seicento e Settecento: musica, poesia, scenotecnica*, Nicolò Maccavino (ed.). *Atti del Convegno Internazionale di Studi (Reggio Calabria, 16–17 maggio 2003)* (Reggio Calabria, 2007). My chapter was written before this publication became available.

The serenata's roots in absolutist spectacle require us not to overlook an important diachronic perspective associated with the genre. In many respects, the serenata vividly captures the spirit of a lingering Baroque culture juxtaposed against the innovation and modernity that characterized the new century of Enlightenment. A sense of continuity exemplified in the maintaining of certain performance rituals and text conventions must be viewed alongside burgeoning elements of progressiveness that are especially evident in the genre's orchestration and musical settings. The serenata's peak period extended from the late seventeenth century through the first third of the eighteenth century; therefore, we must take a broader historical view in order to determine the ways in which legacy, adaptation and decline play out against the serenata's revealing historical trajectory.

Genre parameters

The serenata's variability, as determined by context and surrounding conditions, makes a concise and fixed definition of the genre a challenging exercise. Even where scholars have mined contemporary sources, the genre has been difficult to chart, as many of these sources treat the serenata cursorily and not without some inconsistency.[2]

Giovanni Mario Crescimbeni may be among the earliest in the eighteenth century to come up with a definition of the serenata in an Italian context and to establish how the genre worked propagandistically as political spectacle. He distinguished the serenata from related genres by its public presentation and night-time performances, highlighting the magnificence and splendour of ambassadors, princes and other important personages.[3] Implied in this definition is that the serenata was frequently held outdoors where, as Johann Mattheson suggests, 'one can use various instruments with all their full strength which would sound too violent or deafening in a room'.[4] For Mattheson, the serenata should be concerned with nothing but love, linking the genre's practice to the serenading of a lover. However, several eighteenth-century sources explain that this specific association was no longer present, as did Francesco Saverio Quadrio, who qualified that what had been the amorous

2 For a brief selection of eighteenth-century sources that define the serenata, see Michael Talbot, 'Vivaldi's Serenatas: Long Cantatas or Short Operas?', in *Venetian Music in the Age of Vivaldi* (Aldershot, 1999), pp. 68–70.
3 See 'Delle Feste musicali, e delle Cantate, e Serenate', in Giovanni Mario Crescimbeni, *Commentarj del Canonico Gio. Mario Crescimbeni Custode d'Arcadia intorno alla sua Istoria della volgar poesia* (Rome, 1702), vol. 1, p. 241.
4 For Johann Mattheson's discussion of the serenata, see *Der vollkommene Capellmeister* (Hamburg, 1739), pp. 216–17.

serenata of an earlier period evolved into a more broadly conceived form of evening entertainment.[5]

For some, the structural and generic core of the serenata had always been linked to the cantata, though a special kind of cantata, as Charles Burney explained:

> of considerable length, accompanied by a numerous band … on great occasions of festivity … But these differ essentially from what is usually meant by a cantata or monologue for a single voice, consisting of short recitatives, and two or three airs at most; as they are occasional poems in which several singers are employed; but though in dialogue, they are performed, like oratorios, without change of scene or action.[6]

Attempts to be specific aside, the elements and functions of a serenata appear to have been fluid and flexible, ranging in the eighteenth century from a simple evening form of garden entertainment to a larger and more festive political event, or as *Tafelmusik* for a banquet and, when elaborately performed, resembling opera and other staged entertainment.[7]

During the last few decades, pioneering scholarship on the serenata has led to a more nuanced understanding of its eighteenth-century definition(s).[8] Michael Talbot suggests that the serenata must be treated as a universal term applied to a number of poetic, dramatic, musical and performative parameters: 'no single feature constitutes in itself a decisive criterion of belonging or not belonging; the identity of the serenata emerges from a whole set of typical features, any one of which may be lacking in a particular work.'[9] Beyond eighteenth-century descriptions, scholars have also widened documentation

5 Francesco Saverio Quadrio, *Della storia e della ragione d'ogni poesia* (Milan, 1742), vol. 2, p. 333. Talbot carefully defines the late seventeenth- and early-eighteenth-century vocal serenata as a species of cantata, and thus distinct from the kind of love song implied by 'serenade', which is rooted in turn somewhere between art and folk music. In fact, 'serenata' does not derive from the word for evening (*la sera*), even if in practice the genre was often performed at night, but from the Italian word *sereno* (Latin *serenus*), meaning clear sky, and thus referring to its open-air performances. See Talbot, 'The Serenata in Eighteenth-Century Venice', *Royal Musical Association Research Chronicle*, 18 (1982), pp. 1–2.

6 Charles Burney, *A General History of Music from the Earliest Ages to the Present Period* (1789), ed. Frank Mercer (New York, 1935), 2 vols., vol. 2, pp. 606–7.

7 See Bernd Baselt, 'G. Ph. Telemanns Serenade *Don Quichotte auf der Hochzeit des Comacho*: Beiträge zur Entstehungsgeschichte von Telemanns letztem Hamburger Bühnenwerk', *Hamburger Jahrbuch für Musikwissenschaft*, 3 (1978), p. 92, for his reference to Christian Friedrich Hunold, the early eighteenth-century Hamburg librettist, who similarly captures the sprawling sense of the serenata's function and multi-genre associations.

8 Among the most systematic and noteworthy are Talbot, 'The Serenata in Eighteenth-Century Venice' and Thomas Griffin's study of Alessandro Scarlatti's contribution to serenata composition, 'The Late Baroque Serenata in Rome and Naples: A Documentary Study with Emphasis on Alessandro Scarlatti', PhD thesis (University of California, Los Angeles, 1983). Both authors focus their study on the repertory in a specifically designated area, although each discusses in detail the historical, functional and aesthetic definitions of the genre. I am grateful to Thomas Griffin for his comments and suggestions on various aspects of this chapter.

9 Talbot, 'Vivaldi's Serenatas', p. 72.

by combining information culled from printed librettos (a key source, as many scores did not survive), and fragmentary evidence cited in news reports (*avvisi*), official announcements (*relazione*), diaries and travel memoirs. These additional sources help to highlight the serenata's unique features.

Structurally and stylistically the serenata remained closest to the dramatic cantata; it likewise resembled the oratorio in length, sectional divisions and musical forces used. At the same time, the serenata's association with celebratory and eulogistic events allowed it to draw upon a number of non-musical elements for its presentation, endowing performances with similarities to staged opera. The serenata was not plot-driven or intended for staged action, but with its 'casts' of singers (usually two to four) it was 'dramatic' in the general, Aristotelian sense of using singers to represent characters who expressed themselves without the aid of external narration.[10] These figures were typically pastoral, allegorical, or mythological in character. Serenatas used well-known cultural tropes as symbolic references to real personages, and as ways of constructing the narrative. A serenata's pacing was often shaped by how the topical element was revealed and used as a narrative climax, typically in the form of a contest or debate between different characters who express diverging opinions until finding reconciliation, or in the form of a quest narrative in which each character discovers in stages the importance of the object of celebration.[11] Some serenatas explicitly revealed the individual being honoured, while others made more oblique references to him or her – for example, by providing a veiled pseudonym often as an Arcadian surname. Whatever the dramatic details of the serenata, its form was largely driven by the surrounding festivities, including their length and production value, and by the quality of local musical resources, including the number of singers and the force and variety of instrumentation. The serenata's ensemble was often its most distinguishing feature, as its propagandistic nature encouraged especially grand dimensions of orchestral accompaniment. Cities with abundant high-quality instrumentalists made such distinctive ensembles possible;[12] as a consequence,

10 See Talbot's period conception of 'dramatic', based on eighteenth-century sources, in 'The Serenata in Eighteenth-Century Venice', p. 9.

11 See Talbot, 'Vivaldi's Serenatas', pp. 77–8, for his most comprehensive discussion of the serenata's plot types.

12 We see this especially in a city like Rome, where an excess of musicians seeking employment in the papal capital's various institutions (church, chamber, theatre) made numerous highly skilled string players easy to hire. The eighteenth-century serenata was undoubtedly affected by this Roman legacy, with the rise of large-ensemble music and the prominence of string playing and virtuosity shaped by Arcangelo Corelli. On Corelli's orchestras, see Franco Piperno, 'Le orchestra di Arcangelo Corelli', in Giovanni Morelli (ed.), *L'invenzione del gusto: Corelli and Vivaldi* (Milan, 1982), pp. 42–8; see also John Spitzer and Neal Zaslaw, 'Corelli's Orchestra', in *The Birth of the Orchestra: History of an Institution, 1650–1815* (Oxford, 2004), pp. 105–36.

the core reliance on strings and continuo was increasingly augmented by wind instruments (already a trend witnessed in the late-seventeenth- and early-eighteenth-century serenata). By the mid eighteenth century the term 'serenata' had been gradually overtaken by a wholly instrumental form, now recognized as the 'serenade'. As Michael Talbot has clarified, the rise of the independent instrumental serenade coincided with the demise of the solo cantata with continuo, which allowed the term 'cantata' to be employed unambiguously by any vocal genre that used an orchestra and generally more than one singer.[13]

As much as scholars have worked to consolidate definitions of the eighteenth-century serenata, difficulties and misconceptions still remain. In part, these arise from a propensity for affiliating the serenata with a single genre, as when the serenata is equated with opera, or when it is categorized merely as a variety of cantata.[14] The tendency to view the serenata as separate from seemingly related works, such as those given the name *festa teatrale*, or *azione teatrale*, is also problematic since the serenata in actual fact has connecting points to a myriad of genre labels.[15] Among related vocal types, the serenata's multi-dimensionality was not totally unique. Other genres, intimate and spectacular, shared its adaptability to various contexts and audiences. What made the serenata distinct, however, was the extent to which it could serve a number of performance conditions. Part of this quality is explained by the serenata's historical origins.

Early on in Italy, the serenata acted as a vehicle for both musico-dramatic entertainment and socio-political expression.[16] In other regions, the serenata flourished in similar local courts where artistic talent had long been exported from Italy and where the cultural conditions of social politics favoured

13 Talbot makes this point in several of his publications on the serenata, although the most thorough explanation is found in 'The Serenata in Eighteenth-Century Venice', pp. 2, 12. His research on Venice shows that 'serenata' was the preferred term until around 1720, that from 1720 to 1760 'cantata' and 'serenata' co-exist almost equally and that soon after 1760 'serenata' drops off abruptly, a fact probably attributable to the rise of the instrumental serenade in these decades.

14 Talbot similarly argues that the serenata was neither opera nor cantata but sat uniquely at the interface between both genres. See 'Zelenka's serenata ZWV 277', in Günter Gattermann (ed.) and Wolfgang Reich (collab.), *Zelenka-Studien II. Referate und Materialien der 2. Internationalen Fachkonferenz Jan Disma Zelenka (Dresden und Prag 1995)* (Sankt Augustin, 1997), p. 218, for a tabular comparison of all three genres during the first half of the eighteenth century.

15 Talbot reminds us that several writers of serenata texts, in keeping with the custom of the period, sometimes employed a preferred term on a title page quite arbitrarily, almost in the manner of a trademark. Nevertheless, Talbot does stress the importance of regarding the serenata as a larger 'umbrella term' that encompassed a number of genre permutations, and thus disagrees with authors who try to distinguish similar genres, such as the *festa teatrale*, from the serenata. For his arguments on nomenclature, see 'The Serenata in Eighteenth-Century Venice', pp. 12–13.

16 For a consideration of the serenata's origins and early Italian development, see Griffin, 'The Late Baroque Serenata in Rome and Naples', chapter 1, pp. 1–53.

platforms such as opera and the serenata for propagandistic display.[17] Nonetheless, in every early-modern European centre, the serenata or genres of comparable function bore notable differences. As Malcolm Boyd has argued: 'whatever the similarities that exist between these genres, the nature of individual works was closely dependent on the locality and the tastes of the patron for whom they were composed.'[18] Given the serenata's well-documented local malleability, an attempt at a comprehensive survey of the genre would be difficult. It is more important to determine what the serenata's fluidity and adaptability reveals about eighteenth-century contextual issues - about musico-dramatic aesthetics, about the genre's socio-political role in this period and about the cultural conditions for the serenata's performances. This chapter does not seek to cover all geographical grounds of the serenata's eighteenth-century existence, but rather to see the serenata in a variety of practices. In what follows, I shall draw upon a broader historical understanding of the serenata, viewing its constituent elements - private, public, instrumental, vocal and operatic - as they relate to the serenata's diverse qualities and functions. Each sub-section examines several short examples that collectively disclose the variegated and transmigratory nature of the eighteenth-century serenata.

The serenata as private music

The serenata is an exemplar of eighteenth-century musical culture largely on account of its placement at the interstices of events that were grand, public and quasi-theatrical or those that were non-occasional, exclusive and more intimate in performance. Michael Talbot notes that the serenata 'was adaptable enough to incline to one side or the other without compromising its identity'.[19] One deep strain of the serenata's identity was shaped by the cantata, and more simple performance dimensions. In fact, we need only look back to seventeenth-century Italy to notice that while large, occasional musico-dramatic works with explicit political import were much in vogue, a parallel tradition of intimate

17 Vienna was one such location where the ongoing celebration of the Habsburgs' name days and birthdays, as well as diplomatic occasions, helped to maintain a continuous tradition of serenata performances. For research on the serenata in Vienna, see Herbert Seifert, 'Die Aufführungen der Wiener Opern und Serenate mit Musik von Johann Joseph Fux', *Studien zur Musikwissenschaft*, 29 (1978), pp. 9–27; Fabrizio Della Seta, 'La serenata a sei voci per Carlo VI', in Claudio Madricardo, Franco Rossi (eds.), *Benedetto Marcello: La sua opera e il suo tempo* (Florence, 1988), pp. 161–94; Dagmar Glüxam, 'Zur instrumentalen Virtuosität in der Wiener Hofkapelle 1705–1740', *Österreichische Musikzeitschrift*, 56 (2001), pp. 29–39.

18 Malcolm Boyd, 'The Italian Serenata and Related Genres in Britain and Germany. Some Observations', in Gaetano Pitarresi (ed.), *Giacomo Francesco Milano e il ruolo dell'aristocrazia nel patrocinio delle attivita musicali nel secolo XVIII* (Reggio Calabria, 2001), p. 527.

19 Talbot, 'The Serenata in Eighteenth-Century Venice', p. 31.

and private works termed 'serenatas' also existed. Although some eighteenth-century sources made a distinction between the two, the boundary between public and private, or grand versus intimate, was sometimes blurred.

What, then, distinguished the more private, intimate serenata from other dramatic cantatas? At times, very little, since generic terminology was often used imprecisely and interchangeably. Furthermore, such distinctions are difficult to determine in a musical culture that occurred in private and that mostly lacked substantial description. What little we can glean from documents or scores might best be used to capture the fluidity of the serenata's movement between private and public domains, sometimes capturing both simultaneously.

Though largely associated with outdoor performance, the serenata found a place indoors, too, in palaces as private entertainment, near the tables of grand feasts, or at the end of a meal of no particular occasion, and in social gatherings in salons. It is often quite difficult to reconstruct from scores alone how a serenata may have been used, requiring further documentation – libretti, dedications, or other narrative and visual descriptions – to understand a serenata's context and audience. Take, for example, Alessandro Scarlatti's *Venere, Amore e Ragione* (*c.* 1706), where diminutive proportions and use of obbligato winds or string parts might suggest an intimate setting. As we know from similarly scored Italian serenatas, it is possible that larger orchestras also performed such works. In the case of *Venere, Amore e Ragione*, then, it is important to consider how other characteristics of the serenata may reveal possible connections to a more exclusive circle.

Scarlatti, a frequent composer for Rome's prominent musical patrons (including Cardinals Pietro Ottoboni, Benedetto Pamphili, Queen Casimira of Poland and the Marquis Francesco Maria Ruspoli), was commissioned to write not just cantatas, but serenatas set to Arcadian texts, as in *Venere, Amore e Ragione*, a libretto believed to have been composed by Silvio Stampiglia, a famed poet and founding member of the Academy of Arcadians.[20] Serenatas that drew on allegorical qualities of Arcadian themes enabled the artful expression of ideologies, and would have been especially appropriate for the society's frequent outdoor summer gatherings, where we gather that pastoral poetry and musical settings were recited or performed in literary contests or as entertainment.[21]

20 For a more recent treatment of the poetic and compositional background of this work, see Griffin, 'Historical Introduction' to *Alessandro Scarlatti, Venere, Amore e Ragione, Serenata a 3*, ed. Judith L. Schwartz (Madison, WI, 2000), pp. ix–xviii.

21 In several publications Crescimbeni describes the regular meetings of the Arcadians, known as 'Olympiads'; see especially 'Notizie d'Arcadia', appended to the conclusion of *La Bellezza della volgar poesia* (Rome, 1700), pp. 217–30. Though the word or phrase 'cantare' or 'cantare nel Bosco Parrasio' comes up frequently in both archival and published Arcadian documents, it is somewhat more difficult to determine to what extent the *singing* of poetry took place.

In *Venere, Amore e Ragione*, Cupid and Reason try to convince Venus that Cupid, who has been fraternizing with nymphs and shepherds of the Seven Hills of Rome, is better off for having learned (from the Romans) that adopting reason as a guide is preferable to being directed by sensuality. The merging of love with reason is celebrated in the 'terzetto', which concludes the serenata's first part, pointing to a number of model shepherds who have done the same and are praised in song. It is possible that allusions to iconic Arcadian pastoral names – Nice, Clori, Dorinda, Amarilli, Irene and Fileno – were also references to specific Roman noblewomen and literati for whom such entertainment was often intended.[22] However, the private settings of such serenatas frequently lacked obvious celebration of personages. To those outside the privileged circle, references to living figures would have remained intentionally oblique.

There are several features that made a serenata like *Venere, Amore e Ragione* ideal for a private arena. Compared to a simple cantata, Scarlatti's work offered a lengthier and more elaborate dialogue between characters, more instrumental movements, and dance elements that appear at the end as part of the action.[23] For this private circle, the choice of a serenata also might have served as a critical response to public opera. In line with polemics at the turn of the eighteenth century, the serenata offered in scope and compositional procedure a close analogue to the preferred model of pastoral opera. It exemplified a style that was elegant and avoided any extreme Marinist conceits of complexity. Composers writing serenatas often favoured da capo arias with little contrast between sections, and preferred lyrical lines with conjunct or triadic writing, as well as restrained use of coloratura.[24] In this sense, the serenata's lack of a developed 'plot' was advantageous. Simplicity allowed serenata settings reminiscent of pastoral dramas to resemble an elegant conversation or debate, the kind held in learned societies or academies, and at private noble gatherings.[25]

22 Griffin speculates that Arcadian shepherds mentioned in *Venere, Amore e Ragione* were direct references to specific aristocrats in attendance. See 'The Late Baroque Serenata in Rome and Naples', p. 520.

23 Unusual for most serenatas, the character *Ragione* calls for a final dance after the trio's reconciliation. Judith Schwarz posits that such dance movements were not unlike Lullian divertissements in which a *danse chantée* followed a dance of a similar character. See 'Musical Performance and Style', in *Alessandro Scarlatti, Venere, Amore e Ragione, Serenata a 3*, p. xx.

24 While this style was most typical of Scarlatti's pastoral works associated with the Arcadians, it was not standard for all of his serenata compositions.

25 Talbot notes the importance of the early modern academy (*accademia*) to the cultivation of the serenata, as many such institutions professed a great interest in music, dramatic poetry and forms of entertainment that mirrored or suited rhetorical games and intellectual activity performed by an academy's members. For Talbot's discussion of the Accademia degli Animosi, and their influence on the serenata in Venice, see 'The Serenata in Eighteenth-Century Venice', pp. 26–7.

The serenata as public music

Though partially rooted in private courtly contexts, the eighteenth-century serenata also had deep historical links with the Renaissance and Baroque *festa*, whose public face contained ingredients such as tournaments, pageants and firework displays, all of which might conclude with a musico-dramatic performance in the form of an opera, or more often a serenata. Music and poetry formed only one part of a larger grouping of spectacular entertainment. Nevertheless, the musico-dramatic demands for attentive reception and the serenata's association with exclusive listeners could be accommodated by the *festa*'s inherent cultural divisions. Often an orientation towards the private was maintained despite the pretence of public display.

The manipulation of the *festa*'s multiple components and the serenata's position at the interface between public and private performance was especially apparent on occasions of political propaganda. In such cases, the serenata typically concluded a larger series of celebrations that traversed environments, including lively processions or firework displays in public squares, or exclusive banquets and social gatherings inside palaces. Even within the shared space of outdoor performances, the distinction between public and private access was often clearly demarcated, with invited guests favourably and strategically placed near the performance and the general populace at the periphery.[26] In this highly visible public format, the serenata could accommodate both mass audience and privileged guests, service both public *and* private consumption and maintain an important presentational tension: the serenata's cantata-like core was sometimes retained for public consumption so that a smaller, privileged audience could watch the public watching them engage with the serenata's intricate poetic and musical drama. It exploited spectacular elements to reach the lower, public orders, but demanded of elite audiences a different sort of textualism; this is quite fitting in a society in which access to cultural texts (and political authority) was highly stratified through class prerogative and protected within courtly circles.[27]

26 Some of the most spectacular public occasions with serenatas took place in Rome's many grand piazzas, but most importantly in the Piazza di Spagna in the late seventeenth and early eighteenth century. These memorialized events likely served as models for later performances elsewhere. For iconographic representations that help highlight the simultaneous privileged access and public distance from the performance, see Maurizio Fagiolo dell'Arco, *La Festa barocca. Corpus delle feste a Roma* (Rome, 1997), vol. 1, pp. 409, 512, 533, 539.

27 For a broader discussion of the political and aesthetic implications of the serenata's public–private dichotomy as viewed through Pietro Paolo Bencini's *Le gare festive in applauso alla Real Casa di Francia* (1704), see Stefanie Tcharos, 'The Serenata in Early 18th-Century Rome: Sight, Sound, Ritual, and the Signification of Meaning', *Journal of Musicology*, 23 (2006), pp. 528–68.

The sort of public *festa* especially prominent in Italy at the turn of the eighteenth century, an occasion for which a serenata could be commissioned by princes, cardinals, ambassadors and other dignitaries to celebrate monarchies, political alliances, or military victories, became a model easily exported to other European centres of courtly culture. In England, for example, the Italian model of the public serenata melded fluidly, though not uncontroversially, with other native occasional genres, such as the ode. In several respects, the English ode functioned like a serenata, commissioned by the British royal court to celebrate the King's birthday and New Year's Day celebrations. In some cases, odes came to be referred to as serenatas by immigrant musicians working in London and Dublin, even though musically and conceptually they retained their own unique character, mixing the English verse and choral tradition, traditional English song, overtures (sometimes in the French style) and Italian-styled recitative and aria forms.[28]

The most important surviving examples are by the composer William Boyce who served the royal court during the reign of King George II (1727–60) and through the early years of King George III (1760–1820). As Master of the King's Music from 1755, Boyce primarily provided music for the poet laureate whose work praised the King and his princes, though in 1743 Boyce also famously published a concert piece *Solomon* that he and his librettist, Edward Moore, entitled 'a serenata'. Some contemporaries viewed Boyce's *Solomon* as a competitive response to the dominance of the Italian serenata tradition, marking differences from that tradition rather than similarities to it.[29] Even when the serenata or ode did depart stylistically from Italianate models, their performance clearly recalled Italian serenatas, sometimes by their orchestral scoring or through the events surrounding the musical presentation. In the case of Boyce's ode, *Another Passing Year is Flown* (written to commemorate the fourteenth birthday of Prince George, Prince of Wales, on 25 May 1752), the court arranged for its performance at the Ranelagh pleasure garden in London, which was transformed into a 'Jubilee Ball in the Venetian Manner', a series of events that included a tea, a musical concert followed by fireworks, a

28 Johann Sigismund Kusser, who set many odes for the Dublin Court throughout the 1720s, appears to have had an Italian model in mind, sometimes entitling his works 'serenata', 'serenata da camera', or 'serenata teatrale'. Malcolm Boyd argues, however, that the ode was somewhat different from the serenata, as shaped by its seventeenth-century roots in the verse anthem. See 'The Italian Serenata and Related Genres in Britain and Germany', p. 516.

29 In his *Observations on the Present State of Music and Musicians* (1762), John Potter wrote of Boyce: 'His serenata of *Solomon*, is a great performance, a fine piece of composition! It has a number of beautiful strokes of genius; it is fine, it is elegant and sublime. It stares the Italians in the face, and asks them, with what justice they can claim the art of beautiful modulation alone? How delicate the airs in it, how charming the melody! Can anything be more so? Really it is almost impossible.' See Ian Bartlett and Robert Bruce, 'William Boyce's *Solomon*', *Music & Letters*, 61 (1980), p. 46.

reception with food and drink and dancing.[30] Unusually, by the standards of most serenatas and by those in Italy, Boyce's ode and the surrounding events were repeated several times in the weeks that followed, with admission charged to view the event. This may have afforded a wide range of spectators greater access to the serenata in ways truly more public than other 'public' events often turned out to be.

In addition to activities in Britain, other contexts dictated that the serenata would become an important cultural marker in eighteenth-century Europe. The events that transpired in Dresden for the 1719 union of the Saxon Prince Friedrich August III with Maria Josepha (archduchess and daughter of Joseph I, the Habsburg Emperor) are particularly revealing. The prince's father, Friedrich August II (the Strong), had been responsible for fostering a brilliant and extravagant period of cultural history in Dresden. His son's marriage was a celebration of alliance, an excuse to use music, drama, dance, spectacle and other forms of merriment in order to commemorate a significant tie between the House of Saxony and the House of Habsburg, one that would help to raise August II's rank among European powers.[31]

In light of the impending alliance with the House of Habsburg (Vienna's predominant cultural guise was Italian), August II sought the opportunity to establish Italian opera in Dresden, and in 1717 invited Johann David Heinichen from Venice to serve as one of the court Kapellmeisters, engaging an Italian opera troupe led by composer Antonio Lotti, and a retinue of famous singers and musicians. Of all events, which spanned nearly a month, Heinichen's two 1719 serenatas, *La gara degli Dei* and *Diana su l'Elba*, were among the most spectacular, more so than any opera commissioned for the events. August II planned the celebrations himself by studying previously held festivals, selecting the best qualities of Saxon and Habsburg traditions, the latter famously known for their elaborate Italianate festivities. Both serenatas rank among the most visually resplendent of the eighteenth century.[32]

30 As was common for royal odes, *Another Passing Year is Flown* was advertised in newspapers and periodicals, listing the evening's events and containing the work's text, which was by William Harvard. For quoted documents pertaining to this work and historical background, see Robert J. Bruce's 'Introduction' to the facsimiles of William Boyce, *Three Birthday Odes for Prince George*, in *Music for London Entertainment 1660–1800*, series F, vol. 4 (London, 1989), pp. ix–xiii.

31 For background on the Dresden wedding events of 1719, see Michael Walter, 'Heinichens Serenade *Diana su l'Elba* für die Dresdener Fürstenhochzeit von 1719', in Bernhard R. Appel, Karl W. Geck and Herbert Schneider (eds.), *Musik und Szene: Festschrift für Werner Braun zum 75* (Saarbrucken, 2001), pp. 103–16. On Heinichen's serenatas more generally, see Michael Marker, 'Die Serenaten von Johann David Heinichen', in Günter Fleischhauer, Wolfgang Ruf, Frieder Zschoch and Bert Siegmund (eds.), *Zur Entwicklung, Verbreitung und Ausfuhrung vokaler Kammermusik im 18. Jahrhundert* (Blankenburg, 1997), pp. 101–7.

32 See plate 1 in Heinichen, *La gara degli Dei*, ed. Michael Walter, Recent Researches in the Music of the Baroque Era, 102 (Madison, WI, 2000), pp. ix–xix and plates 1–2 in Heinichen, *Diana su l'Elba*, ed. Michael Walter, Recent Researches in the Music of the Baroque Era, 103 (Madison, WI, 2000), pp. vii–xvii.

The serenata and instrumental music

From the serenata's spectacularity, we now turn to its symbolic significance in sound. The Dresden *Hofkapelle* was already known as one of the most outstanding in Europe, with Johann Joachim Quantz noting in 1716 the orchestra's important use of mixed styles and high refinement in performance.[33] Put to use in Heinichen's compositions – as he was well regarded for his use of tone colour, instrumentation and forward-thinking style – the two serenatas highlight the virtuosity of the instrumentalists and the crucial function that instrumental music served in serenata performances in general. The pairing of instrumental timbre and virtuosity with allegorical qualities embodied by the dramatic personae, had long been a tradition in the serenata. In *La gara degli Dei*, Heinichen matches the god-like strength, skill and virtuosity of Saturn with elaborate soloistic writing for solo horn and theorbo, producing some of the serenata's longest concerto-like ritornellos. What was unusual in this case was the selection of sounds, as theorbo solos were not typical and Heinichen and Lotti were the first composers in Dresden to use the horn in their vocal works. Especially in *Diana su l'Elba*, the horn takes on greater significance through its association with hunting music, Diana's emblematic sonic symbol.[34] In fact, displaying Dresden's technical prowess in wind and brass was not just a sonic effect, but was deeply ingrained in the serenata's aesthetic and social function.

By the eighteenth century, the serenata had requisitioned instrumental music as an essential element for accommodating its acoustic needs. This was, in part, a practical response to outdoor performances encouraged by the increase in players and variety of instrumentation. In addition, there was a political imperative, as both the large number of musicians and the quality of ensemble were symbolic of an event's grandeur and a sponsor's wealth. Facilitated by the serenata's narrative strategy, music thus incorporated visual and aural elements – it was to be heard *and* to be seen. Moreover, music's manifestation as a spectacular effect helped it to remain significantly distinct from the poetic/vocal setting for which it originally served as mere 'dressing'. Reliance on allegory allowed the serenata to contain music, and to mark its delivery, as sonic symbol or even as personified agent of a character represented in the libretto.

33 See the translation of Quantz's description in *On Playing the Flute*, ed. and trans. Edward R. Reilly (London, 1966), pp. xiii–xiv.

34 Walter explains that the connection through sound imagery to hunting was especially important in these festivities as the married couple were both fond of the chase. Keeping with the theme of regal power and potency, it is not surprising that the fireworks celebration following *La gara degli Dei* was prefaced by a fanfare of sixty-four trumpets and timpani. For details see Walter, 'Introduction', in Walter (ed.), *Diana su l'Elba*, pp. ix, xii–xiii.

We can take as an example here Johann Sebastian Bach's *Der zufriedengestellte Äolus: Zerreisset, zerspringet, zertrümmert die Gruft*, BWV 205 (1725), which Bach entitled a 'dramma per musica' but which essentially functioned as a serenata as it was performed as an occasional piece, in the outdoors and unstaged.[35] In the spirit of the festivity, Bach maximized the orchestral strengths and capabilities of Leipzig's collegium musicum, writing for two large orchestras. Strength in sound, especially from the winds, was called for by Picander's light-hearted text, in which Aeolus, God of all the winds, is persuaded by Pomona, Pallas and Zephyrus to hold back the autumn winds to ensure beauty and calm for the August celebration of the birthday of Dr August Friedrich Müller, a beloved professor at Leipzig University.[36] Also typical of a serenata is the fact that this climactic turning point is enhanced musically, as Aeolus in the aria 'Zurücke, zurücke geflügelten Winde' commands the 'boisterous winds' to return to their cave, allowing only soft, warm breezes to remain. In the allegorical tradition of serenatas, Bach endows music with a double level of symbolism. The aria's opening ritornello, scored prominently for three trumpets, two horns, timpani and continuo, is both celebratory fanfare (the moment when Aeolus is convinced to celebrate this occasion), and figurative device, as the 'winds' spend the aria engaging in vigorous battle with Aeolus, who eventually usurps their fanfare, and vocally becomes a trumpet himself, taming the winds into mere sonic punctuations (see example 17.1).

Thus, the substantial opening ritornello heralds more than just celebration. The winds are Aeolus' symbolic marker. They also function as a figurative device, personified as sonic force that consequently sets 'music' *apart* from the rest of the serenata's vocal texture. In doing so, music works as the accessory special effect to adorn this poetic setting but also becomes the pivotal element for the work's symbolic interpretation.

35 Several of Bach's secular cantatas show features similar to those of serenatas. Boyd divides these works into three sub-genres: pieces written as occasional works in honour of individual patrons; similar works commemorating events in the lives of the Saxon royal family; and New Year and birthday cantatas for Prince Leopold at Cöthen. Rarely were any of these works described as 'serenatas' (sometimes called *Tafelmusik*, *Abendmusik*, dramma per musica, or just cantata), though all captured at least some aspect of serenatas, whether in their eulogistic setting, style of scoring, musical divisions, or performance outdoors. For Boyd's discussion of Bach's secular cantatas, including BWV 205 and BWV 215, *Preise dein Glüke, gesegnetes Sachsen* (1734), which was famously documented as a performance taking place in front of a general public gathered before the Apel house, with grand display of artillery spectacle, a torch procession and Bach's *Abendmusik*, see 'The Italian Serenata and Related Genres in Britain and Germany', pp. 520–7. Also see Herbert Pankratz, 'J. S. Bach and his Leipzig Collegium Musicum', *The Musical Quarterly*, 69 (1983), pp. 323–53.

36 *Zerreisset, zerspringet, zertrümmert die Gruft* is scored for three trumpets, timpani, two horns, two flutes, two oboes (one doubling on oboe d'amore), strings (including viola d'amore and bass viol) and continuo. The work was likely performed in front of Professor Müller's residence in Leipzig, on 3 August 1725.

Ex. 17.1. J. S. Bach, 'Zurücke, zurücke geflügelten Winde', from 'Zerreisset, zerspringet, zertrümmert die Gruft', BWV 205, bars 81–9

Music's ascendancy in the serenata was met with some trepidation. At the turn of the eighteenth century, we witness a gradual diminishment of the primacy of vocal music through the increased use in instrumental music of introductory sinfonie and internal ritornelli. This was not just the case for the serenata, but was a feature that can be charted across the musico-dramatic spectrum, as instrumental music, ironically, had become a fully integrated element of vocal music's narrative. However, music's emancipation from word did not come without a struggle. A dominant cultural aesthetic that placed a higher value on poetry than on music lingered on for decades into the eighteenth century. Despite the fact that instrumental music was often strongly foregrounded, and that the sinfonia or an extended ritornello took on increased independence, the signifying potential of instrumental music in this period was shaped first in musico-dramatic writings. As we see in the development of the eighteenth-century serenata, instrumental writings embedded in arias still relied on words to identify the specific nature of the emotion that musical symbols represented.[37] Yet, over time, orchestras became more skilled and more varied, and orchestral ritornellos grew in size,

37 Gloria Staffieri describes this as a 'conditioning process'. Stylizing instrumental language was a means to connect semantic labels embedded in the meaning of texts and allegories to distinct musical gestures. This helped to condition audiences in order to guarantee the absence of words in the future, as these musical gestures would help to recall a host of semantic associations cemented through this word–music relationship. See 'Arcangelo Corelli Compositore di "Sinfonie". Nuovi Documenti', in Pierluigi Petrobelli and Gloria Staffieri (eds.), *Studi Corelliani IV: Atti del Quarto Congresso Internazionale (Fusignano, 4–7 settembre 1986)*, *Quaderni della Rivista Italiana di Musicologia*, 22 (Florence, 1990), pp. 349–50.

competing or sometimes rivalling the length of vocal sections.[38] We could argue that the very tensions played out in serenatas were more broadly reflected in operatic practices in the same period. What the serenata affords, however, is an alternative site for such debates to take place, but perhaps at an exaggerated level on account of the genre's unique juxtaposition of instrumental and vocal forces, and its peculiar allegorical strategies that were heavily shaped by occasion-based performances.

The serenata and opera

Reading opera through the eighteenth-century serenata provides an opportune vantage point from which to re-view the serenata. For much of its history, serenatas were often considered miniature operas, and a significant number tipped effortlessly in the direction of staged drama. Georg Philipp Telemann's and Daniel Schiebeler's *Don Quichotte auf der Hochzeit des Comacho* (1761) was more singspiel than serenata, and Leonardo Vinci's and Pietro Metastasio's elaborate staging and costumed performance of *La contesa de' numi* (1729) closely approached opera practice of the day.[39] In some cases, the difficulty of distinguishing between opera and serenata genres tells an important story in itself.

For example, scholars have long puzzled over the performance history, function and genre identity of Handel's various settings of the Acis and Galatea myth. Perhaps the most insistent question is whether his composition, *Acis and Galatea* (HWV49a), believed to have been written at Cannons in 1718, is 'a little opera' as described at the time, or in fact more like an English masque or a serenata.[40] While research in this area has been informative, we must not overlook the elusive nature of this work's performance history and its cross-cultural and cross-historical implications. Brian Trowell contends that even if Handel's 1732 performance of the serenata, *Acis and Galatea*, for the King's Theatre had consisted of the Cannons', *Acis and Galatea*, and had not been given in costume in front of painted scenes, but had lacked entrances, exits and

38 Talbot suggests that this trend was largely shaped by the Italian style, which by the 1730s affected a growth in size and in increased segmentation of orchestral ritornellos (triggering a matching increase in the length of solo sections), and encouraged deceptive cadences to stave off the conclusion of periods, or the regular reiteration of phrases – all as 'expansionary features [that] characterize the music we call "galant" '. See 'Zelenka's serenata ZWV 277', p. 230.

39 For background on Metastasio's Viennese serenatas, see Talbot, 'Vivaldi's Serenatas'; and on Telemann's *Don Quichotte auf der Hochzeit des Comacho*, see Baselt, 'Georg Philipp Telemanns Serenade *Don Quichotte auf der Hochzeit des Comacho*'.

40 Using Winton Dean's assertion of *Acis and Galatea*'s unique chamber character as his point of departure, Brian Trowell carefully scrutinizes score copies, prints, librettos, performance announcements and descriptions to investigate this very question, and to argue that the work was primarily a serenata. See '*Acis, Galatea, and Polyphemus*: A "serenata a tre voci"?', in Nigel Fortune (ed.), *Music and Theatre: Essays in Honour of Winton Dean* (Cambridge, 1987), pp. 31–93.

extensive performed action, an Italian audience or visitor would *still* have called it a serenata.[41]

When Handel first wrote *Aci, Galatea e Polifemo* (HWV 72) for Naples in 1708, he encountered this elusive Italian occasional genre whose lack of staging was in part practical and in part ideological. In England, new conditions came to affect the composer's choices. For his first extended setting in English verse, it is possible that the work did not befit the 'serenata' title in a context where such a term was relatively unknown. However, Alexander Pope's involvement in writing the libretto, along with his *Discourse on Pastoral Poetry* from 1717, may have influenced Handel's decision to keep to simple and small forces,[42] an aesthetic orientation that mirrored the polemics he likely encountered among Italian Arcadians, whose support of the pastoral *topos* was often evoked in cantatas and serenatas. By 1732, Handel insisted that his revised piece be called a 'serenata'; the new label suited his intention to familiarize the London public with a viable alternative to opera, a dramatic work which, like his oratorios, had no stage action.

The performance history of *Acis and Galatea* recounts just one significant and convoluted example of the serenata's realization in a non-Italian context. It serves to reveal not only the multivalent potential of the serenata's identity and use, but also its ability to refract a variety of aesthetic, cultural and political debates, some new and some re-visited, debates that were all vividly situated at the intersection of genre and ritual. Clearly, the serenata's historical roots shaped this eighteenth-century moment quite considerably for Handel. In his later use, we come to understand that the serenata was decidedly *not* opera – to view the serenata merely as a substitute for opera misses a much larger and more significant history (as outlined briefly above). That the serenata showed important stylistic correspondences to opera is only part of the story. It is equally important to recognize how the larger cultural debates and historical development in musical drama were uniquely illuminated in the serenata, as its own separate and distinct genre.

The serenata's long history

For a genre so deeply rooted in a pre-Enlightenment past, the serenata's eighteenth-century trajectory begs an important question: what conditions prompted a society to *maintain* a genre intermediately positioned between the cantata and opera and intriguingly placed in relation to other genre interfaces as well? In what ways did the serenata continue to be relevant?

41 *Ibid.*, p. 46. 42 *Ibid.*, p. 84.

History provides a number of clues, as revealed in the cases outlined above. In several respects, the serenata reflected a culture that remained in the process of negotiating the move from absolutist exclusion to the emergence of the modern public state.[43] The serenata's malleability, a quality that other genres did not possess to the same degree, thus accommodated a society in transition. In each circumstance, the serenata's 'dressing' was as important as its compositional core. We see how elements – visual, textual and musical – were added or dropped to produce different experiences for different venues. This sense of layering was often fragmented into different segments, as we see with the events surrounding a serenata performed in Naples in 1702 for the celebration of King Philip's name day. In this instance, Alessandro Scarlatti's *Clori, Dorino e Amore* was performed for the King and his entourage within the confines of the Royal Palace as the gala's primary entertainment. Afterwards, though, the King exited to the balcony, to witness and be witnessed by those watching the related fireworks display in the square below.[44] The serenata's malleability also enabled it to traverse class distinctions. In some cases, it moved from merchant class to courtly spheres (rather than in the reverse direction), as witnessed with a serenata written by Johann Mattheson, *Die keusche Liebe* (1715), first for a Hamburg merchant's wedding, then as a re-texted version for a more elevated social occasion.[45]

Beneath the appearance of ritual maintenance, the serenata endured great change and mobility until the peak of its eighteenth-century development. After 1750, however, it began to wane as royalist contexts in connection with absolutist governments slowly declined. It is for this reason that works like Christoph Willibald Gluck's *Tetide* (1760) for the wedding ceremonies of Archduke Joseph and Princess Isabella of Bourbon-Parma, and Wolfgang Amadeus Mozart's *Il re pastore* (1775) written to celebrate the reception of Archduke Maxmillian, son of Empress Maria Theresa of Austria, upon his visit to the Archbishop of Salzburg, began to appear out of step with prevailing currents of European culture. In these decades, the serenata was becoming as much a relic of a passing generation as opera seria. Its effectiveness as elite propaganda and its applicability to noble contexts would soon be replaced by the less aristocratic but equally grand 'theatre' of revolutionary spectacle and emerging Romanticism.

43 Jürgen Habermas, 'Remarks on the Type of Representative Publicness', in *The Structural Transformation of the Public Sphere: An Inquiry into the Category of Bourgeois Society*, trans. Thomas Burger and Frederick Lawrence (Cambridge, MA, 1989), pp. 5–14.

44 Griffin, 'The Late Baroque Serenata in Rome and Naples', pp. 365–7.

45 Steffen Voss, 'Johann Matthesons Hochzeitsmusiken', *Hamburger Jahrbuch für Musikwissenschaft*, 18 (2001), p. 256.

Select Bibliography

Alvarez Martinez, Maria Salud. 'Una serenata de Felipe Falconi para la boda de la infanta Maria Ana Victoria'. *Revista de Musicologia*, 20 (1997), pp. 342–54

Bartlett, Ian and Robert J. Bruce. 'William Boyce's *Solomon*'. *Music & Letters*, 61 (1980), pp. 28–49

Baselt, Bernd. 'G. Ph. Telemanns Serenade *Don Quichotte auf der Hochzeit des Comacho* Beiträge zur Entstehungsgeschichte von Telemanns letztem Hamburger Bühnenwerk'. *Hamburger Jahrbuch für Musikwissenschaft*, 3 (1978), pp. 85–100

Biagi-Ravenni, Gabriella and Carolyn Gianturco. 'The Tasche of Lucca: 150 Years of Political Serenata'. *Royal Musical Association, London. Proceedings*, 111 (1984–5), pp. 45–65

Boyd, Malcolm. 'The Italian Serenata and Related Genres in Britain and Germany. Some Observations'. In Gaetano Pitarresi (ed.), *Giacomo Francesco Milano e il ruolo dell'aristocrazia nel patrocinio delle attivita musicali nel secolo XVIII*. Reggio Calabria, 2001, pp. 515–27

Brito, Manuel Carlos de. 'Portuguese–Spanish Musical Relations During the 18th Century'. In Emilio Casares Rodicio, Ismael Fernández de la Cuesta and José López-Calo (eds.), *España en la Música de Occidente. Actas del Congreso Internacional celebrado en Salamanca, 29 de octubre-5 de noviembre de 1985* (Madrid, 1987), vol. 2, pp. 133–8

Bruce, Robert J. 'Introduction'. In William Boyce, *Three Birthday Odes for Prince George*. In *Music for London Entertainment 1660–1800*, series F, vol. 4. London, 1989, pp. ix–xiii.

Burney, Charles. *A General History of Music from the Earliest Ages to the Present Period* (1789). Ed. Frank Mercer. 2 vols., New York, 1935, vol. 2

Cetrangolo, Annibale E. and Gioacchino De Padova. 'La serenata vocale tra viceregno e metropoli: Giacomo Facco dalla Sicilia a Madrid'. *Quaderni dell'IMLA* 2. Padua, 1990

Clostermann, Annemarie. 'Johann Friedrich Faschs hofische Festmusiken: Eine analytische Studie anhand der Kantata Die Gott geheiligte Freude (1722) und der Serenata Freudenbezeugung der vier Tageszeiten (1723)'. In Eitelfriedrich Thom (ed.) and Frieder Zschoch (collab.), *Johann Friedrich Fasch (1688–1758)*, vol. 1. Blankenburg, 1989, pp. 50–4

Crescimbeni, Giovanni Mario. 'Notizie d'Arcadia'. In *La Bellezza della volgar poesia*. Rome, 1700, pp. 217–30

'Delle Feste musicali, e delle Cantate, e Serenate'. In Crescimbeni, *Commentarj del Canonico Gio. Mario Crescimbeni Custode d'Arcadia intorno alla sua Istoria della volgar poesia*, vol. 1. Rome, 1702, pp. 236–41

Croll, Gerhard. 'Gluck's Serenata *Tetide* (1760) and Mozart: A Supplement to the Preface to the First Edition in the Gluck-Gesamtausgabe'. In László Vikárius and Vera Lampert (eds.), *Essays in Honor of Laszlo Somfai on his 70th Birthday: Studies in the Sources and the Interpretation of Music*. Lanham, MD, 2005, pp. 175–9

Dahms, Sibylle. 'Glucks Serenata *Le nozze d'Ercole e d'Ebe* und das Gastspiel der Mingotti-Truppe in Dresden und Pillnitz'. In Stephan Günther and John Hans (eds.), *Die italienische Oper in Dresden von Johann Adolf Hasse bis Francesco Morlacchi*. Dresden, 1988, pp. 439–49

Della Seta, Fabrizio. 'La serenata a sei voci per Carlo VI'. In Claudio Madricardo and Franco Rossi (eds.), *Benedetto Marcello: La sua opera e il suo tempo*. Florence, 1988, pp. 161–94

Fagiolo dell'Arco, Maurizio. *La Festa barocca. Corpus delle feste a Roma*, vol. 1. Rome, 1997

Fourés, Olivier and Michael Talbot. 'A New Vivaldi Cantata in Vienna'. *Informazioni e Studi Vivaldiani*, 21 (2000), pp. 99–109

Furnari, Antonello. 'I rapporti tra Handel e i duchi d'Alvito'. In Nino Pirrotta and Agostino Ziino (eds.), *Handel e gli Scarlatti a Roma*. Florence, 1987, pp. 73–8

Gemin, Massimo. 'L'Adria Festosa per Federico Cristiano: la lunga visita'. In Giovanni Morelli (ed.), *L'invenzione del gusto: Corelli and Vivaldi*. Milan, 1982, pp. 191–212

Gianturco, Carolyn M. 'The "Staging" of Genres other than Opera in Baroque Italy'. In Susan Parisi (ed.), Ernest Harriss II and Calvin M. Bower (collab.), *Music in the Theater, Church, and Villa: Essays in Honor of Robert Lamar Weaver and Norma Wright Weaver*. Warren, MI, 2000, pp. 113–29

Glüxam, Dagmar. 'Zur instrumentalen Virtuosität in der Wiener Hofkapelle 1705–1740'. *Österreichische Musikzeitschrift*, 56 (2001), pp. 29–39

Griffin, Thomas E. 'The Late Baroque Serenata in Rome and Naples: A Documentary Study with Emphasis on Alessandro Scarlatti'. PhD thesis, University of California, Los Angeles, 1983

'Alessandro Scarlatti e la serenata a Roma e a Napoli'. In Domenico Antonio D'Alessandro and Agostino Ziino (eds.), *La musica a Napoli durante il seicento: atti del convegno internazionale di studi. Napoli, 11–14 aprile 1985*. Rome, 1987, pp. 351–68

'Historical Introduction'. In Judith L. Schwartz (ed.), *Alessandro Scarlatti, Venere, Amore e Ragione, Serenata a 3*. Recent Researches in the Music of the Baroque Era, 104. Madison, WI, 2000, pp. ix–xviii

Habermas, Jürgen. *The Structural Transformation of the Public Sphere: An Inquiry into a Category of Bourgeois Society*. Trans. Thomas Burger with the assistance of Frederick Lawrence. Cambridge, MA, 1989

Heartz, Daniel. 'Haydn's *Acide e Galatea* and the Imperial Wedding Operas of 1760 by Hasse and Gluck'. In Eva Badura-Skoda (ed.), *Joseph Haydn: Bericht über den Internationalen Joseph Haydn Kongress, Wien, Hofburg, 5–12 September 1982*, Munich, 1986, pp. 332–40

Heyink, Rainer. 'Pietro Paolo Bencini, "uno de' piu scelti maestri della corte di Roma"'. *Handel-Jahrbuch*, 46 (2000), pp. 101–24

Hirschmann, Wolfgang. '"Gluckwunschendes Freuden-Gedicht": Die deutschsprachige Serenata im Kontext der barocken Casualpoesie'. In Friedhelm Brusniak (ed.), *Barockes Musiktheater im mitteldeutschen Raum im 17. und 18. Jahrhundert*. Köln, 1994, pp. 75–117

'Musikalische Festkultur im politisch-sozialen und liturgisch-religiosen Kontext: Telemanns Serenata und Kirchenmusik zur Geburt des Erzherzogs Leopold (Frankfurt 1716)'. In Peter Kahn (ed.), *Telemann in Frankfurt: Bericht uber das Symposium Frankfurt am Main, 26./27. April 1996*. Mainz, 2000, pp. 163–95

Hortschansky, Klaus. 'Ein verkapptes Orpheus-Drama? Handels Hochzeits-Serenata *Il parnasso in festa per gli sponsali di Teti e Peleo* für Prinzessin Anne und Prinz Wilhelm von Oranien (HWV 73)'. *Händel-Jahrbuch*, 49 (2003), pp. 127–46

Joly, Jacques. *Les fêtes théâtrales de Mateastase à la cour de Vienne (1731–1767)*. Clermont-Ferrand, 1978

Kagiyama, Yumi. 'Gurukku sakkyoku niyoru win serenata no yoshiki'. *Ochanomizu ongaku ronshu*, 4 (2002), pp. 22–42

Lederer, Josef-Horst. 'Zu Form, Terminologie und Inhalt von Mozarts theatralischen Serenaden'. In *Mozart und seine Umwelt. Bericht uber die Tagung des Zentralinstituts für Mozartforschung der Internationalen Stiftung Mozarteum Salzburg*. Kassel, 1979, pp. 94–101

Lindgren, Lowell. 'Il dramma musicale a Roma durante la carriera di Alessandro Scarlatti (1660–1725)'. In Bruno Cagli (ed.), *Le muse galanti: La musica a Roma nel Settecento*. Rome, 1985, pp. 35–57

Lionnet, Jean. 'Introduction'. In Jean Lionnet (ed.), *La Cappella Giulia, Volume I: I vespri nel XVIII secolo*. Lucca, 1995, pp. xxvi–xxix

Maccavino, Nicolò (ed.). *La serenata tra Seicento e Settecento: musica, poesia, scenotecnica. Atti del Convegno Internazionale di Studi (Reggio Calabria, 16–17 maggio 2003)*. Reggio Calabria, 2007

Marker, Michael. 'Die Serenaten von Johann David Heinichen'. In Günter Fleischhauer, Wolfgang Ruf, Frieder Zschoch and Bert Siegmund (eds.), *Zur Entwicklung, Verbreitung und Ausführung vokaler Kammermusik im 18. Jahrhundert*. Blankenburg, 1997, pp. 101–7

Marx, Hans Joachim. 'Eine wiederaufgefundene Serenata theatrale von John Sigismond Cousser und ihr politischer Kontext'. In Karl Heller and Andreas Waczkat (eds.), *Rudolf Eller zum Achtzigsten: Ehrenkolloquium zum 80. Geburtstag von Rudolf Eller am 9. Mai 1994*. Rostock, 1994, pp. 33–40

Handels Oratorien, Oden, und Serenaten. Göttingen, 1998

'Bemerkungen zu szenischen Aufführungen barocker Oratorien und Serenaten'. *Basler Jahrbuch für historische Musikpraxis*, 23 (1999), pp. 133–50

Oefner, Claus. 'Die "Serenata" als Eisenacher Sonderform des Musiktheaters im fruhen 18. Jahrhundert'. In Friedhelm Brusniak (ed.), *Musiktheatralische Formen in kleinen Residenzen: 7. Arolser Barock-Festspiele 1992 Tagungsbericht*. Cologne, 1993, pp. 73–80

Pankratz, Herbert. 'J. S. Bach and his Leipzig Collegium Musicum'. *The Musical Quarterly*, 69 (1983), pp. 323–53

Petrobelli, Pierluigi. '*Il re pastore*: Una serenata'. *Mozart-Jahrbuch 1984–5*, pp. 109–14

Piperno, Franco. 'Le orchestra di Arcangelo Corelli'. In Giovanni Morelli (ed.), *L'invenzione del gusto: Corelli and Vivaldi*. Milan, 1982, pp. 42–8

Quadrio, Francesco Saverio. *Della storia e della ragione d'ogni poesia*, vol. 2. Milan, 1742

Rushton, Julian. 'Mozart and Opera Seria'. In Simon P. Keefe (ed.), *The Cambridge Companion to Mozart*. Cambridge, 2003, pp. 147–55

Schmalzriedt, Siegfried (ed.). *Ausdrucksformen der Musik des Barock: Passionsoratorium, Serenata, Rezitativ*. Laaber, 2002

Schwarz, Judith L. 'Musical Performance and Style'. In Alessandro Scarlatti, *Venere, Amore e Ragione, Serenata a 3*, ed. Schwartz. Recent Researches in the Music of the Baroque Era, 104. Madison, WI, 2000, pp. xix–xxii

Seifert, Herbert. 'Die Aufführungen der Wiener Opern und Serenate mit Musik von Johann Joseph Fux'. *Studien zur Musikwissenschaft*, 29 (1978), pp. 9–27

Spitzer, John and Neal Zaslaw. *The Birth of the Orchestra: History of an Institution, 1650–1815*. Oxford, 2004

Staffieri, Gloria. 'Arcangelo Corelli Compositore di "Sinfonie". Nuovi Documenti'. In Pierluigi Petrobelli and Gloria Staffieri (eds.), *Studi Corelliani IV: Atti del Quarto Congresso Internazionale (Fusignano, 4–7 settembre 1986)*. Florence, 1990, pp. 335–58

Talbot, Michael. 'The Serenata in Eighteenth-Century Venice'. *Royal Musical Association Research Chronicle*, 18 (1982), pp. 1–50

'Zelenka's serenata ZWV 277'. In Günter Gattermann (ed.) and Wolfgang Reich (collab.), *Zelenka-Studien II. Referate und Materialien der 2. Internationalen Fachkonferenz Jan Disma Zelenka (Dresden und Prag 1995)*. Sankt Augustin, 1997, pp. 217–41

'Vivaldi's Serenatas: Long Cantatas or Short Operas?'. In Talbot, *Venetian Music in the Age of Vivaldi*. Aldershot, 1999, pp. 67–96

'Mythology in the Service of Eulogy: The Serenata *Andromeda liberata (1726)*'. In Metoda Kokole, Barbara Murovec, Marjeta Sasel Kos and Michael Talbot (eds.), *Mediterranean Myths from Classical Antiquity to the Eighteenth Century/Mediteranski miti od antikle do 18. Stoletja*. Ljubljana, 2006, pp. 131–61

Talbot, Michael and Paul Everett. 'Homage to a French King'. In Talbot and Everett (eds.), Antonio Vivaldi, *Due serenate*. Milan, 1995, pp. ix–lxxxvii

Tcharos, Stefanie. 'The Serenata in Early 18th-Century Rome: Sight, Sound, Ritual, and the Signification of Meaning'. *Journal of Musicology*, 23 (2006), pp. 528–68

Thom, Eitelfriedrich. 'Einige Bemerkungen zum Vokalschaffen von Johann Friedrich Fasch am Beispiel der Serenata von 1723 Freuden-Bezeugung der Vier Tages-Zeiten'. In Thom (ed.), *Johann Friedrich Fasch (1688–1758)*. Blankenburg, 1984, pp. 44–51

Trowell, Brian. '*Acis, Galatea, and Polyphemus*: A "serenata a tre voci"?'. In Nigel Fortune (ed.), *Music and Theatre. Essays in Honour of Winton Dean*. Cambridge, 1987, pp. 31–93

Vitali, Carlo and Antonello Furnari; Juliane Riepe (trans.). 'Händels Italienreise: Neue Dokumente, Hypothesen und Interpretationen'. *Göttinger Händel-Beiträge*, 4 (1991), pp. 41–66

Voss, Steffen. 'Johann Matthesons Hochzeitsmusiken'. *Hamburger Jahrbuch für Musikwissenschaft*, 18 (2001), pp. 233–56

Walsh, Thomas Joseph. *Opera in Dublin 1705–1797. The Social Scene*. Dublin, 1973

Walter, Michael. 'Introduction'. In Johann David Heinichen, *La gara degli Dei*, and *Diana su l'Elba*, ed. Walter. Recent Researches in the Music of the Baroque Era, vols. 102, 103. Madison, WI, 2000, vol. 102, pp. ix–xix; vol. 103, pp. vii–xvii

'Heinichens Serenade *Diana su l'Elba* für die Dresdener Fürstenhochzeit von 1719'. In Bernhard R. Appel, Karl W. Geck and Herbert Schneider (eds.), *Musik und Szene: Festschrift für Werner Braun zum 75*. Saarbrucken, 2001, pp. 103–16

Windzus, W. *Georg Friedrich Händel: Aci, Galatea e Polifemo, Cantata von 1708; Acis and Galatea, Masque von 1718; Acis and Galatea, italienisch-englische Serenata von 1732: Kritischer Bericht im Rahmen der Hallischen Händel-Ausgabe*. Hamburg, 1979

Private music in public spheres: chamber cantata and song

BERTA JONCUS

The eighteenth-century secular cantata confronts us with a nest of paradoxes. Though conceived at the beginning of the century as a kind of poetry, the cantata had for decades before been Italy's dominant type of vocal chamber music. Though chamber music, the cantata shared with opera its use of alternating recitatives and arias for solo voice with continuo accompaniment. Though from 1700 bound up with particular social practices of the Italian literati, once disseminated abroad after 1700 the cantata merged and competed with indigenous chamber song – in the process becoming an 'umbrella term' for a wide range of musical forms, some of which were extremely popular. Though once so fêted, cantata music is virtually unknown to listeners today. This study will follow the chamber cantata from its birthplace in Italy through its absorption in France, England and Germany, tracking its metamorphoses as determined by local conditions of production and pre-existing traditions of song, and identifying the contributions of the genre's chief exponents.

The legacy of the Accademia degli Arcadi

From around 1630, the secular cantata superseded chamber song and the madrigal in Italy.[1] Although the form of the cantata changed around 1700, patterns in patronage and production followed those of the previous century. Cantatas were composed for an accademia or other privileged social forum, whose invited members shared views on philosophy, aesthetics and artistic trends. The term 'accademia' could carry four separate meanings: a fellowship under one patron or more; a gathering of fee-paying (traditionally male) members promoting current ideas;[2] a meeting featuring musical performances

1 Gloria Rose, 'The Italian Cantata of the Baroque Period', in Wulf Arlt *et al.* (eds), *Gattungen der Musik in Einzeldarstellungen. Gedenkschrift Leo Schrade* (Bern and Munich, 1973), pp. 655–77.

2 Women are absent from the 'Indice degli Arcadi', in Giovanni Mario Crescimbeni, *Le vite degli Arcadi illustri* (Rome, 1708–14), 3 vols. Describing the Accademia degli Arcadi, he refers to female participants generically ('Ninfe'), rather than by name.

and discussion; and the building where such meetings might take place.[3] Cantatas were used to expound on a proposed topic – usually love – set to music by house or hired musicians, though academy members might also participate. To celebrate current events, such as birthdays and marriages, patrons also sponsored occasional cantatas or 'serenatas' (discussed in chapter 17 of this volume). Similarly, the allegorical moral cantata, such as Handel's *Il Trionfo del Tempo e del Disinganno*, formed an independent genre related to the sacred cantata.[4]

Cardinal Pietro Ottoboni's circle in Rome was an important locus for the development of the secular chamber cantata from 1700. Ottoboni was a Venetian *arriviste* who, with the aid of his great-uncle Pope Alexander VIII, sought to replace the recently deceased Princess Christina of Sweden as Rome's leading patron of the arts. Appointed cardinal and vice-chancellor of the church in 1689, he resided in the Cancelleria, where he held court and housed a prestigious art collection (inherited from his great-uncle) and library (taken over from Princess Christina). Ottoboni drew into his entourage celebrated musicians whom the Princess had supported, such as Arcangelo Corelli, Bernardo Pasquini, Alessandro Scarlatti, Filippo Amadei and the castrato and maestro di cappella of the Sistine Chapel (1710–14) Andrea Adami da Bolsena, who became Ottoboni's personal friend. Adami da Bolsena helped organize musical performances for the Cardinal and his circle.[5]

Ottoboni also followed the Princess in co-founding an academy. Created in 1690, the Accademia degli Arcadi was a literary society that aimed to cultivate simplicity and naturalness in the Italian language. Its rejection of *seicentismo* – extravagance and superfluity in expression – in favour of a *buon gusto* in argument and practice was most influential in the poetry that it spawned.[6] Other literary academies quickly re-styled themselves as 'Arcadians', while 'colonies' – academies declaring allegiance to the Accademia degli Arcadi – proliferated. Giovanni Mario Crescimbeni, one of Italy's first literary historians, reported that in twenty years membership had grown to 1,300, and that 114 associated academies existed outside Rome.[7]

The cantata proved a pliant means for animating poetry created for and by academies and patrons. Cognoscenti demanded both music in which to clothe

3 Michael Talbot, 'Musical Academies in Eighteenth-Century Venice', in *Venetian Music in the Age of Vivaldi* (Aldershot, 1999), pp. 21–66.

4 Carolyn M. Gianturco, '*Il trionfo del tempo e del disinganno*: Four Case-Studies in Determining Italian Poetic–Musical Genres', *Journal of the Royal Musical Association*, 119 (1994), pp. 43–59.

5 Hans Joachim Marx, 'Die Musik am Hofe Pietro Kardinal Ottobonis unter Arcangelo Corelli', *Analecta musicologica*, 5 (1968), pp. 104–77.

6 This taste was visible in Ottoboni's art projects inside and outside his home. Edward J. Olszewski, 'The Enlightened Patronage of Cardinal Pietro Ottoboni (1667–1740)', *Artibus et Historiae*, 23/45 (2002), pp. 139–65.

7 George E. Dorris, *Paolo Rolli and the Italian Circle in London 1715–1744* (The Hague and Paris, 1967), p. 30.

and dramatize highly prized poetry, and demonstrations of the poetry's power to move listeners in performance. More discourse than genre, the poetry and music of the Accademia degli Arcadi – created sometimes in extempore – constructed an idealized realm in which participants could enact 'Olympic games', supported by music.[8] Such 'games' included competitions between authors; in one, 'Tirsi' (the lawyer Giambattista Felice Zappi) and 'Terpandro' (Alessandro Scarlatti) attempted to outbid each other in a contest between poetic and musical invention:

> No sooner had Tirsi finished his recital [of poetry] than Terpandro ... began to transcribe the verses recited, with the music thereto ... the souls of those present received of them so great delight that they not only obliged the singer to repeat the song again and again but also urged both poet and musician to display their skill afresh ... their contention was so close that scarce had the one finished repeating the last line of the new air than the other ended the last stave of his music.[9]

Although opera provided space for a similar dynamic, the chamber cantata differed from opera by ruminating about private passion – love. Typically the solo singer would occupy the perspective either of the third-person narrator or of the lovelorn first-person protagonist, both of whose affective expression was mediated and constrained by accepted practices in decorum, literature and music. An obsessive revisiting of the tropes of Arcadian love – the amorous longings of shepherds, shepherdesses, or mythological figures – fed seemingly on a tension between the desire to explore love outside social imperatives and the social imperative of honouring or revitalizing convention. This tension was reflected in the cantata's twinned viewpoints, shifting between the socially responsible narrator–poet and the socially innocent shepherd.

The Academy enhanced the excitement of pitting passion against restraint by merging the member–poet's identity with that of an Arcadian figure, ruling that every member adopt a pastoral name to be used at meetings. This made it possible for imaginative play to subvert social responsibility, as for instance in George Frideric Handel's cantatas, where homoerotic fantasy found licensed expression.[10] The literary gentleman Giuseppe Baretti observed:

> It is impossible to conceive the eagerness with which this whimsical scheme of turning all sorts of men into imaginary shepherds was adopted both in Rome

8 'Olinto [Francesco Maria Ruspoli] spoke thus to the nymphs ... you will see thus today renewed the true Olympic games ... from three sides the sweetest melody resounded on rustic instruments, over one of which Protico [Bernardo Pasquino] presided, over another Terpantro [Alessandro Scarlatti] and over the third the admirable Arcomelo [Arcangelo Corelli] famous *maestros* in the art of playing and of music. Meanwhile the contestants were admitted, stimulated more by the glory than the subtlety of the playing.' Giovanni Mario Crescimbeni, *L'Arcadia* (Rome, 1708), pp. 267–8. (My translation.)

9 Crescimbeni, *L'Arcadia*, p. 289. Cited in Edward J. Dent, *Alessandro Scarlatti: His Life and Works*, rev. edn. with preface and additional notes by Frank Walker (London, 1960), p. 90.

10 Ellen T. Harris, *Handel as Orpheus: Voice and Desire in the Chamber Cantatas* (Cambridge, MA, 2001).

Illustration 18.1. Pier Leone Ghezzi, Misc. MS. 166, folio 49r; Alessandro Scarlatti, *Cantate*, Gilmore Music Library, Yale University.

> and out of Rome: and how the inflammable imaginations of my countrymen were fired by it! ... Every body who had the least knack for poetry was metamorphosed into a shepherd.[11]

By indulging passions through an Arcadian persona while containing them through the sophistication of their expression, cantatas offered endless scope for re-inventing personae, an act commemorated in cantata manuscripts illuminated by Pier Leone Ghezzi who depicted Roman nobility as pastoral figures (see ills. 18.1, 18.2, 18.3).

Poetry dictated the cantata's musical form. Cantata poets developed what would become conventions of dramma per musica librettos: unrhymed mixed

11 Giuseppe Marc'Antonio Baretti, *An Account of the Manners and Customs of Italy* (London, 1768), 2 vols., vol. 1, pp. 255–7. Cited in Michael Talbot, *The Chamber Cantatas of Antonio Vivaldi* (Woodbridge and Rochester, NY, 2006), p. 40.

Illustration 18.2. Pier Leone Ghezzi, Misc. MS. 166, folio 53r; Alessandro Scarlatti, *Cantate*, Gilmore Music Library, Yale University.

verses of seven- or eleven-syllable lines (*versi sciolti*) and arias divided into two semistrophes of even-number syllables, varied endings and regular rhyme schemes.[12] Musical components came also to be shared with opera. Most importantly, the ostinato bass and strophic repetition that had characterized seventeenth-century cantatas receded. Basso ostinato yielded to basso continuo that not only progressed harmonically but could also share motivic material with the vocal line or, if the cantata was *con strumenti*, with accompanying instruments, including the newly popular obbligato line. The recitative became sharply differentiated from the aria sections to create separate movements. Alternating recitative/aria sections grew in length and diminished in number, with R–A–R–A or A–R–A structures becoming common, although this varied considerably depending on poet, composer and the chosen theme.

12 A verse line could conclude with a stressed followed by an unstressed syllable ('plain' line), a seemingly stressed syllable (a 'truncated' line in which the final unstressed syllable is suppressed) or two unstressed syllables ('sliding' or *sdrucciolo* line). Talbot, *The Chamber Cantatas of Antonio Vivaldi*, pp. 33–7.

Illustration 18.3. Pier Leone Ghezzi, Misc. MS. 166, folio 77r; Alessandro Scarlatti, *Cantate*, Gilmore Music Library, Yale University.

Those cantatas that eschewed Arcadian themes to take up stories from classical mythology or history (so-called 'subject cantatas') were much longer and fewer. The cantata was usually anchored in a home key that opened and closed the work, although exceptions to this – most notably by Alessandro Scarlatti, Handel and Giovanni Bononcini – are legion. Minimum instrumental forces were typically violin (*colle parte* if without an independent part), harpsichord and cello.

As in opera, the soprano voice (castrati or female) dominated; alto and bass voices occupied composers less and the tenor voice almost never. The ternary da capo aria (ABA), although also a component of earlier cantatas, came to dominate aria writing; A and B sections lengthened, grew in contrast, and the A section became the focal point of writing through text repetition. The seventeenth-century cavata – an arioso passage in the recitative elaborated through fughetta writing – gradually disappeared.[13] Melismatic, bravura

13 Colin Timms, 'The Cavata at the Time of Vivaldi', in Antonio Fanna and Giovanni Morelli (eds.), *Nuovi studi vivaldiani: edizione e cronologia critica delle opere* (Florence, 1989), pp. 451–78.

writing prevailed, as did sequential repetition; the bass line differentiated itself from the melodic line through its angularity, more rapid motion, and probably its texture, although instrumentation was usually unspecified. Composers adopted *secco recitative* and the delayed instrumental cadence in which the voice resolves prior to the bass.

Cantata composers modulated boldly in recitative or arioso sections, because in the 'judgement of connoisseurs' the cantata's recitative should 'touch the heart' more than the recitative of other genres.[14] Following a recitative, harmonic rhythm slowed in the cantata aria and progressions related to the aria's home key. After *c.* 1710 the ritornello regularly functioned as in opera: it framed the aria's three sections, exposed thematic material, established tonal areas and introduced or concluded with the melody's material. Cantata arias, more frequently than those in opera, tended to open with a *devise*, a term coined by the nineteenth-century musicologist Hugo Riemann. There were two types of *devise*: the 'false start', in which the voice interrupts and repeats the opening instrumental ritornello, and the 'contrasting start', in which the interrupting vocal phrase differs from the opening ritornello.[15] An aria by Bononcini from his *Cantata e Duetti* (1721) shows the first type of *devise* opening (example 18.1).

The Accademia degli Arcadi not only helped to establish poetic models but also nurtured the genre's most prolific composer, Alessandro Scarlatti, who wrote most of his roughly 800 cantatas for this circle. Scarlatti was prized for the complexity of his counterpoint, the daring of his harmonies, the sophistication with which he reflected words in music and the beauty of his melodies. Other composers, while less prolific, contributed uniquely to the genre: Benedetto Giacomo Marcello, a nobleman whose complex 'subject cantatas' were admired into the following century,[16] Antonio Caldara, who cultivated cantatas for the bass as well the soprano voice,[17] Francesco Gasparini, whose writing for concertized instruments contradicted the *con strumenti* practices of Ottoboni's court,[18] Agostino Steffani, who focused on duet rather than solo cantatas,[19] Tomaso Albinoni, who fused pre- with post-1700 cantata

14 Pier Francesco Tosi, *Observations on the Florid Song* (1702), trans. John E. Galliard (London, 1742), p. 67. Cited in Edwin Hanley, 'Alessandro Scarlatti's *cantate da camera*: A Bibliographical Study', PhD thesis (Yale University, 1963), p. 2.

15 For detailed analysis of the cantata's stylistic features, see Talbot, *The Chamber Cantatas of Antonio Vivaldi*, pp. 44–60.

16 Eleanor Selfridge-Field, 'Marcello's Music: Repertory vs. Reputation', in Claudio Madricardo and Franco Rossi (eds.), *Benedetto Marcello: la sua opera e il suo tempo* (Florence, 1988), pp. 205–22.

17 Monica Centanni, '"Delirante, disprezzato, deluso, accesso amante": variazioni su temi classici in alcune cantate inedite di Antonio Caldara', *Musica e storia*, 7/2 (1999), pp. 403–45.

18 Alberto Cavalli, 'Le cantate opera prima di Francesco Gasparini', *Chigiana*, 25/5 (1968), pp. 200–1.

19 Colin Timms, *Polymath of the Baroque: Agostino Steffani and His Music* (New York, 2003), pp. 264–305, 334–40.

Ex. 18.1. Giovanni Battista Bononcini, 'Misero Pastorello', opening of first aria, in Bononcini, *Cantate e Duetti* (London, 1721), pp. 83–4.

writing,[20] Antonio Vivaldi, whose pregnant themes and active bass lines contrasted with cantata writing elsewhere[21] and, most famously, Handel, who produced a wealth of Italian cantatas that he mined throughout his later career.[22] So vast and varied is the Italian cantata repertory that modern scholars have declared it impossible to present a synoptic view of this music.[23]

Cantatas circulated largely in manuscripts produced quickly, and in staggering numbers, by scribes. 'Collections' consisted of single manuscripts sewn together and seem to have aimed to preserve a composer's output, a singer's repertory or selected performances.[24] Judging by the contents of this material

20 Michael Talbot, 'Albinoni's Solo Cantatas', *Soundings*, 5 (1975), pp. 9–28.
21 Talbot, 'Albinoni's Solo Cantatas', pp. 18–19.
22 Ellen T. Harris, '"Cantate, que me veux-tu?" or: Do Handel's Cantatas Matter?', in Melania Bucciarelli and Berta Joncus (eds.), *Music as Social and Cultural Practice: Essays in Honour of Reinhard Strohm* (Woodbridge and Rochester, NY, 2007), pp. 159–84.
23 Colin Timms, 'The Italian Cantata since 1945: Progress and Prospects', in Francesco Fanna and Michael Talbot (eds.), *Cinquant'anni di produzioni e consumi della musica dell'eta di Vivaldi: 1947–1997* (Florence, 1998), p. 75 and Teresa M. Gialdroni, 'Bibliografia della cantata da camera italiana (1620–1740 ca.)', *Le fonti musicali in Italia*, 4 (1990), pp. 31–131.
24 Michael Talbot, *Benedetto Vinaccesi: A Musician in Brescia and Venice in the Age of Corelli* (Oxford, 1994), pp. 156–60.

and related manuscripts, after 1735 opera arias or excerpts began to replace cantatas in chamber vocal performances, with 'song collections' typically combining cantatas and arias.[25] By 1760 the nature of accademia sociability and music-making had changed. Theorist Giorgio Antoniotto reported that cantatas were 'performed only by ladies of quality, and sometimes by young lords, in which assembly are not admitted the professors of music'. Among these ladies were 'not only many excellent singers but also composers'.[26] Writing in the early nineteenth century, the nobleman Giovanni Rossi divided Venetian academies into those of select and open membership, explaining that the latter permitted nobles, priests and ordinary people to co-mingle.[27] The music of these forums has yet to be studied.

Harmonizing taste: the cantata and song of France

In France, the eighteenth-century cantata was characterized by self-consciousness, rather than the idealized desire of its Italian model. Initially, to import the cantata was to stake out a territory removed from court-endorsed musical styles; later, the genre's French composers claimed to unify French and Italian taste. The cantata was also charged with an aim traditionally linked to the salon: the cultivation of politeness. Through domestic music-making, the cantata became gradually intertwined with a concurrent flourishing of French song. Print circulation worked together with public concerts to transform the cantata from a sophisticated hybrid into a popular kind of music that after 1760 devolved into the truncated form of the *cantatille*.

As the power of Louis XIV waned during the late seventeenth century, taste for Italian music among the nobility flourished in implied opposition to the King's bias towards 'native' styles of composition.[28] The most important early patron of the cantata in France was the King's nephew Philippe, Duc d'Orléans (later Prince Regent), whose real and alleged libertinism stood in stark relief to the piety of the aging King. Philippe cultivated Italian music by hiring Italian and Italian-trained musicians, commissioning Italianate works, collecting Italian music, and composing after the Italian manner.[29] He played harpsichord, flute

25 Reinhard Strohm, 'Hasse, Scarlatti, Rolli', *Analecta musicologica*, 15 (1975), pp. 220–57.

26 Giorgio Antoniotto, *L'arte armonico* (London, 1760), 2 vols. Cited in Talbot, *The Chamber Cantatas of Antonio Vivaldi*, p. 38.

27 ' … dove e nobili e preti mescevansi coi diversi ordini delle persone …'. Giovanni Rossi, 'Storia de' costumi e delle leggi de' Veneziani' (MS, n.d.). Cited in Talbot, 'Musical Academies in Eighteenth-Century Venice', p. 29.

28 Donald James Fader, 'The "Cabale du Dauphin", Campra and Italian Comedy: The Courtly Politics of French Musical Patronage around 1700', *Music & Letters*, 86 (2005), pp. 380–413.

29 Donald James Fader, 'Musical Thought and Patronage of the Italian Style at the Court of Philippe II, Duc d'Orléans (1674–1723)', PhD thesis (Stanford University, 2000).

and viol, studied engraving and spoke several languages. During his military campaign in Italy 1706–7, Philippe may have commissioned the first cantatas in French by composers of Italian cantatas, including Handel.[30] The concentration in his retinue of France's earliest and most important cantata composers – Jean-Baptiste Morin, Nicolas Bernier, Jean-Baptiste Stuck (known as 'Batistin') – attest to his seminal role in cultivating a native version of this imported genre. Lower down the social scale, the domestic music-making of the Parisian parliamentarian Hilaire Rouillé du Coudray independently brought the cantata to France at around the same time. In a report attributed to Voltaire, du Coudray's mistress Marie de Louvencourt possessed a beautiful voice for which Nicolas Bernier wrote 'the first' French cantatas – Bernier's works carried no date – to words by her friend, Jean-Baptiste Rousseau.[31]

As in Italy, poetic rather than musical innovations stimulated cantata composition, but in France the poetry aimed to educate rather than entrance. Jean-Baptiste Rousseau, whose cantata *livrets* pre-dated the compositions for the Duc d'Orléans, articulated this goal. Basing his cantatas on allegorical myths, Rousseau claimed to have 'gained' what Italian cantatas had 'lost': 'the soul or moral' of the airs.[32] Sébastien de Brossard emphasized that 'in choosing subjects ... nothing [should] be against good morals. One may well join agreeableness with utility ... they [cantatas] are not less instructive than diverting.'[33]

As he himself pointed out, Rousseau created the model for later cantatas: a survey of cantatas published from 1706 to 1740 shows remarkable continuity in their subjects – Orpheus, Medea, Circe, Piramus and Thisbe, among others – and in their writing conventions.[34] Tales were mythological and typically narrated in the past tense, concluding with a lesson about love. Myths sat alongside other types of poetry – anacreontic, pastoral, or occasional – but whatever the subject, the French cantata *livret* diverged sharply from its Italian

30 Along with Handel, Francesco Mancini and Pietro Antonio Fiocco composed cantatas to French texts before 1710. Jerome Dorival, 'André Campra et la cantate française', in Jean Lionnet (ed.), *Le Concert des Muses: Promenade musicale dans le baroque français* (Paris, 1997), pp. 322–3.

31 This report appeared in 'Vie de M. J.-B. Rousseau (1738)', and was published in the twenty-second volume of Voltaire's complete works (1869). Cited in Manuel Couvreur, 'Marie de Louvencourt, librettiste des cantates françoise de Bourgeois et de Clérambault', *Revue belge de musicologie/Belgisch tijdschrift voor muziekwetenschap*, 44 (1990), pp. 28–9.

32 'I realized after having written some [Italian-style cantatas] that the poetry had lost what the music had gained.' Preface to Jean-Baptiste Rousseau, *Œuvres diverses du Sieur R.*** (Paris, 1712), pp. xxiii–xxiv. This passage, taken from a 1743 edition of Rousseau's works, is translated in David Tunley, *The Eighteenth-Century French Cantata*, 2nd edn. (Oxford, 1997), p. 18.

33 'En choisissant des sujets ... du moins qui n'ayent rien de contraire aux bonnes moeurs ... qu'elles ne sont mois Instructives que divertissantes.' Sébastien de Brossard, 'Dissertation sure cette espece [*sic*] de concert qu'on nomme Cantate', 'Meslanges et extraits relatifs à l'histoire de la musique', *Fr-Pn* N.a. 5269, f. 75 v.

34 This assessment is based on a survey of editions in the seventeen-volume facsimile reprint series, *The Eighteenth-Century French Cantata*, ed. with commentary by David Tunley (New York and London, 1990–1).

counterpart by representing experience and mediating its meaning, rather than inhabiting an Arcadian persona. A closer parallel to the Italian cantata could be found in French poetic structures: free metric and rhyming schemes were used in recitative sections, while the A and B sections of the air consisted of two *quatrains* that formed one strophe of *huitain* verse.[35]

Early French cantata composers commented on how they adapted Italian taste. In his preface to perhaps the earliest French cantata (1706), Morin explained that he strove 'to retain the sweetness of our French style of melody, but with greater variety in the accompaniments and employing those tempos and modulations characteristic of the Italian cantata'.[36] For his part, Batistin claimed to have safeguarded 'the genius of each language' in 'joining the style of Italian music to French words'.[37] André Campra explained his method of cantata writing as one that perpetuated French operatic recitative – which he considered optimal – while exploring the new fashion for the cantata.[38]

Until mid-century, certain Italian forms persisted: the alternating recitative and da capo aria movements, usually in six parts, the *devise* opening, the ritornello principal, the anticipation of melody by the continuo, the aria's steady harmonic rhythm, the harmonic patterns that determined a vocal line, the obbligato writing (primarily for violin or flute) and the bravura display. As in Italy the majority of compositions were for solo soprano, with some duos and trios; unlike in Italy, however, composers intended that tenors should also perform these works.[39]

Yet these cantatas sound unmistakably French, because the melodic writing remained steeped in French tradition. Leaps, step-wise motion, lack of motives and an avoidance of text repetition perpetuated the aesthetic of *douceur*. In airs, melodic fragments articulated prosody instead of structuring musical statements through sequential treatment, as in Italian arias. In recitative, composers adapted Italian methods to accommodate the traditional drive to reflect scansion: the ever-shifting time signatures of Lully became a bass line of chords which, although held, moved more rapidly than in Italian music to highlight differences in syllables (short, medium, long). Like Campra, other

35 Greer Garden, 'Poetic Design and Musical Structure in Campra's Cantata Airs', *Music & Letters*, 78 (1997), pp. 26–8. Garden surveys the cantatas of Morin, Bernier, Batistin and André Campra.

36 Preface to Jean-Baptiste Morin, *Cantates françoises à une et deux voix* (1706); cited in Tunley, *The Eighteenth-Century French Cantata*, p. 47.

37 Preface to *Cantatas of Jean-Baptiste Stuck (Batistin) (1680–1755): Cantates françoises à voix seule, book 1 (1706)*, in Tunley (ed.), *The Eighteenth-Century French Cantata* (New York and London, 1990), vol. 4.

38 'Cantatas having become fashionable, I have consented … to let the public have some of my own … Above all, I have striven to retain the beauty of our melody, of our expression, and of our kind of recitative, which according to my opinion is the best.' Preface to *Cantatas of André Campra (1660–1744): Cantates françoises, book 1 (1708)*, in Tunley (ed.), *The Eighteenth-Century French Cantata*, vol. 2.

39 David Tunley, 'The French Cantata in Performance', *Eighteenth-Century Studies*, 8 (1974), pp. 47–55.

composers – notably Jean-Philippe Rameau, Louis-Nicolas Clérambault and André Cardinal Destouches – carefully safeguarded Lullian tenets of recitative composition. Music generally reflected, rather than obscured, the caesuras and conclusions of verse lines. *Devise* openings, instead of being fragments, were often self-contained statements. Extremes of tempo were avoided, *notes inégales* appeared in middle or slow tempos, and *agréments* (embellishments) and cadential gestures, particularly the *cadence fermée* – an extended appoggiatura on the penultimate tone, a trill and an anticipation of the final tone – remained *de rigueur*.

Critical commentary identified Bernier, Batistin, Campra, Thomas-Louis Bourgeois, Élisabeth Jacquet de La Guerre, Jean-Baptiste de Bousset and Clérambault as the foremost innovators of the genre. In the first 'history' of the cantata, J. Bachelier judged Clérambault's works unmatched for their 'grace of melody, force of accompaniment, and difficulty of execution'. His musical depictions of Medea, Pigmalion, Leander and Hero were 'admired by all Paris', due probably to Clérambault's unique gift for animating dramatic climaxes through dissonance and surprising progressions.[40]

After a 1713 ruling made it possible for French entrepreneurs to secure a royal *privilège* to publish music – this having been until then a monopoly of the Ballard family – music was sold by engravers and other vendors.[41] Catalogues (1738–67) of the four leading Parisian music shops attest to how popular the cantata became as the century wore on.[42] Cantata poetry circulated freely, with 167 texts appearing between 1711 and 1771 in the monthly *Mercure de France*, where poets invited musical settings.[43]

Women played an important part in popularizing the cantata in France. The legendary soprano Catherine-Nicole Le Maure dominated the *Concerts François* that were a central venue for cantata performance from 1727 to 1732.[44] Besides inspiring the 'first' French cantata, Marie de Louvencourt produced cantata *livrets* that two leading composers took up, and her works earned her a place in Evrard Titon du Tillet's *Le parnasse françois* (1732).[45] The Parisian salon, traditionally a sphere over which women presided, promoted cantatas and

40 Preface to J. Bachelier, *Recueil des Cantates … pour l'usage des Amateurs de la Musique & de la Poesie* (The Hague, 1728).

41 Ballard's rights covered music printed from type; the court ruled in 1713 that others could obtain the *privilège* to print music from engraved plates.

42 Anik Devriès, *Édition et commerce de la musique gravée à Paris dans la première moitié de XVIIIe siècle* (Geneva, 1976), pp. 13–43, 74–7.

43 David Tunley, 'An Embarkment for Cythera: Literary and Social Aspects of the French Cantata', *Recherches sur la musique française classique*, 7 (1967), pp. 110–11.

44 Le Maure performed more than fifty times; her rival, Marie Antier appeared eighteen times. See David Tunley, 'Philidor's "Concerts français"', *Music & Letters*, 47 (1966), p. 132.

45 Evrard Titon du Tillet, *Le parnasse françois* (Paris, 1732), p. 550.

also allowed growing numbers of amateurs *musiciennes* to perform chamber music.[46] Politically powerful women such as the Duchesse du Maine and Maria Leszcinska, wife of Louis XV, commissioned or requested cantatas for private concerts.[47] One of the most innovative composers of the period was Jacquet de La Guerre, whose 'fertility of genius' peaked in her cantatas.[48]

Secular song in France drew from similar musical sources, addressed similar topics and enjoyed a similar dissemination to that of the cantata. The output of song during the century was staggering: in Paris alone over 10,000 song collections appeared before 1750.[49] Here, the Ballard family was able to retain its earlier dominance in publishing, though composers such as de Bousset, Louis Lemaire and Philippe Courbois did hire engravers to issue their collections independently. De Bousset, the era's best-known composer of song, re-used forms developed in this genre when composing cantatas, which may be true of others who contributed to both genres.[50]

Ballard's collections both circulated the new sounds of Italian arias and perpetuated seventeenth-century French song types. Airs could be packaged as collections by single composers or as excerpts from stage productions, but it was miscellanies ('recueils') that were by far the most popular, particularly the monthly series of *Recueil d'airs sérieux et à boire* (1694–1724).[51] In each volume Ballard divided the music into *airs sérieux* (songs about love), *airs à boire* (drinking songs commenting on love, after seventeenth-century *baccanales*) and *airs italiens* (Italian arias). *Airs sérieux* and *à boire* often modelled themselves on earlier song forms such as the *ronde de table*, the *vaudeville* – which flourished independently – and the *brunette*, collections of which also appeared.[52] Airs were typically set as continuo songs, vocal duos without accompaniment, or on one stave. The heterodox nature of these collections is striking: virtuosic rondos, canons and fashionable arias appeared alongside street ballads and

46 Julie Anne Sadie, 'Musiciennes of the Ancien Régime', in Jane Bowers and Judith Tick (eds.), *Women Making Music: The Western Art Tradition, 1150–1950* (Urbana, IL, 1986), pp. 191–223.

47 Records of cantata performances at court and at the nocturnal festivals ('Les grandes nuits de Sceaux') for the Duchess are summarized in Gene Vollen, *The French Cantata: A Survey and Thematic Catalogue* (Ann Arbor, MI, 1982), pp. 23–8.

48 Titon du Tillet, *Le parnasse françois*, pp. 635–6, plate XI (medallion portrait). Her cantatas are unrivalled in their sophistication of text-setting and thematic development, and she was virtually the only French composer to cultivate sacred cantatas. Adrian Rose, 'Elizabeth Claude Jacquet de La Guerre and the Secular *cantate françoise*', *Early Music*, 13 (1985), pp. 529–41.

49 This repertory remains largely unexplored. See Tony Eastwood, 'The French Air in the Eighteenth Century: A Neglected Area', *Studies in Music* (Australia), 18 (1984), pp. 84–107.

50 Greer Garden, 'A Little-Known Contributor to the Early French Cantata: Jean-Baptiste de Bousset (1662–1725)', in Warren Drake (ed.), *Liber amicorum John Steele: A Musicological Tribute* (Stuyvesant, NY, 1997), pp. 357–77.

51 The 1750 inventory of Ballard lists 104 volumes of airs. For the volume titles, see http://rand.pratt.edu/~giannini/ballardnewhtml.htm.

52 Jörg Fiedler, 'Brunettes ou petits airs tendres: Unterrichts- und Unterhaltungsmusik des französischen Baroque', *Basler Jahrbuch für historische Musikpraxis*, 12 (1988), pp. 65–79.

boisterous drinking songs for bass voice (*récits de bass*). Ballard also made Italian airs publicly accessible for the first time in the *airs sérieux et à boire*, and again in the series *Recueil des meilleurs airs italiens* (1699–1708).[53]

Over time, the French cantata's Italian origins became greatly attenuated – first by the formal innovations of its earliest practitioners and then by its gradual absorption into a public sphere in which it consorted freely with indigenous musical traditions. Leading patrons such as the Prince de Conti (Louis François I de Bourbon) and Alexandre Le Riche de La Pouplinière held concerts open to audiences,[54] and the concerts of the Crozat family grew into twice-weekly subscription 'Concerts Italien' featuring cantatas.[55] While they continued, the *Concerts François* founded by Anne Danican Philidor built on the successful sacred music programmes of his *Concerts Spirituels*, though their high ticket prices ensured well-heeled audiences only. More informally, composers such as Clérambault held house concerts and exchanges at cafés.[56] Salons seemed to foster vocal chamber music generally: in 1763, the Comtesse de Rochefort declared, 'we no longer talk but only make song'.[57] In the provinces, cantatas featured in concerts called *académies* in which professionals – the soloists and the director – performed with amateur academy members for paying audiences.[58]

By 1760 the Italian cantata had completed its transformation into the French *cantatille*: a reduced piece of two or three airs joined by recitative. Jean-Jacques Rousseau identified this genre with poetasters and musicians 'without genius', content to repeat 'politeness'.[59] His disparagement reflected the genre's success: from 1740 to 1760 *cantatilles* flooded the market, becoming the province of dabblers.[60] Composers of merit passed over the genre and production tailed off in the 1780s.

53 Catherine Massip, 'Airs français et italiens dans l'edition française (1643–1710)', *Revue de musicologie*, 77 (1991), p. 179.

54 Types of audiences included invited guests, subscribers and ticket-holders. Michel Brenet, *Les concerts en France sous l'ancien régime* (Paris, 1900), pp. 160–4 and Georges Cucuel, *La Pouplinière et la musique de chambre au XVIIIe siècle* (Paris, 1913), p. xi.

55 Knowledge of the Crozart concert programmes is based on the family's music collection that included nineteen cantata editions. See Rosalie McQuaide, 'The Crozat Concerts, 1720–1727: A Study of Concert Life in Paris', PhD thesis (New York University, 1978), p. 184.

56 Brenet, *Les concerts en France sous l'ancien régime*, p. 168 and Dorival, 'André Campra et la cantate française', p. 320.

57 'Nous ne parlons plus, nous ne faisons que chanter.' Letter to Mme de Pailly of 19 July 1763. Cited in Antoine Lilti, *Le monde des salons: sociabilité et mondanité à Paris au XVIIIe siècle* (Paris, 2005), p. 252.

58 Humphrey Burton, 'Les Académies de musique en France au XVIIIe siècle', *Revue de musicologie*, 37 (1955), pp. 122–47.

59 'Le genre [cantatille] vaut moins encore que celui de la Cantate ... comme on n'y peut developper ni passions ni tableaux, & qu'elle n'est susceptible que de gentillesse, c'est un ressource pour les petits faiseurs de vers, & pour les Musiciens sans génie.' Jean-Jacques Rousseau, *Dictionnaire de Musique* (Paris, 1768), p. 73.

60 Tunley, *The Eighteenth-Century French Cantata*, pp. 168–93.

Commercializing leisure: English cantata and song

In Britain, the chamber cantata and song assumed radically different forms than elsewhere in Europe. The early commercialization of entertainment in Britain replaced private patronage with patterns of consumption horizontally dispersed among those with disposable incomes. Initially the English cantata struggled in this market, superseded in publication by the Italian cantata until it absorbed the mid-century vogue for stage ballads. The ballad-style cantata, initially conceived by Henry Carey, became the musical staple of concerts at London's pleasure gardens, where it enhanced the gardens' appeal to pastoral pleasures.

The English cantata was therefore not so much chamber music as theatre or concert music that became domesticated through publication. Composers also produced songs in the Italian style, but these remained marginal within a robust market for English song nourished by both the theatre and by a range of indigenous forms. From 1750 Italianate writing swung back into fashion, first in song and then in cantatas composed for performance by specific stage players. As editions combined cantatas with songs, generic distinctions blurred, although the popularity of the Italianate cantata outlasted that of Italianate song.

From around 1700, impresarios of theatres and concerts and publishers of editions capitalized on English audiences' willingness to 'follow [Italian] Musick and drop their pence freely'.[61] The bi-partite Restoration theatre air gave way to the Italian-style recitative-air or paired declamatory and lyrical airs.[62] The earliest English cantata written 'after the Italian Manner' was a stage novelty at Drury Lane on 13 April 1706.[63] A separate claim to have fathered the English cantata was made on behalf of John Hughes, whose poetry was said to be 'the first in its kind for Compositions in *English* after the manner of *Italians*'.[64] Hughes wrote his 'Essay' to emulate Horatian odes.[65] Like many English men of letters, Hughes believed that the 'End of Vocal Musick' was to

61 Roger North, 'Of Musicall Ayre', f. 75; cited in Michael Tilmouth, 'Some Early London Concerts and Music Clubs, 1670–1720', *Proceedings of the Royal Musical Association*, 84th session (1957), p. 14.

62 Richard J. Goodall, *Eighteenth-Century English Secular Cantatas* (New York, 1979), p. 248. Composers of Italianate song included John Eccles, Daniel Purcell, John Weldon and William Croft.

63 The cantata, performed by Margherita de L'Epine, was probably Daniel Purcell's 'Love, I defy thee'. Goodall, *Eighteenth-Century English Secular Cantatas*, p. 119.

64 'Mr Pepusch having desir'd that some Account shou'd be prefix'd to these Cantata's [*sic*] relating to the Words, it may be proper to acquaint the Publick, that they are the first Essays of this kind, written for the most part several years ago.' John Hughes, 'To the Lovers of Musick', in Johann Christoph Pepusch, *Six English Cantatas humbly inscrib'd to the most noble the Marchioness of Kent* (London, 1710).

65 Quoting Hughes, William Duncombe, who introduced a collection of Hughes' verses that included those for Pepusch, commended his 'Diction, Beauty, Vivacity and Epithets' after Horace. John Hughes, *Poems on Several Occasions* (London, 1735), vol. 1, p. xv.

promote 'Reason', that music required the mediation of native words to achieve this goal, and that Italian cantata verses were 'inferior'.[66] Ambrose Philips counselled poets that the cantata required 'Regularity' and 'utmost Nicety' rather than 'extraordinary Capacity' – a far cry from the aesthetic concerns of his Italian counterparts.[67]

Johann Christoph Pepusch, resident composer of the Duke of Chandos, set Hughes' verses and those of others. Pepusch wedded standard devices – alternating secco recitative–da capo sections (usually two pairs), motivic development, sequential writing, thematic fragmentation, *devise* openings, contrapuntal dialogue – to Corelli's instrumental style. The high quality of Pepusch's cantatas paralleled that of Handel's last Italian cantatas, composed for the same patron (1710–20).[68] But the cantata composers who followed, such as John Ernest Galliard, Daniel Purcell, Nicola Haym and John Eccles, did not work to the same standard.[69] Most glaringly, the piquante harmonic progressions vital to Italian cantatas were lacking, particularly in recitative, an element of the cantata that critics claimed was inimical to English vocal music.[70] From 1721 until the mid-1730s, the operatic composers around Paolo Rolli – Bononcini, Attilio Ariosti, Nicola Porpora and others – dominated the form with Italian cantatas written to target London's Italian opera supporters.[71] Italian cantatas by non-Italians such as Maurice Greene, Willem De Fesch and Thomas Roseingrave followed.[72]

Only Henry Carey composed English cantatas during the 1720s, though in a way that broke sharply with cantata precedent.[73] He merged high with low style, he conceived works to showcase his singing pupil, the soprano Kitty

66 'If Reason may be admitted to have any Share in these Entertainments [Italian cantatas], nothing is more necessary than that the Words shou'd be understood, without which the End of *Vocal Musick* is lost ... in the great number of their [i.e. Italian] *Opera's*, *Serenata's*, and *Cantata's* [*sic*], the Words are often inferior to the Composition'. John Hughes, 'To the Lovers of Musick' (1710).

67 *The Guardian*, 16 (30 March 1713). Cited in Goodall, *Eighteenth-Century English Secular Cantatas*, p. 18.

68 Ellen T. Harris, 'Handel's London Cantatas', *Göttinger Händel-Beiträge*, 1 (1984), pp. 86–102.

69 Comparing Purcell and Galliard to Pepusch, Goodall observes that Purcell lacked Pepusch's 'melodic inspiration, harmonic interest and formal spaciousness' and that Galliard's arias 'suffer from underdeveloped middle sections' and lack of thematic development. Goodall, *Eighteenth-Century English Secular Cantatas*, pp. 149, 153.

70 The attack against English recitative was led by Addison in *The Spectator*, 29 (3 April 1711) and was 'argued for the rest of the century'. See Roger Fiske, *English Theatre Music in the Eighteenth Century*, 2nd edn. (London and New York, 1986), p. 32.

71 The subscription list to Bononcini's *Cantate e duetti* (1721) was full of opera patrons loyal to the Duchess of Marlborough, who supported the composer in his rivalry with Handel. See Dorris, *Paolo Rolli*, pp. 79–81. Elsewhere, the royal family figured as dedicatees: Ariosti's cantatas were titled *Alla Maestà di Giorgio Rè della Gran Britagna* (1728) and Porpora's *All' Altezza Reale di Frederico Prencipe Reale di Vallia* [Prince of Wales] (1735).

72 Maurice Greene composed thirteen Italian cantatas and duets in the early 1730s, Willem De Fesch produced two volumes of 'canzonette' (1733–5) and Thomas Roseingrave published six cantatas (1735).

73 No English cantatas were published between 1720 and 1735 except Carey's *Six Cantatas* (1723) and *Cantatas for a Voice* (1724).

Clive, and he sought to revive past native traditions of vocal writing, in particular by championing the ballad. His new direction in cantata writing received impetus from the astonishing success of *The Beggar's Opera* (1728), whose repertory plundered dance music, Handel arias and broadside ballads alike. Along with vocal music, Carey also cultivated the burlesque, as in the cantata 'The Musical Hodge Podge' or the song 'The Ladies' Lamentation for the Loss of Senesino'. In critical commentary as well as music, Carey articulated his 'ballad style': a binary air of an even number of bars (eight, twelve or sixteen) with *galante* dance metres, cadences in the dominant (or relative major or minor), syllabic word-setting, restrained embellishment, triadic melodies, symmetrical phrasing and frequent appoggiaturas on the bar's first beat (usually a 4–3 suspension).

Carey's ballad style became characteristic of the era's largest English vocal repertory – that of pleasure garden concerts. By mid-century, London's sixty-odd pleasure gardens formed an archipelago of public spaces where higher and lower orders could mix freely. At the most prestigious establishments – Vauxhall, Ranelagh and Marylebone – concerts enhanced consumer pleasure by showcasing the theatre's rising vocal talent and providing pastoral theme music.[74] Songs and cantatas came to revolve around rural love, framed as naïve tableaus 'calculated rather to entertain the Fancy than improve the Understanding',[75] and favouring the indigenous and prosaic over the foreign and mythological; as the century progressed, figures such as Jenny and Jocky came to replace those of Phillida and Damon. Topics also broadened to include nationalist sentiments, advice about or parodies of female conduct – a mainstay of ballad operas – and reflections on personal values.

Theatre singers' pre-eminence at garden concerts – publishers invariably identified the music with the performer ('sung by Mr. Lowe') – suggests that concerts merely extended the urban musical monopoly of London's patent theatres. This use of theatre singers impacted directly on the cantata, with composers routinely showcasing a vocalist's particular skills or reputation. That concerts were performed from bandstands – or, in the case of Ranelagh, inside the giant 'rotunda' – dictated the instrumentation, which typically included strings, woodwinds, horns – hunting horn motifs were a cliché – trumpets, and

74 Berta Joncus, '"His Spirit is in Action seen": Milton, Mrs Clive, and the Simulacra of the Pastoral in *Comus*', *Eighteenth-Century Music*, 2 (2005), pp. 7–40. See also Christopher Hogwood, 'The London Pleasure Gardens', in *Johann Christian Bach: Favourite Songs Sung at Vauxhall Gardens* (Tunbridge Wells, 1985), pp. ix–xv.

75 'The *Poetry* of following *Cantata's*, (which, it is imagin'd, will be more the Subject of Criticism than the *Music*) … are calculated rather to entertain the Fancy than improve the Understanding.' Preface in John Stanley, *Six Cantata's for a Voice and Instruments* (1742) (Alston, 2004; facsimile edn.). Stanley's cantatas were all 'probably first performed' at Vauxhall Gardens. Tony Frost, 'The Cantatas of John Stanley (1713–1786)', *Music & Letters*, 53 (1972), p. 286.

harpsichord or organ.[76] The gardens' most prolific composers, John Stanley, Thomas Arne and William Boyce, made the most of these musical resources and the ballad-style idiom in which they worked.[77] Arne excelled at conjuring images of nature through word-painting and instrumental colour, particularly in recitative, and his melodies superbly match the charm and accents of the words. Uniquely, he used arioso sections to intensify drama in narrated passages. Arne tightened the air's structure by restating the first section's theme and home key in the second section, and he created broad-based tonal schemes to accommodate modulations.[78]

Spearheaded by Arne's collection *Vocal Melody* (1749–52), Italianate song finally found a market that James Hook and other composers were able to tap into.[79] After soprano Charlotte Brent's spectacular 1762 success in his *Artaxerxes*, Arne created bravura cantatas for the pleasure gardens concerts where Brent, his former pupil and then-mistress, appeared. These ushered in the English cantata's final but most popular era, until around 1790. Following Arne, a host of composers supplied works whose bravura writing for principal singers over-rode any other formal demands.

Paired in programmes and editions, the gardens' cantatas and songs after 1750 grew increasingly to resemble each other.[80] Standard song devices such as hunting horn motifs and Lombard rhythms resurfaced in cantatas, as did dance meters such as the minuet and, from *c.* 1770, the rondo. Composers wrote cantatas with airs in binary and da capo form, and songs prefaced by recitative.[81] From roughly 1740, publishers tended to combine cantatas and songs in one volume rather than issuing them separately. The song's ballad-style poetry infiltrated cantatas, and 'ballad cantatas' such as James Oswald's 'The Dust Cart' (*c.* 1755) proliferated as, until 1760, did simplified cantatas – *secco* recitative prefacing binary airs or ballads – by minor composers.[82] From 1750 the

76 Based on newspaper reports (1790–1), the average number of band members was twenty-five. Charles Cudworth, 'The Vauxhall "Lists"', *The Galpin Society Journal*, 20 (1967), pp. 27–9.

77 Although Arne's output was clearly for the pleasure gardens, that of Boyce is less clear, but the music in book III and VI of Boyce's six-book series *Lyra Brittanica* (1745–60) was probably performed there. Robert J. Bruce, Introduction to *William Boyce: Lyra Britannica* (Tunbridge Wells, 1985), p. x.

78 Goodall, *Eighteenth-Century English Secular Cantatas*, pp. 220–37. For exemplary pictures of nature and arioso writing see, respectively, Thomas Arne, *Six Cantatas for a Voice and Instruments* (London, 1755), pp. 47–55 ('The Morning'), and pp. 31–5 ('Bacchus and Ariadne').

79 Christopher Hogwood, 'The London Pleasure Gardens', p. xii.

80 Popular cantata and song publications are listed in Gwilym E. Beechey, 'Songs and Cantatas in Eighteenth-Century England', *The Consort: Annual Journal of the Dolmetsch Foundation*, 49 (1993), pp. 30–40.

81 Stanley's 'Three Songs', Op. 9 are da capo arias with obbligato. See Frost, 'The Cantatas of John Stanley (1713–1786)', p. 288. The songs of J. C. Bach (1766–71) were 'indebted to Bach's operatic music' and used simple sonata patterns. See Stephen Roe, 'J. C. Bach's Vauxhall Songs', in *Johann Christian Bach: Favourite Songs Sung at Vauxhall Gardens* (Tunbridge Wells, 1985), p. xviii.

82 Michael Christian Festing, Thomas Bowman and a 'Gentleman from Oxford' are three of many contributors; Goodall, *Eighteenth-Century English Secular Cantatas*, pp. 206–9.

glee – a through-composed partsong for unaccompanied voices – flourished in London catch-clubs and eventually became a staple of commercial and home performance.[83]

Publishers had from 1730 virtually ceased issuing volumes dedicated to high-style song. Whether preparing miscellanies or a composer's collected works, publishers put da capo or multi-sectional airs together with strophic ballads. The practice had precedents in earlier collections by the leading publishers John Walsh, Thomas Cross and Henry Playford, who had combined theatre and concert songs with glees, Scotch airs and ballads.[84] In England, commerce erased the boundaries of genre, style and location that characterized vocal chamber music in the rest of Europe.

The dialectics of song: Germany and the promise of the Enlightenment

Characteristic of the hundreds of autonomous polities that made up Germany was division: between regions, between court and bourgeois circles, between sovereign cities and absolutist centres of power, between Catholic and Protestant. While German courts imported sophisticated and expensive musicians from Italy, German urban institutions – churches, schools, city councils and societies – cultivated vernacular music. Chamber cantata and song in Germany therefore consisted of very different strands: the Italian cantata, which flourished particularly under the powerful dynasties of Brandenburg-Prussia, Saxony and the Bavaria–Rhenish Palatinate; the German lied, which was cultivated by literati from the seventeenth century onwards; and the German secular cantata, which was influenced by German opera, Lutheran cantata and critical writings on music and poetry. Throughout the era, the urge among German men of letters to theorize was unparalleled. This created another rift, between theory and practice. Although often reporting on current practices, theorists also misrepresented 'histories' or held up ideals that were in practice routinely ignored. The German cantata exemplifies the gulf between the optimism of Enlightenment theory and the reality of the work that was produced.

Without private patrons, the German chamber cantata, like its English counterpart, depended upon consumers. The genre began in Hamburg, a

83 The roughly 300 eighteenth-century publications featuring the glee, together with performances in and outside the home, helped to stimulate interest in native composers and forms. Emanuel Rubin, *The English Glee in the Reign of George III: Participatory Art Music for an Urban Society* (Warren, MI, 2003), pp. 10–14, 111–31. For a list of editions, see *ibid.*, pp. 379–84. For the relationship of the catch to the glee and the rise of glee clubs, see Brian Robins, *Catch and Glee Culture in Eighteenth-Century England* (Woodbridge and Rochester, NY, 2006).
84 David Hunter, *Opera and Song Books Published in England, 1705–1726: A Descriptive Bibliography* (London, 1997).

wealthy independent city-state where civic institutions – a public opera house featuring German operas, five major churches, a nascent concert venue (the Drill House) and esteemed church schools – supplied inhabitants with a rich mix of vernacular music supported by local printers. Hamburg's leading opera composer, Reinhard Keiser, wrote the first German cantatas, *Gemütsergötzung* (1698), which he asserted 'came from the [Italian] theatre' and had 'overtaken German song'.[85] His statement was only partially true. Although 'theatrical', the forms on which these and later cantatas by Keiser drew came from local German opera – for example, their binary airs, French dances (courante, loure), French-style arioso recitative and rich instrumental solos.[86] Keiser's claim for the success of the German secular cantata was fiction, but this did not deter theorists such as Johann Christoph Gottsched from repeating it.[87]

Generally, the wealth of writing about the German chamber cantata – by Christian Friedrich Hunold ('Menantes'), Gottsched, Johann Adolph Scheibe, Johann Mattheson and Johann David Heinichen – misrepresented the importance of this genre, which only seven composers notably cultivated and which had fizzled out by mid-century.[88] This did not deter theorists from constructing histories or developing rules about it. According to Menantes, Erdmann Neumeister's poetic models for the Lutheran cantata were also seminal for German secular cantata poetry. Music and literary theorists set guidelines for writing cantata music and poetry: the number and order of movements (RARA, ARA), how to develop motives, where to modulate, which type of poetry to choose, where to apply tender melodies, etc.[89] Composers followed their own inclinations. Keiser, for instance, extended the length of cantatas beyond four movements, deployed *dramatis personae* and diversified his melodic writing, all in disregard of theorists' prescriptions.

85 'Diese Sing-Gedichte, oder wie sie die Italiener nennen Cantaten, haben die ehemaligen deutschen Lieder ganz verdrängt. Die Erfindung derselben ist aber von den Opern hergekommen.' He states later that in composing his cantatas he writes more 'in the theatrical rather than chamber style' ('in den Theatralischen- als Kammer-stil'). Reinhard Keiser, Preface to *Gemütsergötzung* (1698). Cited in Robert Eitner, 'Cantaten aus dem Ende des 17. und Anfänge des 18. Jahrhunderts', *Monatshefte für Musik-Geschichte*, 16/5 (1884), pp. 50–1.

86 Klaus-Peter Koch, 'Reinhard Keisers gedruckte weltliche Kantaten (1698–1715)', in Bert Siegmund (ed.), *Zur Entwicklung, Verbreitung und Ausführung vokaler Kammermusik im 18. Jahrhundert* (Michaelstein, 1997), pp. 49–63. After 1698, Keiser produced the cantata collections *Divertimenti serenissimi* (1713), *Musicalische Land-lust* (1714) and *Kayserliche Friedens-post* (1715).

87 In 'Von Cantaten', *Versuch einer Critischen Dichtkunst* (1730). Cited in Eugen Schmitz, *Geschichte der weltlichen Solokantate*, 2nd edn. (Leipzig, 1955), p. 262.

88 The composers of German cantatas catalogued are, in addition to Keiser, Georg Philipp Telemann, Johann Sebastian Bach, Carl Heinrich Graun, his brother Johann Gottlieb Graun, Gottfried Heinrich Stölzel, and Johann Heinrich Rolle. These are 'not only the most significant but largely all the names' of those who wrote German secular cantatas. See Schmitz, *Geschichte der weltlichen Solokantate*, p. 301.

89 These writings, including Menantes' observations from *Die aller-neueste Art zur reinen und galanten Poesie zu gelangen* (1706), are summarized in Schmitz, *Geschichte der weltlichen Solokantate*, pp. 260–6.

Only through Georg Philipp Telemann did the German cantata achieve even moderate success. Perhaps the best-known and most highly regarded German composer of his day, Telemann commands our attention as much for his innovations in marketing as for his gifts in composition. Cantatas were only a part of Telemann's vast chamber music output to meet the demands of private worship, domestic entertainment and self-education. He astutely managed the issuing of this huge corpus, testing markets before investing in publications, covering overhead costs through subscriptions, running advertising campaigns, networking with distributors and offering discounts to subscribers.[90] Vital to the success of Telemann's chamber cantatas was talent in blending chamber, theatre and sacred styles. Issued by installment, his *Harmonischer Gottesdienst* (1725–6) and *Fortsetzung des harmonischen Gottesdienstes* (1731–2) were cycles of sacred cantatas 'suited for private domestic service'. Clarity of word-painting, simplicity of coloratura and naturalness of recitative ensured that this music did not exceed amateur abilities. In the *Harmonischer Gottesdienst*, Telemann encouraged users to replace the voice part with a second solo instrument to create trio sonatas out of these sacred vocal works.[91] Conversely, his series *VI Moralische Cantaten* [I–II] (1735–6) made secular music into hymns, albeit to Enlightenment principles such as 'Hope' and 'Happiness', after which he titled movements. In 1739 Scheibe based his rules for cantata composition partly on these works, translating practice into theory.[92]

Telemann's publishing enterprise popularized his lieder as effectively as it did his cantatas. His musical 'newspaper' *Der Getreue Musicmeister* (1728) set didactic texts to melodies, making him one of the earliest composers to adapt the rationalist ideals that would dominate the lied until 1760. In *Singe-, Spiel und Generalbassübungen* (1733–4), he set the poetry of Friedrich von Hagedorn, the pioneer of 'order and nature'. Based on the literary form of the strophic 'ode', the lied opposed a basic tenet of Italianate composition that ruled that melodies must change to reflect a word's meaning. Hamburg literati, followed by Gottsched, maintained that the lied, through its formal simplicity and unity around one idea, represented the essence of rationalist aesthetics.[93] Although

90 Steven Zohn, 'Telemann in the Marketplace: The Composer as Self-Publisher', *Journal of the American Musicological Society*, 58 (2005), pp. 275–356.

91 Richard Petzoldt, *Georg Philipp Telemann*, trans. Horace Fitzpatrick (London, 1974), p. 154.

92 Günter Fleischhauer, 'G.Ph. Telemanns Zyklen VI moralische Cantaten (TWV 20:23–28 und 29–34) im Urteil J. A. Scheibes', in Monika Fink, Rainer Gstrein und Günter Mössmer (eds.), *Musica privata – die Rolle der Musik im privaten Leben: Festschrift zum 65. Geburtstag von Walter Salmen* (Innsbruck, 1991), pp. 315–38.

93 Hamburg's informal societies ('Teutsch-übende Gesellschaft', 1715) and weekly 'moral' publications after English prototypes fired debate on the relation between poetry and Enlightenment principles before Gottsched's *Versuch einer critischen Dichtkunst* appeared (1730). Jürgen Rathje, 'Zur hamburgischen Gelehrtenrepublik im Zeitalter Matthesons', in George J. Buelow (ed.), *New Mattheson Studies* (Cambridge University Press, 1983), pp. 108–11.

other lied composers adhered to these principles after 1730, Telemann was their most prominent early advocate, declaring his debt to this school of thought in the preface to his *Vierundzwanzig Oden* (1741).[94]

After 1750, the centre of song production shifted from Hamburg to Berlin, where King Frederick had assembled a brilliant and tight-knit entourage of composers, poets and critics whose debates about the lied spilled into print.[95] They also visited *bürgerlich* salons and assemblies where lieder were performed. Both debate and amateur performance stimulated lied production, with more than a thousand lieder appearing in print from 1753 to 1768.[96] Like their French counterparts, German salons were generally a semi-public sphere within which women could compose and perform without transgressing rules of decorum. Corona Schröter, who led female lied composition, composed her repertory for domestic use, despite being a stage singer. Because women had no access to formal musical training, miniature forms demanding few resources such as the lied were conducive to female cultivation.[97]

Ruptures between the theory and practice of the lied soon emerged, as they had for the cantata. Perhaps the most successful early lied collection was *Singende Muse an der Pleisse* (Leizig, 1736), prepared by the poet Johann Sigismund Scholze ('Sperontes'), and frequently re-issued (1742, 1743, 1745 and 1751). Because the music was largely recycled from dance tunes, however, contemporaries did not credit the music with contributing to the development of the lied. While Christian Gottfried Krause iterated the lied's neo-classical aim of calling forth joy through noble simplicity, Gotthold Ephraim Lessing reported how lieder reflected the 'wit and taste' of salon audiences.[98] In line with the taste of the king, critics held up French airs as models, urging authors to copy their anacreontic verses and practice of writing for unaccompanied voices. Composers, however, continued to adhere to earlier German traditions of accompanied writing, and poets such as Christian Fürchtegott Gellert expanded their subject matter to include devotional poetry.

One of the period's most celebrated lied composers was Carl Philipp Emanuel Bach. His residency at Berlin (1738–68) coincided with the lied's

94 Siegfried Kross, 'Telemann und die Liedästhetik seiner Zeit', in Günther Fleischauer, Wolf Hobohm and Walther Siegmund-Schultze (eds.), *Die Bedeutung Georg Philipp Telemanns für die Entwicklung der europäischen Musikkultur im 18. Jahrhundert* (Magdeburg, 1983), 3 vols., vol. 2, pp. 31–46.

95 'Ramling, Lessing, Sulzer, Agricola, Krause ... Bach, Graun, in short all those belonging to the Muses and liberal arts, daily got together, either on land or on water.' Johann W. L. Gleim, letter of 16 Aug. 1758. Cited in Hans-Günter Ottenberg, *Carl Philipp Emanuel Bach*, trans. Philip. J. Whitmore (Oxford, 1987), p. 64.

96 Ulrich Leisinger, 'Die Ode in der poetischen Theorie und in der musikalischen Praxis', in Anselm Gerhard (ed.), *Musik und Ästhetik im Berlin Moses Mendelssohns* (Tübingen, 1999), pp. 188–9.

97 Marcia J. Citron, 'Corona Schröter: Singer, Composer, Actress', *Music & Letters*, 61 (1980), pp. 15–27.

98 Gotthold Ephraim Lessing, *Berlinische privilegierte Staats- und gelehrte Zeitung*, 17 November 1753. Cited in Leisinger, 'Die Ode in der poetischen Theorie', p. 194.

efflorescence there. In his autobiography Bach famously declared that he aimed to compose 'as songfully as possible' with a 'noble simplicity of melody'.[99] Lieder allowed him to develop these ideals. His balance of phrase, refinement of gesture and sensitivity to declamation epitomized the aesthetic endorsed by neo-classicists. By writing accompaniment that articulated prosody and commented on the poetry's meaning, Bach enhanced simplicity with emotional immediacy. Particularly in his Gellert lieder, the ode's modest structures – a binary strophic air with I–V–I tonal plan and syllabic setting in which melody dominated over the bass – became a springboard for expressiveness.[100]

The drive among poets to replace Baroque artifice with simplicity and to follow French models also affected cantata poetry. From 1760 German writers took up the mythological subjects popular in France – Cephalus and Procris, Pigmalion, Ino – sometimes translating from the French original. These subjects became the springboard for a new type of dramatic cantata whose interweaving arioso, recitative and aria sections, rich orchestration, dynamic contouring and pictorial effects were designed for formal professional performances.

After 1770, lied poetry embraced folk-style writing for the first time. Johann Gottfried Herder's theories about *Ursprachen*, or primal languages, stimulated interest in the cultural practices of a 'Volk'. Paradoxically, even as poets took up 'folk' paradigms, composers set their verses in increasingly sophisticated ways. Responding to developments in instrumental music, this new through-composed or modified strophic writing with unorthodox modulations, as in the songs of Johann Friedrich Reichardt, or sonata-based forms, as in Joseph Haydn's lieder, established the means through which Franz Schubert would later transform the genre.[101]

Conclusion

Cantata and song repertories throughout the eighteenth century show how local patterns of production and consumption not only determined, but also became embedded within, musical forms. Italian *accademie* and courts created

99 'My chief effort ... has been directed towards both playing and composing as songfully as possible ... the noble simplicity of the melody is not to be disturbed by too much bustle.' See William S. Newman, 'Emanuel Bach's Autobiography', *Musical Quarterly*, 51 (1965), p. 372.
100 'The Gellert Songs', in William H. Youngren, *C. P. E. Bach and the Rebirth of the Strophic Song* (Lanham, MD, 2003), pp. 203–40. See also Gudrun Busch, *C. Ph. E. Bach und seine Lieder* (Regensburg, 1957), pp. 62–5, 380–1 and Ernst Suchalla, 'Carl Philipp Emanuel Bach – Ludwig van Beethoven: *Bitten* – ein Gellert-Lied', in Bert Siemund (ed.), *Zur Entwicklung, Verbreitung und Ausführung vokaler Kammermusik im 18. Jahrhundert* (Michaelstein, 1997), pp. 141–8.
101 Amanda Glauert, 'The Lieder of Carl Philipp Emanuel Bach, Haydn, Mozart, and Beethoven', in James Parsons (ed.), *The Cambridge Companion to the Lied* (Cambridge, 2004), pp. 63–73.

realms where, under Arcadian guise, participants could experiment with pleasure, learning and invention. In France, adapting Italian cantatas to local traditions was a self-conscious way of defining and refining a characteristic taste; what had begun as a hybrid French–Italian genre became indigenous through its cross-fertilization with song and its popularization through salons, concerts and publications. In England, London's entertainment industries turned cantata and song so effectively into commodities that the boundaries separating vocal chamber music from stage or low-style music quickly disappeared. In Germany, the separation of court and bourgeois cultures consigned Italian cantatas to court circles and German cantatas to domestic use, leaving the lied as the vital forum for aesthetic experiment in musico-literary circles whose members moved between royal and other privileged spheres. 'Great works' are the exceptions among myriad eighteenth-century vocal chamber music productions whose contrasts highlight the ways in which very different cultural contexts, economic developments and social practices could shape generic characteristics. These repertories still have much to teach us.

Select Bibliography

Antoniotto, Giorgio. *L'arte armonico*. 2 vols., London, 1760

Arne, Thomas. *Six Cantatas for a Voice and Instruments*. London, 1755

Bachelier, J. *Recueil des Cantates ... pour l'usage des Amateurs de la Musique & de la Poesie*. The Hague, 1728

Baretti, Giuseppe Marc'Antonio. *An Account of the Manners and Customs of Italy*. 2 vols., London, 1768

Beechey, Gwilym E. 'Songs and Cantatas in Eighteenth-Century England'. *The Consort: Annual Journal of the Dolmetsch Foundation*, 49 (1993), pp. 30–40

Brenet, Michel. *Les concerts en France sous l'ancien régime*. Paris, 1900

Brossard, Sébastian de. 'Dissertation sure cette espece [*sic*] de concert qu'on nomme Cantate', 'Meslanges et extraits relatifs à l'histoire de la musique', *Fr-Pn* N.a. 5269, f. 75 v

Bruce, Robert J. (ed.), Introduction to *William Boyce: Lyra Britannica*. Music for London Entertainment 1660–1800. Series F: Music of the Pleasure Gardens, III. Tunbridge Wells, 1985

Burton, Humphrey. 'Les Académies de musique en France au XVIIIe siècle'. *Revue de musicologie*, 37 (1955), pp. 122–47

Busch, Gudrun. *C. Ph. E. Bach und seine Lieder*. Regensburg, 1957

Campra, André. *Cantatas of André Campra (1660–1744): Cantates françoises, book 1 (1708). The Eighteenth-Century French Cantata, II*. Ed. David Tunley. New York and London, 1990.

Cavalli, Alberto. 'Le cantate opera prima di Francesco Gasparini'. *Chigiana*, 25/5 (1968), pp. 53–68

Centanni, Monica. '"Delirante, disprezzato, deluso, accesso amante": variazioni su temi classici in alcune cantate inedite di Antonio Caldara'. *Musica e storia*, 7/2 (1999), pp. 403–45

Citron, Marcia J. 'Corona Schröter: Singer, Composer, Actress'. *Music & Letters*, 61 (1980), pp. 15–27

Couvreur, Manuel. 'Marie de Louvencourt, librettiste des cantates françoise de Bourgeois et de Clérambault'. *Revue belge de musicologie/Belgisch tijdschrift voor muziekwetenschap*, 44 (1990), pp. 25–40

Crescimbeni, Giovanni Mario. *L'Arcadia*. Rome, 1708

Le vite degli Arcadi illustri. 3 vols., Rome, 1708–14

Cucuel, Georges. *La Pouplinière et la musique de chambre au XVIIIe siècle*. Paris, 1913

Cudworth, Charles. 'The Vauxhall "Lists"'. *The Galpin Society Journal*, 20 (1967), pp. 24–42

Dent, Edward J. *Alessandro Scarlatti: His Life and Works*. Rev. edn. with preface and additional notes by Frank Walker. London, 1960

Devriès, Anik. *Édition et commerce de la musique gravée à Paris dans la première moitié de XVIIIe siècle*. Geneva, 1976

Dorival, Jerome. 'André Campra et la cantate française'. In J. Lionnet (ed.), *Le Concert des Muses: Promenade musicale dans le baroque française*. Paris, 1997, pp. 319–31

Dorris, George E. *Paolo Rolli and the Italian Circle in London 1715–1744*. The Hague and Paris, 1967

Eastwood, Tony. 'The French Air in the Eighteenth Century: A Neglected Area'. *Studies in Music* (Australia), 18 (1984), pp. 84–107

Eitner, Robert. 'Cantaten aus dem Ende des 17. und Anfange des 18. Jahrhunderts'. *Monatshefte für Musik-Geschichte*, 16/5 (1884), pp. 45–54

Fader, Donald J. 'Musical Thought and Patronage of the Italian Style at the Court of Philippe II, Duc d'Orléans (1674–1723)'. PhD thesis, Stanford University, 2000

'The "Cabale du Dauphin", Campra and Italian Comedy: The Courtly Politics of French Musical Patronage around 1700'. *Music & Letters*, 86 (2005), pp. 380–413

Fiedler, Jörg. 'Brunettes ou petits airs tendres: Unterrichts- und Unterhaltungsmusik des französischen Baroque'. *Basler Jahrbuch für historische Musikpraxis*, 12 (1988), pp. 65–79

Fiske, Roger. *English Theatre Music in the Eighteenth Century*, 2nd edn. London and New York, 1986

Fleischhauer, Günter. 'G.Ph. Telemanns Zyklen VI moralische Cantaten (TWV 20:23–28 und 29–34) im Urteil J.A. Scheibes'. In Monika Fink, Rainer Gstrein and Günter Mössmer (eds.), *Musica privata – die Rolle der Musik im privaten Leben: Festschrift zum 65. Geburtstag von Walter Salmen*. Innsbruck, 1991, pp. 315–38

Frost, Tony. 'The Cantatas of John Stanley (1713–1786)'. *Music & Letters*, 53 (1972), pp. 284–92

Garden, Greer. 'A Little-Known Contributor to the Early French Cantata: Jean-Baptiste de Bousset (1662–1725)'. In W. Drake (ed.), *Liber amicorum John Steele: A Musicological Tribute*. Stuyvesant, NY, 1997, pp. 357–77

'Poetic Design and Musical Structure in Campra's Cantata Airs'. *Music & Letters*, 78 (1997), pp. 24–44

Gialdroni, Teresa M. 'Bibliografia della cantata da camera italiana (1620–1740 ca.)'. *Le fonti musicali in Italia*, 4 (1990), pp. 31–131

Gianturco, Carolyn M. '*Il trionfo del tempo e del disinganno*: Four Case-Studies in Determining Italian Poetic–Musical Genres'. *Journal of the Royal Musical Association*, 119 (1994), pp. 43–59

Glauert, Amanda. 'The Lieder of Carl Philipp Emanuel Bach, Haydn, Mozart, and Beethoven'. In James Parsons (ed.), *The Cambridge Companion to the Lied*. Cambridge, 2004, pp. 63–73

Goodall, Richard J. *Eighteenth-Century English Secular Cantatas*. New York, 1979

Hanley, Edwin. 'Alessandro Scarlatti's *cantate da camera*: A Bibliographical Study'. PhD thesis, Yale University, 1963

Harris, Ellen T. 'Handel's London Cantatas'. *Göttinger Händel-Beiträge*, 1 (1984), pp. 86–102

Handel as Orpheus: Voice and Desire in the Chamber Cantatas. Cambridge, MA, 2001

'"Cantate, que me veux-tu?', or: Do Handel's Cantatas Matter?' In Melania Bucciarelli and Berta Joncus (eds.), *Music as Social and Cultural Practice: Essays in Honour of Reinhard Strohm*. Woodbridge and Rochester, NY, 2007, pp. 159–84

Hogwood, Christopher. 'The London Pleasure Gardens'. In *Johann Christian Bach: Favourite Songs Sung at Vauxhall Gardens*, Music for London Entertainment 1660–1800. Series F: Music of the Pleasure Gardens, III. Tunbridge Wells, 1985, pp. ix–xv

Hughes, John. *Poems on Several Occasions*. 2 vols., London, 1735

Hunter, David. *Opera and Song Books Published in England, 1705–1726: A Descriptive Bibliography*. London, 1997

Joncus, Berta. '"His Spirit is in Action seen": Milton, Mrs Clive, and the Simulacra of the Pastoral in *Comus*'. *Eighteenth-Century Music*, 2 (2005), pp. 7–40

Koch, Klaus-Peter. 'Reinhard Keisers gedruckte weltliche Kantaten (1698–1715)'. In Bert Siegmund (ed.), *Zur Entwicklung, Verbreitung und Ausführung vokaler Kammermusik im 18. Jahrhundert*. Michaelstein, 1997, pp. 49–63

Kross, Siegfried. 'Telemann und die Liedästhetik seiner Zeit'. In Günther Fleischauer, Wolf Hobohm and Walter Siegmund-Schultze (eds.), *Die Bedeutung Georg Philipp Telemanns für die Entwicklung der europäischen Musikkultur im 18. Jahrhundert*. 3 vols., Magdeburg, 1983, vol. 2, pp. 31–46

Leisinger, Ulrich. 'Die Ode in der poetischen Theorie und in der musikalischen Praxis'. In Anselm Gerhard (ed.), *Musik und Ästhetik im Berlin Moses Mendelssohns*. Tübingen, 1999, pp. 187–216

Lilti, Antoine. *Le monde des salons: sociabilité et mondanité à Paris au XVIIIe siècle*. Paris, 2005

McQuaide, Rosalie. 'The Crozat Concerts, 1720–1727: A Study of Concert Life in Paris'. PhD thesis, New York University, 1978

Marx, Hans Joachim. 'Die Musik am Hofe Pietro Kardinal Ottobonis unter Arcangelo Corelli'. *Analecta musicologica*, 5 (1968), pp. 104–77

Massip, Catherine. 'Airs français et italiens dans l'edition française (1643–1710)'. *Revue de musicologie*, 77 (1991), pp. 179–85

Newman, William S. 'Emanuel Bach's Autobiography'. *Musical Quarterly*, 51 (1965), pp. 363–72

Olszewski, Edward J. 'The Enlightened Patronage of Cardinal Pietro Ottoboni (1667–1740)'. *Artibus et Historiae*, 23/45 (2002), pp. 139–65

Ottenberg, Hans-Günter. *Carl Philipp Emanuel Bach*. Trans. Philip J. Whitmore, Oxford, 1987

Pepusch, Johann Christoph. *Six English Cantatas humbly inscrib'd to the most noble the Marchioness of Kent*. London, 1710

Petzoldt, Richard. *Georg Philipp Telemann*. Trans. Horace Fitzpatrick, London, 1974

Rathje, Jürgen. 'Zur hamburgischen Gelehrtenrepublik im Zeitalter Matthesons'. In George Buelow (ed.), *New Mattheson Studies*. Cambridge, 1983, pp. 101–22

Robins, Brian. *Catch and Glee Culture in Eighteenth-Century England*. Woodbridge and Rochester, NY, 2006

Roe, Stephen. 'J. C. Bach's Vauxhall Songs'. In *Johann Christian Bach: Favourite Songs Sung at Vauxhall Gardens*, Music for London Entertainment 1660–1800. Series F: Music of the Pleasure Gardens, III. Tunbridge Wells, 1985, pp. xvii–xxi

Rose, Adrian. 'Elizabeth Claude Jacquet de La Guerre and the Secular *cantate françoise*'. *Early Music*, 13 (1985), pp. 529–41

Rose, Gloria. 'The Italian Cantata of the Baroque Period'. In Wulf Arlt *et al.* (eds.), *Gattungen der Musik in Einzeldarstellungen. Gedenkschrift Leo Schrade*. Bern and Munich, pp. 655–77

Rousseau, Jean-Baptiste. *Œuvres diverses du Sieur R.***. Paris, 1712

Rousseau, Jean-Jacques. *Dictionnaire de Musique*, Paris, 1768

Rubin, Emanuel. *The English Glee in the Reign of George III: Participatory Art Music for an Urban Society*. Warren, MI, 2003

Sadie, Julie Anne. 'Musiciennes of the Ancien Régime'. In Jane Bowers and Judith Tick (eds.), *Women Making Music: The Western Art Tradition, 1150–1950*. Urbana, IL, 1986, pp. 191–223

Schmitz, Eugen. *Geschichte der weltlichen Solokantate*. 2nd edn., Leipzig, 1955

Selfridge-Field, Eleanor. 'Marcello's Music: Repertory vs. Reputation'. In Claudio Madricardo and Franco Rossi (eds.), *Benedetto Marcello: la sua opera e il suo tempo*. Florence, 1988, pp. 205–22

Strohm, Reinhard. 'Hasse, Scarlatti, Rolli'. *Analecta musicologica*, 15 (1975), pp. 220–57

Stanley, John. *Six Cantata's for a Voice and Instruments* [1742]. Facsimile edn., Alston, 2004

Stuck, Jean-Baptiste. *Cantatas of Jean-Baptiste Stuck (Batistin) (1680–1755): Cantates françoises à voix seule, book 1 (1706)*. The Eighteenth-Century French Cantata, IV. Ed. David Tunley. New York and London, 1990

Suchalla, Ernst. 'Carl Philipp Emanuel Bach – Ludwig van Beethoven: *Bitten* – ein Gellert-Lied'. In Bert Siegmund (ed.), *Zur Entwicklung, Verbreitung und Ausführung vokaler Kammermusik im 18. Jahrhundert*. Michaelstein, 1997, pp. 141–51

Talbot, Michael. 'Albinoni's Solo Cantatas'. *Soundings*, 5 (1975), pp. 9–28

Benedetto Vinaccesi: A Musician in Brescia and Venice in the Age of Corelli. Oxford, 1994

'Musical Academies in Eighteenth-Century Venice'. In *Venetian Music in the Age of Vivaldi*. Aldershot, 1999, pp. 21–66

The Chamber Cantatas of Antonio Vivaldi. Woodbridge and Rochester, NY, 2006

Tilmouth, Michael. 'Some Early London Concerts and Music Clubs, 1670–1720'. *Proceedings of the Royal Musical Association*, 84th session (1957), pp. 13–26

Timms, Colin. 'The cavata at the Time of Vivaldi'. In Antonio Fanna and Giovanni Morelli (eds.), *Nuovi studi vivaldiani: edizione e cronologia critica delle opere*. Florence, 1989, pp. 451–78

'The Italian Cantata Since 1945: Progress and Prospects'. In Francesco Fanna and Michael Talbot (eds.), *Cinquant'anni di produzioni e consumi della musica dell'eta di Vivaldi: 1947–1997*. Florence, 1998, pp. 75–94

Polymath of the Baroque: Agostino Steffani and his Music. New York, 2003

Titon du Tillet, Evrard. *Le parnasse françois*. Paris, 1732
Tosi, Pier Francesco. *Observations on the Florid Song* (1702). Trans. John E. Galliard, London, 1742
Tunley, David. 'Philidor's "Concerts français"'. *Music & Letters*, 47 (1966), pp. 130–4
'An Embarkment for Cythera: Literary and Social Aspects of the French Cantata'. *Recherches sur la musique française classique*, 7 (1967), pp. 103–24
'The French Cantata in Performance'. *Eighteenth-Century Studies*, 8 (1974), pp. 47–55
The Eighteenth-Century French Cantata. 2nd edn., Oxford, 1997
Vollen, Gene. *The French Cantata: A Survey and Thematic Catalogue*. Ann Arbor, MI, 1982
Youngren, William H. *C. P. E. Bach and the Rebirth of the Strophic Song*. Lanham, MD, 2003
Zohn, Steven. 'Telemann in the Marketplace: The Composer as Self-Publisher'. *Journal of the American Musicological Society*, 58 (2005), pp. 275–356

Handel and English oratorio

EVA ZÖLLNER

When we think of eighteenth-century oratorio today, the composer whose name comes to mind almost immediately – and inevitably – is George Frideric Handel. This is less a statement about the indisputable artistic merit of his oratorios than about the extraordinary status Handel's oratorios acquired even in their own time, especially when considered in broad historical context: English oratorio was to all intents and purposes created by Handel, and his creation had a tremendous influence on the musical history of his chosen country of residence long after his death.

When Handel arrived in London in 1712, oratorio was still an unknown musical genre there. In the 1730s and 1740s Handel gradually developed an entirely unique English variant, skilfully combining elements taken from Italian opera and oratorio, the English anthem and other sources. The end result – if Handel can be said ever to have arrived at a 'final' version of the form – was so different from contemporary oratorio on the Continent that it has to be considered on its own.[1] Another factor to be taken into account is that Handel developed English oratorio virtually single-handedly. English composers took an interest in the genre during the 1730s and 1740s, notably Maurice Greene (*The Song of Deborah and Barak*, completed and performed only a few months after the first London performances of Handel's *Esther* in 1732, as well as *Jephtha* (1737) and *The Force of Truth* (1744)), and William Boyce (*David's Lamentation over Saul and Jonathan* (1736) and the serenata *Solomon* (1742)).[2] But Handel never had to face any serious competition and, in consequence, cannot be said to have been influenced by his English contemporaries.

In mid-eighteenth-century England the term 'oratorio' – which was more or less synonymous with Handelian oratorio – denoted a substantial musical

1 The most detailed information about the history of Baroque oratorio in Italy and Germany can be found in Howard E. Smither, *A History of the Oratorio*, vol. 1 (*The Oratorio in the Baroque Era, Italy, Vienna, Paris*) and vol. 2 (*The Oratorio in the Baroque Era, Protestant Germany and England*) (Chapel Hill, NC, 1977).

2 As Winton Dean suggests (*Handel's Dramatic Oratorios and Masques* [London and New York, 1959], p. 226), Handel may have been inspired by Greene's *Deborah* to tackle the subject himself; otherwise the oratorios of Handel's contemporaries unfortunately had very little impact.

entertainment in three acts with an English libretto based on a sacred subject. The overall tri-partite structure followed that of Italian opera, and the forms of aria, recitative and ensemble were clearly derived from operatic models. The two main features that distinguished English oratorio from opera were the sacred or religious nature of the libretto and, most importantly, the addition of a chorus that played a predominant role. Oratorios were usually performed at theatres or in concert halls. Even though most of the oratorios were dramatic in character, they were not acted: vocal soloists, chorus and orchestra were positioned on stage, with a backdrop providing visual interest. Additional important features of oratorio performances were the concertos presented in the two intervals, another tradition instigated by Handel, who from about 1735 onwards used the intervals to present his own organ concertos.[3]

When Handel arrived in England, oratorio was still far from his mind. It is true that during his travels in Italy in the preceding years he had tried his hand at two Italian oratorios, *Il Trionfo del Tempo e del Disinganno* and *La Resurrezione*, which were performed in Rome in 1707 and 1708, respectively. These works were certainly important exercises for Handel, and a sign of greater things to come. However, at this point, a career as an opera composer clearly held greater appeal: during his first years in the English capital, he devoted almost all his energies to Italian opera, and for the time being further oratorio experiments – if indeed he planned any at this stage – had to wait. Only a few months after his arrival he created his first opera for London, *Rinaldo*, and wrote many more in quick succession in the ensuing years. Handel was soon considered the foremost opera composer then resident in London.

The Handelian oratorio tradition as such began about twenty years later and can probably best be dated to the famous 1732 performance of a revised version of *Esther*, a concise work with choral movements that Handel had composed as early as 1718. At that time Handel enjoyed the patronage of James Brydges, Earl of Carnarvon, later to become Duke of Chandos, at his large mansion Cannons Park near Edgeware. Brydges had made a stupendous fortune and was able to afford a princely lifestyle that also included a musical establishment on a grand scale with singers and instrumentalists. As a composer-in-residence Handel apparently stayed at Cannons for periods of time, and, away from the hectic and demanding operatic scene in London, was able to turn his attention

3 The first advertisements announcing this addition appeared in the London newspapers from 1735; see Donald Burrows, *Handel* (Oxford, 1994), p. 18. The influential and long-lasting nature of this tradition is demonstrated by the fact that Handel's direct competitors and even following generations of oratorio entrepreneurs tried to do the same, notably John Christopher Smith, Jr, Thomas Augustine Arne and Michael Arne in the second half of the century; see Eva Zöllner, *English Oratorio after Handel: The London Oratorio Series and its Repertory, 1760–1800* (Marburg, 2002), pp. 29–32.

to other activities. One result was the original version of *Esther*, the first English oratorio, and the first to include a substantial amount of music for chorus.[4] Whereas the circumstances of the first performance of *Esther* went relatively unnoticed by the wider public, its reappearance in 1732 caused a great stir. The oratorio was first performed at London's Crown and Anchor tavern in February of that year and repeated twice in March, promoted by the Philharmonic Society and the Academy of Ancient Music, and sung and performed 'in action' by the Children of the Chapel Royal under their master Bernard Gates. When Handel planned a staged performance later that year at the King's Theatre with the same performers, he encountered objections from Edmund Gibson, Bishop of London and Dean of the Chapel Royal. Whereas an acted performance of a religious work of this kind was still permissible in a non-theatrical context, its presentation in the theatre was considered unthinkable, and Gibson would not agree to such an immoral scheme, especially since the boys of the Chapel Royal were involved. Handel had to agree to a compromise, and the oratorio was eventually given several staged performances towards the end of his 1732 opera season at the King's Theatre in the Haymarket, but 'in *still life*',[5] that is to say, performed in a concert version, with the boys being replaced by professional singers from Handel's opera company.[6] The manner of performance more or less accidentally chosen for *Esther* is significant as it became the standard for all ensuing oratorio performances by Handel and his English contemporaries. The *Esther* performances proved popular, which may have encouraged Handel to pursue this line of composition: the next two oratorios, *Deborah* and *Athalia*, followed shortly after, both completed and premiered at the King's Theatre in 1733. Whereas *Deborah* was first given as part of the theatre season, as *Esther* had been, Handel completed *Athalia* surprisingly quickly towards the end of his opera season. Armed with three oratorios, Handel then set off for Oxford, where all three were performed at a music festival connected with the annual university degree ceremonies.[7]

4 Handel's source of inspiration was an English version of Jean Racine's biblical play *Esther*, originally written in 1689. Thomas Brereton's translation of the play had been published in London in 1715. An account of the legend of Esther who saves the Jews from persecution by the Persian King Ahasuerus, the play contained choruses that had been set to music by Jean-Baptiste Moreau. It seems likely that Handel was interested in the manner in which choruses were integrated into the drama. See also Anthony Hicks, 'Handel and the Idea of an Oratorio', in Donald Burrows (ed.), *The Cambridge Companion to Handel* (Cambridge, 1997), pp. 145–63, esp. pp. 150–1.

5 According to Charles Burney 'Handel had it performed … but in *still life*: that is, without action, in the same manner as Oratorios have been since constantly performed'; see Charles Burney, *An Account of the Musical Performances in Westminster-Abbey and the Pantheon in Commemoration of Handel* (London, 1785; facsimile reprint Amsterdam, 1964), p. 101.

6 On the background of these performances, see Burrows, *Handel*, pp. 165–70.

7 For more on the Oxford performances, see Otto Erich Deutsch, *Handel: A Documentary Biography* (London, 1955), pp. 323–5.

All three works mark the early experimental phase of Handel's involvement with the oratorio format; not yet conceived as genuinely new works created along the lines of a novel concept, the first two are rearrangements of earlier music, adapted to a new text. Both versions of *Esther* contain a number of pieces from the *Brockes-Passion*, a work in the German tradition of the Passion oratorio that Handel had devised for performances in Hamburg,[8] as well as from two of Handel's 1727 Coronation Anthems;[9] *Deborah* is also basically a rearrangement of numbers from the *Brockes-Passion*, *Il Trionfo del Tempo*, the two remaining Coronation Anthems and other works.[10] *Athalia* marks a new stage of development: even though Handel still relies on material from the *Brockes-Passion*, the music is newly composed and demonstrates a noticeable move in the direction of greater dramatic coherence, particularly in the treatment of the choruses: not merely commenting on the action, the chorus is now fully integrated into the drama, representing the Jews and the Baalites. Whereas the former are characterized by church-style movements in solemn counterpoint, the latter are given dance-like numbers in simpler harmonies – a contrasting technique that Handel explores further in his later oratorios.[11] Also, Handel aims at a greater flexibility of form by adding choral sections to some of the arias. *Athalia* is an important work in that it contains in embryonic form many of the elements moulded and developed fully in his oratorios of the late 1730s and 1740s. Yet it is still an early work, touching on but not fully uncovering the full dramatic potential of the genre and remaining much more compact than the theatrical oratorios of Handel's later years.

After this unusual but successful Oxford excursion, Handel returned to his mainstay, opera, allowing five years to pass before tackling a new oratorio. With *Saul* (1739),[12] Handel's first full-scale English dramatic oratorio, he took an important new step. His first collaboration with the librettist Charles

8 This was a setting of Barthold Heinrich Brockes' libretto *Der für die Sünden der Welt gemarterte und sterbende Jesus*, published in 1712. Sent from London to Hamburg, Handel's *Brockes-Passion* is known to have been performed there in Holy Week of 1719 alongside settings of the same text by Reinhard Keiser, Georg Philipp Telemann and Johann Mattheson. The *Brockes-Passion* is an unusual experiment. Nothing is known about why Handel decided to renew his Hamburg contacts at this point, or about why he took such a sudden interest in the Passion oratorio, a form that he never subsequently pursued. It is possible, however, that Mattheson had a hand in proceedings and was the driving force behind the composition; see Walter Eisen and Margret Eisen, *Händel-Handbuch*, *herausgegeben vom Kuratorium der Georg-Friedrich-Händel-Stiftung (HHB)*, vol. 2 (Leipzig, 1984), pp. 60–1.

9 *Zadok the Priest* and *My Heart is Inditing* (HWV 258 and 261). For a complete list, see *HHB*, vol. 2, pp. 99–100.

10 For details see *HHB*, vol. 2, p. 116.

11 It was also taken up by later generations of oratorio composers – yet another indication of the all-pervading influence of Handel's oratorios. For later examples, see Thomas Arne's *Judith* (1761) and John Stanley's *Fall of Egypt* (1774) where Assyrians/Israelites and Egyptians/Israelites are similarly contrasted; see Zöllner, *English Oratorio after Handel*, pp. 108–9 and 143–4.

12 Dates given for Handel's oratorios refer to first performances, not to the completion of the work concerned.

Jennens (1700–73) and his first with a male lead, this was an oratorio conceived and planned as an entirely new dramatic piece destined for the theatre. The subject matter was again taken from the highly dramatic heroic legends of the Old Testament – this time Handel and Jennens chose the well-known story of the conflict between Saul and David – but in *Saul* the characters are strongly drawn, their portrayal resting on solid dramatic foundations, and the tri-partite structure has grown to its fullest, operatic dimensions, with substantial, large-scale choruses and unprecedented orchestral forces to match. Handel obviously brought his operatic experience to bear on this work, employing a very large orchestra that included trombones, timpani and, exceptionally, a 'carillon' or keyboard glockenspiel, which he had commissioned especially for the occasion. Another novel structural feature in *Saul* is the orchestral interludes either underpinning the 'action' or marking the passage of time.

Handel was keen to extend the possibilities of oratorio even further: *Israel in Egypt*, a companion work to *Saul* presented during the same theatre season, follows an entirely different path. With a libretto compiled exclusively from the Book of Exodus and the Psalms, *Israel in Egypt* is a non-dramatic oratorio; whereas in *Saul* (and later in *Judas Maccabaeus*, *Samson*, *Belshazzar* and others), Handel clearly approaches the oratorio concept from an operatic angle, in *Israel in Egypt* he takes his cue from the English anthem – the oratorio includes a few arias, but with about forty choruses it is essentially a choral work. In fact, it almost seems that Handel self-consciously intended it to showcase his choral writing skills: recycling his *Funeral Anthem for Queen Caroline* as the first part of the new oratorio in order to achieve the usual tri-partite layout, and adding two new parts, he employs almost every known form of choral writing, including antiphonal double choruses, choral recitatives, fugues and double fugues. However interesting as a new variation on the oratorio theme, *Israel in Egypt* was a failure with the public: audiences used to oratorios of operatic dimensions and standards were not comfortable with the unusually low proportion of solo numbers. Even though the work found a few admirers in the local newspapers, it had only a brief run of performances.[13]

Nonetheless, Handel continued to experiment. Even though by the late 1730s English oratorio had found its 'classical', most extensive form with *Saul*, the first full-length tri-partite biblical oratorio, Handel repeatedly deviated from this concept. Starting with a revised version of the pastoral *Acis and Galatea* in 1732, he also offered odes and secular dramas performed in concert

13 The *London Daily Post* of 13 and 18 April 1739 carried enthusiastic letters by two anonymous listeners who warmly recommended the work, even in the latter giving a very detailed introduction to *Israel in Egypt* and praising it as 'a sublime Act of Devotion'; see *HHB*, vol. 4 (Leipzig, 1985), pp. 307–9, which quotes these letters in full; see also Deutsch, *Handel: A Documentary Biography*, pp. 480–3.

in his 'oratorio' series. Among these were the ode *Alexander's Feast* (1736), with a text by John Dryden, often combined in performance with the *Ode for St Cecilia's Day* (1739, also by Dryden), and *L'Allegro, il Penseroso ed il Moderato*, composed and first performed in 1740, another hybrid ode–oratorio with a text based on John Milton's twin odes 'L'Allegro' and 'Il Penseroso'. The text of the obligatory third part, titled 'Il Moderato', was again supplied by Charles Jennens. There is no plot as such, merely a continuous dialogue between two opposing moods, personified as L'Allegro (Joy) and Il Penseroso (Melancholy), who are tempered by Moderation (Il Moderato).

Given that he presented both secular and sacred works under the common roof of an 'oratorio' season, Handel probably was not much concerned about 'correct' labelling; instead, variety seems to have been the key factor in his considerations, and he clearly did not see any need to reserve the formal pattern of oratorio only for works with a sacred subject. As we have already seen, in the 1730s he repeatedly turned to the writings of two major English poets, Milton and Dryden. In the case of *Alexander's Feast*, this was certainly attributable to the influence of his librettist Newburgh Hamilton (*c.* 1691–1761), whereas in the case of *L'Allegro*, Handel's Salisbury friend James Harris (1709–80) and later Charles Jennens directed him towards Milton.[14] To some extent, Handel may have been attracted by the idea of establishing himself as a quintessentially English composer (as opposed to a 'mere' composer of Italian operas) setting texts by those English poets who were held in the highest esteem and who were more or less above criticism.

Thanks not least to the detailed correspondence of Jennens and Harris outlining the genesis of *L'Allegro*, it is evident that Handel collaborated quite closely with several librettists. In particular Jennens (*Saul*, *Messiah*, *Belshazzar*, possibly *Israel in Egypt*) and later Thomas Morell (1703–84, author of *Judas Maccabaeus*, *Alexander Balus*, *Theodora* and *Jephtha*) are known to have had close working relationships with Handel, tailoring and continuously reshaping their texts to his demands, but also making musical suggestions. As Donald Burrows observes, Handel met Jennens at strategic stages in the compositional process; the contact with Morell was probably even closer, involving frequent meetings to discuss details.[15]

14 Harris and his family circle were avid supporters of Handel and followed his career closely. The extremely informative Harris correspondence has been edited and published by Donald Burrows and Rosemary Dunhill as *Music and Theatre in Handel's World: The Family Papers of James Harris, 1732–1780* (Oxford, 2002). From December 1739 to January 1740, Jennens and Harris exchanged several letters that give a detailed account of the genesis of the *L'Allegro* libretto (*Music and Theatre in Handel's World*, pp. 82–9).

15 Burrows, *Handel*, p. 322. To date, the most complete study of Handel's librettists and the political and historical background of his oratorios is to be found in Ruth Smith, *Handel's Oratorios and Eighteenth-Century Thought* (Cambridge, 1995).

In 1742 there followed what was to become Handel's most famous oratorio, *Messiah*, the fourth collaboration between Jennens and Handel after *Saul*, *Israel in Egypt* and the ode *L'Allegro*. Originally intended for a London performance in Passion Week, *Messiah* was first given in Dublin in April 1742, the high point of a successful season featuring sacred as well as secular oratorio-style works. In some respects *Messiah* is an entirely logical follow-up to *Israel in Egypt*, in that its libretto is again a scriptural collection; however, it stands out from Handel's other oratorios in not having a storyline as such: parts I and II follow Christ's life on earth, his birth, his suffering and his ascension into heaven. Part III deals with thoughts on the resurrection of Christ and his future return in glory. Only towards the end of part I, where the Nativity is narrated in a more direct manner, with several consecutive numbers taken from the Gospel according to St Luke, does the 'story' progress, mostly via references back to the Old Testament and the Psalms, stressing and justifying Jesus' claim to be regarded as the rightful Messiah expected by the prophets. However, what *Messiah* may lack in direct dramatic appeal it gains in its emotional intensity, particularly in the section dealing with the Passion in part II, and in the assured and exuberant statements of faith in part III.

Messiah was enthusiastically received in Dublin, where it was performed for the benefit of several local charities and drew huge crowds. The admonition to the ladies, published in some of the Dublin newspapers prior to the first public performance, not to come with hooped dresses in order to maximize seating space for a record attendance is legendary,[16] and even Handel himself had to concede that 'without Vanity the Performances were received with a general Approbation'.[17] By contrast, the work was greeted much less warmly at its London premiere in March 1743; objections were initially raised to the presentation of scriptural texts in the context of a theatre by singers primarily associated with the stage and its secular entertainments. This fact may also explain why the work was not officially labelled *Messiah* at first but, rather more cautiously, as 'A New Sacred Oratorio'; incurring the wrath of more conservative parties would thus have been avoided.[18] By 1750, however, such reservations were forgotten, and *Messiah* came to be appreciated as one of Handel's greatest works. As one of the biggest draws among his oratorios, it was duly given every year towards the end of Handel's oratorio season at the Covent Garden Theatre. Handel also established a performance tradition of the work

16 Several newspapers carried notes to this effect; see *HHB*, vol. 4, p. 348, which gives an advertisement from *The Dublin Journal* for 10 April 1742; see also Deutsch, *Handel: A Documentary Biography*, p. 545.

17 In a letter to Charles Jennens, dated 29 December 1741, quoted in *HHB*, vol. 4, p. 341; see also Deutsch, *Handel: A Documentary Biography*, pp. 530–1.

18 See Anthony Hicks, 'Handel and the Idea of an Oratorio', p. 158.

with the Foundling Hospital, an institution set up in order to aid abandoned children: from the 1750s onwards, annual benefit performances were given at the institution's chapel, further reinforcing the work's longevity and outstanding popularity.[19]

At about the time of *Messiah*, Handel finally decided to abandon Italian opera for English oratorio. Throughout the 1730s, he had offered both genres side by side in his theatre programmes at Covent Garden, Lincoln's Inn Fields and the King's Theatre, with the balance veering sometimes to one side, sometimes to the other – it seems that Handel tried to keep both options open in order to be able to react flexibly to the changing tastes of his audiences. By the mid-1740s, the balance had tipped conclusively in the direction of the oratorio. Whereas in the 1730s oratorios had been performed as mere 'add-ons' towards the end of the opera season, by the mid-1740s a performance pattern had developed, with oratorio performances being given during the annual Lenten season in the months of March and April.[20]

Handel's decision to prioritize oratorio is certainly an indication of the financial success of his oratorio performances in the late 1730s. Still, Handel does not seem to have been content with established routines and, as he had done in the 1730s, mixed biblical oratorios such as *Joseph and his Brethren* (1744) and *Belshazzar* (1745) with new secular works: *Semele* (1744) and *Hercules* (1745), advertised for performance 'after the Manner of an Oratorio', were secular dramas, in fact not much different from operas, save for the inclusion of a chorus. However, Handel's innovation did not meet with success: his librettist Jennens clearly disapproved, describing *Semele* as 'a baudy opera',[21] and audiences expecting musical virtuosity in a suitably pious guise appropriate to the Lenten season were dismayed and stayed away, with dire financial consequences. In a letter written in January 1745 and addressed to Handel's friend James Harris, Anthony Ashley Cooper, the 4th Earl of Shaftesbury observed:

> The musicians are charmed with Hercules. However seeing things go on so horribly, the poor man must to save himself from ruin think of retiring, and his

19 On Handel's connection with the Foundling Hospital, see Donald Burrows, 'Handel and the Foundling Hospital', *Music and Letters*, 58 (1977), pp. 269–84.

20 Handel's oratorio performances in the London theatres were not as a rule confined to the Lenten period. He started off with single oratorio performances towards the end of the theatrical season; gradually a regular pattern of oratorio performances developed on the basis of an exceptional rule given by the Lord Chamberlain as early as 1712 that precluded opera and other secular entertainments on the Wednesdays and Fridays during Lent. By offering oratorios on these days, Handel used the regulation to his advantage; see also Zöllner, *English Oratorio after Handel*, pp. 19–22.

21 As given in his famous annotations to a copy of John Mainwaring's *Memoirs of the Life of the Late George Frederic Handel* (1760); a facsimile of the page in question is reproduced in Burrows, *Handel*, illustration no. 9.

friends have it now under consideration (with great privacy) what step he ought to take. I am quite provoked to see people behave so partially.[22]

And just a few weeks later, Charles Jennens summed up the disastrous season:

> For the last two years he had perform'd Oratorios in Covent Garden Playhouse on Wednesday and Fridays in Lent only, when there was no publick Entertainment of any consequence to interfere with him; and his gains were considerable, £2100 one year, and £1600 the other, for only 12 performances. Flush'd with this success, the Italian Opera being drop'd, he takes the Opera-House in the Haymarket for this season at the rent of £400, buys him a new organ, and instead of an Oratorio produces an English opera called Hercules ... His Opera, for want of the top Italian voices, Action, Dresses, Scenes and Dances, which us'd to draw company, and prevent the Undertakers losing above 3 or 4 thousand pounds, has scarce half a house the first night, much less than half the second.[23]

In consequence, from the mid-1740s Handel abandoned all further experiments of this kind (except for *The Choice of Hercules*, in which he recycled music from the incidental music to *Alceste*), and returned instead to the tried-and-tested oratorio formula with a handful of works based on heroic legends from the Old Testament and the Apocrypha. To some extent this emphasis on legends with a heroic flavour was a reflection of the Jacobite rebellion of the mid-1740s, which had repercussions even in the field of public entertainment: *Judas Maccabaeus*, based on the apocryphal story of the Israelite leader Judas Maccabaeus who frees Jerusalem from its Syrian oppressors, was a veritable victory oratorio, conceived and written at a time when, in the autumn of the year 1745, the English victory over the Jacobite rebellion led by Prince Charles Edward Stuart seemed imminent.[24] Even though Handel's librettist Thomas Morell makes no direct references to the rebellion, the work was 'design'd as a compliment to the Duke of Cumberland upon his returning victorious from Scotland'.[25] Similarly heroic notes are struck in the *Occasional Oratorio* (1746), *Alexander Balus* and *Joshua* (both 1748). *Solomon* (1749) was also to some extent a reaction to political events of the time, celebrating the wisdom of Solomon and the restoration of peace – probably, as Ruth Smith suggests, a reaction to the Peace of Aix-la-Chapelle that was being negotiated as Handel was writing the oratorio.[26]

22 Letter from the 4th Earl of Shaftesbury to James Harris, dated 8 January 1745; see Burrows and Dunhill, *Music and Theatre in Handel's World*, p. 210.

23 Letter to Holdsworth, 21 February 1745, *HHB*, vol. 4, p. 386.

24 The Second Jacobite Rising of 1745 (also called 'The Forty-Five' for short) led by 'Bonnie Prince Charlie', the 'Young Pretender' Charles Edward Stuart, had thrown the country into turmoil; it ended in April 1746 at the Battle of Culloden, with the Hanoverian troops under the command of William Augustus, Duke of Cumberland.

25 *HHB*, vol. 4, p. 407.

26 Smith, *Handel's Oratorios and Eighteenth-Century Thought*, pp. 313–14.

In his last three oratorios Handel chose to put human drama centre stage rather than heroic battles and extrovert public grandeur: *Susanna* (1749) is the story of a virtuous heroine, who, accused of infidelity and quickly sentenced to death on the strength of false evidence, is saved by Daniel, who discovers the truth and reunites her with her husband. *Theodora* (1750) outlines the sufferings of two early Christian martyrs and *Jephtha* (1752) focuses on the poignant drama of Jephtha's daughter, who, due to an ill-fated vow made by her father, is to be sacrificed, a fate that is only at a very late stage averted by the appearance of an angel.

Much to Handel's disappointment – the composer is known to have favoured *Theodora* as his best oratorio[27] – these last three works did not appeal to his audiences, and ticket sales did not meet expectations – 'the Town don't like it at all', the Earl of Shaftesbury observed, commenting on *Theodora* in 1750.[28] Morell recorded the composer's poignant and embittered reaction to the lukewarm response to *Theodora*: 'The Jews will not come to it (as to Judas) because it is a Christian story; and the Ladies will not come, because it [is] a virtuous one.'[29] By the early 1750s, Handel's health was declining rapidly; on account of his failing eyesight, he had barely been able to finish *Jephtha*,[30] which was to remain his last new oratorio. The last 'new' work to appear in the oratorio series in Handel's lifetime was *The Triumph of Time and Truth*, but this was an arrangement of his early *Il Trionfo del Tempo* to an English text adapted by Thomas Morell; the music was probably assembled by the younger John Christopher Smith, who helped Handel with the management of his oratorios during his last years. Handel's own contribution is uncertain. In the early and mid-1750s the oratorio seasons mainly included performances of *Messiah*, *Judas Maccabaeus* and *Solomon*, with the occasional lesser-known work thrown in.

The most striking components of Handel's rich oratorial oeuvre were, of course, the choruses, which were much appreciated by an audience familiar with the prodigal English choral tradition; Handel strove here for maximum variety, and the wide range of forms and textures that he used makes it difficult to draw up a brief and yet meaningful list of typical ingredients – it is simply not possible to put them neatly in specific categories. He uses homophonic textures, fugal (with up to three subjects) and *basso ostinato* structures, as well as more flexible imitative forms, all of which are often combined freely in a single piece. The range of expression and function is just as wide: in Handel's

27 See Burrows, *Handel*, pp. 333–4.

28 Letter to James Harris, dated 24 March 1750, quoted in Burrows and Dunhill, *Music and Theatre in Handel's World*, pp. 267–8.

29 Letter dated *c.* 1770, quoted in Deutsch, *Handel: A Documentary Biography*, p. 852.

30 Handel himself noted in German in the autograph score that he had to lay aside the composition because of serious problems with his left eye. His annotations are given in full in *HHB*, vol. 2, p. 406.

dramatic oratorios, choruses are often used to represent and characterize opposing forces, such as the Israelites and their enemies, but could also be more general and anthem-like in nature. The choruses in *Israel in Egypt* are exceptional in that Handel exploited the onomatopoeic potential of his text to the full.

As far as arias and ensembles (most of them duets) are concerned, these are clearly derived from operatic models, in both structure as well as in the expression of affects. However, Handel wrote progressively fewer arias in standardized operatic da capo form until the mid-1740s, preferring to cast them in binary or strophic form instead. Only in his late oratorios *Susanna* and *Theodora* did he again employ a larger proportion of tri-partite arias.

Unlike Continental models, where oratorios were more closely associated with the church and thus closer to the field of sacred music, Handel's twenty-plus oratorios[31] were clearly theatrical creations, even though they were not acted. The sacred-or-secular issue was very important to audiences in Handel's time and, as we have seen, could lead to confusion, irritation and criticism when Handel introduced words from the Scriptures (*Messiah*) or had secular works performed in the context of an 'oratorio season' (*Hercules*, *Semele*).[32] Furthermore, Handel's punctilious librettist Charles Jennens had moral qualms whenever Handel veered too far for his taste from sacred and edifying topics. But it is doubtful that Handel himself was bothered by this, given that he still continued to present secular works alongside his biblical oratorios, which of course prompts the question of Handel's intentions for his oratorios and whether he pursued any particular aesthetic goals. This is a difficult question to answer, especially since we have almost no direct statements from Handel himself that would help to clarify matters.[33] According to one

31 The exact number of Handel's oratorios depends on how we define the term: apart from the two early Italian oratorios *Il Trionfo del Tempo* and *La Resurrezione* and the German *Brockes-Passion*, there are seventeen English oratorios from *Esther* to *Jephtha*, making a total of twenty in all, but this number does not include pasticcios and arrangements (*The Triumph of Time and Truth*), or ode-oratorios (*L'Allegro* and *Alexander's Feast*), or secular dramas (*Semele* and *Hercules*), which were part of Handel's regular oratorio repertory.

32 The debate even continued into the second half of the century. Robert Maddison's *Examination of the Oratorios which have been performed this Season at Covent-Garden* (London, 1763) is a case in point: 'At *one end* of the *Town*, an *Oratorio* is a sort of sober, solemn entertainment; which, by way of *mortification* in *Lent*, is served up to the public on *fish* and *soup* days; and so the admirers of *Acis and Galatea*, and *Alexander's Feast*, have slyly slipped them in under the names of *Oratorios* ... On the contrary, at the other end of the *Town*, an *Oratorio* is a bundle of diverting songs and choirs, tied together, with a little solemn nonsense, during which, you may talk, sleep, or stare, without any interruption, either to your own, or the audience's entertainment' (pp. 3–4).

33 The only authentic remark in this regard refers to his wish to include works sung in English in his theatre programmes since 'that joining good Sense and significant Words to Musick, was the best Method of recommending *this* [music] to an English Audience; I have directed my Studies that way, and endeavour'd to shew, that the English Language, which is so expressive of the sublimest Sentiments is the best adapted of any to the full and solemn Kind of Musick'; see Deutsch, *Handel: A Documentary Biography*, p. 602.

oft-quoted anecdote Handel, referring to *Messiah*, supposedly wished 'to make them [the audience] better'.[34] But this should be taken with a pinch of salt, and certainly not viewed through a nineteenth-century romantic lens that would imply missionary zeal on Handel's part. Rather, Handel was proud of his oratorios (which can also be deduced from his disappointed comments on the failure of *Theodora*). He considered them works of art, and wanted them regarded as such by his audiences.[35]

The whys and wherefores of Handel's oratorios must also factor in basic financial and practical details. When the interest in his operas waned, Handel still took a long time to decide to devote his attention to oratorios. Indeed, had his operas been more successful in the long run, his attitude towards oratorios would likely have been different and would have led to him continuing to produce operas for a longer period. Handel was an entrepreneur in the full sense of the term – he had to shoulder the entire financial risks of his opera and oratorio projects, first by subscription, and later (from 1747[36]) even by day-to-day ticket sales. Several poorly attended performances could put an entire series at risk, and Handel certainly had to react to the financial necessities of such an undertaking. In this respect, oratorios had a number of advantages over operas, including that they did not require elaborate stage designs, sets, costumes, dancers, or supernumeraries. Just one backdrop was needed, which was put up behind the orchestra, a tiered platform had to be erected on stage to seat the musicians, and an organ had to be available for the obligatory concertos in the intervals.[37] Oratorio was thus a medium much easier to control than opera, as no additional personnel such as stage directors were involved; Handel (and indeed other oratorio entrepreneurs too) took high financial risks but – and a definite bonus – had full control of the project in question. Practical considerations aside, oratorio offered a wide range of new musical opportunities; from a compositional point of view Handel surely would have found exploring the dramatic potential of the choruses – which was not possible to so great an extent in opera – an especially rewarding task. Oratorio was an ideal form for him, offering numerous possibilities for secular and sacred works, dramatic and non-dramatic alike.

34 Letter of 25 May 1780 from James Beattie to the Reverend Dr Laing, quoted in Deutsch, *Handel: A Documentary Biography*, pp. 854–5.

35 On this point, see Smith, *Handel's Oratorios and Eighteenth-Century Thought*, p. 53.

36 See Burrows, *Handel*, p. 401.

37 There is a very detailed list for the expenses of the 1779 oratorio series at Drury Lane in the Drury Lane Account Book for that year, down to 'guards', 'candles', 'stationary' and 'coffee' (Folger Shakespeare Library, Washington, DC, W.b. 319), which gives us an idea of the range of costs Handel himself may have had to consider in his time. On the practicalities of Handel's oratorio performances, see Burrows, 'Handel's Oratorio Performances', in Burrows (ed.), *The Cambridge Companion to Handel* (Cambridge, 1997), pp. 262–81.

Handel's contribution to the history of English oratorio in the eighteenth century falls into two easily distinguishable halves: the period covered by Handel's career as an oratorio composer, and the decades following his death. Not surprisingly, Handel's oratorios exerted a powerful influence on oratorios written in the latter half of the century, both on the choice of texts that were set and on their musical realisations. Many of the subjects that Handel himself had favoured, such as legends from the Old Testament and the Apocrypha and excerpts from Milton, reappeared in the works of his successors. Other oratorios were based on biblical compilations in the tradition of *Messiah*. Apart from a few ode-like oratorios, the tri-partite design preferred by Handel remained standard, and, even though *galant* influences gradually made their way into the new oratorios, contrapuntal sections are to be found in late-eighteenth-century works, most noticeably in the choruses; many of these works even include an obligatory 'Hallelujah' chorus. Furthermore, traditional Baroque oratorio elements such as the French overture and da capo aria were long-lived, appearing even in end-of-century works, and thus resulting in a highly eclectic style.[38]

More important than these stylistic influences, Handel gradually acquired the status of national icon from 1760 onwards, not least on account of his oratorios, which were presented to great acclaim in the Handel Commemoration of 1784 and in succeeding festivals as well.[39] Performed with large orchestral and choral forces that reached massive proportions by the turn of the century, the oratorios made ideal material for impressive musical spectacles and, with the added bonus of representing an essentially English art form, were also received as affirmations of national identity and pride.[40]

The uniqueness of this development cannot be stressed enough. As we have seen, Handel's career as an oratorio composer had its ups and downs, and the crisis of the mid-1740s was particularly severe. When John Christopher Smith, Jr (1712–95), John Stanley (1712–86) and their colleagues continued Handel's oratorio series at Covent Garden in the second half of the century, putting Handelian favourites on their programmes and, very occasionally, works of their own, this was not always appreciated, and just a few years before the Commemoration, audiences were intensely bored to the extent that not even the choruses attracted much attention:

38 See Zöllner, *English Oratorio after Handel*, pp. 193–200.

39 This process and its political background is described in detail in William Weber, *The Rise of Musical Classics in Eighteenth-Century England: A Study in Canon, Ritual, and Ideology* (Oxford, 1992).

40 See, for example, the assessment in the *Morning Chronicle* for 24 February 1776, in which oratorio is described as 'the only musical ground which is left for English genius to take root and flourish'.

> Once a year, indeed, a few of the oratorios are performed; but all their thunder, majesty, and strength, is scarcely sufficient to keep the audience awake, which, to say the truth, is for the most part so thin, that it cannot be in the interest of a manager to continue these entertainments any longer.[41]

By 1784 and the Handel Commemoration, however, the pattern was fixed and, as John Stanley had surmised in 1777, '[none] other than Mr Handel's musick would succeed, as people in general are so partial to that, that no other Oratorios are ever well attended'.[42] The end result was that even in the early nineteenth century, English oratorio – now incorporating influences from other sources such as Haydn and Mozart – was still deeply rooted in the Handelian tradition,[43] something even Handel himself could not have foreseen, given the miserable failure of his last three oratorios at their first performances. He would perhaps have been intrigued and surprised to learn that some of his oratorios were still all the rage at the turn of the century, but would certainly have raised objections to having his talents as an oratorio composer reduced to only three works (*Messiah*, *Judas Maccabaeus* and *Samson*, almost the only oratorios performed[44]) and to seeing *Theodora* still overlooked.

Select Bibliography

Bartlett, Ian. 'Boyce and the Early English Oratorio'. *Musical Times*, 120 (1979), pp. 293–7, 385–91

Burney, Charles. *An Account of the Musical Performances in Westminster-Abbey and the Pantheon in Commemoration of Handel*. London, 1785; facsimile reprint, Amsterdam 1964

Burrows, Donald. 'Handel and the Foundling Hospital'. *Music & Letters*, 58 (1977), pp. 269–84

Handel: 'Messiah'. Cambridge, 1991

Handel. Rev. edn., Oxford, 2000

Burrows, Donald and Dunhill, Rosemary (eds.). *Music and Theatre in Handel's World: The Family Papers of James Harris, 1732–1780*. Oxford, 2002

Dean, Winton. *Handel's Dramatic Oratorios and Masques*. 2nd edn., Oxford, 1990

41 *Westminster Magazine* (October 1782), p. 21; as quoted in Weber, *The Rise of Musical Classics*, p. 124.

42 Letter dated 21 April 1784; as quoted in A. Glyn Williams, 'The Life and Works of John Stanley (1712–86)', PhD thesis (University of Reading, 1977), 2 vols., vol. 1, p. 56.

43 See Nigel Burton's chapter 'Oratorios and Cantatas', which presents an overview of the early oratorio repertory written in the early nineteenth century, in Nicholas Temperley (ed.), *The Blackwell History of Music in Britain*, vol. V: *The Romantic Age, 1800–1914* (Oxford, 1988), pp. 214–41. On nineteenth-century English oratorio, see also Barbara Mohn, *Das englische Oratorium im 19. Jahrhundert. Quellen, Traditionen, Entwicklungen* (Paderborn, 2000).

44 For a statistical overview, see Eva Zöllner, '"There will be a great struggle of competition": Die Oratorienserien an den Londoner Theatern von 1760 bis 1784', *Göttinger Händel-Beiträge IX* (Göttingen, 2002), pp. 177–203.

Deutsch, Otto Erich. *Handel: A Documentary Biography*. London and New York, 1955; reprint New York, 1974

Eisen, Walter and Margaret Eisen (eds.). *Händel-Handbuch, herausgegeben vom Kuratorium der Georg-Friedrich-Händel-Stiftung*. 4 vols., Leipzig, 1978–85

Hicks, Anthony. 'The Late Additions to Handel's Oratorios and the Role of the Younger Smith'. In Christopher Hogwood and Richard Luckett (eds.), *Music in Eighteenth-Century England: Essays in Memory of Charles Cudworth* (Cambridge, 1983), pp. 147–69

'Handel, Jennens and "Saul": Aspects of a Collaboration'. In Nigel Fortune (ed.), *Music and Theatre: Essays in Honour of Winton Dean*. Cambridge, 1987, pp. 203–27

'Handel and the Idea of an Oratorio'. In Donald Burrows (ed.), *The Cambridge Companion to Handel*. Cambridge, 1997, pp. 145–63

Hurley, David Ross. *Handel's Muse: Patterns of Creation in his Oratorios and Musical Dramas, 1743–1751*. Oxford, 2001

King, Richard. 'John Christopher Smith's Pasticcio Oratorios'. *Music & Letters*, 79 (1998), pp. 190–216

Marx, Hans Joachim. *Händels Oratorien, Oden und Serenaten: Ein Kompendium*. Göttingen, 1998

Smith, Ruth. 'The Meaning of Morell's Libretto of "Judas Maccabaeus"'. *Music & Letters*, 79 (1989), pp. 27–49

Handel's Oratorios and Eighteenth-Century Thought. Cambridge, 1995

'The Achievements of Charles Jennens (1700–1773)'. *Music & Letters*, 79 (1998), pp. 161–90

Smither, Howard E. 'The Baroque Oratorio: A Report on Research Since 1945'. *Acta Musicologica*, 48 (1976), pp. 50–76

A History of the Oratorio, vol. 1 (*The Oratorio in the Baroque Era, Italy, Vienna, Paris*) and vol. 2 (*The Oratorio in the Baroque Era, Protestant Germany and England*). Chapel Hill, NC, 1977

Weber, William. *The Rise of Musical Classics in Eighteenth-Century England: A Study in Canon, Ritual, and Ideology*. Oxford, 1992

Zöllner, Eva. *English Oratorio after Handel: The London Oratorio Series and its Repertory, 1760–1800*. Marburg, 2002

The overture-suite, concerto grosso, ripieno concerto and *Harmoniemusik* in the eighteenth century

STEVEN ZOHN

Historical narratives of eighteenth-century orchestral music have, with good reason, tended to focus on the ascendancy of the solo concerto and the emergence – and eventual dominance – of the concert symphony. Likewise, instrumental chamber music of the second half of the century has been viewed largely from the perspective of the new string quartet and duo or trio with obbligato keyboard. We need hardly point out that all these types remained of central importance during the nineteenth and twentieth centuries. Often lost in the historiographical shuffle, by contrast, are genres that were equally present in the day-to-day lives of many eighteenth-century musicians and listeners, but which were nonetheless comparatively short-lived: the overture-suite, the post-Corellian concerto grosso, the ripieno concerto (or concerto for strings without soloists) and *Harmoniemusik* for wind band. Besides the lack of continuity between historical eras, there is the fact that few examples of these genres have achieved sustained and widespread popularity. Bach's four overture-suites, Handel's *Water Music*, *Music for the Royal Fireworks* and Twelve Grand Concertos, Op. 6, and Mozart's 'Gran Partita' immediately come to mind. These are the works most likely to be included in pedagogical anthologies; when absent, students may be left with the mistaken impression that after 1700 suites were restricted to French keyboard works, concertos were invariably of the solo (Vivaldian) type and music for wind band was virtually unknown. As this chapter will show, the relatively unfamilar repertories of overture-suites, concerti grossi, ripieno concertos and *Harmoniemusiken* not only harbour treasures, but also reveal much about the richness and diversity of eighteenth-century musical culture.

The overture-suite

> Just as French music is a special art, so it requires special admirers. Their suites sound well during meals ... And whoever is an admirer of them can presently derive great satisfaction from such compositions at many German courts.
>
> Johann Beer, *Musicalische Discurse* (Nuremberg, 1719)

These words by the Weissenfels Konzertmeister Johann Beer, written around 1690,[1] speak to the enthusiastic cultivation of all things French at German courts during the late seventeenth and early eighteenth centuries. Not only French music, but literature, dance, architecture, landscaping, fashion and the language itself became emblems of absolutist power as the German aristocracy sought to emulate the magnificence of King Louis XIV, on full display to the many foreigners who visited Versailles and Paris. Along with opera and ballet, the overture-suite (often called simply 'ouverture' during the eighteenth century) offered an especially potent expression of French cultural prestige, for it combined courtly and theatrical dance music with a large instrumental ensemble governed by an almost militaristic discipline. Ironically, the overture-suite was a quintessentially German phenomenon; although initially modelled on the music of Lully and his followers, it existed in France only as a compilation of pre-existing theatrical music.

Beginning in 1682, collections of instrumental music from Lully's operas were published in Amsterdam by Jean Philip Heus, Antoine Pointel and Estienne Roger. These suites of up to thirty movements apiece reduced the texture from five to four parts and omitted the original indications for wind instruments.[2] As an alternative to these editions, German musicians created their own overture-suites from French opera scores published in France by Christophe Ballard and Henri di Baussen. During the 1710s, for example, the Belgian dancing master and violinist Jean-Baptiste Volumier led the Dresden Hofkapelle in performances of overture-suites arranged from operas by Lully, André Campra and André Cardinal Destouches.

As table 20.1 shows, it was also during this period that the first newly composed overture-suites were published by the German 'Lullists', so named because several – Johann Sigismund Kusser, Johann Caspar Ferdinand Fischer, Rupert Ignaz Mayr and Gottlieb Muffat – had studied with Lully in Paris.[3] By the 1680s there was a well-established German tradition of French-style ensemble suites, such as those published in Johann Caspar Horn's six-volume

1 Johann Beer, *Musicalische Discurse* (Nuremberg, 1719); reprinted in *Johann Beer: Sämtliche Werke*, ed. Ferdinand van Ingen and Hans-Gert Roloff (Bern, 2005), p. 328: 'Die Frantzösische Music/gleichwie sie einer sonderlichen Art ist/also brauchet sie auch sonderliche Liebhaber. Ihre *Suiten* klingen brav bey der Taffel ... Und wer ein Liebhaber davon ist/kan jetzt auf vielen teutschen Höfen grosse *Satisfaction* von dergleichen *Compositionen* ... geniessen.'

2 Herbert Schneider, 'The Amsterdam Editions of Lully's Orchestral Suites', in John Hajdu Heyer (ed.), *Jean-Baptiste Lully and the Music of the French Baroque: Essays in Honor of James R. Anthony* (Cambridge, 1989), pp. 115–16 and 118.

3 The Italian-born Agostino Steffani also visited Paris, and there is some circumstantial evidence that Fischer did as well (Herbert Schneider, 'Johann Caspar Ferdinand Fischers Orchestersuiten, ihre Quellen und stilistische Einordnung', in Ludwig Finscher (ed.), *J. C. F. Fischer in seiner Zeit* (Frankfurt, 1994), pp. 83–4). The table is a modified version of Table 1.1 in Steven Zohn, *Music for a Mixed Taste: Style, Genre, and Meaning in Telemann's Instrumental Works* (Oxford and New York, 2008), p. 18.

Table 20.1. *German Overture-suite publications, 1682–1706*

Composer	Publication [Number of Suites]
Johann Sigismund Kusser	*Composition de musique, suivant la méthode françoise, contenant six ouvertures de théâtre accompagnées de plusieurs airs* (1682) [6]
Rupert Ignaz Mayr	*Pythagorische Schmids-Füncklein, bestehend in unterschidlichen Arien, Sonatinen, Ouverturen* (1692) [7]
Philipp Heinrich Erlebach	*VI Ouvertures begleitet mit ihren darzu schicklichen airs, nach französischer Art und Manier eingerichtet* (1693) [6]
Benedict Anton Aufschnaiter	*Concors discordia, amori e timori* (1695) [6]
Johann Caspar Ferdinand Fischer	*Le Journal de printems consistant en airs, & balets à 5 parties, & les trompettes à plaisir* (1695) [8]
Georg Muffat	*Suavioris harmoniae instrumentalis hyporchematicae florilegium primum* (1695) [7]
Georg Muffat	*Suavioris harmoniae instrumentalis hyporchematicae florilegium secundum* (1698) [8]
Johann Abraham Schmierer	*Zodiaci musici, in XII partitas balleticas* (1698) [12]
Johann Caspar Ferdinand Fischer	*Neu-verfertigtes musicalisches Divertissement, in sechs sehr anmuthig- und Gehör-vergnügenden Ouverturen, Entrée, Air, Gavotten, Sarabanden, Chaconnen, Rondeau, Menueten, Trio Bouréen, & c. bestehend* (1700) [6]
Johann Sigismund Kusser	*Apollon enjoüé, contenant six ouvertures de théâtre accompagnées de plusieurs airs*; *Festin de muses, contenant six ouvertures de théâtre accompagnées de plusieurs airs*; *La cicala della cetra d'Eunomio* (all 1700) [6 each]
Johann Joseph Fux	*Concentus musico-instrumentalis, enthaltend sieben Partiten und zwar, vier Ouverturen, zwei Sinfonien, eine Serenade* (1701) [7]
Johann Caspar Ferdinand Fischer	*Tafel-Musik bestehend in verscheidenen Ouverturen, Chaconnen, lustigen Suiten, auch einem Anhang von Pollnischen Däntzen à 4. & 3. Instrumentis* (1702) [5]
Agostino Steffani	*Sonate da camera à tre* (ca. 1705) [6]
Johann Caspar Ferdinand Fischer	*Musicalische Fürsten Lust, bestehend anfänglich in unterschiedenen schönen Ouverturen, Chaconnen, lustigen Suiten und einen curiosen Anhang Polnischer Täntze mit 3 und 4 Instrumenten* (1706) [5]

Parergon musicum (1663–76) and Georg Bleyer's *Lust-Music nach ietziger Frantzösischer manier gesetzet* (1670); many of these works begin with an abstract movement such as an intrada, sonatina or symphonie (as do a significant minority of the Lullists' works). But Kusser's combination of a French overture with French dances in the *Composition de musique* was novel. Each of his suites is scored for a five-part string ensemble in the Gallic configuration of *dessus*, *haute-contre*, *taille*, *quinte* and *basse*. Not surprisingly, the music owes much to Lully, 'whose works', Kusser tells us in his foreword, 'now entertain all the courts of Europe'.[4] The fact that the *Composition de musique* did not immediately inspire similar publications is probably due more to the unfavourable climate for published music in late-seventeenth-century Germany than to any lack of enthusiasm for the overture-suite. Indeed, such works were composed throughout the 1680s. For example, eleven overture-suites copied in 1689 appear to preserve Stephan Valoix's ballet music for the Francophile Hanover court, and twelve more are possibly by the court's *maître des concerts* Jean-Baptiste Farinelly.[5]

The 1690s saw a steady stream of published overture-suites scored for a four- or five-part string ensemble.[6] In contrast to keyboard suites, these works go beyond the 'classic' suite sequence of allemande – courante – sarabande – gigue to include *galant* social types (bourrée, gavotte and menuet), and those associated with the theatre (canarie, chaconne, loure, passacaille, passepied and 'airs' and rondeaus evocative of opera and ballet). Many other movements include characteristic titles suggestive of a theatrical origin: for example, 'Air Le Sommeil' (Erlebach, *VI Ouvertures*), 'Air des Combattans' (Fischer, *Le journal du printems*) and 'Entrée de Pallas, Junon & Venus' (Kusser, *Apollon enjoüé*). Muffat, who went even further by providing overall characteristic titles for each of his suites, tells us that the *Florilegium secundum* originated as ballet music; the same may be true of the *Florilegium primum*, and indeed of suites by other Lullists.[7]

Early-eighteenth-century written accounts of the French overture are no doubt indebted to the Lullists' suites. Fuhrmann (1706) speaks only of bi-partite

4 Kusser's text is reprinted in *Johann Sigismund Kusser: Suiten für Orchester*, ed. Rainer Bayreuther (Mainz, 1994), pp. [1–2].

5 Erik Albertyn, 'The Hanover Orchestral Repertory, 1672–1714: Significant Source Discoveries', *Early Music*, 33 (2005), pp. 463–8; Herbert Schneider, 'Unbekannte Handschriften der Hofkapelle in Hannover: Zum Repertoire französischer Hofkapellen in Deutschland', in Wolfgang Birtel and Christoph-Hellmut (eds.), *Aufklärungen: Studien zur deutsch-französischen Musikgeschichte im 18. Jahrhundert* (Heidelberg, 1985–6), pp. 180–93; Karen Marie Trinkle, 'Telemann's *Concertouverturen*', PhD thesis (Washington University, 2004), pp. 84–96.

6 On the scoring of these collections, a few of which call for wind instruments, see Hans-Werner Boresch, 'Satz und Besetzung in Fischers Journal du Printems', in Finscher (ed.), *J. C. F. Fischer in seiner Zeit*, pp. 85–101; Schneider, 'Johann Caspar Ferdinand Fischers Orchestersuiten'; and Inka Stampfl, *Georg Muffat: Orchesterkompositionen: Ein musikhistorischer Vergleich der Orchestermusik, 1670–1710* (Passau, 1984), pp. 32–42.

7 Steffani's *Sonate da camera* group eighty-three movements from his Hanover operas into six suites. On the evident theatrical origin of movements in Kusser's *Apollon enjoüé*, see Samantha Owens, 'The Stuttgart *Adonis*: A Recently Discovered Opera by Johann Sigismund Cousser?', *The Musical Times*, 147/1896 (Autumn 2006), pp. 71–5.

overtures (slow – fast), whereas Niedt (1706) and Walther (1708) claim that overtures conclude with a third section resembling the first. Mattheson (1713) acknowledges but disapproves of tri-partite overtures, and further claims (1721) that the third section is 'optional, and nowadays most overtures end with the fast [i.e. second] section, without special ceremony'.[8] All five of the overtures in Muffat's *Florilegium primum* are bi-partite, as are both of the overtures in Mayr's *Pythagorische Schmids-Füncklein*. But mixtures of bi-partite and tri-partite overtures are found, for instance, in Kusser's *Composition de musique*, and the collections of Philipp Heinrich Erlebach, Fischer and Johann Abraham Schmierer.

Although Erlebach thought it unnecessary to describe French performance style in his *VI Ouvertures* because it was then 'rather well known' in Germany, Muffat's *Florilegium secundum* includes a quadrilingual foreword describing the Lullian manner of playing, going into considerable detail about bowing, tempo, rhythmic alteration (*notes inégales*), pitch standards, instrumentation and ornamentation.[9] As invaluable as these instructions are, it is important to recognize that they (and the music to which they apply) are some thirty years removed from the author's experiences in Paris. Muffat says nothing about ensemble size, but Schmierer recommends that each of his instrumental lines be doubled, tripled or quadrupled, as long as the outer parts are 'more heavily manned' than the inner parts; he also gives the option of performing the music with single strings. This last option was probably the most common in late-seventeenth-century Germany, for most courts employed only small groups of instrumentalists.[10] Manuscripts of later works by Bach, Telemann and their contemporaries show that one-to-a-part performance remained a common option.

During the first ten to fifteen years of the eighteenth century, the overture-suite was transformed from an aggregate of brief dance-based movements into a large-scale concert piece of increased stylization. The bi-partite overture, in

8 Martin Heinrich Fuhrmann, *Musicalischer-Trichter dadurch ein geschickter Informator seinen Informandis die Edle Singe-Kunst nach heutiger Manier bald und leicht einbringen kan* (Frankfurt, 1706), p. 86; Johann Mattheson, *Das neu-eröffnete Orchestre* (Hamburg, 1713; reprint Hildesheim, 1993), p. 171; Friedrich Erhardt Niedt, *Handleitung zur Variation* (Hamburg, 1706), 2nd rev. and expanded edn. ed. with commentary by Johann Mattheson as *Musicalische Handleitung zur Variation des General-Basses* (Hamburg, 1721; reprint Amsterdam, 1976), trans. Pamela L. Poulin and Irmgard C. Taylor as *The Musical Guide: Parts I (1700/1710), 2 (1721) and 3 (1717)* (Oxford, 1989), p. 100; Johann Gottfried Walther, *Praecepta der Musicalischen Composition* (1708), ed. Peter Benary (Leipzig, 1955), p. 51.

9 Muffat's foreword is edited and translated in David K. Wilson, *Georg Muffat on Performance Practice: The Texts from* Florilegium Primum, Florilegium Secundum, *and* Auserlesene Instrumentalmusik: *A New Translation with Commentary* (Bloomington, IN, 2001) and Kenneth Cooper and Julius Zsako, 'Georg Muffat's Observations on the Lully Style of Performance', *The Musical Quarterly*, 53 (1967), pp. 220–45.

10 John Spitzer and Neal Zaslaw, *The Birth of the Orchestra: History of an Institution, 1650–1815* (Oxford and New York, 2004), pp. 219–20.

which a slow section featuring dotted rhythms precedes a fast, lightly imitative section, was replaced by a tri-partite plan featuring a much-expanded second section of greater contrapuntal rigour, sometimes resulting in a fully worked-out fugue. No longer conceived primarily for dancing, the following movements also expanded in dimension. More frequent use was made of concertante instruments, including string trios, the *trio des hautbois* or 'French wind trio' of two oboes and bassoon, and recorders, flutes, horns and trumpets.[11] Significantly, the Lullian idiom gave way to a version of the German 'mixed taste', an amalgamation of the French, Italian, English and Polish styles. Symptomatic of this stylistic shift is the frequent presence of ritornello form in the overture's middle section, and the occasional replacement of French 'airs' with Italian 'arias'.

The central figure in these developments, and indeed in the history of the overture-suite after 1700, is Georg Philipp Telemann. He may have begun composing overture-suites as a university student in Leipzig (1701–5); his works were, in any case, known there only a few years later, when Johann Friedrich Fasch successfully fooled Gymnasium students into believing that one of his overture-suites was really Telemann's.[12] During the period 1705–8 Telemann studied the overture-suites of 'Lully, Campra, and other good composers ... not without good success'. He later reckoned that by 1718 he had produced as many as 200 such works.[13] Most of the 125 extant overture-suites by Telemann were undoubtedly written for the *Hofkapellen* he led at Sorau and Eisenach, for the *collegia musica* he directed in Frankfurt and Hamburg, and for courts (principally Darmstadt and Dresden) to which he had close connections. Only ten were published, including three in the *Musique de table* (1733).

Half of Telemann's works are for strings alone, with many others adding two oboes and bassoon. More colourful concertante scorings include pairs of flutes, oboes and violins (TWV 55:e3), three oboes (TWV 55:C6, D15, d3, g4

11 Later in the century, Johann Philipp Eisel (*Musicus Autodidaktos, oder Der sich selbst informirende Musicus* [Erfurt, 1738; reprint Leipzig, 1976, p. 37]) and Johann Adolf Scheibe (*Der Critischer Musikus* [Leipzig, 1745; reprint Hildesheim and New York, 1970, pp. 672–3]) referred to overture-suites with concertante instruments as *Concertouverturen*.

12 Johann Friedrich Fasch, 'Lebenslauf des Hochfürstl. Anhalt-Zerbstischen Capellmeisters, Herrn Johann Friedrich Fasch', in Friedrich Wilhelm Marpurg (ed.), *Historisch-kritische Beyträge zur Aufnahme der Musik* (Berlin, 1757), vol. 3, p. 125.

13 Georg Philip Telemann, 'Lebens-Lauff mein Georg Philipp Telemanns; Entworffen In Frankfurth am Mayn d. 10.[–14.] Sept. A. 1718', in Johann Mattheson (ed.), *Grosse General-Baß-Schule. Oder: Der exemplarischen Organisten-Probe* (Hamburg, 1731; reprint Hildesheim, 1968), p. 174. Looking back at his Sorau years in 1740, Telemann claimed to have written about 200 overture-suites in just two years (Mattheson, *Grundlage einer Ehren-Pforte* [Hamburg, 1740; reprint Kassel, 1969], p. 360). The oft-repeated claim that he composed 600 overture-suites is based on a misreading of another passage in the 1740 autobiography (Mattheson, *Grundlage einer Ehren-Pforte*, p. 368).

and B10), and two oboes with four horns and bassoon (TWV 55:F11). Over a dozen works feature a single, concerto-like soloist (usually violin) playing a leading role in most, if not all, movements. Telemann may have originated this type of concerto-suite hybrid, though antecedents may be found among Handel's overtures and Francesco Venturini's Op. 1 (1714). One of the best-known examples is TWV 55:a2, for recorder and strings. Although Telemann's suites are formally similar to those of the Lullists, he more often groups dances into alternating pairs to create large-scale ternary structures. Dance types include, in addition to those used by earlier composers, the polonaise, angloise, hornpipe and jesting types entitled 'Harlequinade', 'Badinerie' and the like.

In their effective exploitation of the overture-suite's mimetic potential, Telemann's characteristic overture-suites adumbrate the characteristic symphony of the late eighteenth and early nineteenth centuries. Some movements recall the Lullists in referring to stock scenic types in French opera (such as the extraordinary 'Sommeille' of TWV 55:C6 and 'Combattans' of TWV 55:B10), others evoke rustic music-making (for example, the hurdy-gurdy imitation in 'La Vielle' of TWV 55:Es3) and more than a few are humorous, parodistic or satirical. Among the latter, the overture of TWV 55:G2 cleverly pokes fun at convention by quoting musical material from the second section in the first section, and vice versa. Thus the movement constitutes an early example of music about music. A few dozen overture-suites have overall programmes or characteristic titles, many of which are probably inauthentic. Two suites of 'water music' (the *Wasser-Ouverture*, TWV 55:C3, and the untitled TWV 55:F11) celebrate, respectively, Hamburg's status as a prosperous port city and life on the Alster lake, where one hears highly dissonant 'Concertizing Frogs and Crows' and humorously crude 'Village Music of the Alster Shepherds'. The *Ouverture burlesque de Quixotte*, TWV 55:G10, offers character portraits and vignettes of famous scenes from Cervantes' *Don Quixote*. Colourful depictions of commedia dell'arte characters are sketched in the *Ouverture burlesque*, TWV 55:B8, whereas the people of different nations are portrayed in the *Ouverture des nations anciennes et modernes*, TWV 55:G4, and in the untitled TWV 55:B5. Historical and mythological women are the subject of TWV 42:C1, in trio scoring. Telemann retained his taste for characteristic suites into the 1760s: a courtly day built around hunting is the subject of TWV 50:21, and the *Ouverture, jointes d'une suite tragi-comique*, TWV 55:D22, satirizes the public's fascination with contemporary 'self-help' medicine.

Next to Telemann, the most prolific composers of overture-suites are Johann Friedrich Fasch and the Darmstadt Kapellmeister Christoph Graupner, with about eighty works apiece.[14] From the time of his visit to Dresden in 1726–7, Fasch supplied more than sixty works to the court orchestra.[15] The talents of the Dresden musicians are reflected in the elaborately fugal textures and virtuosic wind writing of many overtures. In his suites, Fasch typically provides a five-movement mixture of airs and standard dance types; characteristic movements are few in number. Many Dresden works include pairs of flutes, oboes and horns, and a few feature even larger wind complements. Particularly interesting are late works such as FWV K:B5, which strongly reflect the mid-century symphonic style in their homophonic conception and strong sense of thematicism.[16] Graupner came later to the overture-suite, writing all of his during the period 1729–53.[17] His indebtedness to Telemann's works is clearest in the high incidence of characteristic movements. Also notable is the impressive variety of concertante winds employed, including the semi-exotic flûte d'amour, viola d'amore and chalumeau. For all their ingenuity, however, Graupner's overture-suites seem not to have circulated beyond Darmstadt.

Ironically, those composers responsible for the best-known overture-suites in modern times, J. S. Bach and Handel, appear to have been indifferent towards the genre. Bach likely first encountered the overture-suite through hearing the Celle court orchestra in Lüneburg, and by playing keyboard transcriptions such as those found in the Möller manuscript and Andreas Bach Book. Later models included four overture-suites by his cousin, Johann Bernhard Bach, who was said to have written 'many fine *ouvertures* in the manner of Telemann'.[18] Although all four of Bach's overture-suites are known through manuscripts with a Leipzig provenance, BWV 1066 and 1068–1069 may have been composed at Köthen. Three works survive in revised versions. The B-minor overture-suite, BWV 1067, was originally in A minor, apparently with a violin soloist in place of a flute; alternatively, an early version of the piece may have lacked a soloist of any kind. In the case of BWV 1068, Bach added parts for two oboes, three trumpets

14 Note that these totals far exceed the number of works surviving, or known to have once existed, by contemporaries such as Johann Sebastian Bach (four), Johann Samuel Endler (seven), Christoph Förster (six), Johann Adolf Hasse (four, lost), Johann David Heinichen (two), Pantaleon Hebenstreit (ten, lost), Johann Melchior Molter (fourteen), Johann Christoph Schmidt (four), Gottfried Heinrich Stölzel (three, lost) and Jan Dismas Zelenka (six).

15 Stephan Blaut, 'Zur Überlieferung der Ouverturen-Suiten von Johann Friedrich Fasch in der Sächsischen Landesbibliothek – Staats- und Universitätsbibliothek Dresden', in *Das Wirken des Anhalt-Zerbster Hofkapellmeisters Johann Friedrich Fasch (1688–1758) für auswärtige Hofkapellen* (Dessau, 2001), pp. 59–73, provides a source-critical discussion of these works.

16 On this sub-repertory, see Manfred Fechner, 'Ouverturen-Suiten "auf neue Art": Johann Friedrich Faschs Beitrag zur Fortentwicklung der Orchestersuite – Eine Skizze', in Martin Geck (ed.), *Bachs Orchesterwerke* (Witten, 1997), pp. 329–34.

17 Christoph Großpietsch, *Graupners Ouverturen und Tafelmusiken: Studien zur Darmstädter Hofmusik und thematischer Katalog* (Mainz, 1994), pp. 287–93.

18 Hans T. David and Arthur Mendel (eds.), *The New Bach Reader: A Life of Johann Sebastian Bach in Letters and Documents*, rev. and enlarged Christoph Wolff (New York, 1998), no. 306, p. 298.

and timpani to a piece first conceived for strings alone. Similarly, he added three trumpets and timpani to his original scoring of three oboes, bassoon and strings in BWV 1069.[19]

Bach's overture-suites imbue the genre with a contrapuntal and expressive intensity rarely encountered in works by other composers. This quality is nowhere more evident than in his unusually lengthy overtures, each of which scores the fugal episodes differently: 'French wind trio' in BWV 1066; soloistic writing for violin/flute in BWV 1067; soloistic writing for first violin (as *primus inter pares*) in BWV 1068; and quasi-antiphonal exchanges between winds and strings in BWV 1069. In his suites, Bach deploys just one non-standard dance type (the polonaise of BWV 1067), and mostly avoids characteristic movements. The famous 'Air' of BWV 1068 again places the first violin in the role of soloist. Perhaps BWV 1066 best exemplifies Bach's rigorous approach to the suite for instrumental ensemble. Here, all four second dances in a pair offer a contrasting scoring, none of which is found elsewhere in the suite. Passepied II, like the Polonaise-Double of BWV 1067, high-mindedly combines the first dance's tune with a new countermelody, while energetic quavers beneath the Forlane melody greatly ennoble a dance with humble origins.

On 19 July 1717 London's *Daily Courant* reported that two days earlier King George I had sailed on an open barge from Whitehall to Chelsea, accompanied by another vessel with '50 Instruments of all sorts' playing 'the finest symphonies, compos'd express for this Occasion, by Mr Hendel; which his Majesty liked so well, that he caus'd it to be plaid over three times in going and returning'.[20] The 'finest symphonies' were of course the *Water Music*, an hour-long group of movements written (or perhaps compiled) for a kind of royal photo opportunity on the River Thames. Scored for strings with oboes, flutes doubling on recorders, bassoons, horns and trumpets, the piece opens with a French overture in F major and continues with a suite-like succession of nine movements. The rest of the *Water Music* consists of a dozen more movements in several keys, none fully coalescing into a complete suite but

19 See, among the literature on Bach's overture-suites, Werner Breig, 'Zur Vorgeschichte von Bachs Ouvertüre h-Moll BWV 1067', *Bach-Jahrbuch*, 90 (2004), pp. 41–63; Siegbert Rampe and Domenik Sackmann, *Bachs Orchestermusik: Entstehung, Klangwelt, Interpretation: Ein Handbuch* (Kassel, 2000), pp. 256–76; Joshua Rifkin, 'The "B-Minor Flute Suite" Deconstructed: New Light on Bach's Ouverture BWV 1067', in Gregory Butler (ed.), *Bach Perspectives 6: J. S. Bach's Concerted Ensemble Music, The Ouverture* (Chicago, IL, 2007), pp. 1–98, esp. 12–43, 'Besetzung – Entstehung – Überlieferung: Bemerkungen zur Ouvertüre BWV 1068', *Bach-Jahrbuch*, 83 (1997), pp. 169–76, 'Klangpracht und Stilauffassung: Zu den Trompeten der Ouvertüre BWV 1069', in Martin Geck (ed.), with Klaus Hofmann, *Bach und die Stile* (Witten, 1999), pp. 327–45 and 'Verlorene Quellen, verlorene Werke: Miszellen zu Bachs Instrumentalkomposition', in Geck (ed.), *Bachs Orchesterwerke*, pp. 59–61; and Steven Zohn, 'Bach and the *Concert en Ouverture*', in Butler (ed.), *Bach Perspectives 6*, pp. 137–56.

20 Quoted in Christopher Hogwood, *Handel: Water Music and Music for the Royal Fireworks* (Cambridge and New York, 2005), p. 10.

nevertheless offering considerable variety of mood and scoring. Handel returned to the overture-suite only in 1749, the occasion being a nine-hour fireworks display celebrating the end of the War of the Austrian Succession. Many thousands of spectators heard the *Music for the Royal Fireworks* performed by a band of twenty-four oboes, twelve bassoons, nine trumpets, nine horns and three sets of tympani.[21] Although Handel's score shows the oboes and bassoons doubled by strings, the latter are unlikely to have been used outdoors. Musically, the work's main attraction is the overture, the first section of which establishes a mood of hymnic majesty. Perhaps because of the public setting and military-band instrumentation, Handel follows this section not with a fugue, but with an intrada-like allegro constructed around brief fanfares.

After the 1730s the overture-suite went into rapid decline, as younger composers increasingly turned their attention to the concerto and concert symphony.[22] Quantz lamented the French overture's virtual disappearance by the early 1750s ('Since the overture produces such a good effect, however, it is a pity that it is no longer in vogue in Germany'),[23] and already a decade earlier, Scheibe had attempted to explain why 'many musical connoisseurs ... regard overtures as antiquated and ridiculous pieces':

> One could accuse [the first section] of causing every overture to begin in the same manner. Thus a certain variety is lacking that is otherwise constantly necessary in composition, if all works are not to sound of a piece ... Perhaps this very great similarity that the beginnings of all overtures have with one another has contributed significantly to their no longer being as popular as they used to be.[24]

The last significant overture-suites date from the 1760s, when the octogenarian Telemann composed a group of works for the Darmstadt court.[25] The

21 *Ibid.*, pp. 100–1; Alfred Mann, *Handel: The Orchestral Music* (New York, 1996), p. 108.

22 Among significant composers of overture-suites born after 1700 are Johann Gottlieb Graun, Karl Hartwig, Johann Gottlieb Janitsch, Johann Philipp Kirnberger, Christoph Nichelmann, Johann Pfeiffer, Christoph Schaffrath and Johann Nikolaus Tischer. Most of their works, however, were likely composed before 1740.

23 Johann Joachim Quantz, *Versuch einer Anweisung die Flöte traversiere zu spielen* (Berlin, 1752; reprint Kassel, 1983), p. 301, English trans. Edward R. Reilly as *On Playing the Flute*, 2nd edn. (New York, 1985), p. 316.

24 Scheibe, *Der Critischer Musikus*, pp. 667 and 669–70: 'Was man diesem Satze vorwerfen könnte, ist dieses, daß er verursachet, daß sich alle Ouverturen auf einerley Art anfangen. Es fällt also eine gewisse Veränderung hinweg, die sonst in der Tonkunst durchgehends nöthig ist, wenn nicht alle Stücke wie ein Stück klingen sollen ... Vielleicht daß auch diese sehr große Aehnlichkeit, die alle Ouverturen im Angange mit einander haben, ein großes dazu beygetragen hat, daß sie nicht mehr so beliebt sind, als sie sonst waren.'

25 Wolf Hobohm, 'Bemerkungen zum Konvolut T6 der Deutschen Staatsbibliothek zu Berlin (DDR)', in Carsten Lange (ed.), *Telemann-Beiträge: Abhandlungen und Berichte, 2. Folge: Günter Fleischhauer zum 60. Geburstag* (Magdeburg, 1989), pp. 4–13. That the Darmstadt court remained an important locus for the overture-suite into the 1760s is demonstrated by Joanna Cobb Biermann, 'Johann Samuel Endlers Orchestersuiten und suitenähnliche Werke', in Martin Geck (ed.), *Bachs Orchesterwerke* (Witten, 1997), pp. 341–53.

Ouverture, jointes d'une suite tragi-comique and the 'hunt' suite have already been mentioned; two other works replace the overture with a symphonic allegro (TWV 50:22–23), while four more (55:D21, D23, F16 and g9) can be heard as almost post-modern meditations on the overture-suite's history, which Telemann now effectively brought to a close.

The concerto grosso and ripieno concerto

The posthumous publication in 1714 of Corelli's Op. 6 concerti grossi marked both an end and a beginning for the Roman type of concerto. Having originated during the 1660s and 1670s in the vocal and instrumental works of Alessandro Stradella, the type featured an amplified trio scoring, whereby two violins, cello and continuo were set against a reinforcing body of four-part strings (doubled *ad libitum*) and continuo; in Corelli's concertos, these two groups are called concertino and concerto grosso.[26] Muffat recalled hearing concertos or sonatas by Corelli in Rome during the early 1680s, which inspired him to compose his own works.[27] These were published in 1682 as the *Armonico Tributo*, six 'sonatas' in concerto grosso scoring that mix the Corellian idiom with elements of the French and German styles (an early example of the 'mixed taste'). In 1701 Muffat published revised versions of the sonatas, along with six more recently composed works, as 'concertos' in the *Auserlesene mit ernst und lust gemengte Instrumentalmusik*.[28] Other German exponents of the Roman concerto included Johann Christoph Pez (a student in Rome, 1689–92) and Benedikt Anton Aufschnaiter, whose *Dulcio Fidium Harmonia* appeared in 1703.

Despite the popularity of Corelli's Op. 6 concertos, their musical language was decidedly archaic in 1714. At that time, the works of northern Italian composers such as Giuseppe Torelli, Tomaso Albinoni and Antonio Vivaldi represented the stylistic cutting edge. Yet the Roman concerto style lives on in the works of Giuseppe Valentini (Opp. 7 and 9, 1710 and 1724), Francesco Manfredini (Op. 3, 1718), Pietro Antonio Locatelli (Opp. 1, 4 and 7, 1721–41) and Alessandro Scarlatti (*VI Concertos in Seven Parts*, *c.* 1740). It is also evident in

26 Concerning trio versus orchestral scoring in the early concerto grosso, see Owen Jander, 'Concerto Grosso Instrumentation in Rome in the 1660s and 1670s', *Journal of the American Musicological Society*, 21 (1968), pp. 168–80; Simon Harris, 'Lully, Corelli, Muffat and the Eighteenth-Century Orchestral String Body', *Music & Letters*, 54 (1973), pp. 197–202; and Peter Allsop, *Arcangelo Corelli: 'New Orpheus of Our Times'* (Oxford, 1999), pp. 144–6. Although here I follow other writers in using the term 'concerto grosso' to denote a work with a particular scoring, it appears not to have been construed so narrowly during the late seventeenth and eighteenth centuries. See Richard Maunder, *The Scoring of Baroque Concertos* (Woodbridge and Rochester, NY, 2004), pp. 4–5.

27 Wilson, *Georg Muffat on Performance Practice*, pp. 71–2.

28 In order to mix national styles on a larger scale, Muffat advised that one perform his concertos only following a suite from his *Florilegium* collections (Wilson, *Georg Muffat on Performance Practice*, p. 77).

concertos by the Corelli pupils Pietro Castrucci (Op. 3, 1736), Francesco Geminiani (Opp. 2–3 and 7, 1732 and 1748), Michele Mascitti (Op. 7, 1727) and Giovanni Mossi (Opp. 2–4, *c.* 1720 and 1727). And one still hears Corellian echoes, transmitted via the music of Geminani and Handel, in works by Charles Avison (Opp. 2–4, 6 and 10, 1740–69), Michael Christian Festing (Opp. 3, 5 and 9, 1734–56), Giuseppe Sammartini (Opp. 2 and 5, 1738–47) and John Stanley (Op. 2, 1742). Many of these publications betray their debt to the solo concerto by doing away with the concertino cello, employing ritornello structures and allowing the first concertino violin to dominate.[29] Although both Corelli and Muffat had used the viola soloistically, Valentini was the first to place one explicitly in the concertino, a scoring also adopted by Locatelli, Geminiani, Sammartini and Avison.[30]

As is apparent from these lists of composers and publications, Britain was the one place where the Roman concerto, however modified, remained popular beyond the 1720s. Corelli's Op. 6 was a mainstay of British provincial music societies for decades, and still figured prominently in performances of London's Concert of Ancient Music between 1776 and 1790.[31] Almost as influential as these works were Geminiani's Opp. 2 and 3, the first in a flurry of concerto grosso publications appearing in London during the 1730s and 1740s.[32] Despite many outward similarities to Corelli's Op. 6, Geminiani's are highly individual works that also reflect more recent developments in concerto style. The second movements of Op. 3 nos. 1 and 5, for example, are concerto-allegros in the Vivaldian manner, complete with virtuosic episodes for a solo violin. There are also instances of stylistic mixture: the first two movements of Op. 3 nos. 2 and 4 invoke the French overture, the latter movement pair even including a literal repeat of the fugal section.

But the greatest post-Corellian concertos in the Roman style are Handel's *Twelve Grand Concertos*, Op. 6 (1740).[33] This was not the first publication of concerti grossi to appear under Handel's name: six unauthorized works published as Op. 3 (1734) contain music written mainly during the 1710s and early

29 Allsop, *Arcangelo Corelli*, pp. 168–9 and 184–5.

30 Peter Walls examines the four-part concertino in detail in 'Geminiani and the Role of the Viola in the Concerto Grosso', in Warren Drake (ed.), *Liber Amicorum John Steele: A Musicological Tribute* (Stuyvesant, NY, 1997), pp. 379–413. On this and other issues of scoring in the concertos of Corelli, Valentini, Mossi, Locatelli, Geminiani, Festing, Handel, Castrucci and Sammartini, see Maunder, *The Scoring of Baroque Concertos*, chapters 4 and 10.

31 Allsop, *Arcangelo Corelli*, pp. 197–8.

32 On Geminiani's Opp. 2–3 and the idiosyncratic Op. 7, see Enrico Careri, *Francesco Geminiani (1687–1762)* (Oxford, 1993), chapter 5. Geminiani had already published orchestral arrangements of Corelli's Op. 5 violin sonatas, and would later publish similar elaborations of trios from Corelli's Opp. 1 and 3.

33 Studies of Handel's Op. 6 are surprisingly few. For an overview of the collection, see Mann, *Handel: The Orchestral Music*, chapter 5.

1720s.[34] Yet despite a title closely aping that of Corelli's Op. 6, the concertos have no concertino–concerto grosso division. Handel composed his own Op. 6 between 29 September and 30 October 1739, the hurried pace suggesting that publication was foremost on his mind.[35] It seems possible that he was responding not only to the continuing popularity of Corelli's works, but also to the recent publications of Geminiani, Castrucci, Festing and others. Both for their quality of invention and ingenious handling of instrumental forces, Handel's concertos rank among the greatest of the eighteenth century. The distinction between *da chiesa* and *da camera* works found in Corelli's concertos, and preserved in some of the publications mentioned above, is replaced here by a free mixture of movement types. Perhaps in emulation of Geminiani, Handel opens nos. 5 and 10 with French overtures, the first beginning boldly with a solo violin flourish and the second marked 'Ouverture'. The Polish, French and English styles are represented by a Polonaise (no. 3), Musette (no. 6) and Hornpipe (no. 7). Although Handel uses the traditional three-part concertino, its interaction with the concerto grosso is both complex and varied. However, more than a third of the collection's movements are scored for tutti strings without soloists, and the seventh concerto includes no independent parts for the concertino.

This last work belongs to a sub-type cultivated in northern Italy mainly between the 1690s and 1720s. Referred to variously as the concerto a quattro, concerto ripieno (following Vivaldi's occasional usage) or 'orchestral concerto' (a modern term), such works are scored for tutti strings throughout, sometimes with incidental solo passages. The earliest examples appear alongside sonatas in Torelli's *Sinfonie à tre e concerti à quattro*, Op. 5 (1692); in his *Concerti musicali* Op. 6 (1698), Torelli paired ripieno concertos with the first-known solo concertos. The last years of the seventeenth century saw further published ripieno concertos by Giulio Taglietti (Opp. 2 and 4, 1696 and 1699) and Giovanni Lorenzo Gregori (Op. 2, 1698). But more musically and historically significant are several collections from the following decade: Albinoni's influential Opp. 2 and 5 (1700 and 1707), Henricus Albicastro's Op. 7 (1704) and Evaristo Felice Dall'Abaco's Op. 2 (*c*. 1712). Like Torelli's Opp. 5 and 6, many of these publications mix ripieno concertos with sonatas or solo concertos. Most ripieno concertos follow either a sonata-like SFSF plan emphasizing fugal textures in fast movements, or a FSF plan featuring binary and ritornello

34 Hans Joachim Marx, 'The Origins of Handel's Opus 3: A Historical Review', in Stanley Sadie and Anthony Hicks (eds.), *Handel: Tercentenary Collection* (Ann Arbor, MI, 1987), pp. 254–70. Marx demonstrates that only some of the works in the collection were originally conceived by Handel as concertos.

35 Terence Best, 'Handel's Op. 6 and the European Concerto Tradition', *Göttinger Händel-Beiträge*, 6 (1996), p. 71.

forms.[36] Departing from this norm is Dall'Abaco's exceptionally attractive Op. 5 (*c.* 1721), which reflects French influence through its numerous dances and airs (some in rondeau form).

Vivaldi's approximately forty-five works, composed mostly after 1720, are both the largest and the most important body of ripieno concertos by a single composer.[37] His failure to publish this music (the lone exception being RV 124, in Op. 12 of 1729) may reflect a waning interest in the ripieno concerto during the 1720s. That some works are called 'sinfonia' may indicate their origin as introductions to vocal works; others, such as the two-movement 'Sepolcro' concertos (RV 130 and 169) were doubtless written for performance in church. The ritornello form Vivaldi employs in many fast movements consists of a series of modulating periods, each with the type of modular organization found in the ritornellos of his solo concertos. Also of special interest are a number of vigorous fast-movement fugues.

Non-Italian examples of the ripieno concerto are relatively few. Prince Johann Ernst of Sachsen-Weimar wrote two works that were subsequently recast as solo violin concertos in his *Six concerts à violon concertant*, published by Telemann in 1718. There are also a small quantity of works by Johann Jakob Kress, Fasch (FWV N:d3), Graupner and Johann Melchior Molter. But by far the most significant body of ripieno concertos written outside Italy are the nineteen works by Telemann, apparently dating from the 1710s and 1720s.[38] One might also place Bach's Third and Sixth Brandenburg Concertos, BWV 1048 and 1051, within the ripieno concerto tradition.[39] Indeed, such a classification goes a long way towards explaining the style of the works (including the enigmatic, two-chord middle 'movement' of BWV 1048) and the scoring for strings without independent soloists.

Harmoniemusik

The aristocratic, military and street wind bands referred to by the term *Harmonie* (also *Feldmusik*, *Feldharmonie*, *Harmoniemusik* and *Militärmusik*) flourished from the 1760s to the 1830s, with the years 1780–1810 representing the period of greatest popularity. Although their instrumentation varied

36 Eugene K. Wolf, *The Symphony, 1720–1840*. Antecedents of the Symphony, series A/1 (New York, 1983), p. xvi.

37 Karl Heller, 'Vivaldis Ripienkonzerte: Bemerkungen zu einigen ausgewählten Problemen', in Wolfgang Reich (ed.), *Vivaldi-Studien* (Dresden, 1981), pp. 1–31 and Heller, *Antonio Vivaldi: The Red Priest of Venice*, trans. David Marinelli (Portland, OR, 1997), pp. 192–201.

38 These are TWV 40:200; 43:D5, Es1, E2, e5, F3-5, G7-9, A5-6, a4-5, B1-3; and 44:1.

39 The first writer to connect BWV 1048 with the ripieno concerto was apparently Walter Kolneder, in 'Orchestral Music in the Early Eighteenth Century', in Gerald Abraham (ed.), *The New Oxford History of Music*, vol. 6, *Concert Music (1630–1750)* (Oxford, 1986), p. 281.

considerably, *Harmonien* invariably combined pairs of instruments from the woodwind and brass families. The smallest ensembles contained five or six instruments, typically oboes or clarinets with horns and one or two bassoons; larger ensembles included pairs of all these winds plus one or two flutes, oboes d'amore or trumpets, with bass support provided by double bass, contrabassoon or serpent. The music played by *Harmonien* consisted principally of dances, military pieces (especially marches), multi-movement works such as divertimentos, partitas and serenades, and arrangements of operas, ballets and symphonies. As in the first half of the century, repertories of court and military wind bands overlapped significantly.[40]

Important precursors to *Harmonien*, and sometimes indistinguishable from them in instrumentation, are the oboe bands of the late seventeenth and early eighteenth centuries. One of the five ensembles in Louis XIV's *grande écurie* ('large stable') at Versailles consisted of twelve *joueurs de violons, hautbois, sacqueboutes et cornets*, known informally (and more accurately) as the *douze grands hautbois du roi*. A similar band was formed by combining the four oboists attached to each of the two musketeer companies; these eight *hautbois des mousquetaires* also performed for ballets, plays and balls.[41] In Germany, many courts, towns and military regiments had organized *Hautboisten Banden* by the turn of the eighteenth century. Often modelled directly on the ensembles at Versailles, and likewise called upon to perform in various settings while doubling on a number of instruments, these replaced earlier consorts of shawms and dulcians. Hanns Friedrich von Fleming's *Der vollkommene teutsche Soldat* (Leipzig, 1726) notes that such a band should include two treble oboes, two tenor oboes and two bassoons. But in fact German *Hautboisten Banden* had no standard scoring; a pair of horns or a single trumpet was frequently added to members of the oboe family after 1730.[42]

Much of the surviving music composed for *Hautboisten Banden* consists of suites, concertos and marches for combinations of oboes and bassoons, sometimes with horns.[43] An early work is the 'Marche' for two oboes, two horns and

40 See the many examples of intersections between ensembles and repertories cited in Achim Hofer, 'Harmoniemusik-Forschung: Aktuell situiert – Kritisch hinterfragt', in Bernhard Schrammek (ed.), *Zur Geschichte und Aufführungspraxis der Harmoniemusik* (Michaelstein, 2006), pp. 26–31.

41 Rebecca Harris-Warrick and Carol Marsh, *Musical Theatre at the Court of Louis XIV* (Cambridge, 1995), pp. 5–6 and 68–70; Geoffrey Burgess and Bruce Haynes, *The Oboe* (New Haven, CT and London, 2004), pp. 37–8.

42 Even the late-eighteenth-century octet scoring was subject to much variation: Heinrich Christoph Koch (*Musikalisches Lexikon* [Frankfurt, 1802; reprint Hildesheim, 1964], cols. 737 and 759) mentions that pairs of oboes, clarinets, horns and bassoons are usual, but that this ensemble is often supplemented by a flute, one or two trumpets and a contrabassoon or serpent.

43 A particularly rich collection of such works, assembled around 1720, is documented in 'Des Herren General Major Frey Herrn von Sonsfeldt Musikalisches Cathallogium'. See Jürgen Kindermann (ed.), *Die Musikalien der Bibliotheca Fürstenbergiana zu Herdringen* (Kassel, 1987–8).

bassoon composed around 1711 at the Württemberg court by Johann Georg Christian Störl. At Frankfurt, Telemann composed a ceremonial march in 1716 for three oboes, two horns and bassoon (TWV 50:43), and in succeeding years wrote several overture-suites for two oboes, two horns and bassoon or continuo.[44] Owing to their combinations of paired woodwinds and brass, these and similar works can stake a claim to being the earliest known examples of *Harmoniemusik* in the later-eighteenth-century sense.[45] Perhaps the most extravagantly scored pieces for wind band from the early eighteenth century are Handel's *Music for the Royal Fireworks* (discussed above) and Fasch's concerto for twenty-four instruments (FWV L:D13).

In France during the 1760s and 1770s, private wind bands of clarinets, horns and bassoons were maintained by the Duke of Orléans, the Prince of Condé and the Prince of Monaco; these ensembles performed publicly at the Paris Concert Spirituel, and served as models for military bands (*harmonie militaire*).[46] Following the French Revolution, wind bands expanded in scoring (often adding flutes, piccolos, trumpets, trombones, serpent, double bass and percussion) and size, sometimes involving several dozen musicians. In addition to specially composed overtures, symphonies and marches by Charles-Simon Catel, François-Joseph Gossec and Étienne-Nicholas Méhul, the bands accompanied choruses in hymns, odes and patriotic songs. Some works bear titles describing the occasion for which they were written (for example, Gossec's marches 'lugubre', 'religieuse', 'victorieuse' and 'funébre'), and more than a few had an overtly political dimension.[47]

English military wind bands with oboes, bassoons and horns are documented from the 1750s.[48] Marches appear to have formed the bulk of their repertories, and the connection between theatrical and military music is nicely illustrated by the march in Handel's *Scipione*, which Charles Burney recalled as having been 'adopted by his Majesty's life-guards, and constantly played on the parade for near forty years'.[49] In and around London during the 1760s and 1770s, one could hear music for pairs of clarinets and horns in the Marylebone

44 Achim Hofer, 'Geburtsmomente der Harmoniemusik: Beispiele – Perspektiven', in Bernard Schrammek (ed.), *Zur Geschichte und Aufführungspraxis der Harmoniemusik* (Michaelstein, 2006), pp. 38–47; Wolf Hobohm, 'Telemanns Musik für Hautboisten-Ensembles', in Schrammek (ed.), *Zur Geschichte und Aufführungspraxis der Harmoniemusik*, pp. 69–81.

45 The problems associated with locating the 'beginning' of *Harmoniemusik* in a specific time, place and repertory are considered in Hofer, 'Geburtsmomente der Harmoniemusik', pp. 47–52.

46 Roger Hellyer, 'Harmoniemusik', in Laura Macy (ed.), *Grove Music Online* (accessed 22 July 2007).

47 Achim Hofer, *Blasmusikforschung: Eine Kritische Einführung* (Darmstadt, 1992), pp. 158–62.

48 Edward Croft-Murray, 'The Wind Band in England, 1540–1840', in *Music and Civilization*, The British Museum Yearbook, 4 (1980), p. 139.

49 Charles Burney, *A General History of Music from the Earliest Ages to the Present Period* (*1789*), ed. Frank Mercer (London, 1935), 2 vols., vol. 2, p. 734. Quoted in Croft-Murray, 'The Wind-Band in England', p. 138.

Pleasure Gardens, Finch's Grotto Gardens and Ranelagh Gardens. In the absence of private *Harmonien*, military bands performed publicly from 1770 at St James' and in the nearby park, playing mostly 'military divertimentos' made up of airs, minuets and marches. J. C. Bach's six sinfonias (also called 'Military Symphonies') and four 'Military Pieces', all for two clarinets, two horns and bassoon, represent a more substantial type of *Harmoniemusik*. As on the Continent, the larger English military bands consisted of pairs of oboes, clarinets, horns and bassoons; some also included one or two trumpets and a serpent.[50]

But *Harmoniemusik* flourished in central Europe – particularly in southern Germany, Austria and Bohemia – like nowhere else. Among the earliest significant examples are Haydn's *Feld Parthien* ('outdoor' or 'military' partitas), mostly for two oboes, two horns and one or two bassoons (Hob. II:3–5, 7, 14–15 and 23); these may have been written in 1760–1 for Count Karl Joseph Franz Morzin and Prince Paul Anton Esterházy. Most of Haydn's other surviving *Harmoniemusik* dates from much later in his career. During his London visits, he composed works for pairs of clarinets, horns and bassoons with trumpet and serpent: two 'Marches for the Derbyshire Cavalry Regiment' (Hob. VIII:1–2) and a 'March for the Prince of Wales' (Hob. VIII:3). In the mid-1790s he arranged the slow movement of his Symphony No. 100 ('Military') for *Harmonie*, and wrote a wind-band introduction for the oratorio version of his *Seven Last Words of Our Saviour on the Cross*. Haydn's last completed composition, from November 1802, was the 'Hungarischer National Marsch' for nine winds (Hob. VIII:4).[51]

One of the most important court *Harmonien* in German-speaking lands was maintained by Kraft Ernst, Prince of Oettingen-Wallerstein in Swabia. From 1784 the unusually large ensemble included pairs of flutes, oboes, clarinets, horns and bassoons, with double bass reinforcing the lowest line. Over the next two decades, a mixture of German and Bohemian musicians performed mostly partitas – usually with a four-movement scheme borrowed from the symphony – by court composers Antonio Rosetti, Joseph Reicha, Paul Wineberger and Georg Feldmayr.[52]

50 Stanley Sadie, 'The Wind Music of J. C. Bach', *Music & Letters*, 37 (1956), pp. 107–9; Croft-Murray, 'The Wind-Band in England', pp. 142–6.

51 An overview of this repertory is provided by Hubert Unverricht, 'Joseph Haydns Kompositionen für Harmoniemusik', in Eva Badura-Skoda (ed.), *Joseph Haydn: Bericht über den Internationalen Joseph Haydn Kongress, Wien, Hofburg, 5.-12. September 1982* (Munich, 1986), pp. 457–65.

52 See Sterling E. Murray, '"Grand Partitas with Passages and Minuets": Antonio Rosetti and Harmoniemusik in the Oettingen-Wallerstein Hofkapelle', in Christoph-Helmut Mahling, Kristina Pfarr and Karl Böhmer (eds.), *Zur Harmoniemusik und ihrer Geschichte* (Mainz, 1999), pp. 31–72 and introduction to *Antonio Rosetti: Five Wind Partitas: Music for the Oettingen-Wallerstein Court* (Madison, WI, 1989). The Oettingen-Wallerstein *Harmonie* is captured in a famous silhouette of *c*. 1783, reproduced by Murray.

Mozart's first works for *Harmonie*, the divertimentos K. 186 and K. 166, are scored for the unusual combination of oboes, clarinets, English horns, horns and bassoons. Both date from March 1773, the former written in Milan and the latter in Salzburg. Five further divertimentos for the standard pairs of oboes, horns and bassoons (K. 213, 240, 252, 253 and 270, composed 1773–7), may have served as *Tafelmusiken* for the Archbishop of Salzburg.

But Mozart's most important contributions to the *Harmoniemusik* repertory were all written in Vienna. The city's first private *Harmonien* were established shortly before he moved there in 1781, though informal ensembles had existed for some time; At the 'Golden Ox' inn in 1772, Charles Burney encountered a wind-band of street musicians that 'consisted of French horns, clarinets, hautboys, and bassoons; all so miserably out of tune, that I wished them a hundred miles off'.[53] Both Prince Lobkowitz and the Prince and Princess Schwarzenberg had wind-bands by 1780, and Prince Liechtenstein formed one in 1789 (nothing came of Liechtenstein's 1782 request that Mozart compose works for his as-yet unformed *Harmonie*). Also heard in Vienna were the *Harmonien* of Count Pachta in Prague and Prince Grassalkovich de Gyarak in Pressburg (now Bratislava).[54] These and similar ensembles – including the artillery band, which played both public and private concerts – replaced many of the private orchestras that had flourished in the city before 1780.[55]

The most prominent Viennese wind band was the *Kaiserlich-Königliche Harmonie*, an octet of oboes, clarinets, horns and bassoons founded in April 1782 by Emperor Joseph II. The members of this ensemble were virtuosos who simultaneously held appointments in the Burgtheater orchestra: Georg Triebensee and Johann Nepomuk Went on oboe, the brothers Anton and Johann Stadler on clarinet, Jakob Eisen and Martin Rupp on horn, and Wenzel Kauzner and Ignaz Drobney on bassoon.

The repertory performed by Viennese *Harmonien* included partitas by Franz Aspelmayr, Georg Druschetzky, Franz Krommer, Antonio Salieri, Wenzel Sedlak, Josef Triebensee (son of Georg), Christoph Wagenseil and Went, as well as serenades such as Mozart's K. 375 (1781), 388 (1782 or 1783)

53 Burney, *The Present State of Music in Germany, the Netherlands and the United Provinces*, 2nd edn. (London, 1775; reprint New York, 1969), 2 vols., vol. 1, p. 335.

54 Dorothea Link, 'Vienna's Private Theatrical and Musical Life, 1783–92, as Reported by Count Karl Zinzendorf', *Journal of the Royal Musical Association*, 122 (1997), pp. 225–6; Roger Hellyer, 'The Transcriptions for Harmonie of *Die Entführung aus dem Serail*', *Proceedings of the Royal Musical Association*, 102 (1975–6), pp. 54–5; Wolfgang Suppan, 'Die Harmoniemusik: Das private Repräsentations- und Vergnügungsensemble des mitteleuropäischen Adels zwischen Kunst- und gesellschaftlichem Gebrauchswert', in Monica Fink, Rainer Gstrein and Günther Mössmer (eds.), *Musica privata: Die Rolle der Musik im privaten Leben: Festschrift zum 65. Geburtstag von Walter Salmen* (Innsbruck, 1991), pp. 153–5.

55 Link, 'Vienna's Private Theatrical and Musical Life', pp. 226–7

and 361 (the 'Gran Partita', probably 1783–84).[56] Mozart's works are far more expansive and ambitious than his Salzburg divertimentos, and in fact the *Harmoniemusik* repertory's summit is represented by the 'Gran Partita', scored for the standard wind octet plus an extra pair of horns, a pair of basset horns and string bass. Not only was such music performed by private and military wind bands (Johann Ernst Altenburg observed in 1795 that the partitas of Druschetzky were well known in the imperial army),[57] but it could also be heard on the street. Consider Mozart's report to his father in Salzburg about an open-air peformance of K. 375 in November 1781:

> At night, at 11 o'clock, I was treated to a serenade of 2 clarinets, 2 horns and 2 bassoons – which as it so happens was my own composition ... The 6 gentlemen who performed it are poor devils who, however, played quite well together, particularly the first clarinetist and the two horn players ... During St. Theresia's night it was performed at three different locations – they had no sooner finished playing in one place than they were asked to play it somewhere else – and for money, too. At any rate, these night musicians had asked for the doors to be opened and, after positioning themselves in the courtyard, they surprised me, just as I was getting undressed, most agreeably with the opening chord of E-flat.[58]

Immensely popular with *Harmonien* beginning in the 1780s were arrangements of opera and ballet excerpts, some an hour long. Although these were normally undertaken by the director of the ensemble playing them (Went, Sedlak and Josef Triebensee were especially prolific in this respect), Mozart himself fashioned a *Harmoniemusik* version of *Die Entführung aus dem Serail*.[59] As he explained to his father in July 1782, there was a financial incentive: 'A week from Sunday I have to be done with arranging my opera for wind instruments – otherwise someone else will do it before me – and collect the profits instead of me ... You don't know how difficult it is to arrange an opera for winds – you have to suit the character of each wind instrument, yet not lose the original

56 On the *Harmoniemusiken* of Krommer and Triebensee, see Heinz Ecker, 'Die Harmoniemusik von Franz Krommer (1759–1831) unter besonderer Berücksichtigung ihrer Besetzung, Bearbeitung und Drucklegung', in Christoph-Hellmut Mahling, Kristina Pfarr and Karl Böhmer (eds.), *Zur Harmoniemusik und ihrer Geschichte* (Mainz, 1999), pp. 139–55 and 'Die Harmoniemusik-Kompositionsstil von Franz Krommer', in Schrammek (ed.), *Zur Geschichte und Aufführungspraxis der Harmoniemusik*, pp. 89–100. See also Thomas Krümpelmann, 'Joseph Triebensees Harmoniemusiken: Überlegungen zu ihrem Funktionsusammenhang', in Schrammek (ed.), *Zur Geschichte und Aufführungspraxis der Harmoniemusik*, pp. 149–65.

57 Johann Ernst Altenburg, *Versuch einer Anleitung zur heroisch-musikalischen Trompeter- und Paukerkunst* (Halle, 1795; reprint New York, 1966), p. 58. Quoted in Hofer, 'Harmoniemusik-Forschung', p. 25.

58 Letter of 3 November 1781 to Leopold Mozart; translation from Robert Spaethling, *Mozart's Letters, Mozart's Life* (New York, 2000), pp. 291–2.

59 On Went's activities, see Theodore Albrecht, 'When "Went" Went: The Demise and Posthumous Activities of Viennese Oboist and Wind-Band Leader Johann Went (1745–1801), Including His Previously Unsuspected Son Wilhelm', *Journal of Band Research*, 36/2 (2001), pp. 22–45.

effect.'[60] Whereas most arrangers contented themselves with simple transcription, Mozart composed a substantial amount of new music.[61] Arrangements of operas by Giovanni Paisiello and Vicente Martín y Soler were heard at dinners given by the Schwarzenbergs in 1787–8.[62] Dating from the same time is the most famous example of operatic music for wind band: Mozart's arrangement of his own 'Non più andrai' from *Le nozze di Figaro*, together with arias by Giuseppe Sarti and Martín y Soler, in the Act 2 finale of *Don Giovanni*.

Just how ubiquitous such arrangements were is clear from the music collections of particular *Harmonien*. Arrangements accounted for a third of the music played by the Donaueschingen court *Harmonie* during the 1780s and 1790s. From the 1790s until 1813 the Esterházy *Harmonie* and Grenadier band of Princes Paul Anton and Nicolaus II played more than twice as many arrangements as partitas; a similar percentage may be observed in the repertory of the Schwarzenberg *Harmonie* in 1799.[63] Although wind-band music at the Rudolstadt court was initially heavily weighted towards original compositions, a strong shift towards arrangements occurred after 1817.[64] A particularly interesting case is the *Harmonie* staffed by choirboys at the Augustian monastery in Brno, where an ensemble of oboes, clarinets, horns, bassoons, trumpets and contrabassoon flourished between 1810 and the 1840s. The boys provided *Tafelmusiken* for the Abbot, performed for special occasions and gave concerts for the entire monastery. Although their repertory included dances and partitas, it was especially rich in arrangements of operas and ballets by Auber, Bellini, Donizetti, Mercadante, Mozart, Rossini, Weber and other composers of the period.[65]

The Brno choirboys also played a few works by Beethoven, including an arrangement of the 'Pathétique' sonata. Like most such arrangements, this one was probably not authorized by the composer. But at least two other

60 Letter of 20 July 1782 to Leopold Mozart. Translation from Spaethling, *Mozart's Letters, Mozart's Life*, p. 315. Hellyer ('The Transcriptions for Harmonie', pp. 64–5) plausibly suggests that Mozart was acting to prevent Went from making his own transcription first, which would have deprived Mozart of a fee from Emperor Joseph II.

61 Bastiaan Blomhert, 'Mozarts own 1782 Harmoniemusik based on "Die Entführung aus dem Serail" and its Place in the Repertory for Wind Ensemble', *Mozart-Studien*, 12 (2003), pp. 77–113.

62 Link, 'Vienna's Private Theatrical and Musical Life', pp. 245–8.

63 Bastiaan Blomhert, 'Zur Harmoniemusik am Donaueschinger Hof', in Schrammek (ed.), *Zur Geschichte und Aufführungspraxis der Harmoniemusik*, p. 213; Roger Hellyer, 'The Wind Ensembles of the Esterházy Princes, 1761–1813', *Haydn Yearbook* (1984), pp. 84–90; Jiří Záloha, 'Das Repertoire der Schwarzenbergerischen Bläser-Harmonie zu Ende des 18. Jahrhunderts', *Studien zur Musikwissenschaft*, 44 (1995), pp. 180–7.

64 Axel Schröter, 'Zum Harmoniemusik-Bestand der Rudolstädter Hofkapelle: Repertoireentwicklung und Bearbeitungspraxis in der ersten Hälfte des 19. Jahrhunderts', in Schrammek (ed.), *Zur Geschichte und Aufführungspraxis der Harmoniemusik*, p. 314.

65 Jiří Senhal, 'The Harmonie (Wind Band) of the Augustian Monastery at Staré Brno (Old Brno)', *Journal of Band Research*, 12 (1975–6), pp. 23–8.

Harmoniemusik arrangements (not performed at Brno) were made with Beethoven's approval: wind-band versions of his Seventh Symphony and *Fidelio*. His own original compositions for *Harmonie* mostly date from the early Vienna years: the Octet (originally 'Parthia') Op. 103, possibly begun at Bonn but revised at Vienna in 1793; the 'Rondino' for wind octet, WoO 25 (1793); the Sextet Op. 71 (1796?); and the wind sextet WoO 29 (1797–8).[66] Likewise, Schubert's *Harmoniemusiken* – the Octet, D.72, and the funerary Nonet for pairs of clarinets, bassoons, horns, trombones and contrabassoon, D.79 – date from relatively early in his career (1813). Mendelssohn, too, composed a work for wind band during his teens, the *Ouvertüre für Harmoniemusik*, Op. 24 (1824).

Although most *Harmoniemusik* circulated in manuscript, an increasing number of works were published around the turn of the nineteenth century. Among the most ambitious publications was Josef Triebensee's extensive series of arrangements, *Miscellanées de musique* (1808–13). In 1817 Anton Meysel's *Handbuch der musikalischen Literatur* included no fewer than thirteen pages of published 'Harmonieen fuer Blasinstrumente'.[67] By the 1820s, however, the *Harmoniemusik* tradition was in decline, and the term was fast becoming synonymous with military music.[68] It is telling, in this respect, that Krommer published only marches from around 1818 onwards, and that Johann Heinrich Walch's popular collections of 'Pièces d'harmonie pour Musique militaire' began to appear at this time.[69] Few eighteenth-century-style *Harmonien* survived past the 1830s.

Finally, it is worth noting that *Harmoniemusik* established a foothold in North America. Writing to a European correspondent in 1778, Thomas Jefferson expressed his desire to assemble a private *Harmonie* in Williamsburg, Virginia:

> The bounds of an American fortune will not admit the indulgence of a domestic band of musicians, yet I have thought that a passion for music might be reconciled with that economy which we are obliged to observe ... In a country where like yours music is cultivated and practised by every class of men I suppose there might be found persons of those trades who could perform on the French horn, clarinet or hautboy & bassoon, so that one might have a band of two French horns, two clarinets & hautboys & a bassoon, without

66 Roger Hellyer, '"Fidelio" für neunstimmige Harmonie', *Music & Letters* 53 (1972), pp. 242–53; Bastiaan Blomhert, 'The Harmonie Version of Beethoven's Seventh Symphony', in Wolfgang Suppan (ed.), *Kongressbericht Abony/Ungarn 1994* (Tutzing, 1996), pp. 91–102; Armin Raab, 'Beethoven und die Harmoniemusik', in Christoph-Hellmut Mahling, Kristina Pfarr and Karl Böhmer (eds.), *Zur Harmoniemusik und ihrer Geschichte* (Mainz, 1999), pp. 113–24.

67 Thomas Kiefer, 'Werke Wolfgang Amadé Mozarts in der Bearbeitung für Harmoniemusik von Carl Andreas Göpfert', *Acta Mozartiana*, 42 (1995), pp. 74–5.

68 Hofer, 'Harmoniemusik-Forschung', pp. 21–4.

69 Ecker, 'Die Harmoniemusik von Franz Krommer', pp. 150–1; Achim Hofer, 'Was ist "Harmoniemusik"? Annäherungen an eine Antwort', *Tibia*, 20 (1995), p. 583.

> enlarging their domestic expenses ... Without meaning to give you trouble, perhaps it might be practicable for you in [your] ordinary intercourse with your people to find out such men disposed to come to America.[70]

Jefferson was writing in the midst of the American Revolutionary War, when both British and American regiments maintained wind bands that gave frequent performances. Following the war, wind bands associated with taverns, coffeehouses, theatres and pleasure gardens played arrangements of theatrical and orchestral works, military pieces and patriotic songs.[71] A June 1784 concert at the State House in Providence, Rhode Island promised music performed by 'clarinets, flutes, French horns, bassoons, etc.'. Similar ensembles were heard in a 1786 'Concert of Harmonial Music' at the Pennsylvania Coffee House in Philadelphia, and in 1800 at an open-air performance by the United States Marine Band in Washington.[72]

Harmoniemusik also played a significant role in the musical life of the immigrant Moravian communities in Bethlehem, Lititz and Nazareth, Pennsylvania, and in Salem, North Carolina.[73] Each of these communities supported an amateur *collegium musicum*, one activity of which was a series of outdoor concerts of partitas, divertimentos and opera arrangements for *Harmonie* by European composers such as Adalbert Gyrowetz, Franz Anton Hoffmeister, Ignaz Josef Pleyel, Antonio Rosetti and François Devienne. Also performed were partitas and suites by David Moritz Michael, who directed the *collegia musica* at Nazareth and then Bethlehem between 1795 and 1815. Michael's two suites were written as musical accompaniments to an annual boat excursion on the Lehigh River in Bethlehem. *Bey einer Quelle zu blasen, Suiten* and *Die Wasserfahrt* contain dances, abstract movements and characteristic pieces appropriate to each stage in the two-mile round trip. In both works, the climax occurs at the trip's halfway point, when the boat is momentarily caught in a whirlpool. Thus Michael's suites form a New World counterpart to the 'water music' of Handel and Telemann.

Select Bibliography

Albertyn, Erik. 'The Hanover Orchestral Repertory, 1672–1714: Significant Source Discoveries'. *Early Music*, 33 (2005), pp. 449–71

70 Letter of 8 June 1778 to the Tuscan scientist and civil servant Giovanni Fabbroni. See Thomas Jefferson, *Writings* (New York, 1984), pp. 761–2.

71 Raoul F. Camus, 'Band', §3, iv: 'American Wind Bands', in Laura Macy (ed.), *Grove Music Online* (accessed 25 July 2007).

72 Clyde S. Shive, Jr, 'The Wind Band in the United States, 1800 to 1825', in Bernard Habla (ed.), *Kongressberichte Oberschützen/Burgenland 1988, Toblach/Südtirol 1990* (Tutzing, 1992), pp. 160–1.

73 See Roger Hellyer, 'The Harmoniemusik of the Moravian Communities in America', *Fontes artis musicae*, 27 (1980), pp. 95–108 and Nola Reed Knouse (ed.), *David Moritz Michael: Complete Wind Chamber Music* (Middleton, WI, 2006), introduction.

Albrecht, Theodore. 'When "Went" Went: The Demise and Posthumous Activities of Viennese Oboist and Wind-Band Leader Johann Went (1745–1801), Including His Previously Unsuspected Son Wilhelm'. *Journal of Band Research*, 36/2 (2001), pp. 22–45

Allsop, Peter. *Arcangelo Corelli: 'New Orpheus of Our Times'*. Oxford, 1999

Altenburg, Johann Ernst. *Versuch einer Anleitung zur heroisch-musikalischen Trompeter- und Paukerkunst*. Halle, 1795. Reprint New York, 1966

Bach, Johann Sebastian. *The New Bach Reader: A Life of Johann Sebastian Bach in Letters and Documents*. Ed. Hans T. David and Arthur Mendel; rev. and enlarged by Christoph Wolff, New York, 1998

Baselt, Bernd. 'Die Musikaliensammlung der Schwarzburg-Rudolstädtischen Hofkapelle unter Philipp Heinrich Erlebach (1657–1714)'. In Walther Siegmund-Schulze (ed.), *Tradition und Aufgaben der Hallischen Musikwissenschaft*. Halle, 1963, pp. 105–34

'Philipp Heinrich Erlebach und seine *VI Ouvertures, begleitet mit ihren darzu schicklichen Airs, nach französischer Art und Manier* (Nürnberg 1693)'. In *Die Entwicklung der Ouvertüren-Suite im 17. und 18. Jahrhundert: Bedeutende Interpreten des 18. Jahrhunderts und ihre Ausstrahlung auf Komponisten, Kompositionsschulen und Instrumentenbau: Gedenkschrift für Eitelfriedrich Thom (1933–1993)*. Michaelstein, 1996, pp. 9–30

Beer, Johann. *Musicalische Discurse*. Nuremberg, 1719. Reprint in *Johann Beer: Sämtliche Werke*. Ed. Ferdinand van Ingen and Hans-Gert Roloff, Bern, 2005

Best, Terence. 'Handel's Op. 6 and the European Concerto Tradition'. *Göttinger Händel-Beiträge*, 6 (1996), pp. 70–84

Biermann, Joanna Cobb. 'Johann Samuel Endlers Orchestersuiten und suitenähnliche Werke'. In Martin Geck (ed.), *Bachs Orchesterwerke*. Witten, 1997, pp. 341–53

Blaut, Stephan. 'Zur Überlieferung der Ouverturen-Suiten von Johann Friedrich Fasch in der Sächsischen Landesbibliothek – Staats- und Universitätsbibliothek Dresden'. In *Das Wirken des Anhalt-Zerbster Hofkapellmeisters Johann Friedrich Fasch (1688–1758) für auswärtige Hofkapellen*. Dessau, 2001, pp. 59–73

Blomhert, Bastiaan. 'The Harmonie Version of Beethoven's Seventh Symphony'. In Wolfgang Suppan (ed.), *Kongressbericht Abony/Ungarn 1994*. Tutzing, 1996, pp. 91–102

'Mozart's own 1782 Harmoniemusik Based on "Die Entführung aus dem Serail" and its Place in the Repertory for Wind Ensemble'. *Mozart-Studien*, 12 (2003), pp. 77–113

'Zur Harmoniemusik am Donaueschinger Hof'. In Bernard Schrammek (ed.), *Zur Geschichte und Aufführungspraxis der Harmoniemusik*. Michaelstein, 2006, pp. 213–18

Boresch, Hans-Werner. 'Satz und Besetzung in Fischers Journal du Printems'. In Ludwig Finscher (ed.), *J. C. F. Fischer in seiner Zeit*. Frankfurt am Main, 1994, pp. 85–101

Breig, Werner. 'Zur Vorgeschichte von Bachs Ouvertüre h-Moll BWV 1067'. *Bach-Jahrbuch*, 90 (2004), pp. 41–63

Burney, Charles. *A General History of Music from the Earliest Ages to the Present Period (1789)*. Ed. Frank Mercer. 2 vols., London, 1935, vol. 2

The Present State of Music in Germany, the Netherlands and the United Provinces. 2 vols., 2nd edn., London, 1775. Reprint New York, 1969

Camus, Raoul F. 'Band', §3, iv: 'American Wind Bands'. In Laura Macy (ed.), *Grove Music Online* (accessed 25 July 2007)

Careri, Enrico. *Francesco Geminiani (1687–1762)*. Oxford, 1993

Cooper, Kenneth and Julius Zsako. 'Georg Muffat's Observations on the Lully Style of Performance'. *The Musical Quarterly*, 53 (1967), pp. 220–45

Croft-Murray, Edward. 'The Wind Band in England, 1540–1840'. *Music and Civilization*. The British Museum Yearbook, 4 (1980), pp. 135–79

Ecker, Heinz. 'Die Harmoniemusik von Franz Krommer (1759–1831) unter besonderer Berücksichtigung ihrer Besetzung, Bearbeitung und Drucklegung'. In Christoph-Hellmut Mahling, Kristina Pfarr and Karl Böhmer (eds.), *Zur Harmoniemusik und ihrer Geschichte*. Mainz, 1999, pp. 139–55

'Die Harmoniemusik-Kompositionsstil von Franz Krommer'. In Bernard Schrammek (ed.), *Zur Geschichte und Aufführungspraxis der Harmoniemusik*. Michaelstein, 2006, pp. 89–100

Eisel, Johann Philipp. *Musicus Autodidaktos, oder Der sich selbst informirende Musicus*. Erfurt, 1738. Reprint Leipzig, 1976

Fasch, Johann Friedrich. 'Lebenslauf des Hochfürstl. Anhalt-Zerbstischen Capellmeisters, Herrn Johann Friedrich Fasch'. In Friedrich Wilhelm Marpurg, *Historisch-kritische Beyträge zur Aufnahme der Musik*, vol. 3, 'zweytes Stück'. Berlin, 1757, pp. 124–9

Fechner, Manfred. 'Ouverturen-Suiten "auf neue Art": Johann Friedrich Faschs Beitrag zur Fortentwicklung der Orchestersuite – Eine Skizze'. In Martin Geck (ed.), *Bachs Orchesterwerke*. Witten, 1997, pp. 329–34

Fuhrmann, Martin Heinrich. *Musicalischer-Trichter dadurch ein geschickter Informator seinen Informandis die Edle Singe-Kunst nach heutiger Manier bald und leicht einbringen kan*. Frankfurt, 1706

Großpietsch, Christoph. *Graupners Ouverturen und Tafelmusiken: Studien zur Darmstädter Hofmusik und thematischer Katalog*. Mainz, 1994

Gustafson, Bruce. 'The Legacy in Instrumental Music of Charles Babel, Prolific Transcriber of Lully's Music'. In Herbert Schneider and Jérôme de La Gorce (eds.), *Jean-Baptiste Lully: Actes du colloque/Kongreßbericht Saint-Germain-en-laye – Heidelberg 1987*. Laaber, 1990, pp. 495–516

Häfner, Klaus. *Der badische Hofkapellmeister Johann Melchior Molter (1696–1765) in seiner Zeit: Dokumente und Bilder zu Leben und Werk: Eine Ausstellung der Badischen Landesbibliothek Karlsruhe zum 300. Geburtstag des Komponisten*. Karlsruhe, 1996

Harris, Simon. 'Lully, Corelli, Muffat and the Eighteenth-Century Orchestral String Body'. *Music & Letters*, 54 (1973), pp. 197–202

Hawkins, John. *A General History of the Science and Practice of Music*. Ed. Charles Cudworth, New York, 1963

Heller, Karl. *Antonio Vivaldi: The Red Priest of Venice*. Trans. David Marinelli, Portland, OR, 1997

'Vivaldis Ripienkonzerte: Bemerkungen zu einigen ausgewählten Problemen'. In Wolfgang Reich (ed.), *Vivaldi-Studien*. Dresden, 1981, pp. 1–31

Hellyer, Roger. '"Fidelio" für neunstimmige Harmonie'. *Music & Letters*, 53 (1972), pp. 242–53

'The Transcriptions for Harmonie of *Die Entführung aus dem Serail*'. *Proceedings of the Royal Musical Association*, 102 (1975–6), pp. 53–66

'The Harmoniemusik of the Moravian Communities in America'. *Fontes artis musicae*, 27 (1980), pp. 95–108

'The Wind Ensembles of the Esterházy Princes, 1761–1813'. *Haydn Yearbook* (1984), pp. 5–92

'Harmoniemusik'. In Laura Macy (ed.), *Grove Music Online*. (accessed 22 July 2007)

Hobohm, Wolf. 'Bemerkungen zum Konvolut T6 der Deutschen Staatsbibliothek zu Berlin (DDR)'. In Carsten Lange (ed.), *Telemann-Beiträge: Abhandlungen und Berichte, 2. Folge: Günter Fleischhauer zum 60. Geburtstag*. Magdeburg, 1989, pp. 4–13

'Telemanns Musik für Hautboisten-Ensembles'. In Bernard Schrammek (ed.), *Zur Geschichte und Aufführungspraxis der Harmoniemusik*. Michaelstein, 2006, pp. 69–81

Hofer, Achim. *Blasmusikforschung: Eine Kritische Einführung*. Darmstadt, 1992

'Was ist "Harmoniemusik"? Annäherungen an eine Antwort'. *Tibia*, 20 (1995), pp. 577–85

'Geburtsmomente der Harmoniemusik: Beispiele – Perspektiven'. In Bernard Schrammek (ed.), *Zur Geschichte und Aufführungspraxis der Harmoniemusik*. Michaelstein, 2006, pp. 37–52

'Harmoniemusik-Forschung: Aktuell situiert – Kritisch hinterfragt'. In Bernard Schrammek (ed.), *Zur Geschichte und Aufführungspraxis der Harmoniemusik*. Michaelstein, 2006, pp. 15–36

Hogwood, Christopher. *Handel: Water Music and Music for the Royal Fireworks*. Cambridge and New York, 2005

Jander, Owen. 'Concerto Grosso Instrumentation in Rome in the 1660s and 1670s'. *Journal of the American Musicological Society*, 21 (1968), pp. 168–80

Jefferson, Thomas. *Writings*. New York, 1984

Kiefer, Thomas. 'Werke Wolfgang Amadé Mozarts in der Bearbeitung für Harmoniemusik von Carl Andreas Göpfert'. *Acta Mozartiana*, 42 (1995), pp. 74–85

Kindermann, Jürgen (ed). *Die Musikalien der Bibliotheca Fürstenbergiana zu Herdringen*. Kassel, 1987–8

Knouse, Nola Reed (ed.). *David Moritz Michael: Complete Wind Chamber Music*. Music of the United States of America 16. Middleton, WI, 2006

Koch, Heinrich Christoph. *Musikalisches Lexikon*. Frankfurt, 1802. Reprint Hildesheim, 1964

Kolneder, Walter. 'Orchestral Music in the Early Eighteenth Century'. In Gerald Abraham (ed.), *The New Oxford History of Music*. Vol. 6: *Concert Music (1630–1750)*. Oxford, 1986

Krümpelmann, Thomas. 'Joseph Triebensees Harmoniemusiken: Überlegungen zu ihrem Funktionsusammenhang'. In Bernard Schrammek (ed.), *Zur Geschichte und Aufführungspraxis der Harmoniemusik*. Michaelstein, 2006, pp. 149–65

Link, Dorothea. 'Vienna's Private Theatrical and Musical Life, 1783–92, as Reported by Count Karl Zinzendorf'. *Journal of the Royal Musical Association*, 122 (1997), pp. 205–57

Mann, Alfred. *Handel: The Orchestral Music*. New York, 1996

Marx, Hans Joachim. 'The Origins of Handel's Opus 3: A Historical Review'. In Stanley Sadie and Anthony Hicks (eds.), *Handel: Tercentenary Collection*. Ann Arbor, MI, 1987, pp. 254–70

Mattheson, Johann. *Grundlage einer Ehren-Pforte*. Hamburg, 1740. Reprint Kassel, 1969

Das neu-eröffnete Orchestre. Hamburg, 1713. Reprint Hildesheim, 1993

Maunder, Richard. *The Scoring of Baroque Concertos*. Woodbridge and Rochester, NY, 2004

Murray, Sterling E. (ed.). *Antonio Rosetti: Five Wind Partitas: Music for the Oettingen-Wallerstein Court*. Recent Researches in the Music of the Classical Era 30–31. Madison, WI, 1989

'"Grande Partitas with Passages and Minuets": Antonio Rosetti and Harmoniemusik in the Oettingen-Wallerstein Hofkapelle'. In Christoph-Helmut Mahling, Kristina Pfarr and Karl Böhmer (eds.), *Zur Harmoniemusik und ihrer Geschichte*. Mainz, 1999, pp. 31–72

Niedt, Friedrich Erhardt. *Handleitung zur Variation*. Hamburg, 1706. 2nd rev. and expanded edn. ed. with commentary by Johann Mattheson as *Musicalische Handleitung zur Variation des General-Basses*, Hamburg, 1721. Reprint Amsterdam, 1976. Trans. Pamela L. Poulin and Irmgard C. Taylor as *The Musical Guide: Parts I (1700/1710), 2 (1721) and 3 (1717)*, Oxford, 1989

Owens, Samantha. 'The Stuttgart *Adonis*: A Recently Discovered Opera by Johann Sigismund Cousser?', *The Musical Times*, 147/1896 (Autumn 2006), pp. 67–80

Quantz, Johann Joachim. *Versuch einer Anweisung die Flöte traversiere zu spielen*. Berlin, 1752. Reprint Kassel, 1983. English trans. Edward R. Reilly as *On Playing the Flute*, 2nd edn., New York, 1985

Raab, Armin. 'Beethoven und die Harmoniemusik'. In Christoph-Hellmut Mahling, Kristina Pfarr and Karl Böhmer (eds.), *Zur Harmoniemusik und ihrer Geschichte*. Mainz, 1999, pp. 113–24

Rampe, Siegbert and Domenik Sackmann. *Bachs Orchestermusik: Entstehung, Klangwelt, Interpretation: Ein Handbuch*. Kassel, 2000

Rifkin, Joshua. 'Besetzung – Entstehung – Überlieferung: Bemerkungen zur Ouvertüre BWV 1068'. *Bach-Jahrbuch*, 83 (1997), pp. 169–76

'Verlorene Quellen, verlorene Werke: Miszellen zu Bachs Instrumentalkomposition'. In Martin Geck (ed.), *Bachs Orchesterwerke*. Witten, 1997, pp. 59–75

'Klangpracht und Stilauffassung: Zu den Trompeten der Ouvertüre BWV 1069'. In Martin Geck (ed.), with Klaus Hofmann. *Bach und die Stile*. Witten, 1999, pp. 327–45

'The "B-Minor Flute Suite" Deconstructed: New Light on Bach's Ouverture BWV 1067'. In Gregory Butler (ed.), *Bach Perspectives 6: J. S. Bach's Concerted Ensemble Music, The Ouverture*. Chicago, IL, 2007, pp. 1–98

Sadie, Stanley. 'The Wind Music of J. C. Bach'. *Music & Letters*, 37 (1956), pp. 107–17

Scheibe, Johann Adolf. *Compendium Musices Theoretico-Practicum* (Manuscript, 1728–36). Ed. in Peter Benary, *Die deutsche Kompositionslehre des 18. Jahrhunderts*. Leipzig, 1961, appendix, pp. 5–85

Der critische Musikus. Hamburg, 1740. 2nd rev. edn. as *Critischer Musikus*. Leipzig, 1745. Reprint Hildesheim and New York, 1970

Schneider, Herbert. 'Unbekannte Handschriften der Hofkapelle in Hannover: Zum Repertoire französischer Hofkapellen in Deutschland'. In Wolfgang Birtel and Christoph-Hellmut Mahling (eds.), *Aufklärungen: Studien zur deutsch-französischen Musikgeschichte im 18. Jahrhundert*. Heidelberg, 1985–6, pp. 180–93

'The Amsterdam Editions of Lully's Orchestral Suites'. In John Hajdu Heyer (ed.), *Jean-Baptiste Lully and the Music of the French Baroque: Essays in Honor of James R. Anthony*. Cambridge, 1989, pp. 113–30

'Johann Caspar Ferdinand Fischers Orchestersuiten, ihre Quellen und stilistische Einordnung'. In Ludwig Finscher (ed.), *J. C. F. Fischer in seiner Zeit*. Frankfurt am Main, 1994, pp. 71–84

Schröter, Axel. 'Zum Harmoniemusik-Bestand der Rudolstädter Hofkapelle: Repertoireentwicklung und Bearbeitungspraxis in der ersten Hälfte des 19. Jahrhunderts'. In Bernard Schrammek (ed.), *Zur Geschichte und Aufführungspraxis der Harmoniemusik*. Michaelstein, 2006, pp. 309–52

Senhal, Jiří. 'The Harmonie (Wind Band) of the Augustian Monastery at Staré Brno (Old Brno)'. *Journal of Band Research*, 12 (1975–6), pp. 12–28

Shive, Clyde S., Jr. 'The Wind Band in the United States, 1800 to 1825'. In Bernard Habla (ed.), *Kongressberichte Oberschützen/Burgenland 1988, Toblach/Südtirol 1990*. Tutzing, 1992, pp. 159–79

Spitzer, John and Neal Zaslaw. *The Birth of the Orchestra: History of an Institution, 1650–1815*. Oxford and New York, 2004

Stampfl, Inka. *Georg Muffat: Orchesterkompositionen: Ein musikhistorischer Vergleich der Orchestermusik, 1670–1710*. Passau, 1984

Suppan, Wolfgang. 'Die Harmoniemusik: Das private Repräsentations- und Vergnügungsensemble des mitteleuropäischen Adels zwischen Kunst- und gesellschaftlichem Gebrauchswert'. In Monika Fink, Rainer Gstrein and Günther Mössmer (eds.), *Musica privata: Die Rolle der Musik im privaten Leben: Festschrift zum 65. Geburtstag von Walter Salmen*. Innsbruck, 1991, pp. 151–65

Telemann, Georg Philipp. 'Lebens-Lauff mein Georg Philipp Telemanns; Entworffen In Frankfurth am Mayn d. 10.[-14.] Sept. A. 1718'. In Johann Mattheson, *Grosse General-Baß-Schule. Oder: Der exemplarischen Organisten-Probe*. Hamburg, 1731. Reprint Hildesheim, 1968

Trinkle, Karen Marie. 'Telemann's *Concertouverturen*'. PhD thesis, Washington University, 2004

Unverricht, Hubert. 'Joseph Haydns Kompositionen für Harmoniemusik'. In Eva Badura-Skoda (ed.), *Joseph Haydn: Bericht über den Internationalen Joseph Haydn Kongress, Wien, Hofburg, 5.-12. September 1982*. Munich, 1986, pp. 457–65

Wilson, David K. (ed. and trans). *Georg Muffat on Performance Practice: The Texts from* Florilegium Primum, Florilegium Secundum, *and* Auserlesene Instrumentalmusik: *A New Translation with Commentary*. Bloomington, IN, 2001

Walls, Peter. 'Geminiani and the Role of the Viola in the Concerto Grosso'. In Warren Drake (ed.), *Liber Amicorum John Steele: A Musicological Tribute*. Stuyvesant, NY, 1997, pp. 379–413

Walther, Johann Gottfried. *Praecepta der Musicalischen Composition (1708)*. Ed. Peter Benary, Leipzig, 1955

Wolf, Eugene K. (ed.). *The Symphony, 1720–1840*. Antecedents of the Symphony. Series A/1. New York, 1983

Záloha, Jiří. 'Das Repertoire der Schwarzenbergischen Bläser-Harmonie zu Ende des 18. Jahrhunderts'. *Studien zur Musikwissenschaft*, 44 (1995), pp. 175–90

Zohn, Steven. 'Bach and the *Concert en Ouverture*'. In Gregory Butler (ed.), *Bach Perspectives* 6: *J. S. Bach's Concerted Ensemble Music, The Ouverture*. Chicago, IL, 2007, pp. 137–56

Music for a Mixed Taste: Style, Genre, and Meaning in Telemann's Instrumental Works. Oxford and New York, 2008

· 21 ·

Concerto of the individual

SIMON McVEIGH

The instrumental concerto, a vehicle for solo individualism within a rational framework, was essentially a child of the eighteenth century. The framework contained (yet simultaneously defined) this soloistic expression, a characteristically eighteenth-century tension between the individual and the corporate mass. As a genre, the concerto adapted to vast changes in musical style across the century, yet already in his earliest works Vivaldi captures the essence of the later symphonic concerto: the relationship between soloist and orchestra unfolding across a single span in a unique thematic and tonal argument. In short, the principle of discourse and interaction between these forces, played out in all its diverse richness up to Beethoven and beyond, was there from the very beginning.

Concerto grosso and aria

The early 1710s saw the publication of two monuments of Italian instrumental music. Corelli's Op. 6 (1714) symbolized the culmination of the collaborative Roman 'concerto grosso', while Vivaldi's Op. 3 (1711) introduced the thrilling new Venetian solo concerto, its individualistic display and cantabile melodies set in relief by the driving rhythms of vivid ritornelli. The clarity and order implicit in Vivaldi's ritornello form – structural tuttis alternating with solos that together traverse an expressive trajectory – created for the first time an environment rich in potential for experiment with design on a large scale. In its musical vocabulary, too, the early Vivaldi concerto came to represent a defining instrumental genre, epitomizing the musical idiom of the 1710s (the 'concerto style' of the pioneering historian Manfred Bukofzer).[1]

It is tempting to link the concerto with vocal models, and in some respects the new solo concerto was indeed a three-aria showcase. Unquestionably, slow movements are often vocal numbers in not-so-heavy disguise: an operatic entrance with a *messa di voce* (a swell on a long note) is a commonplace and

1 Manfred Bukofzer, *Music in the Baroque Era* (New York, 1947), p. 222.

there is even the occasional recitative. More fundamentally, the way in which a soloist shifts the argument by a turn of mood or harmony is inherently theatrical, comparable to the interplay of characters in an opera buffa ensemble.

But in truth the aria operates under a different premise. In an opera of interacting characters the aria provides a psychological release, the consummation of a dramatic conflict that has already been played out on stage in the preceding recitative. In the concerto, on the other hand, the drama is instead transferred to the relationship between soloist and orchestra, a collaboration and contention between two purely musical forces that has often been expressed as an anthropomorphic struggle for control. The perception of the concerto as representing a dialogue or dramatic confrontation can be traced back as far as the German theorist Heinrich Christoph Koch, writing of 'a well-worked-out concerto' in 1793:

> There is a passionate dialogue between the concerto player and the accompanying orchestra. He expresses his feelings to the orchestra, and it signals him through short interspersed phrases sometimes approval, sometimes acceptance of his expression, as it were. Now in the allegro it tries to stimulate his noble feelings still more; now it commiserates, now it comforts him in the adagio. In short, by a concerto I imagine something similar to the tragedy of the ancients, where the actor expressed his feelings not towards the pit, but to the chorus.[2]

Furthermore, although the concerto provided a more formal and ordered arena for discourse than the aria, the interactions were actually far more varied, not least because the soloist could accompany or shadow orchestral material in ways simply unavailable to a singer.[3]

Since the concerto soloist is not already 'on stage', how he first presents himself is a defining moment in any concerto, not only in terms of asserting his individual character but also of setting the parameters for each subsequent engagement. During the pioneering years this was a topic of uncertainty and experiment: while in Albinoni's Op. 5 (1707) the solo violinist emerges loosely from a busy tutti texture, in Torelli's Op. 8/1 (1709) the two violinists both open the discussion and initiate each new strand. There was certainly no inherent inevitability to the triumph of Vivaldi's solution – the opening orchestral ritornello heightening anticipation for the dramatised solo entrance – yet it was to prove amazingly durable for over a century.

2 Heinrich Christoph Koch, *Introductory Essay on Composition: The Mechanical Rules of Melody, Sections 3 and 4*, trans. Nancy Kovaleff Baker (New Haven, CT, 1983), p. 209.

3 For comparisons between interaction in Mozart's piano concertos and in his operatic numbers, see Simon P. Keefe, *Mozart's Piano Concertos: Dramatic Dialogue in the Age of Enlightenment* (Woodbridge and Rochester, NY, 2001), pp. 101–46. On formal similarities and dissimilarities, see James Webster, 'Are Mozart's Concertos "Dramatic"? Concerto Ritornellos versus Aria Introductions in the 1780s', in Neal Zaslaw (ed.), *Mozart's Piano Concertos: Text, Context, Interpretation* (Ann Arbor, MI, 1996), pp. 107–37.

In the most radical assertion of independence the soloist ignored the orchestral opening altogether, as in the first movement of Locatelli's Op. 3/5, where all the tuttis outline a C major trajectory and all the solos a C minor one. At the other end of the spectrum, the soloist might reprise the opening motto unaltered, a mirrored acquiescence, as happens in most Tartini concertos and surprisingly often in Mozart.[4] Yet neither of these extremes presents a truly dynamic engagement between orchestra and solo, such as obtains in a third option where the soloist personalises the orchestral material by transforming the motto's mood: whether in a more lyrical vein, as in Bach's A minor violin concerto; or more playfully *galant*, as often in Mozart; or (most decisively of all) more brilliantly assertive in character, as in countless violin concertos from Vivaldi to Viotti, where orchestral hammer-strokes or arpeggio motives are translated into bold chords or high bravura. With the development of powerful grand pianos at the end of the century, this latter device was commandeered by pianists such as Dussek, who favoured a theatrical gesture of two thickly textured solo statements surrounded by rests.

A social drama

Already in the opening minutes of a concerto, then, a question is raised about the relationship of soloist and orchestra, a relationship that can readily be perceived as a metaphor for that between artist and audience, and (by extension) between individual and society. If the concerto plays out a drama in which both display and personal expression are circumscribed – the dangers of the individual voice controlled within agreed limits – then it vividly re-enacts the consensual reconciliation between individual and society enshrined in Rousseau's *Social Contract*, one of the pillars of Enlightenment thought. Furthermore, if this is understood as an interpretative norm, still more challenging readings become possible. In discussing the central peripeteia in the C major Andante of Mozart's K. 453, Susan McClary argues that the precipitous orchestral corralling of the soloist's visionary G-sharp major irrationality back to the tonic represents not so much a blatant sacrifice to overpowering social convention as an oblique critique of Enlightenment reason.[5]

From a slightly different perspective, the concerto might be considered to represent a collision of public and private spheres. Corporate or institutional 'symphonic' writing (the four-square motoric quavers of Vivaldi, the military

4 David Rosen, '"Unexpectedness" and "Inevitability" in Mozart's Piano Concertos', in Zaslaw (ed.), *Mozart's Piano Concertos*, p. 271.

5 Susan McClary, 'A Musical Dialectic from the Enlightenment: Mozart's *Piano Concerto in G Major, K. 453*, Movement 2', *Cultural Critique*, 5 (1986), pp. 129–69.

allusions of Mozart and Beethoven) contrasts directly with the individual expression and solo sensibility of the sonata, thus uniting the public concert milieu with the more intimate world of the salon. Furthermore, as these two genres were increasingly differentiated during the second half of the century, they became strongly gendered (the keyboard sonata being primarily associated with female salon performers); as a result the piano concerto played by a male virtuoso, viewed in a social context, would be considered intrinsically paradoxical.

The solo instrument is therefore in itself a site of social discourse. Even the violin, as the pre-ordained instrument of the orchestral leader or Konzertmeister, can readily be understood as a symbol of established authority, leading Michael Marissen in a provocative exegesis to view the Brandenburg Concertos as an 'unprecedented critical commentary on courtly hierarchy'.[6] Thus in the first concerto the *violino piccolo* plots an erratic solo course, while in the fourth the brilliance of the solo violin is compromised by the expressive counterbalance of 'inferior' recorders and in No. 5 is undermined altogether when the harpsichord, instrument of subservient accompaniment, assumes ever-increasing prominence until it threatens to overwhelm the whole in the disruptive and exaggeratedly long cadenza (greatly expanded in the later version of the work).

These are provocative metaphors, but it is worth recalling that Koch saw the concerto conflict less as an external dispute between the individual and the collective than as a confrontation within the individual's own disposition towards reason or passion[7] – or, in other words, between the soloist's intellectual engagement with the orchestra and individualized, emotional expression. We shall return to this concept after more detailed investigation of the history and role of the solo concerto, beginning with its inception in Venice around 1710.

Experimentation and selection

Critical to the larger instrumental structure was Vivaldi's establishment of a hierarchical chain of tuttis and solos, with each link working both as a response to the previous section and as a springboard to the next. Ritornello form – the preferred option for first movements throughout the century – allowed an interactive argument to unfold across a whole movement, while two further

6 Michael Marissen, *The Social and Religious Designs of J. S. Bach's Brandenburg Concertos* (Princeton, NJ, 1995), p. 10. See also Susan McClary, 'The Blasphemy of Talking Politics During Bach Year', in Richard Leppert and McClary (eds.), *Music and Society: The Politics of Composition, Performance and Reception* (Cambridge, 1987), pp. 13–62.

7 Joel Galand, 'The Large-Scale Formal Role of the Solo Entry Theme in the Eighteenth-Century Concerto', *Journal of Music Theory*, 44 (2000), p. 382.

Table 21.1. *Vivaldian ritornello form*

Key	I	I →	V (→)	→	vi/iii (→)	→	I	I	I
Orch	R1		R2		(R3)		(R4a)		R4b
Solo		S1		S2		(S3)		S4	
[Sonata]		[Exposition]		[Development]			[Recapitulation]		

trajectories were simultaneously played out across tuttis and solos independently (table 21.1).

This table captures the most common elements of Vivaldian ritornello form. Yet already this schema contains a number of elements less obligatory than others (those in parentheses), and in truth the number of permutations across thematic, tonal and textural parameters encompasses an almost infinite variety. Vivaldi must undoubtedly have conceived ritornello form as a dynamic process unfolding in real time, rather than as the static architectural straitjacket sometimes suggested. The hundreds of concertos Vivaldi wrote for the highly professional female orphans of the Ospedale della Pietà, performing in angelic garb behind an iron grille at Mass every Sunday, formed a laboratory for the exploration of the myriad possibilities of the new genre.

Far from settling into some preconceived mould, whose outcome is inexorably determined by the opening motto, Vivaldi's concertos constantly surprise by their individuality and experimental flair: a superficial acquaintance with a few published (and in the case of *The Four Seasons*, not entirely representative) works does scant justice to the rich originality of this huge corpus. In particular, it is easy to neglect the radical shifts in Vivaldi's musical language over more than three decades, as he not only embraced the expressive mannerisms of the *galant* but also began to venture into extremely unsettling discontinuities and contrasts. In many of the late concertos, the opening ritornello strings together fragments of disjointed material in a nervous patchwork quite alien to the certainties of *L'estro armonico* (see below). Vivaldi almost seems to rebel against the comfortably standardized ritornello form that was already emerging: by ostentatiously avoiding the dominant for the second ritornello, by juxtaposing sharply contrasting tempi within a single movement, and even by re-visiting the function of the opening gesture. Thus RV 189 in C major begins with a pompous Larghetto introduction, succeeded immediately by an uneasy and hesitant Allegro in C minor, only for the introduction to return in G major (transcribed into Allegro tempo) later on in the movement. This is a world as challenging to the alert listener, in terms of both genre and expression, as *empfindsam* C. P. E. Bach or Haydn at his most quixotic.

The spread of the Vivaldian concerto: an adaptable concept

Even within the repertory of a single composer, the concerto as a genre proved susceptible to an astonishing diversity of creative experiment. What is perhaps equally remarkable is the way in which the concept permeated musical life throughout the century, not only across the European continent but across the entire range of instruments, drawing imaginatively upon other genres as social context demanded or as musical styles developed.

Rarely in the history of music can a single publication have proved so tellingly influential as Vivaldi's *L'estro armonico* (harmonic inspiration or caprice, Op. 3). Published in Amsterdam in 1711, this set of twelve concertos took Europe by storm, defining the nature of the genre for the remainder of the century. Further sets achieved a similar European currency, some with equally fanciful titles such as *La stravaganza* (extravagance or eccentricity, Op. 4, 1716), *Il cimento dell'armonia e dell' inventione* (The trial of harmony and invention, Op. 8, 1725, opening with *The Four Seasons)* and *La cetra* (The lyre, Op. 9, 1727).

The works of Vivaldi's Italian successors – whether international violinists such as Locatelli in Amsterdam and Tartini with his 'scuola dei nazioni' in Padua, or hitherto neglected masters such as Andrea Zani in Casalmaggiore and Giovanni Platti in Würzburg – insist on being viewed against a shared Vivaldian backdrop. Yet for all their allegiance to certain common procedures, each of these composers developed his own distinctive idiolect. The concertos of the leading Milanese violinist Angelo Maria Scaccia may have ostentatiously revelled in eccentric discontinuities; but others developed specialist traits only detectable in the background. The Parma violinist Mauro d'Alai unusually favoured a third ritornello in the dominant of the dominant, while Tartini experimented with all kinds of fluid tonal structures, showing an idiosyncratic partiality for the minor supertonic. On the other hand, Albinoni held fast to many of his old characteristics – the interplay of sonority and motive in stable tonal blocks – in his concertos for one and two oboes, among the most beautifully crafted and melodically attractive music of the period. Perhaps it was the very ubiquity of the core Vivaldian style that led each composer to exercise his individuality by avoiding or rebelling against norms of the time: even the occasional use of a stock Vivaldian opening can often be regarded more as an act of homage or a gesture of bravado than as mere sterile imitation.

The concertos of Vivaldi and his Italian contemporaries were disseminated north of the Alps not only through their own performances as travelling virtuosi and court musicians, but – much more influentially – through the entrepreneurial opportunism and astute marketing of North European publishers (Roger and his successor Le Cène in Amsterdam, Walsh in London and so on). Successful as Roger's reprints of Corelli sonatas had been, it was his association with the modernity of Vivaldi concertos that truly defined his reputation as the vanguard publisher of his day. It quickly became *de rigueur* for the aspiring concerto composer to achieve Northern publication, and Italians were soon besieging Roger and Le Cène with material – to the extent that, when the business was eventually wound up in 1743, piles of unpublished Italian manuscripts were put up for sale.[8]

Less public, but just as widespread, was dissemination in manuscript. Some of *La stravaganza* must already have reached the Netherlands by 1713, coming to Bach's notice in Weimar in pre-publication versions brought back from Utrecht by Prince Johann Ernst. In 1728 Vivaldi himself presented a set of manuscript concertos to Emperor Charles VI (a second *La cetra*, symbol of Habsburg musicality); and he also sold individual concertos from his house, explaining to an English visitor with typical Venetian relish exactly how much more lucrative this was for the composer than publication.[9] Political ties also encouraged the migration of the Italian concerto repertory – for example, directly from Lombardy to ruling Vienna or, more subtly, infiltrating resistant French territory through links with the House of Savoy. (G. B. Somis, the leading Turin violinist, may well have had a hand in the sumptuous Fonds Blancheton collection – he also taught Leclair, the outstanding French advocate of the Italianate concerto.) In addition, newly Italophile courts such as Dresden – originally modelled on Versailles, but a bastion of Italian opera seria following Hasse's appointment as Kapellmeister in 1730 – built up impressive collections of Italian concertos in manuscript: Johann Georg Pisendel, Konzertmeister from 1728, adapted many works to local conditions, not only supplementing their virtuosity but also adding new wind parts for the large court orchestra.

Both Prince Johann Ernst and Pisendel himself wrote concertos in the newly fashionable Vivaldian manner, and the concept (if not necessarily every detail of the idiom) quickly permeated the German concerto during the early decades of the century. At the King of Prussia's court in Berlin, another flagship of Italian opera seria in emulation of Dresden, Italianate concertos became a standard feature of court concerts. The flautist Johann Joachim Quantz moved from Dresden to Berlin in 1741, adapting his style to the more intimate demands of

8 Rudolf Rasch, 'I manoscritti musicali nel lascito di Michel-Charles le Cène (1743)', in Albert Dunning (ed.), *Intorno a Locatelli: studi in occasione del tricentenario della nascita di Pietro Antonio Locatelli (1695–1764)* (Lucca, 1995), 2 vols., vol. 2, pp. 1039–70.

9 Edward Holdsworth's letter of 13 February 1733, quoted in Michael Talbot, 'Charles Jennens and Antonio Vivaldi', in Francesco Degrada (ed.), *Vivaldi veneziano europeo* (Florence, 1980), p. 71.

the daily chamber concerts, at which the King is said to have played a repertory of some 300 flute pieces in strict rotation. The attraction of Quantz's own concertos is easy to understand, as he adopted the pleasant *galant* manner and short-phrased melody of Hasse's operas, with light textures designed for the mere half-dozen or so players who accompanied; Hasse's own flute concertos were also probably written for the King.

J. S. Bach of course eagerly absorbed the Italian style as early as 1713–14, by transcribing Vivaldi concertos for solo harpsichord and organ, but his original concertos date mainly from his years at the Cöthen court (1717–23). Bach brought his own approach to the concerto, obscuring and deepening the simpler outlines of Vivaldian ritornello form by the interpenetration of contrapuntal textures and recurrent orchestral motives. Often the ritornello framework is merely implicated, the cadential emphasis being sufficient to provide harmonic articulation without the need for separate sections. The effect is frequently to blur the distinction between solo and tutti: for example, in the A minor violin concerto the powerful conclusion of the first solo is ingeniously overlaid with a tutti statement of the opening motto, which does duty as the entire second ritornello. Another Bach idiosyncrasy was the imposition of the large-scale ABA pattern of the da capo aria on to ritornello form. While Vivaldi himself sometimes approaches the recapitulation with a hiatus from the mediant, the full reprise of the entire opening tonic section in Bach's E major violin concerto represents a monumental concept quite alien to Vivaldi's idea of ritornello form.

Bach's concertos clearly illustrate the inter-relationship of genres characterizing the early history of the concerto. We have already touched upon the complex layers in the Brandenburg Concertos, which in truth fit none of the modern (mis-)conceptions of eighteenth-century concerto categorization. In Germany, for example, the very term 'concerto' possessed a multiplicity of meanings, and the 'mix of tastes' there accentuated a genre slippage as characteristic of the solo concerto as of other repertories. Telemann's concertos, for example, are sometimes in three movements, but more often in four, as vestiges of the Corellian 'concerto grosso' intermingle with lively Vivaldian Allegros and more *affettuoso* solos. A still more heterogeneous variety is evident in the published collection *Musique de table* (1733), which adds to the mix movements in French and Italian *galant* idioms.

Elsewhere, too, genre boundaries are by no means as clear-cut as they might appear at first glance, since soloistic breaks infiltrated other instrumental genres. For example, the traditional Roman 'concerto grosso' was neatly adapted for use by virtuoso violinists such as Giovanni Mossi and Antonio Montanari by the simple expedient of downgrading the second part. The resultant solo concertos, often still in four movements, include flamboyant interludes that must have equally astounded Roman churchgoers and cardinal patrons: indeed Montanari's brilliant and well-crafted concertos are the closest the Corelli school ever came to the truly virtuosic violin concerto. Even in Britain, where the pure 'concerto grosso' tradition persisted longer than elsewhere, the solo violinist takes command occasionally, as in Geminiani's Op. 3/1, while the ritornello concept is just one of the many options Handel employs in his dazzlingly magpie Op. 3 and Op. 6 concertos.

By contrast, some of those composers whose normal idiom was at the forefront of modernity could assume the antique manner (*stile antico*) should the occasion demand. Thus in many of the cello concertos they wrote for Count Rudolf Franz Erwein von Schönborn at Wiesentheid, both Zani and Platti don old-fashioned contrapuntal garb in the tuttis in deference to the Count's known partiality for the Corellian manner. Some of Platti's concertos go further still in additionally adumbrating a rich consort texture during the solos. Perhaps the cello concerto in general inspired a more serious, less flashy, mode of expression, befitting the instrument's history and role. It is striking that the earnest and often moving cello concertos of Leonardo Leo, a leader of the Neapolitan opera school, eschew virtuoso breaks and indeed hardly utilize ritornello procedures at all.

The keyboard concerto represents another distinct sub-genre. As Jane Stevens has argued, the harpsichord and organ were there from the very start in Bach's arrangements, which effortlessly absorb violinistic figurations into the normal keyboard style.[10] The Fifth Brandenburg Concerto represented Bach's first original concerto with obligato harpsichord, a fantastically idiosyncratic entry into the genre. His true keyboard concertos followed later. Although most were derived from pre-existing works for other instruments, some were originally conceived, including BWV 1061 for two harpsichords alone and the solo Italian Concerto – neither being particularly exceptional in taking the keyboard concerto out of an orchestral setting.

Bach's keyboard concertos were clearly associated with his directorship of the Leipzig Collegium Musicum from 1729, although some may derive from earlier house concerts with his own family; and it was indeed his three most famous sons (Wilhelm Friedemann, Carl Philipp Emanuel and Johann Christian Bach) who were to bring the genre into sharper focus in the middle of the century. Simultaneously a quite independent development – symptomatic of the evolving place of the keyboard concerto in musical life – was occurring in

10 Jane R. Stevens, *The Bach Family and the Keyboard Concerto: The Evolution of a Genre* (Warren, MI, 2001), pp. 30–2.

London. At his Covent Garden oratorio series in 1735 Handel introduced organ concertos as entr'actes (see below), a popular innovation that soon had crowds flocking to the theatre to hear him; and in *Alexander's Feast* he even included concertos in the plot, gracing St Cecilia with her own organ concerto. Handel's organ concertos are heterogeneous in form and often in more than three movements, but nevertheless many Allegro movements adopt a sprightly Vivaldian texture with unaccompanied solos that Handel must have often simply improvised or extended on the spot: the surviving sources contain frequent *ad libitum* indications, with many a slow movement clearly left to the inspiration of the moment. The organ concerto was a genre that was to be particularly associated with England, not only at oratorio performances in theatres and cathedrals, but also outdoors at the pleasure gardens.

By its very nature, the keyboard can function in a concerto in quite a different way from the violin. Stepping out of its role as the continuo instrument it could independently accompany or interpolate during the tuttis, something comparatively rare in the violin concerto. Yet as soloist it could equally take its own path unaccompanied or set up in direct opposition to the orchestra, especially as more powerful keyboard instruments were devised. Further, its propensity for brilliant arpeggiation between the two hands, even at an early stage of instrumental development, allowed for stormy and powerful accompaniment, or for simultaneous decoration of orchestral material. This rich variety of possibilities encouraged a complexity of textures and relationships that was fully exploited only in the second half of the century.

Adaptation and selection

The concept of the Vivaldian concerto may well have permeated Europe, and broadly the concerto was, like those internationally mobile soloists who propagated it, pan-European both in its style and its appeal. But it also adapted to local conditions and individual propensities in diverse ways within a broadly common approach. Sometimes it is possible to identify local characteristics and variants – the overwhelming preference of G. B. Sammartini and the Milan school for a modulating second ritornello, the standard North German model with a modulating third ritornello leading into the solo recapitulation – but it is rarely possible to speak of a coherent school in the manner of the Mannheim symphonists: even the reputation of Berlin as a centre of the keyboard concerto rested more on the achievements of its main exponents (C. P. E. Bach, Nichelmann, Schaffrath) than on stylistic congruence. More typically, individuals developed their own approaches towards concerto writing, often maintaining their distinctive personal idiolects and procedures throughout their career.

This process of selection set up norms of expectations over time, against which newer voices would begin to innovate, gradually settling on different norms as general consensus was reached.[11] To take a simple example, a solo start was not at all uncommon in the early years of the century: indeed Torelli's Op. 8/1 suggested an alternative ritornello concept of solo answered by tutti. Many Vivaldi concertos have a brilliant solo introduction, while others (by Locatelli and Tartini, as well as Bach) include dialogue with the soloist within the opening ritornello. But this option faded away during the third quarter of the century, so that the insouciant piano response in the second bar of Mozart's K. 271 represents a startling – even shocking – departure. The unaccompanied piano opening of Beethoven's Fourth Concerto was a still more radical assertion of the soloist's right to initiate the thematic exposition (all the more arresting for its hushed reticence), thereby setting the tone of engagement for the entire work.

By contrast, the dominant very quickly came to be regarded as the inevitable initial destination in major-mode concertos, firmly secured in the second ritornello. (Thus Vivaldi's preference for an alternative key in his late concertos already suggests a radical and idiosyncratic gesture.) Yet the idea of a clear solo 'second subject' to be recapitulated later in the tonic was much slower to be adopted across the board. Fleetingly found in Tartini, but standardized only within the Viennese orbit (for example, in Wagenseil's keyboard concertos), it failed to attain universal acceptance until late in the century. On the other hand, sometimes two well-established practices co-existed: the third ritornello modulating from the submediant became the standard North German practice, though largely eschewed by J. C. Bach and Mozart in favour of a tutti recapitulation of the motto in the tonic, the option that eventually came to prevail.

This process of adaptation and selection was clearly related to the reconciliation of ritornello form with the emerging demands of the binary-form sonata principle. Yet in truth, the two concepts were not as intrinsically opposed as might at first appear: both are strongly directional with a powerful cadence-orientated drive, both are articulated by an emerging consensus about the main tonal goals (the central dominant, with instability around vi or iii) and both target an eventual reconciliation through thematic recapitulation in the tonic. It was easy to map the elements of 'sonata form' on to the solos of ritornello form (see table 21.1, p. 587). Indeed, Tartini's final concertos from *c.* 1750 onwards actually superimpose

11 Simon McVeigh and Jehoash Hirshberg, *The Italian Solo Concerto, 1700–1760: Rhetorical Strategies and Style History* (Woodbridge and Rochester, NY, 2004).

a modern binary structure (with repeat signs) on to the expected tutti-solo alternations.

The concerto thus developed in tandem with the emerging symphony and sonata; it would be dangerous to posit it as a reactionary genre ripe to be dragged into some brave new world. True, during the third quarter of the century the concerto sometimes maintained a conservative idiom, as in the concertos of that senior Mannheimer, Franz Xaver Richter, or in the sedate quaver movement of Haydn's C major cello concerto. Yet, at the same time, concertos by other early symphonists – Sammartini in the 1740s, Johann Stamitz in the following decade – already included full-scale, almost independent symphonic ritornelli. Why and how this came about was principally related to the varying roles that the concerto itself was asked to perform.

Professional and amateur

The professional and the public concert

Throughout the century the concerto was virtually ubiquitous across the entire range of music-making. It could be tailored to intimate performances at the music societies of Leipzig or Berlin or to the personal tastes of aristocratic patrons – resulting in both the intricate interweaving textures of J. S. or W. F. Bach and the emergent, simpler *galant* chamber styles. Yet from a very early stage the concerto also took upon itself the mantle of extravagant public display – not just of the performer's own skills and personality, but also of the public magnitude of an occasion. As early as 1712 Veracini played a grand and richly orchestrated concerto at an elaborate ceremony at Venice's Frari church to celebrate the accession of Charles VI. The large expanses of a church were indeed where Italian violinists were often to be heard by the wider public: Tartini, for example, was employed at the huge Basilica di Sant'Antonio in Padua primarily to play concertos at major church festivals.

Quite different in their relationship to a comparatively anonymous audience were the public concerts of the second half of the century, usually aimed at a paying clientele: the Bach–Abel concert series in London, the Leipzig Gewandhaus concerts, the *Concert Spirituel* on religious feast days in Paris, or the large-scale charity benefits in Vienna at which both Mozart and Beethoven appeared. The setting might not necessarily have been larger in terms of scale (J. C. Bach typically performed before an audience of no more than 500), but the dynamic was dramatically different. Here the concerto took on bigger dimensions, not merely in terms of length but in its projection of symphonic sonorities and soloistic bravura; ever-more thrilling gestures were also required to capture the attention of volatile or chattering audiences – or, rather, of those several audiences temporarily united 'into a unique, amalgamated one'.[12]

There can be no clearer representation of the changing environment than the rise of the 'lion of the keyboard' in the last two decades of the century, concert virtuosi such as Clementi, Dussek, Wölfl and Eberl, whose heroic bravura projection and captivating stage presence transcended the domestic connotations of the keyboard sonata, aided of course by the development of the piano itself as a concert instrument. The harpsichord had always been found adequate to the demands of a small concerto for a small space, and despite the occasional criticism of its thin sound[13] the enlarged harpsichord continued as the preferred solo concerto instrument until well into the second half of the century. The expressive potential of the square piano was not matched by a comparable increase in volume, but with the development of more powerful grand pianos – especially in London, with the Backers grand favoured by J. C. Bach in the 1770s, and Dussek's enhanced Broadwood in the 1790s – the potential for engagement between piano and orchestra became much more exciting. Even in Vienna, where the pianos of Stein and Walter possessed a more delicate touch, the concerto became a popular public attraction, as at Mozart's various subscription series during 1784–6: for concerts at the large Viennese theatres, the piano may have been lifted on to the stage in order to project more strongly over the orchestra.[14]

Performer and composer

The virtuoso was usually expected to compose his own concertos, his repertory representing not only an extension of his artistic personality but also an embodiment of the product on offer – in modern parlance, his intellectual property. The autobiography of the violinist Karl Ditters von Dittersdorf makes it abundantly clear that each violinist kept close guard over his most treasured concertos, tailored to show himself off to best advantage against thrusting rivals;[15] and with one solitary exception Beethoven never performed a concerto in public after it had been published.[16] It was as if, by relinquishing a

12 Maynard Solomon, *Mozart: A Life* (London, 1995), p. 293.

13 'The instrument is hardly capable of singing because it seems to be made almost exclusively for accompanying, and the concertos for it are usually so thin that one cannot bear them for long.' Quoted from 'Von dem wienerischen Geschmack in der Musik', *Wienerisches Diarium*, XVIII/84 (18 October 1766), given in Georg Christoph Wagenseil, *Sechs Konzerte: Concerto No. 5*, ed. Rudolf Scholz (Vienna and Munich, 1995), p. 31.

14 Richard Maunder, 'Performing Mozart and Beethoven Piano Concertos', *Early Music*, 17 (1989), pp. 139–40; unless, of course, the entire orchestra was on stage.

15 *The Autobiography of K. von Dittersdorf*, trans. A. D. Coleridge (London, 1896).

16 Leon Plantinga, *Beethoven's Concertos: History, Style, Performance* (New York, 1999), pp. 5–6. The exception was the Fourth, premiered in December 1808 four months after publication.

concerto for all the world to perform, Beethoven also abandoned a claim on its evolution; for every concerto (especially No. 2) went through numerous versions during its performance history prior to publication.

Yet as the century progressed, the solo concerto increasingly came to be regarded as a genre worthy of independent composers. The symphonist Johann Baptist Vanhal, for example, was a prolific composer of concertos for his colleagues in the flourishing Vienna soirée scene of the 1760s and 1770s and the viola-player Carl Stamitz wrote some of the earliest clarinet concertos for Joseph Beer to play at the Concert Spirituel in the 1770s. Haydn's trumpet concerto represents a particularly interesting case: it was commissioned to publicise Anton Weidinger's new keyed trumpet, the melodic potential of which Haydn ostentatiously emphasizes at the very first solo entry.

A particularly pronounced collaboration between composer and performer was celebrated in a genre that first arose in the 1770s: the *symphonie concertante* for two or more solo instruments. Of course, the multiple concerto was not in itself a new concept. Vivaldi's Op. 3 already includes concertos for two and four violins, which take turns in melodic solos and virtuosic breaks, as well as interweaving, shadowing and occasionally accompanying each other; and Bach's double violin concerto follows the same principle. In this way co-operation and friendly rivalry, obviously indebted to the trio sonata, had already been projected on to the wider concerto canvas. Furthermore, Vivaldi, Telemann and many others revelled in creating concertos for the most unlikely groupings, while double concertos for unusual instruments became a staple of travelling virtuosi pairings, such as the horn duo Palsa and Türrschmidt or the Colla brothers on the *colascione* (a type of long-necked lute).

The *symphonie concertante* was no different in kind from these earlier models, but fulfilled a different function: as a concert showpiece for a group of consorting professionals, its ensemble virtuosity was an exact counterpart to the *concertante* chamber music developing at the same time. Though not exclusively French it was particularly associated with Parisian concert life, combining appealing melodies, scintillating brilliance and attractive sonorities with a relaxed approach to thematic coherence and formal development. Such a collaborative approach to virtuosic display enabled local orchestral musicians (as opposed to international travelling virtuosi) to bring their names before the public in a new way, described by Barry Brook as the '"concerted" action of composers and performers working together'.[17] The denomination *symphonie concertante* (Italian *sinfonia concertante*) perhaps suggested a more intense engagement than was customary: it is probably better interpreted as implying

17 Barry S. Brook with Mary Fusco, Introduction, *The Symphony 1720–1840*, Series D, Volume V, pp. xv–xx.

simply an orchestral piece with solos. In reality, the light entertainment style of the works of Cambini and Davaux drew heavily upon the divertimento tradition, and more than half of the oeuvre is in only two movements, with a sectional minuet, rondo, or set of variations as the typical finale.

The new genre was soon popular across Europe: in London, for example, J. C. Bach explored his most colourful and alluring textures in a long series of *concertantes* written for the principals featured in his concerts with Abel. This same tradition inspired the Haydn *sinfonia concertante* for oboe, bassoon, violin and cello, written for the 1792 Salomon concerts, as well as two ambitious works by Pleyel for the rival Professional concerts the same year. It is characteristic of the genre that instruments of the orchestra flit in and out of focus. Even a J. C. Bach string concerto may feature a *cantabile* slow movement for solo oboe or flute. In the early Mozart 'concertone' – usually listed as a concerto for two violins – the solo oboe is of at least equal prominence, and there are incidental passages for the principal cello as well as colouristic interventions for two violas. The unarguably outstanding work of the genre, K. 364 for violin and viola by Mozart, is thus exceptional not only in its symphonic intensity and cogency, but also in the seriousness of its tone, especially in the deeply felt slow movement in C minor, where the two unequally voiced protagonists rise in a passionate embrace well outside the accepted boundaries of the genre.

The amateur market

The concerto was evidently at the heart of a complex matrix of relationships between composer and performer, entrepreneur and patron – whether court aristocrat or paying concert audience. Sometimes composers wrote specifically for wealthy patrons, who understandably kept a close eye on further dissemination; but most sought to maximize their international reputation and income through publication, and in particular to extend the amateur market of home music-making and gentlemen's music clubs.

The violin concerto was of course ubiquitous, but the success of Vivaldi's Op. 10 (1729) provoked an avalanche of undemanding flute concertos directed towards the amateur gentleman, composed by Hasse, the Stamitzes and many others. Handel's organ concertos also proved a publishing triumph, being printed so that the solitary amateur could play the tuttis as well as the solos; in addition the second half of the century witnessed a boom in the publication of harpsichord and piano concertos aimed at the enthusiastic (usually lady) amateur. Wagenseil's attractively modern keyboard concertos were early examples, originally intended for the Viennese court (where in 1749 he was appointed keyboard tutor to Maria Theresa's daughters) but soon widely available across Europe. Even violin concertos were often published in piano versions – perhaps surprisingly in Beethoven's case, given Op. 61's apparent unsuitability for the keyboard.

The question immediately arises as to whether surviving publications accurately reflected what virtuosi themselves performed. Some published concertos (violin concertos by Locatelli, cello concertos by Boccherini) are so technically demanding that the primary objective must surely have been to burnish the composer's international name, rather than to improve an amateur gentleman's shining hour. At the same time, some amateurs were undoubtedly highly skilled, especially women pianists with ample time and social pressure to practise: witness the brilliance of Mozart's K. 449 written for his well-connected Viennese pupil Barbara Ployer, or the unwonted virtuosity of J. C. Bach's Op. 14, probably intended for Madame Brillon de Jouy, intimate of Benjamin Franklin and one of the most accomplished stars of Parisian soirées. Nevertheless, evidence exists that concertos might have been 'toned down' and shortened for publication: J. C. Bach's Op. 7/6 subdues both solo-istic virtuosity and orchestral tuttis in comparison with the longer and more rambling manuscript version.[18] The same applies to certain printed versions of works by C. P. E. Bach, in which public concertos were transformed into more intricate chamber works, prizing interaction with the accompanying instruments over raw power and orchestral grandeur.[19]

This latter transformation may serve as a useful corrective in reminding us of a particular strand of eighteenth-century concerto history, namely its role as an essentially chamber idiom featuring a single instrument to a part.[20] In this context, we can recognize that the lightly accompanied keyboard concerto was not perhaps so very far removed from the domestic 'accompanied' sonata; and indeed the early printed concertos of J. C. Bach may be placed precisely in this tradition. Perhaps under this influence, Mozart's first three Viennese concertos K. 413–415 were deliberately designed for home performance, with optional wind parts and the clear implication that single strings could be used in the accompaniment. Towards the end of his life C. P. E. Bach engaged still more directly with the amateur market. A set of explicitly amateur concertos was published at his own expense in 1772 in which (as a preface explains) the solo parts were made deliberately more playable, the ritornellos transcribed and the cadenzas written out, so that they could easily be essayed domestically as solos without (or with only the merest) accompaniment.

18 Stevens, *The Bach Family*, pp. 203–4. 19 *Ibid.*, pp. 225–6.
20 Richard Maunder, *The Scoring of Baroque Concertos* (Woodbridge and Rochester, NY, 2004).

Symphony and sonata

As has already been suggested, two quite different genres – the symphony and the sonata – impacted equally on the concerto's development, both reflecting the ethos of a changing musical epoch, but one representing the public face and the other the private.[21] Increasingly, the concerto came to embody a conjunction, even a rapprochement, between the demands of the concert hall and the domestic sphere. J. C. Bach's Op. 1 (1763) neatly illuminates this dichotomy with a pair of works designated 'Concerto o Sinfonia' (in three movements) set alongside two-movement pieces more closely allied to the sonata tradition. In his later concertos and in those of his contemporaries in the 1760s and 1770s – the Paris violin school of Gaviniès, Leduc and Giornovichi; the later Mannheimers; and Wagenseil, Dittersdorf and Vanhal in Vienna – these two sides are engaged in constant dialogue. This is not to forget Vivaldi's inspired alliance of ensemble pomp and brio with soloistic lyrical intimacy. But the contrast between the two sides is thrown into still sharper relief by the arrival of the modern symphonic idiom, not to mention the sheer size of the forces involved. For whereas the early concertos were mainly designed to be played in a chamber setting or small church with single instruments to a part – so that the soloist is obliged to emerge from the pack as much by texture and melody as by volume and bravura – the later eighteenth-century concerto was essentially orchestral in conception, with one or two soloists pitted against ever larger symphony orchestras in public concert halls. By the time of Mozart's mature concertos of the 1780s, as well as the piano concertos of Kozeluch, Dussek and Wölfl, the concept of the large-scale symphonic concerto was taken for granted. Beethoven's First Piano Concerto was hardly something you were likely to play at home for solitary domestic entertainment.

Trivial and artistic

J'accuse

Though the solo concerto was everywhere, adapting chameleon-like to every musical and social demand across the century, it was not universally accepted as a serious genre. For some critics the concerto was by its very nature superficial, a parade of virtuoso trickery, thin in texture or shallow in melody, over-dependent on external nature effects or national colour. As such, it could easily be derided as a regrettable example of the trivializing effect of modern, crowd-pleasing

21 See Michael Broyles, 'The Two Instrumental Styles of Classicism', *Journal of the American Musicological Society*, 36 (1983), pp. 210–42.

concerts, to be unfavourably contrasted with the nobler aspirations of Corellian *stile antico* counterpoint.

Throughout the century virtuosity was a subject less of debate than of overt verbal abuse, the tone already captured in J. F. A. von Uffenbach's description of Vivaldi's playing in 1715:

> He added a cadenza that really frightened me, for such playing has not been heard before and can never be equalled: he brought his fingers no more than a straw's breadth from the bridge, leaving no room for the bow – and that on all four strings with imitations and incredible speed. With this he astonished everyone, but I cannot say that it delighted me, for it was more skilfully executed than it was pleasant to hear.[22]

Later in the century, it became a critical and journalistic cliché to say that a concerto was 'more surprising than pleasing', drawing attention to mechanical aspects of performance (significantly, often allied to developing instrumental technologies). Ever faster and more complex figuration, stratospherically high playing on melody instruments and efflorescent ornamentation of slow movements were projected not only as superficial appeals to an unsophisticated and popular audience, but also as inimical to an expression of deeper musical values. Even some composers regarded the solo concerto as a suspect or degenerate genre. Telemann – himself a prolific contributor – wrote that deep down he did not care for the concerto at all,[23] while the internationally celebrated violinist Veracini eventually abandoned it for the more rarified world of the contrapuntal sonata.

But it is all too easy to generalize about the supposedly vacuous nature of the solo concerto. Take Locatelli, the supreme example before Paganini of the demonic virtuoso boasting supernatural powers. Even his notorious Op. 3 concertos, modestly entitled *L'arte del violino*, relegate most of the hand-breaking difficulties to the interpolated solo capriccios. Much of the music is expressive and sensitive, with unusual key schemes and poignant exploration of the minor mode – the violin writing ostentatious only in the unforgiving use of the very high register. Furthermore, by the time of Dussek's piano concertos or Viotti's violin concertos, brilliant or tempestuous solo writing becomes a 'topic' in itself, intrinsic to the energy and drama of the debate as much as a powerful display of dexterity.

22 'er zu letzt eine phantasie anhing die mich recht erschrecket, denn dergleichen ohnmöglich so jehmals ist gespielt worden noch kann gespiehlet werden, denn er kahm mit den Fingern nur einen strohhalm breit an den steg daß der bogen keinen plaz hatte, und das auf allen 4 saiten mit Fugen und einer geschwindigkeit die unglaublich ist, er surprenierte damit jedermann, allein daß ich sagen soll daß es mich charmirt das kan ich nicht thun weil es nicht so angenehm zu hören, als es künstlich gemacht war.' See Eberhard Preussner, *Die musikalische Reisen des Herrn von Uffenbach* (Kassel, 1949), p. 67.

23 Quoted in Pippa Drummond, *The German Concerto: Five Eighteenth-Century Studies* (Oxford, 1980), p. 184.

Another area subject to attack was reference to external material, such as the imitations of nature in Vivaldi's *Four Seasons* or Handel's *The Cuckoo and the Nightingale*. The English composer and aesthetician Charles Avison criticized those who sacrificed 'the Beauties of *Expression*' for 'a still more trifling *Mimickry*':

> SUCH are all Imitations of *Flageolets*, *Horns*, *Bagpipes*, &c. on the Violin; a Kind of low Device, calculated merely to amaze ... The singing of a *Cuckoo*, and the cackling of a Hen, have, in fact, been often introduced into musical Performances. VIVALDI, in his Seasons, or Concertos, so called, has imitated the barking of a Dog; besides many other strange Contrivances; attempting even to describe, as well as imitate, the various Changes of the Elements.
>
> If those Composers, who take such Pleasure in their musical Imitations of the Noise of Animals, will shew their Ingenuity in that Way, I would advise them rather to follow the much more effectual Method of introducing the Creatures themselves.[24]

But, again, external imagery was increasingly sublimated into the musical language. Military images later in the century were a particularly potent symbol of the conflict inherent in the concerto. Sometimes the association was overt, as in Military concertos by Dussek and Wölfl, the latter beginning with a classic 'approaching–departing army' ritornello; Beethoven's First Piano Concerto could almost serve under the same banner. Much more subtly nuanced are the concertos of Mozart, as in K. 453 where the march rhythm is transformed into a melody of exquisite charm and elegance, and K. 467 where the 'toy-soldier' orchestral motto is at first casually ignored by the soloist (in a trill over the top) and later undermined altogether by absorption into an delicately turned chromatic melody.[25]

Contemporary reviews sometimes refer disparagingly to the infiltration of low-culture – by implication, low-life – folk music into concert-hall concertos ('the vulgarity and inefficience of introducing such a street-walker's ballad as "Colin stole my heart away"' into a violin concerto by Salomon).[26] But the simple metrical structure of Scottish folk-songs – not to mention the more exotic polaccas, Russian airs and Hungarian dances – made them ideal for rondo finales, their rustic or 'primitive' origin often pointed up by drone accompaniments and piquant orchestration. Undoubtedly the intention was in part populist, but it was also closely attuned to the contemporary aesthetic of the 'picturesque', subliminally reminding us of Gainsborough's woodcutter set against a sublime landscape. Sometimes, too, there is a political context. In

24 Charles Avison, *An Essay on Musical Expression*, 2nd edn. (London, 1753), pp. 108–9.
25 Joseph Kerman, 'Mozart's Piano Concertos and their Audience', in James M. Morris (ed.), *On Mozart* (Cambridge, 1994), pp. 156–7.
26 *Public Advertiser*, 21 March 1785.

the rondo of Mozart's A major Violin Concerto the comic barbarity of the 'Turkish' episode is flanked and thus tamed by that most explicit symbol of Western aristocratic dominance, the minuet. Most spectacularly of all, in 1794 Cambini built an entire *symphonie concertante* on popular tunes of the revolution such as 'La Marseillaise' and 'Ah, ça ira', creating a grandiose work for two solo violins and large orchestra entitled 'La Patriote'.

Simplicity

It is undoubtedly true that the concerto as a genre encouraged both an approachable idiom and direct melodic appeal. Already in the second quarter of the century the North German school of Quantz, Franz Benda and the Graun brothers (the core of the Berlin court establishment) preferred light Italianate melody and an extreme separation of solo and tutti. The concertos of the next generation – Wagenseil, the Stamitzes and Schroeter – were likewise more agreeable than profound; and it is striking that J. C. Bach completely abandoned the strenuous style of his teacher and half-brother C. P. E. Bach in favour of the more urbane idiom now widely associated with early Mozart.

During the 1760s and 1770s simple sectional forms came into vogue for the second and third movements. There were antecedents here, too – for example, the solo–refrain pattern in some Leclair 'gratioso' Andantes around 1740 or the uncomplicated rondo that closes Bach's E major violin concerto. But it was Giornovichi in his Paris violin concertos of the 1770s who set the seal on the graceful and elegant romance for the central slow movement: a naively unadorned song echoed by a compliant orchestra, its predictability scarcely disturbed by a lightly contrasting central section. The unadorned minuet formed a popular concerto finale for several decades, as in those keyboard concertos by Arne, Wagenseil and J. C. Bach that absorbed the soloist into straightforward exchanges within a binary design. By the 1780s, however, the rondo (sometimes itself in minuet tempo) had become the almost universal finale form, constituting at its simplest an unsophisticated alternation of metrical sections in ABACA pattern.

Yet this picture of empty predictability hardly represents the whole story. In the first place, simplicity – Rousseau's direct expression of the natural voice – could be projected as an artistic aim in itself, a reaction against the excesses of vapid virtuosity and superficial ornamentation. In his late concertos, Tartini pared down the long and complex ritornello structures of his earliest Vivaldian concertos into an idiom of exquisite simplicity, eschewing showy figuration and rococo efflorescence alike in favour of expressive, unadorned melodies with minimal accompaniment. He explicitly allied the new idiom with an expressive singing voice, describing vocal expression as 'la maggior perfezione del buon gusto', its *affettuoso* and cantabile character amplified by the literary mottos that head many of his manuscripts.

The aesthetic of Grecian simplicity itself reflected a widespread reaction in the later eighteenth century against baroque excess, and something of this essence – all superfluous decoration stripped away – can be felt in many slow movements, such as the hauntingly spare Andante of Mozart's K. 488. Particularly evocative are those Adagios evoking a still, hymn-like expression, as in the rapt chordal tutti that opens the original slow movement of Boccherini's Cello Concerto in B-flat. Czerny captured in words the 'holy, distant, celestial harmony' of the Largo in Beethoven's C minor piano concerto, an effect heightened by the choice of a radiantly remote E major – an unexpected major third away from the main key. Indeed the special significance of E major throughout the century is reflected in many a concerto slow movement of similar character: for example, in 'Le calme' in Wölfl's eponymous G major piano concerto and in several Viotti concertos, providing an evocative parallel to his favourite image of the otherworldly sublimity of the Swiss mountains.

There were counter-forces, too, even within the most rudimentary sectional forms. A particular device employed to give depth to the simpler slow movements was a searching harmonic exploration in the central section, eventually resolving into a satisfying return. In Haydn's D major harpsichord concerto, as well as his trumpet concerto, the harmonic richness and textural interplay of the central section enhances the simplest of ternary forms. Similarly, the Larghetto of Mozart's final piano concerto (K. 595) starts as a straightforward romance, only for the central solo to drift away into the most profound uncharted territories.

Rondos, too, proved capable of much more complex trajectories. Most obviously colourful are the sectional rondos of the Mozart violin concertos, with their characteristic folk dances and colourful exoticisms in contrasting meter and tempo. Such sharpness of social reference is turned on its head in the courtly minuets inserted in K. 271 and again (with a distinctive wind band) in K. 482.[27] The rondo also attained new layers of complexity through the interpolation of sonata elements and thematic development, not only (most famously) in Mozart and Beethoven, but also in piano concertos by Kozeluch and Dussek. Multiple returns and symphonic re-workings of the rondo theme, often in unexpected third-related keys, result in enlarged rondos even with such feather-light material as Shield's 'Plough Boy' in Dussek's Piano Concerto

27 For another multi-tempo finale, see the basset horn concerto by Carl Stamitz (ed. Willy Hess [Winterthur, 1982]), where the 2/4 Allegro breaks off first into an Andante minuet and later into a spirited Allegro 6/8.

Op. 15. Viotti, too, delights in transforming rustic matter into large multi-topic movements, as in his Violin Concerto No. 23 in G, where first a drone and then a bagpipe theme are surmounted by a soloist in a sophisticated dotted rhythm, only to be later over-ruled by a strenuously expressive episode in E-flat and moments of *Sturm und Drang*. The long finale of No. 22 must surely be regarded as one of the pinnacles of the classical violin concerto, with its succession of piquant themes and remarkable driving urgency – not to mention its elaborate accompanied cadenza.

Seriousness: Kenner und Liebhaber

At the same time there were explicit attempts to counteract what was perceived as the trivialization of the concerto. The concertos of C. P. E. Bach provide something of a test case, since this was a repertory that even the liberal-minded Charles Burney regarded as beyond contemporary taste. In 1772 he drew a revealing contrast between the more accessible late amateur concertos and the composer's normal style: 'these productions will probably be the better received, for resembling the music of the world more than his former pieces, which seem made for another region, or at least another century when what is now thought difficult and far-fetched, will, perhaps, be familiar and natural'.[28] To Burney, moved though he was by Bach's keyboard-playing, the hyper-expressive and impetuous *empfindsam* style must have seemed nothing less than eccentric in its irregular phrasing, its fragmentation and wild interruptions, its unsettling syncopations, leaps and chromatic inflexions – all working to subvert the elegant natural flow that he regarded as one of the first qualities of modern music.

Yet it was perhaps in the concerto that C. P. E. Bach discovered the natural home for his passionate and disruptive style. Whether in the early idiom of the D minor concerto H. 427 (clearly influenced by his father) or in the more modern symphonic concept of H. 448 in C minor, the orchestra plays a crucial role, often interrupting with unexpected *forte* intrusions or engaging in earnest dialogue with the soloist, even in slow movements. The concerto genre was flexible enough to accommodate the most fragmented eccentricities within its ritornello framework, naturally absorbing the inherent tensions through the spirited drive towards the resolution of the next tutti. Another symptom of C. P. E. Bach's serious-minded approach to the concerto was his avoidance of simpler finale forms, disdaining the minuet and even the rondo (despite his highly experimental exploitation of the form in his solo keyboard music).

28 Percy A. Scholes (ed.), *Dr. Burney's Musical Tours in Europe, Vol. II: An Eighteenth-century Musical Tour in Central Europe and the Netherlands* (London, 1959), p. 220.

Strikingly, he relegated his lighter thoughts in the concerto genre to a new divertimento-like genre, to which he rather misleadingly gave the title 'sonatina'.

C. P. E. Bach's minor-mode intensity was pursued still further by his pupil Johann Gottfried Müthel, and an overtly serious approach is equally evidenced in the concertos of Josef Antonín Štěpán (Steffan) who combined an individual language with an innovative approach: eight of his concertos (very unusually) include a minor-key introduction, to which even the soloist contributes. Another composer with a penchant for the minor mode was the violinist Viotti, whose commanding artistic personality dominated the violin concerto after Giornovichi. In France during the 1780s he developed a boldly dramatic minor-mode idiom, a stormy orchestral style interrupted by tempestuous solos. In the following decade (in London) Viotti's concertos took on a more alluring lyricism, as exemplified by the yearning nostalgia and minor–major poignancy of No. 22 (a favourite of Joachim and Brahms) and the 'ancient' baroque tinges of No. 24 in an unusual B minor. One reviewer perceptively returned to Uffenbach's theme: 'The grand mistake of Musicians has been a continued effort to excite amazement. Viotti, it is true, without making that his object, astonishes the hearer; but he does something infinitely better – he awakens emotion, gives a soul to sound, and leads the passions captive.'[29]

Mozart, who incidentally admired Viotti's E minor Concerto No. 16 sufficiently to add to its orchestration, encapsulated in letters to his father the change that came over the mainstream concerto during the 1780s. On 28 December 1782 he famously explained how in the concertos K. 413–415 he sought to satisfy both *Kenner* and *Liebhaber* (connoisseurs and music-lovers), in music brilliant and natural but not vapid: 'There are passages here and there from which connoisseurs alone will derive satisfaction; but these passages are written in such a way that the less learned cannot fail to be pleased, though without knowing why.'[30] His next concerto led the relationship with his audience in a much more demanding direction. When he wrote on 15 May 1784 that K. 449 was written an 'entirely special manner' he was ostensibly distinguishing its orchestration from its more imposing successors, but he could equally have been signalling his intention to take the concerto into a new dimension, one that engaged the soloist and orchestra in a much more intense relationship than previously attempted.[31] The subsequent series was

29 *Morning Chronicle*, 12 March 1794.

30 See Emily Anderson, *The Letters of Mozart and His Family*, 3rd edn. (London, 1985), p. 833.

31 On K. 449 and its relationship with Mozart's preceding and succeeding piano concertos, see Simon P. Keefe, *Mozart's Viennese Instrumental Music: A Study of Stylistic Re-Invention* (Woodbridge and Rochester, NY, 2007), chapter 1, pp. 19–42.

on a symphonic scale with ever more obligatory winds: when Mozart described K. 450 (his first 'grosses Konzert') and its companion K. 451 as 'concertos bound to make the performer sweat', it was not just a question of mere virtuosity, but also of an innate grandeur and bravura manner, in which the role of the orchestra became almost as crucial as that of the virtuoso.[32]

Discourse and the orchestra: the symphonic first movement

Certainly the most persuasive claim for the concerto to be considered a serious genre lay in the multiplicity of potential relationships between soloist and orchestra. Throughout the century (in Vivaldi just as much as in Dussek) there was a divergence in manner between orchestral and solo sections, between the cogent discourse of the opening ritornello – increasingly symphonic and motivically intricate – and the lyrical melody and show-stopping scintillation of the soloist. Yet many composers still sought integration, or at least greater engagement, between them. One favourite device in the early part of the century was to recall the opening motto within the solo sections. For example, in the second solo of Vivaldi's Op. 8/11, the motto is led around a circle of fifths under solo arpeggiation, already prefiguring a common development procedure in keyboard concertos from Bach (through Wagenseil and Schroeter) to Mozart. A related technique was to set the motto in some kind of dialogue with the solo melody: Telemann's concertos are shot through with orchestral motives, a practice C. P. E. Bach also favoured in the 1740s and 1750s. In one intriguing case (the finale of H. 418) he even alternated the orchestral motto with its own soloistic transformation.[33]

Such solo–tutti interplay became much less common in *galant* concertos around the middle of the century, but it returned in a different guise in the 1770s, as wind instruments began to assume a more prominent role. J. C. Bach was an influential pioneer here: a manuscript Piano Concerto in E-flat dating from around 1772 exploits chamber-style exchanges between three protagonists (piano, winds and strings) and frequently wind instruments alone are allowed to accompany the piano. It was this additional set of relationships that later enabled the rich variety of interaction that so distinguishes Mozart's own piano concertos.

Yet the role of the orchestra amounted to far more than just casual partnership or textural interplay: it was the unfolding relationship overarching an entire movement that provided the opportunity for the most sophisticated debate. Again, this potential had been exploited from the early days of the solo

32 For a discussion of Mozart's first 'grand' concertos set in stylistic context, see *ibid.*, chapter 2, pp. 43–63.
33 Rachel Wade, *The Keyboard Concertos of Carl Philipp Emanuel Bach* (Ann Arbor, MI, 1981), p. 73 and musical examples 1–3.

concerto. Joseph Kerman's off-the-cuff analysis that in Vivaldi concertos the orchestra discourses and the violin displays, whereas Mozart develops a true dialogue and debate through long-term engagement with each others' thematic material, cannot be entirely sustained.[34] In Vivaldi's Op. 4/4, for example, there is a clear sense of a developing relationship across the opening Allegro, with the tutti's thematic role changing in direct response to the unfolding argument.[35] Yet it would be difficult to disagree with Kerman's contention that it is the discursive engagement between solo and orchestra that elevates Mozart's concertos above their models, including those of J. C. Bach and Wagenseil. Simon Keefe has taken this point still further, exploring the notion of the relational dialogue as an instructive intellectual pursuit, analogous to contemporary drama, in which confrontation itself may prove a means of resolving tension. In the most extreme cases, an archetypal trajectory is outlined, leading from competition in the solo exposition through dramatic dialogue in the development section to co-operation and reconciliation in the recapitulation.[36]

Particular demands arose when the opening ritornello was strongly symphonic in character, enforcing a new perspective for the solo entrance. One challenging strategy that deliberately precipitated a different relationship with the orchestra was to introduce the soloist before the return of the orchestral motto, through an independent *Eingang* that might overlap the final bars of the ritornello (K. 364, K. 503) or even present a new solo theme (K. 466). In the latter case, the orchestral motto consists of brooding D minor syncopations impossible for the solo piano to replicate, rendering some kind of lead-in imperative. Yet this has profound implications for the movement as a whole since (when the motto does reappear) the piano can do no more than accompany the orchestra, only gradually asserting its soloistic presence, until it eventually emerges decisively with an independent second theme in the secondary key of F major.

The role of the tutti

This last example raises a crucial question about the nature of first-movement form, one implicit from the genre's earliest days that became increasingly more pressing as the concerto fruitfully elided with the sonata concept later in the century. In short, is the form essentially a series of ritornelli with solos in between, or instead a succession of solos surrounded by a comparatively insignificant frame?

34 Kerman, 'Mozart's Piano Concertos', p. 154.
35 McVeigh and Hirshberg, *The Italian Solo Concerto*, pp. 89–90.
36 In K. 450 and K. 482: Keefe, *Mozart's Piano Concertos*, pp. 63–4.

The latter perception certainly prevailed with late-eighteenth-century theorists such as Vogler and Koch, a somewhat uncomfortable situation for the modern critic in search of a grand symphonic fusion. Still more disconcertingly, composers themselves appeared to reinforce this view. When the apprentice Mozart transformed some J. C. Bach sonatas into concertos (K. 107), he simply added three or four framing tuttis: conversely Clementi turned a piano concerto into a published sonata (Op. 33/3) by the simple expedient of removing the orchestral sections. The relative weight of the tuttis was similarly in transition. Whereas early in the century the three or four tuttis were of roughly equal substance, by its end the opening ritornello was not only always much the longest but generally symphonic in scale and power, with contrasting lyrical and stormy episodes. Often it embraced a move to the dominant – indeed, a contrasting theme in the dominant can be found in concertos from Vivaldi onwards. Ever since Tovey cast judgement upon this stealing of the soloist's prerogative,[37] the issue has taken on an almost moral perspective. It is true that J. C. Bach, Mozart and Beethoven all essay alternative instabilities within the opening ritornello; but a new theme in the dominant or relative major remained an option as late as Beethoven's Third Piano Concerto, tending to corroborate the notion of the opening ritornello as a self-contained entity tacked on to the beginning.

As the opening ritornello gradually became more substantial, subsequent tuttis tended to become shorter or even to disappear altogether: indeed, with the first ritornello excised, some movements by Štěpán or Kozeluch could certainly work as a piano solo. Nevertheless the second ritornello still offered intriguing possibilities. After the enormous build-up of the intervening solo the reassertion of orchestral hegemony implies closure, and in this sense becomes a purely formal gesture whose very formality undermines its significance. Yet at the same time the ritornello's role in the chain intrinsically leads the musical argument into its next phase, and some composers were sufficiently alert to this potential to expound elaborate variants here (Tartini, for one) or to open up a powerful development section. One possibility was to introduce a moment of high drama: thus in an unusual concerto for organ and viola by Michael Haydn the orchestra hammers in at this point with a completely unexpected minor mode (compare the shattering B-flat major explosion in the Beethoven Violin Concerto). Another option, evident throughout the century, was to allow the second ritornello to modulate, a solution completely under-estimated in modern analyses. By no means uncommon in Vivaldi, this became standard practice for several of his successors, including Locatelli, Leclair

37 Donald F. Tovey, *Essays in Musical Analysis* (London, 1936), 3 vols., vol. 3, pp. 16–18 (reproduced from the 1903 article 'The Classical Concerto').

and Sammartini. Later in the mature classical concerto, an unstable second ritornello served to overarch the central articulation of symphonic form – or even to initiate the development section, as in the previous Beethoven example. The overall effect of all such strategies was, of course, to reinforce the powerful status of the orchestra and to reassert its role in taking the movement forward.

Even in his most symphonic concertos Mozart never goes as far as Beethoven down this particular route. Yet the interface between the second ritornello and the ensuing solo becomes of pivotal importance in his late concertos – instead of formal separation, he prefers to divert the ritornello towards a new key and a change of mood, even involving the soloist in a critical process of interaction and dialogue (K. 482). Sometimes an unexpected and arresting solo gesture initiates a much more extended debate, as in K. 503, a *tour de force* of complex motivic development and debate among piano, strings, winds and even brass. Who could imagine such a movement working as a domestic piano sonata?

One particular issue for ritornello form involves the nature of the recapitulation which, across the century, was to remain the single most variable aspect of the concerto concept. All the multifarious options already observable in Vivaldi continued well into the second half of the century, so it is completely misleading to posit simple chronological development, or to associate particular strategies with individual composers on the basis of too small a sample, as has been too often attempted. Occasionally, it is true, one strategy surged to the fore: thus it became North German orthodoxy in the middle of the eighteenth century for a third ritornello to modulate back from the submediant to the tonic for a solo recapitulation. But a quite different option eventually prevailed: the tutti recapitulation of the tonic motto favoured by J. C. Bach, Giardini and Mozart. This scheme has the effect of entirely shifting the recapitulation's dynamic, not only placing the emphasis back on the orchestra – if only for four or six bars – but also subliminally reminding the listener how the soloist was first introduced. J. C. Bach adopted a simple reconciliation: the orchestra typically recalls the motto, with the pianist taking over after a few bars. The remainder of the recapitulation then follows the course of the first solo, merely transposing the dominant material into the tonic.

Other composers attempted a much more complex relationship in the recapitulation, responding to the challenges of the initial tutti–solo exposition. The opportunity to integrate the material of the first ritornello with that of the first solo was fully explored by C. P. E. Bach, as well as by less-renowned experimentalists such as Platti.[38] Mozart, as usual, took the concept to its most sophisticated extreme, constantly challenging the listener by reordering

38 McVeigh and Hirshberg, *The Italian Solo Concerto*, pp. 216–17.

earlier material in new conjunctions and with fresh perspectives. No doubt such subtle reinterpretations were the inspiration behind the unusually complex reordering in the first movement of Kozeluch's Fifth Piano Concerto, certainly one of the most structurally ambitious concertos of the entire period.

One final novelty lay in the ending of the first movement. Whereas Vivaldi and his successors always closed with a final tutti (often including a pause for a cadenza), in the ostentatiously revolutionary K. 271 the soloist both interrupts the lead-in to the cadenza and wittily hints at a rerun of the *Eingang* at the very end. More subtly, in K. 491 the piano unobtrusively accompanies the brief coda, allowing the interaction with the orchestra to continue right up to the muffled close, albeit in uneasy co-existence – an effect extended in Beethoven's own C minor concerto, where the piano emerges quietly out of the cadenza before characteristically flaring up into turbulent confrontation. More extreme in a very different way is Dussek's Piano Concerto Op. 49, which boasts no final tutti at all: instead the climactic trill preparing for the final orchestral return simply fades into a short coda for orchestra and soloist. As with K. 491 the unusual soft ending obscures any sense of closure, thereby paving the way for the ensuing slow movement.

The concerto cycle

So far, we have considered concerto movements in isolation. But these last examples suggest the possibility of a long-range perspective extending across an entire work. To return to the earlier discussion of social drama, Kerman has plotted the overall course of the classical concerto as an archetypal metaphor of the changing relationship between musician and patrons.[39] In this analysis the first movement acts as a collaborative test, a dialogue investigating how the soloist can cope with the conditions laid down by the orchestra; the slow movement embodies a mutual acceptance; and the rondo secures complicity and collusion, symbolized by the blank consensus of the typical tutti repetition of the solo rondo theme. More specifically, it can also be argued that the discursive engagement between solo and orchestra may be played out across all three movements of a Mozart concerto.[40] Certainly there are readily identifiable connections: in K. 466, for example, the central episode of the otherwise placid romance recalls the agitation of the first movement, while the rondo also re-engages with earlier symphonic arguments, emphasized by explicit thematic and harmonic similarities.

39 Kerman, 'Mozart's Piano Concertos', pp. 159–62.

40 For example, K. 453, 459 and 488: Keefe, *Mozart's Piano Concertos*, pp. 158–75.

One way of achieving overall coherence was through the key structure: thus the third ritornello of Wölfl's C major concerto Op. 43 is in an unusual E major that foreshadows the key of the succeeding Andante. Another method was to connect parts of the concerto through thematic transformation. The idea of integrating a slow introduction into the first movement proper (a ploy more usually associated with late Haydn symphonies) has already been observed in Vivaldi's RV 189. Much later in the century in Dussek's Piano Concerto Op. 29 the opening Larghetto in 3/8 is similarly transformed into Allegro 4/4 in order to introduce the recapitulation.

But one set of concertos in particular adopts a much more radical stance. In C. P. E. Bach's last concerto publication, the collection intended for amateurs, each concerto is conceived as a linked cycle, in the same way as some of his late symphonies and trios. Typically each movement is linked to the next, either by a quite unexpected transition or by a catastrophic breakdown – followed by a silence that demands to be filled. Some concertos even re-think the cycle concept altogether by making thematic connections across movements. Thus in No. 5 the introduction provides material for the slow movement, while in No. 3 the central C major Larghetto (a typically unexpected relationship with the home E-flat major) gradually introduces material from the opening Allegro. Most striking of all is No. 4 in C minor, where the first movement is interrupted two-thirds of the way through, first by a slow movement in D minor, and then by a minuet in E-flat, before the first movement resumes where it left off (a further step rise to F minor): the written-out cadenza then neatly ties the whole together with references back to both the intruding movements. This break from ordered conceptions of the concerto genre is perhaps the most radical departure throughout the entire period; yet the fact that it demands to be heard against the background of ritornello form, first established by Vivaldi at the beginning of the century, demonstrates yet again the enduring potency of the solo concerto, the endless options with which almost every composer grappled in order to sculpt works of individuality and intellectual challenge.

Select Bibliography

Berger, Karol. 'Toward a History of Hearing: the Classic Concerto, a Sample Case'. In Wye Jamison Allanbrook, Janet M. Levy and William P. Mahrt (eds.), *Convention in Eighteenth- and Nineteenth-Century Music: Essays in Honor of Leonard Ratner*. Stuyvesant, NY, 1992, pp. 405–29

Boyd, Malcolm. *Bach: The Brandenburg Concertos*. Cambridge, 1993

Clark, Stephen L. (ed.). *C. P. E. Bach Studies*. Oxford, 1988

Dreyfus, Laurence. *Bach and the Patterns of Invention*. Cambridge, MA, 1996

Drummond, Pippa. *The German Concerto: Five Eighteenth-Century Studies*. Oxford, 1980

Dunning, Albert (ed.). *Intorno a Locatelli: studi in occasione del tricentenario della nascita di Pietro Antonio Locatelli (1695–1764)*. 2 vols., Lucca, 1995
Everett, Paul. *Vivaldi: 'The Four Seasons' and Other Concertos, Op. 8*. Cambridge, 1996
Fertonani, Cesare. *La musica strumentale di Antonio Vivaldi*. Florence, 1998
Galand, Joel. 'The Large-Scale Formal Role of the Solo Entry Theme in the Eighteenth-Century Concerto'. *Journal of Music Theory*, 44 (2000), pp. 381–450
Hutchings, Arthur. *The Baroque Concerto*. 3rd edn., London, 1978
Irving, John. *Mozart's Piano Concertos*. Aldershot, 2003
Keefe, Simon P. *Mozart's Piano Concertos: Dramatic Dialogue in the Age of Enlightenment*. Woodbridge and Rochester, NY, 2001
'"Greatest Effects with the Least Effort": Strategies of Wind Writing in Mozart's Viennese Piano Concertos'. In Keefe (ed.), *Mozart Studies*. Cambridge, 2006, pp. 25–46
Mozart's Viennese Instrumental Music: A Study of Stylistic Re-Invention. Woodbridge and Rochester, NY, 2007
(ed.). *The Cambridge Companion to the Concerto*. Cambridge, 2005
Kerman, Joseph. 'Mozart's Piano Concertos and their Audience'. In James M. Morris (ed.), *On Mozart*. Cambridge, 1994, pp. 151–68
Lawson, Colin. *Mozart: Clarinet Concerto*. Cambridge, 1996
Marissen, Michael. *The Social and Religious Designs of J. S. Bach's Brandenburg Concertos*. Princeton, NJ, 1995
Maunder, Richard. *The Scoring of Baroque Concertos*. Woodbridge and Rochester, NY, 2004
McClary, Susan. 'A Musical Dialectic from the Enlightenment: Mozart's *Piano Concerto in G Major, K. 453*, Movement 2'. *Cultural Critique*, 5 (1986), pp. 129–69
'The Blasphemy of Talking Politics During Bach Year'. In Richard Leppert and McClary (eds.), *Music and Society: The Politics of Composition, Performance and Reception*. Cambridge, 1987, pp. 13–62
McVeigh, Simon and Jehoash Hirshberg. *The Italian Solo Concerto, 1700–1760: Rhetorical Strategies and Style History*. Woodbridge and Rochester, NY, 2004
Plantinga, Leon. *Beethoven's Concertos: History, Style, Performance*. New York, 1999
Stevens, Jane R. 'Theme, Harmony and Texture in Classic–Romantic Descriptions of Concerto First-Movement Form'. *Journal of the American Musicological Society*, 27 (1974), pp. 25–60
The Bach Family and the Keyboard Concerto: The Evolution of a Genre. Warren, MI, 2001
Stowell, Robin. 'Viotti's "London Concertos (Nos. 20–29)": Progressive or Retrospective?'. In David Wyn Jones (ed.), *Music in Eighteenth-Century England*. Aldershot, 2000, pp. 282–98
Talbot, Michael. 'The Concerto Allegro in the Early Eighteenth Century'. *Music & Letters*, 52 (1971), pp. 8–18 and 159–72
Vivaldi. 2nd edn., London, 1993
Wade, Rachel. *The Keyboard Concertos of Carl Philipp Emanuel Bach*. Ann Arbor, MI, 1981
White, Chappell. *From Vivaldi to Viotti: A History of the Early Classical Violin Concerto*. Philadelphia, PA, 1992
Zaslaw, Neal (ed.). *Mozart's Piano Concertos: Text, Context, Interpretation*. Ann Arbor, MI, 1996

· 22 ·

Eighteenth-century symphonies: an unfinished dialogue

RICHARD WILL

No genre worked harder in the eighteenth century than the symphony, which opened and closed concerts, punctuated the Catholic mass and introduced plays, operas and oratorios, whose overtures were classified by contemporary writers as 'theatre symphonies' and 'church symphonies'. Meeting all these needs resulted in a vast and varied repertory. 'Chamber symphonies' alone, the focus of this chapter, number several thousand and, as anyone familiar with Haydn's or Mozart's symphonies knows, they draw on every conceivable resource of form, style and mood.

Studies of eighteenth-century symphonies are equally diverse and, after two centuries, almost as numerous as the works themselves.[1] Pedagogues of the time dissected examples by Haydn and others for the benefit of would-be imitators. Critics sought to capture expressive implications by drawing comparisons to odes, choruses, character representations, dialogues and comedies. Some nineteenth- and early-twentieth-century scholars, reflecting the nationalist preoccupations of their age, argued whether the most important predecessors of Haydn came from Italy, Austria, or Germany, while others analysed form, phrasing, harmony and thematic development in an investigation that continues today. Still others have examined how descriptive annotations, conditions of performance, or evocative melodies and rhythms influenced the meanings that symphonies communicated to listeners.

Not surprisingly, when so many perspectives are applied to such a multifarious genre, its history is constantly under revision. Scholars have answered many questions about origins, functions, the development of forms and styles, and the relative influence of composers and places. Yet each time they explore a new method of analysis, or new evidence on meaning, they discover additional possibilities of structure and expression. The publication of previously

1 Bibliographies in Preston Stedman, *The Symphony: A Research and Information Guide*, vol. 1, *The Eighteenth Century* (New York, 1990); Ludwig Finscher (ed.), *Die Musik in Geschichte und Gegenwart*, 2nd edn. (Kassel, 1994–), s.v. 'Symphonie', cols. 148–50; Stanley Sadie (ed.), *The New Grove Dictionary of Music and Musicians, Revised Edition* (London, 2001), s.v. 'Symphony', vol. 24, pp. 831–3.

unknown works changes even the content of the repertory, at least as perceived by the modern beholder: as recently as the 1960s, when a complete edition of Haydn's symphonies finally appeared, few knew the extent or nature of his achievement. And the most familiar pieces are forever being renewed by fresh performances. What defines the eighteenth-century symphony is less an accepted evolutionary narrative than an unfinished dialogue, between musical sources and the interests, experiences and imaginations of those who encounter them.

Origins

The breadth of the genre begins with its ancestry. The most influential early chamber symphonies, written by Giovanni Battista Sammartini, Antonio Brioschi and other Milanese composers in the later 1720s and 1730s, have their most direct precedent in 'ripieno concertos' – that is, concertos without (or with very limited) solo parts, of which several sets were published in the late seventeenth and early eighteenth centuries. As Eugene K. Wolf emphasizes, they share with symphonies a common destiny of concert performance, as well as three-movement cycles, dance-like finales, many binary movement forms and a 'relatively homophonic texture over a basso continuo'.[2] Yet they are not the only works to have inspired the new genre; more widely cultivated progenitors include solo concertos, concerto grossi, partitas, sonatas (sometimes performed orchestrally) and the Italian opera overtures known as 'sinfonias'.[3] All offered models of orchestral pieces in several movements intended, in all but the last instance, primarily for concert use. Each also helped shape the symphony over the course of several decades. The introduction of minuets into German and Austrian symphonies of the 1750s owes a partial debt to the mixing of dance and non-dance movements in the partita,[4] as does the use of extended instrumental solos, found in symphonies through the early 1770s, to the concerto.

Opera sinfonias exerted a special influence, despite being written for the stage. Indeed, they were deemed the motivation for all symphonies – theatre,

2 Eugene K. Wolf, in Barry S. Brook (gen. ed.), *The Symphony 1720–1840*, (New York, 1979–86), 60 vols., vol. A-1, pp. xvi–xviii.

3 Jens Peter Larsen, 'Concerning the Development of the Austrian Symphonic Tradition (*circa* 1750–1775)', in *Handel, Haydn, and the Viennese Classical Style*, trans. Ulrich Krämer (Ann Arbor, MI, 1988), pp. 316–21; Bathia Churgin, *The Symphony 1720–1840*, vol. A-2, pp. xxi–xxiii.

4 Eugene K. Wolf, *The Symphonies of Johann Stamitz: A Study in the Formation of the Classic Style* (Utrecht, 1981), pp. 87–8; Jens Peter Larsen, 'Zur Vorgeschichte der Symphonik der Wiener Klassik', *Studien zur Musikwissenschaft*, 43 (1994), pp. 123–6. Unlike Scheibe (see n. 5), the eighteenth-century commentator Johann Abraham Peter Schulz considered the partita the main predecessor of the symphony; Johann Georg Sulzer (ed.), *Allgemeine Theorie der schönen Künste*, 4 vols., 2nd expand. edn. (Leipzig, 1792–4), s.v. 'Symphonie', p. 478.

church, or chamber – by one of the first writers to discuss them at length, Johann Adolph Scheibe.[5] So frequently were they used as concert works that the boundary between traditions blurs; in his catalogues advertising manuscript copies for sale, Johann Gottlob Immanuel Breitkopf grouped sinfonias and independently conceived symphonies together in one alphabetical listing.[6] The most celebrated sinfonias, moreover, those of the Neapolitan opera, provided models of style and orchestration at several key moments in the development of the chamber symphony. Around 1740 Sammartini began to follow the Neapolitan Leonardo Leo in enlarging his orchestra to include winds as well as strings, and in reducing the dynamics and texture of the second key areas of his fast movements, among other things.[7] A decade later Johann Stamitz, director of instrumental music for the Elector Palatine in Mannheim, took over the crescendo and other orchestral effects from Leo's successors, notably Niccolò Jommelli.[8]

Not that chamber symphonies merely combined the influences of their ancestors. Beginning with Sammartini, they quickly asserted an independent identity, and with the circulation of his and others' works, symphonists could soon look to one another for inspiration as well as to other genres. A closer comparison of Sammartini and Leo shows that the former's movements last longer and incorporate more repetition and variation, particularly the outer movements, in which middle or development sections allow for thematic and harmonic elaborations beyond those of the expositions. Consequently, even the borrowed habit of reducing texture and dynamics in the second key area acquires new significance, for its contrast is more of a shock after a comparatively lengthy first key area, and more of an event thanks to its own expansion. In the first movement of the Symphony in C (Jenkins-Churgin 4, hereafter J-C)[9], the first key area ends with a half-cadence on the dominant for the full orchestra (horns and strings) and two beats of rest. This prepares four bars of the kind of quiet, step-wise, singing theme that often enters at such moments. A similar passage in Leo, in the sinfonia to *Amor vuol sofferenza*, is followed immediately by a tutti cadence that closes off the first half of the movement. Sammartini also proceeds with a tutti

5 *Johann Adolph Scheibes Critischer Musikus* (Leipzig, 1745), pp. 596–7. The sinfonia is accorded comparable importance in Stefan Kunze, *Die Sinfonie im 18. Jahrhundert: Von der Opernsinfonie zur Konzertsinfonie* (Laaber, 1993). Definitions of the symphony are surveyed in Marie Louise Göllner, *The Early Symphony: 18th-Century Views on Composition and Analysis* (Hildesheim, 2004), pp. 9–23.

6 Johann Gottlob Immanuel Breitkopf, in Barry S. Brook (ed.), *The Breitkopf Thematic Catalogue: The Six Parts and Sixteen Supplements 1762–1787* (New York, 1966).

7 Churgin, *The Symphony 1720–1840*, vol. A-2, p. xxiii.

8 Wolf, *The Symphonies of Johann Stamitz*, pp. 354–5; Helmut Hell, *Die neapolitanische Opernsinfonie in der ersten Hälfte des 18. Jahrhunderts: N. Porpora, L. Vinci, G. B. Pergolesi, L. Leo, N. Jommelli* (Tutzing, 1971), pp. 487–501.

9 Authors and numbers following symphony titles refer to thematic catalogues or to the thematic indexes in Brook (gen. ed.), *The Symphony 1720–1840*.

cadence, one that recalls the opening bars of the movement, but then he reprises it *sotto voce* as if to answer, belatedly but in kind, the initial *piano* interlude – only this time the harmony moves to the dominant of the dominant and still another cadence. In short, rather than briefly relieve the tutti excitement, as Leo does, Sammartini writes a series of exchanges that emphasize the contrasts between tutti and strings, vigour and lyricism, first and second key areas. His forms are not simply bigger than the sinfonia's but more active, packed with melodic and harmonic twists.

Two additional characteristics of Sammartini's works are to a greater or lesser extent typical of early symphonies in general. One is the almost breathless quality of the opening movements. Towards the end of the century pedagogues such as Heinrich Christoph Koch would associate symphonies with 'the feeling of a rushing forward passion'.[10] Sammartini's first movements do not always exhibit the grand and unadorned ideas that were held to distinguish the symphony from the more deliberate and ornamental sonata; typically comprising one- and two-bar units that are repeated and varied, his phrases build energy incrementally rather than in the broader spans typical of later-eighteenth-century music. A desire for grandeur is evident, however, in the use of unisons, dotted rhythms and leaping arpeggios, reminiscent of marches or the music of high-born operatic characters. More striking, 'the melody continues to flow' (Koch) in an all but uninterrupted stream. Ideas connect seamlessly together, divisions are bridged by figuration and caesurae tend to come after half-cadences, whose unresolved dominant harmonies project tension through the rests. The brevity of the ideas contributes further to the sense of urgency, since a four- or eight-bar passage may contain several changes of mood; by the eleventh bar of the Symphony in G (J-C 46), one has heard march-like dotted rhythms (1 bar) and repeated notes (1 + 1 bars), a 'singing allegro' of long notes over quick figuration (3 bars), a march-like cadence (1 bar), and brilliant post-cadential turns (3 bars). The effect is heightened by frequent animated counterpoint between the first and second violins (an inheritance of the trio sonata and concerto[11]), and by the absence of repeat signs from a significant number of movements, which ensures an unbroken linear flow.

Sammartini also explores a characteristic mixture of march, song and dance in the three movements of his cycles. First movements may refer to all three. Second movements tend towards lyricism and sometimes 'endeavour to

10 Heinrich Christoph Koch, *Versuch einer Anleitung zur Composition* (Leipzig, 1782–93), 3 vols., vol. 3, p. 384; quoted in Michael Broyles, 'The Two Instrumental Styles of Classicism', *Journal of the American Musicological Society*, 36 (1983), p. 219.

11 Churgin, *The Symphony 1720–1840*, vol. A-2, pp. xxi–xxii.

display all the charms of beautiful song', as Rousseau wrote of the middle movements of sinfonias.[12] While melodies do float over simple bass lines and pulsating inner voices (for example, in J-C 4), the long-breathed themes of Neapolitan slow movements, often in triple meter or siciliano rhythm, are in fact not typical. Like many symphonists throughout the century, Sammartini prefers duple-meter andantes that sing but also move, typically via a bass that suggests walking or very restrained marching. The style can vary from playful (J-C 57), to calm (J-C 46), to *pathétique* (J-C 52, in the minor), but the continuous motion works against the slowing or suspension of time often implied by sinfonia middle movements. Finales bring fresh activity in the form of dance, most often either a fast (usually 3/8) or moderate (3/4) minuet. Many of Sammartini's finales are as fully developed as his first movements, but the events may seem to unfold more slowly since thematic statements in the style of the dance generally avoid bar-to-bar contrast. In addition, the usually joyful affect is balanced by the poised rhythms and balanced phrases of the dance. Along with dance-like movements in duple meter, the minuet would be a popular ending for symphonies through the 1760s, and combined with forward-driven allegros and active andantes it gives many early works a similar if infinitely malleable shape. While remaining lively throughout, they often progress from a continuous and unpredictable action at the beginning towards a more regulated choreography at the end.

Performance

What audiences made of this would have depended partly on how they listened. Symphonies always began eighteenth-century concerts, with a second example (or the finale of the first) often occurring mid-way through or at the end.[13] At the many occasions where music competed for attention with dining, card-playing and other entertainments, symphonies worked especially hard. They were all too easily dismissed, like opera overtures, as preface to the main attraction, in this case instrumental and vocal solos comprising the heart of the programme. At other concerts, however, listening anticipated the nineteenth-century ideal of silent concentration – and at still others, perhaps the majority, it varied from moment to moment. Haydn and Johann Peter Salomon began each half of their London programmes in 1791–5 with symphonies but saved

12 Jean-Jacques Rousseau, *Dictionnaire de musique* (Paris, 1768), s.v. 'Ouverture', p. 357.

13 Programmes and performance conditions are discussed in Mary Sue Morrow, *Concert Life in Haydn's Vienna: Aspects of a Developing Musical and Social Institution* (Stuyvesant, NY, 1989), esp. pp. 141–63; Neal Zaslaw, *Mozart's Symphonies: Context, Performance Practice, Reception* (Oxford, 1989), pp. 517–25; Simon McVeigh, *Concert Life in London from Mozart to Haydn* (Cambridge, 1993), esp. pp. 53–69.

premieres for the second half, by which time the audience could be counted on to have arrived and settled in.[14] The level of attentiveness would have affected reactions. On the one hand, when treated as background music, symphonies were probably thought to enliven social gatherings with rhythm and colour, call audiences to attention, or prepare them for the musical and emotional experiences to come.[15] It is not hard to imagine many early symphonies, exciting but brief, performing any of these functions. On the other hand, when followed carefully symphonies of any length could be taken to express emotions, vary themes, embody unity, broach the infinite, tell jokes or stories – all of which they were heard to do by contemporary commentators. The meanings of the genre would have changed according to whether they arose more from social ritual or individual fantasy.[16]

Sometimes listeners seem to have been struck as much by the performance of symphonies as by the works themselves, which frequently were tailored to fit orchestras that varied widely in size, composition, skill and playing style.[17] Works written for Mannheim, in particular, were associated closely with, and sometimes overshadowed by, an ensemble widely considered the best in Europe. After rhapsodizing about the orchestra – 'Its forte is a thunder, its crescendo a cataract, its diminuendo a crystal brook splashing off into the distance, its piano a spring breeze' – Christian Friedrich Daniel Schubart wrote of its Konzertmeister, Stamitz's student Christian Cannabich: 'As a composer he does not mean much ... the entire character of his compositions consists in bizarre ideas of line, deep study of musical colour, some charming stitched-together fashions.'[18] The music has value primarily insofar as it showcases the performers, a thought echoed by other commentators on the Mannheim style. No other orchestra had quite the same impact, but symphonies, as musical works, would come to be praised for the same combination of power and flexibility that was associated with Mannheim and with good

14 See Haydn's comment in Albert Christoph Dies, *Biographische Nachrichten von Joseph Haydn* (Vienna, 1810), p. 93. The London programmes are collected in H. C. Robbins Landon, *Haydn: Chronicle and Works, vol. 3. Haydn in England, 1791–1795* (London, 1976), pp. 21–320.

15 Cf. Elaine R. Sisman, *Mozart: The 'Jupiter' Symphony No. 41 in C major, K. 551* (Cambridge, 1993), pp. 5–7.

16 For a wide-ranging and imaginative investigation of eighteenth-century listening, see Melanie Lowe, *Pleasure and Meaning in the Classical Symphony* (Bloomington, IN, 2007), esp. pp. 78–163.

17 On orchestras, see especially Adam Carse, *The Orchestra in the XVIIIth Century* (Cambridge, 1940); Zaslaw, *Mozart's Symphonies*, pp. 449–64; John Spitzer and Neal Zaslaw, *The Birth of the Orchestra: History of an Institution, 1650–1815* (Oxford and New York, 2004); George B. Stauffer, 'The Modern Orchestra: A Creation of the Late Eighteenth Century', in Joan Peyser (ed.), *The Orchestra: Origins and Transformations* (New York, 1986), pp. 37–68; Michael Broyles, 'Ensemble Music Moves Out of the Private House: Haydn to Beethoven', in Peyser (ed.), *The Orchestra: Origins and Transformations*, pp. 97–122.

18 Christian Friedrich Daniel Schubart, *Ideen zu einer Ästhetik der Tonkunst* (1806), ed. Jürgen Mainka (Leipzig, 1977), pp. 122, 127; quoted in Christian Schruff, 'Konnte Langweiliges vom Stuhl reißen? Bemerkungen zu Aufführungspraxis und Interpretation der Mannheimer Orchestermusik', in Klaus Hortschansky (ed.), *Traditionen – Neuansätze: Für Anna Amalie Abert (1906–1996)* (Tutzing, 1997), p. 543.

orchestral playing generally. 'Unity in the style of performance and composition' was to some extent a characteristic of the genre.[19]

Performance has also influenced listener perception in the modern era. As the same pieces have been played many times by multiple ensembles, nuances have emerged that would have been difficult to imagine in the eighteenth century, when few if any symphonies remained in the repertory long enough to become as familiar as the works of Mozart and Haydn are today. Many concertgoers now expect good performances to point up previously unheard thematic relationships, formal and rhythmic subtleties, or moods. More obviously, the sound of the eighteenth-century symphony changed radically when, beginning in the 1970s, ensembles such as the Academy of Ancient Music began to apply performance practices based on historical players' manuals and descriptions of orchestras. Using fewer players than most twentieth-century orchestras, and instruments whose timbres were not only different from those of their modern counterparts but more variable in and of themselves, historically inspired performers also took quicker tempos and played with more separation between notes and phrases than was customary. Each ensemble developed its own identity, but the general result was to accent the rhythmic vitality of the repertory and its origins in march and dance, and to offer an alternative to a still-reigning nineteenth-century conception of the symphony as massive and weighty. Powerful when necessary, the new orchestral sonority nevertheless had a transparency approaching that of chamber music, which turned attention from external dimensions toward internal complexities. Orchestras of 'authentic' instruments also took unprecedented interest in the earlier and more lightly scored symphonies of Haydn and Mozart, greatly increasing their visibility on concert programmes and recordings. Some explored other composers as well, revitalizing pieces that had gone mostly unheard since the time of their composition. Today, listeners can hear more eighteenth-century symphonies than has ever been possible, experiencing the history of the genre in ways it could not have been experienced during the period itself. At the same time, the modern history of reinterpretation, much of it preserved on recording, reminds audiences of how fundamentally the repertory's musical and expressive shape is determined by performance.

Mid-century conceptions

By the time Sammartini wrote his last symphonies, in the early 1770s, the genre's centre of gravity had shifted from Italy to Central and Western Europe,

19 Schruff, 'Konnte Langweiliges vom Stuhl reißen?', p. 551.

where a multitude of both public and private concerts created a steady demand for new works. The three capitals of Paris, London and Vienna supported many leading symphonists of the decades surrounding the middle of the century: Louis-Gabriel Guillemain and François-Joseph Gossec in Paris, Johann Christian Bach and Carl Friedrich Abel in London, Georg Christoph Wagenseil, Carlo d'Ordoñez, Leopold Hofmann, Johann Baptist Vanhal and Carl Ditters (from 1773, von Dittersdorf) in Vienna. German-speaking Catholic courts and religious establishments, many of which maintained their own orchestras, employed other influential figures: Stamitz, Cannabich and Anton Fils at Mannheim, Joseph Haydn at Esterháza, Joseph's brother Michael Haydn as well as the Mozarts in Salzburg. A brisk trade in manuscript copies and engraved prints circulated works to and from additional locales, stimulating further demand and impressive productivity. Several of these composers wrote upwards of forty or fifty works within a couple of decades, and when Breitkopf issued his first catalogue in 1762, he could offer no fewer than 446 symphonies (including sinfonias) by forty-eight composers. His first supplement (1766) added 373 titles by 116 composers.[20]

Not surprisingly in light of such numeric and geographic growth, the genre diversified greatly. Least subject to variation was perhaps scoring, since the exchange of works depended on orchestras sharing similar forces. Their foundation remained the four-part string ensemble, sometimes enriched by a second viola line, at other times reduced by the omission of the viola, as in the 'orchestral trios' of Stamitz and others, which are also without winds. In symphonies with winds the usual complement is pairs of horns and oboes, with the oboes occasionally exchanged for flutes or, less frequently, clarinets (in some sources, the choice of woodwind is left to the performers). Depending on the orchestra, one or more bassoons as well as a continuo instrument would have joined the cellos and double basses on the bass part. The winds could be supplemented by flutes, obligato bassoons, trumpets and timpani, and additional horns, but these and more exotic combinations (for example, English horns in Haydn's Symphony No. 22 and trombones in Hofmann's pastoral symphonies) are outnumbered by the 'symphony in eight parts', four strings and four winds.

Less consistent are the number and order of movements. In France, England and northern Germany, three-movement cycles predominate all the way to the end of the century. Elsewhere, preferences waver between three and four movements. In his late works of the 1750s, Stamitz became the first to use regularly the four-movement pattern of fast and slow movement, minuet and

20 *The Breitkopf Thematic Catalogue*, pp. 2–28, 202–23.

finale.[21] Many Austrian and Bohemian composers followed suit, with some, such as Haydn and Dittersdorf, writing only four-movement cycles after an early period of exploiting both possibilities. In Mannheim, however, Stamitz's successors returned to composing mainly three-movement works, examples of which occur among the later symphonies of Austrian and Bohemian figures as well, including Vanhal, Mozart and Michael Haydn. In the 1750s, 1760s and early 1770s alternative tempo orderings were also common, most importantly those that changed the beginning of both three- and four-movement works from fast to slow. Composers prefaced opening allegros with slow introductions, and Ordoñez, Hofmann, Dittersdorf, Gossec and Haydn all began symphonies with complete slow movements, with an allegro following and then a minuet finale, a minuet and a separate finale, or a second slow movement and finale.[22]

Slow opening tempos are one sign of an expressive broadening that renders the progression of excitement, lyricism and dance just one choice among several. A slow introduction turns beginning into a two-stage event and colours perceptions of the allegro, which may seem variously like action after an entrance (Haydn's Symphony No. 7), joy after a lament (Gossec's Symphony in E-flat, Op. 12 no. 5), or reality after a somewhat troubled idyll (Hofmann's Symphony in D, Kimball D7). Opening slow movements go further, reversing the usual flow and balance of energy. The symphonies in which they occur resemble the church sonata with its opening slow movement, although they were no more likely to be played in church than symphonies with opening fast movements.[23] Still, they share the sonata's effort to draw listeners in not with rhythmic bustle or march-like brilliance, but with melody, sonority and texture. The slow movements also bear unusual weight thanks to their position in the cycle and tendency to be longer, slower and more richly scored than those found in the interior of symphonies, especially in Haydn.

At the end of the cycle, new possibilities are created by the expansion to four movements and the use of different types of finale. In a four-movement symphony with its opening movements in the usual order, the minuet postpones and intensifies the return from the slow tempo of the second

21 Wolf, *The Symphonies of Johann Stamitz*, pp. 86–91.

22 G. Cook Kimball surveys Viennese symphonies with slow beginnings in *The Symphony 1720–1840*, vol. B-7, p. xxxiv. For Gossec, see the scores and index in *The Symphony 1720–1840*, vol. D-3.

23 The comparison to church sonatas is drawn repeatedly by Landon, for example, in *Haydn: Chronicle and Works, vol. 1. Haydn: the Early Years, 1732–1765* (London, 1980), p. 286. On symphony performance in church, see Neal Zaslaw, 'Mozart, Haydn, and the *Sinfonia da chiesa*', *Journal of Musicology*, 1 (1982), pp. 95–124; Friedrich W. Riedel, 'Joseph Haydns Sinfonien als liturgische Musik', in Karlheinz Schlager (ed.), *Festschrift Hubert Unverricht zum 65. Geburtstag* (Tutzing, 1992), pp. 213–20.

movement to the quick tempo of the finale, which now comprises an acceleration spanning three movements.[24] Where the finale also uses dance rhythms, usually those of the contradance (2/4) or gigue (6/8), the symphony closes with a strong suggestion of contemporary social habits, since minuets and contradances dominated the later eighteenth-century ballroom. In neither minuet nor finale, however, does reference to dance limit the potential for expressive variation. Some minuets are bold, with unisons, dotted rhythms, or themes arpeggiating triads; others are more mellifluous, with flowing melodies over subdued accompaniments; still others are comic, with folksy tunes or witty contrasts. Trios allow complementary or contrasting affects to be introduced, in many cases the pastoral expressed in melodious interludes featuring the winds. As for finales, while some retain the rhythms, brevity and binary forms of contemporary dance music (among other examples are the minuet-finales that remain common in three-movement works), many others subject dance melodies to elaboration or juxtapose them with other ideas in sonata and rondo forms. Dance may also disappear entirely, or provide only an underlying meter, in finales whose level of contrast and development approaches that of first movements. Stamitz concludes some of his symphonies with a kind of pure nervous energy fuelled by tremolo and crescendos (Wolf D3 and E-flat5a, among others); Hofmann creates a pastoral-inflected heroism with arpeggiating trumpets reinforced by trombones (*Symphonia pastorella*, Kimball D1); Haydn and Vanhal end disquieting minor-mode works with finales in the same vein (see below). Listeners cannot be certain of being left with either choreographic regularity or affective optimism.

First and second movements become equally difficult to predict. If interior slow movements seem generally less substantial than allegros, with fewer ideas and an orchestra that is often reduced to strings alone, they do not necessarily make a weaker impression. On the contrary, in symphonies such as Stamitz's or J. C. Bach's, where the first movements pass quickly thanks to fast tempos and the frequent absence of repeat signs, slow movements are sometimes the longest and weightiest in the work. Through the 1750s and 1760s they also gain in formal complexity and colour. Wind instruments play concerto-like solos in movements by Hofmann, Vanhal, the Haydns and others, and fulfill both solo and accompanimental roles elsewhere. The still-common duple-meter Andante, for strings alone on a lyrical theme over 'walking' lower parts, may well broaden at the second key area into more sustained rhythms and a richer palette of timbres supported by the winds

24 Wolf, *The Symphonies of Johann Stamitz*, p. 90.

(Haydn's Symphonies Nos. 41, 43, 44, or Hofmann's Symphony in D, Kimball D2). While duple-meter andantes remain popular, moreover, other rhythmic foundations along with differing styles in both major and minor keys ensure that slow movements enjoy as much variety as any other part of the cycle.

As modern scholarship has emphasized, the diversity of opening allegros begins with their forms.[25] After expositions that consist of music in the tonic, a transition to a new key (often very quick in shorter pieces), and more music followed by cadences in the new key, continuations vary from simple binary patterns that traverse the same material but end in the tonic, to sonata forms that include development sections and complete tonic recapitulations. Especially popular at the middle of the century are movements with tonic reprises of only the second key area following a developmental middle section. Other variables include the presence or absence of repeat signs at the end of the exposition; the relative length of the sections; the extent to which the recapitulation (whether of both key areas or only the second) preserves or rewrites the exposition; and the strength with which cadences, textural changes and other means set the second key area off from the first.

Equally flexible are the stylistic identities of the formal sections. As will be seen, observers of the mid-century symphony felt that first movements should combine swift-moving energy with 'profound' and 'robust' musical ideas. Many examples fulfilled their expectation – the symphony with martial overtones, in particular, reached a new high point in C major works related to the Viennese trumpet overture.[26] But composers would not be limited to beginning with 'crowd-silencing' power. The vigour of numerous first movements depends on a rhythmic lightness reminiscent of operatic comedy: examples range from the overtly witty Symphony No. 28 in A of Haydn, which plays with metric ambiguities in a staccato texture, to the more generally animated later works of Wagenseil (for example, Kucaba F1, B-flat2, or D2), which scamper through mercurial contrasts atop syncopations, lombardic rhythms, propulsive upbeats and 'drumming' basses (that is, quick repeated notes). Other movements emphasize lyricism, not only in second key areas but also at openings, as in the spacious 'singing allegro' of J. C. Bach's Op. 3 no. 3 in E-flat, or the intimate string-wind dialogue of Haydn's Symphony No. 29 in E. In the years surrounding 1770

25 Overviews in *New Grove, Revised Edition*, vol. 24, s.v. 'Symphony', pp. 814–15; *New Grove, Revised Edition*, vol. 23, s.v. 'Sonata Form', pp. 687–95; Leonard G. Ratner, *Classic Music: Expression, Form, and Style* (New York, 1980), pp. 209–47; Charles Rosen, *Sonata Forms*, rev. edn. (New York, 1988), pp. 98–106, 133–76; James Hepokoski and Warren Darcy, *Elements of Sonata Theory: Norms, Types, and Deformations in the Late Eighteenth-Century Sonata* (Oxford, 2006).

26 A. Peter Brown, 'The Trumpet Overture and Sinfonia in Vienna (1715–1822): Rise, Decline, and Reformulation', in David Wyn Jones (ed.), *Music in Eighteenth-Century Austria* (Cambridge, 1996), pp. 13–69.

Haydn, Vanhal, Mozart and others also began with music that was neither comic nor lyrical but tragic, strident, or melancholic, affirming the symphony's ability to indulge dark sentiments as well as bright.

First movements do continue to share the propulsive continuity of the 'symphony style', but it, too, takes different forms thanks to a general lengthening of phrases and formal sections, and to personal preferences concerning the relationships between phrases and sections. In Stamitz's symphonies of the 1750s, for example, the composer generates relatively little momentum on the small scale; his periods often grow from the literal repetition of two-, three-, and four-bar statements, many of which end on the tonic so that harmonic tension is rarely sustained for more than four bars. However, his ideas connect one to the next as frequently as Sammartini's, and his forms 'show a distinct aversion to large-scale articulation', lacking repeat signs and only occasionally pausing at moments such as the arrival of the second key area or the end of the exposition.[27] The continuities produce a long-range motion that builds right through the tonal return sections at the ends of the movements, which typically reorder earlier materials as if to suggest that the action were still unfolding. By contrast, in J. C. Bach's symphonies of the 1760s and early 1770s, the energy is parsed into waves, each one longer than a typical complex of phrases in Stamitz, but also more separated from its neighbours. The musical ideas are varied and extended more often than repeated, and the harmonic and melodic arrivals tend to fall every four–eight bars rather than three–four. Bach may also combine several ideas into a single span arching sixteen or more bars, particularly at openings (for example, Op. 3 no. 5, or Op. 8 no. 4, both in F). Such passages seem to drive towards a goal, marked by a harmonic arrival and a foreshortening of the bar groupings during the final moments. Once a goal is reached, however, there is usually articulation; Bach nearly always uses strong cadences and caesurae to separate the first and second key areas as well as the exposition, middle section and recapitulation. In addition, he may begin by reiterating an entire opening period (as in Op. 3 no. 3 in E-flat), and end with an exact tonic reprise of the second key area of the exposition. Although the formal similarities with Stamitz extend to Bach also avoiding repeat signs for the most part, the resulting sense of motion differs significantly: the one composer favours continuous restlessness, the other periodic intensity. The discrepancy shows how individual notions of flow and direction can distinguish from one another even those movements that have similar forms and expressive topics.

27 Wolf, *The Symphonies of Johann Stamitz*, p. 144.

Sublimity and nationality

In 1774 an influential encyclopedia of aesthetics, Johann Georg Sulzer's *Allgemeine Theorie der schönen Künste* (*General Theory of the Fine Arts*), tried to capture the momentum of symphony first movements with a literary analogy. Declaring symphonies 'most excellently suited to expressions of grandeur, passion, and the sublime', the *Allgemeine Theorie* compared their first movements to the odes of Pindar, famed for their exalted language and seemingly chaotic syntax: 'The allegros of the best chamber symphonies contain profound and clever ideas, a somewhat free treatment of the parts, an apparent disorder in the melody and harmony, strongly marked rhythms of different types, robust melodies and unison passages, concerting middle voices, free imitations of a theme ... sudden modulations and digressions from one key to another ... strong gradations of loud and soft and especially of the crescendo.'[28] Prefiguring the *Allgemeine Theorie*, a half-century earlier Jean-Baptiste Du Bos cited storms in opera as proof that orchestral music could 'touch us deeply' despite its lack of words.[29] Storms exemplified sublimity in nature as Pindar did in poetry, and as a metaphor they echo through eighteenth-century writing on both symphonies and orchestras (see above). The *Allgemeine Theorie* added a further sublime credential by referring to symphonies as 'instrumental choruses', an obvious comparison given the massed sonorities made possible by the increased use of winds after 1750, and one that evoked the awe-inspiring spectacles and emotions found in the choral sections of religious works. In 1774 most symphonies were still no more than fifteen to twenty minutes long and destined primarily to introduce programmes of instrumental and vocal solos. Nevertheless, they already suggested something beyond 'a splendid display of instrumental music', to borrow a more conventional phrase from the *Allgemeine Theorie*'s description. Particularly in the first movements, there was power, universality, even an

28 *Allgemeine Theorie der schönen Künste*, s.v. 'Symphonie', pp. 478–9; trans. in Nancy Kovaleff Baker and Thomas Christensen (eds.), *Aesthetics and the Art of Musical Composition in the German Enlightenment: Selected Writings of Johann Georg Sulzer and Heinrich Christoph Koch* (Cambridge, 1995), p. 106. See also Sisman, *Mozart: The 'Jupiter' Symphony*, pp. 9–20; Judith L. Schwartz, 'Periodicity and Passion in the First Movement of Haydn's "Farewell" Symphony', in Eugene K. Wolf and Edward H. Roesner (eds.), *Studies in Musical Sources and Style: Essays in Honor of Jan LaRue* (Madison, WI, 1990), pp. 319–31; Nicolas Henri Waldvogel, 'The Eighteenth-Century Esthetics of the Sublime and the Valuation of the Symphony', PhD thesis (Yale University, 1992); Mark Evan Bonds, 'The Symphony as Pindaric Ode', in Elaine Sisman (ed.), *Haydn and His World* (Princeton, NJ, 1997), pp. 131–53. Reactions to the symphony are surveyed in Robert Sondheimer, *Die Theorie der Sinfonie und die Beurteilung einzelner Sinfoniekomponisten bei den Musikschriftstellern des 18. Jahrhunderts* (Leipzig, 1925).

29 Jean-Baptise Du Bos, *Réflexions critiques sur la poësie, la peinture et la musique* (Paris, 1719); trans. in Peter le Huray and James Day (eds.), *Music and Aesthetics in the Eighteenth and Early-Nineteenth Centuries* (Cambridge, 1981), p. 20.

intimation of divinity, attributes for which the genre would later be elevated to the pinnacle of musical art.

The *Allgemeine Theorie* limited the geographic sources of sublime symphonies to composers from German or Habsburg realms, excluding Italian sinfonias, which 'dawdle without energy or expression', and the overtures to French opéra-comiques, in which 'sublimity soon degenerates into bombast'. It is more difficult to distinguish national schools than these judgements suggest, since symphonies by Haydn, Sammartini, or Gossec may all mix 'German' characteristics – generally said to include seriousness, counterpoint and difficult harmony – with 'French' overture rhythms or 'Italian' orchestral brilliance. Nevertheless, others joined the *Allgemeine Theorie* in equating style with compositional origin and in privileging one tradition over another. In 1758 a French publisher gave the title *La Melodia Germanica* to a collection including symphonies by Stamitz, his Mannheim colleague Franz Xaver Richter and the Viennese Wagenseil,[30] and by the 1770s and 1780s, when Haydn and the Mannheimers Cannabich and Carl Joseph Toeschi accounted for most of the symphonies performed in Paris, French critics would associate the whole genre with Germany.[31] Critics in Berlin and Leipzig made a similar but more specific (and judgemental) connection when they described symphonies from the south, Vienna and Mannheim, as having an 'odd mixture ... of the serious and comic, the sublime and the lowly' that differed from the 'more coherent, orderly, solemn' manner of northern composers such as the Graun brothers in Berlin or Pierre van Maldere in the Austrian Netherlands.[32] Such attributions of style to place of origin anticipate the nineteenth century's cultural nationalism, whose ideology would be retroactively applied by scholars who portrayed Haydn's music as an expression of Austrian folk character or an ethnic Croatian 'voice'.[33]

If national and regional identities figured in the meanings associated with symphonies, however, in the eighteenth century those identities were most often evoked independent of a composer's personal ethnicity or national allegiance, chiefly by means of characteristic rhythms or movement types.

30 *Die Musik in Geschichte und Gegenwart*, s.v. 'Symphonie', col. 28.

31 Bernard Harrison, *Haydn: The 'Paris' Symphonies* (Cambridge, 1998), pp. 13–20.

32 Johann Adam Hiller, *Wöchentliche Nachrichten und Anmerkungen die Musik betreffend*, 1 (1766), p. 202 and 3 (1768), p. 107.

33 William H. Hadow, *A Croatian Composer: Notes Toward the Study of Joseph Haydn* (London: Seeley, 1897); Guido Adler, 'Haydn and the Viennese Classical School', *Musical Quarterly*, 18 (1932), pp. 191–207. Nationalist sentiment also figured in the debate over the origins of Haydn's predecessors: Guido Adler, *Wiener Instrumentalmusik vor und um 1750*, in *Denkmäler der Tonkunst in Österreich*, 15/2 (1908), pp. ix–xiii; Hugo Riemann, *Sinfonien der pfalzbayerischen Schule*, in *Denkmäler der Tonkunst in Bayern*, 3/1 (1902), pp. ix–xxx, 7/2 (1906), pp. xv–xxvi and 8/2 (1907), pp. vii–xiv; Fausto Torrefranca, 'Le origini della sinfonia: le sinfonie dell'imbrattacarte (G. B. Sanmartini [*sic*])', *Rivista musicale italiana*, 20 (1913), pp. 291–346, 21 (1914), pp. 97–121, 278–312 and 22 (1915), pp. 431–46.

Several of the most common appear in Dittersdorf's *Sinfonia nazionale nel gusto di cinque nazioni*, where a lightly marching andantino is German; a brilliant allegro, Italian; a contradance, English; a minuet in dotted rhythms, French; and a monotonous minor-key trio, Turkish. If the intent seems mildly polemical, with the German style framing the others as if it were the norm and they the exceptions, still Dittersdorf does not aim to identify himself with any single country. Rather, he exhibits his versatility and lets listeners review the – heavily stereotyped – national or ethnic traits associated with each style. Other references across political boundaries – for instance, the common incorporation of movements 'à la française' in German and Austrian symphonies – reinforce the impression that to represent a nation was less to assert one's roots than to exercise the listener's imagination.

Works that travelled further from Western Europe, or into its countryside, added the frisson of the exotic. Turkish episodes like Dittersdorf's trio communicate a generic sense of 'otherness', employing a 'messy or deficient version of European music' with no real pretensions to sounding authentic.[34] Russian, Polish, Hungarian and other Eastern European references have a firmer basis in regional rhythms or tunes, although to the uninitiated their remoteness from more familiar styles probably mattered as much as their actual sources. The same would have been true for the Ländler and folksong-like tunes used by Stamitz, Haydn, Dittersdorf and others, which may have connoted specific Central and Eastern European regions or a more general rustic flavour, depending on the audience. More 'nativist' employments of national music do become evident following the French Revolution, when dance rhythms and songs expressed patriotic sentiments in symphonies as well as other genres. Yet it is revealing that in August 1789, Haydn would promise a French publisher a (never-written) 'National Symphony', seeing no contradiction, at least at that early date, in an Austrian composer celebrating a renewed French nation.[35] Boundaries would harden in the years to come, but for much of the century symphonists were as ecumenical in the political identities they expressed as in the forms and moods they explored.

Haydn (I)

The sixty-plus symphonies written by Haydn between the late 1750s and the mid-1770s demonstrate like no others the capacity of the genre for structural and expressive variety. They use all the movement orders and forms discussed

34 Mary Hunter, 'The *alla turca* Style in the Late Eighteenth Century: Race and Gender in the Symphony and the Seraglio', in Jonathan Bellman (ed.), *The Exotic in Western Music* (Boston, 1998), p. 51.
35 Dénes Bartha (ed.), *Joseph Haydn: Gesammelte Briefe und Aufzeichnungen* (Kassel, 1965), p. 212.

above and run the gamut of national and other styles. To cite only the most obvious semantic references, they imitate recitatives and arias, quote liturgical melodies and a song by Gluck, depict a sunrise and a storm and choreograph the departure of the orchestra from Prince Esterházy's rural seat in the famous 'Farewell' Symphony (No. 45 in F-sharp minor). And with time they grow longer, adding fresh complexity to every dimension: Haydn eventually adopts four movements as a norm, and enlarges his forms so that by the early 1770s some first movements, in particular, achieve an imposing breadth.

Through it all runs a voice distinctive among mid-century symphonists and exemplary, in many respects, for those of years to come. In the flow of his movements Haydn lies closer to J. C. Bach than to Stamitz, although unlike either composer he prefers sonata forms in two repeated parts with full, if often varied, recapitulations. Nevertheless, the length of his ideas, their frequent organization into units spanning all or part of a formal section, and the generally strong articulation between sections lead to swells and crests of energy not unlike Bach's. The distinguishing features begin with texture and colour. Haydn often writes in only two parts, doubling the treble in octaves to create a sound that drew criticism at first but praise and imitation later on.[36] The spareness of the scoring draws attention to rhythm and phrase patterns as well as to the contrapuntal relationship between the outer voices. The counterpoint itself is unusually active, as evidenced by a general independence of the instrumental lines as well as many imitative passages, including a full-blown fugue in the finale of Symphony No. 40 in F. While the drumming repetitions so familiar from mid-century symphonies play an important role, accompanimental parts regularly engage the melody in dialogue or animate the score with varied rhythmic patterns.[37] Haydn also makes exceptionally ambitious use of the winds, especially after 1761 when he begins writing for the virtuosos of the Esterházy orchestra. In addition to concerto-like solos, the woodwinds and horns present material of many kinds in all movements and sections, and even re-define their customary role of providing colouristic relief from the strings, by taking the lead melodic voice at several beginnings (for example, Symphonies Nos. 6, 24 and 31).

Still more unique is that Haydn, in James Webster's phrase, 'developed musical ideas continually, not to say irrepressibly, in every movement he ever

36 Daniel Heartz, *Haydn, Mozart and the Viennese School, 1740–1780* (New York, 1995), pp. 262–3. There is disagreement as to whether Haydn expected his textures to include continuo: James Webster, 'On the Absence of Keyboard Continuo in Haydn's Symphonies', *Early Music*, 18 (1990), pp. 599–608; A. Peter Brown, *The Symphonic Repertoire*, vol. 2, *The First Golden Age of the Viennese Symphony: Haydn, Mozart, Beethoven, and Schubert* (Bloomington, IN, 2002), pp. 3–4.

37 Eric Weimer, *'Opera Seria' and the Evolution of Classical Style 1755–1772* (Ann Arbor, MI, 1984), pp. 78–92.

wrote'.[38] In the symphonies, an obvious example is the return of opening themes at the beginnings of second key areas, a practice whose modern name, monothematicism, tends to conceal the fact that such thematic returns always entail variation. In Symphony No. 43 in E-flat, what are originally two four-bar phrases punctuated by rests and tutti chords become a single lyrical effusion over a drumming bass. A decade earlier, in Symphony No. 8 in G, the symphony that quotes Gluck, the third section of the quotation is initially a self-contained exchange for violins and flute, but returns in the second key area as a dialogue for oboes and strings whose final bars open out into a half-cadence. Within key areas as well, what the pedagogue Koch summed up as the 'repetition and the variation of repeated melodic sections, both complete and incomplete', helped earn Haydn a reputation for 'unity within diversity'. His symphonies became models for imitation: Koch reprinted the entire second movement of Symphony No. 42 in D in his treatise on composition.[39] The result of Haydn's pervasive elaboration is an unusually chronological quality in the progression from bar to bar and section to section. Thematic continuations and formal arrivals bring familiar identities in new guises, as if to suggest that musical time had the altering or aging effects of real time. Recapitulations often sustain the impression. As in some other monothematic examples, the recapitulation of the first movement of Symphony No. 8 uses a single statement of the Gluck-derived main theme to stand in for both the first and second key areas. This clears the way for fresh developments that include a canonic treatment of the theme and a bizarre unison intensification ending in a fermata on the flattened-sixth scale degree.[40] In such a movement listeners experience not just the rush of the symphony style, but the re-invention of an idea that begins with one shape and ends with quite another.

Webster shows that, on occasion, motivic development combines with other forces to integrate structure and expression across movements.[41] The most ambitious instances are the 'Farewell' Symphony and its companion of 1772, No. 46 in B, in which all four movements are knit together by thematic resemblances and tonal relations (for example, the use of third-related keys

38 James Webster, *Haydn's 'Farewell' Symphony and the Idea of Classical Style* (Cambridge, 1991), p. 198.

39 Koch, *Versuch*, vol. 3, pp. 178–90; Koch, *Introductory Essay on Composition: The Mechanical Rules of Melody, Sections 3 and 4*, trans. Nancy Kovaleff Baker (New Haven, CT, 1983), pp. 141–8. See also Sisman, *Haydn and the Classical Variation* (Cambridge, MA, 1993), pp. 85–7.

40 Cf. the monothematic movements discussed in Eugene K. Wolf, 'The Recapitulations in Haydn's London Symphonies', *Musical Quarterly*, 52 (1966), pp. 72–4. On Symphony No. 8, see Heartz, *Haydn, Mozart, and the Viennese School, 1740–1780*, pp. 271–3; Richard Will, 'When God Met the Sinner, and Other Dramatic Confrontations in Eighteenth-Century Instrumental Music', *Music & Letters*, 78 (1997), pp. 196–208.

41 Webster, *Haydn's 'Farewell' Symphony*, esp. pp. 13–29 (on No. 45), pp. 267–87 (on No. 46).

in the first work, and of the parallel minor in the second). In each case, an unconventional finale caps off the process. The 'orchestral pantomime'[42] of the farewell, an adagio, major-key conclusion to a terse minor-key presto, resolves tonal and expressive tensions that build throughout the symphony, while the reprise of the minuet midway through the finale of No. 46 recalls the relative seriousness of the three preceding movements and thus emphasizes the emotional release offered by the 'presto e scherzando' conclusion. Comparable endings are found in other symphonies associated, like the 'Farewell', with a sequence of events or ideas: Dittersdorf's *Sinfonia nazionale*, for example, finishes with a rondo that reviews the identities represented in the earlier movements. A series of topics need not be present, however, or at least not declared, for Haydn to link multiple movements, as witnessed by other well-integrated symphonies such as Nos. 15, 25, or 49.[43]

Haydn's unusually numerous minor-key symphonies of *c.* 1768–72 have long been associated with the slightly later literary movement of the *Sturm und Drang*, as have contemporaneous minor-key examples by Vanhal, Mozart, Dittersdorf and Luigi Boccherini.[44] Several do exhibit the 'unprecedented vehemence' Daniel Heartz hears in Haydn's Symphony No. 52 in C minor, and they may well represent, if not a proto-*Werther* interest in psychological catastrophe, at least a post-*Orfeo* or *Don Juan* desire to imbue symphonies with the dramatic intensity of Gluck.[45] Boccherini adapted the 'Dance of the Furies' from *Don Juan* as the finale of a D minor symphony entitled *La casa del diavolo* (Gérard 506), and other composers echoed more generally the rhythmic instabilities, harmonic dissonances, orchestral power and religious overtones of Gluck's infernal scenes.

The coincidence of so much minor-key turmoil, however, should not be allowed to obscure the differences between works, nor their role in a transformation that affected all symphonies, whatever their emotional character. Minor-key symphonies followed many affective trajectories. Haydn's Symphony No. 52 begins with stern unisons and racing scales; the more playful, major-key theme of the second key area has difficulty reaching closure and

42 Gerhard J. Winkler, '"Orchesterpantomime" in den Esterházy-Sinfonien Joseph Haydns', in Winkler (ed.), *Das symphonische Werk Joseph Haydns* (Eisenstadt, 2000), pp. 103–16, including discussion of Symphonies Nos. 45, 46 and 60.

43 Webster, *Haydn's 'Farewell' Symphony*, pp. 251–67.

44 First to make the association was evidently Théodore de Wyzewa, in 'A propos du centenaire de la mort de Joseph Haydn', *Revue des deux mondes*, 51 (15 June 1909), pp. 935–46. See also Landon, *Haydn: Chronicle and Works, vol.* 2, pp. 266–84; Landon, 'La Crise romantique dans la musique autrichienne vers 1770: Quelques précurseurs inconnus de la Symphonie en sol mineur (KV 183) de Mozart', in André Verchaly (ed.), *Les Influences étrangères dans l'oeuvre de W. A. Mozart* (Paris, 1958), pp. 27–47; Barry S. Brook, 'Sturm und Drang and the Romantic Period in Music', *Studies in Romanticism*, 9 (1970), pp. 269–84.

45 Heartz, *Haydn, Mozart, and the Viennese School, 1740–1780*, pp. 188, 293–4.

returns subdued, in the minor, in the recapitulation. The second movement is legato but rent by more unisons, and the finale concluded by still more unisons as well as dissonant diminished-seventh chords. By contrast, the 'Farewell' Symphony opens with fierce arpeggios and syncopations that go unrelieved during the first movement, but find eventual resolution in the major-key second half of the finale. Mozart's Symphony in G minor, K. 183, recalls Haydn's No. 52 in its opening unisons and prolongation of a sombre mood through the end of the finale, but the length and periodicity of its second key area theme make the first movement seem comparatively unhurried and stable (see below). Several of Vanhal's minor-key symphonies go further in the same direction, beginning with melancholy but lyrical triple-meter allegros and saving any vehemence for the finales (for example, Bryan Em1, Em2, Cm2, or Gm2).

The minor-key works must also be understood in a context where expanding forms allowed every symphony to broaden and deepen. During the *Sturm und Drang* years Haydn also wrote Symphony No. 42 in D, which elaborates a lyrical impulse in a 'moderato e maestoso' first movement so long that it has room for both a 'second theme' and a 'closing theme' in reduced texture. Comparable spaciousness characterizes the 'cantabile' second movement so admired by Koch. Likewise the first movement of No. 47 in G lends fresh weight to the fanfare openings and pastoral second key areas common among early symphonies, developing dotted rhythms through a substantial first key area and transition, then relaxing into a leisurely oboe solo that returns intact in both development and recapitulation. Similar breadth is evident in some of Mozart's symphonies of 1772–4, including the major-key works K. 134 and K. 200–202 as well as K. 183, and it appears elsewhere around the same time or somewhat later, for instance in Vanhal's Symphonies in D and D minor (Bryan D4 and Dm2) and Dittersdorf's Symphony in D minor (Grave Dm1). Such works seem eager to confirm the opinion of the symphony expressed in Sulzer's *Allgemeine Theorie*. Probing a wide emotional spectrum in forms of increasing length and complexity, they bolster the genre's claim to a position among the most profound in music.

Characters and gender

Asked late in life about 'feelings and ideas' in his music, Haydn answered 'that he had often portrayed moral characters in his symphonies'.[46] Strictly speaking moral characters are personality types, the Melancholics and Irresolutes

46 Georg August Griesinger, *Biographische Notizen über Joseph Haydn* (Leipzig, 1810), p. 117; trans. adapted from Webster, *Haydn's 'Farewell' Symphony*, p. 234.

described by the classical Greek writer Theophrastus and his seventeenth- and eighteenth-century imitators. Haydn sketched 'The Distracted One' ('Le Distrait') in his Symphony No. 60 in C (no later than 1774), originally written as an overture and entractes for Jean-François Regnard's play of the same name. Suggestive of many episodes in the plot and thus more wide-ranging than a Theophrastan essay, the music still reflects the nature of the protagonist at several key moments, most hilariously in the finale when the violins discover they have forgotten to tune.[47] Works by Dittersdorf, Vanhal, Francisco Javier Moreno and others deal with less eccentric figures such as 'Il Superbo', 'L'Umile', and 'Il Vivace'. In so doing, they suggest some broader ramifications for moral characters, who may have been perceived even in symphonies that lacked descriptive labels. For listeners used to encountering personified emotions on stage, or in treatises on personality and manners, it would have been a short step from hearing a symphonic vivace as 'lively' to imagining a depiction of 'The Lively One'. The same goes for any number of majestic opening allegros ('Il Superbo') and pathetic slow movements ('L'Umile').

As the continuation of Haydn's reply shows, the possible characters in a symphony were also not limited to generic types. He cites one of his own movements in which 'God speaks to an unrepentant sinner, and pleads with him to reform; but the sinner in his foolishness pays no heed to the exhortations'. The scenario suggests a dialogue not unlike those found in Dittersdorf's Symphonies on Ovid's *Metamorphoses* (*c.* 1781–6), where protagonists 'speak' to one another through contrasting styles that alternate back and forth, or through instrumental parts that combine contrapuntally.[48] The means of representation are so common in late-eighteenth-century works that one wonders, again, if listeners did not perceive characters even where there was no advertised subject or plot. Encouraging such interpretations, instrumental music was compared to dialogue in many critical writings and musical sources,[49] and while the targets of the metaphor are more often chamber works than symphonies, the latter contain equally suggestive interactions between styles and instrumental parts. Like the moral character, the conversation offered a framework through which instrumental music could be imagined to possess not just meaning, but the didactic force so often demanded of eighteenth-century art. Symphonies did not even need to show God lecturing

47 On this work, see Jacob de Ruiter, *Der Charakterbegriff in der Musik: Studien zur deutschen Ästhetik der Instrumentalmusik 1740–1850* (Stuttgart, 1989), pp. 83–9; Sisman, 'Haydn's Theater Symphonies', *Journal of the American Musicological Society*, 43 (1990), pp. 311–20; Gretchen A. Wheelock, *Haydn's Ingenious Jesting with Art: Contexts of Musical Wit and Humor* (New York, 1992), pp. 154–71.
48 Will, 'When God Met the Sinner', pp. 186–91.
49 Ludwig Finscher, *Studien zur Geschichte des Streichquartetts*, vol. 1, *Die Entstehung des klassischen Streichquartetts* (Kassel, 1974), pp. 285–90.

a sinner in order to be 'moral'; comic portraits like 'Le Distrait' could also edify by illustrating the dangers of extreme temperaments.

For the north German critics who disliked the 'mixed style' of southern symphonies, including Haydn's, part of the problem was the gender of the implied characters. By speaking of grandeur and the sublime, Sulzer's *Allgemeine Theorie* endowed the genre with traditional masculine qualities.[50] Anything thought too feminine drew censure, including 'minuets in symphonies' which, according to Johann Adam Hiller, 'always seem to us like beauty spots on the face of a man; they give the music a foppish appearance, and weaken the manly impression made by the uninterrupted sequence of three well-matched, serious movements'.[51] Hiller deduced the gender of the dance from its steps, small and elegant rather than big and bold as in the march, and from its national source, France, which he and his colleagues considered a wellspring of effeminacy. Thus a symphony without minuet was at once more masculine and more German than a four-movement work. Melodic lyricism suffered a related fate. In the *Allgemeine Theorie*, the 'beautiful songs' of Carl Heinrich Graun's symphonies are said to 'have but a feeble effect', and to show that 'his tender soul lacked the requisite fire' to fuel a properly symphonic energy.[52] Similar values are evident in discussions of the symphony style, which give preference to force and simplicity over grace and ornamentation. In this case, the bias crosses national borders, the French writer Meude-Monpas also detecting an effeminate passivity in melody: 'a pretty tune in a symphony resembles a victim immolated by a number of sacrificial priests.'[53]

Of course, not only Graun but also Haydn, Vanhal, Mozart and many of their contemporaries wrote symphonies in which lyricism extends well beyond its usual domain of the second movement. The symphonic minuet also prospered, despite ongoing complaints from the north.[54] An aesthetic that allowed only for grand symphonies had its limitations (see above) and so, too, did overly strict distinctions between masculine and feminine. The 'French' minuet in Dittersdorf's *Sinfonia nazionale* uses a pattern of dotted rhythms on the second and third beats found also in examples such as Haydn's Symphony

50 Daniel K. L. Chua, *Absolute Music and the Construction of Meaning* (Cambridge, 1999), p. 137.

51 Hiller, *Wöchentliche Nachrichten*, 1 (1766), p. 243; quoted in Matthew Head, '"Like Beauty Spots on the Face of a Man": Gender in 18th-Century North-German Discourse on Genre', *Journal of Musicology*, 13 (1995), p. 144.

52 *Allgemeine Theorie der schönen Künste*, s.v. 'Symphonie', p. 480; trans. in Baker and Christensen (eds.), *Aesthetics and the Art of Musical Composition*, p. 107. German critics frequently demanded that symphonies, overtures, or their composers be 'fiery', for example in *Johann Adolph Scheibes Critischer Musikus*, p. 622; Hiller, *Wöchentliche Nachrichten*, 1 (1766), p. 21; Georg Joseph Vogler, *Betrachtungen der Mannheimer Tonschule* (Mannheim, 1778–81), 3 vols., vol. 1, p. 52.

53 J. J. O. de Meude-Monpas, *Dictionnaire de musique* (Paris, 1787), s.v. 'Symphonie', p. 194; quoted in Broyles, 'The Two Instrumental Styles of Classicism', p. 221.

54 For example, the polemic quoted in Zaslaw, *Mozart's Symphonies*, pp. 415–16.

No. 15 and Mozart's K. 201. The steps are small, and even supplied with *agréments* in Dittersdorf's case, but they nonetheless recall a march in their crisp and vigorous procession. It is not clear which image prevails: the mincing 'femininity' associated with the dance, or the striding 'masculinity' implied by the dotted rhythms. Unisons pose similar questions. Associated by Sulzer with Pindaric exaltation and by C. P. E. Bach with 'manly bearing',[55] they occur at least as often in minuets as elsewhere – indeed, the *forte* unison is a ubiquitous opening gambit in symphonic minuets. Again the impression is of mixed genders – or, in the not uncommon case where unisons provoke a quiet, homophonic response, a dialogue of masculine and feminine. If listeners heard as much gender in symphonies as they did nationality or temperament, these broadest of all character-defining categories were also subject to the greatest inflection.

Mozart

Those who heard characters in Mozart's symphonies met an unusually diverse cast in each work. A famous example is the 'Jupiter' (K. 551 in C), where the finale combines 'learned' counterpoint with *galant* textures and rhythms, and the first movement, in Elaine Sisman's words, 'charts a course from the grand style (first theme), down the stylistic spectrum to the singing style (second theme), then further down still to a comic, popular-style closing theme'.[56] Movements elsewhere traverse similar contrasts, if on a smaller scale and without the synthesis provided by the fugal ending of the 'Jupiter'. During Mozart's most prolific years as a symphonist, 1770–4, the second key areas of his fast movements often feature tuneful phrases in balanced pairs, lombardic rhythms, witty trills and turns, staccato and syncopated accompaniments and dialogues between the strings and winds. These 'popular-style' elements follow first key areas that may be majestic, lyrical, or even stormy: no less fierce an opening than that of the G minor symphony, K. 183, yields to springing turn figures over a tonic pedal in the relative major. The dichotomy is mitigated somewhat by the rhythmic irregularity of the new theme (its consequent is a half-bar shorter than expected) and its eventual recapitulation in the minor. Still, the contrast brings to mind the musical and dramatic oppositions of Mozart's opere buffe, whose dialogues between competing characters, or between

55 Head, '"Like Beauty Spots"', p. 147.

56 Sisman, *Mozart: The 'Jupiter' Symphony*, pp. 47, 68–79. Lowe proposes that a similar 'expressive descent' across three or four movements characterizes the later eighteenth-century symphony generally: *Pleasure and Meaning in the Classical Symphony*, pp. 54–69.

conflicting emotions in an individual, provide illuminating parallels for the stylistic juxtapositions in the symphonies.

Contrast gains force from Mozart's tendency to preserve his musical ideas relatively intact. Many of his recapitulations alter only the key structure and harmonic transition of the exposition. Development sections contain ample fragmentation, counterpoint and harmonic adventure, but ideas often appear in different textures and keys without losing their original identity. None of this diminishes the momentum of the works; initially influenced by the symphonies of J. C. Bach and Abel, Mozart extended their waves of rhythmic energy to unforeseen lengths and punctuated them with powerful arrivals. Yet Wolf and Jan LaRue write aptly that 'elaborate motivic development might blur the characteristic thematic personalities that had been so carefully distinguished in the exposition', and thus developments and recapitulations re-enact more than they re-invent.[57] The passage of time reveals itself not in Haydnesque metamorphosis so much as in the reappearance of familiar shapes in fresh contexts.

Rich orchestration enhances both stylistic contrast and rhythmic drive. The 'Paris' Symphony (K. 297 in D, 1778) is 'in seventeen parts' – four strings, timpani and pairs of flutes, oboes, clarinets, bassoons, horns and trumpets – which would become a common although by no means universal scoring by the end of the century (clarinets were particularly slow to be adopted). Some effects that exploit the larger ensemble, like the orchestral *tirades* at the opening or the inventive use of winds throughout, have parallels in works by Cannabich, Carl Stamitz, Simon Le Duc, Marie-Alexandre Guénin and others active in Mannheim and Paris in the 1770s.[58] In the later symphonies, as in the operas and piano concertos, Mozart continued to create full and often imposing textures, in part by giving the winds a nearly equal role to the strings in both solo and accompaniment. Using fewer winds less ambitiously, the earlier symphonies generate their own opulence with string writing full of tremolo, melodic doubling at the third or sixth, accompaniments in broken arpeggios, and violas divided into two parts. The sound can contribute extra force to passages already propelled by harmonic tension and rhythmic excitement: a Mozartian signature, one that links earlier works such as K. 183, K. 114 in A, or K. 132 in E-flat to the late 'Jupiter' and 'Prague' Symphonies (K. 504 in D), is the sonata- or binary-form transition in which a

57 *New Grove, Revised Edition*, vol. 24, s.v. 'Symphony', p. 830.

58 Alfred Einstein, *Mozart: His Character, His Work*, trans. Arthur Mendel and Nathan Broder (London and Oxford, 1945), p. 227; John Rice, *The Symphony 1720–1840*, vol. D-1, pp. xxii–xxiv; Wolf, 'Mannheimer Symphonik um 1777/1778 und ihr Einfluß auf Mozarts symphonischen Stil', in Ludwig Finscher, Bärbel Pelker and Jochen Reutter (eds.), *Mozart und Mannheim* (Berlin, 1994), pp. 309–30.

melody, often doubled or in imitative counterpoint, unfolds against a multiple-octave spread of tremolo, drumming repeated notes, and long tones in the winds. Both early and late symphonies tend to maintain scorings over many bars as well, building further energy and identifying each successive passage so strongly with its orchestration that the contrast of colour assumes an importance equal to that of style.

By the later symphonies, musical and affective oppositions invade even Mozart's slow movements, otherwise remarkable for their melodic suavity and evocations of vocal music (singing melodies with accompaniment, as in K. 45a in G, K. 134 in A, and elsewhere) and the pastoral ('Paris', 'Prague' and 'Linz' [K. 425 in C] symphonies). In several instances seemingly placid andantes reveal dark undercurrents in their transitional or developmental sections, and in K. 543 in E-flat, a poised and conjunct rondo melody gives way twice to what Peter Gülke terms a 'wild, unchecked lament', etched by jagged arpeggios and 'roiled by syncopations'.[59] As if to maximize disruption, this latter episode appears first in the relative minor of the tonic A-flat (that is, F minor), and later a tritone away in the exceedingly remote minor key of the flattened third (B minor). Such digressions bolstered Mozart's contemporaries in their conviction that his music lacked focus: 'for all their fire, for all their pomp and brilliance [the symphonies] yet lack that sense of unity, that clarity and directness of presentation, which we rightly admire in Jos. Haydn's symphonies.'[60] It did not help that Mozart's abrupt contrasts, advanced harmonies, dense textures and elaborate wind parts posed challenges of execution that few orchestras could overcome.

With higher standards of playing and more intensive listening, later generations found such complexities to be balanced by Mozart's clarity of form and voice-leading, and by rhythmic, melodic and expressive relationships that constitute, if not the systematic variations of Haydn, then a 'thread of connection and succession'.[61] Early commentators were ill equipped to appreciate either the diversity of a work like the 'Jupiter' – recall the proscriptions against minuets, lyricism and mixed style – or its implications for composers and listeners. Some modern scholars hear the disjunctions of Mozart's late symphonies as an assertion of the individual's right to critique pre-conceived rules of

59 Peter Gülke, *Im Zyklus einer Welt: Mozarts letzte Sinfonien* (Munich, 1997), p. 39.

60 *Teutschlands Annalen des Jahres 1794* (Chemnitz, 1795); quoted in Otto Erich Deutsch, *Mozart: A Documentary Biography*, trans. Eric Blom, Peter Branscombe and Jeremy Noble (London, 1965), pp. 472–3; additional comments in Zaslaw, *Mozart's Symphonies*, pp. 529–30.

61 Wye J. Allanbrook, 'Two Threads through the Labyrinth: Topic and Process in the First Movements of K. 332 and K. 333', in Allanbrook, Janet M. Levy and William P. Mahrt (eds.), *Convention in Eighteenth- and Nineteenth-Century Music: Essays in Honor of Leonard G. Ratner* (Stuyvesant, NY, 1992), p. 127. The term 'thread' is from Leopold Mozart.

form and expression.[62] Critics who shared the Enlightenment's faith in universal taste, and who spoke of symphonies articulating choral (that is, communal) sentiment, cannot have approved such a claim to creative autonomy. Nor can they have liked Mozart's frequently 'difficult' counterpoint if, as Sisman suggests, it renders the 'Jupiter' finale representative of a Kantian 'mathematical' sublime, and makes the 'Prague' first movement accessible primarily to '*Kenner*' (connoisseurs).[63] The eighteenth century wanted music to appeal to both connoisseurs and '*Liebhaber*' (music-lovers), something Haydn was said to do by making his most sophisticated passages seem lucid and 'natural'. Mozart would need standards of judgement that arose only after his death, when the early German Romantics began to write of symphonies manifesting genius unfettered by convention, and to view comprehension as a transcendental experience available only to a few (see below). In time, Mozart would be valued more than Haydn, as the older composer's clarity, associated by E. T. A. Hoffmann with 'a childlike and cheerful disposition', was deemed naïve.[64] The comparative opacity of Mozart, which 'leads us into the depths of the realm of spirits' (Hoffmann), would make his works the nineteenth century's model of the symphony before Beethoven.

Characteristic symphonies and interpretations

Through the 1770s, both Mozart and Haydn perpetuated the traditional overlap between chamber and theatre symphonies. Mozart wrote sinfonia-like works in three movements (for example, K. 162, K. 181–182 and K. 184) and adapted one- and two-movement overtures for concert use, while Haydn incorporated overtures and incidental music into symphonies and recycled the music from 'Le Distrait' as Symphony No. 60.[65] In Haydn's case the borrowings often have concrete theatrical associations, not only in No. 60 but also in No. 63 in C, whose second movement, entitled 'La Roxelane', is a character sketch probably drawn from music for Favart's *Soliman II*, and in No. 73 in D, whose finale, 'La Chasse', was originally a hunting overture for

62 Rose Rosengard Subotnik, 'Evidence of a Critical Worldview in Mozart's Last Three Symphonies', in Subotnik, *Developing Variations: Style and Ideology in Western Music* (Minneapolis, MN, 1991), pp. 98–111; Susan McClary, 'Narratives of Bourgeois Subjectivity in Mozart's *Prague* Symphony', in James Phelan and Peter J. Rabinowitz (eds.), *Understanding Narrative* (Columbus, OH, 1994), pp. 65–98.

63 Sisman, *Mozart: The 'Jupiter' Symphony*, pp. 18–20, 74–79; 'Genre, Gesture, and Meaning in Mozart's "Prague" Symphony', in Cliff Eisen (ed.), *Mozart Studies 2* (Oxford, 1997), pp. 47–56.

64 E. T. A. Hoffmann, review of Beethoven's Fifth Symphony, *Allgemeine musikalische Zeitung*, 12 (1810), col. 632. See also Leon Botstein, 'The Consequences of Presumed Innocence: The Nineteenth-Century Reception of Joseph Haydn', in W. Dean Sutcliffe (ed.), *Haydn Studies* (Cambridge, 1998), pp. 1–34.

65 Summaries in Brown, *The Symphonic Repertoire*, vol. 2, pp. 332–40; Webster, 'Haydn's Symphonies between *Sturm und Drang* and "Classical Style": Art and Entertainment', in Sutcliffe (ed.), *Haydn Studies*, pp. 221–2.

Haydn's opera *La fedeltà premiata*. Such movements evidence a broader tendency to use the chamber symphony as a 'stage' in and of itself. Haydn's hunting finale is one of several written between *c.* 1770 and the end of the century. Like other examples it conveys the atmosphere of its subject with galloping rhythms and an actual hunting horn signal, while suggesting particular moments in the chase with crescendos, diminuendos and the placement of the signal in the form. Closely related are tempest finales, which appear *c.* 1750–80 (including in Haydn's Symphony No. 8) and feature shifting dynamics, unstable rhythms and harmonies, and 'lightning' motives.[66]

More ambitious are symphonies that represent a course of action over several movements. Some take their subject from literature, notably Haydn's No. 60 and Dittersdorf's twelve Symphonies on Ovid's *Metamorphoses*. Others expand hunts or tempests into full-fledged scenarios, usually involving the pastoral: the *Sinfonia di caccia* of Gossec (*c.* 1773) has a slow movement depicting a waterside idyll, and the *Portrait musical de la nature* (1785) of Justin Heinrich Knecht represents 'a beautiful countryside' followed by a storm and a hymn of thanksgiving. Still other works depict real or imaginary battles, often in conjunction with other subjects. To mark the Treaty of Campo Formio between Austria and Napoleon, the *Grande Sinfonie caractéristique pour la paix avec la République françoise* (1797) by the Viennese Paul Wranitzky showed in four movements the French Revolution, the death of Louis XVI, the battle of the Revolutionary armies against the Austrians and Prussians and the celebrations of peace.

Never very numerous, and distinguished from ordinary symphonies by unusual movement orders and forms, such works nevertheless prepared the ground for Beethoven's 'Eroica' and 'Pastoral' Symphonies, and revealed a strengthening confidence in the communicative powers of orchestral music. Examples such as Dittersdorf's *Metamorphoses*, premiered at two concerts that consisted of the symphonies and nothing else, bid to satisfy all the musical and dramatic expectations listeners brought to more varied programmes or to opera. Beyond that, they reinforced the association of orchestral music with favourite subjects, especially the pastoral, manifestations of the sublime (storms, hunts, battles), national styles (used in numerous battle pieces) and above all human characters. 'Characteristic' was in fact the most common term for instrumental music with descriptive annotations, and it was appropriate even in its most literal sense, for numerous examples deal partly or wholly in dialogues and the emotions of protagonists. Nor do characters necessarily

66 On hunts, storms and the works discussed in the next two paragraphs, see Richard Will, *The Characteristic Symphony in the Age of Haydn and Beethoven* (Cambridge, 2002).

disappear when the scene shifts to a battle or a storm. Such events are typically shown to affect people sketched in the surrounding movements, who may themselves play a role in the action.

In arranging familiar subjects into dramatic sequences, characteristic symphonies have much in common with what might be called 'characteristic interpretations'. First published in the 1780s, these had the aim of describing the expressive content of individual instrumental works, rather than whole genres as in most eighteenth-century writing on instrumental music.[67] The usual strategy, as formulated by Carl Friedrich Cramer, was 'to imagine some character who could correspond to an excellent piece', and many of the pieces thus described were symphonies.[68] In an 1806 poem by August Apel, a youth experiences first love in Mozart's K. 543. Successive passages suggest naive rapture, a despair that reaches its nadir in the minor-key episodes of the second movement ('Ah, the joys of love have fled'), then yearning, nostalgia and a mature happiness that confirms the eternal power of love.[69] Despite imagery that portends the 'spirit world' of E. T. A. Hoffmann's Mozart, the emphasis on emotional development recalls Dittersdorf's *Metamorphoses* and related eighteenth-century examples. Similar although more mundane is the tale created by Jérôme-Joseph de Momigny for the first movement of Haydn's Symphony No. 103 in E-flat. The 'character' in this instance is a community of peasants seeking social harmony. Following the 'thunderclap' of the opening timpani roll, they pray for deliverance, dance for joy, argue, pray again after the return of the timpani and finish in an 'intoxication of contentment'. Both authors assume that listeners can associate musical events with the twists and turns of a plot, as do, increasingly, analytical discussions of instrumental music – Momigny couples his programmatic narrative with a section-by-section account of phrase structure and form.[70] As they ask audiences to listen more closely, Momigny and Apel also enhance the symphony's aura of profundity. Humble protagonists notwithstanding, Momigny writes of redemption inspired by thundering divinity, and Apel imitates epic, beginning with a Homeric exordium that reads Mozart's slow introduction as a paean to the gods. Symphonies may have been equally capable of essaying

67 *Ibid.*, pp. 11–12; Mark Evan Bonds, *Wordless Rhetoric: Musical Form and the Metaphor of the Oration* (Cambridge, MA, 1991), pp. 169–76.

68 *Magazin der Musik*, 1 (1783), p. 1243.

69 August Apel, 'Musik und Poesie', *Allgemeine musikalische Zeitung*, 8 (1806), cols. 449–57, 465–70; trans. in Bruce Alan Brown, 'Modes of Apprehension in the Classical Symphony: August Apel's "Sinfonie nach Mozart in Es dur" (1806)', unpublished paper delivered at the American Musicological Society National Meeting (Phoenix, AR, 1997).

70 Jérôme-Joseph de Momigny, *Cours complet d'harmonie et de composition, d'après une théorie nouvelle et générale de la musique* (Paris, 1803–15), 3 vols., vol. 2, pp. 586–606; trans. in Ian Bent (ed.), *Music Analysis in the Nineteenth Century* (Cambridge, 1994), 2 vols., vol. 2, pp. 130–40

comedy, as in Haydn's 'Le Distrait', but critics preferred their analogies serious and monumental.

Haydn (II)

Scholars have long judged 'Le Distrait', along with other Haydn symphonies of *c.* 1774–84, to be more popular in style than works of the preceding *Sturm und Drang*. In place of expressive intensity and formal concentration come tuneful melodies, clear textures, stable harmonies, major keys, expansive variation and rondo forms, and excerpts from theatre music. Haydn has been criticized for the change, which is variously attributed to his increased involvement with the stage or a desire to make his symphonies more marketable. However, quite apart from the drawbacks of confining the symphony to a single aesthetic, his turn towards 'entertainment' is defensible in its own right and historically momentous.[71] Even as he invested the later 'Paris' (Nos. 82–87) and 'London' (Nos. 93–104) symphonies with more complex harmony, counterpoint and thematic development, Haydn preserved much of the tunefulness and formal clarity of the post-*Sturm und Drang* works. It was this leavening of the intellectual challenges of the late symphonies, in large part, that allowed him to avoid the charges of obscurity levelled at Mozart.

As H. C. Robbins Landon notes, Haydn's symphonies of the 1770s and early 1780s also influenced several younger composers who would make prominent contributions of their own, among them Adalbert Gyrowetz, Franz Anton Hoffmeister and Haydn's pupil Ignaz Josef Pleyel.[72] All strive for lucid forms and accessible content, while at the same time showing the 'popular' symphony to be as adaptable to individual preference as any other kind. Gyrowetz rarely disturbs the bustling cheerfulness he establishes with triadic fanfares, lyrical and dance-like episodes and accompaniments of sustaining winds and drumming or syncopating strings. Textures and key areas change slowly, and counterpoint and chromaticism appear only briefly. The result has much in common with examples such as Haydn's Symphony No. 63, whose memorable tunes, easily followed variations and bright orchestration are likewise unruffled by any substantial instabilities. Pleyel writes equally striking melodies, some of which, like Haydn's, were given words and published as songs. They are also so numerous, and at times so extended, as to make his movements seem unusually spacious:[73] the principal second key area theme of the first movement of Pleyel's Symphony in D (Benton 147, 1791) lasts at least twice as long as any

71 Webster, 'Haydn's Symphonies between *Sturm und Drang* and "Classical Style"', pp. 218–45.
72 Landon, *Haydn: Chronicle and Works, vol.* 3, p. 507.
73 Raymond R. Smith, *The Symphony 1720–1840*, vol. D-6, pp. xiii–xiv.

comparable passage in the contemporaneous London symphonies of Haydn. Yet Pleyel generates far greater dramatic tension than Gyrowetz through extensive chromaticism, rapid textural change, concentrated thematic development and counterpoint. Similar elements characterize the symphonies of Antonio Rosetti, who lacked Pleyel's direct connection to Haydn but pursued a related aesthetic during the 1780s. While favouring lyricism over humour or grandeur, Rosetti builds considerable energy with melodic and harmonic developments comparable to Pleyel's and a much faster pace of events. His counterpoint can grow especially complicated, as when multiple themes are superimposed in the first movements of the Symphony in C (Murray A9) and the *Sinfonia pastoralis* in D (Murray A15). At the same time, even at such moments a desire for comprehensibility remains evident, in the clarity of the orchestration and the handling of contrapuntal passages as episodes within a governing homophony.

Haydn's own symphonies, having helped to invent a popular idiom, never ceased testing its limits.[74] Slow movements offer the best illustration. After 1780 they focus increasingly on variation, whether of a single theme, in traditional theme-and-variation form; two themes, in Haydn's patented 'double' or 'alternating' variation; or a main subject, in rondo, ternary, or sonata forms.[75] This new emphasis puts Haydn's stylistic hallmark, continuous development, into a form that every listener can understand. Rather than small motives constituting themes or connecting disparate passages, now whole themes, often binary forms in themselves, undergo readily perceptible elaboration. Yet as often as not both the themes and their progress throw up unexpected challenges. As Webster shows, as simple and repetitious a tune as that of Symphony No. 53 in D includes internal variations that make its melodic direction unpredictable, and a tonicization of the second scale-degree that introduces chromaticism and the minor.[76] Equally surprising are the offbeat accents in Symphony No. 84 in E-flat, the extra bar of ticking accompaniment in No. 101 in D and, most famously, the abrupt *fortissimo* that gives the 'Surprise' Symphony (No. 94 in G) its name. In No. 101 the unsettling moment in the theme leads directly to the biggest shock of the variations, a detour to the flattened sixth preceding the final statement in the tonic. Elsewhere the movements reach unforeseen destinations by means of juxtaposition, as when minor-key variations or episodes burst in on major-key themes, or two themes

74 On the popular style and its sources, see Charles Rosen, *The Classical Style: Haydn, Mozart, Beethoven*, 2nd edn. (New York, 1997), pp. 329–37; David P. Schroeder, *Haydn and the Enlightenment: The Late Symphonies and their Audience* (Oxford, 1990), pp. 144–51.

75 Sisman, *Haydn and the Classical Variation*, pp. 168–72.

76 Webster, 'Haydn's Symphonies between *Sturm und Drang* and "Classical Style"', pp. 234–6.

of contrasting mode alternate. The 'Surprise' Symphony, for its part, travels steadily to a point of furthest remove, working through stormy, sprightly, suave and heroic variations to a *fortissimo* coda that stops short on a diminished-seventh chord. The lightly stepping theme returns in the final bars, but with chromatic colourings in the accompaniment that deny its earlier innocence. Haydn took the clarity of variation form as license for extreme transformations, a calculation that brought the symphonies their greatest public success. The slow movements were encored at the London concerts and praised for their superlative expressivity by observers such as Charles Burney.[77]

Seemingly the most accessible of the remaining movements, Haydn's finales derive equally startling consequences from materials that are generally tuneful and in contradance rhythm. Given the speed of the movements and, in rondo-form examples, the many happy iterations of the refrain, minor-key and stormy episodes tend to cause less affective disruption than in slow movements. Instead, listeners are confronted with monothematicism, imitative counterpoint, advanced harmony and other musical complexities that play an especially important role in development sections and in the developmental episodes found mid-way through Haydn's 'sonata-rondo' forms. The incongruity of dance tunes generating fugues or chromatic modulation is pronounced, so much so that the eventual reprise of the theme in something like its original guise stretches credibility; the naïveté thus restored has come to seem impossibly distant. Minuets can have a related effect when their second halves expand to several times the length of the first, as in some of the 'Paris' Symphonies and many works thereafter. Following the elaborations that the extra space allows, the original strain returns, seeming to hold much more nuance than it had at first. Frequently Haydn strengthens the impression with additional development in the reprise itself, not only the harmonic adjustment that may be necessary for a tonally open theme to close in the tonic, but also extensions, interpolations and re-scorings. If minuets had always shared some of the chronological quality of his forms, by the late symphonies their 'characters' experience as much change as in any other movement.

Listeners may have been better prepared for the difficulties of Haydn's first movements, which combine the stylistic variety, contrapuntal depth and developmental invention of his earlier examples with more adventurous tonality and considerably larger forms than all but the most substantial works before 1775. A popular impulse expresses itself in periodic themes

77 Charles Burney, *A General History of Music* (1776–89), ed. Frank Mercer (London, 1935), 2 vols., vol. 2, p. 960. See also A. Peter Brown, 'The Sublime, The Beautiful, and the Ornamental: English Aesthetic Currents and Haydn's London Symphonies', in Otto Biba and David Wyn Jones (eds.), *Studies in Music History Presented to H. C. Robbins Landon on His Seventieth Birthday* (London, 1996), pp. 44–71.

evoking song or dance, as well as in 2/4, 6/8 and *alla breve* meters (for example, in Nos. 67, 88, or 94), which lend a choreographic lilt quite unlike the marching or 'drumming' more typical of symphony openings. But Haydn also poses the new challenge of slow introductions, which begin three of the six 'Paris' Symphonies and all but two subsequent works. Allowing the allegro to start quietly, mid-bar, or even off the tonic, introductions may also obscure the initial direction of the work, through chromatic departures that reach their apex in a tonicization of E minor mid-way through the introduction of Symphony No. 99 in E-flat major. While the allegros bring comparatively bright, stable music in the major (Haydn does not employ introductions in minor-key symphonies), what precedes them, in the words of one contemporary, 'intensifies expectations, which are but gradually fulfilled or surpassed'.[78] Complicating matters, material from the introduction may return in the allegro. Transposed to the major, the ominous minor-mode arpeggio that launches Symphony No. 98 in B-flat becomes the lyrical subject of the first key area and appears later in various permutations. More radically, the equally ominous unisons that begin No. 103 in E-flat, which reminded Momigny of prayer, become a transitional idea in the dancing 6/8 meter of the allegro. Haydn emphasizes the metamorphosis by setting transition and introduction side-by-side when the latter is reprised near the end of the movement. His introductions lengthen the reach of the symphonies, allowing first movements alone to go from prayer to dance, or from majesty, idyll, or lament to places equally far away on the stylistic and expressive spectrum. This initial step echoes long after the introduction itself has concluded, setting the scale against which all ensuing contrasts are heard.

Works that move specifically from majesty to idyll, with or without introduction (for example, Nos. 82, 88, or 104), recall Charles Rosen's much-quoted description of Haydn's symphonies as 'heroic pastoral'. The analogy further captures a paradox underlying the entire oeuvre. Eighteenth-century pastoral has 'a naïveté or simplicity that demands ... to be taken at face value, even though it is belied by everything else in the work' – namely, the skill and artifice of the representation. Likewise Haydn's symphonies, particularly after 1775, protest an innocence that is supported 'by an art learned almost to the point of pedantry'.[79] A similar if less pronounced irony is evident elsewhere, in Rosetti

78 Christian Friedrich Michaelis, 'Einige Bemerkungen über das Erhabene der Musik', *Berlinische musikalische Zeitung*, 1 (1805), p. 180. On introductions see especially Sisman, 'Genre, Gesture, and Meaning', pp. 33–5; Webster, *Haydn's 'Farewell' Symphony*, pp. 162–5; Rosen, *The Classical Style*, pp. 345–50; Marianne Danckwardt, *Die langsame Einleitung: Ihre Herkunft und ihr Bau bei Haydn und Mozart* (Tutzing, 1977), 2 vols., vol. 1, pp. 19–126, 175–210.

79 Rosen, *The Classical Style*, pp. 162–3; also Harrison, *Haydn: The 'Paris' Symphonies*, pp. 60–1; Brown, *The Symphonic Repertoire*, vol. 2, p. 230.

and Pleyel as well as in the second and fourth movements of Beethoven's Symphony No. 1 in C (1800). It bears witness to changing standards of reception. Audiences and critics continued to prize musical sophistication in the symphony, along with evocations of characters and the sublime. By the end of the century, however, they were saving their highest praise for artistry that admitted of easy comprehension. For the content to be moral no longer sufficed; now the medium had to be transparent, capable of edifying a whole society. In London, argues David P. Schroeder, Haydn's studied simplicity allowed concert-goers of diverse background to share a 'process of discovery' that reinforced civic values.[80] The virtues of tolerating difference could not be better demonstrated than by a symphony in which everyone, provided they listened, could hear contrasting ideas spring from the same source and co-exist in tonally closed forms. Haydn's late style may have further suggested that social complexities, like musical, could be reduced to self-evident principles. The symphony that derived fugues from dances, or sublimity from catchy tunes, reassured listeners that the most intricate structures rested upon simple and attractive ideals.

Romanticism and beyond

Symphonies would soon be heard to express darker ironies. For the early German Romantics, the genre summoned an 'infinity' that could encompass the Mozartian spirit domain spoken of by Hoffmann, or an expressive totality imagined by Ludwig Tieck, 'in which no single emotion is depicted, but rather a whole world, an entire drama of human affects is poured out'.[81] The few who could grasp such immensities felt, when they listened, 'as if [the soul] were set loose from the body'.[82] Yet therein lay the irony: their 'intoxication' ended when the music stopped. Symphonies allowed the Romantics to transcend a social reality from which they felt alienated, but in the sad knowledge that the escape was only temporary. Melancholy tinged even the perception of musical wit. Having at first dismissed Haydn's stylistic mixtures as indecorous, eighteenth-century critics came to praise them as 'high comedy', comparable to the brilliant confusion of subjects in Laurence Sterne. The Romantic Jean Paul agreed, but beyond deriving smiles and intellectual stimulation from Haydn's exalted humour, he sensed in it contempt for the

80 Schroeder, *Haydn and the Enlightenment*, p. 199 and *passim*.

81 Wilhelm Heinrich Wackenroder and Ludwig Tieck, *Phantasien über die Kunst* (1799), ed. Wolfgang Nehring (Stuttgart, 1983), p. 85.

82 Wackenroder and Tieck, *Herzensergießerungen eines kunstliebenden Klosterbruders* (1797) (Stuttgart, 1979), p. 107.

everyday.[83] Conjuring a realm in which unfathomable distances could be travelled in an instant, stylistic, tonal and dynamic juxtapositions made the real world seem sluggish and confining.

The Romantics dispelled any lingering doubts about the worth of symphonies, ranking them on a par with the most exalted sacred music and opera – when not higher. They also anticipated much subsequent reception by embracing semantic ambiguity. If symphonies could evoke infinity, it was because even when they used suggestive idioms like the dance, they admitted a far broader range of interpretation than did musical works with text, to say nothing of paintings or literature. Some in the Enlightenment took this as proof that instrumental music was not, in fact, morally efficacious. Succeeding centuries enjoyed the challenge to the imagination and eventually dissociated symphonies from nearly all of the emotional, scenic and narrative content attributed to them in the eighteenth century. Especially in the late works of Haydn and Mozart, meaning was instead sought in form, and more precisely in what was seen as an exemplary, 'Classical' balance of tonal and rhythmic energies. The change of emphasis produced a fresh irony. Symphonies appealed to the Romantics for the mystery surrounding their semantic vagueness. By the terms of the Classical style, however, they represented clarity, as evidenced by well-articulated and tonally stable forms, and by the co-ordination of part and whole within those forms. Thus even as referential meaning disappeared, in its place there returned an unexpectedly familiar metaphorical significance. To the extent that formal principles imply social values, twentieth-century theorists of the Classical style heard some of the same harmony and transparency in symphonies that had been associated with Haydn's works, in particular, before they were veiled in enigma by the Romantics. Coming full circle, the genre was again taken to project a world of tensions resolved and complexities unravelled.

Reception continues to evolve. By the end of the twentieth century the ideal of Classical style was itself being criticized for relegating the innumerable works that do not meet its standards, including 'all pre-1780 music, to a pre-Classical ghetto'.[84] Fresh perspectives have been inspired by eighteenth-century theories of form, by critical and aesthetic texts, by research into sources, playing technique and contexts of performance, and more. Simply by evolving from a slight, overlooked servant of more important events to a

83 *Horn of Oberon: Jean Paul Richter's School for Aesthetics*, trans. Margaret R. Hale (Detroit, 1973; trans. of *Vorschule der Aesthetik*, 1804), pp. 88–94. See also Wheelock, *Haydn's Ingenious Jesting with Art*, pp. 33–51; Chua, *Absolute Music*, pp. 212–17; Bonds, 'Haydn, Laurence Sterne, and the Origins of Musical Irony', *Journal of the American Musicological Society*, 44 (1991), pp. 57–64; Andreas Ballstaedt, '"Humor" und "Witz" in Joseph Haydns Musik', *Archiv für Musikwissenschaft*, 55 (1998), pp. 195–219.
84 Webster, *Haydn's 'Farewell' Symphony*, p. 356.

substantial, recognized centrepiece of concert life, the symphony seems to have guaranteed itself a history of perpetual reinterpretation. Its Cinderella-like transformation was not magical; on the contrary, it resulted from musicians and listeners spending decades exploring different and sometimes competing ideas about composition, performance and interpretation. No succeeding generation has been able to exhaust that legacy. The genre that served so many functions in its own day, and encompassed such panoramas of style and meaning, remains as protean today as it was in the eighteenth century.

Select Bibliography

Bonds, Mark Evan. 'The Symphony as Pindaric Ode'. In Elaine Sisman (ed.), *Haydn and His World*. Princeton, NJ, 1997, pp. 131–53

Brook, Barry S. (gen. ed.). *The Symphony 1720–1840*. 60 vols., New York, 1979–86

Brown, A. Peter. *The Symphonic Repertoire, vol. 2: The First Golden Age of the Viennese Symphony: Haydn, Mozart, Beethoven, and Schubert*. Bloomington, IN, 2002

Broyles, Michael. 'The Two Instrumental Styles of Classicism'. *Journal of the American Musicological Society*, 36 (1983), pp. 210–42

Carse, Adam. *The Orchestra in the XVIIIth Century*. Cambridge, 1940

Danckwardt, Marianne. *Die langsame Einleitung: Ihre Herkunft und ihr Bau bei Haydn und Mozart*. 2 vols., Tutzing, 1977

Gülke, Peter. *Im Zyklus einer Welt: Mozarts letzte Sinfonien*. Munich, 1997

Harrison, Bernard. *Haydn: The 'Paris' Symphonies*. Cambridge, 1998

Hell, Helmut. *Die neapolitanische Opernsinfonie in der ersten Hälfte des 18. Jahrhunderts: N. Porpora, L. Vinci, G. B. Pergolesi, L. Leo, N. Jommelli*. Tutzing, 1971

Kunze, Stefan. *Die Sinfonie im 18. Jahrhundert: Von der Opernsinfonie zur Konzertsinfonie*. Laaber, 1993

Landon, H. C. Robbins. *Haydn: Chronicle and Works*, 5 vols. Bloomington, IN and London, 1976–80

Larsen, Jens Peter. 'Concerning the Development of the Austrian Symphonic Tradition (*circa* 1750–1775)'. In *Handel, Haydn, and the Viennese Classical Style*. Trans. Ulrich Krämer, Ann Arbor, MI, 1988, pp. 315–25

'Zur Vorgeschichte der Symphonik der Wiener Klassik'. *Studien zur Musikwissenschaft*, 43 (1994), pp. 67–143

Lowe, Melanie. *Pleasure and Meaning in the Classical Symphony*. Bloomington, IN, 2007

Schroeder, David P. *Haydn and the Enlightenment: The Late Symphonies and their Audience*. Oxford, 1990

Schwartz, Judith L. 'Periodicity and Passion in the First Movement of Haydn's "Farewell" Symphony'. In Eugene K. Wolf and Edward H. Roesner (eds.), *Studies in Musical Sources and Style: Essays in Honor of Jan LaRue*. Madison, WI, 1990, pp. 293–338

Sisman, Elaine R. 'Haydn's Theater Symphonies'. *Journal of the American Musicological Society*, 43 (1990), pp. 292–352

Mozart: The 'Jupiter' Symphony No. 41 in C major, K. 551. Cambridge, 1993

'Genre, Gesture, and Meaning in Mozart's "Prague" Symphony'. In Cliff Eisen (ed.), *Mozart Studies 2*. Oxford, 1997, pp. 27–84

Sondheimer, Robert. *Die Theorie der Sinfonie und die Beurteilung einzelner Sinfoniekomponisten bei den Musikschriftstellern des 18. Jahrhunderts*. Leipzig, 1925

Spitzer, John and Neal Zaslaw. *The Birth of the Orchestra: History of an Institution, 1650–1815*. Oxford and New York, 2004

Webster, James. *Haydn's 'Farewell' Symphony and the Idea of Classical Style*. Cambridge, 1991

'Haydn's Symphonies between *Sturm und Drang* and "Classical Style": Art and Entertainment'. In W. Dean Sutcliffe (ed.), *Haydn Studies*. Cambridge, 1998, pp. 218–45

Will, Richard. *The Characteristic Symphony in the Age of Haydn and Beethoven*. Cambridge, 2002

Wolf, Eugene K. 'The Recapitulations in Haydn's London Symphonies'. *Musical Quarterly*, 52 (1966), pp. 71–89

The Symphonies of Johann Stamitz: A Study in the Formation of the Classic Style. Utrecht, 1981

Zaslaw, Neal. 'Mozart, Haydn, and the *Sinfonia da chiesa*'. *Journal of Musicology*, 1 (1982), pp. 95–124

Mozart's Symphonies: Context, Performance Practice, Reception. Oxford, 1989

· 23 ·

The string quartet

CLIFF EISEN

By the end of the eighteenth century, the string quartet had achieved a status beyond that of most other instrumental genres, a status that made it appealing as a hook on which to hang historical reputations. And this, in turn, sometimes meant creating convenient histories – or, by the early decades of the nineteenth century, asserting the importance of 'great men', their originality and independence of mind, their historical leadership, in whatever field:

> The following purely chance circumstance had led [Haydn] to try his luck at the composition of quartets. A Baron Fürnberg had a place in Weinzierl ... and from time to time he invited his pastor, his manager, Haydn and Albrechtsberger (a brother of the celebrated contrapuntist, who played the violoncello) to have a little music. Fürnberg requested Haydn to compose something that could be performed by these four amateurs. Haydn, then eighteen years old, took up this proposal and so originated his first quartet which, as soon as it appeared, gained such general approval that Haydn was encouraged to work further in this form.[1]

To be sure, this story is more historically manipulative than accurate, and in fact paints a picture not of the history of the genre but of the importance of Haydn. Nevertheless, Griesinger's anecdote has at least a grain of truth in so far as it asserts that during the 1750s the string quartet was essentially a 'new' genre. Although some Italian composers of the sixteenth and seventeenth centuries – Gregorio Allegri (1582–1652) and Adriano Banchieri (1568–1634) among them – wrote music for four solo string instruments, there was no continuous tradition for this sort of composition from their time to Haydn's. By the same token, the repertory for four-part viol consort, including works by John Jenkins (1592–1678), Christopher Simpson (*c.* 1605–69) and Henry Purcell (1659–95), was 'even more circumscribed in period and influence'.[2]

1 August Griesinger, *Biographische Notizen über Joseph Haydn* (Leipzig, 1810); this translation is modified from the one given in Vernon Gotwals (ed.), *Haydn: Two Contemporary Portraits* (Madison, WI, 1968), p. 13.

2 David Wyn Jones, 'The Origins of the Quartet', in Robin Stowell (ed.), *The Cambridge Companion to the String Quartet* (Cambridge, 2003), p. 178.

Other genres common in the first half of the eighteenth century, however, may be related to the early string quartet, even if indirectly, including repertories that originally included a keyboard continuo, such as trio or ensemble sonatas, and orchestral music in four parts, including both symphonies and concertos, that may or may not have reckoned on keyboard continuo. Alessandro Scarlatti (1660–1752), for example, wrote six works with the title 'Sonata à Quattro per Due Violini, Violetta e Violoncello senza Cembalo', probably before 1725, while in 1740 Louis-Gabriel Guillemain (1705–70) published 'Six concertinos à quatre parties'. Orchestral concertos – or so-called ripieno concertos – are often related, stylistically and in terms of scoring, to early symphonies, many of which were written or circulated in four parts, often with suggestive changes of title: Matthias Georg Monn (1717–50), for instance, wrote fifteen works for four-part ensemble that are called 'sinfonia' in some sources but 'quartetto' in others; symphonies by Leopold Mozart, also in four parts, similarly circulated as both 'sinfonia' and 'quartetto'.[3] Often their style is indistinguishable from one-to-a-part solo ensemble music. By and large, however, the Austrian tradition is transmitted by works titled 'divertimento', a catch-all designation for instrumental ensemble music played one to a part: it was only later, about 1780, that specific titles such as sonata, trio, quartet and quintet became common. Changes in title notwithstanding, early divertimentos for four strings were nevertheless quartets in the modern sense, just as divertimentos for five strings were quintets; the title had no fixed implications for genre, style, number of movements or seriousness of substance – it signified only a broad category of soloistic ensemble music.[4]

Aside from Haydn's early divertimentos for string quartet – including Hob. III:1–4, 6–8, 10, 12 and II:6 – early Austrian, Bohemian and south Germany divertimentos included works by Franz Xaver Richter (1709–89), Ignaz Holzbauer (1711–83), Franz Asplmayr (1728–86), Joseph Starzer (1728–87), Florian Leopold Gassmann (1729–74), Christian Cannabich (1731–98), Carlo d'Ordoñez (1734–86), Leopold Hofmann (1738–93), Carl Ditters von Dittersdorf (1739–99) and Johann Baptist Vanhal (1739–1813).[5] These vary widely in structure and style: Richter's six quartets Op. 5 (generally thought to date from *c.* 1765–7 but possibly as early as the late 1750s[6]) are in three movements, FSF, as are the majority of Dittersdorf's, while Haydn's Opp. 1 and 2 (probably *c.* 1757–62) are in five, with minuets in

3 The symphony Seiffert 3/30 = New Grove A1, for example, survives in a copy from Stift Lambach (now D-Asa, shelfmark MG II 47) as a 'Sinfonia', but in Stift Seitenstetten (shelfmark V27) as a 'Quartetto'.

4 See James Webster, 'Towards a History of Viennese Chamber Music in the Early Classical Period', *Journal of the American Musicological Society*, 27 (1974), pp. 212–47.

5 See David Wyn Jones, 'The String Quartets of Vanhal', PhD thesis (University of Wales, 1978).

6 Jones, 'The Origins of the Quartet', p. 182.

second and fourth place, a central slow movement, and two quicker movements as the first and last. Others, like Holzbauer's quartet in B-flat, are in four movements, a cycle that became common, though not universal, only with Haydn's Op. 9 (1769–70). Textures also vary, from the purely homophonic with dominant upper parts, reminiscent of the trio sonata, to the intensely contrapuntal. Polyphony, once thought to be a distinguishing feature of string quartets only from the 1770s on (and chiefly as a result of Haydn's Op. 20 [1772]), was a regular feature of chamber music throughout the 1760s[7]: it figures prominently in works by Monn, Georg Christoph Wagenseil (1715–77), Johann Georg Albrechtsberger (1736–1809) and Michael Haydn (1739–1806). Slightly later, d'Ordoñez's Op. 1 (published 1777) includes at least one fugal movement in each quartet of the set; indeed, these works nod in the direction of church – or at least conservative – styles on the whole, since in addition to fugues each begins with a slow, *sonata da chiesa*-like movement.[8] Mozart's first Viennese set, K. 168–73 (Vienna, 1773) is indebted to this tradition. Although it is sometimes said to have been influenced by Haydn's Opp. 9, 17 and 20, fugal finales (as in K. 168 and 173), irregular phrase construction and thematic elaboration are common among early 1770s Viennese quartets in general.[9]

Haydn's quartets of the late 1760s and early 1770s (Op. 9, 1769; Op. 17, 1771; Op. 20, 1772) are high points in the early history of the quartet. Characterized by a wide range of textures, frequent asymmetries and theatrical gestures (Op. 17 no. 5), variety of formal and movement types (Op. 20, including three fugal finales), evocations of low or popular style and even gypsy material (Op. 17, finales), as well as harmonic obfuscation (coda to Op. 20 no. 5, first movement), these quartets established the genre's four-movement form, its larger dimensions and, as James Webster notes, its greater aesthetic pretensions and expressive range.[10]

In Italy, quartets were first cultivated on a regular basis by Luigi Boccherini (1743–1805) and Giovanni Battista Sammartini (1700/1–75). Boccherini's first set was composed in 1761 (but not published until 1767), only slightly later than Haydn's first quartets. In general, they are characterized by varieties of texture and thorough-going dialogue among the instruments and lively,

7 Warren Kirkendale, *Fugue and Fugato in Rococo and Classical Chamber Music*, trans. Kirkendale and Margaret Bent (Durham, NC, 1979).

8 In general, see A. Peter Brown, 'The Chamber Music with Strings of Carlos d'Ordoñez: A Bibliographic and Stylistic Study', *Analecta musicologica*, 46 (1974), pp. 222–72.

9 See A. Peter Brown, 'Haydn and Mozart's 1773 Stay in Vienna: Weeding a Musicological Garden', *Journal of Musicology*, 10 (1992), pp. 192–230.

10 Webster, 'Towards a History'. Further, see William Drabkin, *A Reader's Guide to Haydn's Early String Quartets* (Westport, CT, 2000).

syncopated inner parts, and an uncommon manner of phrasing, slurring from weak to strong beats, which lends a 'certain softness and suavity to [his] melodic contours'.[11] Above all, Boccherini makes use of a variety of colouristic devices, including bowed tremolandos, double stops, *bariolage* and *sul ponticello*, among others.[12] Most of his early quartets are in three movements, although from Op. 15 (1772) 'quartettinos' in two movements predominate. Sammartini's most important quartets date from the early 1770s and include unexpected tonal procedures as well as, at times, an engaging lyricism and touches of chromaticism. As the most prominent composer of quartets working in Italy, Sammartini may have influenced Mozart's earliest quartets, K. 80 (1770, Lodi) and K. 155–160 (1772–3, Milan), which are based on Italian models and have little to do with Austrian chamber music traditions, especially as practised and disseminated in Salzburg.

In France, the quartet owed its impetus chiefly to the works of Haydn and Boccherini; no French quartet is known to predate the 1766 Chevardière edition of quartets Op. 3 incorrectly attributed to Haydn and only Antonine Laurent Baudron's (1742–1834) *Sei quartetti* predates Boccherini's Op. 2, published (as Op. 1) by Vénier in 1767. Other early French quartets include those of François-Joseph Gossec (1734–1829), Pierre Vachon (1738–1803), Jean-Baptiste Davaux (1742–1822) and Joseph Boulogne de Saint-Georges (1745–99). These works, closer in spirit to the *galant* Boccherini than to the 'classical' Haydn, are commonly designated *quatuors concertants*, a title found almost universally on the title-pages of contemporaneous Parisian editions. In them, generally song-like thematic material is shared among the four instruments, often with solos for each in turn, and most are in three movements, with a sonata-style first movement, a binary form, ABA or minuet second movement, and a rondo, set of variations or minuet to conclude. Two-movement quartets are common too, including Gossec's Op. 15 (1772) and all but one of Davaux's Op. 9 (1779); four-movement quartets on the other hand, such as Vachon's (published 1772–82), are rare. The most prolific quartet composer active in Paris at the time was Giuseppe Maria Cambini (1746–1825), who had relocated from Italy about 1770; more than 150 of his quartets were published there between 1773 and 1809. Mozart described Cambini's music as 'quite pretty' and his quartets are characterized by variety in the instrumental solos

11 Christian Speck and Stanley Sadie, 'Boccherini', Oxford Music Online (www.oxfordmusiconline.com) (accessed 8 September 2008).

12 See Christian Speck, *Boccherinis Streichquartette: Studien zur Kompositionsweise und zur gattungsgeschichtlichen Stellung* (Munich, 1987) and, concerning Italian quartets generally, F. Torrefranca, 'Avviamento all storia del quartetto italiano, con introduzione e note a cura di A. Bonaccorsi', *L'approdo musicale*, 22 (1966), pp. 6–181.

and richly ornamented cantilenas (as, for example, in the F minor quartet Op. 20 no. 6); the majority of them are in two movements.[13]

Quartets were less cultivated elsewhere in Europe. In London, they were mostly composed and published by expatriate Italian composers, including Tommaso Giordani (1730/3–1806; Opp. 2 and 8, 1772 and *c.* 1775) and, later, Giuseppe Antonio Capuzzi (1755–1818; Op. 1, 1780). Apparently the first quartets published there were the Op. 8 (1769) set by Carl Friedrich Abel (1723–87); the earliest by a native composer were those of Joseph Gibbs (1698–1788), published in 1777 with a figured bass part (the title page reads *Six Quartettos for Two Violins, a Tenor and Violoncello or Harpsichord*); later examples are known by William Shield (1748–1829; Op. 3, *c.* 1782) and John Marsh (1752–1828). Haydn's quartets were especially influential in England: Marsh's quartet of 1795 was written 'in Imitation of the Stile of Haydn's Opera Prima'. In Spain, Gaetano Brunetti (1744–98) composed forty-four quartets (the earliest of them published as Op. 1 in 1774) chiefly for the Spanish court, while Boccherini's almost 100 quartets, mostly published in Paris, were widely influential across Europe (in 1786, Boccherini was appointed *compositeur de notre chambre* to Crown Prince Wilhelm in Berlin, in no small part based on the prestige of his quartets, but he fulfilled his court duties chiefly by correspondence). His quartets are themselves the product of various influences, possibly a result of his early travels: before his move to Madrid in 1768 he had lived and worked in Vienna, Paris and Italy, where he was a member of one of the earliest professional string quartets, called the Quartetto Toscano, founded in Livorno by Pietro Nardini (1722–93), with Cambini and Vincenzo Manfredini (1737–99).[14]

The early 1780s were watershed years for the quartet. In Paris, Giovanni Battista Viotti (1755–1824) published two sets of influential quartets between about 1783 and 1786 (Opp. 2 and 3), models in many respects of the Parisian *quatuor concertant.* Cast in two movements, usually an opening sonata movement

13 In general, see Janet M. Levy, 'The "Quatuor concertant" in Paris in the Latter Half of the Eighteenth Century', PhD thesis (Stanford University, 1971); Philippe Oboussier, 'The French String Quartet, 1770–1800', in Malcolm Boyd (ed.), *Music and the French Revolution* (Cambridge, 1992), pp. 74–92; and Association française pour le patrimoine musical ed., *Le quatuor à cordes en France de 1750 à nos jours* (Paris, 1995). For Mozart's reference to Cambini's string quartets, see Emily Anderson (ed. and trans.), *The Letters of Mozart and His Family*, 3rd edn. (London, 1985), p. 533 (letter of 1 May 1778).

14 Further concerning the early history of the quartet, see Marc Pincherle, 'On the Origins of the String Quartet', *Musical Quarterly*, 15 (1929), pp. 77–87; Ursula Lehmann-Gugolz, *Deutsches und italienisches Wesen in der Vorgeschichte des klassischen Streichquartetts* (Würzburg, 1939); Karl Geiringer, 'The Rise of Chamber Music', in Egon Wellescz and Frederick Sternfield (eds.), *New Oxford History of Music, vol. VII: The Age of Enlightenment, 1745–1790* (Oxford, 1973), pp. 515–73; Ludwig Finscher, *Studien zur Geschichte des Streichquartetts, i: Die Entstehung des klassischen Streichquartetts: von den Vorformen zur Grundlegung durch Joseph Haydn* (Kassel, 1974); Paul Griffiths, *The String Quartet* (London and New York, 1983); Wulf Konold, *Das Streichquartett, von den Anfängen bis Franz Schubert* (Wilhelmshaven, 1980); and Jones, 'The Origins of the Quartet'.

and a rondo, they exploit a style in which each instrument is given prominent thematic material in turn and, in general, they rely on textural change and melodic variation to make structural and affective points.[15] Haydn's Op. 33, published the year of Viotti's début in Paris, also marked a new path in quartet composition; described by their composer as written in a 'new and special manner', this probably referred less to clarity of structure and textural balance, already achieved in Opp. 9, 17 and 20, than to the consistent application of motivic work (*thematische Arbeit*), the re-introduction of a light, popular touch (as in no. 3) and the integration of the movements of varying character into a convincing whole. This is most apparent in the finales, which are differentiated from the opening movements by the use of 'simpler texture, more regular phrasing and harmonic rhythm and a greater emphasis on soloistic passages for the various instruments'.[16] The quartets are remarkably concise and often small-scale: thematic material is frequently pared to a minimum, accompaniment and melody are often identical, interchangeable or easily transformed from one to the other, and transitional figures and phrases are sometimes eliminated almost completely.[17] Often they are witty, even explicitly humorous (as in the 'joke' finale of no. 2). At the same time, however, they are never less than serious art works and they had a profound impact on other composers and on the later historiography of the genre.

Certainly Op. 33 was important for Mozart, who between 1782 and 1785 composed six magnificent quartets that were published with a dedication to Haydn – according to the composer, they were 'the fruit of long and laborious endeavour'. While similarly characterized by textures conceived as a four-part discourse, Mozart's debt to Op. 33 lies more in a general approach to quartet style than in specific modellings.[18] The quartets, broader in scale than Haydn's and more heterogeneous, are characterized in particular by their multiplicity of motifs (K. 428), chromaticism (K. 465 and 428) and a fusion of strict and *galant* styles (K. 387 and 464, finales) to intensify both structure and expression, as well as their elaborate, ornamental slow movements (K. 387, 458). They also draw attention to themselves in obvious but effective ways – the offbeat accents

15 Generally, see Robin Stowell, *Violin Technique and Performance Practice in the Late Eighteenth and Early Nineteenth Centuries* (Cambridge, 1985); Chappell White, *Giovanni Battista Viotti (1755–1824): A Thematic Catalogue of His Works* (Stuyvesant, NY, 1985); and Kurt Fischer, 'G. B. Viotti und das Streichquartett des späten 18. Jahrhunderts', in Lorenzo Bianconi *et al.* (eds.), *Atti del XIV congresso della Società Internazionale di Musicologia, Bologna, 1987: Trasmissione e recezione delle forme di cultura musicale* (Kassel, 1990), 3 vols., vol. 3, pp. 753–67.

16 Orin Moe, 'The Significance of Haydn's Op. 33', in Jens Peter Larsen, Howard Serwer and James Webster (eds.), *Haydn-Studies: Washington, DC 1975* (New York, 1981), pp. 445–50.

17 See Charles Rosen, *The Classical Style* (New York, 1971), pp. 111–42.

18 Further, see Mark Evan Bonds, 'The Sincerest Form of Flattery? Mozart's "Haydn" Quartets and the Question of Influence', *Studi musicali*, 22 (1993), pp. 365–409.

in the minuet of K. 387, the angular unison opening of K. 428 that is then harmonized, the lushness of the varied melodies (K. 464, Andante) and above all the chromatic introduction to K. 465 all tend towards making explicit the artificiality of pieces and the individuality of their composer.[19] Mozart's quartets were widely disseminated and highly influential; Koch described them as best representing 'the concept of a composition with four obbligato principal voices'.[20]

The quartet K. 499 (1786) was a one-off, composed for a chamber music subscription published by his friend Franz Anton Hoffmeister; like the 'Haydn' quartets, it plays with textures, including textural connections between movements – the high register of the end of the first movement, for example, is aurally the jumping-off point for the first violin at the start of the Menuetto. And the three 'Prussian' quartets (K. 575, 589 and 590) are traditionally thought to be all that Mozart completed of a set of six commissioned by Friedrich Wilhelm II in Berlin. Yet there is no unequivocal evidence that he received such a commission and it may be that Mozart wrote them on spec, hoping to secure money from a dedication when they were published. As it is, the set was never completed and appeared in print only after his death, in December 1791. Frequently dismissed as a compositional let-down, the three quartets strike out in new directions and are seemingly motivated by an aesthetic different from the 'Haydn' quartets.[21] Mozart's expressive goal seems to be the exploitation, in any particular movement, of a single affect, rather than the heterogeneity of affect that characterizes his early set. The first movement of K. 575, for example, is frequently 'about' sonorities, especially parallel thirds and sixths; the first movement of K. 590 plays fullness of texture off against emptiness; and the slow movement of the same quartet is a mesmerizing set of variations cast in sonata form.

Haydn's later quartets, on the other hand, combine the equal-voice texture, elaborate counterpoint and solo display of his earlier quartets with the motivic work and cyclic integration of Op. 33. Op. 50 (1787) – like Mozart's 'Prussian' quartets later – was composed for the cello-loving Friedrich Wilhelm II of Prussia but make few concessions in terms of providing solo passages for that

19 In general, see John Irving, *Mozart: The 'Haydn' Quartets*, (Cambridge, 1998). See also Wye Jamison Allanbrook, '"To Serve the Private Pleasure": Expression and Form in the String Quartets', in Stanley Sadie (ed.), *Wolfgang Amadè Mozart: Essays on His Life and Music* (Oxford, 1996), pp. 132–60 and Simon P. Keefe, 'An Integrated "Dissonance": Mozart's "Haydn" Quartets and the Slow Introduction of K. 465', in *Mozart's Viennese Instrumental Music: A Study of Stylistic Re-Invention* (Woodbridge and Rochester, NY, 2007), pp. 89–104.

20 Heinrich Christoph Koch, *Musikalisches Lexikon* (Frankfurt, 1802), col. 1200.

21 On this point, see Keefe, 'Mozart's "Prussian" Quartets: Towards a New Aesthetic of the String Quartet', in *Mozart's Viennese Instrumental Music*, pp. 105–33. See also Cliff Eisen, 'Mozart's Chamber Music', in Simon P. Keefe (ed.), *The Cambridge Companion to Mozart* (Cambridge, 2003), pp. 105–17, esp. pp. 113–17 (and also including reference to the string quintets).

instrument; they are characterized by a broad harmonic palette and an almost single-minded exploitation of thematic transformation, generally avoiding motivically independent, contrasting subjects.[22] The same is true of Opp. 54–55 (1788) and Op. 64 (1790), composed for the violinist Johann Tost, which additionally explore virtuoso violin writing (for example in the slow movement of Op. 54 no. 3), including high positions (the 'Lark', Op. 64 no. 5, with its opening melody high on the E string) and concerto-like passage work (Op. 55 no. 1, Op. 64 no. 2);[23] the chromaticism of Op. 54 no. 1 (Allegretto) and Op. 55 no. 3 is reminiscent of Mozart, whose influence has been claimed. Op. 64, more intimate in character than Opp. 54–55, was performed in London during Haydn's first visit there in 1791–2; Opp. 71 and 74 ('Apponyi', 1793) were composed before the second journey and presumably intended for the coming season's concerts. Perhaps in response to the relative failure in England of the earlier set, and the need to provide music more outspoken in character for public performance, Opp. 71 and 74 again favour the brilliant style, with richer, more orchestral sonorities than any previous Haydn quartets and, particularly in Op. 74, adventurous tonal relationships between movements (and between minuets and their trios).

Other Viennese quartet composers of the 1780s include Dittersdorf, Leopold Kozeluch (1747–1818), Franz Anton Hoffmeister (1754–1812), Ignaz Joseph Pleyel (1757–1831), Adalbert Gyrowetz (1763–1850), Vanhal and Paul and Anton Wranitzky (1756–1808 and 1761–1820). While many of their works are closer in spirit to the Parisian *quatuor concertant* than to the 'classical' string quartets of Haydn,[24] others are ostentatiously virtuosic *quatuors brilliants*, including works by Paul Wranitzky, Gyrowetz and Franz Krommer (1759–1831).[25] Pleyel's Op. 1 quartets, published in 1782–3, were dedicated to his teacher Haydn; Mozart described them in a letter to his father as 'very well written and most pleasing to listen to'.[26] It may be, however, that this was a backhanded compliment and that Mozart, in his own quartets dedicated to Haydn, was at pains not only to flatter his older friend, but also to show up his younger colleague.[27] A favourite gesture of Pleyel's was the

22 See W. Dean Sutcliffe, *Haydn: String Quartets, Op. 50* (Cambridge, 1992).

23 In general on Haydn string quartets, see Floyd K. Grove, 'Concerto Style in Haydn's String Quartets', *Journal of Musicology*, 18 (2001), pp. 76–97.

24 See, for example, Roger Hickman, 'Leopold Kozeluch and the Viennese "quatuor concertant"', *College Music Symposium*, 26 (1986), pp. 42–52.

25 Roger Hickman, 'The Nascent Viennese String Quartet', *Musical Quarterly*, 67 (1981), pp. 193–212 and *idem*, 'The Flowering of the Viennese String Quartet in the Late Eighteenth-Century', *Music Review*, 50 (1989), pp. 157–80; Horst Walter, 'Zum Wiener Streichquartett der Jahre 1780 bis 1800', *Haydn-Studien*, 7 (1998), pp. 289–314.

26 Anderson (ed. and trans.), *The Letters of Mozart*, p. 875 (letter of 24 April 1784).

27 Mark Evan Bonds, 'Replacing Haydn: Mozart's "Pleyel" Quartets', *Music & Letters*, 88 (2007), pp. 201–25.

'soft, wry, comic ending' (for example in the finale of Op. 1 no. 2), a type of gesture also taken over by Vanhal (in Op. 13 no. 2, first movement, for example) who, like most of his contemporaries, devoted as much attention to textural details as to larger formal ones, and to dialogic play.[28]

Haydn's last completed set of quartets, Op. 76 (composed by mid-1797) were written in Vienna; a high point in Haydn's creative output, and in the history of the genre, they were described by Burney as 'full of invention, fire, good taste and new effects'.[29] Among their novel features are the minor-key finales of no. 1 in G major and no. 3 in C major and the rapid scherzos that replace minuets in nos. 1 and 6. The most remarkable of the set, perhaps, is no. 6 in E-flat, which atypically begins with a set of variations followed by a fugue; its slow movement, entitled 'Fantasia' has no key signature but is in the distant B major, exploring a wide range of tonalities; and sonata form is withheld for the finale. Only the two quartets Op. 77 (1799, dedicated to Prince Franz Joseph Maximilian Lobkowitz) and the unfinished Op. 103 (two movements, by 1803) followed; their publication, in 1802 and 1806, respectively, probably signalled Haydn's inability to sustain creative momentum over the course of a traditional set. Op. 77 no. 1 is an especially fine work, a model of idiomatic quartet writing; Op. 77 no. 2, with its remarkable, rapt variation-style slow movement, is often regarded as Haydn's supreme quartet.

By the later 1790s, the *concertants* and *brilliants* styles of Viennese quartets gave way to more theatrical works, typically in four movements and characterized by bold, almost orchestral gestures as well as pervasive counterpoint and motivic development. Among the most successful were those of Paul Wranitzky, Emanuel Aloys Förster (1748–1823) and in particular Andreas Romberg (1767–1821), whose Op. 2 was described in a contemporaneous review: 'Among quartets newly published since the death of the immortal Mozart, it would be impossible to find quartets composed with such care [for the purity of the composition] as these.'[30] Beethoven's first set of quartets, Op. 18, belong to this tradition as well. Composed between 1798 and 1800 for Prince Lobkowitz, they are not likely to have been greatly influenced by Haydn's most recent quartets before 1800, shortly after the publication of Op. 76: that summer, Beethoven revised the already-composed Op. 18 nos. 1–3. To be sure, the final version of Op. 18 no. 1 does show such influence, especially in its motivic concentration; in this respect it is not dissimilar to Op. 76 no. 2. At

28 W. Dean Sutcliffe, 'Haydn, Mozart and their Contemporaries', in Robin Stowell (ed.), *The Cambridge Companion to the String Quartet* (Cambridge, 2003), p. 196.

29 See H. C. Robbins Landon, *Haydn: Chronicle and Works, vol. 4: The Years of 'The Creation', 1796–1800* (London, 1977), p. 483.

30 *Allgemeine musikalische Zeitung* (12 May 1802), col. 536: 'unter dem, seit des unsterblichen Mozarts Tode neu herausgekommenen Quartetten, irgend welche an die Seite stellen dürfen.'

the same time, motivic concentration is typical of Haydn more generally and figures prominently, for example, in Op. 50 no. 3. Beethoven's interest in Mozart, on the other hand, is documented by copies made by Beethoven of K. 387 and K. 464; the latter in particular is seen as the model for Beethoven's A major quartet, Op. 18 no. 5.[31] But it would be generically narrow-minded to think that Beethoven's works were influenced solely by other quartets – and historically narrow-minded to think he was influenced only by the greatest of his predecessors, Haydn and Mozart. It is likely that he took his inspiration more generally from the Viennese quartet repertory and from his own experience writing chamber music for strings, including the string trios composed between 1794 and 1798 (Opp. 3, 8 and 9).

Whatever Beethoven's inspiration might have been, the Op. 18 set marks an appropriate end to the eighteenth century, embracing precedent and originality, seriousness and lightness, the various taxonomies of quartet composition, the variety demanded by both his patrons and the market and Beethoven's own idiosyncratic blend of 'Classicism' and 'Romanticism'. Even Op. 18 no. 1 makes this clear: where the first movement is concentrated and apparently indebted to Haydn, the slow movement evokes the contemporaneous operatic duet with its various dialogues, above a repeating accompaniment, among the instruments. It also evokes literary interest and inspiration: Beethoven apparently told his friend Karl Amenda that it was inspired by the tomb scene of Shakespeare's *Romeo and Juliet*. The one-in-a-bar Scherzo is both new and old, a harbinger of the famous Beethoven scherzos of the future but at the same time a further development of the scherzos in his piano sonatas of the 1790s. The last two quartets of the set differ in some respects from the others: as Scott Burnham notes, their first movements are 'swift, bland and symmetrical, so that the later movements all seem (and were surely meant to seem) weightier or more arresting'.[32] The most famous moment in the set, perhaps, is the chromatic opening to the finale of Op. 18 no. 6, entitled 'La malinconia', although on the whole, most of Op. 18's slow movements are also marked by elaborate textures, complex harmony and intensity of utterance. The quartets were ambiguously received; according to one contemporaneous assessment they 'must be played often and very well, as they are very difficult to perform and not at all popular'.[33]

31 See, in particular, Jeremy Yudkin, 'Beethoven's "Mozart" Quartet', *Journal of the American Musicological Society*, 45 (1992), pp. 30–74.

32 Scott Burnham, 'Beethoven, Ludwig van. §13. Music of the Early Vienna Period', Oxford Music Online (www.oxfordmusiconline.com) (accessed 8 September 2006).

33 See *Allgemeine musikalische Zeitung*, 3 (1800–1), col. 800. For an introduction to Beethoven's quartets generally, see Joseph Kerman, *The Beethoven Quartets* (London, 1967)

Whatever uncertainties critics may have had concerning Beethoven's Op. 18, by 1801, when they were published, the hegemony of the Viennese 'Classical' string quartet was nearly complete; its influence can be seen, for example, in Hyacinthe Jadin's Op. 2 no. 1 (1796), the slow introduction to which is modelled on Mozart's 'Dissonance' Quartet K. 465, and Samuel Webbe's variations on 'Adeste fidelis' 'after the Manner of Haydn's celebrated Hymn to the Emperor' (Op. 76 no. 3). To be sure, the Viennese style did not entirely absorb the *quatuor brilliant*, which survived as a distinct 'species' of quartet, fuelled by a growing interest in virtuosity for its own sake and by instrumental arrangements of popular operatic numbers. Mostly these were written by professional violin virtuosos, among them Rodolphe Kreutzer (1766–1831), Pierre Baillot (1771–1842) and Viotti's pupil Pierre Rode (1774–1830) in Paris, and Ignaz Schuppanzigh (1776–1830) in Vienna. Not coincidentally, perhaps, it was about this time that professional string quartets were first established. Although some professional ensembles were occasionally active in Vienna, Paris and London during the 1780s – or at least that there were public or semi-public performances of quartets – it was not until the early nineteenth century that quartets became a regular feature of concert programmes. (London, where quartets were given in concert as early as the 1770s, was an exception.[34]) Prior to that time, especially in German-speaking Europe, quartets had been intended chiefly for private performance, 'to serve the private pleasure of the regent or the court', as Koch put it.[35] This accounts, at least in part, for the variable style of the repertory: different patrons had different tastes, and publishers – if quartets were to be printed – had specific markets. Emperor Joseph II, for example, held regular quartet performances in his apartments during the 1780s and given his predilection for the learned style, a large number of works composed for him include fugues or extended contrapuntal passages (as noted in works by Gassmann, Starzer, d'Ordoñez and Albrechtsberger). Friedrich Wilhelm II in Berlin, was a violoncellist and it was for him that Boccherini composed a celebrated set of quartets in 1786 with prominent cello parts,[36] while Mozart did the same in his 'Prussian' quartets (even if he never finished the set and the prominence of the cello drops off dramatically, especially in K. 590). Haydn, on the other hand, seems to have emphasized the 'public' nature of his quartets written for the paying public in London, Opp. 71 and 74.

34 Concerning London, see in particular, Simon McVeigh, *Concert Life in London from Mozart to Haydn* (Cambridge, 1993) and Meredith McFarlane and Simon McVeigh, 'The String Quartet in London Concert Life, 1769–1799', in Susan Wollenberg and McVeigh (eds.), *Concert Life in Eighteenth-Century Britain* (Aldershot, 2004), pp. 161–96.

35 Koch, 'Kammermusik', in *Musikalisches Lexikon* (Frankfurt, 1802).

36 Further, see Mara Parker, 'Friedrich Wilhelm II and the Classical String Quartet', *Music Review*, 54 (1993), pp. 161–82.

Whatever demands lay behind the various styles of quartets – and whatever artistic goals composers may have set for themselves in their works – by the early nineteenth century the quartet was understood more broadly as a vehicle of modernity and social cohesion. According to an anonymous article in the *Allgemeine musikalische Zeitung* for 16 May 1810 (and among the earliest taxonomies in print to distinguish between the *quatuor concertant* and *quatuor brillant* on the one hand and the 'Classical' quartet on the other), competency in quartet performance was impossible for 'old, fossilized ripieno players'; what is more, 'It is impossible to hate someone with whom you have once seriously made music; and those who in some winter season have of their own will freely joined together in playing quartets are good friends for the rest of their lives.'[37]

Select Bibliography

Association française pour le patrimoine musical (ed.). *Le quatuor à cordes en France de 1750 à nos jours*. Paris, 1995

Bonds, Mark Evan. 'The Sincerest Form of Flattery? Mozart's "Haydn" Quartets and the Question of Influence'. *Studi musicali*, 22 (1993), pp. 365–409

'Replacing Haydn: Mozart's "Pleyel" Quartets'. *Music & Letters*, 88 (2007), pp. 201–25

Brown, A. Peter. 'The Chamber Music with Strings of Carlos d'Ordoñez: A Bibliographic and Stylistic Study'. *Analecta musicologica*, 46 (1974), pp. 222–72

'Haydn and Mozart's 1773 Stay in Vienna: Weeding a Musicological Garden'. *Journal of Musicology*, 10 (1992), pp. 192–230

Burnham, Scott. 'Beethoven, Ludwig van. §13. Music of the Early Vienna Period', Oxford Music Online (www.oxfordmusiconline.com) (accessed 8 September 2008)

Drabkin, William. *A Reader's Guide to Haydn's Early String Quartets*. Westport, CT, 2000

Finscher, Ludwig. *Studien zur Geschichte des Streichquartetts, i: Die Entstehung des klassischen Streichquartetts: von den Vorformen zur Grundlegung durch Joseph Haydn*. Kassel, 1974

Fischer, Kurt. 'G. B. Viotti und das Streichquartett des späten 18. Jahrhunderts'. In Lorenzo Bianconi *et al.* (eds.), *Atti del XIV congresso della Società Internazionale di Musicologia, Bologna, 1987: Trasmissione e recezione delle forme di cultura musicale*. Kassel, 1990, 3 vols., vol. 3, pp. 753–67

Geiringer, Karl. 'The Rise of Chamber Music'. In Egon Wellescz and Frederick Sternfield (eds.), *New Oxford History of Music, vol. VII: The Age of Enlightenment, 1745–1790*. Oxford, 1973, pp. 515–73

Gotwals, Vernon (ed.). *Haydn: Two Contemporary Portraits*. Madison, WI, 1968

Griffiths, Paul. *The String Quartet*. London and New York, 1983

Hickman, Roger. 'The Nascent Viennese String Quartet'. *Musical Quarterly*, 67 (1981), pp. 193–212

37 *Allgemeine musikalische Zeitung* 12 (16 May 1810), col. 514: 'Man kann keinen Menschen hassen, mit dem man einmal im Ernste musicirt hat, und Menschen, die einen Winter hindurch aus freyem Triebe zum Quartett vereinigt mit einander gespielt haben, sind zeitlebens gute Freunde.'

'Leopold Kozeluch and the Viennese "quatuor concertant"'. *College Music Symposium*, 26 (1986), pp. 42–52

'The Flowering of the Viennese String Quartet in the Late Eighteenth-Century'. *Music Review*, 50 (1989), pp. 157–80

Irving, John. *Mozart: The 'Haydn' Quartets*. Cambridge, 1998

Jones, David Wyn. 'The String Quartets of Vanhal'. PhD thesis, University of Wales, 1978

'The Origins of the Quartet'. In Robin Stowell (ed.), *The Cambridge Companion to the String Quartet*. Cambridge, 2003, pp. 177–84

Keefe, Simon P. *Mozart's Viennese Instrumental Music: A Study of Stylistic Re-Invention*. Woodbridge and Rochester, NY, 2007

Kerman, Joseph. *The Beethoven Quartets*. London, 1967

Kirkendale, Warren. *Fugue and Fugato in Rococo and Classical Chamber Music*. Trans. Kirkendale and Margaret Bent, Durham, NC, 1979

Konold, Wulf. *Das Streichquartett, von den Anfängen bis Franz Schubert*. Wilhelmshaven, 1980

Lehmann-Gugolz, Ursula. *Deutsches und italienisches Wesen in der Vorgeschichte des klassischen Streichquartetts*. Würzburg, 1939

Levy, Janet. 'The "Quatuor concertant" in Paris in the Latter Half of the Eighteenth Century'. PhD thesis, Stanford University, 1971

McFarlane, Meredith, and Simon McVeigh. 'The String Quartet in London Concert Life, 1769–1799'. In Susan Wollenberg and McVeigh (eds.), *Concert Life in Eighteenth-Century Britain*. Aldershot, 2004, pp. 161–96

McVeigh, Simon. *Concert Life in London from Mozart to Haydn*. Cambridge, 1993

Moe, Orin. 'The Significance of Haydn's Op. 33'. In Jens Peter Larsen, Howard Serwer and James Webster (eds.), *Haydn-Studies: Washington, DC 1975*. New York, 1981, pp. 445–50

Oboussier, Philippe. 'The French String Quartet, 1770–1800'. In Malcolm Boyd (ed.), *Music and the French Revolution*. Cambridge, 1992, pp. 74–92

Parker, Mara. 'Friedrich Wilhelm II and the Classical String Quartet'. *Music Review*, 54 (1993), pp. 161–82

Pincherle, Marc. 'On the Origins of the String Quartet'. *Musical Quarterly*, 15 (1929), pp. 77–87

Rosen, Charles. *The Classical Style*. New York, 1971

Speck, Christian. *Boccherinis Streichquartette: Studien zur Kompositionsweise und zur gattungsgeschichtlichen Stellung*. Munich, 1987

Speck, Christian and Stanley Sadie. 'Boccherini' in *Oxford Music Online* (www.oxfordmusiconline.com) (accessed 8 September 2008)

Sutcliffe, W. Dean, *Haydn: String Quartets, Op. 50*. Cambridge, 1992

'Haydn, Mozart and their Contemporaries'. In Robin Stowell (ed.), *The Cambridge Companion to the String Quartet*. Cambridge, 2003, pp. 185–209

Walter, Horst. 'Zum Wiener Streichquartett der Jahre 1780 bis 1800'. *Haydn-Studien*, 7 (1998), pp. 289–314

Webster, James. 'Towards a History of Viennese Chamber Music in the Early Classical Period'. *Journal of the American Musicological Society*, 27 (1974), pp. 212–47

Yudkin, Jeremy. 'Beethoven's "Mozart" Quartet'. *Journal of the American Musicological Society*, 45 (1992), pp. 30–74

· POSTLUDE ·

· 24 ·

Across the divide: currents of musical thought in Europe, *c.* 1790–1810

SIMON P. KEEFE

Early in 1801, Johann Karl Friedrich Triest (1764–1810) surveyed the German musical scene of the previous century in a series of articles in the Leipzig-based *Allgemeine musikalische Zeitung*, entitled 'Bemerkung über die Ausbildung der Tonkunst in Deutschland im achtzehnten Jahrhundert'.[1] Though not without its quirks – including a quaintly nationalistic claim for 'works that only *German* toil and diligence can produce'[2] – it is an important document, poised perfectly at the century divide. Many of Triest's historical perspectives resonate (to a lesser or greater extent) with common twentieth- and twenty-first-century perspectives on eighteenth-century music, including his sub-division into three periods that comprise 'the beginning ... to the death of Joh. Seb. Bach', 'Graun, Hasse, C. P. E. Bach *et al.* to Jo. Haydn and Mozart' and 'Mozart to the end of the century', his appreciation of Bach, Haydn and Mozart's pre-eminence and his identification of the third quarter of the century as an 'interim period'.[3] Triest is also refreshingly self-aware as a historian, recognizing the 'chameleon shapes' of musical development in the late eighteenth century as 'ever more difficult to follow' and the 'present ferment of the *practical* art of music' as an impediment to determining future directions of travel.[4]

Needless to say, 'ferment' at the end of the eighteenth century was not confined to the musical world. The French Revolution sent shock waves across Europe; catastrophic military activities were to follow from the early 1790s

1 See *Allgemeine musikalische Zeitung*, 3 (1800–1801), cols. 225–35, 241–9, 257–64, 273–86, 297–308, 321–31, 369–79, 389–401, 405–10, 421–32 and 437–45. Trans. Susan Gillespie as 'Remarks on the Development of the Art of Music in Germany in the Eighteenth Century', in Elaine Sisman (ed.), *Haydn and His World* (Princeton, NJ, 1997), pp. 321–94. All translations are taken from this source.

2 'Remarks on the Development of the Art of Music', p. 382. For a contextualization of Triest's German nationalism, see John Deathridge, 'The Invention of German Music, *c.* 1800', in Tim Blanning and Hagen Schulze (eds.), *Unity and Diversity in European Culture c. 1800* (Oxford, 2006), pp. 53–5.

3 The three periods are identified at the end of the first *Allgemeine musikalische Zeitung* article ('Remarks on the Development of the Art of Music', p. 328); for the reference to the 'interim period' see 'Remarks on the Development of the Art of Music', p. 353.

4 *Ibid.*, pp. 357, 382.

until 1815. Antipathy between Emperor Franz II and France led to the French declaring war on Austria and Prussia in April 1792; hostilities between France and Britain, Holland, Spain, Portugal and Tuscany began in 1793. A series of pacts, treaties and peace negotiations among European nations in 1795–7 did little to stem the flow of violence, especially because Napoleon emerged as a dominant military ruler in the final years of the century. Countries turned progressively against France, including in a British–Russian–Austrian–Turkish–Portuguese–Neapolitan coalition instigated by William Pitt the Younger in June 1799. Given the volatile situation in Europe, it is no wonder that on the last day of 1799 the great eighteenth-century Viennese diarist Count Karl Zinzendorf recorded his desire for a better society in the next world than the one he was experiencing in this.[5] Aside from a brief period of peace (1802–3), the early years of the nineteenth century were characterized by devastating confrontations between Napoleon-led France and its enemies – the Italians (1800–1), Austrians (1805, 1809), Austro-Russians (1805), British (1805), Prussians (1806), Spanish (1808) and Russians (1812). Defeat at the hands of Britain and her allies at Waterloo (1815) finally put pay to Napoleon's reign. Reflecting on tumultuous events of the time, the German author and politician Ernst Moritz Arndt explained (1804–5): 'It is regularly asserted ...: whoever has lived through the last twenty years has lived centuries. But that just expresses mere amazement about the period ... The era is in flight ... Unimaginable things have happened; the world has suffered great transformations calmly and noisily, in the gentle passing of days as well as during the hurricanes and volcanoes of revolutions.'[6]

Musical 'ferment' *c.* 1790–1810 was no less culturally significant than military ferment was politically significant. As with any extended period of musical activity, determining whether currents of musical and aesthetic change or currents of musical and aesthetic continuity are on the whole more prevalent is a thankless task; writings attempting implicitly or explicitly to do so tend to tell us as much about the orientation of the writer as about the period in question. Disentangling the relationship between a musical–cultural event and past, present and future activities that may or may not relate to it is, of course, an act of interpretation. It is entirely reasonable to argue in any case that continuity and change are two sides of the same hermeneutic coin. From an aesthetic perspective, Ludwig Tieck and Wilhelm Heinrich Wackenroder's

5 Given (in French) in H. C. Robbins Landon, *Haydn: Chronicle and Works. The Years of 'The Creation', 1796–1800* (London, 1977), p. 500.

6 Ernst Moritz Arndt, *Geist der Zeit*, vol. 1 (1804–5), in Arndt, *Sämtliche Werke*, ed. Karl F. Pfau, vol. 8 (Leipzig, 1905), pp. 53–4; as given in Irene Zedlacher's translation in Reinhold Brinkmann, 'In the Time of the *Eroica*', in Scott Burnham and Michael P. Steinberg (eds.), *Beethoven and His World* (Princeton, NJ, 2000), p. 8.

famous essays of 1799, for example, can come to represent a new orientation, beginning 'the chain of aesthetic events that secured the aesthetic value of abstract, non-mimetic instrumental music', but at the same time can be regarded as a logical extension of forty years of reviews in German periodicals that 'hammered home the idea of an instrumental music that could and should be judged on its own terms'.[7] Equally the launch of the *Allgemeine musikalische Zeitung* in 1798 can be interpreted as both a ground-breaking moment in the history of music criticism, *and* a continuation of traditional types of review writing in late-eighteenth-century German periodicals.[8] The new emphasis around 1800 on an idealism that 'gives priority to spirit over matter ... [and] holds that art and the external world are consonant with one another not because art imitates that world, but because both reflect a common, higher ideal' contrasts markedly with 'the eighteenth-century predilection for explaining the emotional power of music in essentially naturalistic or mechanical terms – that is to say, in terms of its effect on the listener'; nonetheless it is foreshadowed in the late eighteenth-century writings of Joachim Winkelmann, Johann Georg Sulzer, Immanuel Kant and Friedrich Schiller.[9] Continuity and change can also be interpreted as mutually dependent from stylistic and reception standpoints. On the one hand, Beethoven's 'heroic' music was processed very differently from the music of his predecessors in the first decade of the nineteenth century, and Beethoven himself departed self consciously from earlier styles in 1801–2; on the other hand, narratives focusing on Beethoven's continuity with the music of his predecessors (especially Mozart and Haydn) were frequently spun in the 1790s, and Beethoven repeatedly used Mozart's and Haydn's works as models up to 1800.[10]

It is surely beyond dispute that music and musical aesthetics travelled a remarkable distance between 1790 and 1810, irrespective of how the complex dynamics of continuity and change are processed. Writing in the middle of the period, Triest admitted finding it difficult to distinguish the star constellations

7 Mary Sue Morrow, *German Music Criticism in the Late Eighteenth Century: Aesthetic Issues in Instrumental Music* (Cambridge, 1997), p. 151.
8 *Ibid.*, p. 154.
9 Mark Evan Bonds, 'Idealism and Aesthetics of Instrumental Music at the Turn of the Nineteenth Century', *Journal of the American Musicological Society*, 50 (1997), pp. 390, 397–8.
10 On narratives from the 1790s that associate Beethoven and his music with Haydn and Mozart, see Tia DeNora, *Beethoven and the Construction of Genius: Musical Politics in Vienna, 1792–1803* (Berkeley and Los Angeles, 1995), pp. 83–114 (chapter 5). Discussions of Beethoven's early modelling include: Carl Schachter, 'Mozart's Last and Beethoven's First: Echoes of K. 551 in the First Movement of Op. 21', in Cliff Eisen (ed.), *Mozart Studies* (Oxford, 1991), pp. 227–51; Jeremy Yudkin, 'Beethoven's "Mozart" Quartet', *Journal of the American Musicological Society*, 45 (1992), pp. 30–74; Lewis Lockwood, 'Beethoven Before 1800: the Mozart Legacy', *Beethoven Forum 3* (1994), pp. 39–52; Elaine Sisman, '"The Spirit of Mozart from Haydn's Hands": Beethoven's Musical Inheritance', in Glenn Stanley (ed.), *The Cambridge Companion to Beethoven* (Cambridge, 2000), pp. 45–63.

from individual stars, but was still able to pick out Haydn and Mozart as 'the two ... of the first magnitude, which shed their light over all of Germany (and even today over distant lands)'.[11] Our own twenty-first-century problem is more likely to be the opposite of Triest's, even taking into account big musicological advances in understanding music of this period as a whole – we often see three stars crystal clear and miss purportedly smaller ones hiding behind them. Whatever the case may be it is difficult to regard the emergence and consolidation of the reputations of Haydn, Mozart and Beethoven as anything less than the defining reception-related event of the last decade of the eighteenth century and first decade of the nineteenth, hindered and inspired as we are by the huge volume of discussion of these composers from the last 200 years. It pays to re-examine how and why the reputations took shape when they did, since the information we glean provides both an instructive platform from which to survey the period in its entirety, and a vivid illustration of the continuity–change dynamic at work. As we learn from our line of enquiry, music reception *c.* 1790–1810 is characterized *inter alia* by the urge to historicize – a process in which composers themselves are involved – by a value-laden set of relationships between the music of different composers and by evolving attitudes to musical popularity.

Mozart, Haydn and Beethoven

An indication of how far Mozart travelled in reputation terms between 1790 and *c.* 1810 – in spite of living only until December 1791 – can be determined by comparing entries for him in two dictionaries of musicians compiled by Ernst Ludwig Gerber, the *Historisch-biographisches Lexicon der Tonkünstler* (*HLT*) (2 vols., Leipzig, 1790, 1792) and the *Neues historisch-biographisches Lexicon der Tonkünstler* (*NHLT*) (4 vols., Leipzig, 1812–14).[12] Though based in Sondershausen in the principality of Schwarzburg-Sondershausen (central Germany) for almost all of his life, Gerber was cosmopolitan by nature, spending time in Leipzig and maintaining an active correspondence with Breitkopf, who sent him numerous publications. The *HLT* is naturally biased towards Germanic musicians, those active in the early and mid eighteenth century in particular, but demonstrates considerable knowledge of foreign musicians as well; it is therefore as reliable a gauge of Mozart's reputation in

11 Triest, 'Remarks on the Development of the Art of Music', p. 357.

12 Though published in 1812–14, work was carried out on the *Neues historisch-biographisches Lexicon der Tonkünstler* from 1792 onwards. It comprises additions made by J. F. Reichardt (1792) and E. F. F. Chladni (1795) as well as notes and materials accrued by Gerber himself between the publications of the *NTL* and the *NHLT*. See Othmar Wessely, 'Gerber, Ernst Ludwig', in Stanley Sadie (ed.), *New Grove Dictionary of Music and Musicians, Revised Edition* (London, 2001), vol. 9, pp. 685–6.

Central Europe in 1790 as we are likely to find in a single source.[13] Mozart fares reasonably well but by no means spectacularly so. Gerber draws attention to his prolific skills at a young age, his youthful tours around Europe including operatic successes in Milan, his move to Vienna after finding Salzburg too small, and his increasing fame in Vienna that culminates in his court appointment in January 1788 (actually, December 1787); the few works mentioned include *Die Entführung aus dem Serail* (an extraordinary success, Gerber tells us), *Le nozze di Figaro*, *Der Schauspieldirektor*, *Don Giovanni* and some chamber works (piano sonatas, a piano trio and string quartets). But the jury on Mozart the composer is still out. He is one of the great pianists of his era, to be sure, but the unpractised (*ungeübte*) ear finds harmonies in his compositions difficult to follow; even knowledgeable musicians must listen to his works several times in order to appreciate them. The length of Mozart's article is roughly comparable to those on Pasquale Anfossi, Wilhelm Friedemann Bach, Carlo Broschi, André-Ernest-Modeste Grétry, Leopold Kozeluch, Josef Mysliveček, Christian Friedrich Daniel Schubart and Carl Stamitz, and significantly shorter than those on the likes of Johann André, Carl Heinrich Graun, Johann Wilhelm Hässler, Reinhard Keiser, Johann Kuhnau, G. E. Nauert, Christian Gottlieb Neefe, Ignaz Josef Pleyel, Giuseppe Sarti and Christoph Gottlieb Schroeter.

The change to Mozart's entry in the *NHLT* twenty years later is dramatic indeed. The *NHLT* in total is slightly over twice the length of the *HLT* and does not replicate a lot of material from the original; short articles on musicians covered in the *HLT*, then, are not necessarily indicative of a diminished reputation. But significantly expanded articles demonstrate that Gerber and his team had accrued additional information on a musician between the *HLT* and *NHLT* and thus give a firm indication of a growing reputation in the intervening years. At almost twenty-four columns, Mozart's new entry marks a thirteen-fold increase on his entry length in the *HLT*;[14] only Haydn fared better, with a twenty-three-fold increase. Other recently deceased or living composers – including André, Georg Benda, Luigi Boccherini, Muzio Clementi, Carl Ditters von Dittersdorf, Jan Ladislav Dussek, Florian Leopold Gassmann, Grétry, Pleyel, Johann Abraham Peter Schulz and Georg Joseph Vogler – have longer entries in the *NHLT* than in the *HLT*, but increases are modest in relation to those of Mozart and Haydn. Predictably, the tone of Mozart's article has changed, too – doubts about his music disappear and hyperbole takes their place. Presumably reflecting on his earlier article, Gerber recognized that Mozart was a 'meteor on the musical horizon' (*ein Meteor am*

13 For the article on Mozart, see Gerber, *HLT*, vol. 1, cols. 977–9. 14 See *NHLT*, cols. 475–98.

musikalischen Horizonte), for which the world was unprepared; paradoxically, he arrived on the stage too early and departed it too early as well.[15] Stylistic features such as his unusual melodies and use of harmony are now regarded by Gerber as having accelerated advances in musical taste by more than half a century; indeed, his genius – one of the greatest in the history of the arts – was responsible for 'a general revolution in artistic taste' (*eine allgemeine Revolution in dem Kunstgeschmack*).[16]

Gerber profited in his *NHLT* from the Mozart industry that sprang up soon after the composer's death and that gathered a remarkable head of steam. His extended list of Mozart's works draws on André's 'full and complete' catalogue and on Mozart's own Thematic Catalogue (the *Verzeichniss*), which he kept from February 1784 until his death, and which Gerber again obtained through André.[17] At the beginning of the article Gerber also recommends bibliographical items to his readers, all published after Mozart's death; several were principal sources for Gerber himself, notably Friedrich Adolph Heinrich von Schlichtegroll's 6,000-word biography in the *Nekrolog auf das Jahr 1791* (Gotha, 1793), Franz Xaver Niemetschek's *Leben des k. k. Kapellmeister Wolfgang Gottlieb Mozart* (Prague, 1798) and Friedrich Rochlitz's anecdotes about Mozart's life (published in the first three years of the *Allgemeine musikalische Zeitung*'s run).

Perhaps the most striking feature of Gerber's article is that he justifies Mozart's exalted status with recourse to musical–historical frames of reference; it is important to Gerber that Mozart took Haydn's works as his model after his move to Vienna and called Haydn his teacher, that he studied Handel's great choral works, that he held in high esteem the work of other great composers such as J. S. Bach, C. P. E. Bach, Handel, Gluck, Joseph Haydn and Michael Haydn and that he possessed the contrapuntal skills of Bach and the dramatic talents of Gluck.[18] We witness a decisive move in Mozart's position in the historical pecking order in the second edition of Niemetschek's biography, too (1808).[19] Revisions to the 1798 edition in 1808 are not particularly substantial, but are revealing in their new emphasis on Mozart's significance. Niemetschek's dedication to Haydn in the 1798 edition reads: 'This little memorial to immortal Mozart is dedicated by the author with deepest homage to Joseph Haydn (Kapellmeister to Duke Esterházy) father of the noble art

15 *NHLT*, col. 494. 16 *NHLT*, cols. 493, 494.

17 *NHLT*, cols. 482–91. Gerber makes reference to other editions of Mozart's music as well, including the extended series from Breitkopf, piano works from Simrock and Speyer in Braunschweig and assorted works from Kühnel (cols. 491–2).

18 *NHLT*, cols. 478, 498.

19 See Franz Xaver Niemetschek, *Lebensbeschreibung des k. k. Kapellmeisters Wolfgang Amadeus Mozart (1808)*, ed. Peter Krause (Leipzig, 1978); the first edn. is Niemetschek, *Lebensbeschreibung des k. k. Kapellmeisters Wolfgang Amadeus Mozart* (1798), trans. Helen Mautner as *Life of Mozart* (London, 1956).

of music and the favourite of the Muses.'[20] No doubt attentive to his own reference to Haydn's pre-eminent position in the musical world, Niemetschek eliminated the dedication in 1808, substituting a brief, self-contained introduction. Here, Mozart's transcendent position in relation to his compositional contemporaries and forefathers is rendered explicit: 'Unique, unsurpassed, a Raphael of his art, he stands above the glorious geniuses of Handel, Cimarosa, Gluck and Haydn; his fame fills the whole cultured world.'[21] Niemetschek's perception of Mozart's even more exalted status in 1808 than in 1798 emerges elsewhere in the second edition, too, such as in his new assessment of the unequalled position of the piano concertos. As in many other fields, Niemetschek tells us, Mozart invented a new model for the genre: 'These works contain an inexhaustible richness of the most excellent thoughts, the most brilliant instrumentation, and exhaust almost all depths of counterpoint.'[22]

Niemetschek affirms Mozart's superlative historical status by adding material to his second edition that illustrates the geographically widespread nature of the admiration for Mozart's music. His operas and piano pieces, Niemetschek explains, are extremely popular in Italy; his symphonies, piano concertos and quartets are greatly admired in France, as was *Die Zauberflöte* (in its adapted form as *Les Mystères d'Isis*, no doubt), although *Don Giovanni* had less success on account of being poorly produced; he is venerated in England, too, where the Requiem is often performed to great acclaim and where sales of the Breitkopf editions of his works are as strong as in France and Germany. Niemetschek asks rhetorically: where do we find musical *Kenner* and *Liebhaber* who are *not* delighted by Mozart's music? Mozart is known in far-flung places where the names of few Europeans are recognized; Niemetschek learns from a famous botanist that Mozart's works are even popular in the Philippines.[23]

Irrespective of the changes noticed and information accrued by Niemetschek between 1798 and 1808, Mozart had already assumed an exalted position for many musicians – especially in Germany and Austria – a few years after his death. The spectre of Mozart looms large, for example, in Johann Ferdinand Ritter von Schönfeld's testimony to the richness of musical life in Vienna and Prague, *Jahrbuch der Tonkunst Wien und Prag 1796*; Mozart is described as 'immortal'

20 Niemetschek, *Life of Mozart*, p. 10.

21 Niemetschek, *Lebenbeschreibung (1808)*, p. 1. 'Einzig, unübertroffen steht er, ein Raphael seiner Kunst, unter den glorreichen Genien Haendel, Cimarosa, Gluck, Hayden, oben an; sein Ruhm erfüllt die ganze gebildete Welt.'

22 Niemetschek, *Lebenbeschreibung (1808)*, p. 114. 'Diese Werke enthalten einen unerschöpflichen Reichtthum an den treflichsten Gedanken, die glänzendste Instrumentation, und erschöpfen fast alle Tiefen des Kontrapunktes.'

23 Niemetschek, *Lebensbeschreibung (1808)*, pp. 64–5.

and 'unforgettable'.[24] For Schönfeld, any association a living Viennese musician in 1796 had had with Mozart, or any point of comparison with his precociousness, reflected extremely positively: Hummel 'may well claim a talent like Mozart's'; 'much is expected' of Fräulein von Seidschek since she was 'one of [Mozart's] strongest students'; and Franz Xaver Süssmayr's status as Mozart's student, and one whom Mozart valued, is the very thing that 'serves to recommend him'.[25] Almost all his chamber works, two-thirds of his piano concertos and one-quarter of his symphonies were available in print by the end of the 1790s and he was second only in popularity to Ignaz Pleyel for the important German publisher Johann André, who produced 118 print-runs of Mozart's music before 1800.[26] The Austro-German craze for *Die Zauberflöte*, the wide dissemination of his Viennese operas in general, the proliferation of arrangements of his works in the 1790s (operatic numbers, in particular), and the initiation of complete editions of his works by the Brunswick-based publisher Johann Peter Speyer and (especially) Breitkopf & Härtel attest to the spectacular increase in Mozart's popularity in the decade following his death.[27] Mozart deification was all too much for some, including a critic writing in the *Teutschlands Annalen des Jahres 1794* only three years after Mozart's death: 'In this year 1794 nothing can be sung or played, and nothing heard with approbation, but that it bears on its brow the all-powerful and magic name of Mozart ... That Mozart to a large extent deserves this applause will be disputed by no one. But that he was still in his years of ferment, and that his ideas were still frequently in a state of flux, as it were – of this there are only too many instances in his works.'[28]

Even though the number of Mozart sceptics soon dwindled in Austria and Germany, two major European nations – Britain and France – remained collectively uncertain about the composer and his music in the 1790s. Interest in Mozart's works in London in 1788 can probably be attributed to the return to their homeland of two of Mozart's English friends, Nancy Storace and Thomas Attwood, but did not fuel further interest in the 1790s. (Performances of Mozart picked up in 1800.[29]) Mozart was similarly slow to find favour in France; he was less popular among Parisian publishers *c.* 1800, for example, than the likes of Haydn, Pleyel, Vanhal and Carl Stamitz.[30] But the sands had shifted

24 See Johann Ferdinand Ritter von Schönfeld, 'A Yearbook of the Music of Vienna and Prague, 1796', trans. Kathrine Talbot in Elaine Sisman (ed.), *Haydn and His World* (Princeton, NJ, 1997), pp. 302, 313.

25 Schönfeld, 'A Yearbook 1796', pp. 302, 313, 314.

26 Gernot Gruber, *Mozart & Posterity*, trans. R. S. Furness (London, 1991), pp. 24–5, 26–7.

27 See Gruber, *Mozart & Posterity*, *passim*.

28 Otto Erich Deutsch, *Mozart: A Documentary Biography*, trans. Eric Blom, Peter Branscombe and Jeremy Noble, 2nd edn. (London, 1990), p. 472.

29 See Simon McVeigh, *Concert Life in London from Mozart to Haydn* (Cambridge, 1993), pp. 127–8 and Gruber, *Mozart & Posterity*, p. 30.

30 Gruber, *Mozart & Posterity*, p. 26.

by the beginning of the second decade of the nineteenth century according to A. Choron and F. Fayolle who, in their two-volume dictionary of musicians from 1810–11, recorded only mediocre success for Parisian productions of *Figaro* and *Don Giovanni* in the 1790s, but far greater success for Mozart's music in general in the subsequent decade.[31] The debt that Choron and Fayolle owe to Gerber's *HLT* has been identified,[32] but is not a major issue where the Mozart entry is concerned, as the bibliographical items cited, and the principal sources for the article (Schlichtegroll, Niemetschek, and a translation of anecdotes by Rochlitz), all go far beyond Gerber's *HLT* article in scope. As with Niemetschek (especially in the 1808 edition) and Gerber (in the *NHLT*), Choron and Fayolle are particularly interested in Mozart's historical position. They defend him against allegations that he did not concern himself with the music of others, citing his extraordinary work and travel schedules to account for any lack of diligence in this respect, and explain in any case that he admired early eighteenth-century composers such as Leonardo Leo, Nicola Porpora, Francesco Durante and above all Handel. They further claim – following Rochlitz – that Mozart had found Martín y Soler's *Una cosa rara* attractive, but had said that no-one would bother with it twenty years later; the implication is that Mozart's music, in contrast, most certainly stands the test of time.[33] Even if Choron and Fayolle are misinformed on Mozart's views here it is revealing that they impart their own historical mindset on Mozart himself. From the article length – very few, except Niccolò Piccinni, fare better in this dictionary – and the detailed focus on the composer, his life story and a number of his works, we gauge that Mozart had come to occupy a special historical place in the French musical consciousness by 1810–11.

Haydn, twenty-four years Mozart's senior, had already firmly secured his position in the musical firmament by 1790, even before his highly successful and much-publicized trips to London in 1791–2 and 1794–5. As Gerber explained in the *HLT*, in a similar vein to other writers of the time: 'When we name Joseph Haydn, we think of one of our greatest men; great in the small things and greater still in the big things; the glory of our era. Always rich and inexhaustible; always new and striking; always elevated and grand, even when he seems to smile.'[34] The praise lavished on Haydn by the English press during

31 A. Choron and F. Fayolle, *Dictionnaire historique des musicians* (Paris, 1810–1), 2 vols., vol. 2, p. 75.

32 Wessely, 'Gerber', pp. 685–6.

33 Choron and Fayolle, *Dictionnaire historique*, vol. 2, pp. 74–5. For Rochlitz's account of this story, see Maynard Solomon, 'The Rochlitz Anecdotes: Issues of Authenticity in Early Mozart Biography', in Cliff Eisen (ed.), *Mozart Studies* (Cambridge, 1991), p. 27.

34 Gerber, *HLT*, col. 610. 'Wenn wir Joseph Haydn nennen, so denken wir uns einen unserer grössten Männer; gross im kleinen und noch grosser im Grossen; die Ehre unseres Zeitalters. Immer reich und unerschöpflich; allezeit neu und frappant; allezeit erhaben und gross, selbst wenn er zu lächeln scheint.'

his visits to London, the widespread distribution of his music in 1790s Europe and the astonishing success of *The Creation*, first in Vienna then across Europe after its first public performance in 1799, make it reasonable to claim the end of the eighteenth century as the Age of Haydn – such fame for a living composer was unprecedented at that time.[35] Even after a dip in popularity in England in the first decade of the nineteenth century – *The Seasons* (1801) remained unperformed there in Haydn's lifetime – the English commented very favourably on his historical position *vis-à-vis* the musical world: the obituary writer for *The Gentleman's Magazine* explained in 1809 that Haydn 'was justly considered the Father of Musick in our day; for although in his youth he diligently studied the works of every great master, antient and modern, his transcendant genius soaring above them all, soon called the attention of the whole musical world upon himself; all admiring him, first for the beauty, boldness, and originality of his works, and afterwards regarding him as the best model for study and imitation'.[36] Meanwhile, one of Haydn's earliest biographers, Giuseppe Carpani – echoing Niemetschek's claim about Mozart's geographically widespread popularity – cited performances of Haydn's music from Mexico to Calcutta and London to Naples as *de facto* recognition of his historical significance.[37]

The tendency to view Haydn and Mozart as composers of monumental historical import – not simply composers of great works, but great composers who supplied lasting testaments to musical achievement – most often manifests itself in couplings of the two composers *c.* 1790–1810 and in associations between either or both of them and Beethoven. In Vienna, publisher Johann Traeg's musical catalogue (1799) described Haydn and Mozart as 'our best masters'; the symphonic contributions to the *Liebhaber-Concerte* (1807–8) featured works exclusively by Haydn, Mozart and Beethoven, including repeat performances rather than works by other composers;[38] and public concerts between 1791 and 1810 included more than three times as many performances of Haydn's works, and almost twice as many of Mozart's and of Beethoven's, than performances of works by any other individual composer.[39] Elsewhere, too, individuals contributed, either self-consciously or inadvertently, to the ossification of the Haydn–Mozart–Beethoven triumvirate. Count Waldstein

35 See, H. C. Robbins Landon, *Haydn: Chronicle and Works. Haydn in England, 1791–1795* (London, 1976); Landon, *Chronicle 1796–1800*; David Wyn Jones, 'First Among Equals: Haydn and His Fellow Composers', in Caryl Clark (ed.), *The Cambridge Companion to Haydn* (Cambridge, 2005), p. 54.

36 *The Gentleman's Magazine*, 79/2 (1809), p. 678.

37 Giuseppe Carpani, *Le Haydine: lettere sulla vita e le opere del celebre maestro Giuseppe Haydn* (Milan, 1812), p. 3.

38 David Wyn Jones, *The Symphony in Beethoven's Vienna* (Cambridge, 2006), pp. 15, 128–9.

39 As determined from the 'Public Concert Calendar' in Mary Sue Morrow, *Concert Life in Haydn's Vienna* (Stuyvesant, NY, 1989), pp. 238–364.

famously sent Beethoven from Bonn to Vienna with the words 'you shall receive Mozart's spirit from Haydn's hands' ringing in his ears; Christian Gottlieb Neefe, Beethoven's teacher, commented even earlier (1783) that 'this youthful genius ... would surely become a second Wolfgang Amadeus Mozart were he to continue as he has begun'; Andreas Streicher, a well-known piano maker, wrote to Breitkopf & Härtel in 1803 of his 'long-held judgement that Beethoven will certainly effect a revolution in music like Mozart'; and the Leipzig-based *Allgemeine musikalische Zeitung* declared as 'generally known and quite evident' that 'the world owes to the Germans the grand, fullvoiced orchestral symphony – first to Haydn and Mozart. It is the embodiment of the supreme and most brilliant pinnacle of modern instrumental music.'[40] After attending a performance of string quartets on 15 December 1808, Johann Friedrich Reichardt issued a classic pronouncement on the relationship between the music of the three composers, Mozart building on Haydn's foundation and Beethoven on Mozart's:

> It was very interesting for me to observe in this succession [Haydn–Mozart–Beethoven] how the three true humorists, each according to his own individual nature, have further developed the genre. Haydn created it out of the pure, luminous fountain of his charming, original nature. In artlessness and cheerful humor he forever remains unique. Mozart's more robust nature and richer imagination gained further ground, and expressed in many a piece the heights and depths of his inner being. He was himself also more of a virtuoso in performance, and thus expected far more of the performers. In addition, he placed more importance in an artfully developed work, and thus built out of Haydn's charmingly imagined summerhouse his own palace. Beethoven settled down in this palace very early, and thus in order for him too to express his own nature in its own forms, he was left no choice but to build a bold and defiant tower on top of which no one could easily place anything more without breaking his neck.[41]

The impulse to historicize Haydn, Mozart and Beethoven's positions is no doubt representative of broader historiographical trends aimed at establishing and reinforcing the permanent nature of select contributions to the musical world; these trends include writings about music history in general (landmark histories by Charles Burney, John Hawkins, Jean-Baptiste De Laborde and

40 As given in the following secondary sources: Elliot Forbes (ed.), *Thayer's Life of Beethoven* (Princeton, NJ, 1967), vol. 1, p. 115; Maynard Solomon, *Beethoven* (New York, 1977), p. 26; Thomas Sipe, *Beethoven: Eroica Symphony* (Cambridge, 1998), p. 87; Brinkmann, 'In the Time of the *Eroica*', p. 14.

41 Translation from Wye Jamison Allanbrook in Leo Treitler (ed.), *Strunk's Source Readings in Music History, Revised Edition* (New York, 1998), p. 1036. For a discussion of E. T. A Hoffmann's comparisons of Haydn, Mozart and Beethoven, beginning with his famous essay on Beethoven's Fifth Symphony in the *Allgemeine musikalische Zeitung* (1810), see Mark Evan Bonds, *Music as Thought: Listening to the Symphony in the Age of Beethoven* (Princeton, NJ, 2006), pp. 34–6, 48–50, 56–7.

Johann Nikolaus Forkel date from the final decades of the eighteenth century), biographies of 'great' composers (J. S. Bach, Mozart, Michael Haydn and Joseph Haydn all received book-length biographies between 1790 and 1810, and Schubart, Grétry and Dittersdorf wrote lengthy memoirs in the same period) and the establishment of canons of musical works.[42] The three composers themselves contributed actively to historically based activities as well. Joseph Sonnleithner enlisted Haydn's editorial services for an extended project advertised in the September 1799 issue of the *Allgemeine musikalische Zeitung* as a 'History of Music in the Denkmählern from the older to the newest times. With the portraits of the most famous composers, according to an historical plan of Herr Doktor Forkel, Music Director at Göttingen under direction of the Herren, Georg Albrechtsberger, Kapellmeister at the Cathedral Church of Saint Stephan in Vienna, Joseph Haydn, Doctor of Music and Kapellmeister to Prince Esterhazy, and Anton Salieri, I. R. First Court Kapellmeister; edited by Joseph Sonnleithner.'[43] Haydn realized that it was a huge but worthy undertaking, as revealed in his letter of introduction for Sonnleithner to Johann Peter Salomon in London (18 May 1799): 'His musical project is one of the most interesting, but I fear that without the help and counsel of many people he will not be able to realize it.'[44] In the early 1780s in Vienna, Mozart went (in his own words) 'every Sunday at twelve o'clock to Baron van Swieten, where nothing is played but Handel and J. S. Bach. I am collecting at the moment the fugues of Handel and Bach – not only of [Johann] Sebastien, but also of [Carl Philip] Emanuel and [Wilhelm] Friedmann.'[45] At the suggestion of this influential diplomat, civil servant, court administrator and music lover, Mozart re-orchestrated four of Handel's works towards the end of his life – *Acis and Galatea*, K. 566 (1788), *Messiah*, K. 572 (1789), *Alexander's Feast*, K. 591 (1790) and *Ode for St Cecilia's Day*, K. 592 (1790). Niemetschek explained that van Swieten arranged private performances of Handel's works as they were 'too strong a diet for the more delicate taste of the day'; in his arrangements Mozart 'was able to give new life to Handel's noble ideas by his ardent feeling, and through the magic of his instrumentation to make them enjoyable to our

42 On canon formations relevant to late-eighteenth- and early-nineteenth-century contexts, see William Weber, 'The History of Musical Canon', and Mark Everist, 'Reception Theories, Canonic Discourses, and Musical Value', in Nicholas Cook and Everist (eds.), *Rethinking Music* (New York and Oxford, 1998), pp. 336–55, 378–402; see also Weber, *The Rise of Musical Classics in Eighteenth-Century England: A Study in Canon, Ritual, and Ideology* (Oxford, 1992). Thomas Tolley discusses late-eighteenth- and early-nineteenth-century biographies of musicians, focusing in particular on Carpani's biography of Haydn from 1812, in *Painting the Cannon's Roar: Music, the Visual Arts and the Rise of the Attentive Public in the Age of Haydn* (Aldershot and Burlington, VT, 2001), pp. 33–50.

43 As given in Landon, *Chronicle 1796–1800*, pp. 463–4.

44 Landon, *Chronicle 1796–1800*, p. 464.

45 Emily Anderson (ed. and trans.), *The Letters of Mozart and His Family*, 3rd edn. (London, 1985), p. 800 (letter of 10 April 1782).

own generation'.[46] Revising old works to render them comprehensible for a contemporary audience surely also accounts for Haydn's revisions to articulation markings in his Op. 20 string quartets (1772) for publication by Artaria in 1801.[47]

The imperative to update may also represent Beethoven's principal motivation for writing cadenzas for Mozart's Piano Concerto No. 20 in D minor K. 466 (WoO 58,1 and 58,2, *c.* 1809). In the first-movement cadenza in particular it is difficult to disagree that 'the touch, the rhetoric, is emphatically Beethoven's'.[48] But Beethovenian rhetoric on Mozart's territory (so to speak) is not necessarily redolent of an 'openly confrontational' attitude on Beethoven's part, revealing 'some deeper antipathy, difficult to define, but surely dyed in [his] lifelong struggle to conquer the rigorous self-control imposed by Mozartean example'.[49] To argue that the self-evident clash of aesthetics and styles is confrontational, we need to presume – but have no reason for so doing – that Beethoven and his contemporaries would have recognized this kind of passage as a throwing down of the gauntlet rather than as a move to update the work to accommodate contemporary tastes. Beethoven does not revise the text of Mozart's concerto in the same way that Mozart revises Handel or that old Haydn revises young Haydn, of course, but does demonstrate similar aesthetically, stylistically and historically based motivations. While Mozart's Viennese piano concertos of the 1780s assiduously balance grandeur (principally orchestral participation, but also piano–orchestra confrontations), brilliance (solo passagework) and intimate grandeur (piano–orchestra dialogue), Beethoven's piano concertos progressively tilt the stylistic scales in favour of grandeur and brilliance – the piano often assumes a grand presence, without relying on confrontational scenarios to do so, and integrates brilliant writing into expressions of grandeur.[50] The intimate grandeur of Mozart's piano–orchestra dialogue is still present in Beethoven's works, but often gives way to a general impression of intimacy unmediated by interaction (in the middle movements, in particular), or acts as a tame conduit to protracted brilliance, or at least is marginalized as a delineator of solo–orchestra relations.[51] And so it is with Beethoven's cadenza to K. 466. In the *pianissimo* statement of the second theme, for

46 Niemetschek, *Life of Mozart*, p. 40.

47 See Landon, *Chronicle 1796–1800*, pp. 549–50 for a brief discussion.

48 Richard Kramer, 'Cadenza contra Text: Mozart in Beethoven's Hands', *19th Century Music*, 15 (1991–2), p. 116.

49 Kramer, 'Cadenza contra Text', p. 128.

50 Simon P. Keefe, 'The Concerto from Mozart to Beethoven: Aesthetic and Stylistic Perspectives', in Keefe (ed.), *The Cambridge Companion to the Concerto* (Cambridge, 2005), pp. 70–92, esp. 79–92.

51 Keefe, 'The Concerto from Mozart to Beethoven', pp. 83–92.

example, the intimate manner of presentation – dialogue between the left and right hands – plays second fiddle to the remarkable key of presentation, B major, one that does not appear in Mozart's movement and that might indeed constitute an 'implausible key ... a misplaced locus for any of the principal themes' in a strictly Mozartean context.[52] In other words, the piano's distinctive sonic presence here is attributable much more to the tonal colouring than to the intimate presentation. In analogous fashion, the statement of the piano theme heard at the soloist's point of entry at the beginning of Mozart's solo exposition – where it features the intimate grandeur of piano–orchestra dialogue[53] – is soon lost to brazen virtuosity (see example 24.1, bars 43–59). The piano stutters over its quavers (bars 49–50) and symbolically asserts the primacy of brilliance over intimacy by using these exact same stuttered notes to launch a tirade of ascending and descending semiquavers. The ensuing succession of delicate lyricism (*piano*) and gushing virtuosity (*fortissimo*) reinforces the same hierarchy (example. 24.1). In his article on Beethoven in the *NHLT*, Gerber explains that readers sceptical about Reichardt's theory of Beethoven building on Haydn and Mozart's achievements should listen to Beethoven's Piano Concerto No. 3 in C minor, or at least consult the lengthy review of the work in the *Allgemeine musikalische Zeitung* (1805).[54] The reviewer in question pays particularly close attention to the first-movement coda, which 'excites the spirits ... through the excellent choice and treatment of the instruments'.[55] This passage neatly captures a fundamental aesthetic and stylistic difference between Beethoven's and Mozart's piano concertos – increasingly elaborate dialogue is not designed to render relations between piano and orchestra increasingly intimate (as in Mozart), but rather to contribute to a process and a goal that are entirely independent of piano–orchestra engagement (on this occasion, generating momentum towards the grand, climatic moment a few bars later).[56] Beethoven's cadenza is an even better encapsulation of his stylistic and aesthetic divergence from Mozart, played out as it is in Mozart's backyard. It is quite possible that Beethoven would have agreed with a later assessment of K. 466 and Mozart's piano concertos generally in the *Haude und Spenersche Zeitung* (1830): 'it was highly interesting to hear at last one of Mozart's pianoforte concertos [K. 466] again, which are remote from our modern virtuosi

52 Kramer, 'Cadenza contra Text', pp. 30–1.

53 Simon P. Keefe, *Mozart's Piano Concertos: Dramatic Dialogue in the Age of Enlightenment* (Woodbridge and Rochester, NY, 2001), pp. 81–2.

54 Gerber, *NHLT*, vol. 1, col. 316. For the review, see *Allgemeine musikalische Zeitung*, 7 (1804–5), cols. 445–57; trans. in Wayne Senner (ed.) and Robin Wallace (trans.), *The Critical Reception of Beethoven's Compositions by His German Contemporaries* (Lincoln, NE, 1999 and 2001), 2 vols., vol. 1, pp. 205–14.

55 *Allgemeine musikalische Zeitung*, 7 (1804–5), col. 450; trans. from Senner (ed.) and Wallace (trans.), *The Critical Reception*, vol. 1, p. 208.

56 See Keefe, 'The Concerto from Mozart to Beethoven', pp. 88–9.

Ex. 24.1. Ludwig van Beethoven, Cadenza to Mozart's Piano Concerto No. 20 in D minor, K. 466 first movement, WoO 58,1.

because there is not enough passage work in them';[57] for Beethoven, the emphasis on brilliance and grandeur in his K. 466 cadenza may have bridged the temporal and stylistic gap between 1785 and 1809. At any rate, the cadenza (viewed in relation to the surrounding concerto) constitutes Beethoven's most explicit historical statement about where the concerto had been, and to where it had progressed some twenty years later. By providing new material for an old work he demonstrates to his contemporaries that the old could continue to prove enjoyable and aesthetically relevant to the new, that an instrumental work from the not-too-distant past could assume historical rather than just transitory significance.

Imitation and popularity

The musical environment and values *c.* 1790–1810 that rendered Mozart, Haydn and Beethoven increasingly successful winners on the European stage resulted in many losers as well. Composers who intentionally or inadvertently found themselves associated with one of the three great figures had to tread a fine line. As we have seen, tutelage from Haydn or Mozart was regarded as a positive endorsement of an individual's potential; equally, too close a musical connection to one of the masters was highly undesirable. For imitation, especially of a cosmetic variety, was roundly condemned. Mozart himself suffered criticism in this respect in a review of one of his orchestral works in London's *Morning Chronicle* (14 November 1788): the work 'owed its success rather to the excellence of the band, than the merit of the composition. Sterne was an original writer, – Haydn is an original musician. It may be said of the imitators of the latter, as of the former, they catch a few oddities, as dashes – sudden pauses – and occasional prolixity, but scarcely a particle of feeling or sentiment.'[58] This type of invective soon died away in Mozart's case, but proliferated in discussions of works by other composers. Carl Friedrich Zelter's article 'Modest Enquiries to Modern Composers and Virtuosi' (*Bescheidene Anfragen an die modernsten Komponisten und Virtuosen*) in one of the earliest issues of the *Allgemeine musikalische Zeitung* (1798–9) sums up the problem in the adroit phrase 'the lion went in front, the tail came behind' (*Der Löwe ging voran, Der Schweif kam hinternach*). Citing individualistic, exciting practices in Mozart's and especially Haydn's music that were over-exploited by subsequent composers to the point of 'revulsion' (*Ekel*) – remote modulations, symphonic *Bizarrerien*, daring pedal points, use of trumpets and drums, for example – Zelter issued a passionate plea: 'Dear People, who want to do

57 Given in Gruber, *Mozart & Posterity*, p. 107. 58 See McVeigh, *Concert Life in London*, p. 128.

everything he [Haydn] does – consider this matter again! I can well believe that it pleases you: but you don't have to imitate it. Look at it just one more time; there is no noise and racket here! Look at it: it's truly not for you.'[59]

The premium placed upon creative genius and originality in the decades before and after 1800 partially explains resistance to imitation, but other factors contributed, too. A common criticism was that imitators mistook, or were incapable of separating, superficial stylistic features of a Haydn or Mozart work from its genuine essence. In 1790s London, audiences noted other composers 'adopting the manner of the master [Haydn] but not capturing the imaginative or intellectual substance'.[60] Asking his readers to 'appreciate [Mozart's] worth', Triest implores: 'may this appreciation never, here or there, be profaned by a blind, *vain rage for imitation*.' This, he continues, is a forlorn hope: 'In almost all the recent German operettas that are not composed in the tone of a Kasperle-theater [puppet-theatre] (and often even in these), the desire is audible to compose in a manner that is *Mozartish*. Quick, vehement digressions, huge finales and the use of all possible instruments for obbligato accompaniment – and presto, you have a piece *à la Mozart*. In other words the shallow and the shell are taken for the body, with little sense of the spirit that animated it.'[61] E. T. A. Hoffmann argued similarly a decade later (1811): 'Even good composers in recent times, fired by the works of Mozart, have made the dangerous mistake of confusing them with the creative inspiration itself, of taking the means of expression for the expression, and have thereby fallen into meaningless rhetoric.'[62] This, according to Hoffmann, accounted for the extremes of the opera under review (Ferdinando Paer's *Sofonisba*), even though Paer had actually done his homework and studied his Mozart. In any case, it was difficult for even a distantly derivative artist to achieve success when Haydn ranked as 'inimitable' (*unnachahmlich*) and Mozart as 'immortal', and when 'Beethoven's individuality is so complete that it suits him alone, and can find favour, also the most skilled imitation, in no-one'.[63]

Underlying much of the criticism is a belief that imitation of the masters represented a cheap and easy pitch for popularity. The Haydn obituary in *The Gentlemen's Magazine* (1809) identified the virtues of his benevolent, generous

59 *Allgemeine musikalische Zeitung*, 1 (1798–99), cols. 152–4. ('Lieben Leute, die ihr alles ihm gleich thun wollet – überlegt euch einmal diese Sache! Ich glaube wohl, dass es euch gefällt: aber ihr müsst's nich nachahmen. Sehet's euch nur noch einmal an; es ist hier nicht mit Lermen und Geräusch abgemacht! Sehet's es euch an: Eure Sache ist das wahrhaftig nicht.')

60 McVeigh, *Concert Life in London*, p. 162.

61 Triest, 'Remarks on the Development of the Art of Music', p. 366.

62 David Charlton (ed.), *E. T. A. Hoffmann's Musical Writings: Kreisleriana, The Poet and the Composer, Music Criticism*, trans. Martyn Clarke (Cambridge, 1989), p. 261.

63 See Gerber's article on Haydn in *NHLT*, col. 559; Schönfeld, 'Yearbook 1796', p. 302; *Allgemeine musikalische Zeitung*, 20 (1818), cols. 294–5, as given in Jones, *The Symphony in Beethoven's Vienna*, p. 183.

disposition and the pernicious way in which the modeller usurped the modelled in the popular imagination: 'Far from being actuated by the impulse of envy, he was never heard to speak of his numerous imitators, whose airy productions, more suited to the indolence of some, and the weak musical capacity of others, seemed to supplant the original in the public esteem, without allowing them all the merit they possessed.'[64] Triest's positive assessment of Hiller pointed out nonetheless that his 'popularization of music led ... to a certain retardation of the higher inner perception that it would probably have attained if it had descended only gradually to the popular level'; the association of the popular with qualitative impoverishment is unambiguous.[65]

Reactions to virtuosity and brilliance offer an interesting critical perspective on musical popularity at the turn of the century. Condemnation of excessive virtuosity – from the concerto soloist, above all – peppered late-eighteenth- and early-nineteenth-century writings, representing a point of continuity from one century to the next. The inference is clear: self-promoting (and self-regarding) composers and performers pander to the worst instincts of the musical public, appealing to their easy admiration of flashy musical trickery rather than their more sophisticated appreciation of expressive, content-rich music.[66] Composer and audience wallow in popular taste, and are thus equally responsible for acts of musical debasement. The line between performance dexterity and overly ostentatious brilliance, however, was a fine one – the former was as desirable as the latter was undesirable. Schönfeld's descriptions of Viennese musicians reflect the typical position at the turn of the century. Performers are praised for their speed and facility in fast passages, but reprimanded for seeking 'beauty in bombast, extreme speed and a superabundance of notes' and for putting 'speed before expression'.[67] Dexterity and brilliance must be a means to an end, rather than an end in itself, or at the very least complement other performance or compositional attributes; this aesthetic 'rule' applied across Europe. Thus, according to *The Times* (London), singers John Braham 'evinced a brilliance of execution, that kept pace with the genius of the composer' and Angelica Catalani possessed 'neatness and rapidity of execution' as well as 'delicacy' and a 'compass and quality of voice, and energy of manner' that were unrivalled;[68] Schönfeld explained that Fräulein von Seidschek 'as well as great speed ... shows much taste and feeling and uses a

64 *The Gentlemen's Magazine*, 79/2 (1809), p. 678.

65 Triest, 'Remarks on the Development of the Art of Music', p. 355.

66 Simon P. Keefe, 'Theories of the Concerto from the Eighteenth Century to the Present Day', in Keefe (ed.) *The Cambridge Companion to the Concerto*, pp. 8–11.

67 Schönfeld, 'Yearbook 1796', pp. 298, 296–7. Praise for performing speedily can be found *inter alia* on pp. 293, 297, 302, 306, 311, 313, 314.

68 *The Times*, No. 5980 (26 March 1804), p. 3; *The Times*, No. 6981 (25 February 1807), p. 2.

good deal of rubato' and that Johann Andreas Streicher 'while playing with great skill and speed ... never disregards lucidity and the most accurate expression'.[69] Channelling brilliance into appropriately profound expression was, indeed, an aesthetic requirement. In 1796, for Schönfeld, Beethoven 'is generally admired for his extraordinary speed and the ease with which he plays extremely difficult [music]. He seems recently to have entered deeper into the inner sanctum of music, and one notices this particularly in the precision, feeling and taste of his work.'[70] Likewise, a circumspect comparison in the *Allgemeine musikalische Zeitung* (1805–6) between a Mr Stein's performance of Mozart's piano concerto K. 466 and Mozart's own leaves no doubt as to the respective positions of brilliance and holistic expressivity in the aesthetic pecking order: while Stein's swift, precise, fiery and brilliant performance garnered acclaim, 'Mozart himself delivered this concerto with more seriousness and imposing dignity. With him the profound, rich spirit of the composition was more noticeable; with Stein, more the brilliant execution of the virtuoso.'[71]

The rise and fall of one composer, Ignaz Pleyel, attests particularly vividly to the ephemeral nature (and ultimate distrust) of easily achieved musical popularity at the end of the eighteenth and beginning of the nineteenth centuries, albeit not specifically in the context of brazen virtuosity. In the last decade or so of the eighteenth century Pleyel was probably the most famous musician in Europe: he surpassed all others in the number of publications of his works in musical centres such as London, Paris and Vienna, as well as in smaller locations, reflecting what Charles Burney called the 'rage' for his music;[72] innumerable editions of his string quartets appeared across Europe for vast public consumption (at least seventy for the Op. 1 set alone, including arrangements for keyboards, wind and even voice);[73] he took a starring role in London's Professional Concert series in 1791–2 in direct competition with his friend and erstwhile teacher Haydn and, accustomed to monetary windfalls,[74] was in the luxurious position of being able to be disgruntled with the huge £1,000 payment he received.[75] Alongside public acclaim – Gerber reports in the *HLT*

69 Schönfeld, 'Yearbook 1796', pp. 313, 314. 70 Schönfeld, 'Yearbook 1796', p. 293.

71 *Allgemeine musikalische Zeitung*, 8 (1805–6), col. 729. 'Mozart selbst dies Konzert mit mehr Ernst und imponirender Würde vortrug. Bey ihm wurde mehr der tiefe, reiche Geist der Komposition, bei Stein mehr der glänzende Vortrag des Virtuosen bemerkbar.'

72 See Charles Burney, *A General History of Music from the Earliest Ages to the Present Period (1789)*, ed. Frank Mercer (New York, 1957), 2 vols., vol. 2, pp. 951–2. For publication numbers, see Gruber, *Mozart & Posterity*, pp. 26–7.

73 See Rita Benton, *Ignace Pleyel: A Thematic Catalogue of His Compositions* (Stuyvesant, NY, 1977), pp. 99–162, esp. 99–105 (for Op. 1). See also Jiesoon Kim, 'Ignaz Pleyel and His Early String Quartets in Vienna', PhD dissertation (University of North Carolina, Chapel Hill, 1996), pp. 28–31.

74 Gerber points out how well paid Pleyel was in France in the 1780s; see *HLT*, vol. 2, col. 161.

75 McVeigh, *Concert Life in London*, p. 170.

that Pleyel's music was 'universally loved' in Germany, Italy and France[76] – came critical acclaim. As early as 1784 Mozart described Pleyel's Op. 1 string quartets as 'very well written and most pleasing to listen to' and continued – perhaps disingenuously given undoubtedly similar aspirations on his own part – that 'it will be a lucky day for music if later on Pleyel should be able to replace Haydn'.[77] The *Magazin der Musik* described him as 'young, spirited and very talented' (1786) and went further a year later (1787): 'He has composed some beautiful keyboard sonatas, which are impatiently asked for here [in Italy]. His agreeable melodies in them are not as difficult as Clementi's and Mozart's sorcery; he is more true to nature, without, however, violating the rules of composition.'[78] Heinrich Christoph Koch placed Pleyel alongside Haydn, Mozart and Hoffmeister as one of the exemplary quartet composers who 'enriched the public the most'.[79] And Georg Vogler reported (1793) that Pleyel 'imitated [Haydn's] great spirit [his breadth of vision and involvement of all instruments] in miniature, that is, fruitfully in quartets.'[80] Writers were also quick to point out, as with Haydn, that Pleyel was a most pleasant individual: musical and commercial popularity went hand-in-hand with personal popularity. He possessed a 'modest and agreeable' temperament, demonstrated 'marvellously agreeable conduct' and a 'congenial, cheery and moreover unassuming demeanour'.[81] So, Pleyel was a winner in every respect in the popularity stakes; to cap it all, shortly before his arrival in London in late 1791 the *Morning Herald* reported him 'becoming even more popular than his master [Haydn]; as his works are characterized less by the intricacies of science than the charm of simplicity and feeling'.[82]

But the very features eliciting praise and garnering popularity for Pleyel in the 1780s and much of the 1790s – the easy charm and simplicity – set the seeds for his subsequent demise. The *Allgemeine musikalische Zeitung* (1799), positioning itself as an arbiter of highbrow musical taste, delivered a stinging attack on Pleyel in a review of his piano trios published by Artaria: the works 'drag on

76 Gerber, *HLT*, col. 160. ('Dieser ist allgemein in Deutschland, Italien und Frankreich geliebte und geehrte junge Komponist'.)

77 Anderson (ed. and trans.), *Letters of Mozart and His Family*, p. 875 (letter of 24 April 1784). On relationships between Mozart's 'Haydn' Quartets and Pleyel's Op. 1 set, see Mark Evan Bonds, 'On Replacing Haydn: Mozart's "Pleyel" Quartets', *Music & Letters*, 88 (2007), pp. 201–25.

78 As given in Benton, *Ignace Pleyel: A Thematic Catalogue*, p. ix and Cliff Eisen, *New Mozart Documents: A Supplement to O. E. Deutsch's Documentary Biography* (London, 1991), pp. 47–8.

79 Heinrich Christoph Koch, *Introductory Essay on Composition: The Mechanical Rules of Melody, Sections 3 and 4* (1787–93), trans. Nancy Kovaleff Baker (New Haven, CT, 1983), p. 207.

80 Georg Vogler, *Verbesserungen der Forkel'schen Veränderungen über 'God Save the King'* (Frankfurt, 1793), p. 9. 'Sein [H's] Schueller: Pleyel ahmte diesem grossen Geist in Kleinen d.i. in Quartetten glücklich nach.'

81 Benton, *Ignace Pleyel: A Thematic Catalogue*, p. ix; Eisen, *New Mozart Documents*, p. 47; Gerber, *HLT*, vol. 2, col. 160 ('angenehmen, munter und dabei bescheidenen Betragens').

82 Landon, *Chronicle 1791–1795*, p. 108.

indefinitely' (*sie ziehen sich gewaltig in die Länge*), are 'actually only for the large houses of vulgar dilettantes' (*sind zwar nur für den grossen Hausen gemeinerer Dilettanten*) and 'distinguish themselves neither by anything new nor by anything else excellent' (*sie zeichnen sich doch ausserdem weder irgend etwas Neues, noch etwas sonst Vorzügliches aus*). More to the point, the reviewer explained, Pleyel was actually recycling old material: 'If this is not musical wretchedness, then there is no such thing. A shame, a great shame, that Mr. Pleyel in the process seems virtually to reach his goal by being a polygraph.'[83] The *Zeitung für die elegante Welt* (1805) was similarly unequivocal: Viennese salons devoted Sunday mornings and Fridays to 'true music', namely the quartets of Haydn, Mozart, Beethoven, Romberg and Wrantizsky; the easier keyboard music of Pleyel (and of Vanhall and Kozeluch), in contrast, was 'entirely out of style'.[84] Gerber's *HLT* contains only commendations for Pleyel, but the later *NHLT* is critical, citing his polygraph tendencies, the routine nature of his works, and qualitative lapses. After listing Pleyel's post-1790 works, moreover, Gerber threw up his hands at the idea of listing the innumerable arrangements: 'who wants to calculate all of them?'[85] Pleyel's extraordinary popularity, then, rendered him unpopular. Even later defenders tended to damn with faint praise. For Jérôme-Joseph de Momigny, reflecting on Pleyel's fall from grace, the composer's quartets were agreeable and easy to play – less profound than those of Haydn and Mozart, but distinct as well from the 'flat and petty' (*plate et mesquine*) music evident in the 1780s. While his fashionability had been 'surprised and deserved', he lost it through 'a powerful cabal [*une cabale puissante*] and through the advances of the Enlightenment' and started up his piano factory: 'he occupied himself with lining the hammers in order to perfect the sound. This reminds us, it seems to me, of those Roman generals who put down the sword to pick up the plough.'[86] The dye had been cast for Pleyel by the early years of the nineteenth century: popular and fashionable, his music was ephemeral. In contrast, Haydn's music, even when popular, demonstrated 'artful popularity [*kunstvolle Popularität*] or popular (easily comprehensible, effective) artfulness [*populäre Kunstfülle*]',[87] thus not detracting from its oft-cited historical import. Pleyel's music, it seems, was quickly consigned to the second of two categories identified by Koch in his essay 'Ueber den

83 *Allgemeine musikalische Zeitung*, 1 (1798–99), cols. 572–3. 'Wenn dies nicht eine musikalische Armseligkeit ist, so giebts gar keine. Schade, sehr schade, dass Hr. Pleyel schlecterdings seine Rechnung dabey zu finden scheint, den Polygraphen zu machen.'

84 From Morrow, *Concert Life in Haydn's Vienna*, p. 9.

85 Gerber, *NHLT*, cols. 735, 737.

86 Jérôme-Joseph de Momigny, 'Quatuor', in Pierre-Louis Ginguené, Nicholas-Etienne Framery and Momigny (eds.), *Encyclopédie méthodique: musique* (Paris, 1818; reprint New York, 1971), 2 vols., vol. 2, p. 298. ('il s'occupe lui-même à en garnir les marteaux pour en perfectionner le son. Cela rappelle, ce me semble, ces généraux romains qui déposoient le glaive pour prendre la charrue.')

87 Triest, 'Remarks on the Development of the Art of Music', p. 373.

Modegeschmack in der Tonkunst' (1795): 'True artistic beauties in works of fine art defy the ravages of time; the imagined beauties of fashion, however, lose their reality like a dream as soon as the fashion that favoured them changes.'[88] Irrespective of Koch's own views on Pleyel's music in the mid-1790s (he certainly had a high opinion of the string quartets a few years earlier), Pleyel has never recovered – deservedly or undeservedly – from his reputational nose-dive.

Pleyel stands as a salutary symbol for the forgotten (or almost forgotten) musical past, for the thousands of European composers diligently plying their trade at the turn of the nineteenth century who were soon airbrushed from music history. Ultimately, it matters not whether twenty-first-century musicians collectively re-rate someone like Pleyel as a discarded gem, a musical charlatan, or even – to follow Salieri's cruel self-mockery in Peter Schafer and Milos Forman's *Amadeus* – a 'patron saint of mediocrities'; all that is important is that more music from the period is exposed, especially music achieving localized or widespread popularity at the time of composition. We cannot lose by listening to more, by re-embracing the one-time musically popular. In all probability we will discover misplaced pearls, best-forgotten fake diamonds and numerous gradations of musical jewel in between. Whatever the case may be we gain immeasurably – in our knowledge of tastes of the time, of the *lingua franca* and regional stylistic predilections (such as they were), of the contextual framework through which value judgements were made. Significant advances have occurred in this area of research in recent times, but much more work remains.

In the seedy atmosphere of a mid-twentieth-century Vienna reeling, just as 140 years earlier, from the cataclysmic effects of military conflict, one of cinema's notorious villains, *The Third Man*'s Harry Lime, issued a famous historical proclamation:

> In Italy for thirty years under the Borgias they had warfare, terror, murder and bloodshed, but they produced Michelangelo, Leonardo da Vinci and the Renaissance. In Switzerland, they had brotherly love; they had five hundred years of democracy and peace – and what did that produce? The cuckoo clock.

1790–1810, indeed, had its Napoleon, its reign of terror, its deep-seated political and fiscal uncertainties and its military barbarity, yet it produced music – and supported musical cultures – of the most glorious kinds. The

88 Koch, 'Ueber den Modegeschmack in der Tonkunst', *Journal der Tonkunst*, 1 (1795), cols. 63–4, as given in David Gramit, 'Selling the Serious: The Commodification of Music and Resistance to it in Germany, circa 1800', in William Weber (ed.), *The Musician as Entrepreneur, 1700–1914: Managers, Charlatans, and Idealists* (Bloomington, IN, 2004), p. 87.

first casualty of war may be truth, but the arts, and artists in general, are understandably high on the conceptual casualty list as well. The rampant inflation of the war years 1790–1815 and the re-direction of expenditure from 'luxury' activities to war-related activities hit musicians hard.[89] Yet they collectively weathered the storm, contributing to the kind of quiet aesthetic revolutions that were 'almost unnoticed by the noisy rabble at the time', according to Friedrich Schlegel in his 'Athenäums-Fragment' (1798).[90] Perhaps many precariously placed musicians at the turn of the century – in the spirit of Count Zinzendorf's diary entry at the end of 1799 – longed for a better life in the nineteenth century than the life they had experienced at the very end of the eighteenth, but they could scarcely have yearned for richer or more vibrant musical cultures. The brightest of musical pasts and presents guaranteed the brightest of musical futures.

Select Bibliography

Allgemeine musikalische Zeitung, ed. Friedrich Rochlitz *et al.* Leipzig, 1798–1848

Anderson, Emily (ed. and trans.). *The Letters of Mozart and His Family*. 3rd edn., London, 1985

Benton, Rita. *Ignace Pleyel: A Thematic Catalogue of His Compositions*. Stuyvesant, NY, 1977

Bonds, Mark Evan. 'Idealism and Aesthetics of Instrumental Music at the Turn of the Nineteenth Century'. *Journal of the American Musicological Society*, 50 (1997), pp. 387–420

Music as Thought: Listening to the Symphony in the Age of Beethoven. Princeton, NJ, 2006

Brinkmann, Reinhold. 'In the Time of the *Eroica*'. In Scott Burnham and Michael P. Steinberg (eds.), *Beethoven and His World*. Princeton, NJ, 2000, pp. 1–26

Burney, Charles. *A General History of Music from the Earliest Ages to the Present Period (1789)*, ed. Frank Mercer. 2 vols., New York, 1957

Charlton, David (ed.). *E. T. A. Hoffmann's Musical Writings: Kreisleriana, The Poet and the Composer, Music Criticism*. Trans. Martyn Clarke, Cambridge, 1989

Choron, A. and F. Fayolle. *Dictionnaire historique des musicians.*, 2 vols., Paris, 1810–1

89 On hardships – financial and otherwise – for musicians in London, see McVeigh, *Concert Life in London* and Deborah Rohr, *The Careers of British Musicians, 1750–1850: A Profession of Artisans* (Cambridge, 2001). The *Allgemeine musikalische Zeitung*, 3 (1800), cols. 68–9 identifies contemporary economic difficulties for Viennese musicians.

90 See Schlegel, 'Athenäums-Fragment', in *Philosophical Fragments*, trans. Peter Firchow (Minneapolis, MN, 1991), p. 46. As Schlegel explained: 'The French Revolution, Fichte's philosophy, and Goethe's *Meister* are the greatest tendencies of this era. Whoever is offended by this juxtaposition, whoever cannot take any revolution seriously that isn't noisy and materialistic, hasn't yet achieved a lofty, broad perspective on the history of mankind. Even in our shabby histories of civilization ... many a little book, almost unnoticed by the noisy rabble at the time, plays a greater role than anything they did.' This quotation is used as the point of departure for Brinkmann in his study of the 'Eroica' Symphony, 'In the Time of the *Eroica*'.

Deathridge, John. 'The Invention of German Music, *c.* 1800'. In Tim Blanning and Hagen Schulze (eds.), *Unity and Diversity in European Culture c. 1800*. Oxford, 2006, pp. 35–60

Eisen, Cliff. *New Mozart Documents: A Supplement to O. E. Deutsch's Documentary Biography*. London, 1991

Everist, Mark. 'Reception Theories, Canonic Discourses, and Musical Value'. In Nicholas Cook and Everist (eds.), *Rethinking Music*. New York and Oxford, 1998, pp. 378–402

DeNora, Tia. *Beethoven and the Construction of Genius: Musical Politics in Vienna, 1792–1803*. Berkeley and Los Angeles, 1995

Deutsch, Otto Erich. *Mozart: A Documentary Biography*. Trans. Eric Blom, Peter Branscombe and Jeremy Noble, 2nd edn., London, 1990

Gerber, Ernst Ludwig. *Historisch-biographisches Lexicon der Tonkünstler*. 2 vols., Leipzig, 1790, 1792

Neues historisch-biographisches Lexicon der Tonkünstler. 4 vols., Leipzig, 1812–4

Ginguené, Pierre-Louis, Nicholas-Etienne Framery and Jérôme-Joseph de Momigny (eds.). *Encyclopédie méthodique: musique*. 2 vols., Paris, 1818; reprint New York, 1971

Gramit, David. 'Selling the Serious: The Commodification of Music and Resistance to it in Germany, circa 1800'. In William Weber (ed.), *The Musician as Entrepreneur, 1700–1914: Managers, Charlatans, and Idealists*. Bloomington, IN, 2004, pp. 81–101

Gruber, Gernot. *Mozart & Posterity*. Trans. R. S. Furness, London, 1991

Hosler, Bellamy. *Changing Aesthetic Views of Instrumental Music in 18th-Century Germany*. Ann Arbor, MI, 1981

Jones, David Wyn. 'First Among Equals: Haydn and His Fellow Composers'. In Caryl Clark (ed.), *The Cambridge Companion to Haydn*. Cambridge, 2005, pp. 45–57

The Symphony in Beethoven's Vienna. Cambridge, 2006

Keefe, Simon P. *Mozart's Piano Concertos: Dramatic Dialogue in the Age of Enlightenment*. Woodbridge and Rochester, NY, 2001

'The Concerto from Mozart to Beethoven: Aesthetic and Stylistic Perspectives'. In Keefe (ed.), *The Cambridge Companion to the Concerto*. Cambridge, 2005, pp. 70–92

Mozart's Viennese Instrumental Music: A Study of Stylistic Re-Invention. Woodbridge and Rochester, NY, 2007

Kramer, Richard. 'Cadenza contra Text: Mozart in Beethoven's Hands'. *19th Century Music*, 15 (1991–2), pp. 116–31

Landon, H. C. Robbins. *Haydn: Chronicle and Works. Haydn in England, 1791–1795*. London, 1976

Haydn: Chronicle and Works. The Years of 'The Creation', 1796–1800. London, 1977

McVeigh, Simon. *Concert Life in London from Mozart to Haydn*. Cambridge, 1993

Morrow, Mary Sue. *Concert Life in Haydn's Vienna*. Stuyvesant, NY, 1989

German Music Criticism in the Late Eighteenth Century: Aesthetic Issues in Instrumental Music. Cambridge, 1997

Niemetschek, Franz Xaver. *Lebensbeschreibung des k. k. Kapellmeisters Wolfgang Amadeus Mozart (1808)*. Ed. Peter Krause, Leipzig, 1978. First edn. (1798) trans. Helen Mautner as *Life of Mozart*, London, 1956

Rohr, Deborah. *The Careers of British Musicians, 1750–1850: A Profession of Artisans*. Cambridge, 2001

Schlegel, Friedrich. 'Athenäums-Fragment'. In *Philosophical Fragments*. Trans. Peter Firchow, Minneapolis, MN, 1991

Schönfeld, Johann Ferdinand Ritter von. 'A Yearbook of the Music of Vienna and Prague, 1796'. Trans. Kathrine Talbot. In Elaine Sisman (ed.), *Haydn and His World*. Princeton, NJ, 1997, pp. 289–320

Senner, Wayne (ed.) and Robin Wallace (trans.). *The Critical Reception of Beethoven's Compositions by His German Contemporaries*. 2 vols., Lincoln, NE, 1999 and 2001

Sipe, Thomas. *Beethoven: Eroica Symphony*. Cambridge, 1998

Solomon, Maynard. *Beethoven*. New York, 1977

Stanley, Glenn (ed.). *The Cambridge Companion to Beethoven*. Cambridge, 2000

Tolley, Thomas. *Painting the Cannon's Roar: Music, the Visual Arts and the Rise of the Attentive Public in the Age of Haydn*. Aldershot and Burlington, VT, 2001

Treitler, Leo (ed.). *Strunk's Source Readings in Music History, Revised Edition*. New York, 1998

Triest, Johann Karl Friedrich. 'Remarks on the Development of the Art of Music in Germany in the Eighteenth Century'. In Elaine Sisman (ed.), *Haydn and His World*. Princeton, NJ, 1997, pp. 321–94

Vogler, Georg. *Verbesserungen der Forkel'schen Veränderungen über 'God Save the King'*. Frankfurt, 1793

Weber, William. *The Rise of Musical Classics in Eighteenth-Century England: A Study in Canon, Ritual, and Ideology*. Oxford, 1992

'The History of Musical Canon'. In Nicholas Cook and Mark Everist (eds.), *Rethinking Music*. New York and Oxford, 1998, pp. 336–55

· APPENDIX I ·

Chronology

DAVID BLACK

Year	Works/Musical Writings	Musical Events	Other Artistic	Historical/Scientific
1700	Corelli: *XII Suonati a violino e violone o cimbalo*, Op. 5 Albinoni: *Sinfonie e concerti*, Op. 2 Kuhnau: *Musicalische Vorstellung einiger biblischer Historien*	Inventory of Medici family documents first piano	Dryden: *Fables, Ancient and Modern*	Great Northern War begins (–1721). Control of Spain passes from Hapsburgs to Bourbons.
1701	Marais: *Pièces de viole, deuxième livre* Muffat: *Auserlesene mit Ernst- und Lust-gemengte Instrumental-Musik*	Philharmonic Society established in Ljubljana	Rigaud: *Louis XIV* Dennis: *The Advancement and Reformation of Modern Poetry*	War of Spanish Succession begins (–1714). Act of Settlement establishes Hanoverian succession in England. Frederick I becomes King of Prussia.
1702	Campra: *Tancrède* Charpentier: *Judicium salomonis* Fischer: *Ariadne musica*	Telemann becomes director of Leipzig opera and founds Collegium Musicum	Mather: *Magnalia Christi Americana*	First regular English-language newspaper, *The Daily Courant*, begins publication. Amontons introduces concept of absolute zero.
1703	D. Scarlatti: *Il Giustino* Brossard: *Dictionnaire de musique*	Vivaldi appointed *maestro di violino* at Pio Ospedale della Pietà	Schlüter: *Elector Frederick William on Horseback*	St Petersburg founded by Peter the Great. Isaac Newton becomes President of Royal Society.
1704	*Dandrieu: *Livre de clavecin* Gasparini: *La fede tradita e vendicata*	Handel and Mattheson duel in Hamburg	Galland: *Les mille et une nuits* (–1717)	British and Dutch capture Gibraltar from the Spanish. Newton: *Opticks* Stanislaus Lesczcynski elected King of Poland.

Year	Music	Musical events	Arts	History and science
1705	Handel: *Almira, Königin von Castilien* Buxtehude: *Castrum doloris*, *Templum honoris* A. Scarlatti: *Al fin m'ucciderete*	Bach walks to Lübeck to visit Buxtehude	Addison: *Remarks on Several Parts of Italy*	Halley correctly predicts return of comet.
1706	Rameau: *Premier livre de Pièces de Clavecin* Marais: *Alcyone*	Corelli, Pasquati and A. Scarlatti admitted to Arcadian Academy in Rome	Dome des Invalides, Paris, completed	*The Evening Post*, first evening paper, issued in London.
1707	Albinoni: Concerti a cinque, Op. 5 A. Scarlatti: *Cain, overo Il primo omicidio* Handel: *Dixit Dominus*	Handel arrives in Rome	Watts: *Hymns and Spiritual Songs*	Act of Union between England and Scotland.
1708	Bach: *Gott ist mein König* Handel: *La Resurrezione*	J. S. Bach appointed organist at Weimar	St Paul's Cathedral, London, completed	Merger of British East India and New East India companies.
1709	Torelli: Concerti grossi, Op. 8 Handel: *Agrippina* Caldara: *Chi s'arma di virtù*	Volumier appointed leader of the Dresden *Kapelle*	Meissen porcelain factory established in Saxony	Darby produces coke-smelted cast iron at Coalbrooke.
1710	Clérambault: *Premier livre d'orgue* Pepusch: Six English Cantatas	First mention of clarinet, in a order from the Nuremberg maker Jacob Denner	Versailles Chapel completed	First copyright legislation, the *Statute of Anne*, becomes effective in Britain.
1711	Keiser: *Croesus* Handel: *Rinaldo* Vivaldi: *L'estro armonico*, Op. 3	John Shore invents tuning fork	Pope: *An Essay on Criticism* Schloss Schönbrunn, Vienna, completed	French capture Rio de Janeiro from Portuguese.
1712	Keiser: *Brockes-Passion*	Early use of 'hairpin' dynamics in Piani's Sonatas Op. 1	Castle Howard, Yorkshire, completed	First commercially successful steam engine developed by Newcomen.

Year	Works/Musical Writings	Musical Events	Other Artistic	Historical/Scientific
1713	Couperin: *Pieces de clavecin, premier livre* Vivaldi: *Ottone in villa* Handel: Utrecht Te Deum	Dance school established at Paris Opéra	Carey: *Poems on Several Occasions*	Peace of Utrecht between Britain, France, Holland, Savoy, Portugal and Prussia.
1714	Corelli: 12 Concerti Grossi, Op. 6 Bach: *Nun komm der Heiden Heiland*	Bach promoted to Konzertmeister in Weimar	Pope: *The Rape of the Lock*	Mercury thermometer invented by Fahrenheit. British parliament establishes Board of Longitude.
1715	Bononcini: *Astarto* Telemann: *Six Sonates à violon seul*	Fux becomes Hofkapellmeister in Vienna	Lesage: *Gil Blas* (–1735)	Death of Louis XIV. Unsuccessful Jacobite uprising in Britain.
1716	Couperin: *L'art de toucher le clavecin* Vivaldi: *Juditha triumphans*	Pisendel studies with Vivaldi in Venice	Construction of Boston Light, the first lighthouse in the United States	Prince Eugene of Savoy defeats Turks at Petrovaradin.
1717	Lotti: *Giove in Argo* *A. Marcello: Oboe Concerto in D minor Handel: *Water Music*	Bach becomes Kapellmeister in Cöthen	Watteau: *The Embarkation for Cythera*	Grand Lodge in London established, beginning modern history of Freemasonry.
1718	Handel: Chandos Anthems	Quantz settles in Dresden	Installation of *Twelve Apostles* at San Giovanni in Laterano, Rome Establishment of Studley Royal Water Garden, Yorkshire	Founding of New Orleans.

1719	Fux: *Elisa* Weiß: Fantasia in C minor	D. Scarlatti appointed *mestre* in Lisbon	Defoe: *Robinson Crusoe*	Prussia conducts Europe's first systematic census.
1720	Marcello: *Il teatro alla moda* Bach: *Sei Solo a Violino senza Baßo*	Debut of Farinelli in Naples	Church of St John Nepomuk, Zelená Hora, completed	Share price of slave-trading South Sea Company collapses in 'South Sea Bubble'.
1721	Bach: *Brandenburg Concertos* A. Scarlatti: *La Griselda* *Zelenka: Six Sonatas	Telemann becomes director of music in Hamburg	Fischer von Erlach: *Entwurf einer historischen Architektur*	Lady Mary Wortley Montagu introduces variolation against smallpox.
1722	Bach: *Das Wohltemperirte Clavier, Erster Theil* Albinoni: Concerti a cinque, Op. 9 Rameau: *Traité de l'harmonie*	Rameau moves to Paris from Clermont	Defoe: *Moll Flanders*	Habeas Corpus Act suspended following discovery of Jacobite plot against George I.
1723	Bach: *Magnificat* Fux: *Costanza e fortezza* Tosi: *Opinioni de' cantori antichi e moderni*	Bach becomes Thomaskantor in Leipzig	Belvedere Palace, Vienna, completed	Louis XV attains majority.
1724	Handel: *Giulio Cesare* Bach: St John Passion Marcello: *Estro poetico-armonico*	Metastasio writes his first original opera libretto, *Didone abbandonata*	Huysum: *Bouquet of Flowers in an Urn*	Philip V of Spain abdicates but is forced to resume throne after the death of his son.
1725	Fux: *Gradus ad Parnassum* Vivaldi: *Il cimento dell'armonia e dell'inventione*, Op. 8 Telemann: *Pimpinone*	Concert Spirituel established in Paris	Vico: *Principi di Scienza Nuova* *Blenheim Palace, Oxfordshire, completed	Guy's Hospital opens in London.
1726	Muffat: *72 Versetl sammt 12 Toccaten* Telemann: *Harmonischer Gottes-Dienst*	Academy of Vocal Music (later, Academy of Ancient Music) founded in London	Swift: *Gulliver's Travels*	Alliance of Russia and Austria against Ottoman Empire.

Year	Works/Musical Writings	Musical Events	Other Artistic	Historical/Scientific
1727	*Bach: St Matthew Passion Handel: Coronation Anthems	Faustina Bordoni and Francesca Cuzzoni fight onstage at performance of Bononcini's *Astianatte*	Menshikov Palace, St Petersburg, completed.	Coronation of George II in London.
1728	Gay: *The Beggar's Opera* Heinichen: *Der General-Bass in der Composition*	Pisendel succeeds Volumier as leader of Dresden *Kapelle*	Pope: *The Dunciad*	Vitus Bering discovers Bering Strait.
1729	*Bach: *Der Streit zwischen Phoebus und Pan*	Bach takes up directorship of *Telemannische Collegium Musicum*	Swift: *A Modest Proposal* Canaletto: *The Stonemason's Yard*	Founding of Baltimore.
1730	*Bach: Six Trio Sonatas, BWV 525–530 Hasse: *Artaserse* Vinci: *Alessandro nell'Indie*	Hasse appointed Kapellmeister in Dresden	Gottsched: *Versuch einer kritischen Dichtkunst für die Deutschen* Marivaux: *Le jeu de l'amour et du hasard* Basilica and Convent at Mafra National Palace, Portugal, completed	Prince Frederick of Prussia (later Frederick the Great) attempts to flee to England, but is imprisoned by his father.
1731	Bach: *Clavier-Übung, Erster Theil* Hasse: *Cleofide*	Completion of Royal Theatre in Mantua	Hogarth: *A Harlot's Progress* Prévost: *Manon Lescaut*	Protestants expelled from Salzburg by Prince Archbishop Firmian.

1732	Handel: *Orlando* Geminiani: Concerti Grossi, Op. 2–3 Walther: *Musicalisches Lexicon* Giustini: *Sonate da cimbalo di piano e forte*	Opening of Theatre Royal, Covent Garden	Canaletto: *View of the Entrance to the Venetian Arsenal*	Colony of Georgia established.
1733	Pergolesi: *La serva padrona* Rameau: *Hippolyte et Aricie* Porpora: *Arianna in Naxo* Telemann: *Musique de table* Locatelli: *L'arte del violino*, Op. 3	Geminiani visits Paris on concert tour	Hogarth: *A Rake's Progress*	War of Polish Succession begins. John Kay invents flying shuttle.
1734	Handel: Concerti Grossi, Op. 3	C. P. E. Bach moves to Frankfurt from Leipzig	Voltaire: *Lettres philosophiques* Pope: *An Essay on Man*	Spanish army under Don Carlos conquers Naples.
1735	Bach: *Clavier-Übung, Zweiter Theil* Pergolesi: *Stabat Mater* Rameau: *Les Indes galantes* Handel: *Alcina* Hasse: *La clemenza di Tito*	Zelenka styled Kirchen Compositeur in Dresden	*Chardin: *Boy with a top* Facade of San Giovanni in Laterano, Rome, completed	Russians capture Danzig (Gdansk) from the Polish.
1736	Mizler: *Neu eröffnete musikalische Bibliothek* Araja: *La gara dell'amore e del zelo*	Italian opera troupe established in St Petersburg	Euler: *Mechanica*	Stanislaus I of Poland abdicates. John Harrison completes first marine chronometer for timing longitude.
1737	Rebel: *Les elemens* Leo: *L'olimpiade*	Opening of Teatro San Carlo in Naples	van Loo: *Halte de chasse* Completion of Karlskirche, Vienna and St Nicholas Church, Prague	Direct male line of Medici becomes extinct on death of last Grand Duke, Gian Gastone.

Year	Works/Musical Writings	Musical Events	Other Artistic	Historical/Scientific
1738	Telemann: *Nouveaux quatuors en six suites* *Bach: Harpsichord Concerti, BWV 1052–1058 Scheibe: *Der critische Musikus* D. Scarlatti: *Essercizi per gravicembalo*	Vaucanson presents automated flute-player to French Academy of Sciences	Voltaire: *Sept Discours en Vers sur l'Homme* Bernoulli: *Hydrodynamica*	John Wesley returns to England from Georgia; beginnings of Methodism.
1739	Mattheson: *Der vollkommene Capellmeister* Bach: *Clavier-Übung*, *Dritter Theil* Muffat: *Componimenti musicali*	*Haydn recruited to become choirboy at St Stephen's Cathedral, Vienna	Boucher: *The Breakfast* Hume: *A Treatise of Human Nature*	Foundling Hospital created by royal charter in London.
1740	Handel: Concerti Grossi, Op. 6 Monn: Symphony in D L. Mozart: *Sonate per chiesa e da camera* Zelenka: *Missa Dei Patris*	*C. P. E. Bach enters Frederick the Great's service	Richardson: *Pamela*	War of the Austrian Succession begins (–1748).
1741	Bach: *Clavier-Übung*, *Vierter Theil (Goldberg Variations)* Handel: *Messiah*	Graun appointed Kapellmeister in Berlin	*Longhi: *La lezione di danza* Branicki Palace, Warsaw, completed	Russia begins settling Aleutian Islands.
1742	Hasse: *I pellegrini al sepolcro di Nostro Signore* C. P. E. Bach: 'Prussian' Sonatas Graun: *Cleopatra e Cesare*	Durante becomes *primo maestro* at Conservatorio di S. Maria di Loreto in Naples	Young: *Night Thoughts*	Anders Celsius proposes temperature scale.
1743	Handel: *Samson*	*Grosses Concert* founded in Leipzig	Batoni: *The Ecstasy of Saint Catherine of Siena*	Founding of American Philosophical Society and University of Erlangen.

1744	*Bach: *Das Wohltemperirte Clavier, Zweiter Theil* Veracini: *Sonate accademiche*, Op. 2	Moravian settlers establish *Collegium Musicum* in Bethlehem, PA	Completion of Residenz, Würzburg Tiepolo: *The Banquet of Cleopatra*	France declares war on Britain and Austria.
1745	Leclair: 6 Violin Concertos, Op. 10	J. Stamitz awarded title Konzertmeister in Mannheim	Piranesi: *Carceri d'invenzione*	Failed Jacobite rebellion in Britain. Frederick the Great begins planning Sanssouci.
1746	Durante: Requiem in C Minor	W. F. Bach appointed organist at *Liebfrauenkirche*, Halle	Gellert: *Fabeln und Erzählungen*	Jean-Étienne Guettard makes first geological map.
1747	Forqueray: *Pièces de viole* Galuppi: *Adamo* Bach: *Musikalisches Opfer*	Bach visits Berlin, meets Frederick the Great	Muratori: *Della regolata devozione dei cristiani* Founding of Załuski Library, Warsaw	Marggraf isolates sugar from beets.
1748	Dehesse/Guillemain: *L'opérateur chinois* Gluck: *La Semiramide riconosciuta* Alberti: *VIII sonate per cembalo*, Op. 1	Renovated Burgtheater opens in Vienna	Montesquieu: *L'esprit des lois* Richardson: *Clarissa* Hume: *An Enquiry Concerning Human Understanding*	Excavations begin at Pompeii.
1749	*Bach: *Mass in B minor* Handel: *Music for the Royal Fireworks*	Haydn leaves St Stephen's Cathedral, becomes freelance musician in Vienna	Oudry: *Clara le Rhinoceros* Fielding: *Tom Jones* Buffon: *Histoire naturelle, générale et particulière* (–1778)	Jacob Rodrigue Péreire invents a sign language for deaf-mutes.

Year	Works/Musical Writings	Musical Events	Other Artistic	Historical/Scientific
1750	Hasse: *La conversione di Sant'Agostino* Handel: *Theodora* Galuppi: *Il mondo alla roversa*	Handel makes final visit to the Continent, travelling to The Netherlands and Germany	Cleland: *Fanny Hill* Gray: *Elegy Written in a Country Churchyard* Bellotto: *New Market Square in Dresden*	Population of Europe reaches 140 million.
1751	Hasse: Mass in D minor Geminiani: *The Art of Playing on the Violin*	Reutter appointed Hofkapellmeister in Vienna	First volume of the *Encyclopédie* Haywood: *The History of Miss Betsy Thoughtless* Boucher: *The Toilet of Venus* Completion of Hofkirche, Dresden	Reform to British calendar establishes 1 January as New Year's Day.
1752	Quantz: *Versuch einer Anweisung die Flöte traversiere zu spielen* Rousseau: *Le devin du village* Wagenseil: Cello Concerto in A	*Querelle des Bouffons* begins in Paris	Voltaire: *Micromégas* Lennox: *The Female Quixote*	Dalibard and Franklin show that lightning is electrical.
1753	Mondonville: *Titon et l'Aurore* Marpurg: *Abhandlung von der Fuge* C. P. E. Bach: *Versuch über die wahre Art das Clavier zu spielen (I)* Jommelli: *Attilio Regolo*	*Hampel and Werner develop *Inventionshorn*	Tiepolo paints frescoes at Würzburg *Residenz* Linnaeus: *Species plantarum*	Founding of British Museum. Leipzig reaches peak eighteenth-century population of 32,384.
1754	Galuppi: *Il filosofo di campagna* Holzbauer: *La Passione de Gesù Cristo*	Jommelli appointed Oberkapellmeister in Stuttgart	Completion of Holy Trinity Column, Olomouc and *Wieskirche*, Steingaden	Founding of St Andrews Royal and Ancient Golf Club, Scotland.

1755	Graun: *Der Tod Jesu* Galuppi: *La diavolessa* Araja: *Tsefal i Prokris* Algarotti: *Saggio sopra l'opera in musica*	J. C. Bach departs Berlin, arrives in Milan	Johnson: *A Dictionary of the English Language* Winckelmann: *Gedanken über die Nachahmung der griechischen Werke* Place Stanislas, Nancy, completed	Lisbon earthquake destroys city and kills up to 90,000.
1756	*Haydn: *Salve regina* in E L. Mozart: *Versuch einer gründlichen Violinschule* Jommelli: Requiem in E flat	Swedish government bans import of musical instruments to encourage native builders	Butler: *The Lives of the Fathers, Martyrs and Other Principal Saints* (–1759)	Seven Years' War begins (–1763).
1757	Graun: *Te Deum* J. Stamitz: 6 Symphonies, Op. 2 Agricola: *Anleitung zur Singekunst*	*Michael Haydn leaves Vienna for Grosswardein	Burke: *A Philosophical Enquiry into the Origin of Our Ideas of the Sublime and Beautiful*	Robert-François Damiens is quartered and burned at the stake after attempted assassination of Louis XV.
1758	Adlung: *Anleitung zu der musikalischen Gelahrtheit* Richter: 3 Symphonies, Op. 10 Avison: 12 Concertos, Op. 6	Clarinettists first engaged at Mannheim	Baumgarten: *Aesthetica* Linnaeus: *Systema naturae* Boscovich: *Theoria philosophiae naturalis*	Jedediah Strutt invents machine to manufacture hose.
1759	Hopkinson: *My Days Have Been So Wondrous Free* *Haydn: Symphony no. 1 Gluck: *Le diable à quatre* Traetta: *Ippolito ed Aricia*	J. C. F. Bach appointed Konzertmeister in Bückeburg	Voltaire: *Candide* Sterne: *Tristram Shandy* (–1767)	Lomonosov states that topography of earth is the result of slow natural activity.

Year	Works/Musical Writings	Musical Events	Other Artistic	Historical/Scientific
1760	Hasse: *Alcide al bivio* Piccinni: *La buona figliuola* J. C. Bach: *Artaserse* Gossec: *Grande Messe des morts*	*Vanhal moves to Vienna from Nemyčeves	Greuze: *The Village Betrothal* Macpherson: *Fragments of Ancient Poetry*	Russians occupy Berlin. Frederick the Great defeats Austrians at Leignitz and Torgau.
1761	Haydn: Symphonies *Le matin, Le midi*, *Le soir* Martini: *Storia della musica (I)*	Haydn appointed Vice-Kapellmeister to Prince Esterházy	Rousseau: *Julie, ou la nouvelle Héloïse* Morgagni: *De sedibus et causis morborum per anatomem indagatis*	Joseph Black conducts experiments on latent heat.
1762	C. P. E. Bach: *Versuch über die wahre Art das Clavier zu spielen (II)* Gluck: *Orfeo ed Eurydice* Arne: *Artaxerxes* Telemann: *Der Tag des Gerichts*	J. C. Bach moves to London	Hamann: *Aesthetica in nuce* Rousseau: *Émile*, *Du contrat social*	Murder of Tsar Peter III, accession of Catherine the Great.
1763	Rameau: *Les Boréades* Eckard: 6 Sonatas, Op. 1 Traetta: *Ifigenia in Tauride*	Mozart begins Grand Tour with his family (–1766)	Febronius: *De statu Ecclesiæ et legitima potestate Romani pontificis* Completion of Villa Albani, Rome	Frederick the Great establishes village schools in Prussia.
1764	Gaviniés: 6 Violin Concertos, Op. 4 Flagg: *A Collection of the Best Psalm Tunes*	Leclair murdered in Paris, most likely by his nephew	Winckelmann: *Geschichte der Kunst des Altertums* Beccaria: *Dei delitti e delle pene* Walpole: *The Castle of Otranto*	Jesuits expelled from France. Mining Academy, Europe's first technical university, opens in Banská Štiavnica. Hargreaves invents spinning jenny for manufacture of yarn.

1765	Haydn: Symphonies *Hornsignal*, *Alleluia*	Galuppi arrives in St Petersburg to work for Catherine the Great Bach–Abel concerts begin in London	Reynolds: *George Clive and his family with an Indian maid*	Stamp Act imposes direct tax on American colonies, but is repealed the following year. Cugnot begins experiments on steam-powered vehicles.
1766	Sacchini: *L'isola d'amore*	Haydn promoted to Kapellmeister to Prince Esterházy	Lessing: *Laokoon* Esterháza Palace first inhabited San Giorgio, Ragusa, completed	Cavendish isolates 'inflammable air' (hydrogen).
1767	Guglielmi: *La sposa fedele* Gluck: *Alceste*	Guglielmi and Alessandri engaged at King's Theatre, London	Mendelssohn: *Phaedon* Lessing: *Minna von Barnheim*	Jesuits expelled from Spanish Empire.
1768	Jommelli: *Fetonte* Hasse: *Piramo e Tisbe* Haydn: *Lo speziale* Rousseau: *Dictionnaire de musique* Boccherini: 6 Violin Sonatas, Op. 5	Esterháza Opera House completed C. P. E. Bach takes up directorship of Hamburg churches	First volume of *Encyclopedia Britannica* Wright: *An Experiment on a Bird in the Air Pump* Completion of Schloss Augustusburg, Brühl	Founding of Royal Academy. Astley stages first modern circus. Spallanzani disproves 'spontaneous generation' theory of cellular life.
1769	C. P. E. Bach: *Die Israeliten in der Wüste*	Jommelli departs Ludwigsburg, returns to Italy	Completion of Royal Palace, Buda, and New Palace, Sanssouci	Cook at Tahiti in First Voyage (–1771). Spanish missionaries establish missions in California. Watt patents improved steam engine.
1770	Mozart: *Mitridate, rè di Ponto* Gassmann: *La contessina* Jommelli: *Armida abbandonata* Daube: *Der musikalische Dilettant*	Charles Burney undertakes musical tour to France and Italy	Euler: *Anleitung zur Algebra* *Gainsborough: *The Blue Boy*	'Boston Massacre' as five civilians die at hands of British troops.

Year	Works/Musical Writings	Musical Events	Other Artistic	Historical/Scientific
1771	M. Haydn: Requiem in C Minor Kirnberger: *Die Kunst des reinen Satzes in der Musik* Boccherini: 12 String Quintets, Op. 10/11	F. Benda promoted to Konzertmeister in Berlin	Sulzer: *Allgemeine Theorie der schönen Künste*	Famine in central Europe kills up to 500,000.
1772	J. C. Bach: *Temistocle* Traetta: *Antigona* Haydn: 'Farewell' Symphony	Burney undertakes tour of Low Countries, Germany and Austria	Lessing: *Emilia Galotti* Basilica of the *Vierzehnheiligen*, Bad Staffelstein, completed Herder: *Abhandlung über den Ursprung der Sprache*	Marine chronometers used to measure longitude on Cook's Second Voyage (–1775).
1773	Burney: *The Present State of Music in Germany, the Netherlands and the United Provinces* Mozart: Symphony in G minor, K. 183 *Gossec: Symphony 'La Chasse' Sammartini: 6 Quintets Schweitzer: *Alceste*	Hasse retires to Venice	Beaumarchais: *Le Barbier de Séville* *Messerschmidt: *Charakterköpfen* Doyen: *Miracle des Ardents*	Jesuits suppressed by Pope Clement XIV. 'Sons of Liberty' throw 45 tons of tea overboard in Boston Tea Party.
1774	C. P. E. Bach: *Die Auferstehung und Himmelfahrt Jesu* Gluck: *Iphigénie en Aulide* Mozart: Symphony in A, K. 201 Gerbert: *De cantu et musica sacra*	Cannabich promoted to director of orchestral music in Mannheim	Goethe: *Die Leiden des jungen Werther* Completion of Royal Crescent, Bath	British Parliament passes 'Intolerable Acts' against American colonies. Discovery of chlorine by Scheele.

1775	Benda: *Ariadne auf Naxos*, *Medea* Engramelle: *La tonotechnie* Haydn: *Il ritorno di Tobia*	Sarti dismissed from Copenhagen service after political intrigues	Sheridan: *The Rivals*	American Revolutionary War begins (–1783). Bushnell invents the 'Turtle', first submarine used in combat.
1776	Sarti: *Le gelosie villane* C. P. E. Bach: *Orchester-Sinfonien*	Prince Nicolaus reorganises theatrical life at Esterháza, establishing regular 'season'. Concert of Ancient Music founded in London	Smith: *The Wealth of Nations* Gibbon: *History of The Decline and Fall of the Roman Empire* (–1789) Paine: *Common Sense* Klinger: *Sturm und Drang*	Joseph II establishes National Theatre in Vienna. Declaration of American Independence.
1777	Gluck: *Armide* Mozart: Piano Concerto in E-flat, K. 271 'Jenamy' Holzbauer: *Günther von Schwarzburg*	Baron van Swieten returns from Berlin, becomes Prefect of the Hofbibliothek in Vienna	Sheridan: *The School for Scandal*	*Scheele, Priestly and Lavoisier discover oxygen and the nature of combustion.
1778	Salieri: *L'Europa riconosciuta* Naumann: *Cora och Alonzo*	Mozart visits Paris Amalgamation of Mannheim and Munich ensembles Opening of La Scala, Milan	Copley: *Watson and the Shark* Beaumarchais: *Le Mariage de Figaro*	Joseph Bramah patents improved water closet design.
1779	Mozart: 'Coronation' Mass, K. 317 Schulz: *Gesänge am Clavier* Gluck: *Iphigénie en Tauride* C. P. E. Bach: *Sechs Clavier-Sonaten für Kenner und Liebhaber*	Haydn signs new employment contract with Prince Esterházy, allowing the composer to sell his music and fulfil outside commissions	Herder: *Volkslieder* Completion of Royal Saltworks, Arc-et-Senans	First cast-iron bridge constructed in Shropshire.

Year	Works/Musical Writings	Musical Events	Other Artistic	Historical/Scientific
1780	Piccinni: *Atys* La Borde: *Essai sur la musique ancienne et moderne*	Clementi embarks on European tour (–1783)	Completion of *Encyclopédie* and Royal Palace, Caserta	Joseph II becomes sole ruler of Austrian Monarchy.
1781	Mozart: *Idomeneo* Haydn: 6 Quartets, Op. 33	Mozart breaks with Salzburg establishment, settles in Vienna	Kant: *Kritik der reinen Vernunft* Schiller: *The Robbers* Fuseli: *The Nightmare*	Patent of Toleration enacted in Hapsburg lands, extends religious freedom to non-Catholic Christians. Founding of Los Angeles. Herschel and Lexell discover Uranus.
1782	Mozart: *Die Entführung aus dem Serail* Koch: *Versuch einer Anleitung zur Composition* (–1793) Paisiello: *Il barbiere di Siviglia* Sarti: *Fra i due litiganti*	Archbishop Colloredo introduces unpopular sacred music reforms in Salzburg	Falconet: *The Bronze Horseman* Laclos: *Les Liaisons dangereuses*	Pope Pius VI visits Vienna, attempts to convince Joseph II to abandon religious reforms.
1783	Pleyel: 6 String Quartets, Op. 1 *Mozart: Piano Sonatas, K. 330–332 Kraus: Symphony in C minor	Opening of Bolshoi Theatre, St Petersburg	Crabbe: *The Village*	Treaty of Paris ends American Revolutionary War. First balloon flight by Montgolfier brothers.
1784	Grétry: *Richard Coeur-de-lion* Salieri: *Les Danaïdes* Paisiello: *Il re Teodoro in Venezia* Wesley: *Missa de Spiritu Sancto*	Handel Commemoration in London (–1791)	Boullée: *Cénotaphe a Newton* David: *Le Serment des Horaces* Schiller: *Kabale und Liebe*	Edmund Cartwright designs power loom. Murdoch designs steam-powered locomotive.

1785	Mozart: Piano Concerto in D minor, K. 466 Mozart: 6 'Haydn' Quartets Schubart: *Ideen zu einer Ästhetik der Tonkunst*	*Tourte perfects 'Tourte bow'	Construction begins on Palacio del Prado, Madrid Schiller: *An die Freude*	Berthollet introduces use of chlorine as a bleach.
1786	Mozart: *Le nozze di Figaro* Haydn: 'Paris' Symphonies Martín y Soler: *Una cosa rara* Dittersdorf: *Der Apotheker und der Doktor* Cimarosa: *L'impresario in angustie*	Cherubini moves from London to Paris	Burns: *Poems, Chiefly in the Scottish dialect* Completion of Schloss Bellevue, Berlin Founding of New Lanark, Scotland	Frederick William II creates National Theatre in Berlin. Grand Duke Leopold abolishes death penalty in Tuscany.
1787	Haydn: *Die sieben letzten Worte unseres Erlösers am Kreuze* Mozart: *Don Giovanni* Martín y Soler: *L'arbore di Diana*	Beethoven visits Vienna, allegedly meets Mozart	Bentham: *Panopticon* David: *La Mort de Socrate*	Assembly of Notables meets at Versailles. United States adopts Constitution.
1788	Mozart: Symphonies, K. 549–551 Salieri: *Axur, rè d'Ormus* Guglielmi: *Debora e Sisara* Forkel: *Allgemeine Geschichte der Musik*	Salieri appointed Hofkapellmeister in Vienna	Kant: *Kritik der praktischen Vernunft* Lagrange: *Mécanique Analytique* Hutton: *Theory of the Earth*	Louis XVI agrees to convene Estates General. Founding of British colony in Australia.
1789	Paisiello: *Nina* Mozart: Clarinet Quintet, K. 581 Wranitzky: *Oberon, König der Elfen* Türk: *Clavierschule*	Hummel embarks on European concert tour	Lavoisier: *Traité Élémentaire de Chimie* Vigée-Lebrun: *Madame Vigée-Lebrun et sa fille* Completion of Pantheon, Paris	Fall of Bastille, promulgation of the Declaration of the Rights of Man. George Washington elected President of the United States.

Year	Works/Musical Writings	Musical Events	Other Artistic	Historical/Scientific
1790	Mozart: *Così fan tutte* *Viotti: Violin Concerto in E minor Gossec: *Te Deum* Haydn: 6 Quartets, Op. 64	Steibelt settles in Paris	Burke: *Reflections on the Revolution in France* Kant: *Kritik der Urteilskraft* Burns: *Tam o' Shanter*	Census of thirteen United States establishes population of 3.93 million; Philadelphia now temporary capital.
1791	Cherubini: *Lodoïska* Mozart: *Die Zauberflöte* Mozart: Requiem Kraus: *Aeneas i Cartago*	Haydn visits London Berlin *Singakademie* founded	Paine: *The Rights of Man* Brandenburg Gate, Berlin, completed Boswell: *The Life of Samuel Johnson*	Vancouver Expedition to Pacific begins (–1795).
1792	Cimarosa: *Il matrimonio segreto* Gossec: *Offrande à la liberté* Haydn: Sinfonia Concertante in B-flat	Beethoven arrives in Vienna	Wollstonecraft: *A Vindication of the Rights of Woman* Jennings: *Liberty Displaying the Arts and Sciences*	First Republic in France. New York Stock and Exchange Board founded. Chappe introduces optical telegraph.
1793	Müller: *Das Neusonntagskind* Gossec: *Le triomphe de la République* Beethoven: Octet, Op. 103	Cimarosa departs Vienna for Naples	David: *La Mort de Marat*	Execution of Louis XVI, Reign of Terror begins. Holy Roman Empire declares war on France.
1794	Eybler: *Die Hirten bei der Krippe* Süssmayr: *Der Spiegel von Arkadien* Billings: *The Continental Harmony*	Haydn visits London for second time	Blake: *Songs of Innocence and of Experience* Paine: *The Age of Reason* (–1807) Casanova: *Histoire de ma vie*	Prussian *Allgemeines Landrecht* promulgated. Fall of Robespierre. *Murdoch introduces gas lighting.

1795	Haydn: 'London' Symphony Salieri: *Palmira regina di Persia* Beethoven: Piano Trios, Op. 1 Beethoven: Piano Concerto No. 1	Founding of Paris Conservatoire	Fichte: *Grundlage der gesamten Wissenschaftslehre* Goethe: *Wilhelm Meisters Lehrjahre* Austen: *Lady Susan*	Polish state extinguished by Third Partition.
1796	Schenk: *Der Dorfbarbier* Haydn: Trumpet Concerto Beethoven: Piano Sonatas, Op. 2 Zingarelli: *Giulietta e Romeo*	Härtel buys Leipzig publishing firm of Breitkopf	Turner: *Fishermen at Sea* Completion of Somerset House, London	Bonaparte conquers northern Italy. Jenner introduces vaccine against smallpox. Cuvier establishes extinction as scientific fact. Trevithick begins to apply steam power to traction. Invention of lithography by Senefelder.
1797	Haydn: 6 Quartets, Op. 76 Cherubini: *Médée* Clementi: 6 Sonatinas, Op. 36	Paer becomes musical director at Kärtnertortheater, Vienna	Wackenroder: *Herzensergiessungen eines kunstliebenden Klosterbruders* de Sade: *La Nouvelle Justine*	Bonaparte conquers Venice. Nelson defeats Spanish navy.
1798	Haydn: *Missa in angustiis* Haydn: *Die Schöpfung* Beethoven: 3 Sonatas, Op. 10	*Allgemeine musikalische Zeitung* founded in Leipzig	Wordsworth and Coleridge: *Lyrical Ballads* Malthus: *Essay on the Principle of Population* Austen: *Elinor and Marianne*	Bonaparte leads Egyptian expedition, Battle of the Nile. French invade Papal States and establish Roman republic. Irish rebellion.

Year	Works/Musical Writings	Musical Events	Other Artistic	Historical/Scientific
1799	Beethoven: 'Pathétique' Sonata Paer: *Camilla* Field: Piano Concerto in E-flat	Zelter and Goethe begin correspondence	Schleiermacher: *Reden über die Religion* Laplace: *Mécanique Céleste* (–1825)	War resumes between France and Austria. Bonaparte seizes power in France. Collapse of Dutch East India Company.
1800	*Haydn: Te Deum Cherubini: *Les deux journées* Beethoven: Symphony No. 1	Cimarosa imprisoned in Naples, moves to Venice upon release	Tieck: *Romantische Dichtungen* Novalis: *Hymnen an die Nacht* *Goya: *La maja desnuda*	Britain passes Act of Union with Ireland. Volta demonstrates first electric battery. Discovery of infrared by Herschel.

Note: * Indicates approximate or conjectural date.

· APPENDIX II ·

Institutions in major European cities

DAVID BLACK

Berlin

Sacred The principal churches supporting sacred music were the Petrikirche, Nikolaikirche and Marienkirche; others, including the Schloss- und Domkirche (completed 1750), Parochialkirche, Sophienkirche, Neue Kirche, Garnisonkirche and the Catholic Hedwigskirche (1773) maintained more modest establishments.

Opera The Königliches Opernhaus, commissioned by Frederick the Great and designed by Knobelsdorff, opened in 1742. Its ensemble included famous singers from Italy, with the repertory dominated by Hasse and the operas of the court Kapellmeister C.H. Graun. After the Seven Years' War the house re-opened in 1764, but the fortunes of the Italian opera declined thereafter. In the late 1770s C.T. Döbbelin began presenting singspiel, and in 1786 his troupe moved to the French Theatre (renamed the Nationaltheater) with a royal subsidy. Until the end of the century the Nationaltheater specialized in German opera, while the royal theatre maintained the tradition of opera seria.

Court The Elector of Brandenburg, Friedrich III declared himself King of Prussia in 1701. Initially encouraged in musical pursuits by his wife Sophie Charlotte, Friedrich maintained a court orchestra of approximately thirty players. Friedrich was succeeded by his son Friedrich Wilhelm I in 1713, after which the ensemble was almost disbanded. With the accession of Friedrich II (Frederick the Great) in 1740, the orchestra was re-established and music became an integral part of daily life at the court. The king was an enthusiastic flautist and employed distinguished musicians including Quantz, C.P.E. Bach and F. Benda. After the Bavarian War of Succession (1778–9) Friedrich mostly withdrew from musical life, but the establishment was maintained to a more limited extent under his successor Friedrich Wilhelm II (1786–97).

Concerts As early as the 1720s, the Cathedral organist Gottlieb Hayne directed an amateur choir and gave public singing lessons. Later in the century, a number of private concert-giving institutions flourished, including the *Concert* of the court composer J.F. Agricola, the *Akademie* of the court double-bass player J.G. Janitsch, the *Musikübende Gesellschaft* of the cathedral organist J.P. Sack and the *Assemblee* of Sack's successor C.F. Schale. In 1770, Agricola and F.E. Benda founded the *Liebhaberkonzerte*, which continued until Benda's death in 1786. A series of *Concerts Spirituels* were organized by J.F. Reichardt beginning in 1783, and in 1787 the publisher J.C.F. Rellstab initiated the *Konzerte für Kenner und Liebhaber*. The court musician C.F.C. Fasch instituted a weekly *Singe Übung* in 1791 with both amateur and professional musicians; with its move to the Akademie der Künste in 1793 it was renamed the *Sing-Akademie zu Berlin* and became the city's leading promoter of sacred choral music in concert.

Publishers Berlin was a leading centre for the publication of theoretical writings, including the works of Kirnberger (*Die Kunst des reinen Satzes*), Agricola (*Anleitung zur Singekunst*), Marpurg (*Der critische Musicus an der Spree* and many others), Quantz (*Versuch einer Anweisung die Flöte traversiere zu spielen*) and C.P.E. Bach (*Versuch über die wahre Art das Clavier zu spielen*).

Dresden

Sacred In 1708, the Elector ordered the establishment of a choir school and the conversion of the old opera house (completed in 1667) into a Catholic court chapel. The institution initially maintained a low profile, but by the 1720s the sacred music provided by the *Hofkapelle* was among the grandest at any Catholic court, featuring works by Heinichen, Zelenka and later Hasse. The new Katholische Hofkirche, begun in 1738, was consecrated in 1751. The city also featured three principal Lutheran churches: the medieval Sophienkirche (destroyed in 1945) and Kreuzkirche (destroyed in 1760 and subsequently re-built), in addition to the new Frauenkirche (1726–34, destroyed in 1945, rebuilt 1993–2005). Students at the Kreuzschule provided music for the Kreuzkirche and the Frauenkirche; holders of the office of Kantor included J.Z. Grundig (1713–20), T.C. Reinhold (to 1755) and G.A. Homilius (to 1785). With the closure of the Lutheran castle chapel in 1737 the Sophienkirche became the Lutheran court church; W.F. Bach was organist there from 1733 to 1746.

Opera An Italian opera troupe was recruited in 1717, and a magnificent new opera house designed by M.D. Pöppelmann was inaugurated in 1719. Hasse and Faustina Bordoni first visited in 1731, and from 1734 to 1756 Hasse provided a steady stream of ambitious new stage works for the Dresden stage. The opera was closed during the Seven Years' War and the Italian company was dismissed thereafter. A small theatre was built in the Zwinger in 1755 which hosted Italian opera buffa, while German-language repertory was heard at the Theater auf dem Linckeschen Bade. In the 1770s various German-language companies were supported by the court, but comic opera in Italian was the most important operatic form. Works in both languages were heard at the Kleines Kurfürstliches Theater, as the Zwinger theatre was now known, under the direction of the Kapellmeister J.G. Naumann.

Court The Saxon Elector Friedrich August I converted to Catholicism in order to become King of Poland (as August II) in 1697. An enthusiastic patron of the arts, Friedrich maintained one of the largest and most renowned musical establishments in Europe, distinguished by its cosmopolitan makeup and technical excellence. Instrumentalists and composers in the Kapelle included Volumier, Pisendel, Buffardin, Quantz, Weiss, Lotti, Heinichen and Zelenka. After 1717 the establishment was divided according to its court, church and operatic responsibilities. J.S. Bach petitioned August's successor Friedrich August II (later August III of Poland) for a position in 1733 and was granted the title of court composer in 1736. August III continued his father's tradition of patronage, supporting lavish operatic productions under Hasse and re-establishing a Kapelle in Warsaw. The Seven Years' War had a disastrous effect on the court music, leading to the dismissal of Hasse and Faustina Bordoni without pensions. Under August III's grandson Friedrich August III the ensemble eventually recovered its former excellence under the leadership of J.G. Naumann. From the 1770s a number of court musicians were involved in public subscription concerts, among them Joseph Schuster and Naumann himself.

Florence

Sacred *Maestri di cappella* at the Cathedral (S Maria del Fiore) included Giuseppe Maria Orlandini (1732–60) and Carlo Antonio Campioni (1763–88). Other church *maestri* active in composition included Bartolomeo Felici at S Marco and Francesco Maria Veracini at S Pancrazio and S Michele Berteldi (S Gaetano). In the first half of the century the Cathedral *maestro* effectively directed the court music as well; of the later court *maestri* the most distinguished was Pietro Nardini (1770–93).

Opera From 1701 to 1718, the Teatro del via del Cocomero alone was permitted to present public opera under the auspices of the Accademia Drammatica degli Infuocati. In 1718, however, the Teatro di via della Pergola was re-opened for regular productions under the protection of the Immobili. The repertory of the two theatres increasingly diverged, with the Cocomero known for comic productions and the Pergola for serious opera. The restriction on new operatic ventures was relaxed from 1759, and new productions were mounted at the Teatro di via S Maria and Piazza Vecchia from the 1760s. In 1779 the Regio Teatro degl'Intrepidi was built, offering a mixture of comic opera, serious opera and ballet. Florence was the operatic capital of Italy by the 1790s, with regular productions in six theatres and frequent premieres involving both Tuscan and international composers.

Patronage In the early part of the century the leading patron of music was Prince Ferdinando de' Medici, son of Duke Cosimo III. He mounted operatic productions, corresponded with composers and supported Bartolomeo Cristofori in the invention of the piano. Aristocratic patronage declined after the Medici line became extinct in 1737, but recovered under the Hapsburg Grand Duke Leopold (1765–90) and his son Ferdinand (1791–1800). From the 1760s, groups of noble and bourgeoisie music lovers known as the Armonici, Faticanti and Ingregnosi organized public concerts. Held at the Teatro di Borgo dei Greci and other theatres, the concerts included both vocal and instrumental items.

Hamburg

Sacred The music for the city's five parish churches – St Petri, St Nikolai, St Katharinen, St Jacobi and St Michaelis – was directed by the Stadtkantor, who also served on the faculty of the Johanneum Lateinschule. Holders of the post in the eighteenth century were Joachim Gerstenbüttel (1675–1721), Telemann (to 1767), C.P.E. Bach (to 1788) and C.F.G. Schwencke (to 1822). Telemann provided a regular series of cantatas for the Sunday morning services but this provision was not continued by Bach, reflecting the decline in the fortunes of Hamburg sacred music. After Schwencke's death the position of Stadtkantor was abolished.

Opera Hamburg's opera house, the first public opera house in Germany, opened in 1678. The dominant figure in the early eighteenth century was Reinhard Keiser, who served as director in 1703–7 and composed operas for the theatre until the 1720s. Telemann served as director from 1722, but declining audiences led to the closure of the company in 1738. Italian opera troupes continued to visit the city, and after the demolition of the old theatre a new Komödienhaus was built in 1765. Its focus was primarily drama, but from 1771 under the directorship of Friedrich Ludwig Schröder it presented operas by Gluck, Mozart and Salieri.

Concerts Keiser directed orchestral concerts at the house of Graf Eckgh throughout the winter of 1700, and public concerts were later held at such venues as the Drillhaus, Kaiserhof and Klefekersche Orangerie. Telemann presented his own passions and oratorios to paying audiences, and both Telemann and C. P. E. Bach contributed substantial works (*Kapitänsmusiken*) to the celebrations of the Hamburg militia. In 1761 the Konzertsaal auf dem Kamp opened, initially hosting a subscription series under the control of Friedrich Hartmann Graf. Further events were organized by C.P.E. Bach from 1768 and Johann Christoph Westphal from 1770. In 1789 the *Harmonie Gesellschaft* began presenting concerts on the model of the Leipzig Gewandhaus orchestra.

Leipzig

Sacred At the head of the town's musical establishment was the Thomaskantor, who was in charge of proceedings at the four principal churches: St Thomas, St Nicholas, the Neue Kirche and (from 1712) St Peter. In his capacity as *director musices* of Leipzig, the cantor also organized music for civic occasions such as town council elections, and as academic musical director provided occasional music for the University Church (St Paul). St Thomas and St Nicholas saw regular performances of concerted music on Sundays and feast days, provided by students of the St Thomas School and the town music company. Since the sixteenth century the cantorate had been occupied by distinguished musicians, and this tradition continued with the appointments of Johann Kuhnau (1701–22) and J.S. Bach (1723–50). Changing fashions in theology and musical taste led to the decline of the importance of the office in the second half of the century, although J.F. Doles (1756–89) and J.A. Hiller (1789–1800) were both fine musicians. In addition to the Lutheran churches of the city, a Catholic chapel existed in the Pleissenburg and held services from 1710.

Opera The first opera house, designed by Sartorio, opened in 1693. In the early eighteenth century the enterprise was directed by Telemann and Melchior Hoffmann, but declined thereafter and was shut in 1720. For the next few decades opera was provided by visiting troupes on temporary stages. In 1766 the Comödienhaus was built for theatre and opera, hosting productions by Bondini (1777–89), Guardasoni (1782–94) and the Seconda brothers.

Concerts In the first half of the century, public concerts were principally in the hands of two private student societies or *collegia musica*. The first, founded by Telemann around 1702, was directed by J. S. Bach in 1729–37 and from 1739 to the early 1740s. From 1723 it was associated with the coffeehouse and garden of Gottfried Zimmermann. The second, founded by J.F. Fasch in 1708, was later directed by J.G. Görner (1723–56) and held concerts at Schellhafer Hall. In 1743 a *Grosses Concert der Kaufleute* was founded that held a subscription series at the hotel *Zu den drei Schwanen*. After the Seven Years' War the ensemble was directed by J.A. Hiller, but in 1775 Hiller founded a new *Musikübende Gesellschaft* that eventually supplanted the *Grosses Concert*. In 1781 a new concert hall in the city-owned Gewandhaus was inaugurated, with Hiller's orchestra as the resident ensemble. From 1785 the Gewandhaus ensemble was directed by J.G. Schicht and developed into one of Germany's leading orchestras.

Publishers The publishing house of Breitkopf was founded in 1719. Initially it published little music, but from the 1750s it produced editions of works by leading German composers using a new moveable type. Breitkopf also maintained a large-scale trade in manuscript music, advertised through thematic and non-thematic catalogues. The firm was bought out by Gottfried Christoph Härtel in 1796 and continued publishing under the name Breitkopf & Härtel.

Lisbon

Under João V (1707–50), the royal chapel included more than sixty singers and four organists, and the royal music library was considered among the most comprehensive in Europe. In 1713 a training school for the musicians, the Seminário da Patriarcal, was founded, and in 1716 the chapel was raised to the status of patriarchal basilica. There was a strong Italian presence in the chapel's membership, with Domenico Scarlatti (1719), Giovanni Giorgi (1725) and David Perez (1752) acting as *mestre de capela*. The organists – Francisco António de Almeida and Carlos de Seixas – were local, however. Opera was produced at the Teatro do Bairro Alto (1733), Academia da Trindade (1735), its successor the Teatro da Rua dos Condes (1738) and to a limited extent at court. José I (1750–77) ordered the construction of a new theatre in 1755, but it was destroyed along with the royal music library in the disastrous earthquake of the same year. Court opera resumed at Ajuda, while the Bairro Alto and Rua dos Condes theatres mounted sporadic productions from 1763 (although women were banned from the stage in 1774). A large new theatre, the Teatro de S Carlos, was completed in 1793 and began staging opera under the direction of António Moreira.

London

Sacred St Paul's Cathedral and Westminster Abbey both suffered declining standards in the eighteenth century, and neither featured regular orchestral accompaniment of the kind found on the continent. The Chapel Royal at St James' Palace had its own resident composers (including Handel), and combined with the royal band of twenty-four musicians to present anthems, birthday odes and other ceremonial music on occasion. Masters of the Music included

John Eccles (1700–35), Maurice Greene (1735–55), William Boyce (1755–79) and John Stanley (1779–86). From the 1770s, Catholic masses were performed at the chapels of the Portuguese, Sardinian and Bavarian embassies.

Opera The principal opera house for most of the century was the King's (originally Queen's) Theatre on the Haymarket, opened in 1705. The first resident company, offering operas mostly in Italian, closed in 1717 after competition from English-language productions at Lincoln's Inn Fields (opened in 1714). Italian opera was resurrected at the King's Theatre in 1720 by the 'Royal Academy of Music' under the direction of Handel. The venture went bankrupt in 1728, but the 'Second Academy' resumed at the end of 1729. A rival venture in Italian opera, the Opera of the Nobility, opened at Lincoln's Inn Fields in 1733. Meanwhile, the extraordinary success of Gay's *The Beggar's Opera* (1728) at Lincoln's Inn Fields had enabled the actor-manager John Rich to build the Theatre Royal at Covent Garden, opened in 1732. Handel produced opera there from 1735, but returned to the King's Theatre in 1737 for a season with the Opera of the Nobility, bankrupted the following year. The King's Theatre continued to present Italian opera under rapidly changing management, while Covent Garden and Drury Lane (designed by Wren and opened in 1674) successfully presented operas and musical entertainments in English. The King's Theatre was renovated in 1782 but was destroyed by fire in 1789. Its replacement opened in 1791 but was not granted an operatic licence, this instead being awarded to the Pantheon, a former exhibition space opened in 1772. The Pantheon itself was destroyed by fire in 1792, after which productions resumed at the King's Theatre.

Concerts Musical societies for the entertainment of gentleman amateurs began to be established in the 1720s, the two most important of which met at the Castle Tavern in Paternoster Row and the Swan Tavern in Cornhill. The Academy of Ancient Music, founded in 1726 as The Academy of Vocal Music, initially explored Italian and English music of the sixteenth and seventeenth centuries. Attracting a crowd of mostly professional musicians, it initially met at the Crown and Anchor in the Strand but eventually broadened both its audience and its repertory. The most important hall for public subscription concerts in the first half of the century was Hickford's Room in James Street, later supplanted by a rival hall on Dean Street. Handel initiated a tradition of oratorios given during Lent at Covent Garden, and supported the benevolent Society of Musicians, founded in 1738. The exclusive Bach–Abel concerts began in 1765 at Carlisle House, but in 1775 moved to a purpose-built room in Hanover Square and remained there until their cessation in 1781. Concerts at Hanover Square were continued by the 'Professional Concert', which faced competition from impresarios such as Salomon – especially after Haydn was brought to London.

A conservative streak remained in the city's musical taste, with the multiple Handel commemorations at Westminster Abbey from 1784–91 and the foundation of the Concert of Ancient Music in 1776 (unrelated to the Academy, which continued until at least 1797). An important supplement to concerts held in the city were those held at the various 'pleasure gardens', notably Vauxhall Gardens in Lambeth, Ranelagh Gardens in Chelsea and Marylebone Gardens.

Publishers In the first half of the century, music publishing was dominated by John Walsh. Active since 1695, Walsh surpassed his competitors in business acumen and the number of prints issued. From about 1730, when Walsh's son became involved in the firm, it was the regular publisher of Handel's works and secured exclusive rights to them in 1739. Prominent publishers in the latter half of the century included Longman & Broderip, John Bland and Robert Birchall.

Madrid

Philip V (1700–46) was an enthusiast for Italian music, and the royal chapel in both its direction and membership featured musicians from Italy. Sacred music, written by such figures as the *maestro de capilla* Joseph de Torres, Antonio de Literes and José Nebra reflected an eclectic mixture of styles. The royal monasteries of San Lorenzo del El Escorial and La Encarnación employed talented musicians, including El Escorial's *maestro de capilla*, Antonio Soler. Domenico Scarlatti followed his royal pupil Maria Bárbara from Lisbon in 1729, and remained in her service until his death. Philip V invited an Italian opera troupe to Madrid in 1703, and with the accession of his son Ferdinand VI (1746–59), lavish productions were mounted under the direction of Farinelli at the Coliseo del Buen Retiro (1640) and Aranjuez (1753). In contrast, Carlos III (1759–88) had little liking for the Italian opera seria produced at the Buen Retiro and the Teatro de los Caños del Peral (1738), and the vernacular zarzuela and tonadilla enjoyed popularity at the Teatro de la Cruz (1743) and Teatro del Príncipe (1745). Boccherini was in the service of Carlos III's brother Don Luis from 1770 to 1785, and was a member of the Real Capilla from 1786. Concerts were held at the Caños del Peral from the 1760s, and Italian opera resumed at the theatre in 1787.

Mannheim

Mannheim became the capital of the Electoral Palatinate in 1720, and under Elector Karl Philipp (1716–42) it began acquiring one of the largest palace complexes in Europe. The Schlosskirche was consecrated in 1731, and as the court was strongly Catholic in orientation the Kapelle under its director Carlo Grua (1734–73) was frequently engaged for masses and other services. The palace theatre was inaugurated with Grua's *Meride* in 1742, but was destroyed by siege in 1795. The Elector died in 1742 and was succeeded by Karl Theodor, an enthusiastic patron of the arts who substantially enlarged the Kapelle and was fond of lavish celebrations. With members such as the Stamitz brothers, Cannabich, Ramm, Wendling and Lebrun, the orchestra was famous for its virtuosity and the precision of its ensemble. Ignaz Holzbauer was appointed 'Kapellmeister für das Theater' in 1753, and succeeded Carlo Grua as Hofkapellmeister in 1773. Both opera seria and comic opera were staged at the court theatre and at the summer residence in Schwetzingen, and there were notable premieres in the 1770s of works by J.C. Bach, Schweitzer and Holzbauer. Most of the musicians moved with the court to Munich after Karl Theodor became Elector of Bavaria in 1778.

Milan

Milan was ruled from 1706 to 1797 by the Austrian Hapsburgs, with the arts and sciences flourishing particularly under the acting governor-general of Lombardy, Count Firmian (1758–82). Like Florence, Milan had strong connections with Vienna, and there was a frequent exchange of music and musicians between the two capitals. The principal opera theatre was the Teatro Regio Ducal (1717), which hosted lavish productions with renowned set designers, singers and dancers until it was destroyed by fire in 1776. The two replacements were the Teatro alla Scala (1778) and the Teatro della Cannobiana (1779), the former becoming one of the most famous opera houses in Italy. The Cathedral employed famous musicians including J.C. Bach and Sarti, and G.B. Sammartini was *maestro di capella* at the city's other leading churches, including the ducal chapel. Noble families held instrumental concerts (*Concerti di Quaresima*) during Lent when the theatres were closed, and Sammartini directed free open-air events at the Castello Sforzesco and the Porta Orientale. In 1758 the Accademia Filarmonica was founded by a mixture of professional musicians and the nobility.

Naples

Sacred Naples was a viceroyalty of Spain until 1707, then of Austria until 1734, then a kingdom ruled along with Sicily by the Bourbon Carlo VII (1735–59) and his son Ferdinand IV (from 1759). The royal chapel, which was increasingly involved in opera, nevertheless continued its liturgical duties and maintained some continuity of membership in the face of these political changes. Among the *maestri di cappella* were A. Scarlatti, Leo, de Majo and Cafaro, with organists including D. Scarlatti, Piccinni and Cimarosa. The city of Naples had a *maestro* responsible for civic celebrations, particularly those associated with the Treasury of S. Gennaro at the Cathedral, and the Cathedral itself had a distinguished ensemble. The Oratorio dei Girolamini (Filippini) sponsored liturgical performances and oratorio, and numerous churches and confraternities made occasional commissions such as Pergolesi's *Stabat Mater* for the Confraternita dei Cavalieri di San Luigi di Palazzo. The four conservatories – S Maria di Loreto, S Onofrio in Capuana, S Maria della Pietà dei Turchini and the Poveri di Gesù Cristo (suppressed in 1743) – were famous centres for the musical instruction of talented youth. Like the Casa dell'Annunziata, which cared for orphans, the conservatories boasted famous teachers and produced composers of international standing. Among the *maestri* and students associated with the conservatories were Cimarosa, Duni, Durante, Feo, Guglielmi, Jommelli, Leo, Paisiello, Perez, Pergolesi, Piccinni, Porpora, Sacchini, Storace, Traetta, Tritto, Vinci and Zingarelli.

Opera With the strong links between the royal chapel and the Teatro S Bartolomeo (1620), many of the singers were common to both institutions, and the works of *maestro di capella* A. Scarlatti were instrumental in establishing a local operatic tradition. The Teatro de' Fiorentini (1707) was the first Italian theatre to hold regular seasons of comic opera, partly in Neapolitan dialect, and was followed by the Teatro Nuovo (1724), Teatro della Pace (1724) and the four conservatories. S Bartolomeo was demolished in 1737 in favour of the lavish new Teatro San Carlo, which was supported by the state and became one of Europe's most famous theatres for opera seria, particularly the works of Metastasio. In 1741 the King banned the performance of comic intermezzos and ordered them replaced at the San Carlo by ballet – an early example of the increasing French influence on Neapolitan opera. Choruses, when required, were supplied by students of the conservatories. Ferdinand IV gave the comic theatres some respectability in the second half of the century by ordering company productions at the royal palace, and a new theatre, the Teatro del Real Fondo di Separazione, opened in 1779.

Paris

Sacred Most churches in the city lacked a choral tradition, but a number attracted large congregations through the illustrious organ-playing of Balbastre, Clérambault, François Couperin, Dandrieu, Daquin and Marchand. Those institutions that maintained choral ensembles, such as Notre Dame, Saints-Innocents and the Chapelle Royale in the Tuileries continued to celebrate major feasts with concerted masses, psalms and motets. With the advent of the Revolution, these activities had ceased by the early 1790s.

Opera The most prestigious company was the Académie Royale de Musique, usually known as the Opéra, which performed at the Palais Royal until the theatre's destruction by fire in 1763. Its replacement, opened in 1770, was again destroyed in 1781, after which the company moved to a new theatre near the Porte-St-Martin. The Comédie-Française, which until 1770 occupied a theatre on the rue des Fossés-St-Germain-des-Prés, was a state-supported enterprise like the Opéra. The Comédie-Italienne was formed in 1716 and performed at the Hôtel de Bourgogne; despite its name, the repertory included French productions. Lowest in prestige but among the most popular were the Fair Theatres (Sant Germain and Sant Laurent), who were known from 1715 as the Opéra-Comique. The Opéra-Comique and the Comédie-Italienne merged in 1762, and the company moved to the new Salle Favart in 1783. A new company, the Théâtre de Monsieur, was formed in 1789 and was based at the new Salle Feydeau from 1791. The relaxation of restrictions on the opening of public theatres in the early 1790s led to a rapid reshaping of Parisian theatrical life, with the Opéra changing its title several times and moving to the Théâtre Montansier in 1794.

Court The court music was organized into three divisions: the Musique de la Chambre, Musique de la Grande Ecurie and Musique de la Chapelle Royale. The Chambre included a small group of singers and instrumentalists in addition to the famous twenty-four Violons du Roi. The Ecurie was a large group of brass, woodwind and string players employed for grand public occasions, while the Chapelle Royale was responsible for sacred music, principally at the Versailles chapel (completed in 1710). Louis XV designated Versailles at the official residence of the court in 1725, and the château was the venue for numerous operatic productions and concerts under the patronage of Louis' consort Marie Leczinska and his mistress Mme de Pompadour. In 1761 the King ordered that the Chambre and Chapelle should be merged and the twenty-four Violons disbanded in response to rising expenses, but a permanent theatre at Versailles was completed in 1770. Marie Antoinette had her own private theatre and took leading roles in productions of opéra comique.

Concerts Paris enjoyed a rich concert life in the early eighteenth century, although most concerts were private events in the homes of the aristocracy. The most significant exception was the Concert Spirituel, established in 1725 by Anne Danican Philidor. Until 1784, these concerts took place in the Tuileries Palace (destroyed in 1871), with the singers and instrumentalists coming from the Opéra and various city churches. Initially the repertory consisted of French instrumental and religious vocal music (especially the *grand motet*), but later expanded to include secular items and works from Italian and German sources. Another enterprise, the Concert des Amateurs, established a subscription series in 1769, and was followed in 1781 by the Concert de la Loge Olympique. With its dissolution in 1789 and that of the Concert Spirituel in 1790, the principal focus of public concerts switched to the theatres. During the Revolution and its aftermath, open-air festivals often included massed vocal and instrumental forces.

Publishers Until the abolition of printing privileges in 1790 the monopoly on printed music was held by the Ballard family, but this privilege was limited to the old-style method of moveable type. Publishing firms using the newer method of engraved plates included Le Clerc, La Chevardière, Sieber, Heina, Leduc and Pleyel.

Prague

Sacred Sacred music was enthusiastically cultivated in Prague at many institutions, including St Nikolaus auf der Kleinseite (1702–52), St Jakob (1702), St Francis Serafin, Kloster Strahov and the Teynkirche. At St Vitus Cathedral, which gained a major new organ in the 1760s, the outstanding *regentes chori* were F.X. Brixi (1759–71) and J.A. Kozeluch (1784–1814). Other prominent directors, organists and composers included B.M. Černohorský, J. Seger, J.B. Kucharž and J. Strobach. The Jesuit Clementinum emphasized musical instruction and educated J. Stamitz, F. Benda and J. Mysliveček, while strong traditions of school drama, oratorio and sepulchre cantata flourished at the colleges and monasteries.

Opera Prague and the Kingdom of Bohemia were ruled by the Hapsburgs, and sporadic productions such as Fux's *Costanza e fortezza* (1723) were mounted for court visits to the city. Count Franz Anton von Sporck employed an Italian company at his garden theatre (1701) from 1725 to 1734, and other noble families such as Clam-Gallas and Thun had their own stages. The Comoedia-Haus, or Kotzen Theatre (1738) was the main venue for Italian buffa productions and later German singspiel, and was managed by the Mingotti brothers among others until its closure in 1783. The Nostitzsches Nationaltheater (1783), known as the Estates Theatre from 1798, was managed by Bondini and later Guardasoni, and saw the premieres of Mozart's *Don Giovanni* and *La clemenza di Tito*. From 1789, Bondini's company presented opera in Czech at the former monastery Hyberner-Haus.

Concerts The city's musicians were organized into three guilds representing the Altstadt, Neustadt and Kleinseite, with membership numbering in the hundreds. Musical life was also well developed in the Jewish quarter, especially at the Maisel Synagogue. Concerts were held at the Saal bei der Eisernen Tür as early as 1713, and Baron Hartig headed an Academy of Music that was similar in intention to the London institution. Travelling virtuosi increasingly visited Prague and performed in the city's theatres during the second half of the century, and noble families such as the Lobkowitz, Černin and Pachta maintained their own ensembles.

Rome

Sacred Many Roman churches maintained musical ensembles, including S Giovanni in Laterano, S Maria Maggiore, Il Gesù, S Lorenzo in Damaso and S Maria in Vallicella (Chiesa Nuova). At S Pietro, the Cappella Giulia was directed by distinguished musicians including D. Scarlatti, Pitoni, Jommelli, Costanzi and Guglielmi. The Cappella Sistina maintained its unusual disposition of about thirty singers with soprano castratos, augmented by opera soloists during the famous Holy Week services. A professional body of the city's musicians, the Congregazione di S. Cecilia, held patronal celebrations at S Carlo ai Catinari and attempted to exercise control over church appointments. From 1716, all musicians working in Rome were required to be members.

Opera From the second decade of the century, operatic productions were held at the Teatro Pace (1694), Capranica (1694), Alibert (Teatro delle Dame, 1717), Valle (1726), Argentina (1731) and Tordinona (1733). All parts were taken by men as female singers were forbidden. During Carnival season, two of the theatres presented opera seria from elsewhere in Italy, while comic opera and intermezzi were more frequently by local figures. The ownership and administration of the theatres varied, with some run by noble families, others run by independent impresarios and one (Tordinona) administered by the government.

Patronage In the early part of the century, the Cardinals Pamphili and Ottoboni and Prince Ruspoli were lavish patrons of music, holding weekly academies and commissioning oratorios and cantatas to their own libretti. Among the composers who worked for them were Corelli, A. Scarlatti, Handel, Caldara and Gasparini. Throughout the century, a number of seminaries including the Collegium Germanicum et Hungaricum and the Collegio Romano supported the performance of oratorio and opera. Foreign ambassadors to the Papal States commissioned new works for family celebrations, and middle-class patrons and musicians held academies in their homes in the absence of a public concert tradition.

Venice

Sacred The standard of music at the Basilica of S Marco declined during the eighteenth century, as the institution faced difficulties retaining performers in the face of more lucrative opportunities in opera. *Maestri di capella* at the

Basilica included Biffi (1702–33), Lotti (1736–40), Pollarolo (1740–46), Saratelli (1747–62), Galuppi (1762–85) and Bertoni (1785–1808). Galuppi was responsible for reforming the ensemble in 1765–6, reducing the choir from thirty-six to twenty-four and modernizing the orchestral make-up. In addition to S Marco, numerous parish churches, confraternities and guilds supported concerted ensembles, although few details are presently known. The four *ospedali* for various disadvantaged members of society – the Incurabili, Mendicanti, Ospedaletto and Pietà – all maintained musical establishments, and engaged distinguished composers including Vivaldi, Porpora, Galuppi, Jommelli and Hasse as *maestri*. The musical activities of the *ospedali* peaked in the middle of the century, but they were largely bankrupt by 1777 and were taken over by the state. In the 1780s and 1790s they did, however, continue to employ *maestri* and commission works from composers such as Bianchi and Mayr.

Opera The main season for operatic productions was Carnival, with shorter seasons in the preceding autumn and (from 1720) during the Ascensiontide Fair. Theatres were usually named after the parish in which they were situated, and were under the control of one or more noble families. Opera was produced at S Cassiano (1637), S Moisè (1639), S Samuele (1665), S Angelo (1677) and S Giovanni Grisostomo (the most prestigious stage, 1678), although the number of productions varied between them. The running of the theatres was entrusted to impresarios (including Vivaldi), and productions generally ran consecutively. From the 1720s the prominence of Neapolitan composers began to increase, and Neapolitan comic opera arrived in the 1740s. S Giovanni Grisostomo ceased productions of opera seria in 1752, and its owners built a smaller theatre for the purpose, S Benedetto (1755), which they were obliged to sell in 1766. In the following decades, S Benedetto hosted opera seria, while S Moisè, S Samuele and S Cassiano were the venues for comic opera. In 1788 the owners of S Benedetto were forced by a lawsuit to give up control of the theatre, and opened their own, La Fenice, in 1792. Initially intended for seria, it eventually became the most famous of all Venice's opera houses.

Vienna

Sacred Concerted sacred music was central to the life of Vienna's churches, and large ensembles were employed at Michaelerkirche, the Schottenstift, the Kirche am Hof, the Universitätskirche and a number of other institutions. At St Stephen's Cathedral, which shared many of its personnel with the Hofkapelle, the Kapellmeisters included Fux (1705–15), Reutter (1738–72),

Hofmann (1772–93) and Albrechtsberger (1793–1809). Under Charles VI (1711–40) the court made regular excursions to city churches on feast days, but the number of such feast days was curtailed somewhat under Maria Theresia (1740–80). In 1783, Joseph II (1765–90) approved a much-reduced order of services for the city that led to the abandonment of many smaller music programmes. Often ignored in practice at the larger institutions, the restrictions on sacred music were eventually lifted in the 1790s.

Opera Until 1744, the principal court venue for opera and other staged musical entertainments was the Teatro Grande, the renovated ballroom of the Hofburg, with further performances in other rooms of the Hofburg and the Favorita Palace. The performers were members of the Imperial Hofkapelle, with the singers sourced from Italy and the repertory dominated by local composers such as Conti, Fux and Caldara. The Kärntnertortheater, built in 1709, was initially put to various purposes, but from 1728 hosted Italian and German intermezzi. In 1741 a former tennis court was renovated for the performance of Italian opera, and as the Theater nächst der Burg it replaced the Teatro Grande as the principal opera theatre. A French theatrical troupe was employed from 1752, and under the directorship of Count Durazzo the theatre hosted opéras-comiques and new works by Gluck, Hasse and Traetta. The Kärntnertortheater was destroyed by fire in 1761 and rebuilt in 1763, and Durazzo was dismissed the following year. The theatres continued to be run by a series of impresarios, until in 1776 Joseph II dismissed the Italian and French companies and took over the management together with his *Musikgraf* Count Orsini-Rosenberg. As the Nationaltheater, the Burgtheater hosted a German singspiel company from 1778 to 1783, and an Italian company with Lorenzo da Ponte as court poet from 1783 to 1791. Under the musical direction of Salieri, with renowned soloists and new works by Mozart, Martín y Soler and Salieri himself, the Italian buffa company was renowned as among the finest in Europe. In 1791, Leopold II removed Salieri from his post as director and instituted a more eclectic repertory that included opera seria, buffa, ballet and later singspiel. Of the city's remaining theatres, the most important were Karl Marinelli's Theater in der Leopoldstadt (1781) and Emanuel Schikaneder's Theater auf der Wieden (1787), both of which presented German popular comedies with variable musical content.

Court With a peak membership of 134 musicians under Charles VI, the Imperial Hofkapelle was responsible for providing theatrical music for the court opera, sacred music for the court chapel, and vocal–instrumental items for court events and private entertainments. Headed by Johann Joseph Fux (1715–41) and his deputy Antonio Caldara (1716–36), the Hofkapelle was an integral component of Hapsburg ceremony. Under Maria Theresia the size of the group was reduced, the opera was contracted out to impresarios and most of the remaining musicians eventually became direct employees of Hofkapellmeister Georg von Reutter (1751–72). The membership declined further under Reutter's successors Florian Leopold Gassmann (1772–4) and Giuseppe Bonno (1774–88), although Joseph II's personal interest in the theatre and the appointment of Salieri as chamber composer ensured lively developments in the operatic scene. A dedicated wind band was established in 1782, and a restructure in 1788 led to Salieri's appointment as Hofkapellmeister. In the later 1790s a particularly enthusiastic patron of music was Empress Marie Therese, wife of Franz II (1792–1835), who organized her own private concerts.

Concerts Vienna lacked a dedicated concert hall in the eighteenth century, and most public performances involving an orchestra took place in one of the theatres. Restrictions in force until 1786 prevented the performance of opera and plays during Lent, and this season consequently provided the best opportunities for the mounting of concerts. Public concerts involving court musicians were first held in the Burgtheater in the 1750s on the initiative of Durazzo, and an increasing number of local and visiting performers mounted benefit concerts for themselves in the second half of the century. The *Tonkünstler-Societät*, founded in 1771 to support the widows and children of deceased musicians, held fundraising concerts every Advent and Lent, and was notable for the enormous size of its orchestra. By the 1780s, performers such as Mozart were heard in non-theatrical venues such as the Augarten, the former chapel of the Trattnerhof, the Mehlgrube casino and Ignaz Jahn's restaurant. Noble patrons such as the Auersperg, Galitzin, Lichnowsky, Liechtenstein, Lobkowitz and Schwarzenberg families supported music and organized their own private concerts, although few details are known of these events. Baron Gottfried van Swieten, the Prefect of the Imperial Library, hosted private chamber concerts and in the mid-1780s founded the Gesellschaft der Associierten Cavaliere, a loose coalition of nobles who financed the performance of oratorio.

Publishers Anton Huberty opened a music engraving and printing business in 1777 and Christoph Torricella began issuing his own editions in 1781. Both were eclipsed, however, by the firm of Artaria, which began a prolific stream of musical publications in 1778 and soon developed productive relations with Haydn and Mozart. Franz Anton Hoffmeister founded a competing firm in 1784, notable for its ambitious publishing agenda. From the 1770s there was a flourishing trade in manuscript copies produced by such dealers as Johann Traeg, Laurenz Lausch and Wenzel Sukowaty.

· APPENDIX III ·

Personalia

DAVID BLACK

Abel, Carl Friedrich (1723–87) Composer and bass viol player. He studied with his father Christian Ferdinand (a former colleague of J. S. Bach) and accepted a position in the Dresden court orchestra around 1743. He left Dresden in 1757–8 and moved to London, where he established a concert series (1765–81) in association with Johann Christian Bach. Abel's compositions are mostly instrumental, and include symphonies, concertos and works for his own instrument.

Agricola, Johann Friedrich (1720–74) German composer and writer on music. A student of J. S. Bach, he moved to Berlin in 1741 and established himself as a leading commentator on aesthetic issues of the day, in addition to producing an important translation of Tosi's singing treatise (1757). He sang the tenor part in the premiere of Graun's *Der Tod Jesu*, and was widely respected as an organist and composer.

Aguiari [Agujari], Lucrezia ['La bastardina'] (1743–83) Italian soprano. She studied initially in her native Ferrara, and made her operatic debut in Florence (1764). After a string of early successes she settled in Parma, where she was appointed *virtuosa di camera* in 1768. She created roles in operas by Paisiello, Gluck and her later husband Giuseppe Colla, and made her final stage appearances in 1782. Possessed of a remarkable range and fine acting ability, she was in demand across Europe.

Alberti, Domenico (*c.* 1710–46) Italian composer and performer. He reportedly studied with Biffi and Lotti, but did not pursue a professional musical career. Known in his own day as a singer and harpsichordist, his fame rests today on the more than forty keyboard sonatas probably written in Rome during his later years. All cast in two movements, they feature the first regular use of the accompaniment pattern known as the 'Alberti bass'.

Albinoni, Tomaso (Giovanni) (1671–1750/1) Italian composer. Of independent means, Albinoni studied violin and singing in his native Venice and had his first opera produced there (*Zenobia*, 1694). A series of important instrumental publications followed (especially the Concerti a cinque, Op. 9, 1722), as did regular commissions for operas, serenatas and cantatas. Albinoni composed prolifically and his works achieved widespread distribution, but he seems to have retired around 1741 and died in obscurity. The famous 'Adagio in G minor' is a twentieth-century construction with no authentic material.

Albrechtsberger, Johann Georg (1736–1809) Austrian composer, theorist and organist. He was a choirboy and student at Melk Abbey, and occupied various provincial positions as an organist. In 1772 he was appointed *regens chori* at the Carmelite Church in Vienna, and in 1793 became Kapellmeister at St Stephen's Cathedral. The author of an important textbook on composition (1790), he was also famous for his organ playing and contrapuntal abilities.

Alessandri, Felice (1747–98) Italian composer, primarily of opera. He studied in Naples, and had his first operas produced in Verona and Venice. In 1767 he visited London and for a short time shared the direction of the Concert Spirituel in Paris (1777–8). In addition to supervising productions in various Italian cities, Alessandri spent time in St Petersburg (1786–9) and Berlin (1789– 92). His final years were spent mostly in Italy.

Algarotti, Francesco (1712–64) Italian poet and writer, variously resident in London, Paris, Berlin, Dresden and his native state. His *Saggio sopra l'opera in musica* (1755) is an important critique of contemporary opera, in which the author argues that musical aspects should be subordinated to poetic considerations. Many composers and librettists of later 'reform operas' took their inspiration directly or indirectly from Algarotti.

André, Johann (1741–99) German composer and publisher. He initially worked in the family business of silk manufacture, but had a successful premiere of an opera in 1773. At about the same time he opened a music printing business and became director of a theatre in Berlin. In 1784 he took over the administration of the music business, and through commercial acumen and technical innovation developed it into one of the leading German music publishers. He was also a prominent composer of lieder.

Anfossi, Pasquale (1727–97) Italian composer, primarily of opera and sacred music. He began his career as an orchestral violinist, but had compositional ambitions and first came to prominence with *L'incognita perseguitata* (Rome, 1773). In the 1770s he was *maestro di coro* at one of the Venetian conservatories, and from 1782 to 1786 served as music director at the King's Theatre in London. He subsequently returned to Italy and in 1792 was appointed *maestro di cappella* at S Giovanni in Laterano, Rome.

Anna Amalia, Duchess of Saxe-Weimar (1739–1807) German patron of music and composer. She studied keyboard and composition with the later Weimar Kapellmeister E. W. Wolf, and her singspiel, *Erwin und Elmire* (to a libretto by Goethe) was premiered in 1776. Under her patronage Weimar became an important centre for the development of German opera and a site of pilgrimage for the artistic intelligentsia.

Anna Amalia, Princess of Prussia (1723–87) German patron of music and composer. She studied initially with the Berlin Cathedral organist Gottfried Hayne, and became proficient on harpsichord and organ. In her mid-thirties she began studying composition with Kirnberger; her works include songs, chamber music and an oratorio *Der Tod Jesu*. She later hosted musical soirées in Berlin and was a supporter of C. P. E. Bach. Her extensive musical library, one of the most important of its kind, is now in the Staatsbibliothek zu Berlin.

Araja [Araia], Francesco (1709–*c.* 1770) Italian composer resident in Russia. He made his operatic debut in 1729 and in the next few years had operas produced in Rome, Naples, Milan and Venice. In the late 1730s he went to St Petersburg as *maestro* to Tsarina Anna Ivanovna and remained until 1762, organizing the first Russian music school and writing several stage works. His *Tsefal i Prokris* (1755) is the first opera in Russian.

Ariosti, Attilio (1666–*c.* 1729) Italian composer and diplomat. Initially a monk, and possibly a priest, he became *maître de musique* to the Electress of Brandenburg in Berlin and later an imperial minister to Joseph I in Vienna. In this capacity he travelled widely while continuing to compose, and made his first London appearance in 1716. From 1723 he received opera commissions from the Royal Academy, alongside Handel and Bononcini.

Arne, Michael (*c.* 1740–86) English composer, son of Thomas Augustine Arne. Active principally as a composer for the theatre and pleasure gardens, he wrote the famous song *The Lass with a Delicate Air* (1762). He also directed the first public performance of Handel's *Messiah* in Germany (1772) and was involved in alchemical experiments.

Arne, Thomas Augustine (1710–78) English composer. He was educated at Eton and from 1733 was active as a composer for the London stage, initially at

Drury Lane and later Covent Garden. His works include the masque *Alfred* (1740, containing 'Rule, Britannia'), the comic opera *Thomas and Sally* (1760) and the serious opera *Artaxerxes* (1762). Arne also composed odes, songs, overtures, concertos and keyboard music.

Avison, Charles (1709–70) English composer and writer on music. He allegedly studied with Geminiani, and was organist at St Nicholas, Newcastle. In 1735 he began the direction of the concert-giving Newcastle Musical Society, a position he retained until his death, and was active elsewhere in Newcastle and Durham. Avison was a leading composer of concerti grossi and the author of a controversial *Essay on Musical Expression* (1752), in which he argued for the primacy of Geminiani and Marcello over Handel.

Bach, Carl Philipp Emanuel (1714–88) German composer and harpsichordist, the second surviving son of J. S. Bach. He was taught by his father and studied law in Leipzig and Frankfurt, and in 1738 was engaged by Crown Prince Frederick of Prussia. Bach accompanied Frederick to Berlin in 1740 and was active in the musical life of the capital. In 1768 he moved to Hamburg as director of sacred music for the five principal churches of the city, remaining in contact with leading figures of the German intelligentsia. Bach developed a distinctive musical style often characterized by dramatic gestures and rapid shifts of emotion, and through his *Versuch über die wahre Art das Clavier zu spielen* (1753–62) and many solo works he occupies a central place in the history of keyboard music.

Bach, Johann Christian (1735–82) German composer resident in England, the youngest son of J. S. Bach. He presumably studied with his father, and later with his brother Carl Philipp Emanuel in Berlin. He moved to Milan in 1755 and was appointed organist at the Cathedral, gaining a reputation as an opera composer at the same time. In 1762 Bach moved to London, writing operas for the King's Theatre and working as music master to Queen Charlotte. He went into partnership with Abel in the famous Bach–Abel concerts and accepted a number of foreign operatic commissions, but his final years were marred by declining health and financial difficulties.

Bach, Johann Christoph Friedrich (1732–95) German composer, son of J. S. Bach. He studied with his father, and was appointed harpsichordist to the court of Bückeburg. In 1759 he was promoted to Konzertmeister, initially concentrating on the composition of instrumental music, but later writing German oratorios. In 1778 he visited his brother Johann Christian in London.

Bach, Johann Sebastian (1685–1750) German composer and organist. He studied in Lüneburg and held organist positions at Arnstadt (1703–7) and

Mühlhausen (1707–8). In 1708 he became organist at the ducal court in Weimar, and in 1714 was appointed Konzertmeister. He moved to Cöthen in 1717 as Kapellmeister to Prince Leopold, and in 1723 was elected Thomaskantor and civic director of music in Leipzig. The finest organist of his day, Bach was also a respected authority on the instrument's construction. His keyboard works, particularly in contrapuntal forms, have served as models of composition since their creation, and the sacred works are among the most original and profound vocal music of the late Baroque.

Bach, Wilhelm Friedemann (1710–84) German composer and organist, the eldest son of J. S. Bach. He studied with his father and was appointed organist of the Dresden Sophienkirche in 1733. In 1746 he became organist at the Liebfrauenkirche in Halle, leaving the post in 1764 but remaining in the city. In 1774 he moved to Berlin, applying unsuccessfully for various positions and composing little. Renowned as an organist, he apparently possessed a difficult personality which harmed his professional opportunities.

Balbastre, Claude-Benigne (1727–99) French composer and keyboard player. He moved from Dijon to Paris in 1750 and studied composition with Rameau. For several decades he performed at the Concert Spirituel and was organist at several Paris churches. Balbastre was also active at court, and taught Marie-Antoinette the harpsichord. His compositions include numerous keyboard pieces and four suites of variations on popular *noëls* (1770).

Beethoven, Ludwig van (1770–1827) German composer and pianist. He studied in his native Bonn with Christian Gottlob Neefe and moved to Vienna in 1792. Here he took lessons with Haydn and Albrechtsberger and developed a formidable reputation as a piano virtuoso. At the turn of the century he began to suffer from hearing loss which eventually progressed into near-total deafness. He relied on aristocratic support and income from publications, and in 1809 was granted an annuity by three of his patrons. His later years were clouded by a guardianship dispute regarding his nephew. Beethoven's contributions to the symphony, piano sonata and string quartet have remained at the centre of the repertory since their composition, and the importance of his example for the Romantic conception of the artist cannot be over-estimated.

Benda, Franz [František] (1709–86) Bohemian composer and violinist, resident in Germany. In 1733 Crown Prince Frederick of Prussia engaged him as a violinist, and he followed Frederick to Berlin after the coronation. He was appointed Konzertmeister in 1771. Benda studied composition with the Graun brothers, and produced concertos, sinfonias, solo sonatas and violin caprices.

Benda, Georg (Anton) [Jiří Antonín] (1722–95) Bohemian composer, resident in Germany. Like his brother Franz, he was a violinist at the Berlin court, and in 1750 he became Kapellmeister to Duke Friedrich III of Saxe-Gotha. He resigned in 1778 and lived in seclusion while continuing to compose sporadically. With *Ariadne auf Naxos* and *Medea* (both 1775), Benda created the first successful melodramas; he also composed singspiels, sacred and secular cantatas, chamber works and orchestral music.

Bertoni, Ferdinando (Gasparo) (1725–1813) Italian composer. He studied with Padre Martini and came to prominence with several successful operas. In 1752 he was appointed organist at S Marco in Venice, and in 1753 became *maestro* of the chorus at the Ospedale dei Mendicanti. He continued to compose for the stage, including a setting of Calzabigi's *Orfeo ed Euridice* (1776), and spent a number of years in London. From 1785 to his retirement in 1808 he was *maestro di cappella* at S Marco.

Billings, William (1746–1800) American singing-master and composer. Thought to have been mainly self-taught in composition, Billings achieved success in Boston through his musical direction in the city's churches. His music, the majority of which was published in six collections between 1770 and 1794 includes hymns, fuging tunes and anthems, all set for unaccompanied four-part chorus.

Billington (née Weichsel), Elizabeth (1765–1818) English soprano. Taught by her musical parents, she made her public debut in 1775. She married her singing teacher James Billington in 1783 and was engaged at Covent Garden from 1786. In the 1790s she sang successfully in Italy, and returned to England in 1801 where she continued to make stage and concert appearances. She was renowned for her intonation and abilities in improvised ornamentation.

Blavet, Michel (1700–1768) French flautist and composer. Self-taught on his instrument, he moved to Paris in 1723 in the entourage of Duke Charles-Eugène Lévis. He had a long and successful career as a performer at the Concert Spirituel, and was later in the service of the court and the Opéra. Universally praised for his performing abilities, Blavet also made important contributions to the early flute repertory through his sonatas.

Boccherini, (Ridolfo) Luigi (1743–1805) Italian composer and cellist, resident in Spain. He studied in Rome and was engaged from 1758 to 1764 at the Burgtheater in Vienna, gaining a reputation as a virtuoso. From 1768 he was in Aranjuez, first in an opera orchestra and from 1770 to 1785 as *compositore e virtuoso di camera* to Don Luis. By 1786 he was a nominal member of the Real

Capilla in Madrid and *compositeur de notre chambre* to Crown Prince Wilhelm of Prussia. He later received the patronage of the French consul in Madrid, Lucien Bonaparte. Boccherini's prolific output includes a large quantity of chamber music in a distinctively personal style, in addition to operas, symphonies, concertos and sacred works.

Böhm, Georg (1661–1733) German composer and organist. He studied initially with his father, and continued his education in Goldbach, Gotha and Jena. In 1697 he was appointed organist of the *Johanniskirche* in Lüneburg, and by 1700 was teaching the young J. S. Bach. Böhm's compositions are chiefly for keyboard instruments and include an important series of organ chorale partitas and harpsichord suites.

Boismortier, Joseph Bodin de (1689–1755) French composer. He held an administrative post in Perpignan and then moved to Paris around 1723. In 1724 he obtained a royal *privilège* and began to publish his own music. Boismortier's publications, great in number and consisting almost entirely of chamber music, were very successful and allowed the composer to maintain a freelance career.

Bonno, Giuseppe (1711–88) Austrian composer. He studied in Naples with Durante and Leo, and in 1739 was appointed court composer in Vienna. He later served the Prince of Sachsen-Hildburghausen, and in 1774 succeeded Gassmann as Hofkapellmeister. Bonno initially made his name as a composer of stage works, but increasingly turned to sacred music in connection with his court duties.

Bononcini, Antonio Maria (1677–1726) Italian composer. He studied in Bologna, and performed with his brother in Rome before moving to Vienna. From 1705 he composed operas, oratorios and cantatas for the Imperial court, but returned to Italy in 1713. In 1721 he was appointed *maestro di cappella* to the Duke of Modena. Bononcini's output includes dramatic and sacred vocal works and a series of sonatas for his own instrument, the cello.

Bononcini, Giovanni (1670–1747) Italian composer, brother of Antonio Maria (above). He studied in Bologna, and after working in Rome he entered the service of Leopold I in Vienna in 1697. After the death of Leopold's successor Joseph I in 1711, Bononcini worked in Rome for the Austrian ambassador. In 1720 he went to London as a composer for the Royal Academy of Music and was initially successful, but departed in 1732 due to cabals against him. In 1736 after further travels he settled in Vienna. Bononcini's works include operas, oratorios, cantatas, sacred music and instrumental sinfonias.

Bonporti, Francesco Antonio (1672–1749) Italian priest and composer. He studied in his native Trent, and later in Innsbruck and Rome. He returned to Trent after 1695 and made unsuccessful attempts to advance his ecclesiastical career, partly through the dedication of his works to prominent patrons. In 1740 he moved to Padua, and remained there to his death. Bonporti's works are almost entirely instrumental; a number of his *Invenzioni da camera* (Op. 10, 1712) were copied by J. S. Bach.

Bordoni (Hasse), Faustina (1697–1781) Italian mezzo-soprano. She studied with Gasparini in her native Venice and made her operatic debut there in 1716. Beginning in 1717 she made successful appearances in other Italian centres, and later in Munich and Vienna. From 1726 to 1728 she was in London, creating a number of Handel roles and pursuing a celebrated rivalry with Cuzzoni. In 1730 she married Johann Adolf Hasse, moving with him to Dresden and becoming a principal interpreter of his music. Faustina retired from the theatre in 1751 and moved with her husband to Vienna and finally Venice. She was particularly noted for her dramatic qualities and ability in improvised ornamentation.

Bortniansky, Dmitry Stepanovich (1751–1825) Russian composer. He was a choirboy in St Petersburg and studied with Galuppi in Venice. In 1779 he returned to Russia as Kapellmeister to Paul, the son of Catherine the Great. When Paul became emperor in 1796, he appointed Bortniansky as director of the Imperial Chapel Choir, a position the composer held until his death. Bortniansky is particularly remembered for his large-scale works for unaccompanied choir, known as sacred concertos.

Boyce, William (1711–79) English composer and organist. He studied with Greene and Pepusch and became composer to the Chapel Royal in 1736. He began composing for the stage, and in 1755 was appointed Master of the King's Musick. He composed many anthems and odes for royal occasions, and published symphonies, violin sonatas and a retrospective collection of English sacred music, *Cathedral Music* (1760–73).

Brixi, František [Franz] Xaver (1732–71) Czech composer and organist. He studied at the Piarist Gymnasium in Kosmonosy and in 1749 moved to Prague, where he was organist at a number of churches. In 1759 he was appointed Kapellmeister at St Vitus Cathedral, Prague, a position he held until his death. A prolific composer of sacred music, Brixi drew inspiration from both Neapolitan and central European traditions.

Broadwood, John (1732–1812) English piano-maker. He went to London in 1761 and worked with Burkat Shudi, going into partnership with the harpsichord-maker and later managing the firm alone. He continued to make harpsichords but concentrated on producing square and grand pianos, patenting a number of design innovations that improved the tone of the instrument. Broadwood's son James joined the firm in 1785 and became a full partner ten years later.

Buffardin, Pierre-Gabriel (*c.* 1690–1768) French flautist, active in Germany. He travelled to Constantinople with the French ambassador and taught J. S. Bach's younger brother Johann Jacob. In 1715 he joined the Kapelle of August II in Dresden and established a reputation as a leading virtuoso. Buffardin's salary was doubled under August III and in 1749 he was pensioned, after which he returned to France.

Burney, Charles (1726–1814) English music historian and composer. A pupil of Arne, he played in London orchestras and from 1751 to 1760 was organist at St Margaret's, King's Lynn. On his return to London he became a fashionable music teacher and composed for the stage. In 1770 and 1772 he undertook journeys to the continent to gather material for a large-scale history of music, producing valuable accounts of the musicians he met *en route*. The *General History* (1776–89) is a landmark in music historiography, and its author produced further writings on music including an account of the Handel commemoration in 1784 and articles for *Rees's Cyclopaedia*.

Caldara, Antonio (?1671–1736) Italian composer, later resident in Austria. He is assumed to have studied with Legrenzi, and was a member of the ensemble at S Marco, Venice. In 1699 he became *maestro di cappella* to the Duke of Mantua and from 1709 held the same post with Prince Ruspoli in Rome. He moved to Vienna in 1716 as imperial Vice-Kapellmeister, a position he held until his death. Caldara's immense output includes operas, oratorios, cantatas and a large amount of sacred music.

Calzabigi, Ranieri [Raniero] (Simone Francesco Maria) [de] (1714–95) Italian librettist. He wrote his first texts for musical setting in Naples, and after time in Paris and elsewhere he moved to Vienna as secretary to Chancellor Kaunitz. He wrote the libretti for Gluck's *Orfeo ed Euridice* (1762), *Alceste* (1767) and *Paride ed Elena* (1770) and penned the famous manifesto for opera reform in the published score of *Alceste*. Calzabigi's later years were spent in Pisa and Naples, where he continued to produce a small number of libretti.

Cambini, Giuseppe Maria (Gioacchino) (1746–?1825) Italian composer and violinist, active in France. He moved to Paris in the early 1770s and established his reputation through opera productions, performances at the Concert

Spirituel and the publication of his instrumental music. He remained in France during the Revolution, but little is known of his late years. Cambini's prolific output includes a large number of string quartets and sinfonie concertante.

Campra, André (1660–1744) French composer, principally of sacred music and stage works. He held a number of directorships in French churches before being appointed *maître de musique* at Notre Dame Cathedral, Paris, in 1694. In 1697 he began writing opéras-ballets for the Académie Royale de Musique, and the success of these works prompted him to leave Notre Dame in 1700. He was granted a pension by Louis XV in 1718, and from 1723 to 1742 he was one of the directors of music at the royal chapel.

Cannabich, (Johann) Christian (Innocenz Bonaventura) (1731–98) German composer and violinist. He studied with J. Stamitz in Mannheim and Jommelli in Rome and Stuttgart. Upon his return to Mannheim he was made joint Konzertmeister by 1759 and became well known in Paris through publications and concert appearances. In 1774 he was appointed director of instrumental music and retained the position after the merger of the Mannheim and Munich orchestras. Cannabich's works include ballets, symphonies, concertos and chamber music.

Carestini, Giovanni (*c.* 1704–*c.* 1760) Italian soprano (later alto) castrato, known as Cusanino. He sang in northern Italian centres before making his Roman debut in 1721. He later sang in Vienna, Venice, Naples and Munich, and went to London in 1733 where he created roles in many Handel operas and oratorios. Carestini's subsequent career was less successful. He was celebrated for the power and virtuosity of his voice.

Cavalieri, Catarina (1755–1801) Austrian soprano. She made her operatic debut in 1775 in Anfossi's *La finta giardiniera*, and joined the new National-Singspiel at the Vienna Burgtheater in 1778. She later sang in a number of Mozart productions including *Die Entführung*, *Davide penitente*, *Der Schauspieldirektor*, the Viennese *Don Giovanni* and the 1789 revival of *Le nozze di Figaro*. She was pensioned in 1793, and little is known of her final years.

Cherubini, Luigi (Carlo Zanobi Salvadore Maria) (1760–1842) Italian composer, conductor and administrator, resident in France. He studied in his native Florence and served an apprenticeship with Sarti in 1778–81, after which he composed operas for various Italian centres. After a season at the King's Theatre in London, Cherubini moved to Paris in 1786 and began writing French operas, in 1795 joining the Conservatoire as an inspector. He was appointed *maître de chapelle* to Louis XVIII in 1815 and director of the Conservatoire in 1822. Admired by Beethoven, Cherubini was a leading figure in the musical life of the French capital.

Cimarosa, Domenico (1749–1801) Italian composer. He studied at the Conservatorio di S Maria di Loreto in Naples and from 1772 composed operas for Naples and Rome. In the 1780s he was organist of the Neopolitan royal chapel and *maestro* of the Ospedaletto conservatory in Venice. From 1787–91 he was in St Petersburg at the court of Catherine the Great, and after a few years in Vienna he returned to Naples. He narrowly avoided execution in 1800 after supporting the French republican cause. Cimarosa was among the most celebrated composers of comic opera in the late eighteenth century.

Clementi, Muzio [Mutius Philippus Vincentius Franciscus Xaverius] (1752–1832) Italian composer, keyboard player, publisher and piano manufacturer, resident in England. Born in Rome, he was taken in 1766 to Dorset where his studies were sponsored by a patron. He moved to London in 1774, working at the King's Theatre and gaining a reputation as a keyboard virtuoso. From 1780 his career was divided between England and the Continent as he pursued opportunities in performance, composition, teaching, publishing and instrument-making. Clementi's prolific output of keyboard music was highly influential on the following generation of pianists.

Clérambault, Louis-Nicolas (1676–1749) French organist and composer. He studied with Raison and Moreau, and became organist at the Grands-Augustins in Paris. In about 1714 he was appointed organist at St Sulpice and at the Maison Royale de Saint-Cyr. Clérambault wrote organ, harpsichord and sacred vocal works, but is best known for five *livres* of French secular cantatas (1710–26).

Conti, Francesco Bartolomeo (1681/2-1732) Italian composer and theorbist. He was serving as associate theorbist at the imperial court in Vienna by 1701, and in 1708 was promoted to principal. Around the time of his promotion he began to be active in composition, and received the additional title of court composer in 1713. He was favoured with commissions for both serious operas and comic intermezzi, but retired in 1726 and spent a number of years in Italy. In addition to his stage works, Conti composed oratorios, cantatas, sacred music and instrumental pieces.

Corelli, Arcangelo (1653–1713) Italian composer and violinist. He studied in Bologna and was in Rome by 1675, where he played in orchestras and cultivated the patronage of Queen Christina of Sweden and Cardinal Pamphili. He later lived in the palace of Cardinal Ottoboni and in 1700 became head of the instrumental section of the *Congregazione di S Cecilia*. His last years were devoted to the revision of his concerti grossi for publication. Although Corelli's works were not great in number, they enjoyed great renown throughout the eighteenth century as 'classic' examples of the solo sonata, trio sonata and concerto grosso.

Corrette, Michel (1707–95) French composer, organist and writer on music. From 1737 he was organist at St Marie in Paris, and fulfilled the same role at the Jesuit College until 1762. He was knighted, and at some stage visited England. Well known as a teacher, Corrette was a prolific composer, and much of his music incorporates popular melodies of the day. He also wrote a number of instrumental treatises which are a valuable source of information on performance practice.

Couperin, François [*le grand*] (1668–1733) French composer, harpsichordist and organist, the most renowned member of a distinguished musical family. He succeeded his father as organist at St Gervais in Paris, and in 1693 was appointed one of the organists at the Chapelle Royale. He was increasingly active at court as a teacher and performer and in 1717 received the post of *ordinaire de la musique de la chambre du roi*. Couperin's four *livres* of harpsichord pieces are among the most important French repertory for the instrument, and the chamber music is notable for its reconciliation of French and Italian styles.

Cristofori, Bartolomeo (1655–1732) Italian harpsichord and piano-maker. In 1688 he was appointed to the Medici court in Florence as a tuner, and by 1716 had become steward of the Medici's instrument collection. Cristofori is commonly credited with the invention of the piano; the earliest known reference to such an instrument is found in an inventory of 1700, where it is called *arpicimbalo*. The three surviving Cristofori pianos all date from the 1720s.

Cuzzoni, Francesca (1696–1778) Italian soprano. A pupil of Lanzi, she made her operatic debut in 1714. After appearing in numerous Italian centres she went to London in 1722, achieving unprecedented success at the King's Theatre in operas by Handel, Ariosti and Bononcini. In 1728 she returned to the continent and sang in Vienna and Italy, but her later visits to London were not as successful and she died in poverty.

Dandrieu, Jean-François (1681/2-1738) French composer and keyboard player. He was organist at St Merry in Paris from 1704, and from 1721 served as one of the *organistes du roi*. Dandrieu's harpsichord music, published between 1705 and 1734, forms an important counterpart to the contemporary works of Couperin and Rameau. He also published a single book of organ music and two collections of instrumental sonatas.

Danzi, Franz (Ignaz) (1763–1826) German composer. He studied composition in Mannheim with Vogler, and in 1784 was appointed principal cellist in the Munich court orchestra. In 1790 he married the soprano Margarethe Marchand and together they toured in Germany, Austria and Italy. On his return to Munich he became deputy Kapellmeister in 1798, followed by Kapellmeister in Stuttgart and later Karlsruhe. Danzi composed prolifically in all forms but is best known for his chamber music.

Da Ponte, Lorenzo [Conegliano, Emmanuele] (1749–1838) Italian librettist. Ordained a priest, he was banned from Venice in 1779 and moved to Vienna in 1781. From 1783 to 1791 he was court poet, writing libretti for Salieri, Soler, Mozart and others. He was based at the King's Theatre in London from 1793, and in 1805 moved to the United States. After working as a merchant and book dealer, he settled permanently in New York in 1819 and was Professor of Italian at Columbia College.

Daquin, Louis-Claude (1694–1772) French keyboard player and composer. An infant prodigy, he studied composition with Bernier and was organist at numerous Parisian establishments. In 1739 he was appointed organist at the Chapelle Royale, and in 1755 became one of the four organists at Notre Dame. A renowned improviser, his published music includes a book of harpsichord music and a collection of organ *noëls*.

Destouches, André Cardinal (1672–1749) French composer. Of a high social status, he led an adventurous youth before studying with Campra. He attracted the attention of Louis XIV and from 1699 his stage works were produced at the Opéra. From 1713 he was *surintendant* and from 1728 *maître de musique de la chambre*. For some years he directed the Académie Royale de Musique and organized concerts for Queen Maria Leszcynska.

Devienne, François (1759–1803) French flautist, bassoonist and composer. From 1780 he served Cardinal de Rohan and made appearances at the Concert Spirituel. From 1789 he was a bassoonist in the Théâtre de Monsieur, and in 1795 become an administrator and professor of flute at the Paris Conservatoire. Devienne published a famous flute method in 1794, and his numerous works for the instrument did much to raise its profile in France.

Dieupart, Charles [François] (?*c*. 1670–*c*. 1740) French violinist, harpsichordist and composer, resident in England. By 1703 he was in London, where he played in opera orchestras and gave concerts. He later played at Drury Lane and worked as a fashionable music teacher. Dieupart was among the earliest composers of French origin to write concertos, and his *Six suittes de clavessin* (1701) were copied by J. S. Bach.

Dittersdorf, Carl Ditters von (1739–99) Austrian composer and violinist. He studied the violin with Trani and composition with Bonno, and after playing in the Burgtheater orchestra in the 1760s he became Kapellmeister to the Bishop of Grosswardein in 1765. From 1769 he directed the musical establishment of Count von Schaffgotsch, Prince Bishop of Breslau. Dittersdorf's works were well received in Vienna but he was unable to secure employment in a major centre. He composed in all forms, achieving great success with the singspiel *Der Apotheker und der Doktor* (1786).

Doles, Johann Friedrich (1715–97) German composer and organist. He enrolled at Leipzig University in 1739 and was a student of J. S. Bach. In 1744 he became Kantor in Freiburg, directing the music at four of the city's churches. In 1756 he was appointed Thomaskantor in Leipzig, and held the office until 1789 when he resigned due to disputes with the authorities. He continued to be active in composition until his death.

Duni, Egidio (Romualdo) (1708–75) Italian composer, resident in France. He studied in Naples, and after writing operas for numerous centres he was appointed *maestro di cappella* to the Duke of Parma. He settled in Paris in 1757 and wrote a successful series of opéras-comiques. From 1761 to 1768 he was music director at the Comédie-Italienne, after which he retired.

Durante, Francesco (1684–1755) Italian composer. He studied in Naples and possibly Rome, but little is known of his life until his appointment in 1728 as *primo maestro* of the Neopolitan Conservatorio dei Poveri di Gesù Cristo. He resigned in 1739 and in 1742 took up the same position at the Conservatorio di S Maria di Loreto. Durante was a renowned teacher and composer of sacred music; among his students were Pergolesi, Traetta and Piccinni.

Durastanti, Margherita (fl. 1700–34) Italian soprano. She was in the service of Marquis Ruspoli in Rome from 1707, and was prima donna at the S Giovanni Grisostomo theatre in Venice in 1709–12. At this stage she had already created roles in a number of Handel cantatas, the oratorio *La Resurrezione* and the opera *Agrippina*. She sang in a number of other Italian centres, and was engaged by Handel in 1720 for the Royal Academy in London. Handel wrote numerous roles for her during this visit and for subsequent seasons in 1722–4 and 1733–4.

Dušek [Duschek], František Xaver (1731–99) Czech composer and music teacher. He attended the Gymnasium at Hradec Králové and studied in Vienna with Wagenseil. By 1770 he was in Prague, where he worked as an influential teacher and received the patronage of the Counts Pachta and Clam-Gallas. In 1776 he married the soprano Josefa Hambacher, for whom Mozart wrote a number of works.

Dussek [Dusík], Jan Ladislav [Johann Ludwig] (1760–1812) Czech pianist and composer. He studied in Kutná Hora and Prague, and from 1779 travelled widely as a virtuoso, visiting The Netherlands, Germany and Russia. He lived in Paris from 1786 to 1789 and in London after the Revolution, establishing an unsuccessful publishing business. He was Kapellmeister to Prince Louis Ferdinand of Prussia from 1804 to 1806 and later served the diplomat Tallyrand. Dussek was one of the earliest travelling piano virtuosi and his sonatas are notable for their technical virtuosity.

Eckard, Johann Gottfried (1735–1809) German pianist and composer, resident in France. Initially a copper engraver, he accompanied the piano-builder Johann Andreas Stein to Paris in 1758 and settled there permanently. He was an early advocate of the piano in France and the first Parisian composer of piano sonatas. Eckard's surviving works, although few in number, were admired by Mozart and formed part of his performing repertory.

Farinelli [Broschi, Carlo] (1705–82) Italian soprano castrato. He studied in Naples with Porpora and made his debut in 1720. In 1722 he began singing in earnest and enjoyed unprecedented success in northern Italian opera houses. From 1734 he was in London and in 1737 moved to Madrid. Here he sang for Philip V and directed opera productions before retiring to Bologna in 1759. Farinelli was the most celebrated castrato of the eighteenth century.

Fasch, Carl Friedrich Christian (1736–1800) German composer and conductor. From 1756 he was second harpsichordist to Frederick the Great, advancing to first harpsichordist in 1767 and conductor of the Royal Opera in 1774–6. In the 1790s he founded the *Sing-Akademie zu Berlin*. Fasch did much to encourage choral singing in Germany and contributed to the Bach revival.

Fasch, Johann Friedrich (1688–1758) German composer, father of Carl Friedrich Christian (above). He was a student of Kuhnau at the Leipzig Thomasschule, and after studying with Graupner and holding positions in Greiz and Prague he became court Kapellmeister in Zerbst. Appointed in 1722, he held the position for the rest of his life. Fasch wrote several cycles of sacred cantatas but is most significant for his overtures and concertos, works notable for their woodwind writing and progressive stylistic features.

Feo, Francesco (1691–1761) Italian composer. He studied at the Conservatorio di S Maria della Pietà dei Turchini in Naples and made his operatic debut in 1713. In 1723 he became *maestro* of the Conservatorio di S Onofrio a Capuana and in 1739 was appointed *primo maestro* of the Conservatorio dei Poveri di Gesù Cristo. He retired in 1743 but continued to compose sacred music for Neapolitan churches.

Fiala, Joseph (1748–1816) Bohemian oboist, cellist and composer. He studied in Prague and from 1774 was an oboist in the service of Prince Kraft Ernst von Oettingen-Wallerstein. In 1778 he became first oboist in the Salzburg Hofkapelle and was friendly with the Mozarts. Dismissed in 1785, he toured St Petersburg and other cities before entering the service of Prince Fürstenberg at Donaueschingen in 1792. Fiala composed symphonies, concertos and a large amount of chamber music.

Fischer, Johann Caspar Ferdinand (1656–1746) German composer. By 1689 he was Kapellmeister to Duke Julius Franz of Saxe-Lauenburg in Schlackenwerth (Ostrov). The state was later divided and from 1715 Fischer served Margrave Ludwig Wilhelm of Baden in Rastatt. He composed instrumental suites and sacred music but is best-known for *Ariadne musica* (1702), a collection of preludes and fugues in most of the available keys.

Forqueray, Jean-Baptiste (-Antoine) (1699–1782) French violist and composer. A celebrated virtuoso on the viol, he was considered almost the equal of his father Antoine (1672–1745) and succeeded him as *ordinaire de la chambre du roi* in 1742. In 1747 he published a collection of *Pieces de viole* ostensibly by his father, although stylistic considerations suggest that he himself was involved to an undetermined extent.

Fux, Johann Joseph (1660–1741) Austrian composer and theorist. He was educated in Graz, Ingolstadt and possibly Italy, and by 1696 he was organist at the Schottenstift in Vienna. In 1698 he was appointed court composer, and from 1705 he fulfilled Kapellmeister duties at St Stephen's Cathedral. Charles VI appointed him Hofkapellmeister in 1715. Fux's large output includes numerous operas, oratorios and sacred works, but he is chiefly remembered for *Gradus ad Parnassum* (1725), the most influential music treatise of the eighteenth century.

Galuppi, Baldassare (1706–85) Italian composer. He studied with Lotti and became involved in the Venetian opera scene while working at the

Ospedale dei Mendicanti. He visited London in 1741–3 and later enjoyed a successful collaboration with the librettist Goldoni. In 1762 he was elected *maestro di coro* at S Marco, and after an invitation from Catherine the Great he worked from 1765 to 1768 in St Petersburg. In his later years Galuppi concentrated primarily on his church duties in Venice. One of the most successful opera composers of the eighteenth century, he also produced numerous oratorios, sacred works, instrumental works and keyboard sonatas.

Gasparini, Francesco (1661–1727) Italian composer. He studied in Rome, and in 1701 was appointed *maestro di coro* at the Ospedale della Pietà, Venice. He left the Pietà in 1713 and in 1716 became *maestro di cappella* to Prince Ruspoli. In 1725 he was named *maestro di cappella* at S Giovanni in Laterano, Rome. A prolific composer of opera, Gasparini also wrote a large body of chamber cantatas, oratorios, sacred vocal music and a treatise on figured bass, *L'armonico pratico al cimbalo* (1708).

Gassmann, Florian Leopold (1729–74) Bohemian composer, active in Austria. He studied in Italy, and the success of his Venetian operas led to his appointment in 1763 as ballet composer at the imperial court in Vienna. The following year Gassmann was made Kammerkomponist, and in 1772 he succeeded Reutter as Hofkapellmeister. His works include operas, symphonies, chamber music and a Requiem thought to have influenced Mozart; he was also the teacher and mentor of Salieri.

Gay, John (1685–1732) English playwright. He collaborated on the libretto for Handel's *Acis and Galatea* in 1718 and wrote a quantity of verse, but scored an unprecedented success with *The Beggar's Opera* in 1728. The production of its sequel *Polly* was banned and it was not staged until 1777.

Gazzaniga, Giuseppe (1743–1818) Italian composer. He studied with Porpora and Piccinni, and during the 1770s wrote operas for several Italian centres. In 1786 he colloborated with Lorenzo da Ponte on *Il finto cieco*, and the following year he produced the work for which he is best known, *Don Giovanni, o sia Il convitato di pietra*. In 1791 Gazzaniga became *maestro di cappella* at Crema Cathedral and held the position until his death.

Geminiani, Francesco (Saverio) (1687–1762) Italian composer, violinist and theorist. He studied with Corelli and possibly A. Scarlatti, and moved to England in 1714. There he enjoyed aristocratic patronage and was active as an art dealer. From 1733 he divided his time between London and Dublin and visited Paris on a number of occasions. His works include solo sonatas, concerti grossi and a number of late treatises of considerable interest.

Giordani, Tommaso (*c.* 1730/3–1806) Italian composer, resident in the British Isles. He travelled across Europe with his family's theatre troupe, performing at Covent Garden from 1753. By 1764 he was in Dublin, where a number of his operas were performed, and after further productions in London from 1767 he settled in Dublin in 1783. Giordani published several sets of keyboard pieces and chamber music in addition to selections from his stage works.

Gluck, Christoph Willibald, Ritter von (1714–87) Bohemian composer, known for his innovative stage works. He studied in Milan with Sammartini and wrote his first operas for Italian centres. In 1745 he travelled to London as house composer to the King's Theatre, and later received commissions from Dresden, Copenhagen, Prague, Naples and Vienna. He settled in Vienna and in 1755 became Kapellmeister at the Burgtheater. Here he produced opere serie, opéras-comiques and ballets, and collaborated with the librettist Calzabigi on the 'reform operas' *Orfeo ed Euridice* (1762), *Paride ed Elena* (1770) and *Alceste* (1767). From 1773 he was often resident in Paris and wrote a series of works for the Opéra, notably *Iphigénie en Tauride*. Gluck returned to Vienna in 1779 and remained in semi-retirement until his death.

Goldoni, Carlo [Fegejo, Polisseno] (1707–93) Italian playwright and librettist. He was professionally active as a lawyer, and from 1734 to 1762 wrote for theatres in Venice. In 1762 he moved to Paris, where he wrote less prolifically for the Comédie-Française. Although Goldoni wrote in many forms, he is best known for his opera buffa libretti, many of which include extended finales designed for continuous musical setting.

Gossec, François-Joseph (1734–1829) Belgian composer, resident in France. He went to Paris in 1751, and worked for Alexandre-J. J. Le Riche La Pouplinière and the Prince of Condé. In 1769 he founded the Concert des amateurs and in 1773 assumed the joint directorship of the Concert Spirituel. From 1780 he was associated with the Opéra, but resigned in 1789 and became the successful director of the *Corps de Musique de la Garde Nationale*. In his later years Gossec was a professor at the Conservatoire and composed little. His works include operas, symphonies, chamber music and revolutionary pieces.

Graun, Carl Heinrich (1703/4–59) German composer. He studied in Dresden and from 1724 worked for the Duke of Brunswick-Wolfenbüttel. In 1735 he went to Prussia as composer to Crown Prince Frederick, and with Frederick's coronation was appointed Kapellmeister in 1741. He composed operas for the newly established court opera in Berlin in addition to concertos, chamber music and the famous oratorio *Der Tod Jesu* (1755).

Graun, Johann Gottlieb (1702/3–71) German composer and violinist, brother of Carl Heinrich (above). A student of Pisendel and Tartini, he worked for the Prince of Waldeck from 1727. In 1732 he joined the Kapelle of Crown Prince Frederick of Prussia, and moved to Berlin with him in 1740. Graun's compositions include sinfonias, concertos, chamber music and cantatas, although there is some confusion between his works and those of his brother.

Graupner, Christoph (1683–1760) German composer. He studied in Leipzig with Schelle and Kuhnau and from 1707 to 1709 worked as a harpsichordist at the *Gänsemarktoper* in Hamburg. In 1709 he became Vice-Kapellmeister to the Landgrave of Hesse-Darmstadt and succeeded to the full position in 1712. He secured the position of Thomaskantor in Leipzig in 1722–3 but remained in Darmstadt after an increase in salary, allowing J. S. Bach to take up the post. Graupner was a prolific composer of operas, suites, concertos, chamber music and sacred cantatas.

Greene, Maurice (1696–1755) English composer. He was a choirboy at St Paul's Cathedral and became organist there in 1718. In 1727 he was appointed organist and composer of the Chapel Royal, and in 1735 Master of the King's Music. He wrote a large number of anthems in addition to oratorios, songs and keyboard music.

Grétry, André-Ernest-Modeste (1741–1813) Belgian composer, resident in France. He studied in Rome in 1760–5, and after some time in Geneva moved to Paris in 1767. Here he produced a successful series of opéras-comiques that established his fame all over Europe, notably *Zémire et Azor* (1771) and *Richard Coeur-de-lion* (1784). He later produced philosophical writings and a valuable collection of memoirs.

Guadagni, Gaetano (1729–92) Italian alto castrato. He went to London in 1748 to sing at the Haymarket Theatre, and created the role of Didymus in Handel's *Theodora*. After further appearances in France and Italy he travelled to Vienna in 1762 and created roles in operas by Hasse and Gluck, including the title role in the latter's *Orfeo*. He later sang in Italy, England and Germany, and after appearing before Frederick the Great in 1776 retired to Padua.

Guarneri, (Bartolomeo) Giuseppe 'del Gesù' (1698–1744) Italian violin-maker. He trained in Cremona with his father, also a distinguished maker, and from the late 1720s was making his own instruments. At the height of his powers in the mid-1730s, Guarneri was crafting violins of a quality comparable to, although very different from, those of Stradivari. The nickname 'del Gesù' derives from the maker's habit of signing his instruments with the Christogram *IHS*.

Guglielmi, Pietro (Alessandro) (1728–1804) Italian composer. He studied at the S Maria di Loreto conservatory in Naples and from 1757 wrote operas for Naples and Rome. He was in London from 1767 to 1772 as director at the King's Theatre, after which he returned to Italy. He was appointed *maestro di cappella* at St Peter's, Rome in 1793. Guglielmi was a prolific composer of both serious and comic opera and achieved particular success with *La sposa fedele* (1767).

Handel [Händel], George Frideric [Georg Friederich] (1685–1759) German composer, later resident in England. He joined the orchestra of the Hamburg Opera in 1703 and began to compose for the theatre. In 1706 he left for Italy, settling in Rome in 1707 and visiting Naples, Florence and Venice. In 1710 he arrived in Hanover as Kapellmeister to the Elector and in the same year journeyed to London, where he settled permanently in 1712. Granted a pension by Queen Anne, he served the Duke of Chandos and for much of the 1720s and 1730s was engaged in the composition and direction of opera at the King's Theatre and Covent Garden. He also began composing oratorios, and from 1742 gave up opera entirely to concentrate on this genre. Handel produced works in all forms but it was his oratorios, above all *Messiah* (1741) that established his iconic position in English musical history.

Hasse, Johann Adolf (1699–1783) German composer. He appeared as a tenor in Hamburg and Brunswick, and in 1722 went to Naples where he converted to Roman Catholicism and studied with A. Scarlatti. The success of his operas led to his appointment in 1730 as Kapellmeister in Dresden, but he spent much of his time abroad on operatic projects, particularly in Vienna and Venice. From the 1740s he was engaged in a fruitful collaboration with Metastasio and together they produced a series of works for Hapsburg celebrations in the 1760s. In 1773 he retired to Venice and continued a long association with the Ospedale degli Incurabili. During his lifetime Hasse was among the most celebrated operatic composers in Europe and also composed prolifically for the church.

Haydn, (Franz) Joseph (1732–1809) Austrian composer. He was a choirboy at St Stephen's Cathedral in Vienna from about 1740. When his voice changed in 1749 he remained in the city as a freelance performer and teacher while studying with Porpora. After a short time in the service of Count Morzin he became Vice-Kapellmeister to Prince Esterházy in 1761, advancing to Kapellmeister in 1766. In the 1780s he began to cultivate relations with other patrons and publishers, and in 1791–5 twice visited London. His last years were spent in Vienna. Although not the 'father' of the symphony and string quartet, Haydn achieved lasting fame in those genres through his creative ambition and prolific output. Of his numerous sacred and secular vocal works, *Die Schöpfung* (*The Creation*) (1798) occupies a central position in the history of the oratorio.

Haydn, (Johann) Michael (1737–1806) Austrian composer, younger brother of Joseph (above). Like Joseph he was a choirboy at St Stephen's Cathedral, and by 1760 he was working as Kapellmeister to the Bishop of Grosswardein. In 1763 he was appointed Konzertmeister to Archbishop Schrattenbach in Salzburg, and in 1782 succeeded Mozart as court organist there. Haydn composed operatic, orchestral and chamber music but was particularly known for his sacred works.

Haym, Nicola Francesco (1678–1729) Italian composer and librettist. He was a cellist in Rome and in 1701 moved to England. There he played in opera orchestras and began adapting operas for the London stage. He provided librettos for Handel, Bononcini and Ariosti and was secretary of the Royal Academy of Music from 1722 to 1728. Apart from his opera adaptations, Haym composed cantatas, chamber music and sacred works.

Heinichen, Johann David (1683–1729) German composer. He was a student at the Leipzig Thomasschule, and later a law student at the University. He combined his legal and musical interests during posts in Weissenfels and Leipzig, and from 1710 to 1716 was in Italy, meeting the leading Italian composers and composing operas for Venice. In 1717 he moved to Dresden as joint Kapellmeister and retained the post until his death. Heinichen wrote a large amount of sacred and secular music, but his most important achievement is the treatise *Der General-Bass in der Composition* (1728).

Hiller, Johann Adam (1728–1804) German composer, conductor and writer on music. He studied in Dresden and Leipzig, and from 1763 was director of the Leipzig *Grosse Concert-Gesellschaft*. He also began writing Singspiele, founded a song school and established the music periodical *Wöchentliche Nachrichten* (1766–70). In 1781 he became director of the Gewandhaus concerts, and after a short time in Breslau succeeded Doles as Thomaskantor in 1789. Many of Hiller's writings are of considerable interest as early examples of musical journalism.

Hofmann, Leopold (1738–93) Austrian composer. He studied with Wagenseil and in 1764 was appointed *regens chori* at St Peter's, Vienna. In 1769 he became Hofklaviermeister to the Imperial family, and in 1772 succeeded Reutter as Kapellmeister at St Stephen's Cathedral. His output includes numerous sacred works, symphonies, concertos and chamber music.

Hoffmeister, Franz Anton (1754–1812) Austrian music publisher and composer. He studied law in Vienna but devoted himself to music, composing extensively and establishing a publishing firm in 1785. In 1799 he embarked on a concert tour and met the organist Kühnel in Leipzig, with whom he established another firm, the *Bureau de Musique*. He sold both businesses in 1805–6 and devoted himself to composition. Hoffmeister issued first editions of works by Haydn, Mozart, Beethoven and others.

Holzbauer, Ignaz (Jakob) (1711–83) Austrian composer. He studied in Vienna and worked for Count Rottal in Holleschau (Holešov). From 1746 to 1750 he composed ballet music for the Burgtheater and in 1751 was appointed Oberkapellmeister in Stuttgart. Following court intrigue he moved to Mannheim in 1753 and in 1773 was appointed Kapellmeister. Holzbauer's greatest success was his opera *Günther von Schwarzburg* (1777).

Homilius, Gottfried August (1714–85) German composer and organist. He studied law at Leipzig University from 1735, and took lessons from J. S. Bach in composition and keyboard playing. In 1742 he was appointed organist at the Frauenkirche in Dresden, and in 1755 became Kantor at the Dresden Kreuzkirche and director of music for the principal churches of the city. A prolific composer of cantatas, passions, motets and organ music, Homilius ranks with Doles and C. P. E. Bach as a leading practitioner of Protestant sacred music in the second half of the eighteenth century.

Hotteterre, Jacques (-Martin) ['le Romain'] (1673–1763) French flautist and composer, the most distinguished member of a large family of woodwind-makers and players. From 1698 to 1700 he was in the service of Prince Ruspoli in Rome, and on his return to Paris received the post of *grand hautbois du roy*. A fashionable teacher, he was appointed *flutte de la chambre de roy* in 1717. Hotteterre published numerous solos and produced an important method, *Principes de la flûte traversière* (1707).

Hummel, Johann Nepomuk (1778–1837) German composer and pianist. A child prodigy, he studied with Mozart and toured Europe with his father. On his return to Vienna he studied with Haydn, Albrechtsberger and Salieri and from 1804 to 1811 directed the Esterházy Hofkapelle. He was Kapellmeister at Stuttgart from 1816 to 1818 and thereafter at Weimar until his death. Hummel was an acclaimed virtuoso pianist and composed keyboard music, concertos, chamber music, operas and sacred works.

Jommelli, Niccolò (1714–74) Italian composer. He studied at the S Onofrio and Pietà dei Turchini conservatories in Naples and made his operatic debut in

1737. From about 1745 he was *maestro* at the Ospedale degli Incurabili in Venice and *maestro di cappella* at St Peter's, Rome from 1750. In 1754 he was appointed Oberkapellmeister to the Duke of Württemberg in Stuttgart, and returned to Italy in 1768. A central figure in mid-century opera, Jommelli was noted for his dramatic abilities and for his ability to combine elements of the various national styles.

Keiser, Reinhard (1674–1739) German composer. He was a student at the Leipzig Thomasschule and by 1694 was in the service of the Brunswick-Wolfenbüttel court. In about 1697 he moved to Hamburg, subsequently becoming director of the Opera, and provided many of his own settings before the company's bankruptcy in 1718. After composing a number of operas for Copenhagen he resumed work in Hamburg in 1722, and in 1728 became Kantor of Hamburg Cathedral. Keiser was the most important composer of Baroque opera in Germany and was the first to set Brockes' influential passion oratorio (1712).

Kelly, Michael (1762–1826) Irish tenor and composer. He studied in Italy and in 1783 was recruited for the new Italian opera company in Vienna. There he became acquainted with Mozart and created Don Basilio and Don Curzio in *Le nozze di Figaro*. In 1787 he moved to London and sang at Drury Lane, later becoming stage manager at the King's Theatre, Haymarket. Kelly's *Reminiscences* (1826) is a valuable source of information on theatrical life in the eighteenth century.

Kirnberger, Johann Philipp (1721–83) German theorist and composer. He studied with Kellner, Gerber and J. S. Bach and spent a number of years in Poland. In 1751 he returned to Germany and worked as a violinist in Berlin, and from 1758 served Princess Anna Amalia. Kirnberger produced vocal and instrumental music but is remembered for his theoretical writings, particularly the composition treatise *Die Kunst des reinen Satzes*.

Kittel, Johann Christian (1732–1809) German organist and composer. He was one of J. S. Bach's last students in Leipzig, and successively organist in Langensalza, the Barfüsserkirche in Erfurt and the Predigerkirche in Erfurt. Renowned as a virtuoso, he composed organ and piano works and produced the important treatise *Der angehende praktische Organist* (1801–8).

Koch, Heinrich Christoph (1749–1816) German composer and theorist. He spent his entire career in the Rudolstadt Hofkapelle, becoming Kapellmeister in 1792. He is remembered for the three-volume *Versuch einer Anleitung zur Composition* (1782–93) and the equally ambitious *Musikalisches Lexikon* (1802).

Kozeluch [Koželuh], Leopold [Jan Antonín] (1747–1818) Bohemian composer and music publisher. He studied music in Prague and went to Vienna in 1778, soon establishing himself as a pianist, composer and teacher. In 1785 he founded a music publishing house and in 1792 was appointed Hofkomponist. Kozeluch's works include oratorios, symphonies, concertos, piano sonatas and chamber music. His cousin Jan Antonín Kozeluch (1738–1814) was Kapellmeister at St Vitus Cathedral in Prague from 1784 to 1814.

Kraus, Joseph Martin (1756–92) German–Swedish composer. He studied music in Mannheim and law in Erfurt and Göttingen. In 1778 he moved to Stockholm, where he was appointed Vice-Kapellmeister in 1781. Gustav III sent him on a four-year grand tour of Europe, and on his return he was appointed Kapellmeister in 1788. An original and inventive voice in late-eighteenth-century music, Kraus composed operas, symphonies, concertos, chamber music and sacred works.

Krebs, Johann Ludwig (1713–80) German organist and composer. In 1726 he enrolled at the Thomasschule in Leipzig and was a student of J. S. Bach over the next decade. In 1737 he was appointed organist at St Marien in Zwickau, and after a move to Zeitz in 1744 became organist to Prince Friedrich of Gotha-Altenburg in 1755. He wrote an important body of organ music in addition to chamber, orchestral and sacred vocal works.

Krumpholtz, Jean-Baptiste [Johann Baptist, Jan Křtitel] (1747–90) Czech harpist, composer and instrument-maker. He studied in Vienna and from 1776 toured Europe as a harp virtuoso. In 1777 he settled in Paris but committed suicide after his wife abandoned him. Krumpholtz made technical improvements to the harp and composed sonatas and concertos for the instrument.

Kuhnau, Johann (1660–1722) German composer and organist. He studied in Dresden and Zittau and in 1684 was appointed organist at the Leipzig Thomaskirche. While in Leipzig he successfully practised law and gained proficiency in mathematics, theology, rhetoric and foreign languages. In 1701 he became Thomaskantor in succession to Schelle. Kuhnau is well known as the composer of the *Biblische Historien* for keyboard, but he also wrote a large quantity of sacred vocal works, now mostly lost, and a satirical novel *Der musikalische Quacksalber* (1700).

La Borde, Jean-Benjamin (-François) de (1734–94) French composer and writer on music. He studied with Rameau and entered the service of Louis XV in 1762, eventually becoming *premier valet du chambre*. La Borde was primarily a composer of opéras-comiques, but he also produced an important if not always reliable *Essai sur la musique ancienne et moderne*. He was guillotined during the Revolution.

Lalande, Michel-Richard de (1657–1726) French composer. Early in his career he was organist at a number of Paris churches, and in 1683 was appointed *sous-maître* at the royal chapel. He became *compositeur de la musique de la chambre* in 1685, *surintendant* in 1689 and *maître* in 1695. Favoured by Louis XIV, Lalande was a leading composer of *grands motets*, ballets and instrumental works.

Lebrun, Franziska [Francesca] (Dorothea) [née Danzi] (1756–91) German soprano. She made her operatic debut in 1772 and was engaged for the Mannheim court opera. She created roles in Holzbauer's *Günther von Schwarzburg* (1777) and Salieri's *L'Europa riconosciuta* (1778), and appeared with her husband in London, Paris, Vienna, Naples and elsewhere. During her residence in London (1779–81) she composed and published two sets of violin sonatas.

Lebrun, Ludwig August (1752–90) German oboist and composer. He joined the Mannheim court orchestra while still a teenager and retained a post there until his death. With his wife Franziska (above) he toured widely as an oboe virtuoso and composed a number of concertos for the instrument.

Leclair, Jean-Marie [*l'aîné*] (1697–1764) French violinist and composer. He studied with G. B. Somis and made his successful debut at the Concert Spirituel in 1728. From 1733 to 1737 he was *ordinaire de la musique du roi*, after which he served Princess Anne of Orange in the Netherlands. He returned to Paris in 1743 and from 1748 directed the private theatre of the Duc de Gramont. Considered the founder of the French violin school, Leclair met an unfortunate end when he was stabbed to death, most likely by his estranged nephew. His brother, also called Jean-Marie (1703–77) was a violinist and composer in his native Lyons.

Leo, Leonardo (Ortensio Salvatore de) (1694–1744) Italian composer. He studied in Naples and from 1720 received a string of operatic commissions. In 1725 he was appointed organist of the viceroyal chapel and in 1737 became *vicemaestro*. By 1741 he was also *primo maestro* at the conservatories of S Onofrio and S Maria della Pietà dei Turchini. A more conservative figure than his Neopolitan rival Durante, Leo composed both serious and comic opera in addition to oratorios, church music and cantatas.

Le Sueur [Lesueur], Jean-François (1760–1837) French composer. He held a number of choirmaster positions, culminating in his election to the directorship at Notre Dame, Paris, in 1786. He left after only a year, and in the 1790s turned his attention to stage works and revolutionary music while holding a position at the Conservatoire. In 1804 he became director of music at the Tuileries Chapel and held the position until the chapel's closure in 1830. Le Sueur wrote several successful operas and was a prolific composer of sacred music.

Linley, Thomas (1733–95) English composer. He studied in London with Boyce and directed concerts in Bath before moving to the capital in 1776. He was one of the proprietors of Drury Lane and joint director of the oratorios there, enjoying success with his harmonizations for Gay's *The Beggar's Opera* (1777). Many of his twelve children were involved in music, including the singers Elizabeth and Mary, and the composers Thomas (below) and William.

Linley, Thomas (1756–78) English composer and violinist. As a child he displayed prodigious musical gifts, playing in concert at the age of seven and studying with Boyce. In 1768 he went to Italy to study with Nardini, and met Mozart in 1770. On his return to England he became leader at Drury Lane, but met his death in a boating accident while on a family holiday. He contributed to three stage works and composed odes, songs and instrumental music.

Locatelli, Pietro Antonio (1695–1764) Italian composer and violinist. In 1711 he went to Rome and played in performances sponsored by Cardinal Pietro Ottoboni and the *Congregazione dei Musici di S Cecilia*. He later spent time in Venice, Munich, Berlin, Frankfurt and Kassel, and in 1729 moved to the Netherlands. There he performed privately and concentrated on publishing his music. The most important of these collections was *L'arte del violino* (Op. 3, 1733), a collection of twelve concertos with twenty-four caprices that make great demands on the soloist.

Loeillet, Jean-Baptiste (1680–1730) Flemish composer and instrumentalist, resident in England. He moved to London in about 1705, and played in the orchestras of Drury Lane and the Queen's Theatre. He was in demand as a harpsichord teacher, and gave a series of concerts in his home that included the first English performances of Corelli's Op. 6. Loeillet composed harpsichord lessons and solo sonatas for flute, recorder and oboe. His cousin, also called Jean-Baptiste (1688–*c.* 1720) published several sets of recorder sonatas.

Lolli, Antonio (*c.* 1725–1802) Italian violinist and composer. In 1758 he was appointed violinist at the Stuttgart court, and was frequently abroad on concert tours in France, Germany and the Austrian lands. From 1774–83 he served Catherine the Great in St Petersburg, after which he continued to tour widely. Although his compositions do not reflect his performing ability, Lolli was one of the most acclaimed violinists of his age.

Lotti, Antonio (1666–1740) Italian composer. He studied with Legrenzi in Venice and became an organist at S Marco. From 1693 he received operatic commissions, culminating in a visit to Dresden where his *Giove in Argo* inaugurated the Hoftheater in 1719. In 1736 he was named *maestro di cappella* at S Marco. Lotti's sacred music demonstrates a refined contrapuntal craft as seen in the famous *Crucifixus*, and his works continued to be performed in Venice throughout the eighteenth century.

Lübeck, Vincent (1654–1740) German organist, composer and teacher. He studied with Caspar Förckelrath and in 1674 became organist at St Cosmae et Damiani in Stade. In 1704 he was appointed organist at the Nikolaikirche in Hamburg, a church whose instrument (destroyed in 1842) was among the largest in the world. Lübeck composed a small but significant number of virtuoso organ works in addition to sacred cantatas and a single collection of harpsichord pieces.

Majo [Maio], Gian Francesco de (1732–70) Italian composer. He was organist at the royal chapel in Naples and in 1759 made a highly successful operatic debut with *Ricimero, re dei goti*. He studied with Padre Martini in 1761–3 and accepted operatic commissions from Vienna, Venice, Turin, Rome, Mannheim and Naples. A number of Majo's operas have 'reform' characteristics and his sacred music is often of high quality.

Manfredini, Vincenzo (1737–99) Italian composer and writer on music. He studied in Bologna and Milan and in 1758 went with his brother to Moscow. After moving to St Petersburg he served Pyotr Fedorovich and was named director of the Italian opera. He returned to Italy with a pension in 1769 and continued to compose and teach. His writings, including the *Regole armoniche* (1775, 1797), are significant as documentation of Enlightenment attitudes towards music.

Marais, Marin (1656–1728) French viol player and composer. He studied with Sainte-Colombe and by 1675 was playing in the Opéra orchestra in Paris. From 1679 he was a member of the *musique de la chambre du roi*, and from 1705 to 1710 was *batteur de mesure* at the Opéra. Marais' five *livres* of viol music are central repertory for the instrument, and his four tragédies en musique are fine works in the tradition of his mentor Lully.

Marcello, Alessandro (1669–1747) Italian composer. Born of a noble family, he combined his musical interests with diplomatic and governmental responsibilities. By 1719 he had become *principe* of the Accademia degli Animosi in Venice, with his publications appearing under his academician name of Eterio Stinfalico. Marcello's most well-known work is an oboe concerto (*c.* 1717), transcribed by J. S. Bach for harpsichord.

Marcello, Benedetto Giacomo (1686–1739) Italian composer, brother of Alessandro (above). Like Alessandro he was a dilettante, and after studying composition with Gasparini he fulfilled various magistracies in his native Venice. In 1730 he was exiled to Pula as provincial governor and spent his final years in Brescia. He composed in most of the standard forms but was particularly influential through the *Estro poetico-armonico* (1724–6), a collection of psalm paraphrases. He also produced the amusing pamphlet *Il teatro alla moda* (1720), satirizing the opera business.

Marchand, Louis (1669–1732) French keyboard player and composer. He moved to Paris by 1689, and was organist at several churches there. In 1708 he was appointed as an *organiste du roi*, but departed France in 1713 for an extended tour of Germany. In 1717 he was to have competed with J. S. Bach at the Dresden court, but apparently departed the city before Bach arrived. On his return to Paris, Marchand resumed an organist position at the Cordeliers and was much in demand as a teacher.

Marpurg, Friedrich Wilhelm (1718–95) German critic, theorist and composer. He spent time in Paris, and on his return to Berlin in the late 1740s became active in music journalism. He contributed the preface to the second edition of Bach's *Kunst der Fuge* and wrote the standard treatise on the subject, *Abhandlung von der Fuge* (1753–4). In his later years Marpurg was director of the Prussian state lottery.

Martín y Soler, Vicente (1754–1806) Spanish composer. In 1777 he moved to Naples as a composer of opera and ballet, and after several years in Venice he settled in Vienna in 1785. Of the three operatic commissions he received there, *Una cosa rara* (1786) and *L'arbore di Diana* (1787) achieved unprecedented success. From 1788 to 1794 Martín was in St Petersburg as Kapellmeister to the Russian court, and he returned there in 1796 after a season at the King's Theatre in London.

Martini, [Padre] Giovanni Battista (1706–84) Italian composer, teacher and writer on music. He studied in his native Bologna and was made *maestro di cappella* at S Francesco in 1725. In 1758 he became a member of the Accademia dell'Istituto delle Scienze and the Accademia Filarmonica. Martini was one of the most famous musical authorities in Europe and corresponded with leading composers. He wrote a large-scale but unfinished *Storia della musica* (1757–81).

Mattheson, Johann (1681–1764) German composer, theorist and writer on music. He received a broad education in Hamburg and sang solo roles at the Opera from 1696. He became secretary to an English diplomat in 1706, director of music at Hamburg Cathedral in 1715 and Kapellmeister to the Duke of Holstein in 1719. Mattheson's critical and theoretical writings, including *Das neu-eröffnete Orchestre* (1713), *Critica musica* (1722–5) and *Der vollkommene Capellmeister* (1739) are of the highest importance for the understanding of Baroque musical culture in Germany.

Méhul, Etienne-Nicholas (1763–1817) French composer. By 1779 he was in Paris, where he worked as a teacher and composed for the Concert Spirituel. In 1790 he made his operatic debut, and in 1795 became one of the inspectors at the Conservatoire. He wrote a number of revolutionary works and was highly favoured by Napoleon during the Consulate and Empire. Méhul's varied output of operas was influential on later nineteenth-century composers.

Metastasio [Trapassi], Pietro (Antonio Domenico Bonaventura) (1698–1782) Italian poet and librettist. A protégé of the jurist Gianvincenzo Gravina, he was active as a librettist from 1720. In 1729 he was appointed imperial court poet in Vienna and wrote extensively for Hapsburg celebrations. He later had a fruitful collaboration with Hasse, but retired from writing for the stage in 1771. Metastasio was the principal representative of eighteenth-century opera seria.

Molter, Johann Melchior (1696–1765) German composer. He was a violinist in the service of Margrave Carl Wilhelm in Karlsruhe, and spent 1719–21 in Italy. On his return he was promoted to Kapellmeister, and in 1734 received the same appointment from Duke Wilhelm Heinrich in Eisenach. He visited Italy again in 1737–8 and returned to Karlsruhe in 1742. From 1747 he was Kapellmeister to the new Margrave Karl Friedrich. Molter composed prolifically in all instrumental forms.

Mondonville, Jean-Joseph Cassanéa de (1711–72) French composer and violinist. He moved to Paris in 1734 and in 1739 joined the royal chapel. He was made its *sous-maître* in 1744 and gained fame from his concert appearances throughout France. From 1748 he was involved with the Concert Spirituel and from 1755 to 1762 served as its director. Mondonville composed stage works and instrumental music but was best known for his *grands motets*, many of which continued to be performed long after his death.

Monn, Matthias Georg (1717–50) Austrian composer. He sang in the choir at Stift Klosterneuburg and from about 1738 was organist at the Karlskirche, Vienna. Although he wrote chamber music and sacred vocal works, Monn became well known in the twentieth century as the alleged composer of a Symphony in D, the first dated symphony in four movements to include a minuet (1740).

Monsigny, Pierre-Alexandre (1729–1817) French composer of stage works. Of noble heritage, he went to Paris in 1749 and from 1759 to 1777 produced a series of successful operas, specializing in opéras-comiques. After 1777 he retired from composition due to a cataract, but was appointed Inspector of Musical Education in 1800. Among Monsigny's most successful works were *Rose et Colas* (1764) and *Le Déserteur* (1769).

Monteclair, Michel Pignolet (1667–1737) French composer and theorist. He went to Paris in 1687 and at some stage travelled to Italy with the Prince of Vaudémont. By 1699 he was playing *basse de violon* in the Paris Opéra orchestra, and in 1721 opened a music shop with his nephew. He published a number of treatises and was well known as a teacher; his works include two operas and numerous secular cantatas.

Mozart, Leopold (1719–87) German violinist, composer and theorist. He studied in Augsburg and Salzburg, and joined the Salzburg Hofkapelle in 1743 as fourth violinist. He was later appointed second violinist, and in 1763 became deputy Kapellmeister. Much of his later career was occupied with the promotion of his talented son, although he continued to fulfill his court responsibilities. Mozart's *Versuch einer gründlichen Violinschule* (1756) is among the most important instrumental treatises of the eighteenth century.

Mozart, (Johann Chrysostom) Wolfgang Amadeus (1756–91) Austrian composer, pianist and violinist, son of Leopold (above). As a child he displayed extraordinary musical gifts, and from 1762 to 1773 spent much of his life travelling Europe in the company of his family. From 1772 he was Konzertmeister to Archbishop Colloredo in his native Salzburg, but became increasingly dissatisfied and visited Mannheim and Paris in 1777–8 in an unsuccessful attempt to secure employment elsewhere. Re-hired in Salzburg as court organist in 1779, he resigned in 1781 and settled in Vienna. Here he relied on income from concerts, publications and operatic productions, and was appointed to a minor court post in 1787. A prolific composer of remarkable versatility and profundity, Mozart has been the continual subject of admiration and debate as much for the nature of his personality as for his music.

Muffat, Gottlieb [Theophil] (1690–1770) German composer and organist. He studied with Fux in Vienna and become court organist in 1717, second organist in 1729 and first organist in 1741. His output consists almost entirely of keyboard music, including versets, toccatas, suites, ricercars and canzonas.

Müller, Wenzel (1767–1835) Czech composer, resident in Austria. He studied with Dittersdorf and in 1782 joined a theatre company in Brno. In 1786 he was appointed Kapellmeister at the Theater in der Leopoldstadt in Vienna, and apart from a stint in Prague in 1807–13 he retained the position until his death. Müller was the most successful composer of his time for the suburban Viennese theatre.

Mysliveček, Josef (1737–81) Czech composer. He studied in his native Prague, and in 1763 travelled to Venice to study operatic composition. His *Bellerofonte* was successfully produced in Naples in 1767, and thereafter he accepted commissions from numerous Italian cities. Mysliveček visited Vienna and Munich in the 1770s, but his final Italian operas were failures and he died in poverty. His music, admired by Mozart, consists primarily of operas, but he also wrote numerous symphonies, concertos and chamber works.

Nardini, Pietro (1722–93) Italian violinist and composer. He studied with Tartini, and after time in Vienna, Stuttgart and Brunswick he was appointed *maestro di cappella* to Grand Duke Leopold of Tuscany in 1770. Renowned for his purity of tone, Tartini composed numerous violin concertos, sonatas and string quartets.

Naumann, Johann Gottlieb (1741–1801) German composer and conductor. After studying with Homilius he travelled in Italy and in 1764 was appointed church composer in Dresden. He was appointed Kapellmeister there in 1776. The following year he went to Sweden at the invitation of Gustavus III, but returned to Dresden in 1776 as Oberkapellmeister. Naumann composed prolifically in all forms and produced two of the earliest large-scale operas in Swedish.

Neefe, Christian Gottlob (1748–98) German composer. He studied with Hiller in Leipzig, and in 1779 joined the Großmann theatre troupe in Bonn as composer and director of music. In 1782 he was appointed court organist in Bonn, by which time he had begun teaching the young Beethoven. The French Revolution harmed Neefe's prospects and he became music director of the

Dessau theatre shortly before his death. He was a prominent composer of lieder and German operas.

Ordoñez, (Johann) Karl (Rochus) von [Carlo d'] (1734–86) Austrian composer and violinist. He pursued a career in the Lower Austrian administration and was named Registrant in 1780. At the same time he participated in chamber music performances and became a member of the *Hofkammermusik* in 1779. Ordoñez was a prolific composer of symphonies and string quartets, and achieved popularity in court circles with his marionette opera *Alceste*.

Paisiello, Giovanni (1740–1816) Italian composer. He studied at the Conservatorio di S Onofrio in Naples and made his operatic debut in 1764. From 1776 to 1784 he was in St Petersburg as *maestro di cappella* to Catherine the Great, and on his return to Naples entered the service of Ferdinando IV. He was made *maestro della real camera* in 1787 and *maestro di cappella* at Naples Cathedral in 1796. From 1802 to 1804 he was in Paris as *maître de chapelle* to Napoleon. Paisiello was among the most successful opera composers of the late eighteenth century.

Paradis, Maria Theresia (1759–1824) Austrian pianist and composer. She became blind in infancy, but thanks to good family connections received an excellent musical training with Salieri and others. From 1783 to 1786 she undertook an extended concert tour and became increasingly active as a composer. In 1808 she started a music school. Salieri wrote an organ concerto for her, and she has also been connected with piano concertos by Haydn and Mozart.

Pepusch, Johann Christoph (1667–1752) German composer and theorist, resident in England. He was employed at the Prussian court and settled in London after 1697, playing in opera orchestras. From 1714 he was musical director at Drury Lane and later served the Duke of Chandos. Pepusch published *A Treatise on Harmony* (1730) and it is to him that the musical arrangement of *The Beggar's Opera* (1728) is attributed.

Perez, David (1711–78) Italian composer. He studied at the Conservatorio di S Maria di Loreto in Naples and from 1740 wrote operas for Naples and Palermo. By 1739 he was *maestro di cappella* of Palermo's Capella Palatina, but left in 1748 to concentrate on his operatic career. In 1752 he was appointed *mestre de capela* to the King of Portugal and held the position until his death. Perez wrote prolifically for the stage, notably with *Solimano* (1757), and produced a large body of sacred music.

Pergolesi, Giovanni Battista (1710–36) Italian composer. He studied at the Conservatorio dei Poveri di Gesù Cristo in Naples and wrote his first opera in 1731. In 1734 he entered the service of the Duke of Maddaloni and became deputy *maestro di cappella* to the city of Naples. Pergolesi's intermezzo *La serva padrona* (1733) and his setting of the *Stabat Mater* (1736) achieved the status of 'classics' even in the eighteenth century.

Peter, Johann Friedrich (1746–1813) German composer and minister, resident in the United States. He was educated at Moravian schools in the Netherlands and Germany, and in 1770 set sail for America. He served Moravian communities in Pennsylvania and elsewhere as a school teacher and assistant, but regularly took responsibility for music. In 1789 he completed six string quintets, the earliest known chamber music written in America, and was also active as a composer of anthems and songs.

Philidor, François-André Danican (1726–95) French composer. He studied with Campra but initially established himself as one of Europe's leading chess players. From 1756 he wrote numerous successful opéras-comiques and divided his time between Paris and London.

Piccinni, (Vito) Niccolò (Marcello Antonio Giacomo) (1728–1800) Italian composer. He studied in Naples and from 1754 wrote prolifically for the Italian stage, achieving particular success with *La buona figliuola* (1760). In 1776 he moved to Paris and wrote both comic and serious opera before returning to Naples in 1791. He was placed under house arrest due to Jacobin associations but moved again to Paris in 1798. Piccinni was among the most popular opera composers of the mid eighteenth century.

Pichl, Václav [Wenzel] (1741–1805) Czech composer, violinist and writer. He studied music, philosophy, theology and law in Prague, and was engaged by Dittersdorf at Grosswardein. In about 1770 he became first violinist at the Vienna court theatre, and in 1777 went to Italy as director of music to Archduke Ferdinando d'Este, Governor of Lombardy. Pichl's output includes symphonies, concertos, sacred works and chamber music, including a notable series of exercises for solo violin.

Pisendel, Johann Georg (1687–1755) German violinist and composer. He studied with Torelli in Ansbach and later at Leipzig University. In 1712 he became a violinist in the Dresden court orchestra, and in 1728 took over Konzertmeister duties on the death of Volumier. Pisendel was the leading German violinist of his time and set new standards in ensemble direction; his works for violin are also of high quality.

Pleyel, Ignace Joseph [Ignaz Josef] (1757–1831) German composer, publisher and piano manufacturer, later resident in France. He studied with Haydn and was assistant Kapellmeister at Strasbourg Cathedral from about 1784. In 1795 he moved to Paris and founded a publishing house that was to produce the first miniature scores (1802). His piano manufacturing firm began in 1807 and was continued by his son Camille. Pleyel's prolific output includes symphonies, concertos and a great many chamber works.

Porpora, Nicola (Antonio) (1686–1768) Italian composer. He studied at the Conservatorio dei Poveri di Gesù Cristo in Naples and wrote his first opera in 1708. From 1725 to 1733 he was *maestro* of the Incurabili in Venice, after which he spent three years in London. He later held posts in Naples, Venice and Dresden, and lived in Vienna from 1752 to 1759 with Haydn as his pupil. His last years were spent in poverty in Naples. Porpora was a celebrated singing teacher, and a number of his operas were very successful.

Portugal [Portogallo], Marcos António (da Fonseca) (1762–1830) Portuguese composer. He studied at the Seminário da Patriarcal in Lisbon and was appointed *maestro* at the Teatro do Salitre in 1785. From 1792 to 1800 he was in Italy, and on his return to Lisbon became *mestre de capela* of the royal chapel and *maestro* of the Teatro de S Carlos. He sailed for Rio de Janeiro in 1811 and continued to serve the Portuguese court in exile. Portugal was celebrated for his Italian comic operas.

Pugnani, (Giulio) Gaetano (Gerolamo) (1731–98) Italian violinist and composer. He studied with Somis and was an orchestral violinist in Turin from 1748. He acquired an international reputation through touring and was conductor at the King's Theatre in 1767–9. On his return to Turin he was made first violinist and director of instrumental music. Pugnani contributed to the development of violin technique and was the teacher of Viotti.

Punto, Giovanni [Stich, Johann Wenzel (Jan Václav)] (1746–1803) Bohemian horn player and composer. He studied in Dresden with Hampel, and after abandoning his former employer Count Thun he toured Europe as a virtuoso. He was in Paris from 1789 to 1799 and in 1800 went to Vienna, where Beethoven wrote a sonata for him. Punto was acclaimed as the greatest horn player of his time.

Quantz, Johann Joachim (1697–1773) German flautist, writer on music and composer. He studied with Zelenka and joined the Polish chapel of Augustus II in 1719 as an oboist. From 1724 to 1727 he visited Italy, France and England, and in 1728 became a regular member of the Dresden chapel, now concentrating on the flute. In 1741 he moved to Berlin and served Frederick the Great as flute teacher, composer and instrument-maker. Quantz's *Versuch einer Anweisung die Flöte traversiere zu spielen* (1752) is a valuable source for flute technique and eighteenth-century performance practice more generally.

Raaff, Anton (1714–97) German tenor. He studied with Ferrandini in Munich and from 1738 lived for a number of years in Italy. He subsequently sang in Bonn, Vienna, Lisbon and Madrid among other centres, and in the 1760s was a principal tenor in Florence and Naples. In 1770 he moved to Mannheim, creating the title roles in operas by Piccinni, J. C. Bach and Holzbauer. His final role was the title character in Mozart's *Idomeneo* (1781).

Rameau, Jean-Philippe (1683–1764) French composer and theorist. He was appointed organist at Clermont Cathedral in 1702, and after holding further organist positions in Paris, Dijon and Lyons he returned to Clermont in 1715. In 1722 he settled in Paris and gained a formidable reputation through the publication of his theoretical and keyboard works. He made his controversial operatic debut with *Hippolyte et Aricie* in 1733, and for the remainder of his career concentrated on dramatic music. He enjoyed the patronage of the rich financier Alexandre-J. J. Le Riche de la Pouplinière and in 1745 was appointed *compositeur de la musique de la chambre du roy*. Rameau was the most prominent French operatic composer of his day, and his *Traité de l'harmonie* (1722) was among the most important music treatises of the eighteenth century.

Rauzzini, Venanzio (1746–1810) Italian soprano castrato and composer. He studied with Porpora and made his debut in 1765. The following year he entered the service of Elector Maximilian III Joseph in Munich and remained there until 1772. That year he created the role of Cecilio in Mozart's *Lucio Silla* and was the intended soloist for the composer's *Exultate, jubilate* in Milan. From 1774 Rauzzini was a singer and composer for the King's Theatre in London, and in 1777 moved to Bath as a concert impresario, composer and teacher.

Rebel, Jean-Fery (1666–1747) French composer. He studied with Lully, and had a long career at the Paris Opéra as a violinist, harpsichordist, *batteur de mesure* (from 1715) and *maître de musique* (*c.* 1727–33). He was also a member and later director of the *24 violons du roi* and served as *compositeur de la musique de la chambre*. Rebel was among the earliest composers of sonatas in France and made an important contribution to ballet music, notably in his last work *Les elements* (1738).

Reichardt, Johann Friedrich (1752–1814) German composer and writer on music. He was appointed Kapellmeister at the Royal Berlin Opera in 1775 and travelled extensively on court business. He was dismissed in 1794 due to Republican suspicions, and was involved in administrative and political activities before serving Jérôme Buonaparte for a short time. Reichardt was a prolific composer of lieder and the author of the influential *Musikalisches Kunstmagazin* (1782–91).

Reutter, (Johann Adam Joseph Karl) Georg (von) (1708–72) Austrian composer. After studying with Caldara and a tour of Italy he was appointed a court composer in 1731. He became Kapellmeister at St Stephen's Cathedral in 1738 and acting court Kapellmeister in 1751, receiving a formal appointment to the latter position in 1769. Reutter was the leading composer of sacred music in mid-century Vienna.

Richter, Franz Xaver (1709–89) Czech composer, resident in Germany. He studied in Vienna, and from 1746 was a singer and chamber composer in the Hofkapelle of the Elector Palatine in Mannheim. In 1769 he was appointed *maître de chapelle* at Strasbourg Cathedral. Richter contributed to the formation of the Mannheim instrumental style and was later a prolific composer for the church.

Righini, Vincenzo (Maria) (1756–1812) Italian composer. He sang in operatic productions as a tenor and by 1777 was in Vienna, where he established himself as a singing teacher and composer. In 1787 he was appointed Kapellmeister in Mainz, and in 1793 moved to Berlin to take up the same position at the Prussian court. Righini's music is primarily operatic, but he also composed a number of sacred works including a coronation mass for Leopold II (1790).

Ristori, Giovanni Alberto (1692–1753) Italian composer. In 1717 he was appointed composer to the comic Italian theatre and director of the *cappella polacca* in Dresden. From the 1720s he composed church music for the Dresden court, and was named Kirchenkomponist in 1746 and vice-Kapellmeister in 1750. In addition to his sacred works, Ristori composed operas, cantatas and a small amount of instrumental music.

Rodríguez de Hita, Antonio (1722–87) Spanish composer. In 1744 he was appointed *maestro de capilla* at Palencia Cathedral and from 1765 occupied the same post at the Monasterio de la Encarnación in Madrid. From 1768 to 1770 he wrote four zarzuelas that established his reputation as a stage composer, after which he concentrated on Latin sacred music. His other works include numerous villancicos and an important treatise, *Diapasón instructivo* (1757).

Roman, Johan Helmich (1694–1758) Swedish composer. By 1711 he was a member of the Swedish royal chapel, and from *c.* 1715 to 1721 was in England. On his return he was named deputy Kapellmeister and in 1727 advanced to the full post. He undertook another European tour in 1735–7 and was semi-retired from 1745 due to increasing deafness. Roman composed orchestral and chamber works, secular cantatas and sacred music, much of it to Swedish texts.

Roseingrave, Thomas (1690/91–1766) English organist and composer. From 1709 to 1713 he was in Italy, where he met D. Scarlatti. He moved to London by 1717 and in 1725 was appointed organist at St George's, Hanover Square. Although he was an excellent performer and teacher he apparently suffered from mental illness, and retired to Dublin in the 1750s. Roseingrave composed anthems, cantatas and keyboard music, and brought out an edition of sonatas by Scarlatti (1739).

Rosetti [Rössler], Antonio [Anton] (*c.* 1750–92) Bohemian composer. In 1773 he entered the service of Kraft-Ernest, Prince of Oettingen-Wallerstein, as a double-bass player. He visited Paris in 1781, and in 1785 was appointed Kapellmeister. In 1789 he moved to Ludwigslust as Kapellmeister to the Duke of Mecklenburg-Schwerin. Rosetti's prolific output includes oratorios, sacred works, symphonies, concertos and chamber music.

Rousseau, Jean-Jacques (1712–78) Swiss philosopher, composer and theorist. He taught himself music using Rameau's *Traité de l'harmonie* and was active from about 1740 as a composer for the stage. Beginning in 1749 he contributed to the *Encyclopédie* and criticized French music in the *Querelle des Bouffons* (1752–4). Rousseau's opera *Le devin du village* (1752) was a great success, but his lasting contribution to music was the *Dictionnaire de musique* (1768).

Sacchini, Antonio (Maria Gasparo Gioacchino) (1730–86) Italian composer. He studied with Durante at the Conservatorio S Maria di Loreto in Naples and in 1761 became *secondo maestro* there. He later lived in Rome and Venice, and in 1772 moved to London. Faced with mounting debts he fled to France in 1781, where his last operas were caught up in the rivalry between the supporters of Gluck and Piccinni. Sacchini was among the leading composers of serious opera in the later eighteenth century.

Saint-Georges [Saint-George], Joseph Bologne, Chevalier de (1745–99) French composer and violinist. Born in Guadeloupe to a French planter and an African slave, he was taken by his father to France in 1753 and became one of the best swordsmen in Europe. He joined the Concert des Amateurs in 1769 and became its director in 1773. In 1781 he founded the Concert de la Loge Olympique, which was later to commission Haydn's 'Paris' symphonies. Saint-Georges composed operas, concertos, symphonies and chamber music.

Salieri, Antonio (1750–1825) Italian composer. Early in his career he was taken to Vienna by Gassmann, who became his teacher and mentor. In 1774 Salieri was appointed Kammerkomponist at the Imperial court and director of the Italian opera. He received operatic commissions from Milan, Venice, Rome and Munich in addition to his work in Vienna, and in 1788 was appointed Hofkapellmeister. In later years he turned increasingly to sacred music, and retired in 1824. A versatile composer and able administrator, Salieri is now increasingly recognized for his contributions to Viennese operatic life in the 1780s.

Salomon, Johann Peter (1745–1815) German composer, later resident in England. He was a court musician in Bonn from 1758, and by 1764 was serving Prince Heinrich of Prussia. In 1780 he left for London, making his début at Covent Garden in 1781. He initially made his name as a violinist, but turned to concert promotion in 1783 and eventually secured Haydn's two visits to London. Salomon was a founder-member of the Philharmonic Society and composed operas, songs, concertos and chamber music.

Sammartini, Giovanni Battista (1700/1–75) Italian composer. He spent his entire life in Milan, where he was *maestro di cappella* at numerous churches. He taught at the Collegio de'Nobili from 1730, and in 1768 became director of the ducal chapel. Sammartini was among the most important figures in the early development of the Classical style, particularly in his cultivation of the symphony.

Sammartini, Giuseppe (1695–1750) Italian oboist and composer, brother of Giovanni Battista (above). He played in several Milanese orchestras and by 1729 was in London. Here he gained a reputation as a virtuoso and had parts written for him by Handel. In 1736 he became music master to Augusta, Princess of Wales. Sammartini's sonatas and concerti grossi were popular in England long after his death.

Sarti, Giuseppe (1729–1802) Italian composer. He studied with Padre Martini and was Kapellmeister in Copenhagen from 1755 to 1765. After a number of Italian engagements he returned to Copenhagen in 1768 but was dismissed in 1775. In 1779 he was appointed *maestro di cappella* at Milan Cathedral, but left in 1784 to become director of the imperial chapel in St Petersburg. Sarti achieved great success with both serious and comic opera and composed a number of works for the Russian Orthodox liturgy.

Scarlatti, (Pietro) Alessandro (Gaspare) (1660–1725) Italian composer. He began his career in Rome, and in 1684 became *maestro di cappella* to the viceroy of Naples. In 1702 he returned to Rome, but after political intrigue and unsuccessful operatic productions in Venice took up the Naples position again in 1708. He remained in Naples until his death, making occasional visits to Rome to supervise new operas. The success of Scarlatti's stage works was variable, but they have achieved a prominent position in modern scholarship.

Scarlatti, (Giuseppe) Domenico (1685–1757) Italian composer, son of Alessandro (above). He joined the Naples royal chapel in 1701, after which his father sent him to Venice. In 1709 he went to Rome to serve the exiled Queen of Poland, and in 1714 was appointed *maestro di cappella* of the Cappella Giulia at St Peter's, Basilica, Rome. João V of Portugal appointed him *mestre de capela* in 1719, and in 1729 he moved to Spain as music master to João's daughter María Barbara. Although he composed in a variety of forms, Scarlatti is chiefly renowned for the hundreds of single-movement keyboard sonatas written for his royal pupil.

Scheibe, Johann Adolph (1708–76) German composer and theorist. He studied law at Leipzig University, but became preoccupied with music and in 1737 moved to Hamburg. There he composed extensively and initiated the publication of *Der critische Musikus*, with its infamous criticisms of J. S. Bach. From 1740 to 1747 he was Kapellmeister to King Christian VI in Copenhagen, after which he worked in Sønderborg and again as court composer from 1766.

Schenk, Johann Baptist (1753–1836) Austrian composer. He studied with Wagenseil and from 1780 was active as a composer of German operas for the Viennese theatres. His first great success was *Der Dorfbarbier* (1796), at which time he was also Kapellmeister to Prince Auersperg. Although Schenk achieved further recognition with *Der Fassbinder* (1802) and continued to compose, most of his later life was occupied with teaching. He is alleged to have taught Beethoven in 1793.

Schikaneder, Emanuel (Johann Joseph [Baptist]) (1751–1812) German actor, singer, impresario and playwright. He joined the Moser acting troupe around 1773 and was made its director in 1778. In the 1780s he began appearing in Vienna, and from 1789 directed the company at the Theater auf der Wieden, commissioning works from Henneberg, Mozart, Süssmayr and others. He opened the new Theater an der Wien in 1801, but his later fortunes in Vienna and Brno were variable and he died in poverty.

Schobert, Johann [Jean] (*c.* 1735–67) Silesian harpsichordist and composer, resident in France. He is first documented in the service of the Prince of Conti in the early 1760s, at which time he began publishing his own music. The young Mozart encountered him in 1764 and was influenced by Schobert's distinctive keyboard writing. Schobert and his family died as a result of eating poisonous mushrooms.

Schröter, Corona Elisabeth Wilhelmine (1751–1802) German singer, actress and composer. She studied with Hiller in Leipzig and achieved success there in public concerts from 1765, expanding her activities to acting in the early 1770s. In 1776 Goethe arranged for her to become chamber musician to Duchess Anna Amalia in Weimar. Schröter created many roles in Goethe's early dramas and composed the first setting of *Der Erlkönig*. She later published two books of lieder and maintained a friendship with Schiller.

Schubart, Christian Friedrich Daniel (1739–91) German poet, composer and writer on music, well known for his lieder. In 1763 he was appointed organist at Geisslingen, and in 1769 moved to Ludwigsburg as organist and harpsichordist to the Duke of Württemberg. He was banished in 1773 and began publishing a periodical, the *Deutsche Chronik*. Schubart was imprisoned for ten years on the orders of Duke Carl Eugen, and while confined dictated an autobiography and wrote the important *Ideen zu einer Ästhetik der Tonkunst*. On his release in 1787 he was appointed court and theatre poet in Stuttgart.

Schulz, Johann Abraham Peter (1747–1800) German composer and conductor. He studied with Kirnberger, and in 1776 was appointed director of the French theatre in Berlin. After holding further operatic directorships he became Hofkapellmeister and director of the Royal Theatre, Copenhagen in 1787. He retired in 1795 after contracting tuberculosis. Schulz is best known for the three volumes of *Lieder im Volkston* (1782–90) and for his essay *Gedanken über den Einfluss der Musik auf die Bildung eines Volks* (1790).

Schweitzer, Anton (1735–87) German composer. He was Kapellmeister to the Duke of Hildeshausen and later musical director of a theatrical company. In 1771 Duchess Anna Amalia of Saxe-Weimar engaged the company, followed in 1774 by Duke Ernst II in Gotha. With Benda's resignation in 1778 Schweitzer became Kapellmeister to the Duke. He is remembered for the opera *Alceste* (1773).

Senesino [Bernardi, Francesco] (d. ?1759) Italian alto castrato. Born in Siena, he sang in numerous Italian theatres from 1707. He was engaged for Dresden in 1717 but dismissed in 1720, after which he travelled to London. Here he was a sensational success and created roles in operas by Handel, Bononcini, Ariosti, Porpora and others. From 1737 to 1740 he sang in Italy.

Silbermann, Gottfried (1683–1753) German organ, harpsichord and piano-builder. He trained in Strasbourg with his brother Andreas, and returned to Saxony in 1710. His instruments included those at Freiberg Cathedral (1710–14), the Sophienkirche and Frauenkirche in Dresden (1718–20, 1732–6) and the posthumously completed Dresden Hofkirche (1755). He was acquainted with many leading musicians including J. S. and W. F. Bach, and played a leading role in the development of the early piano.

Smith, John Christopher [Schmidt, Johann Christoph] (1712–95) German composer, resident in England. Like his father (also John Christopher), he worked for Handel as a copyist and amanuensis. From 1754 to 1770 he was organist at the Foundling Hospital. In addition to his own operas and oratorios, Smith produced several adaptations of Handel oratorios and inherited many of the late composer's manuscripts.

Soler (Ramos), Antonio (Francisco Javier José) (1729–83) Catalan composer and organist. In 1752 he joined the Hieronymite order at El Escorial and later became a priest and *maestro de capilla* at the monastery. He studied with Nebra and possibly Scarlatti, and in 1762 published an important treatise, *Llave de la modulación y antigüedades de la música*. In 1766 Soler was appointed music tutor to the *infante* Prince Gabriel and wrote a number of keyboard sonatas for him. He was also a prolific composer of sacred music and villancicos.

Sorge, Georg Andreas (1703–78) German organist, composer and theorist. He spent almost his entire career as court and civic organist at Lobenstein in Thuringia. From 1741 he began publishing at his own expense a long series of books and pamphlets on composition, organ construction, tuning and improvisation. He was a member of Mizler's *Societät der Musikalischen Wissenschaften* and composed a large amount of keyboard music, some of it under the title *Clavier Übung*.

Stadler, Anton (Paul) (1753–1812) Austrian clarinettist and composer. By 1773 he was in Vienna, where he played in the orchestra of the *Tonkünstler-Societät* and joined the imperial *Harmonie* in 1779. In 1781 he was appointed to the orchestra of the Burgtheater along with his brother Johann. Mozart wrote a number of works for him, and Stadler himself devised a 'Bass-Klarinet' with an extended lower register.

Stadler, Abbé Maximilian [Johann Karl Dominik] (1748–1833) Austrian composer and music historian. He studied at the Jesuit College in Vienna and was ordained in 1772. Appointed successively prior of Melk, abbot of Lilienfeld and abbot of Kremsmünster, he moved to Vienna in 1796 and assisted Constanze

Mozart with the organisation of her husband's manuscripts. He later worked on a history of Austrian music and defended the authenticity of Mozart's Requiem.

Stamitz, Carl (Philipp) (1745–1801) German composer and violinist. He studied with his father and other Mannheim musicians, and after playing in the electoral orchestra moved to Paris in 1770. Here he was active in the Concert Spirituel and served the Duke of Noailles. He toured widely in the 1780s and spent his last years as Kapellmeister in Jena. Stamitz was a prolific composer of symphonies, symphonies concertantes and concertos. His brother Anton (b. 1750) travelled with him to Paris and remained there until his death some time between 1796 and 1809.

Stamitz, Johann (Wenzel Anton) [Jan Václav Antonín] (1717–57) Bohemian composer and violinist, father of Carl (above) and Anton. He studied in Jihlava and Prague and joined the service of the Elector Palatine in Mannheim about 1741. Here he advanced to Konzertmeister in 1745 and director of instrumental music in 1750. Stamitz was among the earliest composers to write four-movement symphonies and was responsible for developing the Mannheim orchestra into one of the most famed in Europe.

Stanley, John (1712–86) English organist and composer. He was blind from an early age, but studied with Greene and became organist at St Andrew's, Holborn in 1726. In 1734 he was appointed organist of the Inner Temple, and in 1779 became Master of the King's Band of Musicians. Stanley is remembered for his organ voluntaries and for the Six Concertos, Op. 2 (1742).

Starzer, Joseph (Johann Michael) (1728–87) Austrian composer. By 1754 he was a violinist and composer at the French theatre in Vienna, writing ballet scores in collaboration with the choreographer Franz Hilverding. He was with Hilverding in St Petersburg from 1759 to 1767, after which he returned to Vienna and worked with Noverre and Angiolini. For some years he was the director of the *Tonkünstler-Societät*.

Steffani, Agostino (1654–1728) Italian priest, composer and diplomat. He studied with Kerll and by 1678 was appointed court organist in Munich. From 1688 he was in Hanover as Kapellmeister of the Italian opera but mostly gave up composition during his subsequent appointment to the Elector Palatine. In 1709 he was appointed Apostolic Vicar in northern Germany, and in the 1720s wrote a number of works for the Academy of Ancient Music in London. Steffani is best known for his chamber duets and for a setting of the *Stabat Mater*.

Storace, Nancy [Ann Selina, Anna] (1765–1817) English soprano. She studied with Rauzzini and Sacchini and went to Italy in 1778. She made her operatic debut the following year and in 1783 was engaged for the Italian opera in Vienna. Here she created roles in works by Mozart, Salieri, Soler and others. In 1787 she went to London and sang at the King's Theatre and Drury Lane. Storace gave her farewell performance in 1808.

Storace, Stephen (John Seymour) (1762–96) English composer, brother of Nancy (above). He studied at the S Onofrio Conservatory in Naples, after which he divided his time between London and Vienna. After his final return to London in 1787 he composed for the King's Theatre and Drury Lane. Storace wrote two Italian operas for Vienna and many English operas for the London stage.

Stradivari, Antonio (1644/9–1737) Italian violin-maker. His early violins show an affinity with Amati, but in the 1690s he developed a more individual construction. Over the next two decades he produced what are now regarded as the finest violins in existence, and also made violas and cellos of the highest quality. He continued to be active in his last years, supervising the work of his son Francesco.

Süssmayr, Franz Xaver (1766–1803) Austrian composer. He was educated at Stift Kremsmünster and moved to Vienna in 1788. In 1791 he assisted Mozart with the preparations for *Die Zauberflöte* and completed Mozart's Requiem the following year. He achieved great success with *Der Spiegel von Arkadien* (1794), written for Schikaneder's Theater auf der Wieden, and composed numerous other operas, instrumental pieces and sacred works.

Swieten, Gottfried (Bernhard), Baron van (1733–1803) Dutch patron of music and diplomat, resident in Austria. He was educated at the Theresianum in Vienna and embarked on a diplomatic career, serving as Austrian ambassador to Berlin (1770–7). On his return to Vienna he was made Prefect of the Imperial Library and encouraged the cultivation of old music. He was instrumental in the establishment of a society for the private performance of oratorios, and compiled the texts for Haydn's *Schöpfung* and *Jahreszeiten*.

Tartini, Giuseppe (1692–1770) Italian violinist, composer, teacher and theorist. Largely self-taught as a violinist, he played in various orchestras before being appointed *primo violino e capo di concerto* at S Antonio, Padua in 1721. In 1727 he started a violin school, attracting students from all over Europe, and became increasingly devoted to theoretical pursuits. Tartini composed hundreds of violin concertos and sonatas and wrote several original treatises influenced by mysticism.

Telemann, Georg Philipp (1681–1767) German composer. He entered Leipzig University to study law but was already professionally active in music. From 1705 he was in the service of Count Erdmann II of Promnitz, and by 1709 was Kapellmeister to Duke Johann Wilhelm in Eisenach. In 1712 he was appointed city director of music in Frankfurt, and in 1721 was elected Kantor at the Hamburg Johanneum and director of music for the city's principal churches. One of the most prolific composers of the eighteenth century, Telemann was a pioneer in the use of publication to promote his music. In its combination of fluent counterpoint and *galant* gestures, Telemann's work represents a synthesis of contemporary stylistic trends.

Toeschi, Carl Joseph (1731–88) German composer and violinist. He studied with Stamitz and Fils and joined the Mannheim court orchestra in 1752. In 1759 he advanced to Konzertmeister and in 1774 became director of music to the Electoral cabinet. His works, almost all instrumental, include symphonies, concertos, chamber music and ballets.

Tomasini, Alois Luigi (1741–1808) Italian violinist and composer, resident in Austria. By 1761 he was first violinist in the Esterházy *Hofkapelle*, and was later appointed Konzertmeister. He was the dedicatee of a Haydn violin concerto, and performed in Vienna, Frankfurt and elsewhere. His works include string quartets, trios, concertos and works for baryton.

Tosi, Pier Francesco (1654–1732) Italian castrato, composer and writer. He served Emperor Joseph I and the Elector Palatine as a diplomat, and spent time in London as a singing teacher. He is remembered for the singing treatise *Opinioni de' cantori antichi e moderni* (1723), which was widely distributed and translated into English and German.

Tourte, François Xavier (1747–1835) French bow-maker. He was apprentice to his father Louis, and in the 1780s made important innovations to the form of the bow in collaboration with Viotti. These changes, including an increased weight and a screw to control the hair tension, laid the foundations for the modern design of the device.

Traetta, Tommaso (Michele Francesco Saverio) (1727–79) Italian composer. He studied with Porpora and Durante in Naples, and after writing operas for various Italian centres was appointed *maestro di cappella* to the Duke of Parma in 1758. Here he produced the French-influenced *Ippolito ed Aricia* (1759) and received commissions from Vienna and Mannheim. In 1768 he went to St Petersburg to serve Catherine the Great, and in 1775 settled in Venice where he continued to compose.

Tritto, Giacomo (Domenico Mario Antonio Pasquale Giuseppe) (1733–1824) Italian composer and teacher. He studied at the Pietà dei Turchini conservatory in Naples, later serving as *maestrino*, *secondo maestro* and finally *primo maestro* of the institution (1799). He also pursued, with variable success, a career as an opera composer, writing more than thirty comic operas in addition to opere serie and sacred music.

Türk, Daniel Gottlob (1750–1813) German organist, theorist and composer. He studied with Homilius in Dresden and Hiller in Leipzig, and on the latter's recommendation was appointed Kantor at the Ulrichskirche in Halle. In 1779 he became director of music at Halle University, and from 1787 was organist and director at the Liebfrauenkirche, the principal church of the city. Türk was a prolific composer of keyboard music and produced an important *Clavierschule* (1789).

Umlauf, Ignaz (1746–96) Austrian composer. By 1772 he was a violist in the Burgtheater orchestra and organist at the Kirche am Hof in Vienna. He was appointed Kapellmeister to the new German National Theatre in 1778, assistant to Salieri at the Italian opera in 1783 and assistant Hofkapellmeister by 1789. A number of Umlauf's early singspiele achieved great popularity in Austrian theatres.

Uttini, Francesco Antonio Baldassare (1723–95) Italian composer, resident in Sweden. He studied with Padre Martini in Bologna and in 1752 became resident composer in the Mingotti theatre troupe. Uttini was invited with other members of the troupe to Stockholm in 1755, and he became Kapellmästare to Queen Lovisa Ulrika. He was appointed Hovkapellmästare in 1767 and retired in 1788. On a commission from Gustavus III, Uttini produced the first Swedish grand opera, *Thetis och Pelée* (1773).

Valls, Francesc [Francisco] (?1665–1747) Catalan composer and theorist. He was successively *maestro de capilla* at Gerona Cathedral (1688), S María del Mar in Barcelona (1696), assistant at Barcelona Cathedral (1696) and finally titular *maestro* there (1709). He is remembered for the treatise *Mapa armónico* and for the *Missa Scala Aretina*, a work whose treatment of dissonance provoked a debate involving more than fifty Spanish musicians.

Vanhal [Wanhal], Johann Baptist (1739–1813) Bohemian composer, active in Austria. He moved to Vienna about 1760, and gained a reputation as a composer while supporting himself as a violinist and music teacher. From 1769 to 1771 he was in Italy on the sponsorship of Baron Riesch, and on his return to Vienna concentrated on disseminating his works through publication while making short visits to patrons. An inventive composer in all the forms of the day, Vanhal is also of interest for the high degree of independence he was able to maintain in his professional life.

Veracini, Francesco Maria (1690–1768) Italian composer and violinist. He played in Venice in 1711–12 and spent time in London, Düsseldorf and Dresden. In 1733 he returned to London, where three of his operas were produced by the Opera of the Nobility. His last years were spent as a church musician in Florence. Veracini is principally remembered for a set of violin sonatas, the *Sonate accademiche*, Op. 2 (1744).

Vinci, Leonardo (*c.*1690/6–1730) Italian composer, mainly of opera. He studied at the Conservatorio dei Poveri di Gesù Cristo in Naples, and made his operatic debut in 1719. Initially concentrating on Neapolitan comic opera, he later turned to the dramma per musica and had a successful collaboration with Metastasio. Late in life he held posts at the Royal Chapel in Naples and the monastery of S Caterina a Formiello. Vinci's emphasis on melody and simple homophonic accompaniment is an early indication of stylistic trends that were later to become dominant.

Viotti, Giovanni Battista (1755–1824) Italian violinist and composer. He studied with Pugnani, and after playing in the court chapel in Turin and touring with his teacher he settled in France. Here he served Marie Antoinette at Versailles and established an opera house in 1788. He fled to London after the Revolution and continued his successful concert career, but was ordered to leave the country in 1798. After returning from exile he worked as a wine merchant and from 1819 to 1821 directed the Paris Opéra. The founder of the 'modern' French violin school, Viotti wrote twenty-nine violin concertos that are among the most important Classical examples of the genre.

Vitali, Tomaso Antonio (1663–1745) Italian composer. He studied violin in Modena with his father, the composer Giovanni Battista Vitali, and counterpoint with Pacchioni. From 1675 he played in the Este orchestra and later led the ensemble, retiring in 1742. His works, all instrumental, resemble those of Corelli.

Vivaldi, Antonio (Lucio) (1678–1741) Italian violinist and composer. In 1703 he was appointed *maestro di violino* at the Pio Ospedale della Pietà in his native Venice. He held the position until 1716 (with an interruption in 1709–11), and was then promoted to *maestro de' concerti*. From 1713 he was active in opera and travelled widely in Italy from 1718. In the 1720s and 1730s he spent time in

Venice, Mantua, Rome and smaller centres, and was *maestro di cappella* at the Pietà in 1735–8. In 1740 he travelled to Vienna, where he died the following year. The hundreds of concertos composed by Vivaldi helped establish the standard Italian form of the genre, and collections such as *L'estro armonico* (Op. 3, 1711) were distributed across Europe.

Vogler, Georg Joseph (Abbé) (1749–1814) German organist, composer and theorist. He studied law, and after musical and religious travels in Italy became second Kapellmeister at the Mannheim court in 1775. After time in Paris and London he was appointed Kapellmeister in Munich in 1784, but after two years took up the same position in Stockholm. After extensive travels he received a generous appointment at Darmstadt in 1807. Vogler produced extensive theoretical writings and proposed reforms to organ design.

Wagenseil, Georg Christoph (1715–77) Austrian composer and keyboard player. He studied with Fux and Palotta and in 1739 was appointed court composer in Vienna. He became Hofklaviermeister to the imperial archduchesses in 1749 and achieved international prominence through the publication of his symphonies, concertos and chamber music. Wagenseil was renowned as a teacher, and although most famous for his instrumental music also composed operas and sacred works.

Walther, Johann Gottfried (1684–1748) German organist, composer and writer on music. He studied in his native Erfurt and after travels in central Germany became organist at the Weimar Stadtkirche in 1707. At Weimar he was friends with his cousin J. S. Bach and taught the musically gifted Prince Johann Ernst. In 1721 he was appointed Hofmusicus at the ducal court. Walther's principal achievement is the *Musicalisches Lexicon* (1732), a music dictionary of great significance.

Webbe, Samuel (1740–1816) English composer and organist. From about 1763 he was active as a composer of glees, catches and canons and in 1775 was appointed organist of the Sardinian Embassy Chapel in London. Webbe was the leading eighteenth-century composer of glees and became secretary of the Noblemen's and Gentlemen's Catch Club in 1784.

Weiß, Silvius Leopold (1686–1750) German lutenist and composer. He studied with his father, and held posts in Breslau and Rome. By 1717 he was in the court orchestra in Dresden, and retained the post until his death as the highest-paid instrumentalist in the establishment. Weiss was the greatest lute virtuoso of the late Baroque and the single-most prolific composer for the instrument, writing more than sixty *Suonate* or dance suites.

Werner, Gregor Joseph (1693–1766) Austrian composer. He was organist at Melk Abbey, and in 1728 was appointed Kapellmeister to the Esterházy court. In 1761, Haydn took over most of Werner's duties while the latter retained responsibility for sacred music. Werner is mostly remembered for his uneasy relationship with his subordinate, although he was a prolific composer of church music, oratorios and chamber works.

Winter, Peter [von Winter] (1754–1825) German composer. He studied in Mannheim and joined the court orchestra, becoming its director with the move to Munich in 1778. He was appointed Vice-Kapellmeister in 1787 and Kapellmeister in 1798. Winter composed orchestral, chamber and sacred music but achieved most success with his opera *Das unterbrochene Opferfest* (1796).

Wranitzky, Anton [Vranický, Antonin] (1761–1820) Czech composer. He studied philosophy and law in Brno, and after moving to Vienna entered the service of Prince Lobkowitz in 1790. He was made Kapellmeister to the Prince in 1797, and later directed the orchestras of the court theatre and the Theater an der Wien. Although he wrote no operas himself, Wranitzky did produce symphonies, concertos and much chamber music.

Wranitzky, Paul [Vranický, Pavel] (1756–1808) Czech composer and conductor, brother of Anton (above). He was educated in Moravia and went to Vienna in 1777. In 1785 he was appointed director of the orchestra at the Kärtnertortheater, and obtained the same position at the Burgtheater in the 1790s. Wranitzky's symphonies are of considerable interest, and his opera *Oberon, König der Elfen* (1789) was highly successful.

Zelenka, Jan (Lukáš Ignatius) Dismas (1679–1745) Czech composer. He spent a number of years in Prague, possibly as a student at the Clementinum, and moved to Dresden in 1710–11 as a violone player in the Hofkapelle. He studied in Vienna with Fux and became increasingly involved in composition for the Dresden royal chapel. From 1735 he was styled Kirchen Compositeur. In addition to his extensive sacred output, Zelenka wrote a small but distinctive body of chamber and orchestral music.

Zelter, Carl Friedrich (1758–1832) German composer and conductor. He initially trained as a mason, and studied composition with Fasch in 1784–6. In 1791 he joined the Berlin Singakademie and became its director in 1800. From 1809 he was a professor at the Akademie der Künste, and in 1822 founded the *Königliche Institut für Kirchenmusik*. Zelter was an advocate for the state support of music education and did much to encourage amateur choral singing in Germany.

Zeno, Apostolo (1668–1750) Italian poet, librettist and scholar. His first libretto was set by Pollarolo in 1696, after which he maintained a prolific output culminating in his appointment as imperial poet in Vienna (1718–29). Zeno was one of the leading providers of opera seria libretti before Metastasio.

Zingarelli, Niccolò Antonio (1752–1837) Italian composer and teacher. He studied at the Conservatorio di S Maria di Loreto in Naples, and after gaining a reputation as an opera composer was appointed *maestro di cappella* at S Casa, Loreto (1796) and St Peter's, Rome (1804). He was subsequently made director of the S Pietro a Majella conservatory in Naples (1813) and *maestro di cappella* at Naples Cathedral (1816). Zingarelli was among the last composers of opera seria, and wrote extensively for the church.

Zipoli, Domenico (1688–1726) Italian organist and composer. He studied in Naples, Bologna and Rome with A. Scarlatti and Pasquini, and in 1715 was appointed organist at the Jesuit church in Rome. In 1717 he sailed to Paraguay as a prospective Jesuit missionary, and completed clerical training in Córdoba. Zipoli is most renowned for a collection of keyboard music, *Sonate d'intavolatura* (1716), but he also wrote numerous sacred works now extant in Bolivian archives.

Zumsteeg, Johann Rudolf (1760–1802) German composer and conductor. He studied in Stuttgart and was friends with Schiller. In 1781 he joined the orchestra of Duke Carl Eugen of Württemberg, became director of German music at the court theatre in 1791 and finally court Konzertmeister in 1793. Although Zumsteeg composed operas, sacred music and concertos he was noted primarily for his lieder and ballads, many of which were admired by Schubert.

Index

Lightning Source UK Ltd.
Milton Keynes UK
UKHW021031260121
377497UK00011B/120